The Conran Cookbook

The Conran Cookbook

Caroline Conran
Terence Conran
and
Simon Hopkinson

Recipe Photography by James Murphy

General Editor: Norma MacMillan

Contents

First published in 1980 as *The Cook Book* by
Mitchell Beazley Publishers
This new edition first published in 1997 by
Conran Octopus Limited
37 Shelton Street
London WC2H 9HN

ISBN 1 85029 897 1

COMMISSIONING EDITOR: Suzannah Gough
PROJECT EDITOR: Kate Bell
ART DIRECTION: Helen Lewis assisted by Sue Storey
ART EDITOR: Alistair Plumb
PRODUCTION: Jill Beed, Suzanne Bayliss

British Library Cataloguing-in-Publication Data
A catalogue record for this book is available from the British Library

Printed and bound by Mohndruck Graphische Betriebe GmBh
Origination by Mandarin Offset, Singapore

Both metric and imperial quantites are given in the recipes in this book. Use either all metric or all imperial, as the two are not necessarily interchangeable.

Page 2: Oysters Rockefeller
Page 6: Roast Partridge with Celeriac

HOW THE BOOK WORKS

The three main sections chart the progress of food from the market to the kitchen to the table. All sections are cross-referenced – for example, when reading about scallops in Part One, the reader will find, at the side of the page, cross-references to the preparation of scallops (also in Part One), the recommended specialist equipment for dealing with scallops (Part Two), and recipes including scallops (Part Three). This system allows the book to be used on many different levels. Novices can explore any subject in depth, while experienced cooks can easily find whatever information they require.

Introduction 6–7

PART ONE – The Purchase and Preparation of Food

Fish and Seafood

Choosing and storing fish 10
Saltwater and freshwater fish 11
Preparing fish 26
Preserved fish 29
Shellfish 33
Preparing shellfish 39
Other seafoods, snails and frog's legs 43
Preparing seafood 47

Meat

Choosing, storing and cooking meat 48
Beef 51
Veal 54
Lamb 56
Pork 58
Offal 61
Preparing meat 63
Ham, bacon and salted pork 68
Cured meat and poultry 71
Sausages and salamis 72

Game and Poultry

Furred game 79
Feathered game 82
Poultry 86
Preparing poultry 91

Eggs, Dairy Foods, Cooking Fats and Oils

Eggs 96
Milk, cream and butter 97
Cheeses 101
Cooking fats and oils 110

Grains, Breads, Pasta and Dumplings

Grains 114
Thickening agents 118
Breads 119
Pasta, noodles and dumplings 121

Vegetables

Dried peas and beans 126
Salad vegetables 129
Greens 132
Brassica 134
Stalks and shoots 137
Pea, beans and sweetcorn 140
The onion family 143
Roots and tubers 145
Vegetable fruit 150
Cucumber, squashes and pumpkin....................155
Mushrooms and other fungi 158

Fruit and Nuts

Apple and pear 162
Citrus fruit 165
Stone fruit 167
Berries and rhubarb 170
Grapes 174
Melon 176
Tropical and Mediterranean fruit 177
Dried and candied fruit 182
Nuts 186

Herbs, Spices and Flavourings

Herbs 190
Spices 196
Salt and pepper 200
Mustard 202
Vinegar 204
Sauces, flavourings and colourings 206
Cooking with alcohol 208
Honey, syrup and sugar 210
Cocoa, chocolate and carob 212

Coffee, Teas and Tisanes

Coffee 214
Tea 217
Tisanes 219

PART TWO – Equipment

Knives 222
Other cutting implements 224
Mincers, mashers and sieves 226
Essential items and useful utensils 227
Bowls 230
Measuring 230
Stovetop pans 233
Ovenware and bakeware 235
Cake and pastry making 236
Electrical appliances 238
Barbecuing 240
Smoking 241
Preserving 241

PART THREE – Recipes

Stocks 244
Soups 246
Sauces 255
Fish 261
Shellfish....................275
Meat 282
Game 294
Poultry 305
Pies and pâtés 314
Eggs 322
Cheese 329
Pasta 332
Rice, grains and pulses 346
Breads 356
Salads 365
Vegetables 372
Desserts and puddings 387
Ice-creams and sorbets 398
Pastries 402
Cakes and biscuits 410
Preserves 417
Planning menus 420

Glossary 422–3
Index 424–2
Acknowledgments 432

Introduction

This book is about food, and is intended as a reference book for cooks. It is significantly different from the many recent cookery books generated by chefs, in that it has concentrated solely on the terms and practices of home-cooking. This is *the* book for home cooks who want practical information and a straightforward approach, and who like food cooked beautifully but without pretension.

It is concerned with food in all aspects – it is about raw ingredients and their preparation, and about the cooking and presentation of food. Fortunately, where food is concerned, the material is always fascinating. Food has a marvellous sensuality about it; even the simplest raw vegetable has a vitality and beauty of its own. The colours, textures and smells of food are all stimulating to the cook, inspiring a desire to cook in the same way that a writer wants to write or a painter to paint. And, like a painter or writer, the cook never knows exactly what will emerge at the end. Good ingredients are so individual – one tomato varying from the next according to the sun, the soil, the season – that there are constant surprises to keep up interest.

Many variations can be made on each theme too. Every time a dish is cooked, there is a feeling that it can be improved upon, that it can be done a little differently from the time before. But to add this dimension to cooking, the cook's response must be both intuitive and well informed; the more one understands the subject, the more one's feeling for ingredients will develop, and the surer one's instincts will become. Therefore the wider the knowledge, the more interesting and successful will be the experiments. This book sets out to provide a knowledge of a vast range of different foods, so that the cook – like someone with an extensive vocabulary – can be fluent and confident. Take, for example, olive oil: you may go to the supermarket and buy an olive oil that has been refined, treated and blended in order to keep the price to a minimum, and which therefore cannot afford to have much character. But, if you first find out about olive oil and then try different qualities and pressings with their strong individual flavours, you will be in a much better position to judge what the true olive oil taste is like, and which particular oil would be best suited to your purpose. Whether it is oils or cheeses, this book will encourage you to learn to hunt for and try individual products sold in specialist shops or markets, and to recognize the quality of foods not manufactured for mass appeal, but produced individually by people who are passionate about maintaining their high standards, and whose products have a unique character of their own.

As a matter of fact, all good food starts with the shopping – certainly living out of a freezer is convenient, but it does away with a good deal of enjoyment. The seasons and their differences are part of the experience of life. If you eat frozen green peas throughout the winter, where is the pleasure when the first young peas appear in the spring?

Obviously it is madness not to freeze or preserve food when it is in abundance, and would go to waste otherwise, but does it make sense to ship or fly food many thousands of miles so that we can eat it all the year through? And surely shopping for fresh food in the market is a much more inspiring and entertaining activity than burrowing in the freezer for anonymous-looking frosty packages.

The recipes we have chosen for this book will provide a basis for everyday cooking. With these recipes, which for the most part are very simple, you can cook throughout the year. There are flights of culinary fantasy – Galantine of Duck for example, and Brisket of Beef with Soy, Sake and Oysters – but we have, in the main, tried to give recipes at a level that one can live with. Nowadays, with life getting more and more complicated, it is good to be both quick and simple whenever possible – simple surroundings and simple food, with the occasional elaborate dish for days when you want to glory in the whole process.

Simplicity does not mean dullness. There are countless enjoyable tastes, flavours and experiences available to people who take the trouble to find and try them. This book is intended to help you to do so.

CAROLINE CONRAN • TERENCE CONRAN • SIMON HOPKINSON

1

The purchase and preparation of food

Fish

fish recipes 261–75
freshwater fish 21–5
preparing fish 26–8
preserved fish 29–32
saltwater fish 11–20

Sabayon Sauce for Fish 256

Fish is a food of tremendous character and charm. To a cook with true feeling for the raw materials, there is great satisfaction to be found in the beauty of form, the shimmering colours of scale and skin, and the distinctive flavours and textures of fish of all kinds.

It pays to look beyond the inevitable cod, haddock and sole – although these are no less good for their predictability. But the seas, rivers and lakes are filled with an extravagant variety of fish, each with its own character. It is comparatively easy to obtain a thick slice of hake, a fresh mackerel or eel, but more of a triumph to find a beautiful sea bass, a bony John Dory or a fresh tuna steak. Cooking becomes more of a pleasure if one can make an occasional experiment or discovery, and among fish there are endless discoveries to be made.

Choosing fish

There is no excuse for bad fish being offered for sale any more, now that refrigerated equipment makes it easy to transport fish for long distances in a freshly caught state. What we are more likely to see in fish shops these days are fresh fish that have been in the shops too long, or fish that have been in and out of the freezer several times, thawed out and sold as 'fresh'. Unfortunately, the tell-tale signs of a thawed-out fish are less easy to detect than those of a stale fish. If you are an expert, the best fish to buy are those you see in a crate, packed in ice and obviously straight from the quayside or wholesale market. These will have been chilled – not blast-frozen – immediately after they have been caught.

However, with frequent visits to the fishmonger it soon becomes easy to recognize the differences between good fresh fish that have simply been chilled, stale fish, and thawed-out frozen fish. Don't be afraid to sniff the fish if you are suspicious, or to ask pertinent questions. Here are the signs to look for – remembering that the fish is likely to be only marginally on the stale side rather than offensively bad.

Fresh fish A really fresh fish looks almost alive and ready to swim away. It gleams, and it slides and slithers springily through your hands as though it would like to escape. Its colour is bright; its flesh is firm and rigid yet elastic to the touch; and the skin shines with a viscous slime that is clear and evenly distributed.
Eyes Bright, bulging eyes with black pupils are a clear indication of freshness. The eyes of stale fish have greyish pupils with red rims, and are dull and sunken.
Gills These should be clean and bright red. Dirty, dark or slimy gills are a sure sign of a bad fish.
Smell Fresh fish smell fresh and pleasant, while, quite obviously, the more offensive the odour, the staler the fish will be.

Frozen fish Commercially frozen fish, usually in fillets, are sold from freezers in shops and supermarkets. But there are other fish that have been frozen and thawed out, and although supermarkets will generally label such fish, these are sometimes sold with no sign to indicate the previously frozen state. This is an unfortunate deception. Genuinely fresh fish must be eaten as soon as possible after they are caught or bought, but these thawed-out fish are usually imported and have travelled some distance. As long as you are aware of their condition, they need not be shunned – often they are the only chance you will have of tasting unusual fish such as tilapia, from far away. To detect a badly thawed-out fish, look for a sad appearance and dull, flabby skin that has lost its natural slime and shininess. If a fish has suffered badly from freezing and thawing it will be unpleasantly watery and woolly.

Fresh fish have bright, bulging eyes and skin that shines with a clear, natural slime (RIGHT). *A fish with dull, discoloured, sunken eyes and lifeless skin is well past its best* (FAR RIGHT).

Storing fish

There is only one essential piece of advice on the storing of fresh fish – don't. If you must keep it overnight, put it, well wrapped in several layers of newspaper, in the coldest part of the refrigerator (but not in the ice-making compartment). Fresh mackerel, herrings and sardines should be eaten the day they are purchased; if this is not possible, put them in the freezer overnight.

Freezing fish Most domestic deep-freezers simply do not act fast enough to prevent large ice crystals forming in the flesh of a fish. The jagged crystals destroy the delicate tissues, resulting in the loss of texture, juices and flavour. So if you want a freezer-load of fish as a standby, you would be well advised to buy commercially frozen fish, which should keep in a domestic freezer for 2 to 3 months.

There is a way to preserve a degree of texture and flavour using a domestic deep-freeze, and this is called glazing. First, clean and gut the fish in the normal way, then place it, unwrapped, in a freezer set to fast freeze. When the fish is reasonably solid, dip it into cold fresh water. A thin film of ice should instantly form. Return the fish to the freezer immediately and, freeze until the ice has set solid. Repeat the process two or three times until the fish is completely encased in a good coating of ice. Then store the fish in a freezer bag in the usual way.

Fish that best withstand the freezing process are those with fine-grained flesh, such as the sole and its flat relations. Salmon, and other fish with flesh that falls into flakes, can be frozen but are decidedly nicer fresh; the flesh becomes a little soft with the freezing and thawing process. The shorter the time any fish remains frozen, the better it will be.

Frozen fish should be defrosted before cooking. If cooked from frozen, the outside may be overcooked before the inside has had time to thaw out.

SALTWATER FISH

Fish from the sea can be roughly divided into those that have white flesh and those that are oily. Within these broad categories exist several natural culinary groups, such as the flat fish, the cod and its relatives, the sea basses and breams, and the oily salmon, mackerel and herring. The great ocean fish have a category of their own, and there is a section for the multitude of fish that do not fall easily into categories.

French names, plus Italian and Spanish in some cases, have been given in case you wish to try an unknown fish from a restaurant menu, before deciding whether to add it to your repertoire.

Flat fish

All flat fish are fine fleshed, white, delicate and lean, and two members of this group – turbot and Dover sole – rank in the top echelon of all sea fish.

Dover sole (*sole, sogliola, lenguado*) The true Dover, or Channel, sole is perhaps the cook's perfect fish, a fact reflected by its prominence on restaurant menus in England and Europe. The flesh is firm, white and delicate and keeps well (in fact, sole tastes better if it is 24 hours old). It lends itself to almost any cooking method, and is excellent with a multitude of sauces, but is at its finest when simply cooked on the bone and served with butter, parsley and lemon. Only poor-quality fish need dressing up in other ways. If you order filleted Dover sole from the fishmonger, remember to take the head and bones home with you – they are the basis of an excellent fish stock.

Buying guide: available fresh all year round in Europe. There is no true sole in American waters – although a number of flounder-like fish are labelled sole – but imported Dover sole is available in larger East Coast cities. Buy whole if serving plainly grilled or fried, or in fillets if serving in a sauce (it is hard to deal with bones in a fish covered with sauce). Each fish provides four good fillets. The price of Dover sole is high; however, a 200–225 g/7–8 oz sole is enough for one person, although vegetables will be needed if it is to be served plain.
Best cooking method: grilled, fried or *à la meunière*, or filleted and poached in sauce.

Flounder (*flet, passera pianuzza, platija*) The European flounder, or fluke, is a fish of poor reputation. It has a dark brown, distinctly rough skin and a pale belly, and

à la meunière 422
filleting and skinning flat fish 26
trimming flat fish 26

Fish Fumet 246
Fried Sole with Lemon and Parsley 261

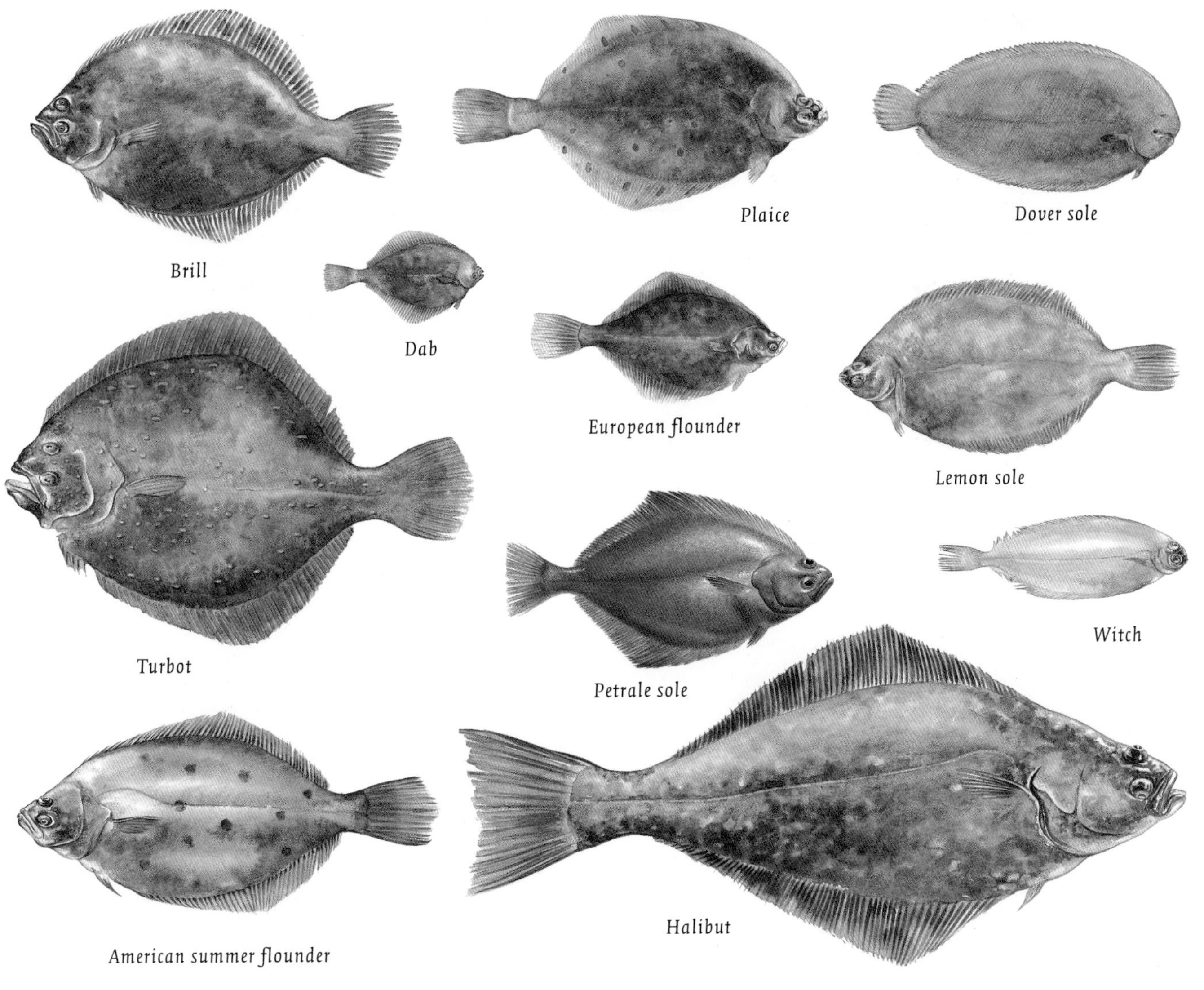
Brill
Plaice
Dover sole
Dab
European flounder
Lemon sole
Turbot
Petrale sole
Witch
American summer flounder
Halibut

burbot 25
coating with egg and crumbs 423
dried cod, stockfish 31
smoked cod's roe 30
smoked halibut 29

Baked Halibut 263
Fish Cakes 265
Fried Plaice 264
Halibut Salad with Capers 368
Hollandaise Sauce 255
Hot and Sour Shellfish Broth 253
New England Fish Chowder 252
Normandy Fish Stew 263
Salt Cod with Potatoes 274
Sauce Tartare 259
Seviche 263
Steamed Cod with Ginger and Spring Onion 264
Turbot Poached in Cider 261

little of the other flat fishes' delicacy of flavour. In North America, however, the flounder family includes the excellent summer flounder (also known as fluke), the winter flounder, the grey and lemon sole, and the fine-textured petrale sole. These are all good eating when freshly caught, and are often used in recipes that call for Dover sole or turbot since they respond to the same cooking methods.
Buying guide: winter months for European flounder; year-round for American, except for fresh summer flounder. Sold whole and in fillets.
Best cooking method: a good-quality thick flounder can be poached like turbot; a thin one should be fried gently in butter or cooked like sole.

Turbot (*turbot, rombo, rodaballo*) Turbot is one of the finest of sea foods. Its flesh is the firmest and most delicate in flavour of all the white fish, and this has to be paid for dearly these days. Despite this, any opportunity to buy it should not be missed. Recognize turbot by its knobbly brown skin. A whole fully grown specimen can weight up to 12 kg/28 lb and makes a handsome centrepiece on the fishmonger's slab, usually white belly uppermost. In the heyday of the turbot, in the nineteenth century, a huge fish could be poached whole in a *turbotière* designed for the purpose. These days, most of us can only manage to cook chicken turbot (a young turbot weighing 900 g–2.5 kg/2–6 lb) in this way, substituting a large pan for the turbot kettle. If you can't manage a whole turbot, buy fillets or steaks, but remember that cooking time is shorter.
Buying guide: available all year, sold whole, in fillets and in steaks. The flesh should be creamy white; a bluish tinge means that it is stale. Imported turbot can be found in large American cities.
Best cooking methods: turbot is so excellent that it suits any cooking method, but is best simply poached or grilled and served with parsley sauce, lobster sauce or hollandaise. It is also very good as a salad.

Halibut (*flétan, halibut, flétan*) A giant among flat fish, the halibut can grow up to 2 m/6 ft long and is not, in fact, particularly flat. It is a medium to darkish brown on top and pearly white underneath. It has almost as good a flavour as turbot, although it is softer and doesn't hold its succulence so well. It is, however, cheaper than turbot.
Buying guide: available all year. Best when small: a young halibut, called chicken halibut, weighing less than 1.5 kg/3 lb is a very good-looking lunch or dinner for 4–6 people, depending on how it is served. Larger halibut are sold in steaks, cutlets and fillets. Avoid frozen halibut, which is dull and dry.
Best cooking methods: poach or bake, and serve with a good sauce – lobster, egg or parsley or hollandaise. Also good when eaten very fresh, as in a seviche.

Lemon sole (*limande-sole, sogliola limanda, mendo limón*) A delicious-sounding fish, lemon and sole being such a good combination of tastes, lemon sole in fact neither tastes of lemon nor is it a sole (it belongs to the dab and plaice family and corresponds to the American yellowtail flounder). A pleasant-looking fish, it is considered to be slightly superior to plaice. It has a fresh salt-and-iodine taste and benefits greatly from total freshness. Soft-textured but pleasant, it is best simply cooked with few additional ingredients.
Buying guide: available all year, sold whole or in fillets. Frozen fillets tend to be somewhat woolly.
Best cooking methods: use simple dab or Dover sole recipes. It is good filleted, egg-and-crumbed and fried.

Plaice (*plie* or *carrelet, passera di mare* or *pianuzza, platija*) Dark brown with russet spots on its upper side and white on its underside, plaice is a mainstay of every British fish and chip shop, its mild, soft flesh heavily encased in batter and deep-fried. It is particularly good when quite fresh. It is also good egg-and-crumbed and fried, or gently poached in milk, when it is an ideal fish for children and invalids. American plaice can be prepared in the same ways.
Buying guide: available all year, sold whole or in fillets.
Best cooking methods: deep fry in batter or egg and breadcrumbs and serve with tomato ketchup or tartare sauce; or poach and cover with a cheese or parsley sauce.

Dab (*limande, limanda, lenguado*) Looking like a small plaice with very rough skin, the European dab is not the most exciting of fish although its flesh is soft, fragile and easily digested. It can grow up to 30 cm/12 in long, but is usually smaller. The American sand dab, or rust dab, is prepared in the same ways.
Buying guide: best in autumn and winter, sold whole or in fillets.
Best cooking methods: grill whole, or fillet, egg-and-crumb and fry.

Brill (*barbue, rombo liscio, rémol*) A very good European fish akin to turbot, the handsome brill has a mixed tweed colouring and is smaller than its cousin. Its flesh is a little softer and not so gelatinous, but it is sweet and delicate to eat.
Buying guide: available all year, sold whole or in fillets.
Best cooking methods: recipes for turbot, halibut and sole suit brill, and it is excellent in a matelote.

Megrim (*cardine, rombo giallo, gallo*) A small, yellowish-grey, rather transparent fish, megrim is also known as whiff, sail-fluke, West Coast sole, white sole and lantern flounder. Not a particularly good fish, it has the advantage of being cheap, and is useful for fish soup.
Buying guide: available autumn and winter, sold whole or in fillets.
Best cooking methods: as for lemon sole or plaice, but probably best filleted and fried with the added texture of crisp breadcrumbs to help it along.

Witch (*plie grise, passera cinoglossa, mendo*) Also known as Torbay sole, witch sole, witch flounder or pole flounder, this long, narrow, cold-water fish is shaped rather like a sole and has sandy-brown colouring. Cook it in exactly the same ways as sole, but as it is a duller-tasting fish, use a little more seasoning, herbs and spices.

The cod family

This large family of white-fleshed fish, including such cornerstones of the fishing industry as cod, haddock and whiting, keep their succulence best when lightly poached, fried in batter or bathed in a good, light home-made sauce.

Cod (*cabillaud, merluzzo, bacalao*) The cod has a skin of greenish bronze dappled with yellow. Once taken for granted as the fisherman's bread and butter, overfishing in northern European and

American waters is now causing it to become more scarce.

Too often cod has been overcooked until dry and grey, and hidden under a blanket of sauce. When treated with care, cod proves to be very fine, but it must be very fresh to be first class. The flesh is succulent and comes in large flakes – a really fresh fish will produce a cheese-like curd between the flakes, rather like salmon. The cod has an excellent roe – used in taramasalata – and its liver produces a disagreeable but effective vitamin supplement. An adult cod can weigh up to 36 kg/80 lb; small cod, also called scrod or codling, just as good, are about 700–1 kg/1½–2½ lb.
Buying guide: available all year, but best in winter. Fresh cod is sold mainly as steaks and fillets. If you are able to choose a cut, pick the middle, which combines the tenderness of the tail with the flavour of the shoulder. Never buy fillets or steaks with yellow or pinkish patches on the flesh. Frozen cod, although reliable, lacks the flavour of really fresh cod, but is certainly a better buy than cod of dubious quality.
Best cooking methods: the flesh falls naturally into large, firm flakes and keeps its texture well. It is splendid poached, and excellent in fish pies, croquettes, salads and fish cakes. Also bake, grill, fry or deep fry with good home-made sauces such as tomato salsa or tartare sauce. In Britain poached cod is traditionally served with slices of lemon and horseradish relish, but nowadays with a whole poached cod you are more likely to be offered aïoli, the mayonnaise heavily flavoured with garlic (cod is robust enough to take strong Mediterranean flavours). In order to whiten and tenderize the flesh, it is a good idea to rub it with a cut lemon half an hour or so before cooking.

Haddock (*églefin* or *aiglefin, eglefino, eglefino*) Fresh haddock is sometimes considered to be preferable to cod simply because it is scarcer and more expensive to buy, but it is really no better a fish. It has a fresh marine flavour and a light, firm texture, and is blessed with fairly good keeping qualities. It is similar in appearance to cod, but has a greyer skin, larger eyes and a marked black lateral line. Haddock is also popular smoked.
Buying guide: available all year, best in winter and early spring. Fresh haddock is usually sold in fillets.
Best cooking methods: deep-fried and served with chips, in fish pie (especially good mixed half and half with smoked haddock), or using any method that is suitable for cod.

Hake (*merlu, nasello* or *merluzzo, merluza*) An elongated, deep-water member of the cod family, hake appears on some French menus as white salmon (*saumon blanc*), and is familiar all over the United States under a variety of names, including ling and white or red hake. Silver hake, from America's East Coast, is a particularly fine fish which also goes under the name of whiting (not to be confused with the European whiting, a lesser fish). Hake is most popular in Spain, fried in beaten egg or in an escabeche – a cold hors d'oeuvre of fried fish in a herby marinade – but it is sadly becoming an increasingly rare sight in the fish shops of northern Europe. No opportunity should be missed to buy it, though it does tend to be expensive. It has tender, soft, pinkish flesh, somewhat lighter than that of cod, with a delicate flavour, and the advantage of possessing few bones, which are fairly easy to remove.
Buying guide: fresh hake must be very fresh and is sold whole, in fillets and in steaks. It is also sold frozen, but beware of imported frozen South American hake, which is a very inferior relation and is really only fit for commercial processing.
Best cooking methods: deep-fried in batter, pan fried, baked with pine nuts, breadcrumbs and cheese, or poached and served on a bed of spinach or sorrel mixed with fresh cream.

Whiting (*merlan, merlano, merlán*) This is a common but unexciting European fish not found in American waters (in the United States whiting is another name for silver hake). It is grey and white with a pointed head and backward-slanting teeth. A really fresh whiting is quite good, light and easily digestible, but a tired and travelled specimen will be dry, dull and tasteless.

Arbroath smokie 30
finnan haddie, smoked haddock 29

Aïoli 259
Creamed Finnan Haddie 275
Fish Chowder 252
Fish Pie 266
Omelette Arnold Bennett 325
Saffron Bouillabaisse with Rouille 253
Salmon Pâté 317
Salsa Cruda 258
Sauce Tartare 259
Taramasalata 275

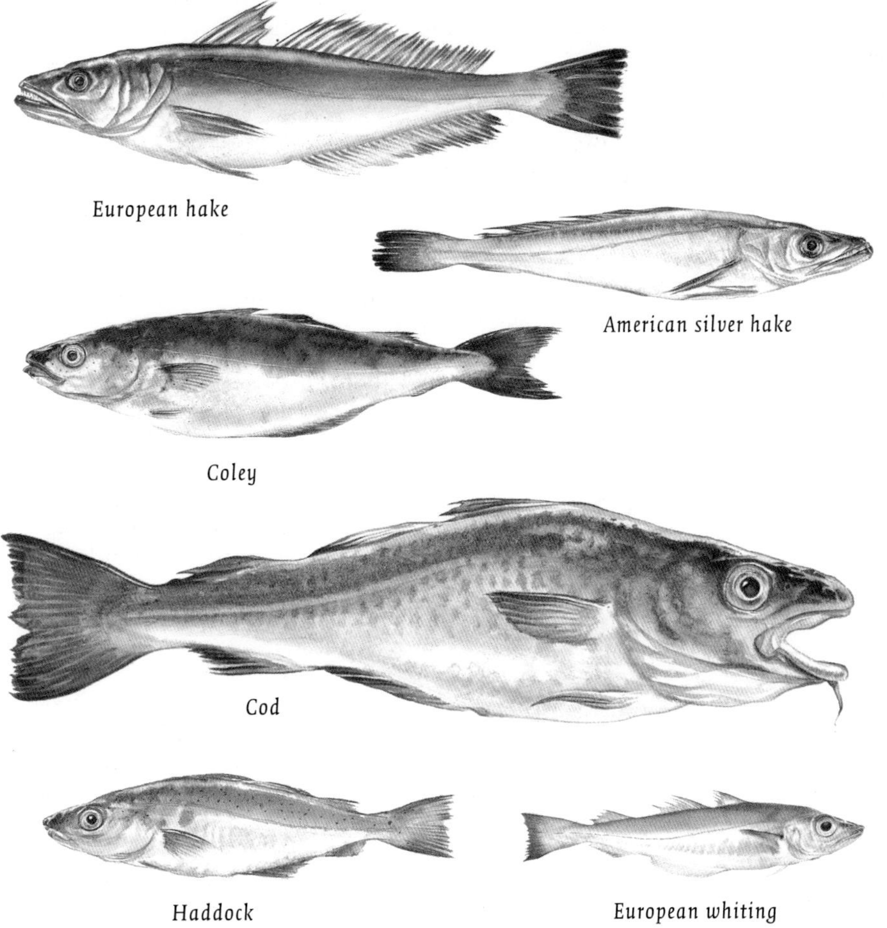
European hake
American silver hake
Coley
Cod
Haddock
European whiting

coating with egg and crumbs 423
freshwater bass 25
freshwater bream 25
julienne 422
scaling round fish 26

Beurre Blanc 256
Fish Mousselines 274
Fish Pie 266
Hollandaise Sauce 255
Salsa Cruda 258
Salsa Verde 258
Sea Bass Pipérade 264
Seviche 263

Buying guide: available all year but best in winter. Sold whole, usually 225–450 g/ ½–1 lb, or in fillets.
Best cooking methods: flake and use in fish cakes; purée for mousses and mousselines; poach and serve with a julienne of vegetables; fry fillets covered with egg and crumbs to improve the texture and serve with fresh tomato sauce.

Coley (*lieu noir, merluzo nero, abadejo*) Regarded as cat food by the uninformed, coley, also called saithe and coalfish, is a useful fish whose worst feature is its colouring and the best its price. The greyish flesh whitens during cooking; more so if rubbed with lemon juice beforehand. Coley is less firm and succulent than cod, but is fine for fish cakes and fish pies. Smoked and served with toast it makes a passable substitute for smoked salmon pâté. In the United States, it is a firm-textured, strong-flavoured fish and a mainstay of the ocean-fresh and deep-sea fillet markets.
Buying guide: available all year, sold in fillets or steaks.
Best cooking methods: in well-seasoned soups, pies and fish cakes.

Pollack (*lieu jaune, merlano nero, abadejo*) This fish, also called lythe, is somewhat short on flavour and needs a little help in the form of a good sauce, such as hollandaise, or interesting seasoning.
Buying guide: available all year, best in autumn and winter. Sold whole, in fillets or steaks.
Best cooking methods: as for cod, but best in pies, fish cakes and fish soups.

Some less sought-after members of the cod family:
Ling (*lingue, molva occhiona, maruca*), when dried, is known as lutfisk and is a traditional Christmas dish in Sweden, boiled and eaten with masses of butter. The flesh of the fresh fish is well flavoured and can be used in fish pies and soups of all kinds.
Cusk or torsk (*brosme* or *loquette*) is used in pies and soups, and sometimes steamed and eaten with a cream sauce.
Pouting should be eaten very fresh indeed as its main claim to fame is that it goes off very quickly – it is sometimes known as 'stinkalive'. Cook like whiting.

Bass, bream and grouper

Firm and white fleshed, these fish all go well with strong Mediterranean flavours – saffron, fennel, olive oil, tomatoes, white wine and garlic. They are delicious when grilled whole over charcoal in the open air, or oven-baked with olive oil and herbs.

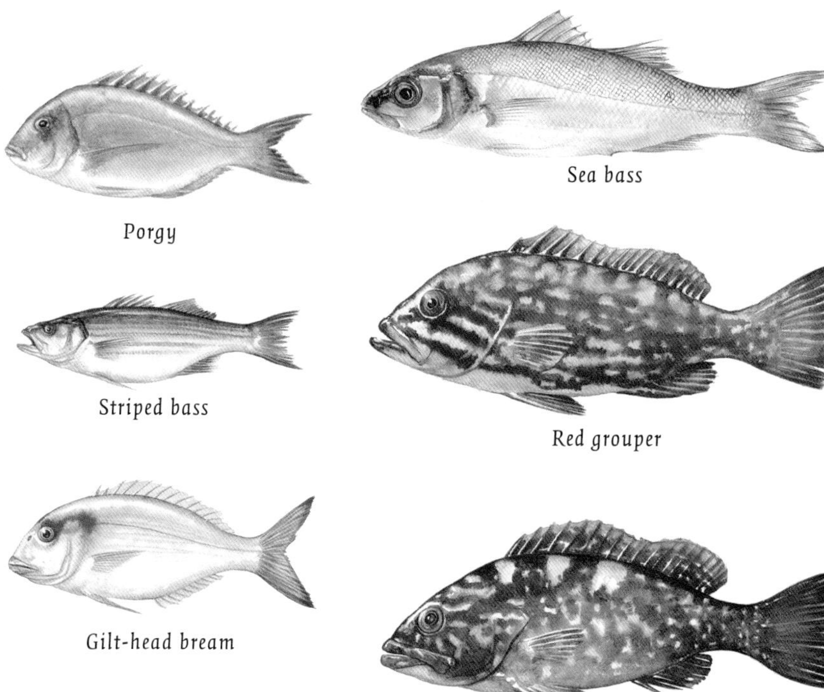

Porgy

Sea bass

Striped bass

Red grouper

Gilt-head bream

Mediterranean grouper

Bass (*bar* or *loup de mer, spigola, lubina*) Sea bass, whether one of the North American varieties – striped bass, black sea bass – or the beautiful silver bass of the Mediterranean and warmer northern European waters, is the ideal fish for a splendid meal at home. It is just the right size for a small family and has delicately flavoured milky flesh.
Buying guide: available all year round, whole and as steaks and fillets.
Best cooking methods: bass up to 900 g/2 lb can be grilled whole – in France they are cooked on charcoal with herbs and a handful of fennel twigs. Bake larger fish, and bake or poach steaks and fillets. Bass is also excellent in salads or a seviche, or steamed on a bed of seaweed. Serve with mayonnaise or beurre blanc, or with salsa verde or raw tomato salsa.

Bream Some species of sea bream are distinctly better than others: the finest is the Mediterranean gilt-head (*daurade, orata, dorada*), with its gold spot on each cheek and its compact body. The red bream (*dorade commune, occhialone, besugo*) is the bream found in northern European waters, a large fish usually sold in fillets and recognizable by its rosy-grey skin. Porgies and scups, the American East Coast bream, are quite small; one species, called red porgy in the US and sea bream in the UK (*pagre* in France, *pagro* in Italy and *pargo* in Spain), is also found in the Mediterranean. All bream have rather coarse but juicy flesh and a pleasant taste that suits fairly strong accompanying flavours. They must be scaled – ask your fishmonger to do this for you, or cook the fish with its scales intact and carefully remove them with the skin just before serving.
Buying guide: available all year but best in autumn. Sold whole or in fillets.
Best cooking methods: season well and grill or bake in foil, or roll in cornmeal or flour and fry briskly in oil. Make two or three slashes on each side with a sharp knife if cooking bream whole, so that the heat can quickly penetrate the thicker parts, thus ensuring that the whole fish cooks evenly.

Grouper (*mérou, cernia, mero*) A delicacy in Mediterranean countries, grouper are not widely available in northern Europe, which is a pity because their flesh is particularly firm and well flavoured.

North America enjoys a number of varieties – red grouper are found from Virginia down to Florida, and the Gulf of Mexico has black grouper and the Nassau. Yellowmouth is also common along the East Coast.
Buying guide: sold whole, weighing up to 6 kg/15 lb, and in steaks and fillets.
Best cooking methods: as for sea bass.

Oily fish and small fry

Absolute freshness is essential – all oily fish are inedible when stale. The traditional accompaniments of mustard for herring and green gooseberry for mackerel counteract their natural oiliness.

Mackerel (*maquereau, sgombro, caballa*) The mackerel is easy to recognize – the taut, steel-blue skin, mottled on the back with blues and greens and a pattern of blackish bands, is so smooth that it looks almost enamelled. The belly is pearly white, the inside of the mouth black. If the natural markings have lost their brilliance and the fish does not shine, do not buy it. The pink-tinted flesh is firm, well flavoured, oily, and rich in vitamins.
Buying guide: at their best in late spring and early summer, when they are in roe. Usually sold whole, weighing up to about 450 g/1 lb, a mackerel will serve one person as a main course or two as a starter.
Best cooking methods: grill, cook over charcoal, or even better a wood or peat fire, or poach in white wine; or roll fillets in oatmeal and fry them like herring. Mackerel are good stuffed; soft roe can be mixed with the stuffing, but a hard roe is better baked under the fish. Sauces for mackerel, apart from gooseberry, include mustard and horseradish.

Horse mackerel, scad (*saurel* or *chinchard, suro, jurel* or *chicarro*) These somewhat off-putting names, and others such as jack mackerel and round robin, belong to a group of fish regarded as poor man's mackerel – rather unfairly to the mackerel, since although horse mackerel have much in common with true mackerel they are not related. They lack the fine markings of the true mackerel and are not considered a high-quality fish, being rather coarse and bony.
Buying guide: available all year. Sold whole – a large one will feed two people, and a small one, one person.
Best cooking methods: treat as mackerel, although they will not respond as well, or braise.

Bluefish (*tassergal, pesce serra, anjova*) Familiar along America's East Coast in summer and in the warm waters around Bermuda, as well as being found in the Mediterranean, the bluefish can be identified by the blue-green sheen along its back. The delicate flesh is rather soft and goes best with sharp accompanying flavours – lemon juice, capers or green gooseberries.
Buying guide: most seasonable in spring, summer and autumn. Usually sold whole (900 g–1.5 kg/2–3 lb is a manageable size, but it can be up to 4.5 kg/10 lb).
Best cooking methods: brush with melted butter and grill (in Turkey, it is grilled on charcoal), or bake with a little white wine and butter, or poach whole and serve with melted butter.

Herring (*hareng, aringa, arenque*) Once plentiful, popular and cheap, herrings are rapidly becoming less available because of overfishing. They are a tasty fish and rich in protein, fat, iodine and vitamins A and D. They need cleaning and may need boning before cooking (this is a simple job), and produce a pervasive smell while cooking.
Buying guide: available all year but best from spring to autumn. Choose herrings that are large, firm and slippery. They are usually sold whole.
Best cooking methods: bone, open out flat, pat with seasoned oatmeal and fry in a little lard or butter; or score with a

Bismarck herring 31
bloater 29
boning round fish 28
buckling 30
cleaning round fish 27
filleting round fish 27
kipper 29
Maatjes herring 31
pickled herring 31
rollmop 31
salt herring 31
smoked mackerel 30
soused herring 31

Grilled Mackerel with Green Paste 266
Herrings in Oatmeal 267
Soused Herrings 267
Spiced Marinated Mackerel 266

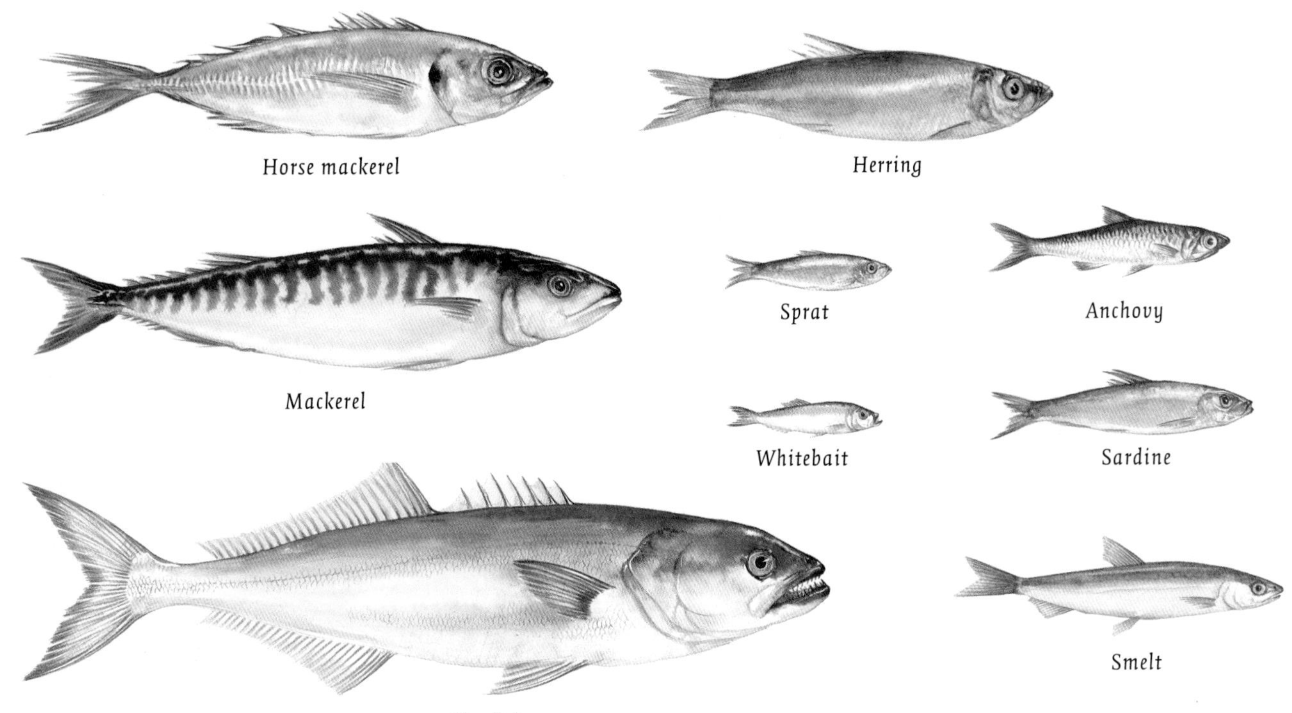

anchovy essence 206
anchovy paste 206
canned sardine 32
canned sprat 32
canned tuna 32
fish sauce 206
Harvey sauce 206
oatmeal 116
salted anchovy 31
smoked sprat 30

Fried Whitebait 267
Garlic and Herb Butter 257
Grilled Tuna with Anchovy 267
Salsa Cruda 258
Salsa Verde 258
Tuna in a Packet with Red Sauce 268

sharp knife, brush with fat and then grill. Never discard the roe of herrings, which is very good to eat.

Smelt (*éperlan*), **argentine** (*argentine, sperlano, pez plata*) **and atherine, sand-smelt** (*prêtre, latterino, pejerrey*) Although unrelated, these bright, silvery, semi-transparent little fish are very similar in size, appearance and taste. About 17 cm/7 in long, they spawn in fresh water. The smelt is superior: it has a delicious scent when very fresh – some say of cucumber, others of violets – but this disappears very rapidly, so if they seem scentless when you buy them it doesn't mean that they are stale. They all need delicate handling – leave the head and tail on and clean them through the gills.
Buying guide: best in winter and spring, but there are good and bad years, so buy smelt when you see them – it may be a long time before you do so again.
Best cooking methods: in France they are strung on a skewer through their heads, dipped in milk and flour, and deep-fried.

Sardine (*sardine, sardina, sardina*) Fresh sardines are a delight, but they must be fresh. They travel badly so are usually only found close to where they are caught, such as the Mediterranean coasts of France and North Africa (the true Mediterranean sardine is named after the island of Sardinia). When you do find them in shops or markets, they are simplicity itself to prepare. Cut the head almost through from the backbone and pull: as the head comes off the gut will come with it.
Buying guide: at their best in spring. Fresh sardines are sold whole; sizes vary so judge by eye how many you need per person. Also sold frozen – the finest are from Portugal.
Best cooking methods: fry in olive oil, or coat lightly with salt and olive oil and grill, preferably over charcoal. Eat them with halved lemons, chilled rough wine and fresh bread.

Anchovy (*anchois, acciuga, boquerón*) Seeing fresh anchovies for the first time, with their slim bodies and sparkling silvery greenish-blue skin, comes as something of a surprise when one's only previous acquaintance with this useful fish has been as canned fillets. Fresh, they can be distinguished from the sardine by their slimmer body and protruding upper jaw. To enjoy their delicate flavour at its best they should be straight from the sea, which ideally means the Mediterranean, although varieties appear in northern European and North American waters.
Buying guide: sold whole.
Best cooking methods: fry or grill as sardines. Also delicious marinated in olive oil and lemon juice with garlic, or boned and fried with garlic and parsley.

Sprat (*sprat, papalina, espadín*) These are worth some attention if only for their superabundance in European waters, which means that they are very cheap. Tiny silvery fish, looking rather like small herrings, but shorter and stouter.
Buying guide: a winter fish, said to be best when the weather is frosty.
Best cooking methods: sprats are very oily so are best when grilled; or they can be dusted with flour or oatmeal and dry-fried in a pan sprinkled with salt.

Whitebait (*blanchaille, bianchetti, chanqutes*) The small fry or young of herrings and sprats, whitebait are the most delicious little fish. Bright, silvery and slender, they are scarcely more than 4–5 cm/just under 2 in long, and have for a long time been one of the summer treats of the British. Whitebait are eaten whole so there is no need to clean them – simply rinse them gently.
Buying guide: traditionally February to August. Allow about 115 g/4 oz per person.
Best cooking method: the best and only way to cook whitebait is to dip them in milk, shake in a bag of flour and then deep fry them. They should be so crisp that they rustle as they are put on the plates. Serve with lemon and fresh bread and butter.

The great fish

The great ocean fish make firm, meaty eating. Their flesh is inclined to be dry, so marinate them in olive oil and lemon juice or white wine with some herbs before cooking.

Tuna and bonito Found in all the warmer waters of the world, the powerful, beautifully shaped tuna family is related to the mackerel, and includes the bluefin (*thon rouge, tonno, atún*), the albacore (*germon, alalonga, albacora*), the skipjack (*bonite à ventre rayé, tonnetto listato* or *listado*) and the yellowfin. Bonito (*bonite à dos rayé, palamita, bonito*) is another close relative. When you see fresh tuna, don't be put off by its reddish colour – this will improve during the cooking process. It needs plenty of oil and seasoning, and great care must be taken not to overcook it or it will be dry. Bonito can be treated in the same way as either tuna or mackerel.
Buying guide: available all year. Sold in steaks; occasionally very small fish are available whole. Avoid tuna steaks with very dark marks, which are an indication of bruising. Look for an even, deep colour: pale flesh is not fresh.
Best cooking methods: grill, barbecue or bake in slices, basting often with seasoned oil; or slice very thinly into small escalopes, dust with flour and fry gently in butter and oil for 2–3 minutes on each side. Serve with fresh tomato salsa or salsa verde.

Swordfish (*espadon, pesce spada, pez espada*) Familiar in Mediterranean waters and popular in North America as 'the steak of the sea', the swordfish is only a very occasional visitor to northern European waters. It makes delicious eating, but the flesh is close grained and can be dry so it is often marinated in wine, oil and herbs before cooking.
Buying guide: sold fresh in steaks; also sold frozen in countries that import it.
Best cooking methods: grill or barbecue and serve with plain or herb butter or tomato sauce; or seal in butter and then bake in a sauce. Also excellent as kebabs.

Sailfish (*voilier, istioforo, aguja de mar* or *pez a vela*), **spearfish** (*makaire, agugliа imperiale*) **and marlin** (*poisson Epieu, pesce lancio, aguja*) Well known to American sport fishermen, these majestic fish are spectacular fighters and highly prized trophies. But if you don't want to put them on the wall, all three make very good eating.
Buying guide: marlin is commercially fished in Hawaii, but not elsewhere; in other parts of the world these fish are occasionally sold as steaks in ports near the fishing grounds.
Best cooking methods: as for swordfish.

Opah (*poisson lune, lampride* or *pesce re, luna real*) Whatever you call this splendid fish – sunfish or moonfish, mariposa or

kingfish – you should never miss a chance to sample it. But a rare chance it will be, for it lives deep in the Atlantic, Pacific and Indian oceans and is only occasionally caught, by accident rather than design. It is thought it might exist in great numbers, but little is known about its habits, and only solitary opahs have been caught. The skin reflects blue, rose, silver and gold, and the texture of the flesh, may have a markedly different taste – and colour – depending on which part of the fish it comes from.
Buying guide: should you ever see one for sale, ask for steaks or escalopes.
Best cooking methods: bake, fry, grill or poach, but take care not to overcook. Serve with hollandaise.

Shark The shark family includes porbeagle (*taupe, smeriglio, cailón*) and its close relative the mako or mackerel shark, dogfish (*petite roussette, gattuccio, pintarroja*), hammerhead (*requin marteau, pesce martello, pez martillo*) and smooth-hound (*émissole, palombo, musola*), as well as angel shark (*ange de mer, squadro, angelote*) and tope (*milandre, cagnesca* or *galeo, cazón*).

All sharks have very firm flesh, scaleless skin and a cartilaginous skeleton (like skate and rays). Not attractive fish, they tend to have an ammoniac smell which disappears in cooking. The flavour and texture are good.

Shark is usually sold minus head, tail and fins, in steaks. The small dogfish is often called euphemistically huss, flake, rigg and even – quite shamefully – rock salmon. The flesh is white or slightly pink and firm textured, and deserves more attention than it gets.
Buying guide: available all year.
Best cooking methods: cut into pieces, dust with seasoned flour and fry gently; or coat with batter and deep fry; or use an oil-based marinade and grill or barbecue.

Barracuda (*brochet de mer, luccio marino, espetón*) A large game fish with vicious teeth, barracuda can reach 68 kg/150 lb. It is found in warmer Atlantic waters, but is caught mainly on North America's Pacific coast. The meaty, very firm flesh is rich in oil. Small barracuda (like the Pacific or California barracuda, weighing 1.8–3.6 kg/4–8 lb) are the best to eat.
Buying guide: available in summer.
Best cooking methods: small fish can be barbecued or baked whole; or cut them into steaks, marinate and then grill them, preferably over charcoal; or egg-and-crumb fillets and fry them.

coating with egg and crumbs 423
dried shark's fin 31

Hollandaise Sauce 255

Assorted fish

Many fish do not fall naturally into a culinary category except that they are good to eat. For many of them their looks are not their greatest asset, but it is a pity that they should be so often passed by in favour of their better known and more comely cousins.

Monkfish, angler fish (*lotte* or *baudroie, rana pescatrice, rape*) This fish is sometimes muddled with the angel fish, which is also known as monkfish but is a member of the shark family. There would be no confusion if the fishmonger would leave the monkfish intact, but it is usually sold headless. Despite its rather endearing ugliness, this is one of the best fish you can buy. The skin is smooth and easy to remove, as is the translucent membrane beneath, and the flesh is

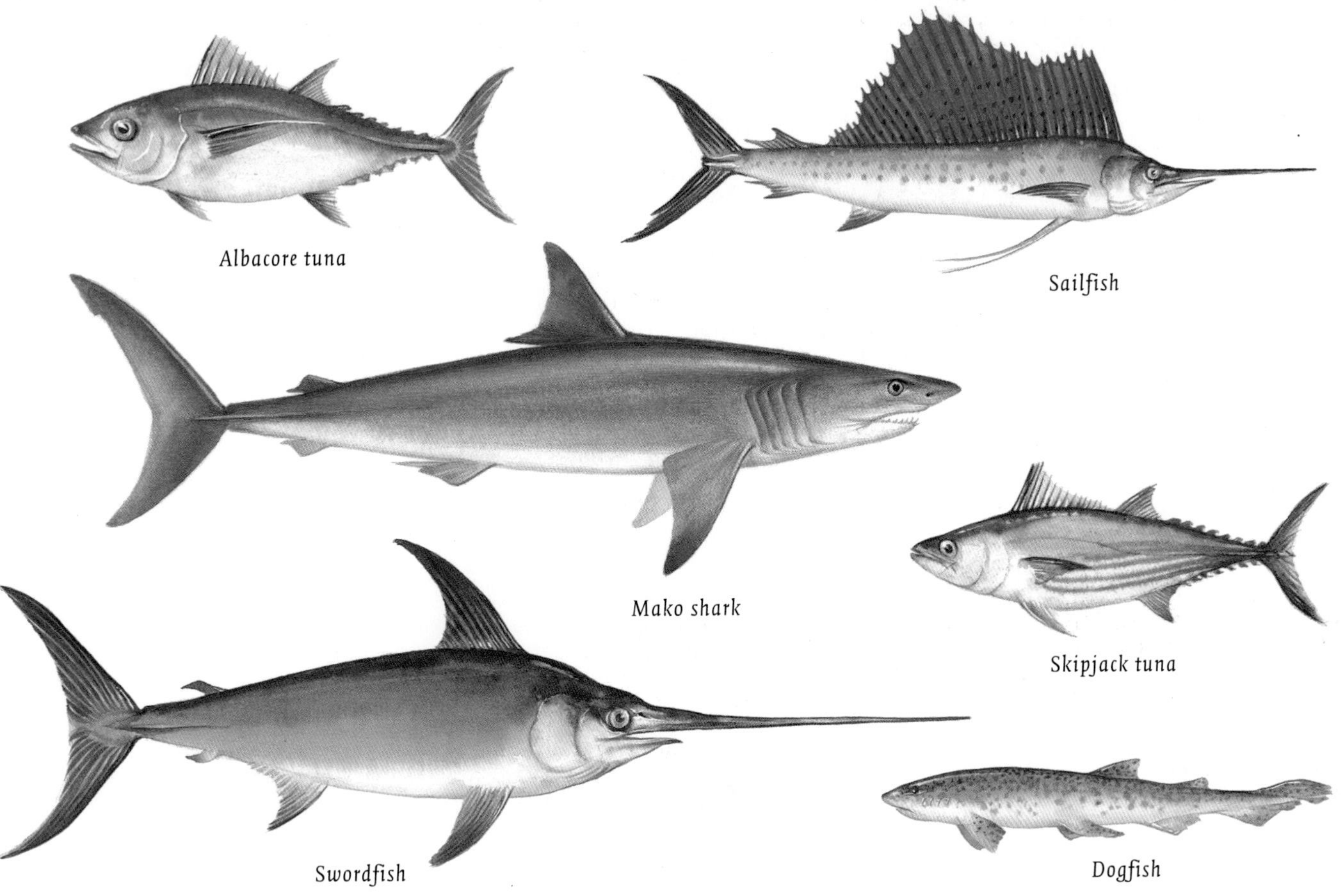
Albacore tuna
Sailfish
Mako shark
Skipjack tuna
Swordfish
Dogfish

scaling round fish 26
shark 17

Normandy Fish Stew 263
Red Mullet en Papillote 270
Saffron Bouillabaisse with Rouille 253
Skate with Black Butter 268

firm, boneless and very white, with the succulence of lobster – its taste is more associated with shellfish than with fish.
Buying guide: available all year. Ask for a good tailpiece – 1.5 kg/3 lb for six people. It can then be sliced or cooked whole.
Best cooking methods: can be treated almost as meat – it is sometimes roasted and called *gigot de mer*. It can also be poached like cod, but allow twice as long for the cooking; or split the tail in half, brush with oil and grill well on both sides. Simplest and best of all are small escalopes marinated in lemon and garlic, dusted with flour and fried in butter.

Skate, ray *(raie, razza, raya)* Only the wings of skate are eaten – they contain no real bones, just strips of gelatinous cartilage from which the flesh comes off in long, succulent shreds. Fresh skate is covered with a clear slime, which reappears when wiped dry, and the flesh should be pearly white, resilient and not flabby to the touch. Large skate are generally kept by the fishmonger for a day or two in chilled conditions because they can be tough when very fresh.
Buying guide: best in autumn and winter. Small wings are sold whole; otherwise choose a thick middle cut. A very faint smell of ammonia is normal and will disappear in cooking.
Best cooking methods: The classic French skate dish, *raie au beurre noir*, serves the fish with browned butter and capers. It can also be grilled, deep-fried or poached. The skin is easy to remove after cooking, if the fishmonger has not done it for you: simply scrape it carefully from the thicker part towards the edge. Because of its gelatinous quality, skate makes a good fish stock or aspic.

Red mullet *(rouget, triglia salmonete, salmonete)* The Mediterranean red mullet (varying in size from 5–8 cm/2–3 in to 18–30 cm/7–12 in) is a superb fish, a shimmering, deep silvery rose, sometimes with faint golden, horizontal stripes along each side. The flavour is quite distinctive, something between prawn and sole. This is the ideal fish to cook with strong Mediterranean flavours – garlic, saffron, rosemary and fennel. Its liver is often left in during cooking and provides an added richness of flavour, giving red mullet its English nickname of sea woodcock.
Buying guide: best in summer. Look for bright colour and transparent, shining eyes. If the fish seem to be bent sideways they have been frozen and have just thawed out. Sold whole (always ask for the liver to be left in). Large fish are less bony than tiny ones.
Best cooking methods: scale before cooking, unless grilling over charcoal. Excellent grilled, baked or *en papillote* and ideal for using in fish terrines, mousses or pâtés.

Grey mullet *(muge* or *mulet, cefalo, pardete* or *cabejudo)* There are several varieties of grey mullet, known variously as striped mullet, thin- or thick-lipped grey mullet, black mullet, jumping mullet and lisa; they are frequently neglected in favour of the more highly prized red mullet, which is no relation.

In North America the term mullet applies to fish of the grey mullet family; fish belonging to the red mullet family which inhabit American waters are known as goatfish. The grey mullet has

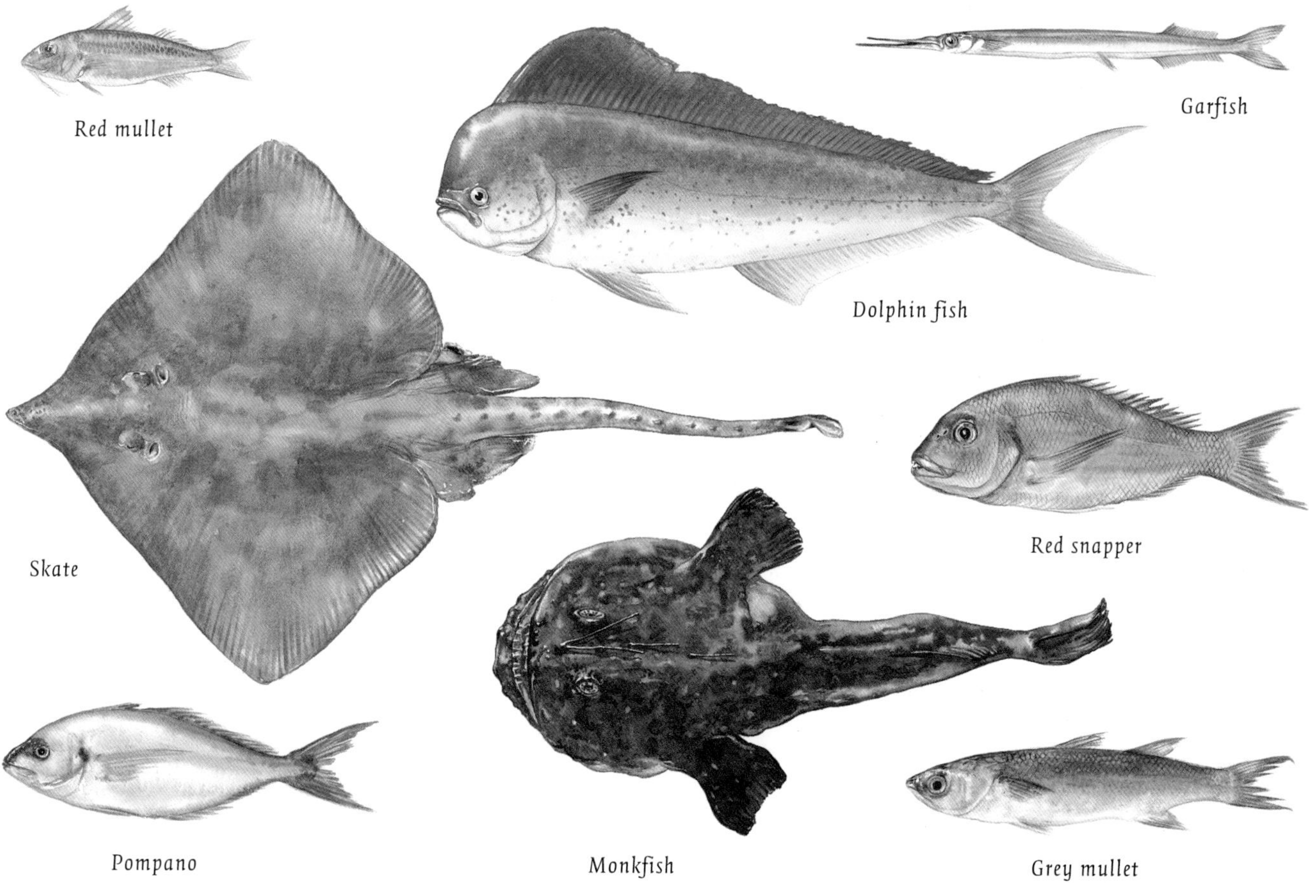

Red mullet

Garfish

Dolphin fish

Skate

Red snapper

Pompano

Monkfish

Grey mullet

large, thick scales and a heavy head with thick, delicate lips. The flesh is coarse and slightly soft, but the flavour is very good, particularly if heightened with fennel or Pernod. The roe is excellent and, used salted, is the proper roe for making taramasalata.
Buying guide: available all year. Sold whole; look for firm fish caught at sea rather than flabby fish caught in estuaries – their flavour will be muddy.
Best cooking methods: slash the sides and grill, preferably over charcoal; or if more than 900 g/2 lb, fill with herbs and garlic, coat with olive oil and bake. Do not cook with water, unless using as an ingredient for a rich fish soup.

Pompano *(palomine, leccia stella, palometa blanca)* One of the finest fish in the sea, with firm, white, meaty flesh, pompano are found fresh in Florida and appear on the menus of expensive restaurants elsewhere – notably in New Orleans, where Antoine's pompano *en papillote* is a speciality. Pompano are now exported to northern Europe from the Mediterranean.
Buying guide: when available, sold whole, approximately 675–900 g/1½–2 lb in weight, or in fillets.
Best cooking methods: brush with melted butter and grill, or poach in white wine. Pompano can also be stuffed and baked. Crabmeat or shrimp sauces make an excellent accompaniment.

Dolphin fish, dorado, mahi mahi *(coriphène* or *dorade tropicale, lampuga, lampuga)* Nothing whatsoever to do with the true dolphin, which is a mammal, the dolphin fish is a Caribbean native. It is also found in the Mediterranean. Easily recognized by its high ridge of fin, it has a strong, excellent flavour.
Buying guide: when available, sold in steaks or fillets. Steaks are better.
Best cooking methods: bake, grill or fry, with lemon and garlic. Serve with fresh tomato salsa.

Red snapper *(vivaneau)* You will need to live close to the southern Atlantic or Gulf coasts of America to enjoy this blushing, large-eyed fish fresh from the sea. These snappers will be weighty fish, pleasantly textured and well flavoured – a 900 g–2 kg/2–5 lb fish, stuffed and baked, makes a delicious meal.
Buying guide: sold whole or in steaks and fillets when fresh; snapper is also available frozen.
Best cooking methods: bake, grill or poach.

Garfish *(orphie, aguglia, aguja)* **or needlefish** *(balaou, costardello, paparda)* The green and silver garfish – no relation to the freshwater species of fish more correctly called gars – is a pleasant fish to eat, although not perhaps of the first order. The flesh is a rather poor greyish-purple in its raw state, but it whitens during cooking. The bones have a rather startling advantage – they are bright copper-green (quite harmless, the colour is caused by a phosphate of iron) and easily picked out on the plate. The saury is similar, with colourless bones.
Buying guide: worth trying whenever you see them. Sold whole.
Best cooking methods: cut the fish into segments, then fry or bake with garlic, or poach and serve with dill or fresh tomato sauce. Highly gelatinous, garfish is also good in fish pie.

Gurnard, gurnet, sea robin *(grondin, capone, arete* or *borracho)* A large family of sweet-tasting fish, despite their armour-plated appearance, the gurnards have several culinary uses and are relatively cheap. The red gurnard – sometimes sold as red mullet – is best.
Buying guide: usually sold whole; ask the fishmonger to do the skinning for you if possible, as they are spiny and tough.
Best cooking methods: excellent in fish soups, gurnards can also be baked with white wine, or egg-and-crumbed, whole or in fillets, fried and served with a Provençal or tomato sauce.

John Dory *(Saint-Pierre, pesce San Pietro, pez de San Pedro)* This grandly ugly fish belies its appearance and is, in fact, one of the most delicious of fish – firm, delicate and excellently flavoured. The dark circles on its sides are said to be the marks of St Peter's fingers, hence its other name, St Peter's fish.
Buying guide: buy whenever you can find it. Remember that almost two-thirds of its weight is taken up by its excessively large bony head and its gut.
Best cooking methods: larger ones can be cooked whole or in succulent, bone-free fillets, as for sole. Small ones are excellent in bouillabaisse.

Pomfret *(fiatole, fieto, pámpano)* This small, coin-shaped fish is found in the Mediterranean, but it does not make good eating. However, the pomfret of the Indo-Pacific is excellent, as is the closely related butterfish of the north-west Atlantic. The off-white flesh is rich and tender with a sweet flavour.
Buying guide: available year round, but best in spring and summer.
Best cooking methods: usually sold whole, pomfret can be baked, grilled or barbecued, fried, poached or steamed. Complement with a piquant sauce.

Red drum The red drum, also known as redfish and channel bass or red sea bass, is part of a diverse family named for the distinctive drumming sounds the fish make – so loud they can be heard on land. Smaller members of the family are called croakers, for the sound they make. The moist, flaky flesh of the red drum is more flavourful than that of its close relative, the black drum. The two fish can easily be distinguished by the black drum's barbels, or small whiskers, along its chin, and the red drum's tail, which has a black spot on either side.

Found off the Atlantic and Gulf coasts of the United States, red drums can be as heavy as 13.5 kg/30 lb or more, but are usually marketed at around 900 g–2.25 kg/2½ lb. Red drum is the fish used for blackened redfish, the Cajun dish that became popular in the US ten years ago or so; the result was overfishing so that red drum became a rarity. Now, however, it is being farmed in Texas, among other places.
Buying guide: available year-round, whole or in fillets.
Best cooking methods: whole fish can be baked, grilled, poached or braised; fillets can be grilled, poached and fried. Red drum is also good when used in fish stews and soups.

Weakfish Another member of the drum/croaker family, the weakfish is found along the Atlantic and Gulf coasts of the US. The weakfish is usually silvery grey in colour but may be multicoloured, spotted, or striped. The delicious flesh is delicate in texture and sometimes has a pinkish hue. Whole fish are usually marketed at about 1–2.5 kg/2–5 lb.
Buying guide: available year-round, whole or in fillets.

coating with egg and crumbs 423
en papillote 422
salted grey mullet roe 31

Braised John Dory with Tomatoes and Fennel 268
Grey Mullet with Fennel 270
Mediterranean Garfish 270
Saffron Bouillabaisse with Rouille 253
Salsa Cruda 258
Taramasalata 275

coating with egg and crumbs 423
freshwater eel 25

Saffron Bouillabaisse with Rouille 253

Best cooking methods: whole fish are good fried (weakfish have no pin bones, making it easy to deal with the whole fish) or baked. Fillets can be grilled, sautéed or shallow-fried, or baked.

Redfish, ocean perch, rockfish (*rascasse, scorfano, gallineta Nórdica*) A fairly good deep-sea fish, found on both sides of the Atlantic and in the Pacific, this has bright red or orange skin and ranges from 1–11 kg/2–25 lb. Its flesh is tender, moist and mild.
Buying guide: available year-round. It comes whole or in steaks or fillets.
Best cooking methods: Eat grilled or fried, with Mediterranean flavours, such as garlic, tomatoes and fennel.

Orange roughy (*hoplostète orange* or *poisson montre, pesce specchio atlantico, reloj anaranjado*) This increasingly popular fish was only discovered about 20 years ago in the deep waters around New Zealand. It is normally sold frozen, but some is air-freighted to British and American markets to be sold 'fresh' (the fish is always cleaned and frozen at sea, then partially thawed later on shore for skinning and filleting). The firm white flesh is moist and tender, with a sweet, mild, almost crab-like flavour.
Buying guide: available all year, most often in fillets weighing about 225 g/8 oz.
Best cooking methods: a very versatile fish, this can be baked, grilled, egg-and-crumbed and fried, coated with batter and deep-fried, steamed or poached. It can also be used in fish soups and stews.

Tilapia, telapia This small African fish, usually only 450–700 g/1–1½ lb in weight, can live in both salt and fresh water. New hybrids are being developed and farmed all over the world, with skin colour ranging from dark grey-black to bright red. The white flesh of tilapia is moist and tender with a sweet flavour.
Buying guide: available year-round, whole and in fillets.
Best cooking methods: whole fish can be baked, with or without a stuffing, or barbecued. Coat fillets with egg and crumbs or a batter before grilling or frying to keep them moist; or poach or steam, notably with Chinese flavourings.

Sea lamprey (*lamproie marine, lampreda marina, lamprea de mar*) A legendary fish that resembles a thick eel, the sea lamprey is distinguishable by the seven holes behind its eyes that have given rise to its nicknames of flute and *sept-yeux*. It has a thick body, dark grey with mottled markings, and no scales. The flesh is richly flavoured, firm and fatty.
Buying guide: best in autumn.
Best cooking methods: prepare and cook as for eel, but scald before skinning and marinate before cooking. It can be pickled in vinegar, or stewed with port or red wine.

Conger eel (*congre, grongo, cóngrio*) The conger is one of two edible sea-water eels – the other is the moray, which is really only suitable for bouillabaisse. Conger makes a good meal, in spite of its long, sharp bones.
Buying guide: spring to autumn. Ask for a thick cut from the head end.
Best cooking methods: use in fish soups, fish mousselines and terrines. A good-sized cut can be roasted, basted with cider and butter, or poached in cider.

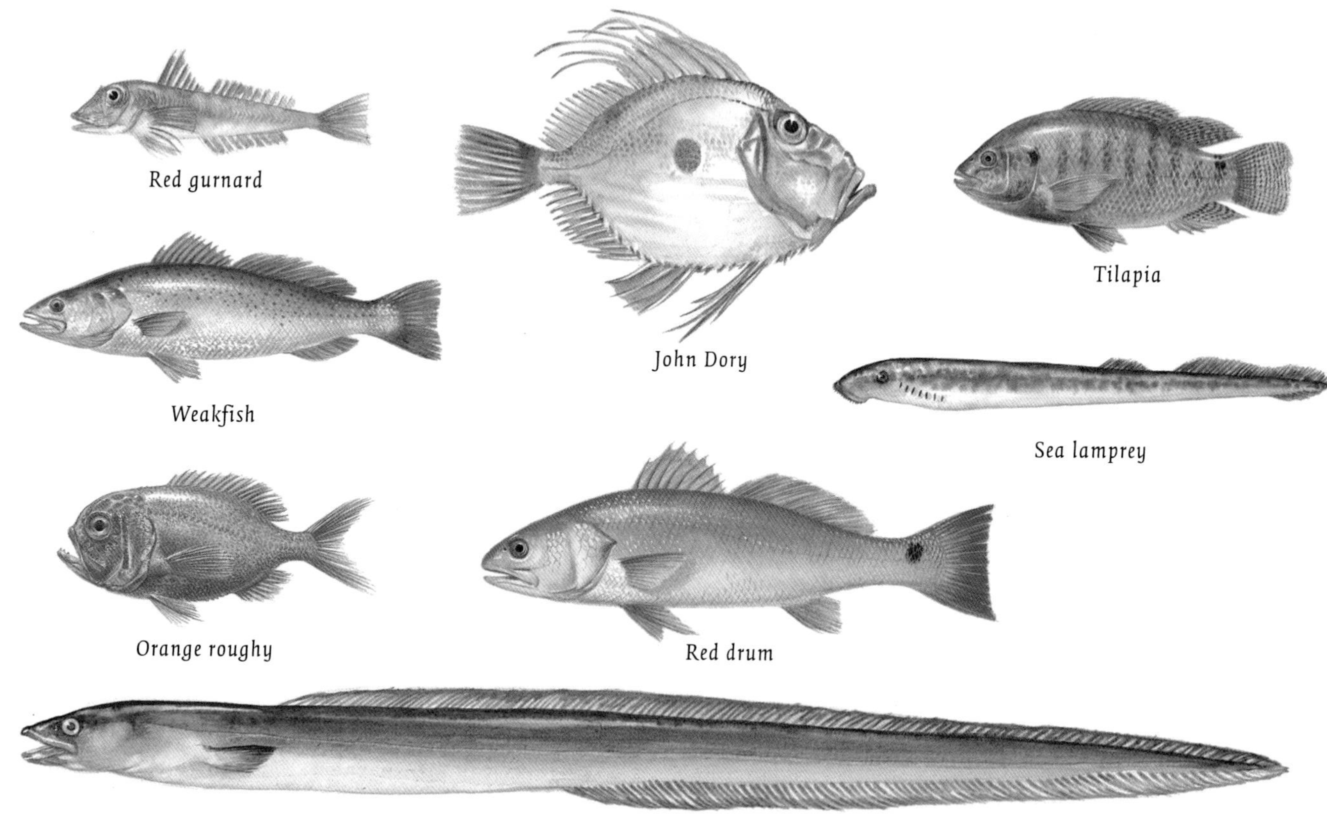

Red gurnard

John Dory

Tilapia

Weakfish

Sea lamprey

Orange roughy

Red drum

Conger eel

FRESHWATER FISH

Lake and river fish are often more frail than sea fish. Their tissues and organs take up a larger proportion of their bodies, and their skin, once scaled, is easily torn. The flesh is much lighter, tends to be dry, and is often riddled with a structure of hair-like forked bones of amazing intricacy. Because of the vulnerable nature of freshwater fish it is imperative that they should be eaten in their freshest possible state.

It has been said that freshwater fish should never touch another drop of water once they have left it, so when they are cleaned and scaled they should be wiped down without washing whenever possible, and baked, grilled or fried in preference to being boiled or poached. If liquids are used they should be wine, cider, or melted butter or cream rather than water.

The exceptions to the no-water rule are the members of the salmon family – these are exquisite poached in a court-bouillon or *bonne-eau*, and eaten warm or cold, but not refrigerated.

When cleaning a freshwater fish, be sure to remove the gills, and see that no weed is left in its throat because this can give a sour and reedy taste. Take particular care to remove the blood that lies along the backbone – this is bitter and must be cleaned away until there is not a trace left.

If you can choose your fish, take those with a silvery or green rather than brownish hue – the brown fish are more likely to have come from slow-moving, muddy haunts. Various remedies have been suggested – keep the fish alive in a tank of clear water for a day or so, or pour a tumblerful of vinegar or a couple of handfuls of salt into its mouth as soon as it is killed, or bake it unscaled in clay, which means that the mud-flavoured skin and scales can be removed all at once. But, in fact, there seems little point in trying to rid fish of their inherent taste, so if you dislike the flavour, choose some other fish that has a different character.

Most freshwater fish need quite a lot of salt and other seasoning – in Spain, river fish are gutted, rubbed with salt and left for several hours, or even buried in salt overnight, to make the flesh firmer and tastier. If your fish has been caught by an angler and there are herbs growing near the pool or river, such as watercress or mint, it is a good idea to gather these and take them home for flavouring the fish – it may have been feeding on them and have a suspicion of their aroma in its flesh.

Small river fish have such a plethora of tiny bones that they are best either soused or pickled, so that the bones are softened by the vinegar, or used in a fish soup or a matelote. If the fish are very small they make an excellent mixed fry of the sort often served in the Dordogne region of France as a *friture de la Dordogne*; then the bones can be happily crunched along with the crisp brown skin.

Salmon *(saumon, salmone, salmón)* Known as the king of fish, the salmon is a majestic creature whose life is mysterious and exhausting. Spawned in fresh water, it spends most of its life in the sea, only returning to fresh water – usually to the river where it was born – to spawn. In fresh water salmon take no sustenance, so on their way back to the sea, when they are known as kelts, they are miserably thin and spent, and certainly not fit to eat.

A Scotch or Irish wild salmon in good condition, caught in early summer, is considered by many to be the best in the world. It is a glossy, steely-blue fish shading to bright silver underneath, with black spots on the head and upper part of the body; the flesh is fine and pink. Choose a short, round one with a small head and broad shoulders (the head can represent a fifth of the total weight of the fish).

Salmon from Norwegian waters are also excellent, and so are those from Greenland. Of the Canadian and American West Coast salmon, the tastiest are the red-fleshed chinook, or king salmon, and the sockeye.

Today, farmed salmon is readily available and a very good buy.

Major Pollard, author of *The Sportsman's Cookery Book*, written in 1926 and published by *Country Life*, said: 'Salmon, which has a particular virtue of its own, is best plain, so do not attempt to better it.' It should be cooked simply and served unadorned, except for an appropriate sauce or mayonnaise and boiled new potatoes. If you are presented with a salmon straight from the river, you will need to clean it, but leave on the head and tail. It is better to cook it a day after it is caught, when it is more succulent, unless you intend to prepare sashimi or sushi and eat it raw. After cooking, skin it very carefully, removing the skin from each side in one piece.

Buying guide: good all year round, but wild salmon is best in spring and summer. Sold whole or in steaks. When really fresh there is a creamy substance between the flakes of flesh which sets to a curd when cooked. Avoid steaks that look soft, greyish, oily or watery. Allow 170–225 g/6–8 oz per person.

Best cooking methods: unless you have a truly enormous fish kettle, the best way to cook a salmon whole is to bake it in foil. If you do have a large fish kettle, or can borrow one, poach the salmon in a court-bouillon at the lowest possible simmering point for a really succulent result. Hot, salmon is best with hollandaise or perhaps mousseline sauce, or with beurre blanc, lobster sauce or plain melted butter, with or without *fines herbes* (chervil, parsley and chives). Salmon steaks can be brushed with butter, grilled and served with the same kinds of sauces. Cold, salmon is best eaten with plain or green mayonnaise or with horseradish in whipped cream, and served with thinly sliced cucumber and boiled potatoes.

Salmon trout, sea trout *(truite saumonée* or *truite de mer, trota salmonata, trucha marina)* Salmon trout – closely related to the brown trout found in rivers and lakes – is perhaps the perfect fish. As the name suggests, it combines the best of both the salmon and the trout: it has the superior texture of trout, being less dense and more succulent than salmon, but has salmon's excellent flavour and pale pink-coloured flesh. Salmon trout is also a much more useful size than salmon for cooking whole as it usually weighs less than 2.5 kg/5 lb, although it can grow to 4.5 kg/10 lb or even more.

The correct name for salmon trout is sea trout and that, too, is apt since the fish is really a trout that has taken it into its head to wander down to the sea to feed, returning to fresh water to spawn. It is a beautiful silver fish with a small head, not as pointed as that of the salmon, and with dark X-shaped spots on the gill cover.

In North America, the steelhead trout, an anadromous rainbow trout, is the

canned salmon 32
char 22
cutting salmon escalopes 28
gravlax 31
salmon caviare 32
smoked salmon 29

Beurre Blanc 256
Hollandaise Sauce 255
Lemon Court-Bouillon with Parsley 245
Mayonnaise 259
Poached Whole Salmon 272
Salmon Coulibiac 271
Salmon Escalopes with Chanterelles 271
Soy-Marinated Salmon Brochettes 273
Salmon Pâté 317
Spicy Green Fish 272

à la meunière 422
boning round fish 28
cleaning round fish 27
filleting round fish 27
salmon 21
smoked trout 30

smoking equipment 241

Lemon Court-Bouillon with Parsley 245
Trout in White Wine Jelly 273
Trout Marinated in Vermouth 273

most similar in appearance to salmon trout, although other brown trout may be called salmon or sea trout. Steelhead may be as small as 450 g/1 lb or as large as 4.5 kg/10 lb or more.
Buying guide: sold whole. Allow 225 g/8 oz per person, although, as it is a filling fish, less will do.
Best cooking methods: salmon trout can be dealt with in the same ways as salmon and is particularly good baked in foil. Poached, it makes a delicious summer lunch. Allow the same cooking time as for salmon, or a few minutes less, and use the same sauces as you would for salmon.

Trout *(truite, trota, trucha)* The rainbow trout is a familiar and delicious fish, and a very neat parcel of food it makes, just the right size for one person, pretty to look at and sweet and succulent to eat. The farm-reared rainbow trout is the most familiar: white fleshed and delicate and deserving better treatment than the usual sprinkling of almonds. A hardy fish, it responds well to freezing, and frozen rainbow trout are quite a good buy. It is often possible, too, to buy extra large rainbow trout up to 1.5–2 kg/3–4 lb. These are farmed trout and may have been fed special food to give a pink tinge to their flesh.

Brown trout, the wild native trout of British rivers and streams, are a beautiful brown with red and dark grey spots. They are usually only available to the families of fly fishermen, which is a great pity, because they are quite delicious. In North America, however, the brown trout has thrived since its introduction at the end of the last century, and is a hardy and popular fish.

Take care when cleaning trout to wipe rather than wash it. Remove the gills but leave the head on – the eyes will turn quite white as the fish is cooking. The skin can be removed after cooking, if wished, in one whole piece.
Buying guide: available all year, fresh (farmed) or frozen. Sold whole. Allow one trout per person, unless the trout are particularly large.
Best cooking methods: trout can be poached in a court-bouillon, served *à la meunière*, baked, grilled or fried, cooked over a fire, or smoked in a home smoker. It can also be cooked in beer with horseradish and served with horseradish sauce. Another good, if surprising, sauce partner is a purée of green gooseberries. In Sweden trout is boiled in a very little salt water and served with butter.

Char *(omble, salmerino, salvelino)* The arctic char of northern Europe and Canada, the char *(omble-chevalier)* of the deep lakes of the French and Swiss Alps, and the Dolly Varden, brook or alpine trout and lake trout of North America (also chars) all belong to the enormous and excellent salmon family.

The arctic char is a silver, salmon-like fish with a pink underside, which flushes deep red during spawning. It has firm, delicate flesh and makes a delicious meal. Arctic char used to be so prolific in the Lake District of northern England that potted char became a famous breakfast delicacy, but these days its numbers have lessened considerably. In France, the *omble-chevalier*, which resembles trout, is eaten throughout the summer, and is definitely worth ordering if you see it on a menu. The Dolly Varden, brook trout and lake trout are also very good table fish and deservedly popular.
Buying guide: the arctic char is best in early autumn; American chars are available all year. Small brook trout are sold whole, each enough for one person. Lake trout are larger, and these and arctic char can be cut into steaks, or cooked whole.
Best cooking methods: as for trout or salmon. Steaks can be poached for a few minutes with bay leaves and eaten cold.

Grayling *(ombre, temolo, salvelino or timalo)* A delicious, thyme-scented fish, called by St Ambrose the flower fish or flower of fishes, grayling should ideally be eaten as soon as it is caught because the delicate flavour is fugitive. It is a graceful fish, silver with finely marked geometric scales and a long, spotted back fin. It cannot survive in even slightly polluted water and only thrives in cold, crystal-clear, turbulent rivers, often

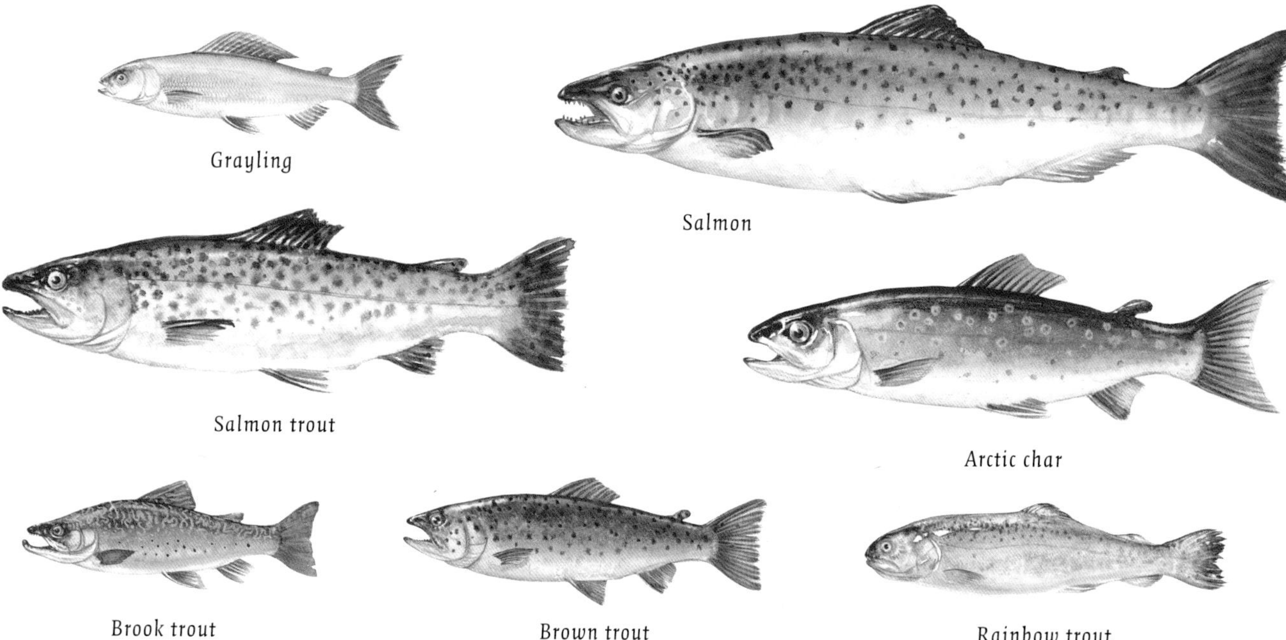

Grayling

Salmon

Salmon trout

Arctic char

Brook trout

Brown trout

Rainbow trout

living alongside trout and eating the same food. A fresh grayling has much in common, in taste and texture, with trout, and bears up well in comparison.

You will probably have to catch your own grayling to try one. Scale it before cooking – scald with boiling water and use a knife or a fish scaler, or try picking the scales off with your fingernails. Grayling never weigh more than 2 kg/ 4 lb, and are usually less than 900 g/2 lb.
Best cooking methods: brush with butter, flavour with thyme – especially if you find thyme near the brook where the fish was caught – and grill; or fry gently in clarified unsalted butter.

Carp (*carpe, carpa, carpa*) One of the hardiest of all fish, the carp is known to have existed in Asia thousands of years ago and is reputed to live to a grand old age. In its natural state it lives in slow and often muddy rivers or lakes, but it can survive well in domestic ponds and is extensively farmed.

The common or king carp is covered with large scales that are difficult to remove, but variants have been bred, such as the crucian, mirror, spiegel and leather carp, with just a few large scales that can be picked off with your fingernails, or with no scales at all. To scale a common carp, pour some boiling water over it first, but better still ask the fishmonger to scale it for you. A compact and meaty fish, carp needs to be cooked with plenty of interesting flavours.
Buying guide: at their best in late summer and autumn. Sold whole, usually a good size for four people.
Best cooking methods: stuffed and baked, or poached and served with horseradish or sorrel sauce. A baked carp can be served on a large dish, surrounded by fried gudgeon if that is what the day's catch has consisted of – the small fish have just their bodies coated with egg and crumbs, leaving their heads and tails free as if they were in a muff, and are then deep-fried. Jewish recipes for carp are excellent, and carp is traditionally eaten in Poland on Christmas Eve.

Catfish (*silure, pesce gatto, siluro*) So-called because of the long barbels that hang about its mouth like drooping cat's whiskers, the catfish is a particularly hardy creature. It is easily transplanted from one region to another, and is very successfully farmed in North America. It should be skinned before cooking.
Buying guide: almost always sold in fillets, and should be white and sweet-smelling.
Best cooking methods: Fillets are often deep-fried and served with tartare sauce; they can also be pan fried and baked and make a good basis for a fish soup that should include plenty of tomatoes, garlic, herbs and white wine.

Pike (*brochet, luccio, lucio*), **pickerel** (*brocheton, luccio giovano, lucio joven*) **and muskellunge** The predatory pike is quite handsome in its way, especially the younger fish, or jack, which has bold markings on a golden brown or greenish-silver background. An adult pike can weigh up to 18 kg/40 lb or more, and the flesh is white and firm. The muskellunge of northeastern and north-central North America can grow even larger, but the pickerel, or chain pickerel, of the eastern and southern United States is much smaller, usually around 2.5 kg/ 5 lb. In France pike is much admired, and *quenelles de brochet*, the lightest of fish dumplings, served with a white wine sauce, is a classic dish.

The theories about cooking pike are many: it should be bled to remove the sharp, reedy taste; it should have quantities of salt forced down its throat and be left to stand overnight to dissolve the bones; it should not be washed because its natural slime keeps it tender. However, a medium-sized pike is perfectly good cooked without any of these refinements. Simply scale it before cooking – pour a little boiling water over it first. Watch out for the bones when you eat it, for they are vicious and plentiful; and don't ever eat the roe, which in some cases can be poisonous.
Buying guide: best in autumn and early winter. If you do see pike for sale, a small, whole one is best. Large pike are usually cut into steaks.
Best cooking methods: pike tends to be dry, and a very large one may also be tough, so a whole fish should be stuffed before baking and steaks should be marinated before being fried or grilled. Small pike can be poached and served with beurre blanc, melted butter, parsley sauce or caper sauce. Best of all, you can make it into quenelles. In Scandinavia, pike is boiled and eaten with horseradish.

Perch (*perche, pesce persico, perca*), **pike perch, sander** (*sandre, sandra, luci perca*) **and yellow perch** (*perche Canadienne, persico dorato, perca Canadiense*) The perch is a beautiful little fish, pale greenish-gold with a white or yellowish belly and superb coral-coloured fins. The back has dangerously sharp spines and the scales are stubborn, but the fish is well worth the trouble of preparing: it is firm fleshed, delicate and light, and has a very good flavour. It is a fish that should only be eaten when it is gleamingly fresh.

Looking somewhat like a cross between pike and perch, with a bony head, thick skin and spiny dorsal fin, the European pike perch is farmed, like trout, in special conditions for fast growth. Even so it is a most delicious fish with firm, white, well-flavoured flesh, more interesting than trout and well worth purchasing whenever you see it. The American pike perch is also known as the walleye, wall-eyed pike or yellow pike.

The yellow perch, abundant in the Great Lakes and throughout the mid-western US, is a popular sport fish. It is closely related to the common perch and can be cooked in the same ways.

To prepare perch and pike perch for cooking, first carefully cut off the spines and fins with strong scissors, then bend the fish over and scrape off the scales which will be raised a little from their usual flat position. The procedure is slightly easier if you hold the fish firmly by the tail with a cloth or paper towel; or you can sprinkle your hands with salt. A pair of stout scissors is also useful for opening the fish to gut it.
Buying guide: these fish are sold whole. Smaller fish are more delicate to eat.
Best cooking methods: perch and pike perch are probably best fried long and very slowly in clarified butter, about 10–20 minutes on each side for a 700 g/1½ lb fish. They can also be baked, boiled or grilled. Perch *maître d'hôtel* is perch split, seasoned and grilled, with a dressing of butter and chopped parsley poured over it before it is sent to the table. This is simple and good. The parsley can be substituted with crisply fried sage leaves.

Shad (*alose, alosa, sábalo*) The shad is a large migratory member of the herring family which spawns in fresh water.

clarified butter 100, 423
gudgeon 25
scaling round fish 26

Beurre Blanc 256
Fish Mousselines 274
Horseradish Sauce 258
Maître d'Hotel Butter 257
Quenelles 274
Sauce Tartare 259

à la meunière 422
caviare 31
sorrel 133
smoked sturgeon 30

Beurre Blanc 256

White fleshed and nutritious, it has a good flavour, but also, unfortunately, a multitude of fine, wire-like bones. The roe is particularly good – it is even classed as an aphrodisiac by more hopeful gourmets.

The allis shad, which can grow up to 60 cm/2 ft long, and the smaller twaite shad (*alose finte, cheppia, saboga*) are caught in the Loire and Garonne rivers of France in the springtime, when they are spawning. The American shad (*alose canadienne*) has been successfully transplanted from the Atlantic to the Pacific, and the roes of this fish are sold both frozen and canned as well as fresh.

Remove as many of the bones as possible before cooking shad, using tweezers if necessary. When the fish is cooked, cut it through in lengthwise parallel strips about 10 cm/4 in apart, and remove any accessible bones before serving, moving your finger over the surface of the flesh to detect the hidden ones.

Buying guide: best in spring when full-roed. Usually sold whole; a 1.5 kg/3 lb shad will feed six. Ask the fishmonger to scale and possibly bone the fish when he cleans it.

Best cooking methods: stuff with sorrel and bake, or bake and serve on a bed of sorrel. If the roe is not cooked with the fish, it can be cooked *à la meunière* or gently baked in butter. Shad can also be filleted, with the skin left on, and gently grilled. Serve with fresh tomato sauce, beurre blanc or sorrel purée mixed with fresh cream.

Sturgeon (*esturgeon, storione, esturión*)
A huge and somewhat prehistoric-looking

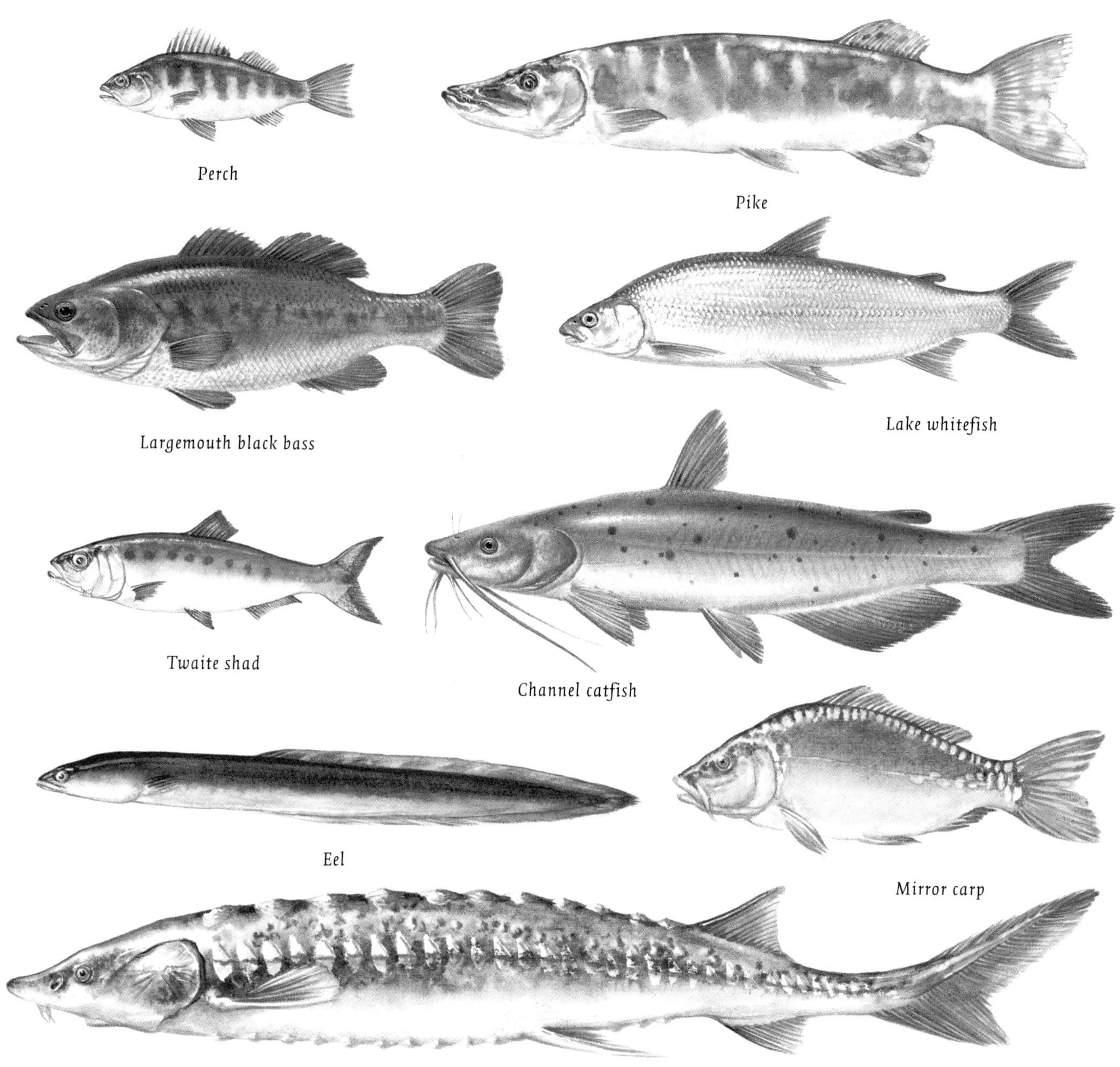

Perch
Pike
Largemouth black bass
Lake whitefish
Twaite shad
Channel catfish
Eel
Mirror carp
Sturgeon

creature, the sturgeon spends most of its life in the sea, but is most sought after when it comes into rivers to spawn. It can grow up to 6 m/20 ft or more, and the beluga sturgeon – usually a more modest size and the source of the most expensive caviare – can live to the ripe age of 100. Sturgeon are still caught in some American and European rivers, but they are most plentiful in the Caspian Sea, using its southern rivers for spawning. Recently sturgeon has begun to be farmed in California.

The flesh of sturgeon is white, very firm, rich and close textured, and is frequently likened to veal. It is inclined to be dry and is improved by being smoked or steeped in a white wine marinade before it is cooked.

Buying guide: best in spring. Usually sold in large pieces or as steaks.

Best cooking methods: grill or fry in butter, like veal; or poach in white wine and serve with a creamy sauce. In France, a luxurious version is sturgeon poached in champagne. It is also very good smoked and cut into thickish slices, eaten with lemon, horseradish and brown bread and butter.

Eel and elver (*anguille, anguilla, anguila*) Eels have a life cycle as strange as that of any fish. The European and American eel is spawned in the Sargasso Sea and promptly travels up to 7,000 km/4,000 miles to find the fresh waters of its ancestors, where it will spend most of its life, only returning to the Sargasso to spawn and then die. (Australian and Japanese eels have spawning grounds that are closer to land, but they still have a very long way to travel.)

By the time they reach the river mouths the tiny baby eels have grown into elvers 5–8 cm/2–3 in long. These little creatures, looking like transparent spaghetti, are good to eat deep-fried, rather like whitebait but not as crisp (they must be soaked for some hours in salted water acidulated with vinegar before cooking). By their second winter in fresh water the elvers have become small yellow eels, which are not so good to eat. These then mature into the familiar silver eels, velvety brown on their backs and silver below, and are excellent – meaty, even textured, succulent and very rich.

Buying guide: elvers appear in the spring; eels are in season all year but are best in autumn. Try to buy live eels – they become tough and go off instantly once killed. If you flinch at the prospect of dispatching a live eel yourself, ask the fishmonger to kill and skin it for you and to chop it into pieces. Fishmongers tend to chop eels into 2.5 cm/1 in lengths, but ask for 8 cm/3 in pieces, which look better and are better able to keep their moisture during cooking; or have it cut into 1 cm/½ in lengths for deep-frying.

Best cooking methods: jellied eels and 'eel pie and mash', with a kind of parsley liquor or sauce, have long been specialities of London's East End, and jellied eels are an English seaside treat. You may prefer to stew your eel in red wine; wrap it in bacon and sage leaves and grill it; or sauté it with a few bay leaves and serve it with salsa verde (an eel dish is always part of the traditional Italian Christmas Eve dinner). Elvers should be washed and tossed dry in a cloth, then dipped in flour and cooked immediately in hot oil with chilli and garlic. In Spain they are served in a fried tangle with a fiery tomato sauce.

Other freshwater fish

Many of the following freshwater fish are not commercially fished or farmed, and are unlikely to be found in a fish shop. These are for the most part fished for sport – they are trophies for the angler rather than the cook.

Bass A collective name for a large family of bony fish with spiny fins, both freshwater and saltwater, which includes the magnificent sea bass and the largemouth black bass. All bass make good eating. Small ones are good cooked whole, baked and stuffed, or grilled with fennel twigs. Fillets from larger fish can be poached or served *à la meunière*.

Bleak This is a small, slim, silvery fish found in the rivers of northern Europe, which can be cooked and eaten whole, just like whitebait.

Bream Freshwater bream needs interesting seasonings and ingredients because the flesh is somewhat dry and tasteless. European bream can be cooked in the same ways as carp.

Buffalofish A popular freshwater fish from the Great Lakes and the Mississippi Valley which makes good eating. It is often smoked, but can be prepared as for carp when fresh.

Burbot This handsome golden fish is the only member of the cod family to inhabit fresh water, and it is found in Europe, Britain and the United States. Burbot has good, firm, fatty flesh and a richly flavoured liver that can be sliced to release its oils and then baked or poached with the fish. The fish may also be cooked in red wine, or served with a tomato, cheese and cream sauce. Burbot is best in summer.

Dace The European and American dace are completely different fish that happen to have the same name, but neither is of much culinary interest. Both may be rolled in flour and deep-fried, or fried in butter (preferably over an open fire on the river bank just after they have been caught).

Gudgeon Found on the sandy bottom of many rivers and lakes in Britain and Europe, gudgeon are delicious little fish that can be crisply fried like whitebait, and served with lemon and chopped parsley.

Roach A quite well-flavoured British and European fish, roach sadly defies much enjoyment because it has such quantities of bones. Larger specimens (around 1.5 kg/3 lb) can be scored and fried in butter, or baked in white wine. The roe, which is greenish, is good, and becomes red when it is cooked.

Tench This fish, which is said to be best when taken from fast-running waters in Britain, must be scaled, cleaned and soaked in cold water before cooking. The flesh is rather flaccid and has a somewhat muddy flavour, but it can be cooked in a matelote together with eel, carp and pike, or fried or baked and served with a sauce that should include such strong flavours as herbs, cloves, garlic or shallots. Tench are in season between autumn and spring.

Whitefish Vendace and powan, known collectively as whitefish, are related to salmon and trout. They are fished in the cool, clear lakes of northern Europe, including the lochs of Scotland and Ireland. Both fish may be treated as for grayling. American whitefish, which include lake whitefish, cisco and chub, are found in deep-water lakes and rivers throughout the northern United States and Canada. They are fished by anglers and commercially, and are sold fresh and frozen as well as smoked. The delicious roe is much prized.

à la meunière 422
carp 23
cod 12
conger eel 20
grayling 22
jellied eel 32
saltwater bream 14
sea bass 14
smoked eel 30

Fried Whitebait 267
Salsa Verde 258

PREPARING FISH

flat fish 11–12

filleting knife 224

kitchen scissors 225

Trimming flat fish

1 Flat fish are usually gutted on the boat as soon as they are caught, so preparing them for cooking is a simple task. First, snip off the tough upper pectoral fin. The fish here is a small halibut.

2 Trim the tail and cut away the dorsal and anal fins.

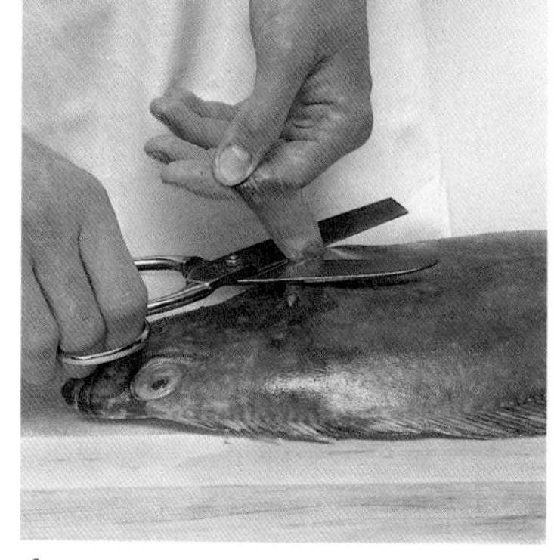

1

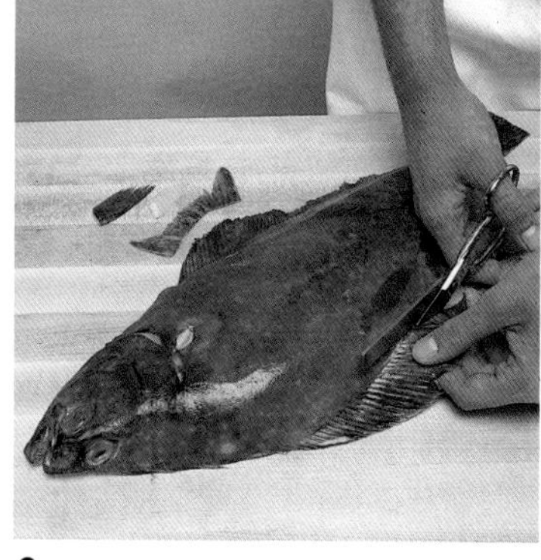

2

3 Cut off the head just behind the gills.

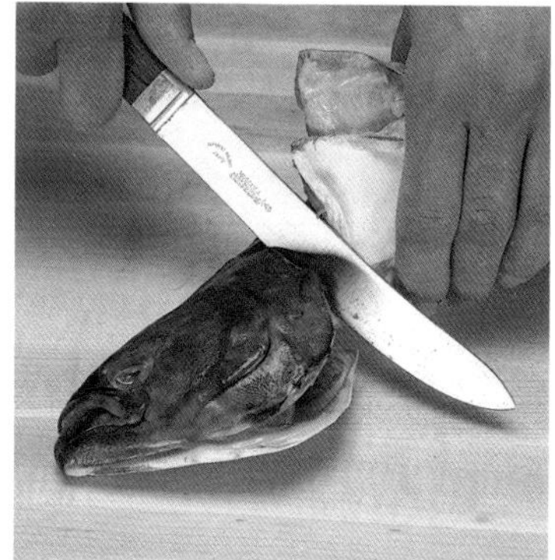

3

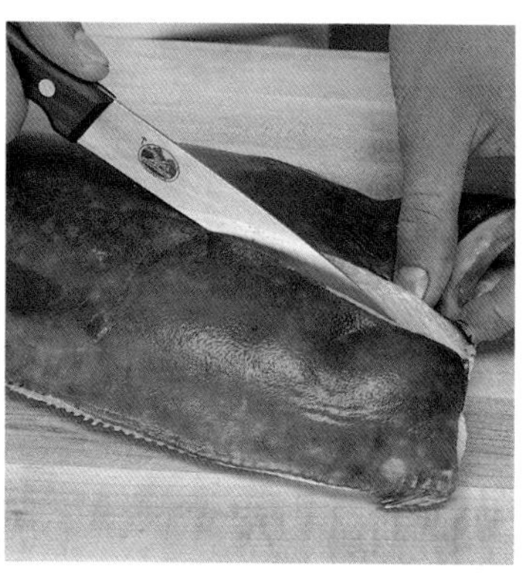

1

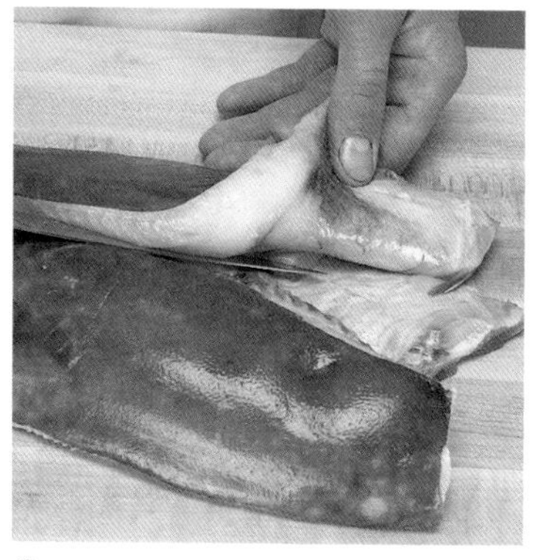

2

3

Filleting and skinning flat fish

(above)

1 With a sharp, flexible knife, make a slit along the backbone from head end to tail.

2 Slice down one side of the fish, sliding the knife between the flesh and the bones. For the second fillet, slice away the flesh from the opposite side. For the third and fourth fillets, turn the fish over and repeat the process.

3 To skin the fillets, hold each firmly by the tail end and work the knife down the length of the fillet, keeping the blade as close to the skin as possible.

Scaling round fish (*left*)

Hold the fish – in this case a red mullet – by the tail. Scrape away the scales with the back of a knife, working towards the head.

round fish 12–16, 18–25

filleting knife 224

Cleaning round fish

1 Before cooking a fish whole, it is important to remove the bitter-tasting gills. Lay the fish – in this case a mackerel – on its back and ease open the gill flaps. Push the fan of gills out from between the gill flaps; sever and discard them.

1

2 Trim off all the fins with scissors.

3 Slit open the fish's belly and ease out the guts. Finally, rinse the fish thoroughly, inside and out, under cold running water.

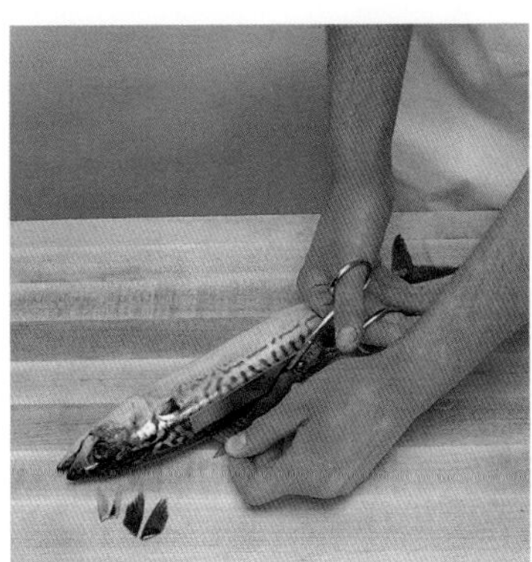

2

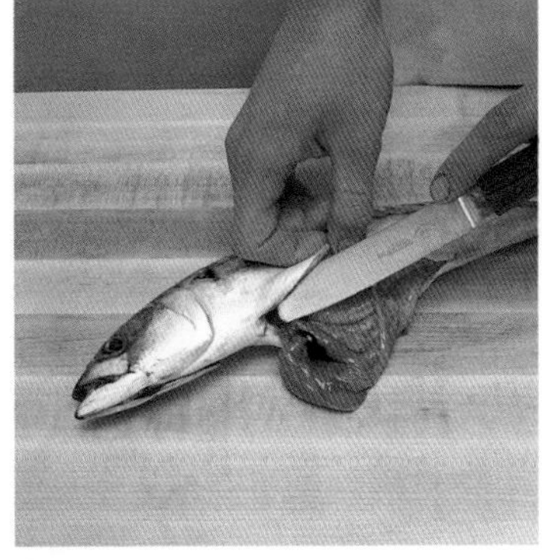

3

Filleting round fish

1 Starting just behind the head, cut into the back of the fish and slide the knife along one side of the backbone to release the fillet, keeping the knife as close to the bone as possible. The fish shown here is a whiting.

2 Continue slicing along the length of the fish, severing the fillet just behind the gills and at the tail.

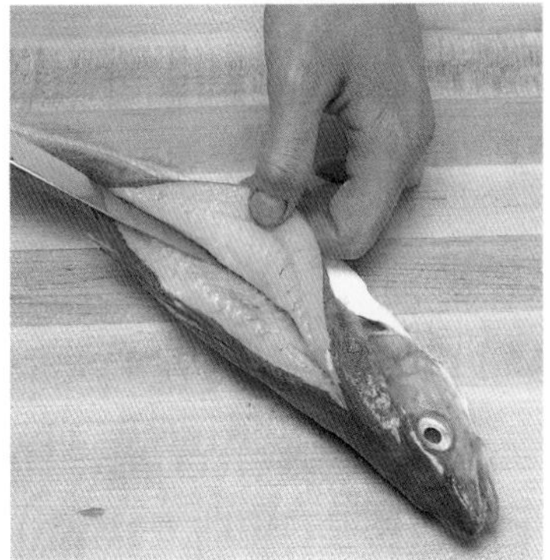

1

2

3 Cut the second fillet from the other side of the fish. Skin the fillets in the same way as illustrated for flat fish.

3

round fish 12–16, 18–25
salmon 21

cutlet beater 226
knives 222–4

Boning round fish

1 Cut off the head behind the gills, without cutting all the way through, then ease the head away from the body, taking most of the guts with it. Remove the rest with the help of the knife. The fish shown here is a trout.

2 Slice along the back of the fish between the flesh and backbone, keeping the knife against the backbone. Do not puncture the belly. Open out the fish like a book.

1

2

3 Turn the fish flesh side down and cut away the backbone and small adjoining bones.

4 This method of boning is particularly suitable when the fish is to be stuffed, or opened flat for grilling or frying.

3

4

Cutting salmon escalopes

1 Take a tail end section of fresh salmon.

2 Slice off the top fillet, starting at the tail and cutting as close to the backbone as possible. Turn the fish over and remove the second fillet. Discard the backbone and skin each fillet as for flat fish.

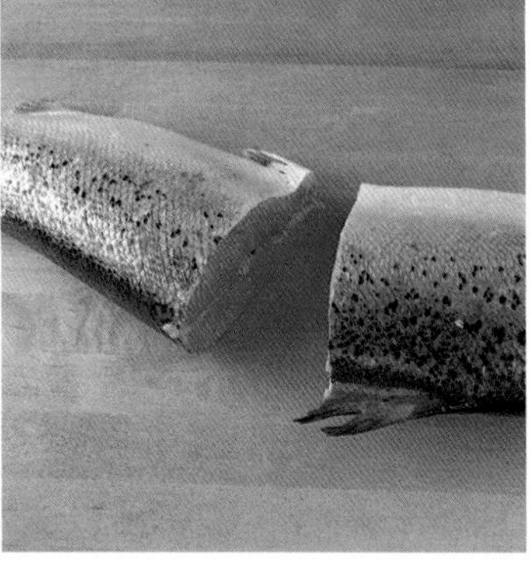

1

2

3 Cut each of the fillets horizontally into two thin slices, using a long, sharp, flexible knife.

4 Place each slice of salmon between two pieces of dampened greaseproof paper. Gently but firmly flatten the fish into escalopes, using a rolling pin or a cutlet beater.

3

4

Preserved Fish

Fresh fish deteriorates fast and has always been a natural subject for traditional preserving methods. Indeed, the smoking, pickling, salting and drying of fish used to be a matter of simple necessity – when fishing boats relied on the wind, and overland transport on the horse and cart, fresh sea fish was practically unknown inland. Moreover, as fish was the prescribed food for the numerous meatless days in the Christian calendar (as many as 12 a month), to preserve it, and to preserve it palatably, was a matter of great importance.

Smoked fish

Fish must be salted before smoking. This process, which entails either soaking the fish in a brine strong enough to keep a potato afloat, or rubbing into it a generous amount of dry salt, improves both the flavour and the keeping qualities. After salting, the fish is dried and then cold- or hot-smoked. The protein content remains unchanged, but calories are diminished.

To find smoked fish you like, try different varieties because they vary enormously, and regional specialities still find their way into shops. Some are pale and oak-smoked, while others are over-salted and artificially dyed.

Store-bought smoked fish will keep for about 3 days, or up to 20 days in a freezer. Home-smoked fish should be eaten at once. Only dried and salted fish keeps indefinitely.

Cold-smoked fish Cold-smoking takes place at temperatures of around 24°C/75°F, which smokes the fish but does not cook it. Products of the cold-smoking process are either eaten raw, like smoked salmon, or may require further cooking, like kippers or finnan haddie (smoked haddock).

Smoked salmon The British think that salmon is best when caught in Scottish waters; Norwegians say that those caught in Norwegian waters are better still; and all agree that Canadian and farmed salmon come third, but can still be excellent when smoked. Smoked salmon should be fresh and succulent, melting away under the knife as it is sliced. The best of all is the pale pink-gold, rather under-salted salmon. A darker red or a deep orange colour usually means dyed or overcured fish, and is not a good sign.

The traditional Scottish way of kippering salmon, as the process used to be called (kippers having merely borrowed the word), involves brining the boned sides of salmon, wiping, drying and oiling them and then covering them in brown sugar. Another wipe with a cloth, often soaked in whisky, another anointing with oil, and another whisky wipe, and then the sides are smoked over a fire of peat and oak chips.

Fresh cold-smoked salmon is usually sliced for you in the shop, but if you can afford the outlay, a whole side works out to be slightly more economical. A side is half the whole length of the fish from shoulder to tail. Buying a whole side has the advantage of giving you both the richer, fattier, lower cuts and the fine-grained middle. To slice the salmon, go across the grain of the flesh – that is, cut from the shoulder towards the tail. You need an extremely sharp, long, flexible knife – one with a wavy edge is best. A nail through the tail helps to keep the fish steady. Or you can buy a side of salmon ready-sliced and layered back into shape.

Scottish smoked salmon is eaten sliced transparently thin, with lemon and thin brown bread and butter. Lox (from the Yiddish word for smoked salmon), which tends to be more heavily cured than other smoked salmon, is eaten with cream cheese and bagels. *Røyktlaks* – Norwegian smoked salmon – is much used for *smørbrød*.

Frozen and canned smoked salmon are available, but both are no more than vividly pink shadows of the fresh variety. However, sliced vacuum-packed and chilled smoked salmon can be perfectly acceptable. And what can be a good buy is 'trimmings' – untidy scraps of fresh smoked salmon with bits of skin and bone attached. Provided they are moist and soft, they are ideal for smoked salmon mousse or any dish requiring chopped smoked salmon.

Kipper Split washed herrings are briefly brined, hung on 'tenterhooks' to dry, and then smoked for 4–6 hours. Many kippers are dyed during brining, emerging mahogany coloured after smoking. There are, however, undyed kippers to be had, notably those from the Isle of Man, which lies in the Irish Sea and has more stringent regulations than the mainland. Delicate Loch Fyne kippers from Scotland are also worth tracking down. Buy a fat kipper – lean kippers tend to be dry. And buy your kippers fresh and loose – frozen kippers, although they keep their texture fairly well, do not taste as good, and boil-in-the-bag fillets make very dull eating.

If you think your kippers will be too salty, put them head first into a jug and pour boiling water over them. Let them stand for a few minutes, then pour off the water and prepare in the normal way – grilled with a lump of butter for breakfast or supper, or cold in salads and pâtés for lunch.

Finnan haddie, smoked haddock Finnan haddie is so called because it was in the village of Findon, not far from Aberdeen in Scotland, that the method of curing this fish, giving it its distinctive pale appearance, was invented. Originally the beheaded fish were dried and cold-smoked in the smoke of seaweed. By a modernized process, finnan haddie is now produced far beyond Scotland, in New England and other places. So are its imitations – fillets of white fish that are artificially dyed a bright, bright yellow and may be chemically treated to taste of smoke. It is easy to tell the true from the false: the colour is a complete give-away.

Smoked haddock is eaten hot. Grill, or poach it for a few minutes in milk or water, then simply serve it with butter or with a poached egg on top and a piece of hot buttered toast; or use it to make dishes such as the creamed finnan haddie that is a favourite in New England, the Anglo-Indian kedgeree, or the poached smoked haddock of Scandinavia which is served together with carrots, hard-boiled eggs and butter. Scotland eats Ham and Haddie, using the palest version of the fish from the Moray Firth and frying it in the fat rendered from a few slices of smoked ham.

Smoked halibut Young halibut are sometimes lightly smoked. Their taste is delicate and their texture firm. Serve in the same way as smoked haddock.

Bloater, *hareng saur* Bloaters are inshore herrings that are lightly salted and then smoked without the gut being removed. The slight fermentation of the enzymes occurring during this process causes the fish to get bloated and develop a gamey flavour. Bloaters are silvery in appearance, and the flesh is soft and moist. They do not keep as long as kippers, and must be gutted before they

freezing fish 10
haddock 13
halibut 12
herring 15
preparing fish 26–8
salmon 21
salt 200
sugar 211–12

slicing knife 222
smoking equipment 241

Creamed Finnan Haddie 275
Fish Pie 266
Omelette Arnold Bennett 325
Poached eggs 322

cod 12
eel 25
haddock 13
herring 15
mackerel 15
sprat 16
sturgeon 24
trout 22

smoking equipment 241

Horseradish Sauce 258
Scrambled Eggs 322
Taramasalata 275

are served. They may be grilled, used to make bloater paste, or simply mashed to make a sandwich filling. The famous *harengs saur* of Boulogne are even more plumped up than the British bloater, and the Swedish *surströmming* is so bloated that it is on the point of explosion. This last is not much exported, but is deeply loved at home, where it is eaten with thin crispbread or potatoes.
Smoked sturgeon If fresh sturgeon, with its fine-grained white flesh, tastes rather like veal, smoked sturgeon resembles nothing so much as smoked turkey both in colour and taste. It is, however, more delicious still, more buttery and melting in the mouth, and of course a great deal more expensive. Eat it like smoked salmon.
Smoked roes Fish eggs from any number of species are smoked and eaten with enjoyment. It should be added that what are called hard roes alone are eggs – soft roes are not roes at all but 'milt', or sperm, from the male of the species. Smoked roes should be firm and moist with no signs of skin breakage. Smoked cod's roe is deliciously grainy and glutinous. Serve it as a first course like pâté, with toast, unsalted butter and lemons, or use it to make taramasalata.

Hot-smoked fish Hot-smoking takes place at temperatures of about 82°C/180°F, and is the method used for eel, trout, buckling and mackerel, which are smoked and lightly cooked at one and the same time. They are bought ready to eat and can also be served hot.
Smoked trout The best smoked trout has gone into brine as soon as it left the water. It is drawn only after it has been drained, and is then ready for smoking. Silver birchwood is said to give it the best and sweetest flavour, and a little peat and a few fir cones make it taste even better. The fish turns golden and then, if left longer, to bronze. Look for springiness in a smoked trout: the flesh should be neither mushy nor dry – the fine, firm texture of a nice plump trout is as much of a pleasure as its delicate flavour. Serve smoked trout for a summer lunch or supper with lemon wedges, thin brown bread and butter, and horseradish mixed with a dash of the thickest cream.
Smoked mackerel Silvery-gold smoked mackerel can be very good indeed. As it is not a very subtly flavoured fish, it emerges from careful kippering tasting straightforwardly of itself and is, usually, rich and juicy. Best bought loose and whole, it is also available filleted and packed in heat-sealed envelopes. Avoid packs that ooze with oil: this indicates that the fish has been stored for too long or at the wrong temperature, and the flesh will be dry. Eat smoked mackerel cold with horseradish sauce or lemon.
Buckling These allegedly get their name from a fourteenth-century Dutchman, William Beukels, who invented this method of preserving ungutted herrings. A good fat buckling can be an almost triumphant rival of a smoked trout. It is good eaten with brown bread and butter and lemon wedges, and is also good mashed to a paste. In Germany buckling is sometimes lightly grilled or gently fried with the roe left in and served with sauerkraut or scrambled eggs.
Sprat, sild and brisling are all small herrings which when smoked are simply served with brown bread, butter, lemon and a glass of beer. As well as being candidates for smoking, they also sometimes find themselves canned as sardines.
Arbroath smokie These are small smoked haddock that have been beheaded and gutted but not split, and hot-smoked in the round. After brining they are placed over birch and oak smoke until pale golden. To serve, open the fish out, put butter and some freshly milled black pepper inside, close it up again and heat it gently under the grill or in the oven. When you peel off the dark skin, you will find a golden outer crust and gradually paling flesh.
Smoked eel Some say that the densely textured smoked eel is even more delicious than smoked salmon. Smoked eel is very rich and filling, and is usually served with pepper, lemon juice and brown bread and butter. Pinky-beige smoked eel fillets laid over a plateful of golden scrambled eggs, bordered with triangles of fried bread,

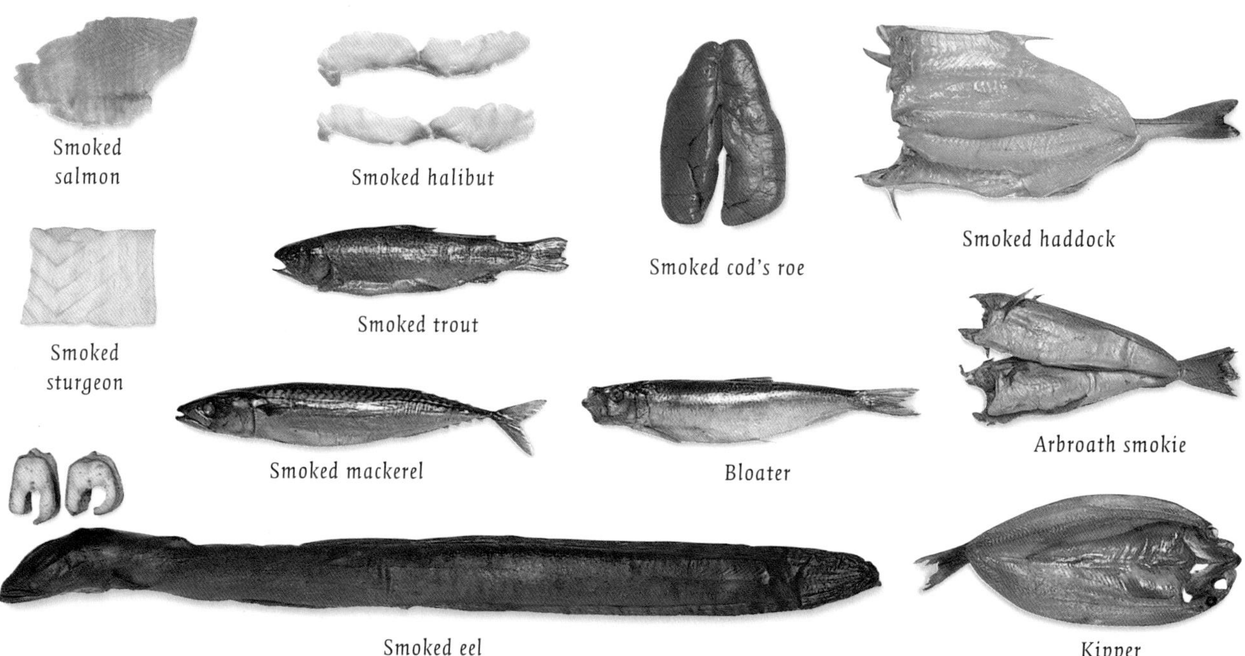

Smoked salmon
Smoked halibut
Smoked cod's roe
Smoked haddock
Smoked sturgeon
Smoked trout
Smoked mackerel
Bloater
Arbroath smokie
Smoked eel
Kipper

make a first course that is especially delicious. Or buy it whole, skin on, if you want larger, more succulent fillets (it is easy to skin), and then serve with horseradish sauce.

Pickled and salted fish

The pickling process is particularly suited to oily fish, such as herrings. They are steeped in a vinegar or brine solution which halts enzyme action in the same way that cooking does.

Gravlax is a most delicious Swedish speciality – it is fresh raw salmon pickled with dill, sugar, salt and white peppercorns. It is traditionally eaten with a rather sweet mustard and dill sauce.

Salt herring These are sold whole. They should be soaked for up to 12 hours, then filleted and chopped for salads or bathed in sour cream for an hors d'oeuvre.

Maatjes herring These are considered to be the best salt herrings. They are lightly salted fat female fish with translucent, slippery flesh of a beautiful old-rose colour. They need no soaking.

Rollmop These are herrings – boned and halved lengthwise – that have been rolled up tightly around peppercorns and slices of onion and fastened with a toothpick before being put into jars to which is added hot, spiced, white wine vinegar. Eat them with an accompaniment of black bread and unsalted butter.

Bismarck herring These herrings, blue of skin and white of flesh, are first steeped in white wine vinegar. They are drawn, boned, topped, tailed and split, and then kept for 24 hours layered in a dish, duly seasoned and interspersed with onion rings and sometimes with a few round slices of raw carrot. Eat them with new potatoes, or bathed in sour cream or a thin mayonnaise dressing.

Soused herring, *bratheringe* Many people like to souse herrings at home by steeping them in a vinegary marinade to which herbs and spices are added. Soused herring (or mackerel) can, however, be found in specialist shops, as can German *bratheringe*, which is first turned in flour and fried golden brown, and only then steeped for 24 hours in a boiled marinade.

Pickled herring These are marinated in spices and vinegar, then often sold in a sour cream sauce.

Anchovy Preserved salted anchovy fillets usually come canned in oil, those in olive oil being the best. Plain salted anchovies, sold direct from a barrel or a large jar, need a brief steeping in fresh water to make them less harsh. An anchovy is the most versatile of piquant ingredients, seasoning dishes without imparting the least hint of fishiness.

Dried fish

Fish that had been hung up to dry in the sun and wind provided an almost indestructible food supply for our ancestors. This earliest method of preserving fish is the precursor of modern freeze-drying. Salting is another way to extract moisture from fish, thus discouraging decay.

Dried cod, stockfish Dried to a flatness and hardness resembling hide, cod and other members of its family – ling, haddock, pollock – spring back to life when they are soaked. This process may take up to 2 weeks, but in Scandinavia, where stockfish – air-dried Norwegian cod – is much eaten, it is now possible to buy it presoaked and even frozen. The revived fish is often eaten with yellow peas, and also appears in a fish pudding, light as a soufflé, which is served with hollandaise sauce. In Holland, Belgium and Germany, stockfish is often soaked in lime water before being cooked.

In Portugal, where *bacalhau* – dried salted cod – is almost a staple food, they boast that they have more than 1,000 ways of cooking it. Some of the best recipes for dried cod are Basque, and include garlic, oil, tomatoes, peppers, onions and potatoes. The French make a rich garlicky purée of salted cod called *brandade de morue*.

Bombay duck This is the most famous of the various Eastern dried fish. It is found in Indian delicatessens, and provides seasoning for the rice that is eaten with curry. Made from cured bommaloe fish, Bombay duck smells awful when you buy it. Toast slowly until its edges curl and no trace of the original smell remains. Then crumble it and sprinkle over cooked rice.

Dried shark's fin This is delicately flavoured cartilage of the fin, which, when you buy it, looks like the tousled beard of Father Christmas. It requires soaking overnight, or even longer, in many changes of water, until it has become like a firm jelly. In China, shark's fin is banquet food: it goes into party soups, into rather liquid party stews and braises, and, shredded fine, into omelettes. Its gelatinous properties have been likened to those of calf's feet.

Salted roes

Into this category fall the costly caviare and its less exotic alternatives.

Grey mullet roe Known as *tarama* in Greece, the salted, dried, pressed roe of the mullet is considered a great delicacy, ranging immediately after caviare and before salmon roe. As the name suggests, it makes taramasalata – one of the 'cream salads' of the Middle East. For this purpose the roe is divested of the membrane that surrounds it, pounded with oil, lemon juice and garlic, and bound with breadcrumbs or mashed potato, and sometimes egg yolk. Smoked cod's roe makes a good substitute.

Caviare The fish that are used for commercial caviare production are the sevruga, the large osetra and the giant beluga, which has a huge roe to match. All are members of the *Acipenser* tribe, and are collectively known as sturgeon, although only the osetra rightfully bears this name. The roes are passed through fine-meshed sieves to separate the eggs, which are then salted. The brining of caviare is a delicate business. The condition of the fish and the size of the eggs both have a bearing on how much salt is required, and the finest grade emerges from the care of the master-tasters as *malassol*, a Russian term meaning 'slightly salted'.

Caviares come in a variety of sizes and colours. Sevruga is small grained and greeny-black. Osetra, larger grained, may be golden-brown or bottle-green or slate-grey; it can also be pale – almost bluish-white. Beluga, the largest and most rare, is grey or, very rarely, golden. The closer to spawning the fish is caught, the paler the roe – and all of these, depending on their quality, make 'first-grade' caviare.

First-grade caviare is sometimes pasteurized, which lengthens its shelf life. Non-pasteurized caviare is kept refrigerated at 0°C/32°F: warmer and it loses its texture and becomes oily; colder and its flavour is ruined. The contents of an open container should be kept, covered, in the refrigerator, but should certainly be eaten within a week.

This also applies to pressed caviare – which is slightly less expensive than the *malassol* but is, in fact, the first choice of

anchovy 16
cod 12
dill 191
herring 15
salmon 21
salt 200
shark 17
sturgeon 24
vinegar 204–5
white peppercorn 201

Grilled Tuna with Anchovy 267
Green Bean Salad with Anchovy-Cream Dressing 367
Lido Pasta Salad 371
Mozzarella in Carrozza 330
Red Peppers with Anchovies 383
Salade Niçoise 368
Salsa Verde 258
Salt Cod with Potatoes 274
Soused Herrings 267
Spaghetti alla Rustica 337
Taramasalata 275

eel 25
salmon 21
sardine 16
sprat 16
tuna 16

Melba Toast 264
Salade Niçoise 368

some caviare experts. It is caviare that has been poured into cheesecloth bags and drained of some of its liquid. The eggs, of course, are squashed in the process, and what emerges is a fairly solid mass, saltier than *malassol*, but tasting more intensely of sturgeon, since 900 g/2 lb of caviare are reduced to make 450 g/1 lb of pressed. Second-grade caviare may be saltier caviare of a single variety, or a mixture of different caviares, some of them highly superior.

To educate the palate, one really needs to eat a lot of caviare, not with tiny special caviare spoons but by the solid mouthful. In Russia, where large helpings of second-grade caviare are fairly unceremoniously served, it is often eaten with blinis – fat little buckwheat pancakes – and sour cream. But as a rule it is best with a little lemon, some fresh Melba toast and unsalted butter: chopped hard-boiled egg and finely chopped raw onion will enhance a small supply.

Keta, red caviare This is made from the roe of the salmon. It is bright orange and large grained, not so much an imitation caviare but a fresh-tasting product in its own right. It, too, is sometimes eaten with sour cream, but usually just with toast, butter and a squeeze of lemon.

Lumpfish roe The pink eggs of the arctic lumpfish are salted, coloured black or sometimes red, and pressed. Sold as German or Danish caviare, it is usually used to make an impression on cocktail party canapés. Alone, it is less interesting than true caviare but is a pleasant experience, served with sour cream and raw onion, and compared with the real thing, it is reasonably inexpensive.

Canned fish

Fish is one of the few foods that stand up well to the business of canning. Canned tuna and sardines, for example, have become foods worth eating in their own right – quite different from their fresh counterparts, but good none the less.

Salmon Canned salmon comes in many grades, from the less good red to a more acceptable pink (the darker, the oilier). It is useful for fishcakes and patties.

Sardine Good brands of sardines have been gently brined, correctly dried and lightly cooked in olive oil, then stored for about a year, so that the flavour of fish and oil are mingled. The sardines caught off the west coast of France are the best and the most expensive. Portuguese and Spanish sardines are less fine but much cheaper. Eat sardines bones and all, with brown bread and butter and a squeeze of lemon juice, or mash them and use in sandwiches or stuffed eggs.

Pilchard These fish, slightly larger than sardines, are not very exciting and never as good as sardines. In order to add a little interest, packers tend to bathe them in tomato sauce before canning.

Tuna The best canned tuna is taken from the albacore, the king of the tunas, which alone is permitted to be described as 'white meat'. Other tuna varieties – skipjack, yellow fin, bluefin – are a little darker, but all make very good salads. Use canned tuna for the classic *vitello tonnato* (cold veal with a creamy tuna sauce). Buy good-quality tuna, which comes in solid pieces, packed in oil rather than water. The cheaper brands are often nothing but broken-up pieces, and are only good for sandwiches.

Jellied eel This traditional Cockney delicacy is difficult to find freshly cooked. But it is sold in cans, and makes a good appetizer: serve it with little bunches of watercress.

Sprat, sild, brisling These are Scandinavian names for young herrings. Small ones are canned and sold under all three names, though they are usually bought as stand-ins for sardines.

Beluga caviare · Sevruga caviare · Osetra caviare · Salted anchovy · Lumpfish roe · Bismarck herring · Maatjes herring · Jellied eel · Soused herring · Rollmop · Dried salt cod · Dried shark's fin · Salt herring

Shellfish

Although overfishing and pollution have taken their toll on shellfish, there are signs that things are improving. Waters that were a hazard to the health of both shellfish and consumers have been radically cleaned up, and new farming methods are making it possible to harvest fast-growing shrimps, prawns and lobsters, for example, in large quantities.

True, the shrimps may not be the small, delicate northern ones but large Pacific varieties; the lobsters may be smaller and softer shelled; and we may find oysters on the market the size of tennis balls that can only be eaten chopped up like large clams and cooked. But we should be able to enjoy more abundant and possibly less costly supplies. And the delicious local varieties of shellfish are still available. Buy them from a dealer who specializes in them and can be trusted to sell them only when they are sweet and fresh.

If you are buying cooked shellfish, a quick sniff should distinguish the freshly cooked from the fading. Shrimps and prawns lose the colour in their shells and become lighter as they dry up. Lobsters and crabs also lose weight – choose heavy specimens with tension in the tail or claws. If they are floppy and unresisting they are likely to be stale. If you want to cook them live, plunge them into fast-boiling salted water, seawater or court-bouillon. Take care not to overcook them – all shellfish toughen and become rubbery if they are cooked for too long.

Crab (*crabe* or *tourteau, granchi* or *granciporri, buey* or *cangrejo*) To pick the meat out of a crab is a labour of love but always worth the effort – the flavour and texture are almost equal to that of lobster, and certainly much less expensive. The large crabs with fearsome claws found all around the British coast, the sweet spider crabs beloved of the French, and the soft green-backed shore crabs which are a Venetian speciality are all delicious, especially if you can choose a female with its berry, a brilliant coral-red roe that tastes and looks superb. In North America the crab really comes into its own, with an abundance of blue crabs from the Atlantic and Gulf coasts, the superbly flavoured Pacific Coast crab, the Dungeness, the Florida stone crabs, the Alaska king crab and snow crab, and the rock crabs and Jonah crabs found all along the Atlantic coasts. Soft-shell crabs are blue crabs that have shed their hard shells and can be eaten shell and all.
Buying guide: alive or cooked, choose crabs that feel heavy for their size and smell fresh and sweet, with no hint of ammonia. About 450 g/1 lb of crab in the shell or 115 g/4 oz of crab meat is usually sufficient for each person, depending on how it is prepared. Soft-shell crabs should always be bought alive.
Best cooking methods: the best crab is the one you boil and dress yourself, eaten cold with mayonnaise and brown bread and butter. Hard-shelled crabs are also good steamed, and can be used to make a very delicious bisque. Soft-shelled crabs – crabs that have just moulted their old shells – can be eaten *à la meunière*, or be grilled or deep fried.

Lobster (*homard, astice, bogavante*) 'There is nothing more delicious in life,' said Byron, 'than the fireside, a lobster salad and good conversation.' With or without the embellishments, lobster is a treat for both the eye and the palate. The colours – creamy-pink flesh, and a shell speckled cream and coral underneath and deep, old brick-red on the back; the texture – firm, delicate and luscious; and the flavour – an appetizing, elusive marine taste – are all highly desirable. And, alas, expensive.

Lobsters from colder waters are generally the finest. The best are the superb Irish and Scottish lobsters and those from Brittany, on the European side of the Atlantic, and the northern lobsters from Maine to Nova Scotia on the American side. The cock lobster is firmer fleshed than the hen and has larger, meatier claws, but the hen has a more delicate flavour, a broader tail and the delicious coral, or roe, which turns scarlet when cooked and makes excellent lobster sauce – if you can bear to use part of this costly creature for making sauce.
Buying guide: fresh lobsters are available all year, but are at their best and most abundant during the summer. Choose a lobster that is heavy for its size and has both its claws – sometimes a claw is lost in a fight, and some of the best meat is in the claws. Alive, the best way to buy lobsters, the shell is dark blue or green; if already boiled, the shell should be bright red. If the lobster is pre-cooked, check that its tail springs back into a tight curl when pulled out straight. This shows that it was cooked when alive. If you are brave enough, give it a sniff underneath, too, to make sure it is quite fresh.

If you intend to cook the lobster yourself, make sure you get a lively specimen and, again, that it is a heavy one – sometimes lobsters get quite thin in captivity waiting for someone to buy them. To keep a live lobster in the refrigerator, but not for more than a day or two, roll it loosely in damp newspaper to prevent it crawling about, enclose it in

à la meunière 422
despatching a live lobster 39
picking a cooked crab 40–1
preparing a cooked lobster 39
shellfish recipes 275–81

lobster crackers, pick and pincer 229

Boiled Lobster 276
Crab Cakes 275
Crab Salad with Thai Flavours 368
Dressed Crab 275
Grilled Lobster with Butter 276
Mayonnaise 259

Live European crab

Blue crab

Dungeness crab

bisque 422
despatching a live lobster 39
preparing a cooked lobster 39

lobster crackers, pick and pincer 229

Boiled Lobster 276
Grilled Lobster with Butter 276
Mayonnaise 259

a paper bag pierced with air holes, and put it in the vegetable crisper.

If called upon to face cutting up a live lobster before cooking, then cut the lobster in pieces, or split it in half lengthwise through the stomach shell and open it out flat, or cut it in half right through the hard back shell. Clean it, removing the sand sac, if it is present, from the head and reserving any coral and the delicious creamy tomalley or liver to use in lobster sauce. Cook the lobster immediately.

Small lobsters are usually the most tender: a 450 g/1 lb lobster will feed one person, so you may have to buy several. Large lobsters are also excellent – and work out less expensive – for salads and sauces. Cooked lobster meat, frozen or in cans, is really best forgotten or used as an ingredient in a shellfish salad. Never have anything to do with a dead, uncooked lobster – the flesh spoils very quickly.
Best cooking methods: the simplest are the best: plain boiled, steamed or grilled, served hot or cold with melted butter and a little lemon juice or a good mayonnaise. Keep the shells to put into fish soup or use them as a basis for lobster bisque or lobster sauce.

Crawfish (*langouste, aragosta, langosta*) Depending on where you find it, this comparatively clawless cousin of the lobster is also known as rock lobster, spiny lobster or crayfish – but do not confuse it with the little freshwater crayfish (*écrevisse*) which, in turn, is sometimes known as a crawfish. Depending, too, on where the crawfish comes from – it thrives in the warm waters of the Pacific, Caribbean and Mediterranean – it ranges in colour from brownish-green to reddish-brown with yellow and white markings. Slightly paler than lobster when cooked, it has dense white flesh, well flavoured but inclined to be coarse. The choicest meat is in the tail, and there is a lively market for frozen tails.

Buying guide: fresh is best, in late spring or early autumn; frozen tails are widely available. Choose specimens without eggs, as those that have eggs are not considered to be wholesome to eat. Otherwise, follow the same guidelines as for buying lobsters.
Best cooking methods: when fresh, they are best eaten simply boiled with melted butter. Anything left makes a fine salad, with mayonnaise, or a very good bisque together with some shrimps or prawns in their shells, and plenty of cream and Madeira or brandy. Otherwise, use the same recipes for crawfish as for lobster.

Crayfish (*écrevisse, gamberi, astaco* or *cangrejo de rio*) A sweet-fleshed miniature of the lobster, the crayfish (alias freshwater lobster, yabby, crawdad and crawfish) is the only edible freshwater shellfish. Once a great feature of country-house tables in Britain, crayfish are still relished both in France and in Scandinavia. To find your own, look in

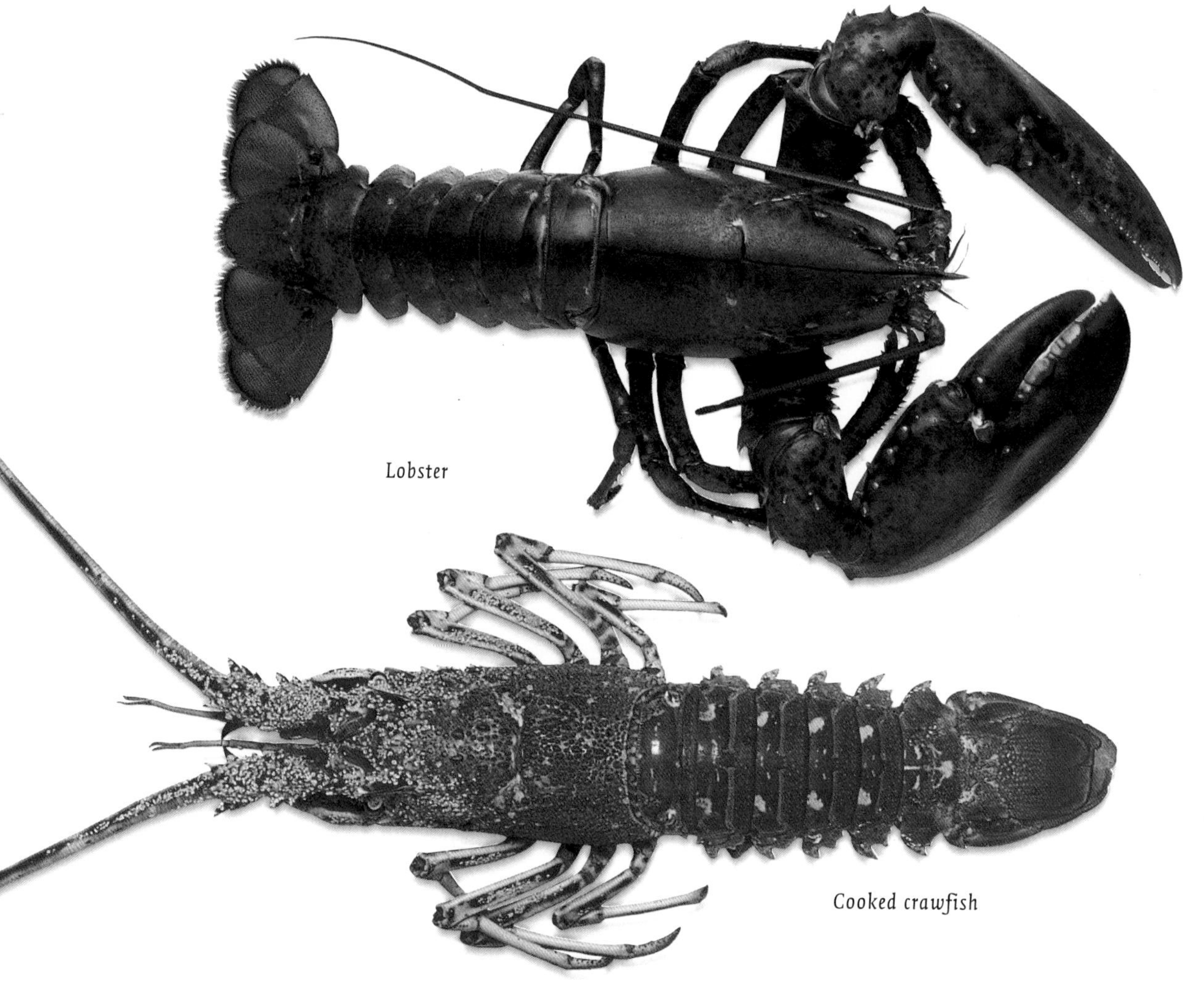

Lobster

Cooked crawfish

clear, unpolluted chalk streams, where they may be found throughout the summer, lurking under the banks. Catch them by knocking out the tip of the inverted cone in the bottom of a wine bottle, baiting the bottle with meat, putting in the cork and lowering the bottle into the water. With luck, the little crayfish will crawl in. Another way is to overturn large stones, pushing a net close by to catch the crayfish; or simply bait a flat, round net with some meat and leave it overnight. Leave them in a bowl under cold running water for an hour before cooking, and remove the thread of intestine by twisting off the middle tail fin, which will bring the intestine with it (or do this after cooking).

Buying guide: apart from the now-scarce native wild crayfish, several cultivated varieties are available from good fish dealers. If you buy them fresh, make sure they are lively – they spoil very quickly once dead. Allow at least 10–12 crayfish per person, depending on your recipe.

Best cooking methods: boiling is best. Put some smooth stones in the bottom of a large pot of water – this will keep the heat up so that the crayfish don't suffer when they are dropped in. Bring the water, into which you have put plenty of salt and fresh dill, to a rapid boil. Drop each crayfish in separately so that the water keeps boiling all the time and cook for about 5 minutes, until they turn bright scarlet. Remove from the heat and let them get cold in their liquor. The French cook them *à la nage* – in a well-flavoured court-bouillon – and serve them in an appetizing scarlet mound with hot melted butter, or cold with mayonnaise. Crayfish are also used to make a beautiful creamy bisque, and for sauce Nantua, the most delicate of sauces, frequently served with *quenelles de brochet* (pike dumplings).

Dublin Bay prawn (*langoustine, scampo, cigala*) Whether you meet them as langoustines or Dublin Bay prawns, Norway lobster (their Latin name is *Nephrops norvegicus*) or Italian *scampi*, these pretty pinky-orange-shelled creatures with their pale claws can be treated as exceedingly large shrimps or very small lobsters, depending on which way you like to look at them. The predictability of finding them in their frozen, ready-shelled form on the menus of bad, expensive and pretentious restaurants has led to their being passed over by many people interested in their food, but cooked with care, and not surrounded by soggy batter, they make many delicate dishes, both hot and cold.

Buying guide: if you are lucky enough to find them fresh, they will most likely be preboiled. Usually only the tails are sold. For four people buy 900 g/2 lb in their shells, half that amount if they are already shelled. They are always available frozen.

Best cooking methods: if raw, cook them in their shells in gently boiling, well-salted water for not more than 10 minutes and eat them with melted butter. Overcooking makes them soggy and tasteless. Preboiled, reheat them gently for a hot dish; never recook them as they easily toughen. Cold, they make a very good salad with oil and vinegar dressing or mayonnaise. In Venice they are dipped in a very light eggless batter, with a few other kinds of small fish and shellfish, then deep fried and served with cut lemons. They are also excellent grilled over charcoal with oil and garlic – even frozen ones are good cooked in this way.

Prawn and shrimp (*crevette, gamberetto* or *gamberello, quisquilla* or *camarón*) There are so many species in this family that anything more than 5–7 cm/2–3 in long is called a prawn in Europe, and it is the discerning French and Italians who award them the distinction of separate names. The *crevette rouge*, or *gambero rosso*, for example, is the large, expensive prawn, very strongly flavoured, much enjoyed by the Italians, who often eat a whole pyramid of them with a bowl of mayonnaise and a bottle of white wine. A clear, deep-coral colour with a violet splotch showing through the transparent shell of the head, it turns a bright pink-red when cooked.

The delicious *crevette rose*, or *gamberello*, is the common large pink prawn, at its best eaten cold with brown bread and butter and lemon juice, or with

peeling, deveining and butterflying prawns 41

Grilled Langoustines 276
Grilled Prawns Wrapped in Bacon 276
Hot and Sour Shellfish Broth 253
Lemon Court-Bouillon with Parsley 245
Marinated Thai Prawns 278
Mayonnaise 259
Normandy Fish Stew 263
Oeufs en Cocotte aux Crevettes 324

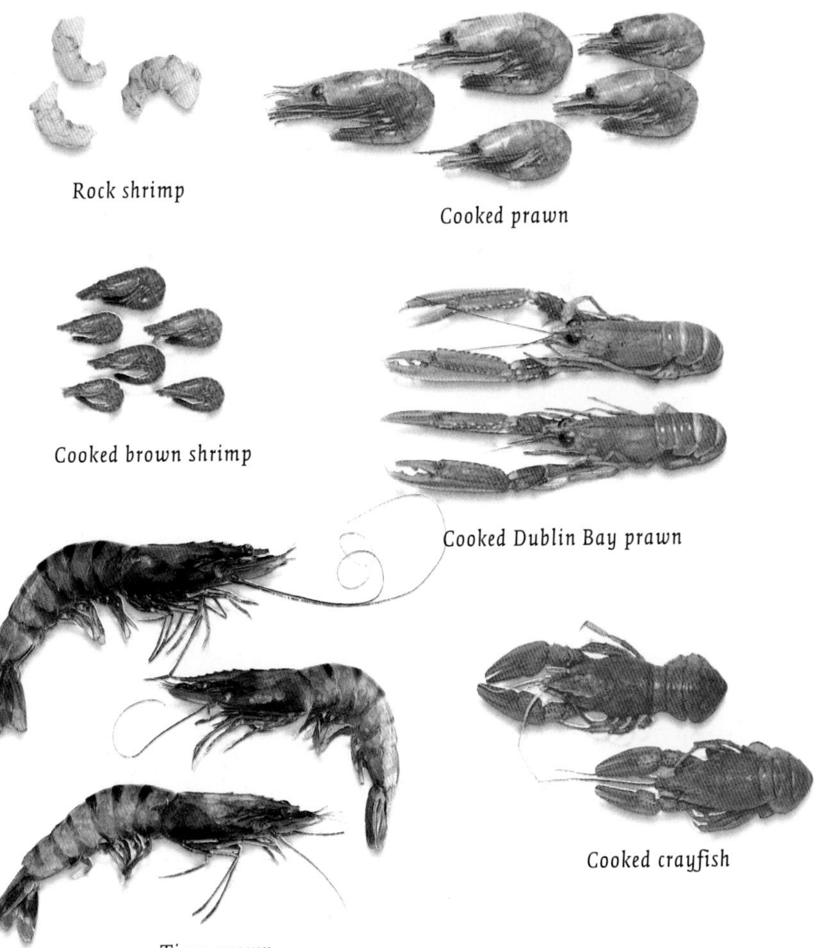

Rock shrimp

Cooked prawn

Cooked brown shrimp

Cooked Dublin Bay prawn

Tiger prawn

Cooked crayfish

peeling, deveining and butterflying prawns 41
shrimp paste 206

Grilled Prawns Wrapped in Bacon 276
Hot and Sour Shellfish Broth 253
Marinated Thai Prawns 278
Normandy Fish Stew 263
Oeufs en Cocotte aux Crevettes 324
Paella 346
Prawn and Fennel Risotto 348
Prawn and Fennel Soup 252
Prawn Omelette 324
Seafood Salad 370

mayonnaise or in a salad. The *crevette rose du large*, or *gambero rosa*, with pretty red markings on its crested head, is one of the best of the prawns, very delicate and much appreciated in northern France, where it is simply boiled, laid on a bed of brown seaweed with ice and halved lemons and served together with brown bread and butter.

In the United States, where more prawns are consumed than anywhere else in the world (and where they are called shrimp in most places), classification is usually by size, from the large and luscious Gulf shrimp (10–12 make 450 g/1 lb) to the tiny cold-water specimens which need 100 or more to tip the scales at that weight. Cold-water shrimp are normally sold cooked, whereas warm-water shrimp, such as those from the Gulf of Mexico and South Atlantic, such as the delicious, hard-shelled rock shrimp, are available raw (frozen or thawed).

Also delicious are the cold-water prawns of Scandinavia, with their firm meat and fresh taste. They are usually boiled in seawater on board the trawler as soon as they are caught, which gives them a mild, sweetish flavour. You will often find these frozen or canned.

Freshly caught and freshly boiled little brown shrimps, *crevettes grises*, *gamberetto grigio* or, in Spain, *quisquilla gris*, are difficult to shell because they are so small, but perhaps it is this fiddly, companionable job that makes the reward so worthwhile. Much more delicate than their larger cousins, these are delicious with lemon and brown bread and butter, or potted and served with lemon and hot toast. Brown shrimps turn browner when cooked; pink shrimps are greyish-brown when caught and turn pink when they are cooked. These are also the little shrimps that are used for open sandwiches and canapés, and go into salads and seafood cocktails.

Large warm-water prawns, farmed by aquaculture methods all over the world, are now widely available raw, in the shell, with or without heads. These include the famed tiger prawn from the Indo-Pacific region, the East Asian king prawn and the Hawaiian blue prawn, a freshwater prawn with a brilliant blue tail.

Buying guide: fresh raw prawns and shrimps should be springy, with bright, crisp shells – avoid any that are soft or limp or have a smell of ammonia about them. They are frequently sold boiled, either in their shells or shelled – give them a sniff to see if they are fresh, and try one to see if it is juicy. Frozen shelled prawns or shrimps should be bought frozen – those thawed-out specimens in trays at the fish market may have been around for some time, and defrosted food spoils much more quickly than fresh food.

Best cooking methods: if you have raw prawns or shrimps, simply drop them into a large pan of boiling seawater or salted water and simmer them for a minute or two, depending on their size – don't overcook them or they will lose their delicate texture. Recooking prawns or shrimps toughens them, so those bought already boiled should be heated gently and for as short a time as possible when being used in a hot dish. They can be shelled and deveined before or after cooking. The larger the species, the better it lends itself to grilling, deep frying and cooking over charcoal.

Oyster (*huitre, ostrica, ostra*) Oysters are a luxury you either love or loathe. To some people they are the height of ecstasy, to others a cause of revulsion. Aldous Huxley said, 'I suppose that when the sapid and slippery morsel – which is gone like a flash of gustatory summer lightning – glides along the palate, few

Blue mussel

Native oyster

Green-lipped mussel

Rock oyster

Atlantic oyster

people imagine that they are swallowing a piece of machinery (and going machinery too) greatly more complicated than a watch.' Perhaps oyster-lovers prefer not to think about it. It is certainly hard to believe that oysters were once the food of the poor: they only became fashionable and expensive as they became scarce, and might have disappeared altogether if a French marine biologist had not discovered the ancient oyster beds at Lake Fusaro, near Naples, and learned how oysters could be artificially reared.

There are three species of European oysters, all of which are farmed by aquaculture. The best British oysters, *Ostrea edulis*, known as natives or flats, include the Whitstable, the Colchester and the Helford. These have rounded shells and a subtle, delicate flavour. In France this type is known as *belon*. Rock oysters, *Crassostrea gigas*, are known as *huitres creuses* in France; these are also found along the west coast of North America where they are called Pacific or Japanese oysters or gigas. They have elongated, crenellated shells; their texture is slightly coarse and they have a sharper, more oceanic flavour. (Whatever name it goes by, any British oyster not called native will be a rock oyster.) The third species, *Crassostrea angulata* or Portuguese oyster, is being gradually supplanted by *C. gigas*, which is thought to be finer. In North America, where most oysters are harvested in the wild, the Atlantic or Eastern oyster, *Crassostrea virginica*, is much prized. Smaller than the rock oyster and milder in flavour, the best known is the Blue Point.

Oysters come in many sizes, and not everyone prefers the largest ones. As a rule of thumb No. 1 is the largest (000 in France) while the smallest is No. 5 (a French No. 5 is much smaller in size than a British No. 5). You will be most likely to be offered a No. 3 in a British restaurant. Rock or Pacific oysters are simply classified as small or large in the UK. There are stringent regulations to keep oysters safe from pollution, but if one tastes bad, spit it out.

Oysters are best eaten raw, on the half-shell. Serve them in the deep halves of their shells, on a bed of crushed ice, and take care not to spill the liquid they contain – it has an exquisite salty, marine flavour with a hint of iodine. Accompany them with halved lemons and, if you like, cayenne pepper, Tabasco or chilli sauce, or with red wine vinegar with a few chopped shallots afloat in it, and brown bread and butter. Drink a chilled Chablis.

Buying guide: oysters are at their best from about the end of October to the end of February, when the sea is coldest. In summer as the sea warms up, they may start breeding and can be milky, fat and soft. Buy and eat them at once. Canned smoked oysters make a good hors d'oeuvre.

Best cooking methods: rock oysters are most often used for cooking. They are delicious in a creamy oyster stew or chowder, in steak and kidney pudding, or in a dry white wine and cheese sauce which is sprinkled with breadcrumbs and browned under the grill.

Scallop (*coquille St Jacques, conchiglie Saint-Jacques, concha de peregrino*) These are a particular favourite among shellfish-lovers, partly because they are such a delight to eat and partly because they are beautiful and symbolic. Often represented in painting (notably in Botticelli's 'Venus'), the scallop shell is a symbol of Christianity and a badge of the pilgrim, particularly those who go to Santiago de Compostela.

Europe can boast the best of the many species of scallop that abound, including

oyster sauce 206
preparing scallops 42
shucking oysters 42

oyster knife 225

Hot and Sour Shellfish Broth 253
Oysters Rockefeller 278
Pan-Fried Scallops with Garlic 279
Scallops with Saffron, Basil and Tomato Vinaigrette 279
Slow-Cooked Brisket of Beef with Soy, Sake and Oysters 284
Steak and Kidney Pudding 283

Queen scallop

Littleneck clam

Cherrystone clam

Chowder clam

Manila clam

Scallop

Cockle

preparing scallops 42
shucking live clams 41
whelk 44
winkle 44

clam knife 225

Hot and Sour Shellfish Broth 253
Lemon Court-Bouillon with Parsley 245
Moules à la Marinière 279
New England Fish Chowder 252
Paella 346
Pan-Fried Scallops with Garlic 279
Sauce Tartare 259
Scallops with Saffron, Basil and Tomato Vinaigrette 279
Seafood Salad 370
Thai Mussels 281

the most common great scallop, the pilgrim scallop and the queen scallop or queenie. These latter, called *vanneaux* in France, *pettine* in Italy and *volandeira* in Spain, are much smaller than ordinary scallops, with two slightly hollow shells rather than one convex and one flat. Small and delicate, they have the texture of butter. American scallops – the large Atlantic deep-sea variety and the small bay scallops – are usually sold without their coral or roe, although in Europe this is considered to be the best part.
Buying guide: at their best in winter, scallops are becoming expensive, but fortunately you do not need many – three or four large ones per person is usually sufficient. If using smaller scallops, allow between 10 and 15 per person. If the scallops you buy have already been shelled and cleaned, ask the fishmonger to let you have some shells, if possible, to use as serving dishes. Scallops identified as 'diver-collected' are prime specimens, hand-picked as the name suggests.
Best cooking methods: be careful not to overcook scallops or they will be tough – small ones only take a few seconds, large ones a minute or two at the most. They can be fried with garlic and parsley or baked in the oven in butter with parsley, garlic and lemon juice; sautéed and served with a little port and cream stirred in to make a sauce; grilled with bacon on a skewer; made into a chowder; or lightly poached or steamed and served in a white wine sauce, sprinkled with breadcrumbs and browned under the grill. When served in a mornay sauce they are known simply by their French name, *coquilles St Jacques*.

Clam (*palourde, vongola, almeja*) North America is the place to appreciate clams: aficionados can delight in steamers, longnecks and littlenecks, cherrystones, Manila clams and razors, surf clams, butter clams and the enormous geoduck. The famous Atlantic littleneck (not to be confused with the Pacific littleneck), cherrystone and steamer clams are not in fact separate species, but are merely different sizes of the hard-shell quahog. Clam chowder is almost a national dish, and a clambake is a serious and favourite pastime, while expressions like 'happy as a clam' are frequently heard along the shorelines. At clambakes the shellfish, plus lobsters and fresh sweetcorn, is steamed on a bed of seaweed over heated stones on the beach. Clambakes are most popular on the East Coast, and here too you can find stands by the side of the road where clams, gathered from the shore at low tide, are sold deep-fried in batter and served with tartare sauce.

In France you may be offered *tellines, clovisses, palourdes, olives* or *praires* (the best, called Warty Venus in England); in Italy, *vongoli* or *tartufi di mare*; in Spain, *almejas, margaritas* or *amayuelas*. In Britain clams are not as difficult to find as they once were, and the large quahogs are sometimes available. These have hard shells and can be difficult to open.
Buying guide: available all year. Since clams vary so much in size from one variety to another, ask the clam-seller how many to allow for each person. Canned clams are also widely available.
Best cooking methods: the soft-shell or long-neck varieties such as razor and Ipswich clams can be eaten raw, like oysters, as can small hard-shell clams such as littlenecks. Larger ones, often called chowder clams, can be steamed and chopped for chowder, fried in olive oil with lemon juice and parsley, grilled with butter, breadcrumbs and garlic, or chopped for the sauce for *spaghetti alla vongole*, which is also good made with tiny littleneck clams.

Mussel (*moule, mitilo* or *muscolo, mejillón*) Clumped in blue-black masses on rocks and piers or attached singly to shingle stones in estuaries, mussels have in the past quite unfairly been considered the poor man's shellfish. Their status, however, has been improving rapidly. In North America, where they are to be found on both coasts and are widely farmed, they have grown steadily in popularity, and in Europe, where they are extremely popular, there are mussel farms around Mediterranean coasts where the mussels are bred on long stakes in clean seawater. If you are collecting your own mussels, make sure that they are living in unpolluted water and known to be safe. Do not collect them in the heat of summer (when there is not an 'r' in the month), and discard any that are even remotely damaged.

Mussels are usually sold cleaned, but wash them in several changes of water to rid them of grit, then scrape the shells clean with the back of a knife, if necessary, and rinse thoroughly in cold water. If the stringy beard is attached, pull it out and cut it off, then rinse the mussels again in a bowl of clean water. Discard any that float to the surface or whose shells are damaged or open.

The French are enthusiastic about raw shellfish and will eat whole platefuls of raw mussels with lemon juice as if they were oysters. The smooth, thin-shelled French species are the best to eat in this way, and they should be from a very pure location.

A more recent arrival is the green-lipped mussel imported from New Zealand. It is larger and meatier than the blue mussel and has a slightly more pronounced flavour.
Buying guide: mussels are happily inexpensive. The medium-size or smaller ones are best; large mussels are not so appetizing. Always buy more mussels than you need, to allow for those you have to discard. For two people, buy a quart (about 900 g/2 lb).
Best cooking methods: one of the best-known recipes for mussels is the excellent *moules à la marinière*. They can also be used, once opened, like snails, grilled with breadcrumbs, garlic, parsley and butter, or in a garlicky tomato sauce, in pasta sauce, seafood salad or deep fried.

Cockle (*coque, cuore, berberecho*) These have long been a favoured shellfish in Britain, traditionally sold with winkles and whelks at the seaside and outside London pubs. Years ago, when vendors did not possess weighing scales, they measured out their pre-boiled wares in their empty pint-size beer mugs, and ever since cockles have been sold by the pint (the equivalent of about 450 g/1 lb).
Buying guide: at their best in the summer, cockles are usually sold boiled. Eat at seaside stalls with salt, pepper, vinegar and brown bread and butter.
Best cooking methods: eat cockles raw, or steam them in a court-bouillon until their shells open. They also make a splendid soup, combined with mussels, garlic, potato, bacon and milk, and are a good addition to risottos and fritters; or they can be stewed with their juices in a thick tomato sauce and served with pasta. In South-east Asia cockles are a traditional ingredient in *char kway teow*, a fried noodle dish, and they are also steamed and served with a piquant dipping sauce.

Despatching a live lobster

In some recipes a live lobster is cut up before cooking. Cover the tail with a cloth and hold it firmly. Insert the point of a heavy, sharp knife into the centre of the cross mark where the head and tail shells meet, and quickly push it down to the board. This severs the spinal cord and kills the lobster instantly. Leave for a few minutes for the reflexes to cease; then cut the lobster in half or into pieces.

lobster 33

lobster crackers, pick and pincer 229
knives 222–4

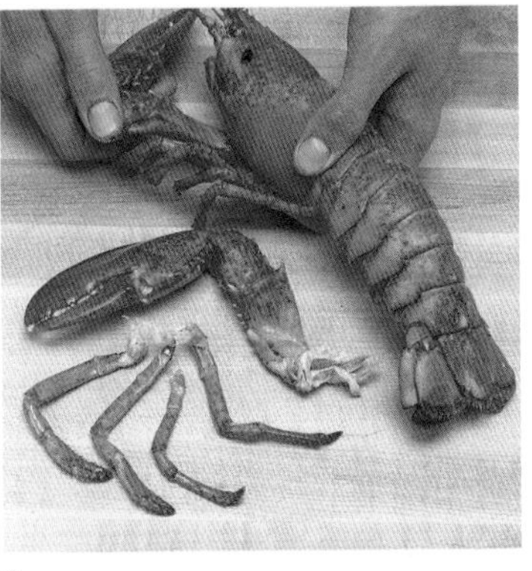

1

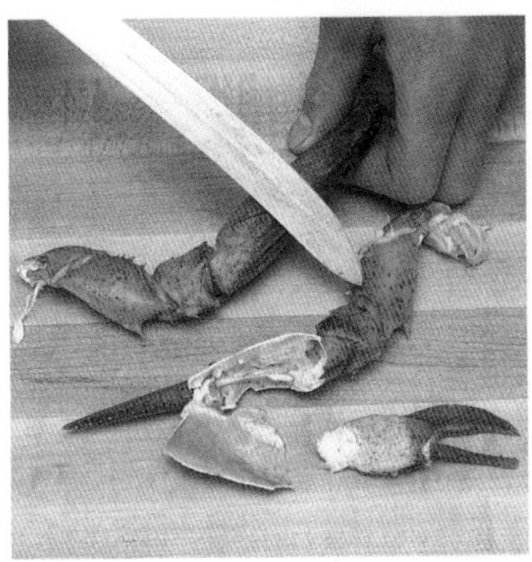

2

Preparing a cooked lobster

1 If you wish to remove the claws and legs, simply twist them off. Dressed lobster dishes are usually presented with the claw meat already extracted.

2 To extract the meat from the claws and legs, crack them open, using the back of a heavy knife, or a nutcracker, lobster cracker or small hammer.

3

4

3 Splitting a lobster in half is easiest to do in two stages (you can prepare an uncooked lobster in the same way). First, draw a sharp knife through the head from the tail section towards the eyes.

4 Reinsert the knife and move it in the opposite direction, cutting down to the tip of the tail and splitting the lobster completely in two.

5

6

5 Pull the halves apart to expose the flesh. This fine female lobster has an excellent red coral, and also some darker external roe, which is unusual. Both are edible and should be reserved.

6 Discard the white gills from the top of the head, and the intestinal tract, which runs down the middle of the tail. As well as the coral, the creamy green tomalley, or liver, should also be reserved to eat or to make lobster sauce.

crab 33

lobster crackers and pick 229
nutcrackers 229

Picking a cooked crab

1 Hold the crab firmly in one hand and give its back underside a sharp thump. This should loosen the body and legs from the shell.

2 Stand the crab on its head and, pushing against the underbody with your thumbs, lever away the back end of the shell with your fingers.

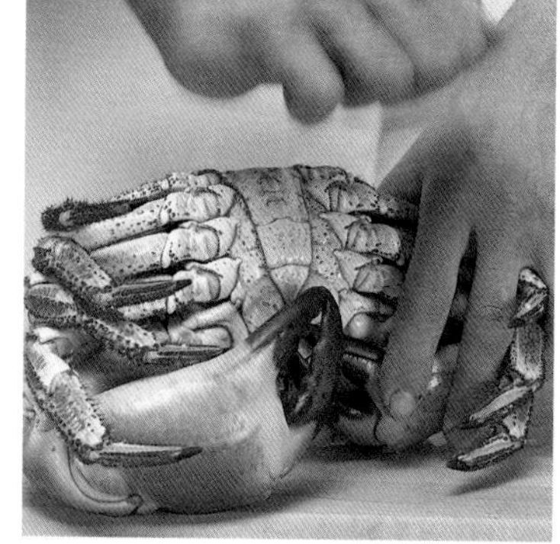

1

2

3 Pull the underbody and the legs away from the shell.

4 Remove and discard the messy bundle of intestines. This will be found either in the shell or still clinging to the body. Comb it gently with a fork to remove any brown meat that is adhering to it.

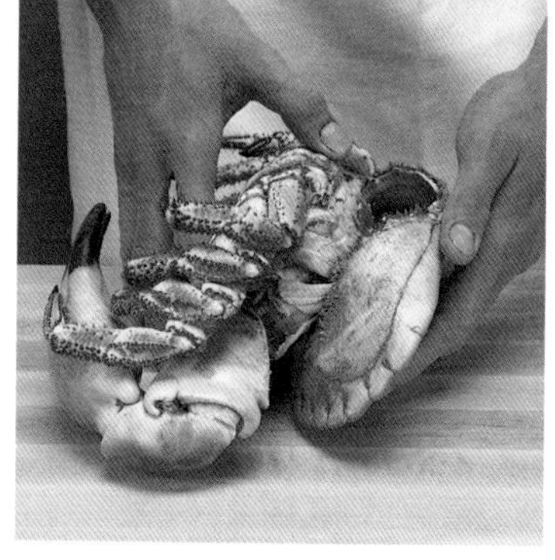

3

4

5

6

5 Scoop out the brown creamy meat from inside the shell.

6 Discard the grey gills, known as dead men's fingers, which lie on either side of the body.

7

8

7 Twist off all the legs and claws. To expose the body's white meat, make two cuts, one on either side of the bony central peak. The two cuts should meet in a V shape at the peak of the body. This divides the body in three. Discard the middle bit, which contains no meat.

8 With a skewer, dig out the white meat from the two outer pieces of the body. Avoid crushing the inner shell. The meat on the plate shows how much you can expect from half the body of a large crab.

clam 38
crab 33
prawn and shrimp 35

clam knife 225

9 Crack open the claws and legs with a hammer, lobster cracker or nutcracker and extract their meat. The meat on the plate is the amount obtained from one claw and one leg.

10 Mix together the white meat from the legs, claws and body, and serve it with the brown meat.

9

10

Peeling, deveining and butterflying prawns

1 Pull off the head and legs with your fingers, then peel the shell away from the body. If you like, leave the last section of tail on the prawn.

2 To devein, use a small knife to cut a shallow slit down the centre of the curved back of the prawn.

1

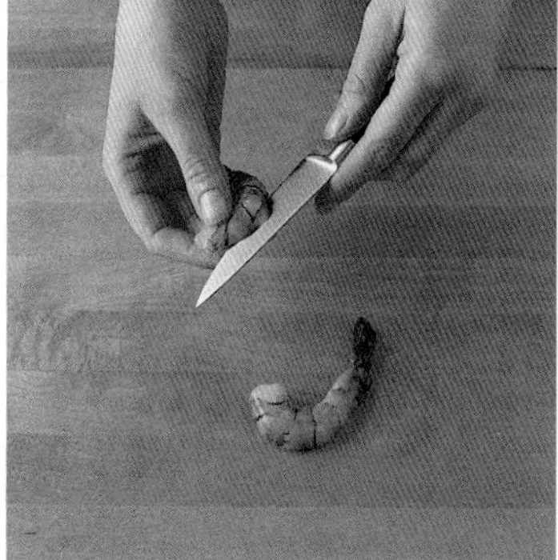

2

3 If the intestinal vein is black or brown, pull it out with the tip of the knife or with your fingers and discard it. (The vein is removed only because of its appearance.)

4 To butterfly, cut into the slit in the back of the prawn to make the cut deeper but without cutting all the way through. Open the prawn flat, like a book.

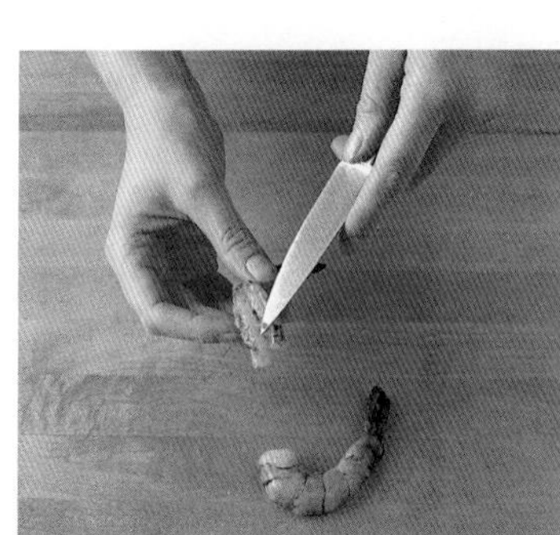

3

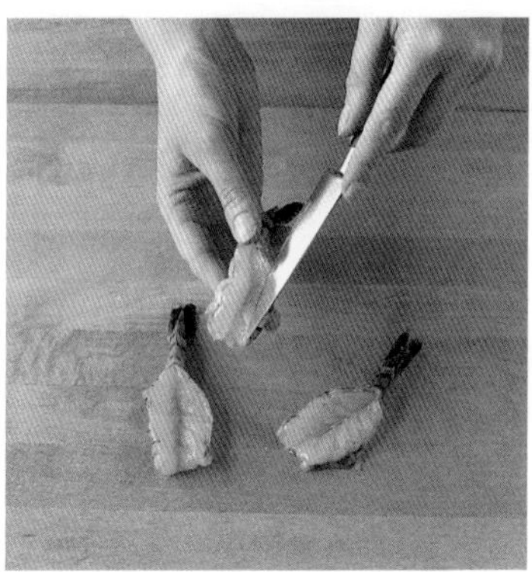

4

Shucking live clams

1 Hold the clam over a bowl, with the hinge of the shell in your palm. Insert the blade of a clam knife between the top and bottom shell, and work it round the shell until you reach the hinge. Do not cut into the shell with the tip of the knife or you may pierce the clam meat.

2 Cut through the hinge muscle and open the shell. Cut the clam free from the top and bottom of the shell, and tip it into the bowl with all its liquor.

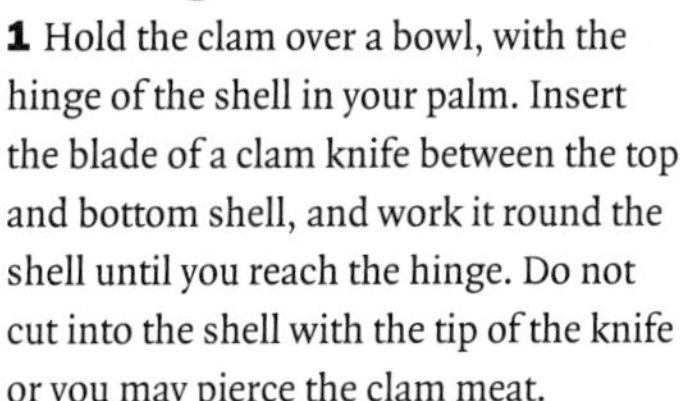

1

2

oyster 36
scallop 37

oyster knife 229

Shucking oysters

1 Hold the oyster steady, cupped side down, and insert an oyster knife between the top and bottom shells, next to the hinge. The oyster shown here is an English Whitstable.

2 Keep a firm grip on the oyster and, pushing against the hinge, carefully work the knife in, twisting it slightly, until the hinge breaks.

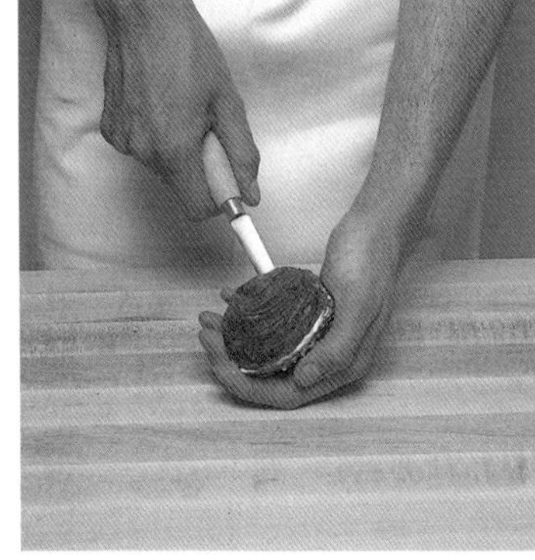

1

2

3 Open the oyster, still keeping the cupped side down to reserve the liquid, and sever the muscle that adheres to the upper shell.

4 Run the knife underneath the oyster to free it from the lower shell. Turn the oyster over to display its more attractive side, and serve it with its own marine-flavoured juices still in the rounded bottom shell.

3

4

Preparing scallops

1 Using a strong, broad-tipped knife, lever the shells apart. Detach the scallop from the rounded shell by carefully sliding the knife underneath the muscle.

2 Rinse the scallop under cold running water. Pull away the surrounding film of membrane, or 'beard', which may contain sand, and discard it.

1

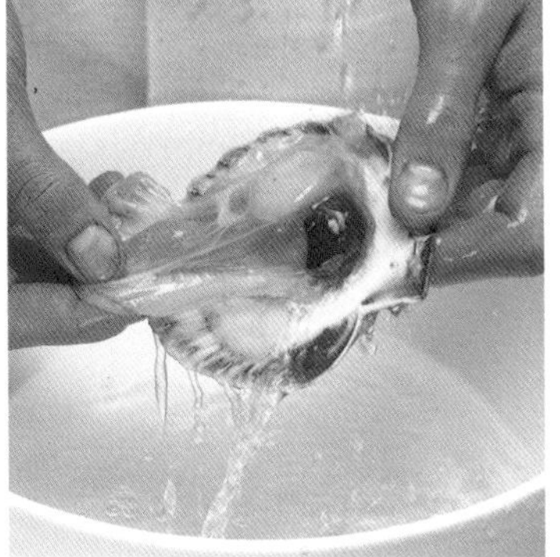

2

3 Keep the scallop under running water and, holding back the white flesh and coral with your thumb, push away the black intestine and sever it. Discard the intestine.

4 The cushion of muscle (the white flesh) and the delicious orange coral attached to it are now ready to cook.

3

4

Other Seafood, Snails and Frog's Legs

Many creatures are so strange and so unlike anything else that they are usually, for want of a better label, called 'miscellaneous'. But unappetizing though they may look to some people, with their spiny, shelly, jelly-like or leathery exteriors, many of us really like them. Some, such as squid, snails, sea urchins and octopus, rank among the most delicious of foods, and all are a challenge to the adventurous cook.

Some seafoods, like limpets, although edible, are not worth marketing and you will have to gather them yourself. Remember that any living thing from the sea and its shores is potentially dangerous if it is from a polluted area, and that many varieties are simply inedible. If in any doubt about the safety of your haul, check with an environmental health officer.

Squid, octopus and cuttlefish

The Mediterranean countries understand best how to deal with these extraordinary creatures, having eaten them in great quantities since the earliest days of civilization. They also play an important role in the cookery of China and Japan. Small ones are the sweetest and tenderest; larger specimens are improved by several hours' marinating in wine vinegar, sliced onion, salt and pepper.

Squid Familiar in Mediterranean dishes as *calmar* or *encornet*, *calamaro*, *calamar* or *kalamári* in Greece, squid is delicious to eat if you understand the principle that the cooking must be either very brief or very long – anything in between and your squid will be as tough as rubber. Once cleaned, the squid can be rapidly grilled; or stuffed with minced meat and the chopped tentacles and baked in a tomato and garlic sauce; or sliced in rings and fried plain or dipped first into a light batter. Larger specimens can be stewed gently with olive oil, wine and tomatoes.

It is a pleasure, in Spain, to be served with two little dishes at the same time, one holding a fragrant stew of the tentacles, with onions and garlic, and the other the sliced, crisply fried rings of the body. Squid can also be cut into rings and boiled very briefly – no more than a minute or two, when they lose their pearly, translucent look – and then put into a seafood salad. The tiniest squid, with fragile bodies no more than 8 cm/3 in long, can be very quickly deep-fried in a coating of beaten egg and flour. Squid ink found in a sac inside can be used in risotto, pasta and sauces.

Octopus (*poulpe* or *pieuvre*, *polpo*, *pulpo*) Octopus can be very tough, and the larger it grows the tougher it gets, so it is a wise precaution, having removed the beak and head (if the fish dealer has not already done so) and turned out the contents of the body, to pound the legs and body with a mallet or a cutlet beater until they are soft. The octopus contains its ink within its liver, and this is sometimes used to make a very strong and heavily scented gravy. The ink can also be used as a pasta sauce. Both octopus and squid ink are available in some large supermarkets and a few good fishmongers.

Octopus can be stewed, or stuffed and baked like squid, but a large specimen will need up to 2 hours or more to become tender. Little ones can also be fried gently

preparing squid 47

cutlet beater 226

Paella 346
Seafood Salad 370
Stuffed Baby Squid 281

Squid

Octopus

Cuttlefish

Whelk

Jellyfish

Abalone

Winkle

Sea urchin

choucroute garnie 422
seviche 423

meat tenderizer 226

New England Fish Chowder 252

in olive oil and make a delicious salad, often eaten warm, with lemon juice, olive oil, garlic and chopped parsley.

Cuttlefish (*seiche, seppia, jibia*) Often gracefully camouflaged by striped markings, the cuttlefish has a larger head than the squid and a much wider, dumpier body. Inside lies the white shell, or cuttlebone, found washed up on beaches and given to pet birds to peck at (ground, it was once used as tooth powder and jewel polish, and as face powder by Roman ladies who wanted to look delicate).

More tender than octopus or squid, cuttlefish can be cooked in the same ways, and very small ones are delicious deep fried. They are cleaned and prepared in the same way as squid. The ink, or *sepia*, can be used to make a sauce in which the cuttlefish can be stewed, and goes into the Italian dish *risotto nero*, black rice.

Single-shelled creatures

These all belong to the same family that includes the familiar garden snail. They are all mobile, moving around on a muscular 'foot', and can go into fish soups, sauces and stews as well as being tasty snacks on their own, accompanied by plenty of vinegar, pepper and brown bread and butter.

Abalone, ormer (*ormeau, orecchia marina, oreja de mar*) 'Delicious ambrosia', an enthusiast wrote in the 1600s about the ormers of the Channel Islands. These white-fleshed shellfish with their curiously ear-shaped shells, the inside gleaming with pearly colours, can still be found fresh around the Channel Islands and the Breton coast at certain times of the year, and in the warm waters off California.

Fresh abalones, even little ones, need to be well beaten to make them tender. Very small abalones can then be eaten raw with a squeeze of lemon juice; larger ones are usually thinly sliced and marinated in white wine, oil, herbs and chopped shallot and then fried very briefly in butter – overcooking only toughens them. They can also be used like clams in soup or chowder. Canned abalone is a good substitute for fresh, but dried abalone is hardly worth the effort of making it edible – it needs to be soaked for 4 days before anything can be done with it.

Winkle, periwinkle (*bigorneau, littorina, bigarro*) There is something homely and comfortable about winkles. Their little dark shells are small enough to make them completely acceptable in a way that many large snails are not. In Britain they are eaten with bread and butter and a pot of tea, and make a tasty snack on seaside piers, accompanied by vinegar. In an Alsatian brasserie you are likely to be given a plate of *bigorneaux* with a glass of kir – cassis and white wine – while waiting for your *choucroute garnie* or your slice of foie gras. Whatever the circumstances, a long pin is indispensable for wheedling the little shellfish out of their shells. To cook winkles, boil them in their shells in salted water for about 10 minutes. Eat only the first part of the body – the second part is easily separated.

Whelk (*buccin, buccino, bocina*) These handsome but decidedly unaristocratic shellfish, with their ribbed, deeply whorled shells, are usually sold already boiled. They are eaten with vinegar and brown bread and butter, like winkles, but are a much more substantial mouthful and easier to remove from their shells. The large 'foot' is the part that is usually eaten. Whelks can also be used in fish soups and stews. On the Scottish island of Iona, where whelks are a traditional part of the islanders' diet, whelk soup is made by thickening seasoned whelk stock with oatmeal and finely chopped onion.

Conch (*conque, conchiglia, concha*) The term conch – pronounced 'konk' – is often used to include the winkle and whelk, but what is usually thought of as being the best of the family is the large Caribbean conch with the graceful spiral-shaped shell in which one seems to hear the sound of the sea. Fresh conch meat needs to be tenderized by vigorous beating and can then be stewed in a wine sauce with herbs and spices, or thinly sliced and deep fried. It also goes into chowders, and in parts of the Caribbean it is used for seviche.

Limpet (*patelle, patella, lapa*) Limpets are exceptionally tough – you can tell they are going to be tough by the strength of the muscle that clamps them to the rocks as soon as they are touched and makes them almost impossible to prise off, unless you can take them by surprise. With persistence they can be gathered at low tide (they are rarely marketed) and eaten raw or used in soup. They can also be fried in butter with parsley, pepper and vinegar, or baked for a few minutes with a little butter in each shell. Smaller ones are better boiled and eaten with vinegar, pepper and bread and butter.

Slipper limpet Native to North America, these are now quite common along the southern coastlines of England. Unpopular with oyster lovers, as they prey on oysters, they are quite good to eat either cooked or raw.

'Fruits' of the sea

Some of the most astonishing candidates for any sort of cuisine are none the less considered delicacies by their devotees.

Sea urchin (*oursin, riccio di mare, erizo de mar*) A menace to the bather but a pleasure to the gourmet, the sharp-spined sea urchin is plentiful in many parts of the world, and its pretty lacy-patterned shell – minus the spines – is often brought home as a memento of seaside holidays. Best for eating are the green sea urchin and the black sea urchin. These can be lightly boiled and are sometimes pickled, but are best eaten fresh, raw and straight from the shell. To accomplish this the sea urchin is cut in half, ideally with a *coupe-oursin* designed for this task. This exposes the rose-coloured or orange ovaries or coral; sprinkle with lemon juice and scoop out with pieces of fresh crusty bread. The crushed coral can also be used in omelettes and as a garnish for fish.

Sea or snake-locks anemone and *tomate de mer* These inhabitants of rocky pools, enticingly waving their multitude of soft arms, are sometimes eaten in Japan, Samoa and France. The sea anemones, known as *orties de mer*, are carefully gathered in France, and then marinated, dipped into a light batter and fried. They also go, together with a few red *tomates de mer* (beadlet anemones) and a great many shellfish, into a Mediterranean soup.

***Figue de mer*, violet** This very odd, leathery-skinned creature, called *limone di mare* or *uovo di mare* in Italy and *probecho* in Spain, is particularly relished in Provence, where it has the proper accompaniment of hot sun and a plentiful supply of white wine. Found anchored to rocks or the sea floor, syphoning water in through one spout and out of the other, it is cut in half and the yellow part inside is eaten raw.

Bêche de mer Also known as sea cucumber, because of its shape, and as sea slug, *trepang* and *balatin*, this warm-water creature is sliced and eaten raw in Japan with soy sauce, vinegar or mustard. Several species are smoke-dried and used in soup. In China it has a reputation as an aphrodisiac. One recipe involves 4 days of preparation and yields 12 Chinese servings or 95 Western servings, which is either a miscalculation or says a great deal about the sea slug's lack of appeal to the Western palate.

Jellyfish The Chinese are great users of dried jellyfish, primarily to add texture to a meal, and dried jellyfish can usually be found in the more specialized Chinese supermarkets. Jellyfish will need to be soaked for some hours in several changes of fresh water. Once soaked, it should be blanched in boiling water briefly, then refreshed in cold water. It can be cut into slivers and stir-fried with chicken, or scalded, which produces crunchy curls that are served with a sauce of sesame oil, soy sauce, vinegar and sugar. In Japan jellyfish is cooked into crisp-textured strips and eaten with vinegar.

Samphire and seaweeds

Apart from being such a pleasure to gather, in the early months of summer when most of them are at their most luxuriant, seaweeds are a rich source of minerals as well as of intriguing textures and flavours. If you gather your own, cut the plant well above its base so that it can grow again, and always wash it thoroughly in fresh water before cooking. Most of the better-known seaweeds can be found dried in health-food stores or oriental supermarkets, and can be restored by soaking.

Marsh samphire (*Salicornia europaea*) This succulent green plant, also known as glasswort or pickle-plant or, in French, as *pousse-pierre* or *saint-pierre*, can be found growing on seaside marshes. It is best at midsummer. The flavour of fresh marsh samphire is salty and iodiney – like seawater; it is the crisp texture that is interesting. When in season, you will occasionally find samphire in good fishmongers.

Samphire can go fresh into salads and is often steeped in vinegar to make a delicate pickle. It is greatly appreciated as a vegetable served with fish, or on its own, simply boiled and dipped in melted butter, then drawn through the teeth like asparagus to strip the succulent part from the thin central core.

Laver (*Porphyra vulgaris*) With its delicate taste of the sea, this reddish-purple seaweed, also known as sloke

mustards 202–3
sesame oil 112
soy sauce 207
sugar 211–12
vinegar 204–5

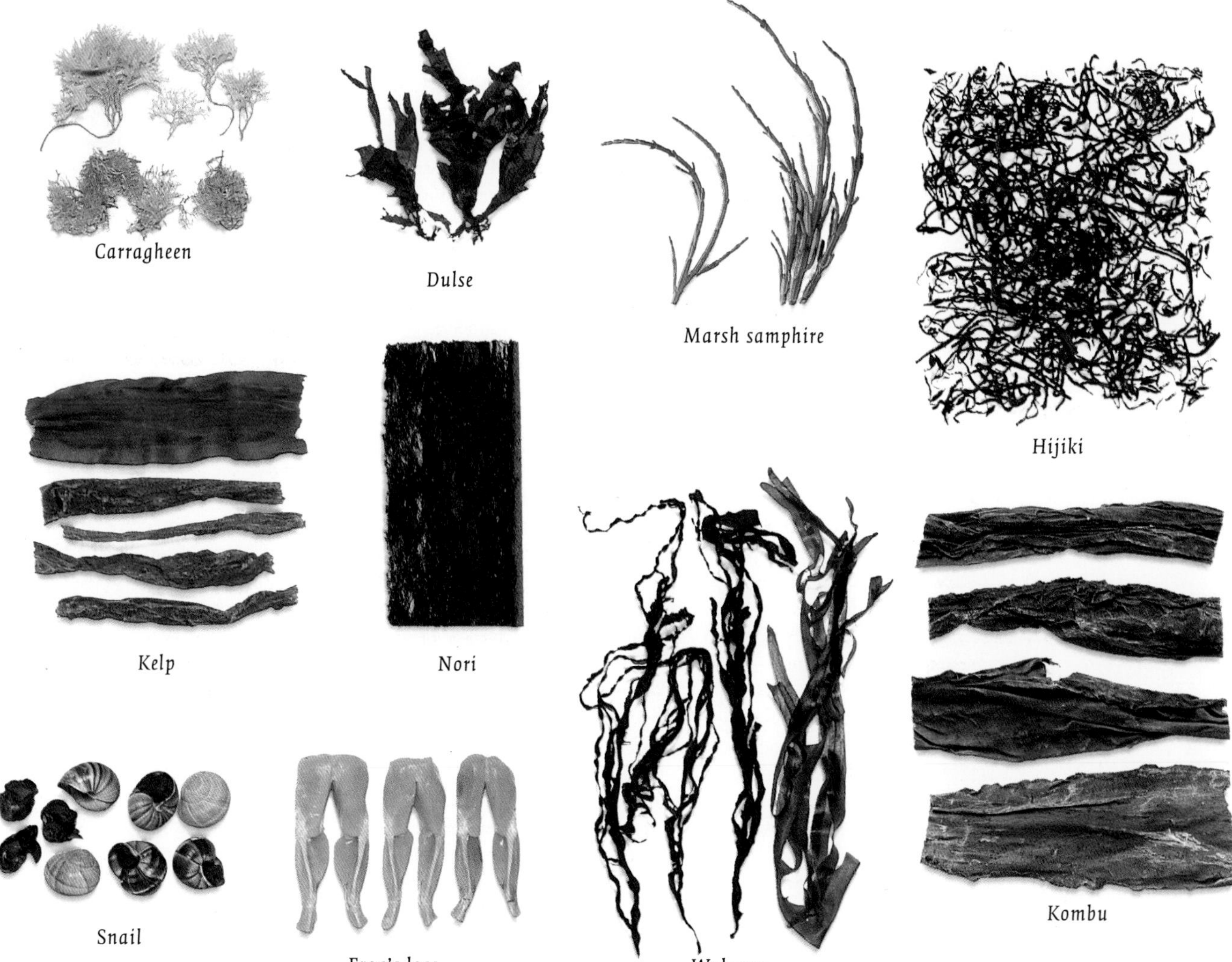

Carragheen

Dulse

Marsh samphire

Hijiki

Kelp

Nori

Snail

Frog's legs

Wakame

Kombu

gelatine 62

Japanese Noodles with Char-grilled Beef 345

or, in France, as *porphyrée pourpre*, was very popular in England in the eighteenth century. Fresh, it is seldom appreciated in the West today, except in Wales, where it is enthusiastically boiled until it turns into the spinach-like pulp called laverbread – although why it should be called bread is a mystery. The pulp is then mixed with oatmeal, shaped into small flat cakes and fried with bacon for breakfast, or heated through with a knob of butter and the juice of an orange or lemon to make a sauce to eat with mutton. In China, laver is dried and then simmered to produce a nutritious jelly. In Japan, where it is cultivated and called *nori*, it is pressed and dried in thin sheets, toasted lightly and wrapped around vinegared rice to make sushi or crumbled over rice as a salty garnish.

Carragheen, Irish moss (*Chondrus crispus*) Although Ireland and the village of Carragheen have given it its most commonly used names, this pretty red-tinged, frond-like plant is common along most northerly Atlantic shorelines growing on rocks and stones. It can be used fresh or dried, when it bleaches to a creamy white, and is an important source of agar-agar, a vegetable gelatine much used in the food industry. The traditional way to make a carragheen jelly is to simmer the moss in milk or water until most of it dissolves, then strain and leave it to set. The result is very nourishing. If you don't like its faint taste of the sea it can be flavoured with vanilla, honey or fruit.

Kelp A number of large seaweeds are popularly known as kelp and have long been used as a source of food and of medicine, being particularly rich in iodine. Much liked in Japan, where it is traditionally dried on sandy beaches and called *kombu* or *konbu*, kelp finds its way to the table as a delicate salad vegetable, a seasoning for root vegetables, a garnish for rice, or fashioned into miniature baskets, deep fried and stuffed with vegetables. It is also used for making soups and stocks, such as *dashi*, or can simply be cooked as a vegetable to accompany fish. Another dried Japanese seaweed, hijiki, is used in the same ways.

To make the stock called *dashi*, cut a piece of kombu into four with scissors and place in a pan with 1 litre/2 pints of water. Bring to the boil, then remove from the heat at once and cool the boiling liquid by adding 4 tablespoons cold water. Add a cup of dried bonito flakes (*katsuobushi*), bring the liquid back to the boil and remove from the heat at once. Skim and strain through a cloth or fine sieve. For a vegetarian version omit the *katsuobushi*.

Dulse (*Rhodymenia palmata*) Another of the familiar purplish-red seaweeds, with fan-shaped fronds up to 25 cm/10 in long, dulse is to be found growing plentifully on rocks and on larger weeds. Known in Ireland as *dillisk*, *algue rouge* in France and *alga roja* in Spain, dulse can be eaten raw as a salad, and around the Mediterranean it sometimes goes into ragouts, but it is a very tough, rubbery plant and needs to be cooked for up to 5 hours. It has a salty, fish-like flavour, and dried, it can be chewed as an unconventional appetizer, or used as a relish.

Wakame A rich source of minerals, this dark green seaweed is much used in Japan. The soft leaves go into salads or are cooked with other vegetables, and both leaves and stems are used in soups.

Snail

The French, of course, are major eaters of snails, and the snails the French prize most are the hefty specimens from the vineyards of Burgundy, where they are fed – like the snails of ancient Rome – on vine leaves until they have grown fat and luscious. The classic way to prepare snails is the Burgundian way, in which case they become *escargots à la bourguignonne*, served sizzling in their shells with great quantities of rich garlic butter and fresh crusty bread for mopping. However, as there are never enough Burgundian snails to meet the demand, the alternative is a smaller striped snail, the *petit gris*, which makes up for its lack of size by being sweet, tasty and tender. A drawback is that the *petit gris* shells, unlike those of the Burgundian snail, may be too fragile to be used once their occupants have been removed, but this is solved by using the little ceramic pots called *godets*, easily washed and always ready to be used again. Other essentials for the dedicated enjoyment of snails are the dimpled plates called *escargotières*, which hold six or twelve snail shells, tongs for picking up the piping hot shells, and special forks which have two prongs for twisting the snails out of their shells.

The business of preparing live snails means that it is much simpler to buy snails canned, or fresh ones that are already cleaned and ready to cook, or cooked and only needing to be reheated and combined with their sauce. As a change from garlic butter, snails are very good simmered in olive oil with garlic, tomato and fresh rosemary or mint – the traditional dish to serve on Midsummer's Eve in Rome.

Frog's legs

Like snails, frog's legs as a delicacy have long been associated with the French. Escoffier, the 'king of chefs', is credited with making them acceptable to the English: in the 1890s, for a party held by the Prince of Wales at the Savoy Hotel, London, he prepared what he called *nymphes à l'aurore*, frog's legs poached in white wine and served cold in aspic with a little paprika to evoke the rose-gold glow of dawn. Presumably he called his frog's legs 'nymphs' out of delicacy of feeling for the English diners. When he wasn't preparing them for the Prince of Wales, Escoffier simply seasoned them with salt and pepper, dusted them with flour and sautéed them in butter, serving them with a squeeze of lemon juice and a sprinkling of parsley.

Today, in the Dombes region of eastern France, those who know their frogs still go frogging in the *étangs* and lakes; however, not all frogs are edible and what appears frozen and canned in the shops and on restaurant menus will have come from special frog farms. They are light and easily digestible, rather similar to chicken in flavour – in China, where frogs thrive in the paddy fields and frog's legs are much enjoyed at banquets, they are known as 'field chickens'.

In North America frog's legs are often big enough to be southern-fried, like chicken legs, but the smaller legs are usually more tender and have a subtler flavour. But Escoffier's way with them is still the best: blanched and skinned, cooked in oil or butter for about 5 minutes until golden brown, and served with lemon and parsley. Alternatively, they can be poached in a little white wine and served hot with a creamy sauce, or prepared *à la provençale*, with garlic and tomato.

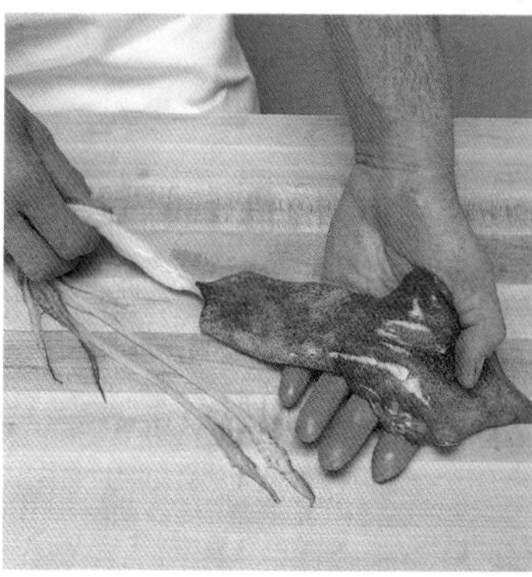

1

Preparing squid

1 Grasp the squid firmly with one hand and with the other reach inside the body and pull the head, tentacles and innards away.

squid 43

knives 222–4

2 Pull off and discard the body's mottled skin.

3 Feel inside the body for the long piece of transparent cartilage, or 'quill', pull it out and discard it.

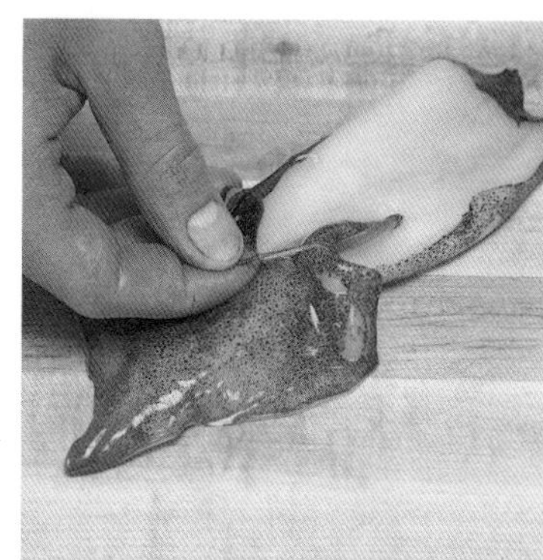

2

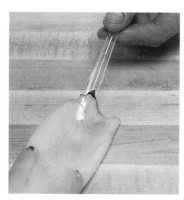

3

4

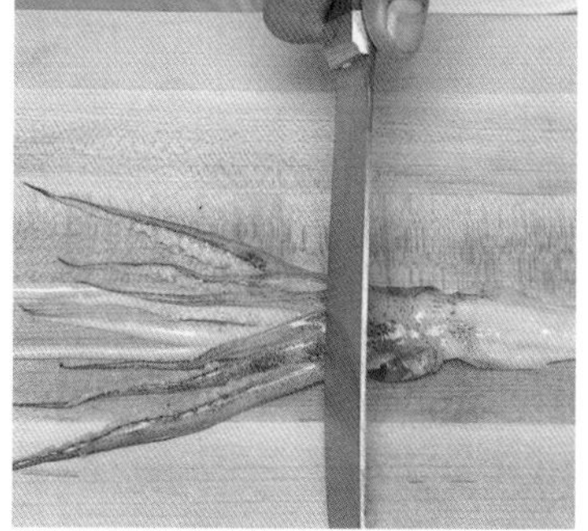

5

4 Wash the body thoroughly, inside and out, under cold running water and then pull off the two flaps from the body. You will find that they separate quite easily, as if held in place only by suction.

5 Cut the tentacles from the head. If the long, narrow ink sac is present and still intact, you will find it attached to the head; remove it carefully and put it aside to use in an accompanying sauce. The head, which contains the entrails, can now be discarded.

6

6 Leave the body whole for stuffing or cut it into thick rings. Slice the flaps in broad strips and cut the tentacles to a manageable size. The squid is now ready for cooking.

Meat

bard 422
beef 51
cooking fats and oils 110–13
cured meat and poultry 71
ham, bacon and salted pork 68–70
hang 422
lamb 56
meat recipes 282–93
offal 61
pork 58
preparing meat 63–7
sausages and salamis 72
veal 54

barbecuing equipment 240–1
cutlet beater 226
frying pan 234
meat tenderizer 226
meat thermometer 233
ridged cast-iron grill pan 233

Meat is such an important part of our diet that it makes sense to buy it as intelligently as possible. If you always go to a high-class butcher (possibly one who raises his own stock or sells organic meat), who hangs his meat until it has reached the peak of juiciness and flavour and who butchers it with finesse, you will seldom have a disappointing piece of meat. You will also be able to buy meat in greater variety, as the butcher will be able to offer you the lesser-known cuts that can go a long way towards making your food more interesting. Because there will be little waste by way of unwanted fat, gristle and awkward bones, his prices will be high, but cooking will be a joy.

Choosing meat

Failing such a paragon, it pays to develop your own expertise when it comes to shopping. Of course, most butchers will give friendly and sometimes disinterested advice when asked. However, at the supermarket there often is no-one to turn to, and the trays of meat can look distressingly similar. Some stores do label their meat 'roasting', 'braising' and 'stewing', and this service is spreading. But many others simply give you the name of the type and cut, sometimes adding a flag saying 'prime', and leave it at that. (In the United States, meat is graded 'prime', 'choice', 'good' and 'standard', but in England the word 'prime' is merely an adjective that is used by the butcher to describe the best meat he has for sale.)

Today, with fat definitely off the menu, special attention is paid to the ratio of fat to lean while the herd is still on the hoof, whilst organic farms, where the animals' diet is carefully supervised, offer the healthiest meat. All beasts are rested before slaughter in the cause of kindness and to guarantee tender meat. The finer the herd, the more care is lavished upon them and as a result the more delicious is their meat.

The look of meat At a really good store all the cuts, even the cheapest, will look appetizing. They should look silky, not wet. All boned, rolled joints should be neatly tied, not skewered, since piercing causes a loss of moisture during cooking and may introduce bacteria into the centre of the meat. Barding should be neat, complete and even. Where there are bones, these should be sawn smoothly, not jaggedly chopped, and meat should be neatly and thoroughly trimmed, particularly ribs, chops and cutlets, with excess fat removed.

The cut surface of meat exposes the grain, or muscle fibres, which are potentially coarser and tougher in an older animal, or in parts of the anatomy, such as the leg or the neck, which have had more active use. However, the fineness or otherwise of grain is not really a reliable indicator of either eating quality or tenderness.

Tenderness When all pieces of meat look equally beautiful, it can be hard to distinguish between the tender and the not so tender, and many factors, apart from anatomy, contribute to this: the age and breed of the animal, the way it was handled before slaughter, the temperature to which the carcass was chilled, the length of time it was hung, the way the meat is cut, and so on.

There are many schools of butchery, producing different cuts of meat not only in different countries but in different regions; in fact, there are as many regional variations and names for the different cuts as there are regional recipes. However, no matter where and how a carcass is divided, most of the best meat of each animal comes from the hindquarter and loin, and the tenderest meat of all comes from the parts that have had the least exercise. Exercise means the development of muscle fibre and of the connective tissue that holds the muscles together in bundles, and it is connective tissue that is primarily responsible for toughness.

The tender cuts with little connective tissue respond to dry heat (roasting, frying and grilling), but the others need slow cooking in moist heat (braising, stewing or boiling), which breaks down the connective tissue into gelatine. Although commercial tenderizers are sometimes used on beef cattle, this is not, fortunately, general practice. Based on papain (from papaya), with its tenderizing enzymes that 'digest' proteins, they may be applied to the tougher pieces by the wholesalers. Although the meat will be more tender, it will also be duller to eat. As the enzymes work on all the flesh, the tender parts as well as the tougher ones, the advantage of the breaking down of connective tissues is often balanced by a general loss in character and flavour – a decided disadvantage. Tenderized meat does not become any less fibrous – the fibre merely becomes soft as it is 'digested'.

There are ways of preparing tough meat in the kitchen so that it arrives at table full of flavour and juice, fit to be cut with a spoon. Try marinating it in a marinade including wine, lemon juice, vinegar, yogurt, or even pulped tomatoes. The acids in these ingredients help to break down connective tissue. Oil, too, is used in many marinades to add succulence, especially in Greece and the Middle East. Of course, lengthy cooking in moist heat must follow to complete the process, but this is no disadvantage since the tougher cuts need time to develop their flavour to the full.

Pounding or scoring is another way to break up connective tissue, thus making tough meat more tender, but then quite a lot of flavouring – chopped onions, garlic, herbs both fresh and dried, spices, seasoning, sharp sauces and relishes – is needed to make it taste good. You can perform the cutting operation yourself with a sharp, heavy knife, chopping the surface of the meat first one way and then the other, or pounding with a rolling pin.

Ageing This improves the taste and tenderness of meat. Carcasses to be aged are hung in a refrigerated store; their moisture evaporates, and enzymes in the meat break down tendons and tough tissues. Beef should be aged for at least 10–14 days, lamb for no less than 4 days. Pork and veal are not aged, nor is kosher meat. Since ageing leads inevitably to weight loss, correctly hung meat costs more than fresh meat but is well worth the difference in price, and a butcher who supplies meat that has been correctly aged is certainly worth cultivating.

Storing in the refrigerator Once bought, transport meat home as quickly as possible. Unwrap and then rewrap meat as soon as you get it home and put it in the refrigerator (be sure that your refrigerator temperature is no higher than 5°C/41°F). All cuts keep best when they are lightly covered and not so tightly wrapped as to rule out the circulation of air. Food wrap, greaseproof paper and foil are all good wrappings. Keep raw meat separate from cooked meat, and store raw meat low in the refrigerator, where it is coldest and where there is no danger of meat juices dripping on to cooked food or vegetables.

Meat for the freezer

It is not easy to freeze meat successfully at home because it must be done very fast – faster than lies within the capacity of any domestic freezer.

Buy meat which has been blast-frozen when it is in season, and at its best and often cheapest, from one of the proliferating freezer-food centres. From the point of view of quality it may be better still, if your butcher offers a freezing service, and many do, to choose correctly hung meat in his shop and ask him to blast-freeze it for you.

Meat for freezing must be correctly aged and of high quality – inferior grades of meat will only deteriorate further, making them scarcely worth the expensive space they are taking up in your freezer. Many independent butchers have blast freezers and will sell you any quantity you require, from a small bag of chops to half a carcass. To save space, bone large pieces and remove excess fat before freezing.

To buy meat by the whole, half or quarter carcass seems an economical way of shopping, but only if you do not eat your way through your investment faster than you normally would, just because it is there, or leave it in the freezer so long that it loses quality.

Storing meat in the freezer Limits are placed on the storage times for meat, not because it will become unsafe to eat but because the quality deteriorates. Meat storage times are determined largely by the fat content, as fat eventually turns rancid even in the freezer. Pork fat turns rancid more quickly than lamb or beef fat, and salted meats (such as bacon or ham) become tough and can retain water. Furthermore, salted meats need to be frozen at a very low temperature.

Meat that has been inadequately wrapped for the freezer will develop freezer burn, which manifests itself as greyish-white or brownish patches on the meat. These are caused by dehydration on the surface, which

APPROXIMATE MAXIMUM STORAGE TIMES FOR MEAT

Uncooked meat	In the refrigerator	In the freezer
BEEF		
joints, steaks	3–5 days	6–12 months
minced, cut up	1 day	3 months
VEAL		
joints	1–2 days	4–8 months
steaks, chops, minced	1 day	3–4 months
LAMB		
joints, chops	3–5 days	6–9 months
minced, cut up	1 day	3–4 months
PORK		
joints, chops	3–5 days	4–6 months
minced	1 day	3–4 months
sausages	1–2 days	1–2 months
OFFAL	1 day	3–4 months
Cooked/processed meat		
HAM	3–5 days	1–2 months
BACON		
unopened package	2 weeks	1 month
opened package	1 week	1 month
ROAST MEAT		
sliced in sauce	2–3 days	3 months
whole joint	3–4 days	2 months
CASSEROLES	2 days	3–6 months
PÂTÉ	1 week	3 months

ROASTING MEAT

Timings for roasting meat can only be a guide, as the shape and thickness of a joint will affect the timing, as will the efficiency of your oven. The most accurate way to test if meat is cooked to your liking is to use a meat thermometer. Before starting to cook, insert the thermometer into the thickest part of the joint, not touching a bone. Take the meat out of the oven when the thermometer registers a few degrees below the final desired internal temperature (joints of meat will continue to cook for 10–15 minutes after being removed from the oven, so during the period of resting before carving they will rise to the required internal temperature).

Meat	Rare	Medium	Well done
Beef*	51°C/125°F	60–65°C/140–145°F	70°C/160°F
Veal			75°C/170°F
Lamb*	55°C/130°F	60–65°C/140–145°F	70°C/160°F
Pork			75°C/170°F

* Because of concern over bacteria in rare meat, current recommendations are to cook beef and lamb to a higher internal temperature: 70°C/160°F for medium and 75°C/170°F for well done.

meat stock recipes 244–5

meat thermometer 233

ovenware and bakeware 235–6

stovetop pots and pans 233–5

results in changes in colour, texture and flavour. The meat will be perfectly safe to eat but will taste dry and unpleasant, so be sure to wrap meat securely in extra-thick moisture- and vapour-proof freezer bags, and do your best to expel all the air before sealing them. Also, ensure that your freezer is kept at -18°C/0°F

Cooking frozen meat All meat is infinitely better if thoroughly thawed before cooking. Joints on the bone and small cuts of beef or lamb may be cooked from frozen without risk to health (pork must always be completely thawed), but inevitably the outside will be overdone before the inside is cooked. For frozen joints you will need a meat thermometer to check on the internal temperature.

For frozen steaks, chops, cutlets and so on, it will be necessary to start the cooking at a lower temperature and to cook for almost twice as long as usual. Boned and rolled joints, however, must never be cooked from frozen, as the inside and outside surfaces of the meat will have been handled when the joint was prepared, and it is therefore important to destroy any bacteria that may be present by thorough cooking.

To thaw large cuts, allow 6–7 hours per 450 g/1 lb in the refrigerator, in its own wrapping. This is much the best way, as the slower the thaw, the more the juices get re-absorbed. Only about 2–3 hours per 450 g/1 lb are needed at room temperature. Cook the meat as soon as it has thawed out – while still cold to the touch. If left thawing longer than necessary, the juices have further opportunity to escape.

Steaks and chops need about 5 hours in the refrigerator to thaw properly – 2–4 hours in the warmth of the kitchen. If you are in a hurry, thawing the meat in cold water helps as long as the package is watertight.

Another means of thawing frozen meat is to use the microwave, but this must be done carefully to ensure that some parts do not start to cook before others have finished thawing. Use the Defrost power level, and follow manufacturer's instructions.

Cooking processes

On the whole, it is wisest to use the correct cooking process for each cut: dry heat for the tender ones, moist for those not so tender. Grilling, frying and roasting come into the first category, braising, pot roasting, stewing and simmering into the second. Of course, delicious results can be achieved by using a superior cut for the humbler processes, but the reverse is not the case.

Grilling This is suitable for small, reasonably thick pieces of best quality meat from the tenderest parts of the animal. The meat, first brushed with butter or oil to prevent drying out, is seared on both sides close to the source of heat to produce colour and flavour. Generally speaking, the thinner the piece of meat, the closer it should be to the heat source. It is then moved a little way from the heat to finish cooking more slowly. Salt should not be added until halfway through the process, as its moisture-retaining properties would inhibit searing and browning. Always allow grilled meat to rest for a few minutes after cooking so that the juices will be evenly distributed. Since with this process there is no juice or gravy, grilled meat is often served with a sauce or a pat of herb butter.

Frying Good quality, flattish cuts are needed for this process. They are fried in a very little hot oil or butter, or a mixture of the two, in a shallow preheated pan so that the meat browns rapidly. The meat can be turned once or twice as it cooks. Do not pierce it while it cooks, and keep a fairly brisk heat going under the pan or the juices will escape too fast (if they do, the meat will boil in its own juice and toughen). Do not overheat the fat because it will burn, and burnt fat imparts an unpleasant, bitter flavour. Fried meat, like grilled meat, should rest for a few minutes after cooking.

Choose a frying pan with a good, thick base, and make sure it is the right size. Meat has a tendency to stew in its own juice in an overcrowded pan, and if the pan is too big, the cooking juices may evaporate too quickly and the meat all too easily burn. A very good reason for not allowing this to happen is that the pan juices, deglazed with a little wine, water or stock, make the best possible accompaniment to fried steaks or chops.

Roasting Top quality meat goes into a hot oven in an open pan so that it is browned on all sides as the outside is seared. The meat can go straight into a dry pan, fat side down, or into a little hot dripping, or can be cooked on a rack in a dry pan or in a pan with a little water or wine in it. Frequent basting with hot fat or the pan juices helps to prevent the meat from drying out. Some people like to put all meat on a rack in a pan, so that the fat collects beneath it, but this is only essential for fatty cuts, especially pork.

Roasting times and temperatures vary according to type of meat, cut and quality, but after the initial searing it is a good idea to lower the oven temperature so that the interior of the meat cooks more slowly. However, top quality cuts will always be tender, no matter how briefly or how fast they may have been cooked. A thermometer that records the internal temperature of a piece of meat as it is roasting is a foolproof gadget for determining the exact moment when the meat is cooked to the required degree.

There are two golden rules for all cuts: do not add salt until after roasting, and let the meat sit in a warm place for at least 20 minutes after it has finished cooking to allow the juices time to settle, making the texture and colour more even and the meat easier to carve. The exception to the no-salting rule is pork crackling, which needs to be well salted or oiled before roasting in order to crisp to perfection.

Braising and pot roasting Large pieces of medium quality meat respond well to these processes, either in the oven or on top of the cooker.

Braising needs a pan with a tight-fitting lid on which the steam from the cooking meat can condense, falling back on to the meat and basting it as it cooks. The meat is browned and placed on a bed of chopped vegetables, which can be tossed in hot oil or butter first, with the possible addition of bacon or salt pork that may have been browned beforehand. Usually stock, tomatoes, water, wine, cider or beer are added – just enough to cover the vegetables. The meat is then slowly cooked in a casserole at a very moderate temperature (170°C/325°F, gas mark 3) until meltingly tender. This usually takes about 30 minutes per 450 g/1 lb, with 30 minutes over, but times vary according to quality. The meat is turned and basted once or twice during cooking, and seasoned halfway through. If the meat is salted at the outset, there is a danger the salt may draw out too much moisture too quickly.

You may find it better to replace the vegetables with a fresh batch towards the end of the cooking time, as the hours they have spent in the pot may well have rendered them lifeless and tasteless.

Pot roasting in a covered pot dispenses with the moisture, and possibly with the vegetables, relying only on the steam from the meat, which condenses on the lid and bastes the meat. Pot-roasted meat needs to be started off with a little fat in the bottom of the pan in order to brown it and to prevent it from sticking and burning. Turn the meat every half hour or so during cooking so that it browns evenly. This operation is made much easier if you have previously tied the meat with trussing string into a neat and compact bundle. Pot roasting takes about the same amount of time as braising.

Stewing A tougher cut of meat does best when cut into smaller pieces and cooked long and slowly in a little liquid – not too much, or the meat will be boiled rather than stewed. The liquid is provided by the meat juices plus whatever is specified in the recipe.

Many recipes call for an initial browning of the meat to give both colour and flavour – usually in fat in which a few vegetables have been gently fried until golden; cooking liquid, flavouring and seasonings are then added. When it is tender (which may take from 1½–3½ hours depending on the type of meat), the gravy may be thickened. If the thickener, usually flour, has been introduced early on, the meat is usually coated with it before or whilst being browned, and care must be taken not to burn it. Stews cooked on the top of the stove will need stirring occasionally to prevent the meat from sticking to the pan.

Boiling Simmering in liquid is the best way to render large pieces of meat tender, but such good things as *boeuf bouilli* and all the other cuts eaten in the rich broth characteristic of the process really need at least a medium quality meat. If you want to keep most of the flavour in the meat, plunge it into unsalted boiling water or, better still, into boiling stock. If, on the other hand, you want a rich, well-flavoured broth at the expense of the meat, put the meat into a pan of cold water and bring it slowly to the boil.

Once the liquid has reached boiling point, turn it down to the gentlest of simmers. If meat is subjected to the intense heat of rapidly boiling water, the gelatinous connective tissue will dissolve and the meat will become tough and dry, while at a gentle simmer the connective tissues melt gradually, keeping the meat succulently moist and tender.

After the scum has been skimmed off, and has ceased to rise, salt, vegetables and herbs are added for flavouring both the meat and broth, and the meat is simmered to tenderness. The slower the simmer, the less cloudy the bouillon will be. Allow 20 minutes per 450 g/1 lb and 20 minutes over for pieces more than 3.5 kg/6 lb in weight, 30 minutes per 450 g/1 lb and 30 minutes over for smaller pieces. Positively all the scum must be removed, but while a bouillon is allowed to be cloudy, a consommé must be crystal clear, which entails a further clarifying process.

BEEF

A beef carcass should be aged by being hung, usually for at least 10–14 days, to reach its peak of flavour and tenderness, but this process results in considerable weight loss, which is reflected in the price, so expect aged beef to be expensive.

Choosing beef

The colour of lean beef varies from coral pink to a deep burgundy-red. The colour variations of the lean indicate the age, sex and breed of the animal, not the eating quality. Freshly cut surfaces of any piece of beef will be bright red, deepening to a brownish-red on exposure to air – thus a well-aged piece of beef will have a plum-coloured crust.

The colour of the fat will vary according to diet – grass-fed beef has yellowish fat, whereas the fat of barley-fed beef is whiter. Something positive to look for is marbling – the lean of good roasting beef should be well endowed with flecks and streaks of fat that melt during cooking, basting the roast from within and guaranteeing tenderness.

The quality of minced beef is fairly simple to judge – it should look red. If it is pink, the proportion of fat will be too high.

As a provider of beef, the bullock (a young castrated male) is the undoubted king. Different countries consider him to be at his peak at different ages – from 10 months to 6 years old – but all agree that a bullock, and perhaps a heifer (a cow that has not calved), produce the most succulent meat. Working animals – bulls and cows – are far less good for eating. Scotch beef is considered the best, with Aberdeen Angus the most highly prized of all.

Cooking with beef

When beef is good and succulent, little is needed by way of added flavours. Horseradish or mustard makes a good accompaniment to roast beef, while the gravy of roast beef is nicest when the pan juices are simply reduced with a little boiling water and perhaps some red wine, and plainly seasoned with salt and pepper.

Most vegetables go with beef – carrots being the traditional accompaniment to British boiled beef, which is also served with dumplings, while the Sunday roast beef comes to the table with roasted potatoes and parsnips and a golden Yorkshire pudding. Indonesian beef rendang uses flank or shin, which is slowly simmered in spiced coconut milk.

Tastes in beef-eating have changed over the years. There was a time when beef was considered at its best when roasted to a crisp. Today many people prefer their roasts and steaks rare, and even raw. The Italians (never renowned as great eaters of meat) have introduced beef carpaccio – raw fillet steak cut almost transparently thin like smoked salmon and served with olive oil and lemon juice or a mustardy dressing.

Grilling and frying Timing depends so much on the thickness of the steak that you can only be sure whether it is done to your liking by pressing it with your finger as it cooks. If the steak feels soft and wobbly, it is rare, or *bleu*; a little give and it will be medium rare, or *saignant*; firm, and it will be well done, or *à point*; hard and it will be quite spoiled.

Roasting The finest cuts of prime beef respond best when roasted at a high temperature, which makes them crisp on the outside and leaves them a tender rosy-pink within. Overcooked beef turns leathery, even when it is meat of the very best quality. For larger, prime cuts such

beef cuts (chart) 52
cow heel 62
internal temperatures for meat (chart) 49
knackwurst 73
kosher frankfurters 73
ox cheek 62
ox heart 62
ox kidneys 62
ox tongue 62
oxtail 62
plockwurst 76
salted and dried beef 71
storage times (chart) 49
teewurst 78
tripe 62

meat thermometer 233

lard 422

Blade Steak with Shallots 282

Japanese Noodles with Char-Grilled Beef 345

Peppered Steak 282

as sirloin, allow 15 minutes per 450 g/1 lb at 220°C/425°F, gas mark 7 for rare meat, and 20 minutes to each 450 g/1 lb for medium.

The coarser cuts, such as thick ribs, make juicier eating when roasted more slowly – allow 20 minutes per 450 g/1 lb at 190°C/375°F, gas mark 5 for thin pieces or for cuts with the bone in; allow 30 minutes per 450 g/1 lb for thick pieces or those that are boned and rolled. Roast beef should be rested for at least 20 minutes after it is removed from the oven and before it is carved.

Pot roasting and braising In general, allow 30–40 minutes per 450 g/1 lb over medium heat, and 40 minutes per 450 g/1 lb in the oven at 170°C/325°F, gas mark 3 for pot roasts. Braises need about the same time, but a great deal depends on the quality of the meat for this and for the other processes.

Boiling The tougher boiling cuts may need up to 1 hour per 450 g/1 lb of beef at a gentle simmer.

The cuts

Because butchering techniques vary from country to country, and indeed from region to region, the various cuts for roasting, pot roasting, braising, stewing and boiling differ slightly all over the world. It remains true, of course, that in the case of beef (as well as the other animals raised for the table) the very best and most expensive cuts come from the back half of the animal, and most of the very best of those from the fleshy hindquarters; but the actual names of the cuts and their shapes differ considerably, as do the direction of the grain and the way the bones are dealt with.

Cuts for frying, grilling and roasting

These are the top quality cuts that respond best to cooking in dry heat.

Loin This provides the tenderest meat that beef or any other animal has to offer. The most luxurious piece of all is the fillet or tenderloin – a tapering strip of practically grainless flesh running inside the rib cage, parallel with the spine. Some butchers offer the fillet in its entirety: it can be roasted, having been larded with strips of fat to keep it moist, or enclosed in a pastry case to make *boeuf en croûte*. In this case a stuffing goes between the pastry and the meat to add moisture. The fillet is often cut into steaks – the centre part makes tournedos; next to these lies the Châteaubriand, a steak so hefty that it is considered a meal for two hungry people.

Raw minced fillet, spiced to taste with cayenne, Tabasco, Worcestershire sauce and capers and bound with a raw egg, makes a classic steak tartare. Cut into fine strips, fillet is the meat to use for *boeuf stroganoff*.

There are many people who consider any part of the fillet too bland, soft and woolly, much preferring for texture and flavour rump steaks, porterhouse steaks, sirloin steaks and T-bone steaks (which include the end of the sirloin and a piece of fillet), and entrecôtes (cut from the thin end of the sirloin nearest the rib cage).

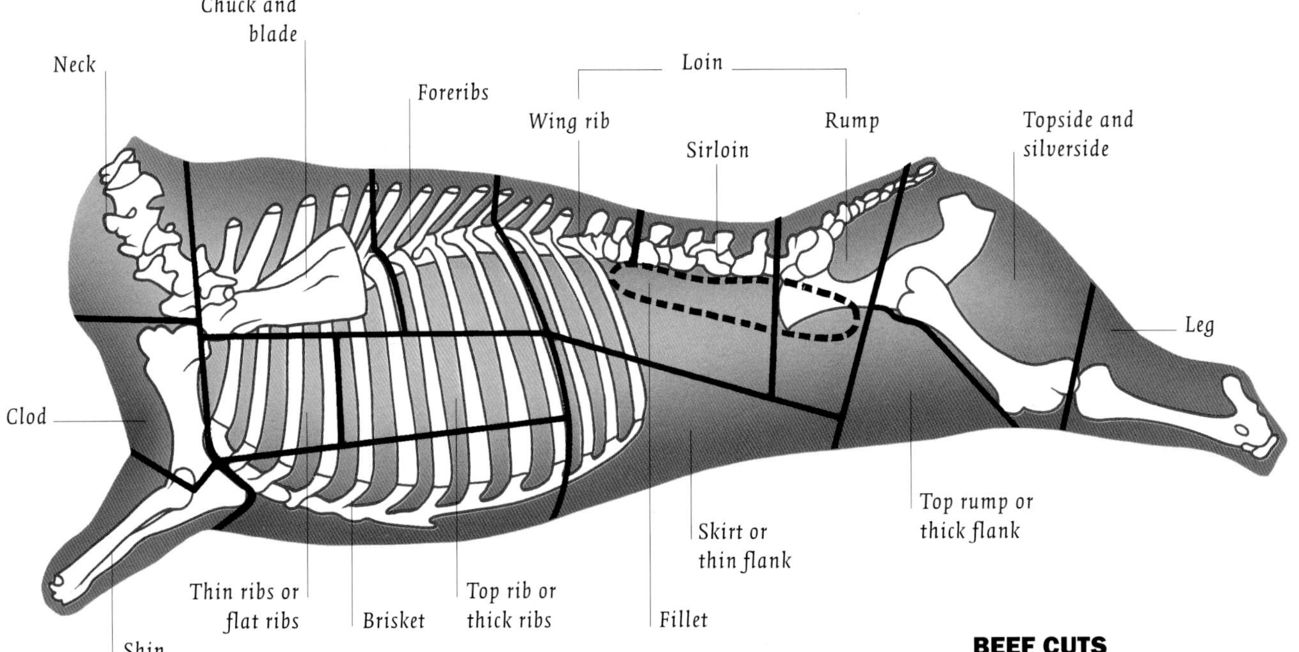

BEEF CUTS

The various national schools cut their steaks differently, some leaving the fillet in place to form part of larger steaks. But this does not really affect the cook, since the principle of cooking steak remains constant, and the various forms of serving it differ only in the presentation. As steaks that are grilled are seared so fast that they do not make their own gravy, it is usual to send them to the table with one of the compound butters. Steaks may also be fried – usually tournedos are cooked by this process, and served on a piece of fried bread to absorb the juices that spurt when the meat is cut. Fried or grilled, steaks are much enhanced by light sauces such as a simple shallot sauce; a light sauce of egg yolks, lemon juice and parsley; a classic hollandaise or béarnaise; or even a raw relish of shallots, lemon juice and oil similar in texture to a salad dressing. Crisp *pommes frites* and a green salad are the best accompaniments.

Sirloin This is part of the loin, and may be sold in a single piece for roasting, either on or off the bone, with or without the fillet, which is then known as the undercut. A sirloin, on the bone and complete with the undercut, makes a wonderful meal, so good in fact that the gourmand King Henry VIII was moved to knight it – hence Sir Loin.

In North America and France the sirloin is often cut into enormous steaks, which are cooked on the bone and carved into slices at the table. In Britain steaks, with the exception of the Châteaubriand, are usually cooked in individual portions.

Rump This yields rump roasts, and beautiful juicy rump steaks for grilling and frying. There will be a few tough sinews running through the meat, and these should be lifted out with a sharp knife before cooking.

Rib When Americans say roast beef, what comes to mind are the great standing roasts from the rib section. The English equivalent to this roast is rib or forerib – the traditional Sunday joint served with Yorkshire pudding, roast potatoes and lightly cooked vegetables, not forgetting the horseradish sauce. This piece may be bought on or off the bone, but with the bone is sweeter. The French rib roast is boned and rolled, and served *au jus* (with its pan juices) accompanied by *pommes frites* and a simple green salad.

Cuts from further down the rib cage – thick ribs – fare best braised or pot roasted, but they can be used for roasting. They are juicier when left on the bone but can be tricky to carve. Below lie the thin ribs, known also as oven busters, with a lot of fat and bone, which can be removed by the butcher. The same applies to the fatty flat ribs from the thin flank.

For stewing, pot roasting and boiling The cuts used for these processes are the tougher pieces that benefit from slow cooking in moist heat.

Topside and silverside Called round in North America, these are boneless cuts from the top of the leg. Together they make the very best *boeuf bouilli*, France's classic boiled beef dish, which is eaten in its bouillon with boiled potatoes and the vegetables that were cooked alongside it; little gherkins called cornichons are often served separately. Topside (the inside leg) is a good braising and pot-roasting meat – being very lean, it usually gets a wrapping of fat. Topside can also be roasted, although it may well be rather on the dry and tough side. Much appreciated in France, where it is called *le rosbif*, it remains much juicier when it is kept very rare, in which case it is also excellent cold.

Fresh silverside (the outside leg) is much like topside in character but coarser. Roasting is not advised, as it is slightly less tender (and slightly cheaper) than topside, but it makes nice pot roasts and good stews. Salted and spiced, silverside makes the traditional English boiled salt beef, eaten with carrots and dumplings.

Top rump Often referred to as thick flank, and called sirloin tip in North America, comes from the underside of the hind leg where leg meets flank. Whole, it can be roasted or pot roasted, and cut into cubes it makes excellent daubes and stews like *boeuf bourguignonne*. Minced, it makes good hamburgers.

Shoulder This area of the carcass is juicy and well flavoured. It is known as chuck or blade in England and chuck in the United States. Blade steak is cut from the flat of the shoulder blade. When scored across with a heavy knife to cut through all the fine connecting tissues, it can be fried like a regular steak. Chuck is excellent for stews, goulash, pies and daubes. Minced, it makes good meat loaves and meatballs.

Neck is a bony, sinewy cut. Trimmed and boned it is used for stews. On the bone it is a good addition to the stock pot.

Brisket is the flesh of the breast, running from between the forelegs to meet up with the forward end of the flank. It is fatty meat that needs pot roasting or braising (it is the favoured cut for a traditional New England boiled dinner), and is nicer when it has been marinated. It is sold on or off the bone and is very economical. It may also be sold salted, in which case it is boiled and often eaten cold, cut into very thin slices.

Flank meat is coarse, and there is plenty of fat. The thinner end of flank is used for stock, curries and stews. Towards the leg end, the flank becomes more tender.

Skirt is a lean muscle from this region. In England it is used with the drier chuck for steak and kidney puddings and pies. In North America this muscle is called flank steak or London broil, and is first scored like the blade steak, then slowly grilled, and sliced thinly across the grain.

Shin, from the foreleg, gives gelatinous stewing meat with a lovely flavour, but takes several hours to cook.

Leg, or hind leg, has a lot of gristle and sinew, but tastes delicious. Slowly cooked it makes a well-flavoured stew.

Marrow This is the delicious soft, fatty substance to be found inside the large bones of beef and veal. In young animals and in the shorter bones of older animals, the marrow is red; in the leg bones of older animals it is yellow, and it is this yellow marrow that is regarded as a delicacy. Beef leg bones are fairly widely available, already cut into pieces.

Marrow makes a wonderful addition to stocks, in which case the split bones are boiled together with the other ingredients to give up their goodness. If you want to use the marrow for sauces or for spreading on toast, the bones should be soaked overnight in cold water, then wrapped in foil and cooked in a fairly hot oven for 45 minutes. The marrow can then be scooped out from the centre of the bones. In Victorian times, marrow on toast was very popular, the bones served wrapped in starched white napkins and the goodness scooped from inside with long narrow marrow spoons. Marrow is an integral part of *osso bucco*, which is made from veal knuckle with its rich supply of marrow.

preparing a fillet of beef 63

Béarnaise Sauce 255
Beef in Beer 284
Burgundian Beef Stew 282
Cornish Pasties 317
Golden Beef Stock 244
Hollandaise Sauce 255
Horseradish Sauce 258
Lasagne al Forno 339
Osso Bucco with Lemon Gremolata 287
Pigeon Pie 321
Ragù alla Bolognese 336
Rich Brown Beef Stock 245
Slow-Cooked Brisket of Beef with Soy, Sake and Oysters 284
Steak and Kidney Pudding 283

bard 422
boudin blanc 74
bratwurst 72
calf's ears 62
calf's foot 62
calf's head 62
calf's heart 62
calf's kidneys 61
calf's liver 61
calf's tongue 62
internal temperatures for meat (chart) 49
lard 422
liver sausage 78
storage times (chart) 49
sweetbreads 61

VEAL

Veal is a light, delicate and versatile meat: a perfect vehicle for flavours subtle and creamy or strong and piquant.

Choosing veal

There are two types of veal: the first comes from milk-fed calves or vealers slaughtered between 8 and 12 weeks of age, and the second from grass-fed calves, which are between 4 and 5 months old.

Milk-fed veal should be pale pearly-pink. It should look firm and moist but never wet, and have bright, pinky-white, translucent bones. Grass-fed veal is a little darker in colour, but never red. Redness is a sure sign that the animal was too old before slaughter. If veal has a brown or grey tinge, it means that it is stale and should be avoided. Veal has a little marbling, which should be hard to spot because the fat is practically the same colour as the meat. If there is too much marbling and too much covering fat, then it means the calf has been overfed. What fat there is should look like white satin, and there shouldn't be much of it except around the kidneys.

Cooking with veal

Because it hasn't much marbling, there is little interior lubrication while the meat is cooking, and veal can be dry unless other fat is added by way of basting, larding or barding for roasting, or by using plenty of butter, good olive oil or fat bacon in sautéed, pot-roasted and stewed dishes.

The flavour of veal is unassertive, so a strongly flavoured garnish is often welcome: the combination of veal and anchovies dates from the earliest times. Lemon and orange often feature in the best sauces, as does white wine and, particularly, Marsala. In Italy, a joint of veal may be studded with strips of anchovies; in Parma, they slit a leg cut of veal and introduce strips of paper-thin *prosciutto crudo*. Escalopes and cutlets of veal may also appear under a slice of mildly cured raw ham on which a generous slice of cheese is gently melting.

Onions have a special affinity with veal, not only because of their taste but because of their texture – they are often put into the pan with a roasting joint. As for accompaniments: any really fresh-looking vegetable is good, as is salad. Veal is pale, so dark green spinach or beans will provide a beautiful background. Potatoes, of course, go with veal in almost any form, and so do rice and noodles. Golden saffron rice is the traditional side dish for *osso bucco*, and a ring of snow-white rice often surrounds a blond blanquette or a fricassée of veal. (A fricassée differs from a blanquette only in the lack of cream and eggs in the sauce.) Tagliatelle is often served with veal in Italy, the slippery texture of the pasta compensating for any possible dryness in the meat.

All veal bones are extremely gelatinous, and give an excellent texture and flavour to sauces and stocks: if the butcher has trimmed the meat for you, be sure to carry a few of the bones home with you and add them to the pot when braising a piece of veal, removing them before you dish up.

Grilling and frying Because of the lack of interior fat, the smaller cuts – chops, cutlets, escalopes, medallions and the like – are more often fried than grilled.

Thin escalopes should be fried quickly over a medium heat; chops should be

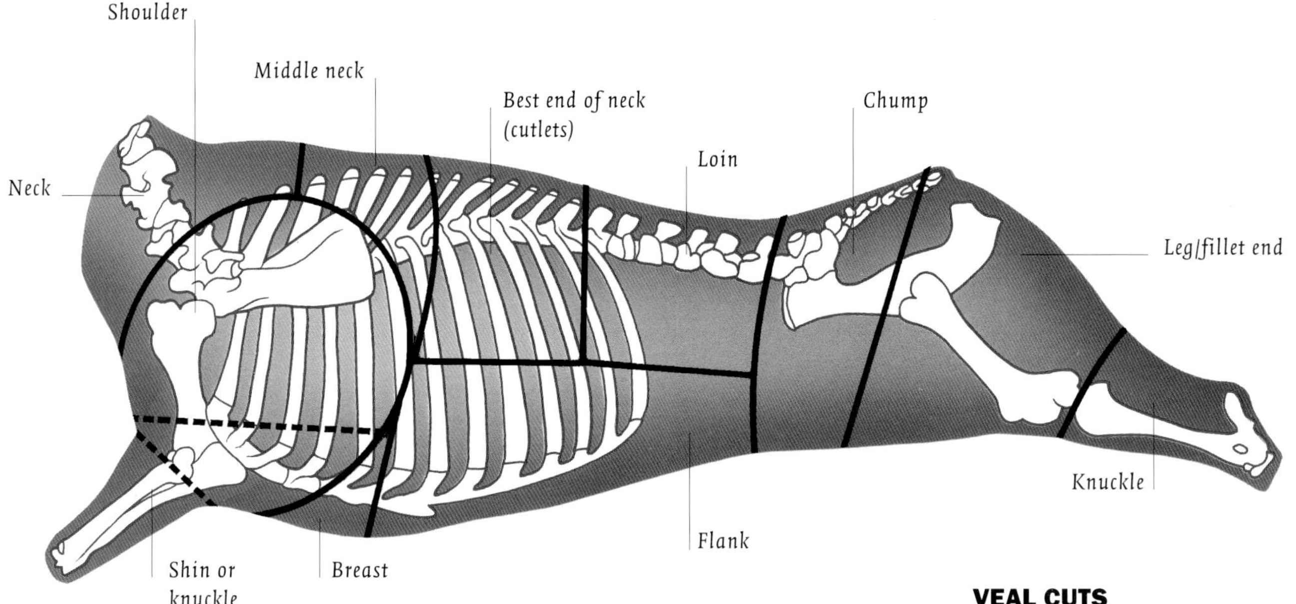

VEAL CUTS

first seared over high heat and then cooked on slowly, otherwise they will become tough and dry. Because of the high temperature of the initial cooking, chops will need to be fried in oil or in an oil and butter mixture as butter alone would burn, but escalopes can be successfully fried in unsalted butter. Serve them with quarters of lemon.

Roasting Baste veal frequently if you do decide to try roasting it – pot roasting and braising are often more successful with this dry meat. Roast for 25 minutes per 450 g/1 lb at 180°C/350°F, gas mark 4 for cuts that are thin or on the bone; allow 30 minutes per 450 g/1 lb at 170°C/325°F, gas mark 3 for those that are thick or boned and rolled or stuffed.

A hefty cut, like a leg, will preserve its succulence better if covered with rashers of bacon before it goes into the oven. The lean little roasts, such as a boned loin, should be threaded through with strips of pork fat (larded) or covered with a layer of pork fat (barded). This extra fat will keep the meat moist.

Pot roasting and braising This is the best method of cooking a large piece of veal. Add some little onions, shallots or carrots to the pot to help produce the moisture that will prevent the veal from drying out. In Italy, a good-sized carrot is sometimes inserted through the middle of the meat for the same purpose.

Allow 40 minutes per 450 g/1 lb at 170°C/325°F, gas mark 3, basting frequently with wine and butter.

Stewing should be done very gently, for well over an hour. Veal is good in a blanquette, stewed in a flavoursome broth which is thickened and enriched at the end of the cooking time with egg yolks and cream.

Boiling, or, more strictly speaking, poaching, should be only a mere simmering: for this process, add a split calf's foot, and reduce the cooking liquid after the veal has been removed to make aspic, having carefully skimmed off the scum rising to the top of the pot at the beginning.

The cuts

Like beef, cuts of veal vary according to the various butchery techniques. However, since calves are smaller than full-grown beef cattle, there is not quite so much scope for variation and not as much difference among the cuts. In fact, most countries follow the economical French style of butchery for veal – and that involves trimming away all gristle and sinew most meticulously and dividing the meat neatly along the natural seams in the muscles.

Cuts for frying, grilling and roasting

Veal needs plenty of additional fat to prevent it from drying out completely in the dry heat of these processes.

Leg Only the hind legs go by this name, as the forelegs are called shin or knuckle. This large and fleshy joint is almost always divided into the hock end and the fillet end. These cuts can be roasted under a layer of fat bacon or, better still, braised with vegetables to keep them moist and juicy.

The fillet end, called round roast in the United States, the top slices of which go by the name of round steak, is the equivalent of an English topside of beef. A fillet end of leg, or cushion as it is sometimes called, is good stuffed with a mixture of pork fat, anchovy fillets and currants and then braised in a web of caul fat.

The most delicate leg meat is from the muscle that runs vertically along the thigh bone. In French butchery it is sold separately as the *rouelle*, but, in general, leg of veal cuts tend to be sliced crossways, containing some of each of the three muscles, which are very similar in taste. So, whether on or off the bone, a cut of centre leg makes good eating. It is this bit that is used for the famous Italian dish *vitello tonnato* – always eaten cool and coated with a sauce of tuna fish pounded to an emulsion with olive oil, lemon juice and capers.

Chump Situated at the point where leg meets loin, the chump, also called rump, is usually boned and rolled for slow roasting and braising.

Escalope It is from the fillet end of the leg that the best escalopes are cut, across the grain and on the bias. Of course, many shops sell thin pink slices of fatless, trimmed veal under the name of escalopes or scallopini from other parts of a calf's anatomy, particularly the ribs, but high-class butchers only recognize those from the leg as the real thing. Ask the butcher to pound the escalopes flat for you for extra tenderness, and when you egg-and-crumb these diaphanous slices, you get the perfect *escalopes panés*. Classically, these are served together with a slice of lemon, perhaps with a rolled anchovy and some chopped hard-boiled egg arranged in a circle around it, plus a few scattered capers.

If you find that you have to pound the escalopes yourself, do take care not to beat the life out of them – a well-cut escalope will only require a gentle flattening. If you don't possess a cutlet beater, then use a rolling pin, or ease the meat into shape with the heel of your hand.

There are many, many ways to serve veal escalopes. This rich diversity is in part due to the fact that the escalope is one of the mainstays of Italian cooking, and it features often in the varied cuisines of France, Germany and Austria. In Italy, for instance, a great favourite is *saltimbocca* – which means literally 'to jump into the mouth'. This is a dish of small escalopes, each one rolled up around a stuffing of Parma ham and fresh sage. *Piccate*, or *scallopini*, are tiny escalopes traditionally dipped in flour and fried in butter. Ideally, they come from the same part of the leg as escalopes; they are usually sautéed and served with a good lemony sauce.

In France, veal escalopes are often simply browned in butter, with the last-minute addition of a handful of finely chopped shallots or spring onions and a slice of lemon. The Germans and Austrians are, of course, famed for their *Weinerschnitzels* – traditionally these are dipped first into flour, then beaten egg, then breadcrumbs before being briefly deep-fried in hot oil.

Loin A lean roasting joint, this contains the tenderloin, which is the equivalent of a fillet of beef. It also sometimes contains the kidneys. But both kidneys and tenderloin are more often removed to be sold separately – the tenderloin to be cut into nice little medallions that look like tournedos. The loin can be divided into chops or sold whole for roasting.

When roasting a loin, keep it very well basted with butter or olive oil, or cook it in a covered casserole to keep it moist.

Best end of neck This rib joint is usually divided into delicious chops, which should not be cut too thin. Chops should be cooked very gently after browning or they may become dry. Escalopes are also often cut from these parts, and both they and chops usually have their garnish sitting on top: a poached egg and a cross of anchovy fillets earns them the suffix

caul fat 62
coating with egg and crumbs 423
preparing veal escalopes 64

cutlet beater 226

Costolette Milanese 285
Veal with Apples and Cream 285
Veal with Mushrooms 285

internal temperatures for meat (chart) 49
smoked mutton 71
veal cuts (chart) 54

Crespolini 341
Golden Veal Stock 244
Osso Bucco with Lemon Gremolata 287
Pâté de Campagne 318
Ragù alla Bolognese 336
Redcurrant Jelly 418

Holstein; and fontina cheese, Parma ham, small white mushrooms and, of course, anchovies may all feature.
Middle neck This provides veal cutlets, which the Americans call shoulder chops and the French *cotelettes découvertes*. Smaller than chops, they are prepared in much the same way, though they are sometimes seared in butter and then enclosed in a foil case together with a *farce* of shallots, onion, mushrooms and parsley and baked in the oven, to be served *en papillote*. Off the bone, the meat of the middle neck is used for pies, *blanquette de veau* and goulash.

For braising, pot roasting and boiling Veal adapts particularly well to moist heat, absorbing both moisture and any flavourings added to the pot.
Shoulder This is a fairly lean cut suitable for slow roasting or pot roasting. Also called oyster of veal, it is almost always sold boned and rolled, sometimes with stuffing, although it is vastly preferable to make your own. For this purpose, good butchers may leave an empty pocket in the centre. Boned and cubed shoulder is a prime candidate for blanquettes and fricassées – especially when mixed with the meat from the breast region. Particularly good is a simple braise made with plenty of oil, garlic, tomatoes and mushrooms.

Minced shoulder, flavoured with marjoram and rosemary and bound together with egg, makes delicious meatballs – made more so with the addition of a sauce of white wine, cream, finely chopped shallots and dill.
Neck Also called collet or scrag, this may be used for stewed dishes as it provides meat that is suitable for long simmering. Minced, it makes good meatloaves, meatballs and stuffings, and can be used in pâtés. Veal mince is an ingredient in many mixtures suitable for stuffing pork fillets, poultry and game birds.
Breast and flank These are often seen boned, and provide a vehicle for some very good stuffings. Traditionally, something green is included in these: spinach, perhaps, or peas, or pistachio nuts. Served cold, a stuffed breast of veal, simmered, gently pressed and allowed to cool in its own gelatine, makes a beautiful summer lunch. A breast is also very good hot – casseroled together with a chunk of fat bacon and some large, juicy onions.

Knuckle, shin This is a gelatinous, sinewy, but well-flavoured piece of meat consisting mainly of bone. Sawn into thick slices and long-cooked, it makes a most delicious veal dish – *osso bucco*.

LAMB

First-grade lamb has rosy flesh. Its bones are slender, and the fat is white, silky and resilient. The very best lamb, meltingly tender but expensive and difficult to find, is milk-fed lamb, with flesh of the palest pink that turns almost white when cooked. It is available only in spring, and is especially good when cooked in the ancient way, herb-strewn on glowing wood embers.

Easter lamb that has been weaned will be much the same size as milk-fed lamb: a whole leg may just feed four people. Summer and autumn lamb has darker flesh than Easter lamb. Lamb only qualifies for the name when it has been slaughtered before its first birthday. After that, it becomes hogget, then mutton.

Yearling mutton or hogget gives delicious meat a little darker and a little stronger tasting than lamb. The expression 'mutton dressed as lamb' arose because all too many butchers used to try to deceive their customers, but there is really no mistaking the two kinds of meat: mutton is dark red, not pink, and there should not be too much fat. Although mutton used to be as despised as lamb was admired, it is just the right sort of meat for the heftier regional dishes. Ironically, now that supplies of good lamb are quite constant – not least because this meat freezes particularly well – people who actually want to buy good old-fashioned mutton often have great difficulty in finding it.

Choosing lamb

When buying lamb or mutton, go for the leanest piece you can see – even the fatty cuts vary greatly in their proportions of fat to lean. Avoid those with fat that looks brittle and crumbly or discoloured – the most appetizing-looking pieces will make the best eating and will have the most flavour.

Where sheep are raised can affect the flavour of the meat. Some of the most delicious lamb comes from sheep that have grazed on salt marshes: the *pré-salé* lamb – 'pre-salted' lamb – of France's Atlantic coast is world famous. Most lamb for the table comes from lowland farms where the sheep are fat, but some prefer the leaner lamb from the hills: Welsh lamb, small and slender boned, is a good example of this. Hillside lamb is a touch gamier in flavour, and there are many recipes for cooking lamb like venison, using the traditional marinades and the same accompaniments: rowanberry or redcurrant jelly, or a compote of cranberries.

Cooking with lamb

Lamb is basically a tender, succulent meat, so take care not to overcook it – grilled, fried or roast lamb should be pink and juicy inside.
Grilling and frying Chops and steaks of lamb, nicely trimmed, are equally good grilled or fried. The timing depends on the thickness of the pieces. Test them by pressing them with your finger during cooking: when they are becoming firmer but are still supple, they are done.
Roasting Much depends on the age of the animal and the quality of the meat. The timing varies according to whether you like your roast rosy-pink or well done.

A leg of lamb should be pink within, most gourmets would agree, although not everyone shares the taste of the French, who like it rose-red in the centre. The best end, saddle and loin are best fairly rare – cook all these cuts at 190°C/375°F, gas mark 5, allowing about 20 minutes per 450 g/1 lb, but test with a meat thermometer or by piercing: when the juice runs red, the meat is rare; rosy, it is fairly rare; and when it runs clear, the meat is thoroughly cooked.

The shoulder and all boned, rolled cuts, including stuffed, rolled breasts, are better when they are well done: cook them at 180°C/350°F, gas mark 4, allowing about 25 minutes per 450 g/1 lb.
Pot roasting and braising is done at an even lower temperature: 160°C/300°F, gas mark 2, allowing about 2 hours for a leg or shoulder, and 1½ hours for casseroling smaller cuts. A lamb stew should be ready for eating after 1½ hours of cooking.
Boiling takes about 30 minutes per 450 g/1 lb for larger cuts of mutton, but it is best to cook them well before they are needed, since they taste nicest reheated. Also, since mutton for boiling tends to be rather fatty, it gives you a chance to lift off the fat, which solidifies when the

dish has cooled. If there is not time to wait for this to happen, the broth can be defatted either by careful skimming, or by plunging ice cubes into the liquid and lifting out the fat when it congeals.

Because all lamb fat congeals so quickly, it is important to take your stew to the table in a preheated dish and to serve it as soon as possible on very hot plates.

The cuts

Most large cuts of lamb can be roasted; even the fattier ones will taste good.

Leg of lamb, gigot This succulent piece, simply roasted on the bone, is one of the greatest cuts of meat there is. It may be subdivided into the shank and the fillet end. The fillet end, in turn, makes leg steaks. Divested of all membranes, this fleshy steak, cut into cubes, makes lovely little kebabs.

The leg is also sold boned. It is usually rolled, but is sometimes opened and cooked flat – this version is called a butterflied leg of lamb and in North America is often cooked on a barbecue or over glowing wood embers. In whatever form, this cut makes a good roast. Leave on the papery outer skin to ensure even cooking, and if you want to make this extra crisp, dredge it with a little flour after basting. Roast lamb should be rested for at least 15 minutes after it is removed from the oven and before carving.

Serve young lamb with mint sauce or redcurrant jelly and spring vegetables, and mutton with root vegetables. If you braise half a leg of lamb on a bed of vegetables and use cream and tarragon in the sauce, it becomes *agneau jardinière*. But what is particularly delicious and all too rarely encountered is a noble, very English, boiled leg of lamb, served with caper or onion sauce.

In France, where rosemary or thyme and garlic are the essential flavourings, the centrebone is sometimes removed from the fillet end of a gigot, leaving only the shank bone in place: this makes carving easier when the meat is served.

Chump end Lying between the leg and the loin, this piece is sometimes sold as a separate cut for roasting. Often it is cut into the juiciest chops – which are expensive, since each leg yields only two or three. In some schools of butchery it simply forms part of the leg itself. The two legs, chump end and the saddle make a very impressive banqueting cut called a baron of lamb.

Loin The single loin may be bought on the bone, but it also comes boned and rolled, often around the kidneys.

The loin is often divided into chops – each with a small T-shaped bone dividing the two pieces of lean. There are a hundred ways of garnishing chops; plain fried or grilled, served pink inside with watercress and mashed potatoes. Loin chops can also be boned and trimmed of any excess fat until only the 'eyes' remain.

Best end of neck This joint, which the French usually call the *carré*, and which in North America is referred to as rack of lamb, lies next to the loin. If you mean to roast or braise it in the piece, ask the butcher to chine it for you, to enable you to carve neat cutlets after cooking. Two best ends placed opposite each other, fat side out, bones in the air and interlinked like swords at a military wedding, make a good party piece called Guard of Honour. A moist stuffing goes in between the two pieces of meat, the same type that you would put into the

boning a leg of lamb 66
butterflying a leg of lamb 67
chine 422
kid 58
lamb's heart 62
lamb's kidneys 61
lamb's liver 61
lamb's tongue 62
preparing a best end of neck 67
sheep's head 62
storage times (chart) 49

Gigot d'Agneau with Haricot Beans 287
Mint Sauce 258
Spiced Stuffed Leg of Lamb 288

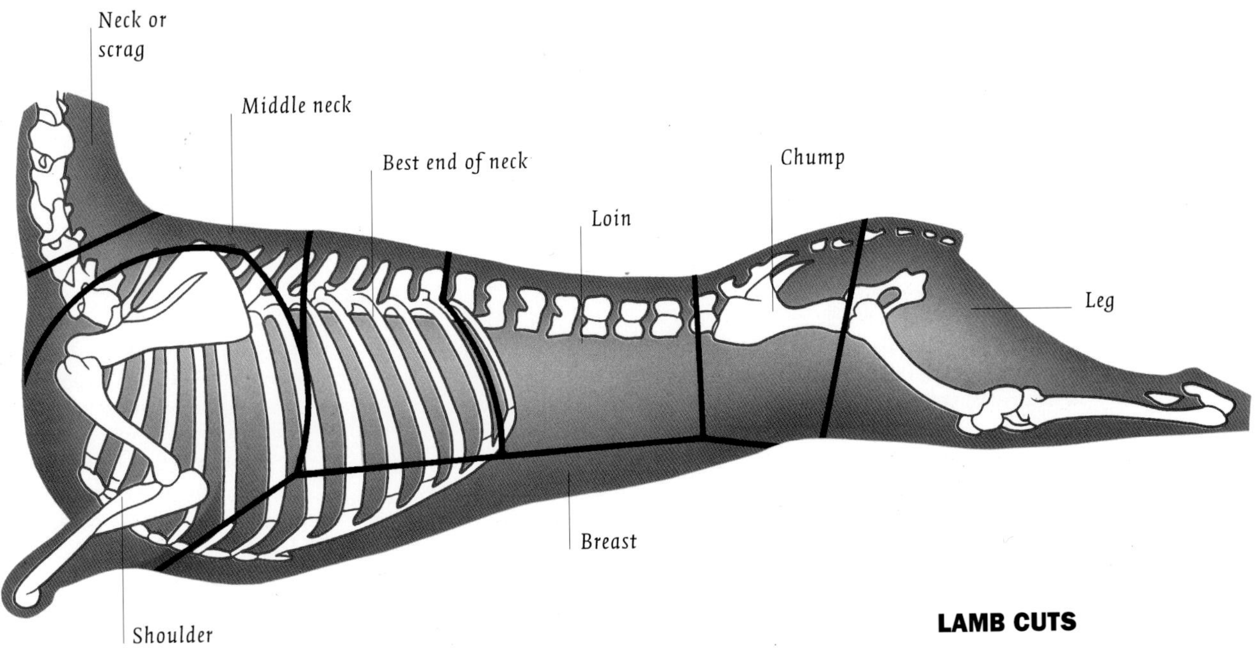

LAMB CUTS

boning a shoulder of lamb 65
burghul 114
coating with egg and crumbs 423
lamb cuts (chart) 57

Garlic-Braised Lamb Shanks with Yellow Peppers 290
Lamb Korma 289
Navarin of Lamb with Potatoes 288

centre of a crown of lamb, which is made from the identical two cuts, joined at both ends. The best end, trimmed and chined and with the ribs removed, can also be rolled and divided into noisettes.

Sliced, the best end gives cutlets that are a fraction less juicy than loin chops, but still very good. When 'frenched' – trimmed with the elegance and care that most French butchers bestow on all the meat they handle, so that in this case the bones are pared of fat – they may come to table with a paper frill at the end, and may be eaten with the fingers. The further back the cutlets lie, the leaner they are; towards the front, they can be quite fatty.

Lamb cutlets may be egg-and-breadcrumbed, but are probably best of all sprinkled with olive oil and lemon, and charcoal-grilled.

Shoulder of lamb Easy to cook, this makes a sweet and juicy roast. It is fattier than the leg, and harder to carve, especially when it is on the bone, but is often a more succulent joint. Boned and tied, it may be stuffed – whether it comes as a long roll or, as in France, in a kind of melon-shaped bundle also known as a ballotine, or *épaule en ballon*. The shoulder also provides Americans with blade and arm chops, good for braising.

Shoulder, trimmed of all fat and membrane, is the cut that is often minced, perhaps together with meat from the foreleg, for use in moussaka, stuffed peppers, vine leaves and the like. In the Middle East this cut of lamb is sometimes pounded to the consistency of an ointment: this smooth paste, which also involves burghul, is called kibbeh and may be eaten raw or cooked.

Middle neck Lying underneath the shoulder blade next to the best end, the middle neck is a decidedly fatty cut, but useful for broth, lamb stew and Lancashire hotpot (unless you make this in the traditional way, with best-end cutlets standing upright in a deep earthenware pot). This is the cut for Moroccan tagines, with apricots or prunes, almonds and spices.

Scrag, neck This is used in the same way as middle neck, but it has more bone, gristle and fat. Use neck to make a good Irish stew – which used once to be made with kid. Neck is fatty, so use plenty of potatoes to soak up the juices. A top layer of thickly cut slices of potato benefits from the rich fat that rises as the meat cooks. A shepherd's pie, with its covering of mashed potatoes, works on the same principle, as do *haricots* of lamb or mutton where dried beans act as the blotting paper. Essentially, *haricot*, *ragout* and *navarin* are all stews. Pilafs, too, use stewing lamb, with rice.

Shank Although full of flavour, this cut from the end of the front leg is tough, and so must be braised slowly to make it tender to eat.

Breast of lamb This thin, fatty cut tastes better when slowly cooked. The breast cage makes riblets for barbecuing; the less bony parts can be boned, stuffed and rolled, or tied flat, like a sandwich, with the stuffing in the middle. Boneless breast can be simmered, cooled, cut into squares, egg and breadcrumbed and fried; these morsels are called epigrams, a charming name and a good dish.

Kid

Athletic lamb from craggy hillsides with no pasture to speak of produces meat that is notable for flavour, but it can be tough or dry. This is where kid, better adapted to such regions, is much preferred to lamb. Cooked in oil and wine with garlic, wreathed in rosemary or myrtle, young kid, creamy white and tender, makes the festive dishes in such places as Corsica and Sardinia, while lamb is for every day. Saudi Arabia, too, feasts on kid: rubbed with coriander, ginger and onion juice, stuffed with rice, dried fruits and nuts, and served with clouds of rice and hard-boiled eggs. Lamb can, of course, be substituted – as far as recipes go, the two kinds of meat are interchangeable. But as the taste of kid is mild, it needs plenty of flavouring.

PORK

Prime, fresh pork should be a lovely pearly-pink and fine textured, and with visible fat that is dense and milk-white. Despite today's pigs being much leaner than they used to be, there is still a good deal of intramuscular fat in any piece of pork. Even a sucking-pig, slaughtered at between 3and 8 weeks old, makes a rich, filling meal, although it has hardly had time to grow stout.

Choosing pork

In the case of meat from animals slaughtered between 4 and 6 months – called, respectively, young pigs and mature hogs by the trade – make sure that there is a good proportion of lean meat to fat; this applies even more to porkers, which is what pigs are called between 6 months and 1 year. By this time, the meat has darkened to rose-pink and the bones, pinkish in young animals, are white.

Deep rose-coloured meat, white brittle bones and rough skin are signs of a porker's unduly advanced age; red meat with a dried-up look is not worth bothering with. If you notice brown or yellowish stains on the skin, or if the meat looks wet and slippery rather than damp, the meat will be of poor quality. If there is any kind of smell, the meat is stale. Ask for free-range pork for the best texture and flavour.

Cooking with pork

Although all cuts of pork taste rich, not all of them are liberally lubricated from within. The leg, for example, does not have much in the way of intramuscular fat, so meat from this part of the animal may appear to be on the dry side: to remain as juicy as possible it should be cooked slowly.

All cuts of pork, without exception, need to be cooked to at least medium doneness, partly because raw pork may contain microscopic parasites – called trichinae – which are killed only when the meat reaches an internal temperature of about 60°C/140°F, and, just as important, because underdone pork tastes less good.

The humbler cuts of pork are cooked and served with plenty of fat on the meat, and so the best accompaniments are mealy – mashed potatoes, beans, dried peas and lentils, which will absorb some of the fat. Chestnuts have the same effect. In Spain and Portugal potatoes are added to braised or stewed fatty pork dishes about half an hour before serving in order to soak up the fat that has risen to the top of the pot.

The more expensive, less fatty cuts of pork – leg and loin – are often served with fruit or vegetables to provide a contrast to the rich, dense meat. Apples are probably the best-known accompaniment, while in Tours, noisettes or medallions of pork are cooked with prunes. In Denmark prunes are used to stuff a loin roast, and a mixture of soaked, dried fruit is used in Poland. In the Rhineland, the mealy and fruity elements are combined in a dish called Heaven and Earth – a mixture of puréed potatoes and apples.

For moistening purposes, beer, wine and stock are occasionally used, but dry cider is the liquid most associated with pork.

By way of herbs, pork takes kindly to the warm flavour of fennel and caraway seeds, as well as to the pungent flavour of sage. Some people in England still make their own sage and onion stuffing for their Sunday roast of pork – much nicer than the ready-made variety. In Italy, pork is often cooked with rosemary or bay leaves; it is good also with juniper berries or whole peppercorns and with thyme. And, of course, a loin of pork is wonderful with truffles.

As for vegetable side dishes, all the members of the genus *Brassica*, led by sweet-and-sour red cabbage, are naturals for pork. The most delicate roasts, such as leg or loin, look most appetizing with something fresh such as little carrots or turnips, leeks, bright green cabbage or spinach. Young peas and artichoke hearts in butter make one of the best combinations. A plain lettuce salad, eaten off the same plate after a grilled or fried chop, and bathed in the meat juices, is extremely delicious to eat.

Grilling and frying A medium chop should take about 15 minutes to cook at medium heat. Turn the chop from time to time as it cooks, and test it by piercing – when the juices run clear, it is ready to serve.

Roasting This must be thorough. Allow 25 minutes per 450 g/1 lb at 180°C/350°F, gas mark 4. If you buy pork with the skin, ask the butcher to score it closely and deeply with his special knife, right through the rind to the fat, to help the heat penetrate to the centre.

In many countries, the skin is peeled off the meat before it is sold and then is supplied separately, to be cooked alongside the joint, enriching the gravy. It turns into the hardest leather by this process. (The Normans found this *cuir bouilli* an effective protection against their enemies' arrows.) So if you like crisp crackling – and many British people, at least, think this the best part of a piece of roast pork – do not allow the meat to sit in the fat in the pan or you render part of the skin inedible. Instead, roast the joint on a rack, having rubbed the skin with oil or salt (but not both together) for extra crispness. Increase the oven temperature a little before the end of the cooking time, and do not baste the crackling during cooking – this will just make it tough.

Braising and pot roasting On top of the stove, simmer pork over a medium heat, or place it in a casserole with a little vinegar, bay leaves and peppercorns and cook slowly in the oven at 170°C/325°F, gas mark 3.

Boiling It is not very usual to boil fresh pork, except for the feet or trotters, but any of the pickled or salted and smoked cuts make perfect candidates for boiling, or rather simmering. These may need soaking beforehand: ask the butcher how long to soak, because he alone knows how long the meat has been salted.

The cuts

There is no single cut of pork that cannot satisfactorily be roasted – the pig is too lethargic a beast to develop much by way of tough muscle and connective tissue. The coarser cuts with little visible fat may be better casseroled or slowly stewed. A coarse, fat cut will still make a lovely braise or stew, provided it is trimmed of most of the fat, which would make the sauce too rich and indigestible.

Leg A whole leg makes a really imposing dish. But even a small one – and one from a pig should weigh no more than 2.5–3 kg/6–7 lb – can be rather daunting, so it

back fat 110
caul fat 62
ham, bacon and salted pork 68–70
internal temperatures for meat (chart) 49
pig's ears 62
pig's head 62
pig's heart 62
pig's kidneys 61
pig's liver 61
pig's trotters 62
sausages and salamis 72–8
storage times (chart) 49
sucking-pig 60

meat thermometer 233

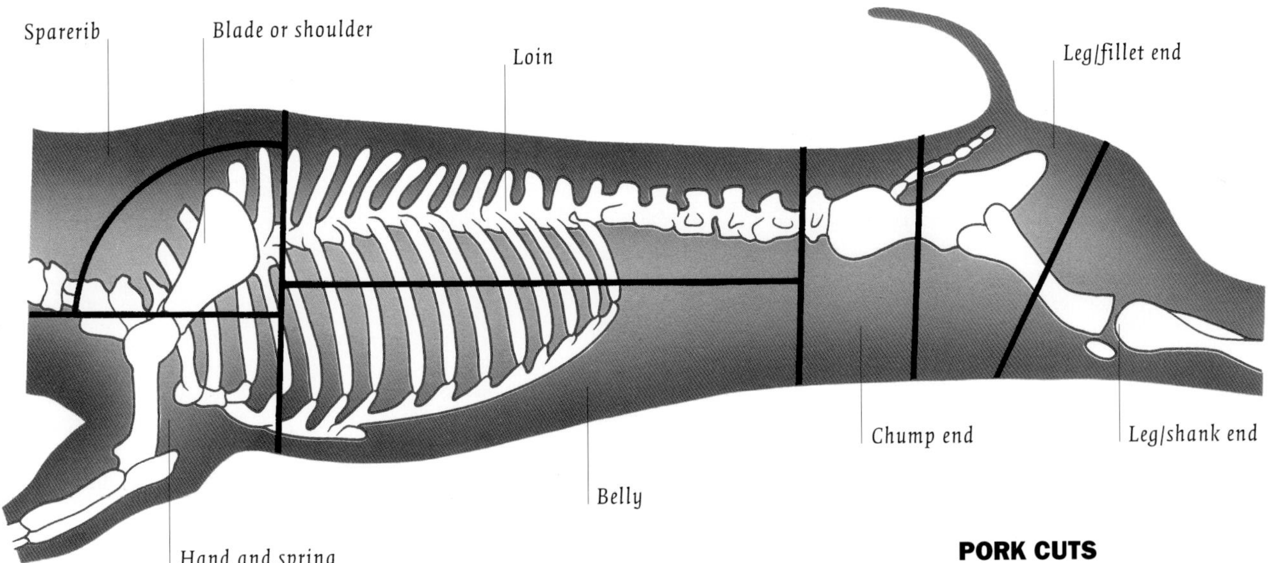

PORK CUTS

pork cuts (chart) 59
preparing a pork escalope 64

Chinese Belly Pork Salad with Boy Choy 371
Fried Pork Chops 291
Old-Fashioned Pork Pie 315
Pâté in a Crust 319
Pork Fillet with Juniper 290
Rillettes of Pork 319
Roast Loin of Pork 290

is usually divided into the shank or leg end and the fillet end, which the French confusingly call *jambon frais* and the Americans refer to as a fresh ham butt.

The shank end is easier to cook evenly when it is boned and rolled, but it then looks less handsome on the platter. When cooking it on the bone, it is a good idea to protect the thinner bony bit by wrapping it in foil halfway through the cooking time, leaving the meatier end exposed to the full heat.

The fillet end of the leg is cooked as a joint, or may be sliced by the butcher into lean slices about 1–2.5 cm/½–1 in thick. Such a slice makes a huge meal – cook it as you would a steak. The fillet end of leg may be cut into cubes to be cooked as kebabs.

A leg is sometimes, especially in Italy, first simmered in milk and then cooked on in the oven, surrounded by quantities of garlic (the milk ends up as a light, golden gravy). Some countries pickle the leg, to be boiled and eaten with the mash of green split peas that is known and loved as pease pudding in the north of England.

Chump end This fleshy part of the loin is usually cut into delicious large chops, but this is another cut that may be roasted on the bone or off, seasoned with sage, rosemary or thyme.

Loin Delicate and very tender, the loin itself makes a wonderful meal if boned, filled with chopped garlic and a few prunes or herbs and mushrooms or even truffles, and rolled and roasted. On the bone, a loin cut is sometimes served sitting on a bed of unsweetened apples and sweet chestnuts.

It is the loin that provides most of the pork chops: to be fried plain or grilled after being lightly brushed with oil, or pounded, egg-and-crumbed and fried *alla milanese*, or braised, moistened with white wine or cider. Chops taken from the hind end of the loin may bring with them a slice of kidney and a portion of the fillet or tenderloin.

Fillet In young pigs the fillet or tenderloin, from the hind end of the loin, is usually much too small to be separated out, but many butchers remove it in its entirety from larger carcasses, where it may weigh up to 450 g/1 lb. Trimmed of its fat, it is good roasted – perhaps scored down the middle and stuffed, or wrapped in bacon and roasted whole like a miniature joint. It may also be cut into medallions or escalopes, but their taste, like that of veal, from which they are almost indistinguishable, is delicate, so some interesting flavouring is needed to give them character.

In France apples or prunes are used as garnish for fillet cuts, which are lovely cooked with crushed allspice berries or fennel seeds, and in Germany they are cooked with caraway seeds or a rich sauce made of sour cream and the delicious pan juices.

Blade, shoulder This rather rich cut can be roasted, or minced and chopped for pork pies or meatballs and for the famous Pennsylvania Dutch scrapple – a cooked mixture of pork and cornmeal, sliced and then fried in either butter or bacon dripping.

Meat from the shoulder can be sliced into steaks that are particularly good when cooked over charcoal.

Hand and spring An awkwardly shaped piece, this is often divided into a variety of cuts for stewing; whole it makes a good, large, economical roast, although the meat is marginally coarser than that of the leg. This is a particularly English cut. It is difficult to carve unless you know exactly how the bones run, but the butcher will advise you if you ask him, or will even bone and roll it for you.

Spareribs These come from the upper part of the rib cage, and are either sold in sheets or separated into meaty single or double bones, each with its cartilage. The sheets of ribs are sometimes cooked sandwiched together with a stuffing in between: the Pennsylvania Dutch like to spread this sandwich with apples, the Germans with cabbage and caraway. The separated ribs are barbecued and often eaten with a sweet-sour sauce, which is said to have been introduced to America by Chinese railway workers, who used to cook this meat as they worked on the line.

Chinese spareribs, as we know them, are not the meaty slices from the upper parts of the rib cage, but the lower ends of the rib bones. These have very little meat on them, but are extremely good braised or barbecued and served with chilli sauce. Eat them with the fingers, allowing about 1.5 kg/3 lb for 2 people because these spareribs are so bony.

Belly of pork The abdominal wall provides rather fatty meat; it is excellent salted and good for enriching dishes of beans, lentils and cabbage. It is useful in pâtés, and, if you don't mind the fat, it can be roasted, or sliced and grilled, or fried, or braised Chinese-style together with star anise.

Sucking-pig

These young pigs, which have been slaughtered between the ages of 3–8 weeks, contain proportionally little meat; however, what there is, is perhaps the sweetest and richest of all pork.

In northern Spain, sucking-pigs are a speciality. These pigs start their short lives on a diet of mothers' milk and wild herbs. They are traditionally roasted in a slow-burning wood oven, and are then served simply with boiled potatoes and apple sauce.

Choosing sucking-pig You will need to order one specially from your butcher. They range in size from 2.5–9 kg/6–20 lb, and a medium-sized one will be a good buy because it will have developed enough meaty parts without sacrificing any of the tender succulence of the smaller pigs. As a rough guide, a 5.5 kg/12 lb pig should feed about 10 people.

Roasting a sucking-pig Sucking-pig, which should have been prepared for you by the butcher, can be stuffed with any stuffing suitable for pork (a combination of breadcrumbs, parsley, onions, sausage, chestnuts and brandy is good), or simply brushed with oil or rubbed with salt and lemon juice and sprinkled with herbs. Place the sucking-pig on a rack and prick the skin before and during roasting to allow the fat to drip out into the roasting pan. It won't need basting, and the skin will turn a shiny crisp brown. A medium-sized stuffed pig will take about 2½–3 hours to cook; an unstuffed one will be ready in 2 hours. Allow 20 minutes per 450 g/1 lb at 180°C/350°F, gas mark 4.

Sucking-pigs are usually reserved for festive occasions, such as the colourful Hawaiian beach barbecues, or luaus, where the central feature is a spit-roasted sucking-pig, liberally basted with barbecue sauce and presented on a tray with a red apple in its mouth.

OFFAL

Some of the best dishes in the world are made with humble pieces of meat that are collectively known as offal. They are treated with special respect in France and the Mediterranean countries, where their distinctive flavours and textures are preserved by careful cooking.

Luckily, many of these meats are among the most economical buys. While some of them, particularly those from veal, may command a high price, only small amounts need to be purchased because of their rich flavour and lack of bones; those from less expensive animals are full of wholesome flavour. Whichever type you buy, make sure it is fresh, and cook it as soon as possible.

Sweetbread A fine delicacy, sweetbreads are sold in pairs, being two parts of the thymus gland, which sits in the throat and chest of young animals. The rounder, fatter one is the better of the two. (The sweetbreads that come from the pancreas gland and that are sometimes referred to as stomach sweetbreads, or beef breads, are coarser than true sweetbreads.) Calf's sweetbreads are the best, especially the very large ones from milk-fed veal. They are whiter and larger than lamb's sweetbreads and less fiddly to prepare, and they have a finer flavour. Pig's sweetbreads are small and not particularly good.

No matter how they are to be cooked, all sweetbreads need to be prepared first to make them white and firm. To prepare sweetbreads, soak them in salted water for 2 hours, changing the water from time to time, until they lose all trace of pinkness and turn white. Put them in a pan of cold salted water, bring to the boil and simmer for 2 minutes. Drain and rinse them under cold running water. This process stiffens the sweetbreads and makes them easier to handle. Peel away the skin, connective tissues and gristle – some sweetbreads will fall naturally into smaller portions. Finally, flatten the sweetbreads between two plates for an hour before cooking.

One of the best ways of cooking them after the initial preparation is to egg-and-breadcrumb them and fry them gently in butter until brown.

Liver Fresh liver is the most nutritious and widely eaten of all offal. It is sold either whole or in slices and is often already trimmed, but if it still has a thin covering of membrane, this needs to be removed or the liver will curl up in the pan. After pulling off the membrane, cut away any fat and gristle from the liver. Less delicate livers, such as pig's liver, will become more tender if they are soaked in milk before cooking.

Calf's liver Pale and plump, liver from milk-fed veal is the most delicious, but is expensive to buy. Liver from grass-fed veal will be thinner, darker and not as mild. Fried liver is delicious if it is cooked very lightly and rapidly and is still rosy inside – overcooking makes liver tough, dry and leathery. In the famous *fegato alla veneziana*, calf's liver is cut into the thinnest slices, fried for mere seconds and served on a bed of golden fried onions. Liver is also good with fried bacon and watercress.

Lamb's liver is a deeper colour than calf's liver and has a less good flavour but is as tender. It is served in the same ways as calf's liver.

Pig's liver is not ideal for frying, as its texture is granular and its taste rather powerful. It is best used in pâtés, or braised in one large piece with wine and vegetables.

Kidney All kidneys, whether they come encased in their fresh white surrounding fat or not, should be firm and smell sweet. Once they have been prepared, they can be grilled or sautéed briefly or simmered slowly and for a long time – anything in between and they will be tough and rubbery.

To prepare kidneys, peel or cut away the surrounding fat and the thin inner membrane. For lamb's kidneys, slice each kidney open and snip out the pale inner core with a pair of kitchen scissors. For calf's kidneys, cut out the gristly core at the centre of the kidney.

Calf's kidneys These multilobed kidneys will be very large and pale when they come from milk-fed veal, and darker and smaller from grass-fed veal. They are best when grilled and served with bacon, or briskly browned in butter to seal in their juices. The piquancy of a mustard and cream sauce is the perfect complement. They can also be roasted, encased in their own fat. This takes about an hour, and the resulting kidneys will be pink and succulent.

Lamb's kidneys These have a mild but delicious flavour, and are excellent fried in butter. They form an essential part of a mixed grill.

Pig's kidneys are larger than lamb's kidneys and thought by some people to be strong flavoured, but they are tender enough to be grilled or fried, and are a favourite dish on the menu in French brasseries. They are also good when cooked slowly in wine and served with boiled potatoes and watercress to offset their richness.

beef 51–3
cayette 75
coating with egg and crumbs 423
faggot 75
lamb 56–8
pâté-type sausages 78
pork 58–60
suet 110
veal 54–6

Braised Liver with Bacon 292
Kidneys with Mustard 293
Lyonnaise Calf's Liver with Onions 292
Spiced Stuffed Leg of Lamb 288

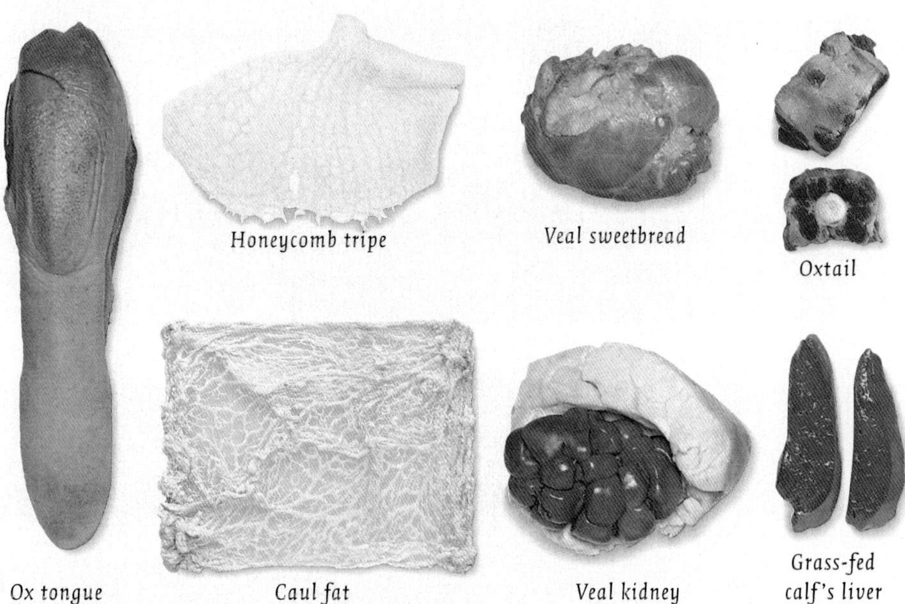

Ox tongue
Honeycomb tripe
Caul fat
Veal sweetbread
Veal kidney
Oxtail
Grass-fed calf's liver

agar-agar (carragheen) 46
choucroute garnie 422
dissolving gelatine 423
faggot 75
haggis 74
lard 110, 422
zampone 73
zungenwurst 76

Salsa Verde 258
Steak and Kidney Pudding 283

Ox kidneys are dark and strong flavoured, and really only suitable for braising. They also provide just the right flavour and plenty of rich gravy in steak and kidney pies and puddings.

Tongue While tongue can be purchased fresh, it is more usual to find it salted and possibly smoked. It is a very smooth meat. Ox tongue is best; calf's tongue, although good, has less flavour; and lamb's tongue is rather dull. Pig's tongue is usually sold with the head.

Whether fresh or salted, choose a tongue that feels soft to the touch. Soak salted tongue overnight if necessary to remove the salt, and then simmer it with vegetables and herbs until tender (this can take 3 hours or more, so allow plenty of time). Skin it carefully and serve it hot with salsa verde, walnut or raisin sauce, and mashed or boiled new potatoes. Cold, it is usually eaten with pickles, horseradish or mustard, and green salad.

Tripe Usually from beef, tripe is the lining of the animal's first and second stomachs. It comes in a variety of textures, some honeycombed, which are considered the best, some just slightly rough, and some smooth. It has to be cleaned and blanched meticulously before cooking, and would take hours to cook if bought fresh – an authentic *tripes à la mode de Caen*, the Normandy dish flavoured with vegetables and Calvados, needs about 12 hours of simmering before it is at its gelatinous best. Thankfully, tripe is usually sold already prepared and partly cooked; always buy tripe that looks white and fresh. In Provence lamb's tripe is made into little parcels enclosing garlic, herbs and salt pork, and simmered with trotters (sheep's feet) to make *pieds et paquets. Menudo* is a hearty Mexican tripe stew.

Caul fat After the fat has been removed to make fine quality leaf lard, a very thin membrane of fat that surrounds the stomach is separated to become the delicious and delicate caul fat, or lace fat. This fat, with its lace-like appearance, is sold in large white sheets in French, German and Chinese shops. It needs to be soaked in warm water until it softens and becomes pliable for cutting into squares with scissors and wrapping around sausages and chopped meats, as in French charcuterie, while the English use it to enclose fresh faggots. In Chinese cooking, caul fat is used to envelop poultry before it is deep fried or baked. The fat provides a basting layer, melts into nothing and leaves behind a delicate, delicious, golden brown crust.

Heart A heart is a hard-working muscle and is never especially tender. Ox heart is particularly tough, and is best sliced and braised with plenty of onions to give it a good flavour. Lamb's, pig's and calf's hearts, being more tender, can be blanched, stuffed, wrapped in bacon and roasted.

To prepare heart, snip out the pipes and tendons from the core with a sharp pair of scissors. Soak the heart in cold water for an hour to draw out the blood, then cook as wished.

Head, tail and feet

Although not always available, heads, tails and feet are often well worth the trouble and the long, slow cooking needed to make them tender and to bring out their velvety, gelatinous qualities.

Head Daunting to look at, the head of a calf, pig or sheep can be a lengthy business to prepare, but an obliging butcher will do this for you and split it into manageable pieces.

Pig's head makes brawn or head cheese (*fromage de tête* in France), the chopped meat suspended in a translucent jelly flavoured with herbs, spices and vinegar (heads are very gelatinous) and eaten cold with mustard and green salad.

Calf's head, cooked, boned and sliced and covered with a vinaigrette containing capers and onions, makes the *tête de veau vinaigrette* sold ready-made in French charcuteries. Or it may be boned, rolled and braised, and eaten hot with salsa verde.

Sheep's head makes a broth much liked in Scotland, and it is a great favourite in Morocco.

Ox cheek – you never see the whole, huge head – looks rather sinister with its prickly surface and layers of dark, dense flesh, but when very fresh it is an extremely good braising piece with a wonderful juiciness and succulence, particularly if marinated in wine before cooking.

Calf's and pig's ears are cartilaginous, and are considered a delicacy by the Chinese. Braised pig's ears sometimes appear in the *choucroute garnie* – garnished sauerkraut – of Alsace, and they can also be coated with egg and breadcrumbs and fried.

Oxtail Oxtail stew, in winter, is one of the very best and most warming dishes. Choose an oxtail with a high proportion of lean, and with fresh, creamy fat. Allow a whole oxtail for two to three people. It will usually be sold jointed and needs only to be trimmed of any large lumps of fat. Generally only the meatier upper joints need trimming.

Oxtail requires long, slow cooking to develop its excellent gelatinous texture. The large amounts of fat that rise to the surface will be easier to remove if the stew is made the day before serving and allowed to get completely cold. Oxtail stew reheats particularly well.

Feet Cow heel, calf's foot and pig's trotters all yield plenty of jelly – use it to top up a home-made meat pie.

Pig's trotters are sold fresh or pickled. They are usually split in half, and can be quite plump and meaty. Often they are just simmered and served hot with sauerkraut or cold in their own jelly. They are also very good cooked and then breadcrumbed and grilled, served with mustard, or fried and served with tomato sauce.

Cow heel A boiled and skinned cow heel, its meat cut into strips, is good in a beef stew, helping to give it a velvety texture.

Calf's foot can be stewed, and goes into the making of jellied stocks and glazes. Traditionally, calf's foot jelly was given to invalids, being both nutritious and easy to eat and digest.

Gelatine Extracted from calf's feet, pig's knuckles and the like, gelatine is sold either in powdered form in individual packets, or in shiny sheets. A good gelatine will have virtually no taste and will dissolve into a clear liquid – so necessary when making galantines, when the meat and vegetables shine through the jelly. Sheet or leaf gelatine is less likely than powdered to go lumpy. Soften gelatine in a little cold water before dissolving it in a hot (not boiling) liquid; or dissolve powdered gelatine in a cup set in hot water. Gelatine does not take kindly to freezing. An alternative to animal gelatine is agar-agar, the jellying agent extracted from seaweed.

Preparing a fillet of beef

1 With the rounded, neater side of the fillet uppermost, start cutting and pulling away the fat from the wide end.

2 Cut away all the fat and gristle that lie along one side of the fillet.

3 Cut off the large lump of fat that is attached to the wide end.

4 Turn the fillet over and pull and cut away the strip of gristle and fat.

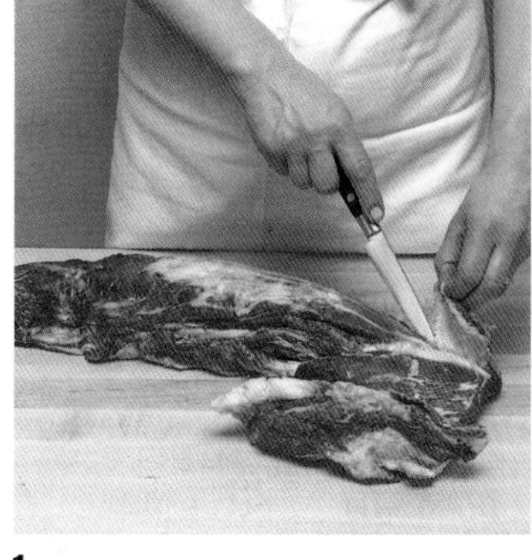

1

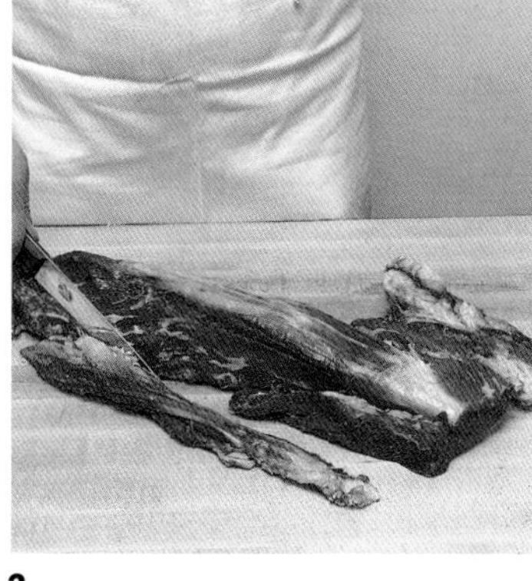

2

beef cuts for frying, grilling and roasting 52–3

knives 222–4

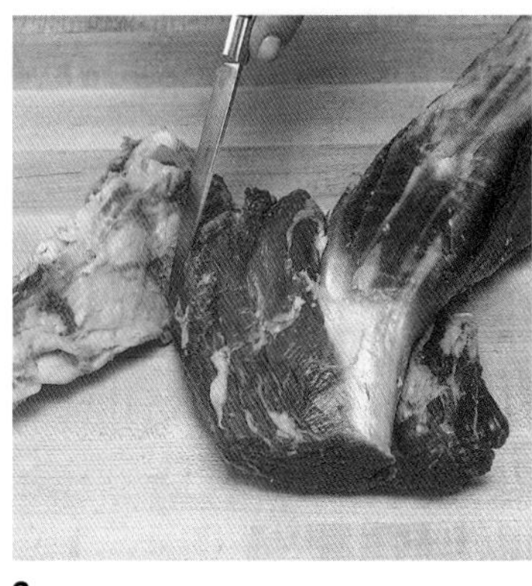

3

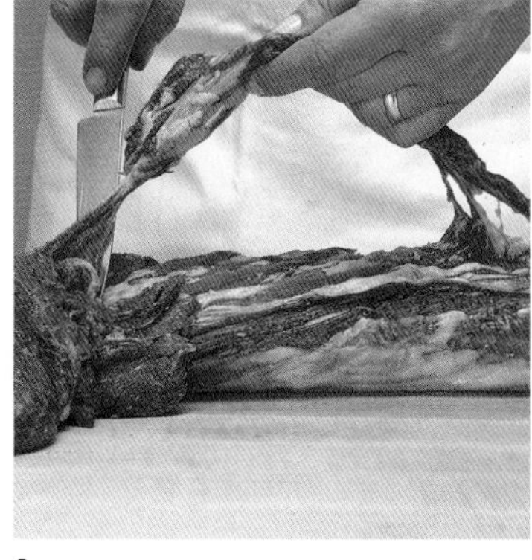

4

5

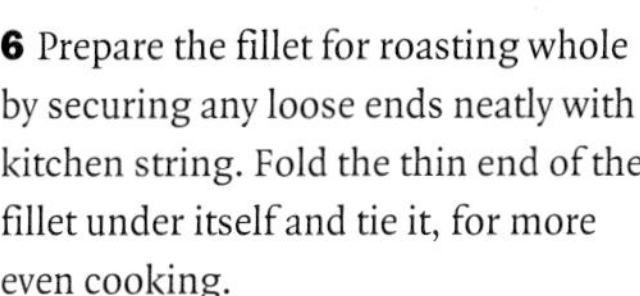

5 Return the fillet to its original position. Using a sharp knife, remove the shiny layer of membrane. This should leave the meat completely free of fat, membrane and gristle.

6 Prepare the fillet for roasting whole by securing any loose ends neatly with kitchen string. Fold the thin end of the fillet under itself and tie it, for more even cooking.

7 Alternatively, cut small filet mignon steaks from the thin end, and medium-size tournedos from the centre. The wide end can be used as a small joint as it is, or prepared for Châteaubriand: wrap it in a clean cloth, turn it on its side and flatten it to half its original thickness.

8 In this way the fillet has been divided into a Châteaubriand (bottom), three tournedos (top) and three filets mignons. Use the trimmings for hamburgers, meat sauce or steak tartare.

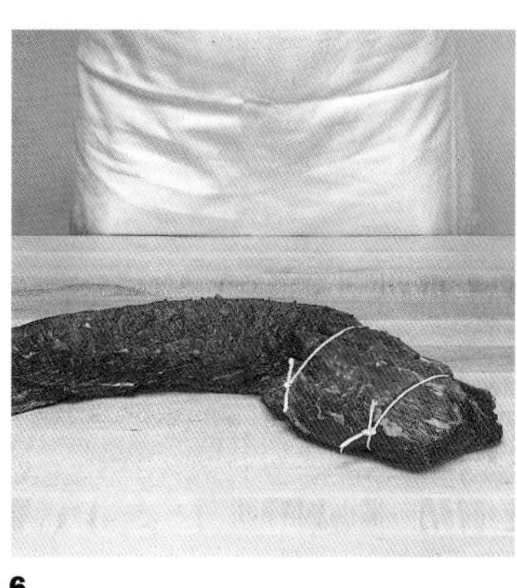

6

7

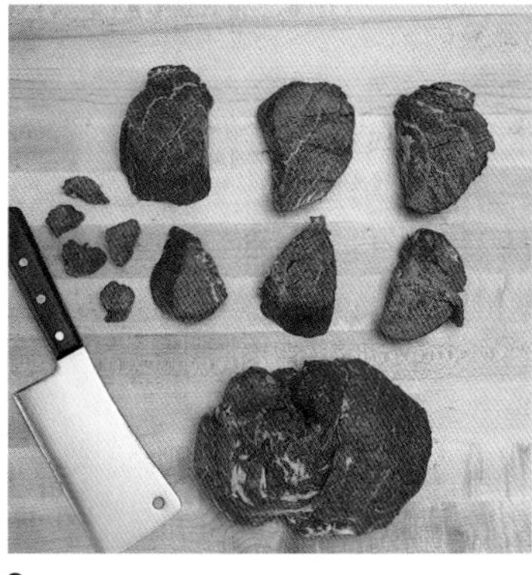

8

pork fillet 60
veal escalopes 55

cutlet beater 226

Veal with Apples and Cream 285

Preparing veal escalopes

1 Cut even slices from a boneless leg cut of veal using a sharp knife.

1

2 Place each slice between two pieces of dampened greaseproof paper, and flatten it gently but firmly using a rolling pin or cutlet beater. Here, a preprared escalope is compared with a freshly cut slice.

2

Preparing a large pork escalope

1 Fillet of pork is normally cooked whole or cut into slices or chunks, but a large fillet can also be flattened and then rolled around a stuffing. Slit the fillet down the middle, being careful not to cut all the way through it.

1

2 Open the meat out like a book and place it on a dampened piece of greaseproof paper.

2

3 Cover the meat with a second piece of damp greaseproof paper, and flatten it gently but firmly with a rolling pin or cutlet beater.

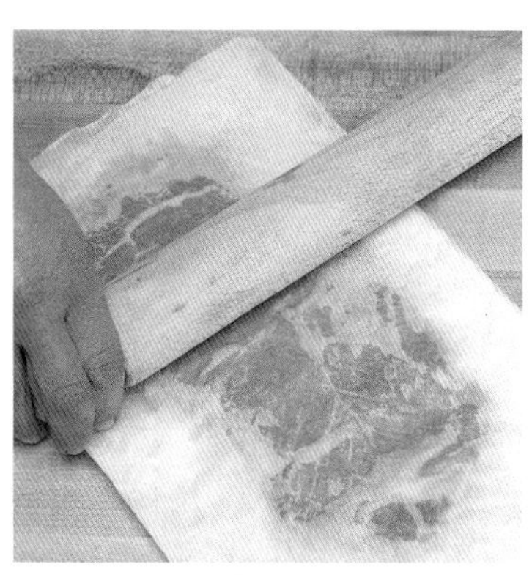

3

4 The escalope can now be stuffed, rolled and tied with kitchen string. Alternatively, cut it into smaller pieces and use as scallopine.

4

shoulder of lamb 58

knives 222–4

Spiced Stuffed Leg of Lamb 288

Boning a shoulder of lamb

1 Lay the shoulder fat side down and take hold of the exposed end of the foreleg. Cut round the bone with a sharp knife, pushing the meat back as you progress towards the joint.

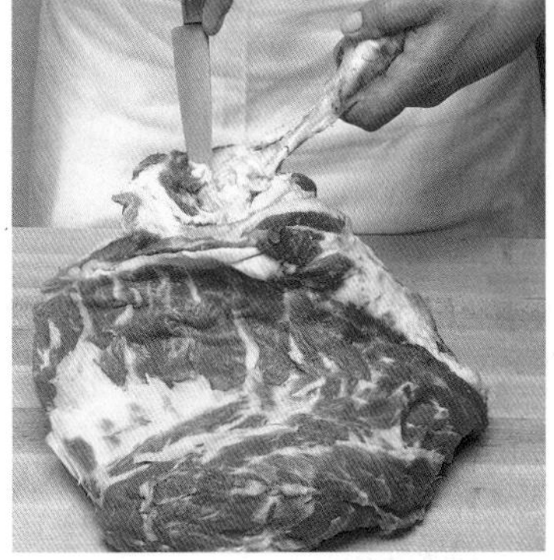

1

2 Cut into the joint between the foreleg and the middle bone, then bend the foreleg back until the joint breaks. Remove the foreleg.

3 Grasp the exposed end of the middle bone and cut back the meat in the same way as with the foreleg, cutting as close to the bone as possible. Avoid piercing the surface of the skin. Pull the middle bone away from the shoulder blade to which it is attached and prise it from the centre.

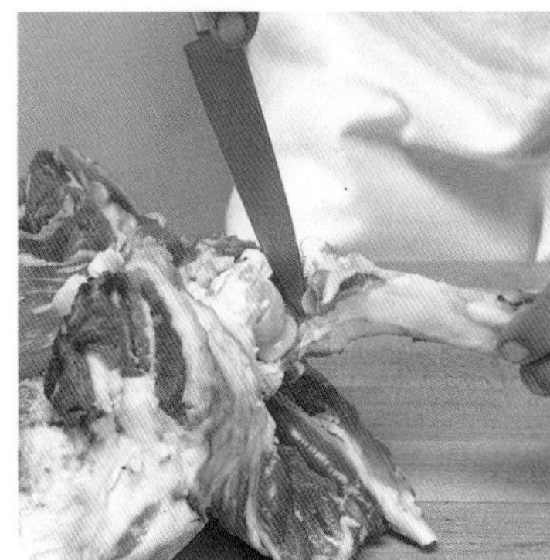

2

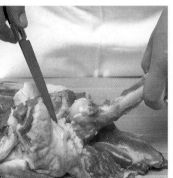

3

4 Turn the meat round so that the triangular shoulder blade is nearest you. Insert the knife into the meat against the bone, and cut the meat away from either side of the flat bone. Pull this last bone out and trim any excess fat from the meat.

4

5 Roll up the boned meat with the skin on the outside and secure it with kitchen string. The three bones that have been removed are, from left to right, the shoulder blade, the middle bone and the foreleg.

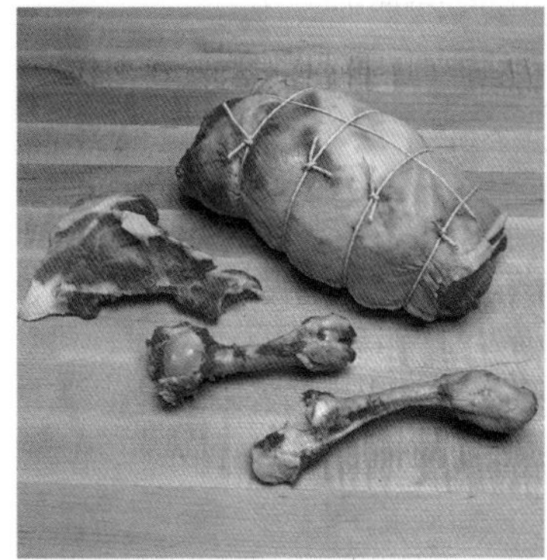

5

leg of lamb 57

knives 222–4

Gigot d'Agneau with Haricot Beans 287
Spiced Stuffed Leg of Lamb 288

Boning a leg of lamb

1 Take hold of the broad, curved hip bone, which protrudes at the wider end of the leg, and carefully run a sharp knife around it, releasing it from the meat and tendons that attach it to the leg bone. Pull out the bone.

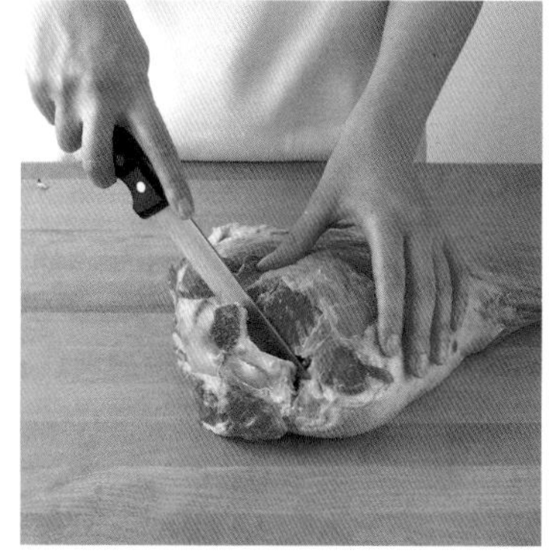

1

2 Grasp the shank bone at the other end of the leg, cut it away from the meat, severing the tendons that attach it, and pull it out.

3 Sit the meat up with the wide end uppermost, and tunnel into the cavity left by the hip bone, cutting as close to the leg bone as possible .

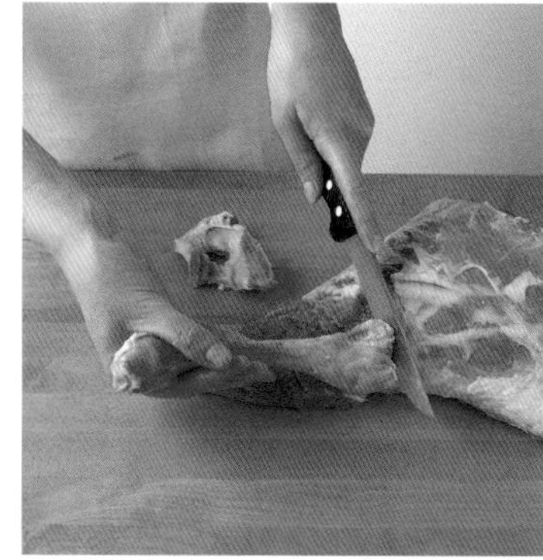

2

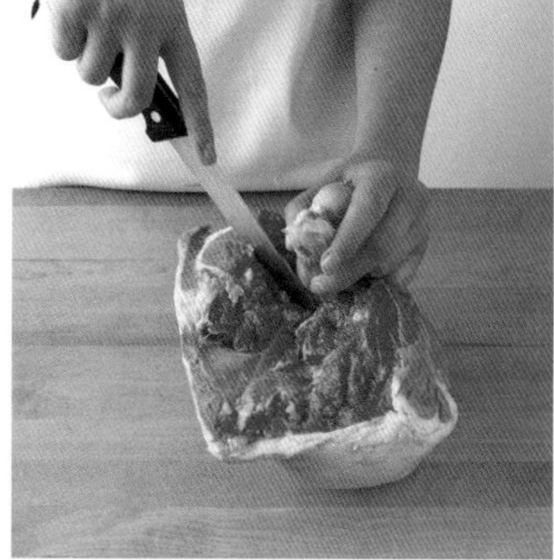

3

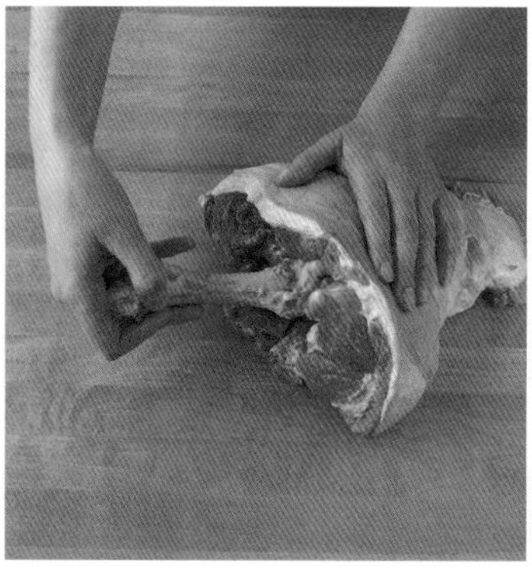

4

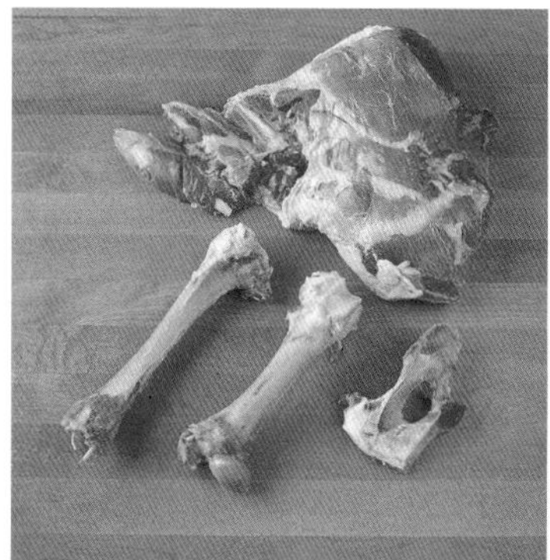

5

4 When all the meat has been cut back from the middle bone, pull the bone out of the hip cavity. Trim away excess fat from the meat.

5 The three bones that have been removed are, from left to right, the shank bone, the middle or main leg bone and the hip bone.

6

6 Tuck the shank end of the meat into the cavity left by the bones and roll up the boned meat to make a neat joint. Tie with kitchen string.

best end of neck 57
leg of lamb 57

Butterflying a leg of lamb

1 Lay a boned leg of lamb skin side down. Cut down to the cavity left by the leg bone and slit open the leg without cutting all the way through. Trim off all excess fat and sinews.

2 Open up the leg and spread it flat. Slash it in the thickest parts so that it will be reasonably even in thickness. Do not cut all the way through the meat.

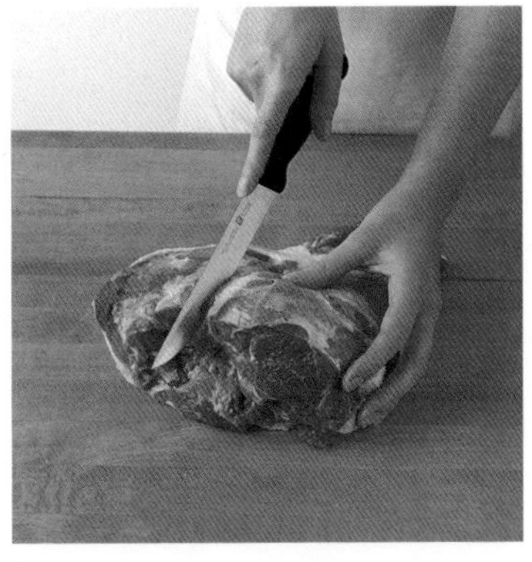

1

2

Preparing best end of neck of lamb

1 If the butcher has not already done so, cut away the backbone, or chine, from the meaty end of the best end, using a strong, sharp knife or a cleaver.

1

2 Peel the fatty skin from the joint, exposing the layer of fat beneath. Trim off most of the fat, leaving a thin layer.

2

3 Cut through the fat across the rib bones, about 5 cm/2 in from the meaty part of the joint, and cut off the layer of fat and meat over the ends of the rib bones.

3

4 Strip the meat and fat from between the exposed rib bones, and scrape the bones clean.

4

Ham, Bacon and Salted Pork

brine 422
fresh pork 58–60
pork cuts (chart) 59
salt 200
saltpetre 200

Cold Chicken and Ham Pie 314
Eggs Benedict 323
Glazed Gammon 292
Ham Omelette 324
Macaroni Cheese with Ham 338
Oeufs sur le Plat 323
Penne with Ham and Tomato Sauce 339

Theoretically, and indeed in practice, every kind of meat can be cured, but pork has long been the prime candidate – not only because of pork's doubtful keeping qualities in the days before refrigeration, but also because this fine-grained and well-lubricated meat emerges from the cure in a succulent and delicious state, and remains so juicy and tender when it is boiled, fried or roasted.

Dry air, salt and smoke are the age-old curing agents. Nitrates and nitrites, added in minute quantities to reinforce the preservative powers of salt, are comparative newcomers, and it is these ingredients that cause the pinkness in cured pork products.

Ham

Pigs used for ham tend to be longer and leaner, as well as older and heavier, than those that yield fresh pork for our tables. Before the cure, their meat is deep pink or clear red, and the fat is firm and white rather than ivory coloured. After the cure, the outside skin may be from creamy-grey to mahogany, depending on whether it has been smoked or not.

Not all hams are smoked: some of the finest are simply salted, either in a bath of brine, often with brine first injected into the flesh to speed up the process before it goes into the bath, or by the dry-salt method, which involves repeated massaging, rinsing and drying. This is a slow process, but ensures that the minimum of salt necessary for preservation penetrates the meat; the brine treatment is faster but tends to introduce more salt into the flesh. In both cases, certain flavouring agents – herbs, spices and sweeteners – may be added. When sugar is added the ham may be labelled 'sweet cure'.

Once salted, all hams are matured. The time and methods for this process vary from place to place (some are buried in wood ash, some hung up in an airy place for months on end) and it is to these differences, as well as to the type and diet of the pigs before slaughter, that we owe our immense variety of hams. There are also differences in the cuts themselves. Strictly speaking, hams are the hind legs of pigs, cut high and at an angle, but there are other parts of the pig's anatomy, such as the loin, the forehock and the shoulder, which are cured in similar ways.

Boiled and boiling hams Whole boiling hams may be bought cooked or uncooked. If you intend to have a stately boiled ham for Christmas, make your enquiries in good time, since you (or your supplier, who usually boils to order) will need time to soak the ham for several days, simmer it for about 40 minutes per 450 g/1 lb, cool it in its own liquid, and then skin it and either glaze and bake it, or simply breadcrumb it.

When buying a whole ham to cook at home, do not be put off by a little bloom or mould on its rind, since this indicates that the ham is cured to perfection. This must, however, be scraped off before the ham is immersed in the cooking liquid.

York ham Firm and tender, this is the best known of the British boiling hams. It is delicately pink, with fat that is white and translucent. It is cured by the dry-salt method, and smoked over oak sawdust until it develops its fine, mild flavour.

Suffolk ham Traditionally cured in brine with spices and honey, this ham is then smoked and hung to mature. During this process it develops its characteristic blue mould and a full, delicate flavour.

Bradenham ham With its coal-black skin and deep red flesh, this is another famous English ham. It is cured with molasses and so has a sweet but robust flavour. If bought uncooked, it should be soaked for several days before cooking, otherwise it will tend to taste very salty.

Gammon or Wiltshire ham Unlike true hams, which are first cut and then cured, English gammon is cured as part of the whole bacon pig, which is then divided into various cuts. It is extremely mild and does not keep as well as most other hams. Like bacon, it is sold smoked or unsmoked, and comes in a variety of cuts such as steaks, the little wedges called slippers, the lean fine-grained corner and the succulent middle gammon, as well as the bony hocks. It is best boiled and served with root vegetables or dried peas or beans.

Virginia ham This is among the so-called 'country-cured' hams of the United States. Pigs destined to become Virginia hams were once fattened on peanuts and acorns, but today they are grain-fed; the meat is usually smoked over scented hickory and applewood.

Smithfield ham Cured and smoked in Smithfield, Virginia, this is probably the

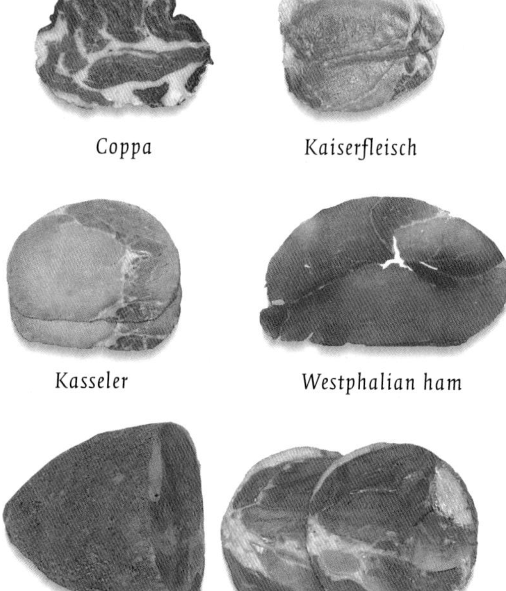

Coppa

Kaiserfleisch

Kasseler

Westphalian ham

Jambonneau

Parma ham

York ham

Jambon de Bayonne

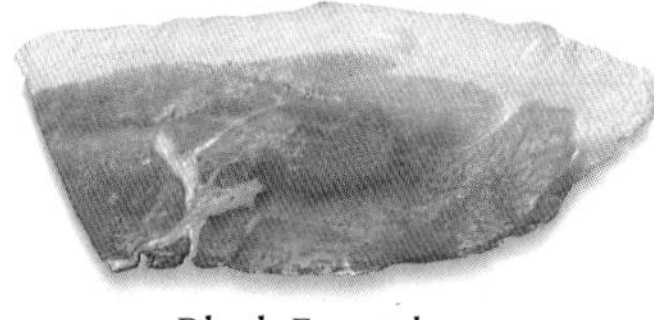

Black Forest ham

most famous of the American country hams. It is spiced with pepper and heavily smoked.

Prague ham is perhaps the most admired of the central European hams. It is traditionally salted and then mildly brined before being lightly smoked over beechwood embers, from which it emerges as perhaps the sweetest of all smoked boiling hams.

Jambon de Paris In France, ham for boiling is sold as *jambon de Paris*, and boiled ham as *jambon glacé*.

Jambonneau, a small ham from the shank part of the leg, is sold covered in breadcrumbs and ready to eat.

Other boiled hams Whole hams are a substantial investment usually reserved for festive occasions, and so ham is usually sold in portions. Like the small jambonneau, 'half-hams' come from the meaty, more expensive butt end of the leg, or from the bonier but cheaper shank portion. Hams are also sold boned, and these are usually bought by the slice. Some are just boiled, while others may have been baked or topped with breadcrumbs. Boneless hams can be bought with the fat and rind, or skinless with the fat trimmed. Skinless hams tend to lack the flavour of hams with their skin and fat still intact.

Hams may also be bought canned, the best known being the Dutch, Danish and Polish. Lean and full flavoured, they are boneless and ready to eat, but taste better baked with cider, brown sugar, mustard and cloves.

Kaiserfleisch and Kasseler Other cured pork products include the delicate smoked Austrian *Kaiserfleisch*, and the *Kasseler* so popular in Germany, Denmark and Poland. Taken from the loin of the pig, these cuts look like a row of pork chops, but they may also be bought by the cutlet, boned or unboned, or sliced. In Germany, *Kasseler* is so popular that pigs have been bred with an extra set of ribs to yield more of this cut. Austria eats its *Kaiserfleisch* with bread-based dumplings and red cabbage. German *Kasseler* is sold uncooked in its native country, but is most often encountered elsewhere cooked and sold by the slice.

Raw hams Local differences in the traditional cures show most clearly in the hams that are not meant to be cooked but are eaten raw.

Parma ham When you go into a shop in Italy to buy prosciutto, you will be asked if you want it *cotto* (cooked) or *crudo* (raw) because *prosciutto* simply means 'ham'. Outside Italy, prosciutto means raw ham, and the best comes from Parma.

Parma ham is lightly salted and air-cured for many months. A crown stamped upon its golden hide tells you that it is the genuine article produced from local pigs. The thousands of hams sent to Parma for the cure from all over Italy are less delicate and do not bear this hallmark.

Eat Parma ham in transparently thin slices, with melon, fresh figs or butter.

Culatello Looking like a half-size Parma ham, culatello comes from the choice rump end of the leg. It is less fatty and more spicy than a whole Parma.

Coppa When Italian recipes specify raw ham, most Italian housewives tend to use coppa. This is the cured shoulder and neck portion of a pig, pressed into a skin, and is fattier and less expensive than prosciutto. It can also be thinly sliced and served as an antipasto.

Bayonne This most celebrated of French hams comes from the Basses-Pyrenees. Wine plays an important part in the curing process, and accounts for its special taste. Locally, Bayonne ham is eaten with eggs or added at the last moment to stews; however, it is most delicious eaten raw like Parma ham, but sliced more thickly.

Westphalian ham is the best known of the German hams and the star of a German *schinkenplatte*, a plate of assorted cold hams. Traditionally, it is cured and then smoked over ash or beech with a bit of juniper. It is a deep golden-pink. Juniper berries used in the cure give it its special flavour. Eat it thinly sliced on dark bread such as pumpernickel.

Black Forest ham, strongly brined and strongly smoked, has well-flavoured flesh and milk-white fat. The robust taste of this ham goes particularly well with sourdough bread.

Jambons de campagne, country hams The Dordogne area of France is well known for its splendid farm-cured hams, often rather salty and hard because the cure is very heavy, but delicious sliced thickly and served with unsalted butter and French bread. Spanish and Italian country hams are also excellent.

Jambon de Grisons This Swiss ham comes from a region with a climate that is ideal for the curing of meats. It is first lightly salted and then dried in the cold, clear air of the Alps.

Lachsschinken, from Germany, is the smoked foreloin of the pig, wrapped in snow-white pork fat and bound with string; it should be pink and moist inside. It can be bought sliced or in its expensive entirety, but should be eaten thinly sliced or minutely diced, with crusty buttered rolls.

Jamón serrano This highly esteemed but chewy ham is cured and air-dried in the Sierra Morena mountains in south-western Spain. It is delicious on rough peasant bread. It is reputed to be the sweetest ham in the world, and although it is produced in other parts of Spain, the variety from the province of Huelva is thought to be the best.

Bacon

Bacon can be bought both smoked and unsmoked, or 'green'. You can tell the difference by the colour of the rind: smoking makes the rind look golden-orange and turns the flesh a nice deep pink. Unsmoked flesh is pale pink, and the rind looks anything from off-white to dark cream. Smoking adds depth and interest to the flavour, but it is a matter of taste.

Bacon joints In those countries, especially England, where entire carcasses of bacon pigs are cured in brine, a number of ham-like cuts appear on the market. The leaner cuts are good hot or cold, boiled with onions and root vegetables, or first boiled and then liberally basted with fruit juice or cider and roasted. Grill or fry bacon chops and steaks, and serve them with apple sauce.

Fat bacon It is the fat of a bacon piece that imparts the most flavour, since it melts slowly, amalgamating with whatever other ingredients are in the pot. Cured flank or belly are therefore the most useful parts to use in cooked dishes. Whether you buy *pancetta*, *lard de poitrine*, *poitrine fumé*, *speck*, *paprikaschinken*, or *tocino*, what you carry home is cured belly of pork which, when sliced, is also known as streaky bacon. Cures and streakiness vary.

Pancetta is pink and white in even proportions, and may be smoked or,

Boiled Bacon and Sausage with Haricot Beans and Garlic Purée 291
Lasagne with Mushrooms, Bacon and Artichokes 340
Pâté de Campagne 318
Rigatoni all'Amatriciana 337
Summer Minestrone 251
Tagliatelle alla Panna 338
Yellow Split Pea Soup 248

back fat 110
bard 422
lardons 422
Bacon and Egg Tart 327
Beef in Beer 284
Boston Baked Beans 354
Broad Beans and Bacon 378
Coq au Vin 305
Frisée and Bacon Salad 366
New England Fish Chowder 252
Pheasant with Chestnuts 298
Pissenlits au Lard 367
Spinach and Bacon Salad 366

more usually, green. *Pancetta stesa* is left flat, in the natural shape; it is used mainly in cooking, in pasta sauces, risotto and bean casseroles. *Pancetta arrolata* is rolled, flavoured with cloves and peppercorns, and eaten as it is or added to cooked dishes.

Lard de poitrine France's version of streaky bacon can be extremely fatty and generally has less lean meat than the pickled *petit salé*. *Lard de poitrine* is given a proper bacon cure and comes smoked, when it is called *poitrine fumé*, or green. It is used to enrich stews and *farces*, and is an essential part of coq au vin and many beef stews. It can also be used to bard roasting birds or dry cuts of meat. Cut into strips it becomes *lardons*.

Poitrine fumé This kind of bacon is splendid sliced and fried, or can be added to omelettes.

Speck, spek This is fat with a thin layer of lean. When it is more striped with lean it becomes *schinkenspeck*. In Germany, Holland, Scandinavia and other northern countries, speck, which can be smoked or unsmoked, appears as a garnish on dishes that need the taste of bacon fat. Speck yields a large quantity of dripping, part of which can be poured off and eaten on bread. The rendered fat is used for frying potatoes or mushrooms, and for browning beef or veal joints before they are roasted.

Paprika speck Translucent white and rindless, powdered on the outside with bright red paprika, this is not used so much in cookery, but may turn up on a platter of cold cuts.

Tocino, the Spanish version of speck, is strong flavoured and stored in salt crystals. It goes into *fabadas* – bean stews with vegetables and sausages.

Breakfast bacon When streaky bacon (cured belly of pork) appears in fried rashers for American breakfasts, it tends to curl up: the pigs' diet causes their fat to be on the soft side, so that it melts easily, causing the bacon to become crisp and crumbly. In other parts of the world, crisping is only possible if streaky bacon is sliced extra thin.

Lean bacon cuts are made from the back of the pig, and those cut from the meaty leg area are considered to be very good. In England, top back rashers are lean; middle-cut bacon rashers have long tails of streaky attached and a good eye of solid pink meat at the top end. The oyster-cut from the hind end of the back comes sometimes in the piece and sometimes sliced, and is beautifully succulent. Shortback, with a nice edge of fat and plenty of lean meat, may come in rashers or in thicker slices, which are meant for grilling. Long back rashers are the leanest and most expensive of all.

When Americans buy their breakfast bacon under the name of Irish bacon, or country style, top back is what is usually offered, while Canadian bacon from the loin is quite lean and smoked and needs a little fat in the pan before frying.

Bacon that has been brine-cured gives off a milky liquid as it cooks, and being thus wet is difficult to crisp properly. So look for dry-salted bacon such as Canadian cure or traditional cure.

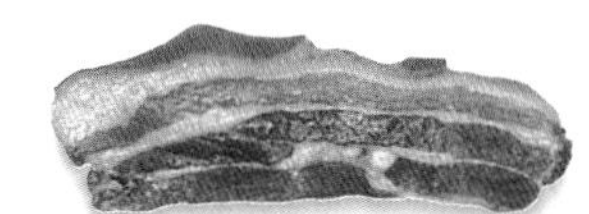
Lard de poitrine

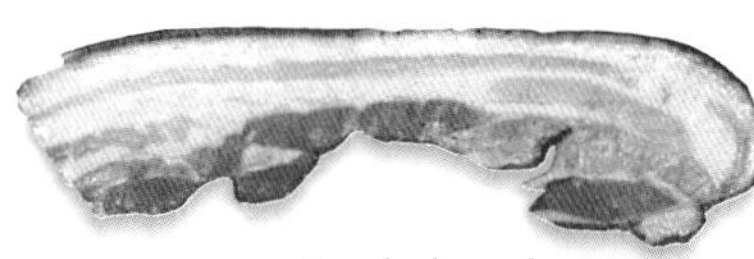
Smoked speck

British unsmoked streaky bacon

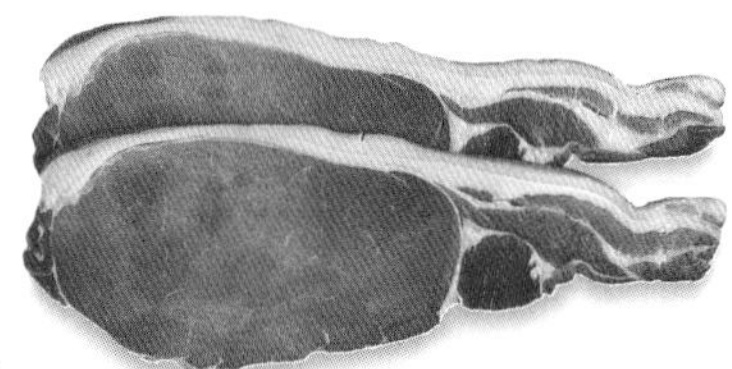
British smoked back bacon

Pancetta

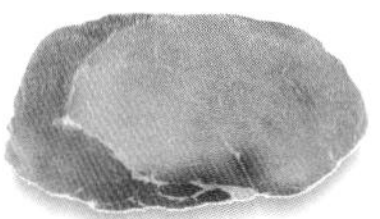
Canadian bacon

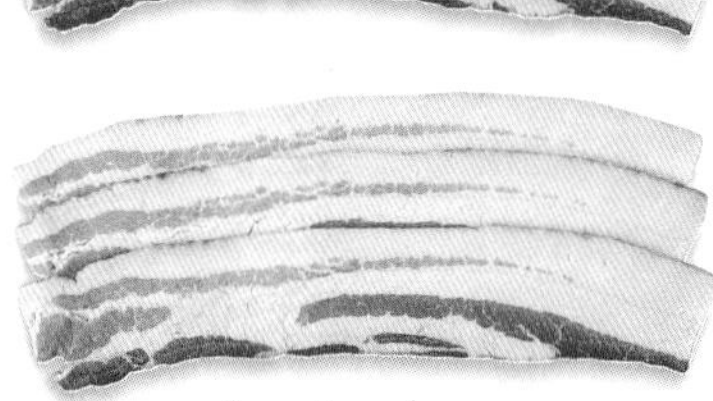
American bacon

Salted pork

The *petit salé* of France, the pickled pork belly of Great Britain, and the salt pork of the United States fall into a category all of their own, being not fully cured but lightly salted in brine.

Petit salé, lightly brined, can be either flank end of belly, or the fatty parts of collar and neck. It is eaten in the traditional French *potée*, a rich cabbage soup containing other cured meats and vegetables. It may also sit in pink-and-white slices on top of puréed peas and beans, or on a dish of cabbage, when it is called *petit salé aux choux*, and it is a vital ingredient in the cooking of sauerkraut.

Pickled pork tends to be slightly more heavily cured in brine, with sugar added. It usually consists of belly, although shanks are sometimes also prepared in the same way. This meat may need soaking before it is simmered with carrots, turnips, swedes and other root vegetables. Pease pudding is another traditional accompaniment.

Salt pork Not to be confused with fat back, salt pork comes from the belly, and may be well streaked or virtually all fat. The streaked salt pork from the leaner end goes into Boston baked beans. Salt pork is also an essential ingredient of a New England clam chowder.

Sylte is pickled belly of pork, rolled around crushed peppercorns and mustard seed. It is delicious thinly sliced and often appears at Scandinavian cold tables.

Bath chap England offers breadcrumbed bath chaps, which come from pig's cheeks. They are cured like hams, and are good if they are not too fatty. In North America, where they are known as jowls, they are usually served with black-eyed beans.

Cured Meat and Poultry

By far the greatest number of preserved meats, whether brined, air-dried, smoked, potted or canned, contain pork and pork mixtures. But other meats, game and poultry also lend themselves to the curing process, producing interesting and luxurious alternatives to ham.

Salted beef There are many ways to treat a salted cut of beef, a number of them a welcome legacy from kosher Jewish cuisine.
Salt beef is simply beef soaked in brine. The addition of saltpetre makes it red – in its natural state it is greyish-brown. Some types of salt beef are so heavily brined that some soaking will be necessary before the meat goes into the pot, while others may be ready for cooking just as they are, so check with your butcher. Salt beef – silverside is the traditional cut – is often boiled with plenty of carrots and served with potatoes and dumplings.
Corned beef Corning is the old term for salting, and corned beef is the term used in the United States to describe the salted and well-spiced briskets that go whole into a New England boiled dinner and chopped into corned-beef hash. To most Europeans, however, corned beef means bully beef, canned, pressed, salted beef, pink in colour and speckled with fat, that is eaten with salad or in fritters or hash.
Pastrami In the Balkans, the word pastrami is used to describe any kind of preserved meat from beef, pork and lamb to goose. Elsewhere, it has come to mean salt beef that has been highly seasoned, usually with black peppercorns, and dry-cured, then smoked. Since Romania, above all other Balkan countries, excels in making pastrami, its methods are the model for the rest of the world, and the words 'Romanian style' often feature on the packaging. Sold fully cooked in slabs or slices, it is delicious with rye bread or hot potato salad.

Dried beef This is beef spiced and salted and then air-dried to the very essence of beefiness.
Bündnerfleisch Grisons in Switzerland is the home of this mountain air-cured beef. As it tends to be rather dry, slivers of it, scraped rather than cut, are eaten with an oil and vinegar dressing.
Bresaola, the Italian counterpart, is a speciality of Lombardy and is eaten thinly sliced. The usual dressing is made with olive oil, chopped parsley and lemon, or the bresaola may be served with olive oil and slivers of Parmesan or white truffle.
Chipped beef is a rather poor American relation sold in jars. It is sometimes served on toast, or is mixed with scrambled eggs.
Biltong, from South Africa, is strips of cured, air-dried beef or game, or, more recently, meat such as ostrich. Biltong can be very good indeed, and will keep indefinitely.
Jerky, the American version of biltong, is usually strips of beef traditionally dried in the sun. It is chewy and salty, but full of flavour.

Smoked mutton 'No sort of meat,' say the Scots, 'is more improved by smoking with aromatic woods than mutton.' The people of Norway are in perfect agreement. Norwegian *fenalar* is smoked and air-dried until it develops a highly concentrated flavour, to be enjoyed with crisp Norwegian *flatbrød* and butter. The Scottish mutton ham has a rich, interesting flavour, and is good sliced and eaten raw, or braised with vegetables.

Smoked poultry and game Unlike hams, poultry and game are always hot-smoked, or first cooked and then smoked. They can be bought whole or sliced and resemble ham in flavour, but are as perishable as fresh-roasted birds. Smoked guinea fowl, smoked chicken and smoked turkey breasts offer plenty of delicate meat; smoked duck is excellent and smoked quail extravagant, but the most prized of all is smoked goose breast from the Baltic coast of Germany, where the geese tend to be the most deep-breasted. Also excellent is smoked reindeer meat from Scandinavia, particularly from Lapland.

Confit d'oie and confit de canard
An everyday food in south-western France, where vast numbers of geese and ducks are fattened for foie gras, *confits* are simply salted or salted and spiced pieces of goose or duck preserved in fat. *Confit* can be bought in jars and will keep for several months, but all that is needed to make it at home is the bird, its rendered fat, coarse salt and patience. The wings and legs are salted for 12 hours, then wiped dry and gently cooked in their own fat, plus extra pork fat if necessary. After this they are placed in jars where they must be completely covered with their own fat. They will keep well in a cool place.

A portion of *confit* is an essential ingredient in a cassoulet, but *confit* can also be eaten on its own, gently sautéed in a little of its preserving fat, and served crisp on the outside, succulent inside, with a green salad dressed with walnut oil.

beef silverside 53
feathered game 82–5
foie gras and goose liver 90
fresh beef 51–3
fresh poultry 86–90
furred game 79–81
mutton 56
ostrich 90
salt 200
saltpetre 200

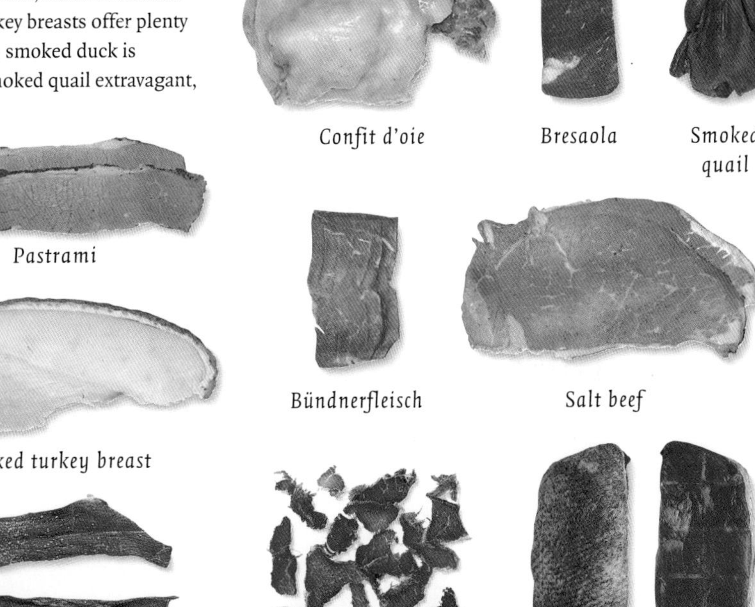

Confit d'oie

Bresaola

Smoked quail

Pastrami

Bündnerfleisch

Salt beef

Smoked turkey breast

Beef jerky

Biltong

Smoked duck breast

Sausages and Salamis

choucroute garnie 422
home-made sausages 75
sausage casings 75

When country people killed their own animals, particularly pigs, to provide themselves with meat, there was always a tremendous amount of work to be done. It was essential to make sure that every part of the animal could be either eaten straight away or, for the most part, stored for later use.

The liver, heart, kidneys and so forth were eaten at once, and legs, bellies, shoulders, trotters and heads were salted for the winter, while certain cuts and all the scraps were gathered together and turned into sausages, with the animals' own guts serving as casings. These sausages were either spiced, to help prolong their life by a few days, and eaten fresh, or dried and preserved by various means, often by salting and smoking, for eating later.

The type of meat, the proportion of fat to lean, and the endless variations of seasonings and cures account for the myriad different sausages we enjoy today. What makes the ideal sausage is largely a matter of regional taste. Some like sausages so coarse that the meat seems to be chopped, not minced; others prefer the stuffing so finely minced that it becomes a paste. But all agree that the meatiest sausages are the best. The seasonings also vary tremendously from country to country and from region to region.

Most interested sausage eaters prefer their sausages in natural casings, true gut being marginally more digestible than the artificial kind, less liable to burst during cooking, and producing a more attractive, rustic, natural-looking result. Natural casing can be recognized by the fine, slim knots between the links; artificial casings tend to be less elastic and to untwist, leaving air spaces between the individual sausages.

Fresh sausages

While fresh home-made sausages are fairly simple to make and easily rival the best store-bought ones, country markets and butchers' and speciality shops now offer some very good fresh sausages. These should be treated like fresh meat and eaten within a few days of purchase. They need really slow cooking – too much heat and they burst their skins, because the contents swell at a faster rate than the casings. Prick them in one or two places before frying in a little pork dripping or oil, and make sure they are cooked right through.

In England, fresh sausages and sausage meat go into sausage rolls, pies and toad-in-the-hole. In Italy and France sausages are poached and boiled and used in soups, *choucroute garnie* and cassoulet, and in France cervelas are sometimes wrapped in brioche dough and then baked. Merguez, heavily spiced lamb sausages, are the favourite for barbecues in the South of France. In Spain blood sausage and chorizo are essential components in richly flavoured bean stews.

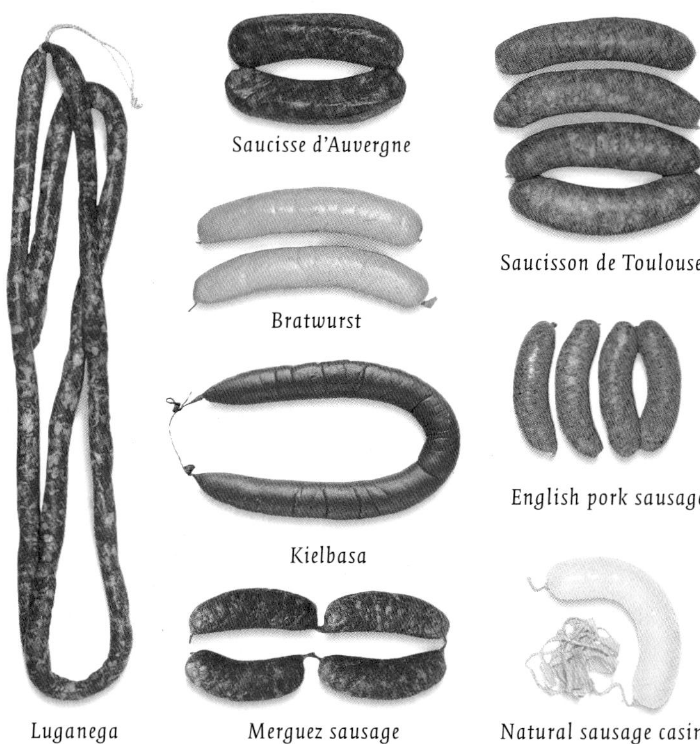

Saucisse d'Auvergne

Bratwurst

Kielbasa

Luganega

Merguez sausage

Saucisson de Toulouse

English pork sausage

Natural sausage casing

English and American sausages

Usually bought by weight, these can be made from fresh pork or, less good, from fresh beef or venison. (Chicken and turkey sausages are also increasing in popularity.) Sage is the traditional seasoning, but new varieties are introduced all the time – one excellent innovation contains pork and leeks. The best are made of pure, coarsely chopped pork.

Accompanied by mashed potatoes, they are called bangers and mash in England and are often eaten with mustard. Grilled and served with fried eggs, fat sausages make a filling and delicious breakfast. (Slender, half-size sausages, filled with pork or beef, are called chipolatas in France and England.)

Unless they are labelled 100 per cent meat, sausages are likely to contain a cereal binder: being descendants of the old *boudins*, or puddings, this cereal was once fresh breadcrumbs, but rusk is now generally used. Sausages may contain a good deal of moisture, since crushed ice may be introduced into the sausage machine to prevent the meat overheating as it is minced.

Cumberland sausage This meatiest of all British pork sausages is made in a continuous spiral, rather than being twisted into links. The filling is coarsely cut and spiced with black peppercorns. It is sold by length and is usually fried.

Weisswurst and bratwurst These fine-grained, pale, almost white sausages – the best known are those from Bavaria and Switzerland – are usually made of veal, though bratwurst sometimes contains pork as well. Called 'frying sausages', they can indeed be fried, or they can be first poached and then briefly grilled so that they are branded with golden stripes. These sausages are of a fine consistency and have a delicate taste.

Saucisses Small fresh sausages in France generally go under the name of *saucisses*, while larger ones are *saucissons*. Regional recipes make for differences of texture and taste, but whether coarse or fine, highly seasoned or not, all are made of pure meat, which is so important when making *saucisses en brioche* and other sausage pastries if the result is to be light and delicate. Throughout France there are any number of excellent locally made country sausages – *saucisses de campagne* – that go into cabbage soups and *farces* as well as being grilled. A wide variety of seasonings is used, ranging from pistachio nuts, chard, truffles or Champagne to sage, peppers or parsley.
Saucisse d'Auvergne These are *saucisses fumées*, or smoked sausages. They are eaten either grilled or fried, and combine their rich flavour beautifully with a hot potato salad.

Saucisson de Toulouse These large, delicately seasoned sausages are made from coarsely chopped pork. They are an essential ingredient of cassoulets, but are also fried or grilled and served with plenty of fried apples and mashed potatoes. A similar but more robust sausage, the air-dried Saucisson de Lyon, makes a good substitute in cassoulet.

Kielbasa In Poland any number of fresh sausages, called kielbasa, are added to hearty *bigos* – cabbage and meat stews – but elsewhere kielbasa refers to a particular garlicky and spicy sausage sold either smoked or fresh, sometimes already fully cooked. It is good grilled and served together with sauerkraut and a mild mustard.

Luganega This sausage from northern Italy, made of pure pork shoulder often seasoned with Parmesan cheese, is made in enormous lengths; it is slim, unlinked and cut to the customer's order. Italian housewives fry it in oil, adding tomatoes or sage, and serve it with polenta, or they may simply scrape all the meat out of the skins and use it as a basis for a thick pasta sauce.

Salsicces Seen hanging in Italian shops, salsicces have a rustic flavour and may be highly spiced with chilli peppers, or very mild, especially if they are made simply with minced pork and pancetta. Salsicces may be seasoned with fennel seeds and garlic – as such they are referred to as Italian sausages in North America.

Loukanika Sliced and served as a Greek *mezze* – hors d'oeuvre – a loukanika usually means coarsely ground pork seasoned with coriander, marinated in red wine, stuffed into casings and sometimes left to air-dry. A loukanika in Greek communities in North America, however, is a combination of minced lamb and pork seasoned with orange zest, and is usually grilled and served at barbecues or for breakfast.

Other cooking sausages

Apart from fresh raw sausages, there are those that have been treated in some way to preserve them. Some, such as the frankfurter, have been fully cooked, but are reheated and served hot. Others have been salted and smoked and then left to mature, but still require further cooking before they are ready to eat.

Frankfurter It is the light smoking that gives the skins of frankfurters their familiar colour. Unless marked kosher, in which case they are made of pure beef, frankfurters contain a mixture of finely minced beef and pork, and are usually quite highly spiced and salted. Genuine frankfurters are always sold in pairs – the best are fresh, while those that are heat-sealed in a vacuum pack come next. Canned varieties are overcooked and lack texture, flavour and robustness. The classic accompaniments to frankfurters are hot or cold potato salad, or sauerkraut and mustard; they are sometimes also added to potato or split pea soup.

In Austria a piece of lean roast beef becomes a *wurstelbraten* when small frankfurter-type sausages called *wurstel* are inserted into the meat before braising. When frankfurters appear in long rolls as hotdogs or dogs (or, possibly, foot-longs), they owe their name to the United States, where they were once known as dachshund sausages because of their shape. They are eaten with mustard.

When heating frankfurters it is best to put them into a saucepan filled with water that is just off the boil and then simmer for 3–5 minutes; too much heat and their thin skins will split.

Knackwurst This short, stumpy smoked sausage is made of finely minced pork, beef and fresh pork fat, flavoured with salt, cumin and garlic. Knackwurst are usually sold in pairs or in long links.

Bockwurst These sausages are prepared in the same way as frankfurters. In Germany they are traditionally made in the spring, when the winter-made bock beer is ready to drink. The Berliner bockwurst is a smoky red sausage, while a Düsseldorf favourite is bockwurst wrapped in bacon with mustard.

Cervelas The best version of this pure pork sausage, which is a type of saucisson, comes from Lyons. It is a large, fine-grained sausage sometimes delicately flavoured with pistachio nuts or truffles and truffled brandy. It is best poached, or wrapped in foil with a few spoonfuls of red wine and baked. It is served hot, sliced, with hot potato salad or *choucroute garnie*. It may also be wrapped in brioche dough and baked. The English version, the saveloy, is a very poor substitute.

Cotechino From northern Italy, this sausage is made of pork moistened with white wine and subtly seasoned with spices. It comes in various sizes and is usually salted for a few days. It is simmered with haricot beans, lentils or other pulses, or is sometimes served simply with rather liquid mashed potatoes. It is one of the essential ingredients of *bollito misto* – an Italian dish of mixed boiled meats.

Zampone and stuffed goose neck
Besides guts, stomachs and bladders, which medieval jesters used indecently to flaunt – accounting for the German Punch-figure's name of Hanswurst and indeed for Mr Punch's own traditional accessory of strung sausages – other parts of animals can be turned into interesting sausages.
Zampone, a speciality from Modena, Italy, is one such example, and is really a cotechino stuffed into a boned pig's trotter. Fresh, it needs soaking and then simmering for an hour, but those that are packaged are precooked and only need heating thoroughly.

farce 422
mezze 422
pancetta 69
pig's trotters 62
polenta 115

Boiled Bacon and Sausage with Haricot Beans and Garlic Purée 291
Brioche Loaf 359
Soft Polenta with Butter and Parmesan 352
Yellow Split Pea Soup 248

morel 159
oatmeal 116
offal 61–2

Stuffed goose neck The fat skin of a goose is used in a similar way. The filling consists of meat and innards – liver, stomach, heart – perhaps morels or truffles, air-cured bacon, breadcrumbs, and an egg for binding it all together. It is sewn up or tied at both ends and may then be fried to a golden brown, or poached, pressed between boards and eaten in slices, or simply poached in stock fortified with a little white wine. A canned version makes an extremely good lunch.

Chinese sausage These narrow sausages are cured and air-dried. Dark red with white bits of fat, they flavour a number of Chinese chicken and vegetable dishes, and are sometimes mixed with rice.

Andouillette and andouille French andouillettes contain beef, pork or veal tripe and chitterlings, which are cooked to a gelatinous tenderness. The skins are made from pig's intestines. Veal andouillettes are the most sought after. They often come covered in lard, and are grilled or fried and eaten with mashed potatoes or fried apples. The larger andouilles, which may be black skinned, are hung to dry, and are sliced and eaten cold.

Cajun andouille This large, rich sausage, from Louisiana, is made with lean pork and pork fat, generously spiced with cayenne or chilli and flavoured with herbs and lots of garlic. It is often heavily smoked, and is the traditional sausage to use in Cajun dishes such as jambalaya and gumbo.

Pudding sausages

These are the ancestors of all the fresh sausages, and contain cereal as well as meat.

Black pudding These get their colour from pig's blood, their richness from cubes of pork fat, and their body from oatmeal – at least it is this cereal that is always used in Scotland and northern England. Elsewhere, other cereals, even breadcrumbs, may be used. In Ireland, lamb's blood goes into the local version, which is called drisheen. The French *boudins noirs* may, variously, also contain onions, apples, chestnuts, eggs, garlic and chard leaves. They are simmered by their makers, but may afterwards be poached, baked or fried. In France, they are sometimes served with fried, thinly sliced onions, but are at their best when grilled and eaten with fried apples.

White pudding, boudin blanc Made of white meat such as chicken, veal, rabbit or pale pork, with breadcrumbs or ground rice, cream and perhaps eggs, these are pre-cooked, and may be slowly fried or grilled, or wrapped in buttered greaseproof paper and baked. They are delicate and should be cooked slowly and at a gentle temperature or they will burst and go brown, losing their succulent softness. As with *boudin noir*, they can be served with fried apples.

Blood sausage These are also known as black sausages, but differ from black puddings in that they have fewer cereal additives and less seasoning. They always contain pig's blood, and come in a great variety.
Blutwurst There are many varieties of German blood sausages, but perhaps the *blutwurst* is the best known. It is made of diced bacon and calf's or pig's lungs, and is seasoned with cloves, mace and marjoram. It is often served with boiled potatoes and cooked apples. Other German blood sausages include *rotwurst*, which is usually sliced and eaten on bread, and *schwarzwurst*, which is smoked and air-dried, and seasoned with garlic, cloves and a sprinkling of pepper and salt.
Morcilla Made and smoked in Asturias, Spain, this blood sausage is made of pig's blood, fat, spices and onions, and is an essential ingredient of *fabada asturiana*, or bean stew. There are two varieties of this sausage – ordinary morcilla, which is the most popular and has a strong, smoky flavour, and *morcilla dulce*, which has a sweeter, spicy flavour that is slightly reminiscent of a rich Christmas pudding.

Haggis Although called a glorified sausage, a haggis is really in a class of its own. In Scotland it is regarded with reverence and solemnly piped in on special occasions such as Burns' Night on 25 January. It is made of roughly chopped, freshly cooked sheep's pluck (liver, lights and heart), toasted oatmeal, onions, suet and herbs, all loosely packed into a sheep's stomach, which is then sewn up. The filling swells as the haggis is boiled, and makes it look like a greyish rugby ball. A bought haggis merely needs to be steamed to heat it

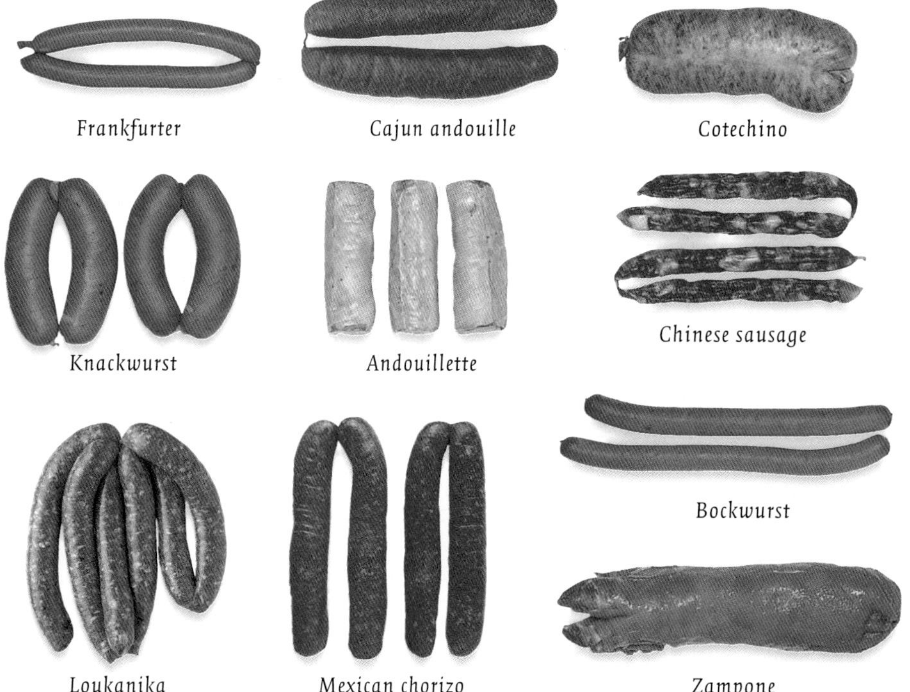

Frankfurter
Cajun andouille
Cotechino
Knackwurst
Andouillette
Chinese sausage
Loukanika
Mexican chorizo
Bockwurst
Zampone

through, but it must be served piping hot in order to be really good.

Faggot These little round parcels are made like crépinettes but contain pig's fry – liver and lights – cereal and fat salt pork or bacon. They are wrapped in caul fat – the lacy, fatty membrane from around the stomach and guts of a pig, previously soaked and softened in warm water – and are cooked slowly in the oven. Also known as poor man's goose or savoury duck, they are best when home-made from good minced meats, with plenty of onion, nutmeg and other spices. If caul fat is a problem to obtain, they can be put unwrapped into the oven, sitting closely together in the tin.

Cayette, caillette These flat, rissole-like sausages from the Ardèche, in France, contain chopped chard leaves, and for the rest they are a mixture of minced pork, liver, garlic, herbs and seasonings, wrapped in caul fat. They are cooked in the oven, like faggots, but are usually far more appetizing.

Home-made sausages

While it may be a fiddly job to stuff the sausage meat into its casings, nothing can be more rewarding than to see links of fresh home-made sausages emerging in your own kitchen. Using a basic chopped or minced pork mixture, any number of delicious varieties of sausages can be made by simply adding various herbs and spices, and if have your own smoking equipment in which to smoke the sausages the possibilities become even greater. Seasonings can range from sage, oregano, marjoram, onions or garlic to sliced truffles or pistachio nuts. Chopped pancetta or bits of ham or smoked tongue can also be added, and the whole mixture can be enriched with eggs. If you don't want to bother with sausage skins, form fresh sausage meat into little patties and fry them.

Sausage meat A basic sausage meat consists of about one-half lean to one-half fat. For pure pork sausages, use lean meat from the shoulder, neck or loin, and add an equal quantity of back fat. For other sausages, veal and game such as hare and venison can be used. Back fat is the best fat to use for any type of sausage, but any scraps of fat from the belly or even the fat trimmed from pork chops or spare ribs can be used. Trim the fat of any rind or gristle, cut it into cubes with the meat and put them through a mincer. Alternatively, you can chop them briefly in a food processor, which works particularly well, especially for the coarser-textured sausages. Take care to remove gristle and sinew from the chopped meat. The minced ingredients should be mixed well before the seasonings are added. The best way to determine how the sausages will finally taste is to fry a little of the mixture and, after tasting it, to adjust the seasonings accordingly.

Casings Some sausages, such as crépinettes – the flat little sausages made in vast varieties in France – cayettes and faggots, are merely encased in caul fat. Others can be skinless, in which case they are bound with eggs or dipped in beaten egg and breadcrumbs or simply floured. Sausage meat can also be poached in a muslin bag or foil, but natural casings are best for neatly bound sausages.

Casings can be bought in small sets from butchers' suppliers or through mail order. The small 3 cm/1¼ in hog casings usually come in approximately 6 m/20 ft lengths and can be cut as required. Store them, layered in salt, in a screwtop jar in the refrigerator.

Stuffing sausages It is not difficult to force the freshly minced, seasoned meat into the casings, and although there is a certain amount of domestic machinery available to help you turn out professional-looking specimens, you really only need a funnel and a pastry bag, some string, a prodder, such as the handle of a wooden spoon, and a tap.

After disentangling and soaking the casing until it is soft (1–2 hours), slip it over the tap and run cold water through it, cutting out any bits with holes. Then cut lengths for convenient handling and wrinkle each one up over the funnel, leaving a good bit dangling at the end. Tie it up and start feeding in your mixture; force out any air bubbles, and tie or twist the casing at intervals. Dry your handiwork for about 24 hours – in an airy place if the weather is cool, on a rack in the refrigerator if it is hot – and then cook in the usual way.

'Slicing' sausages

These sausages are usually either cooked or smoked. They are eaten cold, often in sandwiches or as part of a simple lunch, accompanied by fresh bread, olives and red wine. They are best bought uncut or freshly sliced, although it is important to remember that once they are sliced they will not last particularly well. The varieties of sausage that are sold pre-sliced in vacuum-packed bags in supermarkets are frequently mass produced and of inferior quality.

Mortadella Made of finely minced pure pork, this is the best and most famous of all Italian slicing sausages, patterned perhaps with green flecks of pistachio nuts and white cubes of fat. The best mortadellas, which are made in enormous sizes, come from Bologna, where only the best ingredients are used, and where the flavourings include wine and coriander.

There are, however, other varieties: some good, some pale imitations. Although these have never been seen anywhere near Bologna, they are still called Bologna sausages or, rather contemptuously, baloney. North America is very fond of these sausages, and they come in a variety of shapes: variously sized balloons, rings and sticks, and even a square one to fit bread baked in tins. They vary in texture and flavour depending on whether they are made of pork, beef or veal, or mixtures of these meats, and their taste varies according to the spices used.

back fat 110
caul fat 62
coating with egg and crumbs 423
furred game 78–81
rissole 423
veal 54–6

food processor 238
funnel 229
mincer 226
piping bag 236
smoking equipment 241

Roast Turkey with Two Stuffings 311

Blood sausage

Black pudding

Haggis

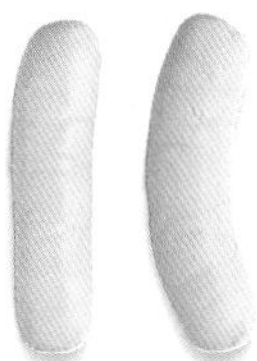

Boudin blanc

cervelas 73
frankfurter 73

Eat mortadella with a plate of mixed salamis or in sandwiches, or use it as part of a meaty stuffing for ravioli.

Garlic sausage Many of the sausages of France, no less than those of Italy, are flavoured with garlic. However, the one known as garlic sausage is different in so far as it is only lightly spiced, so that the distinct taste of garlic predominates.

Jagdwurst This German sausage owes its character to quite sizeable pieces of pork fat and rosy pork meat embedded in its pale pink paste, which is slightly porous due to the fact that it has been made by a process that involves the use of moist heat.

Bierwurst Although much larger in circumference than jagdwurst, this sausage has a similar paste. Ham bierwurst, or *bierschinken*, shows bits of ham in each of its large slices. It is also known as beerwurst in North America (*bier* being German for beer), and is often flavoured with garlic.

German cervelat

Plockwurst

Ham bierwurst

Hungarian brawn sausage

Zungenwurst

Bierwurst

Mettwurst The word '*mett*' is the medieval German name for lean pounded pork. There is *grosse mettwurst*, which is coarse in texture and red, and *feine mettwurst*, which is pink and smooth enough to spread.

Zungenwurst When a blutwurst is interlarded with bits of tongue, it becomes a zungenwurst. Bits of pork fat and a lot of pig's blood, heated carefully to setting point without curdling, make this German black sausage, which does not usually contain any cereal additives.

Hungarian brawn sausage Reminiscent of brawn, Hungarian brawn sausage, also known as presswurst, consists of meat from the pig's head, neck and trotters, blood and seasonings. Cased or uncased, it is cooked, lightly pressed and cooled until the mixture jellifies. Sage is the most usual flavouring.

Sulzwurst Similar to brawn, this sausage is made of large pork pieces. It can be eaten spread on bread, or with sliced onions and an oil and vinegar dressing.

Cervelat sausages

Almost always smoked, cervelats (not to be confused with cervelas) are far less firm than salamis because their maturing time is half as long. There is, however, a slight resemblance between the two. They are always moist, and, being made of finely pounded meat and fat, they have, when cut, a velvety surface and mottled pink colour. Fat or thin, cervelats are always pliable and look rather like large frankfurters.

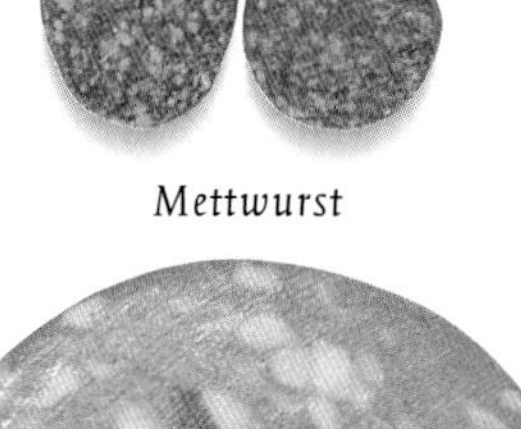

Mettwurst

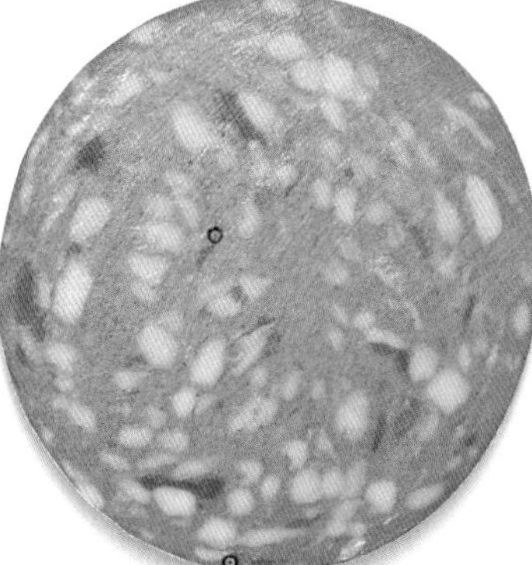

Mortadella

German cervelat Made of finely minced beef and pork, these are very popular in Germany and are exported in various diameters. They are mild, delicate and easy to slice.

Holsteinerwurst Elastic enough to be sold in rings as well as straight, the Holsteinerwurst originated in Holstein on the German-Danish border. Although counted among the cervelat-type sausages, the Holstein is so heavily smoked that it could be categorized among the German country sausages – the sort that once hung above heather, beech or peat smoke in chimneys.

Plockwurst With its smoke-darkened skin and dark meat, which contains a high proportion of beef, this sausage often comes studded with whole peppercorns.

Katenrauchwurst This cottage-smoked German sausage is produced in some quantity and is eaten throughout much of northern Europe. It is made of coarse pieces of pork, is dark and firm, and should be cut diagonally in thick, oval slices.

Danish cervelat Air-dried and hot-smoked, this is rather a bouncy cervelat. Its skin is usually a glossy red.

Thuringer Among the American cervelats – also sometimes called summer sausages because they keep well without refrigeration – is the coriander-spiced variety called Thuringer. It is named after a sausage-producing area in central Germany. In the American Midwest, where many German immigrants settled, dozens of different cervelats are still made today.

Salamis

Among the thousands of traditional sausages, it is the salami, or *salame*, that is perhaps the most celebrated. The

Italian salamis – and there are almost as many regional variations as there are villages in Italy – may be considered by purists to be the only authentic salamis, but it is worth noting that most of central Europe has made this type of tightly stuffed sausage for a number of centuries, so that German and Hungarian salamis, for example, are not pale imitations of the Italian original but indigenous sausages: only the Italian name is borrowed.

Most salamis, wherever they are made, consist of a mixture of lean pork and pork fat and sometimes beef. Occasionally veal takes the place of beef, and sometimes donkey or wild boar is used. They can be flavoured with red or white wine, with rum, with peppercorns, fennel or other herbs or spices, garlic, paprika or chilli and perhaps a few teaspoons of sugar.

Only a few types of salami are smoked, but all of them are matured for periods varying from a few weeks to a few months. During this time they lose a good deal of weight in the form of moisture, while the flavour of the meats and the seasonings – which may include wine, herbs, spices and garlic – becomes more concentrated.

Buy salami that is a fine fresh red or pink, not brown or greasy, on its outside surface. If you squeeze it and it gives a little, you can be sure that it will be fresh and fragrant. The harder the salami sausage, the more thinly it should be sliced. Cut it at an angle, whether you serve it as an hors d'oeuvre, as they do in Italy (where the Genoese eat their local salami with raw young broad beans), or whether you mean to serve it as a meal in its own right with bread and butter, and perhaps a salad.

Genoa salami This is one of the salamis that traditionally contains a high proportion of veal. To make up for the possible dryness of this meat, a little more pork fat than usual goes into the mixture, so that the result is quite fatty.

Cotto salami This is a very garlicky salami that is studded with whole black peppercorns.

Salame di Felino Made near Parma, this pure pork sausage is among the best of all the Italian salamis. Since it is made by hand, it is less perfectly geometrical than most of the others. It contains white wine, garlic and whole peppercorns, and is subtle in flavour and succulent in texture. It does not keep well, but when sent abroad is encased in wax for a longer life.

Salame napolitano Seasoned with chilli pepper, this salami is made with pork and beef. It is usually garlicky and extremely peppery and hot.

Salame finocchiona This pure pork salami has the unusual but very good flavour of fennel seeds. A similar salami, known as *frizzes*, is flavoured with aniseed and comes in both mild-sweet and spicy varieties.

German salami Because this is not usually cured for long, it is fairly moist. It is mild with a whiff of garlic and usually has a medium-fine texture.

Danish salami This is bright pink or red because it usually contains colouring. Made since the fifteenth century, this is one of the types that is salted and then sometimes hung over smoke, which is just cool enough to make the flavour more

broad bean 142
wild boar 81

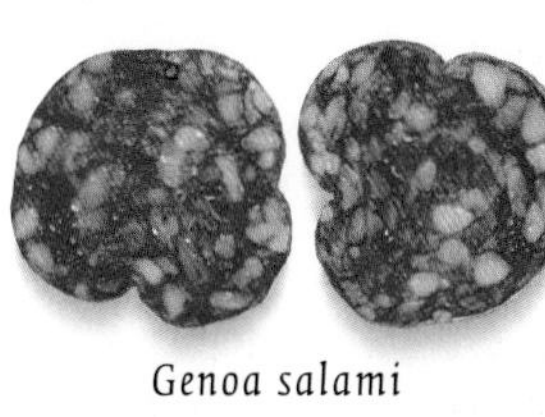
Genoa salami

Salame di Felino

Salame napolitano

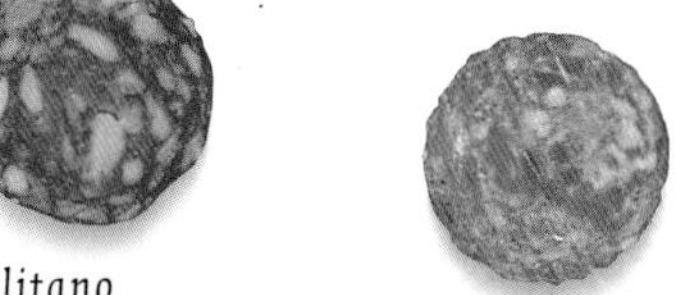
Garlic sausage

Saucisson de Lyon

Rosette

Hungarian salami

Chorizo de Lomo

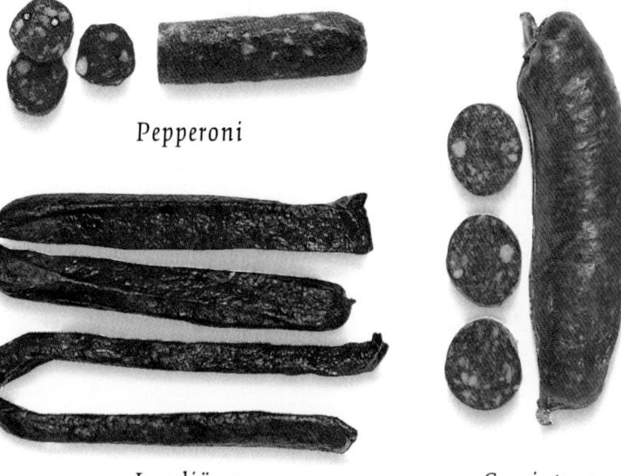
Pepperoni

Landjäger

Cacciatore

Kabanos

black pudding 74
liver 61
paprika 201
rye bread 119

Paella 346

interesting and to brown the casing but not warm enough to cook the meat. Danish salami tends to be fine textured and rather fatty and to have a bland flavour.

Hungarian salami One of the densest of salamis, this is not necessarily made in Hungary. Other countries, especially Italy, also produce this type, which contains paprika as well as other peppers. It is surprisingly mild and is often smoked. Since it is matured for about 6 months, and loses a lot of moisture in the process, it is one of the really hard salamis and ideal for slicing.

Saucisson de Lyon In France, salami is known as *saucisson sec*. Perhaps the most famous of the French salami-type sausages is the saucisson de Lyon, which is made of pure pork or pork and beef flavoured with spices and garlic. Cording is used to keep the salami straight while it dries. It has a medium-fine texture with large cubes of fat, a good rose-pink colour, and an excellent flavour.

Chorizo Widely used in Spanish and Mexican cookery, chorizos are coarsely textured, strongly flavoured with paprika and garlic, and either mild or hot. In Spain they are normally cured or smoked, while the Mexican version is a fresh pork sausage which may be air-dried. Chorizos imported from Spain are usually air-dried and are suitable for slicing or cutting into chunks to be eaten raw or used in a dish; Mexican chorizo is removed from the casing and crumbled before cooking. Chorizo de Lomo is one of the finest Spanish chorizos for slicing and eating.

Salsicha This Spanish sausage is similar to a salami and is usually served as a snack. It is made of finely chopped pork, pork fat and whole white peppercorns.

Rosette Perhaps the finest of the Lyonnaise sausages is the rosette, ridged, large and tapering. It is slowly matured and, due to its extra fat and strong casing, made from the lower end of the pig's intestine, is more moist than other salamis.

Small salamis

These are usually bought whole rather than by the slice, and can be short or long.

Kabanos These slim, garlic-flavoured sausages of Polish origin are smoked until they show wrinkles. Too thin to slice, they are bought whole and eaten in chunks.

Landjäger, gendarmes and cacciatore Landjäger and gendarmes presumably owe their names to uniformed officials who used to patrol and administrate the German and French Alpine regions, carrying a good supply of these hard, salami-type sausages in the pockets of their tunics. The sausages are usually smoked in little frames, which accounts for their strap-like shape. They are normally eaten in chunks.

The Italian version, called cacciatore, or hunter's sausage, is somewhat thicker than the others. It is not usually smoked but briefly cured and matured, and is just about large enough to slice. Chunks of these sausages are sometimes added to Italian stews to enrich and flavour them.

Pepperoni This Sardinian salami can be mild or spicy. It is usually eaten hot, or sliced on to a pepperoni salad or pizza.

Pâté-type sausages

Some sausages, such as liver sausages and teewurst, can be soft in consistency and are meant for spreading, while others such as leberkäse are firm enough in texture to be sliced.

Liver sausage These may be large or small, curved or straight, or finely milled or coarse, and their paste may also contain chunks of fat, bits of liver (which is especially good in the case of goose-liver sausage), truffles, garlic and any number of finely chopped herbs. Some liver sausages are soft and pasty and meant for spreading, while others, such as the Strasbourg liver sausage, which also includes pork meat and is smoked, are meant to be thickly sliced.

All liver sausages can be eaten as they are, but occasionally form an essential ingredient of cooked dishes: the Swedish black soup, for example, needs the Swedish *gåsleverkorv*. Flavourings, besides herbs and truffles, may include nutmeg, cinnamon, browned onions or anchovies; where anchovies predominate, the liver sausage is known as a *sardellenwurst*.

Most liver sausages are made of pig's liver mixed with pork or veal – some may contain other innards as well as liver – but there are also pure liver sausages. Calf's liver sausages are particularly good, and it is also possible to obtain sausages made of goose and other poultry livers.

German liver sausage Authentic German liver sausage is almost invariably smoked. It is prepared by a scalding process, which tends to lead to a harmless whitish film forming on natural casings.

French liver sausage These have more in common with black puddings than with the creamy German liver sausages. They are eaten hot, often accompanied by sautéed apple rings.

Danish liver sausage These are made of pig's or calf's livers to which anchovy is often added. They are excellent spread on dark Danish rye bread, garnished with slices of cucumber.

Leberkäse A mixture of pork and liver baked in an oblong tin, this German sausage has no skin. Sliced, it can be eaten as it is, or it can be fried.

Teewurst This is the name given to small liver sausages of the spreadable type. They are usually made of a spiced, finely pounded mixture of pork and beef.

Leberkäse

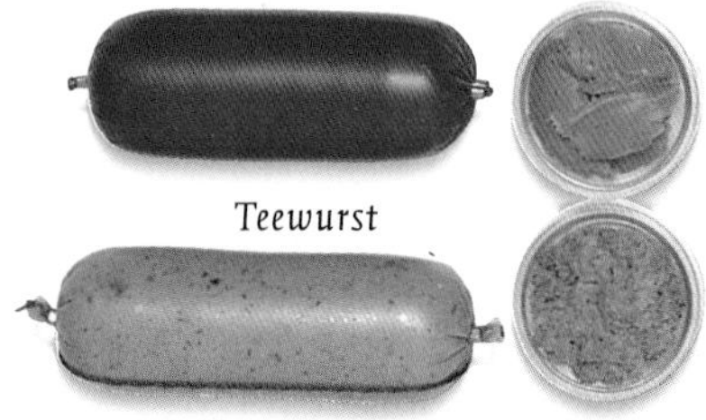
Teewurst

Liver sausage with herbs

Furred Game

In town most game is a luxury, and in winter the best restaurants feature it on their menus. It is usually served carefully carved or boned on its dainty bed of exquisite vegetables.

The situation is different in the countryside where, even if there is no local dealer selling game fairly cheaply during the open season, you are likely to be given some as a present. This time it probably arrives in the kitchen with its fur and guts intact. But once you have mastered the art of preparing it for cooking, this meat above any other is worth your time, skill and attention. Apart from the subtlety of flavour and texture, it is also considered to be one of the healthiest of meats.

To tenderize the more athletic and older creatures, a marinade is useful. This, as a rule, contains vinegar to break down tough fibres, oil to add succulence, and wine, herbs and spices to permeate the meat with flavour. There are cooked and uncooked marinades, the cooked ones being more powerful. The marinade should completely cover the meat, which should be turned periodically during the time it is steeped. This period may vary from a mere 12 hours or so for a hare to at least 2 weeks for a haunch of wild boar.

All game is protected by laws that vary from country to country. These are laid down to prevent the shooting of creatures that are too young, to allow mating and the rearing of young to take place, and also because the game population of any given area varies from year to year. As a further safeguard, the numbers of any species allowed to be shot by each sportsman are also limited in many parts of the world. Some species of game have been hunted almost to extinction – the American buffalo is an example of this, but fortunately it has been reintroduced and is being successfully raised on game ranches.

Venison

Once bagged, deer becomes venison. It does not matter whether it started life in the wild as red deer, roe deer, fallow deer, white-tailed Virginia deer, muntjac or the black-tailed variety called mule deer. The term can even be used for antelope, reindeer, caribou, elk and moose. Nor does it matter if these animals have been bred especially for the table, lived in the wild or, as in the case of roe and fallow deer, in parks; wild or semi-tame, they all become venison.

Venison is now easy to obtain, and prepared with real devotion it makes a memorable meal.

The buck is supposed to be better than the doe, but neither should be eaten too young since the flesh, although tender, will not have had time to develop its characteristic flavour. The tendency these days is towards fresh venison, but if a gamey taste is preferred the animal should hang, head down, in a cool, airy place free of flies for 12 to 21 days, depending on the weather – the cooler the weather the longer it can hang.

The fillet, the saddle, the loin and the haunch, which is the whole leg, make the best roasting cuts. The loin can also be eaten as chops, while the rest of the animal is usually used for sausages, stews, ragouts, game pies and pâtés. The head is rarely used, although smoked reindeer tongue is a delicacy in Scandinavia, as is smoked and salted reindeer meat, and moose in all forms.

When buying venison, make sure that the flesh is dark red and close grained and that the fat is clear and bright (trim off the fat before cooking because it is not good to eat). Venison is by nature a dry meat, and the fat should be replaced by pork or bacon fat before cooking, the venison having been placed first in a marinade of oil, vinegar, spices and plenty of red wine to which juniper berries may have been added. In Italy, venison is sometimes soaked in olive oil with excellent results.

When it is time to cook the meat, lift it out of the marinade and wipe it dry. Brown it in butter or lard in a large frying pan. Then wrap it in a jacket of good white pork fat or, even better, lard it with thick strips of pork back fat, and cover it all over with foil. When cooking venison, it is usual to allow 25 minutes per 450 g/1 lb for the buck and 20 minutes for the doe, in a fairly hot oven. It is cooked when, on piercing the skin, the juices run clear. Any sign of blood indicates that the meat needs more time, unless you wish to eat it rare.

Venison has a strong but muted flavour, sometimes described as lamb that tastes of beef. It needs the encouragement of some sharp, sweet, spicy or piquant accompaniment to taste at its best, so serve it with redcurrant or rowan jelly, cranberry sauce, spiced cherries or Cumberland sauce. Other flavours that marry particularly well with venison include those of thyme, rosemary, Seville orange or lemon juice and spices such as cloves, cinnamon, juniper, mace, allspice and nutmeg.

Among the many dishes that have an affinity with venison are wild rice, which is traditional – but expensive – with game in America; and the noodles or dumplings, made of pasta dough, eaten in southern Germany, Switzerland and Austria, where venison is also sometimes served with a sauce made of sour cream blended with the pan juices. This sauce also accompanies it in northern Germany and in Scandinavia, where it is mopped up with mashed potatoes or potato dumplings. Spiced red cabbage often appears with venison, and chestnut purée is served with it in France, while celery or celeriac suit its taste and texture beautifully.

Hare

The flesh of the hare is a dark mahogany brown regardless of the colour of its coat, which varies from species to species. In the Champagne district of France, the much-prized hares are golden, while northern France offers a mottled variety. German hares are almost russet coloured, English hares are fawn to grey and the Scotch blue hare of the Highlands is the colour of Scotch mist.

The blue Scotch hare is a first cousin of the arctic hare of North America, called the snowshoe rabbit; this name is an example of the linguistic confusion that has overtaken the hare, which is not helped by the fact that the highly palatable, domestically bred Belgian hare is, in fact, a rabbit. Jack rabbits are actually American hares, which becomes clear when it comes to eating them because there can be no confusion between the strong, gamey flavour of hare and the mild, more delicate taste of rabbit.

The hare, a common but usually distant sight in open farmland in autumn, is surprisingly large when seen close to. Its hind legs are heavily built for speed, and it is these and the

hang 422
haunch of venison 80
jointing a rabbit or hare 81
lard 422
marinate 422
nudels, nouilles and dumplings 124
smoked reindeer 71

Char-Grilled Venison 294
Cold Game Pie 316
Cumberland Game Sauce 260
Hare in Sour Cream 295
Pappardelle with Hare Sauce 339
Redcurrant Jelly 418
Roast Haunch of Venison with Pepper Sauce 294
Sweet-Braised Spiced Venison 294

jointing a rabbit or hare 81
lard 422
polenta 115

Braised Rabbit with Tomatoes 295
Cold Game Pie 316
Hare in Sour Cream 295
Pappardelle with Hare Sauce 339
Rabbit with Prunes and Red Wine 297

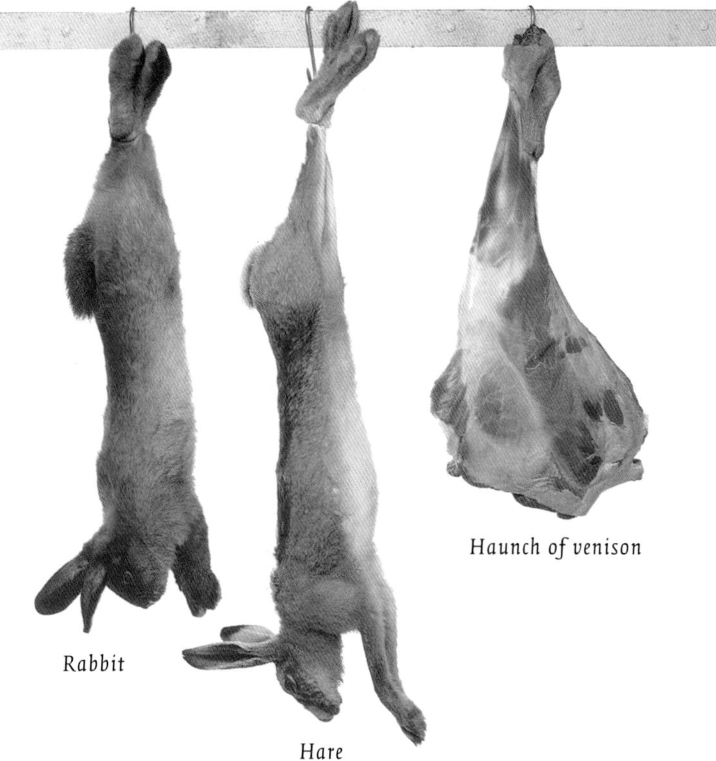

Rabbit

Hare

Haunch of venison

fleshy saddle that are particularly esteemed in haute cuisine. A cut consisting of the back or saddle goes under the culinary name of *râble*, and when the hind legs are included it is called *train de lièvre* or *baron de lièvre*. These are the classic cuts, but a tender, less muscular foreleg can be more succulent than either.

Hare is best eaten when young, and luckily its age is easy to determine. A leveret, as a hare under one year of age is called, has a white belly and pliable ears, easily split skin and a barely noticeable harelip. Its claws are almost hidden under the fur of its paws, and it is also easily recognizable by its fur, which should be soft and smooth – the fur only becomes matted with advancing age. Long, sharp claws and yellow teeth are a definite sign of adulthood.

Leverets are always tender, and although the doe remains so during its second year the buck begins to become tough. A hare is usually hung for a few days by the feet. It is then skinned, after which the inner bluish iridescent layer of muscle that covers the saddle must be removed. If the hare is bought from a game dealer, he will perform this service and probably also joint or truss the animal. Hares are sold minus their heads and innards, but ask for the blood and liver, taking care to remove the gall, which lies between the lobes. You can use the liver to make a forcemeat stuffing, which can be pushed into the diaphragm cavity to make the traditional British 'hare with a pudding in its belly'.

Hare may be marinated and then larded or wrapped in pork fat to counteract its tendency to be dry. Roast it slowly and serve quite rosy if young and tender. The larger the hare, the longer it should be cooked – give it 15–20 minutes per 450 g/1 lb in a medium oven.

Allow about 170 g/6 oz of hare per person if you plan to jug it. The original method was to place it in a jug with herbs, vegetables, spices and port and then to put the covered jug in a pot of boiling water. Nowadays, however, jugged hare is often stewed or braised in the normal way, and it is a good idea to keep the saddle separate and roast it for another meal. Recipes for jugged hare often call for some of the hare's blood. A few drops of red wine vinegar in the blood will prevent it coagulating. If the blood has not been kept or the smell of it is too overpowering, a fine jugged hare can still be made without it.

The flavour of hare, which should never be too high, is improved by the addition of cloves in moderation and red wine in abundance, and also by port, redcurrant jelly, fat bacon, mushrooms, shallots, juniper berries and cream, particularly if it is soured. In France noodles, in Italy polenta and in Switzerland celeriac purée are served with roast or braised hare. In Italy hare makes a superb pasta dish, *pappardelle alle lepre*.

Rabbit

The rabbit is both the ancient enemy and old friend of the countryman; ancient enemy because it eats crops and old friend because it can, in turn, be eaten.

Wild rabbits, still rampant – although reduced in number wherever that unfortunate disease myxomatosis has struck – are stronger tasting and, with age, ranker than farmed ones. They are also less plump and tender. Perhaps the best is a fat, white farmed rabbit that is not too young, when it is tasteless; not too old, when it becomes dry and tough; and certainly not stale, when it becomes yellow and discoloured and loses its resilience and glossiness.

Rabbits are paunched, or drawn, as soon as they have been killed, and can be eaten immediately. They do not have to be marinated or hung, although a large rabbit will develop a good aroma if it is marinated in white wine, olive oil, garlic and herbs. When choosing rabbit in its fur, pick one that is plump and compact rather than heavy, long and rangy. If buying it skinned, try to find one that is not frozen because this tends to make it dry and fibrous. Look for pink meat, and do not be put off by a pearly sheen. Allow half a young rabbit per person.

Although it has a definite flavour of its own, rabbit also makes a good vehicle for other flavours. This works to the cook's advantage in the case of cooking the wild rabbits of Provence, which feed on the tender shoots of wild rosemary and thyme and come with an added herby flavour. Farmed rabbits, however, no longer brought up on lettuce leaves and dandelions, are unlikely to offer unexpected flavours, so it is worth adding a variety of herbs and spices to make them more interesting.

Apart from the famous French rabbit dishes, such as *lapin aux trois herbes* or *lapin à la moutarde*, there are some splendid traditional English recipes, such as rabbit pie, flavoured with salt

biltong 71
chanterelle 159
wild boar salami 77

pork or bacon, grated lemon zest and nutmeg, or rabbit stew with bay leaves, carrots and onions. In some parts of England the stew is moistened with cider, which gives a delicious flavour.

In Spain, rabbit is practically a staple food. When it is not roasted, covered in olive oil and sprinkled with sprigs of rosemary or chopped garlic and parsley, it is stewed in wine or served in a light case of potato pastry. In Italy it is cooked with tomatoes, aubergines, ham or bacon, and Sicilians, true to their early Arab heritage, eat it with pine nuts and an *agrodolce* sauce made with raisins, herbs, stock and vinegar.

Scandinavians roast rabbit like hare and serve it with red cabbage. When rabbits were regarded as everyday 'frontier food' in the United States, pioneers used to enjoy them in a delicate fricassée, whilst in New Orleans they were cooked in red wine with tomatoes and cayenne as *lapin en matelote*.

Wild boar

Any wild pig, male or female, once killed becomes wild boar. Pig sticking, that dangerous sport, is almost a thing of the past, and although wild pigs still roam the woods of the world, notably in the wilder districts of southern France, much of the wild boar – or *sanglier*, as wild boar is also known – found in a butcher's or in a game and poultry shop have been reared in boar pens, an environment as close as possible to the wild woods, but where the animals can be fed and can raise their young successfully.

A young wild boar is called a *marcassin* up to the age of 6 months, after which time it becomes a *bête rousse*. After it is 1 year old it does not make such good eating, and in old age (wild boars can live up to the age of 30) only the head is still considered to be edible.

Wild boar meat should be dark, with little fat. It tastes of pork with strong gamey overtones and, like pork, has a certain natural succulence. While *marcassin* may need only hanging, a *bête rousse* is usually tougher and requires marinating as well as hanging before being cooked. The top part of the leg and the saddle make noble roasts; the smaller cuts such as steaks and cutlets are often grilled or braised. But no matter how you cook wild boar it is a lengthy operation and, again like pork, it must be cooked right through with no trace of pinkness.

In elegant French country restaurants the mounted mask of a ferocious boar with its tusks at a war-like angle may look down on you as you are served, in the autumn, with *marcassin* accompanied by chestnut purée and a *poivrade* sauce, which owes its flavour to wine, spices and Cognac. In German country inns wild boar is served with a sour-cream sauce, plain boiled potatoes and a side dish of golden chanterelles. As with venison, a spicy accompaniment is required, such as cranberry sauce, spiced cherries, or bottled sour cherries in red wine.

Since boar is eaten wherever it is found, and the method of its preparation follows national traditions, it is no surprise that it is made into curry in India. In North America, where boar was introduced from Germany in the early twentieth century, its steaks are grilled and eaten with a sweet pepper and mushroom sauce, flavoured with plenty of garlic and onion. It is also often marinated in cider and served with apple sauce or sautéed apples.

Other game

Bear is now so rare that few of us will be faced with the problem of having to prepare it for the pot. Those who are should know that the paw is reckoned to be the best bit, and that every part of the animal needs to be thoroughly cooked, because bear, like pork, can be dangerous if it is eaten underdone.

Squirrel The squirrel was once highly sought after. A sixteenth-century cook's manual ends its recipe for rabbit pie with the words: 'If you cook for a lord, use squirrel instead of coney – it is the fitter meat for the table.' The squirrel, since the grey superseded the red, is no longer regarded as a delicacy in Europe; indeed it is not eaten at all and as a result has become a destructive pest. In the American South, Brunswick stew and Kentucky burgoo were traditionally made with squirrel (chicken is used today). A Louisianan Creole recipe from earlier this century suggests stewing squirrel (or opossum) with garlic, herbs, red wine and the zest of a lemon.

Buffalo is now being raised on ranches throughout the American West and Canada. The meat tastes much like beef, not at all gamey, but it is leaner and higher in protein.

1

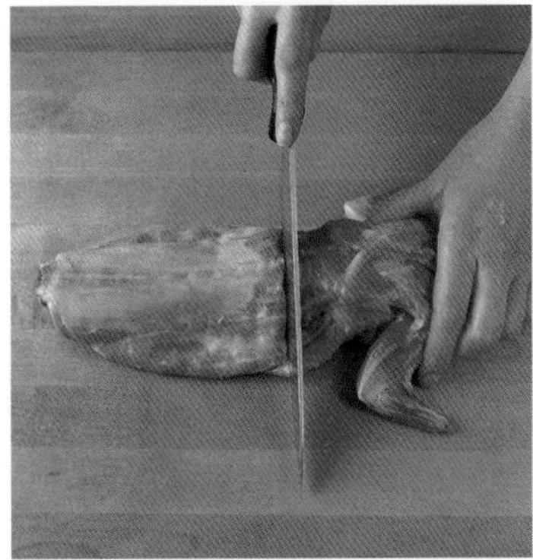

2

3

Jointing a rabbit or hare

1 Cut off the hind legs by inserting a strong, pointed knife into the ball and socket joint, just above each thigh.

2 Cut the forelegs off in one piece, slicing cleanly through the rib cage.

3 Split the forelegs down the middle. The forelegs, saddle and hind legs of this rabbit have been divided into five pieces. If you do not want to keep the saddle whole for roasting, cut it into serving-size pieces.

Feathered Game

bard 422
duck 89
game chips 147
grapevine leaf 195
hang 422
lard 422
quail's eggs 97
smoked quail 71
spatchcocking poultry and game birds 91

Marinated Roast Quails 301
Quails with Thyme and Orange 301
Roast Woodcock 299

One of the great pleasures of autumn is the arrival of game on our tables. In Great Britain shooting begins in August with the open season on grouse – the 'Glorious twelfth' – a red-letter day for those who make an annual expedition to the Scottish moors. By the thirteenth, grouse features on the menu of many a smart restaurant.

However, do not be in too much of a hurry for your first taste. Most game needs time to hang to develop its flavour and tenderness, especially if you like the *haut-goût* – although the day is passing when pheasants were judged fit to eat only when head and tail feathers fell out of their own accord, and when maggots showered down from them like so much rice. Today the ripeness of game birds is judged by smell and by the condition of the bird around the vent. This becomes moist and fragile when the bird is well hung – don't worry about a blue or greenish tint to the skin. A high bird smells powerfully gamey while a bird that is rotten smells bad, like any other bad meat.

Hang pheasant, partridge and grouse heads up; hang wildfowl, including geese, by the feet. Apart from helping the meat to mature slowly and magnificently (especially in cold weather, best for the slow mellowing of game), this helps to retain moisture – and if game has a fault, it is that it tends to be dry. If very smelly once plucked, it is helpful to wipe the meat with a cheesecloth dampened with diluted vinegar.

It is generally accepted that the natural foods of the bird or beast provide the best and most appropriate dressing with which to send it to the table. So cranberries, juniper berries, rowanberries and sweet chestnuts, as well as watercress and celery, play their part in game and fowl recipes.

Wild goose

These migratory birds fly vast distances and as a result are normally less well covered and more muscular than the fat domestic goose. Choose a young bird with bright-coloured legs and a pliable underbill. Like the duck, the wild goose – whichever the species, such as Barnacle, Brent or Chinese – should be eaten within a day or two of being shot. It is best well barded and roasted with a moist stuffing of apples or prunes. An older bird is best stuffed and braised in red wine or cider. Serve wild goose with red cabbage, sour-cream sauce, and any of the tart orange- and chicory-based salads that go so well with waterfowl.

Wildfowl

The mallard is the most common variety of wild duck and also the largest – a fat mallard will feed from two to three people. The widgeon is considered superior to the mallard in flavour. One bird will feed one hungry person, or two at a pinch. The teal is an ornamental duck, tender, and almost too pretty to eat. It will feed one.

Other varieties include the excellent pintail, the Nantais, the blackduck and the American canvasback, which obligingly feeds on wild celery and the aquatic plant tape grass which make the flavour interesting and delicate, lacking any fishy overtones.

Most species of wild duck, however, enjoy a diet of plants growing below the water and so the flavour is, according to their particular biochemical processes, more or less strong, distinctly aquatic and, not to put too fine a point on it, they can taste fishy. This can be countered by placing a raw onion inside the bird for an hour or two (remove it before cooking) or by rubbing the bird inside and out with half a lemon dipped in salt; or you may find that it is enough just to spike the gravy with lemon juice and cayenne or Tabasco.

No matter what the species, the duck is preferable to the drake, which tends to be tougher and may therefore need to be marinated. Wild duck should be cooked within 24 hours of killing, unless it is bled so that bacteria do not have the chance to develop. The two small nodules by the tail, which exude a fluid that helps to waterproof the bird, should be removed as they can give the flesh a musky taste.

Leaner and dryer than domestic ducks, all species of wild duck should be well barded and roasted fairly fast on a rack, alternately basted with fresh butter and whisky, red wine or port. They must be served juicy and slightly pink – the longer they cook the tougher they get. The juices that run out when the bird is cut make the best gravy, mixed with orange or lemon juice, red wine, port and Tabasco. Skim the dripping in the roasting pan and taste – if the juices are not bitter, they too can be added to the gravy. Both duck and gravy must be very hot. Serve with game chips, fried breadcrumbs and a sharp salad of orange, celery and watercress, or chicory and orange. Braised wild duck is good with red cabbage.

Quail

In Egypt and around the Mediterranean, particularly in southern Italy and Sicily, these migrating birds, exhausted by their journey to or from North Africa, are easily caught in their millions. There is some evidence that even quail in fine fettle will stand around just waiting to be killed. It is this that has earned one American breed the name fool-quail. Nowadays, since wild quail are scarce and are even protected all the year round in many parts of the world, most of the birds that find their way into kitchens come from quail farms.

Once their feathers have been removed, quail are so small that unless you have run out of appetite, you will probably eat at least two apiece, supported by small rafts of fried bread or toast. They are best roasted in butter, first on one side, then the other and finally breasts upwards. This keeps the meat moist, what there is of it. Make the gravy with the pan juices and a little Madeira or vermouth, and, if you like, add a few tablespoons of cream or some raisins soaked in Madeira. Or the birds can be rubbed with crushed juniper, allspice and fennel seeds or wrapped in vine leaves and roasted, or cooked in a casserole with shallots and garlic. Quail are very worthwhile, even though their flavour is more delicate than that of other game birds.

Ortolan, woodcock and snipe

Woodcock and snipe are sometimes cooked with their trail – meaning innards – intact. Due to their habit of excreting during every flight they are white and clean inside.

Ortolans are the tiniest of the trio. They are almost too small for the piece of toast on which they are served, plainly grilled or, for preference, threaded like beads on a necklace and cooked on a spit. They can also be wrapped in vine leaves and cooked, tightly packed, in the oven.

Woodcock, gently dappled and speckled with a brown-leaf light-and-shade pattern, has a long, distinctive beak. It eats greedily of almost anything it comes across, and as a result of its omnivorous diet of heather, insects, worms and moss it should be a fat little bird with a fair amount of meat for its size. One bird is just the right amount for one person. It is plainly roasted with its head on, complete with beak, and the head is split after cooking to expose the brains, which are considered a delicacy. It is eaten on toast on which the cooked mashed entrails have been spread.

The snipe is a smaller bird than the woodcock, with a similar beak, and it is often trussed with its beak through its body serving as a skewer. It is cooked like woodcock, but its lesser size has also given it a cooking method of its own: beak threaded through one wing or through the body, it may be encased in a hollowed baking potato that has been cut in two and is then carefully tied together again. When the potato is done, so is the bird. Like woodcock, it is served with its head split open so that the brains can be eaten.

Pigeon

All varieties of pigeon – wood pigeon, mourning pigeon, ring dove, turtle dove, stock dove and rock dove – and squab (specially reared young pigeon) have an agreeable beefy flavour and produce a most appetizing brown gravy. If pigeons have fallen from favour, it is because as they age they become so tough that the work of plucking and drawing them hardly seems worth the pain. Indeed, old wild pigeons, although they may give off a delicious smell, sometimes bounce around on the plate, positively defying you to stick in either knife or fork. The difficulty lies in choosing a young bird. Look at the feet, which should be without scales, soft and supple; if in any doubt perhaps make a stew, pudding or pie instead of braised or roast pigeon. There is, however, an infallible method of softening up a tough old bird: rub it with a dessertspoon of sugar and the same quantity of salt. A liquid will soon form: turn it in this for 2 or 3 days. Alternatively, the birds can be steeped in a red wine marinade.

If you shoot your own pigeons, hang them by the feet and pluck them while still warm, when the job is much easier. A Malaysian recipe recommends that the pigeons be given a final swig of alcohol before their thus intoxicated and unsuspected despatch. This is thought both to be kinder and to improve their taste. They are then rubbed with aniseed inside and honey outside and fried in sesame oil. In the Western world, it is usual to serve pigeons with petits pois, braised onions and mushrooms, cabbage and bacon, or, for a more gamey dish, with braised red cabbage or lentils.

Partridge

These are the round little birds that explode from the stubble in small groups during autumnal country walks. They are always pretty, but are more delicate to eat if they are the native greyish-brown, grey-legged variety. The red-legged partridge is an introduction from France, sometimes referred to as the French infantry. Partridges make the best eating when they are young – about 3 months old, weighing about 450 g/1 lb, most of which is supplied by the plump breast. Allow one bird per person.

Roast partridge is a great delicacy, while partridge *en chartreuse* – a pie of partridge, cabbage, sausage, carrots, onions and cloves covered with pastry – is a tremendous dish for a cold winter's day. Partridge pudding is made with a crust of suet, wild mushrooms, onion and a seasoning of salt and pepper – use old birds for pies and puddings. (Experts can distinguish the old from the young: older birds have

Braised Pigeons and Cabbage 302
Cold Game Pie 316
Partridge with Celeriac 297
Pigeon Pie 321
Roast Partridge with Chicken Liver Toasts 297
Sugo di Carne Toscano 336

Quail

Woodcock

Mallard

Mallard (drake)

game chips 147

Simple Roast Grouse 301

blunt tips to their flight feathers.) Young partridges require only a little hanging, as their delicate taste should not be overpowered by highness. Place a lump of butter and 2–3 sage leaves inside the cavity before roasting. Clear gravy, game chips and watercress are all that is needed with roast partridge, although bread sauce makes a good addition. Cold roast partridge with a green salad is a delicious lunch.

The grouse family

The flavour of grouse is one of the greatest treats of late summer and early autumn. In the controversy about what makes better eating, partridge or grouse, it is the northern British red grouse, *Lagopus scoticus*, that is being held up for comparison. Its numerous cousins all have merit, but none can match the red grouse, which is smaller than any of its relations and tastes richly of game at its gamiest.

Since young grouse look surprisingly like old ones (except that, as with partridges, there is a difference in the tip to their flight feathers), and you can't get to know very much about grouse just by eating it a few times in a decade, it is best to go to a really expert purveyor of game for these expensive little birds.

For all their gamey taste, grouse are very clean-feeding birds whose diet is heather, berries and small insects, and they are quite easy to cook to perfection. Young birds, born in the year they are eaten, need a bacon waistcoat and the plainest of roasting in a quick oven for 20 minutes, until they are pink and slightly underdone. The best way to serve them is to sit them on a piece of toast or fried bread with a few straw potatoes and a little watercress.

Older birds, while very well flavoured, take more time to prepare. They are good in game pie or in a suet-crusted pudding, or braised in red wine and stock with plenty of celery, onions and carrots, and button onions added just before the end of their cooking.

Capercaillie or wood grouse The largest of the grouse tribe. It is almost 90 cm/3 ft long, weighs 3–4.5 kg/7–10 lb, and has spectacular plumage of green, black, red and white. It is a northern bird, and owing to its habit of feeding off the tops of young pine trees it tastes distinctly of turpentine, which is not agreeable. Old English recipes variously suggest that to remove the pungent tang the bird should be soaked in milk or vinegar, or buried in the ground for 24 hours. A good method of improving a cock bird is to stuff it with raw potatoes, which are discarded after cooking.

In Scandinavia cream plays a great part in the cooking process. In Denmark this might take place in a lidded oven dish, the breastbone of the bird having been broken down to make the lid fit. Towards the end of the lengthy cooking time the bird is allowed to brown, and it is served in its sauce with a sharp cranberry jelly, little gherkins and potatoes. In Norway a creamy, cheesy sauce is poured over the carved bird, which has been roasted in the ordinary way.

Blackcock and greyhen The cock will feed three or four people, but the greyhen two at most, because the cock, with his glossy plumage with white bars and his tail feathers curved like a lyre, is twice as large as his wife. Roasted, both need a good lump of butter in the belly to keep the meat moist.

Blackcock can also be casseroled, made into pies and salamis; in fact, it should be treated much like red grouse, although its taste is less delicate.

Ptarmigan Also called the rock partridge, it is getting scarcer. Its size is similar to that of the red grouse, as is its taste, which makes it excellent eating. It is cooked in much the same way as grouse, but in northern Europe, where it is extremely popular, slices of bacon are sometimes inserted under the skin as well as tied over the top. Sour cream goes into the sauce, or there might be a cold sauce of apples cooked in wine, blended with mayonnaise.

Wood pigeon

Red-legged partridge

Red grouse

Pheasant

The pheasant stands out like a target among the quietly feathered birds of the autumn landscape, and a target is just what he is, hand reared with loving care to offer sport for countrymen. And who can complain when pheasants make such delicious eating. The cock pheasant is the more handsome, but the hen, although slighter and less gloriously plumaged, is often the plumper, juicier bird. A hen makes a superlative meal for two; a large cock can almost feed four.

To choose a pheasant in its plumage, feel the width of the breast to see if it is plump, and see that the legs are smooth and the feet soft. It is easy to tell a young cock by its spurs: rounded and without points in the first year, pointed but still short in the second year.

Make sure the bird is hung to your liking before you cook it, as this improves its succulence and flavour. Without hanging – the time depends on your taste and on the weather – pheasant can taste rather like dry chicken (to which it is related). Since pheasant tends towards dryness in any case, it needs a jacket of fat bacon. It also needs basting with butter and bacon fat to keep it moist and make the skin crisp. Traditionally, a young pheasant is served roasted, with Brussels sprouts, braised celeriac, creamed celery or braised chicory, and with watercress, clear gravy, fried breadcrumbs and clove-scented bread sauce.

A plump pheasant boiled, its skin unbroken, on a bed of celery and served with a celery sauce with the merest dash of lemon juice, has been described as a dish for the gods. Roast pheasant with bitter orange is also good: the juice of a Seville orange is used to baste the bird towards the end of the cooking. Spiced cabbage, even sauerkraut, accompanies pheasant in parts of Europe.

Wild turkey

This is almost a different bird from the plump Christmas turkey, with darker flesh and a stronger, more gamey taste. Wild turkey is no longer easy to find in its native North America, although it is being farmed in some parts of the US.

Guinea fowl

This elegantly spotted fowl, of West African ancestry, is an endearing but stupid bird. Looking somewhat like a walking cushion, its feathers are a marvel of pattern, white-spotted on black like old ladies' dresses, or sometimes a delicate lavender. The semi-domesticated breeds are delicious to eat, plumper than their wild counterparts, but both have a tendency to be dry and thus require regular basting during cooking with seasoned butter, or barding and larding with bacon fat. Put a sprig or two of marjoram under the waistcoat of fat if you do not plan to stuff the bird.

Guinea fowl taste like a slightly gamey chicken. Recipes for pheasant, partridge or young roasting chicken will do justice to their delicate flavour, and they make a worthwhile alternative. They are on the market all year round and are at their best in early summer, when the younger birds – guinea-poults – are on sale.

The prime concern when cooking guinea fowl is to keep the flesh moist, so recipes that call for a stuffing of vegetables or butter or fromage blanc under the skin will certainly enhance the texture of the meat. In Poland guinea fowl is rubbed inside and out with ground ginger an hour before roasting and is served with chestnut purée. The traditional British way is to stuff guinea fowl, roast it and serve it with giblet gravy and bread sauce, just like turkey. In the west of England it is braised in cider.

Older birds are good casseroled with stock and cream. Breasts of guinea fowl can be sautéed in butter and served with a sauce of chestnuts, garlic and sweet wine; and a spit-roasted bird, stuffed with buttered fresh breadcrumbs, shallots and marjoram, well larded with bacon, sprinkled with Cognac and served with a well-seasoned 'jus', is French bourgeois cooking at its best.

bard 422
hang 422
lard 422
pheasant eggs 97
smoked guinea fowl 71
turkey 87

Bread Sauce 257
Cold Game Pie 316
Normandy Pheasant with Apples and Calvados 298
Pheasant with Chestnuts 298
Stuffed Guinea Fowl with Leek Purée 302

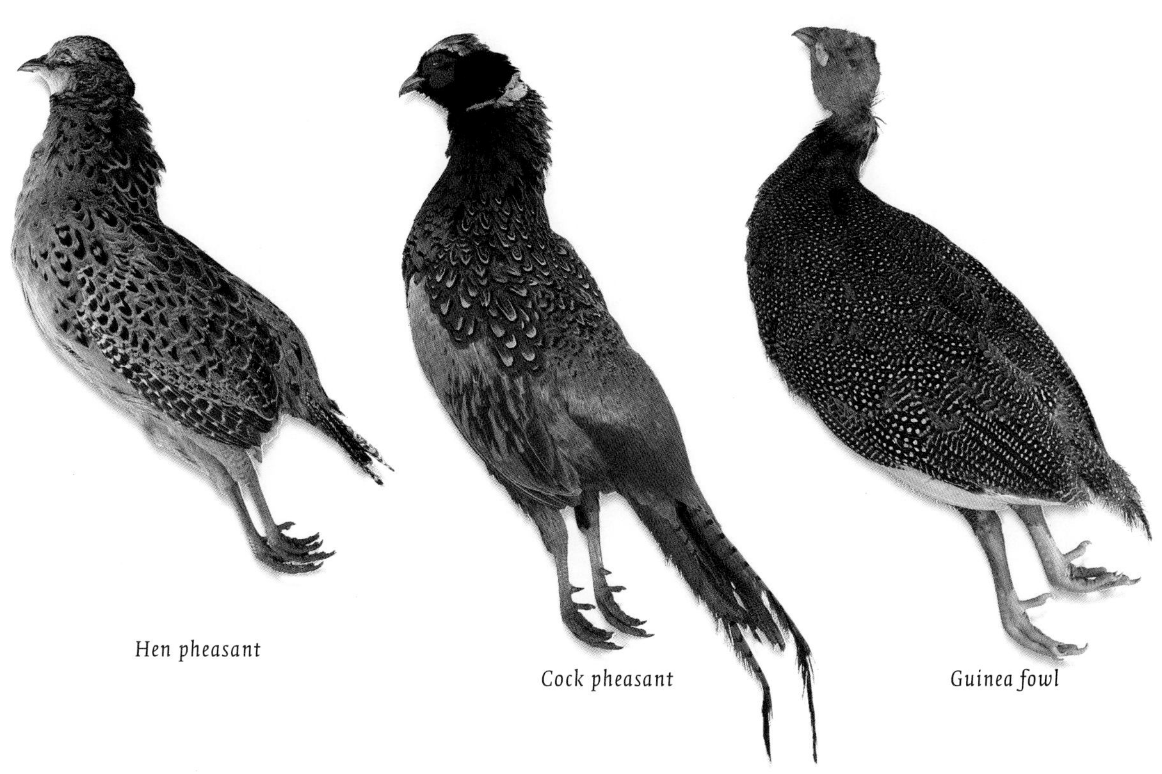

Hen pheasant

Cock pheasant

Guinea fowl

Poultry

boudin blanc 74
chicken recipes 305–8
eggs 96–7
jointing a chicken 92
smoked chicken 71
spatchcocking poultry and game birds 91
stuffing chicken breasts 92
trussing a chicken 91

Chicken Pie with Cream and Mushrooms 317
Chicken Stock 244
Cold Chicken and Ham Pie 314
Coq au Vin 305
Old-Fashioned Chicken Broth 249
Paella 346
Sichuan Chicken Salad 372
Velouté Sauce 255

When Henry IV of Navarre summed up his plans for making his people happy, he wished that all his subjects should be prosperous enough to enjoy a succulent *poule au pot* every Sunday. But in spite of his best intentions, it took a few hundred years to move poultry out of the luxury class.

Chicken

In the days before intensive farming, when chicken was a rare Sunday treat, young farmyard fowls had to be specially fattened for the table. In France a young fowl would be roasted; an older bird, nicely stuffed and boiled with plenty of vegetables, would become *poule au pot*; and a large, heavy cockerel would go into a coq au vin with its heady smell of wine, onions, mushrooms and herbs. The *backhähndl* of Austria (a young roasted rooster) was accompanied by a paprika-sprinkled salad of cucumber cut transparently thin. In England chicken was always stuffed and served roasted, surrounded by sausages, rolls of bacon, roast potatoes and Brussels sprouts or fresh garden peas; with its crisp skin and juicy flesh roast chicken is still always a success. And then, of course, there is the Jewish panacea for any kind of debilitation, from flu to stress – chicken soup made from a fully matured hen, which is by far the best provider of sustaining broth (by the way, it works).

Today we eat chicken often and in a thousand and one ways. Unlike its ancestors, the intensively reared chicken is fattened so fast and killed so young that it does not have time to develop its full flavour. Sad though this is, a modern chicken responds to being enhanced and improved, and makes a good vehicle for any number of different flavours. Even so, it pays to begin with the best chicken you can find. Free-range birds undoubtedly have the best flavour because of the variety of their diet as they scratch happily for their living, and the fact that they have been able to run about in the sunshine gives them altogether more character. But even among the pale, battery-reared supermarket poultry there are varying degrees of taste.

There are, for example, the yellow corn-fed chickens, with richer flesh and an old-fashioned chicken flavour. There is also the fresh-chilled chicken, which may or may not be polythene wrapped and which has been gutted and stored just above freezing point. The giblets (not necessarily its own) are found neatly wrapped inside it. You can cook it at once.

Trussed or untrussed, birds bought from a butcher or poulterer's will not be free range unless specifically advertised as such. The majority will be fresh, intensively reared birds. As the first 24 hours of hanging improves a chicken's flavour, these have the edge over chilled birds.

The polythene-wrapped chicken that has been blast-frozen at a temperature of –18°C/0°F or less is usually the cheapest variety on the market. From the seller's viewpoint it is easier to handle than fresh poultry because no skilled labour is needed for the drawing and trussing. Also, provided the bird is stored at the correct temperature, it will not deteriorate, and the wrapping film not only helps to preserve its bright appearance but substantially retards weight loss through evaporation.

All this is good news for the trade and is also welcomed by economists and nutritionists, because these birds are a cheap source of energy-giving protein. It is not such good news for the cook because frozen chicken can be rather characterless, needing a lot of flavouring to make it taste of anything.

When buying frozen chicken, avoid any with freezer burn (they will be dry and tasteless) and also those with noticeable chunks of ice between them and the bottom of their wrappings – these have at some time been partially thawed and refrozen, which is not good for the quality of the flesh.

All chickens, fresh-chilled or frozen, are drawn through a bath of water as soon as they have been plucked and drawn. In the case of the fresh-chilled bird, the water has dried off before it reaches your kitchen. In the case of the deep-frozen bird, however, the water drains off only when the chicken is defrosted at home, and the bird ends up in a pool of pink liquid.

Thaw your frozen bird most thoroughly and cook it soon afterwards. Not to do so is dangerous, since bacteria develop as the bird is exposed to the warmer temperature, and these must be killed by thorough cooking. Salmonella is always a concern when dealing with chicken, whether it has been frozen or not.

Thawing is best done slowly in the refrigerator. The second-best is to plunge the bird into cold water; change the water every 30 minutes or so as the bird thaws, to keep it cold. Never give a stiffly frozen chicken a bath of warm water: not only does rapid defrosting spoil the texture of the meat beyond redemption, it also promotes bacterial growth. As soon as you can while it is thawing, remove the wrapped giblets from the chicken so that air can get to the cavity. (Never forget to check for the giblet package inside the bird before it goes into the oven. This may sound a little basic, but there have been too many surprise stuffings for the advice not to bear repetition.)

The best way to check if a chicken (or turkey) is thoroughly cooked is to use an instant-read thermometer, inserted into the thickest part of the thigh. The thermometer should register an internal temperature of at least 75°C/170°F.

Poulet and poussin These are small immature birds and are, generally speaking, rather dull. They do not have a great deal of flavour, but can be good split and grilled over charcoal or under fierce heat. They really have to be eaten with the fingers since they are fiddly and bony. Allow one poulet (spring chicken) for two eaters, or one poussin (baby chicken) per head, and marinate in olive oil, lemon and herbs before grilling.

Rock Cornish game hen This is not a game bird at all, but a type of small chicken that is a cross between the Cornish and the White Rock breeds. Very popular in North America, game hens usually weigh 675 g/1½ lb. They are best roasted or spatchcocked and grilled, and benefit from marinating.

Poularde These are fat, neutered young hens, firm and tender and as prized as capons. The most famous come from Bresse, in France, a district so jealous of its superiority that a true *poularde de Bresse* proclaims its provenance by a metal disc clipped to its wing, displayed with great pride at the poulterer's or the restaurant.

Capon These are young neutered roosters fattened on corn, sometimes to an immense girth. Often considered the best chicken available, they are extra succulent because their flesh is marbled with fat, which melts during cooking.

Boiling fowl Once abundant, these are now hard to find, but any of the older recipes that specify boiling fowl can be made at a pinch with a young roasting bird. The boiler is an older bird and therefore a good deal tougher as well as stronger in flavour and cheaper. But treated to long, gentle simmering it can be made tender.

It has both light and dark meat, like a turkey, each with a pronounced flavour of its own. Useful in pies and salads, boiling fowl also provides very good broth.

Roasting chickens and chicken pieces Young roasters are the most popular sort available and can be used for most chicken recipes. Allow a 1.75–2 kg/3½–4 lb roaster to feed 4–6 people.

Of course you can also buy chicken portions in the shape of the legs, or breast and wing, or a mixture of both. These are very convenient if you are short of time. Deep fried with lovely crisp golden batter, chicken pieces eaten with corn bread and fried bananas become chicken Maryland. Chicken breasts wrapped around a piece of chilled garlic butter, egg-and-crumbed and deep fried make chicken Kiev, which spurts hot garlic butter when the eater's fork is inserted.

Cooking with chicken Since chicken is such a good vehicle for flavours, there are as many ways of preparing it as there are regional tastes. In Morocco, it is rubbed with honey and stuffed with ground almonds and sweet basil or with dried apricots and raisins. It is served with peanuts in the West Indies and with almonds in China, and in West Africa it is cooked inside a scooped-out melon. It is poached with truffle slivers under its skin *en demi-deuil* (in half-mourning) in the higher reaches of French gastronomy, and, as one might expect, it comes with tomatoes and garlic in Italy, where, plain roasted, it is also eaten with a *salsa de fegatini* – a sauce made of chicken livers, diced ham, mushrooms, chicken stock and Marsala.

If chicken can be said to have a special affinity with any herb, it is with tarragon. Marjoram or oregano, thyme and, of course, parsley are good too. The best additions and flavourings for cooking a chicken are bacon, garlic, cream, yogurt, olive oil, white wine, sherry, saffron, ginger, cumin or paprika; the best accompaniments: shallots, mushrooms, potatoes and rice. The best fruits and nuts are raisins, walnuts, lemons, apricots, pine nuts and almonds.

Turkey

A British Christmas and an American Thanksgiving would be incomplete without a fine, plump, roasted turkey, served with all the ceremonial trappings. Calculate 450 g/1 lb of oven-ready weight per person – thus a 9 kg/20 lb bird will provide 20 helpings as well as seemingly endless supplies of stock and soup.

The bird to look for is a broad, compact one, hen rather than cock, with a fresh-looking but not moist skin and a pearly white tint to the flesh rather than purple or blue. It should have been hung for at least 3 days, otherwise it will have very little flavour. This makes a fresh turkey your best buy, because although frozen birds can be all right, they are usually frozen as soon as they have been killed, which means that the taste may be undeveloped.

A frozen turkey takes about 48 hours to thaw. Simply put it in the refrigerator 2 days before you want it (3 days if it is extra large) and let it thaw gradually. It won't be cooked in the middle if it isn't completely thawed, and poultry not cooked through is dangerous. Once it has thawed, it should be cooked soon. Resist the temptation to pre-stuff the turkey in order to save time on the day of the dinner, even though there will be so many other traditional bits and pieces to see to. Get the stuffing ready on the eve of the day by all means, but put it in the neck of the bird just before it goes into the oven: if the stuffing sits around inside the bird it may spoil, even if the stuffed bird is kept in the refrigerator.

Cooking with turkey Everybody has a favourite stuffing for roast turkey. Sausagemeat is the usual basis, or a forcemeat of belly of pork, and most people like chestnuts in the mixture. You can also add truffles, mushrooms, celery, oysters or prunes. A plain marjoram and onion stuffing flavoured with lemon rind is good, but might be rather dry unless it has a large lump of butter worked into it. Because there is a risk of food poisoning if turkey is undercooked, you may prefer just to stuff the neck end, leaving the body cavity empty so that heat can penetrate deeply and evenly.

Some people like to cook a turkey simply in butter, starting it off, like a chicken, breast downwards. This is an excellent way of keeping what is by nature rather a dry-fleshed bird succulent. Others like to bard it with bacon; others to roast it wrapped in foil, which must, however, be folded back towards the end of the cooking time to give the breast a chance to become brown and crisp. In very slow cooking, which gives good results, a glass or two of white wine can be added to the juices in the roasting pan halfway through the cooking.

André Simon, the great wine and food expert, compares big birds like the turkey to cygnets and peacocks that once upon a time counted among the greatest delicacies. 'One should be content to meet them occasionally at some friend's dinner table,' he says, 'without troubling to order them when one is the host.' It is easy to agree with him, except on traditional occasions.

For Thanksgiving in the United States the traditional accompaniments are both mashed potatoes and sweet potatoes, creamed onions or creamed celery, succotash (which is a mixture of green lima beans and sweetcorn off the cob) or green beans, creamy giblet gravy and cranberry sauce. For British Christmas dinner, the turkey comes with roast potatoes, Brussels sprouts and chestnuts, clear gravy, bread sauce, bacon rolls and perhaps, if there is no sausage stuffing, a chain of crisp little sausages draped about its bosom, like the Lord Mayor's chains of office. On national holidays in Mexico – the home of the ancestral turkey, from which the domestic variety descends – the bird is eaten with a *mole*, a dark, velvety, not-at-all-sweet chocolate sauce, spiced with chilli. The Spanish, in a festive mood, will stuff their turkey with sweetbreads and truffles.

All these rich meals are best enjoyed once a year and then forgotten until next time. However, we meet turkey with increasing frequency on non-feast days. Supermarkets now sell turkey throughout the year in the form of rolled turkey breasts to be roasted like a Sunday joint, turkey drumsticks, breasts and

bard 422
smoked turkey 85
stuffing and trussing a turkey 93

Bread Sauce 257
Brussels Sprouts with Chestnuts 375
Fresh Cranberry Sauce 260
Roast Potatoes 379
Roast Turkey with Two Stuffings 311
White Devil 312

foie gras and goose liver 90
goose egg 97
goose fat 110
smoked goose breast 71
stuffed goose neck 74
wild goose 82

Goose with Apple Stuffing 312

other portions, and in North America young birds, suitably split, are sold as broilers for summer barbecues.

Goose

Martinmas, on 11 November, is the traditional day for eating goose in northern Europe. It is, presumably, an extended annual punishment meted out to these birds, whose cackling once gave away the farmyard hiding place of the modest St Martin as he was attempting to evade admiring followers who wanted him to be Pope. The raucous cry of geese saved the ancient Romans from barbarian invasion – but that has not stopped the Italians from eating goose, richly stuffed with sausage meat, olives and truffles.

In England goose used to be eaten on Michaelmas. This was not so much because this saint and all his angels had a grudge against geese, but because his day, 29 September, was, like St Martin's, a fast day – one of so many that people were getting heartily sick of being forced to eat fish. Waterfowl – including geese – didn't count as meat and so could be eaten without offence to God or man. Moreover, both saints' days fell in the season when the geese were getting fat, having gleaned the stubble fields since the harvest had been brought in. So Michaelmas geese were the stubble geese, slightly more mature than the green geese of the summer which had fed mainly on grass, but less magnificent than the Martinmas geese, which had an extra 6 weeks to fatten on grain.

When buying a goose for the table, choose a young bird with a pliable breastbone. A well-filled plump breast denotes succulence and value for money. Look for creamy skin with a warm tinge to it, almost pale apricot, without a trace of blue or brown.

A gosling, or green goose, of no more than 3 months old, weighs up to about 2 kg/5 lb and can hardly help being tender and delicate. At 8–9 months old it becomes a goose (in culinary terms it is never a gander), and, weighing 3.5–5.5 kg/8–12 lb, is in its prime. With advancing age it becomes both fatter and tougher, needing longer and longer periods of braising or stewing – very delicious, but perhaps not quite the rare treat that goose is usually expected to be.

You will need to trust in the expertise of your supplier in keeping fresh, chilled or frozen birds in the right condition – he should have plucked the goose and hung it for a few days before gutting it. If by any chance you have to pluck the goose at home, put it into a large bowl and pour boiling water over it to loosen

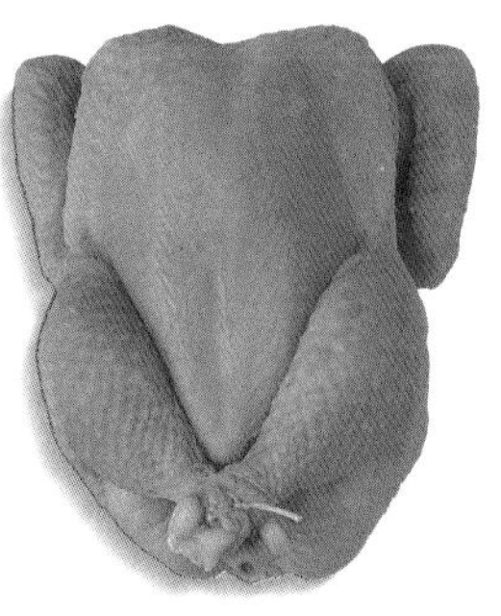

Rock Cornish game hen

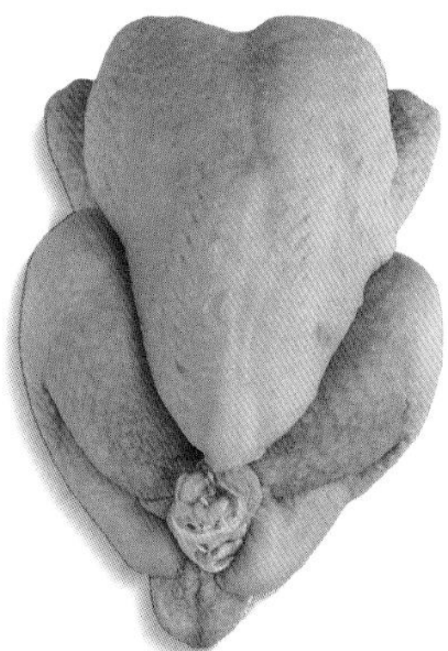

Small roasting chicken

Large roasting chicken

Poussin

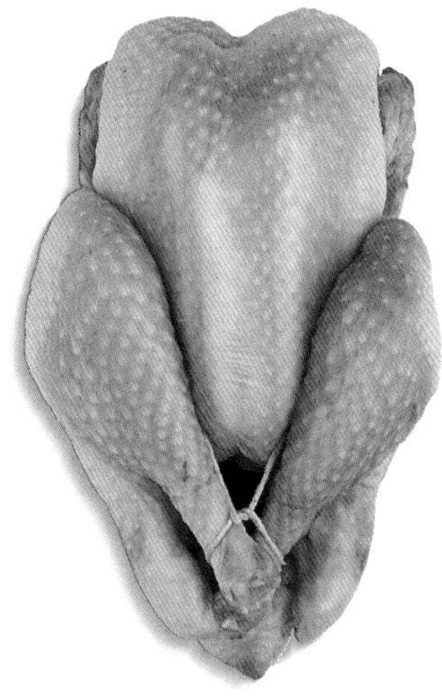

Boiling fowl

Capon

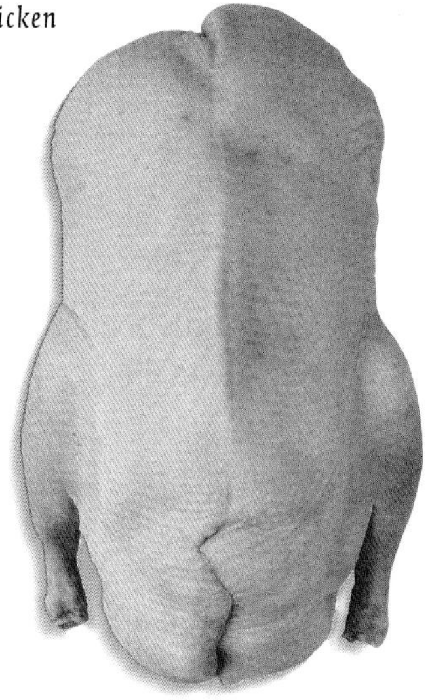

Long Island duck

the feathers, or the job is likely to take you all day.

Cooking with goose Geese are eaten on high days and holidays, especially in northern Europe where goose is the traditional Christmas bird. It comes to the feast magnificently brown, with crackling skin, copious gravy and a stuffing of sharp apples, which may be layered with boiled chestnuts or raisins, or, in Scandinavia, with prunes. (Sausage meat, it is rightly agreed, makes this bird too rich.) In Ireland geese are stuffed with boiled potatoes which sop up the fat, and this method is also known in North America, where rice, wild rice and fruit stuffings are used to the same effect.

The skin of a roasting goose needs to be well pricked, like that of a duck. Pour a kettleful of boiling water over the skin before placing the bird on a high rack in a tin so that it stands clear of the fat that will pour out as it cooks. (Although it is a hot and messy job, it is a good idea to pour off some of the fat halfway through the cooking.)

Shortly before the end, some people like to dredge the top of the bird with a little flour, which forms dark, crusty speckles where it lands. But the best finishing touch is to increase the heat for a few minutes just before the goose comes out of the oven and to splash the bird with drops of cold water. These hiss and evaporate as they would on a hot iron, leaving the skin delicately crisp.

Goose fat rendered into dripping and spread on bread is delicious to eat, and it makes a wonderful cooking medium, particularly good for frying potatoes. It is more highly flavoured than duck fat, and each bird yields so much that in days gone by it was used to good purpose not only in the kitchen but also on the farm: cow's udders were rubbed with it to prevent chapping, as were the hands of the dairymaids; harness and leatherwork were kept supple by its liberal application; and cold plasters made with brown paper coated with goose grease were a common household remedy for colds.

Duck

A duck is an odd-shaped bird: it is a bony, flat-breasted creature covered in fat. When you come to carve it – and here you may come to blows with the bird before you have finished – you will find that there is not enough breast to go round. But hot or cold, duck has such an excellent flavour, richness and succulence that it is well worth the occasional extravagance.

The very best French ducks are the small Nantais and the larger Rouen. The latter is suffocated to retain the blood so that its flesh stays dark, retaining a strong flavour which is something of an acquired taste. The Rouen duck should be cooked within 24 hours of its demise. Roasted very rare and divested of breast, drumsticks and wings, it is this duck which is pressed, together with its lightly cooked giblets, in the great silvery duck presses that are still a feature of some elegant French restaurants, to make the juice for the gravy.

Famous English ducks are the Aylesbury and Gressingham, and the most popular American variety is the Long Island or Pekin duck. These, like the Nantais and the Rouen, are descendants of the Imperial Peking duck, a Chinese snow-white breed of

boning and stuffing a duck 94–5
duck egg 97
duck foie gras 90
smoked duck 71
wildfowl 82

Duck with Coconut Cream and Green Curry Paste 313
Duck with Green Olives 313
Galantine of Duck 320

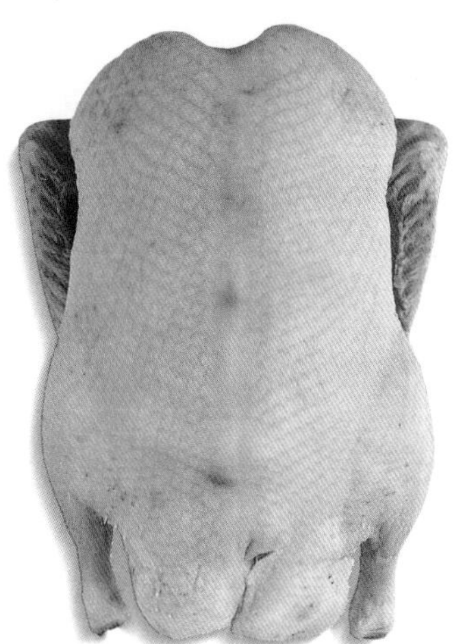

Barbary duck

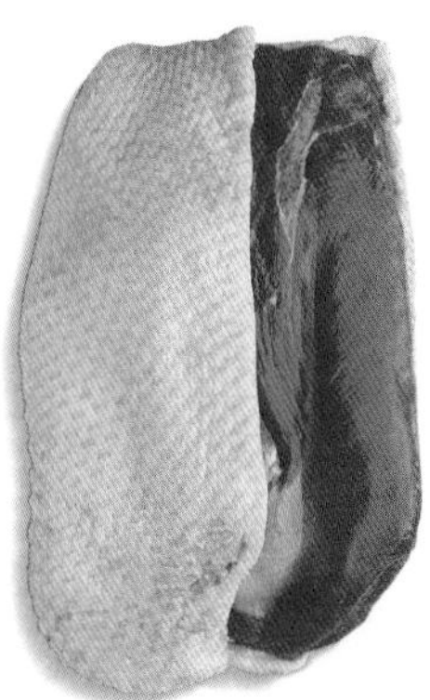

Moulard duck breast

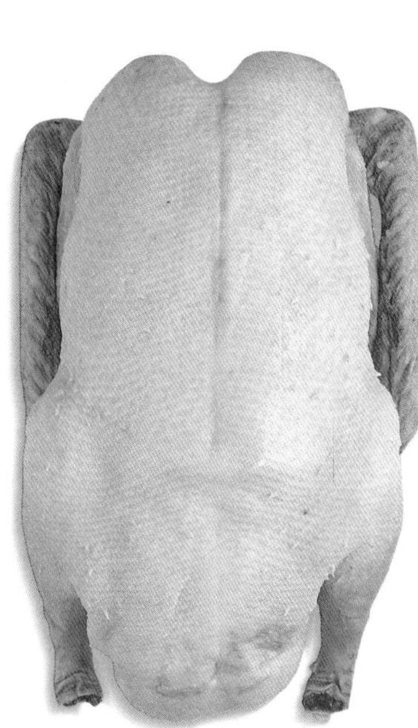

Goose

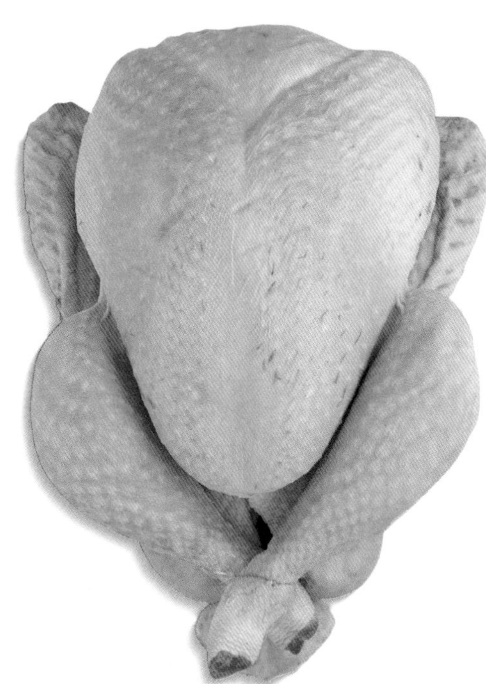

Turkey

duck 89
goose 88
goose liver sausage 78
ostrich egg 97

Blade Steak with Shallots 282
Chicken Liver Risotto 348
Pâté de Campagne 318
Pâté in a Crust 319
Ragù alla Bolognese 336
Sautéed Chicken Livers with Sage 292
Sugo di Carne Toscano 336

special excellence and thin skin, which was once reserved for the Emperor alone.

The Barbary or Muscovy duck, which has a stronger flavour than the Nantais, is a favourite of the French and the Americans. The Moulard is the duck raised for foie gras, both in France and, increasingly, in the United States. The exceptionally plump, meaty breasts of these ducks are called *magrets*.

'Duckling' was once, strictly, the term for birds under 2 months old, but it is now used until the birds are 6 months or so. Duckling sounds more tender than duck, but it is a mistake to invest in too young a bird because it does not have enough meat on its bones to be worth eating. However, the best eating age and weight varies with the breed.

As for how many people a duck will feed, it is hard to say. A wit once observed that the duck was a difficult bird – too much for one, too little for two. However, two people can dine more than well even on a Nantais, and three or even four, if helpings are modest, on a fleshy Aylesbury.

Ducks take quite kindly to freezing – their greater fat content, compared with that of the chicken, assures that when defrosted they retain their succulence, and the stronger flavour is not so easily frozen out. Like the chicken, the duck comes both fresh-chilled and deep frozen, and the same rules regarding thawing apply. Fresh is still a good deal better than frozen, and free-range better than battery. But unlike the intensively reared chickens, who may never have set foot to ground throughout their lives, battery ducklings may have been allowed to waddle about the yard in their youth, before the fattening up process put an end to exercise.

Cooking with duck Before roasting a duck, it is best to prick its skin in all the fatty places so that some of the subcutaneous fat, which serves to insulate the duck against cold water (even though it may never have had a swim in its life), can run out during cooking. This makes a wonderful fat to eat with salt on bread or to use for frying potatoes. To crisp the skin, the bird should be roasted on a rack.

Like chicken, duck is cooked and eaten in countless ways. The Chinese, especially, who domesticated ducks more than 2,000 years ago, have thousands of delicious dishes composed of crisp duck morsels with steamed pancakes. They also have tea-smoked ducks, and deep-fried ducks that are first steamed to remove the fat; sometimes called lacquered ducks, these are a glistening reddish-mahogany colour and so soft that the flesh comes away at a touch. The Chinese even like to chew the brittle bones, saying that the crunchiness is the chief attraction of these vividly glazed ducks, which are often seen hanging in the windows of Chinese restaurants. The Danes and the Swedes boil their ducks with herbs. The Danes serve theirs with mustard and dark rye bread; the Swedes dish up boiled duck with a creamy horseradish sauce.

The classic flavours with duck include oranges, both bitter and sweet, turnips and onions – all designed to offset the somewhat richly flavoured meat. Other classic accompaniments are young peas, morello cherries, green olives, red wine and vermouth. Newer inventions include duck with aubergine and ginger and duck with apples, walnuts and prunes.

Ostrich

Although still a rarity, the meat of this bird is appearing more and more frequently on restaurant menus and occasionally in butcher's shops. Ostrich is rather like slightly sweet beef, with an agreeable texture similar to fillet steak. Because there is very little fat, it is best to cook it like a very lean meat such as fillet steak, and to serve it with a sauce – for example, shallot sauce or something a little sharp and fruity such as a rich red wine sauce with added tomato.

Giblets

The giblets – the neck, heart, gizzard and liver – of most poultry are now removed before packing. However, if you can obtain them, giblets make a wonderful stock for gravy and can be eaten in stews or pies. To prepare them for cooking, remove the yellowish gall-bladder sac from the liver and trim away all yellowish patches, which will give a bitter taste. Trim the fat, blood vessels and membrane from the heart, and discard the outer skin and inner sac containing stones and grit from the gizzard.

When making a giblet stock, it seems wasteful to boil up the liver, which is so good when either pan-fried or used in a stuffing or a sauce.

Poultry livers Chopped chicken livers are a well-known feature of Jewish cooking, and these and other poultry livers are an essential ingredient in many pâtés, terrines and stuffings for poultry. Whole, they are delicious wrapped in bacon, skewered and grilled, or lightly seasoned and sautéed in butter with a dash of dry vermouth and some fresh sage leaves.

Chicken livers, especially, appear in almost every national cuisine: in sauces for spaghetti, in risottos and pilafs, in grand mousses and simple spreads. Much better fresh than frozen, the fine-grained pale livers are considered to be the best.

Foie gras and goose liver The wit of the English Regency period, the Reverend Sidney Smith, defined his idea of heaven as 'eating foie gras to the sound of trumpets'. Indeed, there can be nothing to compare with the exquisite, pale, fattened liver of the goose or duck, for which the birds are expressly bred, particularly in areas of south-western France.

To make foie gras, geese are force-fed until their livers weigh around 2 kg/4 lb apiece. The best comes from a breed known even to the ancient Romans. These geese, unlike table geese, have an extra pleat of skin under the breast, which neatly accommodates the enlarged liver. Ducks are also being bred for foie gras, with the result that fresh foie gras is now much more widely available. Called moulards or mulets, the breed preferred for the '*gavage*' is a cross of the Barbary or Muscovy and the Nantais.

The liver of a goose on a normal diet weighs about 115 g/4 oz. Soaked in milk it will swell a little and become even more tender. It is good sliced and fried and eaten in a risotto or with scrambled eggs. Pounded together with white breadcrumbs, marjoram, chopped mushrooms and diced bacon, and bound with egg, it is used to stuff the fat skin of the neck, which is then tied at both ends and poached in giblet broth and white wine, or fried in goose dripping. In France, no part of a goose is wasted, and in some country areas even the blood is eaten in the form of little cakes flavoured with garlic and poached.

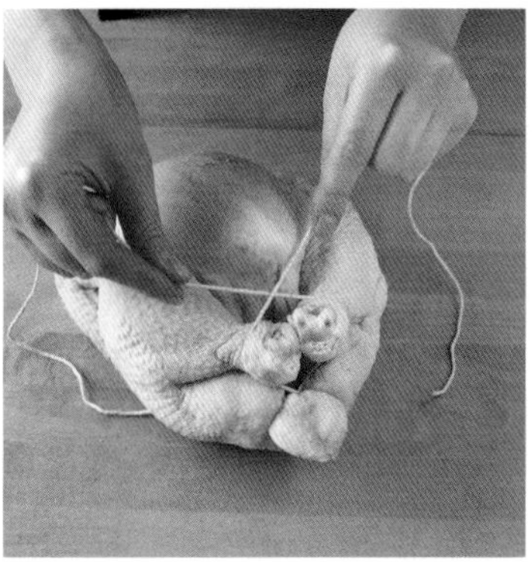

1

2

3

Trussing a chicken

1 Place the chicken breast side up. Take a piece of kitchen string about 1 m/3 ft long, and loop the string, centrally, under the tail. Cross the string over the top of the tail, then bring the string up over the ends of the drumsticks and cross it over them tightly to tie them together and close to the tail.

2 Pull the ends of the string towards the neck end, passing them under the pointed end of the breastbone and over the thighs.

3 Turn the chicken over. Bring the string over the wings, pressing them close to the sides of the body. Tie the string over the neck flap of skin. Small game birds, such as partridge, can be trussed in the same way.

chicken 86–7
feathered game 82–5

knives 222–4
poultry shears 225
trussing equipment 230

Spatchcocking poultry and game birds

1 Place the bird breast side down. With poultry shears or a heavy, sharp knife, cut down along both sides of the backbone, cutting through the skin and bone. Discard the backbone, or keep it for making stock.

2 Turn the bird over. Press firmly on the breastbone with the heel of your hand to break the bone and flatten the breast.

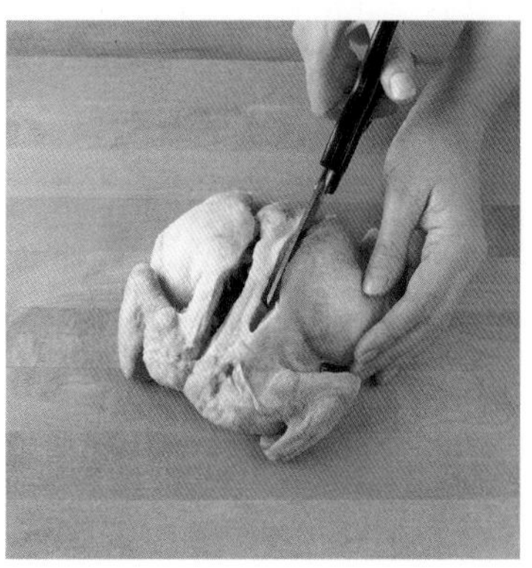

1

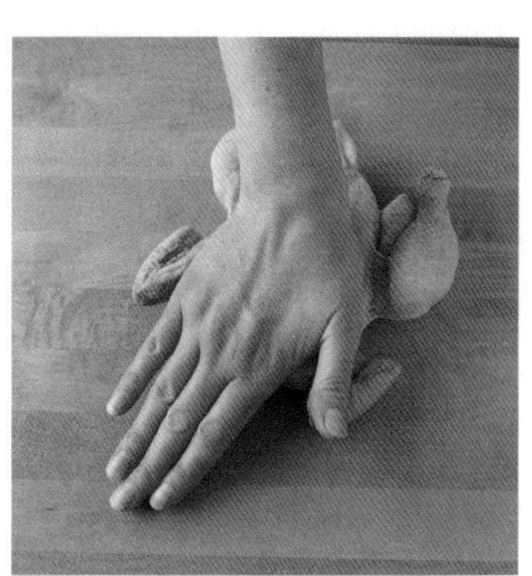

2

3 Make a small slit in the skin on either side of the pointed end of the breast. Insert the ends of the drumsticks in the slits.

4 Tuck the wing tips under the breast. If you like, insert two metal skewers crosswise through the bird, one at the breast and one at the thigh, to keep the bird flat during cooking.

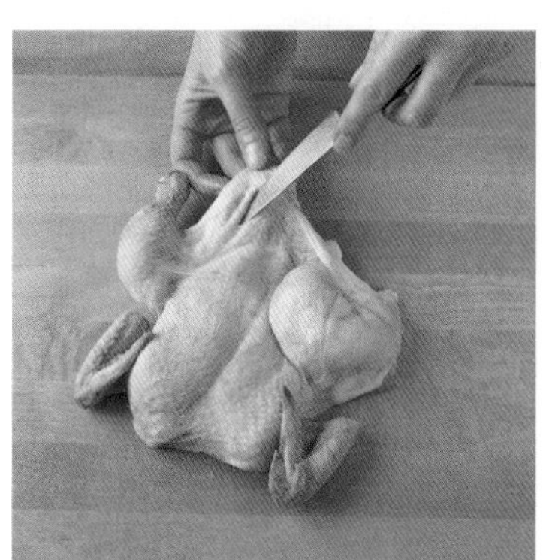

3

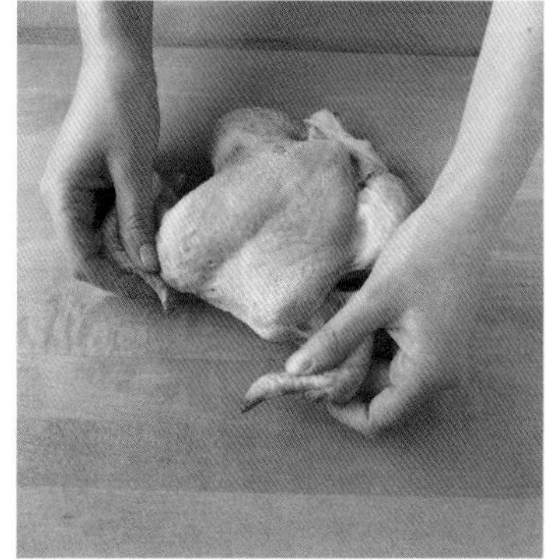

4

chicken 86–7

knives 222–4

Chicken Stock 244

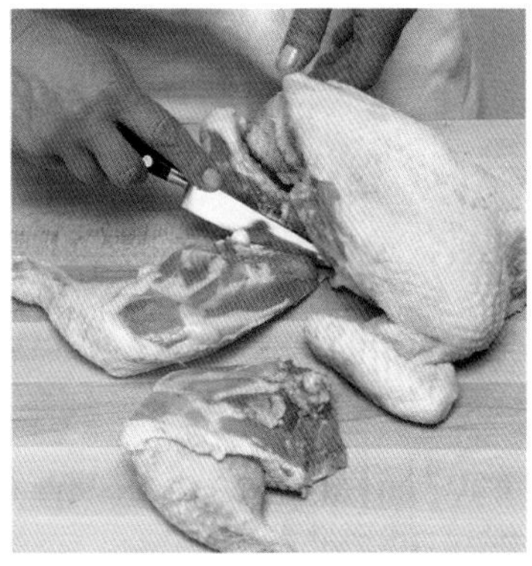

1

2

Jointing a chicken

1 With a sharp knife, cut off each of the legs at the point where they join the carcass. Do this by forcing the tip of the knife blade through the ball and socket joint, and slicing down on either side of the tail.

2 Slide a large, heavy knife inside the bird and make two cuts, one on either side of the backbone and as close to the bone as possible.

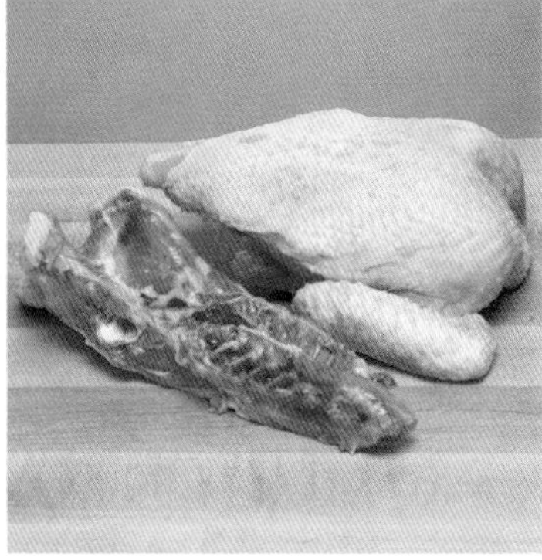

3

3 The backbone, which should be as bare of flesh as possible, can now be withdrawn from the body and reserved for making soup or stock.

4 Turn the bird over and cut along either side of the breastbone.

5 Discard the breastbone or use it for stock, and cut each breast of the chicken in half crosswise.

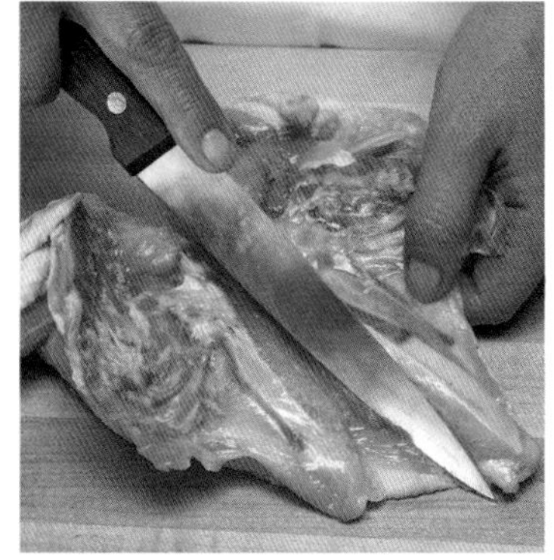

4

5

6 The six resulting portions are two legs, two wings with a portion of breast and two breasts. For eight pieces, the legs may be cut in half to give two drumsticks and two thighs.

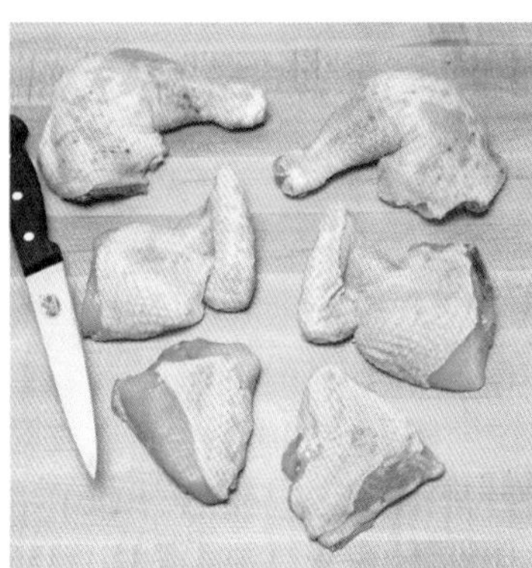

6

Stuffing chicken breasts

1 Take a boneless breast of chicken with wing bone attached, and cut off the wing tip at the second joint. Lay the breast skin side down, and push a spoonful of stuffing (a roll of chilled Garlic and Herb Butter is shown here) under the natural flap of flesh.

2 Seal the flap by pressing the outer edges together; roll the breast up from the tip towards the wing bone. Tie with kitchen string into a neat parcel.

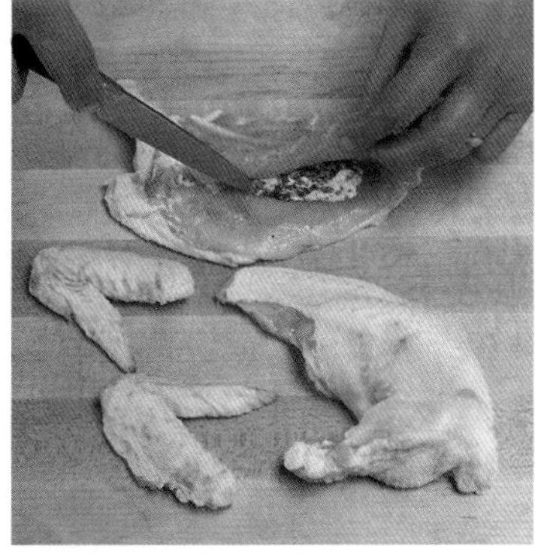

1

2

chicken 86–7
turkey 87–8

trussing equipment 230

Garlic and Herb Butter 257
Roast Turkey with Two Stuffings 311

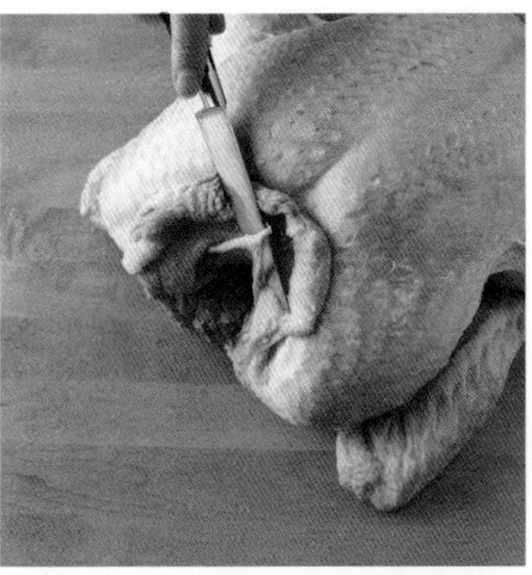

1

2

Stuffing and trussing a turkey

1 With a small sharp knife, cut out the wishbone, which is just under the skin at the neck end. (This will make the breast of the bird easier to carve.)

2 Spoon the stuffing into the neck end of the turkey, putting in only as much as can be covered by the flap of neck skin. If you like, loosen the skin over the breast by easing in your fingers, then press a thin layer of stuffing over part of the breast meat.

3

4

3 Turn the bird over. Pull the neck skin over the stuffing and secure the flap of neck skin to the back with the aid of a small skewer.

4 Turn the bird breast up again. Loosely fill the body cavity with flavourings such as slices of apple or onion or herbs, or with a stuffing.

5

5 With kitchen string, tie the ends of the drumsticks to the tail, looping the string under the tail and crossing it as when trussing a chicken. If you like, tuck the wing tips under the breast as you would do when spatchcocking a bird.

duck 89–90

knives 222–4
trussing equipment 230

Galantine of Duck 320

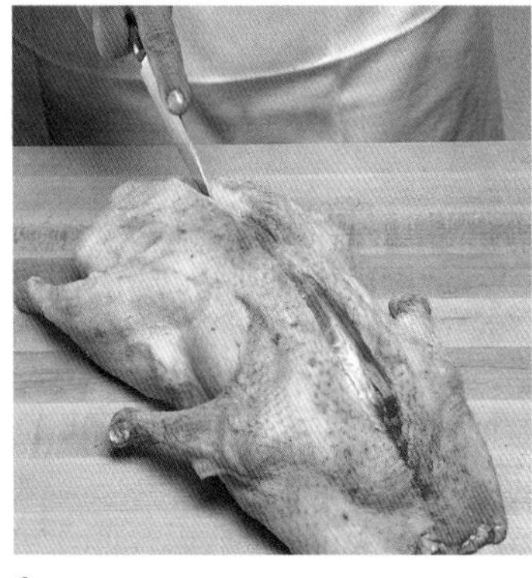

1

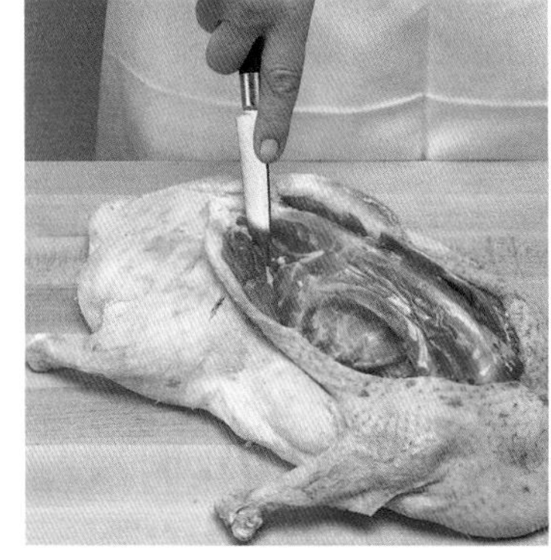

2

Boning and stuffing a duck

1 Lay the duck breast down. Cut off the wings at the second joint (if you like, reserve the wing tips for making stock). With a strong, sharp, short-bladed knife, split the skin down the centre of the back from neck to tail.

2 Cut down along each side of the backbone, starting a little below the neck cavity; feel your way carefully and ease back the skin and flesh until you encounter the ball joint of the thigh bone.

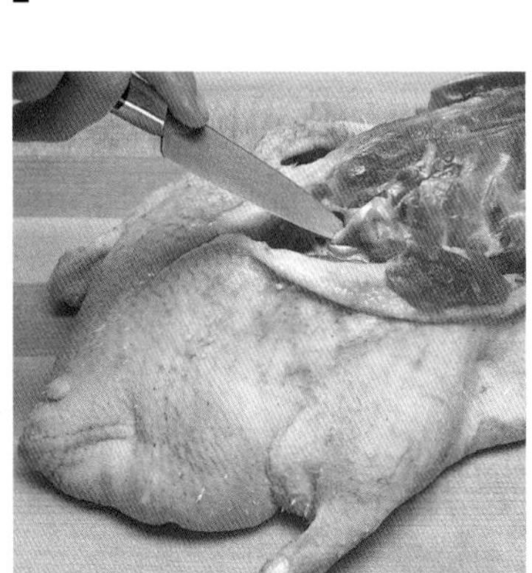

3

3 Place the tip of the knife in the ball and socket of the thigh joint on one side, and twist the knife to sever the thigh bone. Do the same on the other side.

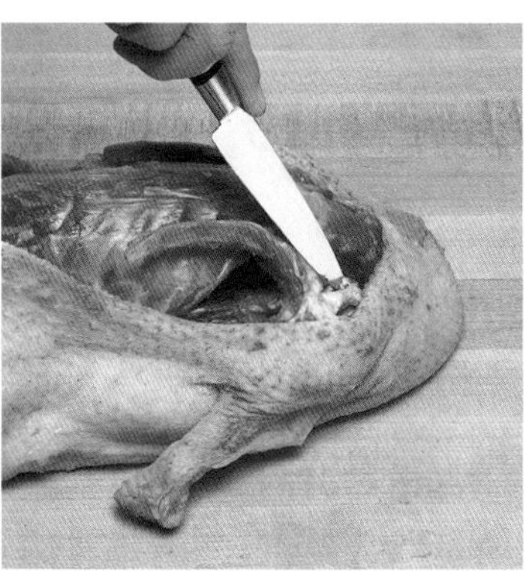

4

4 Slide the knife in the other direction towards the neck until the upper part of the wing is well exposed. Free the other wing bone in the same way.

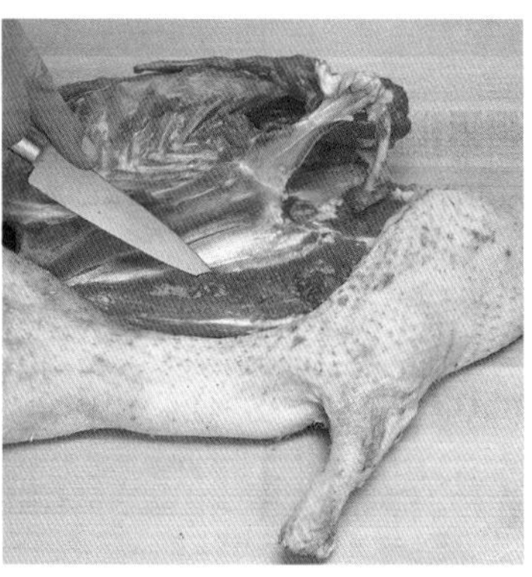

5

5 Cut through the wing joints, and continue to cut carefully, feeling your way and keeping the blade of the knife as close to the bones as possible, until you reach the breastbone.

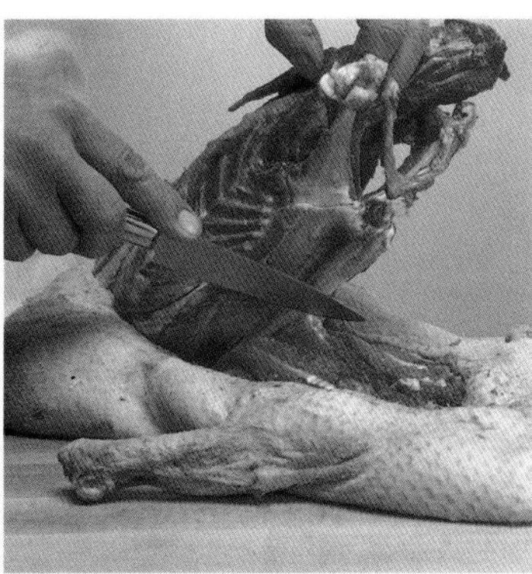

6

6 Lift up the bones, cutting away the remaining flesh. Take care not to puncture the breast.

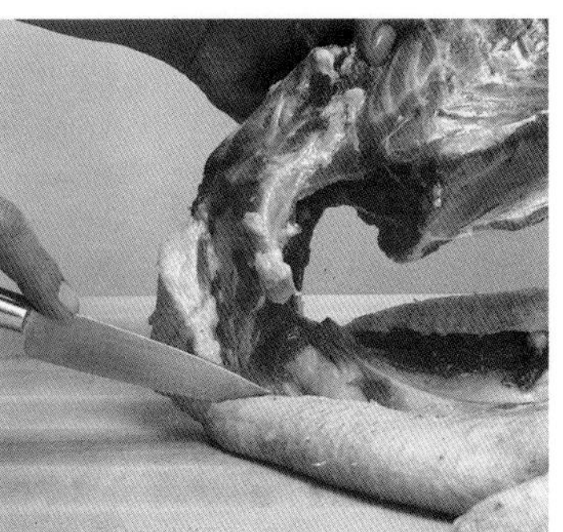

7

8

7 Finally, sever the carcass at the tail, separating it completely from the flesh. Discard the carcass or keep it for making stock if you wish.

8 Free the leg bones from the body, starting from the inside of the duck and pushing down on the flesh, keeping the skin as intact as possible. Once you have reached the 'knob' at the end of each drumstick, chop off the leg bone with a cleaver, leaving the 'knob' in the duck.

9 Slip out each wing bone in exactly the same way as the leg bones, leaving the 'knobs' at the end of the wing joints in the duck.

10 Fill the bird with a stuffing of your choice; do not pack it too tightly or the duck will split during cooking. Sew up the slit with a trussing needle and string.

9

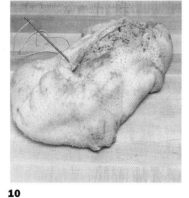

10

11 Press and push the duck into a long, oval shape. Prick the fatty parts of the bird (back end and thighs), just piercing the skin, to allow the fat to run out freely during roasting.

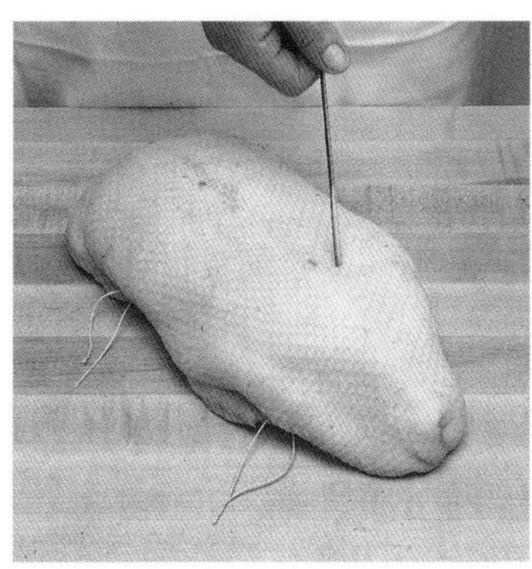

11

Eggs, Milk, Cream and Butter

basic egg cookery 322
egg recipes 322–8
fresh egg pasta 332
ice-cream recipes 398–9

egg slicer 225

Béarnaise Sauce 255
Crème Brûlée 394
Crème Caramel 392
Fresh Egg Pasta 332
Fresh Raspberry Pavlova 388
Dark Chocolate Mousse 394
Grilled Polenta with Poached Eggs, Fontina and Chive Cream 352
Greek Avgolemono Soup 250
Hazelnut Macaroons 413
Hollandaise Sauce 255
Lemon Curd 419
Mayonnaise 259
Pain Perdu 364
Sherry Trifle 392
White Frosting 415
Zabaglione 394

EGGS

For primitive man, with a mind far less tortuous than ours, there was no such thing as a chicken-and-egg dilemma: he recognized the egg as the beginning of life and celebrated it as such. It was in this context that people began to decorate eggs, as a symbol of springtime and fertility.

In the kitchen the hen's egg is celebrated still. Indispensable to the cook and rich in vitamins and minerals, it is one of the most versatile and valuable of foods.

There is a popular misconception that brown eggs are somehow better than white (indeed, the Turks simmer their eggs in coffee to give both flavour and a healthy tan). But shell colour reflects neither flavour nor nutritional content, merely the breed of the laying bird. The best egg, brown or white, large or small, is one that has been freshly laid by a free-range hen, so always check the date on the box.

From the time an egg is laid, the membranes weaken and the flavour changes. The white of a fresh egg is thick (making wonderful fried and poached eggs), getting runnier and thinner as time goes by. The yolk of a fresh egg is round and tight when the egg is cracked and dropped into a plate or pan, while in an older egg the yolk is flatter and more fragile. It is easy enough to tell if an egg is fresh or stale once you get it home. At the rounded end of the egg, between the shell and the membrane, there is an air chamber, all but invisible in fresh eggs, increasingly large as the egg gets older and loses moisture. One way of assessing freshness is to hold the egg upright against a strong light and examine the size of the air space. Another is to weigh it in your hand: the heavier for its size the better. Yet another is to immerse it horizontally in cold water: a fresh egg will stay put; older eggs will tilt; if more than 3 weeks old they will float. If it becomes vertical it is really getting old.

It has been discovered that there is some risk of food poisoning, caused by salmonella bacteria, associated with eating raw or lightly cooked eggs (the yolks are more likely to carry the bacteria than the whites). For this reason, it is recommended that pregnant women, the elderly, infants, and those whose immune systems are compromised should not eat raw or partially cooked eggs. However, the risk is in fact quite minimal, so for most people it makes sense just to be cautious, avoiding any cracked or dirty eggs.

Quail's egg

White hen's egg

Brown hen's egg

Duck's egg

Goose egg

Large eggs are good for breakfast, but when cookbooks specify eggs they generally mean medium-size ones. According to EC regulations, eggs are now graded for size as: XL (very large, 73 g and more), L (large, 63–73 g), M (medium, 53–63 g) and S (small, under 53 g). Eighteenth- and nineteenth-century recipes instructing the cook to 'take three dozen eggs' should cause less amusement than they do, since the average egg used to be a great deal smaller than it is today and was probably laid by bantam hens. There are still dozens of different bantam species, all as pretty as chrysanthemums, and they still make the best 'sitters' – on farms silky bantam hens are sometimes used for hatching eggs of larger hens bred for laying rather than motherhood. But no bantam, however devoted, can be as efficient as a factory farm.

'Factory' eggs are no less nutritious, and their flavour is standard and good, if rather slight, but they are paler and less rich than eggs from contented hens scratching about for their food in the farmyard. These 'free-range' eggs arrive in the shops ready boxed, often with a token bit of down attached. Eat genuine farm-fresh free-range eggs as soon as possible, especially if they have been cleaned, because washing removes the natural protective film from the shell.

Because egg shells are porous they are highly susceptible to neighbouring smells, which is fine if they are intended for truffle omelettes and stored in an egg basket with a truffle, as they are in parts of Périgord, but not such a good thing if their near neighbours are unwrapped, strong-smelling foods such as onions and particularly ripe cheese.

Eggs should be kept in the refrigerator – standing with the rounded end up to allow the air space to 'breathe'. For boiling, some cooking and baking, they should be at room temperature – eggs straight from the refrigerator will crack if plunged into boiling water; a cold yolk will not emulsify reliably, in mayonnaise, for example, and cold whites will not whisk well.

Cooking with eggs A beaten egg will thicken soups, stews and sauces because heat causes the egg to coagulate, thus holding the liquid in suspension. The raw yolk will emulsify with oil or melted butter, holding it in suspension, and to this happy fact we owe such good things as mayonnaise and hollandaise sauce. An egg is sticky and sets when cooked and so will bind mixtures for croquettes and stuffings or rissoles. As for food that is to be deep fried, a dip into a beaten egg will not only keep the breadcrumbs or other coating in place but the film of egg will protect the food from absorbing the oil and becoming greasy. A brushing of beaten egg gives a handsome sheen to pastry, and whole whisked eggs, with millions of tiny trapped air bubbles, give a rise to cakes and batters.

The volume of beaten egg white – so essential for light soufflés and mousses – depends on the eggs being at room temperature before you start and the way you whisk them – electric food mixers are fast, but they produce a dense texture. Big 'balloon' wire whisks, while taking a little more time and energy, do produce a more desirable airy froth.

Apart from omelettes and batters, which are cooked briefly over a high heat, eggs respond best to gentle warmth – too high a heat and too long a cooking time makes them leathery.

Other eggs

No other bird has proved anywhere near so obliging as the domestic hen, which lays up to 250 eggs a year, but hen's eggs are by no means the whole story.

Ostrich eggs (one ostrich egg is equal to two dozen hen's eggs) are rarely sold these days – but Queen Victoria once tasted one made into a giant omelette and declared it to be very good.

Duck's eggs are extremely rich with somewhat gelatinous whites, so although they taste quite good on their own they are best in custards, mousses and other puddings.

Goose eggs are also rich and make very good omelettes, custards and mousses.

Quail's eggs, miniature in size and speckled, come both fresh and preserved. Fresh and hard boiled, they make a good first course served with celery salt. Poached, they look charming on salads.

Gull's eggs are in season briefly in spring, and are eaten hard-boiled with celery salt.

Plover's eggs and pheasant's eggs are sometimes to be found, but in many countries they are, quite rightly, protected from the unheeding gourmet.

MILK, CREAM AND BUTTER

The cow is a good friend to mankind, providing us with one of our most complete foods. Milk contains most of the nutrients required by the human body – proteins, vitamins and minerals, especially calcium – and since cows are so generous with their supply, milk and other dairy products are still very good value for money.

Milk

Most children and quite a number of adults enjoy drinking milk, and it is also used in a variety of ways, including for cooking. In Italy and Germany it is even used for roasting pork, the meat bubbling away under a golden skin that eventually caramelizes with the pan juices into a delicious gravy. In Saudi Arabia lamb cooked with rice in milk is the descendant of an ancient dish. There are also many other sauces and dishes as well as cheeses, yogurts and fermented drinks all over the world that are based on using milk that would not keep for long in the days before refrigeration.

It is said that milk is not so much a drink as a liquid food. There is even an official scale of desirable milk consumption for infants and children: 600 ml/1 pint a day of breast milk or formula for infants aged 4–6 months and 500–600 ml/18 fl oz–1 pint for those aged 6–12 months; 350–600 ml/12 fl oz–1 pint a day of breast, formula or full-fat cow's milk for children aged 1 year. Thereafter there is a gap in advice until the age of 5 and above when it is recommended that two to three servings of dairy products are consumed daily, which includes yogurt and cheese as well as milk.

The majority of milk on the market today is pasteurized. Pasteurization was one of the successes of Louis Pasteur, whose work in the field of microbiology led to the eradication of many animal-borne diseases. It involves heating the milk to a point where any potentially dangerous microorganisms are killed but the flavour of the milk is not affected. Unpasteurized milk is now the exception and is sold as raw or untreated milk. It must always be certified or attested – that is, stringently tested at the farm to make sure that no harmful bacteria are present.

Milk should always be heated slowly and cooked at low temperatures. A skin that is either liked or detested forms on the top when it reaches high temperatures, helping it to boil over the sides of the pan – with the resulting characteristic smell that gives the impression things are getting out of hand in the kitchen. This skin is solidified proteins and milk fat. To avoid it do not boil, but instead scald the milk: that is, remove it from the heat just as it shows a wreath of tiny bubbles around the edge. Non-stick surfaces have made milk-pans much easier to clean, but milk still tends to scorch on the bottom of the pan if it is overheated.

If the recipe calls for the addition of flour or sugar, these, too, help prevent a skin from forming. To prevent the skin that appears on the top of a milk-based sauce such as béchamel as its sits, rub a small piece of butter over the surface on the point of a knife. This makes a protective film and can be stirred in at the last minute. Alternatively, place a sheet of dampened greaseproof paper directly on the surface of the sauce.

Fresh milk There are three main types of fresh milk, which need to be kept as cool as possible.

Whole milk This is milk with its natural cream intact, and has one of the best flavours of all milk sold. In summer the cream rises to the top of the milk in a thick golden layer, while in winter, due to the lack of rich grass for the cows, the cream tends to be paler and thinner. The creamiest milk comes from Jersey and Guernsey cows, but today many farmers are producing good quality milk from Friesians and Holsteins. This used to be thin, watery and blue, but the cows have been bred and re-bred to produce better milk. The cream can be shaken back into the milk or poured off and used in coffee or on breakfast cereals.

Homogenized milk The cream is still present in homogenized milk, but, as the name suggests, it has been evenly suspended throughout instead of being allowed to float to the top as in whole milk. Homogenized milk is good for making ice-cream as it freezes well, but sauces and so forth made with this milk take longer to cook because the heat takes longer to penetrate.

Skimmed and semi-skimmed milk Skimmed milk is milk that has been divested of its rich, delicious cream. Our ancestors went to great pains to

coating with egg and crumbs 423
duck 89
goose 88
ostrich 90
pheasant 85
quail 82
whisking egg whites 423

hand mixer 238
mixer with stand and bowl 239
whisks 227

Béchamel Sauce 255
Cauliflower au Gratin 375
Crespolini 341
Lasagne al Forno 339
Macaroni Cheese with Ham 338
Mornay Sauce 255
New England Fish Chowder 252
Onion Sauce 255
Vichyssoise with Chives 254

cheeses 101–9
making buttermilk 100
soya bean 128

Bacon and Egg Tart 327
Bread and Butter Pudding 394
Cherry Clafoutis 388
Crème Caramel 392
Custard Pancakes 397
Mushroom-Filled Pancakes 328
Scones 364
Vermicelli Milk Pudding with Cardamom and Saffron 395

avoid their milk being skimmed, even to the extent of making the urban dairyman bring his cow to the city streets to be milked on the spot so that the customers could see for themselves the cream going into the jug.

The cream is removed by centrifugal force and the resulting almost fat-free skimmed milk is good in low-fat diets, since it contains only 0.5 per cent fat. In semi-skimmed milk, about half of the cream is left in the milk for flavour, resulting in between 1 and 2 per cent fat. These milks are sometimes given extra milk solids and vitamins to restore something of the nutrients they have lost in skimming.

Long-life milk Heavily sterilized, these milks will keep, unopened, for much longer than ordinary pasteurized milks and are therefore extremely useful for people who are frequently away from home or without refrigeration available.

Pasteurized, homogenized and then held at a high temperature until all the bacteria have been destroyed, they will keep unopened for at least 7 days but have a slightly peculiar taste due to the caramelization of the sugar present in milk, known as lactose. Once opened or reconstituted they need refrigeration and will keep only as long as fresh milk.

UHT (Ultra Heat Treated) milk First pasteurized, this milk is then treated at a temperature of 132°C/270°F for a single second, which means that the lactose does not caramelize to such an extent that the flavour is impaired. It will keep unopened for several months and is an invaluable standby.

Evaporated and condensed milk Evaporated milk is the less sweet and sticky of the two, as it is simply whole or skimmed milk from which 60 per cent of the water has been removed, but the extra sugar in condensed milk helps it to keep better once the can has been opened. Condensed milk tends to taste more like toffee than milk. Both can be used in cooking and can be whipped. Before whipping, chill the milk in the freezer until soft crystals have formed at the edge.

The quality of these milks in cooking is open to controversy; some hold that they enrich foods, while others feel that they impart a strange, oversweet taste.

Dehydrated milk This has a flat but unobjectionable flavour that bears little resemblance to real milk. It can be used in cooking either in reconstituted or dried form and can also be used to make yogurt: a few tablespoons of dried milk powder stirred into the measured quantity of milk before incubating gives a thicker and slightly richer yogurt.

Milk substitutes Merely whiteners, these are used in tea or coffee by those who are allergic to real milk. They are usually made with vegetable or coconut oil or soya beans. Other additives such as artificial colour, emulsifiers and sugar are also often present. Soya milk may be enriched with calcium so that it can be given to young children.

Other milk Although Western society drinks mainly cow's milk, there are many other kinds such as sheep's, goat's and water buffalo's milk. The latter, huge, black beasts with sweeping horns, stand up to hot weather better than cows, and are found in India and the hottest parts of southern Italy. Desert dwellers drink camel's milk, Tibetans drink yak's and ass's milk, while the Kurds like mare's milk, riding along on their milk supply.

Both ewes and goats give milk for delicious cheese such as pecorino, Roquefort and Spanish manchego; buffalo's milk is best for mozzarella.

Goat's milk has the special quality of being highly digestible and is excellent for babies and people with poor digestions and for those who are allergic to cow's milk. It should, however, be avoided by those who are unable to cope with a full cream content: since the cream does not separate as easily from goat's milk as it does from cow's milk only the whole milk is available.

Soured milk products Milk that has been soured is often looked upon as a food. It also makes a drink that is enjoyed in various parts of the world under different names and soured by various methods. *Kefir* is from the Caucasus and is slightly fermented. The Russian *koumiss* is made from mare's milk that turns sour as it hangs in leather bags on the mare's own warm sides. *Villi* is a Finnish sour milk drink. Drinking yogurt has long been a daily food in the Balkans, parts of India, Russia, Turkey, Greece and the Middle East, and is now widely available throughout Europe and the US.

It is the presence of living lactic acid bacteria in milk that makes it go sour. This used to be a real problem before pasteurization, and it was the need to use milk before it became too sour that led to making yogurt and cheese. Pasteurization, however, kills the lactic acid bacteria and now milk, if left, will often not sour but go bad, so a souring culture, such as a tablespoon of buttermilk, must be introduced in order to achieve soured milk products.

Acidophilus milk The bacteria *Lactobacillus acidophilus*, killed during pasteurization, is reintroduced in a dormant state to pasteurized milk to produce acidophilus milk. This milk has been found to be easily digestible even by those who cannot manage ordinary milk and is called 'the milk of the future' by some nutritionists. It looks and tastes like fresh pasteurized milk. The bacteria is said to be extremely beneficial, since it helps to achieve a better bacterial balance in the digestive tract.

Buttermilk This used to be a favourite drink of farmers' children. It had a fresh, slightly acid flavour, and was made from the liquid left over when butter was made on the farm. It was also used in cooking to activate the bicarbonate of soda that

Buttermilk

Crème fraîche

Whipping cream

Clotted cream

was used as a leavening agent in baking to give a soft, tender quality to cakes and scones. The buttermilk sold today is still delicious, but it is thicker than the old farm variety and is made with a culture.

Yogurt Credited with powers of increasing health and prolonging life, yogurt is made daily in those countries where it has a long history. It is eaten as a dessert and is used extensively as a marinade for meat, in soups and salads, and even in cooked dishes. For cooking it must first be stabilized to prevent it from separating (make a little paste with cornflour or potato flour and water; heat the yogurt, stir in the paste and simmer for about 10 minutes until it thickens, then proceed with the recipe).

Commercially made yogurts are made by injecting a low-fat or skimmed milk with a culture of *Lactobacillus bulgaricus*, *Lactobacillus acidophilus* or *Streptococcus thermophilus*. A combination of these strains produces the most acidic yogurts, often considered to have the best flavour. Some, especially the varieties with fruit in them, have had milk solids, sugar, cream, edible gum and/or gelatine added, but none of these contributes to the acid flavour of yogurt, which is particularly desirable in cooking. Heavily sweetened frozen yogurts are becoming an increasingly popular alternative to ice-cream.

Although only some yogurts are labelled 'live', the only ones that are in fact not live are those that have been sterilized.

Cream

Creams vary in thickness and richness according to the amount of butterfat present – the thicker the cream the more butterfat it contains and the richer it will be.

The thickest cream, double cream, is for spooning over strawberries, for syllabubs and for filling cakes, éclairs and so on, and is whipped for decorating cakes and puddings. Thin, light creams are ideal for soups and sauces, for pouring over puddings and desserts and for putting into coffee.

Whipping creams are usually used in soufflés, ice-creams and mousses. A thin cream will not whip no matter how long you work at it, because there is not enough butterfat to trap the air bubbles, so buy double cream or whipping cream (*crème fleurette* in France).

Whipped cream should be light, airy and about doubled in volume – a balloon or spiral whisk will achieve the best result. An electric mixer can be too fast and even a rotary whisk is too fierce. To achieve the right texture, the cream, bowl and whisk should all be cold. A spoonful of cold milk or a crushed ice cube added to each 150 ml/¼ pint of cream as it thickens gives a lighter result. If you add a little sugar to the cream the whipped result will not separate so easily, although it will not be so pure in flavour.

As well as varying in texture, cream can be fresh, which is the best for all purposes; treated with a culture which helps prolong its life; sterilized, when it acquires an odd, flat, sweetish flavour; or treated to a version of UHT, when it has a long life but is not the best choice when the flavour of the cream is important. Fresh cream is obviously the first choice and this will keep, refrigerated, for up to 4 days in summer and 7 days in winter. Some farms still deliver untreated cream to local stores, and this is the cream with the best flavour of all.

Clotted cream This is a speciality of the west of England, where great pans filled with milk are heated, cooled and then skimmed of their thick, wrinkled, creamy crust. This cream is usually eaten in Devon and Cornwall piled on to scones with strawberry jam.

Crème fraîche, crème double This French cream is treated with a special culture that helps it to stay fresh longer and gives it a lively, though not exactly sour, taste. It is this cream that is required when French recipes call for cream.

Soured cream Single or double cream treated with a souring culture is known as sour or soured cream. It is sometimes sold by its Russian name smetana, and in that country it is served on borscht and salads and is used in marinades. Germany, Austria and Scandinavia include it in sauces, which it makes glossy and slightly acid. A plain grilled pork chop eaten from the same plate as a cucumber salad dressed with sour cream produces the most delicious mixture as the meat juices mingle with the dressing. To make your own version of sour cream, simply add a few drops of lemon juice to fresh double cream.

Butter

Experts can tell where butter comes from by the colour, texture, smell and taste. There are some superb French butters, including beurre des Charentes and Isigny. Melted, these resemble cream. Spread on bread, the taste is sweet and nutty and the texture firm and smooth. There are no visible beads of water – if butter has a water content of more than 12 per cent it will not cream well. The aroma is delicate and mild. These are all that a butter could hope to be and are worth buying for a special treat, expensive though they are.

But for normal everyday use we tend to buy butter by brand name or according to country of origin or by price, the cheaper butters being the blended ones. Both for eating and cooking it is always better to buy a good-quality butter, since a low-grade butter can have such an overpowering flavour that it spoils the taste of fresh vegetables and delicate sauces such as hollandaise. Buy only a week's supply at a time and, if possible, take the butter out of the refrigerator some time before using it. Re-wrap what has not been

ice-cream recipes 398–9
making crème fraîche 423
making yogurt 100
whipping cream 423

Chilled Cucumber Soup with Mint 254
Courgettes with Dill and Sour Cream 384
Creamed Finnan Haddie 275
Crème Brûlée 394
Egg Mousse 327
Hare in Sour Cream 295
Fish Mousselines 274
Jerusalem Artichokes with Cream and Parsley 382
Lamb Korma 289
Leeks in Cream 379
New Potatoes Baked with Saffron, Cream and Garlic 381
Oeufs en Cocotte à la Crème 324
Spiced and Fried New Potatoes with Minted Yogurt Dressing 381
Spaghetti alla Carbonara 337
Squash Fritters with Yogurt and Garlic Dressing 386
Strawberry Fool 388
Syllabub 394
Tagliatelle alla Panna 338
Yogurt and Garlic Dressing 259
White Devil 312

beurre noir 422
beurre noisette 422
clarifying butter 423
making beurre manié 423
margarine 110
yogurt 99

Béarnaise Sauce 255
Beurre Blanc 256
Butter Icing (coffee, orange, lemon, chocolate) 415
Fried Sole with Butter and Parsley 261
Garlic and Herb Butter 257
Grilled Lobster with Butter 276
Hollandaise Sauce 255
Horseradish Butter 257
Lemon Curd 419
Maître d'Hotel Butter 257
Skate with Black Butter 268
Soft Polenta with Butter and Parmesan 352
Spinach Gnocchi with Butter and Sage 344
Stewed Broad Beans with Butter and Tarragon 378

Unsalted butter

Salted butter

Ghee

used and keep it well away from strong-smelling foods in the refrigerator, particularly anything flavoured with garlic, and soft fruits such as strawberries – butter absorbs these flavours, and once tainted will not recover. Butter freezes well.

Butter can either be salted or unsalted. Salting used to make all the difference between butter that kept fresh and butter that quickly went rancid. Salt still improves the keeping qualities of butter.

Unsalted butter has a sweeter taste. It makes an excellent table butter and is preferred in cooking. Its delicate flavour lends itself particularly well to cakes, and it is better than salted butter for frying – the deposits in salted butter burn at a fairly low temperature. Unsalted butter has fewer of these deposits and so can withstand higher temperatures.

Butter can be blended with a number of ingredients to make delicious garnishes and fillings for sandwiches. Mix it with garlic to make the classic accompaniment for snails, and with herbs, especially parsley, to serve with fish or meat. With Roquefort cheese it is delicious with steak, and with pounded anchovies, lobster coral or mustard it makes an excellent garnish for fish.

There are many superb butter sauces, including beurre blanc and beurre noir, which, despite its name, should not be black, but, rather, golden brown.

The addition of a little oil will prevent butter from burning when cooking, but perhaps the best butter for frying very delicate foods is clarified butter, from which all the milk solids have been removed. This is the ghee used in India, but only for special occasions – less expensive vegetable ghee is used for everyday cooking. Clarified butter, however, is nowhere near as appetizing on vegetables and potatoes as fresh butter.

Fresh cream butter This can be salted or unsalted and is also known as sweet cream butter, made from unripened cream. The cream is pasteurized, deodorized, cooled and placed in ageing tanks for at least 12 hours before being turned into butter. Salt, which acts as a preservative, can be added during this time. British, New Zealand and American butters tend to be of this type.

Ripened butter This is also known as lactic butter, and like fresh cream butter can be either salted or unsalted. A pure culture of lactic bacteria is introduced to the cream, which is then allowed to ripen to develop a delicious, slightly acid flavour before the butter is made. This butter has a slightly more pronounced taste than fresh cream butter and is also softer.

Making your own dairy foods

Many milk-based products can be made quite easily at home. Starter packets for cultured products such as yogurt can be bought from health-food stores, or use a little of the unflavoured ready-made product. All you then need are very clean, well-covered bowls or jars (not metal), an undisturbed environment and a constant temperature to allow the culture to grow. Store in the refrigerator and set a little aside to start your next batch.

Sour milk Unpasteurized milk will go sour if left out of the refrigerator in warmer weather, and you can make a very basic cheese by straining it through a muslin cloth. The resulting curds can be beaten smooth and flavoured with herbs, garlic and salt.

Buttermilk To make buttermilk, add approximately 2 tablespoons of cultured buttermilk to every 600 ml/1 pint of pasteurized, skimmed milk; cover and leave to stand in a warm place for about 12 hours. Buttermilk can be served as a drink or used to make scones.

Clotted cream This can only be made with fresh, unpasteurized cream, which should be left to stand for 6 hours in summer, 12 in winter, in a heatproof dish. The cream is then scalded, but never boiled, over a low heat until small bubbles appear on the surface. Remove it from the heat immediately and store in a cold place for 12 hours. The thick, clotted cream can then be skimmed off the top.

Yogurt Any kind of milk except condensed or evaporated milk can be used to make yogurt. The milk should be brought almost to the boil and maintained at 75–80°C/170–180°F for 15 minutes, then cooled to about 43°C/110°F. This temperature needs to be maintained throughout the rest of the process so that the bacteria can grow. Stir 1 teaspoon of live yogurt or a packet of culture into each litre/scant 2 pints of milk and leave to stand overnight in a warm place. For a much more reliable alternative, buy a yogurt-making kit. When the yogurt has reached the consistency of thick custard, fruit, nuts and so forth can be added. The yogurt should then be refrigerated immediately.

When heated, yogurt has a tendency to curdle, so if you intend to cook with it you should stabilize it first. Make a little paste with cornflour and water. Heat the yogurt, and stir in the cornflour paste. Then proceed with the recipe.

A delicious fresh cheese similar to fromage blanc can be made by putting yogurt in a muslin cloth and suspending it (attaching it to the taps over the sink is a good method) overnight to drip.

Cheese

There are no set rules about serving cheese at home, but if you want to enjoy this most splendid and noble of foods in all its variations, the first thing to do is to find a good cheese shop run by someone who really cares, where the cheeses are kept in good condition and allowed to ripen to perfection quite naturally. (If cheeses are stored in an over-refrigerated storeroom or cabinet they will not mature properly.)

Having found your shop, buy only one or two types of cheese at a time, taking one generous cheese or piece of cheese in perfect condition, rather than all sorts of bits and pieces. Keep it, if possible, in a cool larder, cellar or cool room rather than in a refrigerator, with the cut surfaces covered. If no such cool place is available, keep it loosely wrapped (in greaseproof paper and then foil, allowing the passage of air) in a large container in the bottom of the refrigerator. Take the cheese out a good hour before you serve it, to give it time to recover from the chill, and do not leave it too long before you eat it.

The serving of cheese varies from country to country. In France it is generally served after the salad, which has then done its job of refreshing the palate. Accompaniments are crusty French bread and good unsalted butter, which sets off the subtlest cheese flavour and will not spoil the most delicate. (Some of the richer Normandy cheeses obviously don't need any butter at all.) The burgundy or claret served with the main course is finished off and appreciated with the cheese.

In Britain cheese is either eaten plain and hearty as a whole meal, with a nice hunk of fresh bread, or, if it is a serious dinner, it can be brought to the table at the end of the meal, after the pudding. There is usually fresh bread or water biscuits or some other neutral biscuits on the table for those who want them, and, again, unsalted butter. A strong cheese may be served with walnuts or celery or perhaps with crisp apples.

When cooking with cheese, it is unwise just to use up any old scraps or ends of mouldy cheese. The best results are obtained by using the best cheese. A piece of good, mature farmhouse Cheddar will be worth any amount of cheap factory-made block cheese – and, whatever the manufacturers may say, it is possible to tell the difference. Another thing to notice is the difference between cheeses made from pasteurized and unpasteurized milk. The unpasteurized cheese will go on developing and maturing because the milk that the cheese was made from was 'alive'; cheese made from pasteurized milk does not have the ability to develop the same subtle flavours and textures.

FRESH CHEESE

These are the simplest of all cheeses. They are made from the curds of soured milk or from milk that has been coagulated with the help of rennet – a curdling substance obtained from the stomachs of unweaned calves or sometimes, in the case of vegetarian rennet, from artichokes. They can also be made from whey, the thin liquid left over from cheese making. The milk used for making fresh cheese has often been skimmed of its fat content, but some fresh 'cream' cheeses have a high fat content and make some of the world's most fattening desserts – cheesecake for one.

These cheeses used to be made on country or mountain farms from surplus milk or milk and cream, but are now usually mass produced in factories from pasteurized milk, and sadly in the process have become rather bland. Some fresh cheeses, however, are left to ripen and ferment for weeks or months, during which time they develop a characteristic bloom and an agreeable sharpness.

Curd cheese, cottage cheese Made from the curds of skimmed milk and therefore having a low fat content, this cheese is popular with people trying to lose weight. The curds are broken into different sizes, and cream is sometimes added, in which case it becomes creamed cottage cheese. Its slightly acid taste makes curd cheese a refreshing accompaniment to a summer fruit salad. In Germany, where a version known as Quark is popular, it is often mixed with fruit purées, while in Provence a similar home-made white cheese is traditionally eaten with tiny new potatoes cooked in their skins. American pot cheese is a cottage cheese allowed to drain longer than usual, which makes it drier; farmer's cheese is drained even longer and is quite firm. Scottish crowdie, also a cottage cheese, is made from fresh sweet milk and butter.

Liptauer, Liptoi Originally from Hungary, this ripened fresh cheese is usually made from goat's or sheep's milk. It has a piquant taste and is delicious when blended with butter, seasoned with salt, paprika and caraway seeds, and spread on rye bread.

Mysost and Gjetost In Norway any cheese that has been made from thickening the whey after it has been separated from the prepared curd is known as Mysost. There are several varieties, but the most popular is Gjetost. It is cooked until it looks like fudge, and has a sweet flavour.

Gomost This Norwegian fresh cheese is made from soured unsalted milk and is similar to the French cheese Caillebotte. White and creamy, it is sometimes mixed with sugar or stewed or fresh fruit.

Pultost This is also a Norwegian curd cheese but is stiffer and stronger than Gomost. It is made from whey or buttermilk and caraway seeds are often added.

Ricotta Traditionally made from the whey left over from making the Italian sheep's-milk pecorino cheese, this can also be made from the whey of other cheeses. Its dryish texture and bland taste makes it ideal for mixing with fruit and raisins, or it can be eaten – as it is in Rome – with salt, or with cinnamon and sugar. It features in many Italian dishes, and is especially good mixed with Parmesan, spinach and chard and used to stuff ravioli.

Fromage blanc Liked by slimmers, this popular creamy-textured French cheese is made from skimmed milk soured with a culture. It is excellent with fresh raspberries or other berries.

Cream cheese Rich and creamy, soft and mild, this cheese can be made from whole milk or a combination of whole milk and cream. It is delicious when mixed with chopped raw vegetables or nuts and raisins, and is also an essential ingredient of American cheesecakes. In France a vast number of fresh cream cheeses are sold, with varying fat contents (*double crème, triple crème*); Explorateur and Brillat-Savarin are two examples. When fresh cream cheese is put into heart-shaped moulds and drained, it becomes *coeur à la crème*, eaten with wild strawberries and sugar.

cream 99
milk 97–9
yogurt cheese 100

cheese knife 225
cheese slicer 225
cheese wire 225

Cheesecake 395
Fresh Sauce Grelette 257
Spinach and Ricotta Ravioli 342
Warm Cheese Bread 363

cream 99
milk 97–9
torta Dolcelatte 109

Aubergine, Pepper and Tomato Pizza 361
Crespolini 341
Lasagne al Forno 339
Melanzane alla Parmigiana 383
Mozzarella in Carrozza 330

Fontainebleau Rarely available outside its native France, this cream cheese is made from a mixture of curd and whipped cream and is usually eaten with sugar. It can be made at home by blending demi-sel or Petit Suisse with whipped cream, but one is unlikely to produce the super-aerated result achieved by commercial manufacturers.
Petit Suisse French in origin, but called Swiss because a French-employed Swiss cowman is credited with its invention, this mild, light little cream cheese is delicious with fruit and excellent in any recipe where cream cheese is required.
Demi-sel Small and square, soft and white, this wrapped cheese is sold under a number of brand names, but is especially good when it has been made in Normandy, where it originated. It has a high fat content and is slightly salted.
Neufchâtel This whole cow's-milk cheese comes from Normandy. It is either eaten fresh, when it has the first growth of a soft white down and a delicate taste, or allowed to ripen until it is firm and pungent with a warm-coloured, bloomy rind. It comes in a variety of shapes.
Mascarpone Originally made in Lombardy and Tuscany, this rich, creamy cheese is enjoyed all over Italy, where it is sold in basins and used in cooking or eaten with fruit or sugar and cinnamon. It is the basis of the dessert, tiramisù.
Mozzarella This fresh white cheese was originally made from water buffalo's milk (*mozzarella di bufala*), but now cow's milk is often used; it is sold swimming in water to keep it fresh, and should be soft and springy. Two popular forms are *boconccini*, or little balls, and a smoked version. Mozzarella is served as an hors d'oeuvre in southern Italy, with olive oil and freshly ground pepper, and is ideal for cooking, being a traditional ingredient of pizza. Keep mozzarella in a bowl of water in the refrigerator.
Feta Crumbly and salty, this is the best known of the white cheeses ripened in brine or salt and known as 'pickled' cheeses. It was originally made from sheep's milk by shepherds in the mountain regions near Athens; today goat's and even cow's milk are used. Feta is popular in Greek cooking, especially in salads with tomatoes, cucumbers and black olives. It can be made less salty by soaking it in milky water.

HARD CHEESE

The word 'hard', when applied to cheeses, means that they have been subjected to pressure to make them dense. They will be softer or firmer according to their age.

Hard cheeses develop their various characteristics according to the milk used and the methods by which they are made. The speed of coagulation, the way the curd is cut, and whether the curd is then left to ripen or cut again, all affect the taste and texture, as does the treatment the cheese receives during ripening.

Some of these cheeses are derivations of more famous originals, but while some remain copies, others have developed a character of their own and deserve to be thought of as cheeses in their own right.

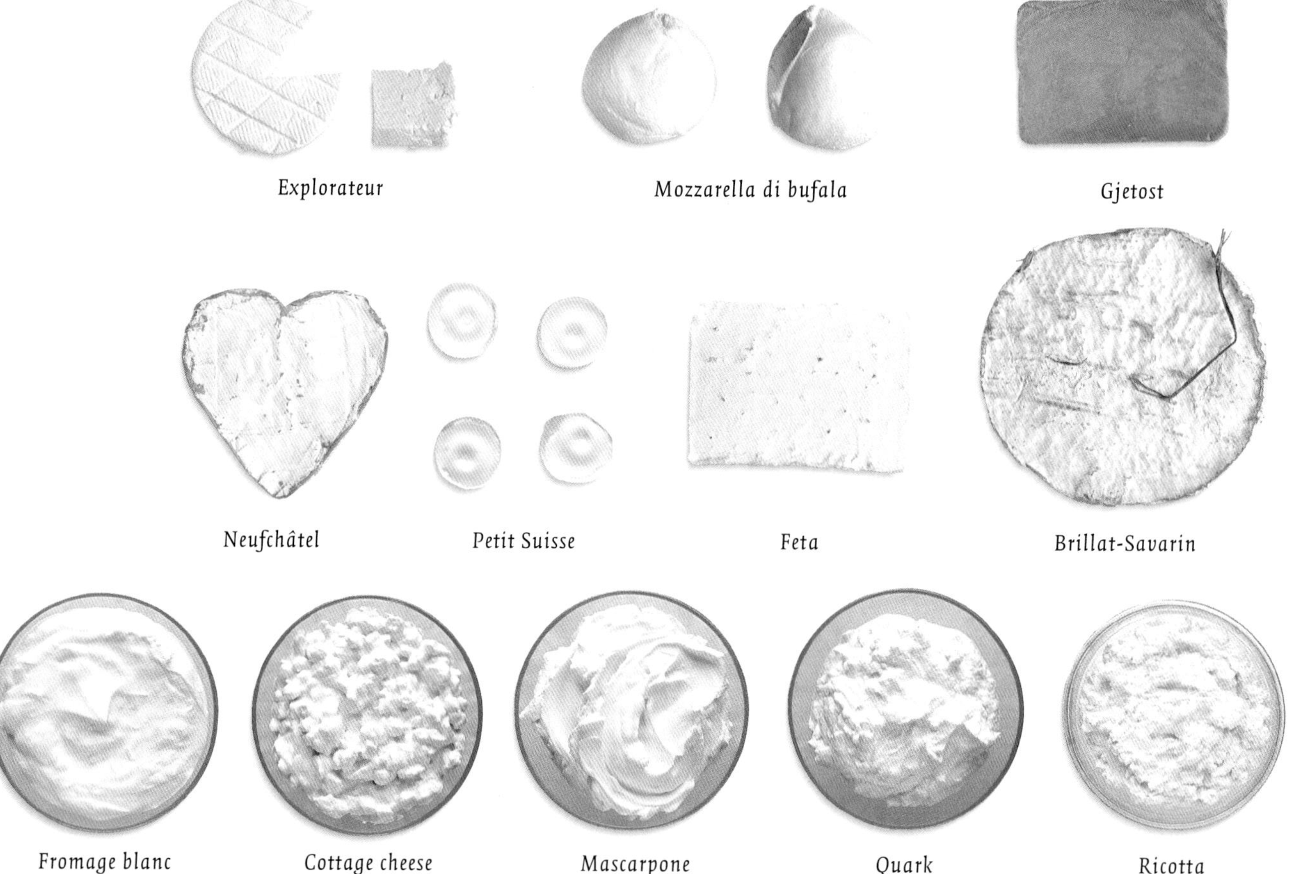

Explorateur · Mozzarella di bufala · Gjetost
Neufchâtel · Petit Suisse · Feta · Brillat-Savarin
Fromage blanc · Cottage cheese · Mascarpone · Quark · Ricotta

Grana cheese

The hard, grainy cheeses known collectively as *grana* are the well-known Italian grating cheeses, familiar to anyone who has ever eaten a plate of pasta or a bowl of minestrone soup. Their slow ageing process and low moisture content give them their long keeping qualities and their crumbly texture. The younger *grana* cheeses are more delicate, and are delicious when broken into chunks and eaten with a glass of white wine.

Parmesan More correctly Parmigiano-Reggiano, this, the most famous and expensive of all the *granas*, is sweet and fragrant. It keeps for years, growing harder and fuller as it ages. When young, it can be eaten at the end of meals. It is an essential ingredient of many of the best and most characteristic northern Italian dishes, and is grated and then scattered on top of soups and pasta.

When buying Parmesan, the name Parmigiano-Reggiano burned in dots on the rind is proof of authenticity. The cheese should be straw coloured and brittle, with a pinprick grain that is scarcely visible but gives it a rocky surface. It should never be grey, sweaty or waxy-looking, and it should always smell fresh. Ground Parmesan is an extremely poor substitute for fresh.

Pecorino A *grana* cheese made from sheep's milk, this is used in much the same way as Parmesan. A pecorino is round, hard and white, with a yellow crust when mature (except for that made in Siena, which is red). The taste is strong, pungent and salty, and there are many varieties that often go by the names of the districts in which they are made. Pecorino Romano is the original variety and is still considered to be the best.

Grana Padano This is made in the Po valley. Since it is cheaper than true Parmesan, it is often used in cooking.

Asiago An ancient Italian cheese from the Veneto region. Young Asiago can be served with biscuits, and the mature version is grated for use in cooking.

Sbrinz This ancient and splendid Swiss cheese is equal in virtue to (although distinct from) Parmesan. Its texture is granular and brittle, and it has an uneven surface with pinprick holes. In central Switzerland it is often shaved in thin slivers and served with a glass of wine. It is also ideal for cooking.

Schabzieger Also known as green cheese, or in North America as sapsago, this cheese from Switzerland is a hard, truncated little green cone. Made from skimmed cow's milk, it ferments naturally, and is mixed with pulverized blue melilot, a sweet clover, which gives it its green colour and characteristic pungent flavour. It smells of coriander or cumin. Grated it is used as a condiment for a variety of dishes.

Cheddar-type cheese

These real grass-roots cheeses are made and eaten all over the world, and used in recipes calling for 'cheese'.

Cheddar No hard cheese has been more widely imitated than English Cheddar, which originated in the small town of Cheddar, in Somerset, and was well established by the sixteenth century. It is a splendid all-purpose cheese, good to eat and to cook with. It has a sweet, full flavour when young and mild, and a sharp nutty flavour (often referred to as tasty) when mature.

Mature English farmhouse Cheddars, still made on some farms and ripened for months or years, are among the world's greatest cheeses. They compress more than ten times their weight of creamy milk when pressed into a cylindrical form and wrapped in a cloth, which may then be waxed. A traditional Cheddar weighs about 22.5–27 kg/ 50–60 lb, while small, whole Cheddars, known as truckles, usually weigh about 6 kg/14 lb. English Cheddar is also made in large blocks, but these do not develop and mature like the traditional aged cheeses.

Smaller Cheddars of various shapes are made outside England, but may vary widely from the true Cheddar flavour. In New York State, the home of the first Cheddar-cheese factory in America, a number of Cheddars are still made in varying sizes – some even come rindless. Wisconsin is also known for the quality of its Cheddars, but most of these, and most other Cheddars, like the Australian and New Zealand varieties, are made from pasteurized milk and lack the authentic taste of the English farmhouse variety. Tillamook cheese, however, from Oregon, is a delicious raw-milk Cheddar. Canadian Cheddars, which are still sometimes made from unpasteurized milk, have a characteristic tangy, nutty flavour. Look for Belleville-Brockville Cheddar (in a plain waxed cloth) or Black Diamond (with a black waxed surface).

Cantal Sometimes called the French Cheddar, Cantal has a smooth texture and, if the truth be told, a duller flavour than Cheddar. It is large, hard and yellow, and is made in cylindrical forms, to which it may owe its old name, 'fourme de Cantal'. Cantal can be good if allowed to mature – it takes as long to ripen as farmhouse Cheddar.

Cheshire Usually known as 'Chester' abroad, and well liked under this name in France and Italy, this is the oldest of the British cheeses. It is crumbly, nutty and salty, and can be red, white or blue. The red, which is dyed with annatto and is a marigold-orange, makes excellent eating as well as first-class soufflés. It is fat and rich, with a special piquancy that is also to be found in the white and blue varieties. The white variety, which is in fact a pale cream, is sharper than the red. It ripens faster but does not keep so well. The blue Cheshire is farmhouse made, and there is also an accidental blue Cheshire, which can start either white or red and is called, rather confusingly, Green Fade.

Gloucester This hard, robust English cheese originated in Gloucestershire and is now made in Somerset. In taste it lies between Cheddar and Cheshire, although there is none of Cheshire's crumble about it. Farmhouse Gloucester, with its natural hard crust, should not be darker than straw coloured. It is a good cooking cheese and makes delicious cheese straws. Single Gloucester is made with partly skimmed milk and is ready for eating within 6–8 weeks. Double Gloucester is made from whole milk and is eaten at 4–6 months.

Caerphilly One of the mildest, softest, crumbliest and fastest-ripening of the British hard cheeses, this was once known as the Welsh miner's cheese because it was the favourite packed lunch at the coal face. The best Caerphilly today, however, is made on Somerset farms. Made from skimmed milk, it is slightly sour and is eaten rather immature. Its melting quality makes it suitable for dishes calling for a mild cheese flavour.

Wensleydale This is similar to Stilton in shape but smaller. White, moist and flaky, it has a delicate buttermilk flavour.

graters 224
Parmesan knife 225

Asparagus Risotto 349
Asparagus Soufflé 328
Bacon and Egg Tart 327
Celery and Parmesan Salad 365
Cheese Omelette 324
Cheese Tart 328
Courgettes au Gratin 385
Crespolini 341
Eggs Florentine 323
Fennel au Gratin 375
Gnocchi Romana 344
Macaroni Cheese with Ham 328
Melanzane alla Parmigiana 383
Mornay Sauce 255
Mushroom Risotto 348
Pesto alla Genovese 336
Pommes Dauphinoise 381
Rigatoni all'Amatriciana 337
Risotto alla Milanese 348
Soft Polenta with Butter and Parmesan 352
Spaghetti alla Carbonara 337

Cheddar cheese 103
milk 97–9

cheese slicer 225

French Onion Soup 249
Swiss Fondue 329

Gruyère

Farmhouse Cheddar

Irish Cheddar

Cantal

Appenzell

Leicester

Parmigiano-Reggiano

Cheshire

Gloucester

Pecorino Romano

Leicester The largest English cheese in circumference, Leicester is a rich orange colour and shaped like a millstone. It is mild and nutty, moist and flaky, and very different from Cheddar in texture, since the curd is shredded rather than milled into knobs, giving it a crumbly consistency. It is ideal for cheese sauce.
Sage Derby Once made for eating at harvest suppers, this farmhouse cheese is a sage-flavoured version of plain Derby, which is similar to Cheddar but closer textured and more distinct in flavour. It should be aged for at least 9 months and be mottled with natural-looking sage-green streaks; at its worst it is heavily marbled with a vivid green, is artificial in taste, and too waxy in texture to even recall the real thing. Sage cheese is a similar cheese, spicy and succulent, made in the state of Vermont.

Gouda-type cheese

Firm and fat, these familiar round cheeses become drier and sharper with age. Those flavoured with cumin or caraway seeds are good with rye bread and wine.
Gouda Made in the town of Gouda, outside Amsterdam, this is the archetypal Dutch cheese. It is creamy, golden and flattish, with a yellow paraffin-waxed protective skin. A mature Gouda will be more pungent than a youthful one and can be very worthwhile. A black coating indicates that it is 7 or more years old, when it becomes known as an *alt* Gouda. Gouda *étuve* has been subjected to a prolonged maturing period or to artificially accelerated ripening. It is a simple eating cheese, which in its native Holland appears for breakfast, and in the kitchen it is fried with potatoes, grated into sauces and melted to make a type of fondue.
Edam Made from partially skimmed milk, Edam, encased in bright red or yellow livery for the export market, has a lower fat content than Gouda and is less smooth and round flavoured. When young it tends to be boring, but once aged and ripened it acquires a rather pleasant mellowness.
Mimolette This Dutch cheese is similar to Edam but bright orange inside, turning a rich red with age. The best Mimolettes are aged for up to 2 years, and look like cannon balls dug up from an Armada wreck. When chipped away at, the best have a glorious rich flavour; however, most are young and flabby.
Leyden Resembling Gouda, this cheese has a sharp, tangy taste. It is usually flavoured with caraway seeds, but varieties with cloves and cumin are also available. It is branded with the crossed keys of the arms of the Dutch city of Leyden.

Gruyère-type cheese

Reminiscent of alpine meadows, these cheeses range from mild flavoured to a rich, full nuttiness. Straw yellow in colour, they are characterized by holes caused by gas forming during ripening. These are the cheeses most popular with French cooks who appreciate their melting qualities, so well suited to the making of gratins and sauces.
Gruyère This Swiss cheese is made of cow's milk and has a fairly smooth rind. Ivory-yellow with tiny pinprick holes spaced far apart, it should have a waxy rather than a velvety surface. It melts well, and is a main ingredient of cheese fondue ; it is also often served after a meal, with grapes, figs or pears.
Comté Made in the Franche-Comté, this is a first cousin to Gruyère. The best,

Emmental Mature Gouda Derby Wensleydale

Havarti Edam Fontina

Jarlsberg Comté Caerphilly

Cauliflower au Gratin 375
Cheese Omelette 324
Eggs Florentine 323
Grilled Polenta with Poached Eggs, Fontina and Chive Cream 352
Mornay Sauce 255
Provençal Soupe au Pistou 250
Spinach Frittata 326
Swiss Fondue 329

'fruitiest' cheeses are made in tiny village dairies, or *fruitières*, to which the village farmers bring their milk, and they can be identified by a green oval plaque on the outside of the whole cheese. These cheeses often have almost no holes at all.

Emmental This is the famous Swiss cheese with the large holes. It comes in huge, shiny golden wheels, and its ivory-coloured paste is riddled with bubbles, which form during its fermentation and cooling period. It has a sweet flavour that grows fuller with age and is excellent for eating and cooking.

Fontina Made in the Piedmont area of Italy and also in Switzerland, Denmark and the US, this is a fat, rich, semi-firm cheese. Experts recommend the Swiss version as a table cheese and the Italian one for cooking. It melts beautifully and is used for Piedmontese *fonduta*, a fondue served with sliced white truffles.

Appenzell, Appenzeller A Swiss relation of Emmental, washed in a mixture of white wine and brine, this makes a tasty element in a fondue when young. Mature, it is firm but buttery with a rich, sweet flavour.

Jarlsberg This popular Norwegian cheese is similar to Emmental but milder and more rubbery in texture. Its taste is slightly nutty.

SEMI-FIRM CHEESE

These cheeses, some of which resemble Cheddar, are characterized by their firm but elastic feel. They are sometimes soft and tender, but, unlikely truly soft cheeses, do not become runny as they mature.

Caciocavallo Made from cow's milk, this is often smoked. An ivory-white cheese with a golden-yellow to grey rind, it is often displayed in pairs joined by a string and is usually eaten at the end of a meal. It is one of the *pasta filata*, or drawn curd cheeses, so named because they are stretched into strands in hot water during their making.

Provolone There are two main types of provolone, a *pasta filata*, or drawn curd cow's-milk cheese: *dolce*, which is young and usually dull, and *piccante*, which is sharp, strong and often very salty, but a good cheese. Provolone is sometimes smoked, and is moulded by hand.

Monterey Jack This pale Californian cheese, with small interior holes, comes in various shapes and degrees of softness. When it has a high moisture content and is quite soft, it is often simply called Jack, while the harder grating varieties are called aged or dry Monterey. The softer versions are often flavoured with chillies.

Colby This cheese of Wisconsin origin is similar to Cheddar but has a more open texture and a soft, mild, bland flavour.

Tilsit German in origin, this yellow cheese is pungent, with a slight smear to its surface. It is sometimes made with caraway seeds.

Havarti A cheese of the Tilsit type, this is named after the farm of one of Denmark's great cheese-makers. Havarti is made in round loaf shapes or in blocks, and has a strong individual taste, somewhat sharp when mature.

Danbo and Samsoe These firm, nutty Swiss-style cheeses are the national standbys of Denmark. (Samsoe is named after the island where it is made.)

Manchego Made in Spain, this cheese has a high fat content, and can be made from cow's or sheep's milk. Young Manchego is called *curado*; aged (*viejo*)

Cheddar cheese 103
Limburger 107
milk 97–9

Maroilles Cheese Tart 329

Provolone

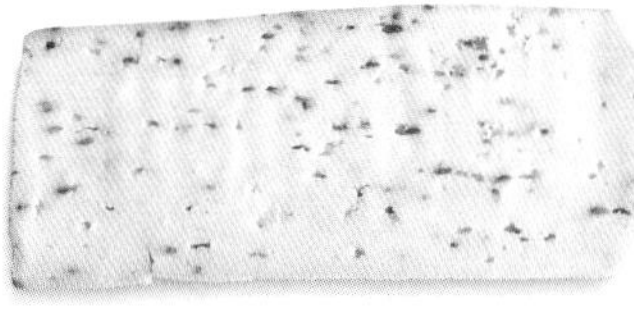
Danbo with caraway seed

Manchego

Tilsit

Colby

Monterey Jack

Manchego may be matured for up to 3 years, sometimes spending a year ripening in olive oil. It may be white or yellow, with or without holes, and varies widely in taste.
Brick An American original, Brick was made in Wisconsin as early as 1875. It has a dry reddish-brown crust and a softish, ivory-coloured interior. The flavour should be mellow, stimulating and somewhat sweet. Depending on its age and ripeness, it is compared to both Cheddar and Limburger.

SOFT CHEESE

The characteristic flavour of the creamy-white soft cheeses comes from bacterial growths, which begin at the outer edges of the cheese and move into the centre. A ripe cheese will be soft at the centre and can be tested by pressing lightly around the waist with the fingers. The bloomy white rinds are also a result of bacterial growth. This is natural in farm or artisan production, where the mould is present in the ripening premises themselves, or induced in many factory-made cheeses by penicillin or other bacteria sprayed on to the crust. (The same applies to cheeses with a russet-brown, washed crust.) If soft cheeses are cut before they are fully ripe and then packaged in portions, the proportion and thickness of crust and consistency of the interior are all affected. Soft cheeses are considered ready for eating when they have a bulge in the middle of the cut surface, although some people prefer them runny. Any smell of ammonia indicates that the cheese is past its best.

The most famous soft cheeses come from Normandy, which has some of the best pastures and produces the richest, creamiest milk in the world (although Normandy farmers say artificial fertilizers are changing the quality of this wonderful milk).
Camembert A farmhouse Camembert is made from raw milk, while the more common factory-produced Camembert is always made from pasteurized milk. The best Camemberts are from Normandy, and are made in rounds weighing 225–255 g/8–9 oz. Camembert is also available in half moons and in portions, but unfortunately it is only reliable if ripened as a whole cheese. A well-made and properly ripened Camembert is smooth and unctuous, even runny.
Brie A whole round, flat Brie usually measures 35.5 cm/14 in across and is sold in wedges. The unliquefied part in the centre of a ripe Brie is called 'the soul of the Brie'. Farmhouse Brie, known as Brie de Meaux *fermier*, is the creamiest variety and has a bouquet that is full and mild. (Nowadays French Bries are mainly produced in factories and there are many imitations, but buy unpasteurized farmhouse Brie from Normandy whenever you get the chance.) The Brie de Melun *affiné*, a smaller cheese, is one of the finest of all. There is now an excellent but pasteurized English Brie made in Somerset, and some decent Bries are also being produced in the US.
Pont-l'Evêque This cheese is square, soft and fat, with a shiny golden or reddish salty rind and warm farmyard taste. It should always have Pays d'Auge and *lait cru* or *non-pasteurisé* stamped somewhere on the wrapping paper or box, proving that it comes from unpasteurized milk.
Livarot This strong, pungent cheese, still made at its village of origin and elsewhere in the Pays d'Auge, is round, weighs about 450 g/1 lb, and is about twice as tall as a Pont l'Evêque. It has a thicker crust and, although it is obviously of the same family, quite a distinct flavour. Traditionally it is tied with reeds or paper.
Vacherin Usually banded with spruce bark, which not only saves it from collapse but also gives it a faint aroma of resin, Vacherin is a seasonal cheese, made in winter by the French and Swiss Comté-producing farms when there isn't enough milk, or transport is too difficult, to produce the Comté they make in summer. Serve it from the centre, digging into the buttery, runny paste with a spoon. It has a sweet, flowery, nutty flavour.
Maroilles Square and strong smelling, this comes from Flanders and is ripened

for up to 4 months, with much crust-washing as it ages. It is delicious with a full-bodied wine, and is used to make *goyère* and *flamiche*, the cheese pies traditional in Flanders.

Reblochon This fine cheese from Savoy is smooth and creamy, with a pinkish-gold crust and a strong farmyard flavour.

Port-Salut Also called Port du Salut – haven of rest – after the Trappist abbey where it was first made, this is a velvety smooth whole-milk cheese, semi-soft or semi-hard, and mildly pungent. One variety, Fermiers-Réunis, is still made by the monks at their Champagne dairy from the unpasteurized milk of their cows. Commercial Port-Salut, made by a farmers' co-operative in a nearby village, is a more rubbery and less tasty affair, as is the Bricquebec – a similar cheese made in the monastic dairy.

Taleggio Made from whole cow's milk, this comes from Lombardy in Italy. It has a smooth pink skin with a straw-coloured interior, and is fruity in flavour. When ripe it is very runny.

Munster, Muenster Originating in the Vosges, this is the national cheese of Alsace. With a firm paste and red rind, it has a pungent smell and flavour, and is traditionally eaten with rye bread, caraway seeds and chopped onions.

Limburger This cheese may take the form of a log, a horizontally corrugated roll, or a little disc or blob, and has a moist, pale rind and an overpowering smell. It is an acquired taste and should be eaten with robust country bread. An American cousin, known as Leiderkranz, is actually more like a pleasant Pont-l'Evêque than an aged Limburger.

Bel Paese The trade name for a soft, cream-coloured cheese of which there are many local and factory-made variations throughout Italy. It is tender and mild.

Tommes This is the family name of a large number of rustic cheeses, made of sheep's, goat's or cow's milk in almost

milk 97–9
rye bread 119

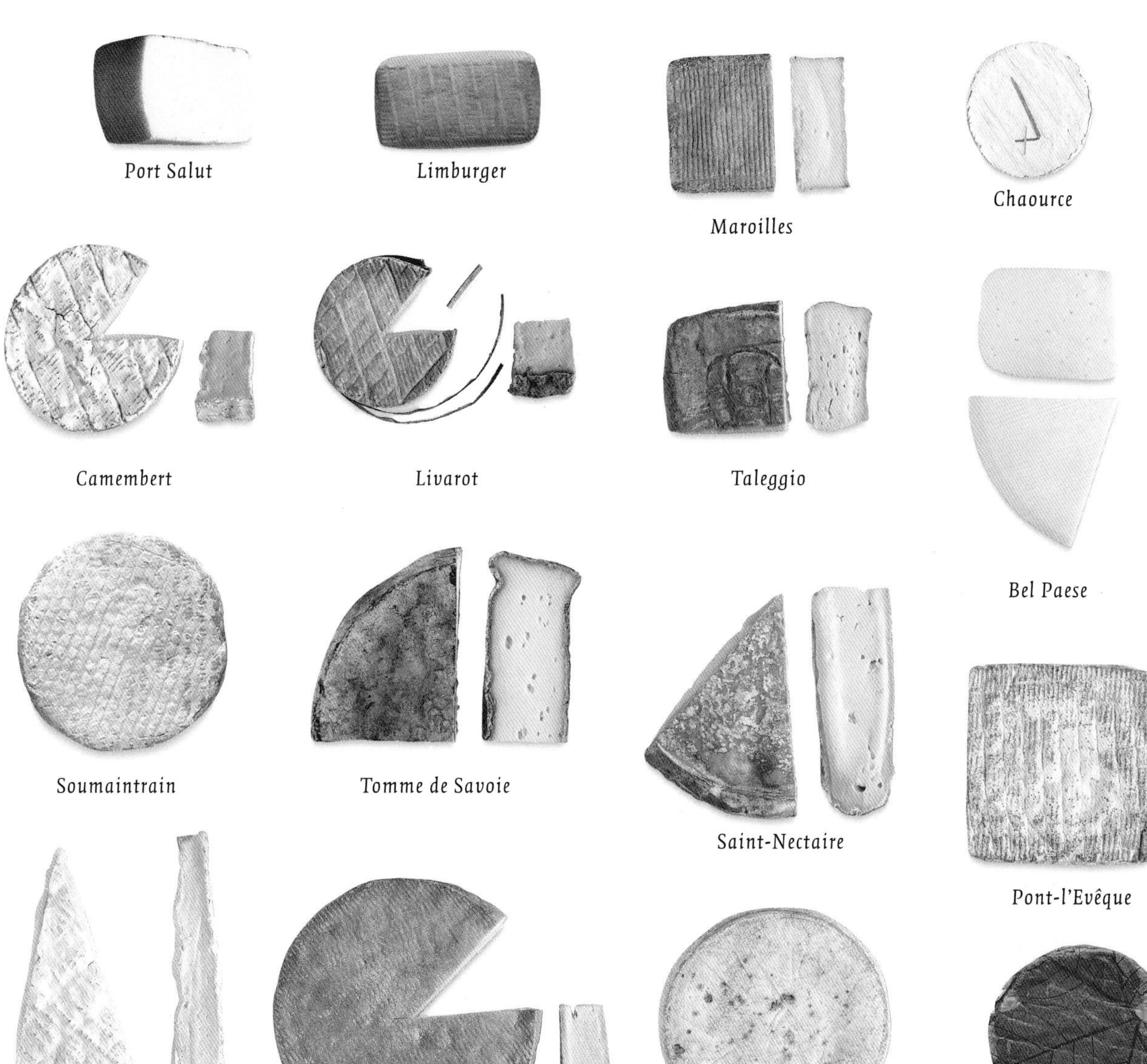

Port Salut

Limburger

Maroilles

Chaource

Camembert

Livarot

Taleggio

Bel Paese

Soumaintrain

Tomme de Savoie

Saint-Nectaire

Pont-l'Evêque

Brie

Munster

Reblochon

Epoisses

marc 422
milk 97–9

Goat's Cheese and Courgette Filo Tart 330
Roquefort Soufflé 329
Warm Cheese Bread 363

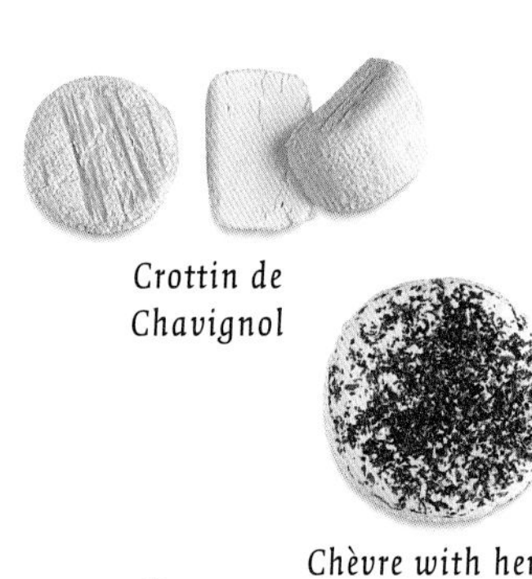

Crottin de Chavignol

Chèvre with herbs and garlic

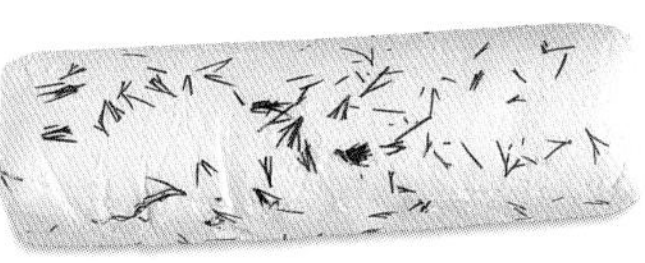

Chèvre with herbs

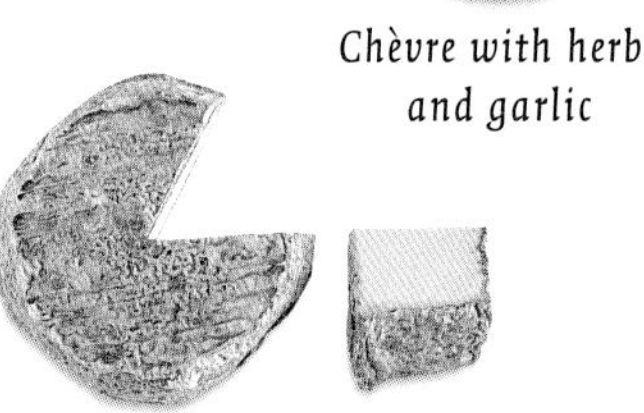

Selles sur Cher

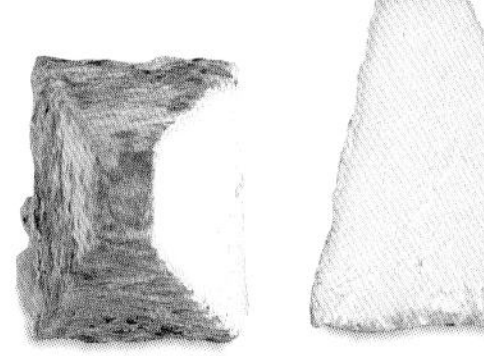

Pouligny St Pierre

any shape. The Tommes were originally from Savoy, the southern mountain ranges of France and the eastern part of Switzerland. Tomme au Marc is coated in fermented grape 'marc' – made from the pressed skins and seeds of grapes left over from wine-making, which gives it its characteristic taste, while Tomme de Savoie has a nutty flavour.

Saint-Nectaire A mountain cheese from the Auvergne, this is a round, flat cheese with a dark rind and a soft, supple but not creamy, straw-coloured inside. It has a nice light flavour.

Epoisses A highly smelly cow's-milk cheese from Burgundy, this is cylindrical and reddish on the outside, and soft, oozy and rich inside, with a strong earthy taste. It is traditionally aged in brine and marc.

Soumaintrain Like Epoisses, this flat, round cheese comes from Burgundy. It is semi-soft, with a sticky red-brown crust, a strong smell and an earthy taste.

Chaource One of those small, white, downy, luxurious-looking cheeses that give a fresh note to an otherwise heavy meal. From Champagne, it has a faintly acid, fruity flavour and a velvety texture.

GOAT'S CHEESE

There are infinite varieties of goat's cheeses, of which the vast majority are simply described as '*chèvres*' and have no distinguishing names. They are made on small farms and dairies all over France and throughout the Mediterranean, and are usually known as '*frais*', which is a fresh cheese; '*affiné*', which has been matured and should be velvety, occasionally creamy and fairly soft; and '*vieux*', which is well aged and varies from soft and creamy to rock hard. They should not be chalky or soapy – often a sign that they have been refrigerated.

The flavours of goat's cheeses vary according to the ripening period, the locality and altitude, which alter the taste and quality of the milk, and the different mould cultures used, which affect texture as well as flavour.

In general, goat's cheeses, whether strong, such as Pouligny St Pierre, or mild, like Selles sur Cher, should taste nutty and sweet with a slight piquancy. Some are flavoured with chives or garlic and other fresh herbs, while others are rolled in sieved wood-ash. Some goat's cheeses are sold sitting on the straw mat on which they have been drained, or wrapped in leaves; they may be coated with herbs or pepper, or preserved in oil.

Crottin de Chavignol, a winter goat's cheese from the Berry region of France, with a reddish or grey crust, has an interior that is white, piquant and full-flavoured. Chabichon, from Poitou, is made in the shape of a cone and has a natural dry rind. Goat's cheeses are also made in Spain, Norway, Britain and North America.

BLUE CHEESE

Blue cheeses first turned blue by a happy accident. Roquefort, the ancestral blue cheese, was once just a humble fresh curd cheese made of sheep's milk. Had it not been for a lovelorn shepherd, who, as legend has it, set off in pursuit of a country girl, leaving his luncheon cheese in a limestone cave, the blue mould might never have happened. However, returning after a week or so of dalliance, the shepherd found that his lunch had changed in texture, colour and taste and become 'blue'. Since that time, the penicillin moulds that turn cheese blue have been isolated and identified, and blue cheeses have multiplied. The cheese's paste itself may be firm or creamy, buttery or brittle, and any colour from chalk white to deep golden-yellow. The only thing that the paste of a blue cheese should never be is brown and dingy.

Roquefort The veining of Roquefort, a sheep's-milk cheese, is due to *Penicillium glaucum* – now better known as *Penicillium roquefortii* – which thrives in the caves high upon the Cambalou plateau in the Aveyron. These ancient caves, cool and damp owing to underground springs, are still used for maturing Roquefort. The blue veining is now accelerated by layering the curd with crumbled bread moulds, but even so, the ripening process still takes about 3 months, and the cheese will not be at its best until it is at least 6 months old.

A Roquefort in its prime is creamy, with green-blue marbling – *Persillé* (parsleyed) is the French descriptive term. It is smooth, firm and buttery when cut, but crumbly owing to the mould, which should be evenly distributed. It is strong, with the fine grain and the extra pungency that sheep's milk produces. It should not, however, be salty – although those for export tend to be over-salted as a precaution against spoilage.

Bleu de Corse A cheese made by Corsican shepherds and sent to the Roquefort caves to become blue and to mature. It is similar to Roquefort in taste.

Gorgonzola Once exclusive to the Italian village of that name, this cheese is now produced all over the lush plain of Lombardy. The squat, cylindrical cheeses, made of cow's milk, are no longer matured in the local caves but rather in the great maturing houses in the district. *Penicillium mycelium* accounts for the streaking. Although Gorgonzola is often described as an early copy of Roquefort, it is softer, milder, creamier and less salty. It should have very little rind, being wrapped in foil, and should be rather smooth and cream-coloured, marbled with blue-grey or blue-green. The cheese should be springy to the touch, and may smell musty, but should not be overpowering. Other Italian blues include the creamy, mild, factory-made Dolcelatte and the smaller Mountain Gorgonzola.

Pipo Crème A cylindrical French cheese, this was originally produced as a competitor to Gorgonzola. It has a quite distinct character of its own.

Danish Blue This is similar to Roquefort, but is made with cow's milk. It can be cylindrical, rectangular or square, and is white with blue veins. It has a high fat content and the saltiness inevitable in this type of cheese.

Bresse Bleu Similar to Gorgonzola, this French soft blue cheese comes from the Bresse region, which also produces a more stodgy blue called, confusingly, Bleu de Bresse, another heavy one called France Bresse, and most recently Belle Bressane, with a hole in the middle.

Torta Dolcelatte Also marketed as Torta di mascarpone, this is a cheese made from layers of mild Dolcelatte and sweet Mascarpone – delicious, like fresh clotted cream.

Bleu des Causses A cheese of high quality, somewhat similar to Roquefort. Made with cow's milk, it is from the same region and has the same mould.

Fourme d'Ambert A naturally blued cow's-milk cheese, this is from the Auvergne. It is exceptional in being almost the only non-English blue cheese to have a hard crust, which is grey flecked with yellow and red. It comes in cylinders weighing about 1.5 kg/3 lb, and is sharp and strong.

Stilton One of the very few English foods to be admired by the French, this is a highly protected cheese made only in Derbyshire, Leicestershire and parts of Nottinghamshire. Although a noble cheese, Stilton is a comparative latecomer and, in fact, was never made at Stilton. But it was first served there, at the Bell Inn in the eighteenth century. Stilton should be a creamy ivory colour with greenish-blue veining throughout. It should be open textured and velvety, never dry, hard or salty.

Stilton is traditionally served with a white napkin wrapped around it, and should be stored wrapped in cloth. Should the cheese become dry in spite of this, it helps to moisten the cloth and to leave it until the dampness restores the cheese's proper consistency. It is not considered a good idea to pour port into a Stilton, as it rots the cheese.

Blue Wensleydale Among the other English blue cheeses, Blue Wensleydale (not made in Derbyshire) is claimed by some to be better than Stilton – creamier, sweeter and nuttier.

Dorset Blue Vinny A hard white cheese with bright blue veining and an agreeably sharp taste. It is made from skimmed milk using vegetarian rennet.

Maytag Blue A tangy and smooth-textured blue-veined cheese made in Iowa, this is one of the best American cheeses. Maytag Dairy Farms is a family operation that has been making its cheese since the early 1940s.

Other blues There are a number of lesser-known blue cheeses made in France and elsewhere, including a rather good blue Brie from Germany.

mascarpone 102
milk 97–9

Danish Blue · Torta Dolcelatte · Bresse Bleu · Maytag Blue · Dolcelatte · Roquefort · Bleu des Causses · Fourme d'Ambert · Blue Wensleydale · Dorset Blue Vinny · Stilton · Gorgonzola

Cooking Fats and Oils

butter 99
caul fat 62
goose 88
kidneys 61
lard 422
render 423
salt pork 70
sausages and salamis 72–8

bulb baster 229
gravy strainer 229

Christmas Pudding 396
Hot-Water Crust Pastry 405
Old-Fashioned Pork Pie 315
Pâté de Campagne 318
Rillettes of Pork 319
Rough Puff Pastry 402
Shortcrust Pastry 402
Steak and Kidney Pudding 283

Every cook in the world uses fat or oil of some kind as a cooking medium. In cool northern regions the fats from grass- and grain-fed animals are traditionally used, while in the hot Mediterranean countries, where the blessed olive tree grows, olive oil is the essential ingredient. Other regions may use goose fat or mustard seed oil, grapeseed oil or sesame oil, each giving its own distinctive flavour to the local dishes.

Today, the limitations of climate count for far less than they used to, and we can obtain and cook with almost any medium we choose. But the flavour of food depends very much on what fat or oil is used, and a good cook will always try to use the right medium for the right dish in order to keep the flavour as authentic as possible.

Unfortunately, the amount of fat, whether animal or vegetable, in our Western diets has come under major criticism from doctors and nutritionists. Not only do we get our chief source of energy from fats that are an 'invisible' part of most foods, but we are all too likely to load up on rich fats in the form of butter and other saturated fats. Many vegetable fats, unlike the traditionally suspect animal fats, contain no cholesterol. Olive oil, sunflower oil and safflower oil are all recommended as particularly healthy and suitable in low-cholesterol diets.

Fats

To the cook, fats were traditionally of animal origin and were either purchased, or collected at home from a roasting joint or bird and then left to solidify. It is this quality of solidifying naturally that distinguishes saturated fats from those rich in unsaturated fatty acids (such as vegetable oils). However, vegetable oils can now be solidified by various chemical processes, so we have solid blocks of vegetable fats at our disposal as well as animal fats, and very often margarines and shortenings are a blend of the two.

Margarine All margarines are made from vegetable oils, and most also contain milk or animal fats (including butter) or fish oils, plus emulsifiers and colouring agents. To make margarine, the oils are 'hydrogenated', or converted from their normal liquid form to a solid. The process of hydrogenation also turns some of the oils' unsaturated fatty acids into what are called trans fatty acids, which some experts believe have the same – or more – harmful effect on the body as saturated fats.

With the exception of the all-important flavour, the characteristics of margarine in the kitchen are similar to those of butter. The main difference is that margarine is not particularly suitable for frying since it splutters and burns easily. Soft tub margarines are also unsuitable for frying, and they are too soft to be rubbed into flour. (When making pastry with this type of fat, mix together the margarine, water and only a third of the flour at the start, then gradually add the rest of the flour until you have a smooth dough that can be rolled out as usual.)

Low-fat spreads, with their high water content, are designed for spreading and cannot be used for cooking.

Suet The word suet comes from the Latin for tallow, and suet was once used instead of wax to make candles: like wax, suet is stiff and melts slowly. It is the firm, white fat that surrounds lamb's or ox kidneys – the latter is the suet you are more likely to find. If you are shredding suet yourself, a little flour sprinkled over the suet will keep it from getting too sticky. Suet has a wide range of uses. It goes into sweet puddings such as Christmas pudding and jam roly-poly, and into savoury ones like steak and kidney and steak and mushroom. A good suet crust, made with self-raising flour and mixed with a light hand, is one of the most satisfying of winter foods. Commercial suet is very easy to use, and for vegetarians a vegetable suet is now produced.

Lard Before technology took a hand lard – rendered pork fat – had to be used fresh, and it had a strong taste and no creaming properties. Now it is usually light and clean tasting. In Britain lard is is used mainly for frying – it was once the traditional medium for deep-frying fish and chips – and for baking, where its creaming properties are appreciated. Lard is the essential ingredient in making a good raised crust for pork pies (when making pastry, a mixture of butter and lard produces a crisp, light, crumbly texture). It also adds lightness to scones. Lard has long been the fat of choice throughout much of South America, and it is coming back into favour in the US as it is recognized as being no less healthful than many other cooking fats.

The best lards are those rendered from the belly fat – the flare or leaf fat – of the bacon pig, and from the fat that lies directly under the skin of the back. Lard made from other pig fat has a stronger taste; it is the lard most widely sold. Add a sprig or two of rosemary to the melted fat to overcome any porky taste when frying potatoes and other delicate foods.

Back fat This is the fat that runs along the back of the pig, over the loin. When cut thinly and beaten into long pieces it is used primarily for larding dry meats, such as veal and game birds, particularly pheasant and partridge. The pieces are tied over the birds like a waistcoat, and the fat bastes the flesh during cooking. Cut into strips called lardons, the fat can be inserted with a special needle into the flesh of dry meat to keep it succulent while it cooks.

Back fat is also used for lining terrines for pâtés, and for rendering lard at home. Rendering is done by cutting the back fat into very small cubes and then gently melting the cubes with a little water in a very low oven or over a gentle heat. When the water has evaporated, the clear liquid fat is poured off into a jar. What is left in the pan are the crisp brown scratchings, or *grattons*, which are sometimes mixed into the lard to give extra flavour and texture.

Dripping and goose fat A good old-fashioned way of acquiring a delicious cooking fat is to strain and reserve the fat that has dripped off a roasting joint or bird. Once this dripping has cooled and solidified, the jelly or juice underneath is removed (it is excellent added to a gravy or stock) and any sediment from the bottom of the cake of dripping is scraped away and disposed of (at one time in Britain it was eaten on toast as a snack).

Drippings from different kinds of meat should not be mixed. Beef dripping can be used to fry the meat for beef stews; pork dripping can be used for any savoury dish. Chicken fat, when rendered, is fine and delicate and is much used in Jewish cooking, where it replaces lard. Use the fat from goose or duck for bean dishes, roast vegetables, poultry and fried potatoes. Lamb dripping smells and tastes rather unpleasant and is only widely used in the Middle East.

Shortening All hard fats are shortenings, meaning that they are capable of producing a crumbly 'short' crust (the greater the amount of fat in the mixture, the greater the shortening effect). However, it is the white cooking fats that are neither pure lard nor dripping which have claimed the name.

White cooking fats may be made of blended vegetable oils or a mixture of vegetable and animal fats or fish oils, depending on what is cheapest on the world market at any particular time. As for margarine, the oils are hydrogenated to make them solid. In taste white fats are bland, in texture light and fluffy. When using white fat for frying, break it into small pieces so that it all heats up at the same rate. The texture of white cooking fat will certainly make creaming and rubbing in easier, but remember that the fat is totally flavourless.

Oils

Unlike fats, oils are liquid at room temperature. They perform the same function as fats in shallow and deep frying, but oils have the advantage of being reusable once or twice, as long as they are not overheated and are carefully strained after each use. (But beware of the taint of overused or overheated oil, which spoils the flavour of so much fried food in restaurants.)

When frying, oils should be heated slowly to the correct temperature. If the oil is not hot enough too much will be absorbed by the food. Overheating is dangerous because an overheated oil decomposes and will start to smoke; eventually, if heated further, it develops harmful toxins, and will finally catch fire. Any oil overheated by accident should be thrown away. A simple rule when heating oil is to wait for a blue haze to rise from it but never to allow it to smoke. Test the temperature of the oil with a thermometer: it should be 180–190°C/350–375°F for raw fish, poultry and meat, and 190°C/375°F for vegetables. Poultry and fish come in between. If you lack a thermometer, fry a small cube of day-old bread in the heated oil: if the bread turns golden and crisp in 1 minute, the temperature is about 180°C/350°F.

The object of deep frying is to seal the surface of the food. The crisp outside crust encloses a food whose inside is cooked in the heat of its own steam. The pieces to be fried should be as nearly as possible of uniform size so that they cook evenly. If you dip the food in batter, let the excess drain off before you put the food into the oil; if you breadcrumb it, press the crumbs on well so that the oil can remain as free as possible of small, dark brown and finally burned crumbs (these will give the oil a bitter flavour).

A good oil should last for up to three fryings. Strain it well after each use. When reused it should neither foam nor smoke excessively: the smoke point gradually decreases with age. It should not smell or look dark or thick. These are definite signs that the oil has reached the end of its useful life.

There are a great many oils in the world. Even without going into such exotics as brazil-nut oil, used as a hair dressing by the inhabitants of the Amazon rain forests, or juniper oil for gin, or even clove oil for toothache, the subject of oils is a complex one. To start with – and this goes a long way to help one make a sensible choice – there is the distinction between oils that are unrefined and refined.

Unrefined oils are those that have simply been cold pressed and then left to clear and mellow for a few months before being bottled. They tend to be cloudy but come to the customer in full possession of their natural flavour and colour. Often called cold-pressed oils, they are – not surprisingly – more expensive than their refined counterparts.

coating with egg and crumbs 423

deep-fat thermometer 233
deep-fryer 239

Margarine

Shortening

Lard

Goose fat

Suet

olive 154–5
peanut 187
sesame seeds 197
sweetcorn 142

Chinese Egg Noodles with Browned Garlic, chillies and parsley 345
Gazpacho 254
Green Bean Salad with Anchovy-Cream Dressing 367
Lebanese Aubergine Salad 365
Mayonnaise 258
Pesto alla Genovese 336
Red Peppers with Anchovies 383
Roast Marinated Chicken Breasts 310
Rouille 258
Saffron Bouillabaisse with Rouille 253
Salsa Verde 258
Seafood Salad 370
Spaghetti alla Rustica 337

Refined oils have been extracted by modern mechanical methods. They may then be degummed, neutralized, heated and blanched, 'winterized' to keep them from going cloudy, deodorized by an injection of steam, and finally given artificial preservatives to make up for those lost in the processing.

Olive oil Indispensable for pasta, salads and many Mediterranean recipes, olive oil, the finest of all oils, varies in character from country to country. Choice is often a matter of personal preference. Generally speaking, Spanish olive oil has a strong flavour, Greek a heavy texture, Provençal a fruity taste and Italian a nutty one.

There are two distinct methods of pressing olives: the artisanal olive mill, where olives are crushed and the oil extracted by pressure in the traditional manner, and the modern mill where the oil is extracted mechanically. ('Cold pressed' and 'first pressing' are terms less frequently used today because with hydraulic presses in modern mills the olive pulp is now pressed once only and requires no heat to facilitate the extraction of the oil.)

The very best and most expensive olive oil, from whatever country, is virgin oil, which is pure enough not to need refining. Virgin olive oils are separated into two grades: 'extra virgin' (with 1 per cent acidity) and 'virgin' (2 per cent acidity). Virgin oil is usually a greenish colour – often helped by putting a few leaves into the press – but may also be golden yellow. The best virgin oils come from green Provençal or Tuscan olives (the town of Lucca is reputed to produce the best Tuscan olive oil). Use virgin olive oil in salads and cold fish dishes, where its beautiful, fruity flavour can be most appreciated.

Cheaper oils, labelled simply olive oil or 'pure' olive oil, have been refined to remove naturally occuring impurities, and are usually blended with one another; they might then be mixed with a small proportion of virgin olive oil to improve the taste. Olive oil has a blander and less characterful flavour and a paler colour than extra virgin and virgin olive oil, but is excellent for cooking. Olive oil is unsuitable for deep frying as it cannot tolerate high frying temperatures.

Groundnut oil Known also as peanut oil, *huile d'arachides* and arachide or arachis oil, this is the favourite cooking oil of those French chefs who do not cling to olive oil. It is often considered a good replacement for olive oil, particularly when used for frying, as it has very little smell and no flavour.

Groundnut oil is used for salads and mayonnaise when a delicate flavour is wanted, although extra seasoning, lemon juice or vinegar may be required. Less refined oil can impart a slight peanut flavour to fried food.

The Chinese, who use this bland oil a great deal in their cooking, like to flavour it by frying a few slices of fresh ginger, garlic or a spring onion in it before use. Chinese oils are generally less processed than Western groundnut oils and so have more peanut flavour.

Corn oil This is one of the most economical oils for shallow and deep frying, having one of the highest smoke points. Corn oil can also be used for salad dressings. Its admirers say it is rich and bland; its detractors find it lifeless, weak and flabby. Unrefined, it has a strong taste of maize about it. Refined, it is practically tasteless when cold, but produces a strong and not very agreeable smell during frying.

Sesame oil There are various types of sesame oil. The thicker and browner the oil, the more aromatic it is; light sesame oil has only a delicate nutty taste. The Chinese use the dark oil, made from toasted sesame seeds, more for seasoning than for frying, as it burns easily. Chinese cooks believe that sesame oil added to seafood before cooking will remove fishy odours, but if it is added after cooking, to lamb, vegetables and sauces, it imparts a pleasant, aromatic flavour.

Ali Baba's efficacious formula 'Open sesame' was based on the fact that sesame pods burst open with a sharp sound to release their seeds. The jars in which the thieves hid were no doubt waiting for that year's sesame oil.

Sunflower oil Sunflower oil is light, mild and thin. Excellent for cooking (although it has a relatively low smoke

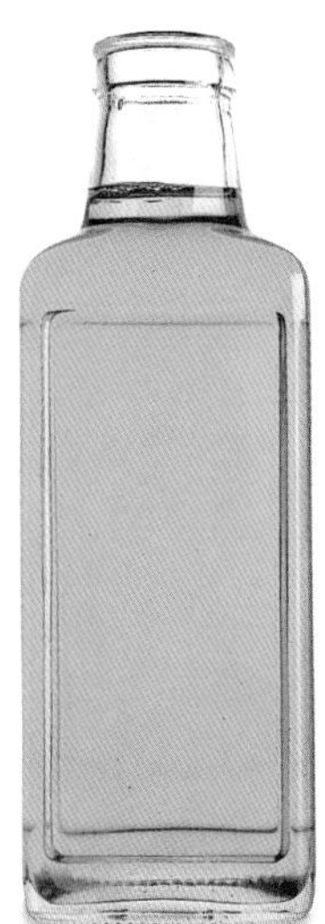
Almond oil

Corn oil

Olive oil

Extra virgin olive oil

Grapeseed oil

Walnut oil

point), it is also good for using with more expensive oils when making delicate salad dressings. It is good for recipes where a fairly neutral oil is required.

Safflower oil This oil, so often confused with sunflower oil, is made from the safflower, a pretty thistle-like plant with orange, red or yellow flowers. Usually a deep golden colour, safflower oil is found refined in supermarkets and unrefined in health-food shops. It is very light and used in the same way as sunflower oil. It is also the oil most recommended for use in the low-cholesterol diets of heart patients.

Mustard seed oil Although mustard seed oil has a distinctive smell and taste when cold, most of this is driven off when the oil is heated. This oil is used in parts of India as an alternative to ghee. It is also used in Kashmiri curries and as a preservative in pickles, including Italy's colourful *mostarda di frutta*.

Rapeseed oil This oil, also known as colza and canola, is widely used in Mediterranean countries and the East for frying and salads. It has become popular in the US because it is the lowest in saturated fats of all oils, and only olive oil has more monounsaturated fat.

Rapeseed oil is also often blended with other oils to make margarine.

Soya bean oil More oil is produced from the soya bean than from any other plant, and most of it goes into the blending of oils, cooking fats and margarines. A good brand, marked 100 per cent soya bean oil, is pleasant in salads, but can be a bit heavy in texture.

Grapeseed oil This light, aromatic oil is a by-product of the wine industry and is popular in France and Italy. The seeds yield a golden oil. Used in salads and for gentle frying, this oil comes into its own as the best cooking medium for *fondue bourguignonne*.

Walnut oil Cold pressed from the new season's walnuts, strong and with a deliciously nutty flavour, this is an unusual salad oil. Best mixed with a lighter oil, or used a little at a time as a flavouring, walnut oil is especially good when used on a fresh spinach salad, with a few shelled walnut halves added.

Walnut oil does not keep well, so should be bought in small quantities and kept in the refrigerator. It is also very expensive, and is not used for frying.

Almond oil When almond kernels are simply pressed they produce a clear, pale yellow oil. A fatty oil obtained from the bitter almond is used at home for confectionery making. When further processed this oil becomes oil of bitter almonds.

Wheat germ oil Extracted by cold pressing, this pleasant, nutty-tasting oil is mainly taken by the spoonful as a vitamin E supplement. It is also used in salad dressings, either by itself or, since it is expensive, blended with other oils.

Vegetable oils The most economical oils on the market are the highly refined, pale golden oils that are a blend of various vegetable products – soya bean oil, cottonseed oil, rapeseed oil, palm oil and coconut oil. They have little taste, but because of their high smoke point they are good for frying. Palm and coconut oil are not recommended in low-cholesterol diets, as, unlike other vegetable oils, they are high in saturated fat.

Flavoured oils There are many flavoured oils available in the shops, many based on olive oil to which flavourings such as herbs, garlic, sun-dried tomatoes and so on have been added. These are good in salad dressings, mayonnaise and other cold preparations – heating can greatly reduce their flavour and aroma. Chilli oil, vegetable oil tinted red by the hot chillies that have steeped in it, is much used in Chinese cookery.

You can make your own flavoured oil by dropping herbs, spices or aromatics – for example, chillies, sprigs of rosemary or fennel, or lemon peel – into a jar or bottle of good olive oil and leaving it to steep for about a month so that the flavouring can permeate the natural oil taste. A good mixture to use for Provençal cooking would be tiny whole chillies, thyme and peppercorns.

almond 186
ghee 100
grape 174–6
margarine 110
mostarda di frutta 203
mustard 202–3
soya bean 128
walnut 188
wheat germ 114

Rocket and Walnut Salad 367
Spiced Marinated Mackerel 266
Spinach and Walnut Salad 367
Spicy Green Fish 272
Trout Marinated in Vermouth 273

Groundnut oil

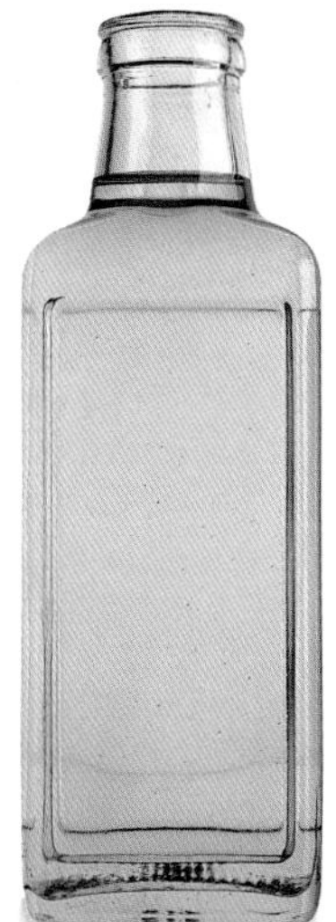
Safflower oil

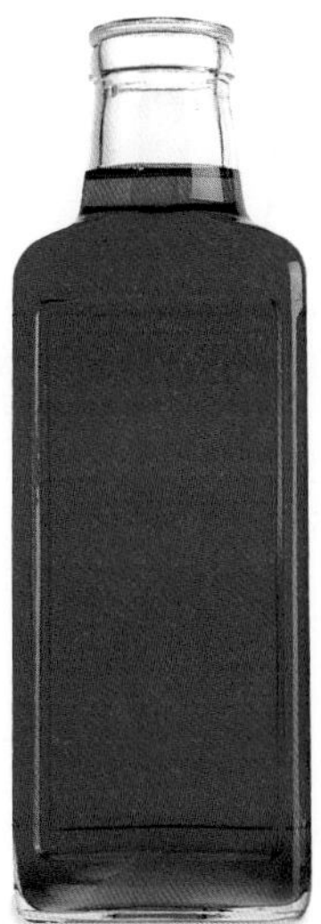
Toasted sesame oil

Sunflower oil

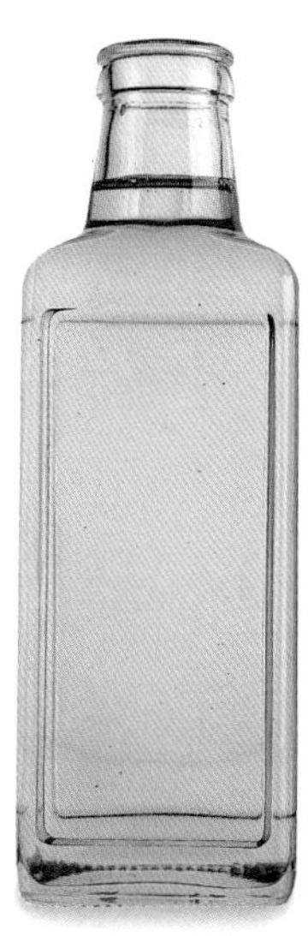
Soya bean oil

Rapeseed oil

Grains, Thickening Agents and Breads

bread recipes 358–64
cake and biscuit recipes 410–14
gluten 422
pasta recipes 332–45
pastry recipes 402–9
wheat germ oil 113

Burghul Pilaf 351
Gnocchi Romana 344
Six-Vegetable Couscous 350
Tabbouleh 351

GRAINS

Besides yielding flour for our daily bread, grains are the staple foods of many countries. The porridge of Scotland, the polenta of Italy, the couscous of North Africa, the kasha of Russia and countless other grain dishes are all basically the same thing: a local grain, in one form or another, cooked in boiling water until swollen and tender, and then eaten on its own or with whatever else makes up the local diet.

Wheat

One of the first cereals to be cultivated, wheat has become the most valuable of all food grains, widely used in all its stages, from whole and unadulterated to finely milled and sifted. When 'flour' is called for in modern recipes it is wheat flour that is meant. The wheat flours can be broadly divided into those made from high-gluten, hard or strong wheats grown in hot, dry areas and used for bread and pasta, and soft-grained or weak varieties grown in temperate places, suitable for cakes, biscuits and general use. The terms 'spring wheat' and 'winter wheat' refer to the time of year the wheat is planted, not to any specific variety.

Wholewheat grain Also called wholewheat berries, this is available in health-food shops. To eat it as a grain, soak it overnight before cooking and then boil it in plenty of water for about 1 hour. Eat it in the same way as rice with meat, fish or vegetables, or mixed into a salad. In earlier times it was cooked overnight at a low temperature, ready to eat as a sort of porridge called 'frumenty', delicious with honey.

Cracked wheat, kibbled wheat Simply the wholewheat grain cracked between rollers, this is eaten in the same way but takes only about 20 minutes to cook. It is also good cooked like porridge as a hot breakfast cereal.

Burghul, bulgur This is wheat grain that has been parboiled, then dried and some of the bran removed before being cracked. The process makes the grain easier to cook and gives it a less pronounced flavour and a lighter texture. Eat it in place of rice, or in the Lebanese salad called tabbouleh – burghul mixed with chopped onions, parsley and mint, with olive oil and lemon juice.

Bran This is the thin, papery outer covering of the wheat grain. It is a by-product of the refining processes of the wholewheat grain and can be bought in health-food shops and supermarkets. For extra fibre, sprinkle it on breakfast cereals, eat plain with milk and sugar, or add it to bread, cake and biscuit mixtures.

Wheat germ The heart of the wheat grain, this is often extracted or destroyed during wheat-refining processes. It can be bought toasted from supermarkets and raw from health-food shops. The raw variety should be kept in the refrigerator, since the oil in the germ quickly goes rancid (it is often extracted from wheat flour to improve the flour's keeping qualities). Sprinkle it on breakfast cereals or mix it with yogurt. When baking bread, sprinkle wheat germ on the sides of the greased bread tin for a nice finish to the loaf.

Semolina When wheat grain is first milled it is separated into bran, wheat germ and endosperm – the floury part of the grain. It is the first millings of the creamy-yellow endosperm that are known as semolina. When medium-ground, semolina is used in desserts, ranging from milk puddings to the powerfully sweet, round Indian cakes, for which the semolina is first fried and then mixed with raisins, nuts and honey. The finest ground semolina is used to make one kind of Italian gnocchi. Flour-coated semolina grains make couscous, part of the excellent North African dish of the same name. Couscous can be purchased precooked. Semolina flour, made from hard durum wheat (*Triticum durum*), is used for most commercial Italian dried pasta.

Wholewheat flour, wholemeal flour This consists of the whole of the wheat grain. Stone-ground flour has a better flavour than roller-milled since the slow grinding of the stones doesn't overheat and destroy the vitamins in the wheat germ; however, stone-ground flour does not keep as well, so do not buy more than a month's supply at a time and keep it in a cool place. Wholewheat flour makes a dense loaf with the warm earthy taste of the wheat. For a less heavy loaf, mix wholewheat flour half and half with strong plain flour or with 80 per cent strong plain flour. For wholewheat pastry, sift the flour first and use the fine part to make the dough. Then when the dough is kneaded and ready for shaping, roll it in the remaining particles of bran.

Wheatmeal and brown flours Flours from which some of the bran and germ have been removed, leaving behind between 80 and 90 per cent of the grain. The resulting flour is lighter in texture than wholewheat flour and so produces a less dense dough. Loaves made from a strong wheatmeal flour rise well, have a smooth crust and still retain some of the sweet nutty taste of the wheat. Soft wheatmeal flour makes good biscuits and scones and can be used for pastry.

Strong plain white flour Usually a blend of soft and hard wheats, this contains virtually none of the grain's bran or germ. However, in the UK refined flours are required by law to be fortified, so some of the lost nutrients are restored during processing. This type of flour is suitable for all yeast baking because its high gluten content gives a stronger crumb structure, and it produces excellent loaves, buns and pizza dough. It is also good for puff and flaky pastry.

Unbleached flour has been allowed to whiten and mature naturally, and has a creamy colour and a better flavour than the bleached variety, which has been whitened artificially.

Plain flour This is the refined and bleached product of soft wheat. Soft wheat flours produce only a small amount of gluten and so give a light, short texture in baking. They are particularly good for cakes, biscuits and shortcrust pastry but are not recommended for yeast baking.

Self-raising flour This is plain flour mixed with baking powder and salt. These chemicals will gradually lose their potency, so it is best to use up a bag of self-raising flour within 2 or 3 months. Use it for making cakes, scones, sponge puddings and suet crusts.

All-purpose flour In the United States, strong plain white flour and plain flour are replaced by this one encompassing all-purpose product. It is milled and refined from a blend of medium to strong wheats. As its name suggests, it is suitable for all types of cooking, from bread to sponge cakes, and for coating and thickening.

Type 00 This Italian flour is the one experts recommend for making pasta dough. It is now available in many supermarkets as well as delicatessens and Italian food shops.

Spelt

This ancient cereal grain, related to wheat, has become popular recently as it is easily digestible and very nutritious, and can be tolerated by people who are allergic to wheat. Apart from baking, spelt is used in soups and stews, and can be cooked like rice.

Corn

Once the generic term for all grains, corn has come to mean maize, and is second in importance only to wheat. There are countless varieties: hard, soft, golden, white, red, or purple.

Popcorn This is a particular variety of maize with hard kernels. When heated, the kernels burst and turn inside out.

Hominy An old Native American name for hulled and dried white or yellow corn. It can be bought either dried or cooked, in cans. The dried grains must be soaked overnight before use. Hominy is also available ground and is then known as hominy grits. The whole grains are cooked and eaten as a side dish, as well as being added to stews. Finer ground grits are used in cakes and puddings and to give body to stews.

Cornmeal, maizemeal, polenta

Ground from white, yellow or blue corn, this is available in coarse and medium grinds. The best cornmeal is ground by the old millstone method, but it does not keep as well as cornmeal ground by more modern processes, so should be bought in smaller quantities and kept in a cool place or the refrigerator.

In the south of France, cornmeal is mixed with wheat flour to make various rough, flattish loaves. The traditional northern Italian dish of polenta is made by boiling coarse or medium ground yellow or white cornmeal until it becomes a supple porridge; this is served soft, or set and then sliced for frying or grilling.

In the United States there are a number of traditional cornmeal dishes such as jonnycakes, deep-fried hush puppies and cornbread. The tortillas of Central America are made from *masa harina* – a fine cornmeal ground from white maize that is soaked in limewater.

corn oil 112
sweetcorn 142
tortilla 120

Corn Bread 362
Fresh Egg Pasta 332
Grilled Polenta with Poached Eggs, Fontina and Chive Cream 352
Soft Polenta with Butter and Parmesan 352
Tuscan Pasta 332

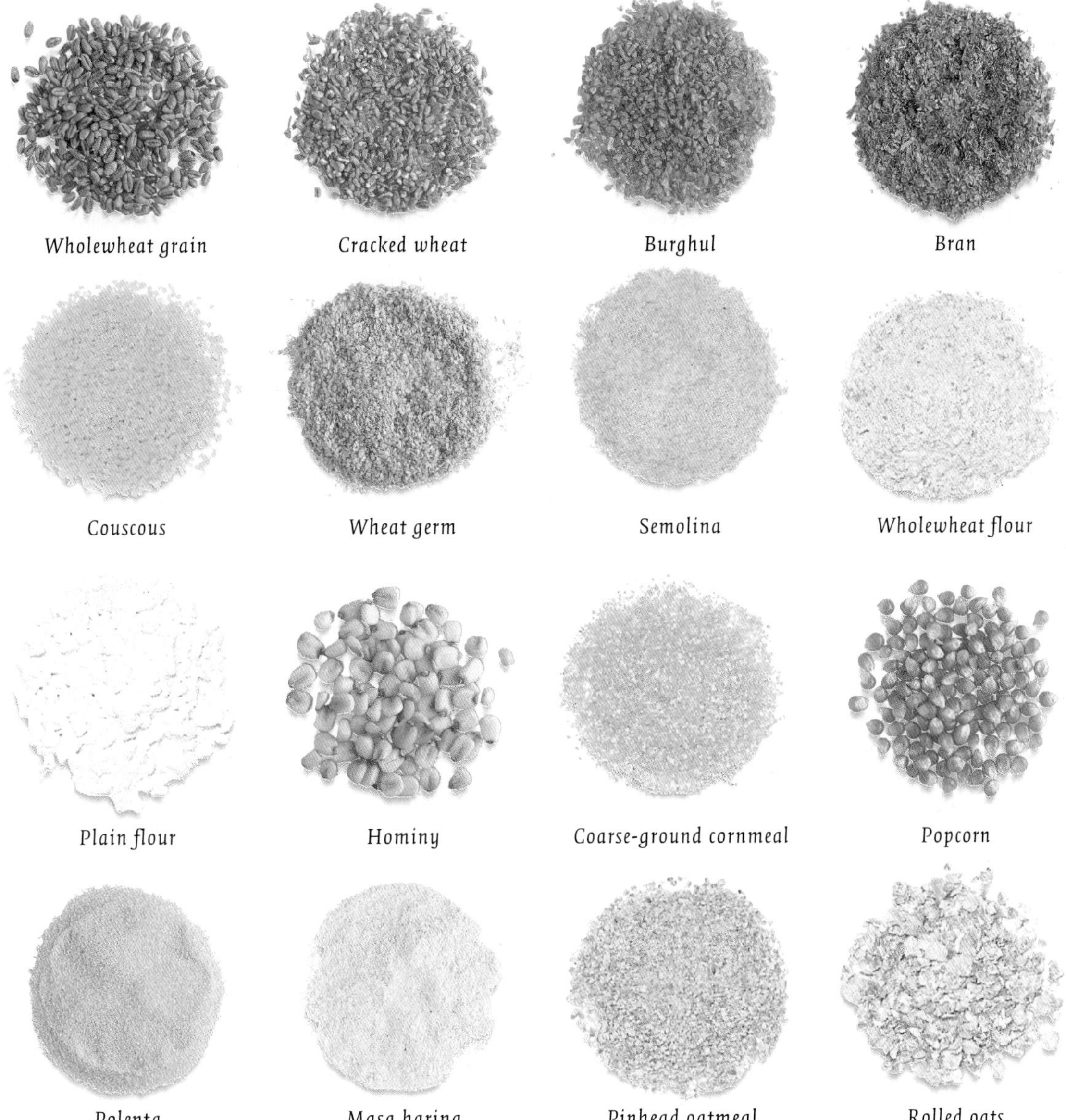

Wholewheat grain · *Cracked wheat* · *Burghul* · *Bran*

Couscous · *Wheat germ* · *Semolina* · *Wholewheat flour*

Plain flour · *Hominy* · *Coarse-ground cornmeal* · *Popcorn*

Polenta · *Masa harina* · *Pinhead oatmeal* · *Rolled oats*

black pudding 74
haggis 74
pumpernickel bread 119
rye bread 119
Scandinavian crispbreads 120

Brown Rice Pilau 346
Flapjacks 414
Herrings in Oatmeal 267
Rye Bread 359

Cornflour The white heart of the maize kernel, ground to a silken powder. In the US it is known as cornstarch. Used primarily as a thickening agent, it can also be added to cakes, shortbread and biscuits to give a fine-textured result. A little cornflour added to an egg custard will stop it from curdling.

Oats

These are among the most nutritious of all cereal grains. Being rich in oils oats soon become rancid, so do not buy more oats or oat products than you can use in about 3 weeks, and store in a cool place.

Oatmeal This comes in three grades: pinhead or coarse, medium and fine. The coarser the meal, the longer it will take to cook. Medium oatmeal is traditionally used to make porridge. It is also used to give bulk to sausages and haggis, and can be added to wheat flour when making bread. Pinhead oatmeal is good in thick soups and stews. Fine oatmeal is used in baking oatcakes, scones and biscuits. Fine-grade meal is also used to make oatmeal pancakes and is good for flouring herrings before they go into the frying pan.

Rolled oats, oakflakes, porridge oats These oats have been steamed and flattened between rollers, a process that makes them quicker to cook. Porridge takes only 10 minutes to make when using rolled oats. They are also used to make English flapjacks – sticky, chewy, teatime biscuits. Uncooked or toasted rolled oats are the main ingredient of the Swiss breakfast cereal, muesli.

Rye

This strong-flavoured, hardy grain is particularly popular in Scandinavia, Russia and Germany.

Whole rye kernels, rye berries These are the whole kernels with only the tough outer hull removed. Boiled until tender, they can be added to stews or mixed with rice.

Rye flour Widely used in bread making in many parts of Europe, this makes a rather heavy, distinctive loaf. Coarse-ground dark rye flour goes into pumpernickel bread, and more finely ground dark rye flour is used for European and Russian black breads. Light-coloured rye breads are made with rye flour and wheat flour mixed. European rye breads are traditionally made with a starter of fermented or sour dough. Rye flour is also used to make crispbreads.

Barley

Although more widely used for brewing than eating, barley has a pleasant nutty taste and can be cooked in a variety of ways.

Pot barley, Scotch barley The whole grain with only the outer hull removed, this requires overnight steeping and several hours' cooking. Eat it like rice or add it to stews.

Pearl barley The polished grain, this is more widely available than pot barley. It will cook to tenderness in about 1½ hours. It is traditionally used in Scotch broth, to which it adds body and a smooth taste. In Ireland it is cooked in buttermilk and eaten as a dessert with treacle.

Barley meal and barley flour The first is ground pot barley, the second is ground pearl barley. Both can be added to wheat flour when making bread.

Rice

At least a third of mankind eats rice as its staple food. There is an enormous number of varieties, each with its own special properties, and it is important to choose the right variety of rice for the right dish.

Brown rice Any rice that has been hulled but has not lost its bran is called brown rice. To the regret of dieticians, polished white rice is usually preferred to brown rice, which contains more nutrients, particularly vitamin B, a deficiency of which causes beriberi. Brown rice is available in short, medium and long grains. Long and medium grains are best eaten as a vegetable, or as a basis for a pilaf. Short grains are delicious in puddings. You may need to cook less brown rice as it is rather more filling than its white counterparts, and it takes longer to cook.

Patna rice This has a long, milk-white grain. It can either be cooked in plenty of salted boiling water for up to 15 minutes, until just tender, or cooked as for

Patna rice

Short-grain rice

Brown rice

Wild rice

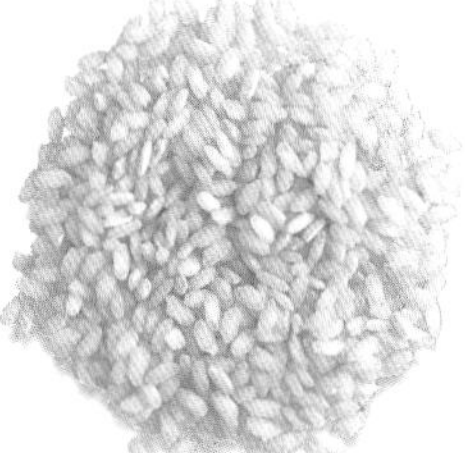
Arborio rice

Basmati rice

Glutinous rice

basmati rice. The centre of each grain, when cooked, should have a slight resistance but no hint of chalkiness. Patna, cooked to perfection, produces a beautiful mound of separate grains, good for pilafs, salads, stuffings and all dishes where the rice is served dry.
Converted rice This is steam-treated long-grain white rice. It is more nutritious than one might think, because it is processed before it is hulled and so has the chance to absorb the bran's nutrients before this is discarded.
Basmati rice Available in Asian food stores and many supermarkets, this is a superior long-grain rice. It is slightly more expensive than patna, but its better flavour and consistency is well worth the extra cost. Before cooking, it sometimes needs to be carefully picked over for any bits of grit and husk and should then be rinsed thoroughly under cold running water to remove excess starch.

Basmati consistently produces good results if cooked in the following way: add one part rice to three parts cold salted water, bring to boiling point, stir, cover the pan and turn down the heat until the water is barely simmering. After 12–15 minutes the rice will have absorbed all the water and, when forked up, the grains will be beautifully dry and separate. It is ideal for pilaus and as a filling and soothing foil for highly spiced Indian dishes.
Thai fragrant rice This aromatic long-grain rice is similar to basmati.
Short-grain rice, pudding rice
This is, in fact, a shortish version of long-grain species. When cooked, the grains swell enormously without disintegrating. They are very suitable for milk puddings, whether baked in the oven until caramel coloured within and brown on top, as in England, or cooked plain on top of the stove and served with sugar and cinnamon as in Germany. In Switzerland the cooked rice is blended with whipped cream and layered with black cherries. These types of rice are also suitable for making moulds and stuffings.
Italian risotto rice This rice has medium-short, roundish grains that are either white or creamy in colour. Varieties include Arborio, which is widely available, Carnaroli and Vialone Nano. Their special asset is that their grains can absorb a great deal of liquid over a long period without becoming soft and mushy. This, and their distinctive flavour, makes them ideal for risottos as well as for any dish such as paella or jambalaya that needs long, gentle cooking. Italian rice is an excellent vehicle for strong-flavoured foods such as squid, white truffles and wild mushrooms.
Glutinous rice Much used in Oriental cooking, this short-grain rice has fat, round, pearly white grains that cook into a sticky mass. It must be soaked overnight before steaming or cooking in water. Black glutinous rice, with its nutty flavour, is used in South-east Asian desserts. Glutinous rice is also ground into flour, to be used for sweet dumplings, cakes and pastries, and it is fermented to make low-alcohol wines, such as the Japanese sake and mirin and Chinese shaoxing, as well as rice vinegar.
Wild rice Grown in North America, this is actually the seed of an aquatic grass related to the rice family. Wild rice is expensive, but it has a distinctive, nutty flavour not to be missed. To cook it, bring to the boil in salted water, then cover and simmer for 45–60 minutes or until the grains are just starting to open. Serve plain or in salads, or mix into stuffings for poultry and game birds.
Ground rice Ground from polished grains, this can be purchased loose or, more usually, packaged. Cook with milk for a fine-textured dessert or add it to a shortcake mixture for extra crunchiness.
Rice flour This is polished white rice very finely ground to a silky consistency. Health-food shops also sell a coarser, off-white rice flour ground from brown rice. A little rice flour can go into a walnut or hazelnut cake of the type that uses no flour, only grated nuts, and is a useful thickener for dishes that are to be deep frozen (wheat-flour-thickened sauces are prone to separating when reheated after freezing).

Buckwheat

Also known as saracen corn or beechwheat, buckwheat, a plant related to sorrel and rhubarb, grows in great

rice flour 118
rice vinegar 205
rice wine (cooking with alcohol) 208–9

Asparagus Risotto 349
Chicken Liver Risotto 348
Moors and Christians 354
Mushroom Risotto 348
Paella 346
Pilau Rice 346
Plain Boiled Rice 346
Prawn and Fennel Risotto 348
Risotto alla Milanese 348

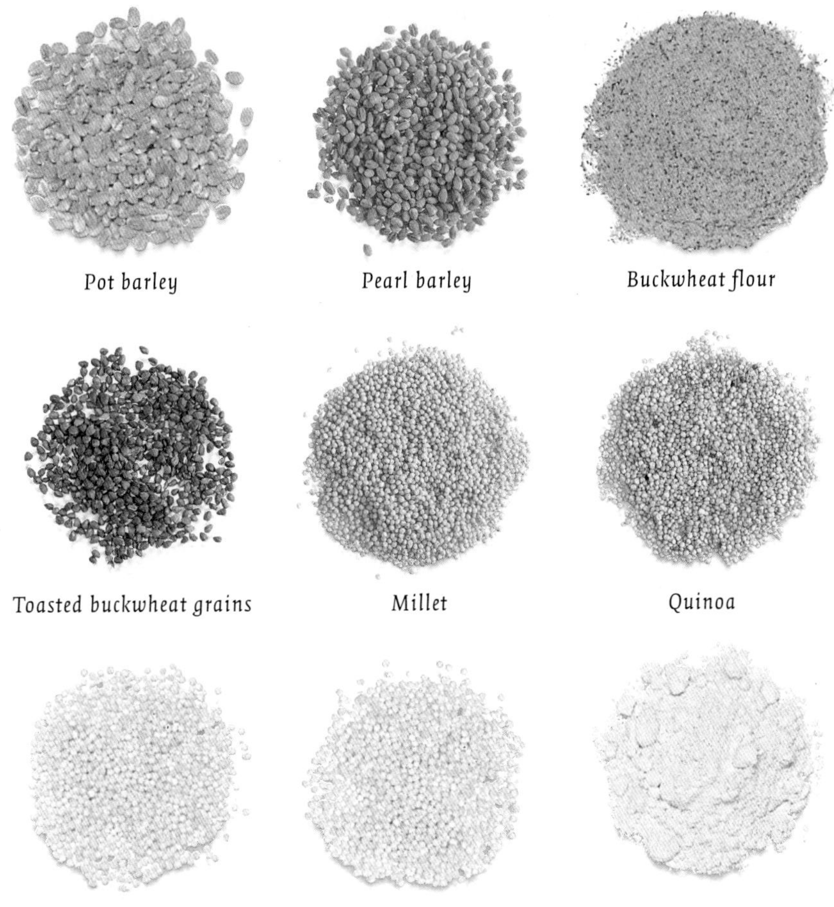

Pot barley *Pearl barley* *Buckwheat flour*

Toasted buckwheat grains *Millet* *Quinoa*

Sago *Tapioca* *Chick-pea flour*

beurre manié 422
buckwheat pasta 123, 125
cassava 147
caviare 31–2
making beurre manié 423
rhubarb 174
roux 423
self-raising flour 114
sorrel 133
sour milk 100

Buckwheat Kasha 351
Indian Millet 351

quantities in north-eastern Europe. The grains, or berries, are sold whole or ground – coarse, medium or fine – and may be toasted or untoasted. When toasted they have a nutty flavour. The grains are used to make a porridge-like dish called kasha, a staple in Russian and Central European cookery. Kasha is perfect with goose and a comforting dish for eating in cold weather. Buckwheat is the correct flour to use for making Russian blini – small, speckled, yeast-risen pancakes that are eaten with caviare. It is also used to make crêpes and can be added to other, lighter flours when making bread. A buckwheat polenta is made in northern Italy.

Millet and sorghum

These are closely related, and are invariably sold shelled because the husk is extremely hard. Their greatest characteristic is that they swell enormously – at least five parts water are needed to one part millet or sorghum. Both have a blandish, slightly nutty taste. They are best cooked and eaten like rice, but bear in mind that a small handful produces a large helping. To reduce cooking time, toast the grains a little in a dry, heavy pan on top of the stove before putting them in the pot to boil. Millet can be toasted, and made, like buckwheat, into kasha, which is excellent with sour cream to accompany chicken. Millet and sorghum flours produce flattish breads.

Quinoa

This tiny South American grain is a healthy addition to the diet, being higher in unsaturated fats and lower in cholesterol than most other grains and being very rich in nutrients. Rinse it well, then cook it like rice and use it in dishes where its subtle, delicate flavour can provide the background for more assertive flavours, just as rice and couscous do.

Sago and tapioca

The starch obtained from the stem of the South-east Asian sago palm, sago is usually exported in pearled form. In Asia and Europe it comes in varying sizes and consists purely of starch. It is most commonly made into sweet milk puddings, which are thought to be easily digestible and so are fed to children and the elderly. In Norway sago is made into a soup with sugar, egg and sherry.

Tapioca, prepared from the tuberous roots of the tropical cassava plant, or manioc, is as tasteless and starchy as sago, and comes both pearled and powdered. Pearled, it is made into creamy milk puddings, while the powder is used as a thickener.

THICKENING AGENTS

All starchy meals and flours will, in the presence of heat and moisture, act as thickeners. They cannot be used indiscriminately, but the cook can experiment with the two broad categories. Finer flours, before being mixed with the liquid to be thickened, must first be blended to a lump-free paste with a little of the liquid or with some butter, to make a roux or beurre manié.

As an alternative to plain flour for thickening soups, stews, gravies and other dishes, try using something more robust, such as fine-ground cornmeal or wholemeal, sorghum, barley or chick-pea flour. These will add flavour and colour as well as body. If you have none of these at hand, a crustless slice of bread or a boiled potato, blended with a little of the liquid, will work too. Chick-pea flour, also known as gram flour or besan, makes a very good batter and is used to make *pakoras*, spicy little Indian fritters.

Fécule is the general French name for starchy powders used in cooking. It is usually associated with potato flour, which is the thickening agent used by cooks in many European countries when making soups and gravies. The other very fine, quick-thickening flours, such as cornflour, arrowroot, tapioca flour and rice flour, are all virtually tasteless. They have double the thickening power of wheat flour, turn translucent when cooked, and are suitable for thickening delicate chicken or game dishes and sauces to accompany sweetbreads. Arrowroot and potato flour are particularly suitable for thickening fruit sauces because they turn completely clear when cooked.

Arrowroot has the added advantage of being ideal for cooking at low temperatures – an advantage when making sauces that contain egg. Take care not to overcook these fine flours as they have a tendency to lose their thickening power.

Yeast and baking powders

When buying flour for baking you will probably also need a raising agent such as yeast for bread, pizza dough and buns, and baking powder for scones and cakes.

Fresh yeast A pale beige, pasty substance, this should be solid but crumble easily, and it should have a clean, sweet, fruity smell. It will keep for a couple of weeks in the refrigerator and for several months if stored in the freezer; if frozen it will need to be thawed thoroughly and brought back to room temperature before it is used.

Dried granular yeast This has virtually replaced fresh yeast. It will keep for several months if stored in a cool, dry place, but it needs a warmer liquid than fresh yeast in which to dissolve. Never use more of this yeast than the recipe calls for or you will find that you have a coarse, sour loaf that will quickly go stale. Easy-blend dried yeast does not have to be dissolved in liquid but can be mixed directly with the dry ingredients.

Brewer's yeast Old cookery books called for brewer's yeast, or ale barm, which was bought at breweries or skimmed off the top of home-made beer and was very temperamental. The brewer's yeast sold these days for home brewing is, however, not suitable for baking purposes.

Baking powder This combines acid (such as cream of tartar) and alkaline (bicarbonate of soda) substances that act together when they come in contact with moisture to create carbon dioxide bubbles; these expand during baking to give a fine, delicate-textured result. Baking powder is sold in airtight containers, and great care should be taken to keep it dry because any hint of moisture will set the chemicals working. When adding the milk or water to a baking powder and flour mixture, work quickly so that the resulting carbon dioxide does not have a chance of escaping. Double-acting baking powder, widely available in North America, is easier to use because it reacts in two stages: first when it is combined with a liquid and then later when it is exposed to the heat of the oven. You can make your own baking powder: use equal quantities of bicarbonate of soda and cream of tartar if sour milk is in the mixture; otherwise use half the quantity of soda to cream of tartar.

Bicarbonate of soda This will work alone as a raising agent in a recipe that

includes an acid ingredient such as buttermilk or orange juice.
Cream of tartar A fine white powder crystallized from grape acid, this is an ingredient of some baking powders. A pinch helps increase the volume and stability of whisked egg whites.
Salt of hartshorn Chemically imitated these days with ammonium carbonate, this is used in Scandinavian countries as a baking powder to produce light biscuits with a crisp texture.

BREADS

The qualities of the plain white loaf are, of course, proper for such things as croûtons, Melba toast and English bread sauce, but there is a host of other breads, of completely different tastes and textures.

French bread, which is most often seen in long sticks or baguettes, has a hard, crisp crust and a wide-holed crumb. When made in the authentic French manner it will only keep a few hours, but it is bread at its very best. A thick slice, plain or toasted, is often floated in soups and consommés.

Malt loaf, a dark, moist, sweet bread, enriched with syrup and malt extract, often comes wrapped and may contain raisins. It is splendid eaten with butter and jam, and keeps well for days.
Light rye bread, with a satisfying sour flavour, is popular for sandwiches, particularly in the United States where it is filled with roast beef, salt beef, pastrami, or ham and cheese. It is also good with smoked fish.
Dark rye bread, pumpernickel and vollkornbrot A dark rye loaf, with its hard, thick crust, will keep fresh for a week or more, while pumpernickel and vollkornbrot (a slightly lighter variety) lose their moisture quickly – they are best wrapped in foil and stored in a cool place. They should all be sliced very thinly and are good served as open sandwiches, with smoked ham, cheese or smoked fish.
Bagel These ring-shaped rolls, which are boiled before baking, are a Jewish speciality. They are particularly good when filled with plenty of cream cheese and smoked salmon. There are endless varieties of these shiny, chewy rolls, including onion and poppy seed.

Croissant These soft doughy crescents, which are such an essential part of the French breakfast, are made from a rich dough of milk and flour interleaved with butter. Eat hot with butter and jam, or plain with a cup of good coffee.
Brioche These are rich, feather-light little loaves with a crisp golden crust, made from a dough of milk, water, eggs and butter; they also come as large loaves. Eat warm with butter and jam, sliced and toasted, or hollowed out and stuffed with sautéed mushrooms or pâté de foie gras.
English muffin Popular in the United States for breakfast or brunch, these are pulled or 'forked' in half and toasted. Toppings may be sweet or savoury.
Crumpet These should be first toasted on the underside and then on the holey top. Eat hot and dripping with butter.
Bap These soft, floury breakfast rolls from Scotland are eaten straight from the oven, split and spread with butter.
Pitta or pita bread, originally from the Middle East, is only slightly leavened and forms flat, hollow rounds or ovals that look like oriental leather slippers. Eaten hot, they are sometimes cut in half and

buttermilk 98, 100
making breadcrumbs 364
rye 116

bread knife 222
bread machine 239

Bread and Butter Pudding 394
Brioche Loaf 359
Eggs Benedict 323
Malt Loaf 362
Marmalade Queen of Puddings 395
Mozzarella in Carrozza 330
Pain Perdu 364
Pan Catalan 364
Rye Bread 359

Brioche
English muffin
Crumpet
Bagel
Croissant
Scandinavian crispbread
Pumpernickel
Pretzel
Naan
Rye bread

masa harina 115
rye 116

Hummus with Tahina 353
Melba Toast 364
Taramasalata 275

filled with grilled lamb and salad. They are always eaten plain with Greek meals, at which it is customary to tear off a bit at a time to use as a scoop for hummus and taramasalata.

Ciabatta, an Italian slipper-shaped bread with a soft, chewy crust, is excellent freshly baked with salads, soups and pasta dishes. It can also be used for sandwiches, particularly those with Italian-inspired fillings.

Focaccia, thought to be Italy's oldest bread, is usually shaped into a flattened round or slab. It was traditionally baked on a hot stone in a wood-fired hearth. The bread can be simply flavoured with salt and herbs or other toppings such as sautéed vegetables, garlic, olives, chopped tomatoes and cheese can be added before baking.

Tortilla The dough for this very thin, round Mexican unleavened bread is made either with *masa harina* or with wheat flour, and it is rolled out and baked on a griddle. Corn tortillas are deep-fried and filled to make *tacos*, or simply fried until crisp to make *tostadas*. Plain wheat tortillas are eaten hot to accompany a main course, or they are filled with meat and vegetables and rolled or folded to make *enchiladas, fajitas, quesadillas*, etc.

Chapati Indian unleavened bread made from *atta* – fine-ground wholewheat flour – chapatis are eaten hot with curries and many Indian savoury dishes, being torn into pieces and used to pick up the food.

Puri This is a deep-fried, puffy chapati. Buy and eat as for chapati.

Paratha is a shallow-fried, butter-enriched unleavened Indian bread.

Naan Teardrop shaped, this rich, leavened Indian bread is traditionally slapped on the side of a charcoal tandoori oven to cook.

Crispbreads

There is a huge array of crispbreads – and their relatives – on the market, ranging from rusks to water biscuits. There are a few varieties, however, which deserve special mention.

Scandinavian crispbreads are generally made from rye. They are popular with slimmers because rye is the most filling cereal grain and so gives one a feeling of satisfaction with relatively few calories. These can be eaten spread with almost anything – sweet or savoury. Available in light and dark varieties, they are sometimes sprinkled with sesame seeds.

Matzo This Jewish, crisp, unleavened flat bread, similar to water biscuits, is traditionally eaten during Passover. Matzos are especially good with cheese. They are completely unsalted.

Poppadom These wafer-thin Indian crisps are available plain or spiced, and need only to be grilled or deep fried for a few seconds. Eat immediately, broken up over curries or with drinks.

Pretzels, often studded with salt crystals, are available twisted into many shapes and sizes. They are usually crisp but some varieties are soft inside. Best served with drinks or as a snack; the soft ones are good with spicy mustard.

Breadsticks, known also by their Italian name, *grissini*, are long, thin sticks of bread with a fine texture, baked and dried until crisp. Eat with drinks, or accompanying an Italian meal instead of bread.

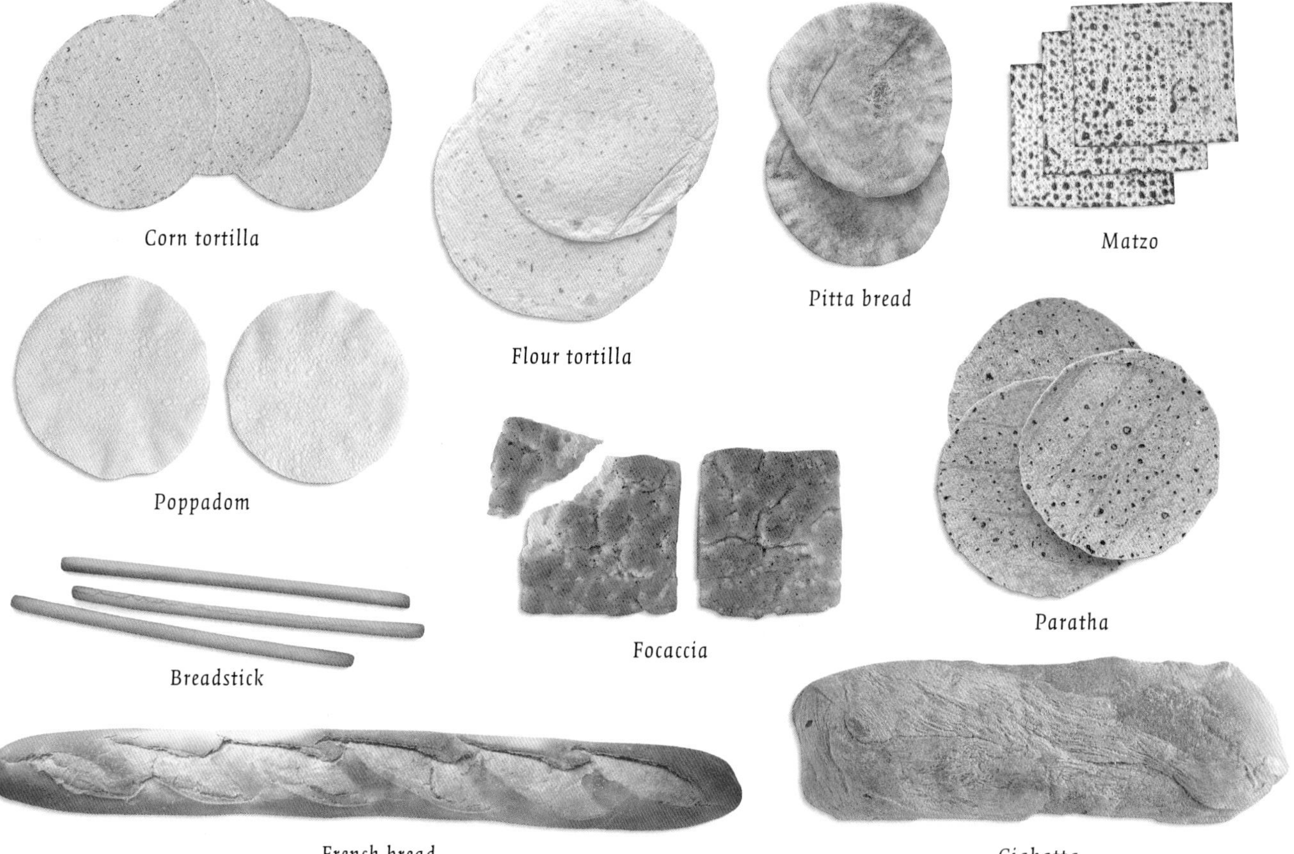

Corn tortilla

Flour tortilla

Pitta bread

Matzo

Poppadom

Focaccia

Paratha

Breadstick

French bread

Ciabatta

Pasta, Noodles and Dumplings

Six hundred or so pasta shapes are made in Italy – most Italians rely on a daily supply of pasta in one form or another to keep up their spirits. Many other types of pasta come from China and Japan, where noodles and stuffed dumplings are an important and ancient part of these classic cuisines.

Pasta

Records show that the Chinese were eating pasta as long ago as the Shang dynasty, some 3,500 years ago, and it was long believed, rather romantically, that Marco Polo brought pasta to Italy in the 1290s from the court of Kubla Khan. But Etruscan murals in Tuscany show all the kitchen equipment needed for pasta making, from the kind of wooden table still used to roll it on (so far laminated plastics have not replaced it in Italian households) to the fluted wheel with which to cut pappardelle, lasagne and ravioli. Even without the murals the story had been put in doubt by the estate of a military man who died in the thirteenth century, leaving among his effects a precious chest of *maccheroni*.

Whatever its origins, the Neapolitans have always been Italy's most serious pasta eaters, and Naples and the surrounding area have long been regarded as the centre of the dried pasta industry. Certainly the best flour for pasta making, milled from the extra hard wheat *Triticum durum*, comes from the hot, dry south. The resulting pasta absorbs the minimum of water as it cooks. The warm, dry, windy climate means, too, that spaghetti can be dried in the open air, swathed like curtains over long canes that are supported on tall stands – although with industrialization, modern factories have taken the place of the old traditional family enterprises.

When buying dried pasta look for that made in southern Italy, especially the Abruzzi, and make sure it is a clear yellow colour without any chalky greyish tinge. Thinner pastas should be translucent when held up to the light, with the exception of dried egg pastas, which should be a sunny bright yellow.

Most pastas can generally be described as long or short; round, tubular or flat; smooth or ridged; solid or hollow. An attempt to classify their shapes by name, however, is a problem, since one shape can have several different names and sizes. The north of Italy insists on one appellation, the south another, and even neighbouring regions cannot reach agreement. Miniature pastas, or *pastine*, which come in every shape possible, from stars to cars to apple pips, are in a category of their own. They can be made from egg pasta or plain pasta (without eggs), and are generally cooked and served *in brodo* – in chicken or beef broth.

The long, round, solid pastas that are coiled around the fork, such as vermicelli, spaghetti and spaghettini, are generally eaten dry (*asciutta*) with oil or butter, a tomato-based sauce or a seafood sauce. Meat sauces, with the exception of *ragù bolognese*, are not generally eaten with these as they do not cling to the pasta well. Short, hollow pastas, such as conchigliette, gnocchi, elbow macaroni, rigatoni or penne, are the ones to serve with meat because the pieces catch easily in the pasta.

The larger short, hollow pastas, such as cannelloni and manicotti, are usually boiled and then stuffed with cheese or meat before baking. Macaroni and rigatoni are sometimes boiled and then baked in a sauce in the oven, perhaps as part of a moulded shape called *timballo* which is among the oldest of all pasta dishes. Two egg pastas, lasagne and tagliatelle, can also be baked in this way, as can farfalle, conchiglie, ruote and lumachine.

Serve cream sauces with short, ridged, hollow pastas, since these catch the cream and do not slip off the fork. Tagliatelle and other flat fresh pastas are generally eaten with rich meat or vegetable sauces, and the same fresh pasta dough is used to make stuffed pastas such as ravioli, anolini, tortelloni, tortellini, conchiglie and lumachine.

Having said all this, of course, one can eat any pasta with any sauce and have a perfectly good meal.

Spaghetti This is the best known of all pastas and always comes in long, straight bundles. It is marketed in a number of widths that go under such names as cappellini, spaghettini, vermicelli, vermicelloni and thin or thick spaghetti. Fusilli is a spiral spaghetti, available in long and short lengths. The thicker ones are better with rich sauces while the thinner ones are better with plainer sauces.

Spaghetti has long been the traditional pasta of Naples, and the traditional way of eating it is still *alla napoletana* – first turned in oil and then topped with a ladleful of tomato sauce. Naples also eats its spaghetti *all'aglio e olio* – pasta bathed in olive oil and mixed with sautéed garlic. Grated *grana* cheese such as Parmesan or pecorino is served with all spaghetti except those with seafood additions such as spaghetti *alla vongole*. This is made with tiny clams and is another Neapolitan speciality, although it is enjoyed all over Italy.

Macaroni It is not known how the idea of making the tubular pasta called macaroni or *maccheroni* started. But the most likely theory is that someone wrapped a piece of rolled-out pasta around a filling, leaving the ends open.

Macaroni comes in an even greater range of sizes than spaghetti. Apart from the long variety, with boreholes that can be measured in millimetres, there are also those that can be measured in centimetres, culminating in cannelloni, but these are despised by purists as too modern an invention, designed solely to make filling our pasta easier. However, we ought to be grateful that we are not obliged, as was the composer Rossini, to fill our macaroni with the aid of a silver syringe. He is said to have used this for filling tubes of pasta with foie gras, for which he had a well-known passion.

Apart from cannelloni there are ribbed rigatoni mafalde, zite, tortiglioni, penne – cut like quills – and elbow macaroni – the curved, short lengths of macaroni used in baked pasta dishes.

Macaroni used to be virtually the only pasta known and loved by English-speaking countries. Called macrow, it had been eaten at the Court of Richard II of England. It fell into decline, but was rediscovered by eighteenth-century Englishmen on the Italian part of their grand tours and taken back to Britain. Soon macaroni cheese became an important high-tea dish, and it is still eaten by many families in Britain and North America.

Egg pasta In northern Italy, until recently, housewives made egg pasta, or *pasta all'uovo*, daily with eggs and flour. Emilia-Romagna, the area with the richest farming land in Italy, was

Chinese noodles 124–5
coloured and flavoured pasta 122
cooking pasta 335
Grana cheeses 103
Japanese noodles 125
lasagne 122
making pasta 332–5
nudels and nouilles 124
pasta recipes 332–45
pasta sauce recipes 335–6
pasta sauces 124
semolina 114
soup pasta 124
stuffed pasta 123
type 00 flour 115
wholewheat and buckwheat pasta 123

pasta machine 229, 239

Fresh Egg Pasta 332
Lido Pasta Salad 371
Tuscan Pasta 332
Vermicelli Milk Pudding with Cardamom and Saffron 395

macaroni 121
making pasta 332–5
pancetta 69
pasta sauces 124
soup pasta 124
spaghetti 121

pasta machine 229, 239

Fresh Egg Pasta 332
Lasagne al Forno 339
Lasagne with Mushrooms, Bacon and Artichokes 340
Ragù alla Bolognese 336
Tagliarini with Fresh Artichokes and Gremolata 338
Tagliatelle alla Panna 338
Tuscan Pasta 332

renowned for its beautiful hand-made pasta, and young women from that region were keenly courted by young men and their mothers for their pasta-making skills. Egg pastas are richer and lighter than ordinary pastas.

Pasta making is a craft, and to see an expert rolling out a golden circle of dough, as thin as fine suede, to the size of a small tablecloth is a wonderful experience. In Bologna, the gastronomic centre of Emilia-Romagna, you can watch it being made in a shop window. It is then turned into tortellini – little stuffed, folded-over pasta triangles – at lightning speed in front of your eyes.

Fresh pasta can be made at home, when it becomes known as *pasta casalinga*, either by hand or with a pasta machine (perfectionists say that the former is better since the machine squeezes the pasta and tends to give it a slippery surface that does not hold the sauce so well).

In fact, a great deal of the *pasta all'uovo* now eaten in Italy and elsewhere is made in factories, where by law it must contain five eggs to each kilo of flour. It is sold in nests or in skeins that loosen when boiled. Buy it wrapped in cellophane or loose, since boxed pasta is expensive. In addition, the size of the box often bears little relation to the contents, and it is impossible to see if the brittle pasta inside is whole or broken.

The best-known egg pasta is tagliatelle, or – as it is called in Rome – fettuccine: those golden strands that were supposed to have been inspired by the long blonde hair of Lucretia Borgia. In Bologna and Parma and all the other places of gastronomic pilgrimage with which northern Italy abounds, the tagliarini (thin tagliatelle) is still normally freshly rolled out every day. Malfatte (which means badly made) are irregular shapes of fresh pasta.

Tagliatelle is, of course, not only eaten *alla bolognese*, even in Bologna, but also *in bianco*, mixed with plenty of melted butter, freshly grated Parmesan and cream, or *al burro*, with the cream left out. Bologna also eats its tagliatelle mixed with strips of delicious sautéed pancetta, or bacon, and grated Parmesan.

Lasagne This can be bought in long, wide, flat strips or in curly-edged pieces that will not stick together as readily as flat pieces do when boiling. It can also be bought as squares, which are easier to fit into a baking dish. In Bologna strips of green lasagne or the narrower lasagnette are layered alternately with plain strips and with Bolognese sauce and rich creamy béchamel sauce. This dish is baked in the oven and emerges, glazed here and there with deep golden flecks, as *lasagne al forno*.

Coloured and flavoured pasta
Lasagne verde and tagliatelle verde prove that spinach has a special affinity with pasta. Both are widely available in this green form, coloured by a small amount of spinach purée that is worked into the dough. Other colourings and flavourings for pasta doughs include tomato purée,

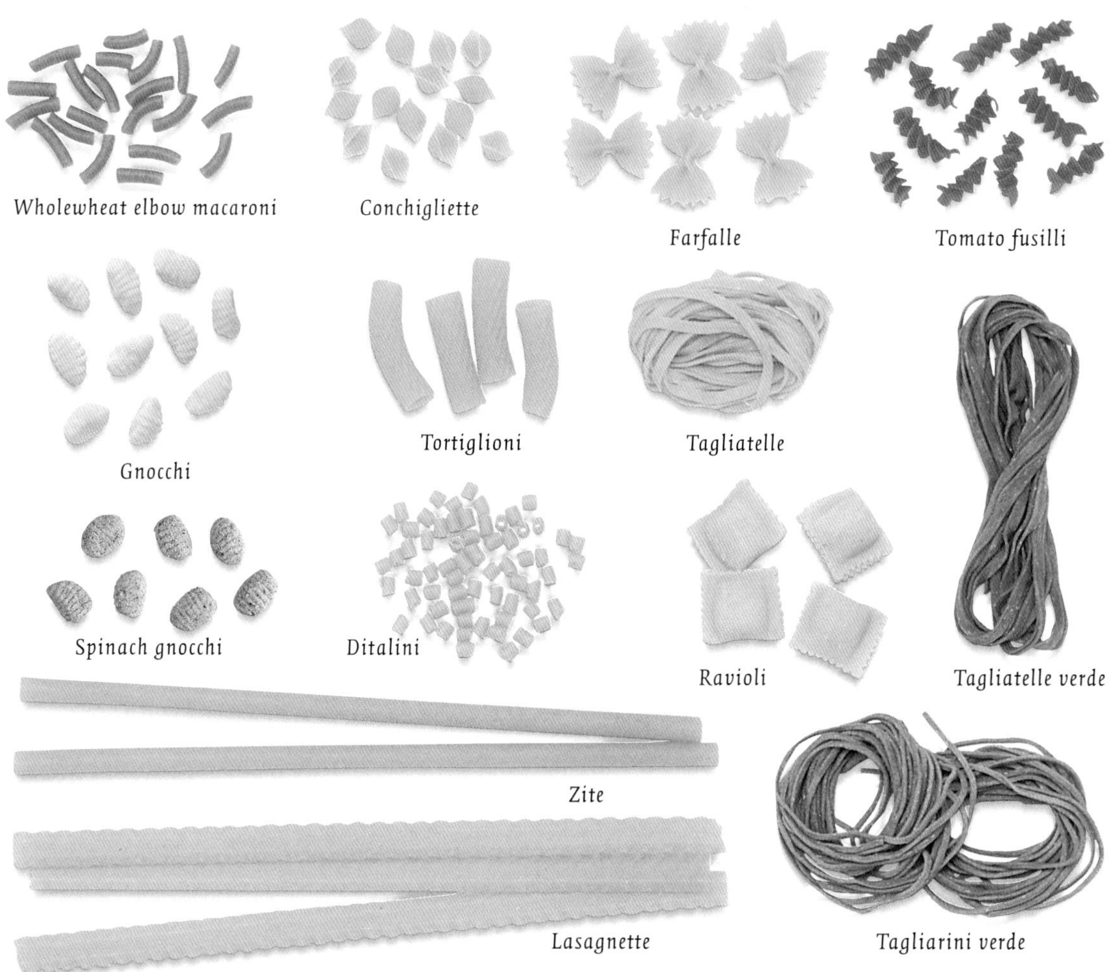

Wholewheat elbow macaroni, *Conchigliette*, *Farfalle*, *Tomato fusilli*, *Gnocchi*, *Tortiglioni*, *Tagliatelle*, *Spinach gnocchi*, *Ditalini*, *Ravioli*, *Tagliatelle verde*, *Zite*, *Lasagnette*, *Tagliarini verde*

saffron, squid ink, herbs and coarse-ground black pepper. Tuscany and Umbria make a pretty mixture of yellow and green tagliatelle or tagliolini, which is called *paglia e fieno*, meaning straw and hay. It is eaten with melted butter and cream and sprinkled with Parmesan.

Wholewheat and buckwheat pasta Although Venice has always had its thick wholewheat spaghetti called *bigoli*, it is not common throughout Italy. There are, however, some relative newcomers in the health-food shops, such as the buckwheat and wholewheat pastas.

Wholewheat lasagne and macaroni and buckwheat spaghetti are some examples. These have a nutty flavour and are richer in vitamins and minerals than the traditional pale pastas. They take longer to cook as they contain far more fibre than pale pasta. The Italian wholewheat pastas are, on the whole, lighter than those made elsewhere.

Wholewheat and buckwheat noodles also feature in Japanese cooking and are often eaten cold as a late afternoon snack.

Stuffed pasta Pasta stuffed with a large variety of finely minced or chopped fillings is eaten throughout Italy. Parmesan cheese and mortadella sausage with pork and veal, diced or pounded and mixed with minced turkey breast, provide the traditional stuffing for tortellini and tortelloni. These are the coiled half-moons that are the famous Bolognese version of ravioli; they are by custom eaten on Christmas Eve and for big celebrations. On these same occasions Perugia, in Tuscany, eats cappelletti, or little hats, whose stuffing includes finely minced veal and sweetbreads or brains. The hollowed shells called conchiglie or the larger

buckwheat flour 118
Japanese noodles 125
making ravioli 334
mortadella 75
wheat flours 114–15

ravioli cutter 225

Ravioli con Funghi Porcini 342
Spinach and Ricotta Ravioli 342

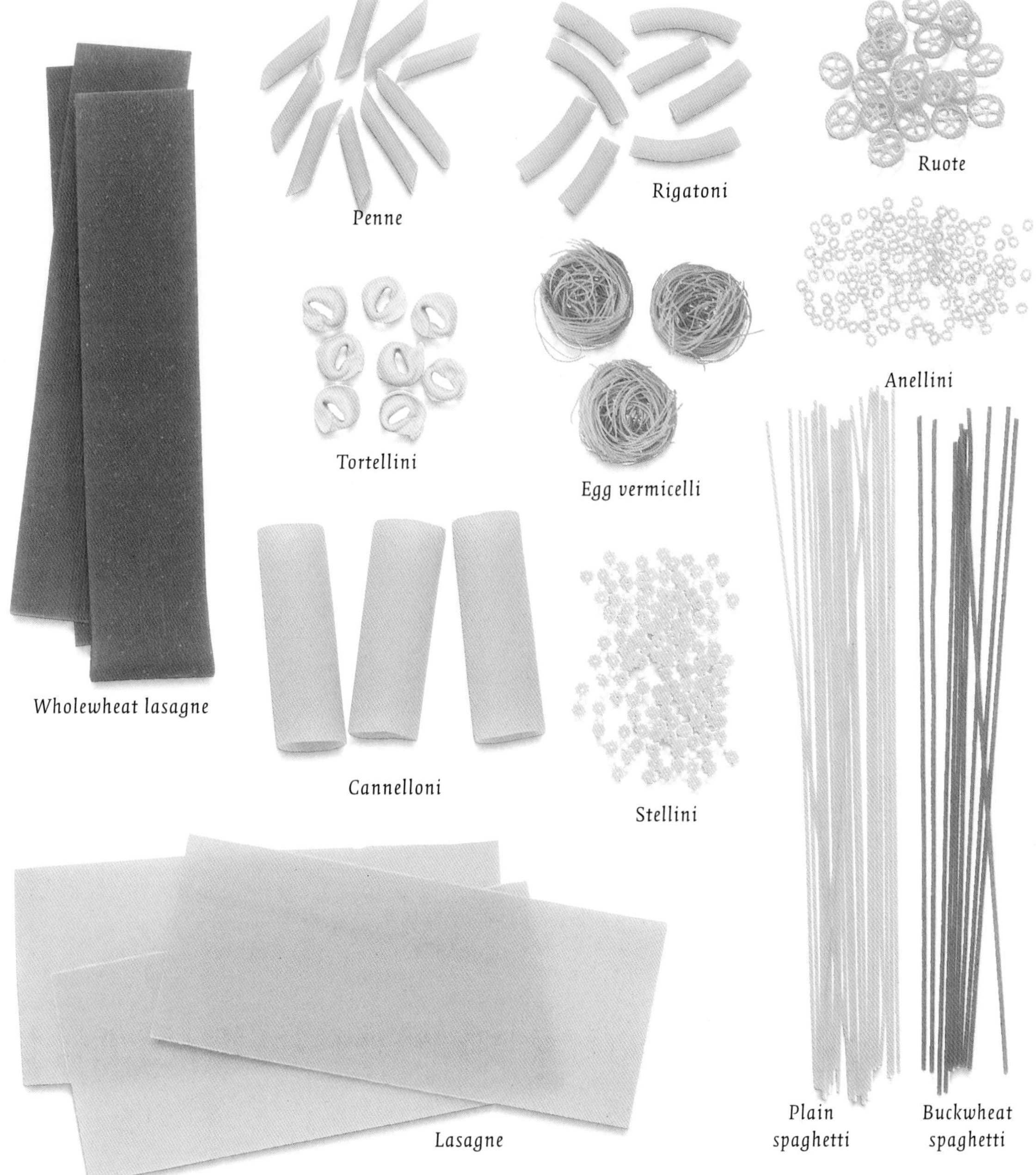

Penne

Rigatoni

Ruote

Anellini

Tortellini

Egg vermicelli

Wholewheat lasagne

Cannelloni

Stellini

Lasagne

Plain spaghetti

Buckwheat spaghetti

chard 140
coloured and flavoured pasta 122
egg pasta 121
lasagne 122
macaroni 121
pasta recipes 332–45
pecorino 103
ricotta 101
spaghetti 121
stuffed pasta 122
truffle 161
wholewheat and buckwheat pasta 122

Gnocchi Romana 344
Pasta e Fagioli 252
Pesto alla Genovese 336
Provençal Soupe au Pistou 250
Ragù Bolognese 336
Ribollita 252
Salsa di Pomodoro 335
Spaghetti alla Carbonara 337
Spinach Gnocchi with Butter and Sage 344
Sugo di Carne Toscano 336
Summer Minestrone 251

conchigloni and even lumache (the largest shells, whose name means 'snails') can also be stuffed.

Throughout the length and breadth of Italy ravioli with delicious spinach, beet greens or chard fillings are to be found. The chopped leaves are mixed with soft white cheese such as ricotta, with Parmesan or pecorino, bound with egg and flavoured with a touch of nutmeg or garlic depending on the local taste. They can also be stuffed with pumpkin or wild fungi, or even lobster.

Soup pasta If the dough and the basic shape of *pasta asciutta* are fairly consistent – allowing for a thousand and one small regional variations – the same cannot be said of soup pastas. The range is vast and includes anellini and stelline, which are used for serving *in brodo*, while the larger varieties such as farfalline, conchigliette and ditalini are used for making hearty soups such as minestrone or *pasta e fagioli*.

Italy garnishes its soups with tiny car radiators, cogs and wheels, with flying saucers, hats, boots, letters and numerals, all made of pasta. The more traditional shapes include grains of rice and melon seeds, twisted bow ties, butterflies, stars, crescent moons, seashells of every description, rings, hoops, elbow macaroni, and noodles that are thinner than matchsticks.

These garnishes are sometimes cooked separately and added to the soup just before serving, as they tend to shed a bit of their starch, which can make a clear broth cloudy.

Pasta sauces Pasta of one kind or another is the main part of most Italians' daily diet, and there are almost as many pasta sauces to be found as there are types of pasta.

All the classic pasta sauces have their origins in regional cookery, and they are made from whatever ingredients are readily to hand. Piedmont, with its famous white truffles, makes a delicious sauce of truffled chicken livers. Tuscany makes a richly flavoured sauce with hare. Pounded anchovy, truffles, garlic, tomatoes and onions go into the sauce that in Spoleto is used to make pasta *alla spoletina*. In Sorrento there is a sauce made of courgettes. Pesto, a mixture of fresh basil, pine nuts, garlic and Parmesan or pecorino, is served with linguine in Genoa, and when Tuscany offers a cream sauce with its tagliarini it saves the sauce from blandness by adding meat glaze.

Spaghetti alla carbonara, despite the story that it was created during World War II to please the Allied armies, with their vast appetites for eggs and bacon, is a traditional speciality of Rome. The sauce consists of pancetta mixed into spaghetti with some Parmesan and a raw beaten egg which partly sets in the heat of the pasta. The secret is not to drain the spaghetti too enthusiastically, otherwise the result will be dry.

In the Abruzzi and Molise regions of central Italy, a favourite sauce is made with lamb and green peppers, another with smoked pork and tomatoes. The pasta eaten here is *maccheroni alla chitarra* – long strands cut on a frame strung with wires like a guitar. In the Marches, black olives preserved in a special brine are incorporated into the sauces, not only for pasta made with the conventional dough but also for a local variation that is made with a yeast-like bread dough. Chick-peas also appear, in a pasta dish called thunder and lightning (*tuono e lampo*).

Towards the south, sauces include red peppers, green peppers and a fiery dash of ground chilli. Since the sea is not far from any spot in Italy, there are often marine accompaniments such as cockles and clams, and, in the Veneto region, a delicious black sauce that is made with squid ink.

Nudels, nouilles and dumplings

In the German-speaking countries, which are supposed to have introduced noodles into Italy in the Middle Ages, flat *nudels* have been eaten for centuries. They are often baked with sultanas and sweetened lemon-flavoured curd cheese and served as a pudding. In Alsace they are known as *nouilles* and are prepared in countless savoury and delicious ways. Coq au vin, for example, is often accompanied by *nouilles*, which are always better when fresh.

In Alsace we also find the ancestral dumpling known as *noque*, while farther south it appears under the name of *nockerln*. By whatever name, it is a pasta dumpling and can be eaten with a variety of sauces.

Gnocchi In Italy, the dumplings known as gnocchi are eaten in the same way as pasta and at the same point in the meal, but they are not strictly speaking pasta. There are several local variations, and they can be made from ricotta cheese and spinach, semolina, mashed potato or potato flour. They are usually poached in boiling salted water until cooked, when they rise to the surface. They are then served with a variety of sauces. Gnocchi are generally made fresh, the semolina variety being particularly easy to make.

Chinese dumplings and spring rolls Chinese dumplings or *wontons* are similar to the Italian ravioli. The delicate ingredients, finely minced and variously flavoured, are wrapped in squares of fine noodle dough. They may be purchased in Chinese supermarkets, but can be made at home in the same way as fresh pasta. The paper-thin wonton dough, cut into squares or rounds, can also be purchased. Boiled or steamed, wontons are often served floating in a clear broth.

One of the prettiest meals available during the day in a Chinese restaurant is *dim sum*, which is often presented in a towering pagoda of baskets. Each one fits into the other and contains bite-size morsels such as steamed buns, savoury pastries and dumplings containing pork, prawns or other meat or fish fillings. *Dim sum* is ideal for a light lunch.

Paper-thin wrappers are also used to make spring rolls, which are filled with a savoury mixture of shredded vegetables and sometimes meat or fish and then deep-fried.

Very thin, semi-transparent rice paper wrappers, or *báhn tráng*, are used to make Vietnamese and Thai spring rolls. The wrappers, which are dried on bamboo mats in the sun, need to be soaked briefly in warm water to soften them before rolling around the filling mixture.

Chinese noodles

Wheat flour, rice flour, arrowroot or ground mung beans are the main ingredients of Chinese noodles. They come in a variety of thicknesses and shapes, some of which can be used interchangeably, and are often tied in bundles or coiled into square packages. The majority, however, are long, as these are thought to symbolize and encourage long life.

Although most Chinese buy their noodles, some do make their own. Fresh noodles are obtainable from Chinese supermarkets and taste best when they are first parboiled and then steamed in a colander over boiling water. Once boiled or steamed, Chinese noodles become part of more elaborate preparations that often involve several cooking methods for one dish, including stir-frying.

Soup noodles These are traditionally served in broth with a topping of finely cut meat or seafood and bright, fresh-looking vegetables. The cooked noodles are put into the bottom of the bowl, the hot broth is poured over them and then the stir-fried meat or seafood and vegetables are added as the garnish.

In the north of China, where wheat is the primary grain, **wheat noodles**, with or without egg, are used. **Egg noodles** are often sold in little nests, while pure wheat noodles may be packaged like Italian spaghetti as well as in square-shaped nests. In the southern districts of China, where rice paddies abound, translucent white **rice noodles** are used. These range from square packets of coiled **rice sticks** to the thin thread-like **rice vermicelli** that comes tied in bundles. White **arrowroot vermicelli** is also available.

Bean thread noodles, also known as **transparent** or **cellophane noodles**, are made from ground mung beans. They are never served on their own, but are used in soups and in stir-fried or braised dishes, adding a distinctive slippery texture.

Fried noodles Crispy fried noodles, known as *chow mein*, are a Cantonese, speciality. Since many Chinese restaurants in the West are Cantonese, these are among the best known of all noodle dishes. They can either be flattened in a frying pan with plenty of seasoned oil and then turned like a pancake, or they can be fried gently with left-over vegetables and meat from a noodle and soup dish.

Bean thread noodles can also be fried if a crisp garnish is all that is required.

Sauced noodles In the West, where Chinese thickeners such as lotus root flour are not readily available, sauced noodles, or *lo mein*, are usually served in sauces thickened with cornflour. Since to the Chinese texture is just as important as taste, a crunchy element is often introduced to these sauces with matchstick slivers of bamboo shoots or crisp stalks of spring onions and leeks. Protein is provided by meat or chicken, shelled prawns or oysters. *Lo mein* and other noodle dishes are usually served at birthday celebrations, as noodles symbolize longevity.

Japanese noodles

There are four main types of Japanese noodle, all of which play an important part in the national cuisine.

Soba are thin, brownish noodles made from buckwheat flour. They are used in soups and sometimes served cold with a garnish.

Harusame are equivalent to the Chinese bean thread noodles and can be deep fried, or soaked and then cooked.

Somen are very fine white noodles – use vermicelli if somen are not available.

Udon are made from white flour and are more substantial.

bamboo shoot 140
buckwheat flour 118
buckwheat pasta 123
mung bean 128
rice flour 117

Chinese Egg Noodles with Browned Garlic, Chillies and Parsley 345
Japanese Noodles with Char-Grilled Beef 345

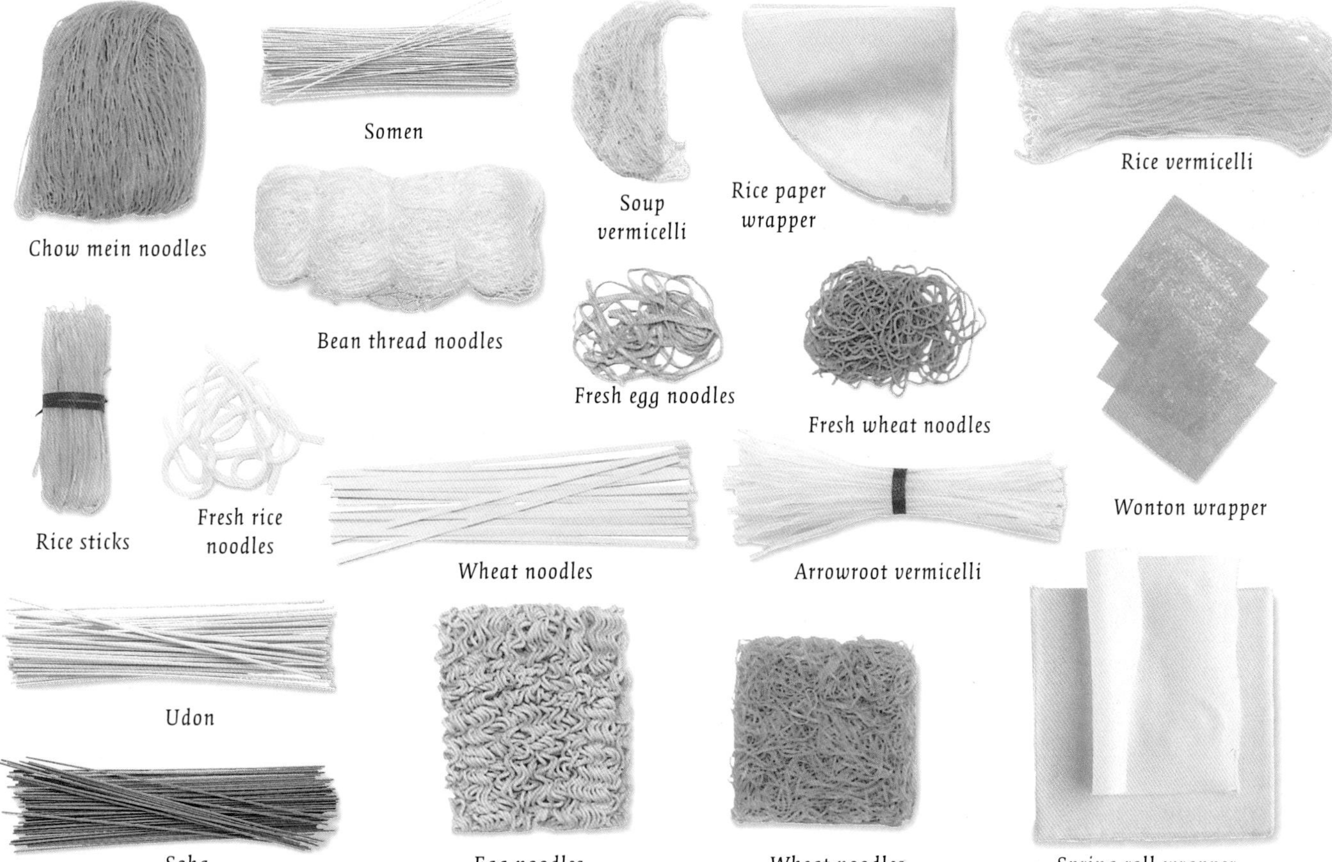

Somen · Chow mein noodles · Soup vermicelli · Rice paper wrapper · Rice vermicelli · Bean thread noodles · Fresh egg noodles · Fresh wheat noodles · Wonton wrapper · Rice sticks · Fresh rice noodles · Wheat noodles · Arrowroot vermicelli · Udon · Soba · Egg noodles · Wheat noodles · Spring roll wrapper

Dried Peas and Beans

cooking pulses 423
tortilla 120

Boiled Bacon and Sausage with Haricot Beans and Garlic Purée 291
Boston Baked Beans 354
Gigot d'Agneau with Haricot Beans 287
Moors and Christians 354
Provençal Soupe au Pistou 250

The dried seeds of podded plants were first popular many thousands of years ago. In Egypt, the pyramids have been found to contain little mounds of dried beans – not only to sustain departed pharaohs on their journey to the next world but also because Egyptians believed beans to be particularly helpful in conveying the soul to heaven.

Unfortunately, apart from being an excellent and sustaining food, very suitable for those about to embark on long journeys, beans have the annoying property of engendering flatulence. Perhaps this characteristic helped lead to their gradual banishment, after medieval times, from Europe's more elegant tables. Another probable reason for their steady decline in appeal was the greater availability of fresh vegetables at that time.

It was not until this century, when the Western world found a new taste for simple, sturdy, regional foods, that dried beans and peas were seriously rediscovered. A growing interest in Indian and Middle Eastern cooking brought Eastern species to Western shelves, and with them the Indian word *gram*, which is one of the collective names for dried beans and peas, particularly the chick-pea.

In Britain the collective name is pulse, originating from the ancient Roman word *puls*, meaning pottage, a thick stew.

Although thousands of species of beans and peas, botanically known as Leguminosae, now exist, they have many common characteristics. Flavour and mealiness may vary, but all have a straightforward earthy taste and satisfying sturdy quality. All are a rich source of protein and, being a healthy and body-building form of food, make a very sound substitute for meat, especially when combined with cereals. Hence their label 'poor man's meat'.

A popular misconception is that dried peas and beans have an indefinite shelf life. In fact, they should not be stored longer than a year for they toughen with age and become difficult to cook. There are two methods of preparing them, both of which help to clean and tenderize them. The most common method is overnight soaking, preferably in soft water, to which all dried peas and beans respond. The dried peas and beans that are prepared for supermarkets are usually quite clean, but it's still best to pick over them for stones or debris. The alternative to overnight soaking, useful when you are short of time, is the quick-soak method: put them into a pan of cold, unsalted water, bring to the boil, then simmer for 5 minutes. Cover the pan, remove it from the heat and allow the peas or beans to cool. Then drain thoroughly and cook them in whatever way the recipe calls for.

All these vegetables should be cooked in soft water – a pinch of bicarbonate of soda will soften hard water – and simmered rather than rapidly boiled. Unless very fresh, they require lengthy cooking. They should be salted towards the end of cooking – if salted at the outset, the skins will split and the insides will harden. A little fat in with the cooking water – salt pork, bacon or oil – improves the texture of all dried peas and beans. When bought canned rather than loose or packaged, they are already cooked and only need rinsing and draining before heating.

Haricot bean The word haricot covers the botanical species of beans *Phaseolus*. It derives from medieval times when dried beans were used chiefly to go into a pot containing a *haricot* or *halicot* of meat – meaning simply that the meat was cut in chunks for stewing. When English and French cookbooks specify haricots, what is meant are white beans, smooth and oval rather than kidney shaped. In the United States they are known, sensibly enough, as white beans.
Soissons, large and white, are generally considered the finest haricot beans. They originated in northern France, but are used to greatest effect in the famous regional dish cassoulet, from Toulouse, cooked with preserved goose, mutton and sausage.
Flageolets, in a semi-dried state, are an important ingredient in another classic French dish, *gigot d'agneau*, but in England they are found only dried. They are a delicate pale green with a subtle flavour.
Cannellini are Italian haricot beans, slightly fatter than the English or French ones. They are popular in Tuscany in various soups and in dishes such as *tonno e fagioli* – served cold with tuna fish in a garlicky vinaigrette.
Navy bean, also known as Yankee beans, small and white, are very popular in the United States, particularly for making Boston baked beans. At one time, these small round beans were served by the US Navy, hence their name.

Butter bean Also known as lima beans, these can be large or small. They are highly prized when fresh, especially in America. The large dried bean easily becomes mushy when cooked and so is best used in soups and purées. When recipes for other dishes call for either haricot or butter beans, it is the smaller bean that should be used.

Red kidney bean Probably best known for their part in chilli con carne – which is not, as it happens, a true Mexican dish – red kidney beans are a staple in Central America. These are the beans that, with black beans, were cooked by the Central American Indians in their earthenware pots (still much the best receptacle for baked beans, which should never be decanted before serving).

After the introduction of lard from Spain, beans were often mashed, formed into a stiff paste and then fried to become *frijoles refritos* – still one of the most popular ways of eating beans in Mexico. In this form they may be used as an accompaniment to a main dish, or as a filling for *tacos* or *tostadas*, those crisply fried corn pancakes which are popular far beyond the borders of Mexico itself. Red kidney beans also appear in many dishes in New Orleans, particularly red beans and rice.

Black bean As well as being used interchangeably with red kidney and pinto beans to make *frijoles refritos*, black beans, also called turtle beans, with their glistening black skins and creamy flesh, are the staple of many soups and stews in South and Central America. There they are often baked with ham or other cured pork and flavoured with garlic, cumin and liberal amounts of chilli and they are an essential ingredient in *feijoada*, the Brazilian national dish. In the United States, black bean soup is a great favourite. The beans are cooked with a ham bone or hock, blended to the consistency of a sauce and served with chopped hard-boiled egg and slices of lemon floating on top.

Borlotti bean and pinto bean Both these beans are often mottled in colour. The pink-splotched pinto bean grows freely all over Latin America and throughout the American Southwest. Like the borlotti bean from Italy, it is an ingredient in many regional stews and is often mixed with rice. The borlotti bean is also mixed with pasta to make the soup *pasta e fagioli*.

Black-eyed bean These white beans with their characteristic black splotch came to Europe and America from Africa, brought over in the late seventeenth century by the slave traders. The bean thrives in warm climates and is a favourite food crop in the southern United States, where it is eaten fresh as well as dried. It is often served with pork and corn bread, and is the essential ingredient in a traditional southern dish called Hoppin' John – a mixture of black-eyed beans, white rice and bacon – traditionally eaten on New Year's Day.

Broad bean Sometimes known as fava beans, these are the strongly flavoured beans that form the basis of the Egyptian *ta'amia* or falafel: deep-fried little patties made with soaked and pounded dried beans and flavoured with garlic, onions, cumin, fresh coriander and parsley. Most often used in their fresh green state, as in the rib-sticking dish called *fabada* from northern Spain – a mixture of beans, cured meats, sausage and plenty of garlic – broad beans become brown when they are dried.

Ful medame or Egyptian brown bean Also known as the field bean in England, these small, brown, knobbly beans, actually a type of broad bean, are grown in South-east Asia and in Egypt, where they are a staple food. In Egypt the cooked beans are usually sprinkled with garlic and parsley, with oil and seasonings handed round separately. They also make a filling for an Arabian bread to become a sort of meatless hamburger, eaten with tomato and onion salad, and they are good when served in a tomato sauce.

The beans require lengthy soaking and cooking.

Chick-pea The botanical name for this pea (which is, strictly speaking, not a pea at all) is *Cicer arietinum* because of its alleged resemblance to the skull of a ram, although to those of us with a less discerning eye it really looks more like a small hazelnut.

The flavour of chick-peas vaguely recalls that of roasted nuts, and indeed they are eaten with drinks in Greece. Large chick-peas are a better buy than small ones because they do not need such long soaking. However, they will still sometimes need as much as 10 hours' soaking and 5–6 hours of gentle simmering to become completely tender.

Once cooked, *ceci*, as they are called in Italy, are very good dressed simply with oil and eaten as a salad. The Italians also make chick-pea soup, and mix them with pasta – a dish known as thunder and lightning. In France, where chick-peas are called *pois chiches*, they are stewed in good stock with herbs to make *pois chiches en estouffade*, and also used in soups and as a garnish. In Spain, *garbanzos* form the basis of *olla podrida* (which means rotten pot), which also includes chunks of meat, pig's

chick-pea flour 118

Egyptian Falafels 353
Hummus with Tahina 353
Israeli Falafels 353
Pasta e Fagioli 252
Ribollita 252
Six-Vegetable Couscous 350
Spinach and Chick-Peas 373
Summer Minestrone 251

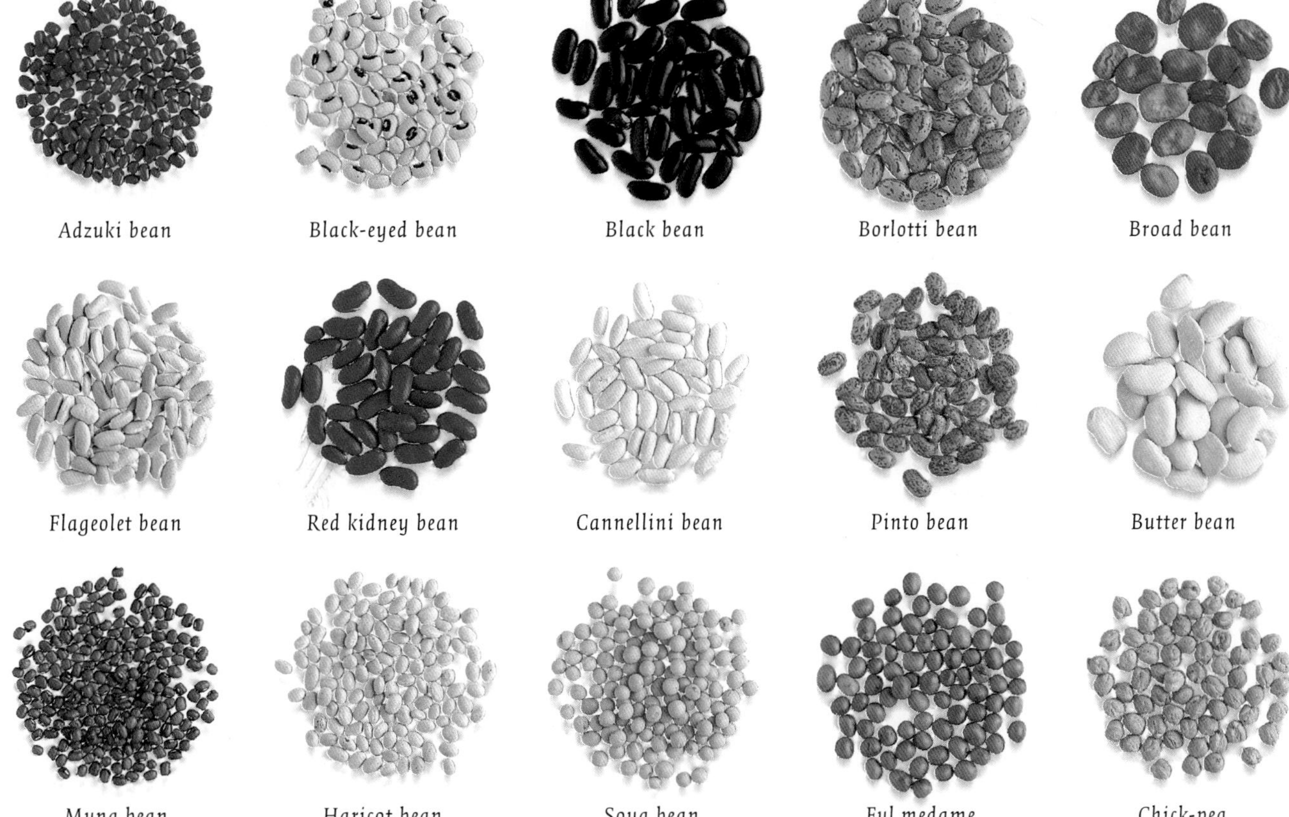

Adzuki bean | Black-eyed bean | Black bean | Borlotti bean | Broad bean

Flageolet bean | Red kidney bean | Cannellini bean | Pinto bean | Butter bean

Mung bean | Haricot bean | Soya bean | Ful medame | Chick-pea

bean sprout 142
Chinese noodles 124–5
dried cod 31
hoisin sauce 206
Japanese noodles 125
miso 207
petit salé 70
poppadom 120
soy sauce 207
soya bean oil 113
soya milk 98
tahina 206

Lentil Dhal 355
Lentil Soup 248
Spiced Lentils 354
Yellow Split Pea Soup 248

trotters or ears, preserved pork, sausages and vegetables; and in Portugal they are combined with spinach and eaten with *bacalhau* – dried salt cod – and other dishes. In the Middle East chick-peas are combined with tahina, lemon and garlic to make the delicious spread, hummus, and Israel uses them for its version of falafel, which is so widely eaten that it has almost become the national dish. Chick-peas are a common ingredient of couscous, and they are also mixed with beef and vegetables to make a rich and filling Israeli dish called *deene* or *daphna*. They are an important crop in India, where they are often cooked with garlic and chillies and turned in aromatics before being fried with herbs and spices in clarified butter.

Split pea Although there are still some dingy-grey whole dried peas to be had, most are now sold skinned, split and bright green or golden yellow. Thick yellow pea soup – *ärter med flask* – is the traditional Thursday evening dish in Sweden, keeping alive the memory of the unpopular King Eric XIV whose last supper on earth, on a Thursday, consisted of this very dish. His brother had contrived to slip a dash of arsenic into this humble food, which would hardly have crossed royal lips had Eric not been imprisoned at the time by his eventual successor.

Green split peas form the basis of a traditional English dish, pease pudding, which is usually eaten in slices with gammon. Although an egg is sometimes beaten into the mushy pea mixture to make it creamier still, it is one of the characteristics of split peas, whether yellow or green, that they turn into a purée by themselves and do not have to be mashed. Nor do they have to be soaked before cooking.

Yellow split pea

Green split pea

Puy lentil

Split red lentil

Brown lentil

Green lentil

Lentil Red, brown and green lentils have all the virtues of dried peas and beans, and the additional one of needing less cooking time, particularly split lentils.

The small red split lentil, originally a native of India, needs no soaking and becomes tender within about 20 minutes' cooking, quickly turning into a mush. The brown lentil, also known as the German lentil, and the green lentil of France, *lentille de Puy*, take a little longer to cook.

Lentils make excellent purées and soups. In Germany they sometimes accompany roast duck, while in France lentils cooked with garlic and flavoured with a squeeze of lemon juice are eaten with a *petit salé* – hot salt pork.

Dhal These are not a particular type of bean but the Hindi word for dried beans and peas. Most packages labelled dhal in the West will contain split varieties such as chick-peas, lentils and the pigeon-pea, which is known as tur dhal. They are not soaked but are cooked for 40–45 minutes and served spiced as a thick purée, or are mashed to make thick soups. Another of the dhals, called urad dhal, is often ground and becomes the basis of the poppadom, without which no curry would be complete.

Mung bean These beans, also called green gram or golden gram, can of course be cooked in the usual way, but they tend to become rather sticky. In India they are ground into a flour, and ground mung beans are the basis of some Chinese and Japanese noodles. In the West they are now chiefly used, like alfalfa seeds and soya beans, for sprouting purposes.

Soya bean The soya is the most nutritious of all beans. Better known for its products than for the bean itself, it is one of the few sources of complete protein. The soya bean has been periodically rediscovered by the West, but was first brought to Europe in the eighteenth century, when it confounded scientists with its amazing qualities. It is still the subject of considerable research today.

But while the West has only recently started turning soya into steaks and processing it into cheese, the Chinese have for thousands of years called soya 'the meat of the earth', and have used soya-bean curd – a bland substance known as tofu, which readily soaks up other flavours – as a substitute for meat, fish and chicken. The extracted 'milk' is used in cooking a wide range of vegetable dishes; soy sauce is used for flavouring; and a fermented paste made from the bean, called miso, is used as a basic seasoning in everything from sauces, soups and salad dressings to casseroles and, when sweetened, in puddings in the manner of jam.

Of the thousand or so known varieties, two soya beans are chiefly cultivated – one sort for commercial purposes, the other to be eaten both fresh (when young) and dried, in which case they are prepared and cooked just like other dried beans. Soya milk is a useful substitute for those allergic to dairy products.

Adzuki bean The adzuki bean, which is also known as the asuki bean and the aduki bean, is one of the most delicious of the dried beans and also one of the more expensive.

A native of Japan, it is small and red with a curiously shaped white-striped ridge. It is a fairly recent arrival in the West and is found mainly in health-food stores. It is cooked in exactly the same ways as other dried beans, both in Japan and abroad, but since it very much sweeter than most other beans its flour is also much used for cakes and pastries in Japan, and the crushed bean is made into puddings and ice-cream by the Chinese. It is one of the most easily digestible of all the dried beans.

Fresh Vegetables

SALAD VEGETABLES

It was that scholarly seventeenth-century English diarist, John Evelyn, who said of a salad that it should be composed like a piece of music, with each ingredient playing its due part without being overpowered by anything of strong taste. Since his time, a salad has come to be widely regarded as an essential part of the everyday diet, so much so that in many countries it is served instead of a vegetable.

Exactly at what point of the meal to serve a green salad is a matter of taste. Ancient Romans, who regarded lettuce as a panacea for all ills, believed that its milky juices 'lined the stomach', enabling people to drink more with their food. Accordingly, lettuce was served as a first course, as it is still sometimes eaten, although hardly for the same reason, in the United States. It is more usual to eat it immediately following the main course, as in France and England, or at the same time, on a side plate or, not so agreeably, on the same plate – although this has something to recommend it in the case of such dishes as chops, steaks or roast chicken because the meat juices mingle so delectably with the dressing.

Green salads should not meet their dressings until they are on the point of being served, since once dressed they rapidly become limp. A good compromise is to prepare the dressing in the bowl, put the crossed salad servers over it and to place the leaves lightly on top, without mixing them. Some people prefer to mix the dressing at the table, while Italians simply pour olive oil and then vinegar on to the salad – they say you need a generous person for the oil, a miser for the vinegar, a judge for the salt and a madman to mix it.

To make sure that your 'sallet herbs', as John Evelyn called them, are fresh and good, see that the leaves look vigorous and show no sign of brown. Inspect the cut parts: they should be sound, neither discoloured nor soggy. The heavier the lettuce the more tightly packed it will be, giving you more leaves for your money.

A salad plant in good condition will stay fresh in the refrigerator if it is wrapped in a plastic bag to retard the evaporation of its moisture. Should it have wilted, it can be refreshed by being plunged into cold water, shaken dry and put into the refrigerator in a plastic bag or wrapped in a damp tea towel.

Shortly before using them, salad leaves should be washed and then thoroughly dried – either by absorbing the moisture by shaking in a clean tea towel or by getting rid of it in a salad shaker or spinner. The leaves should be torn rather than cut, to avoid bruising.

Apart from being used in salads, lettuces and other leafy plants can be cooked. The less substantial the leaf, the faster it collapses, and while heavier leaves may retain a bit of body, lighter ones do not. For braising, choose small, plump lettuces and cut them in half or braise them whole.

Round or cabbage lettuce

These vary greatly in size and crispness but have in common their general round shape. Although there are many varieties of cabbage lettuce, ranging from soft to very crisp, there are three main types.

Butterhead These are light, loosely packed and delicate. A particularly melting one, Bibb, is prized in the United States; Boston is another favourite. Continuity, grown in England, sports leaves with a reddish tinge to them. Butterheads tend to be floppy, a characteristic that is by no means a defect as long as the loose leaves are fresh.

Crisphead Whereas there is not much joy in eating a wilting butterhead, these hearty lettuces, when fading on the outside, may still be full of vitality in the middle. Crispheads, such as Iceberg and Webb's Wonderful, although not strong in flavour, are by far the crispest lettuces. They are often sold without their aureole of outer leaves, looking like tightly wrapped heads of cabbage.

Loosehead These are cabbage lettuces that have no heart at all. Instead of the leaves, which are often crinkled, becoming more tightly packed towards the centre, they all splay outwards from the middle. Some varieties have red-, bronze- or ruby-tipped leaves. Lollo Rosso is a red-tipped, curly and somewhat tough example of a loosehead lettuce. It is a good salad plant, but is often used indiscriminately as a garnish.

Cos lettuce, romaine lettuce

Far more elongated in shape than the round cabbage lettuces is the cos or romaine lettuce. Tall and large, with a nutty flavour to its vigorous leaves, it has a beautifully crisp and tender heart. Its two names – cos in England and romaine in France and the United States – testify to its origins: the Romans found it on the Greek island of Cos and brought it back to Rome, whence it was introduced to the rest of Europe. A popular small variety, Little Gem, shares the same good qualities as Cos, and has a vivid young heart.

Celtuce

This tall Far-Eastern specimen is among the less well-known salad plants. So called because it tastes slightly of celery and looks rather like a head of lettuce, with long pale stalks and a head of leaves, it used also to be called asparagus lettuce. However, it tastes neither like asparagus nor much like celery or even lettuce. The similarity to celery lies mostly in the crunch of the stalks, which, like celery, can be eaten raw, making a good salad when peeled and chopped. The similarity to lettuce is confined to the tender central leaves. The stalks can also be cooked like Swiss chard, and make a similar vegetable dish to be eaten with butter or a creamy sauce, while the tough outer leaves can be cooked like spinach.

Corn salad, lamb's lettuce

This is what you are served when you order a dish of *mâche* in France. The spoon-shaped leaves grow in dark green rosettes, which can be difficult to wash since they harbour sand. It is more substantial than lettuce and has a nutty taste that blends particularly well with the sweetness of beetroot for an excellent winter salad.

Chicory, endive and escarole

Wild chicory, with its pretty blue flowers, is the ancestor of varieties that are now grown primarily for their roots. These are roasted and ground to make a coffee substitute. Its leaves have a bitter taste and are sometimes mixed with other salad leaves.

Chicory First bred in Belgium, and sometimes called by its Flemish name, witloof, this is the best known of the cultivated chicories. It is blanched by being grown in the dark or under peat or sand, and with its tightly furled leaves it resembles a fat white cigar with a pale yellow tip (not green). Sliced across or with the leaves separated, it makes a fresh and interesting salad on its own, or it can

chicory coffe 216
oils 111–13
spinach 132
Swiss chard 140
vinegars 204–5

salad basket and spinner 229
wooden bowl 230

Burghul Pilaf 351
Chicory in Butter and Cream 372
Herb Vinaigrette with Balsamic Vinegar 259
Peas with Lettuce Hearts 376
Rich Vegetable Stock 245
Salade Niçoise 368
Spring Sorrel Soup 247
Tabbouleh 351
Vinaigrette 259
Yogurt and Garlic Dressing 259
Yogurt and Spring Onion Dressing 259

Crab Salad with Thai Flavours 368
Frisée and Bacon Salad 366
Light Watercress Soup 247
Rolled Omelette with Spiced Greens 325
Salmon Pâté 317

be mixed with sliced orange or a little watercress and some oil and lemon juice.

What little bitterness there is in chicory tends to come to the fore when it is cooked, so it is usually blanched in a little stock with a few drops of lemon juice before being braised. In this way it is particularly good with ham, veal, chicken and pheasant.

Radicchio, ciccorio There are several types of this chicory, introduced from Italy. Looking like miniature coloured lettuces, the plants can be either deep ruby-red, cream splashed with a fine wine-red, or marbled pink. When they have not been carefully shaded they look green or dark copper coloured and less pretty.

It is its beauty that recommends radicchio: it tastes much like a lettuce but with more bitterness, and has somewhat tougher ribs. It makes a very beautiful salad mixed with green lettuce and pale yellow-green escarole.

Curly endive and escarole The curly-leaved endive (frisée or frisé) and the broad-leaved escarole are more robust than the lettuce tribe. Although by nature they are bitter, they become less so when the jagged rosettes are shielded from the light and blanched to a succulent pale golden-green. Look for these in winter – they have much more character than most hothouse-reared winter lettuces. Endive looks like a frizzy, pale greenish-white mop, and escarole has broad, crinkled, strap-shaped leaves with a rather leathery texture and a pale yellow centre. Prepare curly endive and escarole as you would any lettuce, but with a more highly flavoured dressing; use them to give texture to a salad made of more delicate leaves or on their own. A few walnuts and some strips of bacon make very good additions, and these are the greens to eat with a Roquefort dressing.

Escarole is often called by its variety name, Batavia, while the different names used for endive must stem from its Latin name, *Chicorium endiva* – in France it is known as *chicorée frisée*, and in the United States it is called chicory as frequently as it is known as curly endive.

Cress

Watercress Dark green, bunched sprigs of watercress make a beautiful garnish for grilled kidneys, chops and game, and little sprigs enhance both the taste and look of a green or an orange salad. A watercress sauce is an excellent and pretty complement for fish, while nothing is fresher-tasting than a good watercress soup. When buying

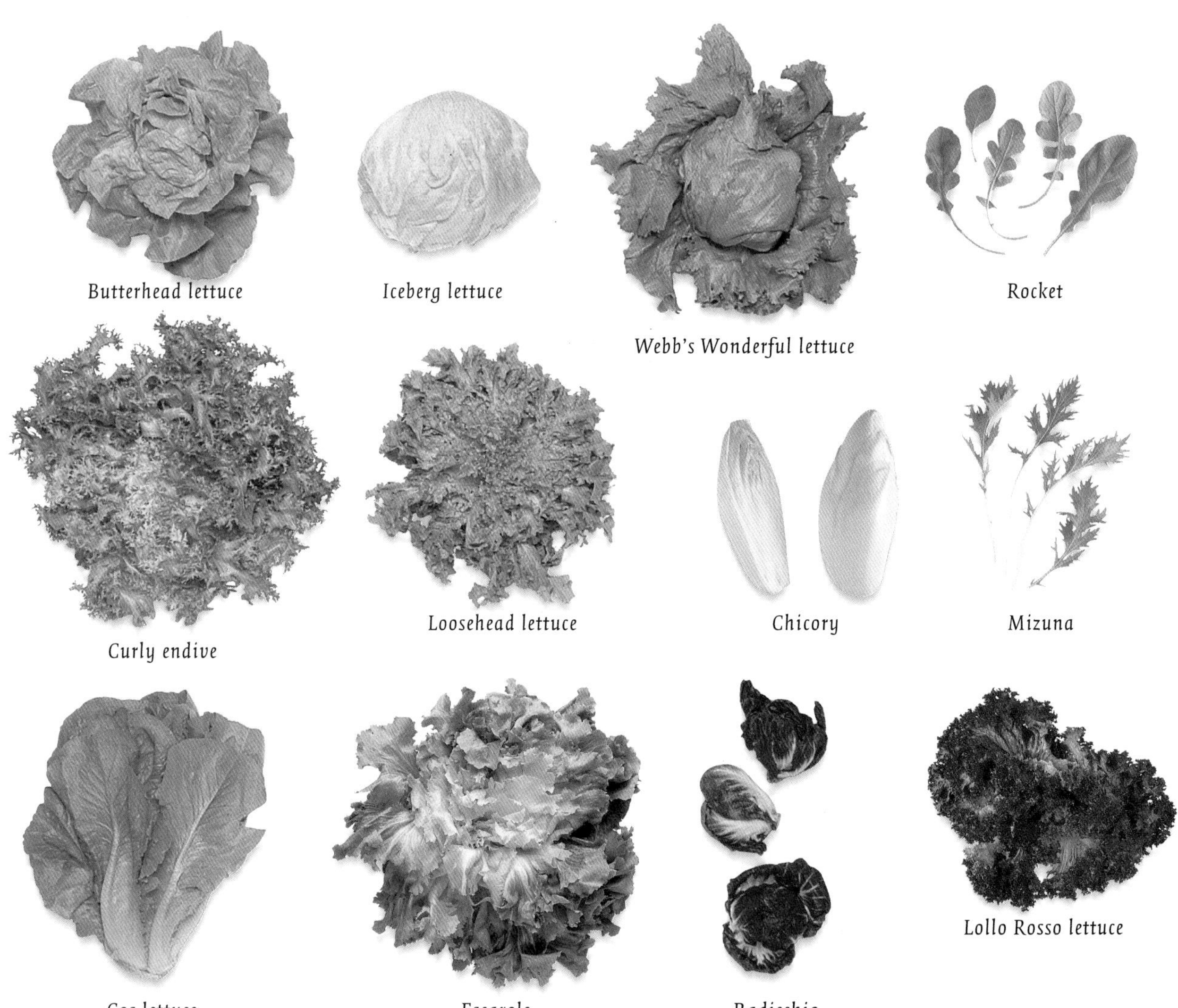

Butterhead lettuce
Iceberg lettuce
Webb's Wonderful lettuce
Rocket
Curly endive
Loosehead lettuce
Chicory
Mizuna
Cos lettuce
Escarole
Radicchio
Lollo Rosso lettuce

watercress, the rule is the darker and the larger the leaves, the better. Use it soon after purchase, keeping it meanwhile in the refrigerator in a plastic bag or in a cool place in water, like a bouquet in a jam jar or even completely submerged in a bowl.

Mustard and cress The tiny embryonic leaves of mustard and salad or garden cress are usually found in the thinnest and most delicate sandwiches – especially those containing egg or chicken, to which they bring a warm, sharp flavour – and as a garnish sprinkled over salads. If you don't grow mustard and cress yourself, what you are most likely to buy growing in punnets is simply cress, the smaller of the two.

Rocket

This salad green, with its pale yellow flowers, looks like a cross beween mustard greens and radish leaves. Also called arugula, *rucola* and *roquette*, it is much used to ornament Italian dishes and on tomato salads. The young leaves give a pungent, peppery taste to plain green salads, and in southern Italy wild rocket is used as an extra flavour in the mixed salads eaten with pasta or veal. But be careful which rocket you use – the name is also applied to a number of other plants, some of them far too bitter to be eaten.

Radish

As a family, these roots belong to the mustard tribe, which, considering their hot pungency, is not surprising. In shape and colour they range from little scarlet or white globes to long red and white types such as the Icicle radish. There is also a black radish, which has snow-white flesh.

Pungency varies not only according to type but also according to the soil in which the plants are grown. The elongated, red and white type tends to be the mildest and goes by the name of French Breakfast, although one has yet to meet a Frenchman who actually eats them first thing in the morning. The most pungent of the pure white radishes is the type offered in Bavarian beer halls to encourage thirst.

Except in the East, where radishes are eaten as a fully fledged vegetable, they mostly provide an appetizer. As they 'carry their pepper within', they can simply be dipped in salt and eaten with crusty French bread and butter, or may themselves be buttered and then sprinkled with sea salt. To serve them this way, wash them, trim off the roots and leaves, leaving a tuft about 1 cm/½ in long, and crisp them in the refrigerator with a few ice cubes on top. In Italy thin white slices of radish with their pretty red edges are scattered over green salads, perhaps with some equally thin slices of carrot.

Winter radish So-called spring radishes, such as the globe, French Breakfast and Icicle, have a short growing season – sometimes only 4 weeks – whereas winter radishes, such as some black radishes, take much longer to mature. Winter radishes are large, and have firm and compact flesh. They are cooked or grated into salads, and can also be curried.

Mouli, mooli or daikon The winter radish from the Far East, the birthplace of radishes, this is long, white, cylindrical and enormous, with a less peppery flavour than ordinary radishes. It can be pickled, dried and salted, cooked, or grated raw and mixed with grated fresh ginger to make a sauce for fried vegetables. It also features in tempura dishes.

pickled radish 207

Crudités with Aïoli 365
Rocket and Walnut Salad 367

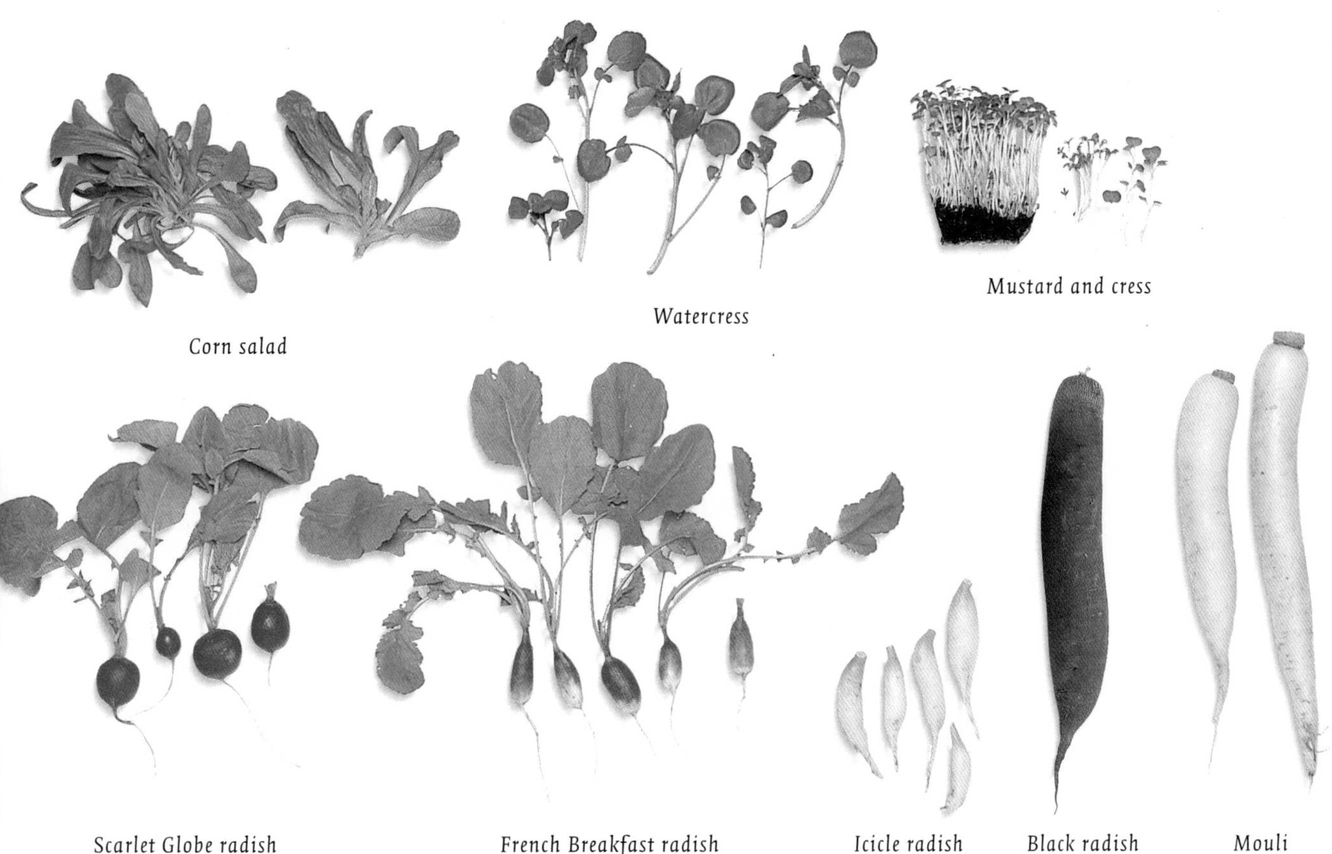

Corn salad

Watercress

Mustard and cress

Scarlet Globe radish

French Breakfast radish

Icicle radish

Black radish

Mouli

Eggs with Spinach and Cheese 323
Mornay Sauce 255
Oysters Rockefeller 278
Sesame Spinach 372
Spinach and Bacon Salad 366
Spinach and Cheese Omelette 324
Spinach and Chick-Peas 373
Spinach and Ricotta Ravioli 342
Spinach and Walnut Salad 367
Spinach Frittata 326
Spinach Gnocchi with Butter and Sage 344
Spinach Tart 328
Stewed Artichokes with Spinach 376

Mizuna

This feathery, delicate salad green has been cultivated in Japan since antiquity. Its flavour is mildly peppery, and it makes a good addition to Provençal *mesclun*, a mixture of young and tender salad leaves.

GREENS

This group of green-leaved vegetables includes several that are now considered to be weeds. Once they were as well known as spinach, which since its wide cultivation has displaced them. But while spinach is the most widely grown and popular of all our leaf vegetables, there should still be a place in the kitchen for its old-fashioned relations, such as Good King Henry and Fat Hen. All greens should be very fresh and need to be bought in generous quantities, as they reduce in volume when cooked.

Spinach

The cultivation of spinach, since its first appearance in Persia (now Iran) many thousands of years ago, has resulted in succulent leaves of a beautiful green, which may be small and rounded – the best for salads – or larger and more pointed, smooth or curly.

Since spinach greatly reduces in volume when cooked, you need to allow 225 g/8 oz for each person. If stalks are coarse they should be removed, and on larger leaves tear the midribs from each leaf, which is done by folding the leaf inwards and pulling the stalk towards the tip. The spinach should be well washed in several changes of water to remove the grit that it often contains. Cook on a low flame, uncovered, with only the water that clings to the leaves after they are washed. As the lower layer softens, stir the spinach, and continue in this way until all the leaves have wilted down. The spinach must be very well drained because it tends to exude water after it is cooked.

Spinach can be used in a multitude of ways. As an accompanying vegetable it can be served simply with masses of butter, or in a mornay sauce, or as a purée with cream. Sweet spinach purée, although it sounds odd, is an ancient dish: Elizabeth I sat down to a pipkin of boiled spinach mixed with rosewater, raisins, vinegar, butter and sugar. And a pastry case filled with spinach and candied orange and lemon peel and bathed in a rich creamy custard is a Christmas dish of southern France.

In Italy there are dozens of lovely spinach recipes: spinach is eaten in soufflés, frittatas and dumplings; mixed with ricotta, Parmesan and nutmeg to make a filling for stuffed pasta; and used to make fresh green pasta, which looks so pretty with a cream or tomato sauce. No wonder that a spinach garnish goes under the Italian name of *alla fiorentina*. Eggs Florentine are eggs arranged on a bed of cooked spinach under a covering of cream or mornay sauce; fish and sweetbreads *à la florentine* have spinach in the sauce.

Spinach can also be eaten raw: delicious salads are made with small, young spinach leaves garnished with pieces of crisply fried bacon and hard-boiled eggs, tossed in a garlic-laden vinaigrette.

There are some wild plants that are reminiscent of spinach in flavour, two of them so close to spinach in taste that they are sometimes cultivated.

New Zealand spinach This fleshy-leaved plant was discovered by Sir Joseph Banks, botanist on Captain Cook's *Endeavour*, who brought it back to Europe. It is still grown outside its native land, flourishing where excessive heat and lack of water would make true

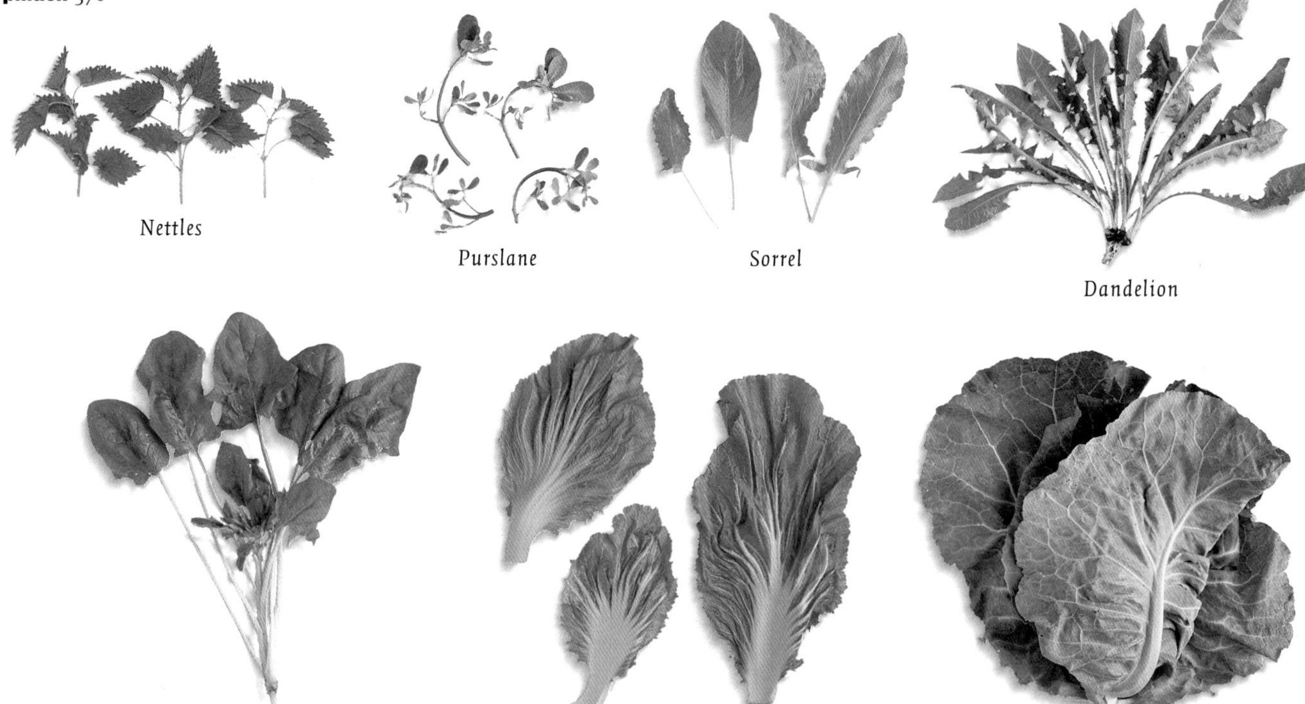

Nettles

Purslane

Sorrel

Dandelion

Spinach

Chinese mustard greens

Spring greens

spinach bolt (run to seed). Somewhat tougher than true spinach, it is often sold in local French markets, where it is called *tetragon*.

Malabar spinach This thrives in tropical Asia and in tropical parts of Latin America. The large, bright, shiny leaves have a distinctive but good taste, and are treated in the same way as spinach. In China it is cultivated for its fleshy berries, which yield a dye that has been used by women as a rouge and by high-ranking officials as a seal.

Cabbage greens

Any member of the cabbage family that does not form a proper head becomes simply 'greens'. They are cheap enough to allow any woody stems, coarse midribs or damaged leaves to be ruthlessly discarded. See that the midribs are crisp and snappy.

Spring and winter greens, collards These are the Cinderellas of the vegetable world, but, like Cinderella, they are good and can be quite splendid when properly dressed. The leaves are particularly tender and delicate when cooked. They are excellent for sustaining dishes such as 'mess o'greens' from the southern United States, which usually contains salt pork or bacon and yields cooking juices referred to as 'pot likker'. These braised greens are eaten with corn bread to mop up the broth.

Beet greens

Curly kale

Kale and curly kale Of the two, curly kale is the better known and certainly the better tasting. Kale, with its smooth, greyish-green leaves, is less succulent than other greens but is good when stir-fried. Curly kale has crimped leaves, like curly endive. It was known by the early Greeks and Romans, whose climate was too warm to grow cabbage. There are many varieties; some are grown as cut-and-come-again plants, and there is even one type whose stems become so hard and woody that when dried they are made into walking sticks. The edible ones taste rather like spring greens but stronger, and can be used for all cabbage recipes.

Cavolo nero An Italian kale with dark green, strong-flavoured leaves, this is much used in vegetable soups or eaten fried in oil with chillies.

Beet greens, spinach beet

The first-century Roman gourmet Apicius included in his book recipes for beet greens with mustard, oil and vinegar, and for barley soup with beet greens. Beet greens are still grown extensively in Italy and in eastern districts of France where, together with Swiss chard, they are known as *blettes* and are used interchangeably with both Swiss chard and seakale beet. They are often mixed with sorrel to counteract the latter's acidity, being themselves very mild but earthy. When cooked, they are used like spinach, and in Italy are a popular stuffing for ravioli or agnolotti, together with ricotta and Parmesan.

Mustard greens

This dark green leaf vegetable, popular in the American South, has a hot taste and is delicious lightly braised with garlic and chilli. The young leaves, which are far less pungent than the larger, older leaves, are a zesty addition to a green salad.

Chinese mustard greens or cabbage (*gai choy*) resemble spring greens in appearance. This vegetable is eaten fresh, simply stir-fried or used in soups, or it is pickled in a sweet-sour brine.

Sorrel, dandelion and purslane

Sorrel Of all the different types of sorrel, it is the cultivated French variety that is best for eating; this vegetable adds an acid, lemony note to salads, soups, purées, sauces and omelettes. The classic *potage Germiny* consists of sorrel cut into delicate ribbons – called a *chiffonade* – cooked in butter and then moistened with chicken stock and emulsified with egg yolk. A purée of sorrel is the traditional accompaniment to grilled shad and is also an exceedingly good foil for salmon. Because sorrel, even more than spinach, is rich in oxalic acid, it should only be eaten in moderation.

Dandelion In some countries, gardeners wage constant, if ineffectual, war against this golden flower, regarding it as a noisome weed. In other places they carefully sow seed and then take great trouble earthing up or blanching the plants with a cover to keep the leaves tender and white for use in salads. In France, where housewives buy dandelion greens on market stalls, they are called *pissenlits*. Another name for them in England is piss-a-bed, illustrating their diuretic properties, so those addicted to dandelions should be warned not to eat them to excess. Their other French name, source of the English word, is *dent de lion*, meaning 'lion's tooth', because of their jagged edge.

Weed though they may be, they are certainly useful. The roots can be used as a caffeine-free coffee substitute, and the leaves make excellent salads. Perhaps the best is *pissenlits au lard*, a bowl of small, fat, juicy, whole dandelion plants in vinaigrette, over which is thrown a panful of sizzling pieces of salt pork or bacon and bacon fat.

You can remove most of the bitterness from wild dandelions by placing a plate or tile over a patch of young plants to blanch them. But the juiciest, least bitter dandelions are those grown from a packet of domestic seed. Blanch them before they start to produce flower buds, and pick them young.

Purslane A native of India, where it has grown wild for thousands of years, fleshy-leaved purslane spread to England in the Middle Ages and was popular pickled and as a salad. It was introduced to North America by the early colonists, but today most people discard it as a weed. In England, too, it was once cultivated in gardens, but is now uncommon. The French are more astute and still consider

beetroot 149
dandelion root coffee 216
seakale beet and Swiss chard 140
shad 23

Corn Bread 362
Pissenlits au Lard 366
Spring Sorrel Soup 247

asparagus 137
haggis 74
spinach 132
watercress 130

purslane – known as *pourpier* in France – to be a salad plant worth cultivating. The succulent leaves can also be boiled, and are good when briskly fried in butter and then used to fill an omelette. In the Middle East, where purslane is also cultivated, it is an important ingredient in *fattoush* – a salad mixture including tomatoes and cucumber eaten with pita bread.

Wild greens

There are still many edible green-leaved plants growing wild and free, which, if nothing else, can be regarded as survival food. However, much enjoyment can be had gathering these plants on country walks and experimenting with cooking and eating them at home. Make sure, though, that you know exactly what you are gathering. If you are uncertain what the plants look like, take an illustrated field guide with you so that you can identify the plants you want to find.

Nettle Northern countries used to prize the nettle, but it is now something most people avoid because of its sting (which completely disappears when the nettle is cooked). In Scandinavia the leaves were boiled like spinach, and the coarse fibres of the stalks used for cloth, in the manner of flax. (This explains, without making it any less sad, the task of the fairy-tale maiden set to stitching nettle garments for her seven brothers, to lift the spell that had transformed them into swans.) Ireland combined nettles and oats in a broth, but her nettle haggis – a purée of nettles, leeks, cabbage, bacon and oatmeal boiled in a bag – would not, one imagines, pass muster with a Scot. Italians still eat nettle purée or soup in the spring as it is supposed to be excellent for cleansing the blood.

Nettles should be picked when they are only about a finger-length high; later on they become bitter and tough. Remember to wear gloves, and use scissors to snip off the leaves.

Goosefoot The two best-known members of this family are the delightfully named Good King Henry and Fat Hen, both of which were staples in antiquity but have now been superseded by spinach. Fat Hen is a tall, stiff-stemmed plant that grows prodigiously wherever there are people – or weeds. It tastes much like spinach but is considerably milder. The leaves of Good King Henry are also treated like spinach, and some suggest that the shoots can be prepared and eaten like asparagus.

Amaranth The green leaves of this species, known in England as pigweed, also have a taste similar to spinach, but are more tender and sweet. The celery-like stalks taste somewhat of artichokes.

Chickweed So called because poultry has a particular yen for it, chickweed grows in all temperate climates of the world. Probably the most common of all edible weeds, it is a tender vegetable that, cooked in butter with chopped onion, goes well with rich meats.

Brooklime This makes a perfectly acceptable, though slightly bitter, substitute for watercress. Brooklime is found by streams and in marshy places in North America and in northern Europe.

BRASSICAS

Cabbages that form into a head are members of the vast *Brassica* genus, which also includes cauliflower, broccoli and Brussels sprouts (as well as turnips and kohlrabi, which are eaten, respectively, for their roots and their swollen stems).

All brassicas are descendants of the wild cabbage, which still grows in coastal regions of Italy and France – a tough, tall plant, almost all trunk. They are rich in vitamin C and minerals, but half the vitamin content is lost when they are cooked. They all contain sulphur compounds, which give them their characteristic 'cabbagey' smell when they are overcooked.

Cabbage

There are three main types of cabbage that form a head, distinguished mainly by texture – crinkled or smooth – and colour: green, white and red.

Green cabbage Early green cabbages are a deeper green and more loosely packed than the later ones, and often have pointed heads. Buy them in the spring, checking that the leaves – frequently curly at the edges – are fresh and crisp; even the outer leaves should be tender. Do not worry about the lack of heart – they have not had time to develop the firmness associated with the later kind.

The later green cabbages are altogether tougher, but have solid hearts. They include the crimped variety, called the Savoy cabbage, which is particularly tender and mild flavoured and needs less cooking than other varieties. The Savoy's head is quite firm, for all its crinkliness, and is a beautiful green with a touch of blue. It stands up well to frosty weather and is therefore readily available throughout late winter. This is the best variety for stuffing.

White cabbage The very palest of green, almost white, this is sometimes called Dutch cabbage. It has smooth leaves, and is quite hard and firm.

Red cabbage Although this is magenta or dark purple, the colour fades during cooking unless a little vinegar is added. The flavour is improved by the added sharpness, too. Red cabbage is best stewed with some kind of fat, plus vinegar, sugar and plenty of spices and flavourings. It is also good eaten raw or pickled.

Buying and storing cabbage When buying cabbages, no matter what kind, look not only at the leaves, which should

Bok choy

Chinese leaves

be sound and unblemished, but also at the core. This should be neither dry and split nor woody and slimy. Those cabbages with wilted outer leaves or a puffy appearance should be avoided.

The firmer the cabbage, the longer it will keep – Savoys can be kept in a cool place for several days; white and red cabbages will keep in a cool place for at least a week.

Cooking with cabbage Red cabbage is cooked very differently from green and white varieties, with such ingredients as wine vinegar, red wine, apples, raisins, onions, brown sugar and spices going into the pot after the cabbage has been gently sautéed in lard, oil, butter or goose fat. A sweet and sour red cabbage dish is also much improved by the addition of some prunes during the cooking. Red cabbage is traditionally served with the Christmas goose in many northern countries and is also excellent with pork or game. Pickled red cabbage is one of the best of all pickles to eat with cold meats or game.

The simplest way to cook a green or white cabbage is to boil it, after removing the core and thickest stalks, and washing it in a bowl of cold water with a tablespoon of salt to deal with the creatures that might lurk between the leaves. Cut into quarters or shreds and cook uncovered for no more than a few minutes – the moment it starts to sink it is ready.

The smell of cooked cabbage is a dreary one, and the sodden leaves that mark overcooked cabbage have to take much of the blame for what was until recently Britain's poor culinary reputation. Yet cabbage that has been carefully cooked and gently but thoroughly drained, and then heated with a generous quantity of butter, makes a delicate, light vegetable dish. Long, slow cooking gives a succulent texture quite different from cabbage cooked fast and served green.

There are several good slow-cooked dishes in which the cabbage is started off with fat and onions and then cooked on with meat: partridges, no longer young, for *perdrix au chou*, and ham, beef or spiced salt beef for Irish-American 'boiled dinners'. Then there are the filling, stock-based cabbage soups, poured over slices of bread, which make complete meals by themselves.

In northern Germany there is the famous hunter's cabbage, made with golden cubes of fat bacon bathed in a piquant sauce, which accompanies the equally famous bratwurst. In Bavaria cabbage is braised with chopped bacon, caraway seeds and white wine. The nineteenth-century king of the dream castles, the eccentric Ludwig, liked to eat his cabbage braised with pike and served with a crayfish sauce.

bratwurst 72
pike 23
salt beef 71

Braised Pigeons and Cabbage 302
Braised Red Cabbage 374
Cabbage with Chestnut Stuffing 374
Colcannon 374
Cumin-Spiced Cabbage 375

Cauliflower

Purple sprouting broccoli

Calabrese broccoli

Savoy cabbage

Red cabbage

Purple cauliflower

White cabbage

Brussels sprout

Green cabbage

Béarnaise Sauce 255
Brussels Sprouts with Chestnuts 375
Cauliflower au Gratin 375
Cauliflower Soup 254
Chinese Belly Pork Salad with Bok Choy 371
Hollandaise Sauce 255

Stuffed cabbages are a subject on their own: stuffings of all descriptions are layered between the blanched and semi-unfurled leaves. Ingredients may include different kinds of meat, bacon, chicken livers, herbs, rice, onions and chestnuts, all bound with eggs and possibly rice or breadcrumbs. Cabbages can also be stuffed after being hollowed out, with their tops cut off but replaced before going into the oven; or the individual leaves can be stuffed and tied into little parcels.

Sweet-sour cabbage dishes are popular with Jewish families and in Russia, where cabbage baked with apples is eaten with smoked meats. From sweet-sour it is only a small step to sour; cabbage ferments and becomes sauerkraut when packed in a barrel with salt. Fresh sauerkraut for immediate use is preferable to the bottled versions. Raw white cabbage makes a good salad either as coleslaw, or simply shredded into a bowl and dressed with oil and vinegar.

Chinese cabbage

A wide variety of cabbages are grown in China, and they frequently end up in large wooden barrels, coarsely chopped and pickled in brine. The pickles are often used for dishes that need a piquancy or bite to them.

The Chinese cabbage with which we are most familiar is a variety called, in Chinese, *pe-tsai*; we know it as Chinese leaves. It resembles a large, pale cos lettuce, and is crisp and delicate with a faint cabbage flavour. Its crinkly inner leaves are best in salads, while the outer leaves, once divested of their tough ribs, can be braised, stir-fried, simmered or treated like ordinary cabbages.

Another Chinese cabbage is the bok choy or pak choi. It has large, dark green leaves at the top of long white stalks. Bok choy is used in soups and stir-fried meat dishes as well as being prepared in the same ways as spinach or cabbage.

Cauliflower

Since early cauliflowers used to be no larger than tennis balls, one can justify the complaint made by six seventeenth-century travellers to Italy who rose from the table in a marble palazzo as hungry as they arrived, having shared among them one cauliflower, a dish of anchovies and three hard-boiled eggs. Modern cauliflowers can be enormous, although ironically a strain no larger than golf balls is being grown once more. One type of cauliflower grown in Sardinia and southern Italy is purple, but turns green when cooked; another is green with a pointed head. A particularly beautiful cauliflower, the Romanesca or Roman cauliflower is bright green all the way through, a more grassy green than broccoli, and its curds grow in whorls.

A fresh head of cauliflower will have a compact cluster of creamy-white (or other colour) florets, or curds – so called because they resemble soured-milk curds – and feel heavy for its size. Loose or spreading florets mean the cauliflower is overmature. When cooking cauliflower whole, start testing for tenderness after 8–10 minutes by carefully sticking a skewer into a side stalk; continue testing until there is little, but still some, resistance. Florets take 6–8 minutes and will cook more evenly.

Cauliflower needs sauce: a light creamy sauce flavoured with cheese or mustard; or perhaps an Italian sauce incorporating chopped onion, capers, olives and anchovies; or fried breadcrumbs and chopped hard-boiled eggs. Cauliflower and cheese have a special affinity: cauliflower au gratin is a classic, and the English nursery dish, cauliflower cheese, can be delicious if cooked well. Serve florets of raw cauliflower as part of a dish of crudités, arranged around a bowl of mustardy mayonnaise; and cold cooked florets in a mustardy vinaigrette dressing as a delicious salad.

Broccoli

Like the cauliflower, broccoli started life in the Mediterranean region where the warm, dry climate encouraged wild cabbages to shoot into buds rather than concentrate on making leaves. The earliest broccoli was the purple sprouting type, with green stalks and loose green rudimentary flowers. The best and most luxurious of the broccolis is calabrese. It is a delicate vegetable and combines the subtle, fresh texture of cauliflower with the succulence of asparagus.

Purple sprouting broccoli This was the type the Romans ate cooked in wine, or dressed in oil and sharp *garum* – a sauce of fermented fish – as well as adding it as a garnish to a soup of chick-peas and lentils, peas and barley. In Sicily broccoli is still cooked in the oven with anchovies and onions. In the rest of Italy it is often parboiled and finished off with oil, garlic and chilli in the frying pan, and perhaps eaten with pasta.

Although less succulent than calabrese, purple sprouting broccoli is a very fine vegetable. Its stalks are usually cooked whole with the small loose flowerbuds and served with butter. White and green sprouting broccoli are treated in the same way. The flavour of all kinds is excellent, but they must be picked young or they become stringy and tough. Purple sprouting broccoli turns green on being cooked; the others keep their original colour.

Calabrese broccoli Called after the Italian province of Calabria, where it was first grown, this beautiful bluish-green broccoli keeps its colour when it is cooked. The large flowerheads sit on succulent spikes. One of the tests for freshness is to see that the spike snaps cleanly, although your eye can also tell whether the spikes are juicy and stiff. Avoid florets that are turning yellow.

Broccoli of whatever kind is best steamed or boiled briefly so that it still retains some crispness, and it can be used for all cauliflower recipes. In fact, a white head of cauliflower looks particularly appetizing when surrounded by green broccoli florets. Broccoli on its own is often eaten with a hollandaise or béarnaise sauce, or simply with butter and a squeeze of lemon juice.

Brussels sprout

At their best, Brussels sprouts look like tiny green buds, at their worst like miniature full-blown cabbages. Developed in Flanders, the vegetable garden of Europe, some time in the Middle Ages, Brussels sprouts grow at the intersection of leaf and stalk on a tall plant that much resembles the old wild cabbage. They have a delicate nutty taste, especially when they are small. Cooked until just tender but not too soft, they are an excellent vegetable.

The ideal size for Brussels sprouts is just a little larger than hazelnuts. These, however, are usually sold at some expense in punnets, while the ordinary medium-sized ones are sold loose or in nets. Do not waste much time before using them – they soon turn yellow. Look for compact green heads and uniform size so that they will cook evenly. Some people cut a cross in the base, but this is really only necessary in large specimens with coarse, wide stalks; fresh small ones do not need such incisions. Prepare by washing and trimming off any yellowing leaves, then cook in fast-boiling well-salted water without a lid so that they preserve their good green colour.

Brussels sprouts traditionally accompany the turkey, together with separately cooked chestnuts, for the British Christmas dinner. On less festive occasions they appear simply tossed in butter, or with brown butter and breadcrumbs. They are also good 'au jus', with the addition of some good clear gravy. If Brussels sprouts are used to garnish a meat dish or game birds in France, the dish is called *à la bruxelloise*. Some people like them with a béchamel or mornay sauce, or with a few slices of crisply fried bacon.

STALKS AND SHOOTS

Although shoots and buds often look appetizing, there are in fact only a handful that make serious eating: the buds of the palm tree are familiar as hearts of palm, and asparagus and bamboo shoots are two of the best vegetables there are – particularly asparagus, one of nature's kindest gifts to man. Stalks are mainly enjoyed in the form of celery and sweet fennel, chard and cardoons, while the globe artichoke, a companion delicacy, is a flower bud.

Fennel

Looking like a short, bulbous celery plant, Florence fennel, also called sweet fennel or finocchio, is a close relation of the herb, and the same feathery leaves can be seen emerging from its fat overlapping stalks. Like the herb, it tastes of anise, and its leaves can be used to flavour court-bouillons for fish dishes. Southern Italians eat it raw, very thinly sliced, and simply dressed with a fruity olive oil or with an aïoli sauce; northern Italians slice and parboil it, then bake it with butter and grated Parmesan. It makes a very good addition to a green salad.

When braising fennel, allow one bulb per person; trim away the stalks and string it as you would celery, and halve or quarter the bulbs. Choose rounded, fat bulbs in preference to long, thin ones which tend to be less succulent. Buy fennel as fresh as possible; it should be white and firm – any yellowness is a sign of age. It will keep crisp in a plastic bag in the refrigerator.

Asparagus

Although there are many species of asparagus, from the thorny ones of Spain to the shiny ones of the Far East, asparagus is always something of a luxury because its season is so short. There are also many differences in the way it is raised: white French asparagus is cut below the sand that covers the crown when the tip has emerged above the soil; English and American asparagus is allowed to grow above the ground, which gives it its green colour all the way down the stalk; Dutch and German ivory-tipped asparagus is always grown under mounds of soil, which helps to blanch it, and it is cut as soon as the tips begin to show.

Whatever the colour, the thick varieties of asparagus are usually the most expensive, although some people prefer thinner types. The fennel of Argenteuil, with their white stalks showing a purple tinge towards the top, and their pointed green and purple heads, are considered to be the very best, certainly in France, but this does not stop England from considering its more modest green asparagus to have a superior flavour. In fact, each of the great asparagus-growing areas – Argenteuil, Lauris, Fribourg, Schwetzingen, Bassano and Norfolk – tends to prefer its own asparagus above all others, because although asparagus travels well it starts to lose flavour from the moment it is cut. It is a revelation to eat asparagus fresh from the garden, cut and cooked within the hour.

Thick or thin, the tips are the best part, and this is the part to inspect when buying asparagus. The tips should be tightly furled, with the scales close together, and none of them discoloured or moist. Loose asparagus, which is

celery 138
fennel seed 196
herb fennel 191

Aïoli 259
Fennel au Gratin 375
Prawn and Fennel Risotto 348
Prawn and Fennel Soup 252

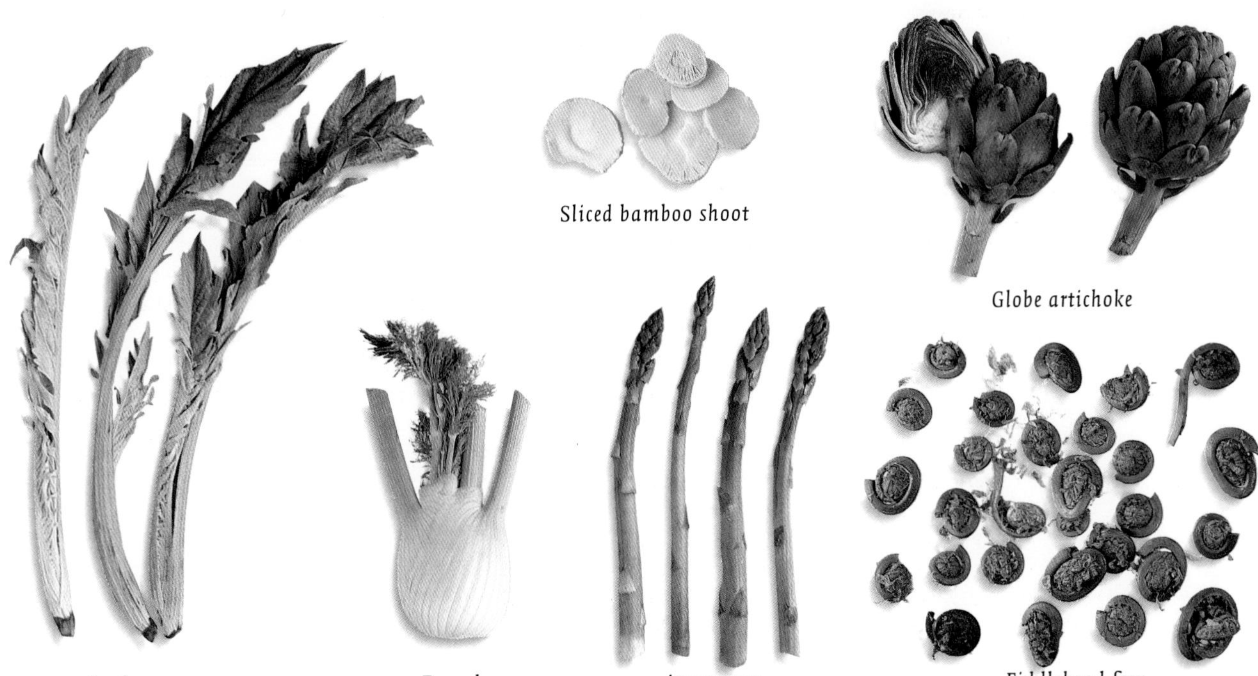

Sliced bamboo shoot

Globe artichoke

Cardoon

Fennel

Asparagus

Fiddlehead fern

beurre noisette 422
celeriac 148

Asparagus Risotto 349
Asparagus Soufflé 328
Celery and Parmesan Salad 365
Hollandaise Sauce 255
Mayonnaise 259
Vinaigrette 259

sometimes thin and often short, and which may be sold as 'grass' or 'sprue' asparagus, is usually well worth having.

The difficulty encountered in cooking asparagus arises from the fact that the tips, being much more tender than the stalks, cook more quickly and may break off when you transfer the asparagus to the serving dish. The answer is to cook asparagus in an asparagus kettle, a special pan with a perforated insert. Failing this, cook them tied together in bundles in a wide, shallow pan. With the second method it is extremely important not to overcook the asparagus or to boil it too fast, or the tips will be damaged.

To prepare the asparagus, wash it well, cut off the hard ends and pare the lower part of the stalks with a knife or potato peeler. Tie the asparagus into bundles, one for each serving, if you are not using an asparagus kettle. Bring well-salted water to the boil in the kettle (or wide pan). Lower the asparagus into the water (in the kettle just the stalks are in water: the tips will be in the steam) and return to the boil as rapidly as possible. Cover and cook for 8–10 minutes or until the lower parts of the stalks are easily pierced with the tip of a knife. Don't overcook them – they should be just tender when pierced and the tips will break up if boiled for too long. Alternatively, asparagus can be steamed over boiling water.

Save the asparagus water and a few token asparagus for making soup. Serve the rest, carefully drained. Thick asparagus is always served as a course on its own, usually at the beginning of the meal.

Served warm, thick asparagus comes with melted or whipped butter, with hollandaise or mousseline sauce, or *à la flamande* with halved hard-boiled eggs and noisette butter served separately. Served *à la polonaise*, the noisette butter – butter heated in a pan until it is a pale hazelnut colour – is poured over the tips that have been sprinkled with finely chopped hard-boiled eggs.

In Italy, asparagus is eaten with Parmesan and butter over the tips, melted for a moment under a grill. If served cold, mayonnaise or vinaigrette are the usual accompaniments. As asparagus contains a certain amount of sulphur it spoils the taste of wine, so save this for other courses.

Swiss chard *Celery*

Thin asparagus makes a good vegetable dish and goes well with delicate, light meats: veal, sweetbreads, chicken breast, slices of turkey, or rosy boiled ham, thinly sliced. And asparagus can also go into quiches or omelettes.

Celery

This can be white, which means that it has been blanched during cultivation or is the self-blanching kind that is naturally golden-white or pink, or it can be green.

You can buy celery washed, or 'dirty', in which case it will need to be scrubbed before use. The stalks should be thick and crisp, the leaves green and full of vitality, and the base sound. You can revive limp celery by wrapping it in moist paper and standing it in a jar of water. Raw celery sticks are often served with cheese, standing in a tall jug with their decorative leaves intact; however, the coarse outer strings should be removed. Do this by cutting partway through the stalk bases and pulling off the attached strings down the length of the stalks.

Raw celery is excellent with cheese and, chopped, it is good mixed with cream cheese as a sandwich filling. Celery also goes into poultry stuffings and sauces, and can be stewed with bacon to accompany game. It is delicious parboiled and served *au gratin*, and is equally good when braised in stock or water, or cold, *à la grecque*.

Globe artichoke

Although not strictly a stalk or shoot but in fact a bud, the globe artichoke is usually considered in the same group as delicacies such as asparagus. While some of its flavour lies in the fat base of each of its leaves, the best part – the heart, or *fond* – lies deep within its centre.

When you buy artichokes – they can be green or purplish – make sure they still have a good bloom on their leaves and that the centres are well closed, not about to burst into great purple thistle-like flower heads. Artichokes do not keep well and should ideally be used at once, but if you must keep them, place their stalks – they may be sold with about 10 cm/4 in of stalk – in water.

To prepare them for cooking whole, twist off the stalks, which will also remove some of the tougher fibres from the base. Then, with a stainless-steel knife, cut the base of each globe flush so that it won't wobble on the plate when it is served; rub the cut surface with lemon to prevent it from turning black. If the leaves are very spiky, cut them into a pretty V shape or simply trim off the ends. Wash the artichoke and then boil it in acidulated water in a stainless pan, perhaps with a piece of lemon tied to its base. Test for readiness by tugging at a leaf: if it comes away and is tender, the artichoke is done and ready to be drained upside down on a rack.

One of the best ways to eat globe artichokes is simply to pull off the leaves with the fingers, one at a time; dip the fleshy part into melted butter, vinaigrette or hollandaise, and then draw it through the teeth, eating the fleshy part and putting the remains of the leaf on to your plate. When you reach the tiny pale leaves in the centre, which seem to be arranged in the form of a little pointed hat, grasp them tightly together at the top and pull off the whole rosette. Then pull away and discard the prickly, straw-like choke, which may come away with one tug or need a bit of scraping. Finally, eat the heart, which is slightly pitted, with a knife and fork.

It is possible to remove the choke before cooking, to form little cups. This is usually done in smart restaurants, where instead of a simple butter or vinaigrette dressing you may be offered various sauces such as puréed shallots reduced in wine. The hearts can also be stuffed, perhaps with a béchamel enriched with egg yolks and Parmesan, or with foie gras, or with a purée of mushrooms. They are usually parboiled before they are stuffed, and then go into the oven, anointed with oil or butter, until the stuffing is cooked. For delicate dishes or when artichoke hearts are required as a garnish, remove the green leaves, keeping the firm white-green part.

Among the many ways of preparing artichokes, the Italians have produced the most inventive. They simmer artichoke hearts in broth or wine, or in wine with oil, tomatoes and garlic, and fry small, tender ones in oil; sometimes they blanch them and then dip them in batter before deep frying them. As elsewhere, artichokes are also eaten cold.

Sliced sautéed artichoke hearts may be mixed with peas and ham or scrambled eggs for an interesting first course, and in France if you are given a soup called *Chatelaine* you will find that it is made of puréed hearts. In the south of France and some parts of Italy, tiny young artichokes are eaten raw, either whole with aïoli or *bagna cauda* – a hot anchovy- and garlic-flavoured dip – or thinly sliced and tossed with Parmesan in olive oil.

Seakale

Highly popular in earlier times, although less often seen now, this European plant is a member of the mustard family. A

Preparing globe artichoke hearts

As you work, rub all cut surfaces with juice from lemon halves to prevent discoloration.

1

1 Snap the stalk off at the base of the artichoke, pulling out the fibres with it.

2

2 Bend a large lower leaf out and over towards the base until the leaf snaps, then pull it off. Continue snapping off all the large outer leaves in this way.

3 Cut off the cone of paler green, soft inner leaves, cutting straight across just above the hairy choke.

4 Using a small knife, trim off all the dark green parts from around the sides and base of the artichoke, trimming it into a neat round shape.

3

4

5

5 Scoop out the hairy choke in the centre using a teaspoon (or do this after cooking the artichoke heart according to the recipe instructions). Cook the artichoke heart immediately, or immerse it in water acidulated with lemon juice, to prevent discoloration.

acidulated water 422
foie gras 90

Aïoli 259
Artichokes alla Romana 376
Béchamel Sauce 255
Lasagne with Mushrooms, Bacon and Artichokes 340
Omelette with Artichokes and Parsley 324
Stewed Artichokes with Spinach 376
Tagliarini with Fresh Artichokes and Gremolata 338

asparagus 137
beet greens 133
blanc 148
bone marrow 53
Chinese noodles 124–5
spinach 132

Béchamel Sauce 255
Mornay Sauce 255
Vinaigrette 259

frail, pale vegetable, it grows wild in English coastal districts, forcing its stalks up through piled-up sand so that they emerge perfectly white. Cultivated seakale is forced in early spring under special pots and cut when its leaves are no more than a yellow frill edged with purple. It is boiled in sea-water, or in salted water by those who are distant from the shore. The juicy but delicate stems are sometimes found in the shops, wrapped in blue tissue paper: once they are exposed to the light they very soon lose both their pallor and their flavour.

Seakale should be boiled or steamed for about 10–12 minutes to become tender, or it can be parboiled and then braised. Plain boiled in little bunches, it makes, like asparagus, a course of its own, and should then be served with melted butter and the same sauces as asparagus. It is also good raw, like celery, with cheese.

Seakale beet and Swiss chard

No relation to the seakale of coastal areas, these forms of *Beta vulgaris* are grown primarily for their pale, wide midribs and crinkly leaves rather than their roots. Their green leaves can be prepared like spinach or beet greens (whose stalks are not big enough to be cooked separately). A variety with bright scarlet stalks, called ruby chard, looks sensational, but unfortunately the colour disappears on cooking.

The large silver seakale beet and Swiss chard stalks have a delicate flavour and, like the smaller seakale beet, are extremely succulent when boiled or steamed. Both can be served *au gratin* or simply dressed with melted butter. In France chard, or *blettes*, are served with béchamel sauce and sausages, while in Italy they are used to make stuffings for tarts and ravioli or are chopped and cooked in risotto.

Cardoon

A relation of the globe artichoke, the cardoon is cultivated for its young leaf stalks and has a flavour that faintly resembles the artichoke. Left to itself, it produces a smaller, spikier head than the artichoke, which in Greece is picked and eaten stewed, but what comes into the shops in winter and early spring are the bottom ends of the plant, looking like overgrown grey-green celery. Like celery, cardoons are earthed up to blanch the stalks, which gives them their delicate texture and delicious flavour.

The finest cardoons are those grown in the region of Tours and near Lyons, but you are most likely to come across cardoons in Italian shops, as Italians enjoy *cardoni* even more than the French.

To prepare them, trim off the skin, which is fibrous and prickly at the ridges, blanch in boiling water and then cook them for about 30 minutes in a *blanc* – like artichokes, cardoons discolour easily when cooked. Serve them with bone marrow or a béchamel or cheese sauce, or *alla piedmontese* – dipped in a sauce of anchovies, oil and garlic – or simply eat them with melted butter. In North Africa they are used to flavour meat stews.

Bamboo shoot and palm heart

Edible young bamboo shoots – and not all bamboos are edible – are bought fresh in the Far East and, stripped of their tough brown outer skins, the insides are eaten. Their texture is similar to celery and their taste to a globe artichoke.

The canned variety is the most readily available kind outside the Far East. It needs no peeling, but it should be rinsed before use, whether packed in brine or water, otherwise it has a pronounced tinny taste. Chopped bamboo shoots can be used in a number of stir-fried vegetable and meat dishes, and as a garnish for clear chicken broth, or served with any sauce suitable for asparagus.

Fresh palm hearts, which are the buds of cabbage palm trees, need to be blanched before being cooked to get rid of their bitter flavour. When boiled, they are eaten with any of the sauces suitable for asparagus; cold, they need a vinaigrette dressing. They are also good in mixed salads. Hot or cold, they are usually served cut in half lengthwise.

Hop shoot

While the dried flowers of hops are used for brewing, the young blanched shoots, cooked and eaten with melted butter, make a useful substitute for asparagus – in France, where they are known as *jets de houblon*, they are considered a delicacy. Like asparagus, they should simply be rinsed well to clean them of any soil and sand, then tied in bundles and boiled. Their delicate flavour goes well with creamy sauces. In Belgium young hop shoots are served with eggs.

Fiddlehead fern

Found in eastern North America, this fern is eaten when young and the shoots are still tightly coiled. They are not, in fact, a particular type of fern, but simply young ferns of any type. The small, rich green shoots have a satisfyingly chewy texture and a flavour that has been described as a mixture of asparagus, French beans and mushrooms. Eat them raw, in a salad, or sauté in butter.

PEAS, BEANS AND SWEETCORN

From the moment they are picked, peas, beans and sweetcorn start converting their sugar into starch. This process subtly alters both their taste and texture, so they should be chosen carefully and eaten the very day they are bought. Freezing, however, arrests these changes, so frozen peas, beans and sweetcorn retain their sweetness and melting consistency well.

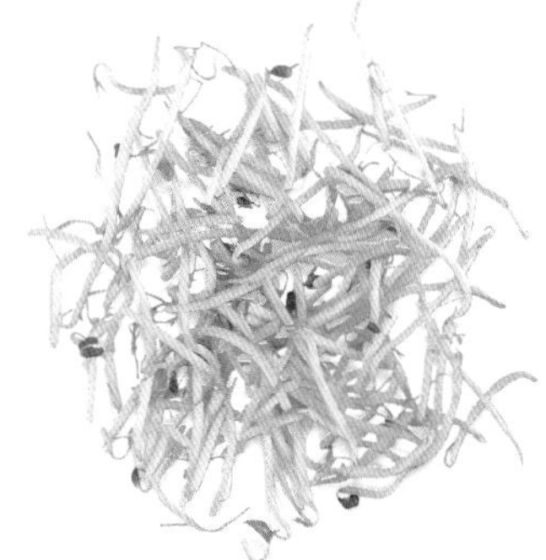

Bean sprout

Sweetcorn

Pea

Once inordinately expensive and considered a great luxury, peas have become one of the best loved of all vegetables. Endless varieties have been developed, especially in England where the climate suits them to perfection.

Garden pea and petit pois
Gardeners make a distinction between two types of garden pea: the larger marrowfat, which is wrinkled when dried, and the varieties that remain smooth when dried. The former is much sweeter and is the one most often frozen.

The reason for the disappearance of many varieties of green pea is, of course, the ubiquitous frozen pea – more expensive to be sure, but a great timesaver.

Garden peas respond to all sorts of treatment: in England they are preferred plain, boiled and bathed in butter, although some cooks like to add a small sprig of fresh mint. In Italy peas are often mixed with fine shreds of raw ham, or with rice, in which case the dish becomes *risi e bisi*. In countries such as France where vegetables are habitually served in a light coating of béchamel sauce, peas, too, are given this treatment. They are often mixed with carrots, *à la flamande*.

Contrary to popular belief, petits pois are small not because they are immature but because they are a dwarf variety. These are the peas canned in vast quantities by the French and Belgians, and they are excellent: tiny, dull green and very sweet, quite unlike most other canned peas. The fat, ugly canned peas, swimming in green dye, that are sold in Britain are best avoided altogether.

Petits pois à la française are peas cooked in a lettuce-lined saucepan with a little sugar, some tiny silver onions, a lump of butter and only as much water as clings to the lettuce leaves after washing. Cooked in this way, the peas turn a delicate yellowish colour and have a most delicious flavour; even larger peas on the mealy side become melting and young-tasting. Really solid older peas are best for fresh green-pea soup or purées.

Mangetout pea, sugar-snap pea and asparagus pea As their name suggests, mangetout peas, which are also called snow peas and sugar peas, are eaten pods and all. There are many varieties, all bred with the minimum of thin, tough membrane that lines the pod of the common green pea, so both the large, flat mangetout pod with immature seeds and the smaller, darker kind make tender eating, provided they are very young. If they have strings at the sides, these should be removed in the kitchen during topping and tailing.

Mangetout peas taste best when they are very briefly boiled or steamed. When cooked, they should still have a little bite to them, and they are best served perfectly plain with enough butter to coat each pod. Very young mangetout are

Green Pea Soup 254
Navarin of Lamb with Potatoes 288
Paella 346
Peas an Indian Way 378
Peas with Lettuce Hearts 376

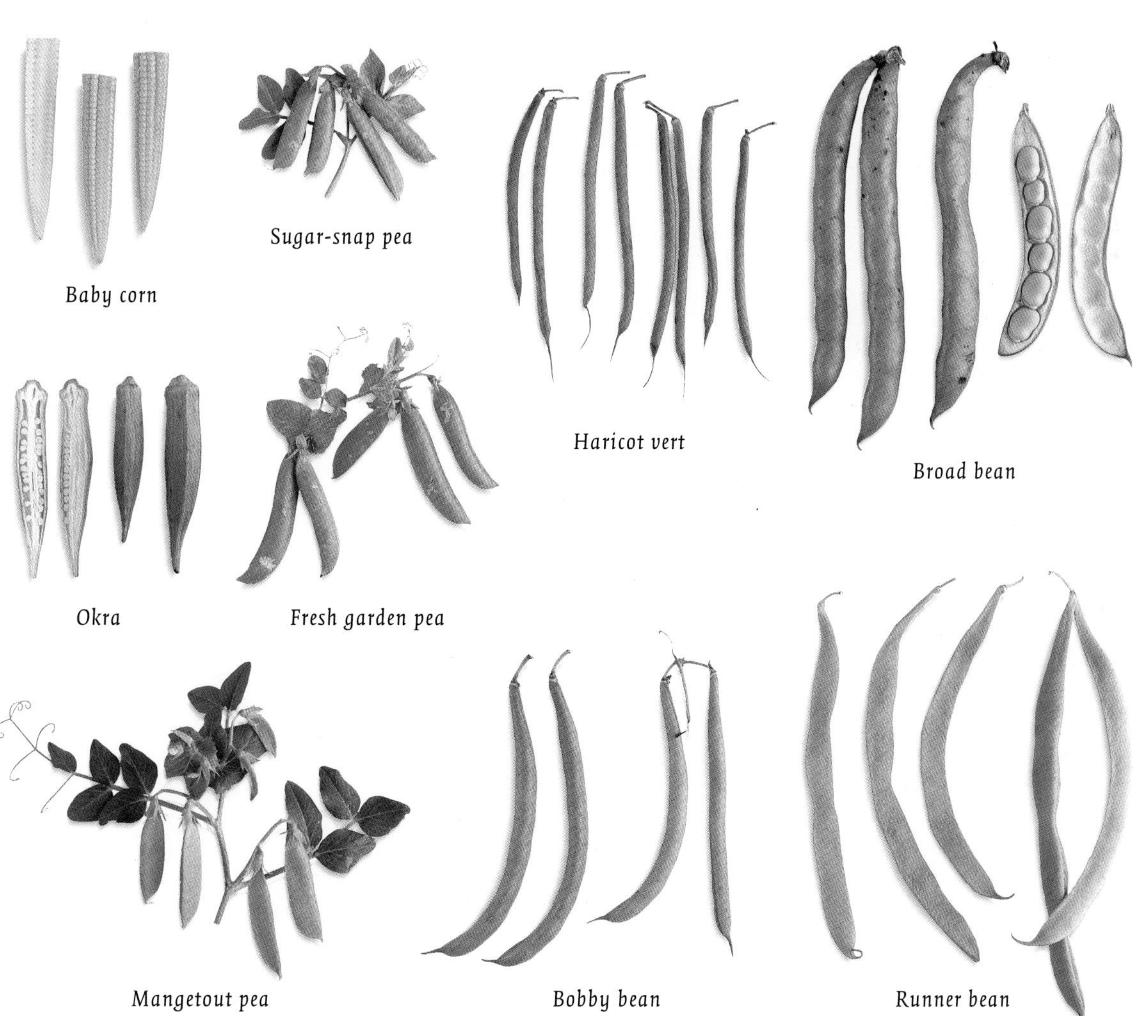

Baby corn

Sugar-snap pea

Haricot vert

Broad bean

Okra

Fresh garden pea

Mangetout pea

Bobby bean

Runner bean

al dente 422
corn (grain) 115
corn oil 112
mung bean 128
soya bean 128

Broad Beans and Bacon 378
Crab Salad with Thai Flavours 368
Gratin of French Beans with Chives 378
Green Bean Salad with Anchovy-Cream Dressing 367
Japanese Noodles with Char-Grilled Beef 345
Six-Vegetable Couscous 350
Stewed Broad Beans with Butter and Tarragon 378

good in salads, and all mangetout peas are also excellent when stir-fried.

Like the mangetout, the sugar-snap pea has an edible pod, but it is eaten after the peas inside have matured and swollen. As a result, the pod is lumpy rather than flat.

Asparagus peas, not a relation of the asparagus but of the cow-pea, and in fact not a true pea at all, are rarely seen these days. They have winged pods which, like the mangetout, are eaten as well as the seed, but they are only good when they are very young and 5 cm/2 in long or less.

Green bean

This is a general term for beans with edible pods, but in fact they come in colours ranging from deep green and purple to pale yellow. The two main types, however, are the French or green beans, and the runner or pole beans.

Of the French beans there are dozens of varieties. Snap or bobby beans, a fairly fat, fleshy variety, should snap in half juicily if they are fresh. The highly prized haricot vert is slim and delicate and should be eaten very young and when no larger than the prong of a carving fork. The yellow wax-bean is also a French bean and is somewhat mild in taste.

Runner beans have long, rough and usually stringy pods, although stringless varieties are available. As their name suggests they are a type of climbing bean, as are the delicious purple-podded beans, which have stringless pods, but turn green when they are cooked (there are also purple bush beans).

Whatever the type, beanpods should be crisp and bright – avoid buying wilted ones or overly mature beans with tough-looking pods. They all need topping and tailing, and some types still need de-stringing. Test for stringiness by keeping the top or tail end just attached to the pod and drawing it downwards: if a portion of stout threat comes away, careful de-stringing is indicated.

All podded beans are cooked in the same way. They should be briefly steamed or plunged into well-salted, rapidly boiling water and cooked until just *al dente* – too often they are overcooked. Once drained, they can be tossed in butter. French beans can be served in a sauce containing shallots, or cream and butter with chives, or bathed in a tomato sauce with a touch of onion.

Broad bean and lima bean

In their first youth, neither broad beans nor lima beans strictly require shelling, but the pods are nearly always discarded to reveal large, flattish seeds.

Broad bean Often called fava beans, these are the original Old World bean, much appreciated in Italy and Spain. These large, lumpy beans with their furry-lined pods should be shelled immediately before going into the pot, unless they are very young. In that case top and tail them before cooking or eating raw, pods and all.

Lima bean Named after the capital of Peru, these are most familiar in North America in their shelled and frozen state, but are at their best when they can be bought fresh and in their pods. They appear in the Native American dish succotash, which also includes sweetcorn. Lima beans are sometimes called butter beans in the southern American states. There are two types of lima bean – the baby Sieva, pale in colour, and the larger Fordhook. The large, European butter bean, a close relative of the lima bean, is rarely found fresh but is instead canned or dried.

For a plain dish of broad beans or lima beans, plunge them into rapidly boiling water and cook until just tender, but not a moment longer. They are also delicious with cooked ham or bacon. Elderly broad beans need skinning after cooking.

Okra

These curved and pointed seed pods came originally from Africa. They travelled to America and feature a great deal in Creole cooking. The flavour resembles that of aubergines, but the texture is mucilaginous, and this is what gives the body to the Creole stews and gumbos to which okra is added.

Crossbreeding has produced a range of colours and surfaces, but the slim, green octagonal okra is the one usually sold in our shops. Look for small, crisp pods and avoid any that are shrivelled or bruised. To cook okra whole, trim off the tip and the cap, but be sure not to expose the seeds and sticky juices inside or the okra will split and lose shape during cooking. Steamed or cooked in boiling salted water until just tender, okra can be served with a tomato sauce or simply tossed in butter, or it can be used in vegetable curries and stews.

Sweetcorn

One of the delights of late summer is the appearance on the market of fresh, tender young sweetcorn. The husks should be clean and green; the silk tassels bright with no sign of dampness or matting; and the kernels pale, plump, well filled and milky, with no space between the rows. Avoid cobs with dark yellow kernels or older large ones that look tough and dry.

With fresh sweetcorn, time is of the essence – the briefer the span between picking and eating, the sweeter and more tender the corn will be. There are now supersweet varieties being bred that will stay sweeter much longer than other types, but even with these, the fresher, the better.

If you can't use sweetcorn immediately, then keep it in plastic bags in the refrigerator for 2 or 3 days. Allow sweetcorn plenty of space – if the cobs are piled on top of each other, this tends to generate warmth and 'cook' the corn.

To cook corn on the cob, strip away the green packaging and silk tassel, then steam, or plunge into briskly boiling water or milk and water. A little sugar can be added for extra sweetness – especially for the sweetcorn grown in Europe, which is never quite as sweet and tender as American corn. Serve with plenty of butter, sea salt and freshly ground pepper, and large napkins to protect the diners' clothes from dripping butter.

Baby corn Imported from Thailand, this is a popular addition to stir-fry dishes. It has a crisp yet tender texture but not much flavour.

Bean sprout

The sprouts that can be bought in plastic bags and are an ingredient in many oriental dishes have usually been sprouted from mung or soya beans. Look for crisp, pale sprouts; even a hint of exuding brown juice means that they are past their prime. Mild flavoured, they add a crunchy texture to salads, or they can be stir-fried briefly over high heat and seasoned with soy sauce, fresh ginger, garlic and spring onions. Serve them immediately or they will lose their crunch. Keep sprouts in a plastic bag or box in the refrigerator while they are waiting to be used.

THE ONION FAMILY

The genus *Allium*, which includes onions as well as garlic and leeks, has a great many members, both cultivated and wild. The onion is an ancient vegetable and has been bred in many forms; while many of these can be used interchangeably, each type has a particular purpose.

Onion

Being both flavouring agent and vegetable in its own right, the onion is something that no kitchen can ever be without. There are few savoury dishes that don't start with a sliced or chopped onion, and few that would be good without it. There are onions in onion soup, creamy or clear; *sauce soubise* or onion sauce to go with lamb; flans like *zwiebelkuchen* from Austria or the French *tarte à l'oignon*; as well as all the garnishes that this versatile vegetable provides. Among these are the glazed, bronzed button onions, good with any roasted meat, particularly veal; fried onion rings that go with steak and liver; little pickled onions; and the smaller, fresh green-tailed onions that are eaten with cheese.

It is a good idea to try to buy onions in assorted sizes, or to choose smaller rather than larger specimens, because once cut they do not keep well. To keep back the tears when peeling an onion, try peeling it under running water.

Chopping an onion into dice can be quite a fast business if efficiently tackled. Peel the onion but do not cut off the root end. Halve the onion through the root and lay the half onion cut side down. Slice down into narrow strips, cutting from tip end to root end, but do not let the strips fall apart. Now, holding the half onion together, cut across the strips, at right angles to the first cuts. Remove the root end and the onion will fall into dice.

Once chopped, the onion is often sweated in hot fat or oil – which means allowing it to become translucent without colouring – or fried to a more or less deep gold to develop its characteristic flavour. It is then incorporated with the other ingredients for the dish in the making.

Globe onion These come in all sizes, from pearly button onions to large coppery spheres, and in a variety of colours – white, gold and red – and shapes: oval, round, slender and flat. All come to a peak at the top, like the domes of the Kremlin, which owe their shape to the fact that the many-layered onion – 'a sky within a sky' – was regarded as a symbol of eternity in its native Asia and beyond.

Yellow onion So called although their outer skin is golden brown rather than yellow, these are considered to be the most pungent of all the globe onions. Look for sound specimens that are dry, with no trace of moisture at the base or the neck, and with no growth of light greenery at the top – a sign that they have

Coq au Vin 305
French Onion Soup 249
Lyonnaise Calf's Liver with Onions 292

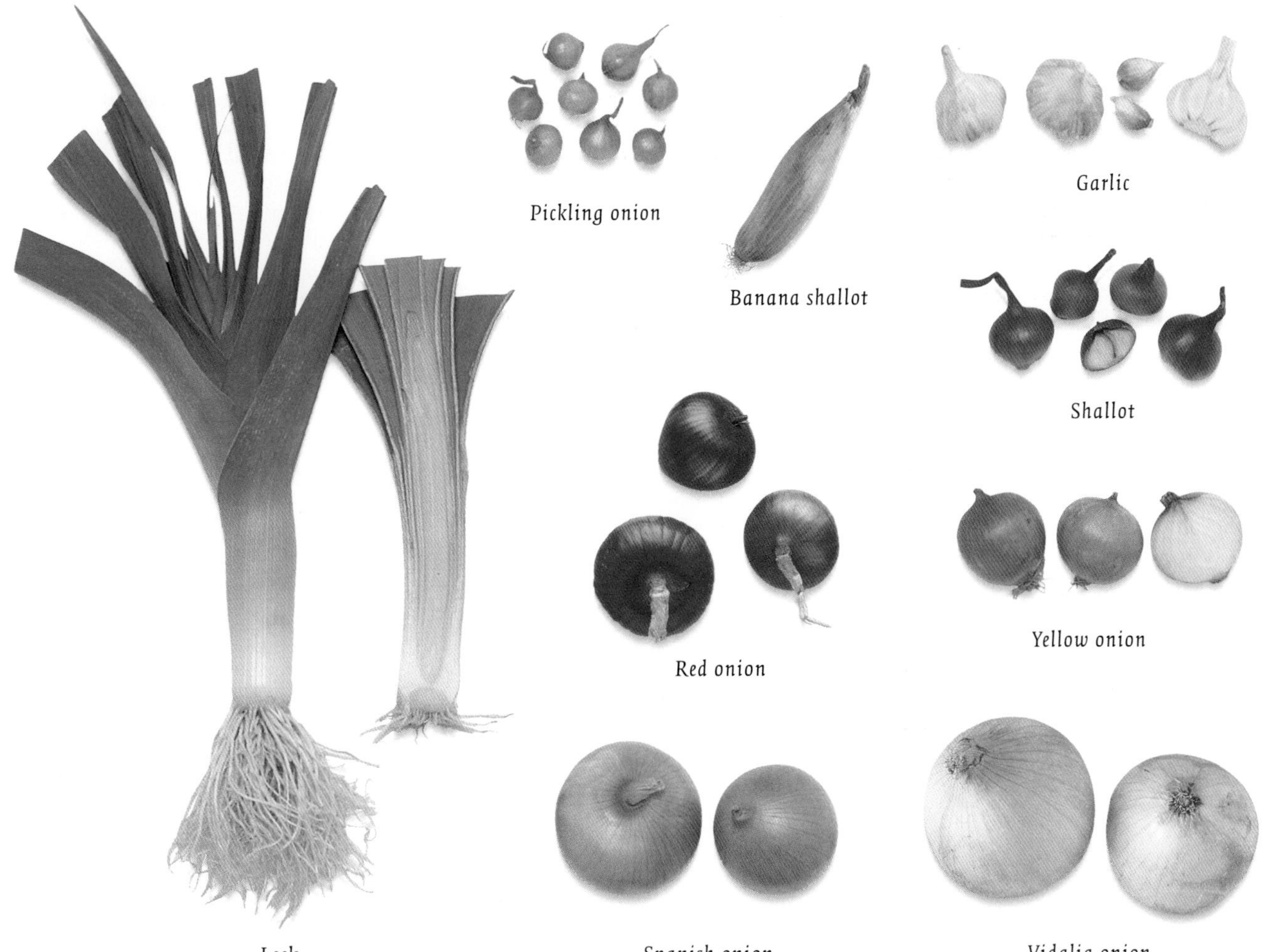

Pickling onion

Banana shallot

Garlic

Shallot

Red onion

Yellow onion

Leek

Spanish onion

Vidalia onion

antipasto 422
Beurre Blanc 256
Blade Steak with Shallots 282
Sichuan Chicken Salad 372
Spanish Onion Tart 328
Steamed Cod with Ginger and Spring Onion 264
Yogurt and Spring Onion Dressing 259

begun to sprout again at the expense of the soundness of their core. Yellow onions are the basic all-purpose onion. The smallest are often offered as pickling onions, but do as well for the pot.

Spanish onion This large, flattened, brown or pale copper-coloured onion is generally inclined to be milder and sweeter than the yellow variety. Its size makes it particularly suitable for stuffing and baking, and its comparative gentleness makes it ideal as fried onions, in salads and for use in dishes that need its substance, such as creamy soups and sauces.

Red onion This is relatively mild and distinguished by its deep red skin and the red-tinged layers below the skin. Sweet in flavour, it can be used for the same purposes as Spanish onions, and is good to eat raw in antipasti and in salads.

Bermuda onion Large but rather squat, this onion can be used in the same ways as red onions and is ideal with hamburgers.

White or silver onion This relatively mild little onion has a shimmery silver skin. It is about the size of a walnut, and is best either added to stews or served in a cream sauce. Very tiny white onions are called pearl or cocktail onions. Sold in jars, these are used as a garnish in various cocktails such as the Gibson – which is what a Martini becomes when an onion replaces the usual olive. Slightly larger white onions are used for pickling, and in many French dishes. They are delicious, too, made into a '*confit*', by slow cooking in a tart-flavoured syrup.

Vidalia onion This very juicy American onion, from Georgia, is much sweeter than the Spanish or Bermuda onion, and is excellent both raw and cooked. Walla Walla onions, from Washington State, and Maui onions, from Hawaii, are similar large, sweet onions. New varieties are being developed all the time.

Green or fresh onions

These are eaten raw in salads, but can also be cooked. There are two types of green onions, so called because of the green leaves that form above the white part. They are spring onions and Welsh onions or Japanese bunching onions.

Spring onion

Welsh onion

Spring onion These may be slim and tiny, like miniature leeks, except that their leaves are tubular, or they may have been lifted from the soil after small silvery bulbs have formed just above the roots. They taste mild and quite delicate, and both the white bottoms and the green tops are used as lively additions to salads and salad dressings. When cooked they are added to some savoury dishes where other onions would be too strong in taste. They are also good chopped finely and mixed with mashed potato, in omelettes and as a garnish on pork dishes.

Welsh onion or Japanese bunching onion If you find spring onions mentioned in Chinese or Japanese recipes, use these onions if you can get them – they are not widely known in the West and certainly not in Wales, despite their name. The other name for the species, Japanese bunching onion, is more precise, since they are very popular in the Far East. Welsh onions grow in a cluster, and if the young leaves are harvested early in the year the bulbs will grow more leaves. Eat the small, young green leaves raw in salads, and the mature stems in any recipe suitable for leeks, and in onion soup.

Tree onion

Also known as rocambole or garlic-onion, the tree onion produces a cluster of little copper-coloured bulbs at the top of the plant, where one normally expects to see only flowers. These are planted in winter or spring and will produce larger bulbs with a good flavour, somewhere between garlic and shallot.

Shallot

This pear-shaped bulb, with a long neck and skin that ranges from grey to pinkish to copper, is intense in taste without being unduly pungent. There are several kinds, including the large banana shallot, or torpedo onion, up to 15 cm/6 in long, that is bright pink. Shallots grow singly or in clusters and are more seasonal than onions, since they do not keep as well. The crisp layers of their flesh are finely textured. Shallots taste sweet and delicate, and are mostly used for flavouring. No other member of the onion family produces such an exquisite flavour in beurre blanc, the butter sauce that features shallots cooked in wine or in wine vinegar.

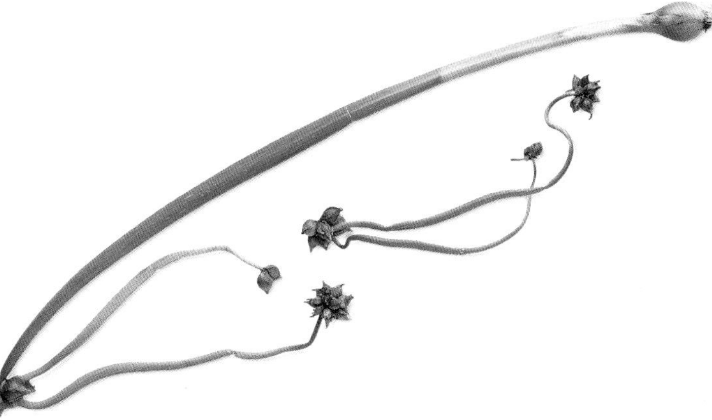

Tree onion

When recipes specify shallots, they should be used. And, although extravagant, you can use shallots instead of onion if you want a lighter, more delicate taste. The exception comes when browning is involved – this makes shallots taste a little bitter – and shallots cook much faster than onions.

Shallots are an important ingredient in the cooking of northern France, featuring in *marchand de vin* sauce, made by reducing shallots to a purée with wine – red wine to go with steak and white wine in fish dishes.

Garlic

By far the most pungent member of the onion family, the garlic bulb or head grows in a cluster of pointed cloves from a single base. Many people are prejudiced against garlic because it stays on the breath, but, by way of compensation when garlic is eaten in company, the nose develops a tolerance of the garlic-laden breath of others. And it is said that vast quantities of garlic eaten at a single sitting will not have much effect on the breath. It is certainly true that a slowly cooked dish using a great deal of garlic – say a chicken cooked on a bed of whole cloves of garlic – or even whole heads of garlic, which can be roasted unpeeled and eaten by picking up the cloves at the end and squeezing the content into the mouth, taste much sweeter and far less garlicky than something like a salad with raw peeled and bruised garlic in the dressing.

Garlic grown in a hot climate is considered to be the most pungent. As a flavouring agent it is therefore most economical in use. But wherever it comes from, and whether it is sold tied in strings or bunches, in little nets or loose, and whether it is snow-white, grey, purple or pinkish, look for fat, round, hard bulbs.

Fresh new-season's garlic, available in the summer, has an especially subtle flavour and, with its suede-like inner skin, is liked by connoisseurs for their salads. However, most garlic is allowed to dry off: it keeps well in a dry, airy place. Too much moisture in the air, and it will start sprouting in due course; too much warmth, and the interior cloves eventually turn to black dust – but this takes a matter of months rather than weeks. In Provence garlic is sometimes smoked to help it keep a little longer, but the white variety, bought in large quantities in September, is considered the longest keeping, lasting up to a year.

To prepare garlic, carefully peel as many cloves as you plan to use. Whether you chop them in the ordinary way, or mash them with salt under the flat of a knife, or crush them in a garlic press is a matter of taste: the finer the result, the more of the pungent oils are released, and it is probably true that the garlic press produces the least subtle taste. If the garlic clove has a green shoot inside, remove it before chopping as it has a bitter taste.

There are many dishes to which garlic gives its essential flavour. It bonds well with meat, particularly lamb, with chicken and fish, with many vegetables, especially the Mediterranean ones such as tomatoes and aubergines, and with mushrooms, whose flavour it enhances. Without it there would be no aïoli, the garlic-laden mayonnaise served in France with fish soups, boiled chicken and every sort of fresh vegetable. And garlic is an essential ingredient in the cooking of southern Europe, of India and South-east Asia, and of China.

Leek

The leek that good Welshmen used to wear in their hats on St David's Day was, in fact, their native non-bulb-forming onion. Leeks were once used interchangeably with onions, but they are, with their flat leaves arranged in chevron formation, more delicate in taste than onions. A leek is certainly a more subtle flavouring for broth, earning it the title of 'king of the soup onions'. Scotland's cock-a-leekie is a justifiably renowned soup composed of chicken and leeks, and the leek's talents were taken to their logical end when the *chef des chefs* of New York's Ritz-Carlton hotel invented his *crème vichyssoise*.

Sadly, many cooks quite ignore the leek's virtues as a plain accompanying vegetable. It is excellent simmered in butter, stewed in red wine, lightly browned and then cooked in a tomato sauce, or eaten cold with a vinaigrette.

If leeks have a drawback, it is that they can be rather a bore to clean. There is no problem when recipes call for chopped leeks, when it is a case of chopping first – after pulling off the outer membrane and trimming the wilted part of the greenery – and cleaning later. This is best done by placing the chopped leeks in a colander set in a bowl and running cold water over them until all the grit has settled at the bottom of the bowl. But when recipes call for sliced leeks, it is necessary to loosen the leaves gently so that the water can run right into the furled vegetable. Most leeks on sale look quite clean, but it is only the outside dirt that has been removed by the growers; in the kitchen make little slits with the point of a knife in appropriate places and rinse until all the grit has gone, or cut them almost in half down the middle if they are very gritty.

When you buy leeks, examine them at both ends. The white part should be firm and unblemished and the green part fresh and lively – the green is useful for soups or stock even if your dish only calls for the white part. When leeks are sold trimmed, without much greenery, you may suspect that they are not only elderly, but so mature as already to have formed a solid tubular flower stalk in the middle. This you will have to discard, being left with a disappointingly hollow stem as a result.

ROOTS AND TUBERS

The root vegetables and tubers – turnips, parsnips and swedes, beetroots, carrots and potatoes – certainly make rather a humble-sounding list when they are all lumped together. It is true they are of the earth, rustic, robust and ordinary, but it is because of this that they have always been so useful.

In hard times, when people couldn't afford bread, or were forced to make it out of whatever roots they could find, including fern roots, it was herbs and root vegetables, particularly turnips, that kept them alive – herbs can be gathered wild and roots, surviving the worst weather, can be stored through winter. In better times, roots were the vegetables that were liked best, alongside a piece of boiled or roasted meat – hence boiled beef and carrots, roast duck with turnips, haggis with mashed swedes and everything with potatoes.

Potato

Potatoes, whose mysterious underground swellings make better use of their patch of ground than any cereal, are one of the

crushing and chopping garlic 423
garlic vinegar 205

Aïoli 259
Boiled Bacon and Sausage with Haricot Beans and Garlic Purée 291
Chicken on a Bed of Garlic 306
Chinese Egg Noodles with Browned Garlic, Chillies and Parsley 345
Garlic and Herb Butter 257
Garlic Mushroom Soup with Cream 246
Leek Tart 328
Leeks in Cream 379
Leeks with Truffles 379
Pan-Fried Scallops with Garlic 279
Quick-Fried Chicken with Garlic and Chilli 305
Stuffed Guinea Fowl with leek Purée 302
Tomato and Leek Soup 246
Vichyssoise with Chives 254
Yogurt and Garlic Dressing 259

potato flour 118

chip cutter 225
potato peeler 224

Navarin of Lamb with Potatoes 288
New England Fish Chowder 252
New Potatoes Baked with Saffron, Cream and Garlic 381
Poulet Paysanne 307
Salt Cod with Potatoes 274
Spiced and Fried New Potatoes with Minted Yogurt Dressing 381
Vichyssoise with Chives 254

world's most important food crops. They are a most obliging and good-natured vegetable. Easy to grow, cheap to buy, simple to cook and tremendously filling, they also seem to be the one vegetable, apart perhaps from tomatoes, that nobody ever seems to get tired of.

There are almost endless varieties of potatoes – about 80 in Britain alone. Popular varieties change rapidly, coming into favour with the growers because they keep well or are resistant to disease, and then being ousted by newer, even hardier kinds with higher yields or fewer eyes. This makes it extremely difficult to prepare a catalogue of varieties.

However, different types of potatoes, round, oval or kidney-shaped, pink, red, white or, more rarely, blue or purple, do have very different qualities, and a well-informed supplier will be able to tell you which variety is which. There are floury or mealy potatoes, ideal for mashing and baking, but annoying if you want to boil them whole as they tend to fall apart in the water. They are also useless for making chips. Waxy potatoes are very firm-fleshed and not at all good for mashing because they become glutinous, but they make excellent potato salads, lovely boiled potatoes, and delicious gratins, when the potatoes are cooked in slices that are supposed to remain whole.

There are also all-purpose potatoes, whose texture is described as firm. These can be used for almost anything, except perhaps potato salads. They don't disintegrate, can be made into good chips and are excellent for baking. But they don't always have the best flavour, so it is a good idea to try different varieties as you come across them, and then keep to the ones you like best.

As well as different varieties there are, of course, new and old potatoes. New potatoes are not a specific variety of potato, but any potato harvested when small and young. Special varieties that go under the name of 'earlies' are usually dug between June and August, while they are still small and sweet. Maincrop, or old potatoes, are lifted from late summer onwards when they are mature and fully grown, and have converted their sugar into starch. Maincrop potatoes can be stored through the winter and until the beginning of the next season, when the new potatoes – always tremendously welcome – reappear.

Buying and storing potatoes New potatoes should be small and faintly translucent under a coating of slightly damp loam; or, if ready-washed, they should be taut and shiny. If the skin is a little ragged and so tender that you can pull it off in strips, so much the better – this shows that the potatoes are fresh and will be easy to scrape. New potatoes do not keep particularly well, becoming more difficult to scrape (in which case scrub them and cook them in their skins). They also lose their flavour after a few days, so buy them in small quantities and keep them in a cool, dark place.

Old potatoes are more amenable and can be stored in a cool, dark, dry place for months on end. Choose dry potatoes with some earth on them, free of sprouts and without the green patches that appear when potatoes are exposed to light – these contain poisonous alkaloids. If your potatoes do have green parts, cut them off. Avoid potatoes that have scaly or rotting patches. If buying washed potatoes in plastic bags, avoid those that look damp or show signs of condensation as you may find that they have an unpleasant, mouldy flavour.

Potatoes for boiling The very best dish in the world is probably new potatoes boiled and served with a good deal of melted butter and a sprinkling of coarse salt. For perfection, choose walnut-sized potatoes, scrape or scrub them and drop them into already boiling salted water. Bring them back to the boil, and after 8–10 minutes of gentle boiling start testing frequently with a thin bladed knife or skewer. Drain as soon as they are tender. A small sprig of fresh mint added to the water heightens the flavour.

For a delicate, but somewhat earthy

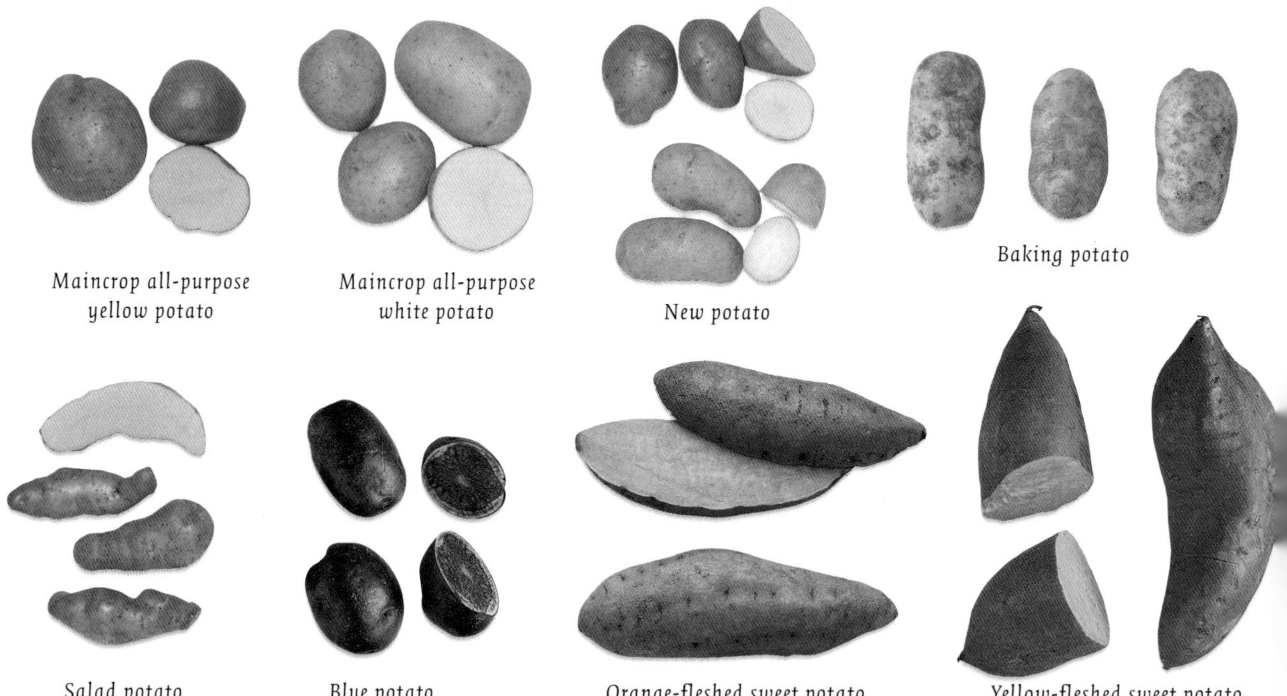

Maincrop all-purpose yellow potato

Maincrop all-purpose white potato

New potato

Baking potato

Salad potato

Blue potato

Orange-fleshed sweet potato

Yellow-fleshed sweet potato

flavour, old potatoes can be scrubbed and boiled in their skins (this conserves the vitamins, too) and then peeled while they are still hot, unless you want to be rustic and serve them with skins on. But peeling the skin from hot potatoes can be painful and tedious, so don't attempt it when you are preparing potatoes for more than two or three people.

If peeling potatoes, do this as thinly as possible because many of the vitamins are concentrated just under the skin. If they are not to be cooked immediately the peeled potatoes must be put straight into a bowl of water or they will dry out; some varieties will discolour on contact with air. But don't soak them too long as this can also lead to a loss of vitamins.

To cook potatoes other than the little new ones, put them in a pan of salted cold water, bring to the boil and then cook fairly gently – fast boiling causes the potatoes to bump against each other, which breaks them up. When they are just tender, drain them thoroughly and return them to the pan. Let them steam for a minute, or leave in the pan covered with a folded napkin to absorb the steam, then drop in a few knobs of butter and turn the potatoes over gently until they are well coated.

Boiled potatoes are very absorbent and good for all dishes with a lot of gravy to mop up. In some countries raw potatoes are placed on the top of stews 25–30 minutes before the end of cooking – the potatoes absorb any fat that has risen to the top of the stew and also help to stretch the dish a bit further.

Potatoes for sautéeing The dry, firm texture of yellow-fleshed maincrop potatoes makes them ideal for sautéeing. Cut them up and drop them into boiling, well-salted water to blanch for about 5 minutes before frying them, or fry them raw, drying them in a cloth before putting them into the hot fat.

Potatoes can also be grated before they are sautéed. *Rösti*, the Swiss national dish, is usually made with potatoes that have been boiled the previous day and kept overnight – traditionally in the snow but the refrigerator will do – to dry them out a little. They are then grated and fried in butter, formed into a pancake, and served inverted on to a plate with the crust uppermost. *Pommes lyonnaise* are potatoes sautéed with fried onions.

Potatoes for frying Whether you call them chips or French fries, choose firm, dry potatoes for frying. The yellow-fleshed varieties are best, although whites are also good. These are also the potatoes to use for game chips, gaufrettes – waffle-cut game chips – matchsticks, ribbons, potato puffs and the many other varieties of fried potatoes.

When frying raw sliced or chipped potatoes, they should be soaked in cold water for at least half an hour to rid them of their surface starch, otherwise the pieces will stick together when fried. Dry them well, since hot fat foams up over wet potatoes and could easily bubble over. Fried potatoes should be salted after cooking, and like other fried foods they will turn soft if covered to keep them warm.

Potatoes for roasting Most maincrop varieties are fine for roasting, but small potatoes should be avoided because roasting tends to dry them out. New potatoes do not roast well (make them into pommes rissolées). Potatoes roast better if they are first boiled in well-salted water for about 5 minutes, then drained and returned to the pan to dry off over a low heat, uncovered, for a minute or two.

Potatoes for mashing Dry, floury, 'old' potatoes are ideal for mashing. Peel and boil them until they are very tender, drain them well and mash them thoroughly or purée in a food mill or potato ricer – but not a food processor as it will ruin the texture. Then add any liquid, which should be hot for best results. Add butter at the end, beat thoroughly and taste for seasoning – potatoes always need more salt. In France, meat juices are sometimes added to mashed potatoes instead of milk.

Potatoes for baking Dry, floury potatoes, such as the long, white-skinned varieties, are ideal for baking. They have a white, fluffy flesh and are usually large or medium sized, which is what is needed for this method of cooking. So-called russet potatoes are also good. Baking potatoes means that no goodness or flavour is lost into water that is then thrown away. They are also a wonderful vehicle for fillings such as cheese, sour cream, bacon bits and chives.

Potatoes for salads The classic potato salad is plainly boiled and sliced waxy potatoes mixed with a simple, sharpish vinaigrette while they are still hot. A little more dressing is added just before serving. Another version mixes the potatoes first with a little dressing while still warm, and then with some good, creamy home-made mayonnaise when cool. Celery, freshly cooked French beans and dill are good additions to fresh potato salad. Serve it with frankfurters or salt herrings – its bland flavour is an excellent foil.

Sweet potato

The tuberous roots of a tropical vine, sweet potatoes have a taste of faintly scented artichoke. The small or medium-sized ones are best: they should be firm and well shaped. Avoid cracks and damp patches.

Sweet potatoes are an important ingredient in Creole cookery. Throughout the American South they are eaten fried, whipped up into soufflés and as an accompaniment to sugar-cured Virginia ham. They are often boiled and mashed with nutmeg as well, or made into a sweet potato pie. Candied, they are a traditional accompaniment for a Thanksgiving turkey. In Australia they are parboiled and roasted with pork.

Yam, taro and cassava

The **yam** belongs to a family of climbing plants that flourish in tropical climates. It comes in a large number of shapes and sizes, and the flesh is white or yellow, with a texture similar to potatoes. In the United States, where true yams are not cultivated, dark-skinned, orange-fleshed sweet potatoes are often erroneously called yams; the other common sweet potato has a pale yellow flesh. The true yam, however, is moister than the sweet potato, although both are usually prepared in much the same ways: boiled or baked and served with butter, nutmeg and other spices as well as apples, oranges and nuts. Like sweet potatoes, yams are delicious when fried.

Looking much like yams (and found in the same markets) are **taro** root (and the edible leaves) and **cassava** or manioc root, the source of tapioca. However, the taro root belongs to the arum family (arum lilies are another member of this family), whilst the cassava belongs to the euphorbia or spurge family. Both taro and cassava

frankfurter 73
salt herring 31
tapioca 118
Virginia ham 68

potato masher 227
ricer 227

Caramelized Sweet Potatoes 382
Colcannon 374
Creamed Potatoes with Parsley 381
Fish Pie 266
Gnocchi Romana 344
Mayonnaise 259
Pommes Dauphinoise 381
Pommes Rissolées 379
Roast Potatoes 379
Vinaigrette 259

potato peeler 224

Crudités with Aïoli 365
Delicate Carrot Soup 246
Glazed Salsify 382
Partridge with Celeriac 297
Sugar-Glazed Carrots 382

Taro

Yam

Cassava

taste similar to potatoes and can be prepared in the same ways, but the taro root will turn a greyish-green colour when boiled. Try them sautéed or mashed with milk and butter and chopped spring onions.

Carrot

These range from slim little slips, pale apricot in colour and no longer than a little finger, to long, stout cylinders, light orange to the deep colour of nectarines.

Young carrots, tender and melting, have a most delicate flavour. Washed and cooked in boiling water for no more than 7 minutes, then simply tossed in butter and sprinkled with parsley, they are one of the celebratory dishes of early summer. Parboiled and glazed in a stout pan with butter and possibly a little sugar to emphasize their natural sweetness, they become one of the essentials of haute cuisine. Young carrots are best boiled in their skins. They can then be drained and eaten with their skins or rubbed in a towel to slip off the skin.

Maincrop carrots are the great standby for winter. They accompany such hearty dishes as boiled beef and dumplings. And it is to carrots, together with onions, celery and leeks, that good warming broths owe their flavour – but don't put in too many or the broth will become so sweet that people will think there is sugar in it. Carrots are also used to make the excellent classic French carrot soup, *potage de Crécy*.

The stubby, bright, almost translucent carrots of uniform size usually found in supermarkets are bred more for the convenience of the seller than the buyer, because they travel well. Although their flavour is a little elusive they are delicious eaten raw, and they make a good dish on their own, either as carrots Vichy – sliced and cooked in Vichy water and butter and sprinkled with parsley – or simply served with butter and parsley.

Buying and storing carrots Avoid specimens that are rubbery, blemished or sprouting little roots. If storing carrots in the vegetable compartment of the refrigerator, take them out of their plastic wrapping. Outside the refrigerator, keep in a cool, airy place to preserve crispness.

Parsnip

Related to the carrot, the parsnip is almost as sweet but blander. It is delicious in soups and stews, and there are many old country recipes for parsnip flans and puddings which make good use of the vegetable's sweetness. This is often emphasized by the addition of ginger, spices and honey. Sweet parsnip dishes are part of the English country tradition, as is parsnip wine, a clear, pale gold drink that is delicious in the year it is made, but even better 12 months on. Boiled parsnips mixed with mayonnaise were once served as mock lobster, but they are probably nicer without the pretentious title.

Available from early autumn until spring, parsnips are at their best in mid-winter, especially when their ivory skin has been touched by frost. They can be bought washed, or with traces of soil still clinging to them, in which case they keep better. Those with brown patches or those that look wizened or dry should be avoided.

Store parsnips in a cool place – the Dutch seventeenth-century paintings that show root vegetables spread around the housewife's feet do not signify untidiness but the fact that the tiled floor of the kitchen was the coolest place. An airy larder or the crisper compartment of the refrigerator is more convenient nowadays.

Salsify

Black-skinned salsify, which has snowy white flesh, is also known as scorzonera; white salsify is sometimes called the oyster plant because its taste is supposedly reminiscent of oysters. In fact, the flavour of both black and white salsify has a nodding acquaintance with that of asparagus – it is just as delicate and therefore at its best when simply boiled or poached and served with a knob of butter, or in a creamy white sauce made from a roux moistened with the cooking liquid and a dash of cream.

Salsify is neither easy to peel nor to clean, so is best boiled in its skin and peeled afterwards, or skinned thinly with a swivelling potato peeler and plunged immediately into a saucepan containing a '*blanc*' – boiling water to which a tablespoon of flour has been added (vegetables cooked in a *blanc* will keep their colour). The white stalks should then be cooked, drained and finished with a little butter. As they are water-retaining, they will not easily burn providing the pan has a well-fitting lid.

When buying salsify, choose those with a topknot of fresh-looking leaves; avoid any that look sad or shrivelled. Or buy canned salsify, since this is one of the few vegetables that lends itself rather well to the canning process.

Celeriac

The edible bulbous root of a member of the celery family, celeriac is not a neat-looking vegetable and needs to be peeled with a sharp knife. Under its brown

Carrot

Parsnip

exterior the flesh is pale, but discolours when exposed to the air so should be plunged immediately into a bowl of acidulated water. Cooked, its texture is similar to that of a potato, but less smooth and with more bite to it. Celeriac is a great standby, not only because soups and broth are often improved by a slight celery flavour and it is milder and less overpowering than celery, but also because *céleri rémoulade* – grated raw celeriac coated in mustardy mayonnaise, one of the delights of French cuisine – cannot, of course, be made without it. Boiled and diced, celeriac is delicious in potato salads, and in Germany it is served with diced apples, potatoes and beetroot in a herring salad. Puréed with potato, it is excellent with game.

Beetroot

Globe-shaped or long and pointed, beetroot comes in bunches with edible greenery at the top when young, and loose and trimmed of leaves when mature. When buying raw beetroots make sure that their whiskers are intact and if possible they have at least 5 cm/ 2 in of stalk at the top – if they are too closely trimmed they will bleed, meaning that they will give up their colour to the cooking water and be no more than pale shadows of themselves when they are cooked. For the same reason, beetroots are never peeled before they are cooked.

When making borscht, the ruby-coloured Russian soup that is as good iced as it is hot, make use of the beetroot's tendency to bleed and don't worry about trimming off most of the stem. It is a good idea, though, to cook one or two specimens whole and cut them into julienne strips to add colour to the soup at the end.

To prepare sliced beetroots as a vegetable dish, sauté them gently, moistening them with wine vinegar to set the brilliant colour and give them a perfect flavour. The greenery attached to young beetroots can be cooked separately and tastes like spinach.

You can also find golden and white beetroot, which taste the same as the red and which are sometimes served with hare and venison. But they are rather disappointing to look at compared to the glorious red ones.

If you are buying beetroots that are already cooked, make sure the skins are still moist. It is best to buy them on the day they have been boiled, while they are still warm and steaming. (Be certain to avoid those that have already been steeped in vinegar – they are violent and indigestible.) In France beetroots are cooked in the oven or in the ashes of a wood fire, which gives a charred skin and an earthy, smoky flavour.

acidulated water 422
beet greens 133
celery 138
haggis 74
julienne 422
spring greens 133

Swede and turnip

Both these roots are, in fact, members of the cabbage family, and are so closely related that it is not surprising to find that their names are sometimes used interchangeably. To add to the confusion, swedes are also called Swedish turnips; in Scotland swedes are known as neeps and are considered to be turnips. However, swedes, with their pale, dense flesh, grow to immense sizes without impairment to taste or texture, while white-fleshed turnips coarsen if they are allowed to become larger than tennis balls. Both swedes and turnips should be heavy for their size, with no spongy patches, worm holes or large blemishes. Samples with side roots should be avoided.

Borscht 249
Cornish Pasties 317
Glazed Turnips 382
Hot Red Beet Salad 379
Mashed Swedes 382

Swede With a warm, strong flavour, swedes make a delicious winter dish when mashed on their own or cooked in stews or Cornish pasties. They are the essential ingredient for 'mashed neeps', a Scottish dish served with haggis, in which the swedes are mashed with potatoes and butter.

Baby turnip Globe-shaped, conical or flattened, with a sweet, mild radishy flavour but not the hot sting, baby turnips are as different from maincrop turnips as new potatoes are from old. They should not be peeled before cooking, but rubbed afterwards: the skin comes off easily and beneath it lies their flavour and goodness. Although it seems a pity to do more to any young vegetable than to boil or steam it for a few minutes, glazed baby turnips are delicious and the classic accompaniment to roast duck. Their fresh greenery can be cooked in the same way as spring greens.

Maincrop turnip These may have a purplish tinge on their nether regions. They need to be peeled before either roasting or boiling.

Kohlrabi

White, pale green or purple, kohlrabi is a brassica that is bred for its bulbous stem. It looks like a horizontally ridged turnip,

acidulated water 422

Chicken with Black Olives and Tomatoes 306
Jerusalem Artichokes with Cream and Parsley 382
Penne with Ham and Tomato Sauce 339
Scallops with Saffron, Basil and Tomato Vinaigrette 279
Stuffed Tomatoes 384
Tomato and Leek Soup 246

and is at its best when young and small, as it becomes coarser with size.

The leaves, which grow on stalks from the spaced-out ridges, can be used in the same way as young turnip tops, but are usually removed before the vegetable reaches the shops. The skin can be peeled easily with a kitchen knife to expose the pale green flesh below. Tiny kohlrabi can be cooked whole, but the larger ones need to be sliced. They can then be eaten, boiled, with fresh butter or a creamy sauce and served with any meat that responds to a delicate cabbagey taste.

Jerusalem artichoke

These knobbly tubers are neither artichokes nor do they come from the Holy City, but from the New World. Related to the sunflower, they were christened *girasole* by the Italians – from whence 'Jerusalem' – because their yellow flowers tend to turn towards the sun.

Jerusalem artichokes are at their best between winter and spring. When buying them, look for neat specimens with the minimum of knobs. Their skin is brownish, like that of potatoes but more delicate. The white flesh must not be exposed to the air because it quickly turns a grey-purple colour. When boiling Jerusalem artichokes, add a squeeze of lemon juice to the water – this will prevent them from discolouring, especially if you plan to make the delicious white soup, sometimes called Palestine soup, which owes its pearly colour as much to the artichokes as it does to the milk or cream that goes into its making. Jerusalem artichokes are delicious roasted like potatoes.

Crosne Also known as Chinese or Japanese artichokes, knotroot or chrogi, crosnes taste similar to Jerusalem artichokes but are nuttier in flavour and more delicate in texture.

These tiny, spindle-shaped vegetables dry out too quickly after being lifted to be widely available commercially. The yellowish patches that tend to develop on fresh white crosnes in no way impair the flavour.

They should be scrubbed – a fiddly job as they are so tiny – and cooked very briefly in boiling salted water, then tossed in plenty of butter.

Jícama, yam bean

A tropical tuber that looks somewhat like a turnip-shaped yam, the jícama has crisp, sweet, juicy flesh. Popular in Mexican and Southwest American dishes, it can be peeled and eaten raw or sliced and stir-fried with other vegetables; it can also be roasted like a potato.

VEGETABLE FRUIT

Glossy black olives, rich purple aubergines, bright scarlet tomatoes and peppers of all colours need hot sun to ripen, and these vegetables bring Mediterranean colour and warmth into the kitchen. Others in this group – avocados, tender summer squashes and huge pumpkins – provide exotic shapes, textures and tastes.

Tomato

Ripened to a marvellous blazing red in the sun, the tomato is one of the cook's most essential provisions. Ideally, one should have tomatoes in the larder at all times, both fresh and in cans (fortunately, tomatoes are one of the very few vegetables that take happily to being canned).

Belonging to the Solanaceae family (as does nightshade), the tomato used to be considered unhealthy and was not eaten raw for many centuries after it arrived in Europe from its native South America.

Jícama

Jerusalem artichoke

Turnip

Beetroot

Kohlrabi

Black salsify

Celeriac

Swede

Spain was the first country to use tomatoes in cooked dishes, and the rest of Europe followed suit, but it was not until the middle of the nineteenth century that tomatoes *en salade* began to appear. Even then they do not seem to have been highly regarded.

Today, however, there is no better salad than a tomato salad, preferably scattered with fresh basil leaves, which have a great affinity with tomatoes. The Italians often add slices of mozzarella, a fresh cheese that goes well with tomatoes. As dressing, a good sun-ripened tomato needs only olive oil, since it provides its own astringency, but a duller one needs vinaigrette. Tomatoes should never be allowed to sit about in their dressing because this will turn them soggy.

Buying and storing tomatoes The best tomatoes are those that have been allowed to ripen slowly on the vine, developing their flavour in the warm sun.

Buy bright red, ripe tomatoes for immediate use; for use in the near future, choose those a paler red colour – after a day or two in a cool spot they will be a vivid red. If tomatoes have been picked when green but after reaching maturity, they are called 'mature green' and will redden well if kept in a drawer or in a brown paper bag (they will ripen faster with a red tomato keeping them company, exuding its ethylene gas, which is responsible for the colour change) or on a light but not sunny windowsill. Tomatoes picked when green and unripe will never turn red naturally, and are best used for making pickles and chutneys.

The large, ridged tomatoes, deep red or orange and green and often quite misshapen, tend to be the best, with rather fewer seeds than the more ordinary globe tomatoes, grown to uniform size and often with very little flavour. Cherry tomatoes can be used whole in salads, while the richly flavoured plum tomatoes, with relatively small seed clusters and pulp that is inclined to be dry, are perfect for sauces and purées.

Fleshy tomatoes, such as beefsteak or beef tomatoes, are best for sandwiches because there is less liquid to turn the bread soggy. Slice them across rather than downwards.

Golden-yellow tomatoes are like red tomatoes in every aspect except colour, and make a pretty salad when mixed with the reds or on their own.

Cooking with tomatoes The traditional tomato dishes include tomato soup, which may be delicate and creamy or rich and strong, perhaps flavoured with basil or chives; tomatoes with stuffings of cooked seasoned rice mixed with lamb, currants, onion and garlic, or with breadcrumb-bound fillings of olives, herbs or mushrooms; and fragrant tomatoes *provençale*, simply grilled with a sprinkling of herbs, garlic and olive oil. *À la provençale* invariably means the presence of tomatoes in a dish, and just as Provençal cookery relies on tomatoes, so does Italian cookery, using them liberally in a vast number of dishes – with pastas and pizzas, with poultry and meat, and in soups and vegetable stews.

Many recipes require tomatoes that have been *concasséed* – skinned, seeded and roughly chopped. In the case of Italian plum tomatoes the skin may come off perfectly easily, but most tomatoes need a quick dip in boiling water first. To seed tomatoes, cut them in half crosswise and squeeze them in the palm of your hand over a bowl, giving a little shake as you do so. You can sieve the contents of the bowl and use the seedless liquid as stock – it will be too watery to serve as tomato juice.

Sun-dried tomatoes These are tomatoes that have been halved and dried – sometimes in the sun. The drying intensifies and sweetens the flavour, and makes the texture leathery. It's much cheaper to buy the tomatoes loose, in bags, rather than packed in oil in jars. Then soak them for an hour before storing in good olive oil with herbs, garlic and chillies. Sun-dried tomatoes are eaten in hors d'oeuvres or accompanying Parma ham or salami in sandwiches. They are also used in cooked dishes, such as meat stews and braised vegetables, in pasta sauces and on pizzas, and in salads – try them snipped over a grilled red pepper and anchovy salad.

skinning and seeding tomatoes 423
tomato ketchup 206
tomato purée 206

Aubergine, Pepper and Tomato Pizza 361
Braised John Dory with Tomatoes and Fennel 268
Braised Rabbit with Tomatoes 295
Delicate Tomato Sauce 256
Green Tomato Sour 419
Roasted Tomato Sauce 256

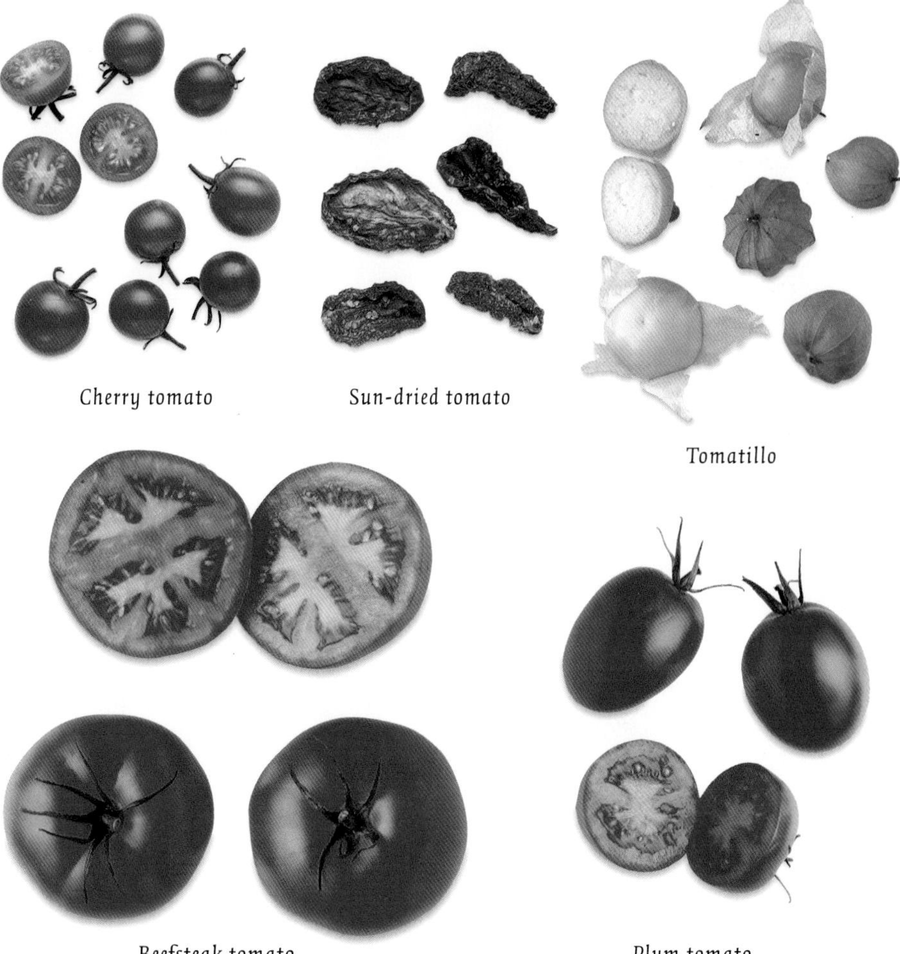

Cherry tomato

Sun-dried tomato

Tomatillo

Beefsteak tomato

Plum tomato

Cape gooseberry 181
paprika 201
skinning peppers 423

Aubergine, Pepper and Tomato Pizza 361
Chakchouka 323
Garlic-Braised Lamb Shanks with Yellow Peppers 290
Gazpacho 254
Ratatouille 383
Red and Yellow Pepper Tart 328
Red Peppers with Anchovies 383
Six-Vegetable Couscous 350
Sweet Pepper Chutney 419
Sweet Pepper Salad 366

Tomatillo

Related to the Cape gooseberry and belonging to the same family as the tomato, the tomatillo does in fact look very like a walnut-sized green tomato, except that it comes wrapped in a thin, papery husk. It is firm in texture, with a flavour like that of a tart apple. Tomatillos are much used in Mexican cookery, in meat stews and green *mole* sauces, and with onion and chillies to make salsa verde, served with *tacos* and *enchiladas*.

Pepper

Peppers may be mild and/or sweet, hot and unbearably fiery, but they are all members of the genus *Capsicum*. The large sweet peppers include the bell (some varieties are called bull-nosed because of their shape), the cubanelle or Cuban pepper, Italian frying and the sweet banana. Sweet peppers may be red, yellow, orange, purple, white or green, and squarish or long in shape.

Chilli peppers add heat and flavour to a dish, although some are quite mild. They can be green, red, yellow or black, and in general the smaller the chilli the hotter it is. To test for heat, just touch a piece of the broken flesh to your tongue.

Most peppers are green to begin with, ripening to red and finally becoming red-brown when dried, although some peppers turn a pale yellow or bright orange when ripe or a deep mahogany colour. Peppers that are sold half ripe – part red and part green – may never ripen to full red. Paprika, cayenne and Tabasco are all made from peppers.

Sweet pepper Bought fresh, large sweet peppers (which are a rich source of vitamin C) are quite light in weight. Red peppers are sweeter than the green ones, and the yellow and orange ones are closer in flavour to red peppers than to green.

Capsicum means box, and the fleshy walls of sweet peppers contain no more than a few ribs and a cluster of seeds. These should all be discarded to the last flat seed, which even in the mildest pepper can occasionally be bitingly hot. The empty boxes can then be filled with any number of stuffings – cooked rice mixed with minced meat and perhaps yogurt, or with a mixture of anchovies, tomatoes and garlic, or olives and capers. They are then put side by side in an oiled pan, sprinkled with oil and baked slowly. Some people like to blanch the peppers in boiling water for a minute or two before stuffing them.

As well as being stuffed, sweet peppers can be cut into strips and used in a variety of dishes. Sicilians make lovely salads with grilled red or yellow peppers, mixing them with anchovy fillets, capers, garlic and olive oil. Yugoslavians have a similar salad, using peppers roasted until they have blistered and then skinning them, and in the south of France there is the beautiful pipérade, a mixture of sweet peppers, tomatoes, onions, garlic and sometimes bacon, to which beaten eggs are added at the last moment. Sweet peppers are also sometimes combined with chillies, as in rouille – the bright orange, fiery sauce that floats in the centre of a bowl of bouillabaisse, and is served with a number of other fish dishes that have their origins in the south of France.

Pimiento, the Spanish word for peppers, has come to mean peeled, seeded and cooked red peppers. They can be bought canned or in jars, but these tend to be softer than those you prepare yourself at home. Once prepared they will keep in the refrigerator, covered, for up to a week.

Chilli pepper When fresh, a chilli should look bright – dullness is a sure sign of over-maturity – with no brown patches or black spots. Chillies can vary in size from 30 cm/12 in in length down to just 5 mm/¼ in, and may be anywhere

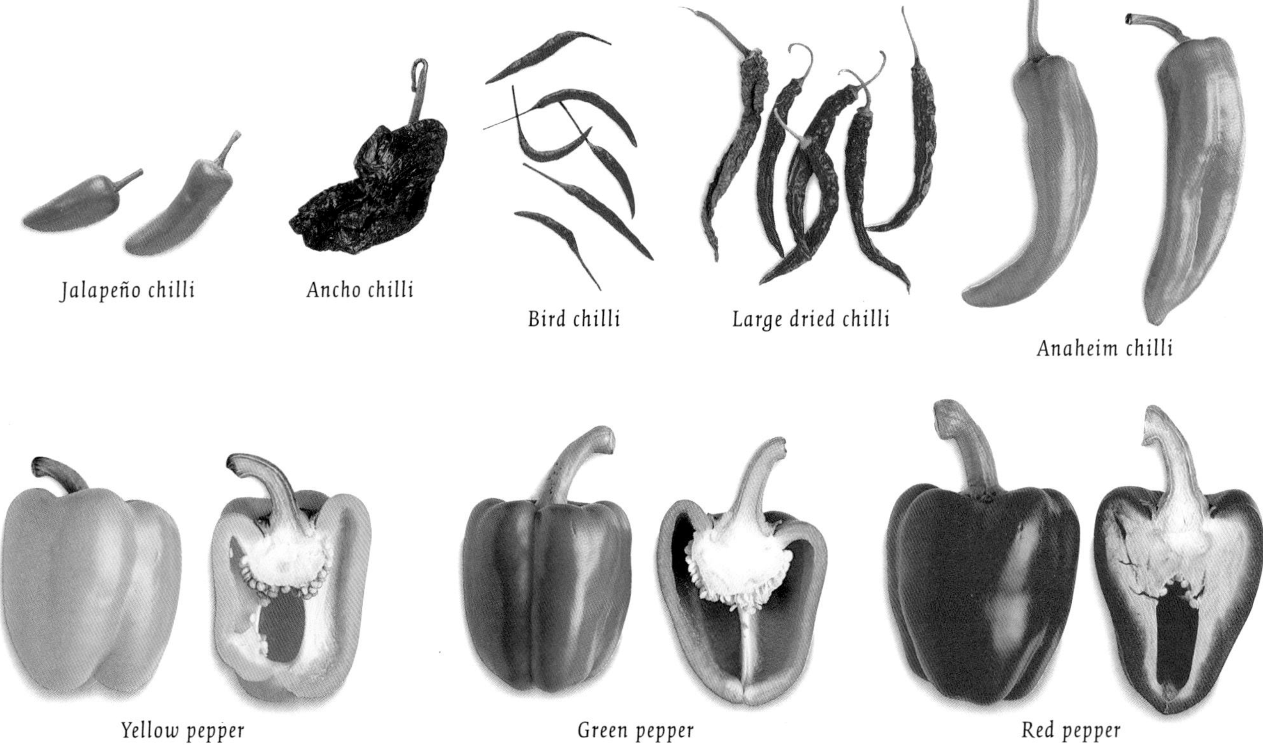

Jalapeño chilli *Ancho chilli* *Bird chilli* *Large dried chilli* *Anaheim chilli*

Yellow pepper *Green pepper* *Red pepper*

from mildly warm to blisteringly hot. As well as fresh, they are sold dried (whole, crushed into flakes or powdered), canned and bottled, often pickled.

In Central America, notably Mexico, chillies are second only to maize in their importance in cooking, and they are widely used in the cuisines of many other countries, including Africa, India, China (Hunan and Sichuan) and Thailand. In most of Europe and North America, hot chillies are generally used sparingly.

Chilli experts, of course, can distinguish between the dozens of varieties, but non-experts tend to differentiate only between the mild, the hot and the unbearable. Large chillies include the mild Anaheim or California (when fresh and green this is used for *chiles rellenos* – stuffed with cheese and deep-fried), the similar but slightly larger New Mexico, the poblano, which can range from slightly hot to hot (when ripened to red and dried this is called an ancho, which is sweet but can be quite pungent), and the Hungarian yellow wax pepper. Among the smaller chillies are the hot to very hot jalapeño (when smoked this becomes a chipotle), the cayenne, Thai and bird (all similar in size and shape and all quite hot), the extremely hot, slender green serrano, the fiery, lantern-shaped habañero and its cousin the Scotch bonnet, and the blistering, tiny red tabasco, which is used to make Tabasco sauce.

With chillies, not only are the seeds hot, but the box itself is pungent. It is a volatile oil called capsaicin, found mainly in the seeds and ribs, that accounts for the heat. Capsaicin irritates the skin and especially the eyes, so keep your hands – even after washing – away from your eyes, lips and other sensitive areas for a while after you have prepared chillies. Also, rinse the chillies in cold water, not hot, or the irritating fumes may rise into your face. To prepare chillies, pull off their stalks and cut each one in half, all under cold running water. Chillies soaked for a while in cold salted water will be less hot, and they can also be blistered under the grill to give them a lovely smoky flavour.

Canned chillies should be rinsed to remove the brine in which they have been preserved. They may be already sliced or diced, or they may need seeding like fresh ones. Dried whole chillies, torn into small pieces, can be used as they are to season dishes, or they can be rehydrated in water first. For a much milder flavour, put dried hot chillies into a pan of cold water, bring slowly to the boil and then drain. They can then be used, more or less discreetly, to heat up dishes such as chilli con carne, for curries and for any number of Creole and Cajun dishes, especially those that include prawns or pork.

Aubergine

This can be long and slim or as fat as a zeppelin, with a glossy purple or almost black skin, or it can be a plump ivory-white oval (to which version it owes its American name, eggplant, instead of the French aubergine). All varieties have the same slightly acrid taste. The difference lies in their consistency: the plump ones, marginally juicier, are the ones to use for such dishes as moussaka, with its golden layers, or the Balkan *okrochka*, similarly layered but without the béchamel or eggs. The long, slim ones, being rather drier, are best for frying.

When buying aubergines, choose those that feel heavy for their size – they are likely to have the smallest seed channels because their flesh will have filled out. They should have smooth, unblemished skins with no rough, spongy patches or brown spots.

It is a good idea to salt aubergines before cooking to sweat out some of the moisture and possible bitterness, although some modern varieties do not really need this treatment. To salt them, cut them into thin slices, sprinkle with fine salt and allow them to drain in a colander for about half an hour, then rinse them and pat them dry.

It is not usual to peel aubergines because the skin contributes to their flavour and colour, and in dishes such as stuffed aubergines it prevents them from disintegrating. But in dishes that involve puréed aubergines, such as 'poor man's caviare', the traditional way of peeling them is to roast them in their skins over a fire or under a grill until they are soft, and then to scoop out the flesh, which will have acquired a delicious smoky taste. (Poor man's caviare, a mixture of puréed aubergines, onions, garlic, oil and lemon, got its name in the region around the Caspian Sea, where it was eaten by the fishermen who had spent the day dealing with caviare, catching sturgeon for city dwellers.)

Although ratatouille – the delicious Provençal stew of aubergines, tomatoes, courgettes, onions and sweet peppers – is one of the great Mediterranean dishes, the best aubergine recipes come from southern Italy and the Middle East. In the Middle East aubergine purées, flavoured with tahina and garlic, are served as a salad, or, with a béchamel sauce and cheese, are served with poultry and meat.

The most famous of the aubergine dishes is the Turkish *Imam Bayildi*, or 'the Imam has fainted', for this is apparently what an *imam*, a Turkish priest, did when presented with an incredibly rich dish of fried aubergines mixed with onions, tomatoes, spices and sultanas, all swimming in oil.

Aubergines may be halved and stuffed, or filled from the stem end after the seeds and a portion of the flesh have been removed to make room for the stuffing. They look very beautiful if they are first peeled in strips so that white flesh and purple skin make handsome stripes around the outside. Fill them with minced lamb or beef, rice, tomatoes, garlic, onions and spices, and their own chopped and cooked pulp. Then sprinkle with oil and bake until tender.

Whether eaten hot or cold, in batter or *à la grecque*, aubergines are often first fried in hot olive oil. Drain them well after frying – they absorb vast quantities of oil. If you fry them fast they do not become so oil laden, but still give you a combination of delicious flavours.

Avocado

The avocado was once called the butter pear because of its consistency, and the alligator pear because its original Spanish name, based on the Aztec, was too difficult to pronounce. It is, strictly speaking, a fruit, but is used mainly as a salad vegetable because its flavour is bland, mild and nutty.

Particularly rich in oils, proteins and vitamins, the avocado was used by the ancient Mayans, Incas and Aztecs both as a food and for skin care. Avocados were a luxury in northern countries until Floridians and then Californians began to cultivate them in the nineteenth century. Some people consider these comparatively northerly avocados to be only pale replicas of those grown in the

cayenne pepper 201
chilli flakes 201
chilli powder 201
chilli sauce 206
chilli vinegar 205
dégorger 422
Tabasco sauce 206

Aubergine, Pepper and Tomato Pizza 361
Aubergine Tart 328
Chinese Egg Noodles with Browned Garlic, Chillies and Parsley 345
Crab Salad with Thai Flavours 368
Duck with Coconut Cream and Green Curry Paste 313
Grilled Mackerel with Green Paste 266
Lebanese Aubergine Salad 365
Melazane alla Parmigiana 383
Quick-Fried Chicken with Garlic and Chilli 305
Rouille 258
Salsa Cruda 258
Spicy Green Fish 272
Stir-Fried Aubergines with Chilli and Coriander 384
Thai Mussels 281
Tuna in a Packet with Red Sauce 268

olive oil 112
pimiento 152
tortilla 120

Chicken with Black Olives and Tomatoes 306
Crudités with Aïoli 365
Duck with Green Olives 313
Guacamole 365
Lido Pasta Salad 371
Salade Niçoise 368
Vinaigrette 259

tropics, but they are still very good, as are the Israeli avocados which supply many European markets in their season.

There are two main types of avocado: those that appear in the summer and those that appear in the winter. The summer variety, of which the Hass is the most common, has a rough, pebbly skin that is green when unripe and purple-black when ripe, and golden-yellow flesh. The winter ones are more pear shaped, usually larger, with smooth green skin and pale green to yellow flesh. With the winter avocados, skin colour is no indication of ripeness, and the test for this is to apply gentle pressure at the thin end: if there is some give, the avocado is ready.

Avocados appear in some unlikely dishes. In Mexico, where they are abundant, they are eaten in soups, salads and stews. They are also the essential ingredient in guacamole – the coarse avocado purée with green chilli, chopped onions and lime or lemon juice, which may be eaten on its own or, as in Mexico, with tortillas. It is best to purée avocado shortly before it is to be eaten because it turns a dirty brown colour when exposed to the air. So does the flesh of a cut avocado, so either halve or slice it just before serving or rub or sprinkle the cut surfaces with lemon.

In the Caribbean avocados baked in their shells are sometimes served with turkey and chicken. But there is no better way to serve them than halved, with a good vinaigrette, or even more simply with a sprinkling of fresh lime juice and salt.

Olive

Groves of gnarled olive trees flourish in the Mediterranean countries and in California, producing a great variety of olives, large and small. Greek and Italian olives are reckoned to be the finest – in ancient Rome olives were eaten both at the beginning and at the end of meals from sheer love of them.

Whether olives are green or black (which may actually be brown or purple) is not a matter of type but of timing: olives picked young are still hard and pale green; black olives have had time to ripen and darken on the tree and have developed more of their oil. In order to make them edible, black olives are soaked in an alkaline solution – traditionally rain water and wood ash (lye), now quite likely to be caustic soda – and exposed to the air to remove their excessive bitterness.

Green olives are treated rather differently, first soaked in running water or steeped in an alkaline solution and then put into tightly sealed barrels of brine and left for up to a year to develop their olive green, smooth succulence. Olives destined for the oil presses are allowed to ripen fully; some of these, looking a little shrivelled and quite small, are also cured in salt and eaten, and can be the best of all.

Of the many olives on the market, among the most commercial and widely available are the green, solid, Spanish ones, called Queens – which are slightly acid and which connoisseurs like to dip in olive oil before eating – and the small, succulent Manzanillas. These are often stuffed with strips of red pimiento or, less frequently, with almonds, anchovies, lemon or orange peel or pieces of black olive – they are meant for cocktail-party offerings, and are not the favourites of olive aficionados.

Olives are preserved in a number of ways. The black ones range from those

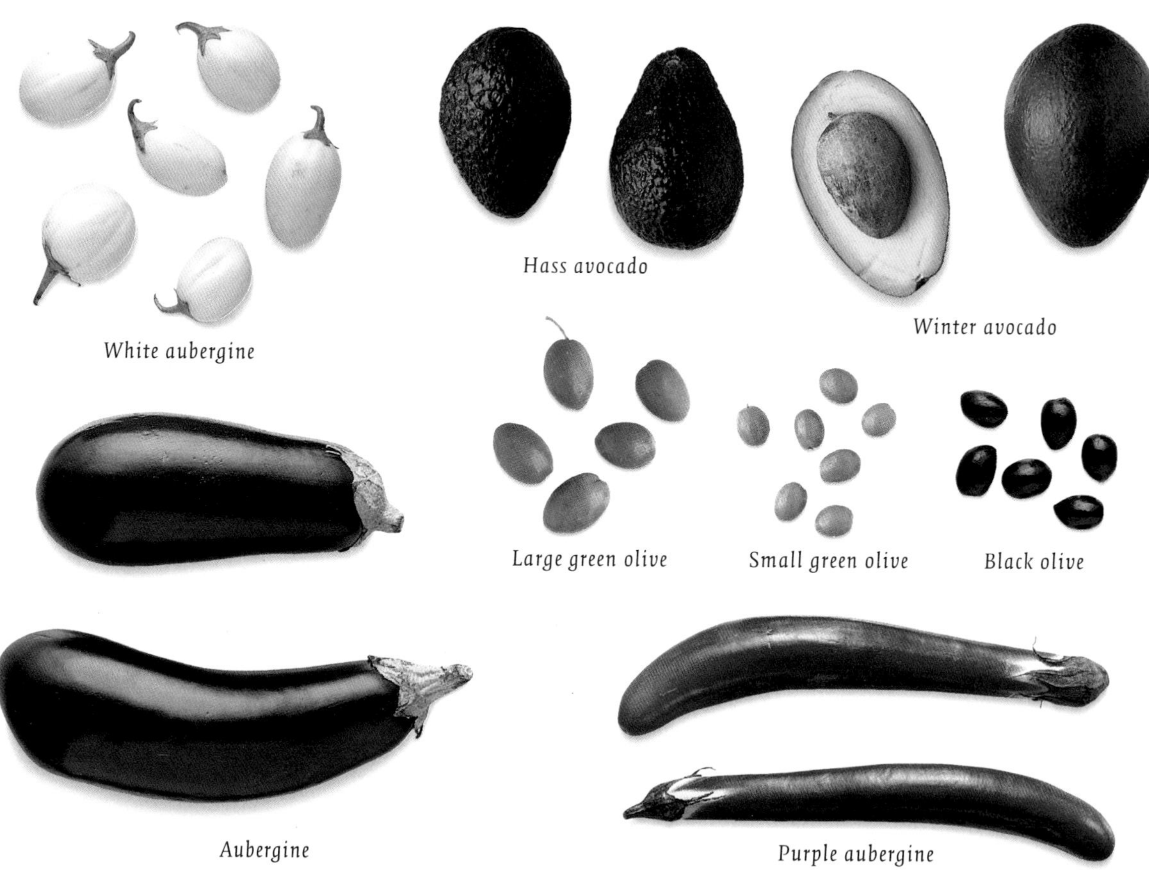

White aubergine

Hass avocado

Winter avocado

Large green olive

Small green olive

Black olive

Aubergine

Purple aubergine

marinated in oil with herbs to those in brine. There are also cracked green olives – which may be plain or flavoured with garlic, spices or herbs – and the stoned, pressed green olives packed with chillies, which are very fine.

Black olives feature in a good many dishes: chopped or whole they go into Mediterranean stuffings with breadcrumbs, mushrooms, anchovies and herbs; moistened with more oil, they make an olive pâté that is popular in the Mediterranean and the Balkans; unchopped, they make beautiful glossy black additions to some rice and pasta dishes and to a great variety of salads. A once famous Parisian restaurant, Chez Allard, teamed mild green olives with roast duck in a delicious sauce.

The Italian olives, such as the large green Cerignola, the black olives from Castellamare and the tiny black wrinkled ones from around Rome, go on top of pizzas. Plump Kalamatas and others from Greece go into a salad with tomatoes and onion rings. And the black olives of Provence are used in rich estouffades and daubes.

Besides the best-known green and black olives, there are also the pale or dark brown ones found in Italy and Cyprus, the tiny, delicate black Niçoise ones, and the popular straw-coloured California olives.

If you buy too many olives and do not use them all at once, store them in the refrigerator, or better still in the larder, in a jar of olive oil or in a mixture of water, oil and vinegar. It is a good idea to roll olives in fresh olive oil, perhaps with a few herbs, chillies or crushed coriander seeds, to liven them up before you eat them. If you want black olives without stones for cooking, use an olive stoner, or *chasse noyau*, or simply split the flesh and remove the stone.

CUCUMBER, SQUASHES AND PUMPKIN

These vegetables belong to the climbing or rambling family that is known as Cucurbitaceae, together with melons and the decorative autumn gourds.

Cucumber and gherkin

Before cucumbers had the bitterness bred out of them they were invariably peeled and salted and drained. This is no longer

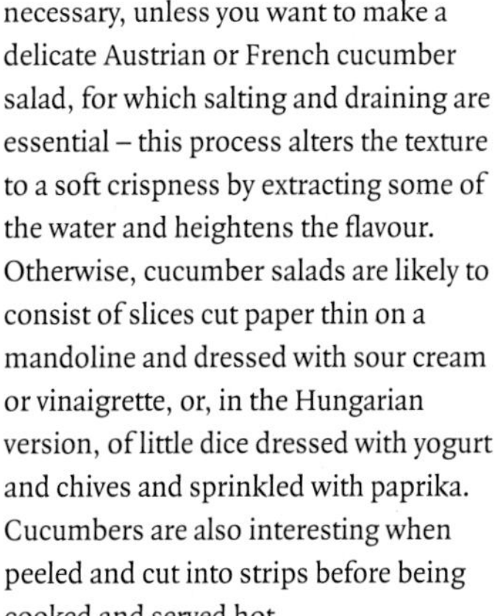

necessary, unless you want to make a delicate Austrian or French cucumber salad, for which salting and draining are essential – this process alters the texture to a soft crispness by extracting some of the water and heightens the flavour. Otherwise, cucumber salads are likely to consist of slices cut paper thin on a mandoline and dressed with sour cream or vinaigrette, or, in the Hungarian version, of little dice dressed with yogurt and chives and sprinkled with paprika. Cucumbers are also interesting when peeled and cut into strips before being cooked and served hot.

Small ridge cucumbers have plentiful seeds and tough, dark green skins (their name comes from the way they are grown on ridges). They usually need to be peeled before they are used. Unpeeled (and unwaxed), they are the cucumbers that are brined, or pickled with a head of dill.

The long, clear green cucumber (known in North America as the English or hothouse cucumber) has fewer seeds and an exceedingly thin skin. It is often sold in a tight plastic jacket to keep it fresh. Largest is the Zeppelin, firm and juicy, that turns a pale yellow when fully ripe. The apple or lemon cucumber, almost round and with crisp, juicy flesh and tough yellowish skin, should always be peeled.

Cucumbers are best when they are young and tender and look as if they are bursting with juice. They can be stored in the refrigerator for about a week at most, but do not like very low temperatures.

Gherkins are usually found pickled in unsweetened vinegar and are eaten with cold meats, with *pâté de campagne* or any fatty terrine, with hot *boeuf bouilli*, or chopped and incorporated in sauces such as tartare sauce. They come in three sizes: the small, rough-skinned ones, also called cornichons, are the ones to eat with pâté, and the middle-sized prickly ones with pickled herrings or salt beef. Large, smooth-skinned gherkins are used to make sweet or dill pickles, and are eaten with salt beef and pastrami.

Squash

Some squashes are soft skinned and for eating when young and tender, which is why they are often known as summer squashes. These should be cooked as soon as possible after they have been

dégorger 422

olive stoner 225

Chilled Cucumber Soup with Mint 254
Cool and Hot Cucumber Salad 367
Crab Salad with Thai Flavours 368
Gazpacho 254
Pâté de Campagne 318
Prawn and Cucumber Curry 278
Sauce Tartare 259
Sichuan Chicken Salad 372

Ridge cucumber

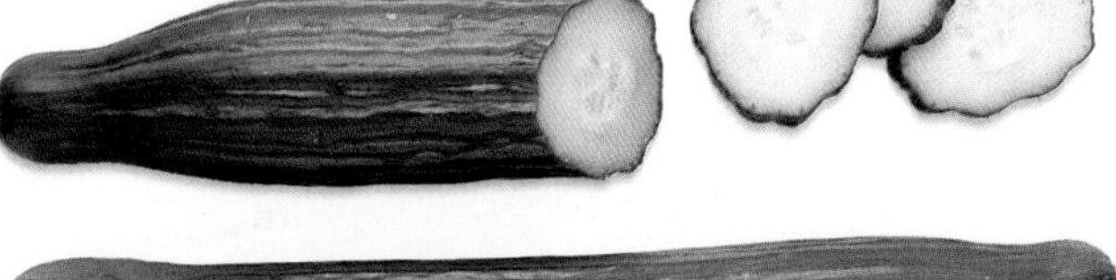

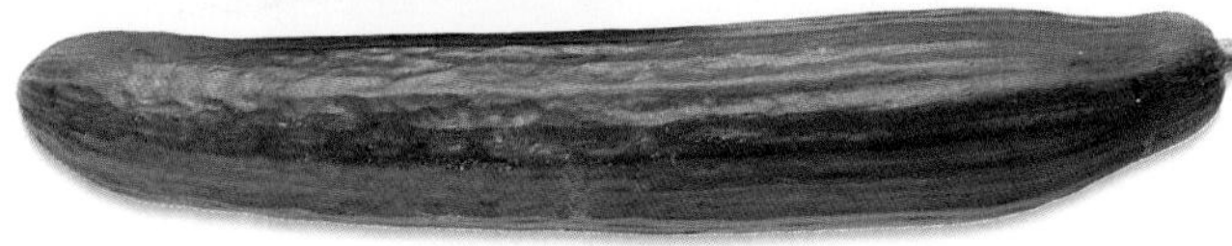

Cucumber

Courgettes au Gratin 385
Courgettes with Dill and Sour Cream 384
Goat's Cheese and Courgette Filo Tart 330
Ratatouille 383
Six-Vegetable Couscous 350
Squash Fritters with Yogurt and Garlic Dressing 386
Stuffed Courgettes 385
Summer Minestrone 251

picked. Winter squashes have bright autumn-coloured or green skins that are tough and inedible, and firm flesh. They are best when they have been allowed to mature slowly.

Courgette These are called by their Italian name, zucchini, in North America. They may have green or yellow skins and have an interesting and delicate taste. There is hardly any work involved in their preparation: just give them a little wash, and then leave tiny ones whole and cut larger ones into circles or slice them lengthwise into halves or quarters. Give them a very few minutes' steaming or frying, add some herbs such as basil or parsley and, perhaps, a dash of cream or a quantity of butter or olive oil, and an extremely good vegetable dish is ready to eat. But don't keep it waiting, because the vegetable continues to soften even after it has been taken off the heat.

Courgettes are excellent deep fried, either plain or in batter, and their big golden flowers are also sometimes stuffed and deep fried in a crisp batter or chopped and used in risotto.

Straightneck and crookneck squashes are like small courgettes in both flavour and texture.

Vegetable marrow The enormous prize-winning and harvest festival specimens are not very delicate as a vegetable and, to some tastes at least, are even less acceptable transformed into jam or chutney. Boiled into a watery mush, medium-size specimens can be equally disappointing, but started off with a little butter and chopped onion and steamed in their own juice, then sprinkled with a generous handful of chopped parsley, they can be fresh looking and delicious, especially when tomatoes are added.

A parboiled or blanched marrow, halved and hollowed out, makes a good vehicle for a minced beef and onion stuffing bound with egg, or a rice and meat stuffing, but both need lively flavouring because the marrow itself has a bland taste.

Spaghetti marrow, vegetable spaghetti This stubby yellow squash is grown with particular attention to its tendency to produce stringy flesh, and is eaten, with sauce, just like spaghetti. It is boiled or baked, the end pierced so that the heat reaches the interior, and is served cut in half lengthwise or the flesh is scooped out. Hand a tomato sauce separately or toss the flesh with the sauce. It is also quite good eaten with butter and grated cheese.

Custard marrow, pattypan squash Usually creamy in colour, although it also comes in shades of yellow and pale green, this tastes rather like a courgette. It is best up to 10 cm/4 in across, when the skin is soft and the interior tender, and the scalloped shape need not be spoiled by slicing. Boil it or bake it whole, then cut off the top, scoop out the seeds and fill the hollow with melted butter; eat with a spoon. It also makes good fritters.

Chayote, christophene, mirliton This small, pear-shaped squash has a large single seed, which in very young chayotes is edible. It features in Central

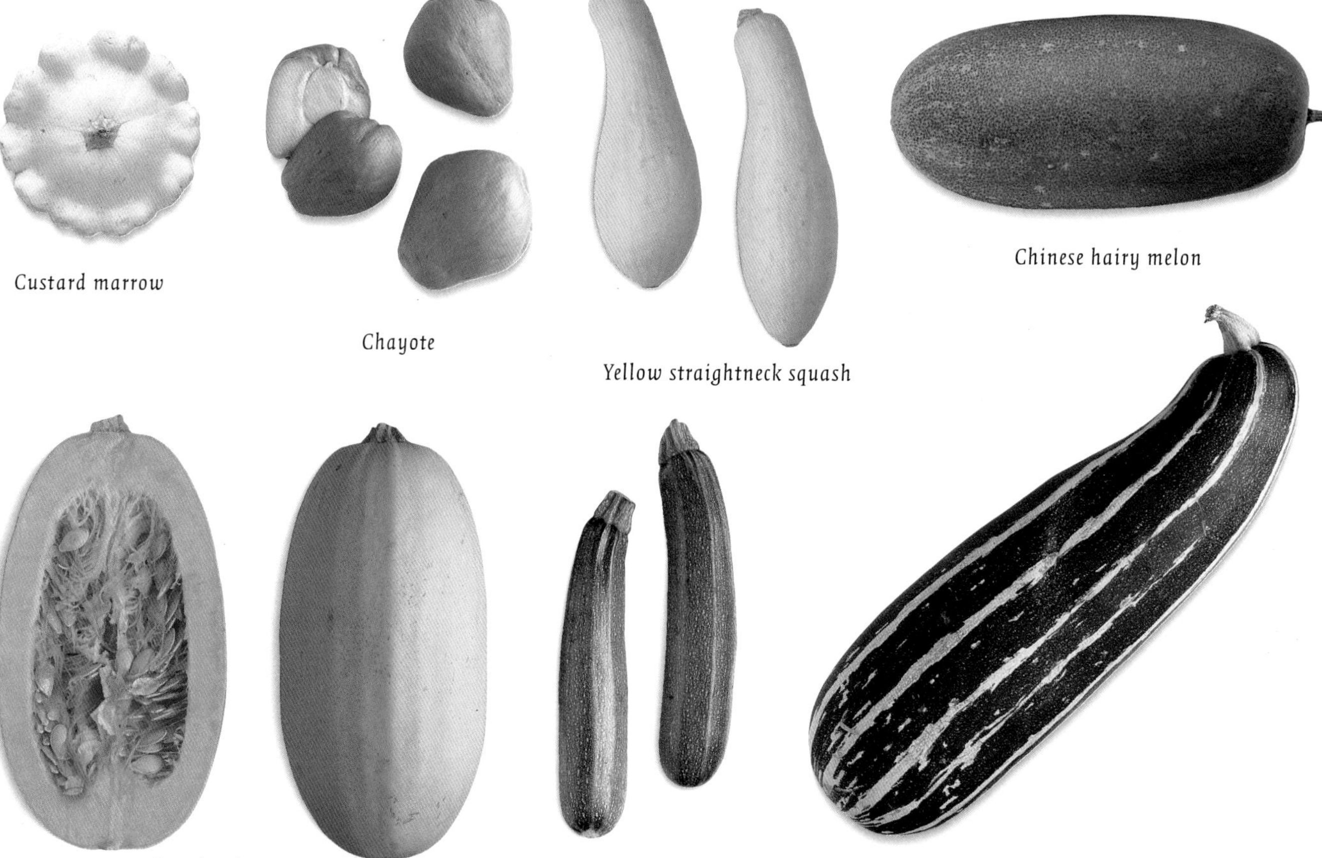

Custard marrow

Chayote

Yellow straightneck squash

Chinese hairy melon

Spaghetti marrow

Courgette

Vegetable marrow

and South American cooking, where besides being used in the same ways as other soft-skinned squashes, it is candied, filled with nuts and raisins, and eaten as a dessert.

Chinese hairy melon, fuzzy melon, wax gourd Looking like a large green or bluish-green torpedo, this can be bought in Chinese supermarkets. When young it is covered with a silky fuzz, which can be scrubbed off under cold running water; however, peeling is usually recommended. In maturity it is usually coated with a white wax-like layer, and needs to be peeled. It has a slight bitterness but is excellent stir-fried, braised and used in soups. A half-ripe specimen makes the best eating. In Chinese cookery it is steamed, boiled, braised, stir-fried or added to soups. In Indonesia it is candied to be eaten with tea, and is used in cakes and biscuits.

Winter squashes A favourite winter vegetable in North America, this group includes the acorn squash, which can be green or orange or a combination of the two; the butternut squash, looking like a huge, pale orange or beige peanut; the bumpy-skinned turban squash and its lighter-coloured cousin, the buttercup; and the large, warty hubbard squash, which is often sold in wedges. When buying, look for firm, unbruised specimens, or wedges that show no signs of softening around the edges.

Peeled, cut into pieces and boiled or steamed for about 20 minutes, winter squash can be served mashed with butter, salt and pepper or a little orange juice. The smaller squashes can be left unpeeled, halved, seeded and baked in the oven for about 30 minutes with butter and brown sugar or maple syrup in their hollows.

Pumpkin

The earliest pumpkin pies were not the familiar spiced golden tarts now eaten at American Thanksgiving. For the Pilgrim Fathers, pumpkin pie was simply a pumpkin with its top sawn off and its seeds removed, with the cavity filled with milk, spices and honey and baked until tender. Nowadays, because of the business of baking, straining, seeding, scraping and puréeing the pumpkin, many people use canned purée – one of the few foods that can be better canned than fresh. For pumpkin soup, which looks so pretty served in a hollowed-out shell, canned purée can also be used, but for baked and fried pumpkins you need fresh ones.

Italians use pumpkin in soups and risotto and as a stuffing for ravioli. English pumpkins are much softer fleshed, and because they cook so readily into a mush they are best used for pumpkin soup. Or they can be combined with potatoes or root vegetables to give them a little extra body when used in vegetable soups.

Calabaza pumpkin Often sold in wedges so as to display its attractive golden-orange flesh, this West Indian variety often features in Caribbean soups; otherwise it can be used for any winter squash or pumpkin recipe.

Pumpkin Pie 407
Pumpkin Soup with Basil 247

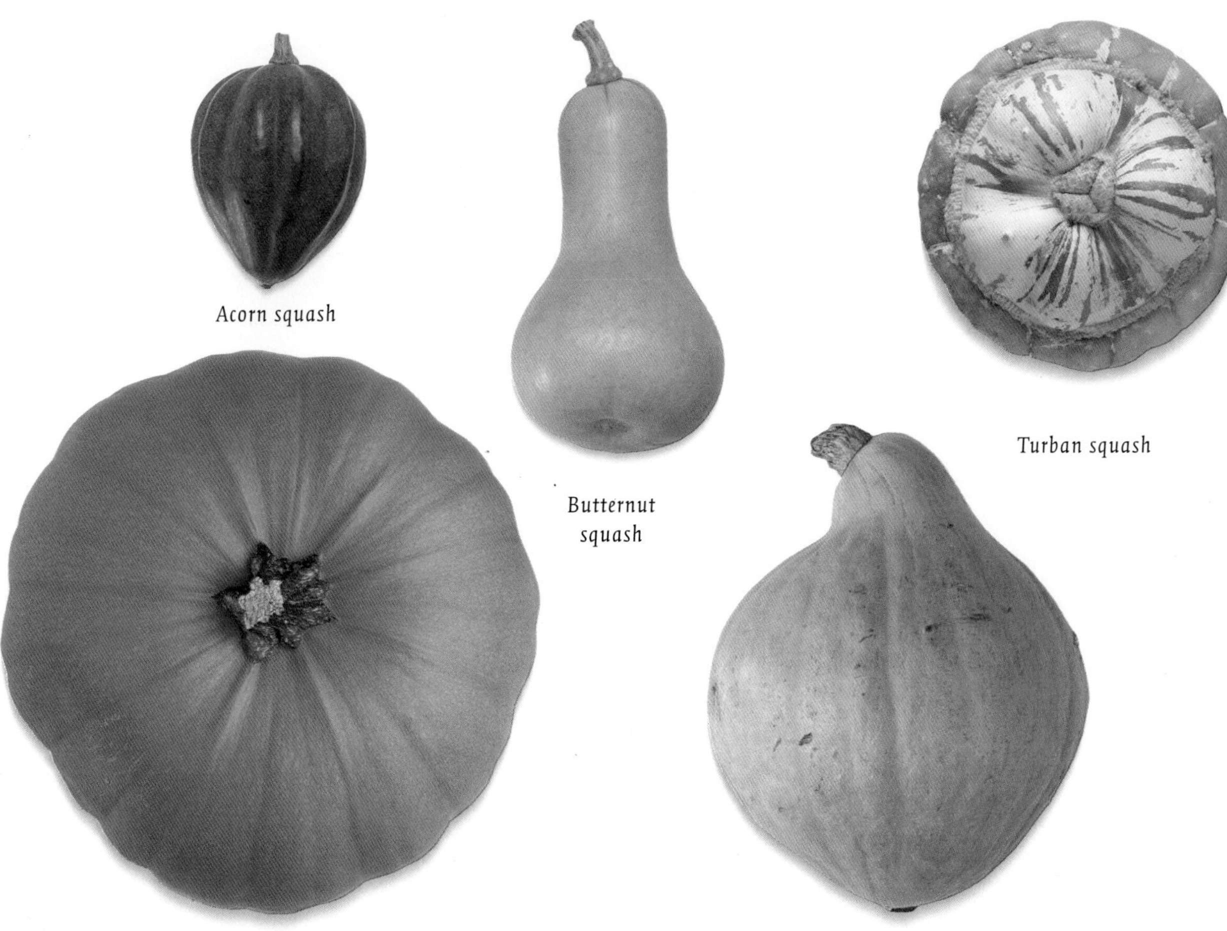

Acorn squash

Butternut squash

Turban squash

Pumpkin

Hubbard squash

Mushrooms and Other Fungi

cultivated mushrooms 160
Japanese and Chinese mushrooms 161
mushroom ketchup 206
truffle 161

In many countries the mushroom forage is an autumn treat, with whole families combing the ground for the 80 or so edible species of fungi which are either sold in the local markets, dried, or enjoyed fresh as a luxurious addition to the normal diet.

Fungi are plants that lack chlorophyll, and cannot therefore use direct sunlight to provide them with energy. Instead they get their energy by decomposing the life around them which contains energy in the forms of sugars and starches. The word fungus covers everything, including the mould that grows from your ceiling or on old jam, so we will use the term mushroom for those that concern us here.

Each species of mushroom inhabits a specific environment. Some types will only grow on pine trees, others only on an oak or birch.

What you see above ground is the fruit of an underground tree. The hidden mycaelium is actually the plant; it grows well in a warm summer. When its season comes, and after a period of high humidity, the fruiting bodies emerge above the ground, fed by the rapid intake of water. The mushroom comes up in a matter of hours; it emerges to release spores when the mycaelium stops growing, as the days shorten and it gets colder. Most mushrooms grow from autumn to the first frosts, September and October being the best months, but as it gets further into autumn, the leaves cover the mushrooms so they are harder to find. The September rain is crucial to many species – it is more important than heat at this time of year. Because they lack chlorophyll, most mushrooms will grow regardless of whether it is light or dark, or the days long or short. Only the first frosts will end their growth.

Essential advice for those considering taking up mushroom hunting for the first time: LEARN YOUR SUBJECT. The means of identifying edible mushrooms and avoiding all poisonous or dubious species is of crucial importance. All writers on this subject praise the beauty of wild mushrooms, and studying them is a great pleasure, using all the senses except hearing. But it is vital to use a guide that gives clear identification information. Take your mushrooms home, lay them out on a table in spirals of different species, and study each sort slowly and thoroughly before you even consider consuming them.

Some common edible wild mushrooms

Cep, penny bun (*Boletus edulis*) This has a dome-shaped cap and bulbous stalk, and is considered by Italians and French to be the king of mushrooms. In Austria it is called *Herrenpilz* (gentleman's fungus). The New Forest and many parts of Scotland, as well as many of the Surrey woods, are excellent hunting grounds for these and other types of boletus, although they are well camouflaged with their caps the colour of dried beech leaves and beige-

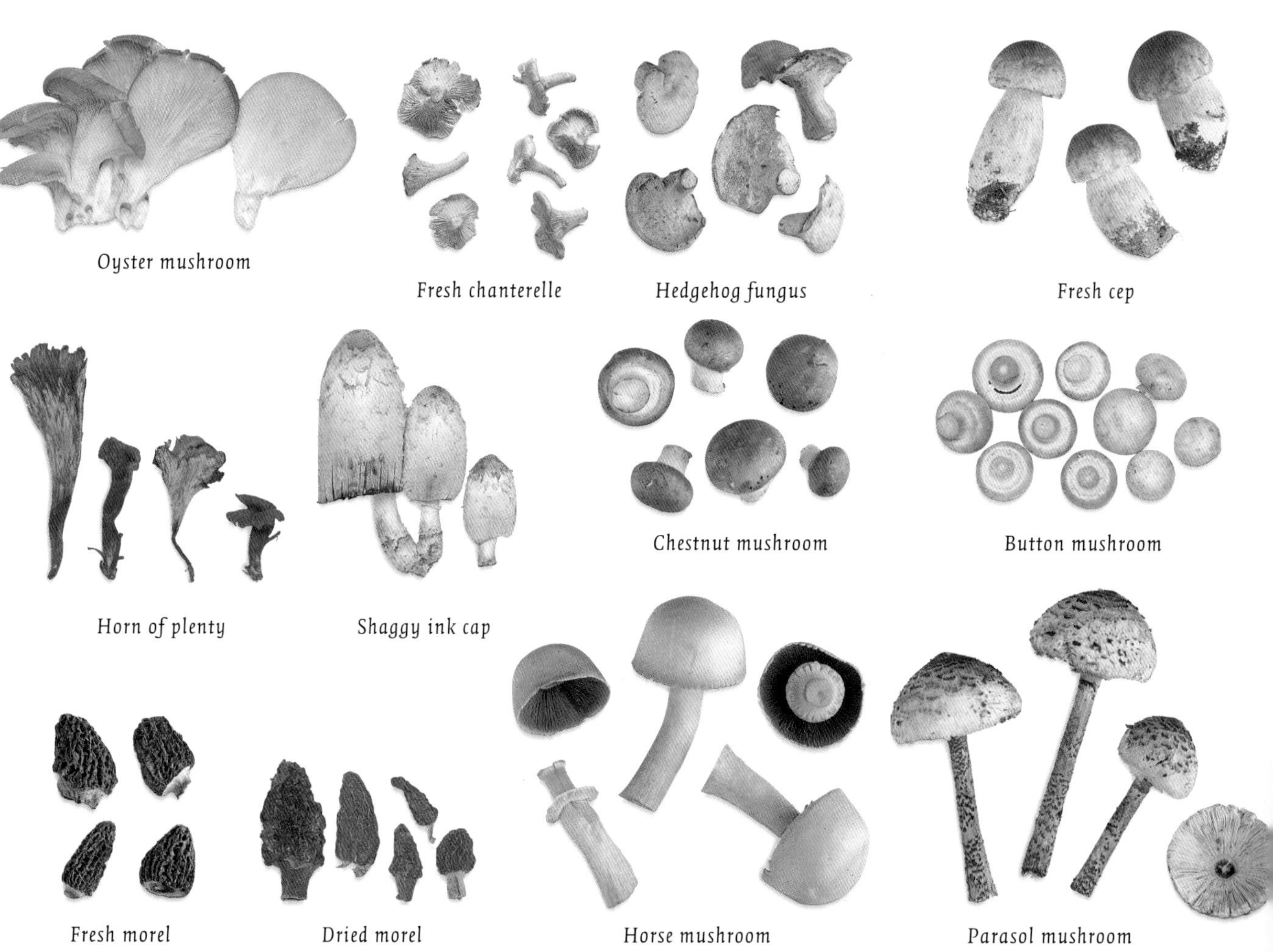

Oyster mushroom
Fresh chanterelle
Hedgehog fungus
Fresh cep
Horn of plenty
Shaggy ink cap
Chestnut mushroom
Button mushroom
Fresh morel
Dried morel
Horse mushroom
Parasol mushroom

white stalks. The flesh is almost white, firm and fleshy, tasting sweet and nutty with a pleasant smell.

Picked when firm, ceps will stay fresh in the refrigerator for up to a week. You can, of course, buy them dried, when they are usually labelled with their Italian name, *porcini*; choose creamy-fawn ones (they blacken with age).

Do not wash ceps, just wipe with a damp cloth. Then, if young, they can be sliced to eat raw in a green salad, possibly dressed with walnut oil. They make the best risotto, and in the Dordogne are eaten in omelettes with garlic and parsley, or fried with potatoes and garlic. Dried ceps must be soaked in warm water for 20–30 minutes before use (use the soaking liquid as stock).

Horn of plenty (*Craterellus cornucopioides*) Also know as Trompette des Morts or Black Trumpet, this mushroom is trumpet- or funnel-shaped and looks like old, dusty black leather. The cap is 2.5–8 cm/1–3 in long, and deep brown to black when the weather is damp, paler greyish-brown in dry weather. It is quite hollow right down the centre when cut and paler inside. The gills are more like radiating folds or wrinkles. It grows in autumn in deciduous woods, sometimes in large colonies beneath beeches, but is often hard to see.

Dried cep (porcini)

Portobello mushroom

Giant puffball

The taste is strong and earthy and the flesh remains black in cooking. Cut down one side to clean them. They should be fried gently in butter with garlic and parsley and used in an omelette, or perhaps in a cream sauce with chicken instead of the more expensive and rare morels, which have a short spring season.

Chanterelle (*Cantharellus cibarius*) In Germany these are known as *pfefferling* or *eierschwamm* on account of their egg-yellow colour. Small ones in France are known as girolles. They are both beautiful and delicious, bright golden-yellow, 2.5–10 cm/1–4 in across, smooth and funnel-shaped, with a margin that is rolled at first and then wavy and irregular. The underside has blunt, gill-like waves and folds. The stalk is short and thick, and the flesh smells of apricots and pepper. They are found in autumn in little clumps in mixed woods, often under moss, and on banks of tracks or among leaves.

They can be confused with the False Chanterelle (*Hygrophoropsis aurantiaca*), which is found in heathy woods of birch and pine. This has a slightly downy cap up to 4 cm/1 ½ in across and is orange. It has repeatedly forked, crowded, thin gills that are soft and easily separated from the cap which is trumpet-shaped, then flat. It is usually considered poisonous but is edible.

Chanterelles are hard to clean, but very good to cook with – any mushroom recipe will be even better done with chanterelles. They are particularly good with scrambled eggs or in an omelette, flavoured with garlic and parsley, and they are wonderful with chicken or pheasant.

There are other good edible chanterelles, such as Yellow Leg (*Cantharellus infundibuliformis*), which has a small, funnel-shaped, dark brown cap and hollow, bright golden stalk. The flesh is yellowish and thin, slightly bitter when raw, and smells aromatic. It grows in autumn in acid soils, in woods – hard to see, but if you find one, look around close by because they tend to grow in clumps.

Horse mushroom (*Agaricus arvensis*) Called in French *boule de neige*, this mushroom does look like a snowball when young, but when fully opened a horse mushroom found in a grassy field looks more like a dish on a green tablecloth. It is large and stout, 10–20 cm/4–8 in across, with a bright, creamy white cap that slowly turns yellowish with age. The cap is smooth and silky and can stain brownish-yellow when handled; the flesh is firm and white and smells of aniseed. The closely packed gills are greyish-white, quickly turning to chocolate-brown and finally black. The stalk is white shaded with rose and up to 2.5 cm/1 in thick; it has a double ring rather like a cogwheel. The base of the stalk does not turn bright yellow when cut. Horse mushrooms can be found in unploughed fields and old grassy meadows from July onwards. They can be seen from a long way off.

This mushroom is very fine. It has a much stronger flavour than its close relative the field mushroom and is less watery. Eat it young as it gets tough and dry with age.

Horse mushrooms can be cooked in all the best ways you might do ordinary mushrooms. I rather like a Swiss recipe that tells us to cook them in butter and then to arrange them on a mound of spinach flavoured with finely chopped onion cooked in butter, to look as if they were growing on a grassy bank.

Morel (*Morchella vulgaris* and *M. esculenta*) These are spring mushrooms, very highly prized by serious mushroom hunters. They are usually seen dried because they are generally scarce and hard to find in western Europe. Characteristically sponge-like, with domed caps 5–13 cm/2–5 in tall and hollow stalks, they come in a range of colours – *M. vulgaris* varying from pale buff to black and *esculenta* being cream-coloured. They appear to like scorched or newly cultivated ground. Dried morels are very good indeed, retaining the rich nutty flavour well; cook them, after soaking, in cream and serve with free-range chicken or veal.

Cauliflower fungus (*Sparassis crispa*) This wonderful cream-coloured mushroom looks like a large sponge, up to 30 cm/12 in across. In Switzerland it is called a Broody Hen; in Britain it is sometimes known as Brain Fungus. It has brittle, wax-like flesh and a pleasant smell; with age it becomes darker and tougher. It is not uncommon and can be found growing on the foot of old conifers

Chanterelles Fried with Dill 386
Lasagne with Mushrooms, Bacon and Artichokes 340
Mushroom Omelette 324
Mushroom Risotto 348
Oeufs en Cocotte aux Champignons 324
Poulet Paysanne 307
Ravioli con Funghi Porcini 342
Salmon Escalopes with Chanterelles 271
Sugo di Carne Toscano 336

lemon 167
sweetbreads 61

Garlic Mushrooms 386

and round pine-stumps. It is good to eat when young, but it needs careful cleaning. Slice it and fry in butter with garlic and parsley. You can also pull it into pieces and, having washed and dried it, dredge it with flour and then sauté in butter with finely chopped onions or shallots.

Giant puffball (*Lycoperdon giganteum* or *Langermannia gigantea*) This lovely fungus ranges in size from a large turnip to almost a metre across, when it can be seen for miles. White at first, it has a kid-glove-like, smooth exterior, taut to the touch when it is young, becoming softer and dingier with age. It is found between May and November but mainly after July, in fields, pastures and gardens; it often reappears faithfully in the same place year after year. Picked young, sliced and fried like fried bread, puffballs have a flavour like a mixture of bacon, mushrooms, aubergine and sautéed potatoes all at once, especially if cooked in bacon fat. Some books say the puffball is exactly like sweetbreads in taste and flavour. You can sprinkle it with lemon juice before or after frying, but don't overcook it. Puffball with bacon is a good start to a day in the country.

Shaggy ink cap (*Coprinus comatus*) Also known as Lawyer's Wig, these tall, white, bell-shaped mushrooms liquefy as they age, and the black fluid has been used as a substitute for Indian ink.

Ink caps are a familiar sight on grass verges and recently disturbed soil. The caps are shaggy, and gills are white at first, then pink and finally black. Collect very young, firm specimens; peel them, rejecting the stalks, and fry them at once in butter with pepper, salt and a last-minute sprinkle of lemon juice, or bake them in cream. They will eat like Dover sole.

Blewit (*Lepista saeva*) This species is one of the few that the English feel it is safe to eat. Called Blue Legs, at one time it was gathered in quantity and could be found in Covent Garden and, more frequently, in country markets. It can be easily recognized by its clay-coloured cap and gills, and stout stalk flushed with a bluish tinge. The dyers of Berwick on Tweed used the stalks to extract a blue dye.

Blewits are found in pastures and meadows. The flesh is fragile and tends to be watery, so they are best fried in butter with softened onions and then stewed, with a lid, for 10 minutes; add sour cream and chives and a little flour, and cook until bathed in a creamy sauce. In England they are sometimes cooked with onions in a white sauce like tripe; in Switzerland they are eaten in white sauce flavoured with paprika, parsley and onion.

The wood blewit (*Lepista nudum*) is a beauty – bluish-lilac or violet when young, with lilac gills. Usually found late in the season in woods, or heaps of garden compost and leaves, it is good to eat if gathered when it is dry and sound; a useful mushroom at the end of the season.

Parasol mushroom (*Lepiota procera*) This handsome mushroom starts as a tight brown dome, quite hard to spot in the shortish grass it favours, and emerges as a glorious tall, shaggy-topped umbrella up to 30 cm/12 in across, which can be seen for miles.

With its characteristic shape and creamy flesh and gills goes a pungent, meaty smell, which makes it easy to identify. However, not everybody is attracted by the strong flavour. Found in many different situations, including sandy, heathy open ground, clifftops or open heathy woods, it should be picked and eaten young. Discard the stalks, and fry with eggs and bacon.

Hedgehog fungus (*Hydnum repandum*) This is a good one for the amateur mushroom hunter as it is very easily identified by the clustered spines underneath the cap, which gave it its name. It is creamy-white, with an undulating top 2.5–10 cm/1–4 in across that sometimes becomes slightly funnel-shaped, and it has a slightly acrid smell. Found in deciduous woods from late summer to autumn, it is pleasant to find and pick, but not particularly distinguished to eat. To cook it, scrape away the gills (some people leave them, but the texture is not good), wipe the caps clean, and fry in butter or use in soups and stews, risottos and pasta sauces which call for a mixture of different mushrooms.

Oyster mushroom (*Pleurotus ostreatus*) This mushroom is now cultivated widely, but is also found growing in the wild. It looks like an ear or a bracket, and grows in tiers on the stumps, logs and branches of hard-wood trees, especially beech trees. Colours vary from oyster-grey to a pale buff, to white, to yellowish-brown, to almost black. The flesh is thick and soft with an almost waxy surface. The stalks are short and tough, and the gills are white to pallid, often fused near the stalk.

There are dozens of varieties of oyster mushrooms and, as they tend to be in season at different times, oyster mushrooms appear almost all year round. They are good to eat when young, but toughen as they age, becoming bitter. The wild ones need long, slow cooking as they can be hard to digest. Several crops may be gathered in one season from the same tree or log: if the log can be carried home and kept moist, it will continue to fruit.

Use a knife to collect them, and tap them sharply to dislodge beetles. Snip off the woody stalks, and either slice and fry until crisp or sauté in butter. They can also be used in stews or stir-fries or pickled. The texture is good, slightly gelatinous and crunchy.

Shiitake mushroom (*Lentinus edodes*) These also grow on trees. First cultivated by the Chinese, and commercially developed by the Japanese, they were originally grown on teak, mahogany or oak logs. Now they are also available in kit form, growing on sterile wood sawdust. The kit simply has to be soaked in water for 24 hours, and within 4–5 days the mushrooms appear. Once these are gathered, the sawdust is allowed to dry out for 2–3 weeks and then soaked again for another crop. This can be repeated up to four times. The kit should be kept under greenhouse staging or indoors with a loose bag over the top.

Shiitake, which have dark brown caps with an inwardly rolling margin and a small tough stalk, do not grow in the wild in Europe. They are, however, extensively cultivated now. If you see fresh ones for sale, bear in mind that they only keep for a day or two. Fresh, shiitakes have a firm and meaty texture to them; the stalks are tough and should be discarded. They are good in tempura, with prawns and vegetables, and in stir-fries. They can used together with dried shiitake to make a good sauce for pasta, or in pilaf and risotto. Dried shiitake are used, soaked for at least 30 minutes, in any recipe where a small quantity of mushrooms is needed for flavouring.

Cultivated mushrooms

Although lacking the pleasing diversity of wild mushrooms gathered by season, cultivated forms have the merit of year-round availability, and are consistent and utterly safe. Most common, of course, is the silky champignon or common mushroom (*Agaricus bisporus*), cultivated relative of the field and horse mushrooms, which is sold in three grades: button, cup, and open or flat.

Now that a wider range of mushrooms is becoming available, large mushroom farms are experimenting with other types: straw mushrooms, which have been grown in China for something like 2,000 years; enoki; and morels, *Morchella* species. Growers are also doing research on the requirements of mycorrhizal fungi, those species such as chanterelles and ceps which can only grow in partnership with another plant.

Button mushroom Small and succulent, these are slightly weaker in flavour than the more mature grades. Remaining pale (although an aluminium saucepan may darken them), they are useful for white sauces and for salads.

Cup mushroom These have a membrane just breaking to expose the gills, and can be kept pale if rubbed with a cut lemon, or if a few drops of lemon juice or white wine are added to the cooking liquor.

Left unpeeled – cultivated mushrooms never need peeling – cup mushrooms are ideal for stews and casseroles. The larger ones can be stuffed or, with the stalks trimmed off level with the cap, the cups can be filled with cream and cooked in the oven.

Open mushroom, flat mushroom These most resemble their wild cousins and are almost as penetrating in taste. Fully mature, these are the kind to eat grilled with bacon, or on toast, having been briskly sautéed with garlic and plenty of black pepper and chopped parsley. They can be used in dark soups or casseroles, but are troublesome cooked with chicken, for example, as they turn it an unattractive grey.

Chestnut mushroom Quite firm and an attractive brown colour, these have a stronger flavour than common mushrooms. These are known as cremini mushrooms in the United States, and mature versions, which range in diameter from 7.5–20 cm/3–8 in, are called Portobello mushrooms.

It is best to buy mushrooms a few at a time and often. Button or closed mushrooms become open cups even in the refrigerator, and their flesh soon starts to shrivel. To limit evaporation keep in brown paper bags. All but the densely fleshed button mushrooms act like sponges when they are cooking, absorbing more than their own weight in liquid, so add them to casseroles towards the end of the cooking time.

Japanese and Chinese mushrooms

Long before mushrooms were first cultivated in Europe, the Japanese were harvesting *take* specially grown in the water-softened bark of various tree trunks. In addition to shiitake, which grow on hardwood (*shi*), and enoki (*Flammulina velutipes*, also called golden needles), the meaty tasting matsutake, grown on pine logs, is a favourite. Unlike the shiitake and enoki, the matsutake has not been successfully cultivated. Available in Chinese supermarkets is the type known as cloud ears, tree ears or wood ears, used for texture rather than flavour. These are dried in small pieces, without stalks; soak for at least half an hour to revive their unusual texture.

Another Chinese mushroom is the tiny straw mushroom (*Volvariella volvaceae*), so-called because it is grown on straw from paddy fields. Occasionally seen fresh in Chinese supermarkets, the straw mushroom is more normally found canned in the West.

Truffles

One of the rarest and certainly the most expensive of all fungi, the black Périgord truffle (*Tuber melanosporum*) grows on the roots of young oak trees. This is the most sought-after of the truffle species, detected beneath the soil by pigs or specially trained truffle hounds.

With its rich, mould-like flavour, a little of the black truffle goes a long way – one of the good reasons it is used sparingly in such things as omelettes or stuffing for roast chicken. The classic dish *truffe sous cendre* – truffle wrapped in bacon fat or pastry, baked (traditionally under cinders) and served with a bottle of St Emilion – is rated by gourmets as the experience of a lifetime. Sadly, truffles found in pâtés often have no flavour at all and were probably canned.

Used somewhat more liberally and with less reverence, the white truffle of Italy's Piedmont is larger and stronger in flavour, and is now as expensive as its French cousin. While the latter is invariably eaten cooked, the Italians use their white truffle raw, grating or slicing it over risottos and salads. One of the great Florentine specialities is a delicate little bridge roll which contains a paste of raw white truffle, Parmesan and butter.

horse mushroom 159

Baked Halibut 263
Burgundian Beef Stew 282
Chicken Pie with Cream and Mushrooms 317
Coq au Vin 305
Garlic Mushroom Soup with Cream 246
Leeks with Truffles 379
Mushroom-Filled Pancakes 328
Red Mullet en Papillote 270
Seafood Salad 370
Soft Polenta with Butter and Parmesan 352
Tarragon Chicken with Mushrooms 308
Veal with Mushrooms 285

Dried cloud ear

Straw mushroom

Fresh shiitake

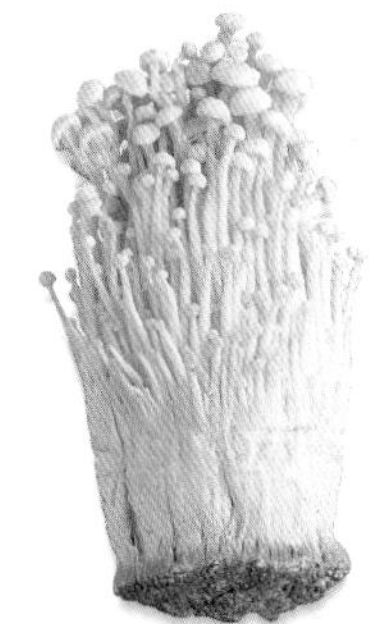

Enoki

Black truffle

White truffle

Fruit

Calvados (cooking with) 208
cider vinegar 204
dried apple 184
fruit teas 219

Apple Sauce 260
Cider Barbecue Sauce 257
Goose with Apple Stuffing 312
Normandy Pheasant with Apples and Calvados 298
Turbot Poached in Cider 261

APPLE AND PEAR

Apples and pears, although frequently bracketed as if they were almost one and the same fruit, could scarcely be more different. Apples are the most common, the most easy-going and the most useful of all fruits, both to eat casually at any time of the day and to cook with – there are more apple puddings than any other sort. Pears on the other hand are a fragile luxury – large, aesthetically pleasing and opulent, they make a grand ending to a grand meal, and speak of sunny orchards and of careful harvesting and marketing.

Apple

Today, unfortunately, the choice and variety of apples is getting smaller and smaller – although there are several thousand different apples cultivated in gardens and nurseries, very few find their way into commercial orchards, where the fruit grown must keep well and be tough, disease-resistant and good at travelling. Of the 7,000 varieties known in the United States only a few dozen are seriously marketed, while in Britain we are generally offered Cox's, Granny Smiths and Golden Delicious, with Red Delicious and Bramley's as runners-up.

It is sad that this is the case, since there are so many aromatic old-fashioned apples that are worth growing. So hunt through country shops and the more enlightened supermarkets, and you may find interesting varieties that are well worth trying. Apples sold as windfalls are also good buys and are perfect for cooking, since unripe apples have plenty of acid, essential to the flavour of apple pies, tarts and crumbles. The best eating apples are those that retain some of their acidity even in their final sweetness, and have a mellow flavour and firm, juicy texture. The eating apples known as reinettes, with their red-flushed golden skins, are especially good.

NAME	APPEARANCE	FLESH	TYPE
Cox's Orange Pippin	small, round, greenish-yellow tinged with red russeting	crisp, juicy, firm, sweet, some acidity	all-purpose, best for eating
Orleans Reinette	small, flat, golden tinged with crimson russeting	crisp, juicy, firm, some acidity	all-purpose
Egremont Russet	medium, round, with brown-orange russeting	soft, very sweet, some acidity	all-purpose
Laxton's Superb	medium, round, greenish-yellow, flushed with red	juicy, firm, sweet, some acidity	all-purpose
Golden Delicious	large, conical, green ripening to yellow	tender, very sweet, no acidity when ripe	all-purpose
Rome Beauty	large, round, thick skinned, shiny red	crisp, firm, juicy, slightly tart	eating, baking whole
Granny Smith	medium to large, conical, green with small whitish flecks	crisp, juicy, mild but acid	all-purpose
Crispin	medium to large, round, yellow-green	crisp, juicy, mild but slightly acid	eating
Bramley's Seedling	extra large, irregular, green, sometimes flushed with red	crisp, juicy acid	cooking
Red Delicious	large, elongated, thick skinned, shiny red	juicy, very tender, no acidity	eating
Worcester Pearmain	medium, round, red, sometimes two-tone red and green	crisp, juicy, sweet, slightly tart	all-purpose
McIntosh	medium, round, firm, two-tone red and green to red	crisp, juicy, slightly tart	all-purpose
Gala	medium, round, yellow flushed and striped with orange and red	crisp, juicy, sweet-tart	eating
Empire	medium, round, dark red	crisp, juicy, slightly tart	all-purpose

Buying and storing apples While obviously one should avoid apples with bruises and soft spots, do not be put off by a few dull, rough, brown patches on sound apples. This is called russeting, and in the case of apples that go by the name of russets this will extend over the whole surface. Russets are splendid with cheese, and cook well.

Those buying for the trade test for ripeness by grasping apples around the waist and applying gentle pressure: if the flesh is firm or the skin only wrinkles slightly the apples are at the peak of perfection. But it takes a bold shopper to emulate this practice. Fragrance is also important when testing for ripeness, and the fruit should be firm.

Apples continue to ripen after they have been picked. If they are to be stored they should be spread out so that they are not touching each other. If you want to buy apples in quantity, at one of the pick-your-own apple farms for example, keep them on racks or in special fibre apple trays in a cool, dry, dark place.

Cooking with apples Selecting the right apples for cooking is important if you do not want your pies to end up watery or your baked apples to collapse in a frothy mess all over the oven. Some apples, such as North America's favourite eating apple, the Red Delicious, are too tender for cooking purposes and lack the acidity that gives apple dishes their delicious flavour. The hard, crisp-textured apples such as the popular Granny Smith or some of the russets will require longer cooking than the softer-fleshed ones.

Apple purée When making this, choose crisp, juicy apples with plenty of acid – adding sugar towards the end of cooking time – as these will quickly turn to a froth. Tart apples give a sweet-acid taste that is delicious with pork, pheasant or goose.

Cooking apple slices Many of the dishes involving apples, such as pies and tarts, turnovers and fritters, depend on apples retaining their shape. Sugar and/or butter added at the beginning of the cooking helps to prevent them from disintegrating. Europe's favourite reinettes and russets, noted for their unique subtle flavour, are excellent for cooking. These are the apples that French cooks use when making *tartes aux pommes*. The Golden Delicious, one of the most popular and common of today's apples, retains its shape well, but lacks the flavour of the reinettes and russets, so cook it with cinnamon and plenty of butter and sugar.

Stewing apples When stewing apples use the same varieties as you would use for pies and tarts. To vary the flavour you can add cloves, cinnamon, or perhaps coriander seeds and grated lemon zest. Rum or Calvados and butter are also good with stewed apples. Some savoury dishes such as Iran's *khoresh* combine apples with cinnamon and onions. In West Germany apples are stewed, sprinkled with breadcrumbs and gently fried, to be served with ham.

Baking apples These are cored with an apple corer and the cavity filled with sugar, butter and perhaps almonds, blackberries or raisins. They are then baked, possibly basted or flamed with Calvados or brandy, and served with thick cream. The best apples for baking are the large ones. Run your knife around the circumference of the apple (to prevent the skin from splitting) before you stuff them and put them in the baking tin. Thick-skinned varieties such as Bramley's Seedling or Rome Beauty are ideal, since their skins are less likely to burst. The harder the apple, the longer it will take to bake: it is done when the top is frothy and seeping with juice.

Frying apples A classic accompaniment to fried or grilled *boudin noir* is peeled, sliced apples fried golden in butter. They are also very good with pheasant.

Raw apples Sliced or chopped apples give a crisp, crunchy texture to salads – the famous Waldorf salad of diced celery, apples and walnuts tossed in mayonnaise is especially good. A squeeze of lemon juice will prevent the apples from turning brown. Any crisp, sharp eating apple will make a good salad.

Crabapple, quince and medlar

These three fruits, like the apple, are related to the rose family and used to be called the fruits of Merrie England.

Crabapple Roasted and still hot, the crabapples that 'hissed in the bowl' in the hot spiced ale punches of Shakespeare's day were most likely the small, sour apples that grow wild or in gardens and which are the ancestors of all our modern apple varieties. These beautiful tiny fruits, which can be yellow,

boudin noir 74

apple corer 225

Apple Crumble 387
Apple Fritters 387
Apple Tart 409
Blackberry and Apple Pie 405
Crabapple Jelly 418

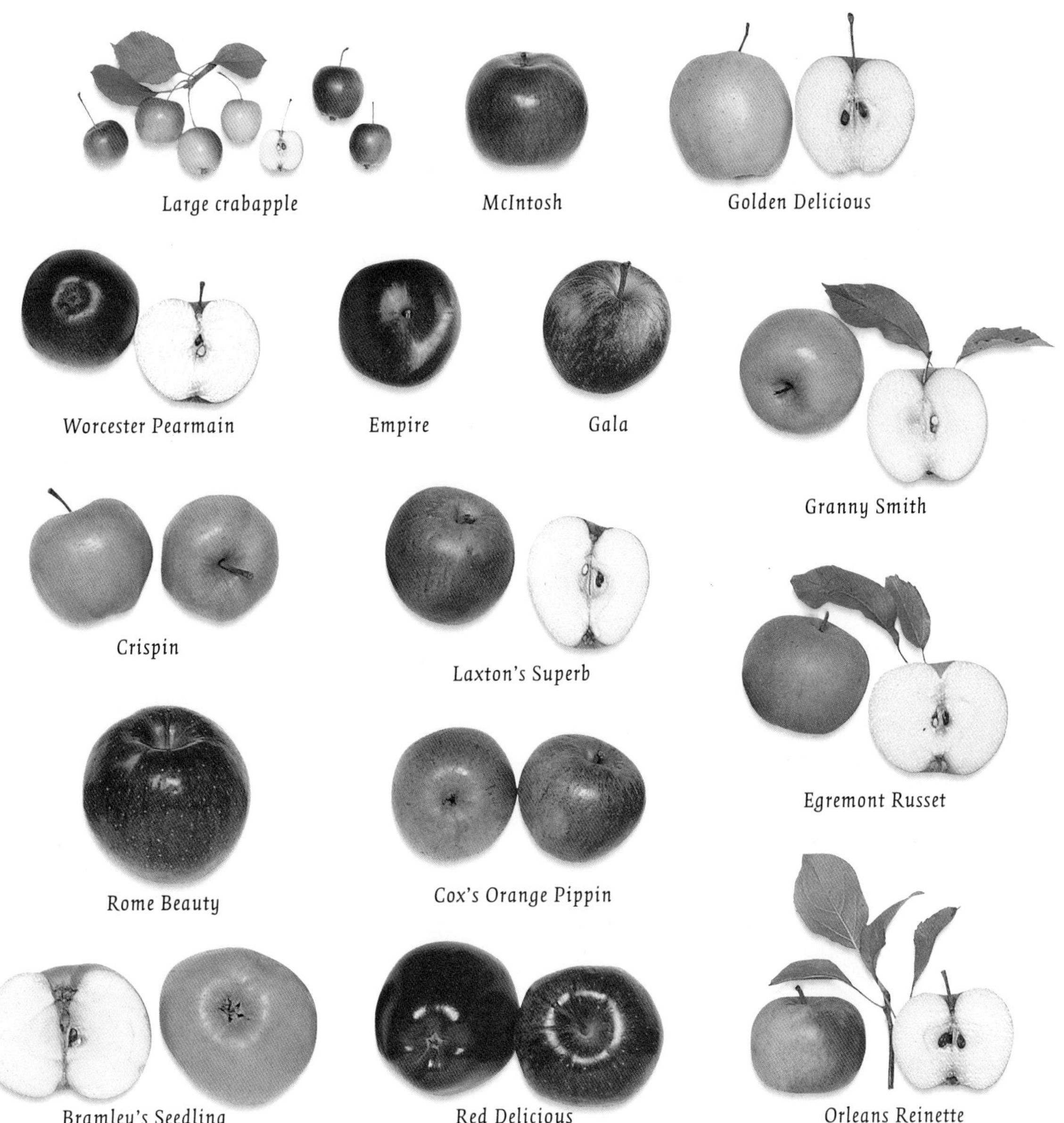

Large crabapple
McIntosh
Golden Delicious
Worcester Pearmain
Empire
Gala
Granny Smith
Crispin
Laxton's Superb
Egremont Russet
Rome Beauty
Cox's Orange Pippin
Bramley's Seedling
Red Delicious
Orleans Reinette

dried pear 184
pear eau-de-vie (cooking with) 208

Clear Quince Jelly 418
Medlar Jelly 418
Quinces in Lemon Syrup 387
Spiced Pears in Red Wine 387

red or green, are no longer eaten (except by birds) because they are generally not worth the bother, being mostly core and often very sour. They make a lovely clear, golden-pink jelly, which is excellent on buttered bread and with Petit Suisse. The larger crabapples, which are slightly sweeter, grow from the seeds of cultivated apples that have become wild. They have a crisp, tart flavour.

Quince Originally from central Asia, yellow-gold and aromatic quinces are a pleasing sight on the kitchen table in autumn. They are usually used to make jellies, jams and cheeses. A slice or two added to an apple pie or tart will give these dishes a delicious scent and flavour. Quinces can also be boiled down with sugar to a thick paste – called *membrillo* in Spain, *cotignac* in south-western France and quince cheese in Britain – which is then dried and eaten as sweets or a pudding.

Medlar Never found in shops, but sometimes cultivated in gardens or seen growing wild in hedges, medlars look like open cups of a warm golden brown and resemble a large rose hip in so far as each is crowned with a five-tailed calyx. Since they do not ripen on the tree they need to be picked and kept until they go soft, in the late autumn, before they are edible. In the past this ripening was done by laying the fruit in straw or packing it in bran. The ripe state is easily recognizable because the unripe fruit is rock hard. Medlars are usually baked, sieved and made into a slightly bitter jam purée or jelly, or the flesh is scraped out of the cup and eaten with sugar and cream. The tart, spicy taste and slightly granular texture are slightly reminiscent of marzipan.

Pear

This fruit, which can be so delicious, is more temperamental than the apple. It has an unpleasant habit of becoming mealy from the core outwards, a state described by fruiterers as 'sleepiness', and it does not keep so well as the apple.

Pears come in almost as great a variety as apples. Europe has about 5,000 named varieties and North America about 1,000, but as with apples only a small proportion reach the market. Three shapes predominate: the ordinary pear shape, the long-necked shape called calabash, and the oval, almost round shape. Colours, too, vary a great deal, from a soft blurred brown, to bright green with dark brown, grey-black or green flecks, to golden with a handsome red-gold flush.

Comice, Doyenné de Comice This is considered to be one of the best pears. It has a perfect balance of sweetness and acidity and a certain spiciness. Its juicy, sweet flesh is buttery – meaning that it is melting and not grainy. Large and greenish-yellow, it has a red blush where it has been exposed to the sun. Its thick, shiny skin is stippled with tiny grey spots and fawn patches.

Williams' Bon Chrétien This pear is known both as the Williams' pear and the Bartlett pear, due to the fact that it was propagated by an English grower named Williams and introduced to North America by an American called Bartlett. It has a sweet, musky flavour and a smooth skin that turns from dark green to yellow as it ripens: eat it when its speckles are still surrounded by a tiny halo of green on an otherwise golden skin. These superb pears are unfortunately bad travellers and extremely perishable.

Packham's Triumph This descendant of the Williams' or Bartlett pear looks somewhat like its distinguished ancestor but is not nearly so delicate. It keeps well and is therefore exported in great numbers from Australia, where it is grown in profusion.

Conference A favourite English pear, this was so named when it won the top prize at a fruit growers' conference because of its fine, tender, melting flesh and delicious flavour. It is slim and calabash shaped, stippled with fawn and grey russeting, and turns pale yellow when ripe. Kept in controlled cold storage by the trade, it is ripened and released as the market demands, so although it is an early pear it may be found late in the season.

Beurré Hardy, Beurré Bosc A number of pear varieties that have the French word

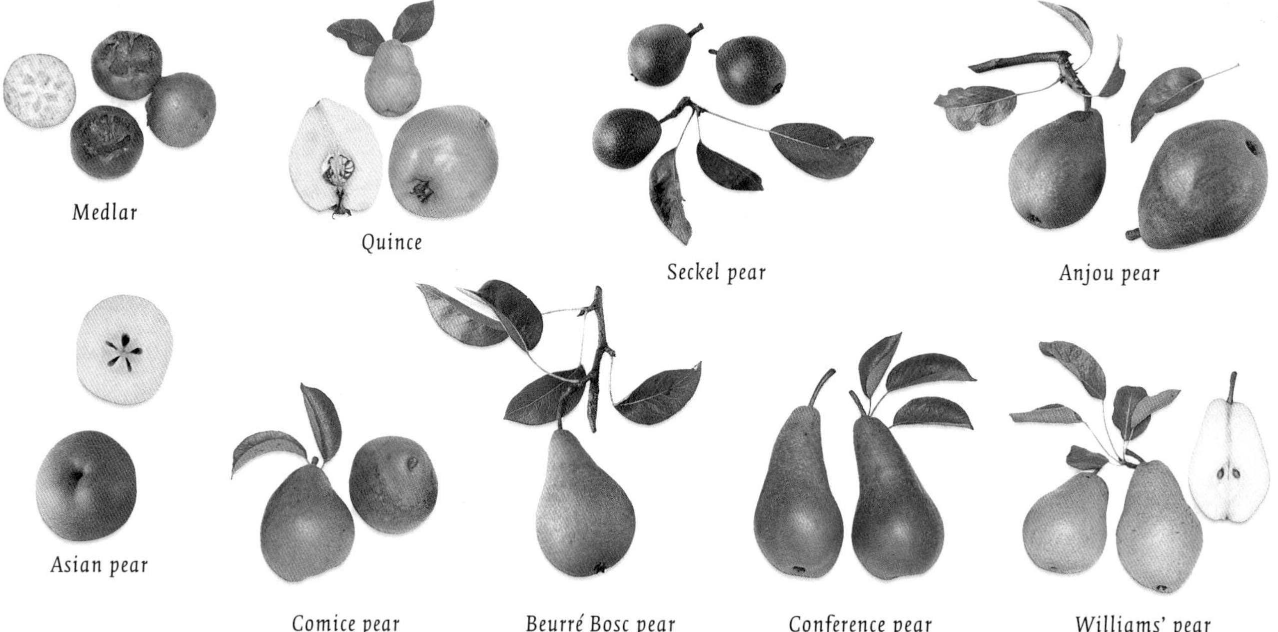

Medlar

Quince

Seckel pear

Anjou pear

Asian pear

Comice pear

Beurré Bosc pear

Conference pear

Williams' pear

for butter (*beurre*) in their names are characterized by their creamy, melting quality. The Beurré Bosc, so named in honour of a former director of the Jardin des Plantes in Paris, who propagated it, is also known as the Emperor Alexander as a compliment to the nineteenth-century Czar. It has a calabash shape and a fine brown russeting. Juicier and plumper than the Beurré Bosc, the Beurré Hardy takes its name from a nineteenth-century Belgian. Both pears in their youth are juicy enough for eating and are also excellent when stewed.

Bonne Louise Properly Bonne Louise de Longueval and d'Avranches, this was named after its grower and the place of its birth in Normandy. It is now also known as Louise Bonne de Jersey, and in German-speaking countries as Gute Louise von Avranches. Good it certainly is, and well known not only in its native country but wherever French pears are exported. Smooth skinned, with the merest speckle of russeting, the Louise tends to be greenish on the shaded side and yellow washed with pink on the side ripened in the sun. It can be stored without loss of flavour and is an excellent dessert pear.

Seckel, Seckle This was discovered growing wild in Pennsylvania by an eighteenth-century trapper. It is small and rather round, with a green to russet skin sometimes tinged with rose. It is sweet, juicy and spicy, and very popular.

Passe crassane This fat, juicy, rounded Italian pear has a lovely flavour and makes an excellent dessert pear. It keeps well and is known as the queen of winter pears.

Anjou One of the most widely grown varieties of pear in the United States, the Anjou remains green even when fully ripe. It has sweet, spicy, juicy flesh speckled with tiny brown spots.

Asian pear The many varieties of Asian pear vary in size, and they may be round like an apple or elongated like a pear. Skin colour is golden-brown or greenish-yellow. The flesh is firm and crunchy when ripe and extremely juicy.

Buying pears Pears for eating or cooking should always be sound. Test for ripeness near the stem end, where there should be more than a little give, and at the blossom end, where there should be no oozing softness, since this usually indicates trouble within. Pears are at their best for a very short time, and although they can be left to mature for a little while they must be inspected frequently.

Cooking with pears Most large pears are eating pears, although some are juicier than others. All pears, however, can also be poached in wine or light syrup, and well-flavoured eaters such as Williams' are, in fact, best for such dishes as pear sorbet and *poires Belle Hélène* – pears served on a bed of vanilla ice-cream and covered with hot chocolate sauce.

Cooking pears, which may be sold as such, are harder and less perfumed than the eaters. Poached in a vanilla-flavoured syrup, they make good compotes and can also be cooked in spiced red wine, in the process of which they become dyed, as the Tudors said, to 'a fine oriental red'. In Italy they are baked in Marsala, the cavity of each half-pear stuffed with a mixture of ground almonds and crystallized fruit. They can also be made into a relish with lemon juice and ginger or with horseradish, mustard seeds and black pepper; or they can be preserved or pickled with sugar, cinnamon and white wine vinegar. Cooked 'brown' with butter and sugar, they used to be served hot with game in Germany. They are still served cold there, poached in lemon juice with cranberries. Pear and spinach purée go well with roast duck.

Around the North Sea pears also go into main dishes: Frieslanders boil them with green beans, potatoes and beef, while in Hamburg they are cooked with beans and bacon or with salt meat. Boiled potatoes mixed with pears and a dash of vinegar are also sometimes served in northern Europe.

CITRUS FRUIT

The beautiful citrus fruits, probably East Asian in origin, all have one thing in common: they ripen while they are still on the tree. Once they have been picked they stop developing and will not get sweeter or improve their flavour. But most of them travel well and remain in good condition for many weeks in the right environment, and only gradually lose weight and pliancy as their juices and oils lose freshness.

Natural untreated citrus fruits are also subject to what is called re-greening. This does not necessarily mean that they are unripe but is simply a matter of temperature; the chlorophyll in ripe fruit fades as the thermometer drops and revives as it rises again. Inside the skin the fruit remains unaffected. However, since green patches are unattractive on citrus fruit that should by rights be orange or lemon-yellow, they are often treated with ethylene gas, which fades the chlorophyll, making the fruit more acceptable to the consumer. When buying citrus fruits, choose those that feel heavy for their size because this means plenty of juice. The fruit should be sound, with no sign of bruising, damp patches or soft spots. If you want to use the peel in cooking or marmalade, try to find fruit that is unwaxed, and wash or scrub it thoroughly to remove any residues of treatments the fruit may have had.

Citron

This fruit is the elder of the citrus tribe. It has a thick corrugated skin and resembles a large, rough lemon in shape. Since its pulp is too bitter to eat, the citron is now mostly grown to make the most beautiful translucently green candied peel used in fruit cakes.

Orange

Oranges may be orange, but can also be green, greenish-yellow and even red. There are three main varieties of orange: the smooth, thin-skinned sweet oranges, such as the Valencias and blood oranges, which range from bright gold to blood red and are full of juice; the larger, rougher, thick-skinned seedless navel oranges, which have the best flavour and are easy to peel; and the bitter oranges, also known as Seville or Bigarade oranges, which are used for making the best marmalade. The bergamot, a small, acidic citrus fruit similar to an orange, yields an essential oil from its rind used in perfumes, confectionery and Earl Grey tea.

Invented in Scotland, orange marmalade owes its origins to a boatload of Portuguese oranges that arrived in Dundee in the eighteenth century and that unexpectedly turned out to be extremely bitter. Bitter oranges still come on to the market in their short New Year season, and marmalade making is about the only occasion on which we boil oranges to good purpose.

candied peel 184
Earl Grey tea 218
glacé and crystallized orange 185
orange liqueur (cooking with) 208
peeling and segmenting citrus fruits 167
zesting citrus fruits 423

citrus zester 224
graters 224
juice extractors 226, 239

Chocolate Orange Mousse 394
Cranberry and Orange Sauce 260
Crêpes Suzette 396
Cumberland Game Sauce 260
Orange Butter Icing 415
Orange Glacé Icing 415
Orange Granita 401
Orange Sorbet 399
Quails with Thyme and Orange 301
Seville Orange Marmalade 418

glacé and crystallized clementines 185
zesting citrus fruits 423

citrus zester 224
juice extractors 226, 239

For the most part, however, we like our oranges fresh. In Trinidad they are sold in the street, halved and sprinkled with salt. Orange juice, freshly squeezed and served with ice, used to be standard refreshment in all countries. In Sicily, a paradise for oranges, the juice is drunk not so much as an appetizer but as a final *bonne-bouche* after a meal, especially the glorious tomato-red juice of blood oranges, which is particularly sweet and full of flavour.

When making orange juice, thin-skinned oranges such as the virtually seedless Valencias are the best choice. This is not so much because navel oranges lack juice but because their size makes them more expensive, and since their skins have a thick padding of pith a lot of what we pay for is thrown away. The navel orange, which can be peeled neatly and is virtually pipless, is the best one to eat as a dessert.

Mandarin and tangerine

These and their many cultivars, such as clementines and satsumas, are the smaller members of the citrus family and their names are sometimes used interchangeably. All are distinguished by having skin that does not cling to the fruit, and flesh that separates easily into segments. They are known as various mandarin cultivars to the botanist but to the shopper as different types of tangerines. Those of North African descent, grown in Tangiers, with loose-fitting skins and perfumed juice, are responsible for the name tangerine. Canned segments are sold as mandarins, although most are, in fact, satsumas.

Clementine Thought by some to be mandarins crossed with the Algerian wild orange, but generally recognized as a variety of tangerine, these are usually tiny, with a very good flavour.
Satsuma These are tangerines grown and exported from Japan and Cyprus; they can be quite sour, but are refreshing.
Ortanique, king, tangor and **murcott (honey tangerine)** Along with many other small hybrids, these are related to both tangerines and oranges. They are often found growing on the same tree, which shows how easily they cross with each other.

Kumquat

This originated in Japan and has recently been cast from the citrus family by botanists, although it continues to look

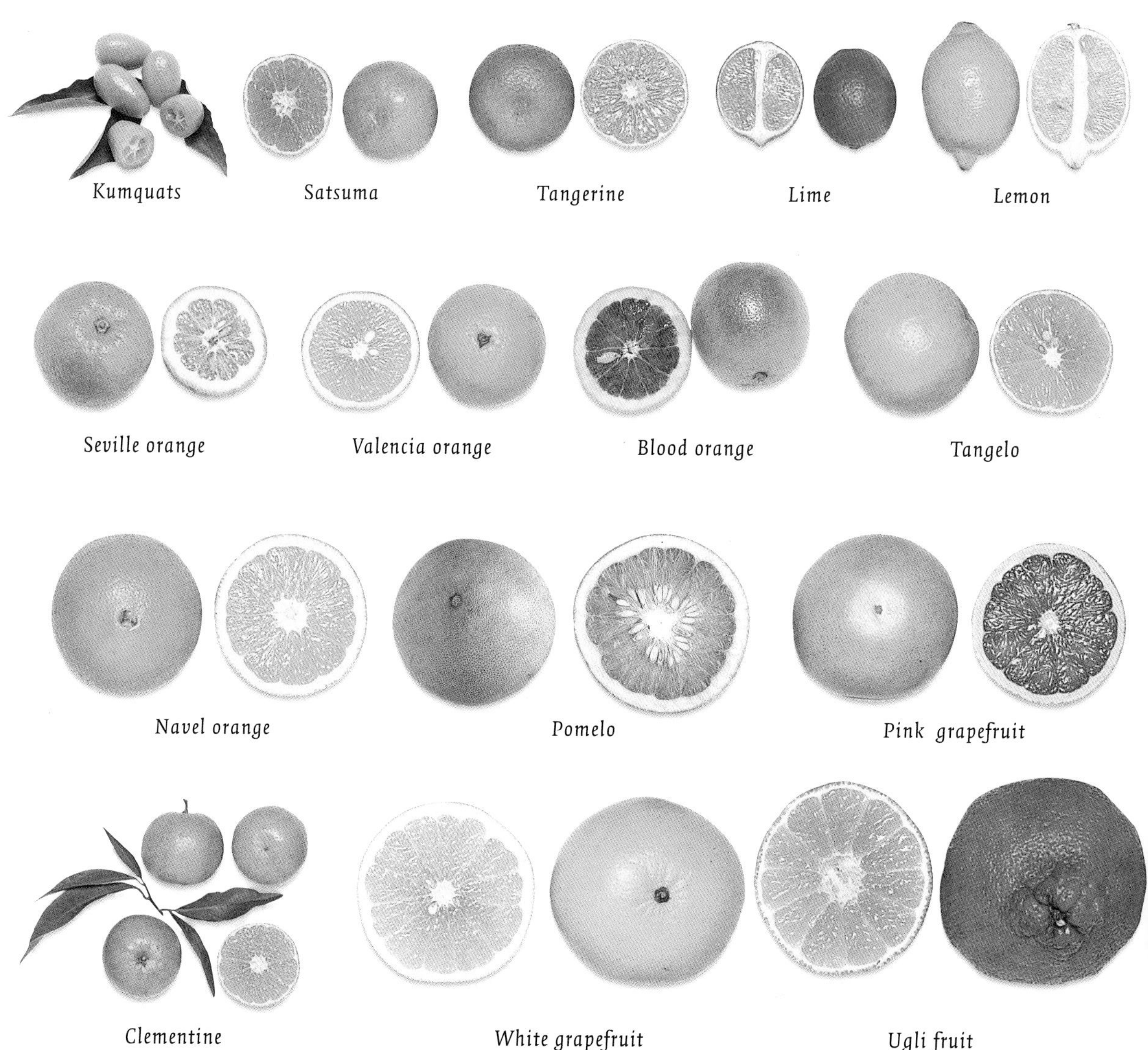
Kumquats Satsuma Tangerine Lime Lemon
Seville orange Valencia orange Blood orange Tangelo
Navel orange Pomelo Pink grapefruit
Clementine White grapefruit Ugli fruit

and taste like a tiny orange. Tart in flavour, kumquats are usually eaten complete with their thin skin, and are often bottled, unpeeled, in heavy syrup.

Grapefruit and pomelo
The large familiar globe of the grapefruit – yellow, when it is called white, rosy, when it is called pink, or ruby-red fleshed inside a yellow or pinky-yellow skin, when it is called ruby – is a descendant of the pomelo, a citrus plant brought from Polynesia to the West Indies in the seventeenth century by an English sea captain. The pink-fleshed pomelo sold today is a cross between a grapefruit and a larger citrus fruit called shaddock. It is refreshing but pleasantly tangy and may need sugar.

The grapefruit is perhaps more popular in North America than anywhere else. It is primarily a breakfast fruit, but also often ends meals in mousses and sorbets, and in between turns up in salads mixed with avocado, or with oranges and mint, and served on beds of lettuce.

Tangelo and minneola
The tangelo is a cross between tangerines and grapefruits. It is loose skinned and somewhat lemon-shaped, and may be stamped 'colour added' when marketed, since its skin does not colour well naturally. The minneola variety is particularly sweet and juicy and easy to peel.

Ugli fruit
No cosmetic colouring treatment is applied to this fruit, which is called hoogli fruit in Jamaica, and its extraordinary bumpy, mottled skin remains greenish-yellow. The light orange flesh is sweet, juicy and delicately flavoured, with a flower-like perfume.

Lemon
Rich in vitamin C, this most indispensable of fruits can be large or small, with a smooth, thin skin or a thick knobbly one. For culinary purposes, such as puddings and sorbets, lemon butters, lemon soups, frothy sauces and for the wedges served with fish and pancakes, it is better to use smooth-skinned lemons as they have more juice.

Choose specimens that are truly lemon-yellow in colour. Butter-yellow lemons may have lost some of their acidity in ripening, and lemons that look dull and do not have a moist-looking sheen may be dry and 'ricy', meaning that the almost invisible little sacs containing the juice have turned grainy through evaporation.

Lemons owe much of their flavour and aroma to the oil in the outer part of their skin, which is known as the zest. When serving lemon quarters they should be cut lengthwise so that when squeezed the juice will be directed downwards on to the food. Whenever possible lemon juice should be added to dishes after they are cooked, to avoid loss of vitamin C, which disappears when the juice is heated.

Apart from flavouring, lemon juice has certain other qualities. When poaching or stewing fruit, a teaspoonful of lemon juice added to each 150 ml/¼ pint of water will help prevent the fruit from breaking up or losing its shape. A few squeezes of juice will help poached eggs to coagulate and boiled rice to keep its colour, and a few drops will acidulate water sufficiently to prevent the discoloration of vegetables such as celeriac and Jerusalem artichokes.

Lemon juice can be used instead of vinegar in salad dressings. And, since it helps to counteract the richness of foods, it can aid digestion when served with fried foods.

Lime
This can be pale or dark green and has a tart, greenish pulp; if the skin is yellowish this usually means that the tang has gone. The West Indian or Mexican lime, which features so much in Creole cooking, is sharp and aromatic, as are the larger Tahitian limes of which the Persian and the Bearss are two types. The Key limes of Florida have a delicious sharpness and are used to make Key lime pie.

Limes are the most perishable of all the citrus fruits: they dry up and shrivel all too fast and develop soft, brown patches on their skins.

They can be used for the same purposes as lemons, and their juice, pale when fresh but often with added green colour when commercially extracted, goes into daiquiris, margaritas and other tequila drinks.

STONE FRUIT

Although hothouse peaches can be found almost all the year round, there is still something wonderfully seasonal about stone fruits. Their year begins with the first cherries and ends with the last of the plums, with outdoor peaches, greengages, damsons, nectarines and apricots in between. All are closely related members of the genus *Prunus*, and when talked about collectively are known as drupes.

acidulated water 422
candied peel 184
lemon balm 194
lemon grass 194
lime leaf 195

grapefruit knife 225

Grapefruit Sorbet 401
Greek Avgolemono Soup 250
Hot and Sour Shellfish Broth 253
Lemon Butter Icing 415
Lemon Court-Bouillon with Parsley 245
Lemon Curd 419
Lemon Glacé Icing 415
Lemon Tart 405
Osso Bucco with Lemon Gremolata 287
Quinces in Lemon Syrup 387
Seviche 263
Syllabub 394

1

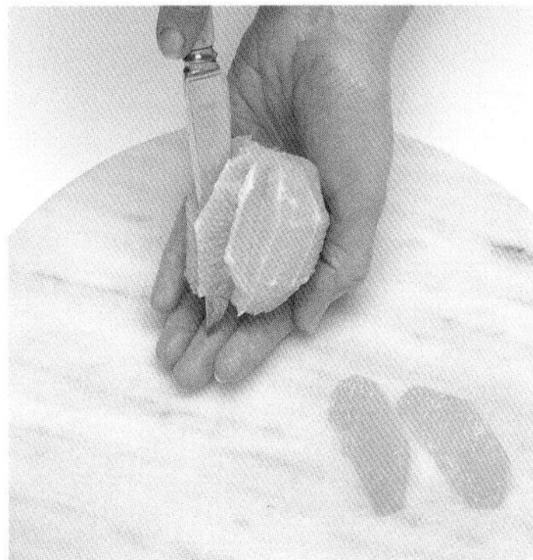
2

Peeling and segmenting citrus fruits

1 Using a serrated knife, cut a slice from the top of the fruit to expose the flesh. Peel the fruit in the same way as you would an apple, cutting just beneath the white pith.

2 Hold the fruit in one hand and cut out each segment, freeing it from its protective membrane as you cut. The resulting segments should be completely free of membrane and pith.

dried cherries 184
glacé and crystallized cherries 185
kirsch (cooking with) 208

Cherry Cake 410
Cherry Clafoutis 388

Cherry

Firmly fleshed or melting, deepest lip-staining black, or the palest cream tinged with a rosy blush, the cherry comes in hundreds of varieties. They are generally classified by their growers as sweet or sour. There is also a third type, which is a mixture of sweet and sour; two of these hybrids are Dukes and Royales. Usually black or translucent red, these are all-purpose cherries and can be both eaten and cooked in a variety of ways.

The wild sweet cherry known as the mazzard is the ancestor of all our varieties.

Sweet cherry Sweet cherries (*Prunus avium*) used to be neatly divided into the hard, crisp bigarreaus and the soft, sweet cherries known as *guignes* in France, geans in England and hearts or heart cherries in North America. Now, however, with the appearance of many hybrids, the distinction has become blurred.

Among the most delicious of the bigarreaus are the Napoleons, or Naps – big, crisp and golden with a red cheek. They are also known as Royal Annes, and in nineteenth-century England were for a time called Wellingtons. This politically inspired name, however, did not catch on, and to restore the balance England named a dark red cherry the Waterloo. A favourite American cherry, the Bing, is also a bigarreau – large, heart shaped and deep red to almost black, with firm, sweet flesh.

Another red-black cherry that is tender and has an excellent flavour is the Black Tartarian, which is a type of *guigne*. This cherry is said to have made its way to Europe from the Caucasus, the seed probably carried by birds. Early Rivers, another of the *guigne* type of cherry, is a prolific variety with red to deep red flesh. The Ranier is a sweet golden cherry with a slight pink blush.

Sweet, juicy black *guignes* are used to make the delicious pudding clafoutis, which comes from the Dordogne region of France; in Kent, England's cherry-orchard county, a similar dish goes by the name of battered cherries. The same juicy type of cherries also goes into the exquisite Swiss black cherry jam, slippery and shiny and full of whole cherries. The cheaper versions, with chopped-up cherry pulp, trying to pass off as the real thing, are best avoided.

Sour cherry If the word sweet is sometimes used too optimistically as far as cherries are concerned, sour is almost an understatement. The dark, short-stemmed, juicy morellos, or *griottes* as they are known in France, are so acid that they are almost impossible to eat. They are small and round, and deep red to almost black. The famous Black Forest cherry cake, *schwarzwälder kirschtorte*, is authentically made with morellos grown in the Black Forest region, and with kirschwasser, the Black Forest version of cherry brandy. Cherries such as the Montmorency, brighter in colour and with pale, clear juice, are so sour that they are not normally eaten uncooked.

Sour cherries (*Prunus cerasus*) go into translucent jams, into pickles to eat with game, pork, poultry, rich meat dishes and pâtés, and into liqueurs and cherry brandies. Duck Montmorency, now something of a cliché, requires cherries for its fruity wine sauce, although they do not necessarily have to be the sour Montmorency cherries of France; any

Napoleon cherry

Gaviota plum

Greengage

Black Tartarian cherry

Bing cherry

Victoria plum

Santa Rosa plum

Black bullace

Sloe

Damson

Apricot

Nectarine

Peach

acid red cherries will do. And cherries set alight in a brandy sauce and poured over vanilla ice-cream make Cherries Jubilee. Morello cherries are often preserved in jars and make excellent tarts and sometimes pies.

Maraschino cherry The sweet, sticky liqueur maraschino is made from a small, wild Dalmatian cherry called damasca, or marasca. Maraschino cherries, however, which were originally preserved by being steeped in the liqueur, are now more likely to be ordinary cherries that have been bleached and then steeped in syrup flavoured with oil of bitter almonds.

Buying and storing cherries Look for brightly coloured fruit; whether heart shaped or spherical, the plump ones are always best. The fruit should be clean and glossy, with unbroken skins and stalks that are fresh and green. Make sure the stalk is attached or the fruit may have been spoiled by moulds or rot in transit. Ripe cherries are perishable, but will keep for a few days in the refrigerator; wash them just before they are to be eaten.

Cooking with cherries Prepare cherries for cooking by pushing out the stones with a cherry stoner or hooking them out with the U-bend of a hairpin or paper clip. If you try to squeeze the stones out, too much juice is lost.

Canned cherries lack firmness and flavour and are best used in sweet dishes rather than savoury, although they still won't be very good. It is best to avoid them if possible.

Plum

No other fruit, said Pliny, has been so cleverly crossed, and since he wrote this some 2,000 years ago, the growers have not been idle. Some plums are grown primarily to be eaten fresh, although many, like the greengages, are equally delicious cooked.

Dessert plums These are usually larger and juicier than cooking plums, with a higher sugar content.

Gage Of all the European plums, none is more sweetly perfumed than the greengage, known in France as the *reine-claude* after Francis I's queen. The old greengage, round and firm fleshed, with a rose-flushed cheek, is still grown, although there are now other varieties such as the Cambridge gage and the juicy Jefferson. There are also many golden descendants of the old French 'transparent gage', large and translucent, with the delicious honeyed flesh that is characteristic of all the gages.

Santa Rosa and Burbank These are pleasantly tart, bright red plums grown largely in California, where the climate suits their warm temperament. Derivatives of the wild Asiatic plum, they are often referred to as Japanese plums, although in fact they were grown originally in China. Others of the Japanese type are the Laroda, with reddish-yellow skin, Friar and Queen Anne.

Gaviota This is one of the newer varieties, grown to giant proportions; it is sweet and juicy, and ruby coloured right through to the stone.

Victoria Golden-red and pink bloomed, the Victoria is one of the most prolific of plums. Oval shaped with golden flesh, it is a favourite in the kitchen as well as being an excellent dessert plum.

Cooking plums These are usually the smaller, drier, sharp-flavoured plums that retain enough acidity to make them delicious when cooked.

Sloe and bullace Dark and mouth drying, the sloe is the wild European plum that grows on spiky hedges and is used for making sloe gin. The bullace, larger than the sloe, is less acid and can be stewed, jellied or preserved.

Damson This plum has a lovely acidity even when ripe, and is used for jams, pies and puddings. In England it may be turned into damson cheese, an old country confection made of sieved fruit and plenty of sugar, which is potted and aged before it is ready to eat. It also used to be dried in slabs and decorated with almonds, and was served with a dousing of port as a pudding. Damson cheese is a close relation to the more pliable *mus* (made from the quetsch plum), which used to be very popular, especially in Germany.

Quetsch Also known as Zwetschen, Switzen or, in the Slavonic languages, slivy, these are small, dark blue plums with a heavy bloom. They thrive in central Europe, where they are made into the plum brandy slivovitz, and in Germany and in Alsace, where they are used to make a potent fruit brandy.

Cherry plum Also called mirabelles or myrobalans, these are very small, with red or yellow skins and golden flesh. They are soft and juicy and are excellent stewed or made into jams. In France they are made into mirabelle, an eau-de-vie.

Beach plum These grow wild along the Atlantic coast of the United States, especially on Cape Cod. The small, tart, dark purple fruits grow in large clusters and are avidly gathered and made into beach-plum jelly.

Buying and storing plums When buying plums make sure that they are firm and free from damage. They should be stored in a cool place, but not for too long; ripened plums do not keep for more than 2 or 3 days. If you buy them unripe, they need to be kept for a day or so in a warm room to ripen.

Cooking with plums All dark plums and some of the lighter varieties such as the small golden-yellow mirabelle, have bitter skins. This makes a delicious contrast to the sweetness of their flesh when cooked. They can be used to make jams and jellies which are transparently luminous when freshly cooked, but darken with overcooking and ageing. They also make a delicious sweet-sour sauce to serve with meat and with the pancakes that accompany Peking duck.

In Austria plums, fresh or dried, go into the middle of lovely deep-fried little dumplings that are rolled in fine sugar mixed with grated chocolate, and also go into strudels. Throughout Germany the plum season means *Pflaumenkuchen* – plums riding on a yeast-based dough that absorbs the juice of the fruit. In Britain, however, many recipes such as plum duff or plum pudding do not require plums at all, the word being used to mean raisins.

Peach

The flesh of peaches ranges from almost silvery white to deep gold or deep red. White-fleshed peaches are tender and juicy, yellow ones slightly coarser but often very good; the little-known red-fleshed *pêches-de-vignes* of France can be the richest in flavour. With some peaches the flesh clings to the stone, hence clingstone peaches, while with freestone varieties the flesh comes away easily and cleanly. In Europe this distinction seems not to weigh so heavily on the shopper, although it is always a shame when too much of the flesh – rightly described as

bitter almond 186
Maraschino (cooking with) 208
plum eau-de-vie (cooking with) 208
plum sauce 206
prune 184

cherry stoner 225

apricot brandy (cooking with) 208
dried apricot 184
dried peach 184
peach eau-de-vie (cooking with) 208
peeling peaches 243

Apricot Tart 409
Peach Conserve 418
Peach Melba 399

voluptuous – refuses to part in any way from the stone.

Known as *Prunus persica*, the peach reached Greece from its native China via Persia, and then Rome and the rest of Europe via Greece. It arrived in America by way of stones carried by Columbus, and the American soil and climate suited the peach tree so well that it spread faster than the settlers. But it is Georgia, especially, that is often known as the peach state. The freestone Belle of Georgia, crimson cheeked, its creamy flesh delicately marbled and its stone sitting in a carmine-tinted pit, comes from seed sent directly from China at the end of the nineteenth century. Elberta, another favourite Georgian, has juicy yellow flesh, firm but tender. It is equally popular fresh or canned. But while canned peaches in heavy syrup are nice enough, they differ almost more than any other fruit from their fresh counterparts. Perhaps this is because canned peaches are cooked in a heavily sweetened syrup, for even the sweetest fresh peach never has a cloying quality.

Buying and storing peaches Large peaches command the highest price but are not always the most delicately flavoured. In China, where peaches symbolize longevity, the venerated ancestor of all the peach trees in the world bears fruit that is relatively small, with large stones, yet its flavour is said to be unsurpassed by any of our hybrids.

Peaches are a fragile fruit and should be handled very gently. They should feel firm with a little give. Greenish fruit should be avoided as it will never ripen at home. Store ripe peaches in the refrigerator; those that are still a little too firm are best kept at room temperature.

Cooking with peaches Some people eat peaches in salads, and spiced or pickled peaches are excellent with ham, but it is in puddings and desserts that peaches come into real use. Peach sorbets and ice-creams are delicate and subtle, and there are scores of coûpes and sundaes made with peaches, the most famous of which must undoubtedly be Peach Melba. Invented by Escoffier for Dame Nellie Melba, the opera singer, this involves a ripe fresh peach gently poached in syrup, served with vanilla ice-cream and fresh raspberry purée. In France, peaches and raspberries are combined in an exquisite salad.

Nectarine

One of the most beautiful of all fruits, with rosy cheeks like blushing girls, the nectarine is smooth skinned like a plum and is very like a ripe plum in texture, but tastes of peach, although it is a little sharper and more scented. Nectarines can be used in all the same ways as peaches, but are usually devoured, messily, as a dessert fruit – much juicier than peaches, they are rarely skinned because their skin is much thinner. Called *brugnons* in France, they are eaten there in vast quantities in July and August, the white-fleshed varieties fetching higher prices than the yellow ones. Nectarines can be purchased under-ripe, as they will ripen at room temperature.

Apricot

Even in the days when fresh fruit was regarded with suspicion, apricots were generally accepted as wholesome food. Known as *Prunus armeniaca* because the Romans obtained them from the Far East via Armenia, they span the spectrum of gentle orangey tones from the very pale to the very rich. Depth of colour, however, is not necessarily an indication of flavour; it merely means that some varieties have more carotene than others and are richer in vitamin A. The deep orange apricot called Moorpark is always sweet and delicious.

The flesh of apricots is much firmer and drier than that of peaches and nectarines, which makes them ideal for cooking as well as for eating fresh – they will not turn into a mush, thereby ruining your pastry or whatever else.

Buying and storing apricots An apricot picked before its time does not sweeten, it only matures a little, so test for ripeness by pressing the fruit between two fingers; it should feel soft. Ripe fruit will keep in the refrigerator for a few days. Unripe, they will keep for longer, and if they are too hard and sour to be eaten fresh, they can be cooked in tarts and fools, or pickled in vinegar with cloves for an excellent relish that is delicious with cold pork or ham.

Cooking with apricots In France large, fresh apricots, arranged on light flaky pastry, make the most mouthwatering flans and tarts, and a compote of apricots, sometimes flavoured with Madeira, is served hot on crisp, golden croûtons. Austria's *knoedels*, or apricot dumplings, are made from fresh skinned apricots individually wrapped in thin pastry, and then poached and eaten with hot melted butter, sugar and cinnamon. And brandied apricots are delicious, the fruit poached with sugar and put up with brandy in equal quantity to the syrup.

BERRIES AND RHUBARB

The arrival of berries heralds the coming of summer, but they will not be so fully flavoured and sweet as later on in the season, and they are also likely to be expensive. In the case of most berries, however, it is a pleasure to buy at least a few early ones for decorating creamy puddings, to which they give an allure that is quite disproportionate to their numbers.

The real feasting begins in the high season, and it is then that most berries taste best, simply dredged with sugar and eaten with creamy milk or cream or possibly sprinkled with wine. Later on, when the first flush of excitement has worn off somewhat, they can be combined with other fruit or made into ice-creams and sorbets.

There are usually at least 2 weeks each summer when a great number of berries are available simultaneously. This is the time to make summer puddings or to offer great bowls of mixed berries, sugared beforehand so that they yield some of their juice. Later in the season, when berries are more abundant – and cheaper – it is time to think about making jams, jellies and syrups.

When buying berries it is important to look not only at the top of the punnet in which they are likely to be packed but also at the underside. Bad staining or wetness underneath suggests squashed, sad fruit below, which will soon go mouldy. Some packers still call to mind the Elizabethan 'strawberry wives' who, according to their monarch, were given to 'laying two or three great ones at the mouth of their pot, and all the rest were little ones'.

If you buy berries loose, ask for them to be weighed and packed 225 g/8 oz at a time since this prevents them being crushed by their own weight on the way home. If you go fruit picking at a farm – every year more of them open their gates to the public – use plenty of small punnets or other containers so that your harvest remains in good condition.

Berries, whether bought or picked, are fragile and perishable, so the sooner you eat them the better. If they must be stored, put them in a darkish, airy place, spreading them out well so that furry casualties do not infect their neighbours. No berries, except perhaps the harder ones that come in the autumn, thrive for long in the refrigerator – although it is cold and dark, it is too humid. Also, the highly scented berries such as strawberries tend to permeate other foods, particularly butter, with their smell.

Strawberry

'Doubtless God could have made a better fruit than the strawberry, but doubtless God never did.' Best loved among the soft fruits, strawberries conjure up all the well-being of summer. In England they are built into the summer way of life – tea at Wimbledon and Henley and garden parties at Buckingham Palace traditionally include what a sixteenth-century writer described as 'strawberries swimming in the cream'.

Somewhat surprisingly, perhaps, the ancestor of the cultivated strawberries we delight in these days was American, introduced to Europe from Virginia by the early colonists. It was smaller than today's prize specimen, but a positive giant compared with the indigenous fragrant wood strawberries (*fraises des bois*) that had long been transplanted into gardens and regarded as a cure for all ills. Alpine strawberries (*fraises des alpes*) have slightly larger fruits and some are completely white in colour. Both these wild varieties have not changed in their intense fragrance and size and still remain the best of all strawberries.

The advent of the Virginian strawberry led to unceasing attempts to grow even larger strawberries. Sadly, it was found that what the fruit gained in size it lost in flavour. It was not until a particularly fragrant strawberry arrived from Chile, and was crossbred with the Virginian, that the balance between size and taste was finally adjusted. This hybrid is the ancestral strawberry of all modern varieties cultivated on both sides of the Atlantic.

Nowadays new varieties of strawberries are regularly introduced and old ones discarded as being too fragile or not sufficiently resistant to disease, or possibly too small: size rather than flavour has been the important factor in marketing, and big strawberries command the highest prices. They may look particularly luscious but from the eater's point of view bigger is not necessarily better; nor do the deep scarlet varieties necessarily taste best.

Do not be put off by the lighter berries or those that have paler tips, but make sure that the strawberries are plump and glossy. They should be bought with their green frills intact. If washing them, do so immediately before hulling. Hulled strawberries yield their juice when sugared. Only in jam making should strawberries be cooked at all. When making strawberry sauce to go with ice-creams or sorbets, simply purée the fresh fruit with sugar and perhaps a little lemon juice.

The way in which strawberries are served is a matter of taste. Some people like them simply hulled and sugared, or, an especially pretty presentation, hulled and arranged in a pyramid with strawberry leaves tucked in here and there. Others prefer them with a dusting of pepper or a sprinkling of orange or lemon juice or balsamic vinegar to bring out the flavour. There is also a school of thought that considers a sprinkling or even a dousing of beaujolais, claret or champagne to be perfection.

Raspberry

This beautiful, velvety berry, from which the liqueur *crème de framboises* is made, is at its best when a deep garnet red. Black raspberries taste much like the red ones, as do the white or golden ones, which do not often find their way on to the market. Raspberries are always sold hulled, which makes them fragile and particularly vulnerable to crushing. When picking them, gently slide the beaded lantern shape off its conical centre, as this turns brown and mushy and quickly spoils the flavour of the fruit.

The flavour of raspberries is intense, and their presence will be apparent even if only a handful is mixed with some other fruit, or the juice of a few is mixed with the juice of, say, redcurrants, for the Scandinavian dessert called *rødgrød*.

balsamic vinegar 205
raspberry leaf tisane 219
raspberry vinegar 205

Fresh Raspberry Pavlova 388
Peach Melba 399
Pouding de Framboises 388
Raspberry Fool 388
Raspberry Granita 401
Raspberry Ice-Cream 398
Strawberry Fool 388
Strawberry Ice-Cream 398
Strawberry Jam 417
Strawberry Tart 405

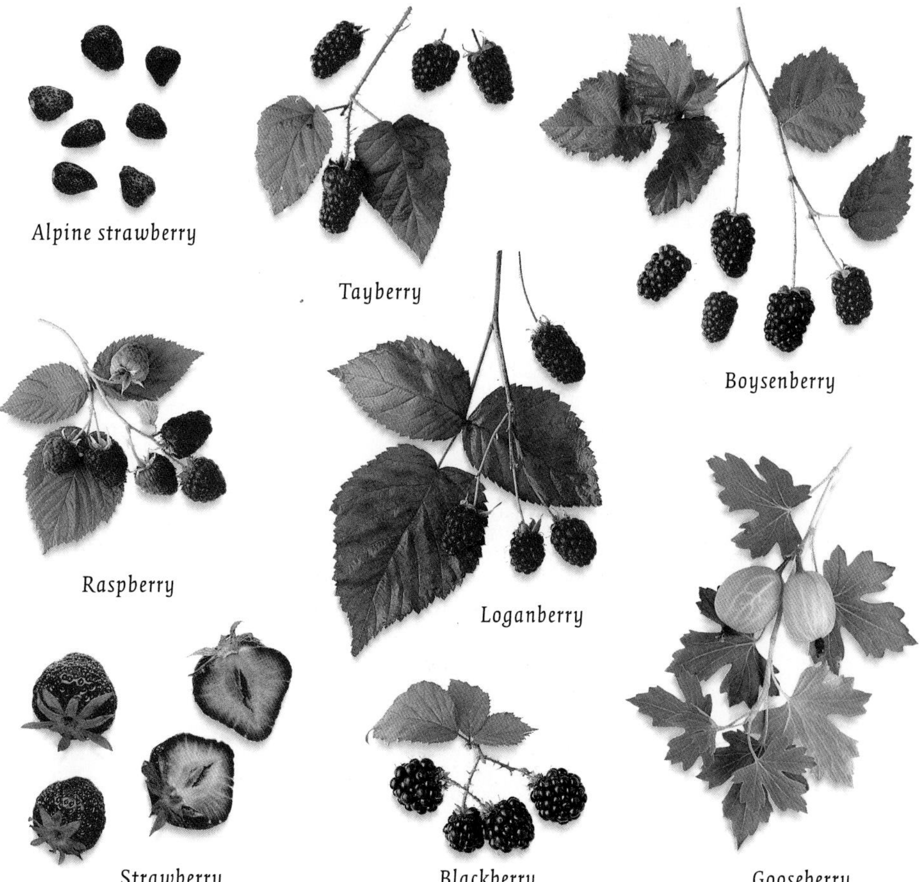

elderflower 174
grouse 84
mackerel 15
muscat grape 174

Blackberry and Apple Pie 405
Gooseberry Fool 388
Gooseberry Jam 417
Summer Pudding 391

Raspberry juice is much loved in Germany and Scandinavia as a refreshing drink. In England raspberry sauce appears at table to be poured over rice puddings, blancmanges and flummeries. And in Berlin when you order a *weisse mit Schuss* in a beerhall, you will be served a goblet containing a shandy-like drink made from pale ale, raspberry syrup and soda. Finally, among the raspberry-flavoured liquids is raspberry vinegar, which is made by steeping crushed berries in wine vinegar. It is a delicious addition to fruit salads, and when mixed with sugar and water and poured over ice it makes a cool, thirst-quenching drink.

A few savoury dishes make use of raspberries – the Scots stuff grouse and blackcock with the wild raspberries that grow in abundance in the hedges. It is in puddings, however, that raspberries come into their own, either served quite plain with a dollop of whipped cream, crushed in fresh sorbets, or puréed with a little sugar and served as a sauce.

Blackberry and dewberry

From the shopper's point of view, the distinction between these two berries is purely academic. From the picker's point of view, these relations of the raspberry are distinguished by their growing habits: upright plants are thought of as blackberry bushes, while trailing ones are described as dewberries.

Although blackberries are generally larger than dewberries, and shiny while dewberries are dull, sometimes with a white bloom, their names are used interchangeably in many places. Neither their taste nor their properties differ, and both are exceptionally rich in vitamin C. Both remain sour for a long time after turning black and are only fully ripe when they are soft to the touch.

The plant, which is a bramble, grows freely, and English hedges tend to be black with berries from September to November. During these weeks pickers are out in full force and kitchens are filled with the aroma of the berries, which, besides preserves, are also made into wine, syrup and any number of puddings. Like raspberries, blackberries can also be eaten with sugar and cream, but this is a success only when the berries are ripe and fresh because, once off the brambles, wild blackberries lose their flavour fast.

Cultivated blackberries are more stable and keep their taste longer. They are always sold with their core but without their green stalks. They, too, make lovely pies, tarts, fools and crumbles. Blackberries are particularly good when cooked with apples, not only because apples give an agreeable texture but also because their mellowness accentuates the blackberry's delicious acid flavour.

Berry crossbreeds

Whether in an attempt to improve the humble blackberry or to make the raspberry more robust, Messrs Logan, Young and Boysen in turn did us a great service in crossbreeding. America's youngberries and boysenberries are used for the same purpose as loganberries, which are more familiar in Europe. All three of these hybrid berries can be made into cooked and uncooked desserts and preserves using any recipe in which raspberries are called for.

Loganberry A cross between a blackberry and a raspberry, this is more acid than the blackberry but less intensely flavoured than the raspberry. It is purple with a delicate bloom, almost conical in shape and has no troublesome seeds. It needs plenty of sugar if it is to be eaten raw.

Youngberry The result of crossing a dewberry with a raspberry, this looks like an elongated blackberry and tastes rather like a loganberry.

Boysenberry This is a cross between a youngberry and a raspberry. Dark red to black and very juicy, it is similar in taste and shape to the raspberry. The size of this fruit causes amazement to those unfamiliar with it, as it is twice or even three times the size of its ancestors.

Tayberry Another blackberry-raspberry cross, bred in Scotland, this is large and scarlet-red, and quite tart.

Marionberry Dark black or scarlet, this sweet-tart berry is a cross between wild and cultivated blackberries.

Cloudberry and mulberry

Cloudberry This is the raspberry's slow-ripening, cold-weather cousin. It has been found as far north as the Arctic Circle, and grows in Siberia, Canada, cold districts of the northern United States and in Scandinavia, where it forms the basis of many fruit puddings and soups. Fully ripe, it is orange, tinged with red where it catches the sun, and resembles a golden mulberry. Its taste is reminiscent of apples with honey – in Canada is called the baked-apple berry.

Mulberry Although not botanically related to the raspberry members of the *Rubus* tribe, the mulberry is used in much the same way. The leaves of the mulberry tree form the silkworm's diet and many trees of great antiquity are to be found in old gardens, dropping their deep purple or white fruit to the ground below. Ripe, sweet-scented and deeply staining, mulberries are good to eat fresh, although sometimes a little musty and watery. They also make delicious ice-creams and sorbets, summer puddings and a superb jam. Take care not to get mulberry juice on your clothes: the stains are hard to shift. One method of removing them, which does work, is to rub the ripe berry juice marks with an unripe mulberry.

Gooseberry

These can be golden, purple, green or red globes, translucent or opaque, covered in whiskers or smooth, and there is one variety that is milky white. The gooseberry is the only berry among the soft fruits that makes the most delicious dishes when it is unripe. No matter what the final colour, immature gooseberries are pea-green.

Cook them, topped and tailed, into a purée with a little water over the lowest heat, adding sugar to taste. They are always sour and require some sweetening even when making the classic sauce for mackerel, to which a little fennel is sometimes added. For pies and crumbles, gooseberries are also best when they are slightly immature. A cream-coloured head of elderflowers laid on top of the fruit is a traditional British addition; it scents the gooseberries and makes them taste a little like muscat grapes.

When fully ripe, the big dessert varieties, full globes of yellow or red, make glorious eating. The common or garden green gooseberries are also good to eat, but are really better for jam making.

Currant

Redcurrants, whitecurrants and blackcurrants are, like gooseberries, of the genus *Rubus*, but here the similarity ends. They hang like tiny translucent grapes in little bunches on the bush, and the longer they hang, the sweeter they become. They are, however, never really sweet and even the ripest retain a good percentage of pectin.

Redcurrant There are those who love eating fresh redcurrants, raked off their stalks with a fork and covered with sugar and milk. Others prefer them in a berry mixture, or bathed in a real vanilla custard to mitigate the acid. They are delicious with melon and an essential ingredient of summer pudding. Perhaps best loved of all redcurrant preparations, however, is redcurrant jelly. Eat it with mutton and lamb, or like jam with croissants and butter. Add a spoonful when cooking red cabbage or when jugging hare. Transform it, with the addition of port and orange juice and zest, into sweet-sharp Cumberland sauce to serve with ham and game.

Whitecurrant Less acid than their red counterparts, these currants can be eaten just as they are, their thin, almost transparent, silver-gold skins liberally dusted with sugar.

Blackcurrant These, too, make lovely jams and jellies, as well as the liqueur *crème de cassis*, but are rarely eaten fresh, except by those who like acid-tasting berries. The Russians, who often add spoonfuls of jam to lemon tea, add blackcurrant jam to the actual brew in cases of colds and coughs. Blackcurrants are rich in vitamin C and a tisane made of their leaves is often taken as a health-giving drink. A few blackcurrant leaves are also sometimes included when making a purée for puddings, and there is a fragrant spring sorbet made with lemons and blackcurrant leaves.

Blueberry and bilberry

These berries, borne by shrubs found on acid soils and in peaty districts wherever heather grows, come from different species of the same genus and are used for similar purposes. Both have a silvery bloom that intensifies their blueness. They can be small or large depending on the soil, although blueberries are usually larger and sweeter than bilberries, and can be identified by their colourless juice.

Both were once so widespread in northern Europe and America that there was little to be commercially gained by putting them under cultivation. But their numbers declined as appetites increased for berry cheesecake and pie, muffins and grunts – delicious concoctions of cooked fruit and dumplings – and now it is possible to buy cultivated berries that are the size of marbles and twice the size of the wild ones. Flavour has suffered considerably with cultivation, but becomes stronger when the berries are cooked and turn to a deep, teeth-staining purple.

The **huckleberry** is a wild American berry that is often confused with the blueberry, which it closely resembles.

Cranberry

In northern Europe where this berry is plentiful it traditionally goes into the sharp fruit relish that accompanies venison and roast game birds. Cranberries used to be as popular in Britain as elsewhere, but with the advent of redcurrants fell out of favour. North America, however, reintroduced the larger, redder cranberry, much eaten as a sauce with turkey at Thanksgiving, and they are still traditional in Britain at Christmas.

When buying cranberries, make sure that they are bright, dry, plump and unshrivelled. They will keep, unwashed, in the refrigerator for up to 2 weeks and also freeze well. When preparing them for fritters, jellies, compotes, sauces, relishes or pies, cook them slowly with plenty of sugar and a little water until they pop their skins and turn into a ruby-coloured purée. They can also be coarsely puréed raw to make a relish.

blackcurrant leaf tisane 219
crème de cassis (cooking with) 208
dried blueberries 184
dried cranberries 184

Blackcurrant Jam 417
Blackcurrant Jelly 391
Cranberry and Orange Sauce 260
Cumberland Game Sauce 260
Fresh Cranberry Sauce 260
Redcurrant Jelly 418
Summer Pudding 391

Rhubarb
Forced rhubarb
Elderberry
Whitecurrant
Cranberry
Blueberry
Redcurrant
Blackcurrant
Rose hip

cooking with alcohol 208–9
currant and sultana 182
grape-vine leaf 195
raisin 182
rose 195

Elderflower Sorbet 401
Rhubarb and Raisin Pie 407

Elderberry, rowanberry and rose hip

These berries are not usually found in the shops, but all are well worth picking.

Elderberry Growing black and shiny in flat clusters, these are a good makeweight for blackberry puddings and ripen at about the same time as those berries. On their own they may be a little sickly, but a syrup made of the berries can add a delicious flavour to apple pies all winter long. Sprigs of the cream-coloured flower heads can be dipped in batter and eaten as fritters; they are surprisingly good, light and delicate. Elderberries also make excellent wine with superb keeping qualities.

Rowanberry The fruit of the mountain ash, which in autumn is a mass of orange-scarlet berries, these are delicious when made into a bitter-sweet jelly to be served with venison or lamb.

Rose hip Either the scarlet ovals that appear in the hedges when the wild roses have blown, or the flat, squat fruits of *Rosa rugosa*, are the essential ingredients of rose-hip syrup, the well-known repository of vitamin C. They also make a delicate, health-giving jelly.

Care must always be taken to strain out the sharp, prickly hairs that surround the abundant seeds in each hip, so after steeping the minced hips in boiling water, pass the liquid at least twice through double muslin or jelly bags.

Rhubarb

Odd man out in the world of fruit, rhubarb is used for the same types of dishes that also call for gooseberries, apples and plums. It is probably best known in pies and crumbles – in fact, it used to be known as the pie plant – and its tart taste combines well with blander, sweeter fruits. When buying rhubarb, look for stalks that are crisp and firm. Use them as soon as possible because they are very perishable, or keep them in the refrigerator until ready to cook them.

Forced rhubarb, with its brilliant pink stalks of a delicate texture, needs only the briefest of cooking as it softens so quickly. Tougher, greenish maincrop rhubarb takes longer. Both need quantities of sugar. If very acid, a teaspoon of redcurrant jelly added to the cooking water often helps. Rhubarb is sometimes sold with its leaves because these prevent it wilting, but the leaves must be discarded before cooking as they contain toxic amounts of oxalic acid.

GRAPES

Grapes can be pale, straw-coloured or amber, shades of green, rose or scarlet, or deepest blue-black with a rich silvery bloom. They can be tear-shaped, oval or round, large or small, in tight or straggly bunches. All of today's grapes are descended from the wild grape-vine.

The main role of grapes, of course, is to provide us with 'God's choicest gift to man' – wine. The grape contains all that is necessary for making wine: it has yeast in its bloom, natural sugar to feed the yeast, tannin in the skin and seeds, and natural acids to help provide the right environment for the yeast to make alcohol.

But grapes have been long, and rightly, celebrated for more than the wine they yield. Fresh grape juice was much used in medieval kitchens. The acid juice that characterizes grapes when they are unripe and sour was pressed out for verjuice – a piquant green liquid used in the place of vinegar for flavouring sharp sauces. The sweet juice of mature grapes, when not concentrated by sun-drying, which transforms the grapes into currants, raisins and sultanas, was boiled down into a syrup that was used as an alternative to honey.

Grape 'cures', too, were once very popular. Edwardian society, after a season's over-eating, would spend a week or so eating nothing but grapes, in an attempt to restore the figure and cleanse the system. These grapes would probably have been huge, perfectly flavoured hothouse muscats – still the most elegant of all the dessert grapes – which became the pride of landowners all over northern Europe as soon as glasshouses appeared in the seventeenth century.

Muscat

These are to be seen in the stores almost all the year round, the hot-house varieties swaddled in cotton wool or tissue paper to protect their yeasty bloom, or hanging in full glory in shop windows. They may be translucent green with a golden tinge, in which case they are known as white muscats, or a deep blue (known as black muscats), or from scarlet to purple (the red muscats). They are all large, with the richly perfumed flesh that makes muscat wines so distinctive, and they all have seeds.

White muscat These include the oval-shaped Muscat of Alexandria, with a bloom that rubs off all too easily unless carefully handled; the prized Golden Chasselas, green with an amber tinge which means that it has developed its full flavour; and the fleshy green Almeria, of Spanish stock.

Black muscat Among these are the delicately flavoured Gros Colmar; the large, round Royal with its heavy bloom, very juicy and sweet; Ribier, oval shaped and sweetly perfumed, with a vine-like flavour; and Black Alicante, oval, firm and not as sweet as the Royal but very juicy.

Red muscat These range from the Cardinal, scarlet and crisp and delightfully aromatic, to the Flame Tokay, a lovely deep red, and the Emperor, red or purple, firm and bland.

Sweetwater

Sweet and juicy to eat, as their name implies, and with thin skins, the sweetwaters include the sturdy Black Hamburgh. A cutting of this type, which was planted at Hampton Court in 1769, flourishes there still.

Seedless grape

These have much less tannin than the varieties with seeds, and make the best canned grapes, since tannin tends to alter the flavour of the grapes in the canning process. Sweet, juicy and green, with smallish fruit, varieties such as Thompson Seedless and the smaller Perlette Seedless, both descendants of the Sultana, are among the most abundant grape varieties in the world, enjoyed both fresh and dried. Flame Seedless is a red-skinned vareity with sweet flesh.

Labrusca and Muscadine

Vitis labrusca – not to be confused with Lambrusco, the sparkling red wine of Lombardy – is the native American vine that thrives in the colder climate of the eastern United States, where more tender varieties of grape refuse to grow. With tough skins that slip easily off the flesh, labruscas, such as the round, blue-black Concord, are rich in pectin and ideal for making grape juice and grape jam. Delaware, small and a lovely pale rose-red, has a juicy, sweet flesh, and Catawba is red-purple and sweet.

Muscadines, such as the large, bronze, sweet-fleshed Scuppernong, are grown mainly in the southern states of America. They have a rich, spicy flavour.

Buying grapes Although some grapes are no longer seasonal, and are issued from storage as the market demands or from greenhouses where they are nurtured all year round, the end of summer is the traditional grape season.

When buying grapes, make sure that the red or black kinds have lost any tinge of green, and that green or white ones have a tone of amber about them. The stems of both kinds should be fresh looking but show at least a few brown patches, with the exception of Emperor grapes whose stems should be woody-brown all over.

From the trade's point of view the perfect bunch consists of grapes that are uniform in size, with no lurking tiny ones, and all of them firmly attached to their stalks. From the consumer's viewpoint, bunches with a tendency to shedding are often the sweetest, as anyone who has bought local grapes from a huge mound in an open market, through a haze of wasps, can testify, for those straggly bunches and loose grapes, can be perfectly delicious and more aromatic than the cosseted sort. But if perfect fruit is desired, it should be plump with no sign of wrinkling in the skin and no brown patches by the stalks. Avoid bunches with little or no bloom, which shows they have been handled too much, or with any small, shrivelled grapes; these are sour.

Storing grapes Grapes will keep in good condition for about 3 weeks in the refrigerator, wrapped in perforated plastic film, or for 2 weeks in a cool larder – a long way on from the barrels in which the Ancient Romans sealed their oil-dipped grapes, hoping to keep them fresh and luscious. But since part of the pleasure of grapes is their appearance, it seems a pity to banish them from sight. A fine bunch in a glass bowl or a basket makes a perfect centrepiece for the dining table: silver epergnes loaded with hothouse grapes were a frequent table decoration at grand Victorian dinners, and talented Victorians would set a bunch of grapes complete with a few leaves and tendrils in a mould of white wine jelly as an edible showpiece.

Serving grapes Grapes are usually served at the end of a meal, either on their own or with one of the soft cheeses from Normandy or perhaps the hard cheeses from Switzerland, where grapes are a frequent accompaniment to cheese. In Italy you may be offered your grapes in a huge bowl of iced water, with a few floating ice-cubes – chilling makes grapes extra refreshing, but room temperature brings out their flavour better.

In the kitchen, grapes are used to make sorbets, jam, jelly and juice, and can also be frosted with egg white and sugar. A Calabrian speciality is a small pastry turnover filled with rum-flavoured grape jam, together with walnuts and grated chocolate. In France, grape juice is sometimes boiled until it is syrupy, and then boiled again with sliced apples, quinces, pears or lemons until it is sticky: such fruit is called *raisiné*.

Sole becomes sole Véronique when the rolled, poached fillets in a light white wine sauce are garnished with scented white muscat grapes. Muscat grapes are good, too, with duck foie gras, sometimes sautéed and eaten hot, and pheasant and guinea hen are sometimes stuffed with peeled, seeded grapes.

Some types of grape slip easily out of their skins, but others may need to be dipped in scalding water for a minute or

duck foie gras 90
grapeseed oil 113
hard cheese 102–5
soft cheese 106–8

Concord

Muscat of Alexandria

Sultana

Thompson Seedless

Emperor

Flame Seedless

cottage cheese 101
prosciutto crudo 69
watercress 130

so. Seeding, too, is simplicity itself if the grapes are first halved. If you want to keep them intact, use the U-bend of a small hairpin or paperclip to extract the seeds.

If you like salads with fresh fruit, try grapes in a mixture of apple and watercress, dressed with oil and lemon. Grapes and cottage cheese also combine well. Make fruit salads prettier with the addition of black grapes, seeded but not peeled, even though the skins of black grapes may be tougher than those of the white varieties. To preserve black or muscat grapes in brandy, prick each grape to make sure that it does not shrivel and then pack the grapes in a jar with equal parts of brandy and sugar. Turn the sealed jar once or twice during the week of maceration. After that, the fruit is ready to eat, poured over ice-cream; the strained brandy can be used in puddings or served in little glasses to accompany the grapes.

MELON

A melon is a luxurious thing. Beautiful and intricately patterned on the outside, a ripe melon no larger than an orange can fill a good-sized room with its fragrance. Inside, cool and full of juice, it quenches your thirst and provides you with a delicate sensation rather like eating snow. 'There is,' say the Arabs, 'a blessing in melons. He who fills his belly with melons fills it with light.'

Sweet melons, ribbed and encrusted with lacy patterns, were brought to Spain by the Moors, who had in turn received them from Persia or from the depths of Africa – both the Middle East and Africa claim to be the home of this honey-sweet fruit, described as 'the masterpiece of Apollo' and celebrated for being as beneficial as the sun itself. Melons appeared in France towards the end of the fifteenth century, to extravagant praise, and were eaten in astonishing quantities by the Court. Served in pyramids and mountains, 'as if it were necessary to eat to the point of suffocation, and as if everyone in the company ought to eat a dozen', they were washed down with draughts of muscat wine.

Melons were taken to the New World by Columbus. At that time, of course, sweet melons were no larger than oranges, but over the centuries they have been cultivated and expanded in both their size and variety.

Musk melon

It is most likely that the musk melon, or 'nutmeg' melon as it is sometimes known, was the kind eaten by the ancient Romans, who served it with a sprinkling of powdered musk in order to accentuate the delicate flavour.

Musk melons are recognized by the distinctive raised netting on the skin, which may be coarse like crochet work or fine like lace. This is why they are also called 'embroidered' melons in France and 'netted' melons in Britain and North America. They may be sharply segmented or grooved, with a green or yellow-orange skin, and the flesh ranges from green to salmon-pink.

Americans know this type of melon as cantaloupe, which is a misnomer. The true cantaloupe melon is not grown commercially in the United States.

Cantaloupe

Named after the Italian town of Cantalupo, this is among the most aromatic of melons. The rind is ribbed and warty, and the flesh is usually a pale orange, rich and juicy. The French prefer to grow this type, especially the Charentais with its deep orange, faintly scented flesh, although new, similar hybrids are always being introduced. The delicate, pale yellow-fleshed Ogen melon from Israel is a small, smooth-skinned cantaloupe hybrid.

Winter melons

These are smooth or shallowly ribbed and less aromatic than the musks and cantaloupes. Principal varieties are the onion-shaped Casaba with its thick golden-yellow skin and creamy-white to golden flesh; the Crenshaw with green-gold skin and aromatic golden-salmon flesh; and the ubiquitous pale green or yellow Honeydew melon with delicate pale green flesh.

Buying sweet melons Whatever type of melon you buy, there are a few sound rules to follow. Choose firm, plump melons with clean scars at the stem ends (a roughness here indicates they were picked before they were fully ripe). Netted melons should have no bald patches – this is a sign that the melon suffered a check during its development. Reject any fruits that are soft or scarred or that show moist bruises on the skin. It is a bad sign, too, if the stem has started to rot; however, light cracking at the stem end is a sign of ripeness. If you press them gently at the blossom end, the cantaloupes and the honeydew melons should feel slightly springy.

If you are able to shake the melon before buying it and you hear a sloshing sound, the fruit is too ripe and may have started to deteriorate. All melons should feel heavy for their size and – most important – ripe melons should have a pleasant, sweet melon scent about them.

Storing melons A cool, airy place is best for storing all types of melons – warmer if you suspect that your melon is not quite ripe. When you think that it is ready to eat, and if you do not want it to scent everything in your refrigerator, put your melon to chill in a tightly closed plastic bag before cutting it.

Serving melons Although the most scented varieties are nicest plain for dessert, melon can be served in salads with leaves of fresh mint and an oil and lemon dressing; with oranges and watercress; or with finely chopped celery, onions, olives and mayonnaise. This last mixture may sound strange, but it rests on an old tradition: a seventeenth-century list of 'sallet' herbs includes the melon, and ideas for eating it with salt and pepper.

Ground ginger mixed with sugar, or a squeeze of lime, have today taken the place of pepper – which had ousted powdered musk – as the melon's usual condiment. Even the sweetest melon will be enhanced by a fine dusting of sugar, but to pour port or other fortified wines into the cavity of a small scented melon, as some do, is a mistake since it ruins both. Fragrant melon slices, resting on the rind from which they have been separated with a sharp knife, beside thin, translucent slices of raw ham – *prosciutto crudo* – is as delicious a starter as one could hope for.

These days, melons have rightly taken a place in the dessert course and are to be met in fruit salads, filled with an assortment of fresh fruit, or diced and mixed with grapes or redcurrants. Or they may appear as melon sorbet or melon ice-cream, made with orange and lemon juice and served, if possible, with wild strawberries. The best melons, of course, really need no dressing up, but a cool and refreshing sweet melon salad can be made with an assortment of melon balls or cubes – orange, white, green and scarlet – sugared and chilled: a feast for the eye and an opportunity for the palate to distinguish between the slightly different flavours of the fruits.

Watermelon

The watermelon – which Mark Twain memorably called 'the food that angels eat' – is a different proposition. Much larger than the sweet melons, and oblong or round in shape, it is an entirely different species that originated in tropical Africa and in India.

Small round watermelons, from 2.5–4.5 kg/6–10 lb, with sweet red flesh and pitch-black seeds, may have deep green rinds with a bloom, as found on the Sugar Baby, or they may be striped on a light green background, such as on the appropriately named Tiger. But the favourites at family picnics are the large spherical or oblong watermelons, often sold in wedges. These may have a paler flesh than the smaller varieties because of their higher water content. There are also yellow-fleshed varieties, as well as seedless watermelons (which usually do have a few small edible seeds).

When buying a watermelon, it should have a bloom on its skin, and the spot where it rested on the ground should be amber coloured, not white or green. It should sound hollow when tapped. If you buy your melon by the piece avoid pieces with visible fibres: the flesh should not have any hard white streaks in it.

Watermelon is usually eaten chilled in slices or as part of a fruit salad.

TROPICAL AND MEDITERRANEAN FRUIT

Before steamships began to cross the seas regularly in the nineteenth century, trading in perishable tropical fruits such as bananas and pineapples was an impossibility. Now, unfamiliar fruits appear by boat or plane and make strange, exotic-looking piles among the more familiar fruits appearing in abundance, just at the time of year when most fresh fruit, apart from oranges, is usually scarce.

banana 178
pineapple 178

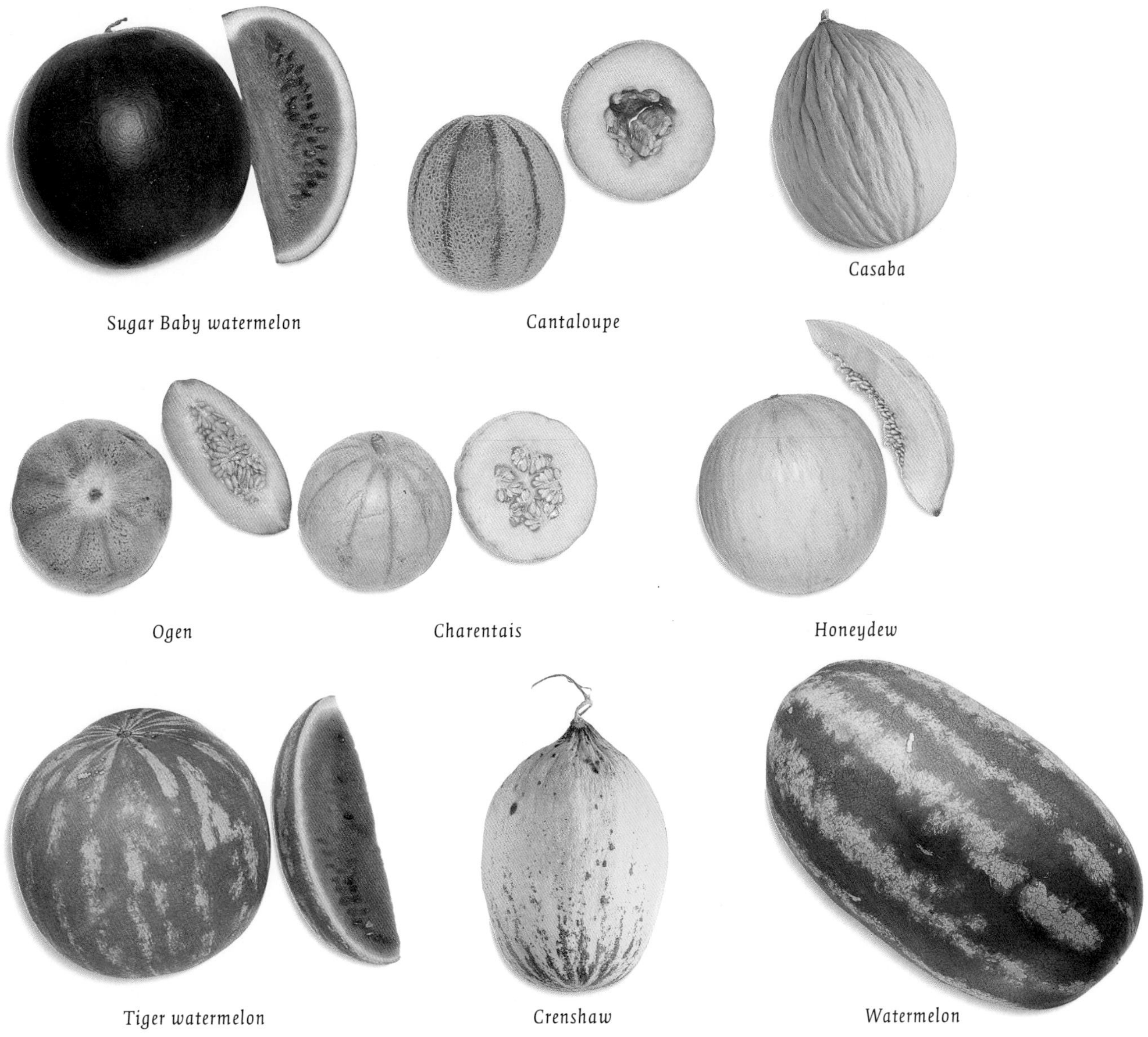

Sugar Baby watermelon

Cantaloupe

Casaba

Ogen

Charentais

Honeydew

Tiger watermelon

Crenshaw

Watermelon

dried banana 183
dried mango 184
dried papaya 184
glacé pineapple 185
mango chutney 207

Coffee Ice-Cream 398
Jamaican Baked Bananas 391
Mango Coulis 260

Banana and plantain

There are many varieties of this perfectly packaged fruit. One is grown only for making beer, and there are red bananas, purple bananas and pink bananas, slim bananas and fat ones. Plantains, also called cooking bananas, tend to be starchier and less sweet than the eating variety and are often used before they ripen.

Bananas for the table are picked while they are still hard and green and may not be perfectly ripe when they reach the shops. They will, however, ripen quickly at room temperature, turning first yellow, when they are ready for eating, then spotted, when they become softer and more scented, and finally black when they can still be used to make banana bread. Buy them in the bunch rather than loose, since the skin of loose bananas may well be ripped at the top, thus exposing the flesh.

The first bananas to reach us came from the Caribbean, and early northern puddings using bananas have a distinctly Creole flavour: demerara sugar and rum, coffee flavouring and rice, or coffee ice-cream feature widely. Bananas are also eaten baked with slices of lemon or plain in their jackets, or fried in batter as banana fritters. Chicken Maryland is often accompanied by peeled bananas fried in butter, and in Central America and the Caribbean ripe plantains are found boiled, fried or baked in many dishes.

Bananas, however, are most enjoyed in their fresh state. Sliced, they form part of many savoury dishes, including curries and Creole rice. In fruit mixtures their slightly scented taste and smooth texture complement juicy or crisp fruits such as oranges and apples. Raw or fried, they also make a perfect pudding.

Pineapple

A whole pineapple on the table is a truly luxurious sight. Fresh pineapples form part of many main courses in their native tropical habitat, where they are plentiful and cheap, and it is in the tropics that the idea of serving them hot as an accompaniment to poultry, pork chops and ham originated.

It is when fresh and simply served with sugar and perhaps kirsch that the pineapple is really at its best, although now that they are imported in quantity they are sometimes fried, grilled, baked in the shell, flambéed with cinnamon and rum, sprinkled with lime juice and used to fill sweet omelettes, or made into chutneys or salsas. They are particularly good in fruit salad.

When buying a pineapple look for one that is fully ripe and fragrant. If the stalk end is mouldy or discoloured, the fruit bruised or the leaves wilting, the pineapple is not at its best. A pineapple will continue to ripen after it is picked, and one that is almost ripe will ripen completely at home, but an unripe pineapple that has no scent and is not uniformly coloured will probably never develop its flavour to the full. Small pineapples often have a more delicate flavour than large ones.

Mango

This beautiful fruit, with its elegant curving shape, may be as large as a melon or as small as an apple. It may be green, gold, rosy or a mixture of all three. The vivid pinky-golden, yellow or orange flesh of the best ripe mangoes (one variety to look for is the small Alfonso) is smooth, juicy and fibreless with a slightly resinous taste that has been compared to that of peaches, apricots, melons and pineapples.

When buying mangoes make sure that they are just soft and have a good perfume. If they are completely green they will not ripen properly, and those with large black areas tend to be overripe.

Mangoes can be embarrassingly difficult to eat. They are usually either scored from top to bottom in several places, peeled and eaten with a spoon, or cut in half by slicing down either side of the large, hairy, flat stone, and eaten with a spoon.

To prepare them 'hedgehog' fashion, cut them lengthways into two pieces, discard the stone and then score the flesh diagonally at 1 cm/½ in intervals in both directions, cutting almost to the skin without piercing it. Turn each half inside out, and the little squares of mango will be easy to eat with a spoon.

Chilled mangoes are sometimes served halved in their shells, sprinkled with lemon juice, sugar, rum or ginger. Pared and cut, they are delicious in fruit salads, and they make excellent sorbets.

It was in India that Britain found its original taste for mango chutney. Green unripe mangoes are used for this, as they are for poached and baked mango dishes.

Papaya, pawpaw

Columbus anticipated Mark Twain – in a different context – by declaring that the papaya, which he called a tree melon, tasted, when ripe, like the 'food of the angels'. The papaya's skin is green to golden, its flesh orangey and its seeds black and shiny. It usually comes on to the market when it is ripening, and is sweet and subtly flavoured.

When buying papaya (which is sometimes called pawpaw) make sure that it is firm, unblemished except for its speckles and just turning yellow, then allow it to ripen at home.

Ripe papaya is distinctive in fruit salads, pies and sorbets, and can also be served simply sprinkled with lemon or

Passion fruit

Kiwi fruit

Pomegranate

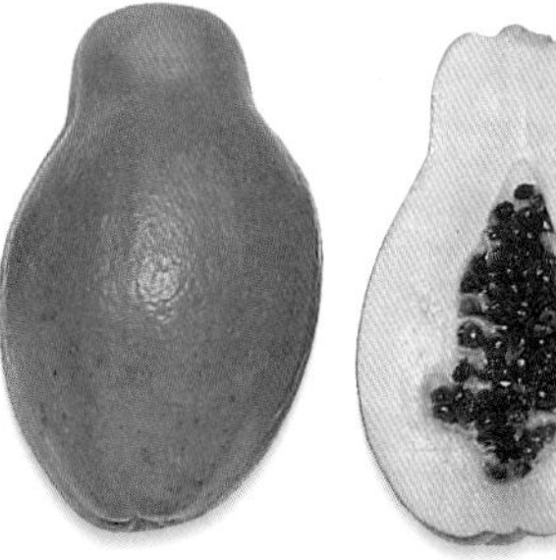

Papaya

lime juice and sugar or ginger. It makes a delicate breakfast fruit when served with a squeeze of lime.

The unripe papaya, also called *lechosa* in Central and South America, is used like a vegetable and tastes like a marrow. It can be served stuffed or baked with butter, added to various salads, or simply pickled. It is also good in chilli-hot salsas.

South American Indians have traditionally wrapped papaya leaves, freshly plucked, around tough meat to act as a tenderizer – the plant contains a powerful enzyme that breaks down protein. A derivative of the leaves, the enzyme papain, is used in commercial tenderizing powders for meat.

Guava

Pink or pale-yellow fleshed, aromatic and sweet, this fruit can be as small as a walnut or as large as an apple. It can be served puréed or baked, or eaten fresh with sugar and cream, and it goes well with other fruit such as pineapple. Guavas are best known, however, for making a jelly, which is served with meat or game as an alternative to redcurrant jelly. If you make guava jelly at home, a few drops of Worcestershire sauce in the juice will give a more interesting flavour. Guava jelly is also delicious spread on hot toast.

Pomegranate

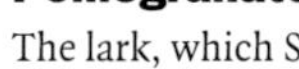

The lark, which Shakespeare's Juliet insisted was a nightingale, 'sang on yon pomegranate tree' – a shrub-like plant that was introduced to the Western world from Persia (now Iran) via Africa. Its beautifully shaped fruit – which is scarlet or golden flushed with crimson on the outside and filled with ruby-coloured beads, each with its central seed – is an intricate construction.

To admire its crimson glory at its best, cut the fruit in half or in segments, slicing through the leather-like skin. Although the juicy pulp surrounding each of the seeds is beautifully refreshing and aromatic it can be rather tiresome to eat. You can take a few grains, suck the flesh off the seeds, discard the seeds and continue to eat and discard until the shell is empty. A much easier way, however, is

pomegranate with rosewater 195
tenderizing meat (use of papain) 48
vegetable marrow 156
Worcestershire sauce 206

Lebanese Aubergine Salad 365

Fuyu persimmon

Hachiya persimmon

Guava

Banana

Pineapple

Mango

apricot 170
guava 179
mango 178
tomato 150–1

to crunch and swallow the seeds, which have a nice texture. Avoid the pale yellow pith, which is bitter.

Persimmon

Looking like a golden-red tomato, the persimmon, when it is completely ripe and plumply soft, is often compared in taste to guavas, apricots, tomatoes and mangoes; however, when less than perfect its astringency 'draws the mouth awry with much torment'. Wrinkled fruit of the acorn-shaped Hachiya type should therefore never be shunned, since by the time it has reached this stage the acidity and tannin will have disappeared. There is also a smaller, rounder variety, called the Fuyu, which is not at all astringent and which remains firm when ripe.

The handsome persimmon stays glossy and plump when it has been plucked early and artificially matured. Provided it is ripe, with cap and stem intact, its tough skin can be cut downwards and peeled back, and the soft flesh eaten as it is or sliced. A seedless variety of persimmon, the Sharon fruit, which was bred in Israel from the Fuyu, has tender, edible skin and a less tannic flavour than the Hachiya.

Kiwi fruit

The brown furry skin covering this egg-shaped fruit hides glistening, translucent green flesh with decorative edible black seeds. Once known as the Chinese or Coromandel gooseberry, it is now best known by the name of New Zealand's national bird, the kiwi. The fruit is used to best effect when it is peeled and thinly sliced, since the pattern of the black pips in the bland but fresh-tasting green flesh is so pleasing.

Kiwis contain huge quantities of vitamin C – one kiwi contains as much as ten lemons. Unripe fruit can be ripened if kept in a plastic bag with a ripe banana, apple or pear; the ethylene gas given off by the ripe fruit accelerates the ripening process.

Passion fruit

This fruit is so called because the flower of the plant is said to symbolize the Passion of Christ. The fruit of some species of the passion flower is also called granadilla (which has yellow skin),

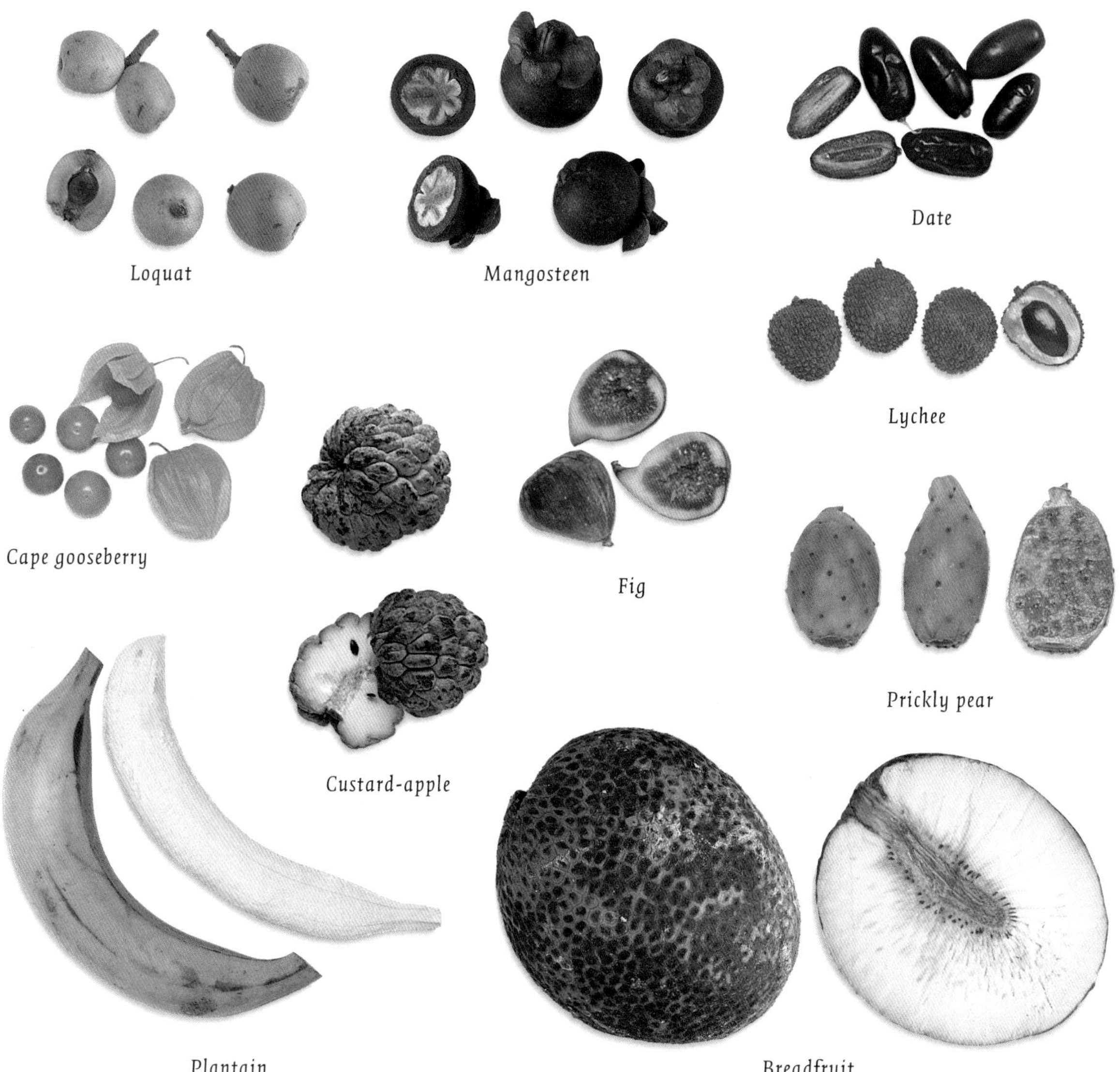

Loquat

Mangosteen

Date

Lychee

Cape gooseberry

Fig

Prickly pear

Custard-apple

Plantain

Breadfruit

or calabesh in the West Indies. The size and shape of an egg, the passion fruit normally has a purple-brown, hard skin that becomes crinkly as the fruit gradually ripens.

The richly perfumed, sweet-sour flesh is inseparable from the many small black seeds, which are edible. The fruit is usually halved and perhaps sprinkled with sherry or cream, or the flesh may be scooped out and mixed in fruit salads. It is delicious made into mousses, sorbets, sauce or ice-cream.

Custard-apple

This is any of the fleshy, round or elongated, thick-skinned fruits of the large family of *Annona* trees of the American tropics. There is the apple-shaped cherimoya, and the llama, whose taste has been compared to that of a banana and pineapple. The soncoya is similar but larger, and the sweet-sop is green, heart shaped and more acid, with a taste similar to that of a blackcurrant. The atemoya is a cross between a custard-apple and the sweet-sop; its delicate flesh tastes of mango and vanilla. All are eaten fresh, often chilled for breakfast, the flesh being spooned from the shell. It can also be used for jam and jelly, in milkshakes and sorbets.

Feijoa

Carambola

Tamarillo

Loquat

Also known as Japanese medlar, the orangey-yellow loquat is the size of a crabapple but more pear-shaped. It contains a few largish shiny pips. Although thirst quenching, it does not have much flavour when raw and is principally used to make jams, jellies and sauces. A few of the seeds are usually included as these give a delicious bitter-almond flavour to any preserve or sauce to which they are added.

Cape gooseberry

Native to South America, this acid-sweet, pleasant, small fruit of the shrub *Physalis peruviana* is encased in a papery balloon shaped like a Chinese lantern. In South Africa the plants are grown on such a large scale that they have come to be known as Cape gooseberries. Golden when ripe, the berries can be eaten in the fingers (peel back the skin to form 'petals' around the golden globe of the fruit for a decorative touch) or coated with fondant and served with *petit fours*, but they are chiefly used to make the most delicious jellies and jams.

Lychee and rambutan

These fruits, encased in brown papery shells with a delicate pink lining, both have translucent colourless flesh enclosing a single brown glossy seed. Lychees when fresh have a delicious perfumed flavour and a refreshing tang that all but disappears when the fruit is canned. In China, the lychee has been cultivated for thousands of years. With its sweet-acid flavour it is used to complement pork and duck dishes in much the same way as apples and oranges are used in the West.

A rambutan has a hairier shell than a lychee. Both fruits can be bought in the West, but should be avoided if they look shrivelled, since this means that their pulp is turning black and their delicate flavour will be lost.

Prickly pear

This is the fruit of a cactus (*Opuntia ficus indica*), and is sometimes known as cactus pear or Indian fig. It is pear shaped, varies in colour from green to rosy and is covered with small clumps of sharp prickles. When buying a prickly pear make sure that it is orange to red, and reasonably bright in colour, and firm but not too hard. It is mild flavoured and sweet, somewhat pear-like in flavour but more melon-like in texture, and is usually eaten raw. The fruit should be slit lengthwise; the prickly skin will come off easily. The flesh can then be eaten with sugar and cream or sprinkled with lemon juice. Take care when handling prickly pears as they are covered in small clumps of prickles which will irritate the skin. Wear gloves or encase your hand in a paper bag before you pick them up.

Mangosteen

This thick-skinned, glossy, dark mahogany fruit is very popular in South-east Asia. The white, soft flesh is segmented like that of an orange, and some segments contain a large pip. Its taste is sweet-sharp, delicate, perfumed and refreshing.

Fig

This is perhaps the most sensual of all fruits with its bloomy, bursting skin and luscious flesh. Ancient Greeks thought figs so health-giving that they formed part of the athletes' diet for the original Olympic games, and so delicious that poets and philosophers sang their praises. White, green, brown or purple, figs are always beautiful. When cut open they reveal their pulpy flesh, deep purple, red or pink, embedded with a mass of seeds, which are in fact tiny fruits.

The entire fruit is edible. In Italy, where the Sicilian figs are most prized, they are served with prosciutto or as a dessert. In France the purple, white-fleshed Barbillone and many other kinds are also served as a dessert. All are good, especially when eaten fresh and ripe. Being perishable, figs will not keep for longer than 3 days in the refrigerator, but should not be served chilled since the cold tends to numb their delicate flavour.

blackcurrant 173
crabapple 163
dried Cape Gooseberries 185
dried fig 183
mango 178
tomatillo 152

dried date 183
grapes 174

Bread and Butter Pudding 394
Chicken with Almonds and Raisins 306
Christmas Cake 412
Christmas Pudding 396
Dundee Cake 412
Pilau Rice 346
Rhubarb and Raisin Pie 407
Six-Vegetable Couscous 350
Twelfth Day Cake 412

Date

In its fresh state, the sumptuous, rich date – called 'bread of the desert' – has a glowing brown skin that promises more juice than the flesh actually delivers, and the plumpest date has a warm, fudge-like consistency. When buying fresh dates make sure that you pick out fat, wrinkly skinned and non-sticky specimens.

Star fruit, carambola

Somewhat cucumber-like in texture, the star fruit, uncut, resembles an elongated yellow Chinese lantern with deep ridges running from top to bottom. When sliced it reveals that the cross-section is a perfect star – very beautiful, but when it comes to flavour it hasn't much to offer. Carambolas can be either sweet or sour and tangy; both are refreshing. The fruit could be eaten with roast duck, but is best either sliced and used in a fruit salad, or poached in a sugar syrup.

Tamarillo, tree tomato

Orangey-red, smooth and glossy, these fruits resemble small oval aubergines in shape, and like them are members of the Solanaceae family, together with potatoes, tomatoes and Cape gooseberries. The orange flesh with its black seeds is sweet-tart, but the skin is intensely bitter and should be removed either by plunging the fruit into boiling water for a minute, like tomatoes, or, if the fruit is very ripe, by peeling. Eat tamarillos raw with sugar or in fruit salads, or use to make chutney.

Feijoa

A round or oval, shiny green fruit related to the guava, the feijoa has a flavour said to resemble pineapple. The soft flesh contains tiny edible seeds. Eat raw by cutting in half and scooping out the flesh with a teaspoon.

Breadfruit

This large and imposing green fruit, covered in short, knobbly spines, can weigh up to 4 kg/9 lb, and may or may not contain seeds. It has a strange smell when unripe. An unripe specimen can be cut up and baked or roasted, while an entirely ripe one may be sliced and eaten raw. Breadfruit is often used in savoury dishes, too.

DRIED AND CANDIED FRUIT

Dried fruit does not so much prolong the taste of summer as provide us with sweetness of a different kind. Drying concentrates the sugar content of the fresh fruit, and although vitamin C is usually lost, vitamin A and the minerals remain. Some dried fruits are completely dried; the larger ones like apricots may need soaking before cooking. Others still contain a percentage of their original moisture. These can be eaten or cooked with straight away and are succulent, but they tend to be heavy on preservatives. The too liberal use of liquid paraffin or sulphur dioxide to keep dried fruit from becoming too dry is a deplorable innovation. The flavour can and occasionally does permeate the fruit and cannot be removed by soaking, so buy unsulphured or organic fruit whenever possible.

Dried fruits such as 'datyes, figges and great raysings' have been valued in Europe since they were imported in the thirteenth century from the Levant, to sit in the larder alongside dried domestic 'prunellas, apricocks and pippins'. There were also dried pears (a special delicacy) and the dried cherries and berries that the medieval housewife would put by in due season. This dried fruit went into a number of what now seem curious dishes. The taste was for the sweet-savoury – the sort of dish still found in countries that were once part of the great Ottoman Empire. In Turkey, Iran, Saudi Arabia, Yemen and North Africa, traditional cookery still allies lamb with prunes, apricots, almonds, honey and spices. Chicken is still simmered with prunes, or with quinces, dates or raisins.

Medieval Europe ate veal tartlets with prunes and dates, pickled fish was enhanced with raisins and figs, and mallards were smothered with fruit. The Great Pyes, without which no great dinner was complete, contained a mixture of beef, chicken, bone marrow, eggs, dates, prunes and raisins, all highly spiced and saffroned before being entombed in the 'coffyn', as the crust was called. The taste for such things lives on. The seventeenth-century recipe for raisin sauce to eat with ham differs very little from that found in modern American cookbooks, or the raisin sauce eaten with boiled tongue in northern Europe. And the eighteenth-century ham stuffed with 'apricocks' is not far from Virginia ham with peaches.

Indeed, that most British of institutions, the plum pudding, is a descendant of the sweet-savoury puddings of the Middle Ages – until the eighteenth century, one of its main ingredients was leg or shin of beef. Now there is the suet to remind us of the old days. Look further back and you find that the Christmas pudding is not English at all, but of ancient Greek origin – a less astonishing fact when you think that the very word currant is derived from Corinth, its place of origin.

Raisin

The large, sweet raisins made from Spanish Muscat grapes and called muscatels used to be the kings of the tribe. Now, similar giants are produced in other places in the world, especially California. It is these that are eaten as a dessert fruit, and are useful in cooking when making pilaus, sauces for quail and hare and in stuffings. Smaller black raisins are sold loose and in packs for cake-making, muesli, Christmas puddings and mincemeat. These are good in couscous, and for stuffed vegetables and onions *à la grecque*. Raisins also come packed together with peanuts, shelled hazelnuts and almonds. This once inexpensive mixture is known as *Studenten Futter* in Germany, because the sugar content of the raisins and the protein content of the nuts quickly revives the energy of poor scholars while they pore over their books.

Currant and sultana

The dried currant comes from the small, black seedless grape that is a native of the slopes around Corinth in Greece, while sultanas are made from the seedless white grapes once grown only in the neighbourhood of biblical Smyrna in Turkey. Although both varieties have long been produced elsewhere, the old names have stuck.

In some parts of the world, currants and sultanas are still sun dried, without the help of chemical treatments. In others, science gives nature a helping hand and the fruit is artificially dried. But welcome the fact that your currants and sultanas, which you can buy separately or mixed and with the addition of finely chopped peel, are likely to have been already washed and tumble-dried. This means that you can forget about picking them over for bits of stalk and grit, and doing your own washing and drying. However, if you mean to use currants or sultanas with yeast for baking, it is a good idea to place the fruit in a sieve over a pot of boiling water for a few minutes beforehand. This warms and moistens the fruit just enough to prevent it from retarding fermentation of the temperamental yeast.

Dried fig

The yellow fig of Smyrna was traditionally the most highly prized, and this is now extensively grown elsewhere, together with many other varieties, including the dark, juicy Mission fig. Although dried figs pack and travel well, blocks of squashed figs can have a depressing look; so if you mean to enjoy figs with dessert wine after a winter dinner, look for those whose plump, cushion shapes are still discernible. In Provence, a dessert that is offered at New Year and known as *les quatres mendiants*, or 'the four mendicants', is a mixture of figs, raisins, hazelnuts and almonds, their colours recalling the habits worn by the four Roman Catholic mendicant orders.

For use in compotes or puddings, dried figs need soaking for a few hours before use: try wine instead of water for a good flavour.

Dried banana

Although often called 'banana figs', dried bananas are quite unconnected with figs and don't have the fig's laxative properties. They are, however, used in the same way as dried figs. Look for them in health-food stores together with slices of dried bananas, which can be eaten as a snack on their own or make up part of 'tropical' mixes with other dried fruits and nuts.

Dried date

The date-palm has flourished in favourable places since 5000 BC, and has always been a good and useful friend to mankind. Only the stickiest, juiciest dates – 'candy that grows on trees' – are sent into the world from their native Middle East and North Africa. Of them all the Tunisian date, the Deglet Noor, 'date of the light', is considered the finest, although some people prefer Medjool dates with their wrinkled skins and rich fudge-like texture. Evaporated dates, soft-dried and hard-dried, black, dark red or golden yellow, are available in winter imported from the Middle East and from California.

Most easily obtained are the shiny or wrinkled dates that have been left on their palm trees to sweeten and mature in the sun, and are then packed in boxes, sometimes with desert scenes on the lid. You used to find them packed 'on the stem', but now the stem is often made

banana 178
candied peel 184
fresh date 182
fresh fig 181
yeast 118

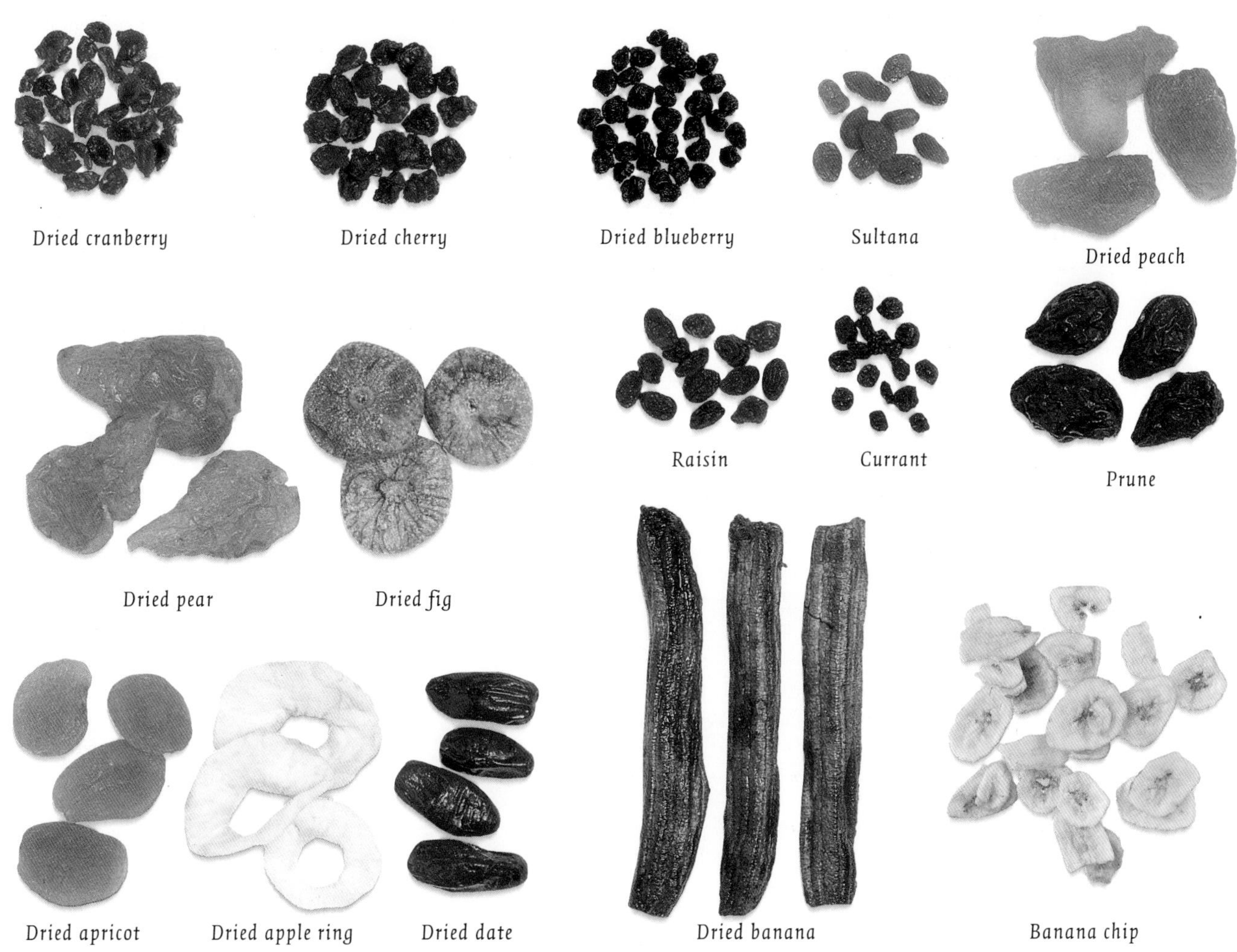

Dried cranberry

Dried cherry

Dried blueberry

Sultana

Dried peach

Raisin

Currant

Prune

Dried pear

Dried fig

Dried apricot

Dried apple ring

Dried date

Dried banana

Banana chip

apple 162
apricot 170
blueberry and bilberry 173
Cape gooseberry 181
cherry 168
citron 165
cranberry 173
lemon 167
orange 165
papaya 178
peach 169
pear 164
plum 169

Blackberry and Apple Pie 405
Madeira Cake 410
Marzipan 415
Rabbit with Prunes and Red Wine 297
Roast Turkey with Two Stuffings 311

of plastic, although the top layer of dates is still 'arranged'. If you plan to stuff dates with nuts or marzipan, making *petits fours* sitting in frilled paper cases to be offered to guests after dinner, you would, of course, use the handsomest dates you could find, while pressed blocks of dates are perfectly adequate to use in breads, puddings and cakes.

Prune

Until the nineteenth century, prunes were far more popular than plums. Traditionally eaten with game, goose and pork, prunes can also be cooked with red cabbage and used to make delicate whips, soufflés and ice-creams. Prunes are essential for *tzimmes*, a traditional Jewish meat casserole. The drying process makes prunes good keepers, and nothing is easier than to reconstitute their plumpness by soaking them overnight. (Better still, keep them in a jar of brandy, ready to eat.)

The finest prunes are from the red and purple plums of Agen and from those of Tours, the orchard of France. It is these varieties that are grown in California and have made the Santa Clara Valley the centre of the excellent American prune industry. Some of the French maintain that the flesh of a California plum is less delicate than that of their native produce, but then in France plum drying has developed into a fine art. There the Perdrigon plum, for example, is not simply dried. It may be either skinned, stoned, exposed to the sun and flattened to become a *pistole*, or scalded in its entirety and slowly dried in the shade to become a *brignole* or *pruneau fleuri*. This is plumper and less wrinkled than the humble grocery prune and somewhat resembles the Karlsbad plum, a glamorous prune with a blue sheen, tasting strongly of fruit, that is on sale around Christmas time packed in handsome wooden boxes. Famous, too, are Elvas plums, semi-dried, and candied greengages from Portugal, a very sweet Christmas treat.

Dried peach, pear and apricot

Dried peaches and pears are most delicious eaten raw: their taste is delicate and does not always survive cooking.

On the tart side even when ripe, dried apricots keep a good deal of their original flavour. Of all the dried fruits, they are the least sickly-sweet. Soaked and cooked, they can be used to make a sharp, fragrant purée, good for puddings, sauces and even jam-making. Roughly chopped, they can go into pilafs; soaked, they make a good stuffing for lamb and poultry.

Apricot paste, a sweetmeat that is much appreciated in Arabian countries, where it is known as *kem-reddine*, 'moon of religion', can be found in the more exotic stores.

Dried apple

This can be reminiscent of faintly scented rings of soft chamois leather; only by shopping around, particularly at health-food shops, can you find dried apples actually tasting of fruit.

Apple rings have only come into fashion during the last century or so. Before that, and before apple-drying became a commercial operation, there were several methods for drying apples whole – all of them considerably more trouble than to simply core, peel and slice apples, soak them for a few minutes in salted water to prevent discoloration, and thread them on to string looped around the ceiling, where air can circulate around them, until the rings are thoroughly dried.

In whatever way apples have been dried, they have many uses. Apple sauce for pork can be made from dried apples that have been soaked and then cooked in plenty of water in a closed pot in the oven. Chopped and mixed with currants and sultanas they usefully stretch a cake mixture. If you use dried apples for a compote, stew them slowly with cinnamon or cloves and add a dash of lemon juice for tartness. If you make your own muesli or mincemeat, you can add chopped dried apple together with the raisins. Indeed, dried apples with any other dried fruit and every type of nut, particularly prunes, blanched almonds and apricots, make nourishing winter fruit salads, steeped in water or a syrup.

Dried cherries and berries

Dried cherries can be made from sweet cherries or sour cherries. The sour ones are bright mahogany-red, and have a sweet-sour tang and an intense flavour. They can be used in sweet sauces and puddings and make a delicious sauce for duck or lamb. Dried sweet cherries are less tangy and lighter in colour than the sour ones. Use them in the same way for cooking or to make a dessert with sugar, lemon juice and cream. Dried sweet cherries can also be eaten like sweets.

Dried blueberries, bilberries or myrtilles These look like dark raisins and almost lose their blueberry taste in the drying. You may need to soak them for an hour or so before using them, raw or sweetened and lightly poached, in blueberry muffins or with apples in apple and blueberry pies and crumbles.

Dried cranberries The dark-rose-coloured dried cranberry is a great deal sweeter than its fresh counterpart and tastes strongly of apples. Cranberries can be eaten raw or soaked and made into sauces and stuffings; alternatively, use them in a fruit salad.

Dried mango and papaya

Golden, leathery dried mangoes can be bought as small pieces, long strips or, best of all, whole mango-sized slices. They need to be soaked for several hours before cooking. Like dried apricots, they can be eaten in their dried state, making delicious chewy snacks with a full, deep, almost parsnippy mango flavour.

Small cubes of dried papaya, pink and glowing, are usually sugared and eaten like sweets. They can also be cut up and used like candied peel in cakes.

Dried Cape gooseberry

With a piercing sweet-sour flavour, these taste more like regular gooseberries dried than they do when fresh. Brownish in colour, they resemble muscatel raisins and could be used in their place to make dried fruit salad, cakes and pilafs. The tiny seeds give a pleasant crunch and are rather preferable to the seeds found in muscatels.

Candied peel

The delicate green variety is the candied, aromatic skin of the citron – the large, scented, extremely thick-skinned cousin of the lemon. It is citron peel that is used to decorate the top of a traditional Madeira cake.

Orange peel – sometimes sold mixed with citron – and lemon peel can also be bought in large pieces. If you buy peel in a large slice, you will find that it has more flavour than the 'cut' peel, not only because there has been less chance for its essential oils to evaporate, but also because only the fattest, juiciest peels are sent to market in their entirety. Peel is perfectly easy to cut into neat dice yourself. If the pieces are very sticky, separate them with a dusting of flour and use that much less flour in your recipe. Store peel in airtight jars to prevent it from becoming tough and difficult to cut. If it becomes hard, steam it to soften it.

Ready-cut mixed peel is sold for use in cakes, puddings and tea breads, but it is always better to chop your own whenever possible.

Glacé and crystallized fruit

Strictly speaking, crystallized fruit is candied fruit that has a coating of granulated sugar. Glacé refers to the glossy coating of sugar syrup found, for example, on cherries, pineapple rings and whole candied fruit such as oranges, clementines and figs. The terms, however, have become almost interchangeable.

Cherries for cakes are candied and glazed with a heavy syrup to aid their preservation. This accounts for their extreme stickiness, and makes it advisable to rinse and dry them before adding them to a cake mixture; alternatively, steam them for 5–10 minutes in a sieve placed over a pan of boiling water and then dry them. Without this precaution, the cherries may sink to the bottom of the cake. A dusting of flour helps to keep them separate and suspended in the mixture.

No need, of course, to wash those cherries you use for decoration – for this, their charm depends on their glistening lusciousness.

Angelica, used primarily for decorating, is quite easy to candy yourself. If you have the plant growing in your garden, gather the stalks in midsummer. Blanch them and peel off the outer skin, then boil the inner stems, ideally adding a few vine leaves to keep them a bright green, in a syrup made of 150 ml/¼ pint water and 225 g/8 oz sugar. When the stems are soft and translucent, let them cool and then soak in the syrup for 2 weeks. Finally, dry the angelica sticks in a cool oven. The same technique works for all sorts of small fruit, as well as for chunks or segments of larger fruit.

Ginger, made with mild, immature ginger in Australia or fiery, hard mature ginger in Asia, is a delicious alternative to chocolates at Christmas time, and one that is far less rich. The Chinese believe that ginger warms and sends energy to the solar plexus, and it cuts the richness after a fatty meal.

Crystallized flowers

To crystallize violets, cowslips, primroses, rose petals or other edible (and non-sprayed) flowers, you need a light hand. First prepare a syrup of 450 g/1 lb sugar and 300 ml/½ pint water, letting it boil to the hard crack stage (146°C/295°F on a sugar thermometer). Draw it off the heat and dip petals or flowerheads into it (in the case of violets, you can dip a little posy at a time). Dry them in a sieve, sprinkling them with icing sugar. Sift off surplus sugar and scatter the flowers over creamy white puddings, or use them to decorate chocolate mousse and trifle.

angelica 194
cherry 168
clementine 166
garden leaves and flowers 195
ginger 199
orange 165
pineapple 178

Cherry Cake 410
Chocolate Mousse 394
Sherry Trifle 392

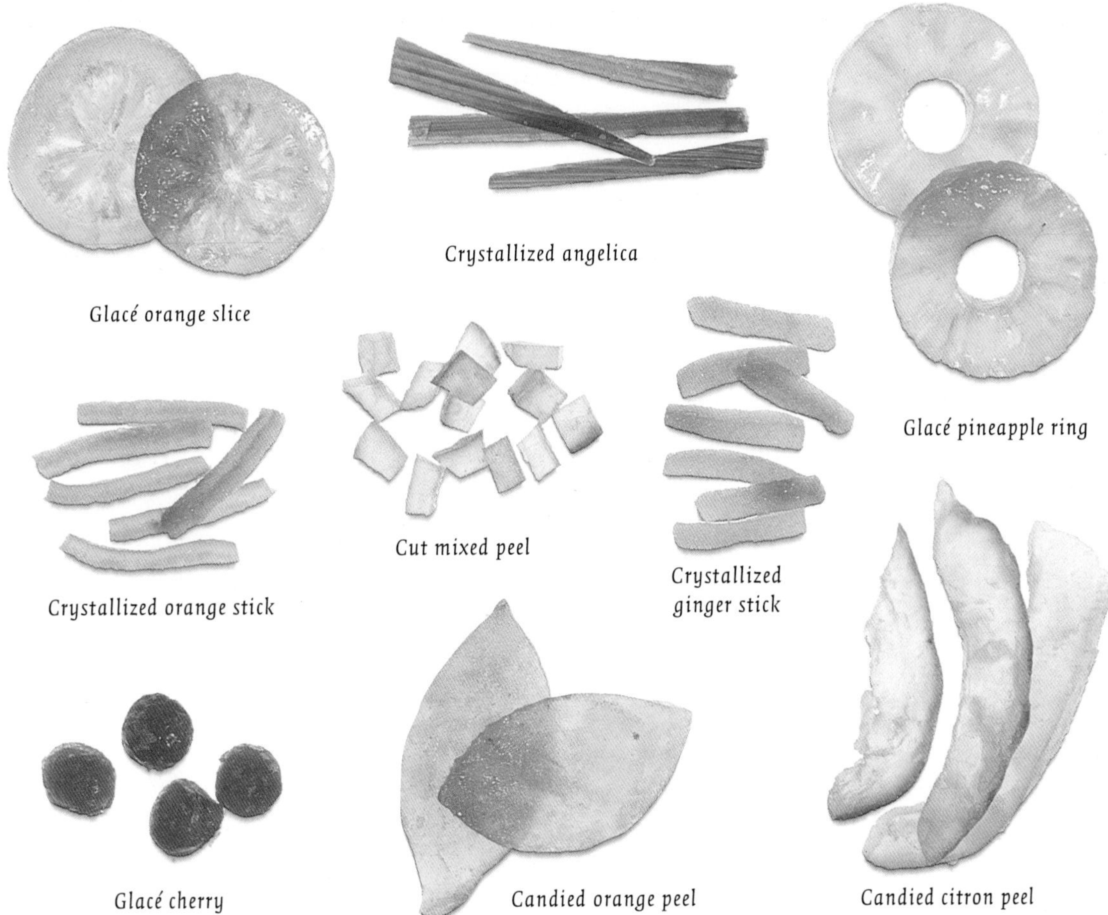

Glacé orange slice

Crystallized angelica

Glacé pineapple ring

Crystallized orange stick

Cut mixed peel

Crystallized ginger stick

Glacé cherry

Candied orange peel

Candied citron peel

Nuts

almond essence 207
almond oil 113
blanching almonds 189
toasting and grinding nuts 423

nutcrackers 229
pestle and mortar 226

Chicken with Almonds and Raisins 306
Christmas Pudding 396
Dundee Cake 412
French Almond Tart 408
Lamb Korma 289
Marzipan 415
Pesto alla Genovese 336
Pilau Rice 346
Provençal Soupe au Pistou 250
Sherry Trifle 392

The sound of cracking nuts has always been a pleasant accompaniment to conversation: 'after-dinner talk across the walnuts and the wine' is Tennyson's description of the ritual, while in the Middle East pistachio nuts and cashews are eaten as part of the varied *mezze*, the morsels that precede a meal, and are 'savoured accompanied by feelings of peace and serenity'.

As well as spreading serenity and tranquil enjoyment, nuts have also been used since earliest times in a huge variety of cooked dishes. Egyptians and Iranians, many of whose favourite recipes have changed very little for almost twelve centuries, may use almonds and pine nuts to thicken their sauces, in stuffings for lamb, chicken and vegetables, and in every kind of pastry and sweet – dates stuffed with walnuts and almonds was one of the earliest sweets invented.

In India, pilaus and rich rice dishes are decorated with almonds or cashew nuts, and coconut is a vital ingredient of soups and curries in many areas, particularly in Kerala in the south-west of India. And peanuts are used throughout Africa in all sorts of stews.

In Europe, chestnuts are much enjoyed with turkey and with game of all sorts. The British love black pickled walnuts, and the Italians use fresh pine nuts to make pesto – the superb green basil sauce for fresh pasta. The French serve wonderful green salads sprinkled with fresh walnuts, and enjoy almonds with trout, while Eastern Europe specializes in rich nut cakes with ground almonds or hazelnuts taking the place of flour. Pecan pie is one of the traditional great American dishes, and of course nut-flavoured ice-creams abound.

Since nuts are so rich in protein, vitamins, calcium, iron and oils (nut cooking oils are used everywhere) and are so extremely versatile, no good cook should be without them. Buy them frequently, in small quantities rather than large, preferably in their shells, and store them in a cool environment (such as the refrigerator), since their high oil content makes them subject to dire alterations of flavour if they get hot or are kept too long. Make a particular point of enjoying fresh nuts in the autumn and early winter when they are sweet and milky.

Cashew (*Anacardium occidentale*) Kidney-shaped cashew nuts come from a tropical tree, which found its way from South America to the rest of the world by way of the early Portuguese explorers. The nuts grow suspended from a large fruit that is liked by monkeys, who ruin the crops in India and Asia. Cashews are widely eaten throughout South America, India and Asia. They often appear – blanched and either plain, roasted or salted – with drinks or as dessert nuts in the colder continents (they are easy to toast and salt yourself at home). Cashews are always sold shelled because the shells are toxic. In Brazil, they are also used for making wine and for the production of the famous *anacard* or cashew-nut vinegar. In Chinese cooking, of course, they often appear as an ingredient, especially in chicken dishes. Use plain cashews for cooking; they are usually fried in oil until golden brown and added to the dish at the last moment.

Pine nut, pine kernel (*Pinus pinea*) This nut actually does come from the beautiful glossy cones of pine trees. It is contained inside hard little torpedo-shaped shells that are covered with a sooty dust. In the Mediterranean the shells can be found lying all over the sand or rocks in September, wherever the handsome umbrella-shaped stone pines grow, and more can be shaken out of the open cones if the weather is dry. In the United States, the nuts come from the piñon pine. Chinese and Koreans use the nut of *Pinus kovaiensis* in various sweets and desserts, and in a rice congée.

Pine nuts are very widely used in Mediterranean cooking. They are delicious in stuffed vegetables – aubergines, courgettes or vine leaves – and are essential for pesto sauce – the smooth green paste of basil that is so irresistible with fresh tagliatelle or linguine. They combine with rice and raisins in a rich stuffing for chicken, duck or turkey, and are mixed with prunes, dried apricots, pomegranate seeds and almonds in *khoshaf* – an exotic dried-fruit salad flavoured with rosewater.

Pine nuts can generally be found in Italian delicatessens and in most supermarkets. Keep them refrigerated, but don't store them for too long because their resinous oil spoils easily and they soon turn rancid.

Macadamia nut (*Macadamia ternifolia*) Sweet and buttery, with a waxy texture, this is of the pre-dinner drinks and dessert-nut variety. Native to Australia, where it is sometimes known as the 'Queensland' nut, it is also grown in Hawaii, California and Florida. The hard shell is cracked open and the kernel roasted in coconut oil before being marketed.

Almond (*Prunus dulcis*) No other nut features as widely in old recipe books as the almond. Milk of almonds – the juice extracted from ground almonds steeped in water – used to take the place of milk on fast days or in hot weather (it is almost as rich in calcium as cow's milk). This technique of dealing with ground almonds is still used in such dishes as almond soup. Slivered almonds, fried golden, were much used for seasoning: they are still sometimes scattered on fried river fish.

Ground almonds do more than provide their liquor. They can be used in the place of flour for rich, moist cakes and for crisp biscuits. Sweet almonds are the chief ingredient of marzipan for coating cakes, and smooth sugared almonds, ovoids in silver, white, pink and pale blue, in silver baskets, traditionally grace French wedding feasts (and confectionery shops). 'Burnt almonds', cooked in sugar until caramelized and the colour of burnt siena – the classic praline – are superb in ice-cream. In delicate Mogul cooking almonds are combined with chicken in a variety of ways, while fresh almonds in their delicate green velvet coats form part of the early autumn *corbeille des fruits* in France and Italy, although these must be soaked in cold water before eating.

Almonds can be bought in their shells or out of them, and also come ready blanched, flaked, shredded, diced and ground. There are also bitter almonds (*Prunus amara*), which some recipes for biscuits and sweets may specify. The pungent taste of bitter almonds – like that of the crushed peach kernels you would add to jam – is related to the same enzyme reaction by which prussic acid is produced. Although they are inedible raw, bitter almonds, like peach kernels, are quite safe to use in cooking, because the poison is highly volatile and evaporates when heated. Once heated, they retain the flavour of ratafia (indeed, ratafia essence and the liqueur by that name rely on the essential oils of both sweet and bitter almonds). One bitter almond can bring out the flavour of a dish using sweet almonds, but store them in a jar apart, well marked to avoid muddles.

Peanut (*Arachis hypogaea*) Whether you know them as peanuts, groundnuts, monkey nuts or goobers, these are the success story of our age. Dry roasted, salted, shelled or unshelled, they come to more cocktail parties than any other nut. In North African countries you will find whole peanuts scattered over couscous; in Indonesia ground peanuts go into salads and sauces; and all over the world pressed peanuts give groundnut or arachide oil – a light, delicate oil for use in cooking and as a salad oil.

Raw peanuts have a faint taste of green beans – not surprising, as the peanut is a member of the legume family. Raw peanuts can be so useful in cooking – you can deep fry, fry or roast them. Try tossing them in heated oil and salt, then toasting them to a light golden colour in a moderate oven. To devil them, coat them in oil with a little chilli powder instead of salt, or season the oil with ground coriander, cumin and cayenne pepper.

When you buy peanut butter you may find the highly nutritious oil sitting on top – stir it in before you start spreading. You can make your own peanut butter by grinding whole shelled peanuts, skins removed, together with a little groundnut oil in a blender. Add a little salt, and do not make too much at a time because fresh peanut butter is inclined to go rancid. However, it will soon be used up if you make peanut butter cookies or use it as a foundation for peanut fudge, in which to encase chopped, blanched nuts.

Pistachio nut (*Pistacia vera*) These exquisite pale green nuts, with usefully half-open shells and papery skins marked with a rosy fingerprint, are the greatest luxury. They are grown in Italy, Iran, Turkey and California, and are usually roasted and salted to eat between meals, or with drinks. Those from the Middle East are sometimes flavoured with rosewater or lemon juice. They are also found, blanched and skinned, in mortadella in Italy, and studding the galantines and terrines and even the sausages in provincial French restaurants (you can use hazelnuts instead in duck pâté). The best halva, Turkish delight and nougat contain pistachio nuts. They make a delicious ice-cream, although the flavour of some commercial pistachio ice-cream may owe more to almond essence and green colouring than to pistachio nuts themselves.

Betel nut (*Areca catechu*) This is the tough little nut much beloved in India. Chopped and mixed with spices, pink-

groundnut oil 112
mortadella 75
skinning pistachio nuts 189

Galantine of Duck 320
Peanut Sauce 258
Spiced Stuffed Leg of Lamb 288

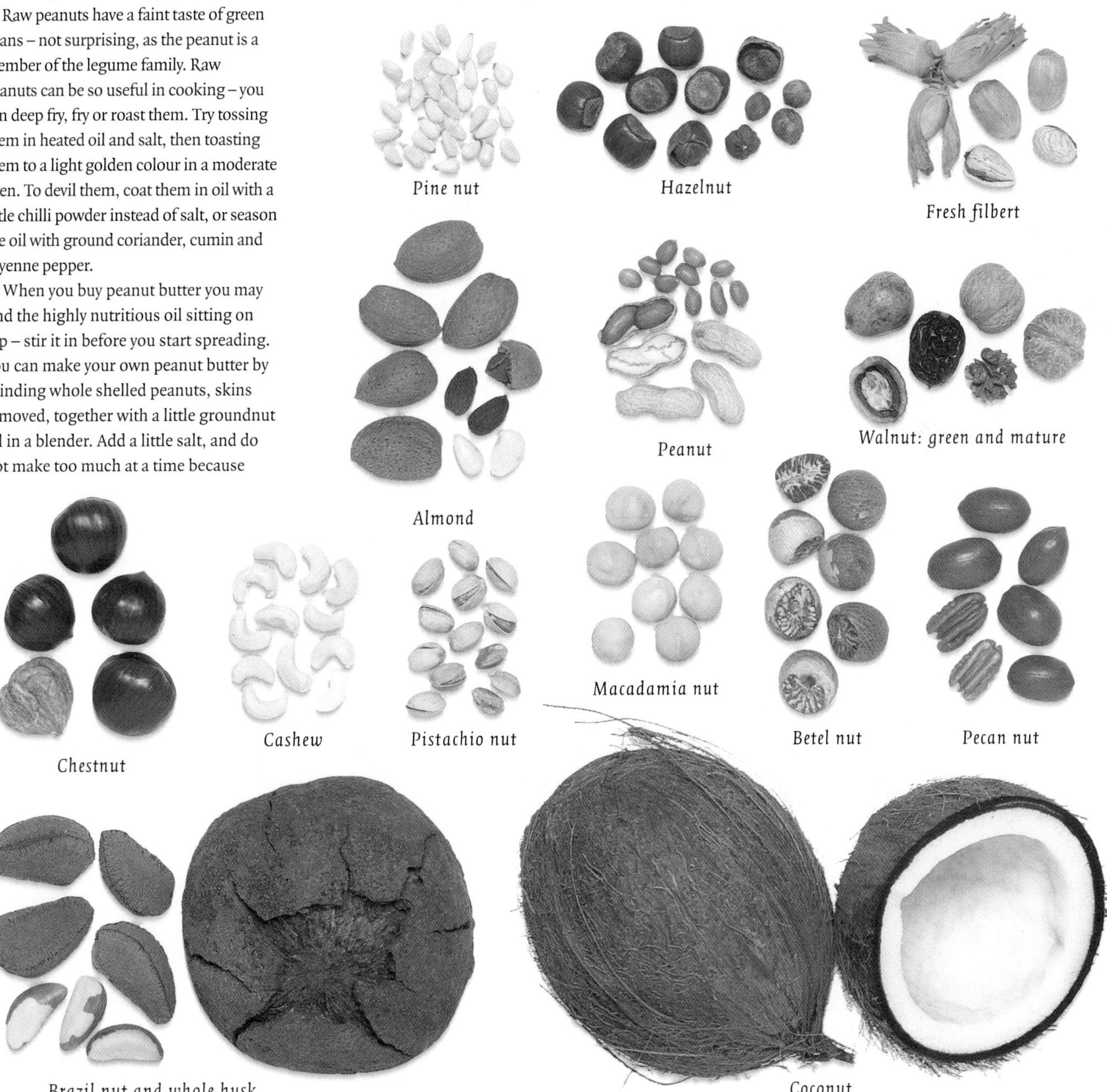

Pine nut

Hazelnut

Fresh filbert

Almond

Peanut

Walnut: green and mature

Chestnut

Cashew

Pistachio nut

Macadamia nut

Betel nut

Pecan nut

Brazil nut and whole husk

Coconut

pickled walnut 207
walnut ketchup 206
walnut oil 113

Brownies 414
Brussels Sprouts with Chestnuts 375
Cabbage with Chestnut Stuffing 374
Hazelnut Cakes 413
Pecan Pie 407
Pheasant with Chestnuts 298
Roast Turkey with Two Stuffings 311
Rocket and Walnut Salad 367
Spinach and Walnut Salad 367
Walnut Bread 358
Walnut Cake 412
Walnut Pie 407

dyed coconut shreds, other nuts, or tiny candy balls, they are wrapped in betel leaves to make the small triangular packages called *paans* that Indian hostesses (and restaurants) may offer to guests after a meal. Chewing these aromatic little parcels is said to aid the digestion and sweeten the breath. It can also turn the mouth an alarming red. Betel nuts can be bought whole (in which case you need a special cutter called a *sarota*) or ready shredded at grocery shops.

Pecan nut (*Carya illinoensis*) Pecans, thin-shelled and richly flavoured, are grown mainly in the United States, their natural home. Their very name is Native American, and the nut was widely used in tribal Indian cookery. Heavier in fats than walnuts, which belong to the same family and which pecans somewhat resemble in taste and in the appearance of their kernels, pecans were particularly cherished for their oil. Their flesh, ground to a fine meal, was used to thicken soups and stews.

Nowadays, pecans are used to enrich cakes, sweets and ice-cream, but their proudest moment comes in toffee-coloured pecan pie – a rich, sweet mixture of syrup, brown sugar, eggs, vanilla and nuts in a buttery pastry shell – which is an American favourite. Pecans can usually be found in most supermarkets, but if they prove to be elusive, walnuts can usually be substituted in recipes that specify pecans.

Hazelnut, cob nut and filbert (genus *Corylus*) These are the joy of the autumn countryside. If you don't have the chance to go gathering your own nuts you can buy them, fresh, moist and juicy, in good stores. By Christmas, the pretty leafy husk will have shrivelled, and the shells hardened and darkened to the familiar hazel colour. The kernels themselves will be less milky, but, in their own way, are still as good to eat and to use in the kitchen.

In England the terms hazel and cob are used for the same nut, while Americans use hazelnut and filbert interchangeably; and the nut known in Europe as the filbert is called in North America the giant filbert. All of these hazelnuts are perfect with goat's cheese and in green salads, but where hazelnuts come into their own is in the preparation of puddings, cakes, ice-cream and chocolates. To make cakes and puddings you need neither flour nor fat: hazelnuts have enough oil, balanced with mealiness, to provide it all. Just combine them, ground, with eggs and sugar and/or cream, as the case may be, and you have a whole repertoire of rich desserts. In grocery shops and supermarkets you can buy shelled hazelnuts whole, ground or chopped. In greengrocers they'll be sold complete with shells – the heavier the nut, the fuller the kernel.

Chestnut (*Castanea sativa*) Edible chestnuts, also called Spanish chestnuts, are first cousins to horse chestnuts. They are a prettier shape, but have none of their cousin's flamboyant mahogany sheen. Their pointed shell encloses a truly delicious nut – good to eat with Brussels sprouts, wonderful for stuffings, and warming roasted over the fire on a winter's day.

Marrons glacés are easy to make, and a great treat, although they do not often look as stunning as those bought, sitting in individual frilled paper cups. Puréed sweet chestnuts make the basis for the creamy and delicious *marrons Mont Blanc* and for iced Nesselrode pudding (invented for the nobleman of that name by his gifted cook). In Italy chestnuts are stewed in wine, and in France these useful nuts, braised or puréed, provide garnishes for chicken, pigeon and young turkey.

When shopping for fresh chestnuts, look for smooth, shiny shells and buy nuts that feel heavy for their size. Preserved chestnuts come vacuum-packed, which saves the laborious business of shelling and skinning them – the inner skin is bitter even when cooked. Less good are those canned in water. They are also preserved in syrup or, of course, in the form of purée, sweetened or unsweetened (which can also be bought in tubes). Chestnuts are also sold dried, ready to be soaked and then cooked to make chestnut purée, a traditional accompaniment for roast game.

Brazil nut (*Bertholletia excelsa*) This is the seed of a mighty tree that towers above the Brazilian jungle. The trees have never been cultivated: their seeds are gathered and buried by the *cotia*, the Amazonian hare, and those that the hare forgets to retrieve take root. The fruit the tree produces is as large as a coconut and a considerable weight; it falls to the ground when ripe. Inside the hard, woody shell are the 12 to 20 triangular seeds, packed tightly together like segments of an orange. These are the brazils that we buy in the shops, either in their shells (don't buy those that rattle or feel light) or shelled in packets. Rich and creamy fleshed, brazils are available all year, but are best in winter. They do not keep well – a high oil content gives them a rich flavour, but soon turns them rancid.

Walnut (*Juglans regia*) Fresh walnuts have flesh that is pearly white and soft, easily peeled inner skins, and shells that still have a trace of moisture about them. These 'wet' walnuts are a great delicacy, eaten raw with cheese – particularly goat's cheese – as soon as possible after you've acquired them so that their moisture has had no chance to evaporate. At an even younger age, before the shells have hardened, green walnuts are suitable for pickling in vinegar, which turns them black. They also make walnut ketchup.

After the first flush of youth, walnuts are kilned to preserve them, and become both drier and more oily in consistency. It is in this state that their kernels, halved or chopped, are used raw in salads or in cooking. Walnuts are good in stuffings, pressed into cream cheese, and baked in buns, breads and cakes. They are an excellent addition to a winter fruit salad of prunes, pears and dried apricots, cooked in spiced red wine. Walnut toffee and walnut fudge are delicious, and so are halved nuts coated in caramel, like praline, to make walnut brittle. In addition, nothing goes better with after-dinner port than a dish of fat walnuts and a pair of nutcrackers.

The common walnut is often known as the English walnut in the US, although it is in fact a native of the Middle East. Black walnuts (*Juglans nigra*) and butternuts or white walnuts (*Juglans cinerea*) are the North American branch of the family. Black walnuts are inclined to be larger than the average European walnut, and their shells are so hard that special nutcrackers need to be used. The kernels give a stronger taste to confectionery, ice-cream and cakes than other walnuts. Butternuts are not as difficult to crack and have a rich flavour.

Coconut (*Cocos nucifera*) The coconut, known to us as a hard, brown, hairy object to be won at fairs, is the basis of a huge international industry. It is harvested when its outer husk is green, its shell pliable and its flesh soft and moist. It is found growing in great clusters on giant palm trees, native to and once found only in Malaysia, but now cultivated on tropical coasts all over the world. This is because, apart from providing an invaluable source of food, the coconut palm also supplies a huge range of products, from coir for rugs and matting to palm wine. And in world kitchens, the coconut proves its worth in any number of ways.

By the time it arrives in our markets, its shell is dark and its flesh thick, and a great deal of the coconut juice – the thin white liquid present in the centre of the unripe nut – will have been absorbed. When you buy a fresh coconut, weight is the factor to watch – the heavier the nut, the juicier it will be. When you have opened it and extracted the juice, which makes a sweet, refreshing drink, you only have to pare away the brown skin with a sharp knife and grate your coconut meat to use in pies, cakes, puddings, sweets and savoury dishes such as curries. You can also mix fresh grated coconut with boiling water and then squeeze the liquid from the shreds to get coconut milk. To make coconut cream, simply use less water, or you can skim the cream from coconut milk that has been allowed to stand for a while, just like cow's milk. Alternatively, you can buy canned coconut milk, or creamed coconut which is sold in slabs, like lard. Use canned milk or fresh, home-made milk in making soups, curries, stews, roasts, drinks, puddings, candies, cakes and even for cooking rice, instead of water.

Coconut is also useful in its desiccated form. This is made from copra – dried coconut meat from which most of the oil has been extracted for other purposes – and has less flavour than the freshly grated flesh, but it can be infused in hot water and then squeezed to produce a quite reasonable coconut milk or cream.

making coconut milk 423

Coconut Ice-Cream 399
Curried Eggs 322
Duck with Coconut Cream and Green Curry Paste 313
Grilled Mackerel with Green Paste 266
Prawn and Cucumber Curry 278
Thai Mussels 281
Wyvern's Chicken Curry with Coconut 308

1

2

3

Splitting a coconut

1 Pierce two of the coconut 'eyes' with a strong, sharp instrument such as a robust kitchen skewer, a screwdriver or, as shown here, a workshop bradawl.

2 Shake out the juice from the coconut. Bake the empty coconut in a hot oven for 15 minutes.

3 Lay the hot coconut down on a board and give the centre of the shell a sharp blow with a hammer; the shell should break cleanly in two.

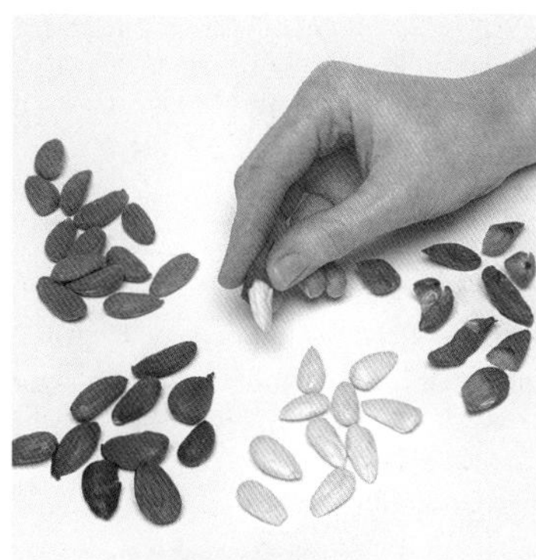

Blanching almonds

Plunge shelled almonds into boiling water and leave for a few seconds, until the skins loosen. Drain the nuts, and then pinch the almonds out of the skins. Pistachios are skinned in the same way.

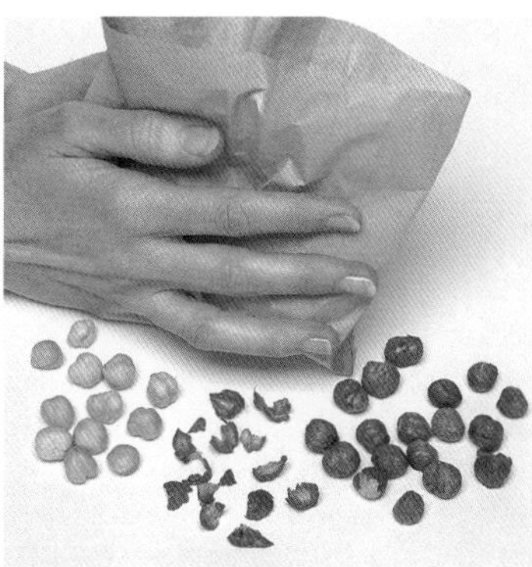

Skinning hazelnuts

Toast shelled nuts under the grill or in a moderate oven until the skins begin to colour and loosen. Put the nuts in a paper bag and rub them against one another to free the skins from the nuts.

Peeling chestnuts

With a sharp, pointed knife, score a cross on the flat side of each nut. Blanch the scored nuts for a few minutes, then drain. While still warm peel away the hard outer shell and the furry inner skin.

Herbs

herb vinegars 205
tisanes (herbal teas) 219

kitchen scissors 225
mezzaluna 224
pestle and mortar 226

Béarnaise Sauce 255
Chinese Egg Noodles with Browned Garlic, Chillies and Parsley 345
Creamed Potatoes with Parsley 381
Fried Sole with Butter and Parsley 261
Gratin of French Beans with Chives 378
Grilled Polenta with Poached Eggs, Fontina and Chive Cream 352
Herb Mayonnaise 259
Herb Vinaigrette with Balsamic Vinegar 259
Lemon Court-Bouillon with Parsley 245
Maître d'Hotel Butter 257
Omelette Fines Herbes 324
Salsa Verde 258
Sauce Tartare 259
Stewed Broad Beans with Butter and Tarragon 378
Tagliarini with Fresh Artichokes and Gremolata 338
Vichyssoise with Chives 254

Each herb used in the kitchen has a special and well-known affinity with certain kinds of food – fresh basil with tomatoes, mint with new potatoes, rosemary with lamb, sage with pork – but there are no rules laid down about these harmonies. Everything is to be gained by improvising with the fresh green flavours that herbs bring to food, playing around to produce sometimes fierce, sometimes delicate tones.

This is especially enjoyable for those who can look out into the garden (or window box) for inspiration and cast their eye over the fresh greenery growing so pleasantly there. The judicious use of dried herbs, too, can lead to some memorable discoveries, so always keep a wide variety at hand – not simply a pot of mixed herbs to fling into everything.

Herbs from the garden can be dried at home, but they must be picked at the right moment, just before they flower, or they lose their strength. Gather them on a dry but grey day and wash them quickly.

Divide small-leafed herbs such as thyme, tarragon and savory into bunches and tie them loosely with string. Either hang them up in muslin bags or spread them on a cloth or on newspaper laid over a rack and leave them to dry in a warm place (but not in sunshine).

Large-leafed herbs such as bay, sage and mint can be tied loosely and dried in the same way, or dipped into boiling water for a minute, shaken dry and dried to a crisp in a very slow oven. Parsley is more difficult, as it is a very juicy herb. Dry it on a rack in a hot oven (200°C/400°F, gas mark 6) for 1 minute, then turn the heat off and leave the parsley in the oven until it is quite crisp.

If you want to crush dried herbs for storage in glass jars, use a rolling pin or whizz them in a little grinder, which will turn them a nice green colour again. Fill the jars loosely to the top and make sure the tops fit properly, to preserve the aroma.

Most of the more tender herbs – mint, tarragon, parsley, chives, dill, basil, chervil and so forth – can be frozen. They will darken in colour when they thaw, but the flavour is well preserved. Since herbs are extremely strongly scented, store them in airtight boxes or bags or they will flavour everything in the freezer.

Bouquet garni Traditionally this is a few sprigs of parsley, some thyme and a bay leaf. Tied with cotton it goes into the soup, stew or whatever dish that calls for it and is discarded when the dish is cooked. When used to flavour a stock the herbs can be tied inside a stick of celery or a leek leaf.

A bouquet garni can also be a mixture of dried herbs tied up in a little square of cheesecloth or muslin. To the basic bouquet can be added a piece of orange peel, a clove of garlic, a few celery leaves, a couple of twigs of fennel or whatever herbs you choose to go with the dish you are making.

Fines herbes This is a delicate mixture of the more tender herbs – parsley, chervil, chives and sometimes tarragon – all chopped very fine. The alchemy of this mixture has a hundred and one uses, from flavouring all kinds of subtly cooked eggs and omelettes to poached sole or any delicate fish with a cream and white wine sauce. *Fines herbes* are delicious, too, mixed into melted butter with a squeeze of lemon, to be poured over roasted, grilled or fried chicken, or veal escalopes. They go into tartare and béarnaise sauce, and can be mixed into mayonnaise to make an excellent sauce to accompany cold poached salmon, prawns and, of course, hard-boiled eggs – the mayonnaise should be green with herbs.

Parsley (*Petroselinum crispum*) The most serviceable of herbs and one that you can always buy fresh, parsley seems to have just as much affinity with garlic and strongly flavoured Sicilian dishes, salty with olives, anchovies, goat's cheese, garlic and capers, as it does with the potato soups and fresh cod of the north, and many a pallid dish has been saved with a sprinkling of this delicious chopped greenery.

Flat-leaf parsley, which is also sold as continental parsley, is tastier and has a better texture than the curled, and parsley root – also called Hamburg parsley – is good for flavouring stews. Use parsley in court-bouillons, soups and, of course, parsley sauce. *Jambon persillé* – a dish of chunks of ham set in a garlic-laden jelly quite solid with green chopped parsley – is a Burgundian dish well worth trying.

To make parsley sandwiches, wash and very finely chop some freshly gathered parsley, mix it with a little butter and spread thickly between two thin slices of buttered brown bread. Put plenty of coarsely chopped flat-leaf parsley in a green salad.

Chervil (*Anthriscus cerefolium*) One of the classic *fines herbes*, chervil has a delicate, aniseedy flavour, so subtle that it needs to be used lavishly. It is good in green salads, with eggs and as a herb butter for steak or sole. In Korea it is used as a salad green instead of lettuce, served by itself or with a dish of grilled or curried prawns. It makes a very good light soup, and chervil and sorrel, both shredded fairly finely, are a traditional garnish for chicken soup. Fresh chervil can be frozen, but it doesn't dry very well.

Chive (*Allium schoenoprasum*) With a flavour faintly redolent of onions but far finer and more delicate, grassy-looking chives are best with eggs, especially omelettes. They are also delicious with potatoes – particularly baked potatoes split open and piled with soured cream mixed with chopped chives – and with raw or cooked tomatoes. As they are such a clean, fresh green they look pretty, cut up small with scissors to prevent bruising, sprinkled over puréed soups – tomato, vichyssoise, avocado, potato or artichoke – as well as in a lettuce salad and as a garnish for potato salad and glazed carrots. Chives freeze well but do not dry.

Chinese chive, garlic chive (*Allium tuberosum*) These garlic-scented and -flavoured chives, also known as *ku chai*, have narrow, flat green leaves and edible white flowers. They are much used in Indian and Chinese cooking, and in South Africa they are used to flavour salads. Usually eaten while still in bud, they can also be picked in full flower and scattered lightly on top of the salad leaves to add beauty and a delicate garlic flavour. The buds may also be fried.

Tarragon (*Artemisia dracunculus*) Like basil and dill, tarragon has an addictive flavour – that is to say, those who have eaten it fresh can't very well get through the summer without it, since it is so delicious. French tarragon tastes sweetly of vanilla and aniseed, and harmonizes completely with all kinds of egg dishes, with cream and with roast chicken or steak. It is good in green salads and potato salad and with cold salmon or trout. Tarragon vinegar makes an excellent mayonnaise for potato salad or chicken, and tarragon is essential for béarnaise sauce. Dried tarragon takes on an uncharacteristic, hay-like flavour, but frozen tarragon is very good.

Russian tarragon (*Artemisia dracunculoides*), unlike the true French herb, has a dull and disappointing flavour.

Dill (*Anethum graveolens*) Scandinavians are as fond of dill as they are of summer, the height of which is the first day of the *krefta* season, when thousands of crayfish are cooked with quantities of dill and served in their scarlet shells on a bed of the green herb, accompanied by numerous glasses of akvavit interspersed with beer. Dill is the flavour that makes Scandinavian cured salmon (gravlax) so delicious, and it is used there as a matter of course together with boiled and mashed potatoes.

In Greece dill is the herb used to flavour broad beans and artichokes. With white fish, serve dill either in melted butter or made into a sauce rather like parsley sauce.

To preserve dill, freeze it in plastic bags, or use dill seeds when fresh dill is out of season.

Fennel (*Foeniculum vulgare*) The sweet herb fennel – not to be confused with the bulb vegetable, Florence fennel – is used both as a herb and for its seeds. A few small twigs are invaluable for bouillabaisse and fish soup and with fresh fish; if you catch your own crayfish and cook them in boiling water with a jungle of fennel, it gives them a most delicate flavour and is a good alternative to the dill the Scandinavians prefer. Burn a few dried twigs when you are grilling fish or lamb outdoors, and put sprigs inside a fish and under it when you bake it in the oven. The anise-flavoured oils will permeate the food with a wonderfully sympathetic flavour. In Sardinia, wild fennel is often used to flavour a bean and pork stew, and is occasionally cooked with lamb.

Coriander (*Coriandrum sativum*) The soft, floppy green leaves of this herb, also called cilantro, look like rather lacy, flat parsley. They don't smell particularly strong unless you bruise them, and their taste, on its own, is harsh with a green note (said by some to be reminiscent of soap), quite unlike the warm flavour of the seeds. But chopped and used in fresh chutneys and salsas, coriander has a superb flavour. It is also an essential flavour in many types of curry, especially prawn and mutton – a very good addition

coriander seed 199
crayfish 34
dill seed 196
fennel seed 196
fennel (vegetable) 137

gravlax 31

Braised John Dory with Tomatoes and Fennel 268
Chanterelles Fried with Dill 386
Courgettes with Dill and Sour Cream 384

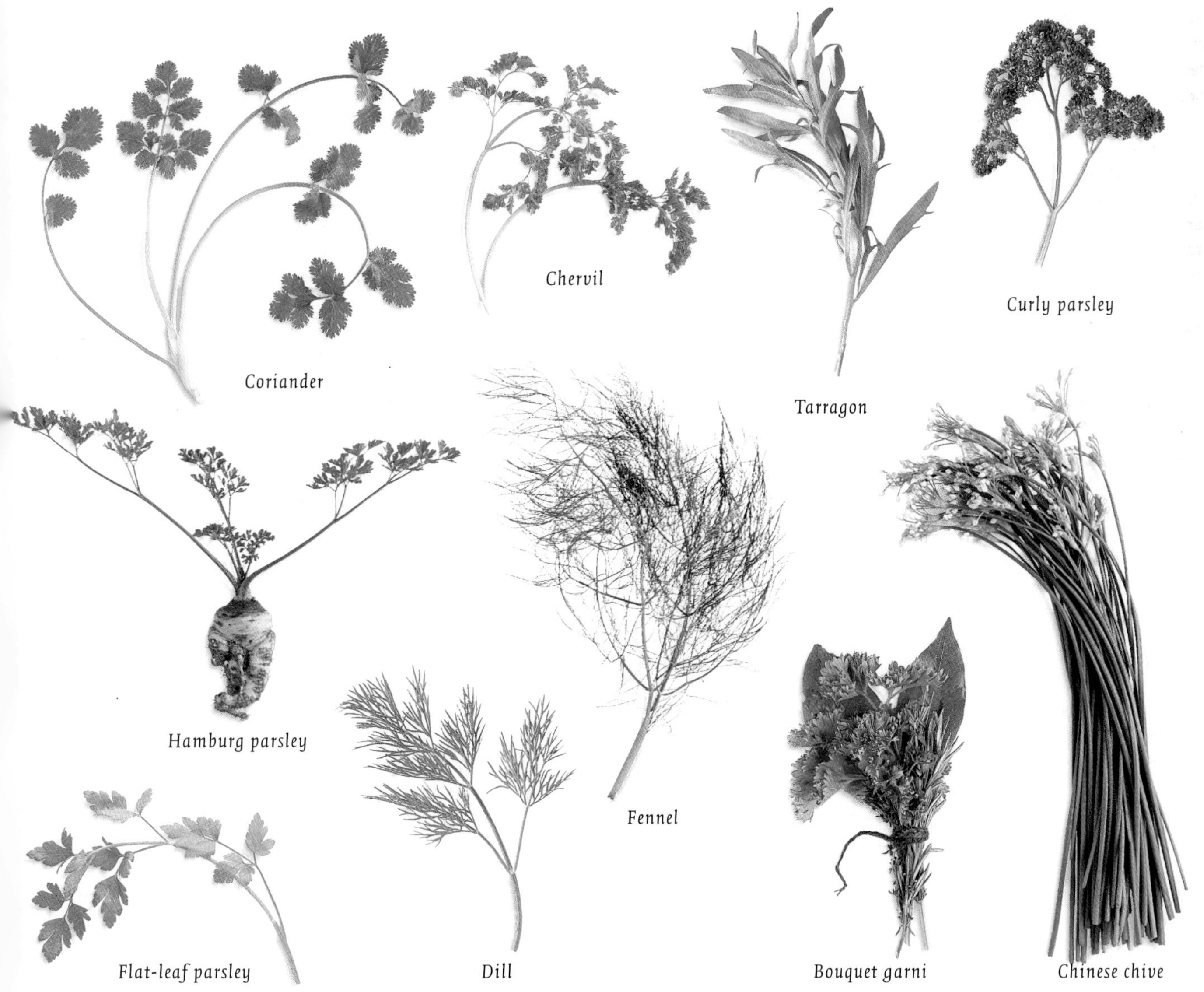

Coriander

Chervil

Tarragon

Curly parsley

Hamburg parsley

Fennel

Flat-leaf parsley

Dill

Bouquet garni

Chinese chive

Chicken with Marjoram 305
Lido Pasta Salad 371
Pesto alla Genovese 336
Provençal Soupe au Pistou 250
Pumpkin Soup with Basil 247
Scallops with Saffron, Basil and Tomato Vinaigrette 279
Spinach and Ricotta Ravioli 342
Stir-Fried Aubergines with Chilli and Coriander 384

to meat or chicken curry is a paste made from fresh ginger, garlic, green chilli and fresh coriander all pounded together. Coriander can be delicious in meatballs and lamb stews, or with lamb or pork kebabs, and in any Mediterranean vegetable dish. It is widely used in Mexican, Thai and other Asian cuisines. It does not dry well, but can be frozen or preserved with salt in oil.

The roots of the coriander plant are also delicious in cooking. In Thailand, the roots are added to dishes that are to be long-simmered and then the leaves are stirred in at the last moment.

Sweet cicely (*Myrrhis odorata*) A pretty, old-fashioned herb, also known as anise chervil, sweet cicely can be used like parsley in salads or as part of a bouquet garni. Both the leaves and the green seeds can be used – they taste fragrant and sugary, somewhere between anise and liquorice. The ripe seeds were once used to make polish to clean and perfume oak floors and furniture.

Basil (*Ocimum basilicum*) Sweet basil, so necessary to the well-being of anyone who loves the warm South, has large, tender leaves that bruise easily and smell sweetly of cloves. It should be picked young and eaten raw, or almost so, since the aroma and flavour are fugitive. Use it lavishly on tomato salad – it has a great affinity with tomatoes – and with aubergines, courgettes and vegetable marrow. In the south of France, a few chopped leaves are sometimes thrust into a dish of ratatouille at the last moment.

The famous *pesto alla genovese* – basil and pine nut paste – is one of the greatest pasta sauces, and *soupe au pistou* would be no more than an ordinary vegetable soup were it not for the '*pommade*' made with oil, garlic and basil pounded together and added to the bowl at the last moment. Fresh basil is also delicious with mozzarella cheese, on a potato salad or a salad of dried haricot beans, and with rabbit and chicken.

There are many varieties of basil in addition to common sweet basil. Small-leaved pot basil is particularly sweet, while Thai or Asian basil has a pungent aniseed aroma, purple stems and sharply pointed leaves – delicious in salads, stir-fried dishes and soups. Handkerchief basil has very large leaves; purple or opal basil has beautiful dark red-purple leaves that have a slightly muted flavour; and lemon basil has a citrus fragrance.

To preserve basil, push the leaves into a jar, sprinkling a little salt between the layers, and fill the jar with olive oil. Both leaves (which become black) and oil are good, and carry the flavour into whatever they are added to. Basil can also be preserved by freezing, after a brief blanching, but the flavour of frozen or dried basil can never compare with that of the freshly picked herb.

Marjoram (*Origanum majorana*) Sweet or knotted marjoram smells very sweet, both when it is fresh and the bees are enjoying it and when it is cut, just after flowering, and dried in bunches like thyme and sage. Use fresh leaves in a salad, on grilled or roast lamb, or in stuffing for chicken or guinea fowl, rabbit or hare; put dried marjoram in spaghetti and tomato sauces and any tomato-based soup or stew.

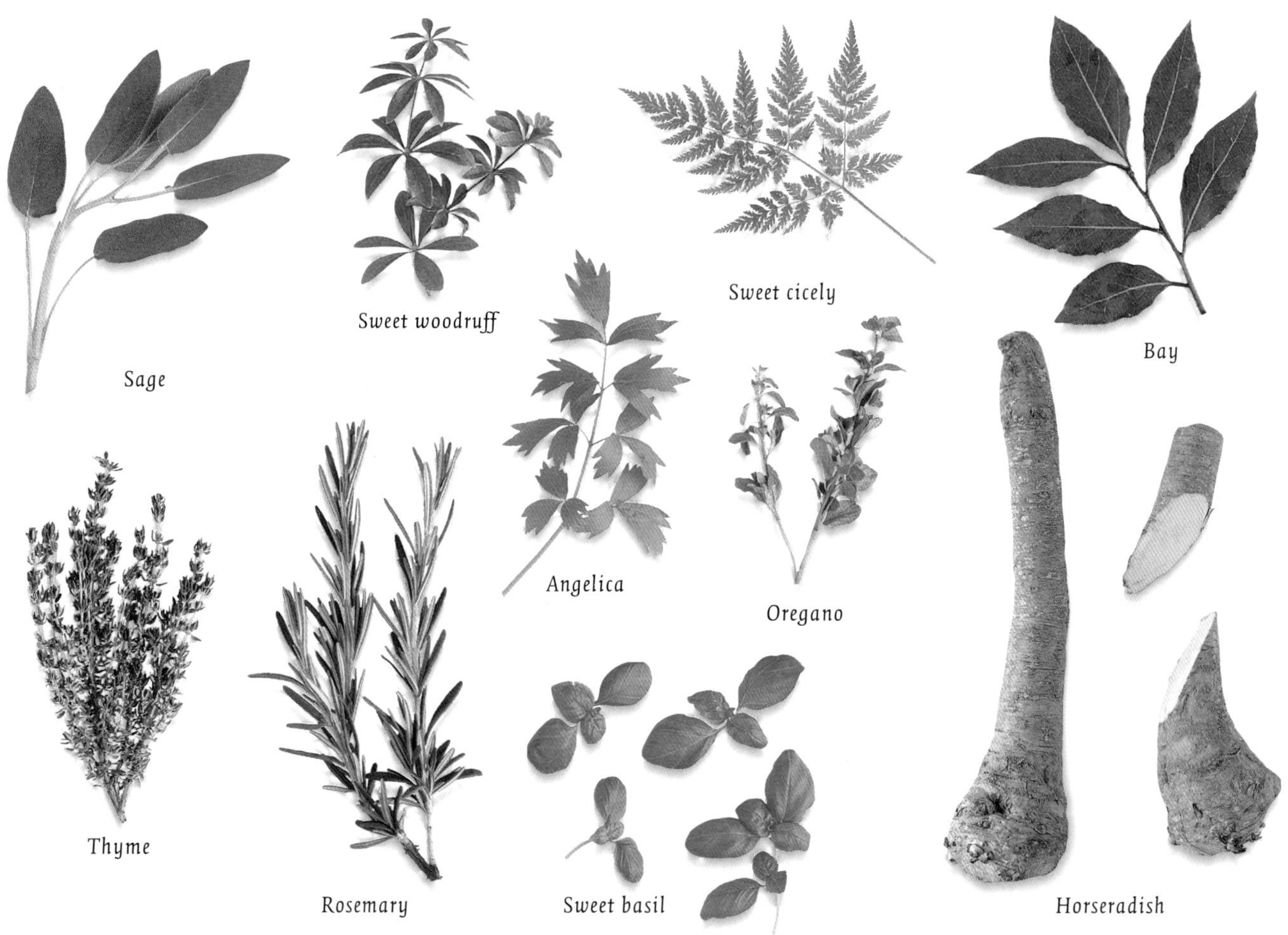

Sage
Sweet woodruff
Sweet cicely
Bay
Angelica
Oregano
Thyme
Rosemary
Sweet basil
Horseradish

Pot marjoram (*Origanum onites*) is slightly less warm flavoured than sweet marjoram but can be used in the same ways.

Rigani is the wild marjoram of Greece. Use the dried flowers rather than the leaves to give the authentic Greek flavour to lamb kebabs and the Greek salad of feta cheese, tomatoes, olives and onions. It is best used dried.

Oregano (*Origanum vulgare*) Sometimes also known as marjoram, this wild Mediterranean herb has a wonderfully warm, heady scent and flavour. In Italy it is used for the same dishes as marjoram. The dried leaves give a strong, spicy flavour to an oil and lemon sauce for fish and roast meat, and to pizza and spaghetti sauces, chicken broth, beef stews and grilled fish, especially red mullet. Oregano is delicious with mozzarella and tomatoes and is one of the flavours in the best chilli con carne. The oregano of Mexico is stronger than the common Mediterranean variety.

Rosemary (*Rosmarinus officinalis*) One of the prettiest of shrubs, rosemary loves the baking heat and dryness of the Mediterranean, but will grow to quite a good size in northern climates if given a warm, dry, sheltered place. It particularly likes the seaside – its name comes from the Latin for 'dew of the sea'. It has a great affinity with veal, lamb and chicken and also with rabbit – put a sprig under a rack or leg of veal or lamb before roasting or into the butter in which you are softening onions for a veal or rabbit stew; drop a sprig into the lard or oil in which you are frying potatoes.

Rosemary is better fresh than dried, and fresh rosemary has the added advantage of staying in one piece in the cooking – which is lucky as it is very disagreeable to eat a mouthful of the dried, needle-like leaves. But be miserly because it is all too easy to overdo the gingery, pungent flavour of rosemary.

Bay (*Laurus nobilis*) Anyone who is familiar with cooking is familiar with the sweet, resinous smell of bay. The leaves and twigs go into court-bouillons for fish, into stocks, broths and marinades, pickles and stews, daubes and spaghetti sauces – in anything, in fact, that demands a bouquet garni. The best decoration for a terrine is a fresh bay leaf, and in the past bay leaves were used to flavour milk puddings – bay infused in boiled milk gives a very agreeable, subtle flavour.

To dry bay leaves, spread them on newspaper and leave them to dry in the dark to preserve their colour. Avoid buying old bay leaves; if they are more than a year old they will have lost their flavour as well as their colour. In France, bay leaves are called *laurier*, sometimes dangerously translated as laurel leaves in cookery books (including Alice B Toklas's famous cookbook, where there is a laurel soup recipe that would fell a horse): leaves of laurels other than sweet bay can be poisonous.

Sage (*Salvia officinalis*) Sage was once believed to give wisdom and prolong life. It is certainly a powerful herb, musky and fragrant. The leaves go into stuffings for roast pork and goose, and sage is an important ingredient – usefully cutting the richness of the fat – in pork pies and sausages. Partridge is sometimes cooked

bouquet garni 190
feta cheese 102
rosemary sugar 211

Char-Grilled Venison 294
Goose with Apple Stuffing 312
Mediterranean Garfish 270
Roast Loin of Pork 290
Sautéed Chicken Livers with Sage 292
Sherry Trifle 392
Spinach Gnocchi with Butter and Sage 344

Burnet, *Lemon balm*, *Marjoram*, *Apple mint*, *Borage*, *Chive*, *Lovage*, *Summer savory*, *Winter savory*

bouquet garni 190
celery seed 197
crystallized angelica 185
***funghi porcini* (cep)** 158
mint tisane 219
wasabi or Japanese horseradish 207

Artichokes alla Romana 376
Aubergine, Pepper and Tomato Pizza with Thyme 361
Chilled Cucumber Soup with Mint 254
Duck with Coconut Cream and Green Curry Paste 313
Horseradish Butter 257
Horseradish Sauce 258
Mint Sauce 158
Peas with Lettuce Hearts 376
Quails with Thyme and Orange 301
Spiced and Fried New Potatoes with Minted Yogurt Dressing 381
Tabbouleh 351
Thai Mussels 281

with sage, and eel and bacon wrapped in sage and grilled makes an extremely good dish. In Italy, fresh sage is fried in the oil in which veal or calf's liver is to be cooked, to give an interesting flavour, and sprinkled on ravioli, sage leaves fried in butter add a warm, satisfying note.

Thyme (*Thymus vulgaris*) Sun loving, tiny leafed but tough, thyme tastes and smells warm, earthy and flowery. Use it in every kind of long-simmered and red-wine dish, with rabbit, veal and chicken in all their tomatoey incarnations, in a bouquet garni, in marinades and – instead of rosemary – with lamb. In Marseilles, thyme is sprinkled into everything including vinaigrette dressing, fried potatoes and over fish to be grilled on a wood fire. It gives pungency to pâtés, terrines and meatballs, and has an affinity with Mediterranean vegetables such as aubergines, courgettes and sweet peppers.

Lemon thyme (*Thymus citriodorus*) is superb in stuffings for pork and veal. Home-dried or frozen thyme is incomparably better than commercially dried or powdered thyme.

Savory (*Satureia*) Aromatic and pleasantly bitter, with a scent a little like thyme, summer savory (*Satureia hortensis*) was used by the Romans to flavour vinegar in much the same way as we use mint in mint sauce today. In France, where it is called *sarriette*, it is used with thyme to flavour rabbit, and fresh sprigs are cooked with broad beans and peas. It is also good in long-simmered stews and daubes. Summer savory dries well, and can be used with a number of other herbs in stuffings for turkey and veal. It is said to be a good antidote to bee-stings.

Winter savory (*Satureia montana*), with its blue flowers, is a tougher herb than summer savory. It has a similar, strong earthy flavour, perfect with rabbit and beef stews, with lentils and with all kinds of stuffing. Its rough, pointed evergreen leaves cannot be eaten raw as they tickle the throat.

Mint (*Mentha*) One of the oldest and most familiar of herbs, mint has almost as many varieties as it has uses. Spearmint (*Mentha spicata*), with its pointed leaves and fresh taste, is the most commonly used. Peppermint has longer, darker green leaves and a more pungent taste. Pretty apple mint (*Mentha rotundifolia*) with woolly, rounded leaves, has a superior, fruitier flavour – its woolliness disappears when it is finely chopped or cooked.

In England, mint is best known in a sauce to accompany roast lamb, and a few sprigs of fresh mint are often boiled with new potatoes, when it is delicious, and with garden peas, when it is a mistake. Mint features a good deal in Middle Eastern cookery, for example finely chopped and stirred into yogurt as a dressing for cucumber salad. In northern India chopped mint is mixed with green chilli and yogurt to make a fresh chutney that is very good with tandoori chicken. In Italy wild mint is used instead of parsley with grilled or fried *funghi porcini*.

Mint is used with shellfish, particularly grilled prawns, and in the making of puddings that contain fresh oranges (with which the herb has an affinity). Sprigs of mint also go into fruit drinks, wine cups and juleps. Sun-brewed mint tea is made by putting mint sprigs and tea bags in a jug of cold water and leaving it to brew in the sun – the resulting tea has no hint of bitterness.

Burnet (*Poterium sanguisorba*) Salad burnet, with its grey-green leaves and cool cucumber flavour, was eaten a great deal by our ancestors. The young leaves are very tender and can be sprinkled into the salad bowl with the lettuce. Used a great deal in France and Italy, burnet can also be used, like borage, in cooling drinks, and is an excellent flavouring for vinegar.

Balm, lemon balm (*Melissa officinalis*) Beloved of bees, balm was the vital ingredient of Paracelsus's *elixir vital*, designed to make man immortal. It now gives its essence to Chartreuse, that green and potent liqueur made by monks, who keep most of the other ingredients a secret. The fresh, lemon-scented leaves and small white flowers are delicious in white-wine cups, and in a German claret cup made with cucumber, orange and soda water. A few freshly picked leaves can also go into a green salad, but the taste is rather overpowering and more bitter than you might expect.

Borage (*Borago officinalis*) A hairy, bristly plant that stings the fingers, borage makes up for the discomfort it inflicts by its flowers, which are a heart-breakingly intense blue. Together with the cucumber-flavoured furry leaves, they complete that fruit salad of a drink called Pimms. The flowers also make a pretty decoration for crab salad.

Sweet woodruff (*Asperula odorata*) A small woodland herb, sweet woodruff has a ravishing hay-like perfume. In Germany it is used in May, before it flowers, to flavour a delicate wine cup: steep the well-washed plants in a jug of white wine overnight in the refrigerator, then add brandy and sugar or Benedictine and serve with a garnish of the green leaves.

Lovage (*Ligusticum officinalis*) This old-fashioned herb looks rather like immensely tall, dark green celery that has got out of hand. It has a very strange, pleasant but heavy smell (it is called the Maggi plant in Holland because the flavour is reminiscent of stock cubes, with monosodium glutamate lurking somewhere in its nuances). It is a strong-flavoured herb and should be used sparingly to season stocks or soups when a meaty flavour is wanted. Lovage seeds can be used like celery seed.

Angelica (*Angelica archangelica*) Nobody knows why angelica is associated with angels, although it has been helpful in its time for curing coughs, colds and colic.

It is best known today as a candied stem used for decorating puddings and cakes. Freshly shredded leaves are a good flavouring for rhubarb, and can be used in jam-making, particularly rhubarb jam.

Horseradish (*Armoracia rusticana*) A fresh, stinging horseradish sauce with roast beef is one of life's pleasures and is very good, too, with hot boiled tongue. In Germany horseradish is grated and mixed with vinegar as a sauce for fish, while creamed horseradish sauce is particularly good with smoked eel and smoked trout, and it can be mixed with mayonnaise to dress hard-boiled eggs. Commercially dried Swedish or American horseradish flakes are a reasonable substitute for the fresh root.

Lemon grass (*Cymbopogon citratus*) Perfumed, spicy and balm-like, lemon grass – called *takrai* in Thailand and *sereh* in Malaysia – adds a light, elusive flavour to many Thai and Indonesian dishes. Tough on the outside, the stalks contain tender inner leaves that are cut in rounds or shredded and used to flavour soups, curry, pork, seafood – particularly crab – and chicken. Lemon grass can be grown in a frost-free place like any other herb. Best fresh, it can also be bought dried: soak for half an hour before use.

Lime leaf, makrut (*Cistus hystrix*) Only the leaves of the evergreen South-east Asian makrut tree and sometimes the peel of its fruit are used in cooking. The glossy, waisted leaves have an aromatic, floral-citrus smell and are used like bay leaves to flavour Thai and other South-east Asian soups and curries. They are usually sold dried, although are occasionally found fresh. The peel can sometimes be found dried, and needs soaking before it is used, like the leaves, to flavour soups, marinades and curries or even marmalade.

Garden leaves and flowers Use only unsprayed leaves and flowers.
Peach (*Prunus persica*) Fresh peach leaves make a delicate flavouring for custard, more interesting than the usual vanilla and tasting faintly of almonds. Pick five or six fresh leaves and infuse them in the milk for 5–10 minutes, then proceed with the custard in the usual way.
Grape-vine leaf (*Vitis*) Every vine that produces edible grapes produces leaves that are edible when young. As dolmades and as a wrapping, with bacon, for little birds such as quail, partridge and snipe, vine leaves impart a delicious, faint lemon flavour. Choose large, tender young leaves; if they are older blanch them in boiling salted water to soften them before they are used. Of course vine leaves in brine are available; rinse them well before using.
Geranium (*Pelargonium graveolens*) The curling, slightly furry leaves of the rose-scented geranium add a delicate rose fragrance to a clear amber-pink crabapple jelly or to lemon water-ice. Pick the larger leaves.
Marigold (*Calendula officinalis*) This pretty golden flower was once used a great deal to colour and flavour fish soups and meat broth and to decorate salads – especially prawn, crab or lobster, but since the petals are surprisingly tough they are best chopped. Mixed with other chopped petals such as borage, rose and hyssop, we are told by Mrs Sinclair Rohde that 'the effect is gay and charming and adds to the wholesomeness of the salad'. Marigold still sometimes colours butter and cheese, and can be used as a substitute for saffron if you don't like saffron's strong flavour. The petals can be fresh or dried, but don't use the flower centres.
Nasturtium (*Trapaeolum majus*) Almost every part of this tender plant has a place in the kitchen. The flowers and young leaves can be used in salads – the leaves taste like watercress, but don't use too many because they are very spicy. The buds and seeds can be pickled to make false capers. Gather the seeds as soon as the blossoms have fallen, before they get hard; rinse them in cold water and soak overnight in cold salted water. Then drain, cover with cold spiced vinegar and seal; keep for 12 months before using.
Rose (Rosaceae) Although much of life was probably far from rosy in medieval days, it must have been a great pleasure, on a fine day, to gather dark red rose petals to make into rose syrup, rose candy and rose vinegar. In the Middle East roses are still definitely the domain of the cook, who will sprinkle rosewater into fruit salads made with pomegranates and make clear, rose-petal jelly with nuts or chewy scented rose-petal jam. In the last century, the American Shakers used their own rosewater to flavour apple pie – an unexpectedly exotic touch for such a 'plain' people.

In England, the Victorians made rose-petal sandwiches – lay deep red petals on and under a large, flat piece of butter in the refrigerator, and the next day spread the butter on to thin slices of crustless white bread; lay a few fresh petals on top and allow them to show around the edges of the sandwich. Cream cheese and cinnamon can also be added. Rose petals are also good in cherry pie.

capers 207
crystallized flowers 185
grapes 174–6
pomegranate 179
rose hip 174
saffron 199
tisanes (herbal teas) 219

Crab Salad with Thai Flavours 368
Crabapple Jelly 418
Hot and Sour Shellfish Broth 253
Marinated Thai Prawns 278
Traditional Custard Tart 407

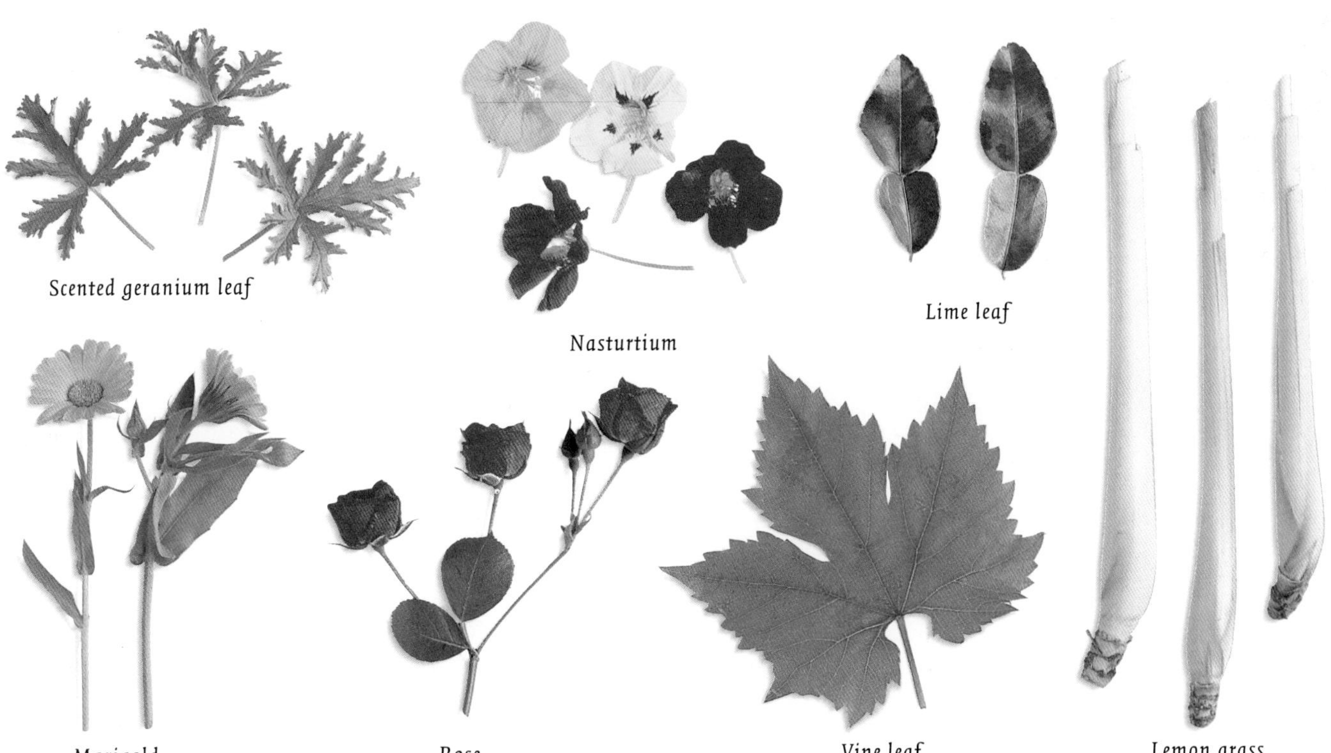

Scented geranium leaf

Nasturtium

Lime leaf

Marigold

Rose

Vine leaf

Lemon grass

Spices

chilli powder 201
dill 191
fennel (vegetable) 191
peppercorns 201
salame finocchiona 77

coffee grinder 226, 239
pestle and mortar 226

Braised Red Cabbage 374
Cold Game Pie 316
Curried Eggs 322
Duck with Coconut Cream and Green Curry Paste 313
Dundee Cake 412
Grilled Chicken Kebabs 307
Prawn and Cucumber Curry 278
Slow-Cooked Brisket of Beef with Soy, Sake and Oysters 284
Wyvern's Chicken Curry with Coconut 308

The spices once used so effectively in Elizabethan dishes rather fell into disrepute in Britain as 'good plain cooking' followed in the wake of Mrs Beeton. Now the heady, aromatic smells of the spice bazaars are back, with the wave of new ethnic food shops, and with them a revived interest in the cooking of India, the Middle East and Far East.

Buy in small quantities and use whole spices whenever possible, pounding or grinding them freshly for each dish that calls for ground spice. A small, specially designated coffee grinder can be used for this purpose, as can a spice grinder, but grinding the spices with garlic and fresh coriander leaves, fresh ginger and chillies in a large pestle and mortar is a pleasure not to be missed.

Mixtures

Pickling spice Ready mixed, this will probably contain a great deal of mustard seed, some small dried chillies, white peppercorns, allspice, cloves, mace, a few coriander seeds and perhaps some ginger. But it is better to use weighed amounts of the individual spices in pickling because appropriate quantities and ingredients vary from vegetable to vegetable and recipe to recipe.

Quatre épices Although called 'four spices' in French, the actual number of spices used in the mixture may vary. The base spices are star anise, cassia or cinnamon, cloves and fennel seeds; the 'extra' spices often added are Sichuan peppercorns, ginger or cardamom.

Sweet mixed spice For use in buns, biscuits, Christmas puddings and mince pies, this is usually a mixture of allspice, cinnamon, cloves, ginger and nutmeg.

Five-spice powder This is a Chinese mixture of powdered star anise, fennel, cloves, cinnamon and Sichuan pepper. Its subtle aniseed flavour is particularly good with roast pork.

Garam masala This Indian mixture of spices is added to a dish towards the end of cooking to enhance the aromas and flavours. It can be bought ready made or ground at home from a mixture of whole spices – a good combination is ½ cup seeds from green cardamom pods, 1 cup cumin seeds, ⅓ cup whole cloves and ⅓ cup broken up cinnamon sticks, to which can be added ½ cup each coriander seeds, black peppercorns and fennel seeds (the fennel could replace the cumin altogether). The powder can be mixed to a paste with water, to use in curry, be stirred into yogurt or eaten with other foods like a condiment.

Other common commercial spice blends include curry and chilli powders.

Anise (*Pimpinella anisum*) Also known as sweet cumin, anise flavours Pernod, ouzo and other addictive drinks of the same genre. From a delicate bush of the hemlock family, the seeds give a sweet, liquorice-like flavour to fish and particularly to mussels, to sweets and creams and, in some parts of Europe, to cakes and bread. In the Middle East, anise flavours figs preserved in syrup, and jam, and it is a flavouring in some Indian vegetable and fish dishes. Buy in small quantities as it quickly loses its strength.

Star anise (*Illicium verum*) The fruit of a small evergreen tree that belongs to the magnolia family, star anise has the same essential oil that gives anise its characteristic flavour but is much stronger and more liquorice like. It is used in Chinese cooking, particularly with pork and duck.

Dill seed (*Anethum graveolens*) Sprigs of dill complete with half-ripe seeds are a familiar sight in jars of pickled gherkins and dill vinegar. Dill seeds are also excellent in a court-bouillon and as a flavouring for poached crayfish and fish soups and stews. In Scandinavia and other parts of northern Europe, they may be used, too, to flavour cakes and breads, much like caraway seeds, although dill is considerably more delicate.

Fennel seed (*Foeniculum vulgare*) These have a sweet, aniseed flavour, and a few seeds chewed after meals will help the digestion and sweeten the breath. In Italy they are used in the manufacture of a marvellous salami called *finocchiona*, and are found in a kind of nougat called *mandorlotto*. Try using them to flavour the liquid in which fish is cooked for fish soup or pie; scatter them on to mashed potatoes; and add them to curry spices.

Juniper berry (*Juniperus communis*) The flavour of the juniper berry, familiar to gin drinkers and especially to those who drink Dutch gin, is strangely harsh and turpentiney on its own. The hard, blue-purple berries, borne on a pretty but prickly evergreen bush, take 2 years to

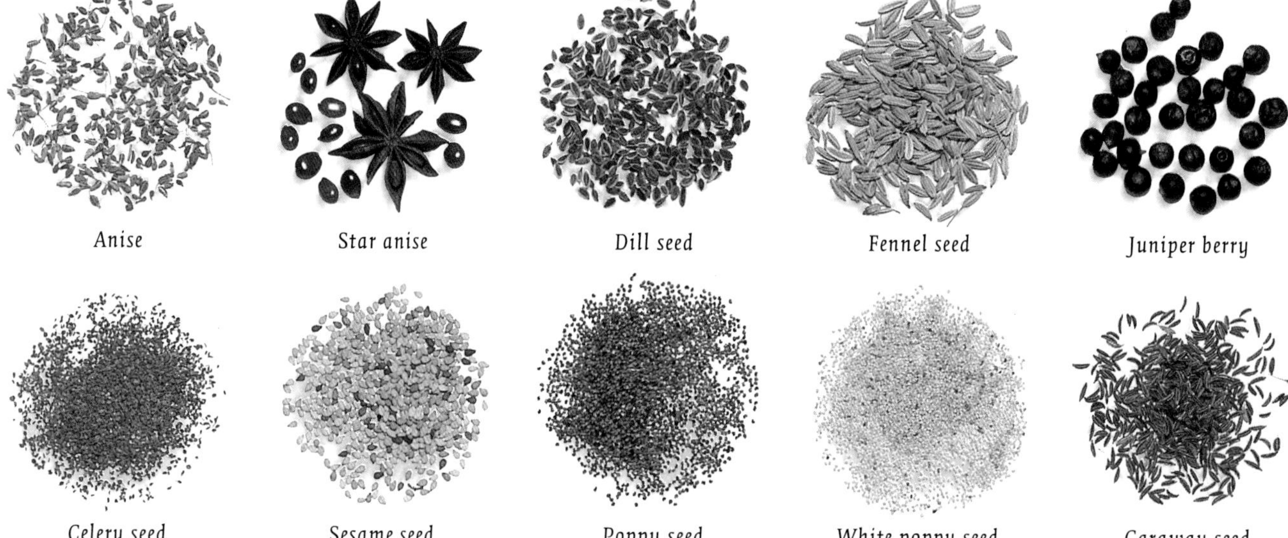

Anise | Star anise | Dill seed | Fennel seed | Juniper berry

Celery seed | Sesame seed | Poppy seed | White poppy seed | Caraway seed ripen, so green and ripe berries appear together. When combined with game, red cabbage, fried pork fillets, stewed rabbit or beef, juniper gives a delicious, rather sombre, spicy background flavour. They are good in pork-based pâté, and in marinades and stuffings for game.

Celery seed (*Apium graveolens*) Although inclined to be bitter, celery seeds give a lift to soups and stews when fresh celery isn't available. They can also go into dishes that combine rice with tomatoes, into savoury bread and into pickling mixtures.

Sesame seed (*Sesamum indicum*) The nutty taste of toasted sesame seeds is probably most familiar topping bread and savoury biscuits, but sesame comes in many guises. Tahina, the oily paste made from finely ground seeds, is used with chick-peas to make hummus, an hors d'oeuvre well known to everyone who has eaten a Middle Eastern meal. Halva, a sweet, compressed, oily bar of crushed sesame seeds, has a delicate scrunch and is good as an unusual dessert. Gomasio – a seasoning popular in macrobiotic cooking – is a Japanese mixture of lightly toasted sesame seeds and sea salt. A delicious Chinese dish is a layer of sesame seeds and ground prawns on bread, deep fried to make an Oriental open sandwich. In the American South, sesame seeds are also called benne seeds (benne is an African name for these seeds, brought to the US by the slaves).

Poppy seed (*Papaver rhoeas*) Although they come from a variety of the opium poppy, there is nothing narcotic about poppy seeds. The blue-grey seeds, scattered over loaves and rolls, add a pretty decoration and have a breadcrumb flavour themselves, warm and dusty. The creamy-yellow poppy seeds used in India are ground to make a floury curry spice that adds texture rather than flavour. Poppy seed chutney, made from the Indian seeds, is delicious freshly made and eaten with all kinds of curry. To make this 'chutney', Mrs Grace Johnson, who wrote for Anglo-Indian Service wives in the 1890s, instructed that 1 tablespoon of poppy seeds fried in ghee (or clarified butter), 2 red chillies, a little tamarind, 2 beads (cloves) of garlic and salt to taste should be pounded well until like a paste.

Caraway seed (*Carum carvi*) It could be the fact that they aid digestion that makes these an ingredient of so much heavy, delicious rye bread. They are also used when making seed cake, with its dry, sandy inside, and treacle sponge – the seeds taste very pleasant with the syrupy part. In Germany caraway is called *kümmel* and gives the typical flavour to the liquor of the same name – a warming and comforting drink. With anise, star anise, fennel and coriander, it also flavours akvavit, the superb but lethal white spirit tossed down in Scandinavia with herrings, crayfish and smoked eel. And there are at least a dozen good cheeses flecked with caraway seeds. However, if you find caraway in a recipe for curry it is probably a mistranslation for cumin, and the confusion is not helped by caraway being known in France as *cumin de prés* – wild cumin – as well as by its correct French name *carvi*.

Clove (*Eugenia caryophyllus*) Cloves have the scent of the Spice Islands, sweet and warm, with a rather numbing quality that has also made them since the earliest days of medicine a sovereign remedy for toothache. They are not, however, particularly pleasant to bite on when found floating in one's dinner, so are usually fixed firmly in an onion – for oxtail stew, jugged hare and other gamey, long-cooked meat dishes – or used ground. Cloves flavour the best bread sauce, spiced beef, hams, pilau rice and curry, and are traditional with cooked apples and pears, in mead, sweet spiced pickles, hot toddies and claret cups. The best cloves are large, dark and plump, and not easily broken.

Cinnamon (*Cinnamomum zeylanicum*) Cinnamon sticks are curled, thin pieces of the bark of a tropical evergreen tree. Use them for flavouring the milk for rice puddings and crème caramel, or put a few pieces in a pilau rice and some curries. The sticks are also used in sweet pickles and in mulled wine.

Ground cinnamon is used in baking – in cinnamon rolls and hot-cross buns – in rum butter and cinnamon toast, and in sweet and savoury spiced dishes all over the Middle East and India. In Italy it appears on doughnuts and in sweet fritters of ricotta cheese, and it has a marvellous affinity with chocolate, a combination particularly liked in Spain and Mexico.

Cassia (*Cinnamomum cassia*) is the inner bark of a relative tree. Mainly produced in China and South-east Asia, it usually

Angostura bitters 207
celery 138
cheeses flavoured with caraway 104–6
cinnamon sugar 211
ghee 100
sesame oil 112
tahina 206
tamarind 199

Apple Fritters 387
Bread Sauce 257
Chinese Belly Pork Salad with Bok Choy 371
Crème Caramel 392
Greek Avgolemono Soup 250
Green Tomato Sour 419
Hummus with Tahina 352
Lamb Korma 289
Pilau Rice 346
Sesame Spinach 372
Spiced Lentils 354

Clove · Ground cinnamon · Allspice

Dried ginger · Fresh ginger · Pickled ginger

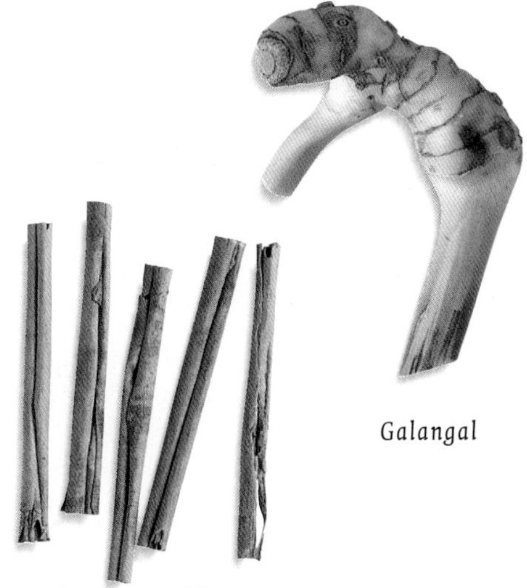

Cinnamon stick

Galangal

chocolate 213
garam masala 196
mignonette pepper 282
salt beef 71

nutmeg grater 224

Braised Pigeons and Cabbage 302
Crème Brûlée 394
Crespolini 341
Custard Pancakes 397
Pâté in a Crust 319
Pumpkin Pie 407
Rich Vanilla Ice-Cream 398
Spinach Gnocchi with Butter and Sage 344
Traditional Custard Tart 407

comes in thicker, harder chunks than cinnamon. Being less delicate, more pungent and less expensive, cassia is better suited to stronger dishes such as spiced meats and curries. Dried cassia buds, which look rather similar to cloves, can be used in much the same ways as the sticks.

Allspice (*Pimenta officinalis*) Allspice, or Jamaica pepper, is a hard brown berry, larger and smoother than a peppercorn. It tastes faintly of cinnamon and strongly of cloves, with a touch of nutmeg, which is why it is sometimes mistakenly thought to be a mixture of spices when it is bought ready ground. It is called *pimienta* in Jamaica, where it is an essential ingredient in jerk seasoning, the spicy paste rubbed on chicken, pork and other meats before grilling them. Pounded, it can go into pâtés, sausages and pork pies, along with coarsely pounded mignonette pepper. It is also used in Christmas cake, in marinades, when pickling pork, with soused herrings and salt beef, and seems to impart something of a peppery as well as a spicy flavour. In autumn when country people make elderberries into a port-like, sweet, dark purple wine, allspice is one of the flavourings used, together with cloves and ginger.

Mace (*Myristica fragrans*) This is the frond-like outer coat, or aril, of the nutmeg, dried to an orange-brown. More delicate than nutmeg, it is invaluable in sausages, pâtés, terrines and pork pies, and in marinades and pickles. Its warm, sweet, spicy flavour is delicious in cakes and puddings, and in Italy it flavours the milk for béchamel and cheese sauces.

Nutmeg (*Myristica fragrans*) Beautifully aromatic, with a warm, slightly bitter flavour, nutmeg is equally at home in sweet and non-sweet dishes. While its pretty outer coating is dried to make mace, the nutmeg or seed is dried slowly in the sun or over charcoal and will keep, whole, for several months and sometimes for years. Buy good-quality, large whole nutmeg rather than ground nutmeg, and grate it as you need it. Use it in sausages, terrines, pâtés and potted meat, in egg dishes, with mashed potatoes and spinach, and in sweet dishes – custards, rice puddings and spiced fruits.

Northern Italians use nutmeg in many of their stuffed pastas, and in India it is a frequent ingredient of garam masala. Nutmeg is also essential in mulled wines, ale and brandy – an excellent sleeping potion, since nutmeg is mildly narcotic.

Vanilla (*Vanilla planifolia*) Vanilla is associated with the exotic because of the drowsy, lotus-eating quality of its perfume. In fact it does have an exotic origin, for it comes from a climbing orchid found in tropical rain forests. It was used to flavour chocolate by the Aztecs, the original chocolate addicts. The vanilla pods are picked unripe, when they are yellow, and are then allowed to cure to a dark brown. When you buy pods they should be somewhat soft, ribbed and pointed at one end, with a frosting of crystals – the vanillin essence. A favourite way of using vanilla pods is to keep them in a jar of sugar, topping up the jar as you use the sugar. Another method, useful when making ice-cream and crème brûlée, is to infuse the bruised or split pod in the milk or cream. The pod imparts a flowery, spicy aroma, and can be gently washed, dried and stored for re-use. There are many easy-to-use substitutes for the vanilla pod, but the only one with a genuine flavour is pure vanilla essence, also called extract, which is extremely concentrated. Vanilla flavouring is synthetic and comes nowhere near the real thing.

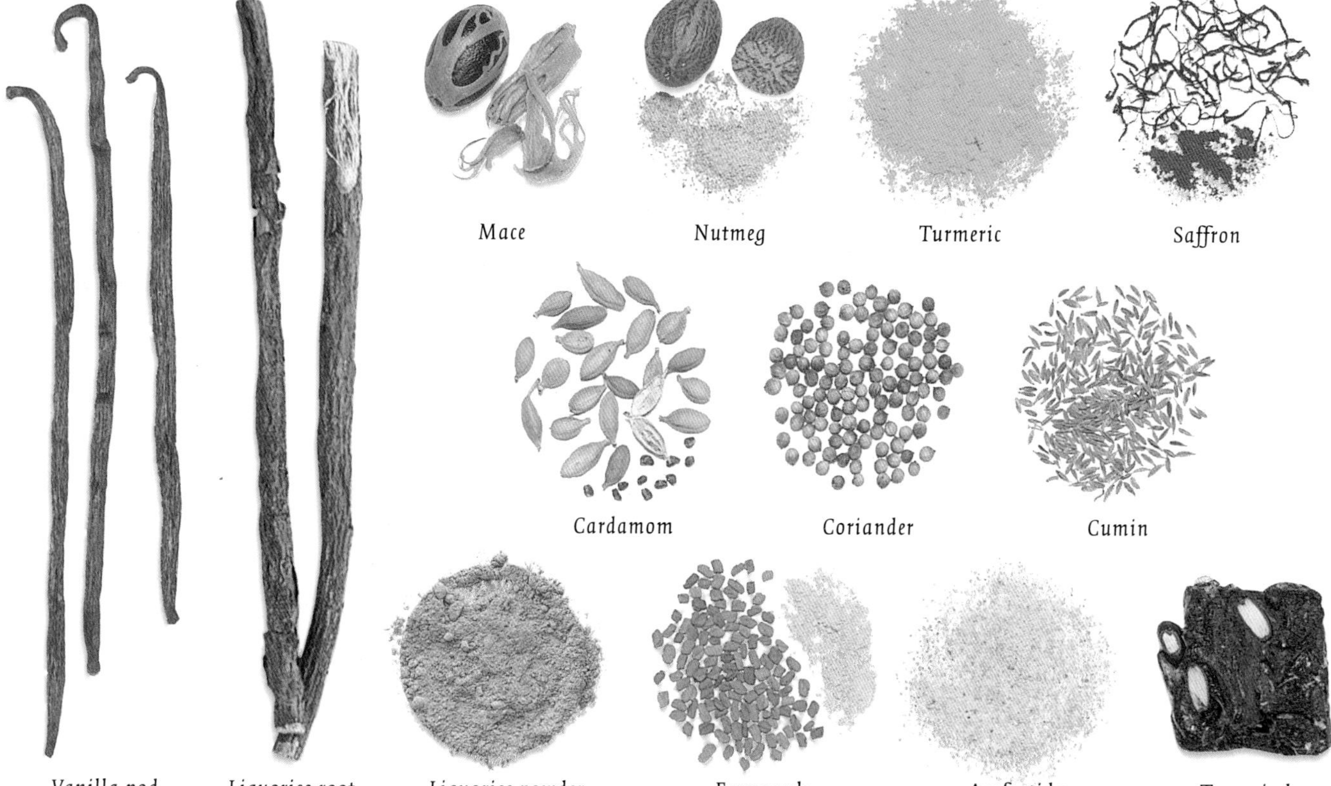

Mace · Nutmeg · Turmeric · Saffron

Cardamom · Coriander · Cumin

Vanilla pod · Liquorice root · Liquorice powder · Fenugreek · Asafoetida · Tamarind

Liquorice (*Glycrriza glabra*) Liquorice root is a natural sweetener and can be made into a strong-flavoured herbal tea. Once given to children to chew instead of sweets, it is supposedly an aphrodisiac, especially for women. Powdered liquorice is used in confectionery.

Ginger (*Zingiber officinale*) This romantic spice is associated with the East. The fresh root (actually a rhizome) is used a great deal in Chinese cooking, with pork, beef, chicken and duck, with fish, prawns and crab. It has a delicious rosemary scent and a crisp texture. In India fresh ginger is a favourite ingredient. Dried root ginger needs to be bruised before it is used to break open its fibres and release the hot flavour. Use it in pickling and to make ginger beer. Powdered ginger – Jamaican is best – goes into ginger biscuits, brandy snaps and gingerbread.

Stem ginger preserved in syrup and packed in Chinese jars goes, with its syrup, into puddings and rhubarb dishes, and over – and sometimes into – ice-cream. **Pickled ginger**, called *gari* in Japan, is made from baby ginger, sliced thinly and cured in vinegar, salt and sugar. It is usually pinky-beige, but may be dyed red. Serve it with sushi or sashimi.

Galangal (*Alpinia galanga*) Galangal, popular in European cooking during the Middle Ages and then forgotten, has recently made a reappearance in Thai and Indonesian supermarkets. An underground rhizome, it takes the place of ginger in Thai cooking. Pounded with lemon grass, chilli, shallots and garlic, it flavours Thai curries and is used, sliced, to spice soups – but don't chew the slices as they release a strong medicinal tang.

Turmeric (*Curcuma longa*) Turmeric has a harsh taste, somehow reminiscent of freshly scrubbed wood, but its colour is indisputably useful – not as golden as saffron, but a deep yellow ochre that turns dishes with dark spices to a warm mahogany colour, and others made with yogurt and pale spices a sharp appetizing yellow. It is delightful with potatoes and other pale vegetables such as cauliflower.

Saffron (*Crocus sativus*) Saffron is fabulously expensive – each red-gold shred is a crocus stigma, and each saffron crocus has only three stigmas to be hand gathered and dried.

It is in Spain that one becomes truly addicted to the flavour of saffron, although it is used a great deal in the south of France for soups, particularly fish soups, and is essential in Milanese risotto. But the Spanish must have it. They like their rice bright yellow, and they have saffron in their fish stews, in vegetable soups, with mussels and prawns. Very little is needed: a pinch soaked in a little warm water or white wine will infuse the liquid with its powerful flavour – which might be described as warm sap, varnish and flowers – and characteristic colour. Saffron is almost always steeped in the liquid with which the dish is cooked, but sometimes, as in certain types of pilau rice, it is stirred in at the end of cooking for a dish of many shades of yellow.

Saffron powder, also expensive and liable to be adulterated, is a substitute for saffron strands. There is a strong Spanish powder, *colorante alimentario* (which contains tartrazine, E102), that adds colour without flavour, for a little economy when making paella.

It is a mistake to substitute saffron and turmeric for each other: saffron is perfect with garlic, fennel, white wine, mussels and fish, while turmeric belongs with vegetables and meat. Both can be used to colour rice.

Cardamom (*Elettaria cardamomum*) Genuine cardamom is costly and has a great many inferior relatives, so it pays to look carefully at what you are buying. The best cardamom pods are the size of peas, pale brown or greenish, and the tiny seeds, when you split a pod open, should be dark, shiny and richly aromatic. The flavour of cardamom is essential in some curries – it has a warm, aromatic but sharp taste, and an anaesthetic effect on the tongue. Sometimes the whole pod is used, but usually the seeds are taken out and freshly ground with other spices. You can buy powdered cardamom, but it has a much more floury flavour than the freshly powdered seeds. In Arab countries cardamom is put into the coffee, which is sweet like Turkish coffee, and in Scandinavian countries it flavours cakes and pastries. White cardamom, once sun-dried, is now more commonly bleached with sulphur dioxide; it is the one to use to flavour hot drinks.

Coriander (*Coriandrum sativum*) These round, brittle, easily crushed seeds are the basis of all that is delicious in home-made curries and vegetables *à la grecque*. They have a warm, faintly orangey fragrance that is much enhanced if they are toasted by gentle heating in a heavy frying pan just before use. Coriander seeds, together with lemon zest, make a delicate and unusual substitute for vanilla in custards and ice-creams, and an excellent flavouring for cooked apples – puréed, or in apple tart or in a pie – and their flavour harmonizes well with lentils.

Cumin (*Cuminum cyminum*) Cumin is an essential spice for the kitchen. Its scent is hard to define: powerful, warm, sweet and slightly oily, but quite unmistakable – which is fortunate, because it looks rather like caraway and the two are often confused. In Spain, cumin is the traditional seasoning for chick-peas; in Mexican cooking it is part of the background in chilli con carne; and in the Canaries it flavours fish soup. In North Africa and countries of the eastern Mediterranean it is used in couscous, on kebabs, with stewed lamb, and to spice rice and vegetable dishes and yogurt. In India it is an inescapable element of every sort of dish. Heating the seeds before grinding releases their aroma and makes them easier to grind.

Fenugreek (*Trigonella foenum-graecum*) Floury, somewhat bitter and smelling of maple or fresh hay, the ground seeds of fenugreek are used in many Indian dishes and are a common ingredient of commercial curry powders and garam masala. The hard seeds need to be lightly roasted before they are ground, but don't over-do it or they become bitter.

Tamarind (*Tamarindus indica*) Sharply sour, the sticky, dried pods of the tamarind tree – also known as Indian dates – are used instead of limes or lemons to add a sour-sweet tang and a bit of body in many Middle Eastern, Indian and South-east Asian dishes. Tamarind makes delicious fresh chutneys. The dried pods are normally shaped into blocks. To obtain tamarind juice, steep the pulp in a bowl of hot water until the sour brown juice can easily be squeezed out or strained. Either vinegar or lemon juice makes a reasonable substitute.

Asafoetida (*Ferula asafoetida*) An ingredient in Indian vegetable dishes, curries and pickles, asafoetida is an evil-smelling resin from equally pungent plants of the giant fennel family. It should be used in exceedingly small quantities, or it can be omitted altogether from recipes that call for it.

coriander 191
crystallized ginger 185
garam masala 196
lemon grass 194
tisanes (herbal teas) 219
Turkish or Greek coffee 216

Chicken with Almonds and Raisins 306
Cornish Saffron Bread 361
Cumin-Spiced Cabbage 374
Gingerbread Men and Women 414
Hot and Sour Shellfish Broth 253
Indian Millet 351
Israeli Falafels 353
Lentil Dhal 355
New Potatoes Baked with Saffron, Cream and Garlic 318
Paella 346
Pilau Rice 346
Rich Vanilla Ice-Cream 398
Saffron Bouillabaisse with Rouille 253
Scallops with Saffron, Basil and Tomato Vinaigrette 279
Soy-Marinated Salmon Brochettes 274
Spiced Marinated Mackerel 266
Steamed Cod with Ginger and Spring Onion 264
Vermicelli Milk Pudding with Cardamom and Saffron 395

Salt and Pepper

brine 422
cooking pulses 126
dégorger 422
ham, bacon and salted pork 68–70
pickled and salted fish 31
salted beef 71
salted roes 31
salting aubergine 153
salting cucumber 155

salt mill 226

Bacon and Egg Tart 327
Boiled Bacon and Sausage with Haricot Beans and Garlic Purée 291
Cold Chicken and Ham Pie 314
Glazed Gammon 292
Green Tomato Sour 419
Salt Cod with Potatoes 274

It has long been considered a measure of a cook's talent as to whether food can be sent perfectly seasoned to the table, and of all the condiments salt and pepper are the cook's greatest allies. But there are two aspects to the proper seasoning of food. One is what goes into the food in the kitchen, the other is what goes on to it at the table.

SALT

One of the properties of salt – which is an invaluable preservative as well as a seasoning – is to draw the moisture out of foods. This is an advantage with vegetables such as aubergines that may have bitter juices; they can be sliced and salted before cooking so that the bitterness is drawn out. Fresh meat, however, should not be salted before frying, grilling or roasting, as the moisture raised on its surface will prevent it from searing and browning; so salt only halfway through cooking, when the surface is seared.

Salt also toughens food, which can be an advantage, for example when pickling with vinegar – food salted before being pickled will not go soft and soggy in the jar. But again this is a disadvantage when braising or stewing meat, and with pulses such as dried beans (start these in unsalted water and do not add salt until at least 15 minutes after they have reached simmering point).

Sea salt This is the best of all salts for both kitchen and table. It is made by evaporating sea water, either naturally by sun and wind or by artificial heat. (Technically, sea salt gained by natural evaporation is called bay salt, but the two terms have become interchangeable.) The result is large crystals of pure salt that retain their natural iodine and have no bitter after-taste. They can be sprinkled directly on to food or ground in a salt mill or wooden mortar. This is also the salt to sprinkle over certain breads, rolls and pretzels before they go into the oven – the crystals dissolve so slowly that they will still be a sparkling presence after baking. Fine sea salt is the best to use in cooking.

Sel gris This coarse, greyish, unrefined French sea salt contains traces of other minerals. Preferred by some discerning cooks, it is for kitchen use rather than at table.

Kosher salt This is widely used in the United States by cooks who prefer its flavour (it is half as salty per volume as common salt) and its coarse-grained, flaky texture. It contains no additives.

Common salt Ordinary domestic salt is made by dissolving the salt found in underground deposits (formed by the drying up of ancient seas) and then drying it in a vacuum. It can be coarse-grained for kitchen use or refined into table salt, in which case it has to be coated with magnesium carbonate or some other additive to prevent it absorbing moisture from the air and to keep it free-flowing. This type of salt, although useful because it can be sprinkled finely, has a decidedly bitter after-taste, but it is better than any other salt for baking.

Iodized salt This is domestic salt to which iodine has been added. It is useful in areas where the water and soil are lacking in this essential trace element.

Rock salt Known in France as *sel-gemme*, this is a hard, coarse, crystalline salt that needs a salt mill or mortar to make it manageable. At its best, it can be the finest flavoured of all the salts, but it must not be confused with non-edible freezing salt, also called rock salt, which is often used in the United States when making home-made ice-creams in an ice-cream freezer.

Block salt Also known as cut lump salt, this is pure, refined rock salt. It is good for all cooking and is the salt to use for pickling, because it has no additives that might spoil the clarity of the pickling liquid. Other names for it are pickling and dairy salt.

Seasoned salts Salts such as garlic salt and celery salt contain extracts of the vegetable – and, in the case of celery salt, the seeds – that give the salt its name, but they add an instantly recognizable 'package' flavour so often found in convenience foods. Many seasoned salts contain flavouring agents plus monosodium glutamate.

Monosodium glutamate The sodium salt of glutamic acid, MSG is a chemical that 'wakes up the palate'. It accentuates other flavours already present in the food and is used extensively in Chinese cooking, but it is a lazy way of giving flavour to food. It can cause palpitations, hot flushes and other allergic reactions.

Saltpetre This is potassium nitrate, a preservative that has been used in the making of brines and dry salt curing mixtures for hundreds of years. It has the culinary quality of turning meat a beautiful pink – in France, many restaurateurs put a pinch of saltpetre in their pâté to keep it a wholesome rosy colour. Potassium nitrate and/or sodium nitrate – a similar preservative – is often present in bacon, ham, sausages, salt beef, salami and so on.

PEPPER

The vine that gives us peppercorns and the pepper or capsicum plants that give us chilli powders, cayenne and paprika are not related, although all these

Crystal sea salt

Fine sea salt

Sel gris

Iodized salt

Rock salt

Kosher salt

seasonings add a pungent heat when added to food.

Ready-ground pepper soon tastes dull and dusty, and inferior brands are sometimes adulterated with such things as powdered date stones, so buy whole peppercorns – they should be evenly coloured, aromatic, free from dust and too hard to be crushed between the fingers. Nothing could be easier than keeping a pepper mill in the kitchen and on the table, and the aroma and flavour of freshly ground pepper, black or white, is quite different from the dry smell and taste of the prepared product.

Peppers vary in pungency and size of peppercorn. Usually they are called after their place of origin – Malabar black, for instance, is one of the best of the black peppercorns. Tellicherry and Lampung are also excellent. Mignonette or shot pepper is a mixture of coarsely crushed black and white peppercorns.

Black peppercorn The dried, shrivelled berries of the pepper vine, *Piper nigrum*, these are picked before they are quite ripe and dried in the sun, where they blacken within a day or two.

White peppercorn These are the ripened berries, soaked, rubbed to remove their husks and then dried. White pepper is slightly less warm and spicy than black pepper, and has a drier smell. It is used in pale soups or sauces, where black specks would spoil the appearance.

Green peppercorn Under-ripe pepper berries, these are milder than dried black peppercorns and have a nice crisp texture. Picked when green, they become black within a day or two and so are rarely found fresh. Freeze-dried and canned green peppercorns in brine, however, are a good substitute. Use them in a sauce for lamb, steak or duck, in pâtés and fish terrines, and with shellfish.

Pink peppercorn (*Schinus terebinthifolius*) Not true pepper but the berries of another tree, these are more subtle than green peppercorns and with little of the hotness associated with pepper. They are much used in the south of France in fish dishes, particularly with red mullet. Preserved in vinegar or water and sold in jars, or freeze-dried, they are quite soft and lend themselves to being mashed.

Sichuan pepper, Szechwan pepper The dried red berries of a small shrub (*Xanthoxylum piperitum*), this spice comes from the Sichuan region in China. Sometimes called anise pepper, it has a peculiar delayed reaction: nothing happens when you bite it, then it floods your mouth with a strong, hot flavour.

Chilli powder and flakes These are dried and ground or crushed chillies, usually red, but also black. Powders can be pungent, mild, tasty or absolutely red-hot, and only by experience can you know what you are getting. Once you have found a good source or brand, or made your own powder or flakes at home by grinding or crushing dried chillies, and have the measure of it – knowing how much or how little to add – it is a good idea to stick to it or you may give yourself some unpleasant surprises. Use chilli powder in curry and chilli con carne, with beans and chick-peas and in couscous (although authentically for couscous you should use harissa, a very hot Tunisian mixture of crushed dried chillies, ground cumin and salt). You can also buy chilli powders that contain spices such as cumin and oregano, made specifically for chilli con carne. Chilli flakes, also called crushed chillies, can be used to heat tomato sauces, and will give a lift to many stir-fried and sautéed dishes. They are excellent combined with garlic and anchovies and used to flavour pasta; quickly fried slices of pork fillet are also splendid with this mixture.

Cayenne pepper Made from ground dried chillies (both pod and seeds are used), cayenne pepper came originally from Cayenne in French Guiana. The red-orange powder is very hot and rather delicious. It is used in dishes such as devilled turkey, with devilled almonds, and in the gravy served with roast wildfowl, particularly mallard.

Paprika Although it may be either sweet or hot, paprika by nature has a sweet flavour and is made from sweet red peppers. In Spain and Portugal it is used in fish stews and with salt cod, as well as in most of the chorizos and salsichas. But it is in Hungary that paprika really comes into its own, so the best to buy is the original mild Hungarian paprika, described as 'noble and sweet'.

chilli pepper 152
five-spice powder 196
garam masala 196
mignonette pepper 282
quatre épices 196
sweet pepper 152

pepper mill 226

Pâté de Campagne 318
Peppered Steak 282
Roast Haunch of Venison with Pepper Sauce 294
Spiced Marinated Mackerel 266

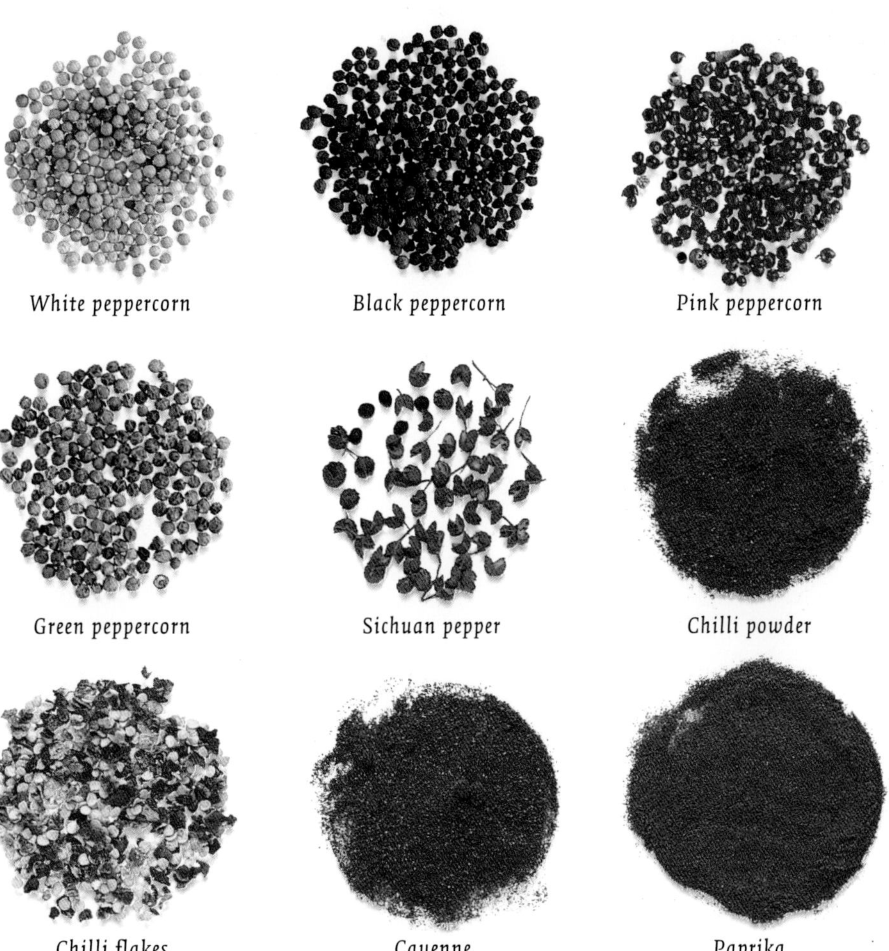

White peppercorn — Black peppercorn — Pink peppercorn

Green peppercorn — Sichuan pepper — Chilli powder

Chilli flakes — Cayenne — Paprika

Mustard

green peppercorn 201
mustard and cress 131
mustard greens 133
mustard seed oil 113

Cumberland Game Sauce 260
Green Tomato Sour 419
Horseradish Sauce 258
Kidneys with Mustard 293
Mayonnaise 259
Vinaigrette 259

Mustard has been adding its hot spiciness to food for thousands of years – the ancient Egyptians and the Greeks and Romans used to crunch the seeds between their teeth during meals, and the Romans used mustard to preserve vegetables – their pickled turnips in mustard were the forerunners of fierce piccalilli.

In the course of time, it was discovered that mustard helps the digestion, and it came to be eaten particularly with pork dishes and with cheese, which was thought to 'sit heavy on the stomach'. It had a place in home medicine, too: hot mustard poultices were applied to relieve aching joints, and sportsmen, when they came home cold and wet from the hunt, used to thrust their feet into a comforting mustard bath to ward off chills.

Mustard as we know it is basically a paste made from the ground seeds of black mustard (*Brassica nigra*), or brown (*B. juncea*), and white mustard (*B. hirta*), which is also called yellow mustard. *Nigra* is hot; *hirta* is cooler.

It is *hirta* that, when young, gives us the tender mustard greens for mustard and cress sandwiches, and, when mature, yields the seeds that are used whole in pickling. The brown variety, also called Indian mustard, is less pungent than *nigra*. It is the seed that is usually called for in recipes for Indian dishes, along with black mustard seeds. And although black mustard seeds were traditionally used in European mustards, they have mostly been replaced by the brown seeds today.

French mustards

The most famous of these are the mustards of Dijon, Bordeaux and Meaux.

In Dijon, mustard centre of the world, the mustard is blended with salt, spices and white wine or verjuice – an acid juice made from unripe green grapes. Some Dijon mustards rival English mustard in strength, but can be distinguished from it by their creamy grey-lemon colour and by a more subtle flavour. Other Dijon mustards are milky pale and delicate rather than sharp. The famous house of Poupon – one of the sights of Dijon – sells dozens of different blends and exports them all over the world.

Most cooks use Dijon mustard in preference to any other: for vinaigrettes, for mayonnaise (which mustard helps to emulsify), for the more delicate creamy sauces to go with kidneys, egg dishes and chicken or fish. As a general rule, when mustard is called for in a recipe it is safe to use a strong Dijon, such as Grey Poupon.

Blended with unfermented claret, Bordeaux mustard is strong, dark brown and both more acid and more aromatic than that of Dijon. It is unsurpassed for eating with steak, complementing rather than overpowering the flavour of the meat. When you are offered a choice of French or English mustard in a restaurant, the French variety is almost certainly Bordeaux, the darkest of them all and the one that differs most, in looks and taste, from the hot, gamboge-coloured English type.

Moutarde de Meaux is an interesting mixture of ground and half-ground seeds, with a grainy texture and an attractive musty taste. It is pleasantly hot, and was described by Brillat-Savarin – the eighteenth-century French *bon viveur* – as 'the gourmet's mustard'. It comes in wide-mouthed stoneware jars, their corks secured by sealing wax, and is made to a formula that has been a closely guarded secret since 1760, when it was handed by the abbots of Meaux to the Pommery family, of Champagne fame. The most superior of the coarse-grained mustards, with a taste all its own, it is best appreciated when eaten with humble food – sausages, bacon, cold meats and pork pies – and it makes an interesting addition to a French dressing.

There are, of course, a thousand other French mustards: sometimes tarragon is added, or a mixture of fresh herbs (which produces a pleasant-tasting but rather alarming-looking green result); there is a red-brown mustard containing tomato purée; and a mustard that is basically mild, but with the bite of crushed green peppercorns, called *moutarde au poivre vert*.

English mustard

Its colour is a hot yellow, it is made of blended seeds, finely ground, and its taste is biting and hot, good with plain English food. For its texture we owe a debt to an eighteenth-century housewife from Durham, who decided to grind and sift her mustard seeds rather than simply pound them. She took her new 'mustard flour' to London, where it was taken up by George I and commercial production soon followed. Mr Colman began milling his mustard powder in 1814.

Today you can buy Colman's mustard in powder form or – more convenient but perhaps not as good – ready-mixed. A straightforward blend of ground and sifted seeds, wheat flour and spices, it contains no wine or vinegar to lessen the natural impact of the seeds.

To mix 'common' English mustard, simply add an equal quantity of cold water to the powder – the water must never be hot or it will release bitter oils that spoil the taste. To be at its best, the mustard should be freshly made up in a small quantity – ¼ teaspoon of mixed mustard per person is usually sufficient. Allow it to stand, well covered, for about half an hour before use, to develop its full flavour and heat.

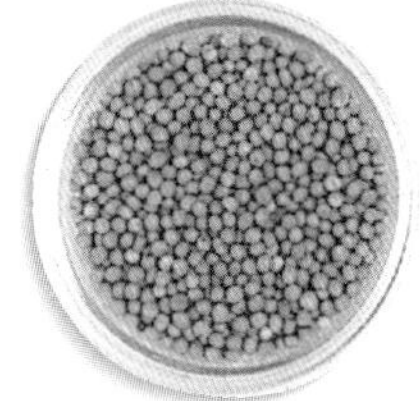
White mustard seed

Black mustard seed

Dijon mustard

Dijon mustard with tarragon

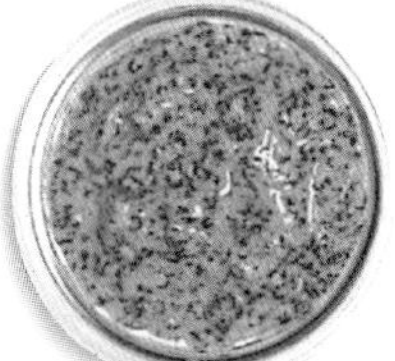
Moutarde de Meaux

Bordeaux mustard

French mustard with tomato

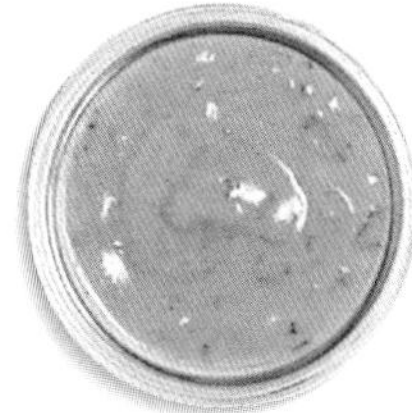
German mustard with herbs

To make a milder mustard, use 1 teaspoon each of milk and cream and a few grains of sugar to 2 teaspoons each of mustard powder and water. To make a thick Tewkesbury-type mustard, which has a delicate flavour and a biting after-taste, moisten the powder with wine vinegar, grape or apple juice, or with claret or ale.

Common English mustard is perfect with roast beef, its classic partner, as well as with other plain roast meat, gammon and ham, pork pie and beef or pork sausages. It goes well with Cheddar cheese (especially in Welsh rarebit) and it is the proper mustard to use when making strong mustard sauce to go with richly flavoured oily fish such as herring or mackerel. But simmered for any length of time in dishes that call for mustard, even English mustard loses some of its taste and piquancy, and in fact mustard sauces of all types benefit from being given a boost of a little more mustard shortly before the end of cooking.

German mustards

Made from a blend of strong mustard flour and vinegar, German mustard – *senf* – generally combines pungency with aroma, and comes halfway between hot, sharp English mustard and the earthy, aromatic flavour of that of Bordeaux mustard. In northern Germany it is ladled out by the spoonful. Stronger palates go for mustard that is *scharf* or *extra scharf* – hot or extra hot.

A lot of mustard is consumed in Germany: it is specifically designed to be eaten with the profusion of sausages of the frankfurter type – knackwurst, bockwurst and of course with frankfurters themselves. So it is not surprising that the Bavarians and other southern Germans, whose pale local sausage is made of veal and called weisswurst, have a mild, pale mustard to go with it: coarse-grained and sweet, it is just right for this bland sausage, which is eaten fried to a golden colour.

So fond is Germany of the condiment that there is even a mustard called Diätssenf – dietetic mustard – that is green and devoid of salt, made for people on salt-free diets.

American mustards

Owing to the wide range of national tastes, every kind of mustard, plain and spiced, can be found in American supermarkets. What is thought of as the true American mustard, however, is yellow (coloured with turmeric), mild and sweet, and has a consistency rather more like a thick sauce than a mustard. It is made from white mustard seeds and is flavoured with sugar, vinegar or white wine, which accounts for its cool character and for the fact that it can be applied in such quantities to hot dogs and hamburgers.

This mustard can be used when making mayonnaise, to give a sweetish mustard flavour. Such mayonnaise is good in salads that contain hard-boiled eggs – potato salad and tuna fish salad being the two main candidates.

A German-style mustard, brown, sweet/sour and spicy, is also very popular in the US, particularly on ham sandwiches.

Mustard preserves

Mostarda di frutta, mostarda di Cremona This is an Italian confection of fruits – figs and cherries, and chunks of pears, lemons and peaches – candied in a syrup containing mustard oil. Enjoyed in Italy from about the sixteenth century on, it is still eaten, like jam, by the spoonful on bread. Its delicate, strange, sweet-sharp flavour makes it an interesting relish for cold and hot meats, particularly boiled beef tongue and zampone (stuffed pig's trotter). *Bollito misto* – mixed boiled chicken, ham, sausage and beef – can be served with *mostarda* on the side.

Mostarda di Voghera Even more special is a mostarda of whole, translucent pale pears, complete with their stalks, in a jar that looks as if it might float off the table; the taste is ethereal too. Eat them with game, particularly game pie or roasted hare or venison, and with the same meats as the *mostarda di frutta*. This also comes as a yellow-brown mush – a less extravagant version.

Piccalilli is a strong mustard pickle with a crunch to it. It includes cauliflower, onions, chillies, ginger and plenty of turmeric to colour it a gorgeous bright yellow. Eaten with pork pie and cold ham, it is very refreshing, cutting the fattiness of the meat.

Making your own mustard

Experimenting with your own blends can be interesting. To grind the seeds, use a small coffee grinder (clean it very well after use) or spice grinder – or, for a coarser mixture, simply pound them in a mortar with a pestle.

The first time you make your own mustard, use equal amounts of black or brown and white seeds and, if necessary, gradually alter the balance according to taste. Moisten the ground mustard with water until just saturated, then add white wine vinegar, salt and the flavourings of your choice – tarragon, green peppercorns, horseradish, honey, etc – and leave to ferment for several days. A little olive oil takes the edge off a hot mixture. Store in a cork-topped jar in a cool larder or in the refrigerator.

To enjoy all mustards at their best, they should be used fairly rapidly. Store them in the refrigerator once opened, and do not keep longer than 3–4 months.

sausages and salamis 72–8
turmeric 199

coffee grinder 226, 239
pestle and mortar 226

Boston Baked Beans 354
Mustard Sauce 256

Hot German mustard

Bavarian mustard

American mild mustard

American spicy brown mustard

Green peppercorn mustard

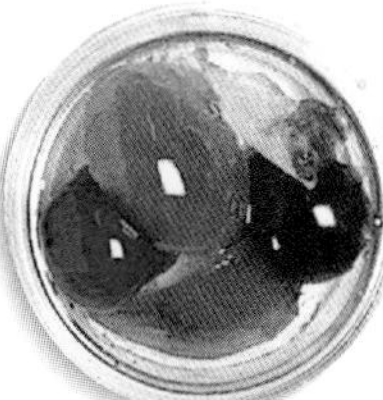
Mostarda di frutta

Ready-made English mustard

English mustard powder

Vinegar

apple 162

Béarnaise Sauce 255
Cider Barbecue Sauce 257
Hollandaise Sauce 255
Horseradish Sauce 258
Lemon Court-Bouillon with Parsley 245
Mayonnaise 259
Mint Sauce 258
Rabbit with Prunes and Red Wine 297
Scallops with Saffron, Basil and Tomato Vinaigrette 279
Sweet Pepper Chutney 419
Vinaigrette 259

***Vinaigre*, the French word for vinegar, means sour wine, and this is what wine vinegar is, being produced by an acid fermentation of fresh wine. By the same process, malt vinegar is made from malt liquor, cider vinegar from cider, and Chinese and Japanese vinegars from fermented rice.**

'The grateful acid', as vinegar was called in the seventeenth century, has had its abuses. In Elizabethan days salads were served dressed in malt vinegar – a condiment much loved by the British – without benefit of either salt or oil. But things have improved. Although vinegary pickles still go well with rich foods such as cold roast pork, the biting character of vinegar has been tempered – by the increased use of wine vinegar, which is an altogether milder affair than malt vinegar, by reducing the quantity of vinegar used in salad dressings and increasing the proportion of oil, and sometimes by the increased use of sugar. (If you want to avoid using sugar in salad dressing, use balsamic vinegar as a base for the dressing or mix red or white wine vinegar half and half with wine of the same colour.)

Apart from its role in salad dressings, vinegar can be used instead of lemon juice in mayonnaise, hollandaise and béarnaise, and is essential in mint and horseradish sauces. It is used in marinades for meat and game, and a little vinegar can improve the flavour of stews and Welsh rarebit. A dash of vinegar can work wonders with a dull sauce. A little vinegar in the water when steaming food stops the pan from discolouring, but vinegar is corrosive, so when cooking with vinegar use stainless steel, glass, earthenware or enamelled pots.

Good vinegars are always worth their price. Cheap vinegars are usually inferior and frequently synthetic, i.e. made from non-brewed or fermented malt liquor.

Wine vinegar The best wine vinegar is made by a slow, gentle process (called the Orléans method) that allows it to mature naturally. The wine vinegars from Orléans are expensive but still probably the best and purest. Wine vinegar can be red or white and is sometimes very powerful, but it has a delicious flavour. If it is stronger than you like, dilute it, for salad dressing, with wine of the same colour.

If you are offered a 'vinegar mother', accept it with alacrity. It is a fungus that lives in wine and will turn all your leftover wine into excellent vinegar. Keep the 'mother' in a warm place in an earthenware jar with a loose-fitting lid, so that air can get in, and add wine as often as you have it to spare. If it is not very active, feed it a large dose of wine and a pinch of sugar.

When the wine vinegar smells sharp and strongly acetic, decant it carefully into a bottle and let it stand for a month to mature and mellow before using it. Red wine seems to produce the best-flavoured vinegar, but that made from white wine is more useful in mayonnaise and even in most vinaigrettes because the red turns them a curious pink colour.

Cider vinegar If we are to believe all we read about it, cider vinegar is a cure for all ills, from indigestion to hair loss. As a seasoning, it has a strong, distinctive taste of cider and in sharpness is mid-way between wine vinegar and malt vinegar. Use it when making pickles and fruit chutneys, especially those with apples in them, and for a refreshing vinaigrette to use with fresh tomatoes.

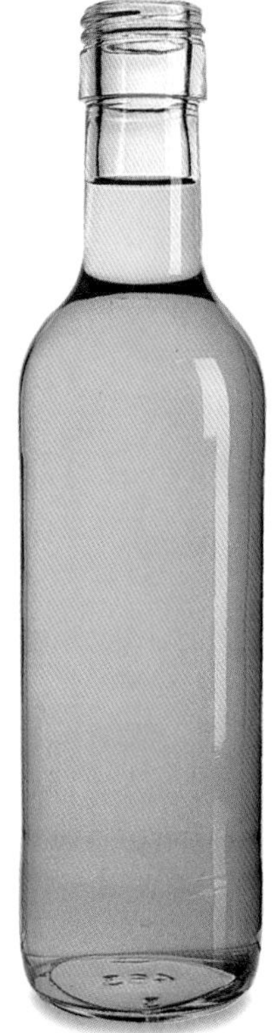
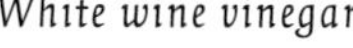

White wine vinegar

Red wine vinegar

Balsamic vinegar

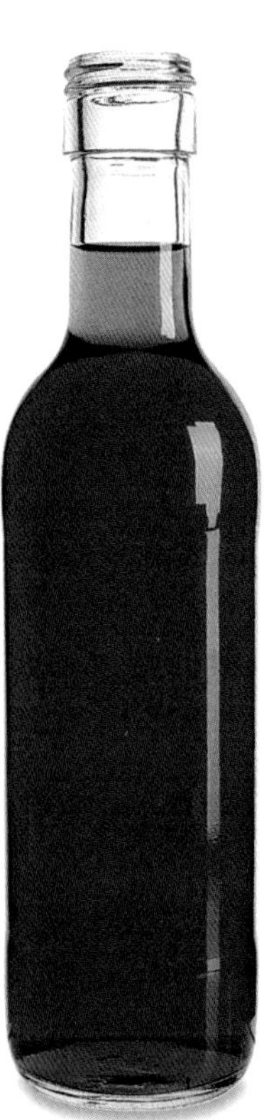

Sherry vinegar

Raspberry vinegar

Malt vinegar Brewed from malted barley, malt vinegar is coloured with caramel to varying shades of brown. (Originally, a deep brown colour indicated a well-matured vinegar, since it was kept in oak barrels that coloured the clear vinegar as it aged.) The best malt vinegar, with an acetic acid content of at least 5 per cent, is excellent for pickling. This is also the best vinegar with fish and chips.

Distilled vinegar Being colourless, this is often labelled white vinegar. It is the vinegar to use for pickling silver onions and for any pickling when colour is important.

Spirit vinegar This is strong and slightly alcoholic – flavoured with lemon, it makes a good addition to a vinaigrette.

Sherry vinegar A delicious vinegar made from sweet sherry, this varies in strength of flavour – a good quality one is worth its place in the kitchen and can be used instead of balsamic vinegar for a slightly drier result. Sherry vinegar used half and half with lemon juice in a vinaigrette gives a nutty taste, almost like walnut oil. French chefs sometimes use sherry vinegar in *poulet au vinaigre*.

Balsamic vinegar A traditional farm-made vinegar from the Modena region of Italy, this is made from the must (the unfermented concentrated juice) of white Trebbiano grapes, boiled until thick and then matured in barrels. Each year for about 5 years, as it reduces in volume by evaporation, it is moved to a smaller barrel made from a different wood; oak, chestnut, mulberry, hornbeam and cherry are favourites. Then it may be left to age for a further 5 years, or for up to as many as 50 years. Sweet, dark brown, highly concentrated and mellow, balsamic vinegar was traditionally used sparingly, and often for medicinal purposes. It is exquisite on salads, cold vegetables, both cooked and raw, on fish and shellfish and on raw steak carpaccio. True balsamic vinegar is expensive; look for '*Aceto Balsamico di Modena Tradizionale*' as there are many imitations.

Rice vinegar This features in Japanese and South-east Asian cooking, where its sweet, delicate flavour is used in *sushi* – vinegared rice – dishes. In China rice vinegar may be 'black', with a rich, smoky, complex flavour; clear pale red, when it is slightly tart; or white and mild – the vinegar for sweet and sour dishes. However, 'black vinegar' may also be made from grains, wheat, millet or sorghum. There is also a sweet rice vinegar that is very dark, thick and aromatic.

Flavoured vinegars Wine vinegar can be flavoured by putting fresh herbs – tarragon, basil, mint, thyme, burnet, for example – into a jar, covering the herb with vinegar and keeping it in a warmish place such as a warm kitchen for a week, giving the jar an occasional shake. Then decant the vinegar, keeping a token sprig of herb to show what's what. Tarragon makes the best home-flavoured vinegar. About 3 good sprigs of fresh herb to 1 litre/scant 2 pints of wine vinegar is ample. Fruits such as raspberries can be used to flavour vinegar in the same way.

To make garlic vinegar, crush the garlic and leave it in the vinegar for 24 hours; use garlic vinegar for salad dressings when sharp flavours such as anchovies and capers are included. For a really good chilli vinegar, the dried chillies need steeping for 10 days, and the jar should be given a daily shake: use chilli vinegar with shellfish, especially lobster salad.

barley 116
chilli pepper 152
garlic 145
herbs 190–3
raspberry 171
rice 116–17

Green Tomato Sour 419
Herb Vinaigrette with Balsamic Vinegar 259
Hot and Sour Shellfish Broth 253
Slow-Cooked Brisket of Beef with Soy, Sake and Oysters 284

Tarragon vinegar

Rice vinegar

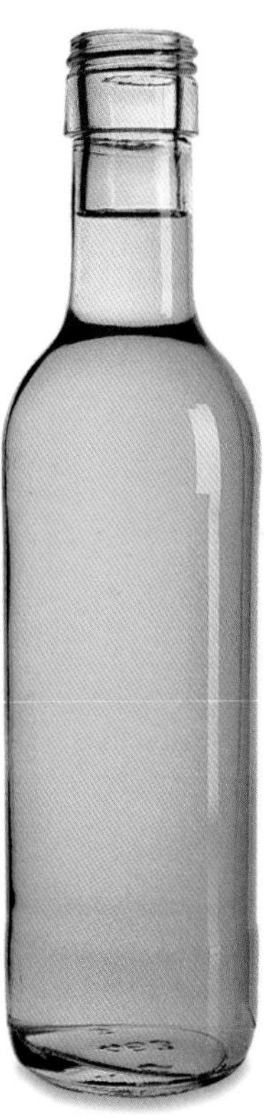
Cider vinegar

Distilled vinegar

Malt vinegar

Sauces, Flavourings and Colourings

anchovy 16
chilli pepper 152
plum 169
sesame seed 197
tamarind 199
tomato 150–1

Chinese Belly Pork Salad with Bok Choy 371
Cider Barbecue Sauce 257
Egg Mousse 327
Hummus with Tahina 353
Marinated Thai Prawns 278
White Devil 312

There is no dispute that sauces, relishes and other condiments are best made at home, but in a busy world it is not possible to brew great batches of ketchups, to crack the secret formula of Worcestershire sauce, or to find the time to extract the essence from an anchovy.

Sauces, ketchups and pastes

Some store-bought sauces have withstood the tests of time and changing tastes, and are to be found in almost every kitchen.

Tomato ketchup This must head the list. Properly made, it is thick and clotted in appearance. It should be bright red and contain no artificial colouring. Home-made ketchup is delicious, of course, but only viable if you grow your own tomatoes; failing this, Heinz make irreproachable ketchup from pure ingredients.

Tomato purée, tomato paste Used in cooking rather than at table, this is highly concentrated – a tablespoonful will improve the taste and texture of Mediterranean casseroles and provide sticky melting juices for Greek braised lamb, a teaspoonful will brighten a sad-looking sauce.

Walnut and mushroom ketchups These were once highly popular condiments. Walnut ketchup used to flavour stews and cheese dishes, while mushroom ketchup came into its own when the menu included a robust sort of meat or a none-too-delicate fish. They are both good used with restraint in dark, savoury sauces, in hearty dishes such as steak and kidney pies and in onion sauce for grilled beef steak.

Worcestershire sauce There is only one true variety, which is of Indian origin, although there are many types of this concoction, including the 'steak' sauces. The real thing is hot, spicy and vinegary and contains tamarind, molasses, sugar, anchovies, garlic, salt and other natural flavours. Besides adding its own ineffable taste, Worcestershire sauce heightens the flavour of whatever is being cooked. It is wonderful in devil sauces, in sauces for reheating cold meat, and in tomato juice. It is essential for a good Bloody Mary.

Harvey sauce More of a relish than a sauce, this includes anchovies, garlic, soy, cayenne and vinegar. It is used in the same ways as Worcestershire sauce.

Chilli sauce Thick and bright red, this can vary considerably in hotness. It is often called Chinese or Sichuan chilli sauce or by its Malaysian name, *sambal oelek*. Use sparingly in stews and as a dip for Chinese and South-east Asian food.

Tabasco sauce An exceedingly hot, peppery liquid made from vinegar, red chillies and salt. The label suggests a multitude of uses: soup, gravy, breakfast eggs, even milk, and insists 'no seafood to be eaten without it'.

Oyster sauce A flavouring used a great deal by the Chinese, this is a thick, brown sauce made with oysters cooked in soy sauce and brine. One of its classic uses is in Cantonese pork-filled dumplings.

Hoisin sauce This anise-flavoured, sweet and spicy, red-brown sauce is, like soy sauce, soya-bean based. The texture varies from a thick, creamy sludge to a sauce that can be poured, and the flavour is inclined to be overpowering, containing as it does garlic, chillies and several spices. However, it is used to advantage, mixed with sugar and sesame oil, with Peking duck, being spread over the pancakes before the cucumber, sping onions and shredded duck are placed on top.

Plum sauce Thick and sweet-tart, this sauce is made from plums preserved with chilli, ginger, vinegar, sugar and spices. It is a popular ingredient in Chinese cookery.

Fish sauce This is made by fermenting barrels of small fish (often anchovies) in brine for several months under the tropical sun. The end result is a strange-smelling, salty brown liquid, highly nutritious, which is a major element of the cooking of South-east Asia. It is called *nam pla* in Thailand and *nuoc cham* or *nuoc mam* in Vietnam and Laos. Fish sauce is mixed with garlic, lime juice, sugar and chilli oil to make a wonderful dipping sauce for fried foods or dumplings. It can be dashed into every kind of food as a sort of alternative seasoning for those who become particularly hooked on the flavour.

Anchovy essence A thick, pinkish sauce, this was once widely used to flavour any kind of savoury dish; now its salty taste cheers up fish pies and sauces. Use it sparingly: a few drops suffice. Mixed with soy sauce it can be used as a substitute for the powerful fish sauces called for in Thai cooking.

Anchovy paste Sold in pots or tubes, this can be spread very thinly on hot buttered toast or used in a sauce for fish.

Shrimp paste Made in Malaysia and Indonesia from dried, salted, fermented shrimp, this paste, called *blachan* or *terasi*, is sold in blocks and cut off in slices to be blended with other ingredients. The pieces may first be wrapped in foil and toasted or fried in a little oil to bring out the flavour. A typical sauce using shrimp paste might contain chopped chillies, spring onions, hoisin sauce and sugar, all fried briefly in oil. This would be served with stir-fried beef. A Chinese version of shrimp paste is the consistency of a thick sauce.

Tahina This is a Middle Eastern, Turkish and Greek staple. A thick, oily beige paste made from ground toasted sesame seeds, tahina resembles medium-fine peanut butter in texture, being rich and dense. It forms the basis of several delicious *mezze*, including hummus and a simple dip of tahina, parsley, garlic and lemon juice.

Tomato purée | Tomato ketchup | Chilli sauce | Anchovy paste

Shrimp paste | Fish sauce | Hoisin sauce | Tahina

Wasabi, Japanese horseradish
Unrelated to our horseradish, although also a member of the cabbage family, grated or powdered wasabi root makes the eye-watering accompaniment that gives *sashimi* such a fresh lift. Powdered wasabi, available from Japanese supermarkets, is mixed with water to make the familiar stiff paste, used – in quite small quantities – together with soy sauce. Wasabi paste is also sold in tubes, but the fresh root is only found in Japan.
Angostura bitters Originally created as a remedy for fever as it contains quinine, Angostura bitters are clove-scented, spiced and pink in colour. Found more often in the bar than in the kitchen, this bitter liquid can do a great deal more than flavour champagne cocktails and tint gin pink. In cooking, it makes a good contribution to several sauces, particularly mustard sauce and tarragon sauce, and a few drops will improve such nourishing mainstays as shepherd's pie, beef stew or baked beans. Oddly enough it can also be good sprinkled into fruit salad.
Soy sauce True soy sauce is a thin liquid distilled from a naturally fermented mixture of soya beans, wheat or barley flour and water. Most commercially prepared brands are chemically fermented from defatted soya bean pulp. When selecting soy sauce, shake the bottle vigorously until bubbles form at the top: naturally fermented soy will form a thick, foamy head that takes quite a while to disperse.

Good soy sauce has a rich aroma and a flavour both salty and pungent. It heightens the flavour of whatever is being eaten with it. In China and Japan it is a staple condiment, used extensively in cooking and at the table in place of salt. In Western cooking it has become a common ingredient in marinades and barbecue sauces.
Tamari is a pure, naturally fermented soy sauce complete with nutritious oils and free from artificial colouring and flavourings.
Light soy sauce, sometimes labelled 'superior soy' is salty, while **dark soy sauce** is thick and sweet. Use light soy for cooking, and dark soy for dipping.
Miso tastes much like soy sauce but is a fermented paste made from soya beans. It is used in oriental cooking to make soups and to enrich sauces.
Teriyaki marinade, which can be bought ready made in bottles, is a mixture of soy sauce, sugar, ginger and spices.

Chutneys and pickles

Chutney The Indian word *chatni* means literally 'to lick something in small amounts', and chutneys form an important part of every meal in India and accompany most basic curries. We are used to seeing chutneys in jars, but they are often freshly made, from a wide range of ingredients. One of the most popular chutneys is mango chutney, which comes in several different guises, some hot, some sweet, but all made from green, unripe mangoes.
Pickles These consist of vegetables and fruits – just one kind or a mixture – preserved in a seasoned and often highly spiced vinegar. Like chutney, they are mainly eaten as a condiment. Commonly pickled vegetables include cucumbers, peppers, beetroots, onions and red cabbage. Other foods that are pickled are ginger and radishes (both popular in Japan), walnuts and herring.
Capers These little green flower buds, pickled or salted, are both a seasoning and a condiment. They are an essential part of Italian and Provençal cooking. Use capers in any sharp sauce to be eaten with fish or tongue, such as *salsa verde*, or with black butter and lemon juice as a sauce for skate. Steak tartare would be almost unthinkable without its seasoning of capers. The large buds imported from Spain are usually called caperberries.
Relish The term often used for pickles made from chopped vegetables and/or fruit. Because of their texture, relishes are ideal in sandwiches.

Flavouring essences

These volatile substances are the essential oils extracted from flowers, nuts, fruits and herbs – think of lemon essence, almond essence and peppermint essence. There are, of course, endless synthetic flavourings which are cheaper than the true essences and are not so hard to find, but if one has ever tasted the real thing one will know and appreciate the difference.

Colourings

In countries where the sun shines brightest – Sicily, for example, and southern Italy, India and South America – food tends to be extravagantly brightly coloured. Shocking pink and silver, bright orange and magenta and glaring yellow and green make the dinner table look like a carnival and the food rather exotic to most of us. Ideally these hues are achieved with vegetable colourings, but even in these locales food may be artificially coloured with chemicals that are potentially harmful.

Cooks at home can avoid using artificial colourings: forget about the garish chemical food colourings and gravy brownings and use the gentler natural colourings. Use onion skins for golden broths; spinach juice or chopped herbs for green sauces and mayonnaise; beetroot juice for a ruby-coloured soup; and tomato paste for reddish-brown stews or delicately pink sauces to accompany shellfish.

clove 197
horseradish 194
mango 178
pickled and salted fish 31
radish 131
soya bean 128
vanilla 198
walnut 188

Halibut Salad with Capers 368
Japanese Noodles with Char-Grilled Beef 345
Marinated Roast Quail 301
Peanut Sauce 258
Salsa Verde 258
Skate with Black Butter 268
Slow-Cooked Brisket of Beef with Soy, Sake and Oysters 284
Soy-Marinated Salmon Brochettes 273

Caper | Sweet pickle | Mango chutney

Pickled walnut | Pickled radish | Wasabi powder

Cooking with Alcohol

maraschino cherry 169

Beef in Beer 284
Cider Barbecue Sauce 257
Coq au Vin 305
Crêpes Suzette 396
Normandy Pheasant with Apples and Calvados 298
Rabbit with Prunes and Red Wine 297
Sautéed Chicken Livers with Sage 292
Sherry Trifle 392
Slow-Cooked Brisket of Beef with Soy, Sake and Oysters 284
Soused Herrings 267
Spiced Pears in Red Wine 387
Trout in White Wine Jelly 273
Trout Marinated in Vermouth 273
Zabaglione 394

In a good restaurant kitchen there will be, within easy reach of the bubbling and simmering pans, a line-up of interesting bottles of wines, fortified wines and eaux-de-vie. This alcohol supply is not for fortifying the cooks but to be used judiciously as an ingredient in cooking – an ingredient as vital as butter, flour, salt, pepper or eggs.

There is no reason why the home cook should not emulate the professional here. Use leftover wine for cooking, and raid the drinks cupboard or buy small bottles of sherry, port, rum, vermouth, brandy and the more exotic spirits. Do not make false economies – 'cooking' sherry, cheap brandy and wine-flavoured concentrates will defeat the purpose, which is not to swamp food in alcohol (which evaporates in cooking anyway) but to add flavour. If a wine or spirit is too awful to drink, then it is too awful to cook with. Use a wooden spoon when cooking with alcohol – the tang of metal is all too easily transferred.

Wine is an important ingredient in marinades. It impregnates food with its flavour and will soften the fibres of meat and draw out the juices from fruit. Wines for cooking should, in general, be young and dry. It is easy enough to find a reasonably priced red, but cheap white wines do tend to sourness – a light French vermouth such as Noilly Prat is an excellent substitute. Cooking with Champagne may seem extravagant, but often a glass or two is all that is required to make a superlative sauce for sole or scallops or an unforgettable sorbet.

Liqueurs and eaux-de-vie will turn a simple dish of fruit into a deliciously alcoholic dessert worthy of any occasion. Apart from the fact that it is fun, flaming Christmas puddings and crêpes Suzette can add to the dish. The purpose of pouring spirits over food and igniting it is, of course, to flavour the food but also to lose the raw taste of neat alcohol.

Liqueurs and eaux-de-vie distilled from fruit or flavoured with it have an obvious affinity with the fruit from which they were made – hence oranges in Grand Marnier – and they share with the parent fruit affinities with certain foods – hence pork cooked with Calvados. The same logic applies to liqueurs flavoured with essences and herbs.

Rice wines are enjoyed in Japan and China. Crystal-clear colourless sake is used in Japanese cooking to remove strong flavours and enhance delicate ones. The Japanese like the lightness of vegetables cooked with sake, and also use it in marinades for chicken and other meats – in one recipe the chicken is pricked all over and marinated in sake, soy sauce and salt for 20 minutes before being steamed with ginger and spring onions. (Although sake is thought of as a wine, this is not really accurate because the rice is boiled and yeast is then added, in a method more akin to brewing than wine-making.)

Mirin, a sweet, lustrous, amber-coloured Japanese rice wine, contains 10 per cent alcohol and a huge 40 per cent sugar. It is used as a seasoning for *sushi* and, together with dark soy sauce, as an ingredient in marinades and for basting grilled foods such as *teriyaki* when it forms a sticky golden glaze.

Shaoxing, a very clear yellow wine, is more like a sherry in colour and flavour than sake. This Chinese wine has been made for thousands of years and is always aged before drinking. It is traditional to buy it when a daughter is born, and keep it to celebrate her coming of age at 15 and her wedding. It is used in stir-fried dishes to moisten the ingredients and in the marinades for cuttlefish and for *char-siu* pork. When drunk it is served warm, as is sake.

Ales have their place in the kitchen, too – the dry taste of beer makes an interesting addition to a soup or a stew, fruity cider complements hare and pork, and bitter-sweet stout is good in beef casseroles.

These charts are not intended to be exhaustive lists – merely a guide to inspire you to tip the right bottle into dishes that will benefit from the added flavour.

Liqueur/Eau-de-vie	Made from	Uses
Advocaat	Eggs and brandy	Whip into cream for trifles and rich custards
Apricot brandy, Abricotine	Apricots	Flame over roast chicken; use to soak dried apricots
Cointreau, Curaçao, Grand Marnier	The rind of bitter oranges, oranges	Chicken, duck; lemon soufflé, chocolate mousse, sweet omelettes, crêpes, fruit salads; apples, pears, figs, strawberries, oranges
Crème de cassis	Blackcurrants	Pour over ice-creams; use in sorbets
Amaretto, Crème d'amandes	Almonds and apricot kernels	Biscuits, icings, cakes, tiramisù
Crème de cacao	Chocolate flavoured with vanilla	Ice-cream, mousses, cakes
Calvados	Apples	Pheasant, partridge; pork and veal dishes; cooked apple desserts
Maraschino (sweet), Kirsch (dry)	Cherries	Black Forest cake, fruit compotes, clafoutis; cheese fondue; fruit salad; strawberries, pineapple, cherries, figs, peaches, apples
Izarra	Herbs and mimosa honey	Jellies, sweet fruity desserts
Kahlúa, Tía Maria, Bailey's	Coffee; coffee and cream	Cakes, gâteaux, puddings, ice-creams
Kümmel	Caraway, cumin, fennel and orris	Cabbage, sauerkraut
Crème de menthe	Peppermint	Pour over chocolate ice-cream; use in chocolate milk shakes and puddings
Pernod, Anis, Pastis	Anise	Trout, sea bass, grey mullet; Florence fennel; pork
Mirabelle, Prunelle, Slivovitz	Yellow plums, sloes, plums	Plum desserts, compotes
Southern Comfort	Bourbon flavoured with peaches	Peach desserts
Poire Williams', Eau-de-vie de poire	Pears	Pear desserts
Eau-de-vie de fraise, de framboise, de pêche	Strawberries, raspberries, peaches	Strawberries, raspberries, melon, sorbets

Wines and Spirits	Soup	Fish and shellfish		Poultry	Game	Meat	Vegetables	Sauces	Fruit and desserts	Cheese and eggs
Red wine	Cherry	Mackerel, salmon, sole		Chicken, duck, goose, guinea fowl	Hare, mallard, pheasant, pigeon, teal, venison; marinades for all game	Beef casseroles, steaks and braises; kidneys, lamb, liver, oxtail, pork, veal, marinades for all cuts of beef	Broccoli, leeks, red cabbage	Gravy (meat); anything *à la bordelaise* (in red wine sauce) such as poached eggs, steak, etc.	Cherries, peaches, pears, prunes, raspberries, strawberries	Poached eggs
White wine (or substitute dry vermouth or dry cider)	Crab and lobster bisque, strawberry	Haddock, herring, mackerel, red mullet, salmon, sole, trout, turbot	Clams, lobster, mussels, scallops, scampi, prawns	Pâtés; chicken, duck, guinea fowl	Pâtés; hare, pigeon, rabbit, teal	Pâtés; beef casseroles; ham, lamb, liver, pork, sausages, sweetbreads, veal	Artichoke hearts, carrots, cauliflower, green beans, leeks, sauerkraut	Court-bouillon; sauces for fish, poultry, vegetables	Peaches, raspberries; sorbet, syllabub	Creamed Brie, fondue
Rosé wine	Prawn	Salmon		Chicken						
Champagne		Salmon, sole, turbot	Oysters	Chicken		Ham, sweetbreads		Sauces for fish, poultry, oysters	Peaches, raspberries, strawberries; sorbet	
Sherry	Asparagus, tomato, chicken consommé, game consommé, pheasant, turtle,	Salmon, white fish; lobster		Pâtés; chicken, chicken livers, duck, turkey, foie gras	Pâtés; pheasant	Pâtés; beef, veal	Stir-fried vegetables; avocados	Apple sauce; gravy (meat), sauce for poultry, seafood sauces	Apricots, oranges; fruit cake, syllabub, trifle	Potted cheese, Welsh rarebit; zabaglione
Port	Duck, hare	Scallops		Duck	Hare, teal		Mushrooms	Apple sauce	Cherries, melon, peaches, plums, prunes, strawberries; trifle	
Madeira	Consommé, kidney, turtle	Crab, lobster		Pâtés; chicken, duck	Pâtés; quail	Pâtés; kidneys, veal		Sauce for veal	Cakes, teabreads, trifle	
Marsala				Chicken livers		Veal escalopes		Sauce for sweetbreads	Pears	Zabaglione
Vermouth		Sole				Pork		Sauce for fish		
Brandy	All bisques	Sole; all shellfish, especially lobster		Pâtés; chicken, chicken livers, duck, guinea fowl, foie gras	Pâtés; grouse, partridge, quail, rabbit, venison, woodcock	Pâtés; beef casseroles and steaks, kidneys, lamb	Mushrooms	Brandy butter, brandy cream, lobster sauce	Apricots, cherries, oranges, peaches; Christmas pudding, mince pies, anything flambéed	Egg custard
Rum		Oysters						Rum butter	Apple desserts, baked bananas, fruit compotes, mixed berries, oranges; rum baba, anything flambéed, ice-cream	Omelettes, soufflés
Whisky		Lobster						Sauce for lobster	Mincemeat, trifle, greengage crumble	
Gin					Quail	Kidneys				

Honey, Syrup, Sugar and Chocolate

jaggery 212
sweetcorn 140

Boston Baked Beans 354
Flapjacks 414
Gingerbread Men and Women 414
Honey Madeleines 414
Malt Loaf 362
Marinated Roast Quails 301
Pecan Pie 407
Quick-Fried Chicken with Garlic and Chilli 305
Spiced Stuffed Leg of Lamb 288
Sticky Golden Sponge Pudding 396

Man was probably born with a sweet tooth. Wild fruits and honey taken from wild bees provided the first sweet foods, and since then the craving for sweet things has continued unabated.

Obviously, any sensible household is now aware that it is unwise to eat too many sweet things, but sweeteners do still have an important part to play in the kitchen. As seasonings and preservatives, they have always been as important as salt to the cook. There are many foods that are simply too bitter, such as Seville oranges and cocoa; too sour, like lemons and sour cherries; too acid, like damsons, rhubarb and gooseberries; or too bland, like apple sauce, to be enjoyable without the addition of sweeteners.

Without sugar it would not be possible to preserve strawberries and raspberries in the form of jam, and there would be no breakfast marmalade.

By using honey, syrups and sugars in their original roles, and cutting down on highly sweetened convenience and other manufactured foods and drinks, it is possible to enjoy sweet things without undue concern.

HONEY

Like all natural things, honey can vary enormously. It can be runny, or gritty, or so stiff that you can hardly dig it out of the pot. It can vary in colour from darkest amber to almost white. Connoisseurs look for a honey with a clean, straightforward flavour, uncomplicated by undertones of bitterness.

For a single pot of honey, bees have to visit a myriad flowers, and the honey's taste, colour and viscosity depend on the sort of flowers they choose. Normally, the bees' main diet will be written on the label – clover, lavender, heather, and so on.

Generally, the paler honeys, gathered from meadow flowers such as clover, have a mild, clean, delicate flavour, although rape-flower honey, stiff and pale, is not liked by many honey enthusiasts. Heather honey is light golden with an aromatic tang to it. Exotic honeys such as California orange blossom, lavender from Provence, or the dark Greek Hymettus honeys have heavily scented flavours. Although not the finest, blended honeys, labelled as coming from various countries, are reliable and consistent.

Clover honey is best for all-round cooking and eating, lovely in honey cakes or rich fruit cakes. If you bake honey yeast buns, note that the presence of honey slightly lengthens the rising time. If you substitute honey for sugar in any recipe, remember that honey is much sweeter than sugar so you need less of it. Frozen yogurt and ice-creams that are made with honey will usually result in a softer consistency than those sweetened with sugar because the freezing point of honey is lower.

Honeycombs give us the honey sealed in the cells with a capping of wax (cut or scoop horizontally so that the honey does not run out); chunk honey includes pieces of the comb bottled in liquid honey. Clear, runny honeys have usually been heat-treated to prevent them from crystallizing – which most honeys will do naturally within a few weeks of being taken out of the comb. If your honey does begin to crystallize, set the opened jar in hot water (but not hotter than 70°C/160°F) until it re-liquifies. Granulated or creamed honeys should be smooth and fine grained, with no coarse or gritty crystals.

Honeycomb

Clear clover honey

Granulated clover honey

Orange-blossom honey

Hymettus honey

Scottish heather honey

SYRUP

Some syrups are made by God, others are made by man.

Maple syrup This is among the former, and is the most delicious of syrups. The grades generally considered to be among the best are light in colour and crystal clear and come from the maples of Vermont and Canada. The clear, thin sap tapped from the trunks of the maple trees is boiled for hours to reduce it to the syrup that goes on to hot buttered waffles and griddle cakes and over ice-creams. There are also various maple-flavoured syrups on the market, less fragrant, less expensive and less good. Maple sugar, produced by boiling the syrup until most of the liquid has evaporated, is much sweeter than ordinary sugar. It is used to make candies in New England.

Palm syrup Another natural syrup, this is the sap of date palms (which also gives us the sugar known as jaggery). Very dark and extremely sticky, it can be bought in Asian grocery stores, and often features in Indian recipes.

Golden syrup A light golden treacle, this is a by-product of sugar refining that has been through its own refining process. Used in cakes and puddings, it is less sweet than sugar, so when it is used in baking, sugar is usually added. It can be useful when making such things as brandy snaps, since it is not as granular as sugar when heated.

Corn syrup Produced from maize or sweetcorn, this can be light or dark (the dark syrup tastes stronger), and is used in the same ways as golden syrup in cakes and puddings. It can also be poured over griddle cakes instead of maple syrup.

Carob syrup Extracted from the pods of the carob tree, mild and sweetly flavoured, this resembles treacle in colour. Rich in vitamins and minerals, it can be used as a sweetener in place of honey or sugar.

Molasses and black treacle These dark, heavy syrups are good friends to the cook. Far less sweet than honey, they go into the making of gingerbreads and hefty fruit cakes – unless brown sugars are used instead – and into such traditional American dishes as Boston baked beans and Indian pudding. A by-product of sugar-refining, molasses comes dark and even darker – the darker the molasses the less sugar it contains.

Being slightly bitter, molasses should be used in smallish amounts for the best flavour. One very good way to enjoy it is on hot porridge with milk. It is much more nutritious than sugar.

SUGAR

Sugar first started to replace honey as a sweetener in European kitchens in medieval times, although it was being used in China and India more than 2,000 years ago. It was introduced into the Americas by Columbus, and it was the first sugar plantations that formed the basis for the slave trade.

While the natural brown sugars still bring us some of the flavour and goodness of the sugar-cane from which they come, the white sugars contain no proteins, no minerals and no vitamins – they are simply instant energy. For the cook, however, sugar, used discriminatingly, is an indispensable ally.

Brown sugars

The natural brown sugars come from raw sugar-cane, and if you like the warm taste of molasses that still clings to them you can use them all the time. Being moist they have a tendency to go hard in the bag or jar, but if covered with a damp cloth for a few hours they soften up again.

Molasses sugar is also known as black Barbados and demerara molasses. Soft, strong-flavoured, fine-grained and very moist, it is good in dark, rich fruit cakes and dried fruit puddings, gingerbread and home-made toffee.

Muscovado Dark muscovado, sometimes called Barbados sugar, can be used in the same ways as molasses sugar. Pale muscovado is excellent for making crunchy toppings, and in pickles and chutneys.

Demerara, gritty with large golden crystals, has been crystallized from partly refined sugar syrup and contains 2 per cent molasses. It can be used in the same ways as pale muscovado. Although, like honey, demerara slightly retards the action of yeast in the early stages of rising, it is particularly good in spiced breads and other yeast baking, giving a nice creamy colour and good flavour.

Turbinado, refined one stage beyond demerara and lighter in colour, can be used in recipes that call for demerara.

Many of the other brown sugars, usually labelled light soft brown or dark soft brown, are simply fully refined white sugars that have been tossed in syrup or molasses. They are usually drier than the natural browns and don't have as much flavour. Coffee crystals, which dissolve slowly in hot liquid, are sugar crystals to which sugar syrup and colourings have been added. The simple way to tell whether brown sugar is natural or manufactured is to read the label: if it lists ingredients and no country of origin, the sugar will be the manufactured sort.

White sugars

All white sugars are equally sweet, but the finer the sugar, the faster it dissolves and the sweeter it seems. There is one thing that white sugars have in common: they taste sweeter hot than cool. This is why ice-cream mixtures, before freezing, need to taste almost too sweet, and why recipes for hot puddings specify, as a rule, less sugar than for cold ones.

Granulated sugar is a highly refined white crystal sugar primarily made from sugar-cane but sometimes from sugar-beet (both are pure sucrose). It is usually used in tea and coffee, with cooked fruit and for making boiled icings, fudges, toffees and fondants. If there is such a thing as an all-purpose sugar, this is it.

Lump sugar Once hacked from a large cone of sugar, this is now granulated sugar pressed into cubes to use in tea or coffee.

Caster or castor sugar is a smaller grained crystal. It is very fine and dissolves easily: use it for soft fruit and meringues, in cake-making, in custards, mousses and crumbles, and whenever it is desirable for the sugar to dissolve before the mixture starts cooking. Use it, too, to make your own vanilla sugar by sticking a vanilla pod or two into a large storage jar of sugar and leaving it for at least 2 weeks.

Make cinnamon sugar – good on pancakes, *pain perdu* and cream cheese – in the same way, substituting cinnamon sticks for the vanilla pods. Or try rosemary sugar: clean and dry sprigs of rosemary, put them in the sugar and shake well; after 24 hours shake again

cake and biscuit recipes 410–15
carob 213
dessert and pudding recipes 387–97
ice-cream and sorbet recipes 398–9
pastry recipes 402–9
preserves recipes 417–19
sweet sauce recipes 260
vanilla, vanilla sugar 198

sugar dredger 237

Beef in Beer 284
Braised Red Cabbage 374
Caramelized Sweet Potatoes 342
Glazed Gammon 292
French Onion Soup 249
Marinated Thai Prawns 278
Mint Sauce 258

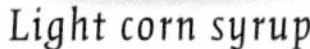
Light corn syrup

Dark corn syrup

Golden syrup

Maple syrup

Molasses

coffee 214–17
palm syrup 210

Brownies 414
Chocolate Butter Icing 415

and then leave for a week. This unusual sugar is good in any milk pudding.

Icing sugar tastes the sweetest of all and dissolves the fastest. Apart from its obvious use making icing for cakes, it is sprinkled (through a sieve to keep it powdery) over pies and sponge cakes and, in the new wave of cooking, over desserts – especially those made with dark red berries and pastry – and over the edges of the pudding plates as decoration. Because it dissolves so quickly it is the sugar to use in sorbets made with uncooked fruit purées.

Preserving sugar is a sugar made for jam-making: the large crystals retain enough air between them to prevent the sugar sinking in a solid mass to the bottom of the pan, so they dissolve evenly and quickly without burning or forming too much scum. Jams, jellies and marmalades will need less skimming, and will be crystal clear. Some preserving sugars have pectin added to them.

Jaggery

In India and South-east Asia, sugar is regarded as quite good for you, and many of the little sweet snacks eaten during the day rather than at meals are intensely sweet. The dark, coarse unrefined sugar used is called jaggery, and it may be processed from the sap of palm trees or from sugar-cane.

COCOA, CHOCOLATE AND CAROB

A century before coffee arrived in the West, the Spanish *conquistadores* had brought chocolate home with them from the New World. They had seen the Aztecs whisk up a hot, frothy drink called *cacahuatl*, 'bitter water', and at the court of Montezuma, the Mexican emperor, they had savoured a thicker, richer brew the Mexicans called *chocolatl.*

Cocoa beans, each the size of an almond, grow 30 or 40 at a time, like the seeds of a melon, in large pods on the *Theobroma cacao*, a tree found in tropical America and Africa. The characteristics of the beans vary enormously depending on the region in which the trees are grown, and one of the closely guarded secrets of the chocolate industry is the formula for handling and blending the different varieties.

Cocoa beans, before treatment, are bitter, and they must undergo fermentation and roasting to make them palatable. Once shelled and ground, a rich liquid – called chocolate liquor – is extracted. The liquor contains a fat called cocoa butter. From this point, cocoa and chocolate undergo separate processes.

Cocoa

In order to make cocoa, a proportion of the cocoa butter – it varies from one manufacturer to the next – is removed from the chocolate liquor. The remaining liquid sets rock hard and is then pulverized. The result, pure, naturally acid cocoa, has a good, bitter flavour but needs to be sweetened before it becomes palatable. 'Dutch' cocoa undergoes a further process to neutralize the acids, making it darker and mellower in flavour.

Cocoa powder contains starch, so when making it into a hot drink it should, like flour, be mixed to a paste with a little milk or water before being added to the hot milk, otherwise it will become lumpy. To improve the flavour and digestibility of drinking cocoa, let it boil for 2 minutes and then whisk it vigorously to a velvety froth before serving. Drinking chocolate, also known as instant cocoa, is precooked cocoa powder to which sugar and flavourings have been added. It blends easily into hot or cold milk without forming lumps and should not be boiled.

Cocoa and drinking chocolate are very popular throughout Europe as well as North America, particularly during the long winters. In France, cream is often added, and in Spain they make a rich chocolate drink thick enough to eat with a spoon. In the United States, steaming cups of cocoa are traditionally topped with whipped cream or a melting marshmallow floating on the top. In Russia and Brazil, coffee is added (when coffee is added to cocoa or chocolate, the resulting flavour is called mocha).

Light soft brown sugar

Dark muscovado sugar

Dark soft brown sugar

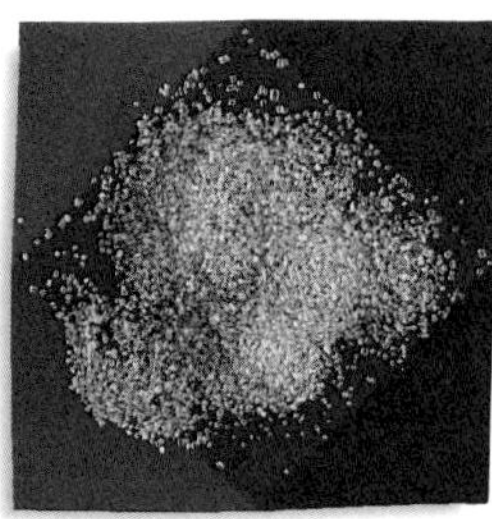
Demerara sugar

Molasses sugar

Granulated sugar

Lump sugar

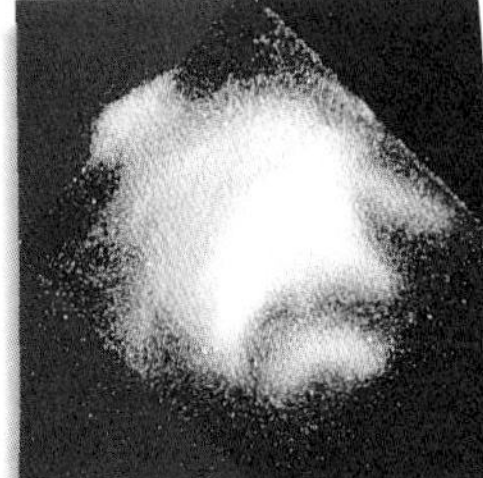
Caster sugar

Icing sugar

Preserving sugar

Cocoa powder can also be used as a flavouring for cakes, biscuits and desserts. When unsweetened cooking chocolate is called for in a recipe, you can substitute 3 level tablespoons of cocoa powder plus 15 g/½ oz of white vegetable fat or unsalted butter for each 30 g/1 oz of chocolate. If bitter chocolate is required, do the same, but add an extra 3 tablespoons of sugar.

When buying cocoa powder, look for the words 'real chocolate' and avoid anything labelled 'chocolate-flavoured'.

Chocolate

The quality of chocolate is a subject of great interest to chocolate lovers and serious connoisseurs alike. Whole books have been written about chocolate, discussing the merits and drawbacks of the many types and the individual characteristics of the beans from which chocolate is made. This is not surprising, though, considering that good chocolate-makers use a blend of as many as twelve different varieties of beans to achieve just the right balance of richness, aroma and depth of flavour.

Unlike cocoa, chocolate may retain all the natural cocoa butter found in the liquor extracted from the beans. In fact, the proportion of cocoa butter varies considerably; in some instances extra cocoa butter is added to the liquor to make the chocolate even richer. The higher the cocoa butter content, the more delectable the chocolate and also the more expensive. Sugar may be added too, and the sweetness or otherwise is another marker: connoisseurs like bittersweet chocolate, whereas more popular by far is chocolate with lots of sugar and, often, milk solids. Chocolate to which sugar and extra cocoa butter have been added ranges from the darkest bitter chocolate to mild milk chocolate.

When cooking with chocolate, it is generally best to use the least sweet variety that you can find (the less sugar that is added to chocolate, the stronger and more chocolatey will be the flavour, and you can always add more sugar). To ensure the best flavour, look for chocolate with at least 50 per cent cocoa solid content; 60–70 per cent is even better, whether it is for cooking or eating. For icings, however, plain or semi-sweet chocolate is preferable because it has a higher fat content than bitter or bittersweet chocolate so is easier to melt, and the sugar in it produces a good sheen when dry. Beware of cheap cooking chocolates, which have often been blended from rather inferior beans.

Great care is needed when melting any sort of chocolate: it should be done in a bowl set over a pan of simmering water or a double boiler – if it is overheated it scorches. It is also important to prevent any steam or the smallest drop of water from coming into contact with the melting chocolate, as this, too, will cause it to 'seize', or become a thick, lumpy mass.

Chocolate is, of course, essential to the making of some of the world's most delicious cakes and sweets, truffles, éclairs and desserts. It has a special affinity with rum and brandy, particularly in mousses and ice-creams. Chocolate cakes, biscuits and sweets should be cooked at a slightly lower temperature than other cakes and sweets because they scorch more easily. To make a particularly rich and glorious drink, melt grated chocolate slowly with sugar and then whisk in hot milk.

Unsweetened chocolate is also used as a flavouring in some extraordinary dishes such as the Mexican national holiday dish, *mole poblano de guajolote* – turkey in Pueblan sauce – while in Spain two casseroles, one of veal tongue *a la aragonesa* and one of braised pigeon, *pichones estofados*, are served in sauce containing chocolate.

White chocolate is made with cocoa butter, milk solids and sugar, and contains no chocolate liquor. It is not suitable for much in cooking except decoration, and is more cloying than proper chocolate.

Carob

Naturally sweet and nutritious, carob provides a satisfying alternative to chocolate. In their natural state carob beans are the long, elegant pods of a Mediterranean tree belonging to the legume family (it is the carob, or locust bean, on which St John reputedly lived in the wilderness).

Carob contains fewer calories than chocolate and none of the substance theobromine, found in chocolate, that can be a cause of migraine. Carob powder, or flour, is ground from the whole pod, which is also very palatable in its natural state. As a flour, carob can be used in the same ways as cocoa in cakes, biscuits and home-made sweets, but carob is sweeter than cocoa so use less sugar or other sweetener with it. Its mild, milk-chocolate taste is particularly good in honey and nut pudding, date loaves, cake icings and ice-creams, but it is not recommended for use in recipes that require a really strong chocolate flavour such as mousses and rich chocolate cakes.

carob syrup 211

Chocolate Ice-Cream 398
Chocolate Orange Mousse 394
Dark Chocolate Mousse 394
Devil's Food Cake 411
Éclairs 409
Malted Ice-Cream 398
Profiteroles 409
Rich Chocolate Cake 410
Rich Chocolate Mousse 394

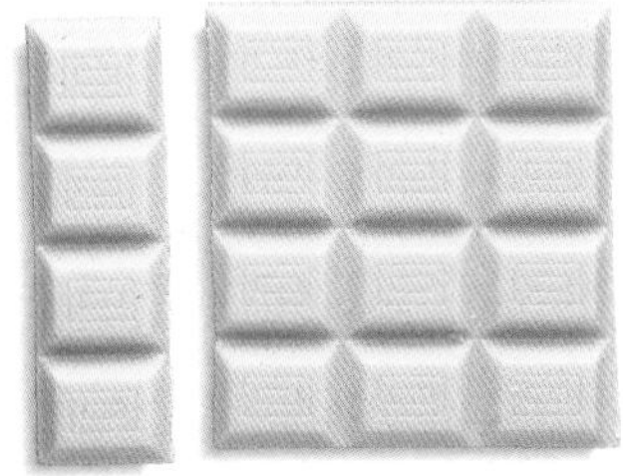

White chocolate

Milk chocolate

Bitter chocolate

Cocoa powder

Carob powder

Carob pod

Coffee, Tea and Tisanes

additives and extractions 216
coffee crystals (sugar) 211
instant coffee 216

coffee grinder 226, 239
coffee machine 239
filter coffee maker 239

Coffee Butter Icing 415
Coffee Granita 401
Coffee Ice-Cream 398
Walnut Cake 412

COFFEE

In the Arab world, where coffee is drunk throughout the day in countless ceremonial cups, the old rule for a good brew is that it should be 'as black as hell and as sweet as sin'.

Good coffee, to suit the Western palate, is made from freshly roasted beans of the particular kind you like best, preferably ground just before brewing. Freshness is vital: coffee rapidly loses quality if exposed to air. There must be a generous amount of beans to the cup, the grind must be suitable for your method of making coffee and the water should be freshly drawn.

The beans

These are, in fact, not beans at all but the twin seeds of the cherry-red fruit produced by the tropical coffee plant. The seeds lie, flat sides facing, in a parchment-like caul. If, as occasionally happens, only one seed develops, it is called a peaberry because of its rounded shape. (This singleton is noted for its even roasting qualities and is therefore especially good for home-roasting.)

Once picked and partially depulped, the fruit is usually, but not always, fermented in water for varying periods. The seeds are extracted from their natural wrappings, dried, washed, dried again, then graded according to size.

Before roasting, coffee beans are quite pale. The type called Mochas are yellowish, small, uneven beans; Bourbon Santos are the same colour but oblong and a little larger; and Martiniques are greenish, rounder and larger still.

True Mocha from the Yemen is now a rarity. There had been hardly enough to go around when only the Arab and Levantine world drank what was described by an astonished British traveller as 'that black liquid called *kahveh*'. But when Europe took to coffee in the seventeenth century, enterprising colonists were quick to spread the tree now known as *Coffea arabica* to new parts of the world. The Dutch were soon providing coffee from plantations in their East Indian possessions, while in France the ever-growing demand for coffee led to its cultivation in Martinique: a young French naval officer introduced a single seedling, which became the ancestral plant of most Central and South American coffee. France was also to grow coffee on its Indian Ocean island of Bourbon (now called Réunion); it is from here that the Brazilians imported the seed for the famous Bourbon Santos coffee.

These *arabica* coffees all do best at high altitudes; they are often labelled 'mountain grown' and are a good deal more temperamental than the group of coffees called *robusta*. The *robustas* can be grown in lower regions and are, as the name implies, hardier, easier to grow and therefore cheaper. Mostly grown in Africa (which also grows *arabicas*), the *robustas* are less delicately flavoured but they are steadily being improved.

However, the *arabicas*, which the trade now also divides into the Brazilians and the Milds (which does not mean that they are not strong), make up most of the quality coffees you are likely to encounter at a specialist coffee merchant's, so always look for the words '100% arabica' or 'Pure arabica' on ready-ground, vacuum-packed coffee.

Brazil The world's largest coffee grower, Brazil produces all grades from exquisite to indifferent. Santos is the word to look out for: the Brazilian Santos, especially Bourbon Santos, give a good, full-bodied cup of coffee. 'Prime Brazilian' on a coffee label is meaningless as far as flavour goes.

Colombia Second only to Brazil as a coffee exporter, Colombia produces some coffees that are quite excellent and that brew so well that you need fewer beans than of other coffee to any given quantity of water. Among the best Colombians are Medellin, mildly acid, which means that it has a much-valued sharpness, just short of being sour; Manizales, a little sharper; and Excelsio, which is slightly bitter.

Jamaica If you find Jamaican Blue Ridge Mountain coffee, which is all too rarely available, you can be sure that it is mellow and 'sweet' – it is rich in natural sugars, which caramelize during roasting. It is also agreeably acid and hailed by many as the best coffee in the world. The Jamaican High Mountain Supremes are a little less full-bodied.

Venezuela Coffee from Venezuela, if it has grown in the mountain districts, can be rich, winy and light in body.

Guatemala Mountain-grown coffees from Guatemala are noted for their acidity and fullness. Antiquas and Cobans are the best. Other regions of Guatemala produce beans renowned for their zest but not for body.

Costa Rica Coffee grown in the high areas of Costa Rica is renowned for its acidity – it has the reputation of being able to curdle the milk in the cup – but other Costa Rican *arabicas* are famed for their fragrance, mild flavour and full body.

Mexico Coffee grown in Mexico is light, mellow and on the bitter side.

Hawaii This is where Kona coffee comes from. It is rich, mellow, full-bodied and full of flavour, with a good, straightforward taste.

Sumatra and Java Sumatran *arabica* coffee is wonderful: sweet, mellow and full-bodied. It is Sumatran coffee that is still most sought after by the Dutch, who take great pride in perfect coffee-making. However, both Sumatra and Java now also grow *robustas*, so ask specifically for a Sumatran *arabica*. Take the same precaution when you buy Java coffee. Old Java ('old' means that it has been stored in tropical conditions for a decade or so) is always of the *arabica* variety; the *robustas* are not worth storing for so long and would not in a hundred years develop the fine special flavour that is associated with Old Java.

Mysore This Indian coffee is velvety, acidy and aromatic. It is delicious, especially when, as is so often the case, it is blended with Mocha.

Malabar Monsooned Malabar from southern India is coffee that has grown throughout the monsoon period, which is supposed to give it a particularly aromatic and mellow flavour. It is indeed wonderful coffee.

Ethiopia This coffee is acid and is also described as 'gamey', which means that its aroma is slightly spicy. A type known as Longberry Harrar is now replacing the traditional descendants of Yemen Mocha, and in this there is a kind of poetic justice: the Yemen's first coffee came from Ethiopia, shortly after a legendary Abyssinian goat-herd observed his goats skipping and dancing after feeding off the hitherto ignored coffee plant growing in the wild.

Kenya The *arabicas* of Kenya are among the quality coffees: one, the Kenya Peaberry, a variant producing a single round bean, is much admired for its flavour and is one of the coffees drunk straight and unmixed with any other.

Although there are these, and many more, distinctive varieties of coffee beans, most coffees are blended, producing a pleasant balance of body, flavour, sweetness and acidity. This is where the skill and knowledge of the specialist coffee merchant is an invaluable help. The names of house blends – Director's Choice, Connoisseur and such like – signify nothing, so it pays to cultivate a discerning coffee merchant who can be relied upon to offer freshly roasted beans, and will explain which combinations of beans constitute his particular blends.

The roast

Roasting brings out the flavour inherent in the bean and determines the mellowness, richness, nuttiness, smoothness or otherwise of the final brew. The roast does not determine the strength of the coffee – this depends directly on the ratio of coffee to water when brewing.

Light roast, also called a light city roast, gives a cinnamon-coloured bean and a brew that is called delicate by those who like it and thin or acid by those who don't. This roast is used for mild-flavoured beans, suitable for breakfast drinking.

Medium roast, brown roast or city roast will give beans a stronger character and more flavour, but the flavour is still on the acid side.

Full roast or full city roast produces dark brown beans and a flavour that is deeper still.

High roast, double roast or continental roast practically burns the beans black, for after-dinner coffee with a strong kick. High roast coffee is a favourite of gourmets.

French roast produces shiny beans, burnt amber in colour, for coffee that is still smooth, but only just.

Espresso roast is dark to the point of carbonization, but can be mellow.

French roast, or Italian or Spanish roast, makes espresso without quite the same kick.

The higher the roast, the lower the acidity of the bean and the less varied the aroma, so the most precious beans are not used for very high roasts. However the high-roasted coffees are distinctly preferred by many coffee connoisseurs who dislike the acid flavours of lightly roasted beans.

Only countries that take their coffee-drinking very seriously indeed go in for large-scale home-roasting, with appropriate machinery. Formerly, drums agitated by a turning handle and heated with spirit lamps set underneath were used; now, electric roasters have taken their place. If you want to try roasting your own 'green' beans (which can be obtained from specialist coffee shops and which will keep, before roasting, in perfect condition for long periods) but lack the apparatus, use a frying pan, shaking it continuously over the heat until the beans are the right colour all over (the spherical peaberries are the easiest beans to handle). However, for the very best coffee it is easier to buy your beans freshly roasted and in small quantities. Store them in an airtight jar to preserve their aroma. In this state they will keep in good condition for up to 3 weeks. You can also freeze them for longer storage.

If you buy your coffee ready-ground in vacuum packs, you may not be told on the pack the exact types of beans that have been used to make the blend, but you should be informed of the degree of roast and grind. Many of these coffees are excellent, blended for consistency of flavour year in and year out, although coffees, like wines, do vary according to weather conditions during the growing season. Once the pack has been opened, store the ground coffee in an airtight jar and use it up within a week if possible, or freeze it.

The grind

Choosing the right grind is essential. The finer the grind, the greater the surface area of coffee that is exposed to the water and the longer the water takes to run through it as it is brewed. A coarser grind has less surface area and the water passes through more rapidly. The various machines for making coffee are designed so that with the right grind the coffee is exposed to the water for just the right length of time. If the grind is not right, it will result in under-extraction, which is wasteful and gives a weak-bodied brew, or over-extraction, which makes coffee bitter and can leave a lot of sediment in the cup. If you don't grind your coffee yourself, tell the shop where you buy the beans by what method you make your coffee and have it ground accordingly.

Turkish grind Powder-fine, this is the grind that is used to make intensely

coffee grinder
226, 239

Unroasted peaberry | Light roast | Medium roast | Turkish grind | Very fine grind

Full roast | High roast | Espresso roast | Drip grind | Regular grind

barley 116
cardamom 199
chicory 129
dandelion 133
fig 181, 183
peppercorns 201
saffron 199

the beans 214
the roast and grind 215

strong, sweet Greek, Arabian and Turkish coffee.

Very fine grind is the grind to use for the paper-filter method. It is too fine to use in an infusion – the fine grounds would turn into an unsievable mud.

Drip or fine grind is the sort to use in an espresso machine and in the drip pot or Napoletana. Brillat-Savarin, the French gastronome, writing on coffee in the early eighteenth century, preferred this one to all others, and it is this the French still call for when they order *un filtre*.

Medium-fine grind is the grind for the popular and successful cafetière method, made with the glass jug with a plunge filter. The coffee comes up through the mesh filter and the grounds stay at the bottom of the jug.

Regular or medium grind is the one to use in a Cona machine, percolator or jug, since it requires an extraction time of 6–8 minutes.

The brew

When making coffee, it is important to use coffee and water in the right proportions. Nineteenth-century visitors to England – then notorious for its awful coffee – were urged by experienced travellers to specify the precise number of beans to the cup, otherwise they would be served with a prodigious quantity of pale brown liquid. 'Waiter, is this tea? Bring me a cup of coffee. Or is this coffee? In that case bring me a cup of tea' – ran a famous joke in *Punch*. Sixty-five beans to the cup was Brillat-Savarin's recipe, but he and his contemporaries liked their coffee extra strong. ('I know it is a poison,' said Voltaire, whose clarity of thought Brillat-Savarin ascribed to copious coffee consumption, 'but it is a slow one.' He was over 80 at the time.)

Today, the recommended amount of ground coffee is 2 level tablespoons per large coffee cup.

There is much controversy among coffee aficionados over which method produces the best brew. Internationally recognized styles of serving coffee include:

Café au lait or café con leche The breakfast drink served in France – traditionally in a bowl – and in Spain, this is made with equal amounts of hot, strong French- or Spanish-roasted coffee and hot milk.

Demitasse This after-dinner coffee is a regular medium-roasted coffee served double strength.

Espresso The Italian favourite, this is a small, strong, foaming cup, the product of a machine that forces steam and boiling water through finely ground espresso-roast coffee. Use a high-roast coffee at double strength to make espresso at home, if you haven't bought espresso roast. It should be drunk as soon as it is made; otherwise, the Italians say, it dies in the cup.

Cappuccino This is espresso served with steaming, frothy milk from the espresso machine (a similar effect can be produced with hot milk in the blender or using a little milk steamer on the stove top). It can be dusted with cinnamon or powdered cocoa. *Café crème* is espresso with milk but without the froth.

Viennese coffee Made with beans that are roasted darker (but not as dark as the French), this brew is topped with sweetened, whipped cream, often spiced with cinnamon and nutmeg. The term Viennese coffee is also used for a brew to which dried figs are added.

Irish or Gaelic coffee This is a strong brew laced with Irish whiskey and topped with floating cream.

Turkish or Greek coffee Usually drunk very sweet and after dinner, this is traditionally made in an *ibrik*, a long-handled copper jug. However, an ordinary saucepan will do. The powdered beans, sugar – plenty of it – and water are slowly brought to the boil and simmered to a froth. This rich, thick coffee is served in a tiny cup and should not be embarked upon until the grounds have settled to a sludge at the bottom.

By long tradition the enjoyment of really good coffee is something of an event. There are still individual flourishes to be seen in Africa and the Middle East. The Moroccans, for instance, add whole peppercorns to the brew for extra kick. The Ethiopians take it with a pinch of salt, and in some Arab countries freshly pounded saffron or cardamom pods are added to a foam called the 'face of the coffee'. Most evocative of all, perhaps, when the Turks gather around the polished *ibrik*, is the practice of taking coffee with extra sugar for happy occasions such as a wedding, but with no sugar at all at sombre gatherings such as funerals.

Additives and extractions

Unless you are positively fond of the taste, avoid coffees that are 'stretched' with additives, or coffee substitutes. The reason for using them is, of course, economy, but chicory 'coffee' and other mixtures that appear in abundance whenever the Brazilian crops are decimated by frost are, even so, quite popular in their own right. In various parts of the world, such things as dandelion roots, toasted and ground, sometimes feature in mass-produced coffee; so do toasted figs and toasted barley, which makes what is called malt-coffee. If you buy packaged coffee, the label will tell you what it contains. 'Coffees' made from chicory, fig and so on are an acquired taste, but worth a try.

Decaffeinated coffee is pure coffee from which the stimulating properties have been extracted. With them, alas, goes a proportion of the aromatics: using the traditional extraction method to get a product that is 97 per cent caffeine free, the beans have to swirl in a solvent and then be dried off 24 times. Nowadays some coffee is decaffeinated using the Swiss water method: rather than using a solvent the beans are steamed and their outer layers – where the caffeine is concentrated – are removed. Decaffeinated coffee beans, which are available ready ground or whole, need a higher, darker roast than unprocessed ones to develop their flavour.

'Gourmet' coffee If tea can be flavoured with anything God can create in the way of fruits, flowers and spices, it would seem to follow that coffee can be too. So we now have designer coffees appearing, with flavours such as vanilla nut crème, Irish crème, chocolate hazelnut and so on. Many coffee-lovers don't seem interested, but if you do like the idea then the time to serve these flavoured coffees is after dinner. Look for those that do not contain artificial flavourings.

Instant coffee

Purists may despise them, but these are nevertheless pure coffee, if not of the most delicately flavoured sort; few (but discriminating) are the people who insist on making the real thing for every cup they drink. Instant coffee is also an asset in the kitchen when you want a coffee flavour but not an extra quantity of liquid.

What is true is that instant coffees vary. Their taste is affected not only by the blends of coffee going into their making (they are made entirely from *robustas*) but also by the way they are produced. The freeze-dried varieties are most like the real thing. For these, brewed coffee is frozen and the resulting ice is ground and vacuum-dried. Other, cheaper varieties are spray-dried at high temperatures, a process that drives away the aromatics; these are sometimes reintroduced by means of a spray of coffee oil, which evaporates as soon as the jar is opened.

Of course, with instant coffee one gains in convenience but loses in excellence of flavour and the delicious aroma that heralds a pot of fresh coffee in the making.

TEA

When, in the early seventeenth century, the Dutch first brought tea to the West – it had been cultivated in China for centuries – it was the rich who savoured its various aromas, not the poor. For another century or more ordinary people continued drinking their habitual cheap ale, wine and sack, while the gentry sipped the costly new brew from the East.

It was not until the middle of the eighteenth century that tea became a popular drink as a result of the British East India Company cutting prices and opening up the trade. Today, still single-minded about their tea, the British lead the field in consumption, drinking three times as much as the Japanese (to whom tea is as much a ceremony as a refreshment) and ten times as much as the Americans, who much prefer coffee. In Russia tea is served very strong, sometimes with lemon but never with milk, while Moroccans like their milkless tea very sweet, adding great quantities of sugar and honey and, frequently, mint leaves. Indian masala tea, brewed with spices – cinnamon, cardamom and so on – and usually made with milk and plenty of sugar, is deliciously reviving for the traveller.

What is a curious anomaly, now that tea is such a universal beverage, is that the terminology under which it is graded and sold remains utterly cryptic to the bulk of the tea-buying public. True, most people readily distinguish black tea, the kind most commonly drunk in the West, from green, which is the favourite in the East. But other terms are for the most part incomprehensible outside the trade. The term Orange Pekoe, for example, on the label of many black teas, simply indicates the size of the leaf and has nothing to do with the taste of the tea.

Although all tea comes from variants of the same evergreen plant, *Camellia sinensis*, it varies noticeably according to the region in which it is grown and after which it tends to be named. The factors mainly associated with superior teas are good soil and water conditions, high elevation, attentive plucking and a favourable harvest season.

Generally, the finest flavours are to be found among what are known as high-grown teas – varieties cultivated on terraced hillsides at high altitude. Scarcer and more difficult to harvest, these hill varieties invariably cost more than the lowland teas.

Following the harvest, what happens to the leaf during processing has considerable bearing on the quality of tea in the cup. Tea processing not only changes the leaf to bring out its inherent qualities but also ensures that the finished leaf will not spoil. And it confirms it in one of the three classifications into which all teas are grouped: black tea, fermented and with the highest concentration of essential oil; green tea, which is unfermented and retains the closest resemblance to the natural leaf; and oolong, which is semi-fermented tea.

Black tea

Rich, aromatic and full flavoured, black teas account for by far the largest proportion of international tea sales. The oxidization that takes place during fermentation largely accounts for their flavour, strength, body and colour – all characteristics that hinge on chemical changes in the tea tannin and the development of the essential oil. The longer tannin ferments, the more colour it has and the less pungent it is to the taste, so that a very black tea might, in fact, have little pungency – in tea terms, astringency without bitterness.

Black teas are graded by the size of the leaf into leaf teas – those with large leaves, which develop flavour and colour more slowly to give a lighter, more fragrant brew – and broken-leaf teas, covering the smaller, broken leaves which yield a stronger, darker, quicker brew.

blended teas 218
green tea 218
oolong tea 218
tisanes 219

kettle 239

Black: Darjeeling

Black: Ceylon spiced with lemon

Black: Keemun

Black: Ceylon

Black: Assam

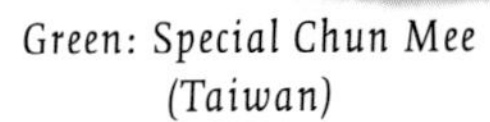

Japanese three-year tea

Green: Special Chun Mee (Taiwan)

Green: Young Hyson (China)

Green: Japanese Sencha (pan-fired)

Green: Gunpowder (China)

bergamot 165
black tea 217

Among the leaf teas, the term Orange Pekoe means that the leaves are long and well defined, perhaps with a few yellow tips or mixed with a few leaf buds. (A thousand years ago, the term *pekoe* – 'white haired' – was applied by the Chinese to teas that showed a touch of white on the leaves and to which they sometimes added orange blossoms for extra fragrance, but the name no longer denotes this agreeable custom.) Pekoe, with smaller and more tightly rolled leaves, produces a brew darker but not necessarily stronger than Orange Pekoe. Souchong, the largest, coarsest leaf picked, makes a tea that is pale and quite pungent.

Of the broken-leaf teas, Broken Orange Pekoe, which gives good strength and colour in the cup, is the one most often used as the mainstay of a blend. Fannings, much smaller, make a strong, quick brew, as does Dust, the smallest grade produced.

Outstanding among the black teas are Keemun, a full-bodied, aromatic tea from North China, which, with its penetrating bouquet, makes a good alternative to after-dinner coffee; and the rich, tarry-flavoured, smoke-cured Lapsang Souchong from South China and Taiwan, which is best without milk.

The classic Indian teas include high-grown Darjeeling, the Champagne of teas and one of the world's most prized, with a rich, pale liquor and exquisite, penetrating aroma; and the full, strong, malty tasting Assam. Ceylon teas are generally softer in character than other blacks, and the high-grown varieties are known for their strength, delicacy of flavour and scented aroma. Dimbula, a rich, mellow Ceylon, makes a good nightcap. Indonesian black teas are taken mainly by Dutch blenders and packers.

Green tea

Primarily from China, Japan and Taiwan, green tea is cool, clean and refreshing. Said to aid digestion, it is often served with highly flavoured or fried foods. It has a mellow, subtle flavour and brews to a pale golden green. But where green tea is concerned pallor does not signify lack of strength: the lighter the liquor, the younger the leaf and the better the brew.

Green tea is steamed and heat-dried but not fermented. It is graded by the age as well as the size of the leaf. The top grades are Gunpowder, young leaves rolled into tiny balls, and Young Hyson, long, thinly rolled leaves. Other grades are Imperial, with loosely balled leaves, and Hyson, a mixture of Young Hyson and Imperial.

Among the Chinese green teas, look for Moyunes, made from soft, tender leaves that give a tea celebrated for its richness and clarity; and Dragon Well, a variety that takes its name from a spring outside Hanzhou – this is considered to be the best green tea in China.

Japan, which meets a good deal of the United States' demand for green tea, grows its finest varieties in the district of Yamashiro, near Kyoto. Sadly, the most prized, Gyokuro or 'Pearl Dew', is not normally exported, nor is the leaf from which Mattcha, the ceremonial tea of Japan, is made. Most of Japan's tea is Sencha, or 'ordinary' tea, which finds its way abroad as pan-fired teas – delicate, light coloured and similar to the Young Hyson of China – and the long-leafed, basket-fired teas, which have been cured to a dark olive green.

The green teas of Taiwan are graded as Special Chun Mee, Chun Mee, Sow Mee and Gunpowder.

Oolong tea

Named after the Chinese words *wu* (black) and *lung* (dragon), the oolongs combine the characteristics of black and green teas. Best known – and the best of all teas, some experts believe – are those from Taiwan, known as Formosa oolongs, with their deep amber colour and magnificent fruity taste. Also very distinctive is Pouchong – oolong mixed with highly scented flowers such as jasmine and gardenia.

Much better than other countries (China included) at cultivating oolongs, Taiwan is the one exception to the high-altitude rule: here on this subtropical island the best teas are grown on the yellow clay soils of the *teela*, or broken lands, many of which are at sea level. It is the summer pluckings that yield the highest grade, rich golden oolongs.

Blended teas

Perhaps not surprisingly, the hub of the tea trade is London. Here firms base their bidding on the verdicts of tea tasters, who are much preoccupied with appearance, aroma and taste. For although there are only three basic types of tea, there are something like 3,000 commercial blends.

Given the fluctuations in price and availability from year to year, the major tea packers mostly market products that are blends using perhaps 15 or 20 varieties. The most distinguished of these blends include English Breakfast, traditionally a straight Keemun but now more likely to be a strong blend of India and Ceylon teas; Irish Breakfast, high-grown Ceylon with hearty Assam; Russian Style (also known as Russian Caravan or Russian Blossom), a blend of Keemun, Assam and China green well suited to the samovar; and Uva, a blended Ceylon, golden when brewed and with a distinctive flowery bouquet.

Another well-known blend is Earl Grey – so called because its secret was

Oolong: Formosa — Blend: Earl Grey — Blend: Uva

Oolong: Pouchong with jasmine — Blend: English Breakfast — Blend: Irish Breakfast

said to have been passed by a Chinese mandarin in 1830 to the Earl Grey, who had it made up for himself by a London tea merchant. Earl Grey is a blend of Indian and Chinese teas scented with oil of bergamot. Ideal for late-afternoon tea, it yields a pale, clear liquor with a slight citrus flavour – a reminder of how well a hint of citrus combines with tea.

Spiced blends on the market, such as the orange-flavoured teas popular in the United States, usually feature a smooth-drinking Ceylon tea with added clove, dried orange peel or lemon. Various teas can also be deliciously spiced with cinnamon, anise or cardamom.

Japanese three-year tea, also called twig tea or *kukicha*, is a natural tea with no caffeine, made from roasted 3-year-old twigs and leaves of the tea bush. It is best sipped slowly after meals.

TISANES

Long eclipsed by ordinary tea, tisanes or herbal teas have made a comeback as more and more people realize that, as well as being refreshing in summer and a fragrant reminder in winter of sunny gardens, tisanes can also be soothing and beneficial. Another advantage, of course, is that they are caffeine-free.

Modern-day tisanes and herbal blends are sold either in packages, complete with instructions, in the ubiquitous tea bag, or loose, by retailers who should be able to advise on their use. The ingredients can also be gathered from the garden, as long as one keeps to the absolutely safe, well-known plants that have not been sprayed with insecticides. The flowers, leaves, seeds or roots can then be used fresh or dried gently, out of the sun, to use later.

Most dried herb, flower and leaf tisanes are infused – made like tea – in a stainless steel or ceramic container (never aluminium or iron). Measure about a teaspoonful of the dried herb or 2 of the fresh (or a few sprigs) per cup of water, add boiling water as if making ordinary tea, cover and allow to stand no more than 5 minutes – long enough to bring out the fragrance, but not too long or the tisane will become bitter.

Strain and, if you like, flavour with lemon or honey. Teas made from seeds, roots or bark are prepared by decoction. Allow 2 tablespoons of seeds or a few roots for each 600 ml/1 pint of water, bring to the boil, cover and allow to simmer gently for about 15 minutes. Strain into a teapot, cover and leave the tisane to steep for a few minutes.

Ginseng (*Panax quinquefolium*) An ancient Chinese cure-all and aphrodisiac, said to be good for the mind, ginseng makes a tisane with a liquorice-like taste. Ginseng root, together with 15 other herbs, features in the powerful, spicy, Japanese *mu* tea.

Lime (*Tilia vulgaris*) Beautifully scented lime flowers are dried to yield relaxing, even soporific lime-blossom tea, a pale amber liquid that can be drunk hot or cold and mixed with lemonade. The leaves also make a good tea.

Bergamot (*Monarda didyma*) Refreshing and relaxing, tea made from the leaves and flowers of bergamot, also called bee balm, has a slightly bitter taste.

Mint (*Mentha* species) A great Arabian beverage, mint tea, which contains both mint and tea leaves, is served hot and heavily sweetened, in glasses, with a sprig of fresh mint. This refreshing tea is stimulating and a good aid to digestion. The many mints include peppermint, with menthol coolness, giving a pungent tea, and sharp, aromatic spearmint.

Camomile (*Anthemis nobilis*) The dried flowers of camomile make a rather bitter but soothing tisane, excellent for settling the stomach and supposed to induce tranquil sleep.

Maté (*Ilex paraguensis*) This stimulating tea, made from the dried and crumbled leaves of a small tropical tree, is a favourite South American drink. Also known as yerba maté or Paraguay tea, it can be drunk hot or cold.

Lemon verbena (*Lippia citriodora*) The lemon-scented leaves make a delicious tea, strongly reminiscent of lemon and excellent for the digestion.

Rose hip (*Rosa* species) Wild rose hips yield a sweet, astringent tea popular for its high vitamin C content; a fragrant tea is also made from rose petals.

Raspberry, blackcurrant The leaves from both bushes make lightly flavoured tisanes that are faintly evocative of the fruits. Blackcurrant leaves, a source of vitamin C, contain tannin.

Fruit teas, refreshing and astringent, are often spiced up with cinnamon or cloves. If you want to sweeten a fruit tea, use honey rather than sugar.

blackcurrant 173
honey 210
marigold 195
mint 194
raspberry 171
rose 195
spices 196–9

kettle 239

Peppermint | Bergamot | Rose hip | Ginseng | Mu

Maté | Lime | Raspberry leaf | Camomile | Lemon verbena

2

Equipment:
How to choose it
and use it

Equipment

Cutting implements, mashers, grinders and sieves
1 mezzaluna
2 carving knife and fork
3, 5 cook's knife
4 slicing knife
6 boning knife
7 serrated knife
8 paring knife
9 Chinese cleaver
10 poultry shears
11 garlic press
12 combined citrus zester and canelle knife
13 swivel-bladed potato peeler
14 bread knife
15 sharpening stone
16 oyster knife
17 chinois
18 sieve
19 biscuit cutters
20 lemon squeezer
21 salt and pepper mills
22 Mouli-légumes
23 rotary grater
24 box grater
25 potato masher
26 mandoline
27 mincer
28 pestle and mortar

KNIVES

A good sharp knife that is comfortable to hold is the most essential tool in the kitchen – one that makes the preparation of food a keen pleasure, rather than a troublesome chore.

Quality and materials

Before selecting the right knife for the particular task you have in mind, it is important to know what qualities raise a kitchen knife into the top-quality class.
Balance It is critical that the weight of a knife should be evenly distributed along the blade and handle, as an unbalanced knife is tiring to use. Knives are balanced by a tang (the metal extending from the base of the blade through the handle), and in the case of heavy-bladed knives, the tang should run the full length of the handle. A full tang will also lend extra strength to a knife designed for tough tasks. Whether the knife is light or heavy bladed, the tang should be securely fixed inside the handle, preferably with rivets.
Machine-ground edge Grinding gives a blade sharpness and strength, and knife grinding is a craftsman's job. The best knives are 'taper' ground with grinding marks at right angles to the cutting edge.
Hollow-ground blades are recognizable by their profile – a thick blade abruptly punched in at the cutting edge. The blade is machined so it cannot be sharpened, and it does not make a good edge for a chopping knife, but hollow grinding does make the hardest serrated edge.
Handles on the best-quality kitchen knives will be either of close-grained hardwood, which will not split or warp – and the slight texture of which gives a secure grip – or of plastic or plastic-impregnated wood, which combines extreme toughness with the natural properties of wood.
Stainless steel is a rust-resisting alloy of iron and chromium. Many people are disparaging of stainless steel, claiming that it is impossible to give it a really sharp edge. This is certainly true of inferior-quality knives stamped out of a flat piece of metal, but those forged from tempered stainless steel with a high carbon content are among the best knives you can buy.

The new 'high-tech', very strong stainless-steel knives and cleavers favoured by some professional chefs – especially the Japanese – are becoming increasingly popular. These knives look very different from traditional knives because they have hollow handles that are integral with their blades. Made from stainless steel, they have molybdenum and vanadium added to them to improve their strength and corrosion resistance, and are ice-tempered until razor-sharp. Their handles are specially weighted to give perfect balance when cutting, and some have engraved textured grips.
Carbon steel has the advantage of being cheaper than stainless steel, and sharpens to a razor edge. The disadvantage is its susceptibility to corrosion and staining, especially from foods with a high acid content, such as lemons and tomatoes, so it needs careful looking after and cleaning.

Shape and size

There are dozens of different knives designed for all the specialist tasks a professional chef may have to perform, but a carefully chosen collection of six or seven will equip most kitchens admirably.
Chopping To chop vegetables, herbs and so on finely, you will need a tough, well-balanced, general-purpose cook's knife with a deep, smoothly curved blade that tapers towards a pointed tip. The handle should be shaped to the grip with a down-turned curve at the end to prevent the hand from slipping backwards. It should have a full tang to balance the weight of the blade and absorb the chopping vibrations.

The bolster (the thicker back end of the blade) must be thick and deep to shield the hand and to allow the full length of the cutting edge to be used without crushing the knuckles against the chopping surface. The way to use this type of knife for fine chopping is to rest one hand on the back of the blade at the tip to keep it in contact with the board, while the other hand rocks the handle up and down, gradually moving the knife across the food. For rougher chopping, raise and lower the whole blade.

For tough chopping jobs a cleaver should be used. This tool relies for its strength on a wide, hefty, full-tanged blade, and is one of the few instances where an imbalance between handle and blade is desirable. Butchers may be seen wielding cleavers with considerable force and accuracy, but ferocious hacking can chip and blunt the cutting edge very quickly. To chop through bones, rest the cleaver in position and knock the back of the blade with a mallet.

Cleavers are traditionally used for all the chopping and shredding that goes into the preparation of oriental dishes. Using the knuckles of one hand the blade is guided across the food, then with a final flourish the pieces are scooped on to the blade and deftly transferred to the pot. This skill takes years of practice, however, and non-professionals should always treat cleavers with respect – and reasonable caution.
Slicing The type of knife you use will depend entirely on what you are slicing.
Bread A long serrated edge is good for cleanly penetrating the rough outer crust. Choose a straight, firm knife with hollow-ground serrations.
Cold meats The compact, tender fibres of cooked cold meats offer little resistance to a sharp knife and thus can be sliced very thinly. Choose a knife with a long, narrow blade, which should be flexible and strong. Special ham-slicing knives have a rounded tip to prevent accidental slashes to the meat, and a fluted edge that gives a little purchase to the first stroke and reduces friction. Fluted smoked salmon knives are also available; they make light work of slicing smoked salmon wafer thin, and are also useful for cutting raw meat and fish for carpaccio.
Fruit and vegetables A small serrated, stainless-steel blade is wonderfully efficient for slicing lemons, tomatoes, cucumbers, peppers and all those other fruits and vegetables with tough or slippery outer skins. The serration pierces the skin so easily that the flesh beneath is not bruised or squashed and each slice will keep all its juice.
Paring, peeling and scraping
Everyone has a favourite little knife that tucks under the forefinger and can be used almost as an extension of the hand. As the hand should be in close contact with the food, choose a light knife with a comfortable, well-shaped handle. The blade should be short, and made of good-quality stainless steel capable of holding a really sharp edge.
Boning This is done in a series of small cutting movements, frequently using the tip of the knife to follow the contours of the bone, so good blade control is important. For lightweight cuts of meat or poultry, a short, rigid knife is best, with a slim, pointed blade and a broad, full-tanged handle. The larger the piece of meat to be boned, the larger and more rigid the blade should be.

1
2
3
4
5
6
7
8
9
10
11
12
13
14
15
16
17
18
19
20
21
22
23
24
25
26
27
28

Filleting Choose a pointed, straight-edged knife with a flexible blade that will feel its way around soft cartilaginous fish bones. The blade should be protected by a bolster and the handle should be full-tanged. This knife is useful for almost every sort of cutting, slicing, carving, etc.
Mincing The Italians have a very practical instrument called a mezzaluna (renamed in France the *demi-lune*). It is a double-handled knife with a crescent-shaped single or double blade that is rocked over herbs, peppers, strips of meat, garlic and sliced vegetables, mincing them to fine bits. Sometimes small mezzalunas are sold together with a herb-chopping bowl.
Carving A good sharp knife is vital for easy carving. So too is a strong carving fork, traditionally used to hold the joint steady while slicing. A chicken can be carved with a small, neat knife, while bulky hot joints with a bone require a straight, sharply pointed knife. It helps when carving meat around a bone if the blade curves slightly upwards towards the tip. The handle should be shaped to the hand, with a full tang and a bolster to prevent the hand from slipping. A slim, slightly flexible blade will enable the carver to slice the meat thinly.

Care and cleaning

Dishwashers can be very unkind to knives. The high temperature and harsh detergents loosen, warp and split the handles, so it is better to wash knives by hand unless they are guaranteed to be dishwasherproof.

Knives should be quickly washed in hot, soapy water and dried immediately. Those made of carbon steel are inclined to go rusty very quickly, so they must be cleaned and dried immediately after use. If the blades do become stained, burnish with a cork sprinkled with an abrasive cleaning powder, or scrub with a plastic scouring pad and a scouring cream.

If by any chance a knife gets put in the dishwasher, you may find that its handle turns out of alignment with the blade. This will be because the tang is fixed to the handle not with rivets but with resin that softens with heat. To realign the knife, put the handle in boiling water for a few minutes, then twist it straight.
Sharpening Knives should always be kept razor-sharp. To help preserve their cutting edges, always chop on a wooden or polyethylene board. A blunt knife is frustrating and dangerous – it performs badly, needing a great deal of force, and it can all too easily slip out of control.

The best way to keep a sharp edge on knives is to use a hand-held steel: draw the blade lightly down the steel at a shallow angle. Repeat, putting the knife first to the front of the steel, then to the back. To resharpen, or hone, a dull blade you will have to use a sharpening stone – a block made of very hard stone.

Stainless steel is harder than carbon steel and will therefore require a harder sharpening steel. Hardness is measured in degrees on the Rockwell scale, and most reputable suppliers will sell a steel to suit the knives in their range.

There are many other devices on the market for sharpening knives, but these usually grind down the blade very quickly and are not recommended.
Storage Kitchen knives should not be stored in drawers where the blades will clash together, bending the tips and dulling the fine edges. Each knife should be separated from the next, and be clearly visible to the cook, who can then easily select the right knife for the job.

The best solution is to slot the knives in a wooden knife block or in a wall-fixed rack within easy reach (but inaccessible to children). Magnetic racks are good, but they may not be strong enough to hold very heavy knives or cleavers.

Carbon steel knives will need a light coating of vegetable oil to protect them from the steamy kitchen atmosphere.

OTHER CUTTING IMPLEMENTS

There are some cutting tasks that are quite difficult to carry out with a straight-bladed knife, however sharp, and over the centuries a wide variety of special tools has been invented to do these jobs more quickly, safely and efficiently. Some, like scissors, are strokes of genius, invaluable in the kitchen and elsewhere. Others are so specialized that you should examine your needs quite dispassionately before acquiring them, or they may spend more time collecting dust than attracting compliments for your prowess.

The following tools, used with a basic collection of knives, should equip the cook to deal with most cutting tasks.

Graters

Choose a sturdy, stainless-steel box or conical grater that will sit firmly in a bowl or on a flat surface without slipping or sliding. Each face should offer a different grating surface, and the grater should be large enough for the food to collect neatly inside without being squashed.

The face with fine holes is useful for Parmesan and other hard cheeses, while the abrading face consists of a series of jagged puncture holes for rasping tough or brittle foods, such as lemon zest and nutmeg. The smoother, directional face cuts smooth slices or slivers from softer cheeses and vegetables. The texture of the grated food is controlled by the size of the cutting holes.

Hand-operated rotary graters are speedy to use, and keep the fingers at a safe handle's length from the grating surface. A curved plate holds the food tightly against the grating drum, which is turned by hand. Choose a model with various drums of fine and coarse gauges.

Small nutmeg graters are nice to have, but not essential. Most come with a compartment in the top, which is very handy for storing the whole nutmeg.

Peelers and corers

Potato peeler It is perfectly possible to peel a potato quickly and easily with a small sharp knife, but the chances are that the discarded peel will contain more nourishment and flavour than the potato on the table. The *raison d'être* of a good potato peeler is to shave off the skin so finely that nothing of value is lost.

Fixed-blade peelers are used in the same way as knives, but left-handed people should make sure they buy a left-handed version. The swivel-bladed peeler is moved quickly to and fro over the potato or other vegetable, in either direction. Some types of fixed-blade peeler have a pointed end for digging out potato eyes.
Citrus zester and canelle knife There are several types of peeler available that will remove only the zest, the thin coloured top layer of citrus peel. A zester has a row of small holes that remove the zest in tiny particles, while a canelle knife has a V-shaped tooth that removes the zest in ribbons or slender filaments – it's especially good for making martini-sized twists. The object of these peelers is to leave behind the bitter pith, which is harder to do when using a knife.

Apple corer The top of this tool should be placed over the target area and pushed firmly through the apple; when it is withdrawn the core will be retained in the centre of the corer. It is a most useful gadget for preparing baked apples, the only drawback being that not every apple has an obligingly straight core of a standard size. Choose a corer with a sharp bottom edge.

Olive or cherry stoner The function of this little gadget is to eject stones from cherries and olives. A sturdy stainless-steel stoner will do the job very efficiently – a boon if you make a lot of cherry jam, or want stoneless olives for cooking.

Slicers

Mandoline This instrument is used for high-speed slicing of firm, crisp foods, such as potatoes, onions, carrots, courgettes or celeriac. While the cutting discs of a food processor can be used for slicing and shredding, they are never as fine and precise as the blades of a mandoline. Professional stainless-steel mandolines have several blades and attachments for a variety of thicknesses and shapes; wooden mandolines usually have just two adjustable blades (preferably of high-carbon stainless steel), one rippled for shredding, crinkle cutting or producing matchsticks, the other straight for slicing thickly or thinly. The mandoline is held firmly in place with one hand while the other hand moves the food over the chosen blade with a regular strumming movement.

Cheese slicer Dutch and Danish slicers are intended for semi-hard cheeses, such as Edam and Samsoe, that are traditionally cut very thinly. They are extremely good once you are accustomed to using them.

Cheese knife This usually has a curved blade and a forked or double-pointed end. It looks attractive when serving a cheese board, and the pointed end helps pick up slices and wedges neatly.

Cheese wire This is only useful if you buy cheese in large pieces. However hard or crumbly the cheese, a stainless-steel cutting wire, drawn taut, will melt through it and leave a clean, straight cut.

Egg slicer Wire slicers are one way of cutting hard-boiled eggs without displacing or crumbling the yolk. Some kinds cut wedges, some slices. Make sure that the wires are of stainless steel.

Chip cutter If you eat a lot of potato chips, then this gadget is quite useful. The whole peeled potato is placed under it, the stainless-steel cutter pushed down, and within a few minutes you have a bowl of neatly cut, chipped potatoes ready for frying. Instruments for cutting raw potatoes must be sturdy, so be prepared to pay for a heavy-duty steel model. A flimsy, cheap cutter is worse than useless.

Scissors and shears

Scissors Kitchen scissors should be very sharp, strong and made of stainless steel with plastic handles, and must be impervious to rust. For tough jobs their power will be strengthened if the lower handle is large enough to take the first three fingers of the cutting hand. A serrated edge is sometimes useful for giving an extra bite to the first cut.

The blades should cut evenly right down to their tips – in fact, especially at the tips because snipping is an important function of this tool. Scissors should be professionally sharpened when they become blunt.

Poultry shears Like garden secateurs, this tool gains its strength from the tension in the coiled spring just below the pivot point of the blades. Usually one blade is serrated to give a sound grip when tackling tough assignments such as small bones, and the pointed tips enable the shears to reach and operate effectively in small awkward places.

Cutters

Graded sets Tinned-steel plain and crinkly edged cutters are basic items of equipment for small pastries and biscuit making; the top edge should be rolled for strength, the cutting edge sharp. For convenient storage, buy graded sets that fit inside each other in their own tin.

Fancy cutters These are usually tinned steel, although occasionally plastic, in every imaginable shape and for every possible occasion. They are fun to use for biscuits, pastry, cake, icing, marzipan, canapés, etc.

Aspic cutters These are miniature shapes in a tiny tin. They were originally only used by professional chefs, but are handy for fiddly decorative work, both sweet and savoury.

Pastry wheel This can cut straight or crimped lines through pastry or through sheets of pasta for parpardelle, ravioli etc with professional panache, dividing dough with a smooth, even pressure.

Ravioli cutter A fluted-edged metal cutter with a wooden handle attached, this is used for stamping out individual rounds of ravioli. Different sizes are available. Ravioli trays are used for sheets of pasta – a rolling pin is rolled over the stuffed sheets and up to 40 small squares of ravioli are cut at one time.

Pizza cutter A wheel with a sharp edge, this is used to cut through cooked pizza dough and its topping to make neat portions.

Specialist knives

Oyster and clam knives These tough knives are designed to open the shells of oysters and clams while they are still alive. The blades of oyster knives have cutting edges on both sides to prize open the shells, and there is usually a guard to protect your hands. Clam knives usually have just one sharp side. Opening the shells of raw shellfish (often called 'shucking') is a tricky task. For safety's sake, choose one of the short, stubby knives, and hold the shellfish in a cloth – this will improve your grip and protect your hand at the same time.

Parmesan knife A special knife for very hard Italian cheeses, this is shaped like a short, fat spear. It is good for gouging and prizing out chunks from blocks of mature cheese such as Parmesan and pecorino.

Grapefruit knife This is a double-edged, serrated knife that is curved to fit the shape of a grapefruit half. It is easier than using a straight-edged knife for separating and removing grapefruit segments from tough membranes.

Sandwich spatula This is similar to a palette knife, but often with a shorter, broader and more flexible blade. It is useful for spreading soft butter, sandwich fillings, whipped cream and icings.

Cleaning

It is an unpleasant fact that behind every meal there looms the inevitable pile of washing up. Even if there is a dishwasher in the kitchen, there will still be a hard core of gadgets, knives and pots to be hand washed. Some of the items listed in this section come into this rather unfortunate category.

Mandolines should be cleaned with a brush, then rinsed and dried quickly to preserve the sharp cutting edge of their blades; wooden ones should never be left to soak or they will warp. Brushing is also the best way to clean graters, although the larger box-shaped ones will usually clean perfectly well in the dishwasher.

Storage

Most of these implements have sharp cutting edges, so do not jumble them all into a drawer. This will ruin the blades and you will most probably cut your fingers as you root about searching for the appropriate gadget. Some can be hung from a rack or a rail on butcher's hooks, while larger items can be kept on a shelf. In all cases, the cook must be able to see and reach them easily.

MINCERS, MASHERS AND SIEVES

When you look at a collection of modern kitchen tools – efficient, easy to use, simple to clean, light and comfortable to hold in the hand – it would be easy to believe that they are all twentieth-century inventions. But most of them have a long and interesting lineage, and this is certainly true of the diverse group of tools in this section, designed to refine or change the texture of food.

Even before the advent of bread our ancestors had realized that seeds and grains could be made more digestible or aromatic by pounding and grinding; pieces of cloth filled with berries and wrung tightly were the first juice extractors, and loosely woven cloths suspended on wooden frames were the predecessors of modern sieves.

Crushers

Pestle and mortar This elegant descendant of the primitive pounding pole is still the most effective tool for pulverizing nuts, garlic, berries, grains, seeds, herbs and spices.

The mortar should have a smooth, regularly curved bowl and a compatibly shaped pestle. The grinding surfaces should be slightly rough to provide the necessary friction and prevent the food sliding away from the pestle.

Pestles and mortars are available in wood, glass, tough unglazed porcelain, stone, metal and marble (which is lovely but very expensive). The small wooden ones are excellent for crushing most things, but because they are fairly lightweight they need a fair amount of force to crush seeds, grains and spices.

The off-white vitrified porcelain pestles and mortars are probably the most handsome and best all-round performers at a reasonable price.

Pepper mill Peppercorns should be ground when and where they are needed so that their fugitive pungency can be enjoyed before it fades.

The mealtime musings of many designers have resulted in an enormous variety of pepper mills to choose from, but perhaps the favourite is still the classic wooden mill with a removable top for easy filling and a highly efficient steel grinding mechanism.

Salt mill Where pepper goes, salt goes too, so most manufacturers make a salt mill to match their pepper mills. They will reduce coarse sea salt to usable size.

Coffee grinder Freshness is the essence of good coffee, and one way to ensure it is to grind your own. Hand-operated mills are preferred by some purists, as the beans are ground rather than cut, and the grind is cooler.

Beaters and pounders

Cutlet beater Thin slices of uncooked meat, such as escalopes of veal that are to be cooked quickly, should be cut across the grain and then flattened to half their original thickness. This is best done with a smooth, heavy beater, gently pounding with a stroking motion, to homogenize the texture of the flesh and break down the fibres (which would otherwise contract when cooked and cause shrinkage and toughness).

Meat tenderizer A mallet with a flat, grid-shaped face is less brutal than the type with small spiky steel protuberances, which cut through fibrous tissues. Only use a tenderizer on thick cuts of meat, never on thin escalopes or tender fillets.

Mincer

A hand-operated mincer should be very strong and have clamps or suction feet for fixing it rigidly to the work surface. The handle turns a small Archimedean screw, which inexorably pushes the food from the hopper on to the rotating stainless-steel mincing plates – these will process almost anything except bones. Make sure that the machine has been designed to come apart completely so that every part can be easily cleaned.

Mashers

Potato masher Choose a strong masher that deals severely with the food and will not collapse under pressure. Traditional-style mashers are extremely efficient at mashing and puréeing cooked potatoes and other root vegetables, and they can be used in the pan in which the vegetables were cooked. Stylish, modern mashers made of coiled stainless steel are quite efficient, but they seem to require more hard work on behalf of the user than the traditional kind.

Ricer Made of chromed steel, this is excellent for making ultra-smooth vegetable and fruit mashes and purées. The food is put into a mesh basket or hopper, then pressed through by means of a metal pusher attached to a handle. The end result is light, dry and fluffy. Buy one that is a decent size, and preferably one that is dishwasherproof as the basket can be a bore to clean by hand.

Garlic press For those who are wary about impregnating a wooden board or a pestle and mortar with the all-pervading odour and flavour of garlic, the press is the answer. Select a sturdy aluminium or stainless-steel press with a fairly coarse mesh – then there is no need to peel the clove of garlic before you squeeze. But beware – crushed garlic is more overpowering than chopped.

Sieves

There are sieves for sifting, sieves for straining and sieves for puréeing: versatility breeds variation, and the sieve family is no exception.

Round-framed stainless-steel sieves are suitable for all sifting and puréeing tasks. They are preferable to the wire- or nylon-mesh type because they do not stain or corrode in contact with acid (an important consideration if you frequently make fruit purées) and they do not wear out so quickly or come apart with constant pushing. To help with puréeing, you can use a wooden mushroom-shaped pestle called (unsurprisingly) a champignon, or the back of a spoon.

Sieves should not be filled too full for sifting. To sift, knock the side of the frame gently against the palm of the free hand to help the contents pass through.

Sieves can be very hard to clean, and for this reason the wood-framed drum sieves are best avoided for puréeing – metal-framed drum sieves are better as they are stronger and can be immersed in really hot, soapy water, or better still left to the dishwasher to cope with.

Chinois For fine puréeing jobs, a stainless-steel chinois, or cone-shaped sieve, is preferable. Look for one with the frame and perforations formed from one piece of metal, with no seams or welds. The food is forced through the perforations by a pumping action using a small ladle or a wooden spoon, or with a long narrow pestle that fits right into the tip. A chinois is also excellent for straining, the tapering point channelling the liquid neatly down in a single trickle into a jug, deep bowl or saucepan.

Mouli-légumes, food mill This rotary sieve produces a range of purées, from the most delicate tomato sauce to a robust vegetable soup. An electric food processor, of course, would do the same, but the Mouli often gives better results as it does not rob the food of its intrinsic texture: it takes out – rather than chops up – lumps, fibres and fine bones. The machine can be dismantled for cleaning or to change the discs for a coarse, medium or fine finish. The best Mouli food mills have bodies of stainless steel.

Juice extractor

A citrus fruit squeezer must be able to extract the maximum amount of juice free from pips, pith and other solids. There are good models available with the reamer and strainer moulded in one piece, which fits on to a container with a lip for pouring. Stainless-steel versions are the most stylish, although plastic ones do the job just as well.

More traditional but not so efficient is the familiar glass version. It has teeth, which only half-heartedly trap the pips and pieces, and a moat that barely holds the juice of one lemon.

For extracting just a few drops of juice without sacrificing a whole lemon or lime there is a very clever little gadget called a spouted reamer. When plugged into the fruit, it will produce the required number of drops.

Ultra-modern citrus presses are made of stainless steel. They look beautiful on the kitchen worktop, and most do the job exceedingly well. The most efficient types have a geared mechanism with sufficient power to squeeze every last drop of juice out of the fruit. Electric juice extractors are also widely available.

ESSENTIAL ITEMS

Some tools are never far from the cook's hand – usually tucked into a jar by the hob ready in an instant to tend those dishes that need stirring, whisking or skimming while they cook. Billowy sauces and soufflés, plump omelettes or luxurious soups can be produced by any cook who has a good sense of timing and the right tools, which will respond instantly and efficiently.

Boards

Wooden boards are tough, but they are porous and so not only stain easily but also take on the flavours of strong foods that are chopped on them. If you choose wooden boards, you need to have several, each one for a specific task – chopping onions and garlic, rolling out pastry, slicing bread, etc. When cleaning wooden boards, they should never be saturated or left to soak in water as this will warp and crack the wood, and they should be kept away from heat.

Polyethylene boards are easier to care for than wood, but wooden boards are often preferred for their natural look.

Whisks

Substances are whisked to lighten their texture by the introduction of air, or to emulsify and blend ingredients, or to thicken those substances that contain fat. Egg whites, for instance, have an almost infinite capacity for trapping air when they are whisked – gently folded into sponges, soufflés or meringues, the air bubbles expand when heated to give the food a texture of honeycombed lightness.

A brisk whisking will rescue a lumpy sauce, and transform egg yolks and oil into a pale golden mayonnaise.

There are many varieties of whisks but the most reliable and effective types are:

Balloon whisk This is made of several loops of stainless steel or wire bound around a handle. It is a simple and effective tool, but it does need a good strong arm to keep up the whisking motion without flagging. Sizes range from large heavy-duty models for egg whites to small, dainty ones for light sauces and delicate dressings.

Rotary whisk This type of whisk can be heaven or hell depending on its quality. A cheap version is really a waste of money; unless the gear mechanism is carefully made of high-quality materials, the whisk will not operate smoothly at high speed. The best types work very well indeed and are less tiring to use than balloon whisks, but they do not achieve the same volume, particularly in the case of egg whites. They occupy both hands, which is sometimes a disadvantage.

Flat coil whisk This is a neat and efficient spoon-shaped tool that can get right into the corners of a pan, or control one or two egg whites so well that they can be whisked on a plate. It is most effective at beating lumps out of sauces.

Spoons

Wooden spoon The wooden spoon is regarded by most people with affection, not only because it is associated with childhood treats like scraping the mixing bowl, but also because it is one of the most useful tools in the kitchen.

A wooden spoon is invaluable for beating, mixing and stirring. It will never burn your hand because wood is a very bad conductor of heat, and it will not scratch or wear away saucepans.

Choose a spoon of close-grained wood like beech or box that is not likely to split. The bowl should have a fairly thin edge that can get right to the bottom corner of deep saucepans – some spoons are specially shaped to help you do this.

Metal spoon Although wooden and metal spoons share the same shape, their functions do not overlap in any way. While wooden spoons are good for stirring and beating, metal ones excel at transferring food quickly from pan to dish, and gently folding together delicate mixtures. A metal spoon should always be used for last-minute taste checks on soups and sauces, as wood can hold a tiny bit of the flavour from its last use.

Perforated and slotted metal spoons are excellent for serving pieces of food cooked in liquid; the excess liquid drains through the holes or slots, keeping the food whole and fairly dry.

Ladle The familiar shape of the ladle is unchanged since very ancient times. Like most classics, ladles are satisfying to use because of their geometric balance, and are pleasing to the eye. Soups and stews can be dexterously served without fear of spilling a drop; just the right quantity of batter can be poured into a crêpe pan for feather-light pancakes; and lipped ladles will transfer punches from serving bowl to glasses with ease.

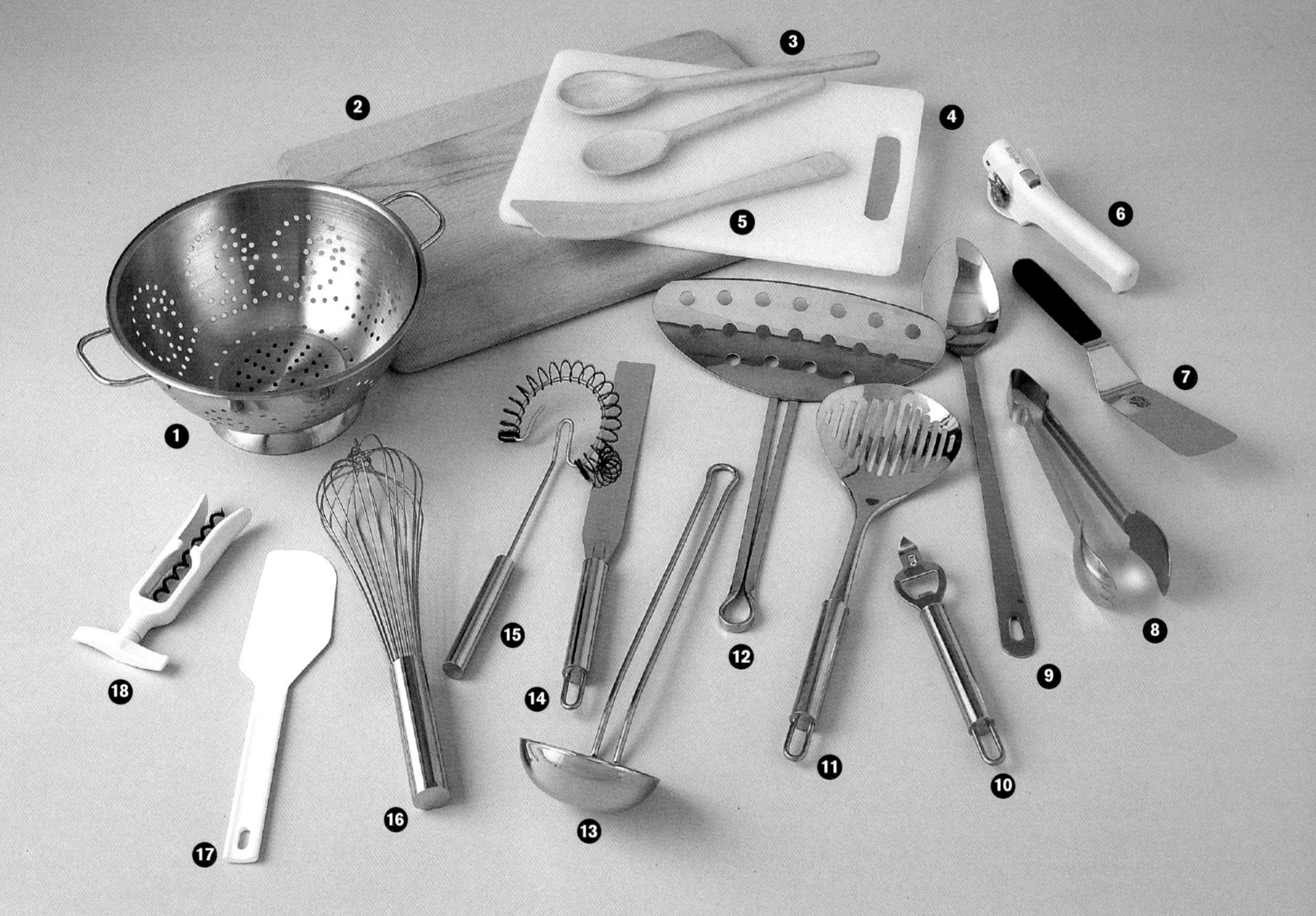

Essential items
1 colander
2 wooden chopping board
3 wooden spoons
4 polyethylene chopping board
5 wooden spatula
6 can opener
7 angled spatula
8 tongs
9 large metal spoon
10 bottle opener
11 slotted turner
12 fish lifter
13 ladle
14 palette knife
15 flat coil whisk
16 balloon whisk
17 plastic scraper
18 'screwpull' corkscrew

Skimmers

A 'spider', a shallow, lightweight wire basket on a long handle, will scour bubbling oil, soup or stock, gathering up impurities or removing food as it cooks. It is also good for scooping up a bobbing doughnut from a pan of hot oil at exactly the right moment to be rolled crisp and hot in sugar.

Solid perforated disc skimmers can both skim liquids and remove pieces of food from their cooking liquid. They are not so good in the deep-frying department, because their bulk lowers the temperature of the oil and the perforations are not large enough to allow the oil to drain freely from the food.

Turners, spatulas and tongs

Metal turner The flexibility of a good turner must be finely judged: it needs to be slim and whippy enough to slide under the food without causing damage, and broad and firm enough – like fish slices and fish lifters – to support it as it is turned or lifted from the pan. Perforations or slots in the blade will allow excess fat or oil to escape, and a sturdy handle will help insulate the hand from the transferred heat of the pan.

Wooden spatula It is strange that this archaic tool should be the perfect companion to the non-stick pan – that culinary spin-off from space-age technology – and although as a turner it is somewhat lacking in flexibility, nothing harsher than wood should be used on this vulnerable finish.

Wooden spatulas are available in rounded spoon shapes, or with a flat blade and a slanted straight end, which fits snugly against the sides of pans and bowls and gathers up everything in its path. You can find pierced or slatted wooden spatulas useful for lifting and draining fried food.

Rubber or plastic scraper or spatula This tool is the delight of a frugal cook's heart. Nothing else can scrape a bowl so clean that washing becomes almost a formality. The rubber or plastic head has a rounded side and an angular edge so that it will fit a wide variety of pots, pans and surfaces. The best ones, called spoonulas, are half scraper, half spoon. Never put rubber utensils in the dishwasher or very hot liquid – the rubber will perish.

Palette knife The long, thin, flexible blade of the palette knife is ideally suited to large-scale spreading jobs – like professionally smoothing a layer of icing on a cake or deftly distributing its filling. It is also a handy tool for turning scones or muffins on a griddle, or lifting and tossing pancakes.

Angled or cranked metal spatula This is useful for removing slices of tart, pie or cake from rimmed tins without breaking, and for lifting and transferring very delicate items like meringues.

Tongs These reach like heatproof fingers into sizzling pots and pans to grip small awkwardly shaped items. They are invaluable for removing individual strands or pieces of pasta from the water to test for doneness, or for serving pasta.

Forks

Metal fork The long two-pronged forks are handy for various tasks, such as removing a whole chicken from a deep pot or turning meat joints. A strong fork with two long tines is necessary for holding meat firmly while it is carved. The best carving forks have a full tang riveted to a wooden or plastic handle; some have a guard to protect the hand.

Wooden fork This friendly giant is ideal for gently swirling spaghetti while it cooks in the pot. Many cooks also find its light touch useful when adding liquid to pastry or dough mixtures.

Colander For the speedy separation of food from liquid, a round, double-handled metal bowl laced with a pattern of perforations and standing on a firm base is the most effective instrument. Choose the most roomy colander you can find so that when you are washing fruit, vegetables or salad greens there is plenty of space to swish them round.

Corkscrew Corkscrews are very personal things – some people swear by one particular type of mechanism, others by another. The coil (or worm) should be an extremely sharp, thin spiral, preferably of a triangular section so that it really cuts into the cork. It should have a comfortable, solid handle to pull upon, and it should be long enough to penetrate the whole cork.

The 'screwpull' corkscrew is very simple. It involves no pulling, and the screw itself is wider than most, making it extremely effective at holding the cork firmly. As you turn the handle, the screw goes into the cork and lifts it out in one action. Good models incorporate a blade for cutting the foil.

The winged or double-lever corkscrew is also easy to use. No pulling is required: the coil is screwed in and the two arms slowly depressed to raise the cork.

The 'waiter's friend' only requires a little strength, and it is quite efficient and reliable if it is inserted and pulled out straight – otherwise it breaks the cork.

The classic corkscrew with a simple wooden crossbar can require a lot of effort, especially if the cork is stubborn.

Bottle opener Choose the simplest and sturdiest shape you can find. Wooden handles have a nice feel to them.

Can opener Easy to use is the type that clamps on the rim of the can and then cuts through the metal by means of two gear-driven cutting wheels, which are turned by means of a butterfly handle. It grips the can very firmly and leaves a very clean cut edge. Dishwasherproof, it is a sophisticated and much improved version of the original all-metal butterfly-action opener. A wall-mounted opener is convenient to use in that the can is slotted into the jaws and held there by a lever. The scythe cutting-action opener has no moving parts to wear out, but it requires a firm pushing action to cut through the lid.

USEFUL UTENSILS

Depending on the kind of cooking you do, you may consider some, or all, of the following to be essential equipment.

Pasta machine This operates a little like an old-fashioned clothes mangle fitted with adjustable rollers, and has attachments to produce different shapes of pasta. The best are made in chrome-plated steel with stainless-steel rollers.

Salad basket and spinner A salad basket, that airy balloon of wire, will contain leafy salad greens with the minimum of restriction while it is whirled around out in the garden by energetic arms to extract the water by centrifugal force. If you don't have revolving arm sockets, or don't like the open-air exercise in mid-winter, there are some ingenious salad spinners, which are operated by a handle.

Bulb baster A useful tool, this looks rather like a large syringe, and acts on the same principle. By inserting the plastic tube of the baster into a liquid and squeezing the rubber bulb at the top, the liquid is drawn up into the tube. It can then be squirted back out again, for basting meat during roasting.

Gravy strainer As a fat separator, this is an alternative to the bulb baster. Invented by the French, it is an ingenious jug with two spouts, one at either side. One of the spouts has a deep funnel that pours the non-fatty (*maigre*) gravy from the bottom of the jug, while the other is shallow and pours the fat (*gras*) that has risen to the surface. The porcelain type, called *maigre et gras* in French, is more often used at the table than in the kitchen, but there are plastic types that are more for kitchen use. These are likely to have just one spout for pouring out the non-fatty pan juices.

Funnel In stainless steel, glass or plastic, this is invaluable for decanting liquids into bottles or other narrow-necked containers. A funnel is also an essential item for preserving.

Lobster crackers These look like nutcrackers in the shape of lobster claws. They are hinged, with ridges on the inside near the hinge, and are indispensable for cracking open lobster and crab claws.

Lobster pick Use this for extracting every last bit of meat from lobsters and crabs, especially from the ends of their legs. The most efficient picks have a kind of two-pronged fork at the end. This helps pull out the meat from hidden crevices.

Lobster pincer A two-in-one tool, this combines both lobster crackers and pick.

Nutcrackers Heavy chromed or silver-plated crackers with a simple squeezing action are the most traditional shape, but people with weak wrists may find them difficult. A wooden version like an old linen press is a worthwhile alternative.

Cake tester Looking like a long needle with a handle, this is inserted into a cake to check if it is cooked.

Cooling rack Raised wire racks are essential for just-baked pastries and cakes: if the steamy moisture is not allowed to escape soon after cooking, it will condense inside the dough or cake, making it leaden. Choose large racks made of good-quality stainless steel.

Toasting fork This looks a bit like Neptune's trident and has an extendable handle so that bread can be safely toasted over a fire without burning your hands.

Blow torch Chefs use this to caramelize the sugared tops of crème brûlée and other desserts. Buy a small one from a hardware store – it will be invaluable for that last-minute professional touch with desserts that might melt or overcook if caramelized by the grill or oven method.

Ice-cream scoop There are two main types. One has a blade that sweeps between the bowl of the scoop and the ice-cream, shaping the ice-cream into a perfect ball. This is the traditional kind used in ice-cream parlours; it is easy to use, but needs to be dunked in water in between each scooping or the ice-cream will stick. It is also useful for serving mashed potatoes and other vegetable purées. A more sophisticated ice-cream

Useful utensils, bowls and measuring equipment
1 gravy strainer
2 meat thermometer
3 combined deep-fat and sugar thermometer
4 bulb baster
5 glass mixing bowls
6 china pudding basins
7 gripstand ceramic mixing bowl
8 wooden salad bowl with salad servers
9 salad spinner
10 stainless-steel bowls
11 blow torch
12 pasta machine
13 lobster crackers
14 nutcrackers
15 lobster pick
16 cake tester
17 wire cooling rack
18 American measuring cups
19 glass measuring jugs
20 funnel
21 electronic scale
22 ice-cream scoop
23 measuring spoons

scoop has no blade mechanism, but inside the handle there is a type of non-toxic anti-freeze fluid. This enables you to scoop out hard ice-cream and sorbets. You must not put this type of scoop in the dishwasher or the anti-freeze will solidify.

Trussing equipment For simple trussing of whole birds, especially small ones, string is sufficient. Metal poultry pins or short skewers are useful for larger birds and those that are stuffed. Trussing with a needle and string will keep a bird in good shape. Trussing needles have very sharp points, and eyes large enough for threading quite thick string. The needle should be at least 25cm/10 in long so that it can pierce a bird from one side to the other, through wings or legs and body in between. Trussing string should be strong, undyed and not plastic-coated.

Larding needle For larding joints of meat with bacon or other fat you need a long, hollow needle with a pointed end and a clasp at the other to hold the fat.

BOWLS

Bowls are used for food preparation, cooking, storing and serving. They are available in a huge variety of materials and sizes, each having qualities suited more to one purpose than another. Like clothes, they reflect their owner's activities – the more varied these are the more choice is needed. Bowls must be suited to the job in hand – too large and the ingredients spread themselves in a film around the sides, too small and the contents overflow.

Every serious kitchen needs at least one huge bowl, suitable for soaking hams and mixing Christmas cake and pudding mixtures. It will also come in useful for serving salads at large parties.

Glass bowls Toughened glass bowls are good for all mixing tasks, and the sets of bowls that fit neatly inside one another are convenient for easy storage. All are heatproof, which is handy for steaming, and some are also ovenproof.

Ceramic bowls The traditional yellow mixing bowl with white interior is still the cornerstone of the bowl collection. Made of stoneware, it is wide enough to allow unrestricted mixing action, and deep enough to contain the mixture that is being stirred, beaten or rubbed. It is also the ideal bowl for dough making. At the bottom of one side there is a small flat area on the outside that acts as a base for holding the bowl steady when tilting it for beating or creaming.

China pudding basin The sides of a pudding basin are steeper and more tapered than those of a mixing bowl because this shape gives support to the centre of the pudding and prevents it from collapsing or sagging when it is turned out. The tough glazed finish will withstand even the high temperatures of a pressure cooker, and its raised rim holds a cover and string firmly in place. Containing steamed puddings is not the only destiny for this versatile crock; it is indispensable for all small beating, whipping and mixing tasks, and for storing food in the refrigerator or larder.

Plastic bowls These bowls are quiet, non-porous, virtually unbreakable and good insulators, but they have to be treated carefully because they are vulnerable to scratching and also to distortion through heat, and of course they cannot be used in the oven or as a pudding basin. A rubber-ringed base will keep the bowl anchored safely in place. Melamine is one of the toughest plastics for mixing bowls, and it can be put in the dishwasher.

Stainless-steel bowls It is not surprising that restaurant kitchens use stainless-steel bowls almost to the exclusion of all others. The conductivity of metal makes these bowls ideal for ingredients that need to be cooled or heated over water; stainless steel is also an excellent alternative to once-popular copper for beating egg whites.

Wooden bowl A handsome wooden bowl is perfect for fresh green leaves. It should be wide and deep enough to contain an exuberant curly salad while it is being tossed. Wooden bowls need to be washed briefly soon after use as they absorb the flavour of food. Use the minimum of detergent, and never soak them or dry them next to direct heat.

Other bowls There are, of course, vast quantities of small porcelain, earthenware, terracotta, stoneware and salt-glaze bowls of both ancient and modern design that are endlessly useful in the kitchen. Hand-made bowls with slightly roughened interiors are good for mayonnaise and vinaigrette – the surface helps the mixture to emulsify.

MEASURING

It is obvious from just a cursory glance at any cookbook that artistry needs to be underpinned by a solid foundation of knowledge. Ingredients must often be measured in exact amounts, assembled and prepared in an ordered sequence, and cooked at precise temperatures for a predetermined length of time. Measuring equipment is therefore an important component of the *batterie de cuisine*, enabling recipes to be perfectly balanced every time.

In these days of international recipe exchanges, measuring is complicated by the different systems used in Europe and America. Americans mete out their ingredients in cups (which sounds like a vague term for what is in fact a precise volume), and only rarely weigh ingredients in ounces and pounds, whereas Europeans measure their dry ingredients by metric weights. To further complicate the issue, the English imperial pints, quarts and gallons are quite different from their American counterparts that share the same names. So whenever possible, buy measuring devices marked with metric and imperial calibrations; if they have American measures too, so much the better.

Scales

Balancing quantities of goods against weights of standard size is a very ancient practice that began in the market place. In these days of high technology, scales are more important than ever, not least in the kitchen, where they are one of the keys to successful cooking.

Balance scale A strong balance scale will last a lifetime because it operates on a simple seesaw principle and there is no complicated mechanism to wear out. The weight is not indicated on a register, but when the weights on the two sides exactly match, a pointer lines up with a central marker on the fulcrum. These scales are usually so sensitive that two or three crumbs added to either side are enough to tip the balance.

Metric or imperial weights may be used according to recipe instructions, and these are available in brass or, less expensively, in cast iron, especially for the heavier weights. The pan for the food should ideally be a pear-shaped brass, stainless-steel or enamel bowl that,

when tipped, will channel its contents neatly into a mixing bowl or saucepan.
Electronic battery-operated scale This has a digital display that shows either metric or imperial weights, and many models incorporate an ingenious device by which the display can be returned to zero when weighing more than one ingredient in the bowl at the same time. The disadvantage of these scales is that they are not very accurate with small amounts under 30 g/1 oz.
Spring-balance scale In this type of scale the weights have been replaced by a metal coil or spring. The ingredients are balanced against the tension stored in the spring and the weight is registered on a calibrated scale, usually marked with both metric and imperial measures. The capacity is limited by the power of the spring, so check before purchase that the scales are not just suited to light loads – the best balance scales will weigh up to 11.7 kg/26 lb. There is a tendency for spring balance scales to wander out of true, so choose scales where accuracy can be restored with an adjustment screw when the scales are at rest.

Measuring jugs and cups

For cooking purposes, liquids are measured in units of litres or pints, in fluid ounces and, in the case of American recipes, in cups.

A toughened glass measuring jug is perhaps the most useful; the glass, which can withstand the impact of boiling liquids, enables the cook to see exactly how much is in the jug, and because it is such a poor conductor of heat the handle always remains cool.

Clear plastic measuring jugs are cheaper, but must be treated more carefully; heat can craze or distort the plastic, and if the shape of the jug alters it may no longer be an accurate measure.

China or stainless-steel jugs have the measure printed or etched on their inner surface, but the cook will often have to peer into their steamy depths to see if the correct level has been reached.
Measuring cups The variety of American cookery reflects the diversity of its origins with contributions from almost every country in the Old World, but the ingredients are almost always measured in cups. This does not mean any old cup picked at random from the shelf – it means exactly 8 fluid ounces, so a special measure is practical and necessary. Cup measures are also available in fractions or multiples of one cup, and the whole set of cups will nest neatly inside one another for convenient storage.

Measuring spoons

Many recipes call for spicy or highly flavoured ingredients to be added by the spoonful. It is occasionally left to the whim of the cook to decide whether these are administered, heaped or unheaped, in mammoth Victorian teaspoons or measured out gingerly in coffee spoons. With many recipes this doesn't matter, but the resulting balance of flavours may be spoiled by a disproportionate amount of one over the other, and in the case of ingredients that are measured in small quantities, such as baking powder, gelatine powder and yeast in dessert and baking recipes, absolute accuracy is vital for success.

A set of measuring spoons is therefore esssential and will accurately dispense small amounts ranging from ¼ teaspoon

1
2
3
4
5
6
7
8
9
10
11
12
13
14
15
16

(1.25 ml) to 1 tablespoon (15 ml). Dry ingredients should always be levelled off with a knife unless the recipe specifies a heaped measure.

Thermometers

A well-equipped kitchen will have a variety of thermometers to cope with the whole gamut of culinary needs, from monitoring the coldest depths of the freezer to recognizing the different stages of sugar boiling.

Precise temperature control is essential for the safety and success of many dishes and methods, such as yogurt-making, custard, yeast cookery, jam-making and deep-fat frying.

Freezer thermometer There are two enemies to be faced when preserving food by freezing: first the bacteria that cause the food to decay, and second the enzymes that break down its structure and impair the flavour. Food that is frozen to -18°C/0°F will be safe from bacteriological activity. You should check that this temperature is constantly maintained, as the enzymes will begin to function at -10°C/14°F.

Sugar and deep-fat thermometers These register the highest temperatures that are encountered in cooking. The secret of successful deep-frying lies in preheating the oil to about 190°C/375°F on a deep-frying thermometer before adding the food, although lesser temperatures suit some delicate foods. At this temperature the oil will seal the food instantly, preventing the escape of any juices or flavour, and conversely the food will not absorb the oil.

When sugar is heated it passes through various stages of crystallization at certain critical temperatures until at 180°C/350°F it becomes caramel. Each of these stages is valuable to the cook, and a sugar or candy thermometer is required to catch the sugar at just the right moment before it passes to the next stage. Most thermometers are made of glass, so warm them in hot water before use to avoid any danger of cracking.

Oven thermometer In a perfect world these would be superfluous equipment, but ovens are notorious for their idiosyncrasies (usually the result of a sluggish thermostat) and temperature variations between the top and bottom shelves and the front and back. The cook can discover the temperature pattern inside a difficult oven by standing or hanging a mercury-filled thermometer in various positions and noting the differences. (Such thermometers are not so successful at measuring the temperature in fan-assisted ovens.)

Meat thermometer This takes all the guesswork out of roasting meat by enabling you to gauge the exact degrees of doneness. A meat thermometer is also vital for checking the internal temperature of whole roast chickens and turkeys – this should be at least 82–85°C/180–185°F to kill any dangerous bacteria such as salmonella.

Some types of 'instant-read' meat thermometers are just used for spot checks, but the most common type is inserted into the meat or poultry before cooking begins, and left until the hand points to the appropriate place on the dial.

Wine thermometer Wine has an optimum temperature at which its flavour is most fully developed. A wine thermometer has a register showing the correct serving temperatures of various types of wine. This is attached to a sensor, which is dipped into the bottle after the cork is drawn.

Timers

Automatic timer Very often it is the sense of smell that alerts a busy person that something is not only cooked but overcooked, but a preset automatic timer will help to avoid disaster.

Sand timer Egg timers and hour glasses have today been largely superseded by automatic timers, but sand timers are quiet and accurate and cost a fraction of the price of their mechanical usurpers.

STOVETOP PANS

Before purchasing, take care to find out what the qualities of good pans are, and the various properties of the metals they are made from. Equipped with this information it is possible to make a selection that will suit all needs and give a lifetime's reliable service.

The materials

Stainless steel The most durable metal in the kitchen, stainless steel will retain a highly polished finish throughout its long life, and is completely impervious to acid or alkali ingredients. Alas, this promising metal is not the best conductor of heat – which is of course an enormous drawback in a pan – but thankfully, modern engineering and technology have found a solution. Good-quality stainless-steel pans now have heavy-gauge bases made of a 'sandwich' of stainless steel with a metal filling that is a good conductor of heat. This may be copper, copper and silver alloy, or aluminium. These types of pans are expensive, but they should last a lifetime.

Care Soak pans to loosen food deposits, then clean with a brush and hot soapy water. Scouring pads and creams can be used without risk of damage.

Steel and iron In spite of its propensity to rust, cast iron is popular for certain pans, such as griddles, ridged grill pans, frying pans, paella pans, waffle irons and blini pans, when cooking the food evenly at high temperatures is important.

Raw steel pans are very susceptible to corrosion and distortion by heat, and although a well-seasoned, heavy steel frying pan, crêpe or omelette pan is a very satisfying thing to use, steel saucepans are only useful if they are covered with sturdy vitrified enamel.

Care Maintenance is a continuous battle against rust. Pans should be thoroughly dried before being stored, and if they are not used very often, coated with a light layer of vegetable oil before being put away. New cast-iron and steel frying pans should be prepared for use by seasoning them: heat slightly and wash thoroughly in hot soapy water to remove any protective coating; dry the pan and heat again, with some vegetable oil in the pan, over fairly high heat, until it smokes. Keep the pan at this high temperature for several minutes, tilting the pan so that the oil runs over the bottom and up the sides until the whole surface is covered. Cool, then vigorously rub and wipe out excess oil with a pad of kitchen paper and some coarse salt.

Enamelled cast iron and steel Enamelled cast iron is a good, even conductor of heat, and it does not rust. It makes very strong, sturdy vessels, excellent for both stove-top and oven cooking – ideal for casseroles and stews started off on top of the stove and then left to simmer in the oven. Allow time for the metal to heat up at the start of cooking, and remember that it retains heat exceptionally well, so it is rare that a high heat need be used. It is for this reason that enamelled cast iron is one of the best materials for casserole dishes and cheese fondue sets.

Stovetop pans
1 pasta pan
2 enamelled cast-iron casseroles
3 gratin and baking dishes
4 ramekins
5 soufflé dish
6 glass custard cups
7 stainless-steel roasting tin with rack
8 non-stick frying pan
9 baking sheet
10 cast-iron griddle
11 long-handled chopsticks
12 wooden spatula
13 wok
14 ridged cast-iron grill pan
15 cast-iron frying pan
16 stainless-steel saucepans

Care Wash in hot soapy water, gently scrubbing off any food that has adhered during cooking. Soaking helps loosen stubborn food stuck on the inside of pans. Plastic scourers can be used, and diluted bleach if all else fails.

Enamelled steel pans need to be treated with care – don't allow empty pans to sit over the heat or they will distort and shed their protective enamel coating, and never clean them with an abrasive substance or you will eventually expose the metal. Harsh scouring powders or pads will destroy the glassy surface and eventually wear through the enamel; any stains can be easily removed by soaking the pan in a dilute solution of liquid bleach. Be careful not to bang or knock these pans, particularly when they are hot, as the enamel may chip. They scorch easily, are not very flat, often warp and are not good conductors of heat, so they are only really appropriate when cooking on gas.

Copper The great advantage of copper is that it is an excellent conductor of heat, and its rich golden-red colour adds a warm glow to the kitchen. But it is expensive and regrettably promiscuous, combining chemically with food, liquids and air to form a poisonous layer of green verdigris. For this reason copper cooking vessels must always be lined to prevent this reaction from occurring and spoiling the food. Tin or silver were the traditional lining materials, but nowadays stainless steel is preferred.

Care Copper needs constant polishing to keep it bright, and for some this is just one chore too many. Salt and lemon halves will keep copper pans burnished – commercial cleaners give a light finish that is difficult to maintain. Avoid using harsh scouring pads, cream or powder when cleaning the copper outside of the pans; the stainless-steel linings are very easy to keep clean (see Stainless-steel Care above).

Non-stick Non-stick surfaces are a gift from modern technology and daily appear in more durable and long-lived forms. They are particularly useful for milk saucepans and frying pans, where eggs and fillets of fish will cook happily with little or no fat and be released completely intact at the end, leaving scarcely a trace in the pan.

Care Clean with a cloth in hot soapy water, rinse and dry. Avoid using metal spoons or spatulas, which will scratch the finish and expose the metal beneath.

The perfect metal Unfortunately no one particular metal is capable of providing the perfect pan, but until a single hybrid alloy can be produced, combining the beauty and conductivity of copper and the stability of stainless steel, the next best thing is to laminate the various metals in such a way as to combine all their best qualities and minimize their negative points. Combinations of metals used for pans that give excellent results are: aluminium sandwiched between an outer layer of copper and an inner lining of stainless steel; copper lined with stainless steel; aluminium lined with a non-stick finish; cast iron coated with enamel; or stainless steel with a thick copper or aluminium base.

Choosing pans

Once you have decided on the best metal or combination of metals, you should then concern yourself with the design and quality of the pan. Look for the following points:

- Thick, heavy-gauge metal, particularly on the base, which will not distort or dent and will spread the heat evenly from the source to all parts of the pan.
- Sides that curve gently into the base so that no part of the pan will be inaccessible to the spoon. This is a good feature to look for in a frying pan – curved sides enable delicate omelettes and crêpes to be rolled gently on to a plate without damage.
- Handles should be strong, securely riveted to the pan and preferably insulated from the heat so they always remain cool enough to hold. They should have comfortable, well-rounded contours – thin angular shapes cut into the hand when you are pouring or lifting heavy pans. Plastic or wooden handles are the best insulators, but may loosen and split if cleaned in a dishwasher, and of course they cannot go in the oven. A ring or hole in the end of the handle is useful for hanging the pan on a rack.
- Lids must give a tight seal and be shaped so that condensed water vapour is returned to the pan and does not escape in trickles down the outside. Lid knobs, like handles, should remain cool enough to touch – again plastic or wood is best.

Storage

If possible, pans should be kept at eye level, or at least above the waist, either hanging from a rack or on a shelf. Crowded, dark, low cupboards infuriate the busy cook – pans get piled together indiscriminately because nothing has a special place, and eventually they get scratched and chipped, or pushed to inaccessible corners.

Useful pans

The following pans make a good 'starter pack' if you are equipping a kitchen from scratch. There are many more pans you can have, but most are suited to specific tasks, so it is best to buy them only if and when you need them. Good-quality pans are expensive but will last a very long time, so are well worth the investment.

Set of stainless-steel pans

A stacking set of three or four saucepans is adequate for most culinary tasks. Sizes vary enormously, so take time and care to choose the ones that suit your needs and size of household. A large capacity pan with two handles is essential even if you normally cook small quantities – you can use it for cooking pasta and making stocks and soups, and it can also double as an oven-going casserole.

Milk pan A most useful small pan, this has a lip for easy pouring and a wide rim to help prevent milk and other liquids from boiling over. Non-stick linings are particularly useful on milk pans, for making scrambled eggs, sauces, etc.

Frying pan Cast-iron frying pans are traditional, especially for sautéeing. They look good, improve with use and age, and can last a lifetime. They are heavy and not always easy to clean, however, so a couple of good-quality, non-stick frying pans will also come in handy. However, these will not last as long as cast iron.

Sauté pan Deeper than ordinary frying pans, sauté pans have straight or slightly rounded sides. A good sauté pan is extremely versatile in that it can be used both as a regular frying pan and for risottos, sautés, stir-fries, sauces, etc.

Pasta pan Made of stainless steel, this has a perforated inner basket. It is expensive, but ideal for cooking pasta in a large quantity of water, and the basket makes for safe and easy draining. The pan itself can serve as a stockpot. Some pasta pans also come with a second insert, for steaming.

Steamer set The best is stainless steel, with one or two steamer compartments that stack on top of each other. It is useful in that the bottom pan can also serve as a conventional saucepan or casserole. An economical – and attractive – alternative is the Chinese stacking bamboo steamer that fits inside a wok, but this has more limited use than its stainless-steel counterpart.

Wok and accessories An inexpensive carbon steel wok from Chinatown is more than adequate, but the slightly more expensive preseasoned carbon steel woks are easier to keep clean. Carbon steel is the best metal because it is such an excellent conductor of heat. The most useful size of wok is 35 cm/14 in in diameter, and comes with a close-fitting, dome-shaped lid. The most useful accessories are wooden spatulas and long chopsticks, plus a long-handled spatula or scoop, a utensil that looks rather like a shovel and is indispensable for stir-frying.

Clean your wok with hot soapy water and a brush, and dry it very thoroughly after each use. To prevent rusting, wipe the inside with a little vegetable oil before putting it away.

OVENWARE AND BAKEWARE

From everyday roasting tins and baking sheets, to country kitchen casseroles, elegant china ramekins and fancifully shaped metal moulds, this section covers items that you will use time and time again, and more specialized equipment that may be used only once a year. Start with the basics and build up your collection gradually as you try new recipes. This will spread the cost and also ensure that your cupboards are not cluttered with equipment you never use.

The materials

Stainless steel This conducts heat slowly, so its use in the oven is generally limited to roasting tins.

Enamel High-quality enamel on steel or cast iron is a most durable, hard-wearing combination – the glassy finish will not be affected by even the most corrosive ingredients. Its weakness lies in the different expansion rates of the enamel and base metal, so it is particularly vulnerable to chipping when it is heated or cooled.

Glass Ovenproof glass behaves in the same way as dark metal surfaces when it is heated, and oven temperatures should be reduced slightly when using glass baking dishes. The brittleness, however, and sensitivity of glass to temperature changes means that careful handling is essential. It is not such a good conductor of heat as metal, so if used for pies and other pastry-based dishes the pastry base will never achieve a very crisp result.

Porcelain The beauty and tempered fineness of this material make it especially suitable for those dishes that must be served straight from the oven. Although porcelain is prone to chipping and cracking and must be handled with reverence, the highly vitrified surface is very tough.

Stoneware This is another tough ceramic with a sturdy quality and the ability to withstand high temperatures in the oven.

Glazed earthenware This has a traditional, rustic simplicity which people find particularly attractive. It is not as highly fired as stoneware, and so it will chip and crack more easily.

Unglazed terracotta Pots of this material, for cooking meats or vegetables without fat, will be essential items for anyone who is diet conscious or who just enjoys the flavour of meat and vegetables that have been stewed in their own juice.

Cake and pastry making

1 loaf tin
2 rolling pin
3 angel cake tin
4 flour sifter
5 bundt tin
6 deep pie dish
7 ceramic flan dish
8 pastry scraper
9 Swiss roll tin
10 pastry brush
11 marble slab
12 pastry blender
13 madeleine tray
14 bun sheet
15 sponge cake tin
16 brioche mould
17 spring-clip tin
18 ring mould
19 loose-bottomed metal flan tin
20 piping bag with metal nozzles

The equipment

Casserole Casseroles require slow, lengthy cooking, so conservation of moisture is of paramount importance. Whatever the material the casserole is made from, it should be heavy so that it absorbs heat slowly and then retains heat and moisture for the longest possible time. Lids must fit the cooking pots very closely to prevent the escape of steam, and the seal must be designed so that condensed water vapour is channelled back into the pot. Handles, which are usually made of the same material as the casserole, should be easy to grip, yet small so that the pot will fit into an oven.

Enamelled cast iron, or other suitable heavy-gauge metals, can be used on top of the stove, both for searing the meat over a high heat (if this is required) and for lengthy simmering. Earthenware or heat-resistant glass casseroles should only be used in the oven.

It is very useful to have a range of casseroles of various sizes because it is important that the contents fill the pot in the right proportion – a small stew in a large pot will dry out long before it is cooked. Different shapes of casseroles are also traditional for certain dishes – the Moroccan meat and vegetable stews called tagines are cooked in an earthenware pot that is narrow at the top and fat at the bottom, while a clay chicken brick is shaped roughly the same as the bird, and bean pots, whether from Tuscany or Boston, are pot-belly shaped.

Terrine Deep enamelled cast-iron or earthenware terrines are traditional for baking pâtés and terrines, but they are by no means essential. They are often long and narrow, which makes for elegant presentation, either when serving slices straight from the terrine or when turning out and slicing.

Roasting tin Tins in one or two sizes are useful, in stainless steel or anodized aluminium, which are both easy to clean – an important consideration with a roasting tin. Buy them with racks that fit inside for keeping meat and poultry above the fat as it runs out during roasting. Racks are especially good for fatty birds like ducks and geese, and long-cooking roasts such as turkey.

Baking sheet Heavy-duty steel sheets are best. Flat and rigid, they are good conductors of heat, and will not buckle or warp in the hottest of ovens.

Soufflé dish These are traditionally straight-sided so the soufflé mixture can rise unimpeded above the edge. Made of porcelain, glass or stoneware, they can be taken straight from oven to table – a crucial factor for serving. Available in different sizes and as individual ramekins, they are also useful for general baking purposes, and for such things as crème caramel and gelatine-set cold mousses and soufflés. The American custard cups are similar to small soufflé dishes, although they have curved sides. They are used for baking individual custards and other puddings.

Gratin and baking dishes It is impossible to have too many of these, in different shapes and sizes, full-size and individual. They are used for vegetable gratins, lasagne and other baked pasta, moussaka and shepherd's pie – in fact any dish with a topping that needs to be crisped and browned at a high temperature. French gratin dishes were traditionally made of copper, but nowadays enamelled cast iron, porcelain and stoneware are more common. They can be put safely under the grill or into a very hot oven and yet look presentable enough to take to the table. Baking dishes may be rectangular or oval in shape and made of porcelain, enamelled cast iron or steel, glass or earthenware or stoneware.

Ovenproof cast-iron frying pan
An ovenproof pan of this kind is useful for dishes that need to start off on top of the stove, finish cooking in the oven and then be turned out for serving. French tarte tatin and potato galette are two such dishes, as are some Italian frittatas. Most frying pans do not have ovenproof handles and so would not be suitable, whereas cast iron is.

CAKE AND PASTRY MAKING

When food is placed in the dry, hot atmosphere of the oven it is cooked equally from all directions, and the containers do not have to withstand and conduct heat from a single source as saucepans do. The function of a baking tin is to mould and contain, and to respond as quickly as possible to the ambient heat of the oven. The shape of tin you use depends entirely on what you are baking and what you want it to look like; the choice of material should be approached more scientifically.

The materials

Some baking tins have bright shining surfaces, which deflect the heat away from the contents so that they will not scorch; others have dark finishes, which absorb and hold the heat and need an oven temperature reduction of 10°C to achieve the same results.

Tin plate This is one of the most widely used materials for baking containers. It is really worth spending money on good-quality baking tins that have the minimum number of seams, as nooks and crannies are difficult to clean and dry. Corrosion is the chief enemy of tin plate, for underneath the shining exterior lurks a metal that is addicted to oxidation through even the smallest pin hole in the tin coating. Never use steel wool or other abrasive cleaning materials, and wash and dry baking tins as soon as possible after use.

A good-quality, well-treated tin will last a lifetime and gradually its surface will acquire a dark patina that acts as a further protection and improves performance. Tin is susceptible to attack from acid foods, so it is not a suitable material for pie dishes.

Aluminium Impervious to atmospheric oxidation, aluminium is a metal that is often used for cake tins, but it is thinner and lighter than tin plate, making it unsuitable for rich fruit mixtures or other cakes that need a long baking time: they are likely to dry out and even burn.

Non-stick silicone surfaces These are a boon and can be applied to either tin plate or aluminium, but the surface will not last if metal utensils are used to cut or scoop out the contents. To clean non-stick surfaces, soak for a few minutes, then wipe with a soapy cloth and rinse.

Aluminium foil If you are baking for the freezer, it is a great nuisance to lose the use of baking containers for weeks on end. Variously shaped aluminium foil dishes are cheap; they can be used in the oven and then transferred to the freezer.

Cake making

Even if you are not a prolific baker or cake maker, a few basic cake tins are very versatile and well worth buying.

Spring-clip tin, springform tin This is one of the most useful tins in that it can be used for most cake mixtures. It can also be used for cheesecakes and for layered mousse cakes. The combination of the spring-clip mechanism and loose bottom makes it an excellent tin for easy unmoulding of delicate or crumbly textures. Some versions come with a removable tube and fluted base and can double as tube tins (see below).

Swiss roll tin Indispensable for making Swiss rolls, this tin is also useful as a small baking tray.

Sponge cake tin This shallow, round tin is for layered sponges and Victoria sandwiches. Shiny metal tins are best for these because they deflect the heat and the cakes cook quickly and evenly.

Deep cake tin This is round or square, for rich fruit and celebration cakes. Buy heavy tinned steel rather than tin plate or aluminium. Loose-bottomed tins facilitate unmoulding. Some tins have double bottoms to help prevent burning during long cooking.

Loaf tin This is available in different sizes, usually 500 g/1 lb and 1 kg/2 lb. Non-stick linings are useful for bread, cakes, pâtés and terrines. There are also hinged tins with drop-down sides.

Bun sheet This usually has 12 cups or holes. The width and depth of cups varies for baking buns, cakes, tarts, cocktail savouries and Yorkshire puddings. Sheets for American-style muffins usually have 6 cups, each 6.5 cm/2⅝ in deep. Non-stick sheets make for easy unmoulding.

Speciality cake tins and moulds

Some traditional and classic cakes require specially shaped tins. Among these is the Austrian kugelhopf tin, a fluted tube tin used for the enriched sweet bread of the same name. The American angel cake tin also has a tube in the centre, but it is not fluted. On the top edge it may have three little feet for keeping air circulating while the cake is cooled, upside down. Bundt tins are fluted tube tins.

Other special tins include those for savarins, brioches and charlottes. All can double as moulds for jellies, mousses and other gelatine-set desserts, so are worth buying to add interest to your culinary repertoire. Trays with depressions for individual madeleines, éclairs and petits fours are more specialized and therefore less generally useful. Moulds for cream horns, castle puddings, coeurs à la crème, darioles, etc, also fall into this category.

Decorating equipment

Desserts, pastries and cakes are often decorated with piping, whether it is writing messages on frosting, making a ring of cream rosettes, or a full-scale cover-up of royal icing. Piping is also used for shaping meringues and choux pastry.

Piping bag These cone-shaped bags are usually made of flexible nylon fabric which can be easily washed and dried. A nozzle is fitted into the opening in the tip of the bag, and the contents are forced through by twisting the top of the bag and then applying gentle hand pressure.

Nozzle A good set of these will contain large, plain round nozzles for éclairs, meringues and profiteroles, large star nozzles for cream rosettes, and a galaxy of smaller nozzles for intricate cake icing.

Revolving turntable When decorating a cake you need the part you are working on facing you – it is all too easy to trail a sleeve across an intricate pattern of wet icing while adding a finishing touch to the far side. Turntables can be rotated with just a flick of a finger as you work.

Pastry making

Anyone who makes pastry needs a good supply of tools, as pastry is not improved by handling.

Rolling pin Some cooks enjoy handling ingredients and are perfectly happy to be up to their elbows in flour; those who have this direct approach will probably opt for a rolling pin made from a single cylinder of wood, which keeps the palms close to the dough. The revolving pin is more likely to suit people who prefer to keep food at a distance. The two handles, which are set on an axle and remain stationary in the hands, guide the pin.

The best rolling pins of either type are heavy and of a good size, made of hard, close-grained wood that has been smoothed to a fine, silky finish. Ceramic and glass rolling pins are also available, but these break easily and do not roll as well as the wooden ones – the smooth surface will not hold a dusting of flour.

Boards and slabs Pastry can be rolled perfectly well on a work surface, provided it is scrupulously clean. A large wooden board can also be used, but to preserve its smooth surface it should only be used for pastry and not double as a chopping board. Polyethylene boards are very good for pastry because they are cool and smooth, and easy to clean. Marble slabs are satin smooth, impervious to flavours and keep the pastry cold while it is being worked.

Dishes and tins

Pie dish For deep-dish pies with a single top crust, choose from earthenware, toughened glass or porcelain. Traditional dishes were always oval for savoury fillings, round for sweet.

Pie plate or tin Those made of metal are best for double-crust pies: the bottom crust of a pie needs metal beneath it to crisp – glass or porcelain does not conduct heat well enough and so results in a soggy crust underneath the filling, especially with wet or juicy fruit fillings.

Flan or tart tin This is for open-faced flans, tarts and quiches. Usually fluted for attractive presentation, they come in different shapes and sizes, and may be made of metal or porcelain. Loose-bottomed metal tins are especially good for sweet, rich pastries that are fragile and likely to break – the bottom is pushed up from the side of the tin so that the tart comes out in one piece.

Flan ring and tart frame An alternative to loose-bottomed flan tins, these come in many shapes and sizes. They are used on a baking sheet and lift off so that the flan or tart can be transferred to a plate.

Other useful equipment

Pastry blender This ingenious tool is most adept at cutting fat into flour and aerating it. It is made of a series of stainless-steel wires curved into a half-oval shape and attached to a handle.

Pastry scraper A piece of flexible plastic, this is used for scraping up rich pastry doughs from work surfaces, and for marking and dividing dough into portions. Some pastry scrapers are rigid with handles, and look just like a decorator's tool for smoothing plaster.

Pie funnel This little china chimney is put in the centre of a pie to prevent the top crust from collapsing into the contents, and to offer a quick way out for steam.

Pastry brush Soft natural or nylon bristles will spread egg wash, glazes, jam, or melted butter without damaging delicate or uncooked pastry.

Sifter and dredger A flour sifter aerates flour as well as blending it with other dry ingredients. Sugar and flour dredgers are used to sprinkle cakes or puddings with sugar or cocoa or to dust a work surface with flour.

Electrical appliances
1 toaster
2 coffee grinder
3 combined espresso, cappuccino and filter coffee machine
4 blender, liquidizer
5 hand-held blender
6 ice-cream maker
7 heavy-duty stand mixer
8 juice extractor
9 hand mixer
10 food processor
11 waffle iron

ELECTRICAL APPLIANCES

There is an ever-increasing choice of electrical appliances for the kitchen. Think hard before you purchase, and don't clutter up valuable space with bulky machines you hardly ever use.

Blender, liquidizer For blending soups and making vegetable purées, pâtés and baby food, a blender gives excellent, smooth results. Many blenders claim to be able to pulverize nuts, chop vegetables and grate cheese, but few have the power and the capacity to do so, and it is often just as quick to use a sharp knife. When buying a blender look for one with blades set low in the container. This way you will be able to blend small quantities such as one or two egg yolks for mayonnaise.

Choose the largest blender you can, as they rarely work well when the container is over half full, and it is time-consuming trying to blend a huge pan of soup in a machine that takes a cupful at a time.

The container should be clear, toughened glass or heavyweight plastic to enable you to see how things are getting on; avoid lightweight plastic which may crack. A small 'trap door' in the lid allows you to dribble in your oil for mayonnaise without spattering.

Hand-held blenders are excellent for puréeing soup in the pan, thus saving on washing up. They are also good for whipping cream, making mayonnaise and blending small quantities of ingredients, particularly baby food.

Food processor The ultimate kitchen machine, this chops, slices, grates, pulverizes and minces, makes pastry and bread dough, and purées soups and pâté mixtures. Some models go even further and, with attachments and different blades, squeeze citrus fruit, grind coffee beans and peel potatoes. They will not beat egg whites effectively, however, so a separate mixer or whisk is still essential.

The more compact the design, the better for work-top storage, but you will still have to find room for the extra blades, discs and attachments.

Choose a model that has a heavy-duty motor and, if possible, one that has a pulse button and a circuit-breaker to prevent it overheating or burning out. Also buy one with a large-capacity bowl because, like blenders, they work better if they are filled no more than half full. Rubber foot pads will make the machine stay put during any operation.

Hand mixer The main advantage of a hand-held electric mixer is that it is faster than a whisk. It also frees one hand to hold the bowl or add ingredients as you beat, and you can beat in every part of the bowl. Choose a mixer with three speeds (high, medium and low) and a switch that is easy to change with a flick of the thumb. The beaters should be easy to remove for cleaning. Unless you want, or already have, a mixer on a stand, buy a hand mixer with a heavy-duty motor and a selection of beaters for tough jobs such as mixing dough.

Mixer with stand and bowl A heavy-duty stand mixer is useful for many jobs besides cake making. Most have a dough hook attachment and some a separate blender and/or coffee grinder.

When a mixer also has such varied attachments as a mincer, a juice extractor, a pasta maker, a potato peeler and a shredder and slicer, it has really moved into the next function and price bracket of the all-in-one food processor. Before buying, check that the motor is capable of coping with heavy-duty jobs and is not just a glorified blender/mixer.

Depending upon the model, the mixer bowl may be plastic, stainless steel or toughened glass; stainless steel or toughened glass is best for durability. In some mixers the beaters are simply inserted into the motor housing and rotate only in one spot. These often leave a ring of unbeaten ingredients around the bowl. The best machines are those with beaters that travel in a circle as they rotate and thus beat every part of the mixture efficiently. Make sure, too, if you can, that the beaters can handle a small quantity such as one egg. Mixers with light plastic bases and bowls may be lighter to move around, but a solid base with a rubber pad or feet will prevent the machine from 'creeping'.

Kettle For most people an electric kettle is an essential. Look for a long guarantee and a non-corrosive body. Automatic cut-outs, which prevent the kettle burning out and the room filling with steam, are fairly standard. The cordless kettle, which sits on an electric base, is very safe and convenient because it has no trailing flex. Look for a model with non-slip feet.

Toaster Toasters are simple electrical gadgets and most do their job efficiently. Some take four slices – a must for the large family – but standard models take two. Some have adjustable slots to take thick slices of bread, muffin and bagel halves, etc. Large catering-style models may have a wide slot with a removable holder for toasted sandwiches. With any toaster, look for a removable crumb tray – and a long guarantee.

Waffle iron The waffle iron consists of two heated griddles joined by a hinge; batter is poured on to one griddle, the other is closed over it and cooking takes only a few minutes. Most griddles have a honeycombed surface. Waffle irons with a non-stick surface are the easiest to use.

Deep-fryer An electric, thermostatically controlled deep-fryer with a lid not only takes the guesswork and odour out of deep-frying, it is also the safest way to deep-fry at home. It brings the fat up to the chosen temperature and holds it there, and the best models have a light that indicates the desired temperature is reached. Deep-fryers come in various capacities and designs, some with non-stick linings that are easy to keep clean. A good design feature in some models is a basket with handles that clip or rest on the pan so that the fat from the fried food can drain into the fryer before serving.

Ice-cream maker Old methods of ice-cream making involved a great deal of cranking and stirring over buckets of crushed ice and rock salt. The latest state-of-the-art ice-cream machines have integral compressors and freezers so they sit on the worktop. This kind is the most convenient to use because it works very fast and doesn't take up freezer space – it also makes the most velvety smooth ice creams and sorbets. Professional-style models make a large quantity in a very short time, and they incorporate mixing blades that allow you to add soft fruits straight into the ice cream as it mixes. Less expensive machines with rotation motors are not quite so convenient because they must be put into the freezer, but they also achieve very good results in a very short time.

Juice extractor These offer effortless juice extraction from fresh fruits and vegetables. An extractor is a worthwhile purchase if you drink a lot of fresh juice, because in the long run it will work out less expensive than shop-bought juices. Models range from simple small citrus juice reamers to large machines with two juicing functions – one for vegetables and fruits such as apples and peaches, the other for juicing citrus fruits. Some models have filters to separate the juice from the pips and pith of fruit.

Pasta machine This is a machine that makes the dough for pasta all in one go, so cutting out all the hard work of kneading and rolling by hand. The dough can be extruded in various shapes according to the cutting disc used – from long and thin spaghetti and tagliatelle to ridged macaroni, flat sheets of lasagne and oriental noodles. Some machines are so versatile that they can even mix pizza and biscuit dough.

Bread machine This mixes all the ingredients, then kneads the dough and bakes it. Most machines are quite compact and sit neatly on the worktop. A programmer allows you to set the time the machine operates, so you can wake up to freshly baked bread in the morning. The machine itself bakes different types of dough in a set loaf shape, but if you want rolls, different-shaped loaves, pizza or pitta bread, etc, you can use the machine just to ready the dough for shaping by hand and then bake it conventionally.

Coffee grinder The advantage of electric coffee grinders over manual is that they are quicker, but they are often noisy. The ideal grinder is quiet, efficient and neat. It is also useful if you can preselect the grind required from powder to coarse ground; if you can't, you will find that you never seem to get the same grind twice. The safest type of grinder will not work unless the lid is on.

Filter coffee maker The electric filter coffee maker is an elaborate version of the filter and jug method. It heats the water to the right temperature and pulses it through the ground coffee into the jug below; a hot plate under the jug keeps the coffee warm. As long as you put the correct type and amount of coffee in the filter, it is really a foolproof way to make decent coffee. Don't leave the jug on the hot plate for too long, however, or the coffee will taste stewed.

Coffee machine The most versatile coffee machine is the type that makes filter coffee into a jug on one side and espresso or cappuccino directly into a cup on the other. Before you buy, check that the instructions are easy to follow. Some espresso and cappuccino machines may look very stylish, but can be fiendishly difficult to use.

Barbecuing
1 large grill
2 hibachi barbecue
3 bamboo and metal skewers
4 fish grill
5 sardine grill
6 long matches
7 long-handled tongs
8 kettle barbecue

BARBECUING

To many, barbecuing is one of the easiest and most enjoyable ways of preparing foods. Devotees of barbecuing will not need to be convinced, but those who have not tried it should not be put off by the vast range of equipment available: the rule is the simpler the better. Food cooked on a piece of chicken wire over a fire on a beach tastes just as good as – if not better than – food prepared on a gas-fired grill with a motorized spit.

Types of barbecues

For those with large gardens, a built-in brick barbecue is worth considering as it allows you to design extra warming cupboards and preparation surfaces.

Heavy-gauge metal and cast-iron grills are less likely to become misshapen with repeated use than lightweight nickel-plated and chrome-plated grills, although these do have the advantage of being rustproof. The grill rods should be fairly close together for grilling sausages, chicken pieces and the like. Most people find it is convenient to cook at table height; so if you buy a small portable barbecue you will need to set it on a table or on a board on two stools. Some ready-made brazier barbecues have very short legs – check that they are high enough to cook on in comfort.

Kettle barbecue These barbecues are totally enclosed by a hinged lid. This may be left open during cooking, but often the food is cooked with the lid down, which reflects the heat like an oven so that even whole chickens and joints of meat can be barbecued. Made from cast aluminium or enamelled steel, kettle barbecues are ideal for a windy garden.

Wagon barbecue Wagons are usually on wheels and sometimes covered. The larger kinds are gas-fired and have all manner of modern cooking aids, such as warming cupboards, electric rôtisseries and thermometers. They are bulky and need storage room in winter, but are ideal when cooking in quantity.

Hibachi These are small Japanese-style, black cast-iron troughs, rectangular or round, with strong wooden-handled grid irons. The height of the grids is adjustable. Especially useful for taking on picnics and other outings, hibachis come with single, double or triple grids, which can be raised to different heights, but are not adaptable for spit-roasting.

Brazier Often made in unsuitably lightweight materials, braziers are basically round or square trays on legs or wheels. Some have hoods, and spits can be fitted, but the main drawback of braziers is that they are often too low to cook on comfortably.
Picnic barbecue This term may be applied to the compact types of brazier that can be easily packed for travel. They may be rectangular or round and are usually made of lightweight metal.

The accessories

There is no need to assemble a battery of gadgets, but some specialized items will aid the cook considerably and some are essential for safety reasons.
Heatproof gloves and apron These are a must when cooking over an open fire. Choose really thick gloves, and avoid plastic aprons.
Bellows or fan Not essential, but most fire-makers find that they are a boon to encourage a reluctant blaze.
Basting brush and bulb baster Succulent barbecued food needs frequent basting. For steaks and chops a long-handled basting brush is easiest to use, but for large spit-roasts a bulb baster allows you to baste over the heat.
Long-handled fork Useful for lifting and turning food over the heat. Those with wooden handles are best.
Tongs Long-handled tongs are useful, both for moving glowing coals and for lifting and turning pieces of food without piercing them. Wooden handles are best.
Skewers Long skewers are preferable because they enable you to leave the handles outside the fire. Those with wooden handles will be easier to use.
Grills Unless your barbecue has bars spaced close together to lay tender fish and crumbly hamburgers on, you need a separate grill to hold them gently while cooking and to keep them in one piece. Made usually of tinned steel, grills consist of two sides of close-set rods hinged together, and two long, flat handles. Steaks and hamburgers are cooked in a flat round, square or rectangular grill; if heated before use, it sears the food with a lovely pattern. Fish grills are curved so that the delicate flesh is not crushed; some have legs on each side to facilitate turning and allow them to stand in the coals. All wire grills need to be greased with oil or butter and heated before use.
Revolving spit-roaster or spit The simplest spit is a long stainless-steel rod with a plastic or wooden handle, and two or four sharp-angled tines that can be adjusted to hold the bird or joint in place. This sort of spit is usually made to slot into the hood of a barbecue. A motor-driven spit with either battery or electrical power is essential for roasting evenly. Make sure the spit is strong enough to take the heaviest roast without bending.
Cast-iron grill plates and racks These are only necessary if you build your own barbecue, as any purchased barbecue has its own grill. Cast iron is best, but it must be dried and oiled after use or it will rust. Always oil it before use, too.

SMOKING

Home smoking – to cook food or to cure it – offers great scope to the adventurous cook. Simply adding aromatic herbs, to enhance the fragrant wood smoke, will produce wonderful flavours.

Hot smoking

Also called smoke cooking, this is a refinement of barbecuing: the food is cooked and smoked at the same time. A covered barbecue can be used, or a special smoker, and sawdust or wood chips are added to create a fragrant smoke to flavour and preserve the food. Favourite woods are apple, hickory and oak, but any hard wood will do. Resinous woods such as pine must never be used because they will make the food taste of disinfectant.

The temperature in the smoker depends on the food you are smoking and on how strong a smoke flavour you want. Fish and shellfish take well to smoking; most is hot-smoked at 50–93°C/120–200°F.

There are many kinds of smoke cooker available, all of which come complete with instructions. You must site your smoker outdoors as there will be a fair amount of smoke and fumes escaping. As it cooks, the food will turn a beautiful light mahogany colour.

Electric smokers are expensive but convenient, and can be used for fish, meat and poultry. Aromatic wood chips are an optional extra, if you like the additional flavour.

Small smokers for the cooker top are also available, and are convenient for smoking small quantities indoors.

Cold smoking

Hot smoking is a method of cooking, but cold smoking, with which it is often confused, does not cook the food but cures it. Before being cold smoked, all foods must be brined and drip-dried. You can make your own cold smoker from a barrel, a few bricks, a pole and a piece of wet sacking, or you can convert a hot smoker to a cold one. Alternatively, hang brined food, away from flames, in a chimney over a hard-wood fire damped with hardwood chips or sawdust.

PRESERVING

Jam jars with airtight plastic lids can be specially purchased for preserving, or you can hoard empty jars all year. Glass is best for jam jars, as it is easy to check that you have not poured the jam in while it is still too hot, causing all the fruit to rise to the surface.

Jam jar covers For jars that you are re-using, keep packs of cellophane covers, waxed sealing discs and elastic bands in stock, plus some self-adhesive labels.
Preserving pan This is a good investment even if you only use it three or four times a year. Large saucepans are not good substitutes, and are likely to cause a good deal of extra work cleaning the burned jam from the pan and stove top.

Preserving pans should have thick bottoms, which heat evenly and quickly conduct the heat away from the source underneath so the contents of the pan does not burn and stick. The pan is deep and wide to allow maximum evaporation and expansion of the contents.

The most practical preserving pans are made of stainless steel with a thick base. The performance of stainless steel is only equalled by copper, but copper reacts with acid foods to form poisonous salts, so these pans should be lined with stainless steel. Never leave fruit or jam in any metal pan for any length of time.
Sugar thermometer This is essential for checking whether the setting-point temperature has been reached.
Funnel Stainless-steel, glass or nylon bottling funnels are essential for pouring jams, jellies or syrups neatly into the jars.
Jelly bag Some coarse or pippy fruits are best preserved as jellies, by straining the cooked fruit through a flannel jelly bag. This catches the pips while letting through all the pectin and flavour.

3

Recipes

Stocks

beef 51–3
bouquet garni 190
poultry 86–95
poultry giblets 90
veal 54–6

sieves 226
skimmers 228
stovetop pans 233–5

Roast Chicken with Marjoram 305

The ingredients for stock need never be expensive. Use bones and pieces of meat the butcher has no use for, or the chicken giblets that many customers don't want, or the remains of a roast chicken. If you haven't any vegetables, you can do without them; if you have only vegetables, you can still make a good stock. Alternatively, you can resort to a shop-bought fresh stock, which can be very good, or to stock made up from powder or a cube.

The yields suggested for the recipes here are just a guideline, as the quantity of stock made will depend on how much evaporation occurs in cooking. Most stocks will keep for 3–4 days in the refrigerator, or up to 3 months in the freezer.

Jellied stock This adds a velvety texture to sauces, gravies and soups. If you make a well-flavoured light chicken or beef stock but include a high proportion of veal bones, or a calf's foot chopped in pieces, or two pig's trotters and other gelatinous things such as skin, heads or feet, you will have a stock that jellies firmly when it is cold.

Meat glazes If you reduce your rich jellied stock, after straining, to one-quarter of its original volume, you will have a syrupy jelly called a glaze, or *glace* in French. It is an important ingredient of French restaurant cooking and the basis of many classic sauces, but most domestic cooking can be absolutely delicious without the bother of making a glaze; just use a good concentrated stock.

CHICKEN STOCK

This is the easiest and quickest stock to make and also one of the best bases for home-made soup. It is made from the bones and carcass of a roast chicken. Use it for most vegetable soups, chicken and rabbit stews, for braising white meats and whenever a light-coloured stock with a good flavour is needed. Chicken giblets and feet, previously boiled for 5 minutes in salted water or scorched under a hot grill and then skinned, or chopped veal bones, can be added to make a stock that will set more firmly. Pieces of fresh chicken, which are now such good value, can also be added to the stock to great effect.

The vegetables that are suggested here can be replaced or augmented by whatever you happen to have in the kitchen – a combination of leeks and celery is particularly good in chicken stock. If you want a very pale stock, peel the onions; otherwise they can be left in their skins, which will give the liquid a clear golden tint. Don't put in cabbage or any of the brassicas because they go sour rather quickly, and don't add too many carrots as they will give an oversweet note to the broth.

MAKES 1.5–2 LITRES/2¾–3½ PINTS

- 1 chicken (or duck) carcass and giblets, preferably from a free-range bird
- chicken feet or chopped veal bones (optional)
- 2 onions or shallots
- 2 carrots
- 2 leeks, halved if large
- 2 celery sticks
- a fresh bouquet garni of thyme, parsley and bay leaf
- 6 black peppercorns
- a wineglass of white wine (optional)
- salt

Put all the bones and, if you have not already used them for gravy, the giblets in a stockpot or other large pan. Add the prepared chicken feet or veal bones, if you are using them. Cover with 3 litres/5 pints of cold water and bring slowly to the boil, skimming off all the scum and froth that rise. Then add the onions or shallots, the carrots, leeks, celery, bouquet garni, the peppercorns and perhaps a glass of white wine. Salt only lightly (or wait until the end) – as the stock becomes concentrated, so does the taste of the salt.

Simmer for 2–3 hours (boiling makes stock cloudy) until it is well reduced, then take it off the heat and strain it into a bowl. If clarity is not important, press the vegetables lightly to extract all the liquid. As soon as the stock is cold, cover and set aside in a cool place or the refrigerator. The fat that solidifies on the surface can then be taken off with a spoon. Store the stock in the refrigerator.

GOLDEN VEAL OR BEEF STOCK

Somewhat stronger, but not such a well-flavoured stock as the pale chicken stock, this is used when making gravy, veal or beef stews, braised veal dishes and daubes, or as a substitute for chicken stock.

The bones from young animals contain the most gelatine, so use some veal bones for a rich, unctuous texture. Beef shin and knuckle bones are the best choice for flavour, neck bones second best. Ideally, use a combination of the two. Long, slow cooking extracts the gelatine, salts and flavour. The stock will have a more interesting flavour if you add some extra meat – shin of beef, a duck or chicken carcass or giblets, and perhaps a piece of calf's liver for flavour and to keep the broth relatively clear.

MAKES ABOUT 1 LITRE/1¾ PINTS

- 1.35 kg/3 lb veal and beef bones, chopped up by the butcher
- 340 g/12 oz shin of beef
- 2 onions, chopped

3 leeks, chopped
2 carrots, chopped
2 celery sticks, chopped
a fresh bouquet garni of thyme, parsley and bay leaf
6 black peppercorns
a wineglass of white wine (optional)
salt

Put the bones and meat in a stockpot or other large pan and cover with 3 litres/5 pints of cold water. Bring slowly to the boil, skimming off the froth and scum that rise. Simmer very gently for 4–5 hours on top of the stove or 45 minutes in a pressure cooker. Or, if you hate the smell of stock cooking, bring it to the boil on top of the stove and then transfer it, covered, to a very slow oven to cook gently. Halfway through the cooking time, add the vegetables, the bouquet garni, peppercorns and wine, if using, plus just a pinch of salt (you can add more later).

Strain, cool and remove the fat as for chicken stock. Store the stock in the refrigerator.

RICH BROWN BEEF OR VEAL STOCK

Brown stock is used for strong beefy soups, such as borscht, onion soup, oxtail soup and goulash soup, and when making stews such as oxtail, English beef stew and hot pot. It is also added to mince dishes such as shepherd's pie. The bones left over from an underdone roast of beef will make a good brown beef stock.

Add onion skins – those from the onions you are using plus an extra one or two – to give the stock a good colour.

MAKES ABOUT 1 LITRE/1¾ PINTS

30 g/1 oz beef dripping or lard
1.35 kg/3 lb beef or veal knuckle bones
340 g/12 oz or more shin of beef
2 celery sticks, chopped
2–3 carrots, chopped
2 onions, unpeeled, chopped
2 leeks, chopped
2 tomatoes
2 cloves
a few sprigs of fresh thyme
1 bay leaf
a wineglass of red wine (optional)
salt

Heat a little of the fat in a stockpot or other large pan and brown the knuckle bones and shin until they are nicely coloured; or put them in an uncovered roasting tin and brown them in the oven preheated to 220°C/425°F, gas mark 7. Pour off the fat from the stockpot. Add 3 litres/5 pints of cold water and bring slowly to the boil, skimming off the froth and scum that rise. Leave to simmer for 2–3 hours, skimming whenever you pass by the stove.

Heat the rest of the fat in a separate pan and fry the celery, carrots, onions and leeks until browned. Drain off the fat and add the vegetables to the stockpot, together with the tomatoes, cloves, thyme, bay leaf, red wine, if using, and a pinch of salt. Simmer for a further 2 hours. (If you add the vegetables at the start of the cooking time for the bones, they can become so overcooked that they make the liquid bitter.)

Strain, cool and remove the fat as for chicken stock. This stock can be reduced to make a glaze. Store in the refrigerator.

RICH VEGETABLE STOCK

This stock may seem to have some strange ingredients, but they are carefully chosen to give a result with a satisfying, savoury taste. Too often vegetable stocks do not have a full rich flavour, or a good after-taste. Use this stock as a substitute for chicken stock or for any recipe using pulses, onions, root vegetables or mushrooms.

MAKES ABOUT 1.2 LITRES/2 PINTS

3–4 very large, flat mushrooms, sliced
2 leeks, chopped
1 red onion, chopped
115 g/4 oz yellow split peas
115 g/4 oz pearl barley
½ teaspoon fenugreek seeds
1 teaspoon black mustard seeds
2 tablespoons light soy sauce
a fresh bouquet garni of parsley and bay leaf
175 ml/6 fl oz dry white wine
a pinch of sugar
salt and freshly ground pepper

Place all the ingredients in a saucepan (add only a little salt at this stage) and add 2.4 litres/4 pints water. Bring to the boil, skimming off all the froth that rises, and simmer for 1 hour.

Strain through a sieve, discarding the last bit of stock which will be dark and cloudy with sediment. Taste for seasoning. Allow to cool, then store in the refrigerator or freezer.

LEMON COURT-BOUILLON WITH PARSLEY

This is the stock in which to poach many types of fish; it is also the basis of many fish soups. Always allow it to cool to blood heat before you put in the fish.

beef 51–3
bouquet garni 190
dripping 110
fenugreek 199
lard 110
light soy sauce 207
mustard seed 202
pearl barley 116
skinning and seeding tomatoes 423
veal 54–6
yellow split pea 128

roasting tin 236
sieves 226
skimmers 228
stovetop pans 233–5

Borscht 249
French Onion Soup 249
Ragù alla Bolognese 336

Stocks/Soups

boning round fish 28
button onion 143
carrot 148
chervil 190
crème fraîche 99
filleting and skinning flat fish 26
filleting round fish 27
fish 10–25
making crème fraîche 423
mushrooms and other fungi 158–61
potato 145

blender, liquidizer 238
food processor 238
sieves 226
skimmers 228
stovetop pans 233–5

Chicken Stock 244
Rich Vegetable Stock 245

MAKES ABOUT 1.5 LITRES/2¾ PINTS
- 2–3 small onions, sliced
- 3 carrots, sliced
- 2 bay leaves
- a small bunch of parsley
- 2 slices of lemon
- 15 g/½ oz butter
- 1 tablespoon salt
- 5–6 black peppercorns
- 600 ml/1 pint white wine or 300 ml/½ pint wine vinegar

Put all the ingredients in a large saucepan together with 1.2 litres/2 pints of cold water. Bring to the boil, then cover and simmer for 20 minutes. If using as the base for a soup, strain the court-bouillon.

FISH FUMET

Reduce this fish stock to use it as the basis of a sauce, or turn it into an aspic with which to glaze fish that are to be served cold. If you cannot obtain sole trimmings, use those from the better-flavoured fish such as cod or plaice (avoid oily, strong-flavoured varieties such as salmon). You can substitute 1–2 wineglasses of dry white wine for some of the water.

MAKES ABOUT 1.8 LITRES/3 PINTS
- the bones and trimmings of 2–3 sole
- 2–3 outside sticks of celery, sliced
- 2 onions, sliced
- 1 carrot, sliced
- 1 bay leaf
- salt

Put all the ingredients in a large pan together with 2.4 litres/4 pints of cold water. Add only a little salt because the liquid will reduce during the cooking process and so the saltiness will become stronger. Bring to the boil and then simmer, uncovered, for 30–45 minutes. Strain.

DELICATE CARROT SOUP

SERVES 4–6
- 6 carrots, coarsely grated
- 2–3 potatoes, peeled and coarsely grated
- 2 onions, coarsely grated
- 30 g/1 oz butter
- 900 ml/1½ pints chicken stock
- 3 tablespoons double cream
- salt and freshly ground pepper
- 2 teaspoons finely chopped fresh chervil or parsley

Put all the vegetables in a large heavy saucepan with the butter and stir them around over a moderate heat until the butter melts. Then cover the pan and leave to cook over a low heat for 10 minutes, removing the lid from time to time to give the vegetables a stir. Add the stock, bring to the boil and simmer for 20 minutes or until the vegetables are very tender.

Purée the soup in a blender or food processor, or through the fine blade of a Mouli-légumes. Pour back into the pan and bring to the boil. Stir in the cream, season and stir in the chervil or parsley. Serve at once.

GARLIC MUSHROOM SOUP WITH CREAM

SERVES 6
- 55 g/2 oz butter
- 8 button onions or shallots, finely chopped
- 1–2 garlic cloves, finely chopped
- 225 g/8 oz mushrooms (button, flat, chestnut, field, oyster, or a mixture), finely chopped
- 2–3 tablespoons dry white vermouth
- 1.2 litres/2 pints chicken stock or vegetable stock
- 3 large or 4 small free-range egg yolks
- 300 ml/½ pint double or whipping cream
- 1–2 teaspoons chopped parsley
- salt and freshly ground white pepper

Melt the butter in a large saucepan and sweat the onions and garlic until soft and translucent. Add the mushrooms and stir them around with the onions for a few minutes, then add the vermouth. In another pan, bring the stock to the boil. Pour the stock on to the vegetables and simmer for 15 minutes or until the taste of the mushrooms has really permeated the broth and the onions are thoroughly cooked.

Beat the egg yolks with the cream in a bowl. Add a few ladles of the soup, then pour the mixture into the saucepan. Add the parsley and seasoning to taste. Heat very slowly, stirring all the time. Do not allow the soup to boil or it will curdle. When the mushrooms are suspended in the soup, serve immediately.

TOMATO AND LEEK SOUP

SERVES 4–6
- 450 g/1 lb tomatoes, quartered
- 2 leeks, white part only, coarsely chopped
- 2 small potatoes, peeled and cubed
- 1.2 litres/2 pints chicken stock
- salt and freshly ground white pepper
- 3–4 tablespoons double cream or crème fraîche

Put the tomatoes, leeks and potatoes in a large saucepan and cover them with the stock. Bring to the boil and simmer for 25–30 minutes – only long enough to make all the vegetables tender. Purée using the finest blade of a Mouli-légumes, or purée in a blender or food processor and then press the soup through a wire sieve. Add seasoning to taste and stir in half of the cream or crème fraîche. Swirl a teaspoonful of cream into each serving at the last moment.

LIGHT WATERCRESS SOUP

SERVES 6

- 30 g/1 oz butter
- 2 large potatoes, just under 450 g/1 lb, peeled and chopped
- 1 onion, chopped
- 2 small leeks, sliced
- 1.2 litres/2 pints chicken stock
- salt and freshly ground pepper
- 2 bunches of watercress
- 150 ml/¼ pint milk
- a little butter or 150 ml/¼ pint double or whipping cream

Melt the butter in a fairly large saucepan and put in the potatoes, onion and leeks. Let them sweat and soften over a low heat for 10 minutes, stirring from time to time to prevent them from browning. Cover with the stock, add a little salt and bring to the boil. Simmer for 10 minutes.

Reserve a sprig or two of watercress for the garnish; coarsely chop the rest, stalks and all. Add to the pan. Taste the broth and add a little more salt if necessary, then simmer until all the vegetables are tender but the cress is still a good green – about 15 minutes.

Purée in a blender or food processor or using a Mouli-légumes; purée coarsely for a green-flecked soup or finely for a soup of a more uniform green. Add some of the milk if the soup is too thick to purée. Return the soup to the pan. Stir in the rest of the milk. Taste for seasoning and reheat.

Either serve as it is with a small knob of butter in each bowlful, or whip the cream to a light snow, until it sticks to the whisk, and at the last moment, whisk it briefly into the pan of very hot soup. To serve, float a leaf or two of raw watercress on top of each bowl.

SPRING SORREL SOUP

Sorrel, when cooked, has a beautiful velvety consistency; the egg yolks make this soup smoother still. It is a refreshing, acid soup that will lift jaded appetites.

SERVES 4–6

- 45 g/1½ oz butter
- 1 onion, chopped
- 340 g/12 oz sorrel, coarsely chopped
- 1 small round lettuce, coarsely chopped
- several sprigs of fresh chervil, coarsely chopped
- 900 ml/1½ pints boiling chicken stock
- salt and freshly ground pepper
- 2 large or 3 small free-range egg yolks
- a little butter or 4–6 tablespoons double cream
- 2–3 tablespoons tiny, freshly made croûtons

Melt the butter in a large saucepan and sweat the onion until soft and translucent. Add the sorrel, lettuce and chervil and allow to wilt; the sorrel melts and changes colour immediately ; the lettuce takes a little longer to wilt. Pour on the boiling stock and add seasoning to taste. Simmer, uncovered, until the vegetables are cooked through, about 10–15 minutes. Purée by pressing through a wire sieve or using the medium blade of a Mouli-légumes, or purée in a food processor or blender, then press through a wire sieve to remove the fine fibres in the sorrel.

Return the soup to the pan and heat through without boiling. Beat the egg yolks in a bowl and stir in a few tablespoons of the soup. Add the egg mixture to the rest of the soup in the pan and stir over a very low heat, without boiling, until slightly thickened. Serve with a knob of butter or a spoonful of cream in each bowl and a spoonful of very hot croûtons.

ALTERNATIVE: **Spinach soup** Substitute 450 g/1 lb spinach for the sorrel and lettuce.

PUMPKIN SOUP WITH BASIL

You can serve this in a pumpkin shell, in which case double the quantities.

SERVES 6–8

- 1 pumpkin or slice of pumpkin, weighing about 450 g/1 lb
- 2 large leeks
- 300–450 ml/½–¾ pint milk
- 1.2 litres/2 pints chicken stock
- 2 sprigs of fresh basil, chopped, or ½ teaspoon dried basil
- a pinch of grated nutmeg
- salt and freshly ground pepper
- 30 g/1 oz butter
- 2–3 tablespoons double cream

Remove the seeds and pith from the pumpkin; cut the flesh away from the skin and then chop the flesh into

basil 192
lettuce 129
pumpkin 157
sorrel 133
spinach 132
sweat 423
watercress 130
whipping cream 423

blender, liquidizer 238
food processor 238
Mouli-légumes 226
stovetop pans 233–5
whisks 227

Chicken Stock 244
Croûtons 264

bouquet garni 190
fresh and cooking sausages 72–4
ham, bacon and salted pork 68–70
yellow split pea 128

blender, liquidizer 238
food processor 238
Mouli-légumes 226
stovetop pans 233–5

BORSCHT

cubes. Reserve the green tops from the leeks, and finely slice the white part. Put the sliced white leek and the cubed pumpkin into a saucepan with a few tablespoons of water, just enough to cover the bottom of the pan. Cover. Set over a gentle heat and allow the vegetables to soften to a mush. Stir from time to time to make sure they do not stick. When they are very tender, purée them in a blender or food processor or using the medium blade of a Mouli-légumes.

Return the puréed mixture to the cleaned saucepan and add the milk, stock, basil, nutmeg and seasoning to taste. Leave to heat through gently.

Meanwhile, finely slice about half a teacupful of the green leek tops (discard the remainder). Melt the butter in a small saucepan, add the green rings of leek tops and sweat until just tender. Stir the leek tops and the cream into the soup and serve.

YELLOW SPLIT PEA SOUP

SERVES 6

1 ham bone or a 225 g/8 oz piece of bacon or salt pork
225 g/8 oz dried yellow split peas
1 carrot, coarsely chopped
2 potatoes, peeled and coarsely chopped
a fresh bouquet garni of a sprig each of thyme and parsley and a bay leaf
1 teaspoon dried marjoram
salt and freshly ground pepper
225 g/8 oz smoked boiling sausage, such as kielbasa, sliced
55 g/2 oz butter or 150 ml/¼ pint double cream

If using bacon, it may need soaking overnight. Put the peas in a large saucepan, cover with water, bring to the boil and boil for 5 minutes. Drain the peas and return to the pan. Add the carrot, potatoes and ham bone, bacon or salt pork. Cover with 2.4 litres/4 pints cold water and add the bouquet garni, marjoram, some pepper and a very little salt. Bring to the boil, skimming off all scum and froth. Leave to simmer for 1¼–1½ hours or until the vegetables are very tender.

Remove the ham bone, bacon or salt pork and the bouquet garni. (If you like you can chop the bacon or salt pork and stir into the soup before serving.) Purée the soup in a blender or food processor or using the fine blade of a Mouli-légumes. Return to the pan and taste for seasoning. Add the sliced boiling sausage and simmer for 15 minutes.

Serve this soup in the traditional way with a knob of butter added to each bowl plus plenty of freshly ground black pepper, or stir cream into it.

ALTERNATIVE: **Lentil soup** Substitute brown or green lentils for the split peas; add 4 celery sticks, coarsely chopped, with the carrot and potatoes; and stir a teaspoon of olive oil into each bowl in place of cream or butter.

OLD-FASHIONED CHICKEN BROTH

The only chicken broth worth eating is the transparently clear, amber-tinted liquid obtained from boiling a whole chicken. It must be good enough to eat on its own, without adornment. It can also be used as the base for countless soups. Chicken broth is understood best by the Italians, who use it in delicate soups such as *stracciatella* or *zuppa pavese*, with eggs stirred or dropped into it, or in soups containing pasta, peas, tomatoes, cubes of custard or a scattering of Parmesan cheese and semolina. In Greece chicken broth is used to make avgolemono soup and sauce, and in England it is the base of a sturdy chicken soup with rice.

SERVES 6

a 1.6–1.8 kg/3½–4 lb boiling fowl or roasting chicken, preferably free-range, together with its giblets
2.4 litres/4 pints pale jellied chicken stock or water
a wineglass of white wine
6 black peppercorns
a large bunch of parsley
2 shallots
2 onions, unpeeled
1 celery stick
1–2 carrots
1–2 leeks
salt

Put the chicken, breast down, in a large saucepan with all the other ingredients. Bring slowly to the boil, skimming off the scum and froth that rise. Simmer gently until the chicken is tender: a roasting chicken will be done quite quickly – in about an hour – but will not give such a rich flavour as a good old boiling fowl, which will need at least 2–2½ hours of slow, steady simmering.

Lift out the bird. Strain the broth, without pressing on the vegetables. When it has cooled, remove all the fat (chicken fat is excellent for frying). Enjoy the chicken at the same time as the broth or at another meal.

BORSCHT

SERVES 6–8

30 g/1 oz butter
2 raw beetroots, finely chopped
½ white cabbage, finely chopped
2 leeks, finely chopped
2–3 celery sticks, finely chopped
2 onions, finely chopped
2.4 litres/4 pints beef stock, well skimmed of fat, or vegetable stock
1 teaspoon caraway seeds
a fresh bouquet garni of a sprig each of thyme and parsley and a bay leaf
salt and freshly ground pepper
a pinch of grated nutmeg
2 tablespoons red wine vinegar
2 teaspoons sugar
a wineglass of red wine
1 cooked beetroot
150 ml/¼ pint sour cream

Melt the butter in a large frying pan and sweat the chopped vegetables in it for about 10 minutes. Add the stock, caraway seeds and bouquet garni and then season sparingly with salt, pepper and nutmeg. Simmer gently for 1 hour. Add the vinegar, sugar and red wine and simmer for a further 20 minutes.

Grate the cooked beetroot or cut it into fine strips. Add to the soup and heat through. Check the seasoning and remove the bouquet garni. Serve, adding a heaped tablespoon of sour cream to each bowl.

FRENCH ONION SOUP

SERVES 4 AS A MAIN DISH OR 6 AS A STARTER

55 g/2 oz butter
450 g/1 lb Spanish onions, sliced
1.2 litres/2 pints beef stock or vegetable stock
2 stalks and leaves of fresh herb fennel
1 clove
salt and freshly ground pepper
1 teaspoon sugar
1 French loaf, cut into thick slices on the diagonal
a dash of brandy
115–170 g/4–6 oz Gruyère, freshly grated

Melt the butter in a large saucepan, add the onions and sweat gently until they are very soft, translucent and golden. Bring the stock to the boil in another pan and pour it on to the onions. Add the fennel, clove and seasoning to taste.

Put the sugar in a long-handled metal spoon and hold it under a hot grill or over a gas flame until the sugar caramelizes and turns deep brown. Stir this into the soup; it will give it a deep, mellow colour. Simmer for 30 minutes. Discard the fennel stalks.

Preheat the grill. Toast the slices of French bread under the grill until they are golden brown on both sides.

beetroot 149
bouquet garni 190
caraway seed 197
chicken 86–7
Gruyère cheese 104
herb fennel 191
lentil 128
semolina 114
sour cream 99
Spanish onion 144
sweat 423
white cabbage 134

skimmers 228
stovetop pans 233–5

Greek Avgolemono Soup 250
Rich Brown Beef Stock 245
Rich Vegetable Stock 245

calf's and pig's foot 62
clarify 423
cooking pulses 423
Emmental cheese 105
haricot bean 126
long-grain rice 116–17
olive oil 112
skinning and seeding tomatoes 423
sweat 423
tomato 150–1
vermicelli 121
whisking egg whites 423

blender, liquidizer 238
food processor 238
pestle and mortar 226
sieves 226
skimmers 228
stovetop pans 233–5

Old-Fashioned Chicken Broth 249
Rich Brown Beef Stock 245

Add the brandy to the soup and ladle it into heatproof bowls. Thickly cover each piece of toast with Gruyère. Float a slice or two of toast in each bowl and then put the bowls under a very hot grill for 1–2 minutes, just until the cheese is bubbling. Serve this extremely filling soup as hot as possible.

CONSOMMÉ

This is a rich, clarified stock, so concentrated that it sets to a firm jelly. It should be delicious enough to eat cold, although it is often served hot, and should have the transparency and tint of sherry, with which it is often flavoured. Consommé can be made with any good stock, but the most usual are chicken and beef.

SERVES 4

ingredients for Old-Fashioned Chicken Broth or beef stock
a calf's foot or 2 pig's feet, cut into pieces
2 free-range egg whites
60 ml/2 fl oz sherry

Prepare the chicken broth or beef stock, with the addition of the calf's foot or pig's feet. Increase the simmering time for chicken broth to 3 hours. Strain and remove all the fat.

To clarify, bring the strained broth or stock to the boil. Stiffly whisk the egg whites, and whisk them into the liquid. Let the whites rise up the pan, carrying all the bits from the liquid with them. Remove the pan from the heat before it boils over, and don't whisk after the egg whites have clotted. Return to a low heat and let the stock simmer under its raft of egg white for 20 minutes. Strain it into a bowl through a wire sieve lined with a layer of damp paper towel or muslin.

Add the sherry, check the seasoning and serve.

ALTERNATIVE: You can add an egg-sized portion of minced beef with the egg whites. This will help to improve the flavour of the consommé, which can be somewhat exhausted by the process of clarification, but allow to simmer for 1 hour before straining.

PROVENÇAL SOUPE AU PISTOU

This soup reheats well, but do not add the pistou until the last moment.

SERVES 4–6

2–3 tablespoons olive oil
1 large onion, finely chopped
450 g/1 lb ripe tomatoes, skinned, seeded and chopped, or a 400 g/14 oz can tomatoes, drained and chopped
salt and freshly ground pepper
225 g/8 oz French beans, cut into short lengths
1 large courgette, cut into small chunks
2 potatoes, peeled and cubed
115 g/4 oz dried haricot beans, cooked until tender (reserve the cooking water), or a 400 g/14 oz can cannellini beans, drained
3 heaped tablespoons broken-up vermicelli
85–115 g/3–4 oz Emmental, freshly grated, to serve

For the pistou:

3 garlic cloves, chopped
a handful of large fresh basil sprigs
3 tablespoons olive oil
salt and freshly ground pepper

Heat the oil in a large saucepan and sweat the onion until soft and translucent. Add the tomatoes and cook for 10–15 minutes, stirring from time to time. Pour in 1.5 litres/2¾ pints of water, add seasoning to taste and bring to the boil. Throw in the French beans, courgette and potatoes. Boil for 10 minutes.

Add the haricot beans with their cooking water (if using canned cannellini beans, add an extra 450 ml ¾ pint water) and the vermicelli. Stir well, then simmer until everything is tender. Taste the soup for seasoning and keep hot.

To make the pistou, put the garlic and basil into a food processor or blender, or use a pestle and mortar, and purée coarsely. Add the olive oil in a thin stream to make an oily green paste. Season to taste with salt and pepper.

Stir the pistou into the soup just before serving, and put a bowl of grated Emmental on the table for each person to sprinkle into their soup bowl.

GREEK AVGOLEMONO SOUP

This is very fresh and light and makes the perfect start to a summer lunch or supper.

SERVES 4

55–85 g/2–3 oz long-grain rice
1.2–1.8 litres/2–3 pints Old-Fashioned Chicken Broth
salt
2 free-range egg yolks
juice of 1 lemon
a large pinch of ground cinnamon

Rinse the rice in several changes of water. Bring the broth to the boil in a large saucepan, add the rice and bring back to the boil. Skim off any scum and froth that rise, then simmer until the rice is just cooked. Season with salt – it needs quite a lot.

Provençal Soupe au Pistou

Beat the egg yolks and lemon juice together in a large bowl. Whisk the soup into the egg and lemon mixture – it must be this way round so that the egg will not curdle – then return it all to the pan. Heat through gently until slightly thickened, but on no account let it boil. Serve the soup sprinkled with cinnamon.

SUMMER MINESTRONE

It is impractical to make minestrone for fewer people than 10, but it does reheat particularly well if you don't eat it all at once. It can also be eaten cool – not cold – in the summer as a very filling sort of bean stew.

SERVES 10

170 g/6 oz dried borlotti beans, soaked overnight
1 tablespoon olive oil
2 large garlic cloves, crushed
2 tablespoons chopped parsley
115 g/4 oz pancetta, salt pork or unsmoked bacon, cut into small pieces
2 onions, chopped
2 carrots, chopped
1 celery stick, chopped
1 potato, peeled and diced
2 courgettes, cut in half lengthways and chopped into chunks
6–7 leaves of Swiss chard or 225 g/8 oz spinach, coarsely chopped
3 tomatoes, skinned and chopped, or 4 canned tomatoes, drained and chopped
1 teaspoon tomato purée
salt and freshly ground pepper
115 g/4 oz penne or elbow macaroni
2 tablespoons chopped fresh basil
freshly grated Parmesan

Cook the soaked beans in 1.2 litres/2 pints water for about 1¾ hours or until almost tender.

In another large saucepan, heat the oil and fry the garlic, parsley and pancetta, salt pork or bacon gently until the fat runs from the pork. Add the onions to the pan and allow them to sweat and soften. Add the beans with their cooking liquid, and the carrots and celery. Bring another 1.2 litres/2 pints of water to the boil and pour into the pan. Simmer until the vegetables are almost cooked.

Add the potato, courgettes, chopped greens and tomatoes to the soup. Return to the boil, then stir in the tomato purée and add seasoning to taste. Simmer for 10 minutes.

Scoop out a large ladleful of beans and vegetables and reserve. Throw the pasta into the pan and let it

borlotti bean 127
cooking pulses 423
pancetta 69
penne 121
salt pork 70
skinning and seeding tomatoes 423
sweat 423
Swiss chard 140

stovetop pans 233–5
whisks 227

al dente 422
blanch 422
cod 12
fennel 137
herb fennel 191
green cabbage 134
haddock 13
penne 121
pinto bean 127
prawn 35
salt pork 70
skinning and seeding tomatoes 423
soup pasta 124
Swiss chard 140

stovetop pans 233–5

Chicken Stock 244
Fish Fumet 246
Rich Vegetable Stock 245

cook while you sieve the ladleful of beans and vegetables to a purée. When the pasta is *al dente*, return the purée to the soup in the pan. Add the basil, check the seasoning and heat through. Serve the soup with a generous bowlful of freshly grated Parmesan.

ALTERNATIVE: **Pasta e fagioli** For this very thick soup, use fresh maltagliate or dried ruotini and double the quantity of beans; omit the meat, courgettes, potato and greens and add a little extra garlic. Purée two-thirds of the cooked beans and vegetables before adding them to the pasta and remaining soup.

RIBOLLITA

This hearty Tuscan soup is called '*ribollita*' because it was originally made with leftover vegetables, which were reboiled with the addition of beans and their liquid the next day. The version here reheats very well. It is traditional to douse chunks of day-old country bread in the soup.

SERVES 4–6

- 4 tablespoons olive oil, plus extra for serving
- 1 red onion, chopped
- a bunch of parsley, chopped
- 2 garlic cloves, chopped
- 225 g/8 oz Swiss chard or large-leafed spinach, coarsely chopped
- 1 loose green cabbage, coarsely chopped
- 4 tomatoes, skinned and chopped
- 3–4 medium-size potatoes, peeled and cut into pieces
- 170 g/6 oz dried pinto beans, cooked and drained
- 2 litres/3½ pints chicken or vegetable stock
- 1–2 yellow courgettes, cut into pieces (green can be substituted)
- salt and freshly ground pepper
- day-old country-style bread, cut into chunks
- freshly grated Parmesan

Heat the olive oil in a large saucepan and soften the onion with the parsley and garlic. Set half the chopped chard and cabbage aside, and add the rest, with all the stalky bits, to the onions. Put in the tomatoes, potatoes and cooked pinto beans too. Stir round for a minute or two to coat the vegetables with oil, then add the stock and bring to the boil. Simmer for 1 hour. Add the courgettes, and season with salt and pepper. Simmer for a further 20 minutes.

Meanwhile, blanch the reserved chard and cabbage by plunging it into a pan of boiling salted water and boiling for 2 minutes; it should be tender but still bright green. Drain and add to the soup. Bring the soup back to the boil.

Put chunks of bread into warm soup bowls and ladle the hot soup over the top. Allow each person to serve themself with olive oil and grated Parmesan.

ALTERNATIVE: Use 115 g/4 oz tubular pasta such as penne instead of bread. Add the pasta to the soup with the courgettes.

NEW ENGLAND FISH CHOWDER

This chowder is a delicious creamy-coloured stew that is slightly thickened by potatoes and cream. It is appetizing in appearance, and is quite cheap to make.

SERVES 6

- 700 g/1½ lb cod or haddock on the bone
- 115 g/4 oz salt pork or unsalted bacon in a piece, cut into small cubes
- 1 large onion, thinly sliced
- 3 potatoes, peeled and sliced
- salt and freshly ground pepper
- 450 ml/¾ pint milk
- 150 ml/¼ pint double cream
- 30–55 g/1–2 oz butter

Remove the bones and skin from the fish and reserve. Cut the fish into large pieces, 2.5 cm/1 in or more across; set aside. Break up the bones and put into a saucepan with the skin. Add 450 ml/¾ pint of water. Bring to the boil and simmer for 15 minutes.

Meanwhile, sauté the salt pork or bacon gently in a frying pan until the fat starts to run. Add the onion and stir, then cover and cook gently for 15 minutes.

Put the potatoes in a large saucepan with 450 ml/¾ pint of water and a pinch of salt. Bring to the boil, cover and cook for 15 minutes. Add the pieces of fish to the potatoes with the milk, strained fish-bone stock, salt pork and onion. Simmer for a further 10 minutes.

Heat the cream in a small saucepan and pour it into the chowder. Add the butter, and season to taste. Heat through gently and thoroughly but do not boil.

ALTERNATIVES: Chopped fresh or canned clams, or oysters, together with their juices, can be added to the chowder at the end and just heated through.

PRAWN AND FENNEL SOUP

SERVES 6

- 450 g/1 lb raw small prawns in their shells
- 1.2 litres/2 pints Fish Fumet
- 1 head of Florence fennel, sliced and green top reserved, or a few sprigs of fresh herb fennel

a sprig of parsley
2 bay leaves
2 onions, sliced
a wineglass of dry white wine
55 g/2 oz butter
a sprig of fresh thyme
55 g/2 oz plain flour
300 ml/½ pint milk
4 tablespoons double cream
1 tablespoon brandy

Peel the prawns and then set them aside. Put the prawn shells and heads in a saucepan together with the fish fumet, and add the green top of the Florence fennel or the herb fennel sprigs, the parsley sprig, 1 bay leaf, half of the sliced onion and the white wine. Bring to the boil, then simmer for 25 minutes. Strain the stock and reserve.

Roughly chop the prawns. Heat all but a little of the butter in another large saucepan and stir in the remaining onion, the other bay leaf and the thyme. When the onion is almost tender, add the prawns and sauté for 2 minutes. Stir in the flour. Gradually stir in the strained stock. Bring to the boil and simmer for 20 minutes. Purée in a blender or food processor and return to the pan. Add the milk.

If using Florence fennel, put the rest of it, with the remaining butter, in a saucepan and cook gently until soft. Add to the soup together with the cream and brandy, heat through gently and serve.

SAFFRON BOUILLABAISSE WITH ROUILLE

SERVES 6–8

1.35 kg/3 lb boneless fish (fillets or steaks), choosing an assortment from rascasse, gurnard, monkfish, conger eel, wrasse, John Dory, cod and haddock
2–3 large tomatoes, skinned and chopped
3–4 garlic cloves, chopped
2 onions, chopped
a large fresh bouquet garni of several sprigs of fresh herb fennel, a few sprigs of thyme, a bay leaf and a piece of orange zest
a wineglass of olive oil
salt and freshly ground pepper
1.5 litres/2¾ pints Fish Fumet
a large pinch of saffron strands, soaked in a wineglass of white wine
4–6 rounds of French bread, dried in the oven
Rouille
115 g/4 oz Gruyère, freshly grated
2 tablespoons chopped parsley

Cut the fish into thick slices or chunks. Combine the tomatoes, garlic, onions, bouquet garni and olive oil in a large saucepan. Season with salt and pepper, and boil rapidly for 5 minutes to soften the onion. Add the fish fumet and saffron-infused wine, and bring to a rapid boil. Allow to boil furiously for 10 minutes – this amalgamates the oil and liquid, which is essential when making proper bouillabaisse. Throw in all the fish and simmer for 4–5 minutes.

Remove the bouquet garni, and ladle the broth into bowls. Spread the rounds of French bread with rouille, sprinkle with Gruyère and float on top of the broth. Serve the fish separately, sprinkled with parsley and accompanied by more rouille. Alternatively, serve it all together in one bowl.

HOT AND SOUR SHELLFISH BROTH

This soup is loosely based on Thai *tom yum* soup, with a little hot and sour Chinese influence thrown in. You can use any kind of shellfish, but mussels are particularly useful for their broth-giving qualities.

SERVES 4

2 tablespoons vegetable oil
2 onions, finely chopped
4 garlic cloves, sliced
900 g/2 lb mussels, scrubbed and debearded
600 ml/1 pint chicken stock
2 stalks of lemon grass, chopped
6 lime leaves, torn into pieces
a 5 cm/2 in piece of fresh root ginger, sliced
a bunch of fresh coriander
3 tablespoons rice vinegar or white wine vinegar
1 teaspoon sugar
juice of 2 limes
4 tablespoons fish sauce
4 scallops, cut into chunks
1 lemon sole, skinned, filleted and cut into strips
225 g/8 oz peeled cooked prawns
1 teaspoon arrowroot, mixed with a little water
3 hot green chillies, seeded and chopped

First make the broth. Heat the vegetable oil in a large saucepan and fry the onions and garlic until they are lightly browned. Add the mussels, cover the pan and cook until the shells open. Lift out the mussels with a slotted spoon and set them aside to cool. Add the chicken stock to the mussel juices in the pan, followed by the lemon grass, lime leaves and ginger. Pull the coriander leaves from their stalks and set the leaves aside; chop the stalks and add them to the pan. Bring the broth to the boil, then simmer for 30 minutes. Meanwhile, shell the mussels.

bouquet garni 190
chilli pepper 152
cod 12
conger eel 20
coriander 191
fish sauce 206
Gruyère cheese 104
gurnard 19
haddock 13
John Dory 19
lemon grass 194
lemon sole 12
lime leaf 195
monkfish 17
mussel 38
olive oil 112
peeling prawns 41
rice vinegar 205
saffron 199
scallop 37
seeding chillies 423
skinning and seeding tomatoes 423

blender, liquidizer 238
food processor 238
sieves 226
stovetop pans 233–5

Chicken Stock 244
Fish Fumet 246
Rouille 258–9

cauliflower 136
chive 190
cucumber 155
green pepper 152
leek 145
making yogurt 100
mint 194
olive oil 112
pea 140–2
skinning and seeding tomatoes 423
Spanish onion 144
whipping cream 423
yogurt 99

blender, liquidizer 238
food processor 238
Mouli-légumes 226
sieves 226

Chicken Stock 244
Croûtons 364

Add the vinegar and sugar to the broth and simmer for a few more minutes. Strain the broth and return to the pan. Stir the lime juice and fish sauce into the broth. Add the scallops and sole. Bring to a simmer and cook for 1 minute. Then add the prawns and shelled mussels. Stir in the arrowroot mixture to thicken the broth slightly. Cook for a further minute or so.

Tip in the chopped green chillies, then chop the coriander leaves and add these too. Remove the pan from the heat, cover and leave the broth to stand for about 5 minutes before serving.

CHILLED CUCUMBER SOUP WITH MINT

SERVES 4–6

1½ cucumbers, chopped (with skin)
300 ml/½ pint sour cream
300 ml/½ pint plain yogurt
450 ml/¾ pint chicken stock, well skimmed of fat
a handful of fresh mint, chopped
salt
whipped cream
paprika or cayenne pepper

In a blender or food processor, purée the chopped cucumber with the sour cream and yogurt. Add the stock, chopped mint and salt to taste, and stir well to mix. Chill the soup in the refrigerator. Top each serving with a dollop of whipped cream and a sprinkling of paprika or cayenne.

GAZPACHO

In its Spanish homeland this soup is made in hundreds of different ways. Sometimes it has breadcrumbs included in the mixture; on other occasions it is a biting, pearly emulsion made only with the vegetables, oil, garlic and water. You can serve the smooth version of gazpacho with bread cubes only, or with just a few cubes of cucumber if you prefer.

SERVES 4–6

3–6 garlic cloves, peeled
½ teaspoon salt
450 g/1 lb tomatoes, skinned
150 ml/¼ pint olive oil
¼ Spanish onion, finely chopped
1 tablespoon wine vinegar
1 green pepper, seeded and cut into small cubes
½ cucumber, cut into small cubes
2 slices of white bread, crusts removed, cut into small cubes

Put the garlic into a bowl and pound it with the salt to make a purée. Reserve one of the tomatoes; chop the rest and press them through a sieve into the bowl. Stir to mix with the garlic. Add the olive oil to this mixture drop by drop, stirring all the time to emulsify it. Then add 600–900 ml/1–1½ pints of water, stirring well.

Soak the onion in the wine vinegar. Cut the reserved tomato into small cubes, and add to the soup together with the green pepper and cucumber. Stir in the onion and vinegar mixture, and put the soup to chill.

Meanwhile, dry out the bread cubes in a very low oven or under a low grill. Add these just as you serve the soup so that they stay crunchy.

VICHYSSOISE WITH CHIVES

This is a particularly fresh and delicate version of vichyssoise, which for a summer soup is often far too rich and heavy.

SERVES 6

55 g/2 oz butter
700 g/1½ lb leeks, white part only, sliced
2 shallots or 1 small onion, chopped
2 small potatoes, peeled and chopped
450 ml/¾ pint chicken stock, well skimmed of surface fat
150 ml/¼ pint dry white wine
salt and freshly ground pepper
a grating of nutmeg
1 litre/1¾ pints milk
150 ml/¼ pint double cream
3 tablespoons chopped fresh chives

Melt the butter in a large heavy saucepan and add the leeks, shallots or onion and potatoes. Let the vegetables wilt and soften, without allowing them to brown, for about 10 minutes. Pour in the stock and wine and bring to the boil. Season with salt, pepper and nutmeg to taste, then simmer for 20–25 minutes or until the vegetables are very tender.

Purée in a blender or food processor or using the fine blade of a Mouli-légumes. Mix in the milk. Let the soup cool, then chill in the refrigerator. Serve topped with the cream and chives.

ALTERNATIVES: **Cauliflower soup** Substitute a cauliflower for the leeks; omit the chives and serve with croûtons.
Green pea soup Instead of leeks and potatoes, use 900 g/2 lb peas, freshly shelled, and a few outer lettuce leaves. Serve the soup with small triangles of fried bread.

Sauces

BÉCHAMEL SAUCE

SERVES 4
45 g/1½ oz butter
30 g/1 oz plain flour
450 ml/¾ pint milk
salt and freshly ground pepper

Melt 30 g/1 oz of the butter in a small saucepan, stir in the flour and leave this roux to cook gently for 1–2 minutes without browning. Add the milk little by little, stirring with a wooden spoon after each addition until it has been absorbed. When all the milk has been incorporated and the sauce is smooth and creamy, season. Cover the pan and simmer for 15 minutes, stirring from time to time to prevent the sauce catching on the bottom. Beat in the remaining butter in small pieces to give the sauce a velvety texture.

ALTERNATIVES: This sauce can also be made with hot milk instead of cold. For a particularly good flavour, warm the milk and infuse for 10 minutes with a sliced onion, a bay leaf and a few cloves. Allow the roux to cool a little before you stir in the hot milk. Bring the sauce to a simmer, then cover and cook gently for 15 minutes.
Mornay sauce Add 30 g/1 oz freshly grated Parmesan and 30 g/1 oz grated Emmental to the béchamel sauce. Use less salt in the béchamel as the cheese is salty. Season with cayenne pepper and a touch of nutmeg.
Velouté sauce This is a domestic recipe as made in French households, not the more complicated restaurant version. Make a basic béchamel, substituting 750 ml/1¼ pints good chicken stock for the milk. When all the liquid has been incorporated, season with salt, pepper and nutmeg, then cover and simmer, very gently, for about 25 minutes, skimming from time to time. Velouté sauce can be made richer by adding a little white wine and a bouquet garni.
Vouvrillonne sauce This special velouté, served with quenelles, is made by replacing some of the stock with Vouvray or another dry white wine, and adding lightly cooked onion and mushrooms, a little lemon juice and some double cream at the end of cooking.

ONION SAUCE

Serve hot with roast lamb and lamb chops.

SERVES 4–6
30 g/1 oz butter
225 g/8 oz onions, thinly sliced
30 g/1 oz plain flour
450 ml/¾ pint creamy milk or chicken stock
salt and freshly ground pepper
a pinch each of grated nutmeg and sugar
a good pinch of cayenne pepper

Melt the butter in a saucepan and sweat the onions gently for 10–15 minutes without browning. Stir in the flour and cook for 2 minutes, then gradually add the milk or stock, stirring as it thickens. Season with salt, pepper, nutmeg, sugar and cayenne. Leave to simmer for 15–20 minutes, stirring occasionally to prevent the sauce from catching at the bottom.

Purée the sauce in a blender or food processor, or press it through a sieve. Taste for seasoning.

BÉARNAISE SAUCE

Serve with beef and lamb.

SERVES 4
2–3 shallots, finely chopped
3 tablespoons white wine vinegar
12 black peppercorns, coarsely crushed
2–3 sprigs of fresh tarragon
3 free-range egg yolks
140 g/5 oz unsalted butter, softened and cut into cubes
salt

Put the shallots in a small saucepan with the vinegar, peppercorns and tarragon and bring to the boil. Reduce rapidly over a brisk heat until you are left with no more than 1 tablespoon of liquid. Allow to cool, then strain. Return to the pan and beat in the egg yolks. Place the pan over a larger pan of hot water – a bain-marie – on a gentle heat and slowly increase the heat, whisking all the time. When the mixture has thickened a little and is creamy, start adding the butter, dropping in a piece at a time and whisking until it has been fully incorporated into the béarnaise before adding the next piece. When all the butter has been incorporated, season the sauce with salt and keep it warm over the bain-marie – away from the heat so that the sauce does not get too hot and coagulate around the edges. If the sauce gets too thick, add a few drops of cold water to cool it down.

HOLLANDAISE SAUCE

Serve warm with poached fish, particularly salmon, salmon trout and shellfish. It is also good with plain cooked vegetables, such as asparagus or broccoli.

SERVES 4
1 tablespoon white wine vinegar or lemon juice
2 free-range egg yolks
115–140 g/4–5 oz slightly salted butter, softened and cut into small cubes

bain-marie 422
bouquet garni 190
Emmental cheese 105
infuse 422
Parmesan cheese 103
reduce 423
roux 423
salmon 21
salmon trout 21–2
shallot 144–5
sweat 423
tarragon 190–1

blender, liquidizer 238
food processor 238
sieves 226
whisks 227

Chicken Stock 244
Quenelles 274

bain-marie 422
basil 192
mustard 202–3
reduce 423
shallot 144–5
skinning and seeding tomatoes 423
tarragon 190–1
tomato 150–1

blender, liquidizer 238
food processor 238
Mouli-légumes 226
sieves 226
whisks 227

Chicken Stock 244

Take a double boiler or a bain-marie and heat some water in the bottom section. In order to lessen the risk of the sauce curdling while it is cooking, you must keep the water well below the boil and make sure that it doesn't actually touch the base of whatever contains the sauce.

In the bowl or pan that is to go over the water, beat the vinegar or lemon juice with the egg yolks. Set this mixture over the hot water and, stirring all the time with a wooden spoon, add the cubes of butter one at a time, letting each one melt before you add the next. Keep scraping the egg down from the sides of the pan or bowl. If the sauce shows any signs of thickening too fast or curdling, immediately remove the bowl or pan from over the hot water and set it in a bowl of cold water, stirring gently all the time. In contrast, if the sauce refuses to thicken, turn up the heat a little.

Taste the sauce; if you find it too salty, add a small amount of unsalted butter. Hollandaise should be smooth and creamy in texture. If it has become too thick, add a few drops of cold water or top of the milk and stir gently to mix.

ALTERNATIVE: **Mustard sauce** Stir 1 or 2 teaspoons of freshly made English mustard into the hollandaise at the last moment. Serve with gammon, pig's trotters and boiling sausage.

SABAYON SAUCE FOR FISH

Based on a recipe by Michel Guérard, this is suitable for delicate fish.

SERVES 4

1–2 bay leaves
a bunch of parsley
the leafy tops of 2 celery sticks
150 ml/¼ pint clear pale chicken stock or boiling water
salt
2 free-range egg yolks
1 tablespoon lemon juice

Put the bay leaves, parsley and celery tops into a measuring jug and pour in the stock or boiling water. Leave to infuse and cool, then season lightly with salt and strain.

Half-fill the bottom of a double boiler with hot water and put the egg yolks in the top pan. Set the double boiler over a gentle heat. Add the herb infusion and whisk until the egg yolks foam and thicken to a light sauce. Add the lemon juice and serve immediately.

The sauce will keep well in the top of the double boiler, away from the heat, for up to half an hour. Whisk again just before serving.

BEURRE BLANC

SERVES 4

3–4 shallots, finely chopped
3 tablespoons white wine vinegar
3 tablespoons dry white wine
115 g/4 oz unsalted butter
salt and freshly ground pepper
a few drops of lemon juice

Put the shallots in a small saucepan with the vinegar and wine. Bring to the boil and reduce until you have 1–2 tablespoons of the liquid left. Remove the pan from the heat and leave to cool a little while you cut the butter into small cubes, each about the size of a walnut. Add the butter to the shallot mixture one cube at a time, whisking well until it becomes creamy. After you have added two or three pieces, place the pan over a low heat. Continue whisking and adding pieces of butter until it is all incorporated. Season the sauce, add a few drops of lemon juice and serve hot.

If you are not ready to serve the sauce immediately, keep it warm over hot water in a double boiler away from the heat. For a more refined sauce, strain before serving.

DELICATE TOMATO SAUCE

Serve with grilled meat or fish, gnocchi and pasta.

SERVES 6–8

55 g/2 oz butter
900 g/2 lb tomatoes, skinned, seeded and coarsely chopped
salt
2 teaspoons chopped fresh basil or 1 teaspoon dried basil
1 teaspoon chopped fresh tarragon or ½ teaspoon dried tarragon

Melt the butter in a saucepan over a low heat, add the tomatoes and cook very gently for 10 minutes. Purée in a blender or food processor or using the fine blade of a Mouli-légumes. Season with salt and stir in the herbs. Allow to stand for at least 10 minutes before serving so that the flavour of the herbs can permeate the sauce.

ROASTED TOMATO SAUCE

SERVES 4–6

900 g/2 lb ripe tomatoes
55 g/2 oz butter
2 teaspoons chopped parsley
salt and freshly ground pepper

Preheat the oven to 200°C/400°F, gas mark 6.

Place the tomatoes in a roasting tin and roast for 30 minutes or until split and blackening. Remove and leave until cool enough to handle. Then slip off the skins, and purée the tomato flesh in a blender or food processor.

Turn the puréed tomatoes into a small saucepan. Add the butter and stir until it has melted. Stir in the parsley and season with salt and pepper. Serve warm.

BREAD SAUCE

The longer you cook bread sauce, the smoother it becomes, although lumpy bread sauce is quite nice. The French make bread sauce with cream, which isn't nearly so good as using milk – the sauce becomes far too bland and rich.

SERVES 4–6

2 small onions, peeled
2 cloves
1 blade of mace
1 bay leaf
300 ml/½ pint milk
55 g/2 oz unsliced white bread, crusts removed
salt and freshly ground white pepper
30 g/1 oz butter

Stick a clove in each onion and put them in the top pan of a double boiler with the mace, bay leaf and milk. Place the top pan directly on a low heat and simmer gently, without boiling, for 10 minutes. Crumble the bread fairly finely and add it to the milk. Season the mixture. Set over the bottom pan of the double boiler, filled with hot water, and cook very gently for 30 minutes to 1 hour, stirring occasionally.

Remove the onions, mace and bay leaf. Beat in the butter and check the seasoning.

ALTERNATIVE: If you like, you can chop the onions or sieve them and return them to the sauce; however, to complement the subtle taste of grouse or partridge bread sauce should not be too highly flavoured.

CIDER BARBECUE SAUCE

Eat with chops and hamburgers or spread it over spare ribs or kebabs before cooking them.

SERVES 4

1 garlic clove, crushed
140 g/5 oz tomato purée
300 ml/½ pint dry cider
1 teaspoon soy sauce
3 large drops of Tabasco sauce
2 tablespoons soft brown sugar
2 tablespoons cider vinegar
¾ teaspoon salt

Put all the ingredients for the sauce into a small saucepan and then simmer for about 20 minutes, stirring occasionally.

MAÎTRE D'HÔTEL BUTTER

Serve small spoonfuls of this butter on top of piping hot grilled mackerel, fried sole and plaice, and grilled kidneys, steaks and chops.

SERVES 4

115 g/4 oz unsalted butter, softened
4 large sprigs of parsley, finely chopped
juice of ½ lemon

Put all the ingredients in a bowl and work them together with a fork until they are thoroughly combined. Cover the bowl and place in the refrigerator to firm up the butter slightly before you use it.

ALTERNATIVES: **Garlic and herb butter** Add 1 shallot and 2 garlic cloves, pounded together to a paste; use finely chopped parsley or tarragon.
Horseradish butter Add some grated horseradish and a little Dijon mustard and wine vinegar, all to taste, to the butter.

FRESH SAUCE GRELETTE

Serve this sauce with plainly cooked cold fish and shellfish or with fish pâté.

SERVES 4

4 tomatoes, skinned, seeded and cut into small cubes
1½ tablespoons fromage blanc
2 tablespoons double cream
1 teaspoon Dijon mustard
juice of ½ lemon
4 sprigs of parsley, chopped
6 fresh tarragon leaves, chopped
salt and freshly ground pepper
a few drops of Tabasco sauce

Put the tomato cubes in a colander to drain. Combine the fromage blanc, double cream and Dijon mustard in a bowl and then whisk them together. Gradually add the lemon juice, whisking all the time, then mix in the tomatoes and herbs. Season to taste with salt, pepper and Tabasco.

bay 193
cider vinegar 204
fromage blanc 101
grouse 84
horseradish 194
mace 198
mustard 202–3
parsley 190
partridge 83–4
skinning and seeding tomatoes 423
soy sauce 207
Tabasco sauce 206
tarragon 190–10
tomato purée 206

blender, liquidizer 238
colander 229
food processor 238
roasting tin 236
sieves 226
whisks 227

anchovy 16, 31
capers 207
chilli flakes 201
chilli pepper 152–3
coriander 191–2
hard-boiled eggs 322
mint 194
olive oil 112
peanut butter 187
red onion 144
red pepper 152
seeding chillies 423
skinning and seeding tomatoes 423
soy sauce 207
stem ginger 199
toasted sesame oil 112
tomato 150–1
vinegars 204–5
zesting citrus fruits 423

blender, liquidizer 238
food processor 238
sieves 226

Crab Cakes 275
Saffron Bouillabaisse with Rouille 253
Sichuan Chicken Salad 372

PEANUT SAUCE

Use this to dress Sichuan Chicken Salad, or serve it with crab cakes or satay.

SERVES 4

- 340 g/12 oz smooth peanut butter
- 100 ml/3½ fl oz soy sauce
- 5 tablespoons lemon juice
- 5 tablespoons toasted sesame oil
- 3 pieces of stem ginger
- 3 tablespoons syrup from the jar of stem ginger
- 1 teaspoon dried chilli flakes (or less or more, according to taste)
- 2 garlic cloves, crushed

Put all the ingredients in a blender or food processor and add 100 ml/3½ fl oz of water. Whizz until smooth. Push through a fine sieve into a bowl. The sauce should have the consistency of bottled salad cream; if it seems too thick, stir in a little more water.

You can store this sauce in a screw-top jar in the fridge for up to 10 days.

SALSA CRUDA

Eat with grilled or steamed vegetables or with grilled meat, fish or chicken.

SERVES 4–6

- 3 large tomatoes, skinned, seeded and chopped
- 3 Serrano chillies, seeded and finely chopped
- ½ red onion, finely chopped
- 2 garlic cloves, finely chopped
- 2–3 tablespoons chopped fresh coriander
- salt
- a dash of red wine vinegar (optional)

Combine all the fresh ingredients in a bowl. Season to taste with salt and a little vinegar if you feel it is needed.

HORSERADISH SAUCE

Eat this with roast beef or with smoked trout or eel.

SERVES 4

- 3 tablespoons grated horseradish
- 150 ml/¼ pint whipping cream
- 1 teaspoon Dijon mustard
- 1 tablespoon white wine vinegar
- a pinch of caster sugar

Whisk all the ingredients together in a bowl. Taste and add more vinegar or an extra pinch of sugar if you think it needs it.

ALTERNATIVE: For a mild horseradish sauce omit the vinegar and add a little more sugar.

MINT SAUCE

Eat with hot or cold roast lamb. Malt vinegar is the traditional one to use, but white wine or cider vinegar will give a mellower flavour.

SERVES 4

- 3 tablespoons finely chopped fresh mint
- 4 tablespoons vinegar
- 1–2 teaspoons sugar, according to taste

Put the chopped mint in a bowl and add 2 tablespoons boiling water to moisten it. Let it get cold, then add the vinegar and sugar. Allow to stand for at least 1 hour before serving, to give it time to develop its flavour.

SALSA VERDE

This Italian sauce is good with all boiled meat, or with boiled or poached chicken or fish.

SERVES 4–6

- 1–2 garlic cloves, finely chopped
- 4 spring onions, finely chopped
- 8 anchovy fillets, finely chopped
- 2 tablespoons finely chopped capers
- 3 tablespoons mixed finely chopped fresh flat-leaf parsley, chervil and chives
- 1 hard-boiled free-range egg, chopped
- finely grated zest of 1 lemon
- ½ tablespoon wine vinegar or juice of ½ lemon
- 6 tablespoons olive oil
- salt

Put the garlic, spring onions, anchovies, capers, herbs, egg and lemon zest in a bowl. Mix in the wine vinegar or lemon juice, then add the oil in a thin stream, beating all the time. Season with salt.

ROUILLE

Serve with fish soup or bouillabaisse.

SERVES 4

- 1 red chilli, dried or fresh
- 1 red pepper
- 1 slice of white bread, crusts removed
- 3–4 garlic cloves, chopped
- 1 free-range egg yolk
- salt
- 150 ml/¼ pint olive oil

Skin and seed the chilli and red pepper, then chop them. Moisten the bread with a little water and squeeze it dry. Put the chilli, red pepper, bread, garlic and egg yolk in a blender or food processor together with a pinch of salt and blend to a paste; or work the ingredients together with a pestle and mortar. Gradually add the oil in a thin stream, beating it in as if you were making mayonnaise. The finished consistency of the sauce should be like that of mayonnaise.

MAYONNAISE

Serve with cold vegetables, shellfish, hard-boiled eggs, chicken and cold fish.

MAKES ABOUT 300 ML/½ PINT

2 free-range egg yolks
½–1 teaspoon Dijon mustard
salt
300 ml/½ pint olive oil
1–2 tablespoons lemon juice or white wine vinegar

Put the egg yolks, mustard and a generous pinch of salt into a bowl and beat them together with a wire whisk, a fork or a wooden spoon – the whisk gives the quickest results, but some people prefer the feeling of working the yolks with a wooden spoon. When they are well beaten, start adding the oil, about ½ teaspoon at a time. Work each ½ teaspoon of oil thoroughly with the egg yolks before adding more. Increase the amount of oil added until, as the mayonnaise thickens, you are adding about 2 teaspoons at a time. When the mayonnaise is thick, add enough wine vinegar or lemon juice to thin it a little, then continue adding the oil. By this stage it is virtually impossible to curdle mayonnaise and you can finish it quite fast.

Taste the mayonnaise for vinegar and salt and eat immediately, or keep in the refrigerator and revive with a whisk. It should be eaten within 24 hours.

ALTERNATIVES: For a lighter mayonnaise, use sunflower oil, groundnut oil, or a mixture of olive oil and groundnut oil.

Sauce tartare Make the mayonnaise as usual, and stir in a good bunch of parsley, finely chopped, 1 small shallot, finely chopped, 2 tablespoons chopped sweet pickled cucumber, 2 chopped hard-boiled eggs and 2 tablespoons capers, chopped.

Aïoli Make the mayonnaise as usual, using half groundnut and half olive oil, but mix 3 crushed garlic cloves with the egg yolks before adding the oil.

Herb mayonnaise Flavour and colour the mayonnaise a good green with chopped and pounded fresh herbs. Use a mixture of tarragon, parsley, watercress and chives.

VINAIGRETTE

SERVES 4–6

½ tablespoon Orléans white wine vinegar or tarragon vinegar
½ tablespoon dry white wine
¾ teaspoon Dijon mustard
1 large garlic clove, sprinkled with salt and crushed
5 tablespoons virgin olive oil
salt and freshly ground pepper

Put the vinegar (good wine vinegar is essential for vinaigrette) into a small bowl. Add the white wine, then stir in the mustard and the crushed garlic. Add the olive oil gradually, beating it in with a teaspoon or a fork, so that it makes an emulsion with the vinegar, mustard and garlic. When you have added all the oil, season the vinaigrette with more salt, if necessary, and with pepper. (Some people also like to add a pinch of sugar.)

HERB VINAIGRETTE WITH BALSAMIC VINEGAR

Use for salads of delicate green leaves, but not for those with strong flavours, such as watercress or rocket. The dressing is perfect for salads containing special ingredients such as foie gras and lobster.

SERVES 4–6

1 teaspoon lemon juice
1 teaspoon balsamic vinegar
salt and freshly ground pepper
2 tablespoons olive oil
2 tablespoons light oil such as sunflower
1 shallot, finely chopped
1 teaspoon chopped fresh tarragon
1 teaspoon chopped fresh chives
1 teaspoon chopped fresh parsley or chervil

Mix the lemon juice and balsamic vinegar in a bowl. Whisk in a little salt and pepper, then the two kinds of oil and, lastly, the shallot and herbs.

YOGURT AND SPRING ONION DRESSING

This dressing is perfect for new potato salad.

SERVES 4

a bunch of fat spring onions – about 6
salt
115 g/4 oz cream cheese
140 g/5 oz plain goat's yogurt
1 teaspoon chopped fresh dill

capers 207
cream cheese 101
garlic 145
hard-boiled eggs 322
herbs 190–5
oils 111–13
shallot 144–5
skinning peppers 423
yogurt 99

blender, liquidizer 238
food processor 238
pestle and mortar 226
whisks 227

apple 162–3
blanch 422
cranberry 173
curd cheese 101
lemon 167
lime 167
mango 178
mustard 202–3
orange 165–6
zesting citrus fruits 423

blender, liquidizer 238
citrus zester 224
food processor 238
potato peeler 224

Redcurrant Jelly 418

Slice the spring onions into fine rounds and sprinkle with salt. Leave for 20 minutes, then drain, rinse and dry on a cloth or kitchen paper. The onions will have become somewhat limp and soft, and their flavour will be mellow.

Whisk together the cream cheese and yogurt until you have a smooth cream. Stir in the spring onions and the chopped dill. Taste the dressing, and add more salt if necessary.

ALTERNATIVES: Use Greek yogurt instead of the plain goat's yogurt, or substitute curd cheese for the cream cheese.
Yogurt and garlic dressing: Use 115 g/4 oz each Greek yogurt and cream cheese; replace the spring onions with 2–3 garlic cloves, sprinkled with a little salt and finely crushed.

CUMBERLAND GAME SAUCE

This is a recipe from cookery writer Ambrose Heath. Serve with cold ham and with game.

SERVES 4

- 1 orange
- ½ lemon
- 2 shallots, finely chopped
- 4 tablespoons redcurrant jelly
- 60 ml/2 fl oz port
- 1 teaspoon Dijon or made English mustard
- a large pinch of ground ginger
- salt

Pare the zest from the orange and lemon as thinly as possible using a citrus peeler or a potato peeler, and slice the zest into fine strips (or use a citrus zester to take fine strips from the fruit). Drop the zest into a pan of boiling water to blanch for a couple of minutes, then drain. Pour boiling water over the shallots and drain thoroughly, pressing out the excess water. Melt the redcurrant jelly in a small saucepan and add the port, shallots and orange and lemon zest. Squeeze the juice from the orange and half lemon into the pan, and add the mustard and ginger. Simmer for a few minutes, stirring occasionally. Season with salt to taste. Serve hot or cold.

APPLE SAUCE

SERVES 4–6

- 450 g/1 lb cooking apples, preferably Bramley's
- 1 teaspoon sugar
- 30 g/1 oz butter

Peel, quarter and core the apples. Put them in a small saucepan with the sugar, butter and 2–3 tablespoons of water. Cover and cook gently until the apples are a soft fluff, then beat until smooth with a wooden spoon.

FRESH CRANBERRY SAUCE

Cranberries have a sweet-acid, slightly spicy taste that is very good with turkey, pheasant and hare.

SERVES 4

- 170 g/6 oz cranberries
- 3 tablespoons soft brown sugar

Pick over the cranberries, discarding any that are soft. Put them in a small saucepan with the sugar and 3 tablespoons of water and bring to the boil. Simmer for 15 minutes or until the berries burst. Allow to cool, then mix to a ruby-coloured mush.

ALTERNATIVE: **Cranberry and orange sauce** Use orange juice instead of water and add the grated zest of 1 orange.

MANGO COULIS

This is excellent with tropical fruit salad or with mango or passion fruit ice-cream or sorbet. The slightly resinous flavour of mango is also excellent with plain yogurt.

SERVES 4

- 2 very ripe mangoes, preferably the large, golden ones (Alfonsos)
- juice of 2 limes
- 55 g/2 oz caster sugar

The slim, flat stone of a mango lies horizontally across the entire centre of the fruit, joined to the flesh by many fibres. To remove the flesh from the stone, use a very sharp filleting knife, or other flexible-bladed knife. First make an incision round the edges of the mango. Then, holding the fruit flat on a board, slide the knife halfway across the top of the flat stone, cutting close to the stone. Turn the mango round, keeping the same side up, and repeat so that the two cuts meet in the middle; remove that half of the flesh. Turn the mango over and cut away the remaining half in the same way.

Cut the mango flesh away from the skins and put it into a blender or food processor with the lime juice and sugar. Reduce to a fine purée. Taste to see if the balance of sugar and acid is right. Keep in the refrigerator until needed.

Fish

Cooking fish

Heat is applied to a fish to develop its flavour, not to make it tender, and cooking beyond the moment when the flesh has just turned from translucent to opaque will make the fish tough and dry. A fish is cooked the moment the flesh flakes when a knife is inserted into the fleshiest part. Start testing halfway through the recommended cooking time – if the moment passes, your succulent fish will be spoiled.

Poaching Boiling extracts flavour from fish, which is fine for soups and stocks but ruinous for a poached salmon. Fish must never be allowed to boil. The poaching liquid, which must be well salted, should barely shiver, never bubble.

Steaming Only steam fish that is absolutely fresh. Season it well, otherwise it will have the bland flavour of hospital food, and place the fish, covered, on a buttered plate over a pan of simmering water.

Baking The important thing to remember is that the fish must not dry out, so always put the fish into a preheated oven, about 200°C/400°F, gas mark 6, and either wrap the fish in foil, bake it in a sauce or stuff with a moist buttery mixture. Leave the head and tail on if you are baking a whole fish: the fish looks better and will retain more moisture.

Frying For the best flavour, fish should be fried as quickly as possible. Shallow fry in clarified butter, but only just enough to stop the fish sticking to the pan, and be especially frugal with fat when frying oily fish such as herrings. Deep fry fast at 190°C/375°F. Large pieces of fish should be sealed in a coating of batter or egg and breadcrumbs. Little fish, such as whitebait, only need a quick dip in milk and seasoned flour.

Grilling Always preheat the grill, or prepare a charcoal fire in good time so it is at the right temperature for cooking. To speed up the cooking process, make diagonal cuts in the thickest part of the fish to allow the heat to penetrate more easily. Brush the fish with oil or clarified butter (steaks or fillets without skin will need more lubrication than whole fish complete with skin). Grill whole fish with head and bones – they will remain juicy and moist. Fillets do not need to be turned over halfway through grilling, but whole fish and cutlets do.

Marinating Marinate well-flavoured, very fresh fish in fresh lemon or lime juice to eat raw. Always marinate fish in a glass or ceramic dish, never in metal, because the marinade will pick up a tinny flavour.

FRIED SOLE WITH BUTTER AND PARSLEY

FOR EACH PERSON

- 1 Dover sole
- salt
- plain flour for coating
- 55 g/2 oz butter
- a sprig of parsley, chopped
- juice of ½ lemon

Make a nick in the skin across the tail end of the fish on the darker side. Run a finger up either side of the fish between the skin and the flesh. Ease the skin away from the flesh, pulling it off towards the head. If you want to remove the white skin from the reverse side, turn the fish over and repeat the process.

Sprinkle the fish with salt, then coat lightly with flour. Heat half the butter in a large frying pan. When it turns brown, slide in the fish and let it sizzle for 5 minutes on each side, and for a further minute or so on each side if it is a thick fish. If it sticks to the pan, slide a palette knife slowly underneath to detach the browned layer. The fish should be a good dark brown in the centre, paling to the sides, with white flesh showing in places. Drain and put on a hot plate.

Add the parsley and lemon juice to the pan. Add the remaining butter and swirl it around. When it has melted, pour everything over the fish and serve.

If you are cooking several fish, fry each one in turn, adding a little more butter for each. Keep them hot, and add the juice of a whole lemon and a generous knob or two of butter to the pan at the end.

ALTERNATIVES: Use lemon sole, dab, brill or plaice.

clarified butter 100, 423
coating with egg and crumbs 423
Dover sole 11
marinate 422
trimming flat fish 26
turbot 12

barbecuing equipment 240–1
deep-fat thermometer 233
palette knife 228

TURBOT POACHED IN CIDER

SERVES 4

- 30 g/1 oz butter
- 1 small shallot or ¼ onion, finely chopped
- 4 slices of turbot, cut about 2.5 cm/1 in thick
- salt and freshly ground pepper
- 300 ml/½ pint dry cider
- 2 free-range egg yolks
- 150 ml/¼ pint double cream
- juice of ½ lemon
- 1 tablespoon chopped parsley

Melt the butter in a frying pan and gently soften the shallot or onion. Remove the pan from the heat and put in the slices of turbot. Season them with salt and pepper and turn them in the butter until they are well

coated. Pour in the cider and put back over a gentle heat. Poach at a slow simmer for 10–15 minutes.

Remove the fish to a serving dish and keep warm. Reduce the cooking liquid by half. Whisk the egg yolks and cream together in a small saucepan, then add the reduced cooking liquid and whisk over a gentle heat until slightly thickened. Add the lemon juice and parsley and taste for seasoning. Spoon the sauce over the turbot and serve accompanied by steamed new potatoes.

ALTERNATIVES: Use halibut, brill, flounder or John Dory instead of turbot.

NORMANDY FISH STEW

SERVES 4

- 900 g/2 lb brill or monkfish
- 900 g/2 lb mussels
- 2 onions, finely chopped
- 85 g/3 oz butter
- 300 ml/½ pint dry white wine or dry cider
- 30 g/1 oz plain flour
- 2 tablespoons chopped parsley
- 16–20 peeled cooked prawns
- juice of ½ lemon, if needed
- salt and freshly ground pepper

Skin the fish and cut it in large pieces. Scrub and debeard the mussels; put them in a large saucepan with 3 tablespoons of water. Cover the pan and shake it over a fierce heat until all the mussels have opened. Strain the liquid into a bowl. Allow the mussels to cool, then shell them.

Sweat the onions gently in 30 g/1 oz of the butter in a large saucepan until they are soft and translucent, but not brown. Add the liquid from the mussels and the wine or cider and heat to simmering point. Put in the pieces of fish, which should just be covered by the liquid (add water if necessary). Simmer gently for 5–8 minutes or until the fish is just cooked.

Work the flour into the remaining butter to make a paste and add it to the simmering liquid, letting it dissolve and thicken the liquid – this will take 3–4 minutes. Add the parsley, prawns and shelled mussels. Season with lemon juice, salt and pepper. Simmer for a few more seconds, just long enough to get the shellfish piping hot without cooking them any further, which would make them tough. Serve in a big tureen with plenty of bread or with croûtons fried in butter.

NORMANDY FISH STEW

ALTERNATIVES: This rich stew can also be made with a mixture of either sea fish or freshwater fish, or with a single kind of fish such as turbot or eel.

SEVICHE

The fish in this dish is 'cooked' only by the action of the lemon juice. Whatever fish you choose, it must be very fresh and in perfect condition.

SERVES 4

- 700 g/1½ lb turbot, completely free of skin and bone
- juice of 2 lemons
- salt
- 1 dried red chilli, seeded and finely chopped or flaked
- 1 teaspoon olive oil
- a few sprigs of fresh coriander, chopped

With a very sharp, flexible knife, cut the fish into thin slices, then cut the slices into strips the size of your little finger. Put them into a bowl, squeeze the lemon juice over them and leave for 45 minutes. Then season with salt and add the red chilli. Leave to marinate for a further 15 minutes.

To serve the seviche, divide the fish among four plates and sprinkle with a few drops of olive oil and a little chopped coriander. Serve with a plain tomato salad, simply dressed with a mixture of olive oil and lemon juice.

ALTERNATIVES: Use sea bass, red snapper, halibut or any firm white fish, or fresh salmon, instead of turbot.

BAKED HALIBUT

SERVES 4

- 55 g/2 oz butter
- 3–4 shallots, sliced
- 115 g/4 oz button mushrooms, sliced
- 1 chicken halibut, weighing 1.1 kg/2½ lb
- a wineglass of white wine
- salt and freshly ground pepper
- 2 tablespoons double cream (optional)

Preheat the oven to 180°C/350°F, gas mark 4.

Melt half the butter in a gratin dish, add some of the shallots and a few sliced mushrooms, and let them absorb the butter for a minute. Lay the halibut on top and pour over the white wine. Lay the rest of the sliced mushrooms and shallots on top, sprinkle with salt and pepper and dot with thin slices of butter. Cover the dish with foil. Bake for 40 minutes (allowing 15 minutes per 450 g/1 lb).

brill 12
button mushroom 161
chilli pepper 152–3
coriander 191–2
filleting and skinning flat fish 26
halibut 12
making beurre manié 423
monkfish 17–18
mussel 38
prawn 35–6
seeding chillies 423
sweat 423

gratin dish 236
sieves 226
whisks 227

Croûtons 364

clarified butter 100, 423
cod 12
dried breadcrumbs 364
ginger 199
light soy sauce 207
plaice 12
rice vinegar 205
sea bass 14
skinning and seeding tomatoes 423
sweat 423
sweet pepper 152
toasted sesame oil 112
trimming flat fish 26

gratin dish 236
sieves 226
steamer set 235

Delicate Tomato Sauce 256
Salsa Cruda 258
Sauce Tartare 259

Take out the halibut and keep warm. Strain the cooking liquid. If you would like a rich dish, add the cream to the liquid and simmer for 2–3 minutes until slightly thickened. Serve the halibut, skinned and taken off the bone, putting a nice piece on each plate and pouring the sauce over and around the fish. Accompany with new potatoes and fresh vegetables.

ALTERNATIVES: Use 4 halibut steaks, or turbot, cod, hake, John Dory or brill instead of halibut.

FRIED PLAICE

SERVES 4

4 plaice
30 g/1 oz plain flour
1 free-range egg, beaten
55 g/2 oz home-made fine, dried breadcrumbs
salt and freshly ground pepper
30 g/1 oz clarified butter, or 15 g/½ oz butter and 1 tablespoon groundnut or sunflower oil
Delicate Tomato Sauce, Salsa Cruda or Sauce Tartare, to serve

Remove the black skin from the plaice, if the fishmonger has not already done so. Put the flour, egg and breadcrumbs in three separate dishes.

Season the plaice with salt and pepper. Dip each one first in flour, then in beaten egg and lastly in breadcrumbs, patting them on well and coating the fish all over. Use one hand for the flour and crumbs and the other for the egg, so that you do not get crumbs stuck to your fingers.

Heat the clarified butter or butter and oil in a frying pan. When it is hot but not smoking fry each plaice for 5 minutes per side.

ALTERNATIVES: Use haddock fillet, lemon sole, dab, megrim, witch, whiting or gurnard instead of plaice.

STEAMED COD WITH GINGER AND SPRING ONION

You might find this style of dish in any number of Cantonese restaurants all over the world, the only difference being that they would probably use the more costly sea bass, sole, lobster or crab instead of cod. However, cod is a triumph cooked like this.

SERVES 4

2 whole small codling, each weighing about 450 g/1 lb, or 4 thick cod fillets, each weighing about 170 g/6 oz (leave the skin on in either case)
2 tablespoons vegetable oil
1 teaspoon sesame oil
2 tablespoons light soy sauce
1½ teaspoons dry sherry
2 teaspoons rice vinegar
a 5 cm/2 in piece of fresh root ginger, cut into thin matchsticks
6 spring onions, shredded on the bias
4 sprigs of fresh coriander

Place the cod or fillets on a plate that will fit into a steamer. Pour over the oils and set the plate in the steamer. While the fish begins to cook, combine all the other ingredients, except the spring onions and coriander, in a saucepan and simmer for 2 minutes. Pour this mixture over the fish. Steam for 15 minutes for the whole fish, 8–10 minutes for fillets. Sprinkle over the spring onions for the final 2 minutes.

Lift the cod out of the steamer, garnish with coriander sprigs and serve.

SEA BASS PIPÉRADE

SERVES 4

3 tablespoons olive oil
2 onions, sliced
2 red or yellow peppers, seeded and cut into strips
2 garlic cloves, chopped
2–3 tomatoes, skinned and roughly chopped
salt and freshly ground pepper
4 small fillets or slices of sea bass, each weighing about 115–170 g/4–6 oz
12 black olives

Preheat the oven to 180°C/350°F, gas mark 4.

Heat 2 tablespoons of the olive oil in a saucepan and sweat the onions until soft and translucent. Add the peppers and garlic and let them cook gently with the onions for 10 minutes. Stir in the tomatoes and season with salt and pepper. Simmer the mixture until the liquid from the tomatoes has evaporated enough to give a good thick sauce.

Meanwhile, heat the remaining tablespoon of oil in a frying pan and fry the pieces of bass, seasoned with salt and pepper, until they are lightly browned all over. Transfer them to an oval gratin dish. When the pipérade is ready, spoon it over the top of the fish and bake for 15 minutes or until it is heated right through. Put the olives on top a few minutes before the dish is cooked, and sprinkle a little fresh olive oil over the pipérade.

ALTERNATIVES: Use sea bream, turbot, brill, cod, haddock, hake, grouper or John Dory instead of bass.

Sea Bass Pipérade

FISH CAKES

SERVES 4

- 45 g/1½ oz butter
- 45 g/1½ oz plain flour
- scant 150 ml/¼ pint milk
- 340 g/12 oz cooked boneless cod, flaked
- 2 hard-boiled free-range eggs, chopped (optional)
- juice of ½ lemon
- salt and freshly ground pepper
- beaten egg
- fine dried breadcrumbs
- oil for frying

Melt the butter in a small saucepan, stir in the flour and then let it cook gently for 1–2 minutes, but without allowing it to brown. Gradually stir in the milk (or use a mixture of milk and cooking liquid reserved from the fish) to make a very thick, smooth sauce. Stir into this the flaked fish and the chopped hard-boiled eggs (if using) and add a good squeeze of lemon juice. The mixture must be thick enough to be formed into shapes when it is cold. Season with salt and pepper. Spread the mixture on an oiled plate in a layer about 1 cm/½ in thick and then leave it to get cold.

When the mixture has set, cut into 2.5 cm/1 in squares and then form these into the shape you like the best – small flat cakes and cork shapes are the most traditional. Dip each fish cake into beaten egg and then into the dried breadcrumbs.

Heat 1 cm/½ in of oil in a large frying pan and fry the fish cakes, turning them once during cooking, until they are a deep golden brown colour all over. Drain briefly on kitchen paper. Serve the fish cakes very hot with Delicate Tomato Sauce, or on their own if they are for breakfast.

ALTERNATIVES: Use haddock, salmon or any cooked white fish instead of cod. You can also add mashed potato to the mixture.

coating with egg and crumbs 423
cod 12
dried breadcrumbs 364
hard-boiled eggs 322

Delicate Tomato Sauce 256

avocado 153–4
chilli pepper 152–3
cleaning round fish 27
coriander 191–2
creamed coconut 188–9, 423
cumin 199
haddock 13
hard-boiled eggs 322
mackerel 15
marinate 422
mint 194
seeding chillies 423
smoked haddock 29

barbecuing equipment 240–1
gratin dish 236
pie dish 237
whisks 227

FISH PIE

SERVES 4–6

340 g/12 oz fresh haddock fillet
1 small whole smoked haddock, weighing about 450 g/1 lb
150 ml/¼ pint milk
1 bay leaf
900 g/2 lb potatoes
55 g/2 oz butter
15 g/½ oz plain flour
4 hard-boiled free-range eggs, chopped
3–4 sprigs of parsley, chopped
butter and milk for mashing
salt and freshly ground pepper

Preheat the oven to 170°C/325°F, gas mark 3.

Put both kinds of fish into a baking dish with the milk and 150 ml/¼ pint water and add the bay leaf. Poach in the oven for 15 minutes. The fish should be just cooked, with a creamy curd coming to the surface.

Meanwhile, start the potatoes cooking in salted water.

Turn the oven up to 220°C/425°F, gas mark 7, or preheat the grill.

Remove the fish from the liquid and flake, taking care to remove the skin and all the bones; reserve the liquid. Melt 30 g/1 oz of the butter in a small saucepan, stir in the flour and gradually stir in the fish cooking liquid to make a sauce. Drain the potatoes, adding some of their cooking liquid to the sauce to make it the consistency of thick cream. Taste it to see if it needs more salt – it probably won't. Mix the flaked fish, hard-boiled eggs and parsley into the sauce. Mash the potatoes and season well.

Put the fish mixture into a pie dish or gratin dish and cover with an even layer of mashed potatoes. Dot the top with thin slivers of butter. Then either bake for 15–20 minutes until nicely browned, or brown under the grill.

ALTERNATIVES: Use cod, plaice or coley instead of fresh haddock, and smoked cod instead of smoked haddock. You can replace the eggs with small button mushrooms sautéed in butter, or with peeled cooked prawns or lightly poached scallops.

SPICED MARINATED MACKEREL

This marinade, with an aroma reminiscent of the spice-stalls of North Africa, can be used for any fish. It is particularly good with strong-flavoured fresh mackerel.

SERVES 4

150 ml/¼ pint vegetable oil
2 teaspoons sweet paprika
2 teaspoons hot paprika
2 teaspoons ground cumin
3 garlic cloves, crushed
juice of 1 lemon
salt
a small bunch of fresh coriander
4 medium-size mackerel, cleaned and trimmed
2 lemons, halved

Whisk together the oil, 85 ml/3 fl oz water, paprika and cumin. Add the garlic, lemon juice and salt to taste. Remove coarse stems from the coriander; finely chop or pound the leaves and add to the marinade.

Make several slanting incisions in both sides of each fish, to help the flavours of the marinade to penetrate. Put the marinade in a glass or earthenware dish and slide in the fish, spooning the marinade into the incisions. Cover and leave to marinate in the refrigerator for several hours.

Preheat the grill or prepare a charcoal fire.

Grill the mackerel, turning once or twice and basting with the marinade, until cooked (mackerel is one of the few fish that is best when very thoroughly cooked). Serve either hot or cold, with halves of lemon for squeezing over the fish.

GRILLED MACKEREL WITH GREEN PASTE

This green paste is remarkable – at once sharp and pungent, cool and spicy-hot, yet also smooth and creamy. The combination with the crisp hot mackerel is excellent, but the paste is also good with other fish, particularly salmon. It is also a fine complement to grilled lamb cutlets.

SERVES 4

4 mackerel, cleaned and heads removed
1–2 tablespoons vegetable oil
coarse sea salt
sprigs of fresh coriander
lime wedges

For the green paste:

85 g/3 oz fresh coriander leaves (plus the roots if possible)
45 g/1½ oz fresh mint leaves
8 garlic cloves, crushed
2 teaspoons ground cumin
1 teaspoon sugar
1 teaspoon salt
85 ml/3 fl oz lime juice
5 small green chillies, seeded and chopped
100 g/3½ oz creamed coconut
½ avocado, peeled and diced

First make the green paste. Put all the ingredients in a blender or food processor and work to a completely smooth purée. Transfer to a bowl, cover and chill.

Preheat a ridged cast-iron grill pan, or prepare a charcoal fire in a barbecue.

Brush the fish on both sides with a little oil and sprinkle with sea salt to taste. Place the mackerel on the hot grill pan or on the grill over the barbecue and cook for 5–7 minutes on each side or until the skin is well blistered and crisp.

Arrange the mackerel on a serving dish and garnish with coriander sprigs and lime wedges. Hand the green paste separately at the table.

HERRINGS IN OATMEAL

Traditionally, herrings in oatmeal are prepared without egg so that the oatmeal absorbs the oil from the fish, but a coating of egg makes them crisper and a little more delicate in flavour.

SERVES 4

1 free-range egg
fine oatmeal or rolled oats for coating
salt
4 herrings, scaled and boned
lard or butter for frying
2 lemons, quartered

Beat the egg in a small dish. Mix the oatmeal or oats with salt in another dish. Dip the herrings first in the egg and then in the lightly salted oatmeal, patting this on to make a good coating. Fry in hot lard or butter for about 8 minutes on each side. Herrings are much nicer overcooked than undercooked, so fry them until they are very crisp and brown. Keep them hot in the oven on kitchen paper if you need to, and serve them with lemon quarters and mustard or Mustard Sauce.

ALTERNATIVES: Use mackerel or sea bream instead of herring.

SOUSED HERRINGS

SERVES 6

6 plump herrings, each weighing about 225 g/8 oz, scaled and cleaned
300–450 ml/½–¾ pint cider vinegar
300–450 ml/½–¾ pint dry cider
2 bay leaves
4 sprigs of fresh thyme
12 black peppercorns
6 allspice berries
4 cloves
2 blades of mace
salt
cayenne pepper
fresh dill or fennel to garnish

Preheat the oven to 180°C/350°F, gas mark 4.

Cut off the heads and fins from the herrings and trim the tails. Put any roes back inside the fish. Lay the herrings in an earthenware or enamelled iron pie dish or gratin dish. Cover with the vinegar and cider (the amount of liquid needed depends on the size and shape of the dish used). Push the herbs and spices in among the fish, and season with salt and cayenne. Cover the dish with a sheet of foil and set it in a bain-marie or a large roasting tin. Pour enough boiling water into the bain-marie or tin to come halfway up the side of the gratin or pie dish. Bake for 30 minutes.

Allow to cool, and serve garnished with fresh dill or fennel. Eat soused herrings within a day or two.

FRIED WHITEBAIT

SERVES 4

450 g/1 lb whitebait, fresh or frozen
oil for frying
150 ml/¼ pint milk
85 g/3 oz seasoned flour
2 lemons, halved

If the whitebait are frozen, let them thaw completely and then dry with kitchen paper.

Start to heat the oil in a deep-fat fryer or large saucepan. Put the milk in a dish and the seasoned flour in a paper bag. Dip the fish in milk, drain and then shake them, a few at a time, in the bag of seasoned flour. Deep fry, still a few at a time, until golden and crisp – they take 2–3 minutes. Drain well and serve immediately in a rustling mound with halved lemons and fresh bread and butter.

ALTERNATIVE: Use elvers instead of whitebait.

GRILLED TUNA WITH ANCHOVY

SERVES 4

900 g/2 lb fresh tuna steak
4 anchovy fillets
6 tablespoons olive oil
6 tablespoons lemon juice
1 teaspoon chopped fresh marjoram
salt and freshly ground pepper

anchovy 16, 31
bain-marie 422
boning round fish 28
cider vinegar 204
cleaning round fish 27
herring 15–16
lard 110
mace 198
oats 116
scaling round fish 26
tuna 16
whitebait 16

barbecuing equipment 240–1
blender, liquidizer 238
deep-fat thermometer 233
food processor 238
gratin dish 236
pie dish 237

Mustard Sauce 255

blanch 422
brill 12
capers 207
chilli pepper 152–3
cumin 199
herb fennel 191
John Dory 19
lard 422
marinate 422
seeding chillies 423
skate 18
skinning and seeding tomatoes 423
tuna 16

Delicate Tomato Sauce 256
Lemon Court-Bouillon with Parsley 245
Salsa Cruda 258

Lard the tuna by cutting a few slits in the flesh and pushing anchovies into the slits. Put the tuna in a dish with the olive oil and lemon juice and marinate for about an hour, or longer. Marinating will help prevent the tuna from drying out during cooking.

Preheat the grill until very hot.

When ready to cook, shake the tuna to remove most of the marinade, place it on a foil-lined baking tray and sprinkle with marjoram, salt and pepper. Grill for 7–8 minutes on each side, basting with the marinade from time to time; a very thick tuna steak will need a little longer. Serve very hot with Roasted Tomato Sauce or Salsa Cruda.

ALTERNATIVES: Use bonito, swordfish, sailfish or shark instead of tuna.

TUNA IN A PACKET WITH RED SAUCE

Adapted from a North African recipe, this is a richly aromatic, boldly coloured dish.

SERVES 4

4 garlic cloves
salt and freshly ground pepper
4 tuna steaks, each weighing 115–170 g/4–6 oz
1 teaspoon ground cumin
3 red peppers
3 yellow, orange or green peppers
4 tablespoons olive oil
700 g/1½ lb tomatoes, skinned, halved and seeded
2–3 green chillies, seeded and chopped
shredded fresh mint
2 lemons, quartered

Crush 2 of the garlic cloves to a paste with ½ teaspoon salt. Rub the tuna steaks with the garlic paste and the cumin. Leave them in the refrigerator to absorb the flavours while you make the sauce.

Skin and seed the peppers, then cut them into narrow strips. Reserve some of the strips, in different colours, for the garnish and chop the rest fairly small. Crush the remaining garlic cloves.

Heat the oil in a frying pan and throw in the tomatoes, chillies and garlic. Fry fairly fast, turning occasionally, until the mixture is no longer watery, and is caramelizing and beginning to stick to the pan. Add more oil if necessary. Crush the tomatoes with a spoon, then stir in the chopped peppers and season with salt and pepper. Set aside.

Preheat the oven to 200°C/400°F, gas mark 6.

Cut out four squares of foil, each large enough to enclose a tuna steak. Put a heaping tablespoonful of the pepper and tomato sauce in the centre of each square of foil, set a tuna steak on top and cover with the remaining sauce. Fold the foil edges together to make sealed parcels. Bake for 15–20 minutes.

Turn the tuna and sauce on to heated plates. Place a few strips of pepper and some shreds of mint on top. Serve with quartered lemons and fried potatoes.

ALTERNATIVES: Use swordfish or any firm-fleshed fish instead of tuna.

SKATE WITH BLACK BUTTER

SERVES 4

4 wings of skate
2.4 litres/4 pints Lemon Court-Bouillon with Parsley
55 g/2 oz butter
1 teaspoon wine vinegar
salt and freshly ground pepper
1 teaspoon chopped parsley

If the skate wings are large and thick, blanch them by dropping them into boiling water for 7 minutes. Remove the fish, drain well and take off the skin.

Bring the court-bouillon to simmering point, put in the pieces of skate and bring back to simmering point. Cover the pan, remove from the heat and leave the skate to cook in the retained heat for 15 minutes. Remove the fish, drain and keep hot on a serving dish.

Heat the butter in a small frying pan until it turns a hazelnut brown. Pour in the vinegar and season. Add the parsley and pour the mixture over the skate.

ALTERNATIVE: Add capers to the browned butter and use vinegar from the caper jar rather than wine vinegar.

BRAISED JOHN DORY WITH TOMATOES AND FENNEL

SERVES 4

1 whole or 2 smaller whole John Dory or brill, weighing 1.3–1.8 kg/3–4 lb
3–4 garlic cloves, halved lengthways
½ lemon, sliced and slices halved, or a few sprigs of parsley
2–3 tomatoes, skinned and quartered
2 small onions, sliced
4 tablespoons olive oil
salt and freshly ground pepper
a few stalks and leaves of fresh or dried herb fennel

TUNA IN A PACKET WITH RED SAUCE

button mushroom 161
cleaning round fish 27
en papillote 422
fennel 137
garfish 19
grey mullet 18–19
herb fennel 191
oregano 193
red mullet 18
scaling round fish 26
skinning and seeding tomatoes 423

Velouté Sauce 255

Preheat the oven to 180°C/350°F, gas mark 4.

Clean, trim and scale the fish, then rinse it under cold water and carefully pat dry. With a sharp knife make two or three deep diagonal slashes on both sides of the fish. In each slash wedge half a clove of garlic and either a half slice of lemon, peel side outwards, or a sprig of parsley. Put a half clove of garlic in the head and another in the belly.

Place the fish in a buttered ovenproof dish and surround it with the quartered tomatoes and the onions. Sprinkle with oil, salt and pepper and bake near the bottom of the oven for 20 minutes. Scatter stalks and leaves of fennel over the fish and bake for a further 15 minutes or until cooked. Serve hot with steamed young vegetables, or cold with a home-made garlicky tomato sauce.

ALTERNATIVES: Use red mullet, grey mullet, red snapper, sea bream or grouper instead of John Dory.

GRILLED GREY MULLET WITH FENNEL

SERVES 4

- 2 medium-size grey mullet
- salt
- ½ lemon, sliced
- a handful of dried herb fennel twigs
- a little olive oil
- 4 tablespoons Pernod or anis (optional)

Preheat the grill to moderate, and preheat the oven to 190°C/375°F, gas mark 5.

Clean the fish, leaving their heads on. Season them inside and out with salt and then, using a sharp knife, slash their sides in two or three places. Cut each slice of lemon into four pieces and push a piece into each of the cuts in the fish. Put the remaining pieces of lemon and a few of the fennel twigs inside the fish. Put the rest of the fennel in an earthenware baking dish, lay the fish on top of the fennel and then sprinkle all over with olive oil. Grill for 5 minutes, then transfer to the oven and bake for an additional 20 minutes. The fish should be white and succulent under their slightly crisp skins, with a wonderful flavour of the sea. You can cook them entirely under the grill if you prefer, but, if you choose this option, turn the fish once so that both sides cook evenly.

Some people like to flame the fish with a little heated Pernod or anis after grilling; doing so will increase the fennel flavour.

ALTERNATIVE: Replace the grey mullet with the larger red mullet.

RED MULLET EN PAPILLOTE

SERVES 4

- 4 red mullet, each weighing about 225 g/8 oz (the livers can be left in)
- salt and freshly ground pepper
- 115 g/4 oz button mushrooms, finely chopped
- a squeeze of lemon juice
- 30 g/1 oz butter plus extra for the paper
- 2–3 shallots, finely chopped
- 1 tablespoon chopped parsley

Preheat the oven to 190°C/375°F, gas mark 5.

Season the fish inside and out with salt and pepper to taste. Slash the sides of the fish to help them cook quickly and evenly.

Sprinkle the chopped mushrooms with a little lemon juice to keep them white. Melt the butter in a small saucepan, add the shallots and mushrooms and stir them over a moderate heat until the liquid that exudes from the mushrooms has evaporated and the mixture is rather dry. Season well with salt and pepper and stir in the chopped parsley. Keep this duxelles on one side.

Cut out four rounds of greaseproof paper or foil, each about 25 cm/10 in in diameter (place the fish on the paper to get the right size). Brush the paper with softened butter, leaving the borders unbuttered. Spoon some of the duxelles on half of each round of paper, place a fish on top and cover with more duxelles. Fold the paper over the fish and pleat the edges together twice to seal them. Arrange the parcels on a baking sheet and bake for 10–15 minutes, or longer if the fish are large.

Serve the fish in their paper parcels, on their own or with velouté sauce into which you can stir any duxelles that may be left over.

ALTERNATIVE: Use trout instead of red mullet.

MEDITERRANEAN GARFISH

SERVES 4

- 1–2 garfish, weighing about 700–900 g/1½–2 lb in all, cleaned and skinned
- 4–5 tablespoons olive oil
- 4 onions, sliced
- 2 garlic cloves, crushed
- 450 g/1 lb tomatoes, skinned and chopped
- 1 teaspoon chopped fresh oregano or ½ teaspoon dried oregano
- salt and freshly ground pepper
- 4 slices of white bread, cut into triangles

For the marinade:
2 tablespoons olive oil
1 tablespoon white wine
a few sprigs of fresh thyme

Cut the garfish into pieces about 5 cm/2 in long. Put the pieces in a bowl with the marinade ingredients and set aside for 1–2 hours, turning the pieces from time to time.

Preheat the oven to 190°C/375°F, gas mark 5.

Heat a little of the oil in a pan and soften the onions and garlic. Stir in the tomatoes and oregano, and season with salt and pepper. Put the pieces of fish, together with the marinade, in an ovenproof dish. Pour the sauce over them and mix it around. Bake for 30 minutes.

Fry the bread triangles in the remaining oil until golden brown on both sides. Arrange them around the cooked fish and serve.

ALTERNATIVES: Use gurnard or 4 tuna or swordfish steaks (do not cut them into pieces). You can add a little saffron to the sauce, and replace the oregano with chopped fresh herb fennel.

SALMON COULIBIAC

This very grand Russian dish is as delicious cold as hot. If the mushrooms are not very white, peel them before chopping – this onion and mushroom mixture should be as pale as possible.

SERVES 6–8
700 g/1½ lb fresh salmon, skinned and boned
115 g/4 oz butter
55 g/2 oz very fine Chinese rice vermicelli (use rice if you cannot obtain the vermicelli)
1 large onion, finely chopped
225 g/8 oz very white button mushrooms, chopped
3 hard-boiled free-range eggs, chopped
a handful of chopped fresh dill
salt and freshly ground pepper
Flaky Pastry made with 450 g/1 lb flour
beaten egg for brushing the pastry
melted butter for serving

Cut the salmon into small cubes. Melt 85 g/3 oz of the butter and toss the salmon cubes in the butter to coat. Put aside to cool and set. Cook the vermicelli in boiling salted water until tender. Drain and chop it, then set aside to cool. Sweat the onion gently in the remaining butter until soft. Stir in the mushrooms and allow the mixture to cool. Mix the hard-boiled eggs with the chopped dill and season well.

Preheat the oven to 200°C/400°F, gas mark 6.

Roll out the pastry into a large oblong measuring about 40 x 30 cm/16 x 12 in. Trim off the thick edges and roll out another, small oblong from the trimmings. Lay the large oblong on a greased baking sheet. Spread the salmon pieces down the middle. Put the chopped vermicelli on top, followed by the mushroom and onion mixture and, finally, the egg and dill mixture. Brush the small oblong of pastry with beaten egg and lay it on top of the filling, egg side down. Bring the sides of the bottom piece of pastry up and pinch them together with the top to form an oblong pastry case. Decorate the top with fish shapes made from pastry trimmings and make a small hole in the centre. Brush all over with beaten egg. Bake for 30–35 minutes.

Pour a couple of tablespoons of melted butter into the hole in the top of the pie and serve hot, or set aside to cool. Serve coulibiac with a fresh green salad.

ALTERNATIVE: Use sturgeon instead of salmon.

button mushroom 161
chanterelle 159
cutting salmon escalopes 28
dill 191
hard-boiled eggs 322
horn of plenty 159
rice vermicelli 125
salmon 21
sweat 423

Flaky Pastry 402–4

SALMON ESCALOPES WITH CHANTERELLES

SERVES 4
1 tail piece of salmon, preferably wild salmon, weighing 340 g/12 oz
salt and freshly ground white pepper
225 g/8 oz fresh chanterelles or horns of plenty
juice of ½ lemon
30 g/1 oz butter
150 ml/¼ pint double cream
12 fresh tarragon leaves (optional)

Cut the salmon into four escalopes and season on both sides with salt and pepper. Slice the larger mushrooms, and sprinkle them all with the lemon juice.

Melt the butter in a frying pan large enough to take all the escalopes side by side. Put in the mushrooms and let them cook gently without browning for 10 minutes, stirring them from time to time. Pour in the cream, season with salt and pepper and add the tarragon, if using. Allow to cook gently for 5–10 minutes. Push the mushroom mixture to the side of the pan.

Place the salmon escalopes in the pan and cook extremely gently for about 2 minutes on each side. Lift them out carefully and put them on heated plates. Taste the sauce for seasoning, then spoon it delicately over the salmon. Serve with boiled new potatoes.

ALTERNATIVE: Use white button mushrooms, sliced, instead of chanterelles.

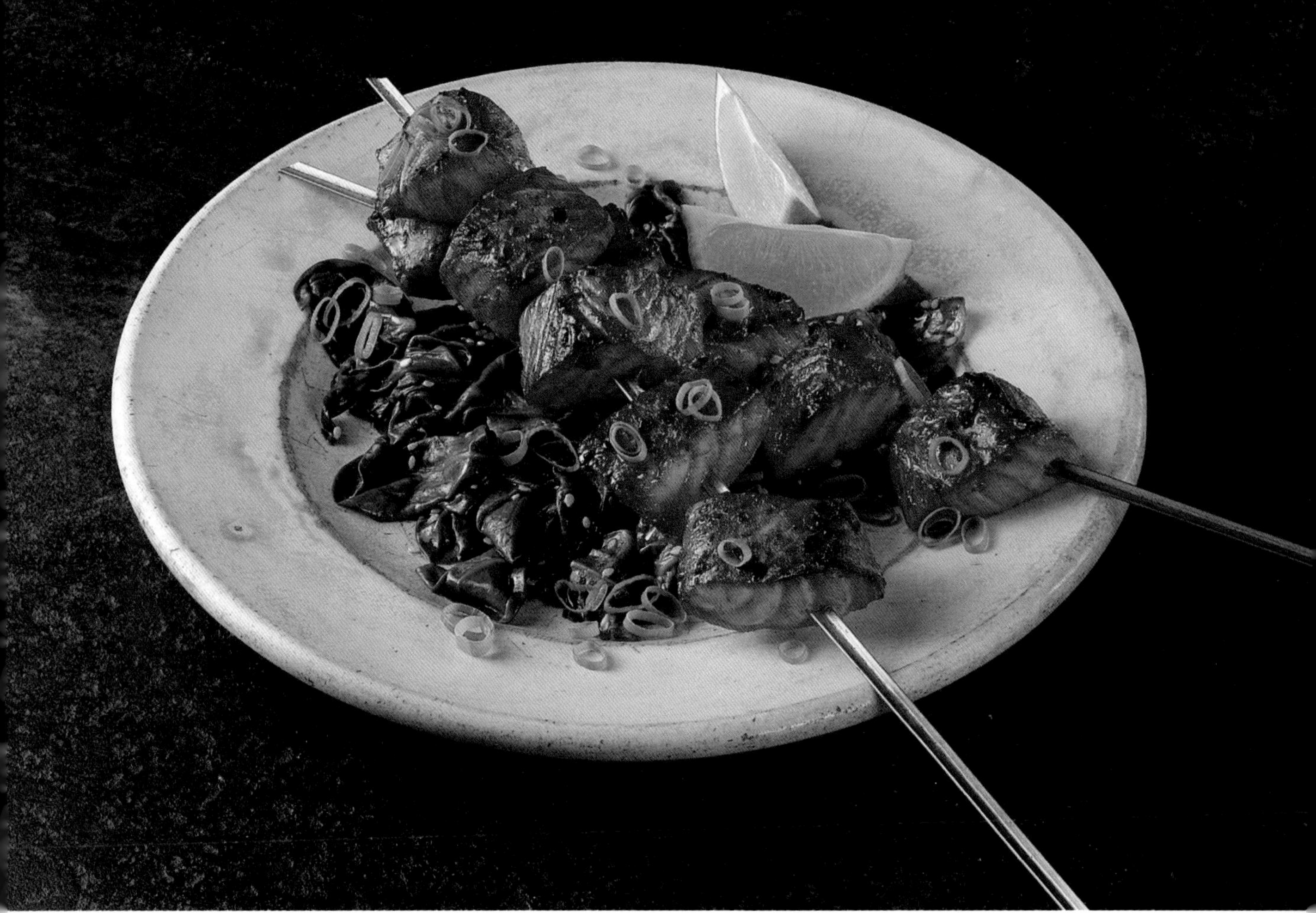

Soy-Marinated Salmon Brochettes

chilli pepper 152–3
chive 190
cleaning round fish 27
coriander 191–2
flat-leaf parsley 190
seeding chillies 423

food processor 238

Hollandaise Sauce 255
Lemon Court-Bouillon with Parsley 245
Mayonnaise 259

POACHED WHOLE SALMON

SERVES 6–8

- 1 salmon, weighing approximately 1.35–1.6 kg/ 3–3½ lb
- 4.8 litres/8 pints Lemon Court-Bouillon with Parsley
- 2 wineglasses of white wine

Clean the salmon, remove the gills and wipe with kitchen paper to remove any blood. When the court-bouillon has cooled to blood heat, add the white wine. Slide in the fish; the liquid should just cover the fish. Bring the liquid back to simmering point. From this point it should simmer gently for 5–6 minutes per 450 g/1 lb (a smaller fish needs a shorter cooking time). Never let the liquid boil.

Lift the fish out on to a rack, set it over the pan of hot liquid (off the heat) and cover with a clean cloth. Leave for 5 minutes to drain and set. Serve hot with Hollandaise Sauce, new potatoes and peas, or cold with mayonnaise.

ALTERNATIVES: Use salmon or sea trout, char, pike or perch instead of salmon.

SPICY GREEN FISH

This is based on an Indian recipe, and is extremely quick and easy to make.

SERVES 4

- 4 pieces of salmon fillet, each weighing 140 g/5 oz
- juice of 1 lemon
- salt
- a bunch of fresh coriander
- a bunch of fresh flat-leaf parsley
- a bunch of fresh chives
- 3 green chillies, seeded
- 3 garlic cloves
- 150 ml/¼ pint Greek yogurt
- 120 ml/4 fl oz sunflower oil

Squeeze lemon juice over the salmon and season with salt. Leave to sit for an hour or more in the refrigerator.

Remove the coarser stalks from the coriander and parsley. Finely chop the herb leaves with the chives, chillies and garlic, or blend them all together to a mush in a food processor, adding a little water if necessary. Put the herb mixture into a flat dish. Spoon the yogurt into another dish.

Heat the oil in a frying pan just large enough to hold all the pieces of salmon. Dip each piece first into yogurt and then into the herb mixture. Lower quickly into the very hot oil (take care as the oil may spit). Cook for 3–4 minutes on each side.

Remove the fish carefully, drain and serve with new potatoes and more yogurt, plus lime pickle if you like.

SOY-MARINATED SALMON BROCHETTES

Salmon is a perfect fish for grilling, due to its inherent oiliness. Barbecuing this dish will intensify the flavour. Serve on a bed of Sesame Spinach.

SERVES 4

- 1 piece of thick salmon fillet, weighing 700 g/1½ lb, skinned and any bones removed
- 4 garlic chives or spring onion tops, finely chopped
- 1 lime, cut into thin wedges

For the marinade:

- 4 tablespoons light soy sauce
- 4 tablespoons rice wine or dry sherry
- ½ teaspoon five-spice powder
- 2 teaspoons chilli oil
- ½ teaspoon dried chilli flakes
- a 5 cm/2 in piece of fresh root ginger, unpeeled, thinly sliced
- thinly pared zest and juice of 1 lime
- 1 tablespoon syrup from a jar of stem ginger

Mix together all the marinade ingredients and pour into a shallow dish. Cut the salmon into 2.5 cm/1 in chunks and immerse them in the marinade. Leave to marinate at room temperature for 2 hours, turning the salmon in the marinade from time to time.

Preheat a ridged cast-iron grill pan, or prepare a charcoal fire in a barbecue. (Or, if necessary, preheat an overhead grill.)

Thread the salmon chunks on to small skewers. Cook the salmon brochettes on the grill pan or barbecue for 5 minutes on one side, then turn them over and cook the other side for 3–4 minutes. The outside of the salmon should be nicely charred and blistered.

If you like, warm the marinade in a small pan and brush it over the salmon to give a glossy finish. Sprinkle the brochettes with the garlic chives and arrange the lime wedges around.

TROUT IN WHITE WINE JELLY

This makes an extremely pretty party dish.

SERVES 6

- a bottle of dry white wine
- 2 onions, sliced
- 115 g/4 oz carrots, sliced
- 2 celery sticks, chopped
- 24 black peppercorns
- a bunch of parsley
- salt
- 6 trout, cleaned
- 1 free-range egg white
- 7 g/¼ oz powdered gelatine
- sliced cucumber or carrot or fresh tarragon to garnish

Combine the wine, vegetables, peppercorns, parsley and 300 ml/½ pint of water in a wide saucepan. Add a small amount of salt (bear in mind that this liquid will be reduced later). Bring to the boil, then cover and simmer for 20 minutes.

Meanwhile, trim the trout tails neatly with scissors. Add the trout to the pan and poach gently, uncovered, for 10 minutes. Turn them over and allow them to cool in the liquid. When cold, remove the trout and keep them in the refrigerator while you make the jelly.

Strain the cooking liquid. Bring it to the boil and let it reduce to just under 600 ml/1 pint. Stiffly whisk the egg white and use it to clarify the cooking liquid. Soften the gelatine in a little water and stir it into the hot (not boiling) liquid until completely dissolved. The liquid will be a beautiful, pale topaz colour. Leave it to cool. When it is syrupy but not yet set, use to glaze the trout. Chill until set. Chill the remaining jelly too.

Before serving, chop the remaining jelly and place it around the trout. Garnish with sliced cucumber or carrot or fresh tarragon.

ALTERNATIVE: Simply serve the trout hot, straight from the poaching liquid, rather than cooling and glazing it with jelly.

TROUT MARINATED IN VERMOUTH

A recipe from the Val d'Aosta.

SERVES 6

- 6 small fresh trout, cleaned
- plain flour for dusting
- oil for frying

For the marinade:

- 6 tablespoons sunflower oil
- 2 tablespoons olive oil
- 2 onions, sliced
- 2 garlic cloves, sliced
- 3 tablespoons white wine vinegar
- 85 ml/3 fl oz white vermouth
- 4 strips of lemon zest
- 4 fresh sage leaves
- a sprig of fresh rosemary
- 1 teaspoon black peppercorns, crushed
- salt

chilli flakes 201
chilli oil 113
clarify (see Consommé recipe) 250
cleaning round fish 27
dissolving gelatine 423
five-spice powder 196
garlic chive 190
light soy sauce 207
marinate 422
rice wine 208
rosemary 193
sage 193–4
whisking egg whites 423
zesting citrus fruits 423

barbecuing equipment 240–1
ridged cast-iron grill pan 233
whisks 227

Sesame Spinach 372

bain-marie 422
dried salt cod 31
marinate 422
pike 23
potato 145
saffron 199
whiting 13–14

cocotte 422
food processor 238
Mouli-légumes 226
ramekin 236, 422
sieves 226

Roasted Tomato Sauce 256–7
Velouté Sauce 255
Vouvrillonne Sauce 255

You will need to prepare this dish a day ahead.

Dust the trout lightly with flour. Fry in hot oil until they are golden and just cooked through – this will take about 6 minutes on each side. Drain the fish well and then arrange them side by side in an earthenware dish.

To prepare the marinade, heat the sunflower and olive oils in a small saucepan, and cook the onion and garlic over a moderate heat until soft and translucent but not brown. Add all the other marinade ingredients and bring to the boil. Pour the hot marinade over the trout. Allow to cool, then leave the fish to marinate in the refrigerator for up to 3 days, turning them from time to time.

ALTERNATIVE: Use strips of orange zest instead of lemon and add 1–2 tablespoons seedless raisins.

FISH MOUSSELINES

SERVES 4

450 g/1 lb pike fillets or other white fish, skinned
1 small free-range egg
salt and freshly ground pepper
cayenne pepper
300 ml/½ pint double cream
juice of ½ lemon
a dash of brandy (optional)
a dash of sherry (optional)
Vouvrillonne, Velouté or Roasted Tomato Sauce

Remove as many of the remaining bones as possible from the fish, then chop the fillets very finely in a food processor. Put through a Mouli-légumes or sieve to remove fibres and any remaining bones.

Return the fish to the processor. Add the egg and season with salt, pepper and cayenne. Process until very fine. Slowly dribble or spoon in the cream and then the lemon juice, continuing to process until the mixture is very light and fine. Taste it and heighten the flavour as much as you feel you can, adding the brandy and sherry now if using. Spoon into a bowl, cover and chill for at least an hour.

Preheat the oven to 170°C/325°F, gas mark 3.

Brush the inside of 8 cocottes or ramekins with butter and fill them two-thirds full with the fish purée. Put the cocottes in a bain-marie or stand them in a roasting tin half-filled with boiling water. Cover the bain-marie or tin loosely with a sheet of foil and bake the mousselines for about 30 minutes. They are ready when they are just set in the centre.

To serve, fill each cocotte up to the brim with vouvrillonne, velouté or tomato sauce.

ALTERNATIVES: Use whiting or other firm white fish instead of pike.

Quenelles Use two spoons to mould the mixture, which is very soft, into little torpedo shapes about 8 cm/3 in long. Put these on to a very lightly floured plate and either chill them thoroughly in the refrigerator, or freeze them briefly to firm them up. Preheat the oven to 190°C/375°F, gas mark 5, or, if you are in a hurry, preheat the grill. Meanwhile, bring a wide, shallow pan of salted water to the boil. Turn down the heat until the water is just gently simmering, and poach the quenelles for 6 minutes, turning them over halfway through the cooking time. Remove them carefully with a slotted spoon and transfer them to a heated gratin dish. Cover with vouvrillonne, velouté or roasted tomato sauce and bake until lightly glazed, or glaze to a golden brown under the grill.

SALT COD WITH POTATOES

SERVES 4

450 g/1 lb dried salt cod fillet, soaked for 24 hours in 2–3 changes of cold water
plain flour for coating
2–3 tablespoons olive oil
450 g/1 lb onions, sliced
900 g/2 lb potatoes, peeled and sliced
4 tomatoes, skinned and sliced
1 garlic clove, chopped
1 tablespoon chopped parsley
salt and freshly ground white pepper
a good pinch of saffron threads

Put the cod into fresh cold water in a frying pan or saucepan and bring it slowly to the boil. Remove the pan from the heat and allow the fish to cool in the cooking liquid.

Drain the cod and cut it into squares. Coat the squares in flour. Heat the olive oil in a flameproof casserole and fry the squares of cod until golden brown on all sides. Remove them with a slotted spoon and keep warm.

Add the prepared onions, potatoes, tomatoes and garlic to the oil in which the fish was cooked. Stir them over a gentle heat for a minute or two, and then add the chopped parsley and just enough boiling water to cover the vegetables. Season with a pinch of salt, if needed. Cover the casserole and simmer for approximately 15 minutes or until the potatoes are almost cooked.

Put in the pieces of cod and the saffron threads, season with white pepper and stir. Simmer for a further 10 minutes.

CREAMED FINNAN HADDIE

SERVES 4

- 340 g/12 oz finnan haddie (smoked haddock on the bone)
- 30 g/1 oz butter
- 15 g/½ oz plain flour
- 150 ml/¼ pint milk
- 1 hard-boiled free-range egg, chopped
- 150 ml/¼ pint single cream
- salt, if needed
- cayenne pepper
- hot toast

Preheat the oven to 180°C/350°F, gas mark 4.

Put the haddock in a baking dish , cover with water and poach in the oven for 15 minutes.

Meanwhile, melt the butter in a saucepan and stir in the flour. Cook for 2 minutes over a low heat, then gradually add the milk, stirring all the time, to make a smooth sauce. Leave to simmer, covered, while you drain the haddock and strip all the flesh from the skin and bones. Flake the fish and add to the sauce with the chopped egg and the cream. Heat through. Taste the mixture, and season with salt if necessary and a sprinkling of cayenne.

Serve the creamed finnan haddie on hot toast.

TARAMASALATA

SERVES 4

- 170 g/6 oz salted grey mullet roe or smoked cod's roe, preferably soft and pliable
- 2 thick slices of white bread, crusts removed
- 1 large garlic clove, chopped
- juice of 1½ lemons
- 120 ml/4 fl oz olive oil or half olive oil and half sunflower oil
- cayenne pepper

If using cod's roe, split it open down one side and scrape out the soft pink part inside. Soak the bread in a little water so that it is moist but not wet, and crumble it.

Purée the roe with the bread, garlic and lemon juice in a food processor. Reserve about half a tablespoon of olive oil, and slowly add the rest to the processor, plus a tablespoon or so of water if the purée becomes too thick. When you have a smooth, light purée, taste it and add more garlic or lemon juice if necessary. Transfer the mixture to a bowl and pour the reserved olive oil on top. Sprinkle with cayenne, and serve with hot pitta bread and radishes or black olives.

DRESSED CRAB

SERVES 4

- 1 large crab, weighing 1.35 kg/3 lb, or 2 small crabs, each weighing 900 g/2 lb
- salt and freshly ground pepper
- 1 teaspoon fresh breadcrumbs (optional)
- ½ teaspoon English mustard powder
- cayenne pepper
- 1 lemon, quartered, or 150 ml/¼ pint mayonnaise

Pick the crab, putting the white meat and the brown into separate bowls. Season the white meat lightly with salt and pepper. If the brown meat seems too wet, mix in the breadcrumbs, mashing well with a fork. Add the mustard and a little salt and cayenne pepper and mix well.

Arrange the white meat around the brown on a serving dish. Serve with quarters of lemon or, for a richer dish, with mayonnaise, and brown bread and butter.

CRAB CAKES

This recipe is incredibly quick and easy to make. The bread binds the crabmeat together lightly and seems to disappear. Serve the crab cakes with Roasted Tomato Sauce.

SERVES 4

- 115 g/4 oz day-old white bread (sliced or steam-baked bread will not do), crusts removed
- 350 g/12 oz fresh white crabmeat
- 55 g/2 oz butter
- 1 onion, grated
- 1–2 garlic cloves, finely chopped
- ¼ teaspoon dried thyme
- 2–3 generous pinches of hot paprika or cayenne pepper
- 1 tablespoon chopped parsley
- salt
- a little plain flour
- 1 lemon, quartered
- Roasted Tomato Sauce

Moisten the bread with a little water and crumble it into a bowl. Stir in the crabmeat.

Melt half the butter in a small pan. Add the onion and garlic and sprinkle with the thyme and paprika or cayenne. Sweat until the onion is soft and translucent. Drain off excess fat, and stir into the crab mixture. Mix in the parsley and a little salt.

With floured hands, form the crab mixture into small cakes. Fry in the remaining butter until golden brown on both sides. Serve with quarters of lemon and roasted tomato sauce.

crab 33
finnan haddie 29
fresh breadcrumbs 364
hard-boiled eggs 322
oils 110–13
picking a cooked crab 40–1
salted grey mullet roe 31
smoked cod's roe 30
sweat 423

food processor 238
gratin dish 236

Mayonnaise 259
Roasted Tomato Sauce 256

despatching a live lobster 39
langoustine 35
lobster 33–4
peeling and deveining prawns 41
prawn 35–6
preparing a cooked lobster 39

barbecuing equipment 240–1
whisks 227

GRILLED LOBSTER WITH BUTTER

SERVES 4

2 live lobsters, each weighing about 700–900 g/1½–2 lb
3 tablespoons olive oil
salt
a pinch of cayenne pepper
115 g/4 oz butter

Preheat the grill.

Kill the lobsters, then cut them in half and clean them thoroughly. Lay the lobster halves, with the cut sides up, in a large roasting tin. Brush them liberally with olive oil and season with salt and cayenne pepper. Grill the lobster halves for about 5 minutes, then turn them over and grill on the shell side for a further 5 minutes.

Meanwhile, melt the butter. Turn the lobster halves over again so that the cut sides are facing upwards, and spoon some of the melted butter over the top. Grill for a further 5–6 minutes, spooning on a little more butter every 2–3 minutes. Serve the lobsters immediately, with the melted butter remaining in the pan poured over the top.

BOILED LOBSTER

SERVES 2

1 onion, finely sliced
1–2 carrots, finely sliced
4–5 parsley stalks
a large wineglass of white wine
1 tablespoon salt
6 black peppercorns
1 live lobster, weighing about 700–900 g/1½–2 lb
melted butter to serve

Put all the ingredients except the lobster and melted butter into a large saucepan. Cover with 1.8 litres/3 pints of fresh cold water, bring to the boil and boil rapidly for 10 minutes. Plunge the lobster head first into the boiling liquid, then cover the pan and hold the lid on tightly. Return the water to the boil as rapidly as possible over a high heat, then turn down the heat and simmer the lobster for approximately 15 minutes, by which time it will have turned a marvellous brick red in colour.

Lift out the lobster and use a sharp knife to split it in half. Remove the gills and intestinal canal, and discard them. Serve the lobster accompanied by plenty of melted butter.

GRILLED LANGOUSTINES

For a barbecue, grill the langoustines over wood embers or charcoal.

SERVES 4

900 g/2 lb large raw langoustines in the shell
salt and freshly ground pepper
juice of 1 lemon
4 tablespoons olive oil

Preheat the grill.

Lay the langoustines, in their shells, on their backs and use a sharp knife to split them in half, cutting from head to tail; avoid piercing the shell along the back. Carefully open each langoustine out like a butterfly. Season the exposed flesh with a little salt and pepper. Whisk the lemon juice and olive oil together with a fork and brush the langoustines all over with half of this mixture.

Thread them on to skewers, keeping them flat. Grill for 3 minutes on each side, brushing each side with more oil and lemon after 2 minutes. Serve very hot and eat with your fingers, not forgetting to eat the soft tomalley in their heads.

GRILLED PRAWNS WRAPPED IN BACON

SERVES 4

16 large raw tiger prawns or raw langoustines, peeled (leaving the last tail section on) and deveined
a large pinch of cayenne pepper
juice of ½ lemon
8 rashers of unsmoked streaky bacon
olive oil for brushing
1 lemon, quartered

Preheat the grill – a charcoal grill is best.

Season the prawns or langoustines with cayenne pepper and a few drops of lemon juice. Flatten and stretch the bacon rashers with the flat side of a knife blade so that they are as thin and long as possible, then cut each rasher in half across the middle.

Wrap half a rasher of bacon around each prepared prawn or langoustine. Thread on to four skewers and brush all over with olive oil. Grill for about 5 minutes, turning frequently during the cooking. Serve with lemon quarters.

ALTERNATIVES: Use Parma ham or pancetta instead of the bacon.

GRILLED PRAWNS WRAPPED IN BACON

chilli pepper 152–3
coconut milk 189, 423
coriander 191–2
fish sauce 206
fresh breadcrumbs 364
garam masala 196
ginger 199
lime 167
lime leaf 195
marinate 422
mint 194
oyster 36–7
peeling and deveining prawns 41
prawn 35–6
rock salt 200
seeding chillies 423
spinach 132–3
turmeric 199

barbecuing equipment 240–1
blender, liquidizer 238
food processor 238
ridged cast-iron grill pan 233
sieves 226

MARINATED THAI PRAWNS

During grilling, the shells of the prawns scorch and blacken, leaving the flesh inside moist. Serve with a salad of thinly sliced cucumber, seasoned with salt and sugar and a tablespoon of white wine vinegar.

SERVES 4

a small bunch of fresh coriander
20 raw king or tiger prawns in the shell

For the marinade:

3 tablespoons vegetable oil
4 tablespoons fish sauce
2 tablespoons syrup from a jar of stem ginger
a 5 cm/2 in piece of fresh root ginger, unpeeled, thinly sliced
4 lime leaves, torn into pieces
4 small green chillies, chopped
2 shallots, sliced
2 garlic cloves, sliced
juice of 2 limes

For the dipping sauce:

12–15 fresh mint leaves
2 garlic cloves, crushed
3 small green chillies, seeded and chopped
2 teaspoons sugar
juice of 3 limes
5 tablespoons fish sauce

In a deep bowl, mix together all the marinade ingredients. Pull the coriander leaves from the stalks and set aside; coarsely chop the stalks and add to the bowl. Immerse the prawns in the marinade and turn to coat them thoroughly. Leave to marinate for at least 6 hours, or overnight, turning them occasionally.

To make the dipping sauce, put all the ingredients together with the coriander leaves in a blender or food processor. Add 5 tablespoons of water. Work until well mixed but not puréed. Pour into 4 small dishes and place on the table.

Preheat a ridged cast-iron grill pan or an overhead grill, or prepare a charcoal fire in a barbecue.

Thread the prawns on to four skewers. Grill for 4–5 minutes on each side or until the shells are blackened and blistered. Serve with the dipping sauce.

PRAWN AND CUCUMBER CURRY

SERVES 4

675 g/1½ lb raw tiger prawns in the shell
a few spring onions and garlic cloves
1 large cucumber
70 g/2½ oz butter
3 garlic cloves, finely chopped
4 cm/1½ in piece of fresh root ginger, finely chopped
1 large onion, thinly sliced
1 teaspoon turmeric
2 teaspoons garam masala
1 teaspoon mixed ground cloves and cinnamon
1 teaspoon sugar
½ teaspoon salt
1 tablespoon plain flour
300 ml/½ pint thick coconut milk
3 green chillies, cut into thin strips
1 tablespoon lemon juice

Peel the prawns and devein them; set aside. Make a broth by simmering the prawn heads and shells with the spring onions and garlic in water to cover for 20–30 minutes; strain and reserve 300 ml/½ pint of this broth. Cut each prawn in half lengthwise.

Quarter the cucumber. Cut the quarters lengthwise into quarters and then across into 5 cm/2 in pieces. Put them into a pan with plenty of salted water and 15 g/½ oz of the butter and simmer for approximately 5 minutes or until half cooked. Drain the cucumber and keep it on one side.

Melt the remaining butter in a saucepan and soften the garlic, ginger and onion without browning. Stir in all the spices, the sugar and salt and cook for 2 minutes, then stir in the flour. Slowly pour in half the coconut milk and half the prawn shell broth, stirring. Bring to the boil, then simmer for about 10 minutes. Remove from the heat. Add the prawns with the cucumber and chillies and stir to mix. Leave to marinate for 30 minutes.

Return the pan to the heat and stir in the remaining coconut milk and broth and the lemon juice. Simmer for a further 3–5 minutes. Serve with rice.

ALTERNATIVE: Use 350–450 g/¾–1 lb peeled cooked prawns instead of raw tiger prawns, and chicken stock instead of the prawn shell broth. Add the prawns to the curry, with the lemon juice, for the final 5 minutes.

OYSTERS ROCKEFELLER

SERVES 4

24 fresh oysters in the shell
a few handfuls of rock salt
115 g/4 oz butter, softened
3 shallots, finely chopped
1 celery stick, finely chopped
1 tablespoon chopped parsley
½ tablespoon chopped fresh chervil or tarragon
225 g/8 oz spinach, finely chopped
2 tablespoons fresh white breadcrumbs

1 tablespoon Pernod or pastis
a dash of Tabasco sauce
a dash of Worcestershire sauce
salt and freshly ground pepper

Preheat the oven to 220°C/425°F, gas mark 7. Open the oysters, leaving them on the half shell. Scatter a layer of rock salt in two large roasting tins, making a steady bed on which to set the oysters.

Melt 30 g/1 oz of the butter in a pan and stir in the shallots, celery, parsley and chervil or tarragon. Soften for 3–4 minutes. Add the spinach and let it wilt down. Purée this mixture in a blender or food processor. Add the remaining butter, the breadcrumbs, Pernod or pastis, and Tabasco and Worcestershire sauces, and blend until smooth. Season with salt and pepper.

Put a tablespoon of the spinach mixture on each oyster and set them firmly on their salt bed. Bake for 4–5 minutes or until they are just beginning to turn golden brown. Serve on the salt bed.

ALTERNATIVE: Use 48 large mussels (12 per person) instead of oysters.

PAN-FRIED SCALLOPS WITH GARLIC

The scallops should be tender and melting, so take care not to overcook them.

SERVES 2–4

8 large or 12 medium-size scallops
30 g/1 oz butter
plain flour for dusting
2 garlic cloves, chopped
1 tablespoon chopped parsley
juice of ½ lemon
salt and freshly ground pepper

Prepare the scallops, removing them from their shells if necessary, and pat them dry on kitchen paper. Heat the butter in a heavy frying pan until it turns nut brown. Quickly and lightly dust the scallops with flour and put half of them into the pan. (If you put them all in at once they lower the heat too much and instead of frying they will boil in their own juices.) Add half the garlic and half the parsley. Fry briskly for 2–3 minutes, turning the scallops over in the butter. When they are golden brown all over, remove them to a heated dish.

Add more butter to the pan if necessary, heat it and fry the rest of the scallops with the remainder of the garlic and parsley. Remove them to the dish. Add the lemon juice to the pan and swish it around, then pour it over the scallops. Season with salt and pepper and serve very hot.

SCALLOPS WITH SAFFRON, BASIL AND TOMATO VINAIGRETTE

Use the very best extra virgin olive oil and the best vinegar you can find for the dressing.

SERVES 4

10 large scallops
salt and freshly ground pepper
2 tablespoons olive oil (not extra virgin)

For the vinaigrette:

2 tablespoons good-quality red wine vinegar
½ garlic clove, sprinkled with a little sea salt and crushed to a paste
freshly ground white pepper
6 tablespoons extra virgin olive oil
1 teaspoon saffron threads
8 large fresh basil leaves, coarsely chopped
2 ripe tomatoes, skinned, seeded and neatly chopped

First make the vinaigrette. In a bowl, whisk together the vinegar, garlic and pepper to taste. Still whisking, add the extra virgin oil, a little at a time, until the dressing is emulsified. In a small dish, infuse the saffron in 2 tablespoons hot water for a couple of minutes, then stir into the dressing (do not use a whisk, or the saffron threads will become entangled in it). Stir in the basil and tomatoes.

Remove the scallops from their shells if necessary, then cut them in half horizontally. Season.

Heat the olive oil in a non-stick or well-seasoned frying pan until smoking hot. Add the scallops and fry briefly until golden brown and crusted on each side. You may need to do this in two batches, as overcrowding can cause the scallops to sweat rather than fry.

Divide the scallops among four warmed plates and spoon over the vinaigrette. Serve at once.

basil 192
infuse 422
mussel 38
olive oil 112
saffron 199
scallop 37–8
shucking oysters 42
skinning and seeding tomatoes 423
Tabasco sauce 206
vinegars 204–5
Worcestershire sauce 206

blender, liquidizer 238
food processor 238
frying pan 234
whisks 227

MOULES À LA MARINIÈRE

SERVES 4

3–4 shallots, chopped
1 onion, chopped
300 ml/½ pint dry white wine or vermouth
1.8 kg/4 lb mussels, scrubbed and debearded
150 ml/¼ pint double cream (optional)
salt and freshly ground pepper
2 tablespoons finely chopped parsley

Put the shallots and onion in a large saucepan with the wine or vermouth. Bring to the boil and then boil for 8 minutes. Add the mussels, cover the pan and steam over a high heat for 3–5 minutes or until all the shells have opened, stirring and turning them over

occasionally. There will usually be one or two recalcitrant mussels that stay firmly shut – discard them if you feel doubtful about them. Spoon the mussels into a deep bowl.

To eliminate sand and grit, you may need to strain the cooking liquid through a sieve lined with muslin. However, if the liquid doesn't look particularly sandy, pour it carefully into another pan, leaving any sand and grit behind at the bottom of the first pan. Heat the liquid to boiling point, add the cream, if you are using it, and heat through. Season to taste. Pour over the mussels, sprinkle with chopped parsley and serve.

ALTERNATIVE: To make a simpler version, use half wine and half water and leave out the cream.

THAI MUSSELS

The wonderfully aromatic flavourings in this recipe add a whole new dimension to the cooking of mussels, and are a world away from the more familiar onions, white wine and parsley of moules à la marinière. Despite their exotic nature, they do not mask the delicate flavour of the shellfish.

SERVES 4

2.3 kg/5 lb mussels, scrubbed and debearded
a bunch of fresh coriander
3 tablespoons fish sauce
150 ml/¼ pint double cream

For the Thai flavourings:

a 5 cm/2 in piece of galangal or fresh root ginger, peeled and sliced
6 spring onions, chopped
4 large green chillies, seeded and chopped
2 stalks of lemon grass, chopped
6 lime leaves
1 garlic clove, crushed
juice of 2 limes
400 ml/14 fl oz thin coconut milk

Put the mussels in a large saucepan and add 300 ml/½ pint of water. Bring to the boil, then put the lid on the pan and steam the mussels for 3–5 minutes, shaking the pan from time to time. When all the shells have opened, drain the mussels in a colander set over a clean saucepan to catch the juices. Reserve the juices.

Allow the mussels to cool slightly, then remove and discard the empty half of each shell. Put the mussels on their half-shells into a bowl and set aside. Pull the coriander leaves from the stalks and set the leaves aside; chop the stalks. Add the coriander stalks and the Thai flavourings to the reserved mussel juices. Set the pan over a low heat and simmer gently for 30 minutes. Strain the liquid through a fine sieve into the large pan in which you cooked the mussels. Stir in the fish sauce, cream and chopped coriander leaves.

Add the mussels on the half-shell and bring to a simmer. Heat through gently for about 5 minutes. Serve in shallow soup plates.

THAI MUSSELS

STUFFED BABY SQUID

SERVES 4

12 small squid

For the stuffing:

1 large onion, finely chopped
1–2 tablespoons olive oil
2 garlic cloves, chopped
3 large or 4–5 small tomatoes, skinned, seeded and chopped
salt and freshly ground pepper
a chunk of bread the size of a fist, softened in milk
a few sprigs of parsley, chopped
2 free-range egg yolks

For the sauce:

3 tablespoons olive oil
1 onion, chopped
1 bay leaf
1 garlic clove, crushed
2 teaspoons plain flour
a wineglass of white wine
salt and freshly ground pepper

Preheat the oven to 170°C/325°F, gas mark 3.

Clean the squid, remove the tentacles and put the bodies to drain on kitchen paper. Chop the tentacles fairly small.

To make the stuffing, soften the onion in the olive oil. Add the garlic, squid tentacles and tomatoes, and season with salt and pepper. Add the bread, squeezed dry, and the parsley. Stir well, then take off the heat and mix in the egg yolks, to make a thickish stuffing. Use to stuff the squid bodies and skewer the ends closed with wooden cocktail sticks. Put the squid in an oiled gratin dish.

For the sauce, heat the olive oil in a small saucepan and soften the onion with the bay leaf and garlic. Stir in the flour. Add the wine and an equal amount of hot water, stirring well. Season. Bring to the boil and simmer for 15 minutes. Pour the sauce over the stuffed squid. Bake for 1 hour, basting occasionally.

ALTERNATIVES: Use cuttlefish or small octopus instead of squid.

chilli pepper 152–3
coconut milk 189, 423
coriander 191–2
cuttlefish 44
fish sauce 206
galangal 199
lemon grass 194
lime leaf 195
mussel 38
octopus 43–4
preparing squid 47
seeding chillies 423
skinning and seeding tomatoes 423
squid 43

colander 229
sieves 226

Meat

beef top rump 53
black peppercorn 201
blade steak 53
bouquet garni 190
button mushroom 161
button onion 143
entrecôte steak 52
reduce 422
shallot 144–5
streaky bacon 70

casserole 236
frying pan 234
knives 222–4
pestle and mortar 226

Chicken Stock 244
Creamed Potatoes with Parsley 381

BLADE STEAKS WITH SHALLOTS

This shallot sauce is delicious with any grilled or fried beef steak.

SERVES 4

- 4 blade steaks, each weighing about 225 g/8 oz
- 7–8 shallots, chopped
- 115 g/4 oz butter
- 2 tablespoons olive oil
- a wineglass of white wine
- salt and freshly ground pepper
- 1 tablespoon chopped parsley

To tenderize the steaks, take a very sharp, heavy knife and score each steak in both directions, cutting almost through to the middle. Make the cuts close together so that all the fine, tough connecting tissues are cut through in both directions.

Put the shallots in a small pan with 30 g/1 oz of the butter and 1 tablespoon of the oil. Let them cook gently until tender. Pour in the white wine and season lightly with salt and pepper. Bring to the boil and boil quite rapidly until the liquid has reduced to 2 tablespoons and become a little syrupy. Set the pan on one side but keep hot.

Heat another 30 g/1 oz of the butter and the remaining oil in a large frying pan, and cook the steaks to your liking over a brisk heat. When they are ready, put them on four hot plates. Stir the remaining butter and the parsley into the shallot mixture until the butter has melted. Divide among the steaks, spreading a generous spoonful over the top of each one. Serve with creamy mashed potatoes or chips.

ALTERNATIVES: Use rump steaks or entrecôtes. These tender steaks do not need to be scored.

PEPPERED STEAK

SERVES 4

- 2 scant teaspoons black peppercorns
- 4 entrecôte steaks
- a little olive oil
- 30 g/1 oz butter
- salt
- a generous 150 ml/¼ pint chicken stock
- a dash of sherry
- 2 teaspoons brandy

Crush the peppercorns coarsely using a pestle and mortar, until they are the texture of fine breadcrumbs. This is a mignonette pepper, and the flavour is best if the peppercorns are freshly crushed. Rub the steaks on both sides with a very little olive oil, then press the mignonette pepper on to the surfaces with your fingers.

Heat half the butter in a cast-iron frying pan and, when it browns, put in the steaks. Fry them fairly rapidly but without allowing the butter to blacken, turning them over now and then. When the steaks are cooked the way you like them, transfer them to a heated plate. Sprinkle with salt and keep warm. Put the remaining butter in the frying pan and let it melt but not brown. Add the stock and bring to the boil, scraping up the juices from the bottom of the pan. Season with a little salt and add the sherry. Allow the stock to reduce to half its volume. Stir in the brandy and boil for a further 30 seconds, then pour over the steaks and serve immediately.

BURGUNDIAN BEEF STEW

This rich stew makes a substantial main dish.

SERVES 6

- 115 g/4 oz streaky bacon, in a piece
- 1.35 kg/3 lb top rump of beef or other stewing steak
- 30 g/1 oz seasoned flour
- 4 tablespoons olive oil
- ½ bottle of red burgundy
- about 300 ml/½ pint beef stock or water
- a fresh bouquet garni of thyme, parsley and a bay leaf
- salt and freshly ground pepper
- about 20 button onions
- 30 g/1 oz butter
- 225 g/8 oz button mushrooms
- 1 teaspoon sugar

Preheat the oven to 180°C/350°F, gas mark 4.

Cut the bacon into little sticks and blanch them in boiling water for 5 minutes – this makes the flavour milder. Meanwhile, cut the beef into large cubes, about 4 cm/1½ in across; if you make the pieces smaller than this, they seem to lose some of their succulence before they are tender. Coat the pieces thoroughly with seasoned flour.

Drain the bacon and pat dry. Heat half the olive oil in a flameproof casserole and brown the bacon. Remove the bacon with a slotted spoon and set aside. Brown the meat in the same fat, adding a little more oil if necessary; put in only a few pieces at a time, just enough to cover the bottom of the pan – you can then make sure they are all evenly browned. Keep the heat very brisk for this. If there is any fat left at the end, pour it out, and return all the meat to the pan together with the bacon. Add the wine and bring it to the boil. Add just enough of the stock or water to the pan to leave the top halves of the uppermost pieces of meat

showing above the liquid. Add the bouquet garni, stir the meat around and season with salt and pepper. Cover and simmer in the oven for 2 hours.

While the meat is cooking, simmer the onions in the remaining stock or water for 5 minutes. Drain. Heat the remaining oil and the butter in a frying pan, add the onions and mushrooms and sprinkle with sugar. Cook, stirring, until browned. Stir into the casserole and cook for a few more minutes. Check seasoning, and serve.

STEAK AND KIDNEY PUDDING

SERVES 6

700 g/1½ lb boneless beef – two thirds chuck, one-third skirt
225 g/8 oz ox kidney
1–2 tablespoons seasoned flour
115 g/4 oz button mushrooms
2 shallots, chopped
1 teaspoon each anchovy essence, Worcestershire sauce, mushroom ketchup and tomato purée
a small wineglass of red wine
salt and freshly ground pepper

For the suet crust:
340 g/12 oz self-raising flour
170 g/6 oz shredded suet

Cut the beef into pieces about 1 cm/½ in across, trimming away fat and sinews. Remove the central core from the kidney and cut it into pieces about the same size as the beef. Coat the meat thoroughly in the seasoned flour. Mix together the meat, mushrooms and shallots in a bowl.

Next make the suet crust. Mix the flour, suet, and some salt and pepper in a bowl. Mix in 7–8 tablespoons of cold water to make a pliable dough. Roll out two-thirds of the dough on a floured board, and use it to line a greased large pudding basin.

anchovy essence 206
beef chuck 53
beef skirt 53
button mushroom 161
mushroom ketchup 206
ox kidney 62
self-raising flour 114
suet 110
tomato purée 206
Worcestershire sauce 206

pudding basin 230

beef brisket 53
chilli flakes 201
cinnamon stick 197
ginger 199
lard 110
leg of beef 53
oyster 36–7
sake 208
sherry vinegar 205
soy sauce 207
star anise 196
streaky bacon 70
zesting citrus fruits 423

casserole 236

Pile the beef mixture into the lined basin. Mix the anchovy essence, Worcestershire sauce, mushroom ketchup, tomato purée, wine, 300 ml/½ pint of water, and salt and pepper to taste in a jug. Pour into the pudding basin, adding enough extra cold water so the liquid comes just below the top of the meat.

Roll out the remaining dough into a round. Brush one side with water and put it loosely over the top of the meat filling, dampened side down. Press the edges with your fingers to seal the lid to the dough lining the basin. Trim away any excess dough from the edges. Cut a large round of foil, grease it and make a pleat in the centre. Place it loosely over the pudding, and tie tightly with string just below the rim of the pudding basin. Tie a string handle across the top of the basin so that it can be removed easily from the pan of water.

Take a large saucepan with a well-fitting lid, and half fill it with water (to which you can add a dash of vinegar to prevent staining the saucepan with long boiling). Bring the water to the boil and lower in the pudding – the water should come up to about 2.5 cm/1 in below the string. Cover the pan tightly – this is most important – and boil gently for 4½ hours, topping up with more boiling water as necessary.

Lift the basin out of the pan and remove the foil. Pin a neatly folded white napkin around the basin. Put it on a plate, place it on the table and plunge in the serving spoon to release a cloud of scented steam.

ALTERNATIVES: You can add a few oysters to the mixture of steak and kidney, or you can poach some oysters and drop them in as you serve the pudding.

BEEF IN BEER

Serve this hearty stew with plain boiled potatoes and a green salad.

SERVES 6–8

1.35 kg/3 lb boneless leg of beef
4–5 tablespoons lard or olive oil
3 onions, sliced
115 g/4 oz streaky bacon, cut into little sticks
2 tablespoons plain flour
600 ml/1 pint pale ale
1 teaspoon sugar
1 garlic clove, sliced
2 bay leaves
1 tablespoon wine vinegar
salt and freshly ground pepper

Cut the beef into cubes about 2.5 cm/1 in across. Heat the lard or oil in a flameproof casserole and fry the meat – a few pieces at a time – until well browned; remove to a large plate as each batch is browned. When all the meat is browned, turn down the heat, add a little more lard or oil to the casserole if you need it and start to fry the onions and bacon.

Preheat the oven to 150°C/300°F, gas mark 2.

When the onions and bacon have started to brown, stir in the flour and let it bubble for a minute or two. Gradually add the pale ale, stirring to keep the liquid smooth while it thickens. Return the meat to the casserole with its juices. Add the sugar, garlic, bay leaves, vinegar, some salt and plenty of pepper. Stir to mix and bring to the boil. Cover and simmer in the oven for 2 hours or until the meat is tender.

SLOW-COOKED BRISKET OF BEEF WITH SOY, SAKE AND OYSTERS

Brisket is one of the most succulent and flavoursome cuts of beef, thanks to its strata of meat and fat.

SERVES 4–6

1 joint of fatty beef brisket, weighing 1.35 kg/3 lb
12 large, fat rock oysters
salt and freshly ground pepper
4 spring onions, thinly sliced on the bias
½ teaspoon dried chilli flakes
a few sprigs of fresh coriander

For the aromatics and braising stock:

3 star anise
½ cinnamon stick
10 garlic cloves, peeled
2 large knobs of fresh root ginger, sliced
4 strips of orange zest
2 dried red chillies
175 ml/6 fl oz soy sauce
100 ml/3½ fl oz sake or dry sherry
1 teaspoon sugar
2 tablespoons sherry vinegar

Preheat the oven to 140°C/275°F, gas mark 1.

Put the brisket in a large pan, cover with cold water and bring slowly to the boil. Boil for 2 minutes, then drain. Rinse under warm running water and pat dry.

Put the beef in a heavy flameproof casserole that is just large enough to hold the meat snugly, but with enough room to spare for the aromatics and oysters. Add all the aromatics and braising stock ingredients to the casserole. Bring to a gentle simmer over a low heat. Move everything around with a spoon so that it is all evenly distributed and the meat does not stick to the bottom of the casserole. Simmer for 5 minutes.

Cover the casserole tightly and place in the oven. Cook for about 3 hours or until the meat is extremely tender when pierced with a skewer; it should be soft enough to cut with a spoon. If the liquid needs topping up during cooking, add a little water.

Meanwhile, remove the oysters from their shells, and reserve with the juices.

Carefully lift the beef out of the casserole on to a heated serving platter. Cover with foil and place in the turned-off oven, leaving the door ajar. Strain the now-syrupy braising stock through a fine sieve into a clean pan. Add the oysters with their juices. Warm through for 1–2 minutes until they have become firm and springy. Check the seasoning (the soy sauce and oysters should have provided enough salt).

Spoon the sauce and oysters over the meat. Sprinkle over the spring onions and chilli flakes and garnish with coriander sprigs. Serve with boiled potatoes.

VEAL WITH APPLES AND CREAM

SERVES 6

- 4 green eating apples, peeled, cored and cut into cubes
- 6 veal escalopes
- salt and freshly ground pepper
- juice of 1 lemon
- 55–85 g/2–3 oz butter
- 3 shallots, chopped
- 60 ml/2 fl oz brandy or, even better, Calvados
- 300 ml/½ pint single cream

Put the apples in a covered saucepan with a little water and leave to cook gently until just tender.

Season the escalopes on both sides with salt and pepper and sprinkle with a few drops of lemon juice. Heat one-third of the butter in a frying pan and, when it begins to brown, put two escalopes in the pan. Cook them for about 2 minutes on each side and then for a further 3 minutes on each side. Put the cooked escalopes on a hot dish, and repeat with the remaining escalopes.

Add the shallots to the pan and soften them. Stir in the brandy or Calvados. Add the apples and stir in the cream, adding just enough to make a smooth sauce. Taste for seasoning. Pour the rich creamy sauce over the escalopes and serve with a crisp chicory salad.

VEAL WITH MUSHROOMS

This is the perfect way to keep veal succulent.

SERVES 6

- 1 boned loin or shoulder of veal, weighing 1.35 kg/3 lb, rolled and tied
- salt and freshly ground pepper
- a sprinkling of dried thyme or 2 sprigs of fresh thyme
- 85 g/3 oz butter
- 3 thick rashers of streaky bacon, cut into little sticks
- 340 g/12 oz firm white button mushrooms
- 20 white button onions
- 2–3 tablespoons veal or light beef stock, white wine or water

Preheat the oven to 170°C/325°F, gas mark 3.

Rub the veal with salt, pepper and thyme. Melt 55 g/2 oz of the butter in a flameproof casserole into which the veal will fit nicely. Fry the sticks of bacon gently in the butter until they have given up all their fat. Put in the veal and brown it on the ends and on all sides, without letting the butter get too brown. Cover the casserole and transfer to the oven to cook for about 2 hours, turning the meat over from time to time. Test by piercing the meat with a skewer to see if it is tender.

While the veal is cooking, sauté the mushrooms in the remaining butter; set aside. Blanch the onions in boiling salted water for 5 minutes. Drain them and put them into the casserole 30 minutes before the veal is ready. Add the mushrooms 15 minutes later.

When the veal is cooked, put it on a serving dish with the onions, mushrooms and bacon. Keep hot. Skim excess fat from the gravy and, if you like, stir in a little stock, white wine or water to thin it. Taste for seasoning and allow to bubble for a minute or two. This thin gravy has a most delicious flavour. If you prefer it thick, whisk in a little beurre manié.

ALTERNATIVE: Use ordinary small onions instead of button onions; brown them in the fat with the meat and cook for the same length of time as the meat.

COSTOLETTE MILANESE

At the end of cooking, the butter will be very dark and ruined, but the chops – if you have not let them burn – will be perfectly crisp outside, delicate and juicy within.

SERVES 4

- 4 veal chops on the bone, taken from the loin
- 1 free-range egg
- 85 g/3 oz fresh white breadcrumbs
- 45–55 g/1½–2 oz butter
- salt
- 1 lemon, quartered

Beat the chops with a cutlet beater or rolling pin to flatten them and make them thinner. Beat the egg in a large, shallow dish, and spread the breadcrumbs on a plate. Sit the chops in the beaten egg, turning to coat them on both sides. Heat the butter in a wide frying pan

apple 162–3
beurre manié 422, 423
blanch 422
button mushroom 161
button onion 143
coating with egg and crumbs 423
fresh breadcrumbs 364
preparing veal escalopes 64
shucking oysters 42
thyme 194
veal cuts 55–6

casserole 236
cutlet beater 226
frying pan 234
sieves 226–7

Golden Veal or Beef Stock 244

that is large enough to hold all four chops (or use two pans if necessary). When the butter has started to brown, pick up the chops, shake off any excess egg and dip them in the crumbs, patting them on well all over. Fry the chops rather fast on each side for a minute, to brown them, then turn the heat right down so they are just sizzling. Leave them to cook for a further 6–10 minutes on each side, depending on their thickness, until they are cooked through. Drain the chops well, sprinkle with salt and serve with wedges of lemon.

OSSO BUCCO WITH LEMON GREMOLATA

SERVES 3–4

½ teaspoon saffron strands
a wineglass of white wine
55 g/2 oz butter
1.3 kg/3 lb osso bucco (slices of veal knuckle, each about 4 cm/1½ in thick and enclosing a piece of bone)
2 tablespoons plain flour
1 onion, finely chopped
1 celery stick, finely chopped
1 carrot, finely chopped
450 g/1 lb tomatoes, skinned and chopped
1 tablespoon tomato purée
thinly pared zest of ½ lemon
salt and freshly ground pepper
2 teaspoons finely chopped parsley
1 large garlic clove, finely chopped
2 anchovy fillets, finely chopped (optional)
100 ml/3½ fl oz veal or light beef stock (optional)

Put the saffron strands to soak in the white wine. Melt half the butter, or a little more than this, in a heavy pan or a flameproof casserole. Roll the slices of veal in flour and brown them all over in the butter. Remove them and set aside. Fry the onion, celery and carrot in the same pan, adding more butter if necessary. Return the slices of veal to the pan. Add the saffron-infused wine and let it sizzle until it has evaporated almost completely. Add the tomatoes, tomato purée, 2 strips of the lemon zest, and some salt and pepper. Cover the pan and leave to simmer for 1½–2 hours, adding a little water from time to time if necessary but keeping the mixture fairly dry.

Meanwhile, finely chop the remaining lemon zest and mix with the parsley, garlic and anchovies to make a *gremolata*. When the meat is tender, sprinkle in half of the *gremolata* and cook for a further 2–3 minutes, turning the pieces of meat over once.

Put the veal on a heated serving dish. Add the remaining butter to the sauce. If it seems too thick, stir in the stock. Heat through, taste for seasoning and pour it over the veal. Sprinkle with the remaining *gremolata* and serve.

Osso Bucco with Lemon Gremolata

GIGOT D'AGNEAU WITH HARICOT BEANS

SERVES 6

340 g/12 oz dried haricot beans or green flageolets, soaked overnight
1 ham bone or a 450 g/1 lb piece of bacon or salt pork
3 garlic cloves, chopped
a handful of parsley, chopped
85 g/3 oz butter
1 leg of lamb, weighing 1.8 kg/4 lb, boned
salt and freshly ground pepper
1 tablespoon pork dripping, or butter and oil mixed
1 large onion, finely chopped
2 tablespoons tomato purée or 3–4 tomatoes
a wineglass of white wine

Put the drained haricot beans or flageolets in a heavy saucepan together with the ham bone or whatever piece of pork or bacon you have. Cover with plenty of cold water, bring to the boil and simmer gently for 1–1½ hours.

Preheat the oven to 220°C/425°F, gas mark 7.

Cook the chopped garlic and parsley gently in a little of the butter, without allowing the garlic to brown. Allow this mixture to cool, then push it into the cavity in the leg of lamb. Season with salt and pepper and add a lump of the remaining butter. Roll up the leg and tie it at 4 cm/1½ in intervals with string. Rub the outside with the last of the butter and some salt and set it in a roasting tin. Roast for 30 minutes, basting and turning from time to time. Turn down the heat to 180°C/350°F, gas mark 4, and roast for a further 40 minutes. Remove from the oven and allow to rest in a warm place.

Meanwhile, heat the pork dripping or butter and oil in a large saucepan and soften the onion. Stir in the tomato purée and let it bubble, stirring, for 2–3 minutes. (If you are using fresh tomatoes instead of tomato purée, skin and chop them, remove their seeds and then reduce them considerably before adding them to the softened onions.) Add the white wine to the onion and tomato mixture, together with a cupful of the beans' cooking liquid. Simmer for a minute or two. Drain the beans and discard the ham bone or piece of bacon or pork. Add the beans to the tomato-wine sauce and stir. Leave them to simmer very gently until the meat is ready.

anchovy 16, 31
boning a leg of lamb 66
dripping 110
flageolet bean 126
ham, bacon and salted pork 68–70
haricot bean 126
infuse 422
osso bucco 56
saffron 199
skinning and seeding tomatoes 423
tomato purée 206
zesting citrus fruits 423

casserole 236
citrus zester 224

Golden Veal or Beef Stock 244

almond 186–7
boning a leg of lamb 66
boning a shoulder of lamb 65
bouquet garni 190
breadcrumbs 364
chilli powder 201
ginger 199
lamb cuts 57–8
lamb's kidney 61
lamb's liver 61
Lyonnaise sausage 78
marinate 422
nuts 186–9
pistachio nut 187
potato 145
raisin 182
tomato purée 206
yogurt 99

casserole 236
skimmers 226

Chicken Stock 244

Remove the lamb from the roasting tin. Spoon all the fat from the juices in the tin, then stir these juices into the beans. Season the beans and transfer them to a heated dish. Carve the lamb and lay the slices down the middle of the dish of beans.

ALTERNATIVES: Sprinkle the slices of lamb with a mixture of breadcrumbs and finely chopped garlic and parsley, then quickly brown under the grill. You can also add sliced Lyonnaise sausage to the beans. But perhaps best of all is plain gigot and beans bathed in their own excellent sauce.

NAVARIN OF LAMB WITH POTATOES

SERVES 6–8

- 900 g/2 lb each boned shoulder and middle neck of lamb
- 2 tablespoons sunflower oil
- 1 large onion, chopped
- 3 garlic cloves, crushed
- 20 g/¾ oz plain flour
- 2 tablespoons tomato purée
- salt and freshly ground pepper
- a fresh bouquet garni
- 450 ml/¾ pint dry white wine
- 450 ml/¾ pint chicken stock
- 700 g/1½ lb potatoes, peeled and sliced

Trim the meat and cut into large pieces, eliminating most of the fat. Heat the oil in a large flameproof casserole and brown the meat over a brisk heat. Remove the pieces as they are browned. Then brown the onion in the same oil, together with the garlic. Stir in the flour and cook for a minute before adding the tomato purée, some salt and pepper and the bouquet garni.

Preheat the oven to 170°C/325°F, gas mark 3.

Return the meat to the casserole. Add the wine and stock, stir to mix and bring to the boil. Cover and transfer to the oven to cook for 45 minutes.

Uncover the casserole and skim the fat from the surface of the liquid. Add some salt. Push the sliced potatoes into the stew, covering the surface with a thick layer. Replace the lid and cook for 45 minutes or until the potatoes are almost tender. Then remove the lid, turn the oven up to 190°C/375°F, gas mark 5, and cook for a further 20–30 minutes. The potatoes will absorb all the remaining fat from the top of the navarin, and turn an appetizing golden brown.

ALTERNATIVE: Cast a handful of freshly shelled or frozen peas into the navarin just before you cover it with the sliced potatoes.

SPICED STUFFED LEG OF LAMB

This is a really fine dish for a dinner party, and looks as beautiful as it tastes. Surround the lamb with boiled rice that has been cooked in salted water with 4 cardamom pods and 2 cinnamon sticks. The cooking juices are rather rich with all the honey, yogurt and onion, but taste good on this simple spiced rice.

SERVES 6

- 2 garlic cloves
- 1 teaspoon ground ginger or a 2.5 cm/1 in piece of fresh root ginger
- 1 teapoon chilli powder
- salt
- 1 onion, very finely chopped
- 300 ml/½ pint plain yogurt plus an extra 1–2 tablespoons
- juice of 1 lemon
- 1 leg or shoulder of lamb, weighing 1.8 kg/4 lb, boned
- 115 g/4 oz lamb's liver
- 2 lamb's kidneys
- 30 g/1 oz shelled pistachio nuts, skinned and chopped
- 55 g/2 oz blanched almonds, chopped
- 115 g/4 oz seedless raisins
- 55–85 g/2–3 oz butter
- 1 tablespoon clear honey

Start a day ahead.

Mash the garlic, ginger and chilli powder with a little salt. Mix them with the onion, 300 ml/½ pint yogurt and the lemon juice. Prick the boned lamb here and there with a skewer, to allow the flavours of the marinade to penetrate the meat. Spread the yogurt paste over the lamb, inside and out. Leave it to marinate in the refrigerator overnight.

The next day, before you commence preparations, preheat the oven to 170°C/325°F, gas mark 3.

Boil the liver and kidneys in salted water until firm, then drain and chop finely. Mix them with the nuts and raisins, and add a large pinch of salt and the extra yogurt. Spread this mixture over the inside of the lamb and press it well down on to the meat. Roll up the lamb and use skewers to hold it while you tie it with string at 2.5–5 cm/1–2 in intervals to keep the stuffing in. Sprinkle the joint with salt and put it into a deep casserole with the butter and yogurt paste marinade.

Cover the casserole and roast for 1 hour. Then turn the joint over and add the honey. Roast for a further hour, turning the joint and basting with the honey and juices in the casserole every 30 minutes. Take the lid off for the last 30 minutes.

Remove the string and carve the lamb into fairly thick slices. Arrange on a heated dish. Skim the fat from the cooking juices and serve them separately.

ALTERNATIVE: Omit the liver and kidneys from the dish, and increase the quantity of pistachios used to 140 g/5 oz.

SPICED STUFFED LEG OF LAMB

LAMB KORMA

This rich, mild and very delicious curry was a firm favourite with the Madras Club in the nineteenth century. Although the korma would originally have been made with mutton, or even with goat, it is even better when lamb is used instead.

SERVES 6–8

- 1.8 kg/4 lb shoulder or neck of lamb
- a 5 cm/2 in piece of fresh root ginger, cut into fine slivers
- 45 g/1½ oz butter
- 1 large onion, finely chopped
- 2 garlic cloves, finely chopped
- 1 tablespoon ground coriander
- 1 teaspoon turmeric
- ½ teaspoon ground cardamom
- ½ teaspoon ground cloves
- ½ teaspoon ground cumin (optional)
- ½ teaspoon freshly ground black pepper
- 150 ml/¼ pint plain yogurt
- salt
- juice of ½ lemon
- a handful of cashew nuts, lightly toasted and coarsely chopped

Remove the meat from the bones and cut it into large pieces. Mix in the slivers of ginger.

Melt the butter in a large pan and sweat the onion and garlic until soft and translucent. Add the spices and black pepper and fry for a minute, stirring well to mix with the onion. Add the meat and fry it, turning

cardamom 199
cashew 186
clove 197
cumin 199
garlic 145
ginger 199
lamb shoulder or neck 58
sweat 423
turmeric 199
yogurt 99

chine 422
fennel seed 196
garlic 145
juniper berry 196–7
lamb shanks 58
pork fillet 60
pork loin 60
preparing veal escalopes 64
red onion 144
rosemary 193
skinning and seeding tomatoes 423
sweat 423
sweet pepper 152
tomato 150–1

casserole 236
cutlet beater 226
frying pan 234
sieves 226–7

Chicken Stock 244

the pieces around until they are browned on all sides. Stir in the yogurt and a little salt.

Cover the pan and leave to simmer gently for about 1½ hours or until the lamb is tender and the curry is almost dry. Add the lemon juice and cashew nuts. Cover again and cook for a further 15 minutes.

GARLIC-BRAISED LAMB SHANKS WITH YELLOW PEPPERS

Cooking the meat on the bone in this recipe gives a wonderful sauce and makes the meat unusually sweet and delectable.

SERVES 6

- 2 red onions
- 340 g/12 oz ripe tomatoes, skinned, seeded and chopped
- 6 tablespoons olive oil
- 6 lamb shanks
- 20 garlic cloves, peeled
- 1 teaspoon dried oregano
- 85 ml/3 fl oz red wine
- salt and freshly ground pepper
- 4 yellow peppers, seeded and cut into large pieces

Preheat the oven to 170°C/325°F, gas mark 3.

Cut the onions in half from top to bottom. Set each half cut side down and slice coarsely lengthways, to obtain crescent-shaped slices. Put the tomatoes in a sieve to drain.

Heat half the oil in a large flameproof casserole and brown the lamb shanks over a moderate heat. Remove them to a dish. Add the onions and garlic to the casserole, sprinkle with the oregano and sweat in the same oil until they start to brown. Stir in the tomatoes and allow to cook for a few minutes, then add the wine. Put the lamb shanks on top and bring to simmering point. Season with salt and pepper. Cover the casserole, transfer to the oven and braise for 45 minutes, turning the meat occasionally.

Fry the pieces of pepper in the remaining oil until lightly browned. Add them to the casserole and continue to cook, covered, until the lamb is tender and melting. This will take a further 30–40 minutes, depending on the size of the lamb shanks. If it takes longer than this, turn down the heat for the last part of the cooking.

Remove the lamb shanks to a heated dish. Reduce the sauce if it is too liquid; it should be velvety in texture. Pour the sauce over the shanks and serve.

ALTERNATIVE: If more convenient, you can braise the lamb shanks in a covered casserole on top of the cooker.

PORK FILLET WITH JUNIPER

SERVES 6

- 2 whole pork fillets
- juice of 1 lemon
- 20 juniper berries, crushed
- salt and freshly ground pepper
- 30 g/1 oz butter
- 1 tablespoon sunflower or olive oil
- 2 garlic cloves, sliced
- a wineglass of red wine

Cut the fillets across into little round slices 2 cm/¾ in thick. Beat these between two pieces of damp greaseproof paper until quite thin and flat. Sprinkle them with lemon juice. Mix the juniper berries with some salt and pepper, and pat this mixture into the little pork escalopes.

Heat the butter and oil in a heavy frying pan. Fry the escalopes quickly, not more than 2–3 minutes on each side; halfway through, add the garlic to the pan.

When the escalopes are done, put them on a heated dish and keep hot. Pour the wine into the frying pan and let it bubble, scraping the sediment off the bottom of the pan. Pour this sauce over the pork and serve immediately.

ALTERNATIVE: Use fennel seeds instead of juniper berries.

ROAST LOIN OF PORK

SERVES 6–8

- 1 loin of pork, weighing about 1.6 kg/3½ lb
- 2 nice sprigs of fresh rosemary
- 2 garlic cloves
- a little wine vinegar or lemon juice
- salt and freshly ground pepper
- a wineglass of white wine or dry cider
- 2 teaspoons plain flour
- 150–300 ml/¼–½ pint chicken stock

Preheat the oven to 180°C/350°F, gas mark 4.

The loin should be on the bone, but chined by the butcher. Score the skin well in parallel lines at 1 cm/½ in intervals. Place the loin, skin side up, on a rack in a roasting tin. Tuck the rosemary under the pork and push the unpeeled garlic cloves between the meat and the fat or next to the bone. Rub the surface with vinegar or lemon juice and fine salt but no oil or other fat.

Roast the pork, without basting, for 2 hours, moving it low in the oven if the crackling is getting too dark on the top. Remove the meat to a heated dish, cover loosely with foil and leave it to rest for at least 15–20 minutes. (This makes the meat juicier and easier to carve.)

Meanwhile, make the gravy. Spoon most of the fat from the roasting tin and remove the rosemary. Retrieve the cloves of garlic and squeeze them from their skins into the tin. Add the wine or cider, and stir and scrape over a rapid heat to dissolve the meat juices and sediment on the sides and bottom of the tin and to crush the garlic. When the wine has reduced considerably, add the flour to the pan and stir it around, breaking up the lumps. Still stirring, pour in the stock. Simmer the gravy for a few minutes, then season it and strain. Serve the loin of pork with this gravy, and with Apple Sauce and Roast Potatoes.

FRIED PORK CHOPS

The trouble with cooking pork chops is that very often by the time they are done right through, which of course they must be, they have become dry. Prepared this way, however, they should be perfectly cooked, tender and juicy.

SERVES 4

4 pork chops
1 tablespoon sunflower or olive oil
2 garlic cloves, crushed
salt and coarsely ground pepper
2–3 sprigs of fresh thyme

Preheat the oven to 180°C/350°F, gas mark 4.

Trim skin and excess fat from the chops, then rub them with a little oil and the crushed garlic. Season them with pepper and a few thyme leaves but no salt yet.

Choose a frying pan large enough to hold all the chops side by side, and pour in just enough oil to coat the bottom thinly. When the oil is really hot, put the chops in the pan. Sear them quickly on both sides, then reduce the heat slightly and fry until they are a little more resistant but still slightly soft to the touch. Transfer the chops to a baking dish, stacking them one on top of the other. Cover lightly with foil. Put them in the oven to cook for 10 minutes, keeping the door slightly open.

Season the chops with salt just before serving.

BOILED BACON AND SAUSAGE WITH HARICOT BEANS AND GARLIC PURÉE

Any combination of boiled or braised salt pork or sausage with starchy beans never fails to seduce the lover of good, sustaining fare. There is something comforting about such dishes, and the floury plainness of the beans makes the perfect foil for the richness of the bacon and sausages.

SERVES 4

340 g/12 oz dried haricot beans, soaked overnight
2 tablespoons goose or duck fat, lard or dripping
2 large onions, chopped
1 tablespoon tomato purée
a wineglass of dry white wine
a fresh bouquet garni
550 g/1¼ lb unsmoked streaky bacon, in one piece, complete with rind
1 vacuum-packed cotechino or zampone sausage
3 tablespoons chopped fresh flat-leaf parsley

For the garlic purée:

30 large garlic cloves, peeled
6 tablespoons olive oil
salt and freshly ground pepper
a squeeze of lemon juice

Put the drained beans in a large saucepan, cover with fresh cold water and bring to the boil. Drain in a colander, rinsing off any clinging scum. In the same pan, heat the fat, lard or dripping and fry the onions until golden. Stir in the tomato purée and cook with the onions until they are rust-coloured. Add the wine and bubble for a few minutes until slightly reduced. Tip in the blanched beans, and push in the bouquet garni and bacon so they are buried in the beans. Cover with water to a depth of 5 cm/2 in. Bring to a simmer, then leave to cook gently for 1 hour. (Do not be tempted to add salt at this stage because it makes the bean skins tough and hard.)

Meanwhile, boil the sausage according to the instructions on the packet (it should take about 30 minutes). Keep warm.

To make the garlic purée, put the garlic cloves in a saucepan, cover with water and bring to the boil. Drain, and repeat the process. Drain again and return the garlic to the pan. Add the oil and just cover with water. Cook until the garlic is very soft. Purée in a blender or food processor. Season with salt and pepper and add a squeeze of lemon. Transfer the purée to a bowl, cover and keep warm over a bain marie or pan of hot water.

Test the bacon with a skewer to see if it is done (it should be by now). Remove it from the pan, cover with foil and keep warm in a low oven while you finish the beans. They should have a sloppy consistency, but not be swimming in liquid. If they seem too wet, drain off the excess liquid. Season to taste.

To serve, stir the parsley into the beans and pile into a serving dish. Surround with thick slices of sausage and bacon. Hand the garlic purée separately.

bacon 69–70
bain-marie 422
cotechino 73
dripping and goose or duck fat 110
flat-leaf parsley 190
garlic 145
haricot bean 126
lard 110
pork chops 60
reduce 423
thyme 194
tomato purée 206
zampone 73

blender, liquidizer 238
colander 229
food processor 238
frying pan 234
sieves 226–7

Apple Sauce 260
Roast Potatoes 379

bouquet garni 190
clove 197
demerara sugar 211
gammon 68
offal 61–2
onion 143–4
poultry livers 90
sage 193–4
sherry vinegar 205
streaky bacon 70

casserole 236
knives 222–4
roasting tin 236

Lentil Soup 248
Yellow Split Pea Soup 248

GLAZED GAMMON

SERVES 4–6

1 joint of cured, unsmoked gammon, weighing 1.35 kg/3 lb, ready to cook

For the glaze:

115 g/4 oz demerara sugar
1 tablespoon dry or medium sherry
3 tablespoons sherry vinegar
6 cloves, pounded and crushed
1 teaspoon English mustard powder

If necessary, soak the gammon to remove excess salt. Then put it in a large pan of cold water, bring to simmering point and simmer gently for 45 minutes.

While the gammon is cooking, mix together the ingredients for the glaze in a bowl.

Preheat the oven to 170°C/325°F, gas mark 3.

Remove the gammon from its cooking liquid, which can be used for making pea or lentil soup. Carefully cut or peel away the rind. Make diagonal cuts into the fat, scoring it every 5 mm/¼ in across from the top to bottom corners. The scoring should be deep into the fat, but not all the way through. Place the gammon in a large roasting tin.

Pour the glaze over the gammon. Bake for 30 minutes, basting frequently with the glaze that will have run into the tin. Then turn up the heat to 220°C/425°F, gas mark 7 or put under a preheated moderate grill to make the fat golden and crunchy. (If using the grill, go gently or the glaze will burn.)

Allow the gammon to rest for at least 15 minutes before carving, or serve cold.

LYONNAISE CALF'S LIVER WITH ONIONS

SERVES 6

30 g/1 oz butter
1 teaspoon olive oil or lard
4–6 onions, sliced
450 g/1 lb calf's liver, thinly sliced
salt and freshly ground pepper
1–2 tablespoons red wine vinegar

Heat the butter and oil or lard in a large frying pan. Add the onions and cook over a gentle heat until starting to brown. Cover the pan, turn down the heat and leave the onions to cook gently for 10–15 minutes or until they are very soft. Push them to one side of the pan or use a slotted spoon to remove them to a plate.

Season the slices of liver with pepper. Put them in the pan and then fry over a moderate heat for about 3 minutes on each side. Spoon the onions on top of the slices of liver. Splash the vinegar into the pan and let it sizzle, then season with salt and more pepper. Serve straight away.

BRAISED LIVER WITH BACON

SERVES 6

3 carrots
2 onions
1 celery stick
10 rashers of streaky bacon
2 garlic cloves, crushed
salt and coarsely ground pepper
1 pig's liver, in one piece, weighing 900 g–1 kg/2–2½ lb
2 tablespoons olive oil
a fresh bouquet garni of parsley and thyme
a large wineglass of red wine

Cut the carrots, onions and celery into strips about the size of your little finger. Cut 4 of the bacon rashers into pieces 4 x 2 cm/1½ x ¾ in. Press the garlic into the pieces of bacon and season them liberally with coarsely ground pepper. Roll up each piece into a little roll. Make rows of deep, short cuts in the liver and insert the rolls of bacon, pushing them in with your finger.

Preheat the oven to 180°C/350°F, gas mark 4.

Heat the oil in a flameproof casserole. Add the vegetables, cover the pan and sweat the vegetables gently for 5–10 minutes. Put the liver on top and arrange the remaining rashers of bacon over the liver. Add the bouquet garni, wine, a little salt and pepper and any leftover garlic. Cover and cook in the oven for 1 hour.

Discard the bouquet garni. Remove the liver and bacon to a deep serving dish and keep hot while you reduce the sauce over a high heat until it is slightly syrupy. Cut the liver into slices and serve with the bacon, sauce and mashed potatoes.

SAUTÉED CHICKEN LIVERS WITH SAGE

Prepared this way, chicken livers are very savoury and fragrant.

SERVES 4

450 g/1 lb chicken livers
1 tablespoon olive oil
30 g/1 oz butter
2 onions, chopped
60 ml/2 fl oz Marsala
a little sage, fresh or dried
salt and freshly ground pepper

Glazed Gammon

Trim the livers and dry them on kitchen paper. Heat the oil and butter in a frying pan and sweat the onions until soft and starting to brown. Pour the Marsala into the pan and boil until almost completely evaporated. Add the chicken livers and season with sage, salt and pepper. Sauté over a moderate heat – hot enough to prevent the juices from running out of the livers, but not so hot that the onions are burned – until the livers are firm but still moist inside.

Serve with rice and a green or young spinach salad.

KIDNEYS WITH MUSTARD

The flavouring of juniper is unexpected, but very good.

SERVES 4

2 calf's kidneys, each weighing about 340 g/12 oz
6 juniper berries, crushed
salt and freshly ground pepper
45 g/1½ oz butter
1 tablespoon olive oil
1 tablespoon brandy
1 tablespoon Dijon mustard
4 tablespoons double cream

Remove the fat from the kidneys and then strip off the thin, transparent membrane that covers them. Using a sharp knife, cut the kidneys in half lengthways. Trim away the cores and slice each half thinly. Scatter the crushed juniper berries over the kidneys and press them in well with your hands. Season with salt and freshly ground pepper.

Heat the butter and olive oil together in a frying pan. Throw in the sliced kidneys and let them brown rapidly, turning them so that they colour evenly. After about 4 minutes, pour in the brandy and let it bubble up for a few seconds. Mix the mustard into the cream, add to the pan and stir well until the kidneys are nicely coated with this sauce.

Serve at once, accompanied by fresh spinach and mashed potatoes.

calf's kidneys 61
Dijon mustard 202
juniper berry 196–7

Creamed Potatoes with Parsley 381
Plain Boiled Rice 346

Game

allspice 198
bay 193
beurre manié 422, 423
lard 110
malt vinegar 205
marinate 422
peppercorns 200–1
rosemary 193
venison 79

barbecuing equipment 240–1
casserole 236

Chicken Stock 244
Redcurrant Jelly 418
Rich Brown Beef Stock 245

CHAR-GRILLED VENISON

SERVES 6

1 venison steak cut from the leg or loin, weighing 900 g–1.35 kg/2–3 lb
1 teaspoon salt
½ teaspoon coarsely crushed pepper
½ wineglass of red wine
2–3 fresh rosemary or juniper branches (optional)

Make up the fire so that it is glowing nicely – if you do not have a charcoal grill, an open fire will do equally well.

Heat the barbecue rack. Rub the meat all over with the salt and pepper and put it over the fire on the rack. After 5 minutes, brush the steak with red wine and turn it over. After another 5 minutes, brush it with wine and turn again. Continue to brush and turn frequently, cooking it for about 25 minutes altogether.

Remove the meat from the rack and wrap it in foil. Let it rest for 7–8 minutes. Freshen the charcoal fire and put the rosemary or juniper on the coals to smoulder and smoke. Unwrap the meat, put it back on the rack and let it cook and smoke for a final 5 minutes to give the outside a nice smoky flavour. The meat should be rosy red but not rare.

Carve the steak at the table, cutting it into fairly thick slices. Serve with a salad, baked potatoes filled with sour cream and chopped fresh chives or dill, and good bread.

ALTERNATIVE: Use 6 venison fillet steaks instead of a large steak. Sear both sides, then continue grilling for 3–5 minutes for medium-rare meat.

SWEET-BRAISED SPICED VENISON

Serve with small potatoes cooked in their skins, redcurrant jelly and puréed celeriac.

SERVES 6

1 boned shoulder joint of venison, weighing 900 g/2 lb
30 g/1 oz butter
1 tablespoon olive oil
salt
1 teaspoon black peppercorns, coarsely crushed
300 ml/½ pint stout
2–3 tablespoons malt vinegar
1 teaspoon brown sugar or 1 tablespoon redcurrant jelly
150 ml/¼ pint chicken or beef stock
2 onions, chopped
8 allspice berries
4 cloves
3–4 bay leaves
2 tablespoons double cream
a knob of beurre manié, if needed

Trim the venison. Heat the butter and oil in a flameproof casserole and brown the joint on both sides. Season with ½ teaspoon of salt and the crushed peppercorns. Add the stout, vinegar, sugar or redcurrant jelly, stock, chopped onions, allspice, cloves and bay leaves. Bring to the boil, then leave to simmer, covered, for 1–1½ hours or until the meat is tender.

Remove the venison from the casserole and keep it hot. Discard the bay leaves. Add the cream to the juices, which should be much reduced. Thicken the sauce lightly with the beurre manié if it seems too thin.

Carve the shoulder into slices. Serve the sauce separately.

ALTERNATIVE: Use moose instead of venison, and serve it with blackcurrant jelly instead of redcurrant jelly.

ROAST HAUNCH OF VENISON WITH PEPPER SAUCE

Before you cook the venison, marinate it for 24 hours to help keep it moist. The marinade here, which has no vinegar, gives the venison a delicious rich flavour.

SERVES 6–10

1 small haunch of venison
30 g/1 oz lard
150 ml/¼ pint chicken or beef stock or water
2 celery sticks, chopped
2 teaspoons plain flour
1 teaspoon green peppercorns or 1 teaspoon coarsely crushed black pepper
salt

For the marinade:

1–2 tablespoons olive or groundnut oil
2 onions, sliced
2 bay leaves
a bunch of parsley
2 wineglasses of red wine
2 teaspoons black peppercorns

To make the marinade, heat the oil in a saucepan and fry the onions until they start to brown. Add the bay leaves, parsley, wine and peppercorns. Bring to the boil and boil for 5 minutes. Pour in 600 ml/1 pint of water and bring back to the boil. Cover and boil the mixture for 15 minutes. Let it cool completely.

Pour the marinade into a flat earthenware dish. Add the venison and leave it to marinate in a cool place for 24 hours. Turn the meat from time to time.

When you are ready to roast the venison, preheat the oven to 190°C/375°F, gas mark 5.

Remove the meat from the marinade – which you keep for the sauce – and wipe it dry. Wrap it completely in oiled foil and place it in a roasting tin. Put the haunch in the oven and roast for 25 minutes per 450 g/1 lb, or 20 minutes per 450 g/1 lb for a haunch weighing over 4.5 kg/10 lb. Then remove the foil, reserving the juices that are inside it, rub the joint with lard and roast it for a further 30 minutes.

Meanwhile, simmer the marinade with the stock or water and the celery for 25 minutes.

When the venison has finished cooking, remove it from the roasting tin and allow to rest. Stir the flour into the fat and juices in the tin and cook, stirring, until browned. Strain the marinade and reserved juices into the tin, stirring to make a nice gravy. Add the green peppercorns or pepper and reduce the gravy to a syrupy consistency. Sprinkle the meat with salt just before serving, with the gravy.

ALTERNATIVES: You could add a little double cream to this gravy, thereby making it even richer. This recipe is also suitable for hare: allow 45 minutes roasting at 180°C/350°F, gas mark 4.

HARE IN SOUR CREAM

SERVES 2

1 saddle of hare
1 onion, thinly sliced
1 carrot, thinly sliced
1 celery stick, thinly sliced into crescents
a small fresh bouquet garni of thyme, parsley and a bay leaf
6 black peppercorns
a wineglass of red wine
4 thin rashers of streaky bacon
1 teaspoon plain flour
150 ml/¼ pint sour cream
salt and freshly ground pepper

Start a day ahead.

Trim the saddle, removing the thick outer membrane and the flaps. Put it in a small earthenware dish. Put the onion, carrot and celery in a small saucepan together with the bouquet garni and peppercorns. Add 150 ml/¼ pint of cold water and the red wine. Bring to the boil and simmer for 5 minutes. Pour this hot marinade over the saddle and leave to marinate for 24 hours.

When you are ready to cook the saddle, preheat the oven to 190°C/375°F, gas mark 5.

Take the hare out of the marinade and wipe it dry; reserve the marinade. To prevent the saddle from curling up while it cooks, puncture the spinal column in several places with the point of a sharp knife. Wrap the saddle in the rashers of bacon and put it in a small roasting tin. Roast for 20 minutes, basting frequently with a tablespoon or two of the strained marinade. (You should add a wineglass of liquid altogether.)

Mix the flour with the sour cream. Add to the juices in the roasting tin and stir in. Season with salt and pepper. Transfer to the oven to cook for a further 10 minutes.

Put the saddle on a heated serving dish, arrange the bacon around it and keep hot. Bring the sauce to the boil. Add more marinade if it is too thick, or boil it for a minute or two if it is too thin. When it is the consistency of cream, pour it through a sieve over the saddle. Serve with small steamed or boiled potatoes, redcurrant jelly and sprigs of watercress.

BRAISED RABBIT WITH TOMATOES

SERVES 4

3–4 tablespoons olive oil
1 onion, chopped
1–2 carrots, finely chopped
2 celery sticks, finely chopped
1 garlic clove, crushed
1 farmed rabbit, jointed
plain flour for dusting
salt and freshly ground pepper
120 ml/4 fl oz red wine
450 g/1 lb tomatoes, skinned and chopped
a fresh bouquet garni of parsley, thyme, marjoram and a bay leaf

Heat the oil in a flameproof casserole and fry the onion, carrots and celery with the garlic until they are soft and beginning to brown. Dry the pieces of rabbit and dust them with flour. Put them in with the vegetables, turning up the heat. Try to get them in contact with the bottom of the pan so they will brown. Frying the rabbit with the vegetables, rather than separately, gives it a more intense flavour.

When the pieces of rabbit are more or less brown all over, season them with salt and pepper and add the red wine. Let it bubble until the smell of wine has disappeared, then add the tomatoes and the bouquet garni. Cover the casserole and simmer for 45 minutes to 1 hour – or longer for a tough rabbit.

ALTERNATIVE: Add some stoned black olives towards the end of the cooking.

bouquet garni 190
hare 79
jointing a rabbit 81
marinate 422
olives 154–5
rabbit 80
skinning and seeding tomatoes 423
soured cream 99
streaky bacon 70
watercress 130–1

casserole 236
knives 222–4
roasting tin 236

Redcurrant Jelly 418

RABBIT WITH PRUNES AND RED WINE

This is a Belgian recipe.

SERVES 4

- 1 farmed rabbit, preferably with its liver and kidneys, jointed
- plain flour for dusting
- 30–55 g/1–2 oz butter
- 1 onion, chopped
- 200 ml/7 fl oz red wine
- 225 g/8 oz plump prunes
- salt and freshly ground pepper
- a little chicken stock (optional)

For the marinade:

- 400 ml/14 fl oz red wine
- 200 ml/7 fl oz wine vinegar
- salt
- 6 black peppercorns
- 2 garlic cloves, crushed
- a sprig of fresh thyme
- 1 bay leaf
- a few sprigs of fresh or dried herb fennel

Mix together the ingredients for the marinade in a bowl. Place the rabbit in it, together with its liver and kidneys, and turn it once or twice. Leave to marinate for a few hours, but not more than 12 hours.

Drain the rabbit, liver and kidneys and wipe dry; dust the rabbit joints with flour. Melt the butter in a sauté pan and brown the rabbit joints, liver and kidneys on all sides. Remove to a plate. Add the onion to the pan and soften it. Return the pieces of rabbit to the pan and add the red wine and the prunes. Season with salt and pepper. Cover the pan and simmer for 30 minutes, turning the pieces of rabbit from time to time. Then simmer, uncovered, for a further 15–40 minutes or until the rabbit is very tender (this will depend on the quality of the rabbit).

Taste the sauce; if it is too rich, add a little stock or water. It should be fairly strong, not too sweet and very well flavoured. Check the seasoning before serving, with small steamed or boiled potatoes.

ROAST PARTRIDGE WITH CHICKEN LIVER TOASTS

SERVES 4

- 4 plump young partridges, plucked and cleaned, with their livers
- salt and freshly ground pepper

RABBIT WITH PRUNES AND RED WINE

- 1 chicken liver
- 4 small slices of white bread, crusts removed
- 1 garlic clove, cut in half
- 85 g/3 oz butter, softened
- 8 small thin rashers of streaky bacon
- ½ tablespoon sunflower oil
- 6 tablespoons white wine
- a bunch of watercress

Preheat the oven to 220°C/425°F, gas mark 7.

Season the partridges inside and out with salt and pepper. Mash the partridge livers and the chicken liver well with a fork, removing any fibres. Rub the slices of bread with the halved clove of garlic. Spread them with butter and then with the crushed livers. Season lightly with salt and pepper. Roll up the pieces of bread, liver side inwards, and push one inside each partridge. Truss the birds neatly, covering each carefully with 2 rashers of bacon.

Heat the remaining butter with the oil in a roasting tin and brown the birds all over for 5 minutes. Then transfer the tin to the oven and roast for 10 minutes. Remove the covering of bacon and roast for a further 5 minutes to finish browning the birds. Take them out, remove the trussing strings and put the birds on a serving dish. Turn down the oven to 150°C/300°F, gas mark 2. Put the birds back into the oven to keep hot while you make the gravy.

Skim some of the fat from the juices in the tin. Add the wine and 3–4 tablespoons of water to the tin and boil over a moderate heat while you stir and scrape up the juices. When the liquid has reduced by half, pour it into a small gravy jug. Arrange sprigs of watercress around the partridges on their serving dish and serve.

PARTRIDGE WITH CELERIAC

SERVES 4

- 4 shallots
- 4 fresh sage leaves
- 170 g/6 oz butter
- salt and freshly ground pepper
- 4 plump young partridges, plucked and cleaned
- 4 rashers of streaky bacon
- 1 medium-size celeriac, weighing about 450 g/1 lb
- 1 small potato
- 4 tablespoons white wine
- juice of ½ lemon

Preheat the oven to 200°C/400°F, gas mark 6.

Put a peeled shallot, a crushed sage leaf, a little butter and some salt and pepper inside each partridge. Lay a rasher of bacon over the breast of each bird.

celeriac 148–9
herb fennel 191
jointing a rabbit 81
marinate 422
partridge 83
prune 184
rabbit 80
sage 193–4
shallot 144–5
streaky bacon 70
thyme 194
trussing a chicken 91
watercress 130–1
wine vinegar 204

roasting tin 236
sauté pan 234
skimmers 228
trussing equipment 230

apple 162–3
bouquet garni 190
chestnut 188
juniper berry 196–7
oils 110–13
pheasant 85
pigeon 83
Spanish onion 144
streaky bacon 70
thickening agents 118–19

bulb baster 229
casserole 236
gratin dish 236
mashers 226
roasting tin 236
slotted spoon 227
whisks 227

Spread 55 g/2 oz of the remaining butter over the birds and put them in a roasting tin. Roast for 15 minutes, then turn down the oven temperature to 170°C/325°F, gas mark 3. Remove the bacon and roast the birds for a further 10 minutes, basting occasionally with the juices in the tin.

While the partridges are roasting, peel the celeriac and potato and cut them into pieces. Put them in a pan of cold salted water, bring to the boil and simmer for about 25 minutes or until completely tender. Drain well. Mash and then whisk to a very soft purée with the rest of the butter. Season lightly with salt and pepper and keep hot.

When the partridges are tender, take them out of the oven and put them on a board. Do not turn the oven off. Cut off the breasts and legs and put these pieces on a heated dish. Sprinkle them with the white wine and lemon juice. Discard the carcasses or reserve them for making stock. Skim most of the fat from the juices in the roasting tin and mix the juices into the celeriac purée. Transfer this to an oval gratin dish. Put the pieces of partridge on top and season with salt and pepper. Put the gratin dish into the oven to cook for a further 10–15 minutes or until heated right through.

ALTERNATIVE: Use young pigeons instead of partridges, and allow an extra 10 minutes roasting time.

PHEASANT WITH CHESTNUTS

SERVES 2–3

- 30 g/1 oz butter
- 6 thick rashers of streaky bacon, cut into little sticks
- 1 pheasant, plucked and cleaned, with its giblets
- plain flour for dusting
- 2 Spanish onions, sliced
- 2 shallots, sliced
- 6 small carrots, sliced
- 120 ml/4 fl oz red wine
- 300 ml/½ pint stock, made with the pheasant's neck, heart and liver, 1 onion, 2 carrots and a bay leaf
- salt and freshly ground pepper
- a fresh bouquet garni of a sprig each of thyme and parsley and a bay leaf
- 6 juniper berries, coarsely crushed
- 225 g/8 oz chestnuts, shelled and skinned
- 1 teaspoon arrowroot or cornstarch

Preheat the oven to 170°C/325°F, gas mark 3.

Melt the butter in a flameproof casserole and fry the sticks of bacon until they are firm. Dust the pheasant with flour, add it to the casserole and brown it on all sides. Remove the pheasant and the pieces of bacon and set aside. Fry the sliced vegetables lightly in the fat remaining in the casserole without browning them. Pour in the red wine and let it bubble for a few minutes. Return the bacon to the casserole. Put the pheasant, on its side, on top of the vegetables. Pour on the stock, season with salt and pepper, and add the bouquet garni and juniper berries. Cover the casserole and transfer it to the oven to cook for 30 minutes.

Put the chestnuts into the casserole around the pheasant. Turn the bird over on to the other side and replace the lid. Cook for a further 30 minutes.

Remove the pheasant to a board and leave to rest in a warm place. Take the chestnuts and vegetables out of the casserole with a slotted spoon and keep them hot. Skim the fat from the juices, tipping the casserole to make this easier. Mix the arrowroot or cornstarch with 1 tablespoon of water in a cup and stir into the juices. Simmer for 2 minutes, stirring from time to time. Taste for seasoning.

Carve the pheasant. Arrange it with the vegetables and chestnuts on a deep serving dish and pour on the lightly thickened sauce.

NORMANDY PHEASANT WITH APPLES AND CALVADOS

SERVES 4

- 55 g/2 oz butter
- 1 tablespoon groundnut oil
- 1 plump young pheasant, plucked and cleaned
- 60 ml/2 fl oz Calvados
- 3–4 tablespoons chicken stock
- 150 ml/¼ pint double cream
- 3 apples – Golden Delicious or other green eating apples are best
- salt and freshly ground pepper

Heat half the butter and the oil in a flameproof casserole and brown the pheasant all over. Then cover the casserole and leave the pheasant to cook gently for 40 minutes, turning it over from time to time.

Remove the pheasant to a board and carve it into four pieces. Arrange the pieces on a serving dish and keep them hot. Skim the fat from the juices in the casserole. Pour the Calvados into the casserole and let it boil for a minute, stirring. Add the stock, followed by the cream. Bubble this sauce, stirring, until it thickens.

Meanwhile, peel, quarter and core the apples. Heat the remaining butter in a frying pan and fry the apples to a golden brown.

Season the sauce; pour over the pheasant. Arrange the fried apples around the edge and serve very hot.

ROAST WOODCOCK

SERVES 4

4 woodcocks, plucked but not cleaned
85 g/3 oz butter
4 slices of white bread
salt and freshly ground pepper
½ tablespoon brandy
4 tablespoons white wine or dry vermouth

Preheat the oven to 220°C/425°F, gas mark 7.

Truss the birds by passing their long beaks through their bodies beneath the wing, and tying the legs close in to the body. Cover the birds with 55 g/2 oz of the butter, and put them in a roasting tin. Roast for 15–25 minutes, according to how pink you like the meat, basting the birds once or twice with the juices in the roasting tin.

Meanwhile, cut a large disc from each slice of bread. Fry the discs gently in the remaining butter to a pale golden colour. Drain them on kitchen paper and keep them hot.

When the woodcock are done, carefully scrape out their insides with a teaspoon. Discard the pip-shaped gizzard. Season the rest of the entrails with a little salt and pepper, and chop them on a board. Spoon half the fat from the roasting tin, then add the chopped 'trail', brandy and wine to the roasting juices. Bring to a simmer, stirring and scraping up the juices from the bottom of the tin. When the liquid has reduced somewhat, rub the sauce through a sieve into a heated sauceboat.

To serve the woodcock, remove the beaks from the bodies, and then cut the heads in half so that you can eat the brains as well. If you can't face this, simply remove the heads and necks before serving. Put the pieces of fried bread underneath the birds and hand the gravy separately.

ALTERNATIVE: Snipe can be cooked in exactly the same way, but roast for 12–15 minutes only.

snipe 83
woodcock 82

chopping board 227
cutters 225
roasting tin 236
sieves 226–7

SIMPLE ROAST GROUSE

SERVES 4

115 g/4 oz butter
salt and freshly ground pepper
4 young grouse, plucked and cleaned
a few sprigs of fresh lovage (optional)
plain flour for dusting
1–2 rashers of streaky bacon
150 ml/¼ pint game or chicken stock

Preheat the oven to 220°C/425°F, gas mark 7.

Put a knob of butter, rolled in salt and pepper, inside each bird, plus a sprig of lovage if using. Dust the outside of the birds with flour. Put 55 g/2 oz of the remaining butter and the bacon into a roasting tin (the bacon fat will mix with the butter and prevent it from burning). Put the tin into the oven. When the fat is very hot, put the grouse into the tin and baste them with the fat. Roast for 10 minutes, then baste again. Turn down the oven temperature to 180°C/350°F, gas mark 4, and roast the birds for a further 10–15 minutes if you like them pink and juicy, or 20 minutes if you like them well cooked.

Remove the grouse and keep them hot. Skim the fat from the roasting juices. Add the stock to the juices and boil to make a thin gravy. Taste it for seasoning. Serve the grouse with the gravy. Watercress tastes particularly good with these juices.

ALTERNATIVES: If they are available, a few ripe rowanberries or raspberries could be pushed into the grouse before roasting, to keep them moist and improve the flavour and colour of the gravy. If there isn't any gravy – no game stock, rowanberries or pan juices – serve the grouse simply with plain melted butter.

MARINATED ROAST QUAILS

These birds are best eaten with the fingers. They could be barbecued over charcoal for an even better flavour.

SERVES 4

8 quails, plucked and cleaned
sprigs of fresh coriander
lime wedges

For the marinade:

120 ml/4 fl oz light soy sauce
150 ml/¼ pint rice wine or dry sherry
2 tablespoons runny honey
1 teaspoon five-spice powder
1 teaspoon freshly ground white pepper
1 tablespoon toasted sesame oil
thinly pared zest and juice of 1 orange
4 tablespoons hoisin sauce
1 teaspoon dried chilli flakes
a 5 cm/2 in piece of fresh root ginger, unpeeled, thinly sliced
1 garlic clove, crushed

Put all the marinade ingredients in a food processor and work for 30 seconds. Tip the marinade into a large, deep bowl. Immerse the quails in the marinade. Cover the bowl and refrigerate for 24 hours, turning the birds in the marinade occasionally.

Preheat the oven to 220°C/425°F, gas mark 7.

Remove the quails from the marinade and shake off any clinging particles. Place the birds on a rack in a heavy roasting tin, spacing them well apart. Pour about 300 ml/½ pint water into the roasting tin, to prevent the drippings from burning.

Strain the marinade through a fine sieve into a saucepan, and simmer until syrupy. Spoon a little marinade over each quail; don't use it all at this stage. Put the quails in the oven to roast for 5 minutes. Remove them and spoon over a little more marinade. Return to the oven to roast for a further 10 minutes, then spoon over the remaining marinade. Roast the quails for a final 5–10 minutes or until they are a rich, glossy golden brown, with a few scorched patches.

Transfer the quails to a serving dish and keep them warm in the turned-off oven, leaving the door ajar. Strain the watered-down marinade from the roasting tin back into the small saucepan and reduce it to a syrupy sauce, stopping before it gets too salty. Serve the quails garnished with sprigs of coriander and lime wedges, and anoint each bird with a little of the sauce.

ALTERNATIVE: Pigeons can be prepared in the same way, but will need a longer cooking time.

QUAILS WITH THYME AND ORANGE

This is a superlative way of cooking quail – they need the sweet and sour of the orange, raisins and eau-de-vie.

SERVES 4

a handful of seedless raisins
60 ml/2 fl oz eau-de-vie, marc or brandy
8 sprigs of fresh thyme
8 quails, plucked and cleaned
55 g/2 oz butter
4 strips of orange zest
salt and freshly ground pepper
juice of 1 orange

chilli flakes 201
eau-de-vie 208
five-spice powder 196
ginger 199
grouse 84
hoisin sauce 206
light soy sauce 207
lovage 194
orange 165–6
pigeon 83
quail 82
raisin 182
rice wine 208
thyme 194
toasted sesame oil 112
watercress 130–1
zesting citrus fruits 423

bulb baster 229
food processor 238
roasting tin 236
sieves 226–7

Chicken Stock 244

MARINATED ROAST QUAILS

allspice 198
bay 193
belly of pork 60
cabbage 134–6
cider vinegar 204
guinea fowl 85
ham 68–9
juniper berry 196–7
leek 145
pigeon 83
rabbit 80
sweat 423
truffles 161

bulb baster 229
casserole 236
food processor 238
Mouli-légumes 226

Béchamel Sauce 255
Chicken Stock 244

Soak the raisins in the eau-de-vie, marc or brandy (or grappa, fundador or other grape spirit) to plump them up. Drain, reserving the eau-de-vie.

Preheat the oven to 190°C/375°F, gas mark 5.

Push a couple of raisins and a sprig of thyme into each bird, together with its liver if possible. Melt the butter in a large flameproof casserole. When it starts to brown, put in the birds and brown them all over. Add the orange zest and the remaining raisins, and season the birds with salt and pepper. Cover the casserole and put into the oven to cook for 10 minutes. Add the orange juice, cover the casserole again and cook for a further 10 minutes.

Turn the oven temperature up to 220°C/425°F, gas mark 7. Pour the eau-de-vie into the casserole and baste the birds well. Return to the oven, uncovered, and cook for a final 5–10 minutes. This will emulsify the juices into a fragrant, smooth gravy instead of separate layers of sediment, juices and fat.

BRAISED PIGEONS AND CABBAGE

SERVES 4

4 pigeons, plucked and cleaned
plain flour for dusting
salt and freshly ground pepper
45 g/1½ oz butter
1 tablespoon sunflower or other oil
2 onions, sliced
1 cabbage, white or green, cored and finely sliced
2–3 rashers of streaky bacon, cut into squares
2 tablespoons cider vinegar
120 ml/4 fl oz white wine
150 ml/¼ pint chicken stock
4 allspice berries
6 juniper berries, crushed
1 bay leaf
2 teaspoons caster sugar

Dust the birds with flour and season with salt and pepper, inside and out. Melt 30 g/1 oz of the butter with the oil in a flameproof casserole that is large and deep enough to hold the birds on their layer of cabbage. When the fat is sizzling, brown the birds all over rather gently. Remove them and put on one side.

Preheat the oven to 170°C/325°F, gas mark 3.

Add the rest of the butter to the casserole and put in the sliced onions. Let them soften and brown very lightly. Add the cabbage and bacon to the onions and stir them around. Cover and sweat for about 5 minutes. Add the vinegar, wine, stock, allspice and juniper berries, bay leaf and sugar. Season with salt and pepper. Put the pigeons on top of the cabbage mixture. Bring the liquid to the boil, then cover the casserole tightly and transfer to the oven to cook for 1–1½ hours. (For farmed pigeons reduce cooking time to ¾–1 hour.)

STUFFED GUINEA FOWL WITH LEEK PURÉE

SERVES 2–4

1 guinea fowl, plucked and cleaned, with the giblets
3 tablespoons Cognac
a bunch of fresh thyme
200 g/7 oz boneless rabbit, finely chopped or minced
150 g/5½ oz fat belly of pork, finely chopped or minced
1 thick slice of cooked ham, finely diced
grated nutmeg
salt and freshly ground pepper
300 ml/½ pint Béchamel Sauce made with 30 g/1 oz each butter and flour and 300 ml/½ pint milk
45 g/1½ oz butter
6 leeks, sliced

The evening before you cook the guinea fowl, sprinkle it inside and out with a little Cognac, and put the thyme inside the bird to perfume the flesh.

The next day, mix together the rabbit, pork and ham. Finely chop the guinea fowl liver and heart, and add to the mixture. Flavour with the rest of the Cognac and season with nutmeg, salt and pepper. Add about a tablespoon of béchamel sauce to bind the stuffing.

Preheat the oven to 200°C/400°F, gas mark 6.

Remove the thyme from inside the guinea fowl. Fill the bird with the stuffing and skewer the body cavity closed. Melt the butter in a small roasting tin, add the guinea fowl and brown on all sides. Transfer to the oven and roast for 1 hour 10 minutes, occasionally basting the bird with the juices in the tin. To test if the guinea fowl is cooked, pierce the thigh with a carving fork or skewer: the juices should be clear.

Meanwhile, cook the leeks gently, covered, in a little water for 1 hour. Drain them, then purée in a food processor or with a Mouli-légumes. Add to the béchamel sauce, and adjust seasoning. Reheat gently.

Remove the guinea fowl from the tin to a hot dish. Skim the fat from the roasting tin, then pour the juices over the bird before serving.

ALTERNATIVES: Use chicken breast instead of rabbit. You can add some sliced truffle to the leek purée; truffle is also recommended for the stuffing.

BRAISED PIGEONS AND CABBAGE

Poultry

COQ AU VIN

SERVES 4

1 plump young chicken, weighing 1.35 kg/3 lb, preferably free-range
a 115 g/4 oz piece of unsmoked streaky bacon
55 g/2 oz butter
1 tablespoon oil
plain flour for dusting
2 garlic cloves, crushed
a fresh bouquet garni of thyme and parsley
½ bottle of red wine
salt and freshly ground pepper
12 button onions
12 white button mushrooms
about 30 g/1 oz beurre manié

Preheat the oven to 180°C/350°F, gas mark 4.

Cut the chicken into 8 pieces. Cut the bacon into little sticks about 5 mm/¼ in across and 4 cm/1½ in long. Heat half the butter and the oil in a flameproof casserole and put in the sticks of bacon. When they are starting to brown, dust the pieces of chicken lightly with flour and add them to the casserole. Sauté until they are nicely browned all over.

Add the garlic and cook for a minute or so, then add the bouquet garni and the wine. Season with salt and pepper. Bring to the boil. Cover the casserole, transfer to the oven and cook for about 1 hour or until the chicken is almost tender when pricked with a fork or skewer.

Meanwhile, cook the onions in a saucepan of boiling salted water for 10 minutes. Drain. Melt the remaining butter in a frying pan and sauté the onions until they are lightly browned. Remove them with a slotted spoon; set aside. Sauté the mushrooms in the same butter until lightly cooked. Add to the onions. With a slotted spoon, remove the chicken and bacon from the casserole, and set aside with the mushrooms and onions. Discard the bouquet garni, then boil the cooking liquid for 5 minutes to reduce it. Whisk in the beurre manié, to thicken the liquid. Return the chicken, bacon and vegetables to the casserole and simmer for 5–10 minutes to reheat. Serve with plain boiled potatoes or turnips, and a green salad.

QUICK-FRIED CHICKEN WITH GARLIC AND CHILLI

Chicken drumsticks and thighs give much more succulent results here than breast meat (although this is easier to prepare). Ask the butcher to do the chopping for you, or do it yourself using a heavy knife or cleaver. Be sure to check the chicken for small shards of bone before cooking it.

SERVES 4

4 large chicken legs, preferably free-range
6 tablespoons soy sauce
3 tablespoons dry sherry
1 tablespoon runny honey
½ teaspoon ground white pepper
100 g/3½ oz cornflour
groundnut oil for frying
10 garlic cloves, sliced
5 large red chillies, seeded and sliced
salt
crisp lettuce leaves

Cut the chicken legs in two at the joint. Chop the thighs into three pieces and the drumsticks into two, leaving the skin on. Put the pieces in a shallow dish. Mix the soy sauce, sherry, honey and pepper. Pour over the chicken and marinate for at least 2 hours, turning the pieces in the marinade occasionally.

When ready to cook, heat a wok or large frying pan over a moderate heat. Drain the chicken pieces and pat dry with kitchen paper. Dip them in the cornflour, coating each piece well, and place on a plate. Pour oil into the wok or pan to a depth of about 5 mm/¼ in. Heat until smoking, then add the chicken pieces. Do not overcrowd the pan; fry in two batches if necessary. Turn the chicken over when crusty, and fry until the pieces are deep golden brown all over. Place the chicken on a plate.

Add the garlic and chillies to the hot oil and fry until crisp and slightly browned. Return the chicken to the pan and toss to mix it thoroughly with the garlic and chillies. Tip into a wire sieve to drain off any excess oil. Put the chicken on a heated serving platter, sprinkle with a little salt and serve with a separate bowl of well-chilled crisp lettuce leaves.

ROAST CHICKEN WITH MARJORAM

SERVES 4

1 chicken, weighing about 1.6 kg/3½ lb, preferably free-range
55 g/2 oz butter

For the stuffing:

½ onion, finely chopped
45 g/1½ oz butter, softened
2 thick slices of day-old white bread, crusts removed
1 tablespoon chopped fresh marjoram or 1½ teaspoons dried marjoram
salt

beurre manié 422, 423
bouquet garni 190
button mushroom 161
button onion 143
chicken 86–7
chilli pepper 152–3
cornflour 116
garlic 145
jointing a chicken 92
marinate 422
marjoram 192–3
reduce 423
sauté 423
seeding chillies 423
soy sauce 207
streaky bacon 70

casserole 236
cleaver 222
knives 222–4
sieves 226
slotted spoon 227
whisks 227
wok 235

COQ AU VIN

almond 186–7
cashew 186
chicken 86–7
garlic 145
guinea fowl 85
long-grain rice 116
pine nut 186
raisin 182
saffron 199
sweat 423
trussing a chicken 91

bulb baster 229
gratin dish 236
roasting tin 236
sauté pan 234
trussing equipment 230

Preheat the oven to 190°C/375°F, gas mark 5.

Sweat the onion in a little butter until soft and translucent but not browned. Grate the bread to make fairly coarse crumbs. Mix these with the onion and its butter, the marjoram, a little salt and the remaining softened butter. Stuff the chicken loosely with this.

Put the bird in a roasting tin and spread the butter all over the breast and legs. Roast for 1 hour, basting often with the juices in the tin.

ALTERNATIVE: In France guinea fowl is often prepared this way.

CHICKEN ON A BED OF GARLIC

This is a simple way of improving a dull bird.

SERVES 4

- 1, 2 or even 3 large heads of garlic (not cloves but whole heads, containing up to 15 cloves each)
- 55 g/2 oz butter
- 1 chicken, weighing 1.6–1.8 kg/3½–4 lb, preferably free-range
- salt and freshly ground pepper

Preheat the oven to 190°C/375°F, gas mark 5.

Peel each clove of garlic one by one. Put a couple of cloves of garlic and a knob of the butter inside the chicken and season it inside and out with salt and pepper. Put half the remaining butter in an oval gratin dish. Set the chicken in the dish and spread the rest of the butter over the chicken.

Roast the chicken for 30 minutes. Then throw all the remaining garlic cloves into the dish around the chicken and roast for a further 30 minutes, basting the bird often with the juices in the dish. The basting is important because the butter is permeated with the flavour of the garlic and by basting you will transfer it to the chicken. The garlic cloves will become mild, soft and delicious to eat.

Serve the chicken in the dish with the garlic and cooking juices. It is wise to serve beautifully mashed potatoes to sop up the butter.

CHICKEN WITH ALMONDS AND RAISINS

This is a very happy combination, often found in Middle Eastern cooking – meat with fruit and nuts.

SERVES 4

- 1 chicken, weighing 1.35 kg/3 lb, preferably free-range, with the giblets
- salt and freshly ground pepper
- 55–85 g/2–3 oz butter
- 1 small onion, peeled
- ½ lemon
- 115 g/4 oz blanched almonds
- 85 g/3 oz seedless raisins
- 3 tablespoons olive oil
- 3 shallots, finely chopped
- 340 g/12 oz long-grain rice
- 1 small packet of saffron strands, soaked in 120 ml/4 fl oz dry vermouth or white wine
- 1 heaped tablespoon chopped parsley

For the stock:

- 120 ml/4 fl oz dry vermouth or white wine
- a few sprigs of parsley
- 1 onion, quartered

Preheat the oven to 190°C/375°F, gas mark 5.

Season the chicken inside and out with salt and pepper, and put a large knob of butter and the onion inside. Squeeze the lemon half over the chicken and rub the juice into the skin with the remaining butter. Roast for 1 hour, basting from time to time with the juices in the roasting tin.

Meanwhile, make 1.2 litres/2 pints of stock by simmering the giblets with all the stock ingredients in water for about 40 minutes. Strain.

Slice the almonds in half lengthways and toss them with the raisins in a dry frying pan until toasted.

Heat the olive oil in a sauté pan and soften the shallots without browning, stirring. Add the rice and stir for 3–4 minutes, then add the raisins, almonds and enough giblet stock to cover the rice. Leave to simmer, without stirring, for 25 minutes or until the rice is tender. Add more of the stock as necessary. Stir in the saffron mixture and cook for a few more minutes. Finally, mix in the parsley. Put the rice into a hot serving bowl.

Take the chicken out of the oven and put it on a heated serving dish. Pour all the juices, including the butter, from the roasting tin over the rice, stir it well and serve immediately with the chicken.

ALTERNATIVES: Use cashew nuts or pine nuts instead of almonds. For a spicier dish, fry 2–3 cloves and a piece of cinnamon stick with the shallots and rice.

CHICKEN WITH BLACK OLIVES AND TOMATOES

SERVES 4

- 1 chicken, weighing 1.35 kg/3 lb, preferably free-range
- salt and freshly ground pepper
- 3–4 tablespoons olive oil
- a wineglass of white wine

1–2 garlic cloves, chopped
6 tomatoes, skinned and chopped
12 black olives
a few sprigs of fresh basil, or some dried basil or oregano

Cut the chicken into 4 pieces and season them with salt and pepper. Heat the olive oil in a large frying pan. Add the pieces of chicken and brown them on all sides. Then turn down the heat and let the chicken cook gently for 30 minutes, turning the pieces frequently. Remove them to a heated dish and keep warm.

Pour the white wine into the frying pan and bring to a simmer, stirring and scraping with a spoon to collect all the delicious sediment. Add the garlic, tomatoes, olives and basil or oregano. Let the sauce simmer for 15 minutes. Taste for seasoning, pour over the chicken and serve.

POULET PAYSANNE

SERVES 4

1 chicken, weighing 1.35 kg/3 lb, preferably free-range, with the giblets
55 g/2 oz butter
3 tablespoons groundnut oil
18 small new potatoes, a bit larger than a walnut, scraped or scrubbed
115 g/4 oz wild mushrooms such as chanterelles or oyster mushrooms, sliced
salt and freshly ground pepper
1 tablespoon chopped parsley
2 garlic cloves, chopped

Use the chicken giblets to make 150 ml/¼ pint stock (or use chicken stock).

Cut the chicken into 6 pieces. In a wide shallow pan, heat half the butter and 2 tablespoons of the oil. Put in the pieces of chicken, side by side, and cook gently for about 15 minutes or until they are golden, turning them from time to time.

Meanwhile, heat the remaining butter and oil in a smaller pan. Dry the potatoes in a cloth, then add them to the pan. Let them brown, shaking the pan occasionally to turn them over. When the potatoes are evenly coloured, add the sliced mushrooms and mix them in. Cook for a minute or two, then add the potatoes and mushrooms together with their butter to the chicken. Season with salt and pepper. Cover the pan and cook gently for about 30 minutes or until the chicken is tender and the potatoes are cooked through.

Remove the lid. Sprinkle in the chopped parsley and garlic and stir around. Cook for a further 3–4 minutes. Remove the pieces of chicken, the potatoes and mushrooms to a deep serving dish and keep them hot. Spoon the fat off the cooking juices. Add the giblet stock to the pan, and scrape and stir to dislodge any cooking juices that have become caramelized on the bottom. Bring to the boil and reduce the liquid by about half. Pour over the chicken, and serve very hot.

GRILLED CHICKEN KEBABS

These are prepared in much the same way as everybody's favourite, chicken tikka. It is best to use thigh meat, which is juicier than breast meat. Spiced Lentils are a perfect accompaniment.

SERVES 4

8 large chicken thighs, preferably free-range
½ teaspoon salt
juice of 2 small limes
a 5 cm/2 in piece of fresh root ginger, roughly chopped
1 small onion, roughly chopped
3 garlic cloves, halved
1 teaspoon turmeric
1 teaspoon ground coriander
2 teaspoons ground cumin
1 teaspoon paprika
1 teaspoon garam masala
¼ teaspoon ground cloves
¼–½ teaspoon chilli powder, to taste
½ teaspoon freshly ground black pepper
150 ml/¼ pint plain yogurt
8 sprigs of fresh coriander
1 lime, cut into 4 wedges

Skin and bone the chicken thighs, and cut them into 2.5 cm/1 in chunks. Put these in a shallow dish with the salt and lime juice, and marinate for 30 minutes.

Place all the other ingredients, except the fresh coriander and lime wedges, in a blender or food processor. Whizz until smooth, adding a little water if the mixture proves difficult to process. Push the paste through a sieve. With your fingers, mix the paste with the chicken. Leave to marinate for at least 3 hours.

Preheat a ridged cast-iron grill pan or an overhead grill, or, best of all, prepare a charcoal fire in a barbecue. Thread the chicken pieces on to 8 small metal or wooden skewers.

When the grill pan or fire is very hot, grill the kebabs on one side for 4–5 minutes. Let them cook undisturbed on the first side before turning them over; moving them too soon may cause them to stick and lose their all-important crust. Turn them over and cook for another 4–5 minutes.

Serve garnished with coriander and lime wedges.

basil 192
chicken 86–7
coriander 191
ginger 199
jointing a chicken 92
lime 167
marinate 422
potato 145
seeding and skinning tomatoes 423
spices 196–9
tomato 150–1
wild mushrooms 158–60
yogurt 99

barbecuing equipment 240–1
blender, liquidizer 238
food processor 238
ridged cast-iron grill pan 233
sieves 226

Spiced Lentils 354–5

button mushroom 161
chicken 86–7
clarified butter 100, 423
coconut milk 189, 243
jointing a chicken 92
mustard seed 202–3
reduce 423
spices 196–9
tarragon 190–1

food processor 238
knives 222–4
saucepans 233–4

Chicken Stock 244

WYVERN'S CHICKEN CURRY WITH COCONUT

This is an Anglo-Indian recipe from 1878. Wyvern was the *nom-de-plume* of Colonel Kenney Herbert, a cavalry officer in the Indian army in the late nineteenth century. Seeing the young English mem-sahibs struggling to feed their households and entertain guests in impossibly difficult conditions, with unfamiliar ingredients and servants from a totally different culture who were cooking in the most appalling filth and heat, he wrote several books of recipes and advice for them. He later opened the 'Commonsense Cookery Association' and a school in Chelsea propounding the virtue of simplicity in all aspects of cooking. This delicious curry recipe exemplifies his straightforward approach.

SERVES 4

1 nice young chicken, preferably free-range, with the giblets
55 g/2 oz clarified butter
300–450 ml/½–¾ pint thick coconut milk
salt
2 teaspoons lemon juice

For the curry powder (enough to use on two occasions):

2 teaspoons turmeric
4 teaspoons ground coriander
1 teaspoon ground cumin
½ teaspoon poppy seeds
1 teaspoon ground fenugreek
½ teaspoon ground ginger
¼ teaspoon mustard seed
½ teaspoon chilli powder
½ teaspoon freshly ground pepper

For the curry paste:

2 small onions
3 garlic cloves
a piece of fresh root ginger, about the size of a large walnut
¼ teaspoon ground cloves
¼ teaspoon ground cinnamon
¼ teaspoon ground mace
¼ teaspoon ground cardamom
a few sprigs of fresh coriander
3 or 4 blanched almonds

Cut the chicken into joints and skin them. Use the giblets to make about 150 ml/¼ pint stock (or use chicken stock). Mix together the ingredients for the curry powder.

Put the ingredients for the curry paste in a food processor and reduce to a purée. Fry the paste gently in half the clarified butter until it is just starting to brown. Add a heaped tablespoon of the curry powder and stir well. Fry the mixture for 2–3 minutes, then slowly add half the coconut milk, stirring. Leave the curry sauce to simmer for about 15 minutes.

In a separate pan, fry the pieces of chicken in the remaining clarified butter until they are golden brown all over. Transfer them to a heavy saucepan. Pour the curry sauce over the chicken and leave it to marinate for 30 minutes.

Season with salt and put the pan over a moderate heat. Simmer very gently for 45 minutes to 1 hour. Add a little giblet stock if the sauce is getting too thick. When the chicken is cooked, stir in the lemon juice and the remaining coconut milk; taste for seasoning and adjust this if necessary. Heat through gently before serving.

TARRAGON CHICKEN WITH MUSHROOMS

This is an excellent recipe – simple to make and yet very luxurious.

SERVES 4

1 chicken, weighing 1.6 kg/3½ lb, preferably free-range, with the giblets
a small bunch of fresh tarragon or parsley
55 g/2 oz butter
1 carrot
2 shallots or 1 onion, quartered
225 g/8 oz button mushrooms
1–2 tablespoons sherry
150 ml/¼ pint double cream
salt and freshly ground pepper

Preheat the oven to 190°C/375°F, gas mark 5.

Put the herbs inside the chicken and put it into a flameproof casserole with the butter. Cover and cook in the oven for 1 hour, turning it from time to time.

Meanwhile, make a little stock by simmering the giblets with the carrot and shallots or onion in water to cover for about 30 minutes. Strain.

Add the mushrooms to the casserole and stir them into the cooking juices. Cook for a further 10 minutes. Remove the chicken and mushrooms to a dish and keep them hot. Reduce the juices a little, then add the sherry and 150 ml/¼ pint of the giblet stock (or chicken stock). Simmer for 2 or 3 minutes. Pour in the cream and tip the casserole back and forth to mix the cream with the juices. Simmer for a further 5 minutes. Taste for seasoning. Serve the chicken whole, with the sauce, or, if you prefer, carve the chicken into pieces and pour the sauce over them.

WYVERN'S CHICKEN CURRY WITH COCONUT

chicken 86–7
ginger 199
rice vinegar 205
toasted sesame oil 112

barbecuing equipment 240–1
frying pan 234
roasting tin 236

Peanut Sauce 258

ROAST MARINATED CHICKEN BREASTS

Partially boned chicken breasts do not shrink in cooking and retain their succulence better than those that are completely boneless.

SERVES 6

- 6 partially boned chicken breasts, preferably free-range
- 3 tablespoons vegetable oil
- Roasted Tomato Sauce, made without butter

For the marinade:

- 4 tablespoons dark soy sauce
- 4 tablespoons light soy sauce
- 2 tablespoons demerara sugar
- 2 teaspoons toasted sesame oil
- 3 garlic cloves, sliced
- a 5 cm/2 in piece of fresh root ginger, sliced
- 1 tablespoon rice vinegar or sherry vinegar

Mix all the marinade ingredients together in a bowl. Arrange the chicken breasts side by side in a shallow earthenware dish. Pour on the marinade. Leave in a cool place for 2 hours to absorb the flavours, turning the pieces of chicken from time to time.

Drain the chicken breasts, reserving the marinade. Preheat the oven to 180°C/350°F, gas mark 4.

Heat the oil in a large frying pan and brown the chicken breasts on each side; they will turn a wonderful golden mahogany colour. Remove the breasts to a large roasting tin and roast them for 15–20 minutes, basting them at frequent intervals with the marinade.

Remove the chicken breasts to a heated dish, cover with foil and keep warm in the turned-off oven. Pour the tomato sauce into the juices in the roasting tin (if the sediment on the bottom of the tin is at all burned, transfer the juices to a small saucepan). Bubble for a minute or two, stirring with a wooden spoon. Serve this sauce with the chicken.

ALTERNATIVE: For a delicious barbecue flavour, grill the chicken breasts over charcoal, basting them at frequent intervals with the marinade, and serve with Peanut Sauce.

ROAST TURKEY WITH TWO STUFFINGS

A traditional roast turkey should be a really splendid dish. Two kinds of stuffing keep the bird succulent and give it an interesting flavour. Serve the turkey with bread sauce or cranberry sauce (or both), roast potatoes, creamed onions and Brussels sprouts with chestnuts.

SERVES 8

- 1 turkey, weighing 3.6–4.5 kg/8–10 lb, with the giblets
- 85 g/3 oz butter, softened
- 3 tablespoons olive or groundnut oil

For the chestnut stuffing:

- 450 g/1 lb fresh chestnuts or 210 g/7 oz vacuum-packed chestnuts
- 15 g/½ oz butter
- 1 heaped tablespoon chopped onion
- 2 celery sticks, sliced into crescents
- 8 soft prunes, stoned and roughly chopped
- salt and freshly ground pepper
- 1 free-range egg

For the sausagemeat stuffing:

- 1 onion, finely chopped
- 30 g/1 oz butter
- 700 g/1½ lb sausagemeat
- 55 g/2 oz fresh white breadcrumbs
- 1 free-range egg
- 2 heaped tablespoons chopped parsley
- 2–3 tablespoons dry white wine
- finely grated zest of 1 lemon
- ½ teaspoon grated nutmeg
- salt and freshly ground pepper

For the gravy:

- 750 ml/1¼ pints good stock, made with the turkey giblets except the liver
- 1 tablespoon plain flour (optional)
- 1–2 wineglasses of white wine

First make the chestnut stuffing. If using fresh chestnuts, remove the shells, put the chestnuts in a saucepan and just cover them with turkey giblet stock (later to be used for the gravy). Boil for 15–20 minutes or until tender, then drain (reserving the stock) and remove the skins. Slightly break up the fresh or vacuum-packed chestnuts and put into a bowl. Heat the butter in a frying pan, add the onion and celery and soften for 5 minutes. Mix into the chestnuts with the prunes. Season with salt and pepper. Add the egg and mix it in well. Use the mixture to stuff the neck cavity in the turkey; skewer the neck flap to secure it.

Preheat the oven to 170°C/325°F, gas mark 3.

Next make the sausagemeat stuffing. Sweat the onion gently in the butter in a small frying pan until tender and translucent. Mix it into the sausagemeat in a bowl. Chop the turkey liver and mix this in too, then add all the rest of the stuffing ingredients and work them together thoroughly. Stuff the body of the turkey with this mixture, and skewer the rear opening closed. (Or put the stuffing in a buttered baking dish and cover with foil. Put it in the oven with the turkey about 1 hour before the end of cooking.) Tie the ends of the legs together and tuck the wingtips under the bird.

Spread the softened butter all over the turkey – the breasts, legs and wings should all get their share. Put it into a roasting tin and pour on the oil. Place the tin fair and square in the centre of the oven, and roast for about 20 minutes per 450 g/1 lb. It will take about 3 hours, depending on your oven; the bird is roasted rather slowly so that it will cook evenly throughout. Baste it frequently with the juices in the tin. When it is an even golden brown all over, cover it loosely with foil to prevent it from getting too dark. To test whether the bird is cooked, stick a skewer deep into the thigh; a bead of clear or cloudy, colourless liquid will emerge (if it is a reddish colour, the bird is not yet done); a foolproof way of checking for thorough cooking is to use a meat thermometer (see below). Turn off the oven, leave the door slightly open, and let the bird rest inside for about 20 minutes to firm and set. This will make it easier to carve.

Take the turkey out of the roasting tin, set it on a heated platter and keep it hot. Spoon most of the fat from the roasting tin (you can use it for frying potatoes on some other occasion). Then, if you like a slightly thickened gravy, stir the flour into the juices and fat remaining. Pour in the wine and let it boil for a few minutes over a moderate heat, scraping up all the brown sediment and caramelized juices from the tin. Add the giblet stock and boil for about 10 minutes. Taste the gravy and season it with salt.

ALTERNATIVE: For a cream gravy, use a wineglass of dry sherry instead of the wine, and a mixture of 600 ml/1 pint giblet stock and 150–300 ml/¼–½ pint double cream instead of the stock.

Timing a roast turkey The information given overleaf is for stuffed turkeys, and is only a rough guide, since oven temperatures can vary considerably. To prevent disaster – and the margin for error increases with larger birds and longer cooking times – check frequently during the last part of the cooking. An unstuffed turkey will take 20–30 minutes less than a stuffed bird. To ensure that the bird is thoroughly cooked, it is a good idea to use a meat thermometer to check the internal temperature. Insert the thermometer in the thickest part of the thigh; the bird is done when the temperature registers 75°C/170°F.

At an oven temperature of 170°C/325°F, gas mark 3, the following roasting times are recommended:

chestnut 188
fresh breadcrumbs 364
peeling chestnuts 189
prune 184
sausage meat 75
stuffing and trussing a turkey 93
sweat 423
turkey 87–8
zesting citrus fruits 423

bulb baster 229
meat thermometer 233
roasting tin 236
trussing equipment 230

Bread Sauce 257
Brussels Sprouts with Chestnuts 375
Chicken Stock 244
Fresh Cranberry Sauce 260
Roast Potatoes 379

apple 162–3
cream 99–100
dripping and goose fat 110
duck 89–90
goose 88
mustard 202–3
salt pork 70
Tabasco sauce 206
thyme 194
turkey 87–8
Worcestershire sauce 206

bulb baster 229
gratin dish 236
roasting tin 236
sieves 226–7
trussing equipment 230

Chicken Stock 244
Roast Turkey with Two Stuffings 311

2.7–3.6 kg/6–8 lb	2½–3 hours
3.6–4.5 kg/8–10 lb	3–3½ hours
4.5–5.4 kg/10–12 lb	3½–4 hours
5.4–6.3 kg/12–14 lb	4–4½ hours
6.3–7.2 kg/14–16 lb	4½–5 hours
7.2–8.1 kg/16–18 lb	5–5½ hours
8.1–9 kg/18–20 lb	5½–6 hours

WHITE DEVIL

This is an excellent way of bringing cold roast poultry back to life. A devil can be light or dark – this is a light version.

SERVES 6

12–18 slices of cold roast turkey
450 ml/¾ pint double cream
2 tablespoons Worcestershire sauce
2 teaspoons made English mustard
2 tablespoons sherry
a generous dash of Tabasco sauce
salt and freshly ground pepper

Preheat the oven to 180°C/350°F, gas mark 4.

Lay the slices of turkey in the bottom of an oval earthenware gratin dish. Mix all the rest of the ingredients in a saucepan and heat to boiling point. Pour the mixture over the turkey. Heat in the oven for 20 minutes.

If necessary, put the dish briefly under a hot grill until brown, glazed and bubbling. Serve with a refreshing salad of lettuce, crisped in the refrigerator, which is excellent for mopping up the juices left on the plate.

GOOSE WITH APPLE STUFFING

In Germany it is traditional to eat potato dumplings and braised celery with this dish. The copious amount of goose fat that runs out during roasting is an excellent medium for frying potatoes, and keeps well in a closed jar in the refrigerator.

SERVES 8

1 goose, weighing about 5–5.4 kg/11–12 lb, with the giblets
salt and freshly ground pepper
900 g/2 lb russet or Golden Delicious apples – not Cox's
600 ml/1 pint stock made with goose giblets, or chicken stock
a wineglass of sweet white wine
1 onion, sliced
1 tablespoon dried sage
1½ tablespoons plain flour

Preheat the oven to 220°C/425°F, gas mark 7.

Pour a kettleful of boiling water over the breast and legs of the goose. Leave to drain. Then salt the goose inside and out, removing any stray quills. Core the apples, leaving them whole and unpeeled, and fill the goose with them. Sew up or skewer closed the bird's rear cavity and neck flap.

Pour the stock and white wine into a roasting tin. Add the onion and sage. Put the goose on a rack in the tin, breast downwards. Roast for 1 hour, basting with the liquid in the tin and pricking the skin with a fork to let the fat run out. Then turn the bird over and reduce the oven temperature to 180°C/350°F, gas mark 4. Roast for a further 2 hours, continuing to baste and prod the goose with a fork, but not too deeply or you will make the juice run out of the meat.

When the goose is done, remove it to a hot dish. Put it back in the turned-off oven to keep hot while you make the gravy. Pour off most of the copious fat from the roasting tin. Add the flour to the juices remaining in the tin, stirring it around until it has dissolved. Simmer until thickened. Taste the gravy for seasoning, and add a little boiling water if it is too concentrated. Strain into a gravy boat.

Serve the goose with the gravy and the apples from the inside of the bird – they will have collapsed into a delicious stuffing.

ROAST DUCK

SERVES 4

1 duck, weighing about 1.8 kg/4 lb with the giblets
1 orange, halved
1 carrot, chopped
1 onion, chopped
a small bunch of fresh thyme
salt and freshly ground pepper
3 shallots or button onions, finely chopped
a 55 g/2 oz piece of salt pork or streaky bacon, finely chopped
a sprinkling of olive oil
a wineglass of white wine
about 2 teaspoons plain flour

Preheat the oven to 220°C/425°F, gas mark 7.

Put the duck's giblets, except the liver, into a small pan and add half the orange, the carrot, chopped onion, thyme and a little salt. Cover with 1.2 litres/2 pints of water and bring to the boil, skimming well. Then turn the heat down and leave the stock to simmer gently while you cook the duck.

Finely chop the duck's liver and mix with the shallots and salt pork or bacon. Score the skin of the remaining orange half, and rub and squeeze the juice over the outside of the duck. Rub the inside and outside of the orange half with salt. Push the piece of orange inside the duck, together with the salt pork, shallot and liver stuffing. Prick the skin of the duck here and there so the fat can escape during roasting. Sprinkle the duck with olive oil and put it on a rack in a roasting tin. Roast it for 15 minutes, then turn down the oven to 180°C/350°F, gas mark 4. Roast for a further 1¼–1½ hours, according to the size of the duck, basting alternately with white wine and the fat in the roasting tin.

Remove the duck to a dish and keep it hot. Spoon all the fat from the roasting tin (duck fat is good for frying potatoes). Sprinkle the flour into the juices remaining in the tin – just enough flour to take up any remaining fat – and stir well, cooking the mixture on a low heat. Strain in the stock, stirring all the time over a moderate heat. Simmer for a few minutes. Taste for seasoning, then pour the gravy into a boat. Carve the duck, putting a little of the stuffing on each plate.

DUCK WITH GREEN OLIVES

SERVES 4

- 1 duck, weighing 1.6–1.8 kg/3½–4 lb
- 450 ml/¾ pint chicken stock
- 1 teaspoon tomato purée
- a fresh bouquet garni of parsley, thyme and a bay leaf
- salt and freshly ground pepper
- 170 g/6 oz stoned green olives
- 2 teaspoons potato flour or cornflour
- 60 ml/2 fl oz Madeira or dry sherry

Preheat the oven to 230°C/450°F, gas mark 8.

Prick the skin of the duck here and there so that the fat can escape during cooking. Put the bird into a flameproof casserole and roast for about 15 minutes, turning the bird so that it browns evenly. Pour off the fat from the pan. Add the stock, tomato purée, bouquet garni and a generous seasoning of salt and pepper to the casserole. Cover and continue roasting the duck for 1 hour and 10 minutes. Test to see if it is tender by piercing the thickest part of the thigh with a skewer.

Meanwhile, blanch the olives in a large pan of unsalted boiling water for 5 minutes. Drain them.

Take the duck out of the casserole and carve it into joints. Put them on a heated serving dish and keep hot. Spoon off most of the fat from the sauce in the casserole, and add the olives. Put the casserole over a gentle heat. Mix the potato flour or cornflour with the Madeira or sherry and stir into the sauce. Discard the bouquet garni, and simmer the sauce gently, stirring constantly, until it thickens and coats the back of the spoon. Taste for seasoning, then pour the sauce over the duck. Serve with plain boiled potatoes.

DUCK WITH COCONUT CREAM AND GREEN CURRY PASTE

Although the duck is initially roasted in the normal way, the final simmering produces a completely different dish. The meat becomes soft and unctuous, and the creamy coconut milk together with the spices in the curry paste give the dish a certain sparkle. The green paste recipe comes (slightly adapted) from Jennifer Brennan's excellent book on Thai cooking. If you cannot obtain galangal, use more root ginger.

SERVES 4

- 1 duck, weighing about 1.8 kg/4 lb
- salt
- 200 g/7 oz creamed coconut
- 2 cans coconut milk
- 2 large mild green chillies, seeded and sliced
- 12 fresh basil leaves, coarsely chopped
- leaves from ½ bunch of fresh coriander, coarsely chopped
- 2 tablespoons fish sauce
- 20 fresh lychees, peeled and stoned, or canned lychees, drained and rinsed

For the green curry paste:

- 1 teaspoon coriander seeds
- 1 teaspoon caraway seeds
- 12 black peppercorns
- 4 cloves
- 1 whole nutmeg, crushed
- a 7.5 cm/3 in piece of galangal
- a 2.5 cm/1 in piece of fresh root ginger
- 2 stalks of lemon grass, chopped
- 2 tablespoons chopped fresh coriander roots, or 3 tablespoons chopped coriander stalks
- 2 tablespoons chopped garlic
- 6 lime leaves, chopped
- 8 small green chillies, chopped – remove seeds for a milder flavour
- 1 teaspoon shrimp paste
- 1 teaspoon salt
- 4 tablespoons vegetable oil

Preheat the oven to 230°C/450°F, gas mark 8.

Season the inside of the duck with salt, and prick the skin all over with a small skewer; this will allow the excess fat to drain off. Set the duck on a rack in a roasting tin. Roast for 20 minutes, then reduce the oven temperature to 180°C/350°F, gas mark 4. Roast for a further hour, draining off the fat from time to

basil 192
blanch 422
bouquet garni 190
chilli pepper 152–3
coconut 188, 423
coriander 191–2
duck 89–90
fish sauce 206
galangal 199
lemon grass 194
lime leaf 195
lychee 181
olive 154–5
seeding chillies 423
shrimp paste 206
thickening agents 118–19
tomato purée 206

bulb baster 229
casserole 236
roasting tin 236
sieves 226–7

Chicken Stock 244

bouquet garni 190
chicken 86–7
covering a deep pie dish with pastry 404
dissolving gelatine 423
gelatine 62
ham 68–9
reduce 423
zesting citrus fruits 423

blender, liquidizer 238
coffee grinder 226, 239
food processor 238
funnel 229
pastry making equipment 236–7
sieves 226
skimmers 228
terrine 236

Flaky Pastry 402
Rough Puff Pastry 402

time into a bowl. Remove the duck from the oven and leave to cool completely.

While the duck is roasting, make the green curry paste. The quantities given will yield about 150 ml/¼ pint; it really is not worth making any less, and you can keep the excess, covered, in the fridge for up to a month. Grind the five dried spices to a powder in a coffee mill or spice grinder. Put all the other ingredients in a food processor or blender, add the ground spices and work to a smooth paste.

Remove the duck legs and breasts from the carcass, using a sharp knife. Divide the legs in two at the joint, and cut the breasts in half. Set aside.

Break up the creamed coconut and put it in a large, heavy-based saucepan with a little hot water. Melt extremely gently until the oil starts to exude from the cream and sizzles. Add 4 tablespoons of the curry paste and cook very gently for 5 minutes, taking care not to scorch the paste. Pour in the coconut milk and bring to a simmer.

Add the duck pieces to the pan. Simmer for 15–20 minutes, stirring gently from time to time, until the sauce has thickened slightly. Add the chillies, basil, coriander and fish sauce. Taste for seasoning and stir in the lychees. Cook for a further 5 minutes. Serve hot, accompanied by rice.

MAKING PIES AND PÂTÉS

Recipes for pies and pâtés often specify more seasoning than seems reasonable. This is because their taste becomes muted once the pie or pâté is cold. Another point worth remembering is that it is the depth of the tin or terrine rather than the surface area that determines the cooking time of pâtés.

After baking, most pies and pâtés en croûte have stock added to them through the hole in the lid, to fill any air holes and gaps between the filling and pastry. The easiest way to do this is to use a funnel and a jug. With large pies, it is sometimes difficult to pour in the stock, so if the pie is very long, make a hole at each end or, for a round pie, make another neat hole near the edge. As the pie or pâté cools, the stock sets to a savoury jelly.

Make your pie or pâté at least one day – and preferably 2 or 3 days – before it is wanted, to give the flavours time to mature. Keep pies and pâtés, covered, in the refrigerator, but do not freeze them – the texture will be hopelessly spoiled. They are best served at cool room temperature. A distinction is often made between pâtés and terrines, although nowadays they are considered to be the same thing, the word terrine referring to the type of dish used.

COLD CHICKEN AND HAM PIE

SERVES 6

1 chicken, weighing 1.35–1.6 kg/3–3½ lb, preferably free-range
1 carrot
1 onion
1 celery stick
a fresh bouquet garni of thyme, parsley and a bay leaf
a wineglass of white wine
salt and freshly ground pepper
15 g/½ oz powdered gelatine
2 tablespoons chopped parsley
1 tablespoon chopped fresh chives
¼ teaspoon grated nutmeg
grated zest of ¼ lemon
340 g/12 oz sliced ham, preferably carved off the bone
Flaky or Rough Puff Pastry made with 225 g/8 oz flour
1 free-range egg yolk, beaten with a few drops of water and a pinch of salt

Put the chicken in a large saucepan with the carrot, peeled onion, celery and bouquet garni. Add the wine, cover with water and bring to the boil. Turn down the heat at once until the water is just simmering, and skim the surface. Add 1 teaspoon salt. Simmer for 50 minutes or until the chicken is just cooked. Allow to cool in the liquid. (If you don't have time for this, it doesn't matter too much, although the chicken will be more succulent if it cools in its cooking liquid.)

When the chicken is cold, remove all the meat and slice it; discard the skin and bones. Strain the stock and simmer to reduce it to 600 ml/1 pint. Soften the gelatine in a little water, then add to the hot stock and stir to dissolve the gelatine completely. Taste for seasoning.

Put a layer of sliced chicken in a large pie dish and sprinkle it with some of the herbs, nutmeg and grated lemon zest. Then put in a layer of ham. Continue making alternate layers of chicken and ham to fill the dish, sprinkling each layer with the remaining flavourings and finishing with a layer of ham. Pour in half the warm stock and leave to cool.

Preheat the oven to 220°C/425°F, gas mark 7.

Roll out the pastry dough to about 5 mm/¼ in thick. Use to cover the pie dish and brush the pastry lid with the egg yolk glaze. Decorate with leaves and flowers cut from the trimmings and brush again with the glaze. Make a hole in the centre large enough to take the end of a funnel.

Bake for 15 minutes, then turn the temperature down to 180°C/350°F, gas mark 4. Bake for a further 25–30 minutes. When the top of the pie is nicely browned, cover it with foil or dampened greaseproof paper to prevent it from getting too dark. When the

pie is ready, remove it from the oven and pour in the remaining stock. Stop when you can see that the pie is full of liquid. Allow to set in the refrigerator overnight before cutting. The flavour improves if the pie is kept for 24 hours before serving.

OLD-FASHIONED PORK PIE

SERVES 6

- 700 g/1½ lb boneless pork – half belly, half blade, bones reserved
- 3 rashers of unsmoked bacon
- 3 fresh sage leaves, chopped, or ½ teaspoon dried sage
- 1¼ teaspoons salt
- 15 g/½ oz freshly ground pepper
- 1 free-range egg, separated

For the jellied stock:

- 1 onion
- 1 pig's trotter
- 1 carrot
- 1 celery stick
- salt

For the pastry:

- 70 g/2½ oz lard
- 15 g/½ oz butter
- a pinch of salt
- 340 g/12 oz plain flour

First start making the stock. Put the pork bones into a saucepan together with the peeled onion, pig's trotter, carrot, celery and 1.8 litres/3 pints water. Bring to the boil, skimming the surface well, and then simmer for 2–3 hours. Strain the resulting stock – you will need 600 ml/1 pint for the pie. If there is too much stock, reduce it by boiling, and then season with salt. Set the stock aside.

While the stock is simmering, chop the pork and bacon into little pieces the size of peas; you can do this by hand or in a food processor. The meat should be chopped rather than minced to keep its succulence. Add the sage, salt and pepper.

Preheat the oven to 180°C/350°F, gas mark 4.

bacon 69–70
lard 110
pig's trotter 62
pork belly 60
pork blade 60
reduce 423
sage 193–4

food processor 238
knives 222–4
sieves 226–7

allspice 198
dissolving gelatine 423
hare 79–80
juniper berry 196–7
mace 198
pheasant 85
pigeon 83
pig's trotter 62
pork belly 60
salt pork 70

deep cake tin 237
funnel 229
loaf tin 237
mincer 226
sieves 226–7
skimmers 228
soufflé dish 236

Hot-Water Crust Pastry 405

To make the pastry, bring 150 ml/¼ pint of water to the boil in a saucepan. Stir in the lard, butter and salt and boil, stirring, until the fat melts. Put the flour in a large bowl, and pour in the boiling hot mixture. Mix with a wooden spoon at first, as the mixture is very hot, then knead to a stiff dough with your hands, adding a little more water if necessary. The dough must be used while it is still hot.

It is easiest to make this pie in a mould – a medium-sized soufflé dish or round deep cake tin is ideal. Reserve a lump of the dough for the lid of the pie, wrapping it in a tea towel to keep it warm. Roll out the rest of the dough into a large disc and use to line the mould, working the dough into place with your fingers. Trim the edge, leaving the dough just hanging over the edge of the mould. Fill with the pork mixture. Roll out the reserved dough to make the lid and put it in place. Lightly beat the egg white and use it to stick the lid to the pastry case. Decorate the top with flowers and leaves cut from the pastry trimmings, and make a hole in the centre large enough to take the end of a funnel.

Bake for 1 hour, covering the top loosely with foil when it has turned a nice golden colour. When the pie is cooked, take it very carefully out of the mould and set it on a baking tray. Beat the egg yolk with a few drops of water and brush this over the top and side of the pie. Put it back in the oven to bake for 10 minutes or so, to give it a golden glaze. Lastly, insert a small funnel in the hole in the top and pour in enough of the warm, liquid stock to fill the pie. Allow the pie to cool, then leave it for 24 hours before eating.

COLD GAME PIE

SERVES 8–10

2 pigeons, plucked and cleaned
1 pheasant (an older bird will do), plucked and cleaned
1 hare (the saddle can be kept for roasting)
225 g/8 oz fresh belly of pork
115 g/4 oz salt pork or unsmoked streaky bacon
2 shallots, chopped
a small strip of orange zest, finely chopped
6 juniper berries, crushed
½ teaspoon ground allspice
½ teaspoon ground mace
60 ml/2 fl oz port
1 tablespoon brandy
2 teaspoons salt
coarsely crushed peppercorns
Hot-Water Crust Pastry made with 450 g/1 lb flour
1 free-range egg yolk, beaten with a few drops of water and a pinch of salt

For the jellied stock:
2 pig's trotters
1 onion
1 carrot
1 celery stick
1 bay leaf
4 peppercorns
a little salt
15 g/½ oz powdered gelatine

Cut the breasts from the pigeons; remove the meatiest parts of the pheasant; and cut the meat off the bones of the hare. Set all the meat aside. Put the carcasses and trimmings into a large saucepan with all the ingredients for the jellied stock except the salt and gelatine. Cover with cold water and bring to the boil, skimming well. Season very lightly with salt and leave to simmer for about 3 hours or until there is no more than about 600 ml/1 pint of liquid left. Strain the liquid. Dissolve the gelatine in it and allow to cool.

While the stock is simmering, cut the pheasant breast meat into fairly large cubes, about 2 cm/¾ in across. Chop the remaining meat – from the pheasant, pigeon and hare – into pieces no smaller than large peas. Mince or chop the fresh and salt pork, and mix with the chopped game and cubes of pheasant breast in a bowl. Add the shallots, orange zest, juniper berries, spices, port and brandy. Season with the salt and plenty of coarsely crushed black pepper. Leave in a cool place to mellow for 2–3 hours, or overnight.

When you are ready to make the pie, prepare the pastry and preheat the oven to 220°C/425°F, gas mark 7.

Grease a large loaf tin with hinged sides or a round deep cake tin with a removable base. Use two-thirds of the warm pastry dough to line the tin smoothly, making quite sure there are no holes. Put in the meat mixture. Brush the edges of the pastry case with water. Cover with the remaining pastry dough and press the edges together to seal. Decorate the top with the trimmings formed into geometric shapes or oak leaves, overlapping them like scales. Make a hole in the centre large enough to take the end of a funnel. Brush the top and decorations with the egg yolk glaze.

Bake for 20 minutes, then turn the temperature down to 180°C/350°F, gas mark 4. Bake for a further 1 hour and 40 minutes, covering loosely with foil when the top is well browned. Allow the pie to cool a little, then pour in the stock through the hole in the lid, filling the pie almost to the top (if the stock has set, warm it slightly until it is liquid). Allow the pie to cool and set in the tin for at least 24 hours before taking it out.

ALTERNATIVES: Use a casserole grouse or 2 casserole partridges instead of the hare.

CORNISH PASTIES

MAKES 8

340 g/12 oz chuck steak
2 small potatoes
1 small onion, finely chopped
salt and freshly ground pepper
Shortcrust Pastry made with 340 g/12 oz flour

Trim the steak of all fat and sinews, and cut it into small pieces, about 5 mm/¼ in across or even a little less. You will need a small very sharp knife to do this. Peel the potatoes and cut them into very fine, small flakes (this is called shripping). Mix the steak, potatoes and the finely chopped onion in a bowl with salt and lots of pepper. Add a teaspoon or two of water to moisten the mixture.

Preheat the oven to 220°C/425°F, gas mark 7.

Roll out the pastry dough fairly thinly. With a blunt knife, cut out 15 cm/6 in rounds using a saucer as a guide. Put some of the steak mixture in an oval shape on the middle of each round. Dampen the edges and fold the dough over the filling. Starting at one end, roll the edges together, pinching them at 1 cm/½ in intervals, to give a rope effect. Pinch the ends to a point.

Place the pasties on a greased baking sheet. Bake for 15–20 minutes or until nicely browned. Then reduce the temperature to 180°C/350°F, gas mark 4 and bake for a further 30 minutes.

ALTERNATIVE: Add a small quantity of shripped swede to the potato.

CHICKEN PIE WITH CREAM AND MUSHROOMS

SERVES 4–6

1 boiling fowl or roasting chicken, weighing 1.35–1.6 kg/3–3½ lb, preferably free-range
2 onions, sliced
3 carrots, sliced
2 celery sticks, sliced into crescents
3 sprigs of parsley, tied together
1 bay leaf
salt and freshly ground pepper
45 g/1½ oz butter
45 g/1½ oz plain flour
115 g/4 oz button mushrooms
115 g/4 oz lean sausagemeat, rolled into marble-size balls
150 ml/¼ pint double cream
Shortcrust or Rough Puff Pastry made with 170 g/6 oz flour
1 free-range egg yolk, beaten (optional)

Put the fowl or chicken into a large saucepan with the sliced vegetables and the herbs. Cover with cold water and bring slowly to the boil, skimming off the froth and scum. Leave to simmer for 30 minutes.

Add a little salt, and continue simmering until the chicken is cooked – this will take 45 minutes to 1 hour longer. Let it cool in its broth if there is time, then remove the bird and take the meat off the bones. (If you prefer, leave wing and leg bones in to make a more substantial pie.)

Make a sauce with the butter, flour and 450 ml/¾ pint of the strained chicken broth. Season it well. Stir in the mushrooms. Leave to cook gently while you lightly fry the sausage meatballs in a small frying pan for a few minutes. Drain them on kitchen paper. Stir the cream, the meatballs and the chicken meat very gently into the sauce. Place a pie funnel in a large pie dish, pour the mixture into the dish around the funnel and allow to cool.

Preheat the oven to 200°C/400°F, gas mark 6.

Roll out the pastry dough to about 5 mm/¼ in thick. Use to cover the pie dish, making a hole in the pastry lid over the funnel. Brush the pastry lid with the egg yolk or the last few drops in the cream pot.

Bake for 12–15 minutes. Then turn the oven down to 180°C/350°F, gas mark 4, and bake for a further 15–20 minutes.

SALMON PÂTÉ

Serve this layered fish pâté with Fresh Sauce Grelette.

SERVES 6–8

450 g/1 lb fresh salmon fillet, skinned
a wineglass of white wine
salt and freshly ground white pepper
2 small bunches of watercress
1 shallot, chopped
225 g/8 oz butter, softened
450 g/1 lb whiting fillet, skinned and chilled
2 free-range eggs

Cut the salmon fillet into long strips. Put them in a small dish with the white wine and season lightly with salt and white pepper. Leave to marinate in the wine for an hour or so.

Meanwhile, trim away the rooty parts of the watercress stalks and wash the sprigs. Bring a pan of lightly salted water to the boil and drop in the watercress. Let it blanch for a minute, then drain, refresh under cold water and pat dry.

Soften the shallot, without browning, in 15 g/½ oz of the butter. Cut the whiting into cubes and put into a food processor with the softened shallot. Blend for

blanch 422
button mushroom 161
chicken 86–7
chuck steak 53
covering a deep pie dish with pastry 404
marinate 422
potato 145
refresh 423
salmon 21
sausage meat 75
swede 149
watercress 130–1
whiting 13–14

food processor 238
knives 222–4
pie dish 237
pie funnel 237
rolling pin 236
sieves 226–7

Fresh Sauce Grelette 257
Rough Puff Pastry 402
Shortcrust Pastry 402

Pâté de Campagne

back fat 110
bain-marie 422
chicken livers 90
fresh breadcrumbs 364
neck of veal 56
pork blade 60
quatre épices 196

food processor 238
mincer 226
terrine 236

3–4 minutes or until completely smooth. Add the eggs and season with salt and white pepper. Blend for another minute, then add the remaining butter and blend for 30 seconds. Take two-thirds of the mixture out of the food processor and set aside. Add the watercress to the remaining third and purée briefly until it is a beautiful bright green. Chill both mixtures for 30 minutes.

Preheat the oven to 140°C/275°F, gas mark 1.

Make a layer of half the white mixture in a lightly oiled oblong terrine – a long, narrow, enamelled iron terrine 25 x 9 cm/10 x 3½ in is the best size (or you can use a large loaf tin if you don't have a terrine). Put in a layer of half the drained salmon strips, then cover them with all the green purée in a neat layer. Put in the remaining salmon strips and spread over the rest of the white purée. Cover with buttered foil and the lid and then set the terrine in a bain-marie or a large roasting tin half filled with water. Cook in the oven for 2–2½ hours. Allow to cool and then chill overnight in the refrigerator.

PÂTÉ DE CAMPAGNE

SERVES 8

- 340 g/12 oz chicken livers
- 225 g/8 oz unsmoked streaky bacon
- 225 g/8 oz pie veal (neck) or pork (blade)
- 2 garlic cloves, crushed
- 15 peppercorns, crushed
- a wineglass of dry cider or white wine
- a dash of brandy
- 1 extra large free-range egg
- 55 g/2 oz fresh white breadcrumbs
- 1 scant teaspoon each dried sage and thyme
- ½ teaspoon quatre épices or ground allspice
- ½ onion or 2 shallots, very finely chopped
- 55 g/2 oz butter
- 1½ teaspoons salt
- 115 g/4 oz pork back fat

Pick over the chicken livers, removing strings and any greenish parts, and chop fairly finely. Mince the bacon and veal or pork coarsely or chop in a food processor. Transfer to a bowl. Add the livers, garlic, peppercorns, cider or wine, brandy, egg, breadcrumbs, herbs and spices. Mix everything together well and leave to mature for 2–3 hours.

Preheat the oven to 180°C/350°F, gas mark 4.

Sweat the onion or shallots in the butter in a small pan until tender and translucent. Add to the meat mixture and season with the salt. Put the mixture into a 1.5 litre/2½ pint terrine.

Beat the pork back fat until quite thin, using the side of a cleaver, and cut into strips. Arrange them in a lattice over the top of the pâté. Cover the terrine and cook in the oven for 1 hour. Then remove the lid and cook for a further 30 minutes uncovered. Allow to stand overnight, or longer, before cutting

PÂTÉ IN A CRUST

SERVES 8–10

Hot-Water Crust Pastry made with 450 g/1 lb flour
1 free-range egg yolk, beaten with a few drops of water and a pinch of salt

For the filling:

450 g/1 lb chicken livers
a small wineglass of dry white vermouth or dry white wine
340 g/12 oz minced pork – one-third fat belly and two-thirds blade
450 g/1 lb chicken hearts or pig's liver, minced
3 rashers of streaky bacon, finely chopped
1 shallot, finely chopped
1 garlic clove, chopped and crushed
1 free-range egg, lightly beaten
½ teaspoon ground mace
½ teaspoon ground allspice
salt and freshly ground pepper

For the jellied stock:

2 large onions
2 pig's trotters
900 g–1.35 kg/2–3 lb veal or pork bones and trimmings
1 large carrot
1 celery stick
1 bay leaf
½ wineglass of medium dry sherry
1 teaspoon salt
½ teaspoon coarsely ground pepper
2 teaspoons sugar

The day before you make the pâté, clean the chicken livers, cut them in half and put them in an earthenware dish. Pour the dry white vermouth or the white wine over them.

In another bowl, mix together the minced pork and chicken hearts or pig's liver, the bacon, shallot, garlic and egg. Season the mixture with the spices and some salt and pepper. Stir well.

Let the two mixtures stand overnight in a cool place so that the flavours can mellow.

The following day, make the pastry dough and use two-thirds of it to line a large loaf tin with hinged sides or a round deep cake tin.

Preheat the oven to 220°C/425°F, gas mark 7.

Take the chicken livers out of the vermouth, and mix the vermouth into the meat mixture. Put a layer of this forcemeat into the pastry-lined tin and lay the chicken livers on top, pressing them in gently. Spread the remaining forcemeat on top, trying not to leave any air gaps. Cover the pie with the rest of the pastry dough, sealing the edges together with water. Brush the lid with the egg yolk glaze. Cut lozenges or other shapes from the pastry trimmings and use to decorate the top; glaze these too. Make a hole in the middle of the top that is large enough to take the end of a funnel. Bake for 1½ hours, covering the top with foil when the pastry is nicely browned. Allow to cool in the tin.

Meanwhile, make the stock. Put all the ingredients except the salt, pepper and sugar in a saucepan and pour in 1.5 litres/2½ pints water. Bring to the boil and simmer for 2 hours. Strain and then reduce to about 750 ml/1¼ pints. Skim off the fat, and clarify the stock if you want perfection. Add the salt and pepper. Caramelize the sugar by holding it in a ladle over the heat, and add it to the clear stock to give it a good colour. Allow to cool.

Pour the still liquid stock into the cooled pie using a funnel. Keep the pie in the refrigerator overnight or longer before taking it out of the tin. Cut into wedges and serve with a salad.

RILLETTES OF PORK

Rillettes is good for a cold lunch or snack. It will keep for a week in the refrigerator.

SERVES 8

115 g/4 oz flare fat
450 g/1 lb lean boneless pork
450 g/1 lb fatty boneless pork
salt and freshly ground pepper
a grating of nutmeg

Preheat the oven to 140°C/275°F, gas mark 1.

Cut the fat and pork into 4 cm/1½ in cubes and put them into a heavy casserole with 3 tablespoons of water. Season with salt and pepper. Cover and cook in the oven for 4 hours.

Drain off the fat and liquid and reserve. Purée the meat briefly in a food processor, or wait until it is cool

chicken giblets 90
chicken livers 90
clarifying (see Consommé recipe) 250
forcemeat 422
flare fat 110
pig's trotter 62
pork belly 60
pork blade 60
sweat 423

casserole 236
cleaver 222
food processor 238
funnel 229
loaf tin 237
mincer 226
round deep cake tin 237
sieves 226–7
skimmers 228

Hot-water Crust Pastry 405

boning and stuffing a duck 94–5
clarifying (see Consommé recipe) 250
duck 89–90
ham 68–9
hard-boiled 322
mace 198
pistachio nut 187
zesting citrus fruits 423

casserole 236
sieves 226–7
trussing equipment 230

but not cold and then shred it with two forks, removing any cartilage. (This is a lengthy job, but there is no better way; you are aiming at fine, soft threads of meat in a creamy, spicy base.) Season very well with salt, pepper and nutmeg. Return the fat and liquid to the meat and reheat until it bubbles. Pack into stoneware jars or china or earthenware dishes and refrigerate. Serve at cool room temperature, not chilled.

ALTERNATIVES: You can add pieces of rabbit or goose at the beginning, but the mixture should be at least half fatty pork.

GALANTINE OF DUCK

SERVES 6–8

- 1 duck, weighing 1.6–1.8 kg/3½–4 lb, with the giblets
- 60 ml/2 fl oz brandy
- fresh tarragon leaves, red pepper, hard-boiled egg and cucumber to decorate

For the stock:

- 2 onions
- a strip of orange zest
- 1 carrot
- 2 celery sticks
- 1 bay leaf
- salt
- 6 peppercorns

For the stuffing:

- 1 shallot, finely chopped
- 30 g/1 oz shelled pistachio nuts, skinned
- 225 g/8 oz minced pork with plenty of fat – about one-third fat to two-thirds lean
- 225 g/8 oz minced veal
- 30 g/1 oz cooked ham, cut into 5 mm/¼ in cubes
- 1 free-range egg
- a strip of orange zest, finely chopped
- a small wineglass of white wine
- 2 very generous pinches of ground mace
- 2½ teaspoons salt
- 15 white or black peppercorns, coarsely crushed
- 3 chicken livers

For braising:

- 30 g/1 oz butter
- 2 onions, chopped
- 4 carrots, chopped
- 3 celery sticks, chopped

Bone the duck (reserve the bones and giblets). Sprinkle the inside with a little brandy and put it on one side.

Put the duck bones and giblets, except the liver, in a large saucepan. Add the ingredients for the stock, except the salt and peppercorns, and cover with 1.2–2.4 litres/2–4 pints of water. Bring to the boil, skimming well. Season lightly with salt and add the peppercorns, then leave to simmer for about 2 hours.

Meanwhile, take some leg and breast meat from the inside of the duck and chop this and the duck's liver into cubes. Mix with all the stuffing ingredients, except the chicken livers. Add the remaining brandy. Take a little piece of the mixture, fry it and taste it so that you can check the seasoning. Put a layer of the stuffing on the duck. Lay the chicken livers down the middle and cover with the remaining stuffing. Roll up the duck tightly and sew it into a long sausage. Tie it with string in two places to keep it in a nice shape.

Preheat the oven to 175°C/340°F, gas mark 3½.

Melt the butter for braising in a braising pan or flameproof casserole and soften the braising vegetables for 10 minutes. Lay the duck galantine on top. Pour on the strained stock and cover the pan. Braise in the oven for 2 hours, uncovering the pan for the last 30 minutes of cooking so that the galantine becomes an appetizing brown. If it bursts along the top, don't worry – it means you have put in a bit too much stuffing; simply cook it uncovered until the burst place has healed, basting it from time to time. (You can hide the splits with decorations before you put on the jelly.)

Let the galantine cool in its liquid, then remove it and put it to chill in the refrigerator so that it becomes firm. Strain the liquid and allow it to get completely cold. It should set into a nice jelly with a layer of fat on top. Remove the fat and then clarify the jelly. Let it cool, but do not allow it to set completely.

Remove the string from the galantine and place it on a white oval serving dish. Decorate it with flower patterns made from tarragon leaves, pieces of red pepper, hard-boiled egg and cucumber peel and so forth. Pour the half-set, rather syrupy jelly over the galatine – it is probably best to pour it through a tea-strainer so that you can guide it to where you want it to go. Give the galantine two layers of jelly – experience is the only way to make this an easy operation; it is hard to catch the jelly at the crucial moment as it is turning from a liquid to a solid. It helps if you have the galantine very cold and do the operation in a cold place. Any jelly that runs off, or is left over, can be chilled and then chopped to put on either side of the galantine. Chill before serving.

Make the first cut right across the middle of the galantine as the ends are not so impressive. Give everyone a generous slice.

ALTERNATIVE: If you prefer you can serve the galantine without first coating it with the jelly.

PIGEON PIE

You can use older birds for this pie, and it will taste just as good.

SERVES 4–6

- 2 pigeons, plucked and cleaned
- 340 g/12 oz chuck steak, cut into smallish cubes
- plain flour for dusting
- 3 tablespoons sunflower oil
- 1 large onion, chopped
- 1 teaspoon Worcestershire sauce
- salt and freshly ground pepper
- 1 bay leaf
- Shortcrust Pastry made with 170 g/6 oz flour
- 1 free-range egg yolk, beaten with a pinch of salt and a few drops of water

For the stock:

- 1 onion, sliced
- 1 carrot, sliced
- 1 celery stick, chopped
- a fresh bouquet garni of parsley, thyme and a bay leaf
- ½ wineglass of red wine

GALANTINE OF DUCK

Cut the legs and breasts from the pigeons. Put the carcasses into a saucepan with the stock ingredients. Add 300 ml/½ pint of cold water. Bring to the boil, skimming, then cover and simmer for 1 hour.

Dust the pigeon joints and beef cubes generously with flour. Heat the oil in a frying pan and brown them, a few pieces at a time, sprinkling with a little more flour. As they brown, transfer them to a pie dish. Brown the chopped onion in the same oil, and add to the pie dish. Place a pie funnel in the middle. Strain the stock, mix it with the Worcestershire sauce and pour it over the meat and onions. Allow to cool. Season with salt and pepper, and put in the bay leaf.

Preheat the oven to 220°C/425°F, gas mark 7.

Roll out the pastry dough, cover the dish and decorate with trimmings. Brush with egg yolk glaze. Bake for 15 minutes, then at 150°C/300°F, gas mark 2 for 1½ hours, covering the pie with doubled damp greaseproof paper, or foil, once it is nicely browned.

bouquet garni 190
chuck steak 53
covering a deep pie dish with pastry 404
pigeon 83
Worcestershire sauce 206

pie dish 237
pie funnel 237
sieves 226–7
skimmers 228

Shortcrust Pastry 402

Eggs

arrowroot 118
coconut 188–9, 423
curry powder 196
egg size for recipes 422
eggs 96–7
Parma ham 69
truffles 161

frying pan 234
non-stick pans 234
sauté pan 234
sieves 226–7
slotted spoon 227

Chicken Stock 244

Basic egg cookery

Soft-boiled eggs The remark about not being able to boil an egg is really no joke. Often the egg cracks and the white pours out, and often the yolk somehow gets overcooked. Many people do not know that eggs should be simmered, not boiled, to prevent the white toughening. Soft-boiled eggs take 3–5 minutes from the time they are lowered into the simmering water, new-laid eggs taking perhaps a minute longer to cook than shop-bought eggs.

A foolproof way to boil an egg is to coddle it. Put the egg in a pan of cold water and bring to the boil, then take it off the heat, cover and leave for 5 minutes.

Hard-boiled eggs These take 10–12 minutes; simmering longer will give a dark grey ring around the yolk, since the iron in the yolk and the sulphur compounds in the white are released to form ferrous sulphide. As soon as the time is up, plunge the eggs into cold water or rinse them under the cold tap, whether you are going to peel them at once or not. If you are, it helps to cool them enough to handle, and if you are not, it prevents them continuing to cook in their stored heat. And it makes them easier to shell.

Poached eggs Use the freshest eggs you can obtain. Use either a shallow sauté pan or a heavy frying pan, rather than a saucepan, which is difficult to get the eggs in and out of. Fill the pan with enough water to cover the eggs. You can add a little vinegar to hasten the setting, but no salt, as this will toughen the white. Bring the water to the boil, then turn down the heat a little so the water is just rolling. Break the eggs in one at a time, keeping your hands very close to the pan. Let the eggs poach until the whites have lost their translucent look. If the yolks are not quite covered, spoon the water over them to cook the tops.

When they are done, lift the eggs out one at a time with a slotted spoon, taking care as you slide it under each egg that you do not break the yolk. Let the eggs drain on the spoon for a few moments before putting them on a warm dish. If you are not ready to serve them immediately, they will keep fresh in a bowl of cold water and can be reheated.

For a neat egg, trim off the untidy edges. A fresh egg has a definite rounded shape with a few trailing bits around the outside which are easily trimmed away with a knife or scissors. Fresh eggs poach best; eggs that are not fresh will spread out and disintegrate.

Scrambled eggs To make scrambled eggs that are creamy and rich, you need patience, butter and, if possible, a non-stick pan (to help with the washing-up).

Away from the heat, break the eggs into the pan and season with salt and freshly ground pepper. Add a good knob of butter – about 30 g/1 oz for every 3–4 eggs. (If you don't possess a non-stick pan it is better to melt the butter a bit before breaking in the eggs.) Put the pan over a low heat. Take a wooden spoon to the mixture and stir it with intelligence – that is, moving every bit of egg around, not just following a clockwise track. Gradually the eggs will thicken. While they are still just runny, remove the pan from the heat and continue to stir until they become a soft, creamy mass. Serve scrambled eggs straight away, on hot buttered toast, or they will harden at the bottom.

You can add chopped fresh parsley or chives to the eggs before you start to scramble them, or flaked cooked haddock, finely grated black or white truffles, or finely chopped ham or Parma ham. Or, when the eggs are cooked, put them on to hot buttered toast and place two fillets of smoked eel or some smoked salmon on top.

CURRIED EGGS

SERVES 4

8 free-range eggs
55 g/2 oz butter
1 large onion, finely chopped
2 tablespoons curry powder
300 ml/½ pint good chicken stock
salt and freshly ground pepper
1 teaspoon arrowroot
150 ml/¼ pint double or whipping cream
3 tablespoons desiccated coconut or freshly grated coconut
juice of ½ lemon
fresh coriander to garnish

Preheat the oven to 180°C/350°F, gas mark 4.

Boil the eggs for 12 minutes, then cool them under cold running water. Shell carefully and put on one side.

Melt the butter in a small saucepan and add the onion and curry powder. Fry, stirring, until the onion is tender and translucent. Add the stock and season with salt and pepper. Simmer for 10 minutes. Mix the arrowroot into the cream and stir into the curry sauce. Simmer for a few more minutes.

While the sauce is simmering, pour 150 ml/¼ pint boiling water on to the coconut in a bowl. When it has cooled, strain the liquid into the curry sauce, pressing the coconut in the sieve with a spoon to extract all the liquid; discard the coconut. Add the lemon juice to the sauce and taste for seasoning.

Slice the eggs into rounds or halve them. Put them in an ovenproof dish and pour the curry sauce over them. Cover the dish loosely with foil and put in the oven to heat through for 10–15 minutes. Serve garnished with coriander.

EGGS BENEDICT

SERVES 4

4 slices of white bread
55 g/2 oz butter
1 teaspoon vegetable oil
4 free-range eggs
4 slices of cooked ham
hot Hollandaise Sauce made with lemon juice

Preheat the grill.

Trim the crusts off the slices of bread, or cut a large disc from each slice. Heat the butter and oil in a frying pan and fry the bread until crisp and golden brown on both sides. Keep the bread hot while you poach the eggs lightly. When the eggs are ready, add a cup of cold water to the hot poaching water to stop them from cooking any further. The eggs can then be left in the water for a moment or two.

Trim the ham and lay a slice on each piece of fried bread. Drain the eggs well, trim off any uneven edges with kitchen scissors and lay one on each piece of ham. Spoon the hollandaise over so that it completely covers eggs, ham and bread. Brown for a minute under the hot grill, and serve as soon as possible.

ALTERNATIVES: At one time, London's Savoy Hotel liked to use a toasted crumpet instead of fried bread, and in the United States a split and toasted English muffin is used, but this is a matter of choice.

EGGS WITH SPINACH AND CHEESE

SERVES 4

700–900 g/1½–2 lb spinach
salt
15 g/½ oz plain flour
a pinch of grated nutmeg
2–3 tablespoons double cream
4 free-range eggs
450 ml/¾ pint hot Mornay (cheese) Sauce

Wash the spinach and shake it gently. Put it into a pan, making sure that there is still a little water clinging to the leaves. Cover with a lid and start cooking over a gentle heat. As the spinach wilts down, add a pinch of salt and turn the heat up. Cook until the spinach is just tender, then drain very thoroughly and return to the pan.

Stir the flour and nutmeg into the cream and mix into the spinach. Simmer over a low heat, stirring from time to time, until the mixture has thickened and the flour has absorbed any water that was running from the spinach. Keep hot.

Preheat the grill.

Poach the eggs. Meanwhile, put the creamed spinach in an oval gratin dish. Drain the eggs, lay them on top of the spinach and pour the mornay sauce over them. Brown the top quickly under the grill.

OEUFS SUR LE PLAT

SERVES 4

55 g/2 oz butter
4 slices of cooked ham
8 free-range eggs
salt and freshly ground pepper

Preheat the oven to 180°C/350°F, gas mark 4.

Divide the butter among four individual enamel gratin dishes or flameproof earthenware dishes or, failing those, saucers. Melt the butter over a gentle heat. Put a slice of ham into each dish and break 2 eggs on top. Sprinkle with a little salt and plenty of pepper. Bake for 10–15 minutes or until the whites of the eggs are set. You can finish cooking the tops of the eggs under the grill, if you like.

ALTERNATIVES: Instead of ham, put slices of chorizo in the dishes, or use finely sliced, lightly fried courgettes or a thin layer of Ratatouille.

CHAKCHOUKA

Chakchouka is originally a Tunisian dish, now widely eaten in many Middle Eastern countries. A version is also found in the South of France where it is known as *pipérade basquaise*, but in the Basque country the eggs are scrambled rather than cooked whole as here.

SERVES 2–4

2 tablespoons olive oil
1 garlic clove, crushed in its skin and then peeled
1–2 green or red peppers, seeded and cut into strips
225 g/8 oz tomatoes, skinned and finely chopped
salt and freshly ground pepper
4 free-range eggs

Heat the oil in a frying pan. Add the garlic and fry until it is golden brown. Put in the strips of pepper and let them stew gently in the garlic-flavoured oil until soft. Stir in the tomatoes and season with salt and pepper. Simmer for 15 minutes, covered with a tilted lid.

Taste the mixture and add more salt and pepper if you think it is needed. Break the eggs on top, cover the pan and cook until the eggs are just set. Serve straight from the pan, as soon as possible.

chorizo 78
ham 68–9
poached eggs 322
skinning and seeding tomatoes 423
spinach 132–3
sweet pepper 152

cutters 225
gratin dish 236

Hollandaise Sauce 255
Mornay Sauce 255
Ratatouille 383

acidulated water 422
bain-marie 422
cocotte 422
Emmental cheese 105
fines herbes 190
mushrooms and other fungi 158–61
Parmesan cheese 103
prawn 35–6
preparing globe artichoke hearts 139
spinach 132–3

whisks 227

Croûtons 364

OEUFS EN COCOTTE À LA CRÈME

SERVES 4

15 g/½ oz butter, cut into 8 slices
salt and freshly ground pepper
4 very fresh free-range eggs
4 tablespoons double cream

Preheat the oven to 200°C/400°F, gas mark 6.

Divide half the butter among four small ovenproof cocotte dishes and add a pinch each of salt and pepper. Break an egg into each dish and season with more salt and pepper. Pour a tablespoon of cream over each egg and add the remaining butter.

Put the cocotte dishes in a bain-marie or a roasting tin and pour enough boiling water around them to come halfway up the sides of the dishes. Place in the oven and bake for 7–8 minutes. Test the eggs by gently shaking the cocotte dishes – the whites should be just set and the yolks still runny.

ALTERNATIVES: **Oeufs en cocotte aux champignons** First stew 115 g/4 oz quartered or sliced wild or cultivated mushrooms in the butter, and divide these among the cocotte dishes before adding the eggs and cream. Season with salt, pepper and a grating of nutmeg.
Oeufs en cocotte aux crevettes Put a few small peeled cooked prawns into each cocotte dish with the butter before adding the eggs.

OMELETTE FINES HERBES

SERVES 1

2 free-range eggs
salt and freshly ground pepper
1 teaspoon chopped fresh chives
1 teaspoon chopped parsley
1 teaspoon chopped fresh tarragon
1 teaspoon chopped fresh chervil
½ tablespoon freshly grated Parmesan
15 g/½ oz butter for frying

Whisk the eggs lightly in a bowl, just enough to break them down. Season with salt and pepper. Add the herbs and cheese and whisk lightly once again to spread the herbs evenly through the mixture.

Heat the butter in an omelette pan that is about 25 cm/10 in diameter. When it starts to brown, pour in the egg mixture. Stir it round for a minute, tipping the pan and lifting the edges as they set, so that the liquid egg can run underneath. When the omelette is set and brown underneath, but still creamy and runny on top, flick one half over towards the middle and then roll the omelette on to a heated plate so that it is folded in three. It should look like a plump golden cushion. Eat at once: speed is essential for both the cooking and the eating of omelettes.

OMELETTE FILLINGS

Omelettes can be filled with almost any cheese, shellfish, vegetable or herb as well as with some meats such as bacon and ham. Among the nicest omelette fillings are:
Cheese omelette A handful of grated Emmental or a mixture of Emmental and Parmesan.
Mushroom omelette Slice a few button or wild mushrooms and lightly fry in butter with chopped parsley and a little crushed garlic.
Prawn omelette Lightly cook a few peeled prawns in a little cream and flavour with chopped fresh chives.
Spinach and cheese omelette Cook chopped spinach in butter, then stir into the beaten eggs with a little freshly grated Parmesan.
Ham or bacon omelette Cut ham or bacon into little strips and sizzle in butter, then stir into the beaten eggs with a little grated cheese.
Portuguese omelette Shake croûtons in a paper bag with grated Parmesan, finely chopped parsley and cayenne pepper.
Parsi omelette Fry sliced onions and potato until tender and golden brown, then season with paprika, turmeric and chopped fresh coriander.

OMELETTE WITH ARTICHOKES AND PARSLEY

You can make one large omelette if you wish, or four individual ones (these are easier to manage).

SERVES 4

8 large globe artichokes
juice of 1 lemon
140 g/5 oz butter
1 small garlic clove, bruised
salt and freshly ground pepper
1 tablespoon chopped parsley
8 free-range eggs

Trim off all the leaves from the artichokes, and remove the hairy chokes. Then pare the artichokes down to the hearts and slice them thinly, dropping the slices into a bowl of cold water acidulated with the lemon juice as you go.

Pat the slices dry. Melt half the butter in a large frying pan, add the artichokes and garlic, and season with salt and pepper. Stew gently until the artichokes are golden brown and tender. Stir in the parsley. Tip the artichokes on to a plate and keep warm.

Lightly beat 2 eggs in a bowl and season with salt and pepper. Heat one-quarter of the remaining butter in a 15–20 cm/6–8 in omelette or frying pan until it starts to brown, then pour in the eggs. Stir them round for a minute, tilting the pan and lifting the edges as they set, so that the liquid egg can run underneath. When the omelette is set and golden underneath, fill with one-quarter of the artichokes, fold over, roll on to a heated plate and serve immediately. Make three more omelettes in the same way.

ALTERNATIVE: To make an Italian-style frittata, cook the omelette as above, leaving the surface quite runny. Then spread the artichokes over the omelette and flash under a preheated hot grill to finish cooking the omelette and slightly toast the artichokes. This is delicious hot or cold and makes great picnic food.

ROLLED OMELETTES WITH SPICED GREENS

These look attractive served on plain white plates.

SERVES 4

6 extra large free-range eggs
6 tablespoons double cream
a large bunch of fresh chives, finely chopped
2 tablespoons olive oil
sprigs of fresh coriander
2–3 tablespoons sour cream
1 lime, cut into wedges

For the spiced greens:

2 tablespoons olive oil
1 small onion, chopped
3 garlic cloves, chopped
375 g/13 oz young spinach leaves
a bunch of watercress, stalks removed
½ bunch of fresh coriander, stalks removed, coarsely chopped
2 green chillies, seeded and chopped
¼ teaspoon caster sugar
salt and freshly ground pepper

First make the spiced greens. Heat the oil in a large, deep frying pan, add the onion and garlic, and fry until pale golden. Put in the spinach and watercress leaves and cook until completely wilted. Tip into a colander and leave to drain for 10 minutes. Then squeeze out any further excess moisture with your hands. Tip the greens into a food processor. Add the coriander leaves and chillies and process in short bursts to achieve a coarse purée, which must be neither too sloppy nor too smooth. Add the sugar and season with salt and pepper.

Preheat the grill.

Beat the eggs with the cream, chives and seasoning. Pour the beaten egg mixture into a measuring jug; there should be about 340 ml/12 fl oz, allowing approximately 85 ml/3 fl oz per omelette.

Heat 1 teaspoon oil in an 18–20 cm/7–8 in non-stick frying pan. Pour in enough egg mixture for one omelette and turn the heat right down to very low. Allow the omelette to set on the base without colouring, then transfer the pan to the hot grill for a few seconds to set the top. Slide the omelette on to a double thickness of kitchen paper and leave to cool until lukewarm, but definitely not cold.

Transfer the omelette to a square of foil. Spread over about 1 tablespoon of the spiced greens and roll up the omelette tightly, like a Swiss roll. Wrap in the foil and twist the ends to make the parcel even tighter. It should resemble a fairly long, fat Christmas cracker. Make three more omelettes in the same way, then refrigerate them all for 1 hour to firm up.

To serve the omelettes, unwrap them, cut on a short diagonal into 1 cm/½ in thick slices and arrange on individual plates. Scatter over some coriander sprigs and serve with the sour cream and lime wedges.

chilli pepper 152–3
chive 190
coriander 191–2
Gruyère cheese 104
seeding chillies 423
smoked haddock 29
spinach 132–3
watercress 130–1

colander 229
food processor 238
non-stick pans 234

FLAT OMELETTES

A **frittata** is a sort of cake made of eggs and lightly cooked vegetables. It is cut like a cake, too, and may be eaten hot, cold or warm – a temperature Italians quite like for certain dishes. It should be a fairly solid, golden disc, nicely crusted on top.
A **tortilla** is the Spanish version of the frittata, containing a mixture of fried sliced onions and potatoes. It can also contain little slices of hot paprika sausage, green or red peppers and garlic. It is eaten hot or cold – wedges of cold tortilla are an essential part of the appetizers available in every tapas bar.

OMELETTE ARNOLD BENNETT

SERVES 4

1 medium-sized smoked haddock, weighing about 700 g/1½ lb
generous 150 ml/¼ pint milk
1 bay leaf
55 g/2 oz butter
30 g/1 oz plain flour
8 free-range eggs
55 g/2 oz Gruyère or Emmental, grated
salt and freshly ground pepper

Emmental cheese 105
spinach 132–3

frying pan 234
sieves 226–7
whisks 227

Béchamel Sauce 255

Bacon and Egg Tart

Preheat the oven to 170°C/325°F, gas mark 3.

Put the smoked haddock into a baking tin with the milk, 150 ml/¼ pint of water and the bay leaf. Put it into the oven. After 15 minutes the fish should be just cooked through. Drain the fish, reserving the liquid, and set aside.

Make a béchamel sauce with half the butter, the flour and 300 ml/½ pint of the strained cooking liquid. Flake the haddock into the sauce, discarding skin and any bones.

Break the eggs into a bowl. Add the haddock mixture and half the cheese and beat well until the eggs are frothing and the sauce has combined with them. Season with salt and pepper.

Preheat the grill.

Heat the remaining butter in a heavy 28 cm/11 in frying pan until starting to brown. Pour in the egg mixture and cook, shaking the pan to keep the omelette loose. When it is half cooked, sprinkle on the remaining cheese and put the pan under the grill. After 1–2 minutes, the omelette should be brown on top but still creamy in the middle. Serve in wedges.

SPINACH FRITTATA

SERVES 4

- 2 tablespoons olive oil
- 2 garlic cloves, crushed
- 225–340 g/8–12 oz spinach, stalks removed
- salt and freshly ground pepper
- 6 free-range eggs
- a pinch of grated nutmeg
- 2 tablespoons double cream
- 85 g/3 oz Emmental, finely grated

Preheat the oven to 180°C/350°F, gas mark 4.

Heat half the olive oil in a large frying pan and throw in the garlic. Let it brown slightly, crushing it into the oil, then add the spinach. Scatter a pinch of salt over the top and stir the spinach around, letting it wilt down. Cook for 10–15 minutes or until most of the moisture has evaporated. Let the spinach cool, then drain and chop it roughly. Put into a bowl and keep on one side.

Beat the eggs in another bowl. Season with salt, pepper and nutmeg, and whisk in the cream, cheese and spinach. Heat the remaining olive oil in a round 28 cm/11 in baking dish or a small roasting tin. Pour in the egg mixture. Bake for 15–20 minutes or until set and cooked through – the time will vary according to the thickness of the frittata. Either eat it hot, or allow it to cool for 15 minutes, then turn it out on to a board or dish and allow to get completely cold. Cut in slices or wedges and serve with small, juicy black olives handed round separately.

EGG MAYONNAISE

SERVES 4

- 4 free-range eggs
- 2 tablespoons single cream
- 300 ml/½ pint mayonnaise, made with groundnut oil or half groundnut and half olive oil
- a sprinkling of cayenne pepper

Boil the eggs for exactly 12 minutes, then cool them under cold running water and shell them carefully. Cut them in half and put them rounded sides up in an oval dish. Stir the cream into the mayonnaise, to make it more liquid, and taste to make sure it is well flavoured. Spoon it over the eggs. Sprinkle lightly with cayenne pepper and serve.

ALTERNATIVES: Instead of cayenne pepper, decorate the tops of the eggs with anchovy fillets. Or blanch a bunch of watercress, purée or finely chop the leaves, and use to flavour and colour the mayonnaise.

EGG MOUSSE

SERVES 4 AS A MAIN COURSE OR 6 AS A STARTER

- 6 free-range eggs
- juice of ½ lemon
- 115 g/4 oz white button mushrooms, cut into 5 mm/¼ in dice
- 55 g/2 oz butter
- 2 teaspoons powdered gelatine or 3 leaves of gelatine
- 150 ml/¼ pint hot consommé – home-made or canned
- 2 tablespoons Worcestershire sauce or 3 tablespoons dry sherry
- 300 ml/½ pint double or whipping cream, chilled
- salt and freshly ground pepper
- 6 fresh tarragon leaves or 6 sprigs of flat-leaf parsley

Boil the eggs for 12 minutes, then cool them under cold running water. Shell and then chop or slice.

Squeeze the lemon juice over the mushrooms to prevent them from browning. Melt the butter in a small frying pan and cook the mushrooms gently for 3–4 minutes. Transfer to a wire sieve to drain.

Dissolve the gelatine in the consommé. Add the Worcestershire sauce or sherry (or both if you like). Allow to cool but not set. Whip the cream until it is a soft snow. Reserve 3 tablespoons of the consommé mixture and mix the remainder with the whipped cream, eggs and mushrooms. Taste for seasoning. Pour the mixture into a 1 litre/2 pint soufflé dish and leave to set in the refrigerator.

Place the tarragon leaves or parsley on top of the mousse. Pour on the reserved consommé, just melted, and allow to set. Serve with Herb Mayonnaise.

BACON AND EGG TART

This very simple but extremely good tart, something like a quiche Lorraine, is delicious hot or cold, and is very good for picnics.

SERVES 4

- 4–5 rashers of streaky bacon
- 2 free-range eggs
- 150 ml/¼ pint milk
- 3–4 tablespoons cream
- 55 g/2 oz Parmesan, freshly grated
- salt and freshly ground pepper
- a pinch of grated nutmeg
- Shortcrust Pastry made with 170 g/6 oz flour

Preheat the oven to 200°C/400°F, gas mark 6.

Cut the bacon into little strips about 2.5 cm/1 in long and 1 cm/½ in wide. Fry, with the trimmed off rinds, in a small pan until the fat runs and the pieces start to brown. Discard the rinds.

Break the eggs into a bowl. Add the milk and cream and beat well. Add the cheese and season with a little salt, pepper and nutmeg.

Roll out the pastry dough and use to line a 17.5 cm/7 in fluted flan tin. Bake the pastry case blind for 10–12 minutes.

Arrange the pieces of bacon on the bottom of the pastry case. Pour in all the melted bacon fat and the egg mixture. Put the tart in the middle of the oven and bake for 10 minutes. Then lower the heat to 190°C/375°F, gas mark 5, and bake for a further 25–30 minutes or until the filling is puffy and browned.

TART FILLINGS

Open tarts, often called quiches, can be filled with a great variety of ingredients. Here is a selection of some of the more interesting ones. The basic tart filling is made in the same way as the egg and bacon tart above, with 2 eggs, 150 ml/¼ pint milk, 3–4 tablespoons of cream and seasoning.

anchovy 16, 31
bacon 69–70
baking blind 404
blanch 422
button mushroom 161
cayenne pepper 201
cream 99–100
dissolving gelatine 423
hard-boiled eggs 322
lining a flan tin with pastry 403
olives 154–5
Parmesan cheese 103
watercress 130–1
whipping cream 423
Worcestershire sauce 206

pastry making equipment 237
sieves 226–7
soufflé dish 236

Consommé 250
Mayonnaise 259
Shortcrust Pastry 402

Eggs/Cheese

asparagus 137–8
aubergine 153
cheese 101–9
clarified butter 100, 423
leek 145
olives 154–5
plum tomato 150
saffron 199
skinning and seeding tomatoes 423
skinning peppers 423
Spanish onion 144
spinach 132–3
sweet pepper 152
tart case and basic tart filling 327

gratin dish 236
soufflé dish 236

Cheese The kinds that can be used are innumerable. Practically any piece of English cheese will be strong enough to make an interesting taste, provided it is neither blue nor just plain mouldy. Gruyère and Emmental are both good too, and grated Parmesan is an excellent addition to any other cheese – it seems to give a more pungent flavour. Perhaps best of all is a mixture of Parmesan and fontina, which melts into a delicious light and gooey mess.

Red and yellow pepper Grill and skin 1 or 2 peppers, then slice them. Add them to the basic tart filling with 55 g/2 oz freshly grated Parmesan and some chopped fresh basil.

Aubergine Add a fried sliced aubergine and 2 skinned plum tomatoes, also sliced and fried, to the basic tart filling with cheese and either fresh thyme or basil.

Spinach Add a handful or two of spinach wilted in butter and some grated goat's cheese to the basic tart filling. Season with 3 chopped spring onions.

Leek Add 2 sliced cooked leeks and a large pinch of saffron threads to the basic tart filling with 2–3 tablespoons grated Gruyère and some chopped parsley.

Spanish onion Fill the pastry case with a mass of thin onion rings cooked in butter and a little oil until they are very soft. You can add a few halved black olives too. Then pour over the basic tart filling.

PANCAKES

Pancakes can be stuffed with all sorts of fillings – both savoury and sweet – and then quickly baked.

SERVES 4 (MAKES 12)

- 140 g/5 oz plain flour
- a pinch of salt
- 1 free-range egg
- 300 ml/½ pint milk and water mixed
- 30 g/1 oz butter, melted
- groundnut oil or clarified butter for frying

Put the flour and salt in a bowl. Break in the egg and add a little of the milk and water mixture. Beat to a smooth paste, then pour in the rest of the milk and water mixture and the melted butter. Beat well to make a smooth, creamy batter. Allow to rest for half an hour or so.

Heat a 24 cm/9 in crêpe pan or frying pan, and brush with oil or clarified butter. Pour in a little batter and tip and rotate the pan so that the batter covers the bottom in a thin layer (don't worry about small holes). When the underside of the pancake is lightly browned, turn or flip it over and cook the other side. Slide the pancake on to a plate and keep warm while you make the remaining pancakes.

MUSHROOM-FILLED PANCAKES

SERVES 4

- 340 g/12 oz mushrooms
- 55 g/2 oz butter
- a squeeze of lemon juice
- salt and freshly ground pepper
- a pinch of grated nutmeg
- 30 g/1 oz plain flour
- 300 ml/½ pint milk
- 4 tablespoons double cream
- 12 pancakes
- 1 mozzarella cheese, weighing 115–150 g/4–5 oz, grated

Cut the mushrooms into quarters if small or chop coarsely if large. Melt half of the butter in a small pan and add the mushrooms with the lemon juice and a generous sprinkling of salt, pepper and nutmeg. Cover and simmer gently for 7–8 minutes.

Meanwhile, melt the remaining butter in a small saucepan, stir in the flour and let it bubble for a minute. Then add the milk, stirring it in gradually to keep the mixture smooth. Simmer for 5 minutes over a low heat, stirring from time to time. Stir in the cream. Add half of this sauce to the mushrooms.

Preheat the oven to 220°C/425°F, gas mark 7.

Place one pancake flat on a plate, spread some of the mushroom mixture over the top and roll up. Place in a buttered gratin dish. Repeat with the remaining pancakes, packing them into the dish in one layer. Sprinkle the mozzarella over the pancakes and cover with the remaining sauce. Heat in the oven for about 20 minutes or until bubbling and the cheese has melted.

ASPARAGUS SOUFFLÉ

SERVES 4

- 225 g/8 oz fresh or frozen asparagus
- 55 g/2 oz butter
- 45 g/1½ oz plain flour
- 300 ml/½ pint milk
- 45 g/1½ oz Parmesan, freshly grated
- salt and freshly ground pepper
- 4 free-range eggs, separated

Cook the asparagus in boiling salted water until tender, about 8–10 minutes according to thickness. Drain and keep on one side.

Preheat the oven to 200°C/400°F, gas mark 6. Butter a 1 litre/2 pint soufflé dish.

Melt the butter in a saucepan. Stir in the flour and cook gently for a minute or two, stirring. Gradually add the milk, stirring all the time, to make a thick, smooth sauce. Simmer gently for 5 minutes, stirring frequently to prevent the sauce from sticking to the bottom of the pan, and then remove from the heat. Add the cheese and stir it around until melted into the sauce. Season.

Cut the tips off the asparagus and set aside. Put the stalks and egg yolks into a blender or food processor and reduce to a light golden-green purée. Mix this into the cheese sauce.

Whisk the egg whites to a fine snow. Stir a heaped tablespoon of the whites into the asparagus mixture in order to lighten it, then fold in the rest of the whites lightly and thoroughly. Put half the mixture into the soufflé dish, scatter the asparagus tips on top and cover with the rest of the mixture. Bake for about 20 minutes or until well risen but still moist in the centre. Serve immediately, on its own or with melted butter.

ROQUEFORT SOUFFLÉ

SERVES 4

55 g/2 oz butter
45 g/1½ oz plain flour
300 ml/½ pint milk
140 g/5 oz Roquefort
a pinch of salt
cayenne pepper
4 free-range eggs, separated
1 free-range egg white

Preheat the oven to 200°C/400°F, gas mark 6. Butter a 1.5 litre/3 pint soufflé dish.

Melt the butter in a saucepan. Stir in the flour and let it cook gently for a minute or two, then add the milk gradually, stirring gently until you have a smooth, thick sauce. Cook over a low heat for several minutes, stirring frequently to prevent it sticking to the bottom of the pan.

Grate the Roquefort on the coarse side of a grater. Add to the sauce and let it melt. Roquefort is often quite salty, so taste the sauce before adding salt. Season quite highly with cayenne pepper. Allow to cool slightly.

Beat the egg yolks into the sauce one at a time. Whisk the 5 egg whites until they hold their shape and stand up stiffly on the end of the whisk. Stir a heaped tablespoon of the whisked egg whites into the sauce to make it a little looser, then fold the rest of the egg whites gently but thoroughly into the rest of the mixture until well combined.

Spoon the mixture lightly into the soufflé dish. Bake for 20–25 minutes or until well risen but still moist. Serve immediately.

SWISS FONDUE

Special fondue sets include long-handled forks, a stoneware or enamelled iron pot to hold the cheese and a little burner to keep the cheese hot and bubbling. If you don't have this arrangement, you can improvise with a plate warmer. Traditionally white wine is drunk with fondue, or hot, unsweetened tea as an aid to digestion – never cold water.

SERVES 6

2 garlic cloves
a wineglass of dry white wine
565 g/1¼ lb Emmental, or mixed Emmental and Gruyère or fontina, grated
1 teaspoon flour, preferably potato flour
freshly ground black pepper
a pinch of grated nutmeg
60 ml/2 fl oz kirsch
a drop of corn oil
plenty of French bread, cut into quarters lengthwise and then into 2.5 cm/1 in cubes

Crush one clove of garlic with the side of a knife, and rub an earthenware dish with it; discard the garlic. Pour the wine into the dish and add the remaining whole clove of garlic, peeled. Heat the wine gently. Add the grated cheese and sprinkle with the potato flour to ensure a smooth finish. Stir with a wooden spoon until the cheese has melted to a cream. Add a little more wine if it seems too thick. Add a pinch of pepper, the nutmeg and the kirsh mixed with the corn oil.

Carry the dish to the table and place it over a gentle burner. When the fondue begins to bubble, the guests can start dipping their bread into it on the end of their forks. Twist the forks round to prevent the cheese dropping off in long strings. When the bottom of the fondue starts to make a crust, those who like it can scrape this up with their spoons. Turn the heat down to prevent it burning.

MAROILLES CHEESE TART

Called *goyère* in France, this tart is made with Maroilles, a somewhat smelly cheese. Eat this as a first course, a light lunch or even instead of cheese at the end of a meal. It is wonderful with a good red burgundy.

SERVES 4

Shortcrust Pastry made with 170 g/6 oz flour
200 g/7 oz well-ripened Maroilles
200 g/7 oz fromage blanc
2 free-range eggs, beaten
salt and freshly ground pepper
butter

Emmental cheese 105
fontina cheese 105
fromage blanc 101
Gruyère cheese 104
potato flour 118
Roquefort cheese 108
whisking egg whites 423

blender, liquidizer 238
food processor 238
graters 224, 226
soufflé dish 236
whisks 227

Shortcrust Pastry 402

anchovy 16, 31
baking blind 404
courgette 156
filo pastry 422
goat's cheese 108
Gruyère cheese 104
lining a flan tin with pastry 403
mozzarella cheese 102
Munster cheese 107
pecan 188
ricotta cheese 101
walnut 188

graters 224, 226
pastry making equipment 236–7

Preheat the oven to 200°C/400°F, gas mark 6.

Roll out the pastry dough fairly thinly and use to line a 24 cm/9½ in flan or tart tin. Bake blind for 12–15 minutes or until just cooked through and set but not brown.

Cut the Maroilles into small cubes, discarding the rind. Beat the fromage blanc lightly, and incorporate the eggs. Stir in the cheese. Season, adding plenty of pepper but a very little salt as the cheese is salty.

Pour the cheese mixture into the pastry case. Bake for 15–20 minutes, then reduce the oven heat to 150°C/300°F, gas mark 2. Continue baking for 25 minutes or so, until the filling is puffed and golden but not set too firmly.

Dot the top with pieces of butter and serve at once.

ALTERNATIVES: If you cannot obtain Maroilles you can use another strong cheese such as Munster. Or you can use grated Gruyère, although this will change the flavour and character of the tart.

MOZZARELLA IN CARROZZA

SERVES 4

- 1 mozzarella cheese, weighing about 140 g/5 oz, cut into 4 slices
- 8 slices of white bread, crusts removed
- 8 anchovy fillets (optional)
- 3 free-range eggs
- salt
- oil for shallow frying

Cut each slice of cheese and each slice of bread in half. Make eight little sandwiches with the bread and cheese, adding an anchovy fillet to each one if you like. Beat the eggs in a bowl with a pinch of salt. Heat about 1 cm/½ in of oil in a frying pan.

Dip each sandwich into the beaten egg, then place in the hot oil. Fry until golden, turning them over as they fry so that they brown on both sides. Drain on kitchen paper. Sprinkle with salt and serve very hot.

GOAT'S CHEESE AND COURGETTE FILO TART

The size of the sheets of filo pastry govern the size of tart that you can make. Two small tarts will feed 4–6 people.

MAKES 2 TARTS

- 450 g/1 lb courgettes – preferably a mixture of yellow and green, grated
- salt and freshly ground pepper
- 2½ tablespoons olive oil
- 1 medium-size onion, chopped
- 1 garlic clove, sliced
- 100 g/3½ oz shelled pecans or walnuts
- 140 g/5 oz soft goat's cheese
- 140 g/5 oz fresh ricotta
- 1 teaspoon lemon juice
- 1 free-range egg
- fresh thyme leaves or dried thyme
- a few fresh basil leaves, shredded
- 10 sheets of good-quality filo pastry, defrosted if frozen
- 55 g/2 oz butter, melted

Put the grated courgettes in a bowl, sprinkle them with salt and mix them around. Leave for about 20 minutes, and then squeeze out as much juice from the courgettes as possible, using both your hands cupped together.

Heat 2 tablespoons of the olive oil in a small pan and soften the onion and garlic. In a separate pan lightly toss the shelled pecans or walnuts in the remaining olive oil and toast them lightly. Chop the nuts coarsely. Fork the goat's cheese, ricotta, lemon juice and egg together in a bowl. Mix in the courgettes, onion, herbs and half the nuts. Taste for seasoning; there may be enough salt from the courgettes.

Preheat the oven to 170°C/325°F, gas mark 3. Butter two 11 cm/7 in tart tins with removable bottoms.

Keep the filo pastry covered with cling film and a damp tea-towel while you are working with it, to prevent it from drying out and crumbling. Remove one sheet of pastry at a time. Lay the sheet across one of the tart tins and brush all over with melted butter. Repeat with a second sheet, laying it loosely over the first one so the points of the corners do not meet, and sprinkle with some of the remaining nuts. Continue adding sheets of pastry, laying them so their corners are at different points of the compass, and brushing with butter and sprinkling with nuts, until you have four or five layers of pastry. Tuck loosely into the tin: the edges of the pastry should hang over the sides. Fill the tart with half the goat's cheese mixture, then fold the edges of the pastry loosely over the top, so they form a crown with the inner leaves covering the filling completely. Make a second tart in the same way.

Bake for 45–50 minutes. Remove the cooked tarts, cover them lightly with a damp cloth and leave like this for 10 minutes. Then slip off the sides of the tins and transfer the tarts to a wire cake rack. Allow them to cool slightly, uncovered. Serve warm, with a crisp salad of lettuce hearts.

MOZZARELLA IN CARROZZA

Pasta

cooking pasta 335
cutting tagliatelle 334, 335
eggs 96–7
making farfalle 334, 335
making pasta shapes 335
making ravioli 334
pasta, noodles and dumplings 121–5
semolina 114
serving pasta 335
wheat flours 114

flour dredger 237
food processor 238
pasta machine 229, 239
rolling pin 237

FRESH EGG PASTA

Fresh free-range eggs are best for pasta making; battery eggs don't seem to have the right sticky texture or the golden yolks that give the pasta its lovely yellow colour.

SERVES 4–5 AS A STARTER

250–280 g/9–10 oz plain flour
3 free-range eggs

Put the flour in a bowl or on a board and make a well in the centre. Break the eggs into the well. Using the fingers of one hand like a fork, break up the eggs and start mixing in the flour. Continue drawing in the flour until you have a thick mass. You want to end up with a moist, pliable – but not sticky – dough that you can knead. There may be some flour left over, since eggs vary tremendously in the amount they will absorb. Allow to rest, wrapped in cling film, for 30 minutes

ALTERNATIVE: Make the dough in a food processor: whizz the eggs for 30 seconds, then add the flour and whizz for 30 seconds more.

TUSCAN PASTA

SERVES 4 AS A STARTER

225 g/8 oz plain flour
1 tablespoon olive oil
2 free-range eggs
1 tablespoon milk

Follow the method for the previous recipe.

Kneading and rolling pasta by hand

Wash your hands, if you have made the dough by hand, and clean the work surface if necessary. Dust it with flour or fine semolina. Cut the pasta dough into as many pieces as there are eggs in the mixture. Work with one piece at a time, and keep the others covered to prevent them from drying out. Using both hands, start kneading the dough, sprinkling on a little more flour if it gets too sticky. After 5 minutes or so of kneading, the dough should be really smooth and silky. Wrap it in a sheet of cling film and let it rest for half an hour, but not in the refrigerator – pasta does not like to get too cold.

There is a special technique for rolling pasta dough so that you stretch it at the same time. Always roll away from you, starting in the centre and rolling only the half that is farthest from you. Keep turning the sheet, lifting it on your rolling pin and rotating it by 45 degrees. As the sheet of dough gets larger, let the part nearest to you hang down over the edge of the table or counter – this helps to stretch it. Work as fast as you can: you must finish before the dough gets too dry and becomes unmanageable. As the dough begins to look thin, like a sheet of suede, increase the stretching action, rolling the far edge up around the rolling pin and pushing it away from you, running your hands from side to side over the dough on the rolling pin as you do so. Keep turning, rolling and stretching until the sheet of dough is so fine that you can see your fingers through it when you slip your hand underneath. The surface should be faintly textured like fine leather – this is what makes hand-rolled pasta superior to machine-made pasta, which has a smooth, slippery surface that doesn't hold the sauce so well or feel so sympathetic to the palate.

If you are using the dough to make tagliatelle, tagliarini or other noodles, spread it out and cover it lightly with a dry tea towel. Let it dry for half an hour, turning it over after 15 minutes, before starting to cut it. If you are making stuffed pasta, start cutting it immediately, keeping everything, except the piece you are working on, well covered with a slightly damp cloth so that the dough does not dry out, otherwise the edges of the pasta will not stick together properly.

Kneading and rolling pasta in a machine

Rolling out pasta dough with the help of a pasta machine is quick and easy, and gives excellent results.

Make sure the machine is very clean, and turn the rollers to their widest setting. Cut the pasta dough into as many pieces as there are eggs in the mixture. Flatten one piece into an oblong shape and feed it through the machine (keep the rest of the dough covered to prevent it from drying out). Fold the rolled piece of dough in three lengthwise, and feed it through the machine again. Continue folding the dough and feeding it through, doing this several times – this has the effect of kneading the dough.

Now move the rollers one notch closer together, and feed the dough through again. Move the machine up another notch and feed the dough through once more, holding it up in your hand above the rollers. As you gradually move the rollers closer and closer together, the pasta ribbon will get progressively longer and thinner. Continue until you reach the finest setting on the machine.

If you are making tagliatelle, tagliarini or other noodles, spread the dough strips out on the work surface, cover lightly with a cloth and leave to dry for 15–20 minutes. For stuffed pasta use the dough as quickly as possible before it becomes dry, keeping the strips (except the one you are working on) completely covered with a slightly damp cloth.

Making pasta

1 Put the flour in a large bowl and make a well in the centre of the flour. Add the eggs to the well.

2 Using your fingertips like a fork, break up the eggs in order to mix them. Gradually mix the flour into the eggs, to make a moist, pliable dough. The dough can now be kneaded and rolled by hand, or using a pasta machine.

flour dredger
237
pasta machine
229, 239

Fresh Egg Pasta
332
Tuscan Pasta
332

1

2

3 Turn the dough on to a lightly floured work surface. Cut the dough into three portions (or as many pieces as there are eggs in the dough). Work with one piece at a time and keep the others covered to prevent them from drying out.

3

Kneading and rolling by machine

1 To knead the dough, turn the rollers on the pasta machine to the widest setting. Flatten the dough and feed it through the rollers, then fold the dough into three.

2 Feed the dough through the rollers again. Do this several times, folding it into three each time.

1

2

3 To roll the dough, turn the rollers one notch closer. Feed the dough through again, but do not fold it into three. Keep moving the rollers together, one notch at a time, and feeding the dough through, rolling it gradually into a long, thin strip.

4 To cut noodles, leave the dough strip to dry until it looks leathery. Fit cutting rollers on the pasta machine. Feed the dough through the rollers, and catch the emerging noodles on your hand.

3

4

kneading and rolling pasta in a machine 333, 334
kneading and rolling pasta by hand 333
making pasta 333

knives 222–4
pastry wheel 225
ravioli cutter 225

Fresh Egg Pasta 332
Tuscan Pasta 332

Cutting tagliatelle *(right)*

Roll up the sheet of pasta loosely, like a Swiss roll. Using a sharp knife, cut across the roll at 5 mm/¼ in intervals. Unroll the little spirals of dough.

Making farfalle *(far right)*

With a fluted pastry wheel, cut the sheet of dough into strips 5 cm/2 in wide, then cut across the strips to make 5 cm/2 in squares. Pinch the middle of each square between your thumb and forefinger, to make a butterfly shape.

Making ravioli

1

1 Roll the pasta dough as thinly as possible. With a fluted pastry wheel, cut the pasta sheets into strips about 8 cm/3 in wide.

2

3

2 Put dabs of the filling down each strip, spacing the mounds of filling about 4 cm/1½ in apart and about 2 cm/¾ in from one long edge. Dampen the pasta dough around the filling, then fold the dough over the filling.

3 Press the long edges together, and press all around the mounds of filling to seal the layers of pasta together.

4

4 With the pastry wheel, cut between the mounds of filling to form the little ravioli parcels.

Making pasta shapes

Tagliatelle is pasta cut in narrow ribbons. They are eaten with all sorts of sauces – creamy, tomato or meat-based. To make tagliatelle by hand, roll up the sheet of pasta like a Swiss roll and slice across at 5 mm/¼ in intervals all the way along the roll. You will now have dozens of little spirals of dough. Unroll them and hang them on a cloth placed over the back of a chair. You can also cut tagliatelle by feeding the strips of dough through the wide cutters on the pasta machine.

Tagliarini is pasta cut in very narrow strands, a third the width of tagliatelle. They are usually eaten in soup, or sometimes with a creamy sauce. Tagliarini are usually cut with a pasta machine because doing it by hand is such a fiddly job. Fit the machine with narrow teeth and turn the handle, feeding in the dough one strip at a time. Use short lengths of dough or the tagliarini may stick together.

Pappardelle are long, wide strips. Using a fluted or plain pastry or pasta wheel, cut the pasta dough into strips 2 cm/¾ in wide and about 30 cm/12 in long.

Farfalle, butterfly-shaped pasta, are eaten with the same sauces as tagliatelle. Using a fluted pastry wheel, cut the dough into 5 cm/2 in squares. With the forefinger and thumb of one hand, pinch each square together across the middle in an even fold, to give a sort of butterfly or bow-tie effect.

Lasagne are large strips that are cooked and then layered with meat or vegetable sauces, cheese and béchamel sauce. The assembled lasagne is then baked until it is bubbling and browned. Cut the dough with a fluted pastry wheel into 10 x 25 cm/4 x 10 in strips.

Cannelloni are made from strips half the size of lasagne. These are cooked and then rolled up around a stuffing. The rolls are arranged side by side in a shallow earthenware dish, dotted with butter, baked and served with tomato sauce. Cut the pasta dough into rectangles 10 x 12 cm/4 x 5 in.

Maltagliate (literally, badly cut) are irregular pieces, about the size of postage stamps, cut from a sheet of dough with a knife. They are normally used in soups.

Cooking pasta

The amount of pasta to cook per person is, of course, based on appetite as well as on the sauce used to dress the pasta, but in general allow 115 g/4 oz of dried pasta per person if you are serving it as a main dish, less if serving as a starter. For every 450 g/1 lb of pasta, use 3.6 litres/6 pints of water and 2 level tablespoons of salt. Bring the water to a rapid boil. Put in the pasta all at once. Long spaghetti should be pushed down as it softens until only a little is left sticking out of the water. This is then pushed under the water with a wooden spoon. Stir the pasta for 1–2 minutes to keep it separate, then leave to cook. Boil spaghetti and other dried pasta for about 12 minutes and fresh pasta for about 4 minutes. When ready, the pasta will be *al dente*, that is, tender but resilient when you bite it.

Take the pan off the heat. To serve, either scoop out the pasta with special pasta servers or tongs and transfer it to a heated white earthenware bowl, or pour it into a large colander, shake it around to drain and then turn it straight away into a heated bowl. Leave a tiny amount of water on the pasta – if it is too well drained it will stick together. Sheets of lasagne and cannelloni should be removed from the boiling salted water with a fish slice, dipped into a bowl of cold water containing a teaspoon of oil and then drained flat on a damp cloth.

Serving pasta

Add a large knob of butter or, if you are having an oily sauce, 2 tablespoons of olive oil to the heated bowl, and mix it around to coat all the pasta. You can add some grated Parmesan at this point if you want to. Now add the sauce, or half the sauce, and mix it in briefly. Serve immediately in wide heated soup bowls. Serve any remaining sauce separately and provide a bowl of freshly grated Parmesan too (unless you have dressed the pasta with a fish sauce, which in Italy is never accompanied by Parmesan).

SALSA DI POMODORO

This is a domestic everyday tomato sauce of northern Italy, where every day means once or even twice every single day. Italians make enough to last a week and eat it with all kinds of pasta, with semolina gnocchi and with polenta. Freshly grated Parmesan is served alongside. In Italy the puréed sauce is very often heated in a frying pan until it bubbles. Drained pasta is then stirred around in it for a few minutes before serving.

SERVES 6

- 4 tablespoons olive oil
- 2 onions, finely chopped
- 3 garlic cloves, finely chopped
- 2 carrots, finely chopped
- 2 celery sticks, finely chopped
- 700 g/1½ lb fresh ripe tomatoes, skinned and roughly chopped, or a 400 g/14 oz can chopped tomatoes
- salt and freshly ground pepper
- 150–300 ml/¼–½ pint chicken stock or water (optional)
- 45 g/1½ oz butter

Heat the olive oil in a thick-based saucepan. Add the finely chopped vegetables and sweat until soft and starting to colour. Add the tomatoes and season with

olive oil 112
Parmesan cheese 103
skinning and seeding tomatoes 423
tomato 150–1

colander 229
fish slice 228
knives 222–4
pasta machine 229, 239
pasta pan 234
pastry wheel 225
polenta recipes 352
wooden fork 228

Chicken Stock 244
Fresh Egg Pasta 332
Gnocchi Romana 344
Tuscan Pasta 332

basil 192
cannelloni 121, 335
chicken livers 90
olive oil 112
Parmesan cheese 103
pigeon 83
pine nut 186
porcini (cep) 158–9
ravioli 124, 334
spaghetti 121
tagliatelle 122, 334, 335

blender, liquidizer 238
food processor 238
frying pan 234
Mouli-légumes 226
pestle and mortar 226

Chicken Stock 244
Fresh Egg Pasta 332
Gnocchi Romana 344
Tuscan Pasta 332

salt and pepper. Simmer for 1 hour, stirring occasionally and adding a little stock or water from time to time if the sauce becomes too dry.

Put the sauce through the medium blade of a Mouli-légumes, or purée in a food processor or blender. Add the butter and taste for seasoning.

ALTERNATIVE: Leave the sauce unpuréed.

PESTO ALLA GENOVESE

Serve this fragrant basil sauce stirred into hot tagliatelle or spaghetti (mixing in just enough of the pasta cooking liquid – a few spoonfuls – to make a smooth sauce), dot with little slips of butter and sprinkle with freshly grated Parmesan and coarse pepper. This makes a memorable dish, especially if the pesto has been made in a mortar and pestle and has a rather coarse texture.

SERVES 4

a large bunch of fresh basil, stalks removed
2 large garlic cloves, chopped
1 teaspoon coarse salt or a pinch of fine salt
3 tablespoons pine nuts
2 tablespoons freshly grated Parmesan
6 tablespoons olive oil

Tear up the basil leaves and put them into a mortar or food processor. Add the garlic and salt and pound or work with the basil leaves until you have a moist purée.

Shake the pine nuts in a cast-iron frying pan over a high flame until they are toasted to a pale brown. Add them to the basil purée and pound or process. Throw in the cheese. Start adding the oil drip by drip, pounding or working all the time, until you have a thick green sauce, glistening with oil, from which rises the most incredibly delicious smell, pungent and aromatic.

RAGÙ ALLA BOLOGNESE

The classic bolognese meat pasta sauce.

SERVES 6

3 tablespoons olive oil, or half olive oil and half butter
1 onion, finely chopped
2 garlic cloves, finely chopped
1 large carrot, finely chopped
1 celery stick with its leaves, finely chopped
225 g/8 oz minced veal or beef
225 g/8 oz minced pork
3 chicken livers, cut into small pieces
3 large ripe tomatoes, skinned and chopped
a large sprig of fresh thyme, chopped
salt and freshly ground pepper
150 ml/¼ pint chicken stock
a wineglass of red wine
2 tablespoons double cream

Heat the oil in a heavy-based saucepan. Add the onion, garlic, carrot and celery and sweat until softened. Add the minced meats to the pan. Turn up the heat and brown the meat, stirring to crush the lumps. Add the chicken livers, tomatoes and thyme, and season with salt and pepper. Cook until most of the liquid from the tomatoes has evaporated.

Add a little of the stock and red wine and stir. Leave the sauce to simmer gently for about 1½ hours, adding more stock and wine as it is needed, using water if you run out of these. When ready the sauce should be rich and smooth. Remove from the heat, stir in the cream and taste for seasoning.

SUGO DI CARNE TOSCANO

This exquisite pigeon and chicken liver sauce, fundamental to the Tuscan kitchen, makes a delicious change from *ragù alla bolognese*. It is ideal with spaghetti and tagliatelle, for stuffing ravioli and cannelloni, and with gnocchi.

SERVES 4

2 pigeons
2 chicken livers, coarsely chopped
1 onion, chopped
2 carrots, chopped
1 celery stick or 55 g/2 oz peeled celeriac, chopped
6 fresh basil leaves, chopped
4 tablespoons olive or groundnut oil
salt and freshly ground pepper
a large wineglass of red wine
about 300 ml/½ pint chicken stock or water
15 g/½ oz dried porcini
3 fresh or canned tomatoes, skinned and chopped

Cut the pigeons into pieces about the size of a large walnut, leaving the bones in – these are removed later. Put the pigeons and chicken livers in a medium-size saucepan with the onion, carrots, celery or celeriac and basil. Still off the heat, add the oil and a little salt and pepper. Put the pan, uncovered, over a brisk heat and fry, stirring from time to time with a wooden spoon. If the vegetables stick to the bottom so much the better, but don't let them burn. When everything is browning nicely, pour in the wine. Keep the heat very brisk. Scrape the bottom of the pan carefully to mix in the pieces that have caramelized on the bottom, and blend them with the wine. This is very important.

Continue cooking so that the wine reduces and loses its smell but doesn't totally evaporate. Add the chicken stock or water. Lower the heat, cover and simmer for 1½ hours or until the pigeons are tender.

Soak the dried mushrooms in lukewarm water until soft. Drain, reserving the liquid, and chop roughly.

When the pigeons are cooked, scoop the pieces out and remove the bones. Chop the meat coarsely – it is this that gives the sauce its character. Return the meat to the sauce together with the mushrooms and their soaking liquid and the tomatoes. Simmer gently for 15 minutes, stirring frequently and adding more stock a little at a time if necessary, to obtain a nice rich sauce. If the sauce seems too thin, cook it slowly until it has a rich, thick consistency.

ALTERNATIVES: Instead of pigeons use 225–280 g/ 8–10 oz rabbit, lean beef, or half beef and half chicken.

SPAGHETTI ALLA RUSTICA

This garlic and anchovy sauce provides a particularly fine way of eating spaghetti. It is important not to overcook the pasta as it does not have a thick, disguising sauce.

SERVES 4–6

- 3 garlic cloves, crushed with the side of a knife
- 6 tablespoons olive oil
- a 55 g/2 oz can anchovy fillets, drained and chopped
- 2 teaspoons dried oregano
- 450 g/1 lb spaghetti
- salt and freshly ground pepper
- 2–3 tablespoons coarsely chopped parsley
- freshly grated pecorino or Parmesan (optional)

Fry the garlic in the oil in a small saucepan. When the garlic has browned and smells nutty, remove and discard it. Turn the heat down as far as it will go. Add the anchovies to the garlic-flavoured oil and let them melt down to a mush. Stir in the oregano.

Cook the spaghetti in a large pan of boiling salted water until it is *al dente*. Put the drained spaghetti into a heated dish. Stir in the anchovy sauce, season and sprinkle with the parsley. Serve with plenty of pecorino or Parmesan if you like.

SPAGHETTI ALLA CARBONARA

SERVES 4 AS A STARTER

- 115 g/4 oz *pancetta stesa* or unsmoked bacon, in 2 thick slices
- 30 g/1 oz butter
- 2 free-range eggs
- 3 free-range egg yolks
- 115 ml/4 fl oz double cream
- salt and freshly ground black pepper
- 340 g/12 oz spaghetti
- 55 g/2 oz Parmesan, freshly grated

Cut the pancetta or bacon into little sticks. Heat the butter in a small frying pan and fry the pancetta or bacon over a gentle heat until brown. Remove from the heat and keep the pancetta or bacon and the fat hot. Put the eggs and egg yolks into a bowl. Add the cream and a generous quantity of black pepper and beat together.

Bring a large pan of salted water to the boil and cook the spaghetti until it is *al dente*. Drain it and put it into a heated bowl or return it to the hot pan in which it cooked. Stir in the pancetta or bacon and its fat. Next add the beaten egg mixture and turn the spaghetti over several times with a wooden spoon and fork until it is well coated. Lastly, mix in the grated Parmesan. All these steps must be done extremely fast so that the pasta can be served hot.

RIGATONI ALL'AMATRICIANA

SERVES 4–6

- 1½ tablespoons olive oil
- 115 g/4 oz *pancetta stesa* or unsmoked streaky bacon, cut into little dice
- 1 small onion, finely chopped
- a good sprinkling of dried chilli flakes
- a 400 g/14 oz can tomatoes, drained
- salt
- 450 g/1 lb rigatoni
- 55 g/2 oz freshly grated pecorino or Parmesan

Heat the olive oil in a saucepan. Add the pancetta or bacon and fry over a brisk heat until lightly browned. Remove with a slotted spoon and keep hot. Sweat the onion in the oil and bacon fat until softened, adding the chilli flakes.

Meanwhile, cut the tomatoes in half, remove the seeds and chop the flesh. When the onions start to brown, add the chopped tomatoes and season with salt. Cook for 10 minutes, stirring occasionally. Add the pancetta or bacon to the sauce.

Bring a large pan of salted water to the boil and cook the rigatoni until *al dente*. Drain it and put into a heated bowl. Stir in the sauce and then add the cheese, mixing it in well. The rigatoni should be a delicate pink – not bright red. Serve immediately, with more freshly grated pecorino or Parmesan if you like.

al dente 422
anchovy 16, 31
chilli flakes 201
cooking pasta 335
olive oil 112
pancetta 69–70
Parmesan cheese 103
pecorino cheese 103
rigatoni 121
serving pasta 335
spaghetti 121
sweat 423

colander 229
pasta pan 234
slotted spoon 227
wooden fork 228

al dente 422
breadcrumbs 364
Cheddar cheese 103
cooking pasta 335
globe artichoke 138
macaroni 121
making tagliarini 335
meat glaze 244
olive oil 112
Parma ham 69
Parmesan cheese 103
preparing globe artichoke hearts 139
serving pasta 335
zesting citrus fruits 423

colander 229
gratin dish 236
pasta machine 229, 239
pasta pan 234
wooden fork 228

Béchamel Sauce 255
Consommé 250
Fresh Egg Pasta 332

TAGLIATELLE ALLA PANNA

This recipe is extremely rapid and simple to make and is extraordinarily good. Parma ham will give a wonderful flavour to the pasta, but cooked ham makes a very good substitute.

SERVES 4 AS A STARTER

- tagliatelle made from Fresh Egg Pasta dough, or 340 g/12 oz dried tagliatelle
- 300 ml/½ pint double cream
- 45 g/1½ oz butter
- salt and freshly ground pepper
- a grating of nutmeg
- 115 g/4 oz Parma ham or cooked ham, sliced and cut into tiny strips
- freshly grated Parmesan

Bring a large pan of salted water to the boil and cook the tagliatelle until just *al dente*.

Meanwhile, put the cream and butter into a large saucepan and season with salt, pepper and grated nutmeg. Heat through.

When the pasta is cooked, drain it well in a colander or sieve and then put it into the pan with the cream and butter mixture. Turn it over until well coated. Add the ham and stir to mix. Cook over a gentle heat for 2 minutes.

Serve in a large dish accompanied by a bowl of freshly grated Parmesan.

ALTERNATIVES: Add a tablespoon of meat glaze or consommé to the cream and butter mixture (the jelly left in the bottom of the dripping bowl is perfect). This will prevent the sauce from being too bland. If you wish, you can also put the pasta, mixed with its sauce, into a gratin dish, sprinkle the top with grated Parmesan and then bake until bubbling and the top is golden brown.

TAGLIARINI WITH FRESH ARTICHOKES AND GREMOLATA

This is the simplest of combinations, but most pasta dishes are at their best when made with the minimum of ingredients. Artichokes cooked this way are also excellent in a risotto.

SERVES 4 AS A STARTER

- grated zest and juice of 1 lemon
- 4 garlic cloves, thinly sliced
- 2 tablespoons chopped parsley
- 8 large artichoke hearts
- 4 tablespoons olive oil
- salt and freshly ground black pepper
- tagliarini made from Fresh Egg Pasta dough, or 250 g/9 oz dried tagliolini
- 2–3 tablespoons extra virgin olive oil
- freshly grated Parmesan

Preheat the oven to 130°C/250°F, gas mark ½, and put a large bowl and four serving plates in the oven to warm. Mix together the lemon zest, garlic and parsley. Set this *gremolata* aside.

Slice the artichoke hearts thinly. Heat the olive oil in a large frying pan, put in the sliced artichokes and fry until golden. Season with salt and pepper, and continue to cook for another minute or two. Squeeze in the lemon juice. Place the pan in the low oven, with the door ajar, to keep warm.

Cook the pasta in a large pan of boiling salted water until *al dente*. Drain well, and tip into the heated bowl. Add the extra virgin olive oil and plenty of black pepper and toss well. Divide the pasta among the four hot plates. Top each serving with artichokes, sprinkle over the *gremolata* and serve immediately. Hand the Parmesan separately.

MACARONI CHEESE WITH HAM

The point with this popular Victorian English supper dish is to make plenty of sauce and not to put in too great a quantity of macaroni, so that the result is moist and succulent.

SERVES 3–4

- 115 g/4 oz macaroni
- 45 g/1½ oz butter
- 30 g/1 oz plain flour
- 450 ml/¾ pint creamy milk
- salt and freshly ground pepper
- a pinch of grated nutmeg
- 115 g/4 oz Cheddar, grated
- 55 g/2 oz lean ham, chopped
- 30 g/1 oz fine home-made breadcrumbs

Preheat the oven to 190°C/375°F, gas mark 5.

Bring a pan of salted water to the boil and cook the macaroni until almost *al dente*. Don't overcook it or it will go flat and will not absorb the sauce. Meanwhile, make a béchamel sauce with 30 g/1 oz butter, the flour and milk. Season with salt, pepper and grated nutmeg. Add the cheese and ham and stir until the cheese has melted. Drain the macaroni and mix into the sauce. Taste for seasoning.

Pour the mixture into a buttered baking dish. Sprinkle the top with the breadcrumbs and dot all over with pieces of the remaining butter. Bake for about 20 minutes or until the top is golden brown.

PENNE WITH HAM AND TOMATO SAUCE

SERVES 4

1 small onion
1 celery stick
1 carrot
2 tablespoons olive oil or 15 g/½ oz lard
85 g/3 oz cooked ham, cut into little strips
a small wineglass of red wine
450 g/1 lb ripe tomatoes, chopped, or a 400 g/14 oz can chopped tomatoes
2 tablespoons tomato purée
a pinch each of dried marjoram and thyme
salt and freshly ground pepper
340 g/12 oz penne
85 g/3 oz Parmesan, freshly grated

Chop the onion, celery and carrot together finely to make a *battuto* (a mixture of chopped vegetables). Heat the oil or lard in a saucepan and lightly brown the *battuto*, stirring. Add the ham and stir it around for a few minutes. Then add the wine and let it reduce until it has almost all evaporated. Stir in the tomatoes, tomato purée and herbs, and season with salt and pepper. Bring to the boil. Turn down the heat and simmer for 30 minutes.

Drop the penne into a large pan of boiling salted water and cook until *al dente*. Drain and put into a heated bowl. Mix in 3 or 4 tablespoons of Parmesan and stir in half the sauce. Serve the remaining sauce and cheese separately.

PAPPARDELLE WITH HARE SAUCE

This rich hare sauce is traditionally served with the wide pasta strips called pappardelle.

SERVES 4

565 g/1¼ lb hare on the bone
5 tablespoons olive oil
115 g/4 oz butter
1 celery stick, finely chopped
1 onion, finely chopped
1 carrot, finely chopped
2 thick slices of *pancetta stesa* or 2 rashers of unsmoked streaky bacon, cut into strips
salt and freshly ground pepper
1 bay leaf
1 tablespoon plain flour
450 ml/¾ pint dry red wine
1 tablespoon tomato purée
pappardelle made from fresh Tuscan Pasta dough
85 g/3 oz Parmesan, freshly grated

Chop the hare into small pieces with a cleaver. Heat the oil and half the butter in a saucepan and put in the hare, chopped vegetables and pancetta or bacon. Add a seasoning of salt and pepper and the bay leaf. Stir over a brisk heat until the hare starts to brown. Sprinkle in the flour and stir it in, then gradually add the wine, stirring well. When this comes to the boil, add the tomato purée and stir to mix. Cover the pan and simmer for 2 hours over a gentle heat, stirring occasionally and adding more liquid if the sauce is becoming too dry.

Take the sauce off the heat. Remove the bones from the hare and put the meat back into the pan. Simmer the sauce for about 15 minutes longer, then taste for seasoning.

Meanwhile, cook the pappardelle in a large pan of boiling salted water until *al dente*; drain and put into a heated bowl. Dress the pasta with the remaining butter and the Parmesan. Pour the hare sauce over the top and serve at once.

LASAGNE AL FORNO

SERVES 6

4 tablespoons olive oil
2 onions, chopped
450 g/1 lb minced beef
225 g/8 oz minced pork
340 g/12 oz fresh tomatoes, skinned and roughly chopped, or a 400 g/14 oz can chopped tomatoes
3 garlic cloves, crushed
1 heaped teaspoon dried oregano
1 heaped teaspoon dried basil
150–300 ml/¼–½ pint chicken or beef stock (optional)
salt and freshly ground pepper
lasagne made from Fresh Egg Pasta dough, or 225 g/8 oz dried lasagne
900 ml/1½ pints milk
1 bay leaf
85 g/3 oz butter
85 g/3 oz plain flour
a pinch of grated nutmeg
450 g/1 lb mozzarella, grated
85 g/3 oz Parmesan, freshly grated

Heat the oil in a large saucepan. Add the onions and sweat them until soft and translucent. Add the minced meats and fry until crumbly, stirring to break up lumps. Add the tomatoes to the pan with the garlic and herbs and let them soften. If they do not make enough liquid to cook the meat in, gradually add a little stock, but always a bit less than you think you

al dente 422
cooking pasta 335
hare 79–80
making lasagne 335
making pappardelle 335
mozzarella cheese 102
Parmesan cheese 103
penne 121
serving pasta 335
skinning and seeding tomatoes 423
sweat 423
tomato 150–1
tomato purée 206

colander 229
cleaver 222
pasta machine 229, 239
pasta pan 234
wooden fork 228

Chicken Stock 244
Golden Veal or Beef Stock 244
Fresh Egg Pasta 332
Tuscan Pasta 332

al dente 422
cooking pasta 335
field mushroom 159
lasagne 122
pancetta 69–70
Parmesan cheese 103
preparing globe artichoke hearts 139
sage 193–4
sautéed artichoke hearts 338
serving pasta 335

fish slice 228
gratin dish 236

might need – you can add more later if necessary. Season with salt and pepper. Cook gently for about 1 hour, stirring from time to time.

Preheat the oven to 180°C/350°F, gas mark 4.

Cook the lasagne in a large pan of boiling salted water until almost *al dente*. Remove, dip into a mixture of water and oil, and leave to drain on a damp cloth.

Put the milk in a small saucepan with the bay leaf and infuse over a gentle heat for a few minutes; discard the bay leaf. Make a béchamel sauce with the butter, flour and warmed milk. Season with nutmeg, salt and pepper.

When everything is ready, assemble the lasagne in a buttered wide gratin dish or casserole: put a layer of about one-third of the meat sauce on the bottom, then add a layer of one-third of the béchamel, a layer of half the mozzarella and half the Parmesan, and a layer of half the lasagne. Add more meat sauce, more béchamel and the rest of the lasagne. Then make layers of the remaining meat sauce and béchamel, and finish with the rest of the grated cheeses. Bake for about 45 minutes or until browned on top.

LASAGNE WITH MUSHROOMS, BACON AND ARTICHOKES

LASAGNE WITH MUSHROOMS, BACON AND ARTICHOKES

This is deceptively rich and constitutes a meal in itself, served with a crisp, lightly dressed green salad.

SERVES 6

140 g/5 oz dried lasagne (about 6 sheets)
450 g/1 lb large, flat black field mushrooms
2–3 tablespoons olive oil
juice of ½ lemon
2 garlic cloves, sliced
170 g/6 oz sliced *pancetta stesa* or unsmoked streaky bacon rashers
1 tablespoon chopped fresh oregano
6 artichoke hearts, sliced and sautéed in olive oil
2–3 tablespoons freshly grated Parmesan
85 g/3 oz butter
8–10 fresh sage leaves

For the béchamel sauce:
600 ml/1 pint milk
3 cloves
1 onion, chopped
2 bay leaves
salt and freshly ground pepper
55 g/2 oz butter
55 g/2 oz plain flour
150 ml/¼ pint single cream
a pinch of freshly grated nutmeg

Make the béchamel sauce, first warming the milk and infusing it with the cloves, onion, bay leaves and a little salt for about 30 minutes. Add the cream and nutmeg to the sauce. Taste for seasoning and simmer very gently for a further 5 minutes. Cover to prevent a skin from forming, set aside and keep warm.

Preheat the oven to 200°C/400°F, gas mark 6. Preheat the grill.

Cook the sheets of lasagne in boiling salted water until almost *al dente*. Remove, dip into a mixture of oil and water, and spread out on a damp cloth to drain.

Arrange the mushrooms in a roasting tin in which they will just fit, tightly packed. Drizzle a little olive oil over each mushroom and sprinkle with the lemon juice. Tuck the garlic slices under the mushrooms and season with salt and pepper. Bake for 30–40 minutes or until well cooked. Leave to cool, then slice the mushrooms in half horizontally. While the mushrooms are cooking, carefully grill the pancetta or bacon until crisp.

To assemble the lasagne, take a rectangular metal tin or shallow plastic box measuring at least 30 x 20 cm/12 x 8 in. Spread a thin smear of béchamel over the bottom. Make a layer of one-third of the lasagne and coat thinly with béchamel. Sprinkle on half of the oregano and cover with half the mushrooms. Add a little more béchamel, then half the pancetta or bacon and half the sliced artichoke hearts. Cover with a second layer of lasagne. Repeat the layers, ending with one of lasagne, well covered with béchamel. Cover the surface with cling film and refrigerate for at least 6 hours or overnight.

When ready to cook, preheat the oven to 200°C/400°F, gas mark 6.

With a sharp knife, cut the lasagne into six equal portions. Carefully lift out each one with a fish slice and place it on a baking sheet, spacing the portions well apart. Evenly sprinkle the surface of each with Parmesan. Bake for 30 minutes or until the tops are bubbling and golden.

Meanwhile, melt the butter in a frying pan until foaming, and fry the sage leaves until crisp. Season with a little salt.

Transfer the lasagne portions to individual heated plates and spoon over the sage leaves and butter. Hand more Parmesan separately if you wish.

ALTERNATIVE: Made without pancetta or bacon, this lasagne is a perfect dish for vegetarians.

CRESPOLINI

This dish is time-consuming to make, with its three separate components, but the light and delicate result makes the effort well worth while.

SERVES 4

For the meat sauce:
1–2 tablespoons olive oil
1 onion, finely chopped
225 g/8 oz minced pork
225 g/8 oz minced veal
2 garlic cloves, sliced
150 ml/¼ pint red wine
1 heaped teaspoon chopped fresh thyme
340 g/12 oz fresh tomatoes, skinned and chopped, or a 400 g/14 oz can chopped tomatoes
salt and freshly ground pepper

For the pancakes:
140 g/5 oz plain flour
a pinch of salt
2 free-range eggs
300 ml/½ pint milk
1 tablespoon brandy
15 g/½ oz butter, melted
olive oil for frying

For the cheese sauce:
15–20 g/½–¾ oz butter
15 g/½ oz plain flour
450 ml/¾ pint milk, heated
1 large or 2 small bay leaves
1 blade of mace
salt and freshly ground pepper
30 g/1 oz each Parmesan and mozzarella, freshly grated

Start by making the meat sauce. Heat the oil in a saucepan and sweat the onion until softened. Add the meat, turn up the heat as high as it will go and let it fry for 1–2 minutes. Stir it well, then let it fry again. Repeat this until the meat is well browned and there is a good brown crust forming on the bottom of the pan. Add the garlic, wine and thyme. Stir well and let it bubble up. Add the tomatoes, and season with salt and pepper. Leave to simmer gently, uncovered, for about 1 hour, adding more liquid (wine, stock or water) if the sauce becomes too dry.

al dente 422
cooking pasta 335
infuse 422
mace 198
mozzarella cheese 102
Parmesan cheese 103
skinning and seeding tomatoes 423
sweat 423
thyme 194
tomato 150–1

fish slice 228
pasta pan 234
roasting tin 236

Béchamel Sauce 255

basil 192
cannelloni 335
cooking pasta 335
field mushroom 159
flat-leaf parsley 190
Parmesan cheese 103
porcini (cep) 158–9
ricotta cheese 101
sage 193–4
serving pasta 335

colander 229
electric mixers 238, 239
food processor 238
frying pan 234
gratin dish 236
pasta pan 234
pasta machine 229, 239
ravioli cutter 225

Fresh Egg Pasta 332
Pancakes 328

To make the pancake batter, sift the flour and salt into a bowl. Add the eggs and beat them in. Gradually add the milk, beating well to get rid of the lumps before the mixture gets too thick. You can most easily do this with an electric mixer on a low speed. Add the brandy and melted butter and beat well. Set aside for 30 minutes to an hour.

While the batter is resting, make the cheese sauce. Melt the butter in a thick-bottomed saucepan and stir in the flour. When it begins to seethe around the edges, gradually stir in the heated milk. (This is a very thin béchamel, the consistency of pouring cream.) Drop in the bay leaves and blade of mace and season with salt and pepper. Leave the sauce to cook for about 5 minutes, stirring from time to time. Discard the bay leaves and mace, and add the cheeses. Stir until melted and smooth. Keep the sauce warm until you need it.

Preheat the oven to 220°C/425°F, gas mark 7. Butter an oval gratin dish, about 30 x 20 cm/12 x 8 in.

Using an oiled 18 cm/7 in frying pan, fry 2–3 small, thin pancakes for each person. Keep them warm until all are made. (It is best to leave the making of the pancakes to the last, so they will not have time to become soggy. They should be tender and light.)

Lay a pancake flat in the buttered gratin dish. Spoon a line of meat sauce along the middle and roll up the pancake. Place it at one end of the dish. Stuff all the pancakes in this way, arranging them side by side in the dish. Ten pancakes will fit into a dish of this size. When the dish is full, pour the cheese sauce all over the top. Bake for about 30 minutes or until bubbling and the top is brown.

ALTERNATIVE: Use cannelloni instead of pancakes.

RAVIOLI CON FUNGHI PORCINI

SERVES 4

Fresh Egg Pasta dough
115 g/4 oz butter
3 large garlic cloves, sliced
15–20 fresh sage leaves
freshly grated Parmesan

For the filling:

55 g/2 oz dried porcini
55 g/2 oz butter
1 onion, chopped
3 garlic cloves, chopped
115 g/4 oz flat field mushrooms, chopped
115 g/4 oz fresh ricotta
a small bunch of fresh flat-leaf parsley, chopped
salt and freshly ground pepper

Soak the porcini in 300 ml/½ pint warm water for 30 minutes. Drain and chop them.

Melt the butter in a frying pan and fry the onion until golden brown. Add the garlic and cook for another minute or two. Put in both kinds of mushrooms and stew over a gentle heat for 20 minutes or until any excess moisture has evaporated and the mushrooms are slightly coloured. Tip on to a plate to cool.

Put the mushroom mixture in a food processor with the ricotta, parsley and salt and pepper to taste. Process briefly until coarsely chopped, then scrape into a bowl and set aside.

Roll out the pasta dough as thinly as you dare. Cut into 6 cm/2½ in squares. Place a scant teaspoon of filling in the centre of half of the squares. Dab a little water around the edges with your finger and top each with another square of pasta. Press the edges together to seal. (Don't worry if you have more pasta than you need; it freezes well.)

Bring a large pan of salted water to the boil. Add half of the ravioli and cook for about 5 minutes; the best way to test if they are done is to pinch the edge of one with your fingers for tenderness. Drain and keep the first batch of cooked ravioli warm in a steamer or covered with foil in a low oven while you cook the remaining ravioli.

Put the ravioli in a large heated serving dish. Melt the butter in a frying pan, toss in the garlic slices and cook until the garlic is pale golden brown. Add the sage leaves and fry until crisp. Spoon the mixture over the ravioli and serve immediately. Hand round the grated Parmesan separately.

SPINACH AND RICOTTA RAVIOLI

SERVES 4

Fresh Egg Pasta dough
freshly grated Parmesan

For the filling:

450 g/1 lb spinach
140 g/5 oz ricotta or curd cheese
4 tablespoons freshly grated Parmesan
10 fresh basil leaves, finely chopped
¼ teaspoon grated nutmeg
salt and freshly ground pepper

For the sauce:

150 ml/¼ pint single cream
30 g/1 oz butter
salt and freshly ground pepper

Ravioli con Funghi Porcini

blanch 422
cooking pasta 335
making ravioli 334
nutmeg 198
Parmesan cheese 103
refresh 423
ricotta cheese 101
rolling pasta 332, 333
sage 193–4
semolina 114
serving pasta 335
spinach 132–3

gratin dish 236
pasta machine 229, 239
pasta pan 234
pastry wheel 225
slotted spoon 227

Delicate Tomato Sauce 256

To make the filling, wash the spinach thoroughly in several changes of cold water to remove any grit and dirt in the leaves. Put the spinach into a large saucepan and cook in the water that clings to the leaves until just tender. Drain well, then chop it finely. Mix with the cheeses, basil and nutmeg. Season with salt and pepper.

Roll out the pasta dough as thinly as possible – this is important with ravioli as it has a double thickness along the edges of each little square, and this would otherwise be too thick. Cut the pasta dough into strips about 8 cm/3 in wide. Put dabs of filling 4 cm/1½ in apart all down one side of each strip, 2 cm/¾ in in from the edge. Lightly dampen the dough around the filling with a little water. Fold the other side of the pasta strip over the top, so that the two long edges come together. Press down all around and in between the dabs of filling, sealing the long edge carefully. Cut between each little parcel.

Preheat the oven to 180°C/350°F, gas mark 4.

Bring a large pan of salted water to the boil. In another pan, heat the cream and butter together, and season lightly with salt and pepper.

When the water is boiling, drop in a few of the ravioli. Let them cook for 3–4 minutes, then remove them with a slotted spoon and transfer to a hot serving dish. Keep them warm while you cook the remaining ravioli. Sprinkle each layer of ravioli with the cream sauce before putting another layer on top. When all the ravioli are cooked and in the dish, pour the remaining sauce over the top. Heat through briefly in the oven.

Sprinkle the ravioli with freshly grated Parmesan and serve immediately. Place another small bowl of Parmesan on the table so that people can help themselves if they wish.

GNOCCHI ROMANA

In Italy this is eaten just as it is, without any sauce, because the flavour of the gnocchi is rather delicate and therefore can easily be overpowered. However, if you feel that it needs an accompaniment, serve with Delicate Tomato Sauce. Gnocchi can also be made from a dough of mashed potatoes and flour, in which case they are poached and then baked in the oven with butter and cheese.

SERVES 4–6

- 600 ml/1 pint milk
- 1 bay leaf
- 1 onion, peeled
- a pinch of grated nutmeg or 1 blade of mace
- 140 g/5 oz semolina
- 1 free-range egg yolk
- 55 g/2 oz Parmesan, freshly grated
- 55 g/2 oz butter
- salt and freshly ground pepper

Put the milk in a saucepan with the bay leaf, onion and nutmeg or mace. Heat very gently until bubbles start forming around the edge. Spoon the flavourings out of the pan as the milk comes to the boil, then pour in the semolina, stirring constantly. Stir well for 2–3 minutes or until it is really thick. Turn the heat right down, cover the pan and cook gently for about 15 minutes, stirring often. Take the pan off the heat. Stir the egg yolk, half the cheese and half the butter into the semolina mixture. Season with salt and pepper. Wet a large tray or oven dish with cold water, and pour the mixture on to it. Spread out the mixture evenly with the palm of your hand to about 1 cm/½ in thick or less. Leave to cool and set.

Preheat the oven to 170°C/325°F, gas mark 3.

Cut the cooled gnocchi mixture into 4 cm/1½ in rounds with a wineglass, re-forming the left-over bits with your hands and cutting more rounds until it is all used up. Lay the little gnocchi, slightly overlapping, in a buttered gratin dish. Dot with the remaining butter and sprinkle with the rest of the cheese. Bake for 30 minutes or until nicely browned.

ALTERNATIVE: If you are in a hurry, cut the gnocchi into squares or triangles to make a very easy dish.

SPINACH GNOCCHI WITH BUTTER AND SAGE

When the texture is just right, gnocchi is sublime beyond belief. Just like making good pastry, the secret of success is a light touch, so work quickly and do not over-process the mixture.

SERVES 4

- 700 g/1½ lb spinach
- 115 g/4 oz fresh ricotta
- 3 free-range egg yolks
- 125 g/4½ oz Parmesan, freshly grated
- ¼ nutmeg, grated
- salt and freshly ground pepper
- a little plain flour for coating
- 115 g/4 oz butter
- 16 fresh sage leaves
- 1 lemon, cut into quarters

Blanch the spinach in boiling water for a couple of minutes. Drain and refresh under very cold running water, then squeeze in a tea-towel until completely dry. In a food processor purée the spinach with the ricotta, egg yolks, 85 g/3 oz of the Parmesan, the nutmeg, and salt and pepper to taste. Spread the mixture evenly in a shallow tray. Cover with a sheet of cling film and place in the refrigerator to firm up for at least 2 hours.

Using two dessertspoons, form the mixture into small egg shapes. Roll these in flour. As you work, place the gnocchi on a floured tray.

Bring about 2 litres/3½ pints lightly salted water to the boil in a large saucepan. Reduce to a simmer, then drop in the gnocchi, about six at a time. Poach gently for about 5 minutes or until they are swollen and floating buoyantly on the surface. Using a slotted spoon, transfer them to a heated serving dish. Keep warm in a low oven while you cook the rest of the gnocchi.

Melt the butter in a frying pan and continue cooking until nut-brown. Add the sage leaves and turn them in the butter until slightly crisp. Spoon the sage and butter over the gnocchi and sprinkle with the remaining Parmesan. Serve with lemon wedges.

CHINESE EGG NOODLES WITH BROWNED GARLIC, CHILLIES AND PARSLEY

This is the ultimate quick dish for supper or lunch.

SERVES 4

- 450 g/1 lb Chinese egg noodles
- 6 tablespoons groundnut oil
- 2 tablespoons toasted sesame oil
- 1 head of garlic, cloves separated, peeled and thinly sliced
- 2 large green chillies, seeded and sliced
- a small bunch of fresh coriander, stalks removed, coarsely chopped

Cook the noodles in boiling salted water until just tender, then drain.

In a wok or large non-stick frying pan, heat the oils until moderately hot. Add the garlic and fry gently until golden brown. Add the chillies and stir around for a second or two. Tip in the drained noodles and toss with the garlic and chillies. Stir in the coriander, tip into a heated bowl and serve straight away.

ALTERNATIVES: Fresh flat-leaf parsley can be used instead of coriander and 2 teaspoons dried red chilli flakes instead of the fresh green chillies, to give the dish a more Mediterranean feel. If using parsley and chilli flakes, omit the sesame oil. You can hand freshly grated Parmesan with this if you wish. You could also use dried Italian pasta or home-made tagliatelle instead of Chinese noodles.

JAPANESE NOODLES WITH CHAR-GRILLED BEEF

Japanese noodles are best for this dish, but, failing these, good quality thin Italian pasta, such as tagliolini, will be fine. The garnish of chopped coriander is not traditional for this dish, but it goes very well with all the other flavours.

SERVES 4

- 2 sirloin steaks, each weighing about 225 g/8 oz, trimmed of all fat
- 6 tablespoons teriyaki marinade
- 1 tablespoon sesame seeds
- 340–400 g/12–14 oz Japanese wheat noodles, such as somen
- 2 sachets of dashi powder
- 6 tablespoons soy sauce
- 4 tablespoons mirin
- 225 g/8 oz bean sprouts
- 1 teaspoon dried chilli flakes
- 4 spring onions, finely sliced
- 1 sheet of nori, cut with scissors into 4 strips, then into thin matchsticks
- leaves from a small bunch of fresh coriander, coarsely chopped

Marinate the steaks in the teriyaki marinade for at least 2 hours, turning them occasionally.

Put the sesame seeds in a small hot frying pan over moderate heat and stir until toasted to a light brown. Tip them on to a plate to cool.

Prepare a charcoal fire, heat a ridged cast-iron grill pan or preheat the grill to hot.

Cook the noodles in boiling salted water until tender but still with some bite; drain and keep warm in a large bowl.

Make up the dashi according to the packet instructions, and keep hot.

Grill the steaks for 3–4 minutes on each side or until medium-rare. Leave to rest in a warm place such as a very low oven with the door open.

Add the soy sauce, mirin and bean sprouts to the hot dashi and stir well. Pour over the noodles and stir to mix, then divide among four warmed shallow soup plates or bowls.

With a very sharp knife, thinly slice the steak on the bias. Arrange one-quarter of the steak slices over each serving of noodles. Sprinkle with the toasted sesame seeds, chilli flakes, spring onions, tiny strips of nori and chopped coriander and serve immediately, preferably with pairs of chopsticks.

ALTERNATIVE: Use 240 ml/8 fl oz light chicken stock instead of dashi.

bean sprout 142
Chinese noodles 124–5
chilli flakes 201
chilli pepper 152–3
coriander 191–2
dashi 46
Japanese noodles 125
making tagliatelle (see Tagliatelle alla panna recipe) 338
mirin 207
nori (kelp) 46
seeding chillies 423
sesame seed 197
sirloin steak 53
soy sauce 207
teriyaki marinade 207
toasted sesame oil 112

barbecuing equipment 240–1
food processor 238
pasta pan 234
slotted spoon 227
wok 235

Chicken Stock 244

Rice, Grains and Pulses

blanching almonds 189
chicken 86–7
chorizo 78
clarified butter 100, 423
jointing a chicken 92
mussel 38
pea 140–2
prawn 35–6
preparing squid 47
saffron 199
skinning and seeding tomatoes 423
skinning peppers 423
squid 43

kettle 239
sauté pan 234
sieves 226–7

Chicken Stock 244

PLAIN BOILED RICE

If you soften the rice grains and remove some of their surface starch before cooking, it helps to prevent them sticking together. You can do this by soaking the rice for half an hour before you cook it, by rinsing it in a sieve under cold running water for several minutes, or by pouring a kettleful of boiling water over the rice, in a sieve, before lightly rinsing it. Prepared in any of these ways, rice cooks very quickly and very well.

55 g/2 oz long-grain Patna or Basmati rice per person
salt

Simply throw the rice into a large pan of boiling, well-salted water, stir it and let it boil for about 10 minutes. Test after 8 minutes to make sure that it is not already cooked. Drain it well and serve very hot.

BROWN RICE PILAU

SERVES 4

225 g/8 oz brown rice, soaked for 2 hours in cold water
55 g/2 oz butter
2 tablespoons olive oil
900 ml/1½ pints chicken stock
salt

Drain the soaked rice thoroughly in a wire sieve. Heat the butter and oil in a shallow saucepan or sauté pan. Put in the rice and stir it around for a minute or so until it is glistening and thoroughly coated with butter and oil. Start adding the chicken stock, a little at a time, stirring the rice around so that it absorbs the stock gradually and the grains remain separate. Add more stock as it is absorbed. Cook gently, uncovered, for about 40 minutes, stirring frequently and keeping the rice just moist. When tender, remove the pan from the heat, cover and let the rice steam for 5 minutes before serving.

PAELLA

SERVES 4–6

1 small chicken, weighing about 900 g/2 lb, preferably free-range
450 g/1 lb mussels
225 g/8 oz small squid, cleaned
2 pinches of saffron threads
1.2 litres/2 pints chicken stock
3–4 tablespoons olive oil
1 onion, finely chopped
2 garlic cloves, finely chopped
1 red pepper, skinned, seeded and cut into strips
225 g/8 oz tomatoes, skinned, seeded and chopped
340 g/12 oz Italian risotto rice
salt and freshly ground pepper
1 bay leaf
115 g/4 oz peas, preferably freshly shelled
12 cooked prawns in shell
a handful of black olives
1 lemon, sliced

Joint the chicken. Cut into 4 cm/1½ in pieces, keeping the drumsticks whole. Scrub and debeard the mussels. Put them into a heavy saucepan with 150 ml/¼ pint boiling water and shake over a brisk heat until all the shells have opened. Drain, reserving the liquid, and put to one side. Cut the squid body into rings and the flaps and tentacles into pieces. Soak the saffron in the stock.

Heat the olive oil in a heavy-based paella pan or wide, deep frying pan and sauté the pieces of chicken over a brisk heat until browned. Add the onion, garlic and red pepper and cook for 5 minutes to soften. Add the tomatoes, squid and the saffron-infused chicken stock. Bring the liquid to the boil. Add the rice, and season with salt and pepper. Spread everything out evenly. When the liquid returns to the boil, add the bay leaf. Turn down the heat and cover the pan (if the base of the pan is thin use a heat diffuser). Simmer very gently for 20 minutes or until the rice is becoming swollen and tender.

Stir in the peas. Place the prawns and mussels on top of the rice and the black olives all around the edge. Add the mussel cooking liquid. Cover again and cook for a further 5 minutes or until the rice is completely tender and the grains are separate. Serve with a slice of lemon on each plate to add a touch of tartness.

ALTERNATIVE: Add chunks of chorizo to the pan with the squid, in which case you may not want prawns.

PILAU RICE

SERVES 4

225 g/8 oz long-grain basmati rice
4 cloves
8 cardamom pods
a 5 cm/2 in piece of cinnamon stick
55 g/2 oz clarified butter
1 onion, cut into very thin rings
2 bay leaves
30 g/1 oz blanched almonds
55 g/2 oz seedless raisins
salt

PAELLA

button mushroom 161
Italian risotto rice 117
Parmesan cheese 103
porcini (cep) 158–9
saffron 199

frying pan 234
ladle 227
sauté pan 234

Chicken Stock 244
Golden Veal or Beef Stock 244

Rinse the rice thoroughly under cold running water and leave to drain. Bruise the cloves, cardamom pods and cinnamon stick. Melt 15 g/½ oz of the butter in a wide saucepan and fry the onion rings, stirring occasionally, until they are a deep cinnamon-brown. Lift them out of the pan with a fork and keep them hot.

Add the remaining butter to the pan and stir in the spices and bay leaves. Add the rice and cook gently for 7–8 minutes, stirring the rice around until it becomes translucent. Pour in about 450 ml/¾ pint of water and stir to mix. Add the almonds and raisins, and season with salt. Bring to the boil, then cover the pan and simmer over a gentle heat for up to 15 minutes or until the rice is tender, adding a little more water if necessary.

Scatter the browned onion rings over the rice and serve as an accompaniment to curries or spiced chicken.

RISOTTO ALLA MILANESE

SERVES 4

- 2 small packets of powdered saffron
- 1 litre/1¾ pints chicken or beef stock
- 2 tablespoons olive oil
- 55 g/2 oz butter or more
- 1 small onion, finely chopped
- 225 g/8 oz Italian risotto rice
- 55 g/2 oz Parmesan, freshly grated
- salt and freshly ground pepper

Dissolve the saffron in the stock in a saucepan and bring just to the boil.

Meanwhile, heat the oil with half the butter in a frying pan or sauté pan. Add the onion and cook until it is tender. Add the rice, stirring it around until it becomes a little translucent, but do not allow it to brown. Add a ladleful of the boiling stock to the rice. It will hiss and bubble violently, but will then bubble and simmer fairly quietly after this initial boiling has died down. Keep stirring all the time – this is an important part of making good risotto. When the rice has absorbed almost all the stock, add another ladleful. When this, too, has been absorbed add another, and so on, stirring continuously. The rice should never be really wet; adding the stock gradually allows the rice to swell and cook slowly, and the liquid becomes creamy with the starch released from the rice.

The risotto is ready when the rice is tender but still has a slight firmness to the grain; this will take 25–30 minutes. Stir in the Parmesan and the remaining butter. Season. Remove from the heat and allow to settle for 2–3 minutes before serving.

ALTERNATIVE: **Chicken liver risotto** Omit the saffron, and throw some chopped fresh sage leaves into the stock. Fry a few chopped chicken livers with the onion, and add 60 ml/2 fl oz Marsala or vermouth before the first ladleful of stock.

MUSHROOM RISOTTO

SERVES 4

- 30 g/1 oz dried porcini
- 3 tablespoons olive oil
- 55 g/2 oz butter
- 225 g/8 oz button mushrooms, sliced
- 2 garlic cloves, chopped
- 2 tablespoons chopped parsley
- 225 g/8 oz Italian risotto rice
- a wineglass of dry white wine
- 600 ml/1 pint chicken stock, boiling
- 30 g/1 oz Parmesan, freshly grated
- salt and freshly ground pepper

Soak the porcini for half an hour in 450 ml/¾ pint of hot water. Squeeze them dry, keeping the liquid to use when cooking the rice. (If there appears to be some grit in the bottom of the bowl, carefully strain the liquid through a coffee-filter.)

Heat the oil and half the butter in a large frying pan. Add the porcini and fresh mushrooms, together with the garlic and parsley, and fry until the fresh mushrooms have exuded some of their juice. Add the rice and fry it for a minute or so, stirring it around until it becomes slightly translucent. Pour in the white wine and let it bubble until it has almost all evaporated. Add a ladleful of the boiling stock and stir the rice until the liquid is almost all absorbed and becoming creamy. Add another ladleful of stock and, when that has been absorbed, add a ladleful of the liquid in which the porcini were soaked. Continue adding the stock and soaking liquid alternately, stirring the risotto continuously.

The risotto is ready when the rice is tender, with a slight firmness, and bathed in a creamy sauce. Stir in the grated cheese and the remaining butter. Taste for seasoning, adjusting as necessary. Remove from the heat and let the risotto settle for 2–3 minutes before serving.

PRAWN AND FENNEL RISOTTO

You must buy prawns in the shell for this recipe, as the broth is made from the shells. If you can obtain fresh or frozen raw prawns with their shells, so much the better, otherwise cooked prawns can be used quite successfully. Do not make the popular mistake of adding Parmesan to this risotto; it just does not work and is regarded as complete heresy in all Italian shellfish dishes! The Pernod, of course, is not an Italian addition, but it brings out the aniseed flavour of the fennel.

SERVES 4–6

700 g/1½ lb prawns in the shells, preferably raw (buy the size that gives 40–50 prawns per kilo)
5–6 tablespoons olive oil
a good slug of Pernod
½ bottle of dry white wine
a 400 g/14 oz can chopped tomatoes
a fresh bouquet garni
2 onions, finely chopped
2 large fennel bulbs, cut into thin strips
4 ripe tomatoes, skinned, seeded and chopped
200 g/7 oz Italian risotto rice
1 large garlic clove, very finely chopped
1 teaspoon grated lemon zest
3 heaped tablespoons coarsely chopped fresh flat-leaf parsley
salt and freshly ground pepper

First make the prawn broth. Peel the prawns and remove the heads (if they are still there); set the prawns aside. Heat 2 tablespoons of the olive oil in a large saucepan and fry the prawn shells and heads until pale golden. Add the Pernod and ignite with a match. Allow the flames to die down, then pour in the wine. Add about 600 ml/1 pint of water together with the canned tomatoes and bouquet garni. Bring to the boil and simmer for 40 minutes, skimming off any scum that forms on the surface.

Strain the broth through a colander into another pan. Put the prawn shells into a blender, add about 300 ml/½ pint of the broth and process for 30 seconds. Tip the mixture into the remaining broth in the pan. Bring back to a simmer and cook for 5 minutes. Then strain through a fine sieve and measure the liquid; you will need about 900 ml/1½ pints. Keep this at the merest simmer.

Heat the remaining olive oil in a wide pan and fry the onions and fennel until soft but not coloured. Tip in the chopped fresh tomatoes and cook for 10–15 minutes or until the mixture has reduced somewhat and is no longer wet. Add the rice and stir until well coated with the tomato mixture. Add a ladleful of the hot broth and cook, stirring, until the rice has absorbed the liquid. Add another ladleful of broth. Continue cooking in this way, adding the stock gradually, until the rice is tender but still has the slightest firmness to the grain.

About 5 minutes before the risotto is ready, stir in the prawns and cook gently until they turn opaque (or just heat through if they are already cooked). Add a final splash of broth, then stir in the garlic, lemon zest and parsley. Heat through once more, then check the seasoning and serve immediately.

ASPARAGUS RISOTTO

Ideally, this risotto should be made during the English asparagus season when 'sprue' (the very thin variety that does not come into the category of 'select') is available. It costs very little, but tastes just as good as the larger spears.

SERVES 4

450 g/1 lb asparagus sprue
900 ml/1½ pints chicken stock, made with 1–2 wineglasses of wine as well as water
55 g/2 oz butter
2 onions, finely chopped
200 g/7 oz Italian risotto rice
1 heaped tablespoon chopped fresh mint or tarragon
salt and freshly ground pepper
2–3 tablespoons freshly grated Parmesan

Cut off the top 8–10 cm/3–4 in of each asparagus spear. Cut these tips into three equal pieces and set aside. Remove any woody ends from the stalks and finely chop the tender green parts. Put in a saucepan, add the stock and bring to the boil. Cover and simmer for 20 minutes. Strain, discard the chopped asparagus stalks and return the stock to the pan. Bring it back to the boil. Add the asparagus tips and cook them for 3–4 minutes. Strain the stock again. Reserve the asparagus tips on a plate, and bring the stock just back to a simmer before you start cooking the risotto.

Melt the butter in a wide pan and fry the onions until soft but not coloured. Add the rice and cook gently until each grain is coated with butter and is slightly translucent. Add a ladleful (about 85 ml/3 fl oz) of the hot stock and cook, stirring, until the rice has absorbed the liquid. Add another ladleful of stock. Continue cooking in this way, adding the stock gradually, until the rice is tender but still has a little firmness to the grain. Just before it is ready, add the asparagus tips and herbs. Stir to heat through as the risotto finishes cooking. Add seasoning if necessary.

Traditionally, Parmesan is stirred into risotto before serving, but it can also be served separately. More butter can be added for an extra-rich result.

ALTERNATIVE: For a vegetarian dish, use vegetable stock instead of chicken stock.

asparagus 137–8
bouquet garni 190
fennel 137
flat-leaf parsley 190
Italian risotto rice 117
mint 194
Parmesan cheese 103
peeling prawns 41
prawn 35–6
skinning and seeding tomatoes 423
tarragon 190–1
zesting citrus fruits 423

blender, liquidizer 238
colander 229
graters 224, 226
ladle 227
sieves 226–7

Chicken Stock 244
Rich Vegetable Stock 245

acorn squash 157
chick-pea 127–8
chilli flakes 201
cooking pulses 423
courgette 156
couscous 114
cumin 199
French bean 142
harissa 201
skinning peppers 423

Six-Vegetable Couscous

SIX-VEGETABLE COUSCOUS

This can be made well ahead and kept in a cool place. Put the herbs on at the last moment.

SERVES 4–6

1 acorn squash, weighing 450 g/1 lb
225 g/8 oz French beans
4 yellow or green courgettes, sliced into 1 cm/½ in rounds
45 g/1½ oz butter
1 teaspoon salt
340 g/12 oz instant couscous
1 teaspoon cumin seeds
½ teaspoon dried chilli flakes
115 g/4 oz seedless raisins
2 tablespoons vegetable oil
340 g/12 oz chick-peas, cooked
10 spring onions, chopped
2 red peppers, skinned, seeded and cut into pieces
chopped fresh coriander
chopped fresh flat-leaf parsley

For the harissa dressing:

2 teaspoons harissa sauce
2 tablespoons lemon juice
6 tablespoons sunflower oil
2 tablespoons olive oil
salt and freshly ground pepper

Preheat the oven to 180°C/350°F, gas mark 4.

Bake the acorn squash for 30 minutes, then remove the peel, seeds and fibres and cut the flesh into chunks. While the squash is baking, cook the French beans in boiling salted water for 4 minutes; drain and refresh under cold running water. Steam the courgettes for 4–5 minutes, leaving them slightly crisp; drain well. Mix the dressing ingredients.

Put 340 ml/12 fl oz of water in a saucepan with the butter and salt and bring to the boil. Pour the couscous into the pan. Stir, then cover and remove from the heat. Allow to swell for 5 minutes.

Meanwhile, fry the cumin seeds, chilli flakes and raisins in the oil until the cumin seeds turn light brown. Return the couscous to a gentle heat and stir for 2–3 minutes to separate the grains. Stir in the cumin mixture, together with one-third of the harissa dressing. Put the couscous in a large dish.

Combine the French beans, chick-peas, squash, courgettes, spring onions and red peppers in a bowl. Spoon the remaining harissa dressing over the vegetables and toss gently. Arrange them on top of the couscous, and sprinkle the herbs over the top.

BURGHUL PILAF

One good way to eat this excellent pilaf is to put a pile of crisp lettuce leaves on the table and to scoop up the pilaf with the leaves, eating them both together.

SERVES 4

- 2–3 tablespoons olive oil
- 1 small onion, chopped
- 2 garlic cloves, chopped
- 225 g/8 oz burghul wheat
- 750 ml/1¼ pints chicken stock
- a pinch of cayenne pepper
- salt
- 4 tablespoons chopped parsley
- juice of 1–2 lemons
- 150 ml/¼ pint plain yogurt

Heat the olive oil in a large frying pan and sweat the onion until it is tender and a pale golden colour. Add the garlic and cook for a few minutes more. Stir in the burghul, coating it well with the oil. Add half the chicken stock, the cayenne and a little salt and bring just to the boil. Cover the pan and cook gently for 10 minutes. Add the rest of the stock, cover again and continue to simmer gently for a further 10 minutes or so.

Taste for seasoning. Stir the burghul, then remove from the heat and cover the pan with a tea towel and the lid. Let the burghul steam for 10 minutes longer or until it becomes light and separate. Stir in the chopped parsley and season well with lemon juice. Serve, hot or cold, with the yogurt.

TABBOULEH

Serve this garnished with olives and radishes, and with lettuce leaves or pitta to scoop it up.

SERVES 4

- 170 g/6 oz fine burghul wheat
- a bunch of spring onions, finely chopped
- 2 tomatoes, skinned and chopped
- 4 tablespoons chopped parsley
- 4 tablespoons chopped fresh mint
- 3 tablespoons olive oil
- juice of 2 lemons
- salt and freshly ground pepper

Put the burghul in a bowl, cover it with cold water and allow to soak for 15 minutes. Take it out by the handful, squeezing out the water as you do so, and put it in a clean, dry bowl. Mix in the spring onions, tomatoes, parsley and mint. Add the olive oil and lemon juice and stir. Taste the salad and add more oil or lemon juice if it is needed. Season.

BUCKWHEAT KASHA

Serve with meat dishes, especially pork and goose.

SERVES 4

- 250 g/9 oz toasted buckwheat (kasha)
- salt
- 2 tablespoons goose or duck fat, or 55 g/2 oz butter

Put the buckwheat in a saucepan. Add 600 ml/1 pint of boiling water and stir it around, then add ½ teaspoon of salt. Cover the pan, bring to the boil over a gentle heat and simmer for a few minutes. The kasha will become porridge-like. Stir in the goose or duck fat or butter. Continue to cook, covered, for about 10 minutes.

Remove the lid and fork up the kasha, turning it to separate the grains. Leave it to cook over a very low heat, uncovered, for about 1 hour, tossing and turning it over lightly with a fork every 5 minutes or so. At the end of this time the kasha will be light, separate and tender.

INDIAN MILLET

This dish makes a delicious and extremely healthy lunch.

SERVES 6

- 2 onions
- 55 g/2 oz butter
- ½ cauliflower, chopped into small pieces
- 2 courgettes, chopped into small pieces
- 225 g/8 oz millet
- 4 cardamom pods
- 1 teaspoon cumin seeds
- 4 cloves
- 2 garlic cloves, chopped
- salt and freshly ground pepper

Slice one of the onions very finely into rings. Heat half the butter in a large frying pan and fry the onion rings over a moderate heat, stirring occasionally, until they

buckwheat 117
burghul wheat 114
cauliflower 136
cardamom 199
clove 197
courgette 156
cumin 199
goose and duck fat 110
millet 118
mint 194
olive oil 112
parsley 190
skinning and seeding tomatoes 423
spring onion 144
sweat 423
yogurt 99

Chicken Stock 244

acidulated water 422
chive 190
cream 99–100
fontina cheese 105
Gorgonzola cheese 108–9
Parmesan cheese 103
poached eggs 322
polenta 115
reduce 423
truffles 161

potato peeler 224
ridged cast-iron grill pan 233
whisks 227

are dry and a nice deep cinnamon-brown. Remove them to a plate and keep them in a warm place.

Chop the remaining onion. Heat the rest of the butter in the frying pan and sauté the chopped onion with the cauliflower and courgettes until lightly browned. Add the millet, spices and garlic, and stir everything around for 3–5 minutes. Add enough water to cover and season with salt and pepper. Bring to the boil, then reduce the heat and simmer for 20–25 minutes or until the millet is just cooked through. During cooking stir and fork up the millet from time to time to help keep it light and separate.

Remove from the heat, cover with a tea towel and the lid, and allow to steam for 5 minutes. Then fork up again and serve with the brown onion rings scattered on the top.

SOFT POLENTA WITH BUTTER AND PARMESAN

Coarse-grain polenta has a flavour and texture that are quite different from the 'instant' type. Contrary to popular belief, polenta does not need to be stirred constantly for hours; 30 minutes cooking is usually sufficient. If possible, use a heat diffuser to prevent scorching.

Simply prepared with butter and cheese, this polenta is divine. However, although expensive, a fresh truffle shaved over the still-warm polenta transports the dish in the direction of the firmament.

SERVES 4

- 2 teaspoons salt
- 310 g/11 oz coarse-grain polenta, weighed into a bowl
- 85 g/3 oz unsalted butter, chilled and thinly sliced
- 1 small fresh black or white truffle (optional)
- 55 g/2 oz Parmesan, freshly grated

In a large, heavy-based saucepan, bring 2 litres/3½ pints water to the boil with the salt. Start stirring the water with a large whisk. Hold the bowl of polenta in your other hand and tip it to allow the polenta to flow into the water like sand in a fine, steady stream. Whisk continuously until all the polenta has been added to the water. Then reduce the heat as low as possible, or place the pan on a heat diffuser. Substitute a wooden spoon for the whisk and continue to stir the polenta often with this while it cooks gently for about 30 minutes. When it comes away from the sides of the pan, it is ready to serve.

Pour the polenta into a large warmed serving dish. Scatter the butter over the surface and shave on the truffle using a truffle shaver or potato peeler. Sprinkle over a thin dusting of Parmesan and hand the rest separately. Serve immediately.

ALTERNATIVES: Instead of topping the soft polenta with butter and Parmesan, stir them into the polenta; omit the truffle. Or stir in chopped ham, chopped fresh herbs and so on to flavour the polenta. Instant polenta takes only 5 minutes to cook, and is a good substitute when you are short of time

GRILLED POLENTA WITH POACHED EGGS, FONTINA AND CHIVE CREAM

Rather than eating polenta soft and unctuous, as in the previous recipe, you can leave it to cool and set firm, then cut into pieces and grill or fry them. Serve with a crisp green salad dressed with lemon juice and olive oil.

SERVES 4

- 310 g/11 oz coarse-grain polenta
- 1 tablespoon olive oil
- 300 ml/½ pint whipping cream
- a bunch of fresh chives, chopped
- salt and freshly ground pepper
- 4 very fresh free-range eggs
- 1 tablespoon vinegar
- 4 thin slices of fontina cheese
- 1–2 tablespoons freshly grated Parmesan

Cook the polenta as in the previous recipe, then pour it into a straight-sided rectangular tin or dish. Cover with cling film and leave to cool. When it has set, cut it into four squares.

Preheat a ridged cast-iron grill pan. Lightly brush the polenta squares with olive oil and grill until they are nicely charred on both sides. Put the pieces of polenta into an ovenproof dish just large enough to hold them snugly, but leaving a little room for the cream sauce. Keep warm in a low oven.

Preheat the grill.

Pour the cream into a small saucepan and reduce until thick enough to coat the back of a spoon. Add the chives and season with salt and pepper. Set aside. Poach the eggs in water acidulated with the vinegar, removing them just before they are completely done. Drain on a triple thickness of kitchen paper.

Place a poached egg on each polenta square, drape over a slice of fontina and spoon over the cream sauce. Place under the hot grill until the cheese has melted and is beginning to bubble, with specks of golden blisters. Sprinkle with Parmesan and serve at once.

ALTERNATIVES: Fry the squares, or smaller pieces, of polenta in butter until golden brown and crisp, then top with slices of Gorgonzola, or spoon over wild mushrooms stewed in butter. Fried or grilled slices or squares of polenta can be eaten with game and stews.

Soft Polenta with Butter and Parmesan

HUMMUS WITH TAHINA

SERVES 4

225 g/8 oz dried chick-peas, cooked and drained
2 garlic cloves, crushed
5 tablespoons tahina
juice of 2 lemons
salt
2 tablespoons olive oil
a generous sprinkling of cayenne pepper
1 tablespoon chopped parsley

Purée the chick-peas through the fine blade of a Mouli-légumes or push them through a sieve (this removes the skins). Alternatively, reduce to a purée in a food processor, and then sieve if you like.

Add the garlic to the chick-pea purée, and beat in the tahina, the lemon juice and up to 5 tablespoons of cold water. The aim is to make a fairly smooth cream, the consistency of thick mayonnaise. Add salt if necessary. Put the mixture into a serving bowl and flatten the top. Pour on the olive oil, then sprinkle with cayenne pepper and chopped parsley.

ALTERNATIVE: Stir in 1 teaspoon chilli powder and 2 teaspoons ground cumin.

ISRAELI FALAFELS

These are much enjoyed in the Middle East. They are sometimes served with a light sauce prepared from tahina, crushed garlic and water.

SERVES 6 AS AN APPETIZER

450 g/1 lb dried chick-peas, soaked overnight
1 garlic clove, chopped
½ onion or 2 shallots, chopped
½ teaspoon baking powder
4 free-range eggs
a large handful of parsley, finely chopped
1 teaspoon salt
4 teaspoons cumin seeds
½ teaspoon coriander seeds
oil for deep frying

chick-pea 127–8
cooking pulses 423
coriander seed 199
cumin 199
parsley 190
tahina 206

food processor 238
Mouli-légumes 226
sieves 226–7

black bean 126
broad bean 127
cardamom 199
chilli pepper 152–3
English mustard 202
haricot bean 126
lentil 128
long-grain rice 116–17
molasses and black treacle 211
navy bean 126
salt pork 70
seeding chillies 423
tomato purée 206

deep-fryer 239
food processor 238
Mouli-légumes 226

casserole 236

Drain the chick-peas. Put them in a food processor with the other ingredients, except the oil, and run the machine until everything is well chopped – the texture should be like moist, very fine breadcrumbs. Alternatively, you can use a Mouli-légumes. Allow the mixture to stand for about 30 minutes.

Form into small flat or round cakes about the size of a walnut – the mixture is rather crumbly but it will make cakes if handled carefully. Using a slotted spatula, lower the cakes, a few at a time, into a pan of hot oil and fry until a deep brown on all sides. Drain on kitchen paper, and eat hot.

ALTERNATIVE: **Egyptian falafels or ta'amia** Use dried white broad beans (*ful nabed*) instead of chick-peas.

BOSTON BAKED BEANS

SERVES 4

- 340 g/12 oz small dried haricot or navy beans, soaked overnight
- 30 g/1 oz butter
- 115 g/4 oz salt pork or streaky bacon, cut into thick slices
- 1 onion
- 2 tablespoons black treacle or molasses
- 2 tablespoons tomato purée
- 1 tablespoon made English mustard
- 1 teaspoon cider vinegar
- 1 teaspoon salt

Put the drained beans into a large saucepan and cover with fresh cold water, which should come 2.5 cm/1 in above the level of the beans. Bring to the boil and simmer for about 1 hour or until tender. To see if they are cooked, take out a spoonful of beans, pour off the liquid and blow lightly on the beans. The outer skin will curl if they are ready. Drain them, reserving the cooking liquid, and put them in a special bean pot or, if you do not have a bean pot, a heavy, deep casserole.

Preheat the oven to 150°C/300°F, gas mark 2.

Melt the butter in a frying pan and fry the slices of salt pork or bacon to brown lightly on both sides. Transfer them to the casserole or bean pot, together with their fat, and half-bury them in the beans. Push the peeled onion into the middle of beans. Mix the cooking liquid from the beans with the treacle or molasses, tomato purée, mustard, vinegar and salt and pour it over the beans. Cover the pot and bake for 2–3 hours, adding more water if necessary. Remove the lid for the last 30 minutes to brown the top.

MOORS AND CHRISTIANS

Beans with rice is a daily food of many Central and South American peoples. This is a Cuban recipe.

SERVES 6

- 170 g/6 oz dried black beans, soaked overnight
- 2 tablespoons olive oil
- 1 large onion, chopped
- 1–2 dried or fresh red chillies, seeded and coarsely chopped
- 1 small green pepper, seeded and coarsely chopped
- 1 garlic clove, chopped
- 115 g/4 oz long-grain rice
- 2 tomatoes, skinned and chopped
- salt

Put the drained beans into a saucepan and cover with fresh water to come 2.5 cm/1 in above the level of the beans. Bring slowly to the boil, then turn down the heat and simmer for about 1½ hours or until tender.

Heat the olive oil in another large saucepan and fry the onion until nicely browned. Add the chillies, green pepper and garlic and allow to sweat gently for 5 minutes. Add the rice and stir it around for a minute or two, then add the tomatoes.

Mix in the beans with the water in which they were cooked. Pour in enough fresh water so that everything is covered with liquid. Season with salt. Simmer for 15–20 minutes or until the rice is just tender. Add a little more water if necessary; the beans should be moist and bathed in a light sauce.

SPICED LENTILS

You can use any lentils, but the small brown ones are best here.

SERVES 4

- 55 g/2 oz butter
- 1 onion, finely chopped
- 2 garlic cloves, finely chopped
- 4 cardamom pods
- 4 cloves
- a 7.5 cm/3 in piece of cinnamon stick
- 1 teaspoon tomato purée
- 2 green chillies, seeded and chopped
- 225 g/8 oz brown lentils, rinsed
- ½ chicken stock cube
- 1 bay leaf
- salt and freshly ground pepper

Melt the butter in a saucepan and fry the onion and garlic until they start to turn golden. Add the spices and cook for a few minutes more. Stir in

Moors and Christians

the tomato purée and cook until the mixture is a rusty brown. Add the chillies and lentils. Pour in 450 ml/¾ pint of water, and add the stock cube and bay leaf. Bring to a simmer and cook for 20–30 minutes, or until the lentils are porridgy but hold their shape. Add more water if necessary. Check the seasoning and serve.

LENTIL DHAL

Dhal, or dal, is an indispensable companion for curry, but can also be a main dish, served with boiled rice or Indian breads. It reheats well; if it is too dry, add some chicken stock or water.

SERVES 4

115 g/4 oz lentils
600 ml/1 pint chicken stock or water
salt
½ teaspoon turmeric
1–2 tablespoons oil or melted butter
1 onion, sliced
3 garlic cloves, sliced
1–2 green chillies, sliced
½ teaspoon chilli powder
1 teaspoon cumin seeds
a handful of fresh coriander, chopped

Rinse the lentils in several changes of cold water, then drain well. Put it in a pan with the stock or water, a pinch of salt and the turmeric, and cook until tender. The time varies according to how you like the dhal – dry like rice or smooth and moist – and on the type of lentils you are cooking.

When it is almost cooked, heat the oil or butter in a frying pan and fry the onion with the garlic, chillies, chilli powder and cumin seeds until the onion is golden brown. Add the lentils and the chopped coriander. Cook over a low heat for 5 minutes, stirring constantly. Taste for seasoning, adding a little more salt if necessary.

chilli pepper 152–3
chilli powder 201
coriander 191–2
cumin 199
lentil 128
turmeric 199

Chicken Stock 244

Breads

breads 119–20
gluten 422
yeast 118
yeast dough recipes 358–62

bread machine 239

Baking bread

Baking bread is a craft – once you have learnt it, nothing could possibly be easier or more enjoyable. If you have never baked before, start with a brown wholemeal or wheatmeal loaf because making a good white loaf only comes with practice. (Wholemeal bread has a good, strong taste and the texture is expected to be dense or heavy, but in a plain white loaf texture is very important.)

Using yeast Fresh yeast is called for in the recipes here, although dried yeast can always be substituted. Just remember that, weight for weight, dried yeast is twice as potent as fresh (so where a recipe calls for 30 g/1 oz fresh yeast, use 15 g/½ oz dried yeast), and the directions on the packet should be carefully followed. When using dried yeast, reactivate it by dissolving it in a little tepid water with a pinch of sugar (to get the temperature of the water right, use one part boiling water to two parts cold). Add any more liquid called for in the recipe at the same time as you add the frothy yeast. Easy-blend dried yeast can be mixed with the dry ingredients, and then all the water added at once.

Kneading This develops the gluten and distributes the yeast evenly. Put the dough on a lightly floured board and, with a rhythmic, regular action, pull it towards you with bent fingers, then push it away with the palm of your hand and fingers closed. Continue doing this until the dough is smooth and elastic – about 5–10 minutes.

Rising and knocking back After kneading, the dough is put into an oiled or buttered bowl, turned to coat on all sides with oil or butter (so that it will expand and stretch easily as it rises) and left to rise, covered, in a warm place such as an airing cupboard or near a fire or central heating boiler. When the dough has roughly doubled in size it should be punched down with the fist to expel the air and then kneaded briefly until it is even in texture and returned to its original size.

Proving For this final stage before baking, the dough is shaped or put into tins, then allowed to stand again in a warm place until it is taut, puffy and well risen. Not all breads require this second rising or proving stage.

Baking To test if a loaf is cooked through, tip it off its baking sheet or out of its tin and tap it on the base with your knuckles. It should should hollow, like a drum. If it does not sound hollow, return the loaf to the oven, putting it on its side, directly on the oven rack, and bake for a further 5–10 minutes.

1

2

3

Making a yeast dough

1 If you are using fresh yeast, mix it with a little tepid liquid to make a thin cream, then leave it in a warm place until it froths. Ordinary dried yeast also needs to be reactivated in this way. Easy blend yeast can be added directly to the dry ingredients.

2 Put the flour and other dry ingredients in a bowl, make a well in the centre and pour in the frothy yeast mixture and the other liquids.

3 With your fingers, start mixing the flour into the liquid. (If using the 'sponge' method, mix in enough flour to make a smooth batter, then leave for about 20 minutes to allow the batter to become aerated.) Continue mixing in the remaining flour to make a rough dough.

4

5

6

kneading 356
proving 356
rising and knocking back 356
shaping a pizza base 358
shaping a round loaf 358
yeast dough recipes 358–62

loaf tin 237

4 Turn the dough on to a floured surface. Start kneading by pressing and then pushing with your palm, stretching the dough away from you.

5 Turn the dough over itself back towards you into a ball, then rotate it slightly, and press and push it away again. Continue the kneading.

6 After 8–10 minutes of kneading, the dough will have become smooth and elastic. Shape it into a ball.

7 Put the dough in a greased bowl and turn the dough over to grease all sides. Cover with plastic wrap and leave to rise in a warm place.

8 The dough will double in size. When it has risen enough a finger pressed down into the centre will leave an indentation.

9 Punch the dough to knock out the air, then turn it on to a floured surface and knead it briefly. The dough is now ready to be shaped.

7

8

9

1

2

Shaping a tin loaf

1 Pat and press out the dough into a flat oblong or disc a little longer than the length of the tin. Roll up the dough like a Swiss roll.

2 Tuck the ends of the roll under the seam side and place in the tin, seam side down. Cover and leave the dough to prove before baking.

baking bread 356
kneading and rising 357
making a yeast dough 356
molasses 211
shaping a tin loaf 357
sutstituting dried and easy-blend yeasts for fresh yeast 356
walnut 188
wheat flours 114–15

baking sheet 236
knives 222–4
loaf tin 237
rolling pin 237

Shaping a round loaf *(left)*
Form the dough into a large, smooth round and place it on a greased and floured baking sheet. Cover and leave to prove. Before baking, slash a cross in the top using the tip of a sharp knife.

Shaping a pizza base *(right)*
Roll out the dough to a thin round to fit your baking sheet or pizza pan. Transfer to the floured baking sheet or pan. Push up the edge all round with your fingertips to make a rim.

WHOLEMEAL BREAD

This bread is delicious, wholesome and nutty.

MAKES 3 LOAVES

- 450 g/1 lb wholemeal flour
- 700 g/1½ lb granary flour
- 225 g/8 oz coarsely ground wholemeal flour
- 1 tablespoon molasses
- 45 g/1½ oz fresh yeast
- 1 heaped tablespoon salt

Mix all the flours together in a large bowl and let them warm slightly for a few moments in a low oven. Mix the molasses into 900 ml/1½ pints tepid water in a measuring jug. Put the yeast in a bowl with a few tablespoons of the molasses and water and mix it to a thin cream. Leave in a warm place until it froths. Add the salt to the remaining molasses and water.

Make a well in the middle of the flour and pour in the molasses and water mixture. Add the yeast mixture. Mix thoroughly to a dough. Turn on to a lightly floured work surface and knead until the dough is smooth and elastic. Return the dough to an oiled bowl. Cover with a sheet of cling film and a cloth. Leave to rise in a warm place for 1–1½ hours or until the dough has doubled in size.

Prepare three 16 x 11 cm/6½ x 4½ in loaf tins, greasing them lightly with sunflower oil or butter.

Knock back the dough, then turn it out of the bowl on to a floured work surface. Knead it briefly. Cut it into three pieces. Knead one piece into a ball, then flatten the ball into a thick disc. Roll up the disc like a Swiss roll, tuck the two ends of the roll underneath and drop into a greased loaf tin. Shape the other two loaves in the same way. Cover the tins loosely with oiled cling film and a cloth, and leave in a warm place to prove. When ready, the dough will be puffy and risen almost to the top of the tin.

Preheat the oven to 220°C/425°F, gas mark 7.

Bake the loaves for 15–20 minutes, then turn down the heat to 180°C/350°F, gas mark 4. Bake for a further 40 minutes or until the loaves sound hollow when tapped on the base. After 20 minutes of this time, check that the loaves are not becoming too brown; if they are, cover them loosely with foil. When the loaves are cooked, leave them to cool on a wire rack.

ALTERNATIVE: **Walnut bread** Substitute about 115 g/4 oz coarsely crushed walnuts for some of the flour, mixing the nuts in well before adding the yeast and the liquid.

PLAIN WHITE LOAF

MAKES 1 LARGE LOAF

- 15 g/½ oz fresh yeast
- a pinch of sugar
- 450 g/1 lb strong white bread flour
- 2 teaspoons salt

Put the yeast and sugar in a small bowl. Add 3 tablespoons of tepid water taken from 300 ml/½ pint, and cream with the yeast until dissolved. Put the flour in a warm bowl, mix in the salt and make a well in the centre. Pour in the yeast mixture. Flick a little flour over the yeast and put the bowl in a warm place until the yeast froths and the flour on the surface cracks.

Add the remaining warm water and mix everything together to make a rough dough. Turn it out on to a lightly floured board and knead it well until it is smooth and elastic, adding a little more flour if it seems sticky. Form the dough into a ball and put it into an oiled bowl. Cover with a sheet of cling film and a cloth. Leave to rise in a warm place for about 1½ hours or until almost doubled in size.

Prepare a 20 x 13 cm/8 x 5 in loaf tin, greasing it lightly with sunflower oil or butter.

Knock back the dough once more, then flatten it into a thick disc. Roll it up like a Swiss roll and tuck the two ends of the roll underneath. Drop it into the loaf tin. Push down round the sides of the tin to give the top of the loaf a good shape. Dust the top with flour. Cover loosely with oiled cling film and leave to prove for half an hour or so, until well risen and puffy.

Preheat the oven to 220°C/425°F, gas mark 7.

Bake for 10–15 minutes, then turn down the oven to 180°C/350°F, gas mark 4. Bake for a further 30 minutes or until the loaf sounds hollow when tapped on the base. Cool on a wire rack, and eat the same day.

RYE BREAD

MAKES 1 LARGE OR 2 SMALL LOAVES

- 450 g/1 lb rye flour
- 340 g/12 oz strong white bread flour
- 2–3 tablespoons wholemeal flour
- 30 g/1 oz fresh yeast
- 1 teaspoon sugar
- 2 teaspoons salt
- 1 tablespoon plain yogurt
- 15 g/½ oz caraway seeds (optional)

Mix the flours together thoroughly in a large bowl. Cream the yeast with 150 ml/¼ pint of tepid water in another mixing bowl, add a pinch of the sugar and stir in 4–5 tablespoons of the flour. Cover and leave this sponge to rise for about 2 hours.

Stir the salt, yogurt and the rest of the sugar with 300 ml/½ pint tepid water. Make a well in the bowl of flour. Add the caraway seeds if you are using them. Pour in the foamy, well-risen sponge and the yogurt mixture, and mix to a rough dough with a wooden spoon. If the dough seems to be rather too sticky, add a little more flour.

Turn on to a floured board and knead well until smooth and elastic. Shape the dough into a ball and put it in an oiled bowl. Cover with a sheet of cling film and a cloth and leave in a warm place to rise for 3–4 hours – or, even better, leave it overnight.

Knock back the dough, then shape it into 1 large or 2 small loaves. Put them on well-floured baking sheets, and dust the tops with flour. Allow to prove for about 1 hour, lightly covered with a sheet of cling film.

Preheat the oven to 220°C/425°F, gas mark 7.

Put the loaves into the oven and bake for 15 minutes, then turn down the heat to 180°C/350°F, gas mark 4. Bake small loaves for a further 40–45 minutes and a large loaf for a further 1–1¼ hours, or until the loaves sound hollow when tapped on the base. Cover the loaves lightly with foil if they are becoming too brown. Bake for a final 5 minutes off the baking sheets. Cool on a wire rack.

BRIOCHE LOAF

Brioche is the lightest, richest bread imaginable. It is exquisite for breakfast and makes very good toast.

MAKES 2 LOAVES

- 30 g/1 oz fresh yeast
- 2 tablespoons sugar
- 4 free-range eggs
- 5 tablespoons tepid milk
- 2 teapoons salt
- 565 g/1¼ lb strong white bread flour
- 115 g/4 oz butter, softened
- beaten egg to glaze

Cream the yeast with 5 tablespoons of tepid water and add ½ teaspoon of the sugar. Leave in a warm place to start working and become frothy. Beat the eggs with the milk, salt and the rest of the sugar in another bowl, and leave in a warm place.

Warm a large mixing bowl and put the flour in it. Make a well in the centre and pour in the yeast and egg mixtures. Mix thoroughly to a rough dough. Turn the dough on to a clean work surface and knead until smooth, sprinkling on a little more flour if the dough feels too sticky and unmanageable. When you have a smooth ball of dough, cover loosely with cling film and let it rest for a few minutes before you start incorporating the butter.

This is a messy business, but all the butter will be absorbed eventually. Flatten the dough and put a few dabs of butter over the surface (about 15 g/½ oz or a bit more). Then fold up the dough and knead it well until the butter is smoothly worked in. Let the dough rest for a minute, covered with cling film, then repeat. Keep on adding butter, kneading and resting the dough as before, until all the butter has been mixed in. Let the dough rest again, then knead to a smooth ball and put into a buttered bowl. Cover with a sheet of cling film and a cloth and leave to rise in a warm place for 1½ hours.

Knock back the dough and knead it for a minute, then re-form it into a ball. Return it to the bowl, cover with oiled cling film and a cloth as before and leave to rise a second time for 1–1½ hours.

Butter two 20 x 13 cm/8 x 5 in loaf tins. Divide the dough in half and knead each piece into a round disc. Roll up the discs like a Swiss roll, tuck the two ends underneath and put into the buttered tins. Cover again and leave to prove until they are well risen and rounded.

baking bread 356
caraway seed 197
kneading and rising 357
making a yeast dough 356
rye flour 116
shaping a tin loaf 357
substituting dried and easy-blend yeasts for fresh yeast 356
wheat flours 114–15

loaf tin 237

Preheat the oven to 200°C/400°F, gas mark 6. Glaze the top of the loaves with beaten egg, then bake for 30–35 minutes or until they sound hollow when tapped on the base. Leave to cool on a rack, and eat warm or cold.

ALTERNATIVE: Form the dough into the traditional brioche shape: divide each portion of dough into a large ball and a much smaller ball. Put each large ball in a buttered fluted brioche tin, brush with beaten egg and set a smaller ball in the centre on top; glaze this with egg too. Prove and bake as above.

CORNISH SAFFRON BREAD

Saffron bread is particularly good with fish soup, and with shellfish such as potted shrimps, crab or mussels.

MAKES 1 LOAF

- 15 g/½ oz fresh yeast
- ½ teaspoon sugar
- 800 g/1¾ lb strong white bread flour
- 1 small packet saffron strands
- 1 small packet saffron powder
- 2 heaped teaspoons salt
- 1 free-range egg, beaten
- 3 tablespoons olive oil

Mix the yeast with 150 ml/¼ pint tepid water, the sugar and 7 tablespoons of the flour. Leave the mixture in a warm place until it is frothy and well risen.

Meanwhile, soak all the saffron in 300 ml/½ pint tepid water.

Warm the remaining flour in a low oven and put it in a large, warmed bowl. Sprinkle over the salt and make a well in the centre. Pour in the yeast mixture and add the beaten egg, the warm saffron-flavoured water and the olive oil. Mix with a wooden spoon to make a rough dough. Turn the dough on to a lightly floured work surface and knead thoroughly until smooth and elastic.

Put the dough into an oiled bowl and cover loosely with a sheet of cling film and a folded cloth. Leave to rise in a warm place until doubled in size.

Knock back the dough and knead it again briefly. Form it into a large round loaf. Put it on a greased and floured baking sheet and cover with a sheet of oiled cling film and a cloth. Set aside to prove until the loaf is well risen, puffy and taut.

Preheat the oven to 220°C/425°F, gas mark 7.

Slash a cross in the top of the loaf with a sharp knife. Bake for 10–15 minutes, then turn down the heat to 180°C/350°F, gas mark 4. Bake for a further 30–40 minutes or until the loaf sounds hollow when it is tapped on the base. Leave it to cool on a rack.

CORNISH SAFFRON BREAD

AUBERGINE, PEPPER AND TOMATO PIZZA WITH THYME

You can make three large or six miniature pizzas from these quantities. The base can be used to make any type of pizza you like. For example, you could top it with olive oil, fresh rosemary, anchovies and mozzarella to make *pizza in bianca alla romana.*

SERVES 3–6

- 400 g/14 oz strong white bread flour
- 1 packet easy-blend dried yeast
- 1 teaspoon salt
- 1½ tablespoons olive oil
- a few tablespoons of fine-grained semolina

For the topping:

- 1 large aubergine, sliced
- 3 medium-size ripe tomatoes, sliced
- fresh or dried thyme
- olive oil
- 1 garlic clove, peeled
- 1 red and 1 yellow pepper, seeded and cut into strips
- salt
- 170 g/6 oz mozzarella, sliced into strips
- 24 anchovy fillets, drained
- 24 black olives (use the oily ones)
- 2 tablespoons capers

Start to make the dough 2 hours ahead.

Set aside 3 heaped tablespoons of flour; put the rest in a large bowl and mix in the yeast and salt. Make a well in the centre. Measure 300 ml/½ pint tepid water in a jug and stir in the olive oil. Pour into the well in the flour, mixing as you pour. Work the liquid into the flour, first with a wooden spoon and then with your hand, until you have made a sticky dough. Form it roughly into a ball and leave for a minute or two so the flour can absorb the liquid.

Turn the dough on to a floured work surface and knead for about 8 minutes or until smooth and elastic, working in the reserved flour if necessary. Form the dough into a ball, coat it lightly with oil and replace it in the cleaned bowl. Cover with cling film or a damp cloth and leave to rise in a warm place for 1 hour or more, until tripled in size.

Meanwhile, make the topping. Sprinkle the aubergine and tomato slices with plenty of fresh or a little dried thyme. Heat 2–3 tablespoons of olive oil in a frying pan and fry the clove of garlic until it browns.

anchovy 16, 31
aubergine 153
baking bread 356
capers 207
kneading and rising 357
making a yeast dough 356
mozzarella cheese 102
olives 154–5
olive oil 112
saffron 199
shaping a round loaf 358
substituting dried and easy-blend yeasts for fresh yeast 356
sweet pepper 152
tomato 150–1
wheat flours 114–15

brioche tin 237
frying pan 234
pastry brush 237
rolling pin 237

baking bread 356
baking powder 118
bicarbonate of soda 118
cornmeal 115
kneading and rising 257
making a yeast dough 356
molasses 211
shaping a pizza base 358
substituting dried and easy-blend yeasts for fresh yeast 356
sultana 182–3
wheat flours 114–15

baking sheet 236
flour sifter 237
loaf tin 237
pastry brush 237
pizza cutter 225

Remove and discard it. Fry the peppers and slices of tomato and aubergine, a few at a time, in the garlic-flavoured oil until lightly browned, adding more oil as necessary. Remove carefully and drain them on kitchen paper, then sprinkle lightly with salt.

Preheat the oven to 200°C/400°F, gas mark 6. Scatter some semolina over the bottom of three baking trays or sheets.

Knock back the dough. Cut off one-third and put it on a floured work surface; keep the rest of the dough covered. Mould the piece of dough into a ball with floured hands, then flatten it. Roll out into a 25 cm/10 in disc. Transfer the disc to one of the baking trays.

Using about one-third of the topping ingredients, cover the pizza base with slices of cheese, and arrange anchovies and then fried vegetables on top. Decorate with olives and capers. Sprinkle with thyme and a little salt. Make two more pizzas in the same way. Bake for 20 minutes or until the pizza bases are golden brown and the cheese has melted.

MALT LOAF

Children love this excellent teabread.

MAKES 2 MEDIUM-SIZE LOAVES

- 30 g/1 oz fresh yeast
- a pinch of sugar
- 225 g/8 oz strong white bread flour
- 450 g/1 lb stone-ground wholemeal flour
- a large pinch of salt
- 115 g/4 oz sultanas
- 55 g/2 oz butter, melted
- 3 tablespoons malt extract
- 1 tablespoon black treacle or molasses
- sugar and milk for glazing

Cream the yeast with the sugar and a little tepid water and leave it in a warm place to froth up. Mix the flours, salt and sultanas in a large warmed bowl. Make a well in the centre and pour in the creamed yeast. Add the butter, malt extract, treacle and a scant 450 ml/¾ pint warm water. Mix and knead to make a somewhat slack dough. Put into an oiled bowl, cover and leave to rise in a warm place for 2 hours or until the dough has doubled in size.

Prepare two 20 x 13 cm/8 x 5 in loaf tins by greasing them lightly with sunflower oil or butter. Knock back the dough, then cut into two pieces. Knead each piece into a ball and flatten the ball into a thick disc. Roll up the disc like a Swiss roll, tuck the two ends of the roll underneath and drop into a loaf tin. Press down well, shaping the top so that it is nicely rounded. Cover and allow to prove for 45 minutes or until puffy.

Preheat the oven to 190°C/375°F, gas mark 5.

Bake the loaves for about 50 minutes, turning the tins round halfway through and covering the loaves with foil if they start to look too black. Boil a little sugar and milk together, and glaze the loaves with the mixture 5 minutes before the end of the baking time.

KILKENNY BROWN SODA BREAD

Eat this soda bread on the day it is made as it is best when very fresh.

MAKES 1 LARGE LOAF

- 700 g/1½ lb 81% plain brown flour
- ½ heaped tablespoon bicarbonate of soda
- 1½ teaspoons salt
- 55 g/2 oz butter
- 1 free-range egg, beaten
- about 450 ml/¾ pint milk mixed with 1 tablespoon molasses

Preheat the oven to 190°C/375°F, gas mark 5.

Put the flour in a bowl, sift over the bicarbonate of soda and salt and mix them in. Rub in the butter. Add the beaten egg, keeping back a little to brush the top of the loaf if a shiny finish is wanted. Mix in the milk, adding enough to make a wet and quite slack dough.

Turn the dough on to a floured board and knead lightly until smooth. Quickly shape the dough into a round flattish loaf, handling it lightly. Put it on a baking sheet and cut almost through in quarters. Brush the top with egg to glaze, or sprinkle with more flour for a matt finish. Leave to rest for 5 minutes before putting into the oven.

Bake for 10 minutes, then lower the heat to 180°C/350°F, gas mark 4. Continue baking for another 40–50 minutes, covering the loaf with foil if it starts to brown too much. To prevent the crust from becoming too tough, you can wrap the loaf in a cloth when you take it out of the oven.

ALTERNATIVE: **White soda bread** Substitute strong white bread flour for the wheatmeal flour. This bread is excellent at tea time and tastes rather like a large scone.

CORN BREAD

MAKES 1 LOAF

- 115 g/4 oz yellow cornmeal (maize flour)
- 170 g/6 oz plain flour
- 2 teaspoons caster sugar
- 1 teaspoon salt
- 1 level teaspoon baking powder

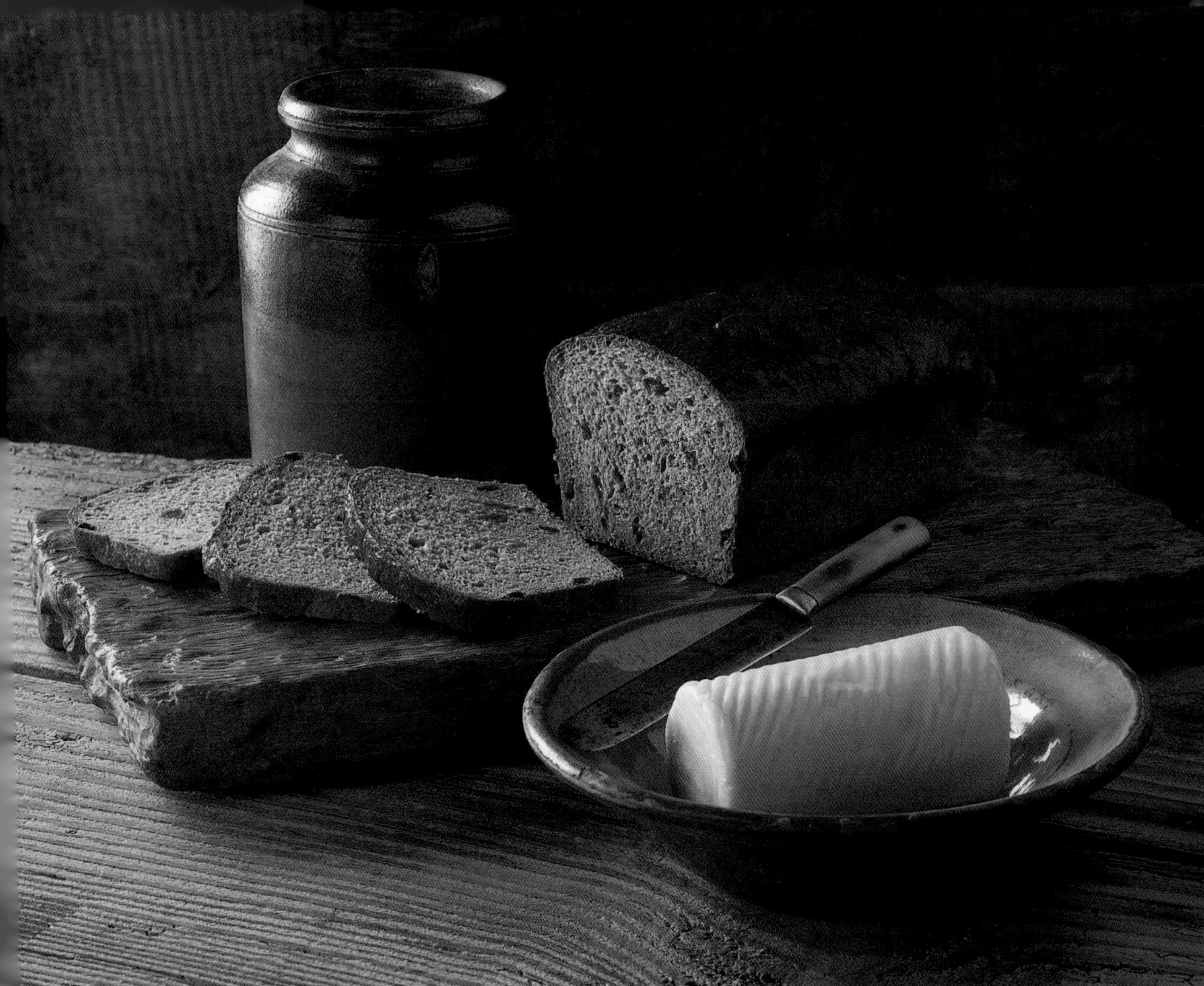

MALT LOAF

1 free-range egg
350 ml/12 fl oz milk
55 g/2 oz butter, melted

Preheat the oven to 220°C/425°F, gas mark 7. Butter a round or square 20 cm/8 in baking tin

Sift the cornmeal, flour, sugar, salt and baking powder into a bowl. Beat the egg and milk and pour into the cornmeal mixture with the butter; mix well. Transfer to the tin and bake for 30–35 minutes. Test with a skewer; if the mixture has not set in the middle, bake for a further 5–10 minutes. Allow to cool on a rack. Serve warm or cold, cut in slices and buttered.

WARM CHEESE BREAD

This bread comes from the former Yugoslavia. The flavour seems modest at first, but people soon find that they cannot stop eating it. Originally it would have been made with curd cheese and feta. It is delicious eaten with a salad of tomatoes, green peppers and onions, or instead of cheese scones for tea, spread with butter.

MAKES 1 SMALL ROUND LOAF
85 g/3 oz self-raising flour
85 g/3 oz instant fine polenta
a pinch of salt
55 g/2 oz cream cheese or low-fat curd cheese
55 g/2 oz fresh goat's cheese
85 g/3 oz Greek yogurt
6 tablespoons olive oil
2 free-range eggs, beaten

Preheat the oven to 190°C/375°F, gas mark 5. Lightly oil an 18 cm/7 in sandwich tin. Just before you are ready to bake the bread, heat the tin in the oven for 1–2 minutes.

Mix the flour, polenta and salt together in a bowl. In another bowl, beat the cream cheese, goat's cheese and yogurt until smooth. Stir in the oil and a tablespoon or two of the flour mixture. Add the eggs,

cream cheese 108
goat's cheese 108
polenta 115
self-raising flour 114
yogurt 99

sieves 226–7
tins 236–7

bicarbonate of soda 118
buttermilk 98, 100
clotted cream 99, 100
maple syrup 210
olive oil 112
self-raising flour 114
soured milk 100
tomato 150–1

baking sheet 236
barbecuing equipment 240–1
cooling rack 229
cutters 225
food processor 238
graters 224, 226
ridged cast-iron grill pan 233
rolling pin 237
sieves 226–7

Strawberry Jam 417

then lightly fold in the rest of the flour and polenta. Transfer the mixture to the heated cake tin. Bake for 20 minutes or until golden brown and a skewer inserted into the centre comes out clean. Eat hot or warm, cut in slices like a cake.

PAN CATALAN

Like its Italian cousin, *bruschetta*, the Spanish *pan catalan* is the most wonderful food – the simplest ingredients combined to make a perfect *bonne-bouche*.

SERVES 4

- 4 thick slices of country bread
- 2–3 garlic cloves, peeled
- 1–2 large, ripe tomatoes, cut in half
- best olive oil
- salt
- a few fresh basil leaves, shredded (optional)

Prepare a wood or charcoal fire.

Grill the bread over the fire until it is toasted and very slightly charred on both sides. Rub one side of each slice fiercely with garlic; the rough surface of the grilled bread will grate the garlic and the bread will absorb all the garlic juices. Rub the surface with the cut side of a tomato half. Drizzle good olive oil all over the pieces of tomato-soaked toast and sprinkle with salt. Scatter over some shreds of basil, and eat at once.

ALTERNATIVE: Use an overhead grill to toast the bread, although this won't give it the same flavour. Or toast the pieces on a ridged cast-iron grill pan or Aga.

SCONES

Eat these warm, split in half, with plenty of butter, or cool with clotted cream and raspberry or strawberry jam. The lightest scones are those made with buttermilk, although you can substitute soured milk .

MAKES 12

- 250 g/9 oz self-raising flour
- ¼ teaspoon bicarbonate of soda
- a pinch of salt
- 45 g/1½ oz butter
- 150 ml/¼ pint buttermilk, or 150 ml/¼ pint soured milk and 2 tablespoons cream

Preheat the oven to 190°C/375°F, gas mark 5.

Sift the flour, bicarbonate of soda and salt into a bowl. Rub in the butter with your fingertips until it is in very coarse crumbs. Add the buttermilk, or milk and cream, and mix to a soft dough.

Turn the dough on to a lightly floured work surface and roll it out to a thickness of about 1 cm/½ in. This should be done quickly, and with a light touch. Cut out rounds from the dough with a 5 cm/2 in plain or fluted cutter. Dust the tops with flour and put them on a baking sheet. Bake for 10–15 minutes or until puffed and golden brown. Cool on a rack.

CRUMBS, CROÛTONS, TOASTS

Fresh breadcrumbs Cut thick slices of day-old white bread, remove the crusts and cut the slices into large cubes. Reduce them to crumbs in a food processor. Alternatively, you can use a grater.

Dried breadcrumbs Put all your leftover ends of bread in a very low oven and bake them until they are dry, golden and biscuity. Wrap the dried pieces in a clean cloth and pound them with a rolling pin, using a rolling motion once they begin to break down. Sieve the resulting crumbs – any lingering bits and pieces should be pounded again.

Croûtons Cut crustless slices of white bread into small neat cubes and fry them in a mixture of hot butter and oil, tossing them frequently, until they are an even golden brown. Remove them with a slotted spoon and drain them on kitchen paper. Or spread out the bread cubes on a baking tray and bake in a moderate oven until crisp and lightly browned. Croûtons can be reheated in a low oven.

Melba toast Toast slices of white bread, with their crusts on, until they are brown on both sides. Then slice each piece horizontally in half. Scrape away the soft untoasted inside, cut off the crusts and dry the wafer-thin pieces for a few minutes in a low oven until they begin to curl and brown. Serve with hors d'oeuvres, caviare and pâté.

Pain perdu Moisten slices of white or brown bread in beaten egg, then shallow fry the slices in butter until they are nicely browned on both sides. Serve hot, sprinkled with sugar and cinnamon, or, alternatively, with a spoonful of maple syrup and crisp rashers of bacon. Pain perdu, also known as French toast, makes an excellent breakfast dish.

Salads

CRUDITÉS WITH AÏOLI

This is a delicious and simple dish, traditionally eaten in the south of France before a whole baked fish, or even as a main course.

SERVES 6–8

1 cucumber
2 celery sticks
225 g/8 oz carrots
225 g/8 oz small courgettes
225 g/8 oz French beans
1 red pepper, seeded and cut into narrow strips
225 g/8 oz firm tomatoes, sliced
a bunch of radishes, trimmed
2 heads of chicory, leaves separated
115 g/4 oz black olives
300 ml/½ pint Aïoli

Peel the cucumber, slice into 5 cm/2 in pieces and cut these into sticks, removing the seeds. Cut the celery and carrots into 5 cm/2 in strips about the width of the beans. Cook the courgettes very briefly, then cool and slice lengthways. Cook the beans briefly, refresh under cold water and drain. Blanch the pepper strips; drain.

Put all the vegetables and olives into separate little dishes, or lay them in groups on a large white platter, and chill before serving. The vegetables should be eaten with the fingers and dipped into the rich aïoli. Coarse brown bread and butter is good with this.

ALTERNATIVES: Use any vegetables in season, such as cooked small new potatoes, freshly boiled beetroots, small boiled leeks, tiny raw globe artichokes the size of walnuts, sticks of celeriac, young raw broad beans, quartered lettuce hearts, sliced Florence fennel and small boiled turnips.

CELERY AND PARMESAN SALAD

Serve this as a separate course after roast veal or pork, or as a starter.

SERVES 6

1 head of fresh celery, trimmed
55 g/2 oz fresh, softish Parmesan in a piece
4 tablespoons olive oil
juice of ½ lemon (optional)
salt and freshly ground pepper

Cut the celery into fine crescents. Slice the Parmesan into the thinnest possible flakes. Mix together the celery and Parmesan in a bowl. Dress with olive oil only, or with olive oil and a squeeze of lemon juice. Season lightly with salt and add plenty of pepper.

GUACAMOLE

Good guacamole should taste both hot and cool at the same time.

SERVES 6–8

3 ripe avocados
juice of 1 lime
4–6 green chillies, finely chopped
1 spring onion, finely chopped (optional)
1 tomato, skinned and chopped
about 5 tablespoons olive oil
salt and freshly ground pepper
a dash of Tabasco sauce (optional)

Remove the flesh from the avocados and mash it with the lime juice, mixing well. Pound the green chillies and spring onion to a paste using a pestle and mortar, or purée in a food processor. Add the mashed avocados and the tomato. Slowly incorporate as much of the olive oil as you can, drop by drop, whisking with a fork or blending in the food processor. Season with salt and pepper and a little Tabasco. Chill briefly, then serve with toast or tortilla chips.

LEBANESE AUBERGINE SALAD

This aubergine purée, often called monk's salad, has a very good and interesting smoky flavour. Serve it cold with brown bread and butter or hot toast or pitta bread, or as a salad with other quick salads, such as tomato salad or cucumber salad. It also makes a good lunch with some slices of salami and a few black olives, or with dolmades.

SERVES 4 AS AN HORS D'OEUVRE

2–3 aubergines
½ small onion, finely chopped (optional)
2 small tomatoes, skinned and chopped
1–2 garlic cloves, crushed to a pulp
6 tablespoons olive oil, or more if needed
a squeeze of lemon juice
salt and freshly ground pepper
spring onions and chopped flat-leaf parsley to serve

Preheat the grill, or preheat the oven to 220°C/425°F, gas mark 7.

Put the aubergines under the grill or in the oven. Grill or bake until the skins have blackened and the insides are becoming soft – about 20 minutes, depending on their size. Then turn them over and continue grilling or baking until they are completely soft inside.

Once the aubergines have cooled a little, cut them open and scoop out all the flesh on to a board, using a teaspoon to scrape the skins. Chop the flesh finely

aubergine 153
avocado 153–4
celery 138
chicory 129–30
chilli pepper 152–3
cucumber 155
olive oil 112
olives 154–5
Parmesan cheese 103
radish 131
refresh 423
seeding chillies 423
skinning and seeding tomatoes 423
sweet pepper 152
tomato 150–1

food processor 238
Parmesan knife 225
pestle and mortar 226

Aïoli 259

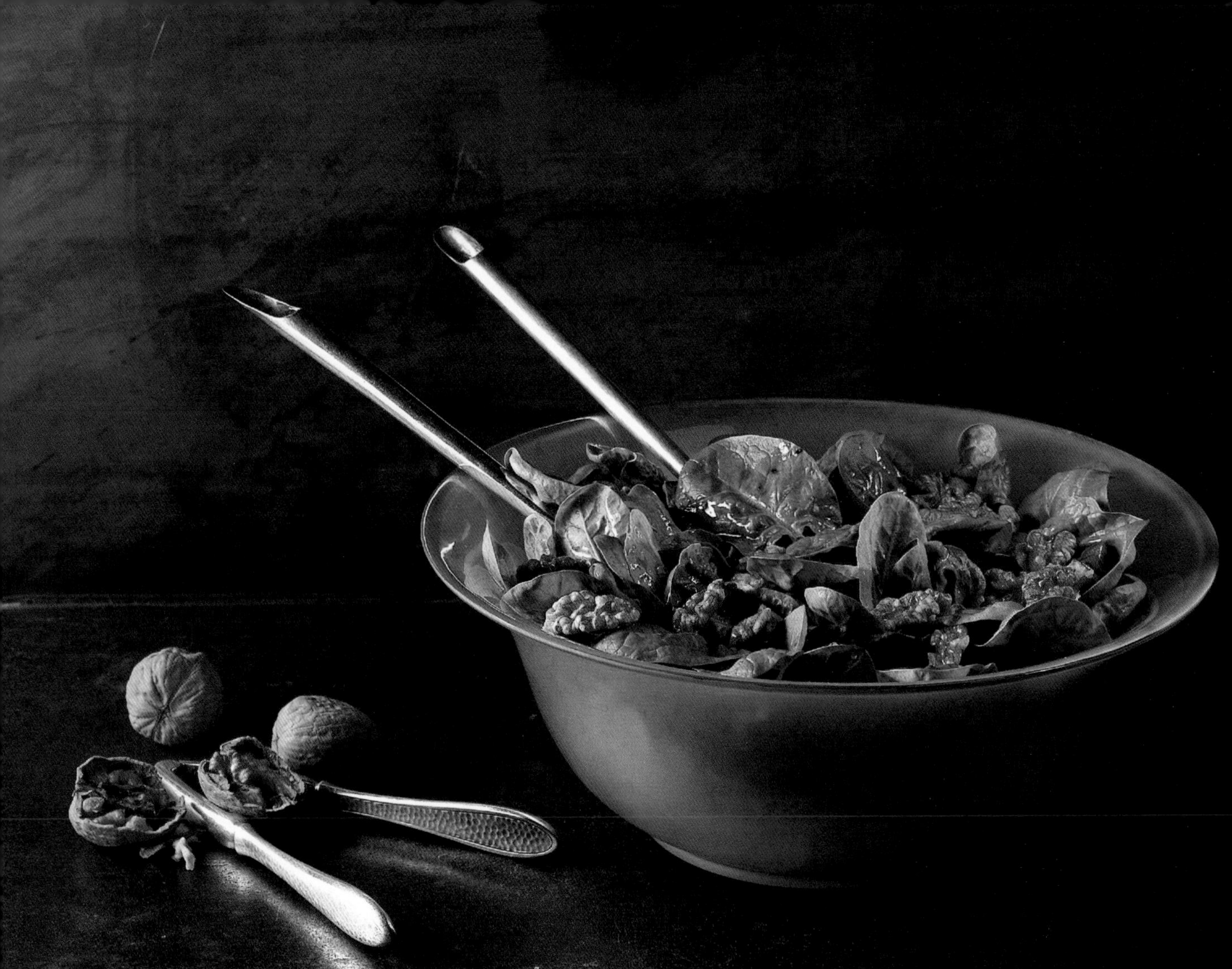

anchovy 16, 31
basil 192
cumin 199
curly endive 130
olive oil 112
pomegranate 179–80
salt pork 70
skinning peppers 423
sweet pepper 152

and put it into a bowl. Mix in the onion, tomatoes and some of the garlic. Gradually add the oil, as if you were making mayonnaise. Taste the mixture and add a few drops of lemon juice, more garlic, and salt and pepper as necessary. Serve with spring onions and chopped flat-leaf parsley.

ALTERNATIVE: Add 1 teaspoon of cumin seeds, toasted and crushed, or sprinkle the salad with fresh pomegranate seeds.

SWEET PEPPER SALAD

Grilling peppers makes them sweet and mellow.

SERVES 4

- 4 peppers, 2 red and 2 yellow
- 4 tablespoons olive oil
- salt
- a small bunch of fresh basil

Preheat the grill. Grill the peppers until black all over, then remove the skins and cut the peppers into 2.5 cm/1 in wide strips. Lay them all facing the same way on a plate – this is simple food and does not need smart serving. Pour the olive oil over the peppers, sprinkle with salt and turn the pieces over in this dressing. Scatter leaves of basil over the peppers and serve lukewarm or cool.

ALTERNATIVES: Add some lemon juice to the dressing. If you like the taste of anchovies, arrange some fat anchovy fillets over the top and sprinkle with a little chopped garlic.

FRISÉE AND BACON SALAD

This is a version of *salade lyonnaise.*

SERVES 4–6

- 450 g/1 lb frisée (curly endive), separated into leaves
- 6 thick rashers of streaky bacon or salt pork, cut into strips
- 1 teaspoon olive oil

For the dressing:
4 tablespoons olive oil
1 tablespoon white wine vinegar or sherry vinegar
a small pinch of caster sugar
salt and freshly ground pepper

Make the dressing first, by mixing the ingredients together with a fork. Wash, drain and dry the frisée, shaking it well in a cloth, a third at a time, or using a salad spinner to get all the moisture off the leaves.

Fry the bacon in the olive oil until crisp and brown. Meanwhile, put the frisée into a salad bowl and dress it lightly with the salad dressing. When the bacon is brown, pour it – still sizzling – with all its fat over the salad. Toss, and serve at once.

ALTERNATIVES: **Spinach and bacon salad** Use fresh young spinach leaves instead of frisée. If you like, add an avocado, cut into thin slices or fairly small dice. **Pissenlits au lard** Use cultivated dandelion leaves instead of frisée – this is a classic French dish.

SPINACH AND WALNUT SALAD

SERVES 4
280 g/10 oz fresh young spinach leaves
115 g/4 oz freshly shelled walnuts
Vinaigrette, preferably made with 4 tablespoons walnut oil and 1 tablespoon olive oil

Wash and drain the spinach leaves. Shake them dry in a cloth, a third at a time so that they do not get crushed or damaged. Put them into a bowl. Scatter the walnuts over the spinach. Dress lightly with the walnut oil dressing just before serving.

ALTERNATIVES: Add a chopped hard-boiled egg to the spinach after you have tossed it in the dressing. **Rocket and walnut salad** Use rocket instead of spinach for another delicious salad.

COOL AND HOT CUCUMBER SALAD

This simple salad is delicious served with grilled oily fish, such as salmon, mackerel fillets and herrings. The combination of hot fish and the cool, spiced cucumber is very pleasing, particularly when eaten out of doors on a hot day.

SERVES 4
1 large cucumber, peeled and not too thinly sliced
2 teaspoons coarse salt
cayenne pepper

For the dressing:
1 tablespoon finely chopped fresh coriander
10 fresh mint leaves, finely chopped
1 garlic clove, finely chopped
½ teaspoon ground cumin
1 teaspoon caster sugar
2 teaspoons lime juice
2 small green chillies, seeded and finely chopped
2 tablespoons plain yogurt

In a colander, mix the cucumber and salt together with your hands, then leave to drain for 1 hour, to draw out the bitter juices. Rinse the cucumber lightly under cold water and dry in a tea-towel.

Whisk all the dressing ingredients together in a bowl. Mix in the cucumber. Transfer to a dish and dust with a little cayenne pepper.

GREEN BEAN SALAD WITH ANCHOVY-CREAM DRESSING

In Italy, salads of green beans make a regular appearance during the summer. This anchovy dressing is often found spooned over other cold green vegetables too, especially broccoli.

SERVES 4
450 g/1 lb extra fine French beans
1 large shallot, very finely chopped
extra virgin olive oil
lemon wedges (optional)
For the dressing:
1 tablespoon Dijon mustard
1 tablespoon red wine vinegar
½ garlic clove, finely crushed
freshly ground pepper
150 ml/¼ pint groundnut oil
150 ml/¼ pint extra virgin olive oil
a 55 g/2 oz can anchovy fillets

First make the dressing. Put the mustard, vinegar, garlic, 4 tablespoons of warm water and pepper to taste in a blender. Whizz until smooth. With the motor still running, add the groundnut and olive oils in a thin stream, blending until the dressing is homogeneous and has the consistency of salad cream. If it becomes too thick, thin it with a little more warm water. Add the anchovy fillets and their oil, and blend until smooth. Tip the dressing into a bowl.

Drop the beans into a large saucepan of boiling salted water and cook briskly for 4 minutes. Drain, and then immediately refresh under very cold running water. Drain the beans again and pat them dry with a tea-towel. Divide the beans among four plates, arranging them

anchovy 16, 31
avocado 153–4
chilli pepper 152–3
coriander 191–2
cucumber 155
dandelion 133
French bean 142
hard-boiled eggs 322
mint 194
oils 110–13
refresh 423
rocket 131
seeding chillies 423
spinach 132–3
walnut 188

blender, liquidizer 238
colander 229
salad basket and spinner 229
whisks 227
wooden bowl 230

Vinaigrette 259

anchovy 16, 31
bean sprout 142
capers 207
crab 33
fish sauce 206
halibut 12
hard-boiled eggs 322
lemon grass 194
lettuces 129
lime leaf 195
olives 154–5
picking a cooked crab 40–1
potato 145
radish 131
red onion 144
refresh 423
skinning peppers 423
tuna 16, 32
watercress 130–1

pestle and mortar 226
potato peeler 224
salad basket and spinner 229

Mayonnaise 259

loosely in piles. Spoon over the dressing. Sprinkle on the chopped shallot and drizzle over a generous amount of olive oil. Serve with good bread and lemon wedges, if you like.

SALADE NIÇOISE

SERVES 4–6

1 small Cos lettuce
1 frilly Oak Leaf lettuce
225 g/8 oz small French beans, trimmed
450 g/1 lb ripe tomatoes, sliced
3–4 small waxy new potatoes, freshly boiled, cooled and sliced
2 red peppers, skinned, seeded and cut into strips
1 yellow pepper, skinned, seeded and cut into strips
3 hard-boiled eggs, halved
a handful of large capers
a handful of black olives
12 fat Spanish anchovy fillets packed in oil, drained
½ red onion, sliced into crescents
a sprinkling of fresh basil leaves

For the dressing:

1 tablespoon wine vinegar
6 tablespoons olive oil
1 garlic clove, sprinkled with a pinch of salt and crushed
freshly ground pepper

Wash and dry the lettuces. Discard any damaged outer leaves, and separate the inner leaves. Cook the beans briefly, then drain and refresh them under cold water.

Lay the lettuce leaves round the edge of a large serving dish. Place the tomato and potato slices in rings in the middle of the dish. Arrange the pepper strips, radiating outwards, over the lettuce leaves. Add bunches of French beans here and there, and the egg halves pointing outwards from the centre. Put little piles of capers here and there, and the olives among the tomato slices. Place the anchovies on the eggs. Make the dish look as full and beautiful as you can.

Make a good dressing with the vinegar, oil and garlic and season with pepper. Pour over the salad. Scatter the onion and basil leaves on top.

ALTERNATIVES: Add sliced cooked artichoke hearts, sliced cucumber, radishes or raw Florence fennel, or cherry tomatoes. Cold cooked peas and chicory are also sometimes included, and cold cooked haricot beans are quite good too. You can add a can of tuna fish in oil to this salad, placing the flaked tuna in the centre with the potatoes.

CRAB SALAD WITH THAI FLAVOURS

Yum or *yam* is the generic name for Thai salads. Many ingredients can be used to garnish the basic salad, which may comprise thinly sliced carrot, cucumber, bean sprouts, any sort of salad leaf, sliced red onion, radishes and herbs. Chillies (usually green) are also thrown into the dish.

SERVES 4

115 g/4 oz bean sprouts
1 large carrot, cut lengthways into strips with a potato peeler
a bunch of watercress, divided into sprigs
2 round lettuces, hearts only, separated into leaves
½ cucumber, peeled and sliced
1 small red onion, sliced into thin rings
8 radishes, sliced
8 fresh mint leaves, roughly torn
15–20 fresh coriander leaves
340 g/12 oz fresh white crabmeat, flaked

For the dressing:

6 lime leaves, cut into thin strips
3 stalks of lemon grass, thick and tender bulbous part only, thinly sliced
3 garlic cloves, finely chopped
3 tablespoons fish sauce
2 tablespoons lime juice
2 teaspoons sugar

Mix all the salad vegetables and herbs together. Arrange on a large platter and distribute the flaked crabmeat over the surface.

If possible, make the dressing using a pestle and mortar – gently crushing the ingredients releases more of their natural oils and juices. You can use a food processor, but the result will not be quite as aromatic. Work the ingredients together until quite smooth. The dressing should have the consistency of slurry, so add a little water if necessary. Spoon the dressing over the salad and serve immediately.

HALIBUT SALAD WITH CAPERS

SERVES 4 AS A STARTER

700 g/1½ lb halibut in a piece, preferably from a large fish
salt
a few sprigs of parsley
a handful of Italian capers in wine vinegar
150 ml/¼ pint thick mayonnaise

SALADE NIÇOISE

chilli flakes 201
chilli pepper 152–3
clam 38
green peppercorn 201
hard-boiled eggs 322
langoustine 35
mussel 38
prawn 35–6
preparing squid 47

Preheat the oven to 180°C/350°F, gas mark 4.

Lay the halibut on a large piece of foil, sprinkle with salt and then place the parsley on top. Wrap the fish closely in the foil. Place on a baking tray and bake for 20–25 minutes. After this time, carefully open up the foil parcel and test the fish with the point of a sharp knife to see whether the flesh flakes apart and comes easily away from the bone. If it does not, put the halibut back into the oven to bake for a further 5–10 minutes.

Remove the parsley, close the foil around the fish once again and leave it to cool for about 30 minutes or so. When it is cool, put it in the refrigerator until it is chilled right through. As it does so, the halibut will set in its own delicious jelly. Remove from the refrigerator and flake on to a dish, together with the jelly, discarding all skin and bones.

Stir the capers into the mayonnaise together with 2 teaspoons of their vinegar. Mix the mayonnaise with the flaked fish. Serve in individual dishes.

ALTERNATIVES: Instead of capers, you could add one of the following: a few well-rinsed green peppercorns packed in brine; chopped hard-boiled eggs and black olives; a handful of cooked and peeled prawns; or a mixture of pounded garlic and chopped fresh parsley, chervil and tarragon.

SEAFOOD SALAD

SEAFOOD SALAD

SERVES 6

36 mussels
a few small clams
8–10 baby squid
24 langoustines, fresh or frozen
225 g/8 oz peeled prawns – large Mediterranean prawns if possible
1 tablespoon lemon juice
6–7 tablespoons olive oil
½ dried red chilli, finely chopped, or dried chilli flakes to taste
salt and freshly ground pepper

Scrub and debeard the mussels. Put them in a large pan with the clams and 300 ml/½ pint boiling water, and shake over a moderate heat until all the shells have opened. Scoop the clams and mussels out of the pan with a slotted spoon, reserving the liquid.

Clean the squid and cut the bodies into rings, keeping the tentacles whole. Bring the mussel liquid back to the boil, adding a little boiling water if there seems to be too little. Drop in the pieces of squid and let them cook gently for 1–2 minutes. Remove them quickly with a slotted spoon. If you are using raw langoustines or prawns drop them into the same liquid and poach for 3–4 minutes or until opaque; drain.

Shell the mussels and arrange them with the clams, squid, langoustines and prawns on a dish. Squeeze over the lemon juice, then pour on the oil. Scatter the chilli over the top and season with salt and pepper.

ALTERNATIVES: Substitute raw mushrooms, finely sliced, for the squid and let the salad marinate for at least 2 hours before serving. Add chopped fresh herbs – parsley, oregano or dill – with the chilli.

LIDO PASTA SALAD

This is pasta to eat in the summer, on the beach or in the garden. It is so easy to make – the secret to its success is using good ingredients.

SERVES 4–6

115 g/4 oz dill-marinated Kalamata olives, stoned
55 g/2 oz salted capers, rinsed
1 red onion or a bunch of spring onions, chopped
4 garlic cloves, finely chopped
6 tablespoons olive oil
juice of 1 lemon
340 g/12 oz penne or rigatoni
450 g/1 lb cherry or baby plum tomatoes, halved
2 tablespoons coarsely chopped fresh basil
1 tablespoon coarsely chopped fresh mint
2 tablespoons coarsely chopped parsley
salt and freshly ground pepper

Put the olives, capers, chopped onions and garlic in a big salad bowl. Mix in the oil and lemon juice.

Cook the pasta in a large pan of boiling salted water until *al dente*. Drain the pasta and throw it straight into the salad bowl. Toss thoroughly with the olive mixture. Keep back a couple of handfuls of tomatoes and some of the herbs; add the remainder to the salad and stir in lightly. Taste for seasoning (the olives and capers are salty). Scatter the reserved herbs and tomatoes over the top and serve warm or cold.

ALTERNATIVE: Add 20 anchovy fillets, cut into pieces, with the olives.

CHINESE BELLY PORK SALAD WITH BOK CHOY

Although it seems an unlikely proposition, thin cold slices of crisp pork belly are one of the nicest things to eat. The preparation of the pork sounds as though it will be rather time-consuming, but the end result is a fabulously crisp and tasty skin, so it is well worth the effort involved.

SERVES 4

700 g/1½ lb fatty belly pork
1 heaped tablespoon five-spice powder
2 teaspoons ground white pepper
1 tablespoon coarse salt
8 heads of baby bok choy
1 tablespoon sesame seeds, toasted in a frying pan until golden
sprigs of fresh coriander

For the stock:

85 ml/3 fl oz soy sauce
85 ml/3 fl oz dry sherry
1 tablespoon plum sauce
a small bunch of spring onions, chopped
3 garlic cloves, smashed
1 teaspoon dried chilli flakes
4 strips of orange zest

For the dressing:

1 heaped teaspoon mustard powder
1 tablespoon Dijon mustard
1 teaspoon caster sugar
1 tablespoon smooth peanut butter
½ teaspoon tahina
2 teaspoons toasted sesame oil
1 tablespoon chilli sauce

Start the recipe the day before you want to eat it.

Ask the butcher to score the pork skin finely, and to remove and chop the bones into smaller pieces.

Place the belly pork, skin side up, on a rack set over a deep roasting tin. Gradually ladle about 3 litres/10 pints of boiling water over the pork skin, discarding the water from the roasting tin when necessary. Turn the pork over on to a large tray. Sprinkle the five-spice powder and pepper over the meat and rub them in, working them in well with your fingertips. Turn the pork over once more and rub the coarse salt into the skin. Hang the pork to dry in a cool, draughty place overnight.

Preheat the oven to 240°C/475°F, gas mark 9.

Mix all the stock ingredients in a bowl and stir in 900 ml/1½ pints of water. Pour into the deep roasting tin. Add the bones from the pork. Place the rack on top of the tin once again. Lay the pork on this, skin side up. Roast for 8 minutes. Lower the oven temperature to 180°C/350°F, gas mark 4, and roast for a further 30 minutes.

Remove the tin from the oven. Top up the stock with more water if it has reduced too much, and turn up the oven temperature to its highest setting. When it is back to full temperature, return the pork to the oven

al dente 422
anchovy 16, 31
belly pork 60
bok choy 136
capers 207
chilli flakes 201
chilli sauce 206
five-spice powder 196
mustard 202–3
olives 154–5
peanut butter 187
pennette rigate 121
plum sauce 206
red onion 144
sesame seed 197
soy sauce 207
tahina 206
toasted sesame oil 112
tomato 150–1
zesting citrus fruits 423

colander 229
ladle 227
pasta pan 234
roasting tin 236

chicory 129–30
chilli flakes 201
chilli pepper 152–3
ginger 199
sesame seed 197
soy sauce 207
spinach 132–3
star anise 196
toasted sesame oil 112

sieves 226–7
whisks 227

Chicken Stock 244
Peanut Sauce 258

and roast for a final 5 minutes or so, until the skin is extremely crisp.

Allow the pork to cool to room temperature on the rack set over a tray. Strain the stock from the roasting tin into a bowl. (It can be frozen for future use, and will get better each time.)

Whisk together the dressing ingredients. Add enough of the stock, a spoonful at a time, to give the dressing the consistency of pouring cream.

Steam the heads of bok choy until tender. Slice the bok choy into manageable pieces and spread over a serving dish. Using a sharp serrated knife, slice the pork as thinly as possible. Lay it over the warm bok choy in overlapping slices. Spoon over the dressing, without covering the meat completely. Sprinkle with the sesame seeds and decorate with coriander sprigs.

ALTERNATIVE: If bok choy is unavailable, use Swiss chard or coarse spinach.

SICHUAN CHICKEN SALAD

This is a variation of bang-bang chicken, a dish often found in Chinese restaurants. It is an ideal way of using up left-over roast chicken.

SERVES 4 AS A MAIN DISH

- 4 large chicken thighs, preferably free-range
- 2 teaspoons sesame seeds
- Peanut Sauce
- ½ teaspoon dried chilli flakes
- 2 teaspoons toasted sesame oil
- sprigs of fresh coriander

For the poaching broth:

- 3 tablespoons soy sauce
- 2 teaspoons toasted sesame oil
- 4 slices of fresh root ginger, unpeeled
- 2 garlic cloves, smashed
- 4 spring onions, sliced
- 2 tablespoons vinegar
- 2 star anise
- 2 green chillies, roughly chopped

For the salad:

- 1 cucumber, peeled, seeded and cut into matchsticks
- 1 large carrot, cut into matchsticks
- a bunch of spring onions, shredded lengthways
- ½ teaspoon caster sugar
- juice of 1 lime
- salt

Put all the ingredients for the poaching broth into a saucepan just large enough to hold the chicken thighs snugly. Put in the thighs and add water to cover. Move the liquid and chicken around with your hands to disperse everything evenly. Place the pan over a low heat and bring to a simmer. Cover and cook very gently for 30 minutes. Remove from the heat and leave the chicken in the broth until completely cold.

Lift out the chicken. Discard the skin and any excess fat, and lift off the meat from the bone in one piece if possible. Shred the meat into strips, place on a plate and cover. Strain the poaching broth (keep it in an airtight container in the fridge for future use, or freeze it for when you make this dish again; it will become progressively more intensely flavoured).

Put the sesame seeds in a small hot frying pan over moderate heat and stir until toasted to a light brown. Tip them on to a plate to cool.

Put the salad vegetables in a serving bowl and toss with the sugar, lime juice and a little salt. Scatter the shredded chicken on top. Spoon over the peanut sauce. Sprinkle on the toasted sesame seeds and chilli flakes, drizzle over the sesame oil and decorate with sprigs of coriander.

CHICORY IN BUTTER AND CREAM

SERVES 4

- 4 plump fresh heads of chicory
- 30 g/1 oz butter
- juice of ½ lemon
- a few tablespoons chicken stock
- a pinch of salt
- 6 tablespoons double cream

Cut the heads of chicory lengthways into strips 1 cm/½ in wide. Cut each strip in half across the middle to give you little ribbons of chicory about 5–6 cm/2–2½ in long. Put them in a wide pan with the butter, lemon juice, just enough stock to cover and the salt. Bring to the boil and cook until the stock has almost evaporated.

Stir in the cream and boil gently, shaking the pan from time to time, until the liquid thickens and clings to the chicory, bathing it in light sauce. Serve very hot.

If you are not ready to serve the chicory straight away, it can be reheated at the last moment.

SESAME SPINACH

SERVES 4

- 700 g/1½ lb spinach
- 1 tablespoon toasted sesame oil
- 1 garlic clove, bruised
- 1 tablespoon sesame seeds
- salt

Rinse the spinach thoroughly and drain well. Discard any tough stalks.

Heat a large frying pan or wok, add the sesame oil and garlic and heat gently. When the garlic starts to colour remove it. Add the sesame seeds to the pan and fry until golden. Throw in the spinach and cook briskly until it is wilted but not soggy, tossing and turning it so it cooks evenly. Season with salt to taste.

Drain in a sieve, pressing with the back of a large spoon to remove excess moisture. Turn into a serving dish and serve hot.

SPINACH AND CHICK-PEAS

This is a fragrant vegetable stew with a deep, sumptuous flavour, substantial enough to make a whole meal. It is very good for a cold day.

SERVES 4–6

450 g/1 lb spinach
salt
4 tablespoons olive oil
1 slice of country bread
1 onion, chopped
3–4 tomatoes, skinned and chopped
1 garlic clove, peeled
1 tablespoon paprika
225 g/8 oz dried chick-peas, cooked and drained

Wash the spinach thoroughly, dry it well and then sprinkle with salt.

Heat half the oil in a small frying pan and fry the slice of bread until golden on both sides; remove and put to one side to cool. Fry the onion in the same oil until golden brown, then stir in the tomatoes; set aside. Pound the garlic to a paste in a pestle and mortar. Add the fried bread and pound again.

Heat the rest of the oil in a large saucepan and stir in the paprika. Add the spinach. When it has wilted down, add the chick-peas, garlic and bread paste, and the tomatoes and onion. Moisten with a wineglass of

SICHUAN CHICKEN SALAD

chick-pea 127–8
paprika 201
skinning and seeding tomatoes 423
spinach 132–3

frying pan 234
pestle and mortar 226
sieves 226–7
wok 235

apple 162–3
black-eyed bean 127
blanch 422
cabbage 134–6
chestnut 188
juniper berry 196–7
leek 145
mace 198
peeling chestnuts 189
rice 116–17
sweat 423
wine vinegar 204
zesting citrus fruits 423

casserole 236
colander 229
electric mixers 238–9
potato masher 226

Chicken Stock 244

water. Cover the pan and simmer for about 30 minutes, adding a little more water if the mixture becomes too dry.

ALTERNATIVE: Use black-eyed beans instead of chick-peas.

COLCANNON

If you have any colcannon left over the next day, you can shape it into small cakes and fry in bacon fat until crisp and brown.

SERVES 4

- 700 g/1½ lb green cabbage, quartered
- 450 g/1 lb potatoes, peeled
- 2 small leeks, or the green tops from a bunch of spring onions, chopped
- 200 ml/7 fl oz milk or single cream
- a pinch of ground mace
- salt and freshly ground pepper
- 55 g/2 oz butter, melted

Cook the cabbage in boiling salted water until just tender, then drain. When cool enough to handle, cut the cabbage quarters into shreds, discarding the core. Cook the potatoes in boiling salted water until tender; drain well and mash them. Keep hot.

Simmer the leeks or onion tops in the milk or cream until tender. Add to the mashed potato and beat until smooth, then add the shredded cabbage. Beat the mixture over a low heat until fluffy and piping hot. Season with mace, salt and pepper.

Pile into a heated serving dish. Make a well in the centre and pour in the melted butter. Serve very hot.

CABBAGE WITH CHESTNUT STUFFING

SERVES 4

- 12 chestnuts, shelled and skinned
- 600 ml/1 pint chicken stock
- 1 Savoy or other green cabbage
- 30 g/1 oz butter
- 1 onion, chopped
- 2 celery sticks, thinly sliced
- 55 g/2 oz long-grain rice
- 1 free-range egg, beaten
- 115 g/4 oz minced veal
- 115 g/4 oz minced pork
- a large pinch of ground mace
- salt and freshly ground pepper
- a 400 g/14 oz can chopped tomatoes
- a liqueur glass of brandy or kirsch

Cook the chestnuts in the stock until tender, adding more liquid if needed. Drain them, reserving the stock, and mash roughly. Drop the whole cabbage carefully into a pan of boiling salted water and boil it for 5 minutes. Drain in a colander.

Melt the butter in a frying pan and soften the onion and celery. Add the rice and stir until it is well coated with butter. Turn the mixture into a bowl and mix in the egg, minced pork and veal, chestnuts, mace, salt and pepper. Moisten with a little of the reserved stock.

Preheat the oven to 140°C/275°F, gas mark 1.

When the cabbage is cool enough to handle, open it out like a flower, turning back each leaf like a petal. Put a spoonful of the rice stuffing into an inner leaf and pat it back into its original shape. Continue filling leaves with stuffing, one by one, patting them back into place. Tie up the cabbage like a parcel with cotton tape. If you haven't any tape, use folded strips of foil.

Put the cabbage in an earthenware pot or casserole. Add the stock from the chestnuts and the tomatoes. Cover the pot tightly and cook in the oven for 2½ hours, basting occasionally. Add more stock if needed.

When the cabbage has finished cooking, remove the tapes or strips of foil and pour the brandy or kirsch over the cabbage. Taste the sauce for seasoning.

ALTERNATIVE: After blanching the whole cabbage, separate the leaves, fill each one with stuffing and fold and roll up into parcels. Arrange the parcels in an ovenproof dish and pour over the stock and tomatoes.

BRAISED RED CABBAGE

This is excellent with roast pork and game stews.

SERVES 4

- 15 g/½ oz pork dripping or butter
- 1 onion, finely chopped
- 1 red cabbage
- 2 apples – russets if possible, peeled, quartered and cored
- a strip of orange zest
- 5 tablespoons wine vinegar
- a wineglass of red wine
- 2–3 tablespoons brown sugar or more to taste
- 3–4 juniper berries, crushed
- 2 bay leaves
- salt and freshly ground pepper

Preheat the oven to 170°C/325°F, gas mark 3.

Melt the pork dripping or butter in a flameproof casserole. Add the onion and sweat it until soft.

Meanwhile, cut the cabbage in half and cut out the core. Slice the halves vertically from top to bottom into

5 mm/¼ in slices. Cut the longer slices across in half. Put the cabbage into the pot with the onion and stir it around to coat it with the fat. Add the apples, orange zest, vinegar, red wine, sugar, crushed juniper berries, bay leaves, and some salt and pepper. Stir to mix.

Cover the pot with foil or greaseproof paper and a lid. Put it into the oven and cook for 1½–2 hours or until the cabbage is beautifully tender. If the casserole is properly sealed, there will be enough liquid; however, stir the cabbage from time to time and if it does seem to be getting too dry add a little more red wine or water. Taste it about 30 minutes before the end of cooking; if it seems too bland, add more vinegar and sugar – this depends very much on the quality of the cabbage. Some are pale and insipid, others are dark and have a wonderful rich flavour.

CUMIN-SPICED CABBAGE

Use a very hard white cabbage for this dish.

SERVES 4

85 g/3 oz butter
1 large onion, thinly sliced
1 small white cabbage, or ½ large white cabbage, cored and finely shredded
1 tablespoon cumin seeds
2 tablespoons white wine or chilli-flavoured vinegar
salt and freshly ground black pepper
1 tablespoon snipped fresh chives

Melt the butter in a large saucepan, add the onion and fry until softened. Tip in the cabbage and stir it around, then put on the lid. Cook over a very low heat for about 20 minutes or until the cabbage is limp and soft, stirring occasionally.

Meanwhile, toast the cumin seeds in a hot frying pan for about 1 minute. Transfer them to a mortar and bruise them with a pestle. Add the cumin to the cabbage with the vinegar, and season with salt and plenty of black pepper. Increase the heat and stir-fry the cabbage for 3–4 minutes so that some of the vinegar evaporates. Put the lid back on the pan, reduce the heat to almost nothing and stew for a further 15 minutes.

Tip the cabbage into a hot serving dish and sprinkle over the chives.

CAULIFLOWER AU GRATIN

SERVES 4–6

1 large cauliflower, broken into florets
55 g/2 oz butter
30 g/1 oz plain flour
450 ml/¾ pint milk
150 ml/¼ pint single cream
85 g/3 oz Emmental, Gruyère or Parmesan, freshly grated
salt and freshly ground pepper
55 g/2 oz fresh white breadcrumbs

Cook the cauliflower in boiling salted water for 8–10 minutes. Drain and keep hot.

Make a mornay sauce with half the butter, the flour, milk, cream and most of the cheese – the sauce should be fairly thin but creamy. Season with salt and pepper.

Preheat the grill.

Melt the remaining butter in a frying pan. Add the breadcrumbs, sprinkle with a little salt and fry until they are nicely browned and crisp. Add the cauliflower and mix it around until every piece is coated with the fried breadcrumbs. Transfer to a gratin dish.

Pour the sauce around the cauliflower, sprinkle with the rest of the cheese and brown under the grill.

BRUSSELS SPROUTS WITH CHESTNUTS

Serve with roast turkey or with game.

SERVES 4

450 g/1 lb Brussels sprouts
225 g/8 oz shelled and skinned fresh chestnuts or vacuum-packed chestnuts
55 g/2 oz butter
salt

Trim the outside leaves from the sprouts; if they are very large, you can cut a cross in the base, but otherwise do not bother.

In two separate pans of boiling water, cook the sprouts for about 12 minutes and the chestnuts for 12–15 minutes. Both must be just tender, but not soft and mushy. Drain them thoroughly and put them into a clean saucepan. Add the butter. Toss over a low heat for a few minutes until piping hot and well coated with butter. Season with salt.

ALTERNATIVE: Cook the chestnuts in chicken stock instead of water for a stronger flavour.

FENNEL AU GRATIN

SERVES 6

3 plump fennel bulbs
salt
55 g/2 oz Parmesan, freshly grated
55 g/2 oz butter

Brussels sprout 136–7
cabbage 134–6
cauliflower 136
chestnut 188
cumin 199
Emmental cheese 105
fresh breadcrumbs 364
Gruyère cheese 104
Parmesan cheese 103
peeling chestnuts 189
vinegars 204–5

frying pan 234
gratin dish 236
pestle and mortar 226

Chicken Stock 244
Mornay Sauce 255

acidulated water 422
garlic 145
globe artichoke 138
lettuces 129
mint 194
olive oil 122
pea 140–2
preparing globe artichoke hearts 139
savory 194
sorrel 133
spinach 132–3

colander 229
gratin dish 236
knives 222–4

Slice each of the fennel bulbs across into fairly thin slices, or, alternatively, simply cut each one into quarters if you prefer. Bring a large pan of salted water to the boil and then plunge in the fennel slices or quarters. Cook for 5–8 minutes or until the fennel is tender but still slightly firm in texture. Drain thoroughly in a colander.

Preheat the oven to 190°C/375°F, gas mark 5.

Butter an oval gratin dish and put in a layer of the cooked fennel. Sprinkle this with a small amount of the Parmesan cheese and dot all over with a little of the butter. Continue making layers of fennel, Parmesan cheese and butter until you have used up all the ingredients, and finishing with a generous layer of Parmesan and plenty of butter. Bake for 20–25 minutes or until golden.

ARTICHOKES ALLA ROMANA

SERVES 4 AS A STARTER

8–12 very small globe artichokes
juice of 1 lemon
150 ml/¼ pint olive oil
4 garlic cloves, chopped
3 tablespoons chopped fresh mint
salt and freshly ground pepper

For this recipe, the stalks of the artichokes need to be left on. Peel the stalks and lower parts of each artichoke with a small stainless-steel knife, cutting away the outer layer of leaves. If the artichokes are more than 5 cm/2 in across, they will contain spiny chokes; these should be removed in the same way as when preparing artichoke hearts. Put each prepared artichoke immediately into a bowl of water acidulated with the lemon juice.

When you have prepared all the artichokes, heat 1 tablespoon of the oil in a small pan and fry the garlic gently with the mint for 2–3 minutes. Remove the artichokes from the water and shake them dry. Spoon some of the mint and garlic mixture into the middle of each one, if you have scooped out the chokes; if the artichokes are still whole, stuff the mixture in among the leaves. Put the artichokes in a heavy pan into which they will just fit. Pour on the remaining oil and add 300 ml/½ pint of water. Season lightly with salt and pepper. Cover and cook over a low heat for about 45 minutes.

Remove the lid and finish cooking over a brisk heat for 15 minutes or until the cooking juices are well reduced. Spoon the juices over the artichokes and serve them either hot or cold, accompanied by plenty of fresh bread.

STEWED ARTICHOKES WITH SPINACH

This was originally made with sorrel, as a spring dish, but is equally good made with young spinach. It is the most wonderful mixture of flavours.

SERVES 4

500 g/1 lb 2 oz young spinach leaves
10 fresh artichoke hearts or two 400 g/14 oz cans artichoke hearts in water (not oil)
30 g/1 oz butter, cut into small pieces
2 tablespoons olive oil
1 garlic clove, peeled
a pinch of sugar
salt and freshly ground pepper

Wash the spinach thoroughly and then remove any coarse stalks. If you are using canned artichoke hearts, drain them. Cut the fresh or canned artichokes into quarters.

Put the pieces of butter in a heavy-based saucepan or flameproof casserole. Add a layer of wet spinach, then a layer of about 10 artichoke pieces. Continue making layers of spinach and artichoke until all are in the pan. Add the oil, garlic clove, sugar and a little salt and pepper. Cover the pan and simmer very, very gently, without stirring, for 1 hour or more (or 30 minutes if using canned artichoke hearts). Check often to make sure the bottom layer isn't burning, and add a little water if necessary. If, on the other hand, there is too much liquid, remove the lid for the last few minutes of cooking.

Serve hot, either on its own or with plain grilled meat or fish.

PEAS WITH LETTUCE HEARTS

SERVES 4

a few sprigs of fresh savory or thyme
2 lettuce hearts
340 g/12 oz shelled fresh peas – about 900 g/2 lb peas in their pods
55 g/2 oz butter
salt
a pinch of sugar

Tuck the savory or thyme into the lettuce hearts and put them in a saucepan with the peas, butter and half a tumbler of water. Season with a little salt and add the sugar. Bring to the boil, then cover and simmer gently for 15 minutes. Drain well and serve hot.

ARTICHOKES ALLA ROMANA

bacon 69–70
blanch 422
broad bean 142
chilli pepper 152–3
chive 190
clarified butter 100, 423
coriander 191–2
cumin 199
French bean 140
ghee 100
pea 140–2
refresh 423
shallot 144–5
sweat 423
tarragon 190–1
zesting citrus fruits 423

colander 229
sieves 226–7

PEAS AN INDIAN WAY

In traditional Indian cuisine peas are often cooked with very little liquid, or with no liquid at all. As a result, they come out deep green in colour and rather strongly flavoured.

SERVES 4

- 3 tablespoons ghee or clarified butter, or 15 g/½ oz butter and 2 tablespoons oil
- 1 large onion, finely chopped
- ½ teaspoon ground cumin
- 340 g/12 oz shelled fresh peas – about 900 g/2 lb peas in their pods
- 1 green chilli, finely chopped
- a small bunch of fresh coriander, chopped, or a few crushed coriander seeds
- salt

Heat the ghee, clarified butter or butter and oil in a shallow pan with a lid. Add the onion and cumin and leave them to sweat until the onion is soft and golden, but not brown. Add the peas together with the chopped chilli and coriander and stir them around in the fat for 1–2 minutes. Add 4 tablespoons of water and a little salt. Cover the pan and cook until the peas are nice and tender, which will take 10–20 minutes, depending on their age. Do not drain the peas before serving them.

BROAD BEANS AND BACON

This is a particularly good recipe to make at the time of year when there are so many broad beans about that you just don't know what to do with them. The bacon fat used here makes a very delicious change from butter. When broad beans are older the outer skins become rather tough and unappetizing; in this case, you should remove the skin from each bean either before or after cooking.

SERVES 6

- 1.35 kg/3 lb broad beans
- salt
- 6 rashers of streaky bacon, cut into small strips
- a knob of butter

Shell the broad beans, and cook them in boiling salted water until tender.

Just before the beans are ready, fry the bacon, starting it off in a little butter to prevent it from sticking to the pan. When the beans are ready, drain them thoroughly in a colander and then put them into a heated bowl. Mix in the bacon with all its dripping and serve.

STEWED BROAD BEANS WITH BUTTER AND TARRAGON

This simple dish should only be made at the beginning of summer, when broad beans are at their most young and tender. The beans are particularly good with spring lamb or boiled gammon.

SERVES 4

- 2.3 kg/5 lb young and tender broad beans, shelled
- 85 g/3 oz butter
- ½ garlic clove, bruised
- 3 strips of lemon zest
- leaves from 4–5 sprigs of fresh tarragon, chopped
- salt and freshly ground pepper

Bring a pan of salted water to the boil. Drop in the broad beans. When the water is just about to boil again, drain the beans in a colander and refresh under cold running water.

Gently melt the butter in a saucepan. Add the garlic and lemon zest. Stir in the broad beans and tarragon, and season with salt and pepper. Warm through and serve.

GRATIN OF FRENCH BEANS WITH CHIVES

This is excellent with roast chicken or a delicate fish such as brill or sole.

SERVES 4–6

- 700 g/1½ lb French beans
- 150 ml/¼ pint double cream
- 150 ml/¼ pint milk
- 2 shallots, sliced
- ¼ teaspoon freshly ground white pepper
- salt
- 2 extra large free-range egg yolks
- a bunch of fresh chives, chopped

Blanch the beans in boiling salted water for 2–3 minutes. Drain and refresh them under cold running water. Leave to dry on kitchen paper.

Combine the cream, milk, shallots, pepper and a pinch of salt in a small saucepan and heat until bubbles start to form around the edge. Leave on the very edge of a low heat for 30 minutes, to allow the liquid to absorb the flavour of the shallot.

Preheat the oven to 170°C/325°F, gas mark 3.

Slice the beans into little pieces the size of peas. Beat the egg yolks lightly in a bowl. Set the pan containing the cream mixture directly on the heat; just before it simmers (when it is at scalding point) pour the mixture through a sieve into a jug. Now pour it slowly on to the egg yolks, whisking lightly – you don't really want bubbles. Stir the beans and chives into the mixture.

Spoon into a buttered gratin dish that is about 28 x 20 cm/11 x 8 in, and set this in a roasting tin. Pour boiling water into the tin to come halfway up the sides of the gratin dish. Bake for about 1 hour or until just set; test by shaking the dish gently – the gratin should still wobble a bit in the centre when it is ready. Remove from the oven and allow the gratin to stand for a few minutes before serving.

LEEKS IN CREAM

This is a rich yet delicate way of cooking leeks.

SERVES 4

- 6 fat leeks
- 55 g/2 oz butter
- salt and freshly ground pepper
- a grating of nutmeg
- 4 tablespoons double cream

Cut the leeks in half lengthways, then into pieces about 1 cm/½ in long. Melt the butter in a heavy saucepan and add the leeks. Season with salt, pepper and nutmeg and stir them around. Cover and cook gently for 15 minutes. Stir in the cream and cook for a minute or two more, until the cream thickens slightly.

ALTERNATIVE: **Leeks with truffles** Add a very thinly sliced small truffle (preferably fresh) with the cream.

HOT RED BEET SALAD

SERVES 4–6

- 4–5 raw beetroots
- 1 tablespoon olive oil
- 55 g/2 oz butter
- salt and freshly ground pepper
- juice of 1 lemon
- a handful of parsley, chopped

Cook the beetroots whole in boiling salted water for 1½–2 hours. Drain and rub off their skins while they are still hot. Slice the beetroots.

Preheat the oven to 190°C/375°F, gas mark 5.

Put the oil in the bottom of an ovenproof dish. Arrange the slices of beetroot in the dish, dotting each layer with butter and seasoning with salt and pepper. Squeeze the lemon juice over the beetroot and dot the top with more butter. Bake for 15 minutes.

Spoon the juice over the top of the beetroot, sprinkle with the chopped parsley and serve hot.

ROAST POTATOES

If you are roasting a large joint at the same time, you can add the potatoes to the tin with the meat and roast them in the drippings.

SERVES 4–6

- 8–12 medium-size floury potatoes
- salt
- 85 g/3 oz butter or goose fat
- 4 tablespoons sunflower oil

Preheat the oven to 200°C/400°F, gas mark 6.

Peel the potatoes and, if they are large, cut them in half. Put them into a saucepan of cold salted water and bring to the boil. Let them simmer, covered, for 5 minutes. Drain, return them to the pan and dry over a low heat, uncovered, for a minute or two. Now shake the pan to give the potatoes a rough surface.

Heat the butter or goose fat and oil in a roasting tin. Put in the potatoes and baste them with the hot fat. Roast for 45 minutes to 1 hour, turning them from time to time. Remove them from the fat with a slotted spoon and serve.

ALTERNATIVES: After parboiling the potatoes, sprinkle them with flour. Then put them in the hot fat and baste well. Or omit the parboiling and put the peeled raw potatoes straight into the hot fat; roll them to coat with the hot fat, then roast as above – surprisingly they do not need any more time.

POMMES RISSOLÉES

Eat these with veal or with almost any roast meat with which you would normally serve plain new potatoes. The best pan for cooking these delicious little potatoes is a sauté pan with a lid.

SERVES 4

- 700 g/1½ lb new potatoes the size of walnuts
- 85 g/3 oz butter
- salt

Wash, scrub or scrape the potatoes, but don't peel them; dry them well in a cloth. Melt the butter in a wide-bottomed pan – it should be large enough for every potato to touch the bottom. Throw in the potatoes and let them brown fairly rapidly, shaking the pan to turn them. When they are browned all over, sprinkle with salt and cover with a lid. Turn down the heat and cook gently for 30 minutes or until the potatoes are tender (test with the point of a knife).

Remove the lid, turn up the heat and crisp the potatoes a little. Serve very hot.

beetroot 149
goose fat 110
leek 145
potato 145
truffles 161

gratin dish 236
roasting tin 236
slotted spoon 227

NEW POTATOES BAKED WITH SAFFRON, CREAM AND GARLIC

This dish is similar in its taste and richness to the classic Pommes Dauphinoise, but the addition of saffron lends another dimension. Prepared this way, the new potatoes become wonderfully soft and creamy.

SERVES 4

- 20 small new potatoes
- 150 ml/¼ pint milk
- 150 ml/¼ pint whipping cream
- 2 garlic cloves, finely chopped
- ½–1 teaspoon saffron threads
- salt and freshly ground black pepper
- ½ tablespoon snipped fresh chives

Preheat the oven to 180°C/350°F, gas mark 4. Lightly butter an ovenproof dish just large enough to accommodate the potatoes in one layer.

Cook the potatoes, in their skins, in boiling salted water for about 8–10 minutes or until half cooked. Drain. When they are cool enought to handle, peel them. Turn into the buttered dish.

Combine the milk, cream, garlic, saffron and a little salt in a saucepan and heat until bubbles start forming around the edge. Remove from the heat and leave for 5 minutes to allow the saffron to infuse and colour the liquid.

Spoon the saffron cream evenly over the potatoes. Bake for 30 minutes or until the top is pale golden, the cream mixture has thickened considerably and the potatoes are cooked through (check with a skewer).

Scatter over the chives and grind over plenty of pepper before serving.

CREAMED POTATOES WITH PARSLEY

These pale green-flecked creamed potatoes go very well with poached or grilled fish. They also make the perfect topping for a fish pie.

SERVES 4

- 900 g/2 lb potatoes
- leaves from a large bunch of fresh flat-leaf parsley
- 115 g/4 oz butter
- 300 ml/½ pint whipping cream
- salt and freshly ground pepper

Peel the potatoes and cook in boiling salted water until tender. Drain and mash, then keep warm.

NEW POTATOES BAKED WITH SAFFRON, CREAM AND GARLIC

Blanch the parsley leaves in boiling water for about 1 minute; drain and refresh under very cold running water. Squeeze dry. Put the butter and cream in a small saucepan and bring to the boil, then immediately tip into a blender. Add the parsley and seasoning, and blend until smooth. Mix the parsley cream with the mashed potatoes until thoroughly blended. Serve hot.

POMMES DAUPHINOISE

SERVES 4–6

- 900 g/2 lb good waxy potatoes
- 30 g/1 oz Parmesan, freshly grated
- about 55 g/2 oz butter, cut into small pieces
- salt and freshly ground pepper
- 1 large garlic clove, chopped and crushed
- 150–300 ml/¼–½ pint single cream

Preheat the oven to 180°C/350°F, gas mark 4.

Peel the potatoes and slice them finely, either with a mandoline or in a food processor. Butter a wide, shallow ovenproof dish. Cover the bottom of the dish with a layer of potatoes. Sprinkle with a little of the grated cheese, dot with some of the butter, season and add a tiny sprinkling of garlic. Pour on a little cream. Repeat these layers, finishing with neat layer of potato moistened with cream and sprinkled with the last of the cheese. Dot the surface well with butter.

Bake for 1¼ hours. Pommes dauphinoise should be very moist – it should not be allowed to dry out during cooking – so, if necessary, cover the dish with foil.

ALTERNATIVE: Omit the cheese for a plainer dish.

SPICED AND FRIED NEW POTATOES WITH MINTED YOGURT DRESSING

Potatoes are often included in Indian dishes to soak up spices and herbs fried with onions and garlic. Serve these potatoes with barbecued meats.

SERVES 4

- 20 small new potatoes
- 4 tablespoons vegetable oil or clarified butter
- 1 large onion, thinly sliced
- 4 garlic cloves, thinly sliced
- a 2.5 cm/1 in piece of fresh root ginger, grated
- 2 teaspoons ground coriander
- 1 teaspoon ground cumin
- 2 large green chillies, seeded and chopped
- salt and freshly ground black pepper
- juice of ½ lime
- 2 tablespoons chopped fresh coriander

blanch 422
chilli pepper 152–3
clarified butter 100, 423
coriander 191–2
coriander seed 199
cream 99–100
cumin 199
flat-leaf parsley 190
ginger 199
infuse 422
Parmesan cheese 103
potato 145
refresh 423
saffron 199
seeding chillies 423

food processor 238
mandoline 225–6

Fish Pie 266

acidulated water 422
carrot 148
Jerusalem artichoke 150
mint 194
potato 145
salsify 148
swede 149
sweet potato 147
turnip 149
yogurt 99

Mouli-légumes 226
potato masher 226
ricer 227
sieves 226–7

For the yogurt dressing:
150 ml/¼ pint plain yogurt
2 tablespoons chopped fresh mint
½ teaspoon cayenne pepper
salt

Cook the potatoes, in their skins, in boiling salted water for 8–10 minutes or until half cooked. Drain. When they are cool enough to handle, peel them.

Make the yogurt dressing by stirring the ingredients together in a small bowl. Set aside.

Heat the oil or clarified butter in a pan and cook the onion and garlic until golden. Add the ginger, ground coriander and cumin and cook gently for 5 minutes. Stir in the chillies, and season with salt and pepper.

Add the potatoes to the spice mixture and stir carefully to coat them all over. Add 120 ml/4 fl oz water and allow to stew very gently for 15 minutes or until the water has almost all evaporated. Stir in the lime juice and fresh coriander. Turn up the heat and fry briskly for 2 minutes, moving the potatoes round in the pan.

If you think there is too much excess oil, drain the potatoes in a sieve. Serve warm rather than hot, with the dressing spooned over the potatoes.

CARAMELIZED SWEET POTATOES

These are perfect with hot boiled gammon or with roasted pork or venison.

SERVES 4–6
900 g/2 lb sweet potatoes
salt
3 tablespoons sugar
55 g/2 oz butter

Find a saucepan large enough to take the sweet potatoes, fill it with plenty of water and bring to the boil. Add some salt. Put the unpeeled potatoes in the water and cook for 20–25 minutes or until just tender. Drain. When the potatoes are cool enough to handle, peel off the skins and cut the potatoes into 4 cm/1½ in slices. Keep hot while you make the caramel.

Sprinkle the sugar into a large frying pan and cook over a moderate heat until the sugar melts and caramelizes to a golden mahogany brown. Add the butter. When it is foaming, swirl it around the pan to mix with the caramelized sugar. Quickly rinse the slices of sweet potato under the cold tap and put them carefully into the pan. Turn them so that they are glazed with the golden caramel on both sides, and heat through.

ALTERNATIVE: Use ordinary potatoes instead of sweet potatoes – the result is delicate and surprising.

SUGAR-GLAZED CARROTS

Prepared this way, young carrots are sweet and succulent and have a very good flavour.

SERVES 6
700 g/1½ lb young carrots
salt
2 teaspoons sugar
55 g/2 oz butter

Scrape the carrots or peel them thinly. Cook in boiling salted water until just tender. Drain off all but about 2 tablespoons of the water. Add the sugar and dissolve it over a gentle heat. Add the butter and cook briskly until the butter and sugar mixture starts to brown, rolling the carrots so they are coated with this glaze.

ALTERNATIVES: **Glazed turnips** Use young turnips instead of carrots; cook in the same way. **Glazed salsify** Use salsify instead of carrots. As each one is peeled, drop it into a bowl of water acidulated with vinegar to prevent it from turning brown. Salsify is best cooked in a *blanc* (1 tablespoon flour dissolved in 1.8 litres/3 pints water with 1 teaspoon salt) to keep it white.

MASHED SWEDES

SERVES 4
450 g/1 lb swede, cut into chunks
450 g/1 lb potatoes, preferably floury, peeled and cut into chunks
30 g/1 oz butter
3–4 tablespoons double cream
salt and freshly ground pepper

Put the swede and potatoes in a saucepan of cold water, bring to the boil and boil until completely tender. Drain the vegetables in a colander. Mash them, then put through the medium blade of a Mouli-légumes. Or mash the vegetables using a ricer.

Return the purée to the cleaned saucepan and beat in the butter and cream. Season with salt and plenty of pepper. Heat through and serve very hot.

JERUSALEM ARTICHOKES WITH CREAM AND PARSLEY

SERVES 4
900 g/2 lb Jerusalem artichokes
30 g/1 oz butter
salt and freshly ground pepper

1.2 litres/2 pints chicken stock or water
2 tablespoons chopped flat-leaf parsley
150 ml/¼ pint double cream
a grating of nutmeg
a squeeze of lemon juice

Peel the artichokes and slice them thinly, a little thicker than a coin. Melt the butter in a large heavy frying pan and put in the artichokes. Season with salt and pepper. Cook gently for 5–6 minutes, stirring so that each slice is well coated in butter. Add enough stock or water to come just to the top of the artichokes. Simmer, uncovered, until just tender.

Add the parsley and the cream and continue to cook gently until the artichokes are bathed in a creamy sauce. Taste and add salt, pepper, nutmeg and a squeeze of lemon juice. Serve hot with game or roast pork.

RATATOUILLE

Ratatouille comes from the south of France where the dish varies from a delicate mixture of lightly cooked vegetables to a really dark brown stew, floating with oil. Ideally it should be rich and moist with different vegetables just distinguishable in a smooth tomato sauce. Frying the vegetables separately from the tomatoes, as here, helps them to remain intact.

SERVES 6

150 ml/¼ pint olive oil
900 g/2 lb tomatoes, skinned, seeded and chopped
salt and freshly ground pepper
2 pinches of sugar (optional)
2–3 onions, sliced downwards fairly coarsely
3 garlic cloves, sliced
2 red or green peppers, seeded and cut into strips or squares
450 g/1 lb courgettes, cut into 5 mm/¼ in slices or quartered lengthways
1 large aubergine, sliced and slices quartered

Heat half the olive oil in a small pan. Add the tomatoes and season with salt and pepper. If the tomatoes are not very ripe and sweet, add the sugar. Simmer for 10–15 minutes.

Meanwhile, heat the remaining oil in a heavy-based saucepan. Add the onions and garlic and fry gently until soft. Throw in the peppers, then the courgettes and, finally, the aubergine. Season with salt and pepper. Cook over a low heat until the vegetables are shining and beginning to soften. Gently stir the vegetables around frequently, otherwise they will cook unevenly and stick to the bottom of the pan.

Add the tomatoes, which will have collapsed to a fairly moist sauce. Continue cooking until all the vegetables are soft and tender. Ratatouille reheats very well.

ALTERNATIVES: Add sprigs of fresh thyme or basil, some black olives or extra garlic.

RED PEPPERS WITH ANCHOVIES

This recipe originally appeared in Elizabeth David's book *Italian Food*, published in 1954, since when it has been cooked all over the world.

SERVES 4

4 red peppers, halved and seeded
4 garlic cloves, sliced
salt and freshly ground pepper
4 large ripe tomatoes, skinned and halved
120 ml/4 fl oz good quality (but not extra virgin) olive oil
16 anchovy fillets

Preheat the oven to 190°C/375°F, gas mark 5.

Arrange the pepper halves in an ovenproof dish, cut side up, and distribute the garlic among them. Season with a little salt and pepper. Push a halved tomato into each pepper, cut side down. Season with pepper only, and spoon over the olive oil.

Roast for about 1 hour or until the edges of the peppers are well scorched and their flesh is soft and collapsing slightly. Remove from the oven, and immediately arrange 2 anchovies in a criss-cross over each pepper half. Allow to cool to room temperature before serving. Serve with plenty of crusty bread.

MELANZANE ALLA PARMIGIANA

SERVES 4–6

900 g/2 lb aubergines
plain flour for coating
generous 150 ml/¼ pint sunflower oil
5–6 tablespoons olive oil
1 onion, chopped
2 garlic cloves, chopped
900 g/2 lb tomatoes, skinned, seeded and chopped
12 fresh basil leaves, torn into shreds
2 tablespoons chopped parsley
salt and freshly ground pepper
340 g/12 oz mozzarella, cut into small cubes
1 teaspoon dried oregano
30 g/1 oz Parmesan, freshly grated

Cut the aubergines lengthways into slices about 5 mm/¼ in thick. Sprinkle them with salt and leave to drain for half an hour. Then pat them dry and dust

anchovy 16, 31
aubergine 153
basil 192
courgette 156
dégorger 422
flat-leaf parsley 190
garlic 145
mozzarella cheese 102
olive oil 112
Parmesan cheese 103
parsley 190
skinning and seeding tomatoes 423
sweet pepper 152
tomato 150–1
thyme 194

Chicken Stock 244

anchovy 16, 31
aubergine 153
balsamic vinegar 205
chilli flakes 201
courgette 156
dégorger 422
dill 191
fresh breadcrumbs 364
ginger 199
olives 154–5
pickles 207
soured cream 99
soy sauce 207
tomato 150–1

colander 229
graters 224, 226
gratin dish 236
roasting tin 236

them with flour. Heat the sunflower oil in a large frying pan, add the aubergine slices, a few at a time, and brown them on both sides. Drain them well on kitchen paper.

Heat the olive oil in a saucepan, throw in the chopped onion and garlic and sweat until softened. Add the tomatoes, half the basil and half the parsley. Season with salt and pepper. Simmer for about 30 minutes or until the sauce is well reduced.

Preheat the oven to 180°C/350°F, gas mark 4.

Butter an oval gratin dish. Make a layer of half the aubergine slices in the dish, cover with half the tomato sauce and scatter over half the mozzarella cubes. Sprinkle most of the remaining basil and parsley and some of the dried oregano into the dish, then repeat the layers of aubergine, sauce and mozzarella. Sprinkle the Parmesan and the rest of the herbs over the top. Bake for 25–30 minutes or until hot and bubbling and beginning to brown on top. Leave to stand for 5 minutes, then serve hot.

STIR-FRIED AUBERGINES WITH CHILLI AND CORIANDER

This vegetable dish is just as good cold or warm as it is hot. It can be served on its own, either as a first course, or as an accompaniment for grilled lamb cutlets or liver.

SERVES 4

4 tablespoons vegetable oil
450 g/1 lb aubergines, cut into 2.5 cm/1 in cubes
4 tablespoons balsamic vinegar
2 tablespoons soy sauce
2 tablespoons finely shredded spring onions
1 tablespoon grated fresh root ginger
1 teaspoon dried chilli flakes (or slightly less if you prefer)
salt and freshly ground pepper
sprigs of fresh coriander

Heat the vegetable oil in a large (and preferably non-stick) frying pan until the oil is smoking. Put in the aubergines and fry briskly until well coloured on all sides. Tip them on to a double thickness of kitchen paper to drain.

Pour the vinegar and soy sauce into the pan and heat until bubbling. Return the aubergines to the pan and cook gently for 5 minutes, stirring occasionally. Stir in the spring onions, ginger and chilli flakes. Cook for another couple of minutes, then season with salt and pepper.

Turn into a serving dish and allow to cool a little before serving, garnished with coriander sprigs.

STUFFED TOMATOES

Serve these on their own as an hors d'oeuvre or with a simple salad as a delicious lunch.

SERVES 4–6

6 large tomatoes
1 large garlic clove, chopped
8 green olives, chopped
6 anchovy fillets, chopped
55 g/2 oz fresh white breadcrumbs
55 g/2 oz butter, melted
1 teaspoon chopped fresh basil or marjoram
salt

Preheat the oven to 170°C/325°F, gas mark 3.

Cut the tomatoes in half across the middle and scoop out the insides. Discard the seeds from this flesh, then put it in a bowl. Add the garlic, olives, anchovies and breadcrumbs. Moisten the mixture with the melted butter and add the basil or marjoram and a little salt. Stuff the mixture into the tomato halves. Arrange them in an oiled roasting tin and bake in the top of the oven for 40 minutes or until tender.

ALTERNATIVES: Stuff the tomatoes with a mixture of cooked minced lamb, cooked rice and chopped herbs; or with sautéed chopped onions and garlic, chopped or minced ham and breadcrumbs; or simply with chopped garlic, parsley and breadcrumbs doused in olive oil.

COURGETTES WITH DILL AND SOUR CREAM

SERVES 4

8 large courgettes, grated
2 teaspoons salt
85 g/3 oz butter
1 large onion, thinly sliced
2 large kosher or Polish dill pickles, sliced and cut into shreds
6 tablespoons dill pickle vinegar, from the jar
300 ml/½ pint sour cream
1 heaped tablespoon chopped fresh dill, plus extra for serving
freshly ground white pepper

Put the grated courgettes in a colander. Sprinkle over the salt, mix with your hands and leave to drain for 1 hour.

Melt the butter in a large shallow pan and sweat the onion until soft and translucent. Tip the courgettes into a tea-towel and squeeze out the juices until completely dry. Add the courgettes to the onion and cook gently for 15 minutes or until soft and limp.

Stuffed Tomatoes

Increase the heat. Add the shredded dill pickles with their vinegar and cook briskly to evaporate the vinegar. Once the mixture is drier, add the sour cream and dill. Bring just to a simmer, then cook very gently for about 10 minutes or until thick and unctuous.

Pour into a hot serving dish. Grind over plenty of white pepper and sprinkle with more chopped dill.

ALTERNATIVE: Try using a marrow instead of the courgettes – you may even prefer it.

COURGETTES AU GRATIN

SERVES 4

700 g/1½ lb courgettes
salt and freshly ground pepper
30 g/1 oz butter, cut into small pieces
55 g/2 oz Parmesan, freshly grated

Preheat the oven to 220°C/425°F, gas mark 7.

Peel the courgettes in stripes with a potato peeler, then slice them into rounds 5 mm/¼ in thick. Put them in a colander, sprinkle lightly with salt and leave them to drain for 30 minutes.

Dry the courgettes slices on kitchen paper. Drop them into a pan of boiling salted water, bring back to the boil and boil for 1 minute. Drain them thoroughly in a colander.

Butter an oval gratin dish. Put in a layer of courgettes, season with salt and pepper, dot them with half the butter and sprinkle generously with cheese. Repeat the layers, ending with a layer of cheese. Bake for 15–20 minutes or until bubbling and the top is a pale golden brown. Serve piping hot.

STUFFED COURGETTES

In Italy these are eaten as a first course before a beef steak or a baked fish – the only other vegetables would be in the form of a mixed salad of lettuce, little leaves of rocket and a few finely sliced rounds of radish – but they also make a very light and appetizing summer lunch.

courgette 156
dégorger 422
Parmesan cheese 103
vegetable marrow 156

colander 229
gratin dish 236
potato peeler 224

courgette 156
dill 191
garlic 145
mushrooms and other fungi 158–61
Parma ham 69
Parmesan cheese 103
pattypan squash 156
shallot 144–5
soured cream 99
sweat 423
whisking egg whites 423

colander 229
deep-fryer 239
gratin dish 236

Béchamel Sauce 255
Hummus with Tahina 353
Israeli Falafels 353
Yogurt and Garlic Dressing 260

SERVES 4

900 g/2 lb courgettes
55 g/2 oz Parmesan, freshly grated
55 g/2 oz Parma ham or cooked ham, sliced and cut into 1 cm/½ in squares
thick Béchamel Sauce, made with 40 g/1½ oz each butter and flour and 250 ml/8 fl oz milk
salt and freshly ground pepper
a pinch of grated nutmeg (optional)

Cut the courgettes in half lengthways and scoop out the seeds with a teaspoon. Drop the halves into boiling salted water and cook for 5–8 minutes or until just tender but still firm. Drain the courgettes very thoroughly in a colander.

Preheat the oven to 220°C/425°F, gas mark 7.

Stir most of the Parmesan cheese and all the ham into the béchamel sauce. Taste the sauce to check the seasoning, adding a little nutmeg if you like. Allow to bubble for 15 minutes.

Arrange the courgette halves, side by side, in an earthenware gratin dish. Using a teaspoon, fill them with the béchamel mixture. Bake for 15 minutes.

Preheat the grill.

Sprinkle the stuffed courgettes with the remaining cheese and brown quickly under the grill.

SQUASH FRITTERS WITH YOGURT AND GARLIC DRESSING

Serve this on its own or as part of a mixed hors d'oeuvres with hummus, falafels, Greek salad and so on.

SERVES 4 AS A STARTER

450 g/1 lb young pattypan or other thin-skinned summer squash
oil for frying
salt
Yogurt and Garlic Dressing

For the batter:

140 g/5 oz plain flour
2 tablespoons sunflower or other light oil
1 free-range egg white

To make the batter, put the flour in a bowl and stir in the oil and 175 ml/6 fl oz of water. Beat well until smooth, then allow to rest for half an hour.

Cut the squash into 5 mm/¼ in slices, cutting downwards rather than across. If you find that the seeds have started to develop, you will need to peel the squash and remove the seeds.

Heat a deep pan of oil to 177°–182°C/350°–360°F.

Whisk the egg white until fairly stiff and fold it lightly into the batter. Dip each slice of squash into the batter, shake off excess and drop into the hot oil. Fry, a few slices at a time, until pale straw-coloured on both sides. Do not allow them to darken any further. Remove to a plate covered in kitchen paper to drain.

Sprinkle the fritters with salt and serve hot with the yogurt and garlic dressing.

GARLIC MUSHROOMS

Serve these delicious mushrooms on their own as a starter, or with a roast chicken, grilled chops, grilled steak or roast beef.

SERVES 4

450 g/1 lb large button mushrooms or oyster mushrooms
a little lemon juice
85 g/3 oz butter
1 tablespoon olive oil
3 garlic cloves, coarsely chopped
2 tablespoons chopped parsley
salt and freshly ground pepper

Slice the mushrooms or cut them in quarters. Sprinkle them with a few drops of lemon juice to keep them white. Melt the butter with the oil in a large frying pan and throw in the mushrooms. Fry until the mushrooms exude their juices, stirring them around all the time with a wooden spoon. Add the garlic and parsley, and season with salt and pepper. Leave to cook over a moderate heat for about 5 minutes more, stirring from time to time. Serve hot.

CHANTERELLES FRIED WITH DILL

Serve as a starter or with roast chicken.

SERVES 4

55 g/2 oz butter
1–2 shallots, finely chopped
340 g/12 oz fresh chanterelles
plain flour for dusting
salt and freshly ground pepper
6 tablespoons sour cream
1 teaspoon chopped fresh dill

Melt the butter in a frying pan and sweat the shallots until soft and golden. Dust the chanterelles with flour. Add them to the pan, and season with salt and pepper. Fry gently for about 10 minutes without browning, so that the mushrooms exude their liquid and then partially reabsorb it.

Stir in the sour cream and dill and allow to bubble gently until creamy. Serve hot.

Desserts and Puddings

APPLE FRITTERS

SERVES 4–6

115 g/4 oz plain flour
45 g/1½ oz unsalted butter, melted
8 eating apples
55 g/2 oz caster sugar
a large pinch of ground cinnamon
a large pinch of ground cloves
a pinch of salt
oil for deep-frying
1 free-range egg white

Make the batter about an hour before it is needed. Mix together the flour and melted butter and gradually add 250 ml/8 fl oz of lukewarm water. Leave to stand in a cool place.

Peel and core the apples and slice into rings. Mix together the caster sugar, cinnamon, cloves and salt. Sprinkle the apple slices with some of the spiced sugar.

Heat a deep pan of oil to about 180°C/350°F. Whisk the egg white until stiff, then fold into the batter. Dip the apple rings in the batter and gently shake off the excess. Deep-fry the rings in the hot oil, putting in just a few at a time, for a minute or two or until golden brown on both sides. Drain on kitchen paper. Sprinkle the fritters with the remaining spiced sugar and serve hot, with cream.

APPLE CRUMBLE

If you like, you can add blackberries to the apple mixture in the autumn.

SERVES 4

450 g/1 lb cooking apples, peeled, quartered and cored
2 strips of lemon zest
115 g/4 oz caster sugar
115 g/4 oz unsalted butter
85 g/3 oz plain flour
1 teaspoon ground cinnamon
a pinch of salt

Preheat the oven to 180°C/350°F, gas mark 4.

Put the apples in a small baking dish with 1–2 tablespoons of water, the lemon zest and 30 g/1 oz of the sugar. Toss gently to mix. Dot with 15 g/½ oz of the butter.

Mix the remaining sugar with the flour, cinnamon and salt. Add the remaining butter and rub it in with your fingertips until the mixture is the texture of fine breadcrumbs. Sprinkle the mixture in a thick layer over the apples. Bake for 40 minutes or until well browned on top. Serve hot, with cream or custard.

SPICED PEARS IN RED WINE

SERVES 4

600 ml/1 pint red wine
55 g/2 oz sugar, preferably vanilla sugar
6 cloves
1 cinnamon stick
2 strips of orange zest
4 large juicy pears
½ lemon

Put the wine in a small saucepan with the sugar, cloves, cinnamon and orange zest. Bring it to the boil and simmer for 5 minutes.

Peel the pears carefully, leaving their stalks on, and rubbing them with the lemon half as they are peeled to prevent them from browning. Arrange the pears, on their sides, in a saucepan or flameproof casserole that will just hold them comfortably. Pour on the spiced wine. Cover the pan and then poach the pears over a very gentle heat for 1 hour, turning them over halfway through cooking so that they become evenly coloured a nice reddish-brown.

Remove the pears with a slotted spoon. Reduce the cooking liquid until you have about 150 ml/¼ pint left. Serve the pears hot or cold with some of the liquid and a jug of cream.

QUINCES IN LEMON SYRUP

SERVES 4

170 g/6 oz caster sugar
2 strips of lemon zest
450 g/1 lb quinces
3 cooking apples

Put the sugar, 150 ml/¼ pint of water and the lemon zest in a saucepan. Dissolve the sugar over a gentle heat, then bring the syrup to the boil and continue to boil for 5 minutes. Remove the syrup from the heat and leave it to cool a little.

Meanwhile, peel and core the quinces and cut them into pieces, each approximately the size of a large sugar lump. Put them into the syrup. Simmer gently for 1 hour, covered at first and then, when the quinces are tender, uncovered.

Peel and core the cooking apples, and then cut them into pieces the same size as the pieces of quince. Add the apple pieces to the quinces and continue simmering until the apples are cooked and all the pieces of fruit are bathed in a golden-pink syrup. Remove the strips of lemon zest, and serve the quinces either warm or cold.

apple 162–3
pear 164–5
quince 164
spices 196–9
vanilla sugar 198, 211
whisking egg whites 423
zesting citrus fruits 423

apple corer 225
deep-fat thermometer 233
deep-fryer 239
slotted spoon 227

cherry 168–9
eau-de-vie framboise (cooking with) 208
gooseberry 172
kirsch 168
milk 97–8
raspberry 171–2
strawberry 171
whipping cream 423
whisking egg whites 423

baking sheet 236
cherry stoner 225
electric mixers 238–9
gratin dish 236
piping bag and nozzle 237
sieves 226–7
whisks 227

CHERRY CLAFOUTIS

This French speciality is delicious hot or cold. The blacker the cherries are the better this will be.

SERVES 6–8

- 85 g/3 oz plain flour
- a pinch of salt
- 3 free-range eggs
- 750 ml/1¼ pints milk
- 60 ml/2 fl oz kirsch
- 3 tablespoons caster sugar
- 700 g/1½ lb black cherries, stoned

Preheat the oven to 190°C/375°F, gas mark 5.

Put the flour in a bowl with the salt and make a well in the centre. Break in the eggs and beat them lightly. Add the milk slowly, stirring with a wooden spoon to make a smooth batter. Stir in the kirsch and sugar. Beat the batter well for several minutes using the spoon.

Butter a medium-sized gratin or baking dish and put the cherries in the bottom. Strain the batter over them. Bake for 50 minutes or until the batter is set. Sprinkle with a little extra sugar, and serve with cream if you like.

STRAWBERRY FOOL

SERVES 4

- 450 g/1 lb strawberries
- 170 g/6 oz caster sugar
- 300 ml/½ pint double cream

Keep 2–3 of the best strawberries on one side. Hull and chop the rest, and put them in a bowl with half the sugar. Leave for 30 minutes to allow them to exude their juices. Then crush them finely in their syrup using a fork.

Whip the cream with a balloon whisk until soft and thick, gradually adding the rest of the sugar. Do not overwhip or the cream will separate.

Stir the crushed strawberries into the cream. Put the mixture into a nice serving bowl and top with the reserved strawberries, whole or halved.

ALTERNATIVES: **Raspberry fool** Substitute raspberries for strawberries.
Gooseberry fool Use 450 g/1 lb cooked sweetened gooseberry purée instead of the strawberries.

FRESH RASPBERRY PAVLOVA

This is an extravagant Australian concoction. Both bowl and whisk must be spotlessly clean for whisking the egg whites: any trace of grease will prevent the whites from rising properly. A balloon whisk will give more volume than an electric mixer, although a mixer is less labour-intensive.

SERVES 4–6

- 4 egg whites
- a pinch of salt
- 280 g/10 oz caster sugar
- 450 g/1 lb fresh raspberries
- 1 teaspoon eau-de-vie framboise (optional)
- 300 ml/½ pint double cream

Preheat the oven to 130°C/250°F, gas mark ½. Dust a non-stick baking sheet very lightly with flour, and then set a 25 cm/10 in diameter plate, upside down, in the centre so that it marks a ring on the flour. Remove the plate.

Put the egg whites and salt in a spotlessly clean bowl and whisk until the whites are a very firm snow. Add about 115 g/4 oz of the caster sugar and whisk until the egg whites are firm again. Fold in another 115 g/4 oz sugar very lightly but thoroughly using a rubber spatula.

Fit a piping bag with a 1 cm/½ in plain nozzle and fill with the meringue mixture. (Or you can use a large clean plastic bag, such as a freezer bag, and cut off one corner to make a hole about 1 cm/½ in across.) Starting in the middle of the ring marked on the baking sheet, pipe out a flat disc of meringue. Squeeze the meringue gently through the hole in the bag, and coil the meringue around on itself like a snail shell. Pipe a ring of meringue on to the edge of the disc, so that you have a flan-shaped meringue case.

Bake for 2 hours or until the meringue is just cooked enough to handle. It will still be very delicate, so take care with it; leave it on the baking sheet to cool and crisp before you move it to a plate.

A short while before serving, fill the meringue case with raspberries. Sprinkle them with the remaining sugar and – if you are using it – the eau-de-vie framboise. Whip the cream to a light snow, and spread over the raspberries in a nice thick layer.

POUDING DE FRAMBOISES

This looks very festive.

SERVES 4–6

- 6–8 tablespoons kirsch or Cognac
- 300 g/10½ oz boudoir biscuits
- 500 g/1 lb 2 oz raspberries

CHERRY CLAFOUTIS

Dilute the kirsch or Cognac with an equal quantity of water. Dip about one-third of the biscuits in the liquid just to moisten them, and arrange them side by side, as close as possible, on the bottom of a large bowl or soufflé dish that is about 20 cm/8 in diameter. If necessary, trim the ends of the biscuits with a knife to make them fit more snugly.

Spread half of the raspberries over the biscuits. Add another layer of moistened biscuits, and cover with the rest of the raspberries. Finish with a layer of moistened biscuits. Set a plate on the top layer of biscuits and weight it lightly. Chill for 7–8 hours.

Run a palette knife round the pudding, to loosen it from the bowl or mould, then turn out on to a plate. Serve with crème fraîche or iced vanilla custard.

ALTERNATIVE: Use sliced strawberries instead of the raspberries.

BLACKCURRANT JELLY

Serve this with warm honey madeleines.

SERVES 6

- 450 g/1 lb fresh blackcurrants
- 225 g/8 oz sugar
- 4 gelatine leaves
- 150 ml/¼ pint port
- 2 tablespoons crème de cassis

Strip the blackcurrants from their stalks; there is no need to top and tail them. Place them in a stainless steel or enamelled saucepan and add the sugar and 300 ml/½ pint of water. Bring to the boil, then lower the heat and cover the pan. Simmer very gently for 10 minutes.

Tip the contents of the pan into a sieve suspended over a bowl and leave to drain and drip for at least 2 hours. Do not be tempted to force the syrup through the sieve; pressing the fruit could make the jelly cloudy.

Soak the gelatine leaves in cold water for a few minutes, until soft and soggy. Pour the blackcurrant syrup into a saucepan and warm it over a low heat. Drain the gelatine leaves, then add to the blackcurrant syrup and stir until completely melted. Remove from the heat, and stir in the port and crème de cassis.

Line the bottom of six ramekins with dampened greaseproof paper (or dampen six individual jelly moulds). Divide the blackcurrant mixture evenly among the ramekins. Chill for at least 6 hours, or preferably overnight, to set the jellies.

BLACKCURRANT JELLY WITH HONEY MADELEINES

ALTERNATIVES: You can use frozen blackcurrants instead of fresh; they give very successful results. Fresh or frozen blueberries would also work well.

SUMMER PUDDING

This is a prince among puddings.

SERVES 4–6

- 450 g/1 lb raspberries
- 400 g/14 oz caster sugar
- 225 g/8 oz each redcurrants and blackcurrants
- 1 small tin loaf of white bread

Put the raspberries in a saucepan with 170 g/6 oz of the sugar, and the red and blackcurrants in two separate pans with 115 g/4 oz of the sugar in each. A teaspoon of water in the bottom of each pan before it is put on the heat will prevent burning and sticking. Cook briefly and gently until the fruit exudes some juice. Do not stir the fruit – just swirl it carefully in the pan once or twice to dissolve the sugar – and do not let it become too mushy.

Cut the loaf of bread lengthwise into large slices, and remove the crusts. Use these large slices to line a 1 litre/2 pint pudding basin, cutting the slices to fit and leaving no gaps. Make alternate layers of currants and raspberries in the basin. Do not add much of the fruit juice – this should be put in a jug. Cover the top layer of fruit with more bread, then put a weighted plate on top. Allow the pudding to stand for 24 hours.

Turn out the pudding. The bread should all be pink with the juice from the fruit filling. If there are white patches, moisten with some of the juice reserved in the jug. Serve with the rest of the juice and with cream.

JAMAICAN BAKED BANANAS

This gorgeously sticky dessert will appeal to anyone with a sweet tooth. For a really deep, rich flavour, use muscovado sugar.

SERVES 4

- 115 g/4 oz salted butter
- 8 small ripe bananas, peeled
- 115 g/4 oz muscovado or demerara sugar
- juice of 1 lime
- 3–4 tablespoon dark rum
- Coconut Ice-cream to serve

Preheat the oven to 220°C/425°F, gas mark 7.

Melt the butter in a flameproof baking dish, preferably cast iron. Put in the bananas and turn them in the butter until lightly coated all over. Sprinkle over

banana 178
blackcurrant 173
crème de cassis (cooking with) 208
crème fraîche 99, 423
dissolving gelatine 423
gelatine 62
raspberry 171–2
redcurrant 173
strawberry 171
sugar 211–12

palette knife 228
pudding basin 230
ramekin 236, 423
sieves 226–7

Coconut Ice-Cream 399
Honey Madeleines 414

almond 186
bain-marie 422
bay 193
blanching almonds 189
cinnamon stick 197–8
crystallized angelica 185
crystallized flowers 185
glacé cherry 185
infuse 422
milk 97–8
raspberry 171–2
vanilla pod 198
vanilla sugar 198, 211
whipping cream 423
zesting citrus fruits 423

ramekin 236, 423
sieves 226–7

Strawberry Jam 417

the sugar. As it dissolves into the butter, turn the bananas to coat them in this sticky mixture. Squeeze over the lime juice. Place the dish in the hot oven and bake for 10 minutes

Remove the dish from the oven and put it back on the hob. Pour in the rum – take care as it may splutter. Allow the butter, sugar and rum to amalgamate, swirling the mixture around in the dish. Return the dish to the oven and bake for 5 minutes to give the bananas a final colouring, or pop the dish under a hot grill for a few minutes. Serve hot with coconut ice-cream.

SHERRY TRIFLE

SERVES 6

5 slices of sponge cake
a small wineglass of sherry
115 g/4 oz blanched almonds, cut into slivers
raspberry or strawberry jam, or fresh raspberries
150 ml/¼ pint double cream
15 g/½ oz caster sugar
a few crystallized violets or glacé cherries and angelica, or fresh raspberries or strawberries for the decoration

For the custard:

450 ml/¾ pint milk
2 tablespoons vanilla sugar, or 2 tablespoons caster sugar and a large strip of lemon zest
1 bay leaf (optional)
4 free-range eggs

Put the slices of sponge cake in a beautiful serving bowl (cut glass is traditional). Moisten with the sherry and allow it to soak in. Sprinkle with half the almond slivers. Spread over the jam, or scatter on some fresh raspberries.

Next make the custard. Put the milk and vanilla sugar, or caster sugar and lemon zest, in a saucepan or the top of a double boiler. Some people also add a bay leaf, which gives custard a very good but somewhat unexpected taste. Heat until bubbles form around the edge. Remove from the heat and leave to stand for 10 minutes so the milk can absorb the flavours. Beat the eggs in a small bowl. Pour on to them the now slightly cooled milk in a thin stream, stirring all the time. Strain the mixture back into the pan. Set over another saucepan of hot, not boiling, water and cook, stirring from time to time, until the custard thickens enought to coat the back of the spoon. Allow the custard to cool, then pour it into the bowl on top of the sponge cake. When it is cold, it should set fairly firm but by no means solid.

Whip the cream with the sugar to a soft snow. Pile it on top of the cold custard. Stick the remaining almond slivers into the cream like a hedgehog's prickles. Decorate the top of the trifle with crystallized violets, or glacé cherries and angelica, or fresh strawberries, or, best of all, raspberries. Chill for about 30 minutes, but no longer than 1 hour . (To prepare in advance, the trifle can be made up to the point of adding the custard, and then the cream piled on top and the decoration added at the last moment.)

CRÈME CARAMEL

A well-made crème caramel has a beautiful velvety texture. It should be shivery and tender, not a solid mass.

SERVES 6

170 g/6 oz caster sugar
600 ml/1 pint milk
a sliver of lemon zest
a 2.5 cm/1 in piece of cinnamon stick or a piece of vanilla pod
2 free-range eggs
1 free-range egg yolk

First make the caramel. Dissolve 85 g/3 oz of the sugar in 120 ml/4 fl oz of water, then bring to a rapid boil. Do not stir the sugar syrup after it boils. When it starts to brown, watch it carefully and tip the pan gently so the caramel turns an even gold. Pour the caramel quickly into a rice-pudding dish, a white china pie dish or some other round or oval dish with sloping sides which you have just rinsed in cold water. Swirl the caramel around a little to coat the sides.

Preheat the oven to 170°C/325°F, gas mark 3.

Put the milk in a saucepan and add the lemon zest, the rest of the sugar and the cinnamon or vanilla. Heat to just below boiling point, when small bubbles start forming around the edge of the pan. Reduce the heat to very low and leave the milk to infuse for 5 minutes.

Beat the whole eggs and egg yolk together in a bowl. Pour on the milk, stirring all the time. Strain the mixture into the dish on top of the caramel. Set the dish in a bain-marie or a large roasting tin half filled with water and bake for about 1 hour. Test the custard to see if it is cooked by sliding in the point of a knife; if it makes a clean cut, the custard is ready. Allow to cool for some hours before turning on to a dish.

ALTERNATIVE: For individual crème caramels, divide the caramel and then the custard among 5–6 ramekins or other small baking dishes. These will take 15–20 minutes to cook.

SHERRY TRIFLE

chocolate 212–13
cream 99–100
garden leaves and flowers 195
infuse 422
lemon 167
orange 165–6
vanilla pod 198
vanilla sugar 198, 211
whipping cream 423
whisking egg whites 423

blowtorch 229
graters 224, 226
gratin dish 236
ramekin 236, 423

CRÈME BRÛLÉE

SERVES 4–6

- 450 ml/¾ pint double cream
- 1 vanilla pod, split in half lengthways
- 4 free-range egg yolks
- 1 tablespoon caster sugar plus more for the top

Pour the cream into a saucepan, or the top of a double boiler, and add the vanilla pod. Heat until bubbles form around the edge, then remove from the heat and leave for 10 minutes to infuse. Meanwhile, beat the egg yolks with the sugar until the mixture is light and a little thickened.

Pour the hot cream on to the egg yolks in a thin stream, stirring all the time until they are well mixed. Return the mixture to the pan. Set over another pan of hot but not boiling water. Stir the custard until it thickens enough to coat the back of the spoon thickly.

Discard the vanilla pod. Pour the custard into ramekins or a gratin dish. Allow to cool, then cover and chill until cold and set.

Preheat the grill to very high.

Sprinkle caster sugar evenly over the top of the custard in a layer that is a little less than 5 mm/¼ in thick. Place the dish under the hot grill to melt and caramelize the sugar. It will colour unevenly, making it look like tortoise-shell, ranging prettily from golden to almost black. Leave the caramel to cool and set before serving.

ALTERNATIVES: Use 1 tablespoon vanilla sugar instead of the caster sugar and vanilla pod.
Trinity cream This was invented at Trinity College, Cambridge. It is made in the same way as crème brûlée, but the cream is not sweetened.

ZABAGLIONE

To make this for more than one, just multiply the ingredients by the number of people.

FOR EACH SERVING

- 1 free-range egg yolk
- 2 tablespoons Marsala
- 1 tablespoon caster sugar
- grating of lemon zest

Put all the ingredients in the top of a double boiler or in a heatproof bowl set over a pan of hot but not boiling water. Beat together well with a wire whisk. Keep whisking the mixture until it has trebled in volume and is light and frothy all the way through.

Pour into a warmed glass and eat immediately.

SYLLABUB

Syllabub should be light in texture and just lemony enough to avoid being over-rich. If you like, decorate with fresh flowers such as primroses, violets or violas.

SERVES 6–8

- 2 lemons
- 3 tablespoons caster sugar
- a wineglass of dry white wine or sherry
- 600 ml/1 pint double cream

Grate the zest from the lemons on the fine side of the grater. Mix with the juice of one of the lemons, the sugar and the wine or sherry. Leave to steep overnight.

Next day, put the mixture into a large bowl and add the cream. Whip until it stands up in soft peaks. Do not overwhip or the cream will separate. Spoon into small glasses and serve chilled, with ratafias.

DARK CHOCOLATE MOUSSE

SERVES 4–6

- 3 free-range eggs, separated
- 100 g/3½ oz best-quality dark chocolate, grated
- 55 g/2 oz caster sugar
- 150 ml/¼ pint plus 1 tablespoon double cream
- a tiny pinch of salt

Put the egg yolks in the top of a double boiler with the chocolate, sugar and 150 ml/¼ pint of cream. Whisk together until light. Set over the lower pan containing hot but not boiling water and cook the mixture, stirring from time to time, until it is thick and creamy. Cool before stirring in the salt and remaining cream.

Whisk the egg whites in a clean bowl until stiff. Stir a tablespoon of the whites into the chocolate mixture to lighten it, then fold in the rest, lightly but very thoroughly, using a metal spoon or a rubber spatula. Turn the mixture into little pots. Chill until set.

ALTERNATIVES: **Rich chocolate mousse** Omit the egg whites, and fold 300 ml/½ pint of whipped cream into the lukewarm chocolate mixture.
Chocolate orange mousse Stir the zest of ½ orange into the chocolate before adding the egg whites.

BREAD AND BUTTER PUDDING

SERVES 4

- 6 slices of bread – white, brown or currant loaf, crusts cut off
- softened unsalted butter

a handful of seedless raisins or sultanas
2 free-range eggs
1½ tablespoons caster sugar
a large pinch of ground cinnamon
150 ml/¼ pint milk
150 ml/¼ pint single cream

Generously butter the slices of bread. Lay the bread in layers, buttered side up, in a buttered pie dish, sprinkling the raisins or sultanas between the slices. Whisk together the eggs, 1 tablespoon of sugar and the cinnamon, then whisk in the milk and cream. Pour over the bread. Leave to soak for an hour.

Preheat the oven to 140°C/275°F, gas mark 1.

Just before putting the pudding in the oven, sprinkle it with the remaining sugar. Bake for 1–1½ hours (at the bottom of a low oven if you are cooking something else). The pudding will puff up and the top will become a delicious golden brown crust.

MARMALADE QUEEN OF PUDDINGS

This is one of those evergreen nursery puddings that almost everybody loves. The substitution of marmalade for the more usual jam is a truly wonderful notion.

SERVES 4
300 ml/½ pint milk
grated zest of 1 orange and 1 lemon
125 g/4½ oz caster sugar
a pinch of salt
55 g/2 oz fresh white breadcrumbs
2 free-range eggs, separated
3 heaped tablespoons good-quality marmalade, warmed until runny

Heat the milk with the orange and lemon zests until bubbles appear around the edge. Take the pan off the heat and cover. Leave to infuse for 30 minutes.

Add 30 g/1 oz of the sugar, the salt, breadcrumbs and egg yolks to the flavoured milk and whisk together thoroughly. Pour into a lightly buttered baking dish. Leave for 15 minutes to allow the breadcrumbs to absorb the milk and swell.

Preheat the oven to 180°C/350°F, gas mark 4.

Bake the pudding base for 20–25 minutes or until set and firm to the touch. Leave to rest for 10 minutes. Meawhile, whisk the egg whites until stiff. Gradually add 85 g/3 oz of the sugar in a thin stream, whisking constantly. Continue whisking until the meringue is thick and glossy.

Spoon the marmalade over the baked pudding base, spreading it evenly over the surface. Pile the meringue on top. Use the back of a spoon to shape the meringue into soft peaks. Sprinkle over the remaining sugar. Return the pudding to the oven to bake for 7–10 minutes or until the meringue is pale golden with a crusted surface. Serve warm, with very cold pouring cream.

VERMICELLI MILK PUDDING WITH CARDAMOM AND SAFFRON

Indian menus often include a milk pudding, perhaps as a left-over tribute to the British Raj. This version using vermicelli is unusual and has a delicious silky texture.

SERVES 4
750 ml/1¼ pints milk
½ teaspoon saffron threads
grated zest of 1 lemon
4 green cardamom pods, bruised
115 g/4 oz vermicelli
4 free-range egg yolks
85 g/3 oz sugar
150 ml/¼ pint double cream
a pinch of salt
30 g/1 oz unsalted butter, softened

Combine the milk, saffron, lemon zest and cardamom in a saucepan and heat until bubbles appear around the edge. Remove from the heat, cover and leave to infuse for 30 minutes.

Preheat the oven to 180°C/350°F, gas mark 4.

Add the vermicelli to the flavoured milk. Return the pan to the heat and bring to a simmer. Cook until the vermicelli is tender, stirring once or twice. Tip into a bowl and leave to cool slightly.

Beat together the egg yolks and sugar. Stir in the cream and salt. Add to the vermicelli mixture and mix thoroughly. Pour into a buttered ovenproof dish. Dot the butter over the surface. Bake for 30 minutes or until the pudding is just set. For an attractive finish, flash the pudding under a hot grill until it turns golden brown. Serve it with pouring cream if you wish.

ALTERNATIVE: Use short-grain (pudding) rice instead of vermicelli.

CHEESECAKE

SERVES 4–6
For the crust:
225 g/8 oz digestive biscuits, finely crushed
115 g/4 oz butter, melted
¼ teaspoon grated nutmeg
¼ teaspoon ground cinnamon
45 g/1½ oz caster sugar

cardamom 199
infuse 422
milk 97–8
raisin 182
saffron 199
short-grain rice 117
sultana 182
vermicelli 121
whisking egg whites 423
zesting citrus fruits 423

deep pie dish 237
whisks 227

Seville Orange Marmalade 418

blanching almonds 189
candied peel 184–5
cream cheese 101
crème fraîche 99
fresh breadcrumbs 364
glacé cherry 185
golden syrup 210
orange 165–6
raisin 182
self-raising flour 114
soured cream 99
spices 196–9
suet 110
sultana 182–3
vanilla sugar 198, 211
zesting citrus fruits 423

pudding basin 230
spring-clip tin 236
whisks 227

For the filling:
450 g/1 lb cream cheese
200 g/7 oz sour cream or crème fraîche
6 tablespoons sugar – vanilla if possible
4 free-range eggs
juice of 1 lemon
85 g/3 oz sultanas

Mix the digestive biscuit crumbs with the melted butter, spices and sugar. Press the mixture firmly and evenly over the bottom and up the sides of a well-buttered 23 cm/9 in spring-clip cake tin. Chill in the refrigerator until the crumb crust is set.

Preheat the oven to 180°C/350°F, gas mark 4.

Beat the cream cheese to soften it. Add the sour cream or crème fraîche and the sugar, then beat in the eggs one at a time. Finally, add the lemon juice and sultanas. Pour the mixture into the crumb crust. Bake for 45 minutes.

Allow the cheesecake to cool, then chill for 1–2 hours. To serve, carefully remove the cheesecake from the tin.

STICKY GOLDEN SPONGE PUDDING

SERVES 4–6
115 g/4 oz unsalted butter, softened
115 g/4 oz caster sugar
2 free-range eggs
115 g/4 oz self-raising flour
2–3 tablespoons milk
6–8 tablespoons golden syrup

Cream the butter and sugar together until smooth and pale in colour. Beat in the eggs one at a time, alternating with a little flour. Stir in the rest of the flour. Add enough milk to lighten the mixture and give it a soft, dropping consistency.

Butter a 1 litre/2 pint pudding basin. Put the golden syrup in the bottom and turn the sponge mixture into the basin. Cover with greaseproof paper and foil, pleated in the middle to allow for the expansion of the pudding, and tie on securely with string. Set the basin in a pan half full of boiling water, cover and steam for 2 hours. Top up with more boiling water as necessary.

Turn out the pudding on to a dish. If you wish, hand a jug of golden syrup separately.

CHRISTMAS PUDDING

Like all Christmas puddings, this is best made a month or so ahead, and improves with keeping. The recipe is based on the British royal family's Christmas pudding.

MAKES 2 PUDDINGS, EACH SERVING 8 OR MORE
225 g/8 oz shredded suet or grated butter
225 g/8 oz demerara sugar
225 g/8 oz large seedless raisins
225 g/8 oz sultanas
115 g/4 oz chopped candied peel
½ teaspoon mixed spice
¼ teaspoon grated nutmeg
225 g/8 oz fresh white breadcrumbs
115 g/4 oz plain flour
115 g/4 oz blanched almonds, cut in half
115 g/4 oz glacé cherries
4 free-range eggs
150 ml/¼ pint milk
½ wineglass of brandy

Mix the first eleven ingredients together in a large bowl. Whisk the eggs well in a small bowl and add the milk. Pour into the large bowl and mix thoroughly with the dry ingredients. Let the mixture stand for 12 hours in a cool place.

Add the brandy. Divide the mixture between two well-greased 1.5 litre/2½ pint pudding basins. Cover tightly with muslin, or with greaseproof paper pleated in the middle to allow for the expansion of the pudding, and tie on securely with string. Set each basin in a pan of boiling water, cover and steam for 8 hours or longer. Allow to cool, then replace the covering with fresh muslin or paper and an outer covering of foil. Store in a cool, dry place.

Before serving, steam again for 2–3 hours. Turn out to serve, flamed with brandy if you like.

CRÊPES SUZETTE

Here is the all-time classic flambéed dessert.

SERVES 4
For the pancake batter:
115 g/4 oz plain flour
a pinch of salt
1 free-range egg
1 free-range egg yolk
finely grated zest of ½ orange
275 ml/9½ fl oz milk
55 g/2 oz unsalted butter, melted, plus extra for frying
For the sauce and final cooking:
2 large juicy oranges
8 sugar cubes
55 g/2 oz caster sugar
juice of 1 lemon
115 g/4 oz unsalted butter, at room temperature
2 tablespoons Cointreau
2 tablespoons Cognac

First of all, make the pancake batter by simply putting all the ingredients into a blender and blending them well. Strain the batter into a jug and leave to stand for at least 30 minutes.

To make the pancakes, melt a small knob of butter in a 15 cm/6 in frying pan until the butter is hot and sizzling. Pour in just enough batter to cover the bottom of the pan, and swirl it around to make a very thin, even layer. Cook the pancake for about 1 minute, or until it is golden on the base, and then flip it over with the help of a palette knife and cook the other side for another minute or so.

The first pancake is often rather a mess; if so, throw it away and start afresh (in any case, this action is good for 'seasoning' the pan). Continue in the same way, using the batter to make about 12 pancakes, as thin as you dare, laying them out on a dry tea-towel as soon as they are cooked. You should not need to use too much butter to cook the pancakes; just add a trace now and again as the pan becomes dry (the melted butter already in the batter mixture usually provides sufficient lubrication).

Preheat the oven to 80°C/175°F, gas mark ¼, then lightly grease an oval serving dish and place it in the oven to warm.

To make the sauce, hold the oranges over a large frying pan and rub the sugar cubes over the orange skins to absorb the zest. When the sugar cubes start to collapse, drop them into the pan. Squeeze the juice from the oranges and then strain it into a bowl. Add the caster sugar to the sugar in the frying pan and set it over a moderate heat. The sugar will slowly melt and start to caramelize. As soon as it turns pale brown, add the orange juice, the lemon juice and half the butter. Bring the sauce to a gentle simmer, stirring it all the time.

Lay one pancake flat in the sauce, then flip it over on to its other side. Fold the pancake in half, then in half again to make a quarter-moon shape. Lay the folded pancake at one end of the warmed serving dish, and keep the dish in the oven with the door ajar while you prepare all the pancakes in the same way. As each one is ready, lay it neatly in the serving dish, slightly overlapping them to create a nice effect.

The sauce will have reduced during this time. If it looks too sticky, add a little more orange juice. Bring it up to a fast boil, and add the rest of the butter in small pieces, swirling the sauce around in the pan as you go. When the sauce is glossy, add the Cointreau and whisk it in. Pour the sauce over the pancakes and leave to soak in for a few minutes.

Pour the Cognac into a ladle and hold over a gas flame to warm it. Light it with a match and immediately pour it over the pancakes. Serve without delay.

CUSTARD PANCAKES

These pancakes make a delicious dessert. The original recipe for them comes from the cookbook of Harry's Bar in Venice.

SERVES 4

12 pancakes (see Crêpes Suzette)
1–2 tablespoons caster sugar
4–5 tablespoons Cointreau

For the custard cream filling:

400 ml/14 fl oz milk
½ vanilla pod, split lengthways
2 strips of lemon zest
3 extra large free-range egg yolks
115 g/4 oz caster sugar
40 g/1½ oz plain flour

First make the custard cream. Combine the milk, vanilla pod and the strips of lemon zest in a heavy-based saucepan and bring just to the boil. Take the pan off the heat and leave the flavours to infuse for several minutes. Remove the vanilla pod and lemon zest (if you like, wash and dry the vanilla pod and store it in a jar of caster sugar so that it can flavour and perfume the sugar).

In a bowl, whisk the egg yolks with the sugar until the sugar has dissolved. Whisk in the flour, adding just a little of this at a time and then whisking it in, until the mixture is smooth. Still whisking, pour in the flavoured milk in a steady stream. When this is well blended, pour it into the saucepan. Cook over a low heat, stirring constantly with a wooden spoon, until the custard is very thick. Continue to cook for a few more minutes, still stirring all the time (it is best to do this on a heat diffuser, if you have one available). Allow the custard cream to cool.

Preheat the oven to 230°C/450°F, gas mark 8. Lightly butter an oval oven-to-table dish.

Lay out the pancakes flat, with the better-looking side downwards so that the pancakes will look their best when they are arranged in the serving dish. Place a rounded tablespoon of the custard cream in the middle of each pancake. Fold the pancake over in half, then carefully fold again into an open fan shape. Arrange the filled pancakes in the buttered dish and sprinkle lightly with caster sugar. Bake for 5–10 minutes. The sugar will melt and become crunchy on the surface, the custard will warm through and the edges of the pancakes will scorch a little.

Take the dish out of the oven. Immediately spoon over the Cointreau and then light it with a match. Tilt and swirl the dish about so that the alcohol mingles with the butter and sugar and forms a sauce. Serve straight away.

eggs 96–7
infuse 422
vanilla pod 198
vanilla sugar 198, 211
zesting citrus fruits 423

blender, liquidizer 238
frying pan 234
palette knife 228
sieves 226–7
whisks 227

Crêpes Suzette 396

Ice-creams and Sorbets

chocolate 212–13
coffee 214–17
coriander seed 199
cream 99–100
eggs 96–7
milk 97–8
raspberry 171–2
strawberry 171
vanilla pod 198
vanilla sugar 198, 211
whipping cream 423
zesting citrus fruits 423

electric mixers 238–9
food processor 238
ice-cream maker 239
ice-cream scoop 229
Mouli-légumes 226
whisks 227

RICH VANILLA ICE-CREAM

This ice-cream is a beautiful creamy yellow, and is soft and smooth in texture, just the way ice-cream is supposed to be. The lemon and coriander used in this recipe are both traditional flavourings for vanilla ice-cream.

SERVES 4–6

6 free-range egg yolks
115 g/4 oz caster sugar
300 ml/½ pint milk
300 ml/½ pint single cream
1 vanilla pod, split lengthways
a strip of lemon zest
15 coriander seeds
150 ml/¼ pint double cream

Beat the egg yolks and sugar together for 5 minutes or until the sugar dissolves and the mixture becomes pale and frothy.

Put the milk and single cream in the top of a double boiler and add the vanilla pod. Heat until bubbles appear around the edge, but do not boil. Remove the vanilla pod, and pour the liquid in a fine stream into the egg yolks, beating all the time. Transfer the mixture to the top of the double boiler. Return the vanilla pod, and add the lemon zest and coriander seeds. Set over the lower pan containing very hot but not boiling water and stir until the custard thickens enough to coat the back of a wooden spoon. Pour into a bowl and allow to cool.

Whip the double cream lightly. Strain the cooled custard on to the cream, and whisk them together. Freeze in an ice-cream maker. Or pour into a freezer tray and freeze for about an hour, then whisk well or whizz in a food processor until all the ice crystals have disappeared; return to the tray and freeze again. Repeat the whisking two more times; the ice-cream takes about 3 hours or longer to set.

COFFEE ICE-CREAM

SERVES 4

3 free-range egg yolks
55 g/2 oz vanilla sugar
150 ml/¼ pint single cream
300 ml/½ pint strong black coffee
1 teaspoon good instant coffee powder
150 ml/¼ pint double cream

Beat the egg yolks with the sugar until pale and frothy. Add all the remaining ingredients and whisk well. Transfer the mixture to an ice-cream maker. Or pour into a freezer tray and freeze to a slush, then whisk or whizz in a food processor to a fine-textured snow; return to the tray and freeze until firm.

Transfer the ice-cream to the refrigerator about 20 minutes before serving, to allow it to soften. Eat this ice-cream within 2–3 days of making it.

ALTERNATIVE: **Chocolate ice-cream** Use 450 ml/¾ pint single cream, and replace the coffee with 115 g/4 oz grated plain chocolate. Heat the milk and chocolate together until the chocolate melts, allow it to cool a little and then whisk it into the egg and sugar mixture. When cool, add the cream and freeze as for coffee ice-cream.

STRAWBERRY ICE-CREAM

SERVES 4–6

3 free-range egg yolks
140–170 g/5–6 oz caster sugar
150 ml/¼ pint milk
150 ml/¼ pint double cream
450 g/1 lb ripe strawberries, hulled

Put the egg yolks and 140 g/5 oz sugar in a bowl and whisk them together until the mixture becomes light and pale. Set the bowl aside.

Heat the milk and cream in the top of a double boiler to just below boiling point. Pour in a thin stream into the egg and sugar mixture, beating all the time. Transfer the mixture to the top of the double boiler and set over the lower pan containing hot but not boiling water. Cook, stirring from time to time, until you have a smooth custard that is thick enough to coat the back of the spoon. Leave to cool completely.

Purée the strawberries in a food processor or put them through the medium blade of a Mouli-légumes. Fold into the cold custard. Taste the mixture and add more sugar if necessary. Ice-cream tastes less sweet after freezing, so the mixture should be fairly sweet when it goes into the freezer. Transfer to an ice-cream maker and freeze. Or pour into a freezer tray and freeze, whisking the mixture or whizzing it in a food processor once or twice to prevent the formation of large ice crystals.

ALTERNATIVE: **Raspberry ice-cream** Use raspberries instead of strawberries, and add 1 teaspoon of eau-de-vie framboise if you like.

MALTED ICE-CREAM

This is an extraordinarily rich ice-cream. The addition of crunchy pieces of Malteser is not essential, but makes the ice-cream particularly delectable.

SERVES 4

300 ml/½ pint double cream
300 ml/½ pint milk
6 free-range egg yolks
85 g/3 oz malted milk powder
225 g/8 oz good-quality milk chocolate, broken into pieces, at room temperature
20 Maltesers, coarsely crushed

Heat the cream and milk in a heavy-based saucepan until bubbles appear around the edge. Beat the egg yolks with the malted milk powder. Add to the hot cream and mix. Cook very gently, stirring constantly, until the custard has thickened enough to coat the back of a wooden spoon. Remove from the heat and stir in the chocolate until melted. Cool completely

Pour into an ice-cream maker and freeze until softly set. Alternatively, freeze the mixture in a plastic container until half-set, then place in a food processor and whizz for 1 minute.

Tip the ice-cream into a chilled bowl and fold in the crushed Maltesers. Spoon into a plastic container and freeze until needed. Transfer the ice cream to the refrigerator 30 minutes before serving.

COCONUT ICE-CREAM

SERVES 4

300 ml/½ pint milk
½ vanilla pod, split lengthways
pared zest of ½ lime
5 free-range egg yolks
115 g/4 oz caster sugar
200 g/7 oz creamed coconut
150 ml/¼ pint whipping cream
a tiny pinch of salt

Heat the milk, vanilla pod and lime zest in a heavy-based saucepan until bubbles appear around the edge. Give the mixture a brief whisk, then remove from the heat and cover the pan. Leave to infuse for 30 minutes.

Beat together the egg yolks and sugar until thick and pale. Add the flavoured milk, whisking well. Mix in the creamed coconut. Pour into the saucepan and cook over a low heat, stirring constantly, until the custard has thickened enough to coat the back of a wooden spoon. Strain the custard into a bowl. Stir in the cream and salt. Leave to cool.

Pour into an ice-cream maker and freeze. Alternatively, freeze the mixture in a plastic container until half-set, then whisk well or whizz in a food processor for 1 minute; return the mixture to the container and freeze again until set.

Transfer the ice-cream from the freezer to the refrigerator 30 minutes before you wish to serve it, so that it has time to soften.

PEACH MELBA

This is a truly great dessert. Legend has it that the singer Dame Nellie Melba lent her name to this concoction, thrown together by Escoffier in a fit of passionate expression to celebrate the diva's art.

SERVES 4

2 large ripe peaches, preferably white-fleshed, or 4 small ones
170 g/6 oz caster sugar
300 ml/½ pint white wine
170 g/6 oz fresh raspberries
Rich Vanilla Ice-cream

Bring a large saucepan of water to the boil. Drop in the peaches and blanch them for 10 seconds. Lift them out and allow to cool, then peel. Cut the peaches in half and remove the stones.

Combine the sugar and wine in a saucepan that will hold the peach halves snugly. Bring to the boil and simmer for 5 minutes. Drop in the peach halves and poach gently for 10 minutes. Leave them to cool in the syrup.

Lift out the peach halves and place on a plate. Reduce the poaching syrup by half, then pour it into a blender. Add the raspberries and purée. Pass through a fine sieve into a bowl and chill.

To serve, put a scoop of vanilla ice-cream in four chilled glass dishes. Perch one large or two small peach halves on each scoop and cover generously with the raspberry sauce.

ORANGE SORBET

SERVES 4

6 oranges
1 lemon
115 g/4 oz icing sugar

Squeeze the oranges and lemon to make just over 600 ml/1 pint of juice. Stir in the icing sugar, whisking it in thoroughly so that it dissolves. Transfer to an ice-cream maker and freeze. Or pour into a freezer tray and freeze to a slush, then whisk well or whizz in a food processor so that the sorbet becomes very light and fine grained; return to the tray and freeze until firm.

Transfer the sorbet to the refrigerator about 30 minutes or so before eating, to let it soften.

chocolate 212–13
cream 99–100
creamed coconut 189
eggs 96–7
infuse 422
lemon 167
lime 167
milk 97–8
orange 165–6
peach 169
peeling peaches 423
raspberry 171–2
reduce 423
sugar 210–12
vanilla pod 198

blender, liquidizer 238
food processor 238
ice-cream maker 239
ice-cream scoop 229
juice extractors 226–7, 239
sieves 226–7
whisks 227

Rich Vanilla Ice-Cream 398

GRAPEFRUIT SORBET

SERVES 4–6
115 g/4 oz caster sugar
4 grapefruit (use pink grapefruit if you like)

Dissolve the sugar in 3 tablespoons of water in a small saucepan. Bring to the boil and boil for 5 minutes, then allow to cool. Meanwhile, squeeze the juice from the grapefruit. Add the cooled syrup to the grapefruit juice. Strain it into an ice-cream maker and freeze. Or strain into a freezer tray and freeze to a slush, then whisk well or whizz in a food processor to a fine snow; return to the tray and freeze until firm.

Transfer the sorbet to the refrigerator at least half an hour before serving, to let it soften.

MELON SORBET

SERVES 4
2 honeydew or small cantaloupe melons, each weighing about 450 g/1 lb
juice of 2 lemons
225 g/8 oz icing sugar

Cut the melons in half and discard the seeds and fibres from the centre. Scoop out all the flesh with a sharp spoon. Put the melon flesh in a food processor and add the lemon juice and sugar. Whizz to a smooth purée. Pour into an ice-cream maker or a freezer tray and freeze. If using a freezer tray, freeze to a slush, then whizz the sorbet in the food processor until smooth, to prevent any large ice crystals from forming; return to the tray and freeze until firm.

ELDERFLOWER SORBET

This sorbet has a delicate, summery flavour.

SERVES 4
3 large sprays of fresh elderflowers
115 g/4 oz caster sugar
2 large grapefruit
1 lemon

Rinse the elderflowers briefly. Dissolve the sugar in 300 ml/½ pint of water in a small saucepan. Bring to the boil and boil for 5 minutes. Remove the pan from the heat and plunge in the elderflowers, stalk upwards. Leave, uncovered, to infuse and cool.

Squeeze the juice from the grapefruit and lemon, and pour it into the cold elderflower infusion. Strain into an ice-cream maker and freeze. Alternatively, strain into a freezer tray and freeze to a slush, then whisk well or whizz in a food processor to prevent large ice crystals from forming; return to the tray and freeze until firm.

ORANGE, GRAPEFRUIT AND MELON SORBETS

COFFEE GRANITA

This is the refreshing late-morning favourite that many Italians and tourists alike enjoy at the myriad pavement cafés in Rome and other cities.

SERVES 4
115 g/4 oz sugar
600 ml/1 pint very strong hot coffee, preferably espresso
300 ml/½ pint double or whipping cream, lightly whipped
2 tablespoons Tia Maria (optional)

Dissolve the sugar in the hot coffee. Allow to cool, then pour into a shallow metal tray. Freeze for 30 minutes.

Remove the tray from the freezer and, using a fork, bring the partially frozen coffee from the edges into the still liquid centre. Do not be tempted to use a whisk; the whole idea is to coax ice crystals into forming, and this is best done with a fork. Return the tray to the freezer. Freeze for 20 minutes, then repeat the forking process. Continue freezing and forking over a period of about 2 hours, until the mixture has become soft crystals of coffee ice, all separate, opaque and pale brown in colour.

Serve the granita in well-chilled goblets, layered up with whipped cream. If you wish, dribble some Tia Maria on to the layers of cream as you build them up.

ALTERNATIVES: **Strawberry or raspberry granita** Dissolve 85 g/3 oz sugar in 150 ml/¼ pint of water and boil for 2 minutes. Leave to cool. Purée 250 g/9 oz strawberries or raspberries with the sugar syrup and the juice of ½ lemon. Strain, then freeze as for coffee granita. Serve these fruit granitas without the whipped cream.
Orange granita Rub 55 g/2 oz cube sugar over the skins of 2–3 oranges to absorb the zest, holding the oranges over a bowl so that the sugar falls into the bowl as it starts to disintegrate. Squeeze enough oranges to yield 500 ml/18 fl oz juice and add it to the bowl. Whisk in 250 g/9 oz icing sugar until the mixture is completely smooth. Strain, then freeze as for coffee granita.

cream 99–100
elderflower 174
espresso
coffee 216
grapefruit 167
infuse 422
lemon 167
melon 176–7
orange 165–6
raspberry 171–2
strawberry 171
sugar 210–12
whipping cream 423

food processor 238
ice-cream maker 239
ice-cream scoop 229
juice extractors 226–7, 239
sieves 226–7
whisks 227

Pastries

butter 99–100
dehydrated milk 98
lard 110
plain flour 114
strong white bread flour 114

food processor 238
pastry making equipment 237

SHORTCRUST PASTRY

The secret of making shortcrust pastry is to handle it as little as possible. If you prefer, you can make the dough in a food processor, but take care not to overwork it. Use shortcrust for sweet and savoury pies, flans and tarts.

170 g/6 oz plain flour
a pinch of salt
85 g/3 oz cold butter
30 g/1 oz cold lard

Put the flour and salt into a bowl. Add the butter and the lard. Using a knife, cut and stir the pieces of fat into the flour until they are about the size of peas. Then very briefly rub the flour-coated pieces of fat between thumbs and fingertips, raising your hands well above the bowl as you do so, so that the smaller pieces fall back in a shower. Stop rubbing as soon as the fat looks rather like cornflakes. Do not try to get the mixture to look like fine breadcrumbs because this will make the pastry dense.

Add just enough very cold water to bind the mixture – about 3–4 tablespoons – and mix it in with a knife or fork until it starts to clump together. Quickly gather into a ball with your hands and put the dough in a plastic bag. Chill for at least 20 minutes.

ALTERNATIVE: For sweet flans, add 1–2 teaspoons of caster sugar to the flour.

PÂTE BRISÉE

This pastry is used for sweet tarts and flans. The milk powder makes it a little richer and lighter.

170 g/6 oz plain flour
1 teaspoon caster sugar
15 g/½ oz dried milk powder
a pinch of salt
115 g/4 oz butter, softened
1 tablespoon brandy or lemon juice
1 free-range egg

Mix the flour in a bowl with the caster sugar, dried milk powder and salt. Make a well in the centre. Cut the butter into small cubes and put them into the well with the brandy or lemon juice and egg. Mix well with your fingers, crushing the butter and incorporating it thoroughly with the other ingredients, to make a sticky dough.

Turn the dough on to a floured board. Sprinkle it with flour and smear it across the board with the heel of your hand. Do this two or three times, until the butter is evenly blended in. Roll the dough into a ball, with floured hands, and put it in a plastic bag. Chill for at least 30 minutes before using.

ROUGH PUFF PASTRY

Use as an alternative to flaky pastry.

85 g/3 oz butter, chilled
85 g/3 oz lard, chilled
225 g/8 oz strong white bread flour
a pinch of salt

Put the butter and lard on a floured board and cut into cubes the size of small hazelnuts. Combine the flour and salt in a bowl and add the cubed fat. Mix in about 120 ml/4 fl oz of iced water with a knife, adding it a little at a time until the dough is just holding together – it may not need all of the water. Chill the lumpy dough for 15 minutes.

On a well-floured board roll out the dough into a rectangle. Fold it over in thirds, like a business letter, and press the outside edges together with the rolling pin to seal in the air. Chill for 15 minutes. Roll out again into a rectangle, fold over, press edges together and chill as before. Roll out and fold once more. You now have 27 layers of paper-thin pastry. Chill for the last time, then roll out, fold into thirds and pinch the sides together. You will now have 81 thin layers of pastry with air in between.

FLAKY PASTRY

This pastry, which is also known as *pâte feuilletée*, is used for light tarts, pies and pastries.

225 g/8 oz strong white bread flour
280 g/10 oz butter
1 teaspoon salt

Put the flour, 55 g/2 oz of the butter, the salt and just under 150 ml/¼ pint of cold water into a food processor. Work until a dough is formed that can be formed into a ball. Place the ball of dough in a plastic bag and put it to rest in the refrigerator for 1–2 hours. At the same time chill the remaining butter – it should be at the same temperature as the dough.

Take the chilled dough and butter out of the refrigerator. Put the butter into a loose plastic bag and beat it with a rolling pin into a rectangle about 2 cm/¾ in thick. Roll out the dough, which will be rather elastic and difficult to roll, into a rectangle large enough to envelop the flattened butter completely. Place the butter in the middle of the rectangle

Making shortcrust pastry

1 Combine the flour, salt and fat in a bowl. With a knife, cut the fat into pieces the size of a pea, tossing to coat them with flour. Then lightly rub the fat into the flour with your fingertips until the pieces look like small cornflakes.

2 Add a little very cold water, tossing with a fork – just enough water so the mixture will clump together.

baking blind 404
covering a deep pie dish 404

pastry making equipment 237

Shortcrust Pastry 402

1

2

3 Gather into a ball of dough and put into a plastic bag. Leave the dough to rest in the refrigerator for at least 20 minutes before using.

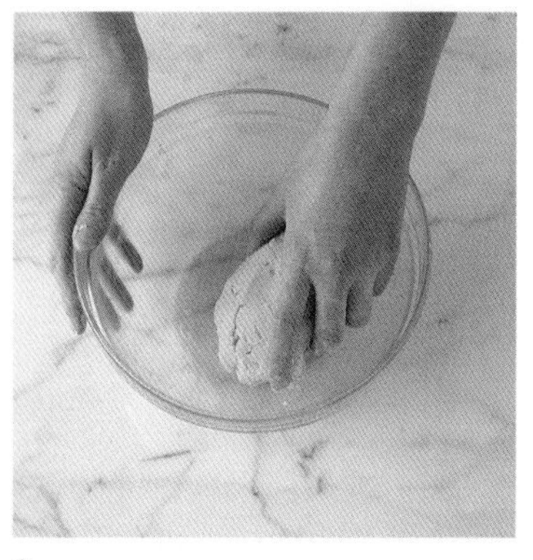
3

Lining a flan or tart tin

1 Roll out the dough on a lightly floured surface to a round that is approximately 3 mm/⅛ in thick.

1

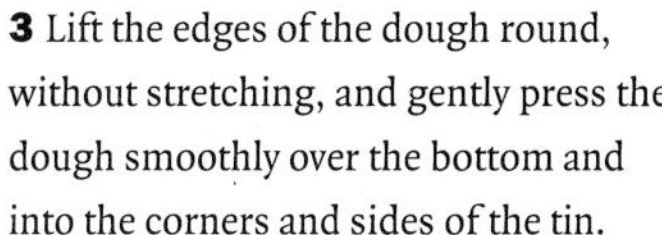

2 Roll up the dough loosely around the rolling pin, then unroll it over the tin, draping it gently over the centre.

3 Lift the edges of the dough round, without stretching, and gently press the dough smoothly over the bottom and into the corners and sides of the tin.

2

3

4 Roll the rolling pin over the top edge of the tin to cut off excess dough.

5 Neaten the edge of the pastry case, pushing up the sides slightly and into the flutes on the side of the tin.

4

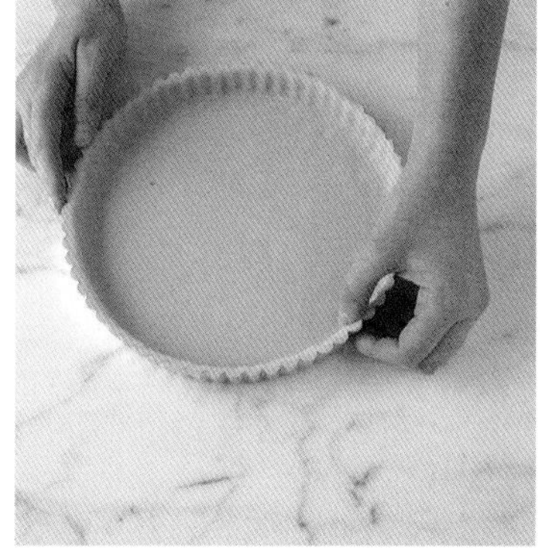
5

butter 99–100
eggs 96–7
lining a tart tin 403
making shortcrust pastry 403
pastry recipes 402
plain flour 114

pastry making equipment 237

Shortcrust Pastry 402

Baking blind
Prick the bottom of the pastry case with a fork, then line with baking parchment or greaseproof paper, crumpling up the paper and then pressing it smoothly over the pastry dough. Fill to the brim with dried beans or with ceramic baking beans. Bake until the pastry case is set, then remove the paper and beans and bake for a few more minutes, to cook the bottom of the case.

1

2

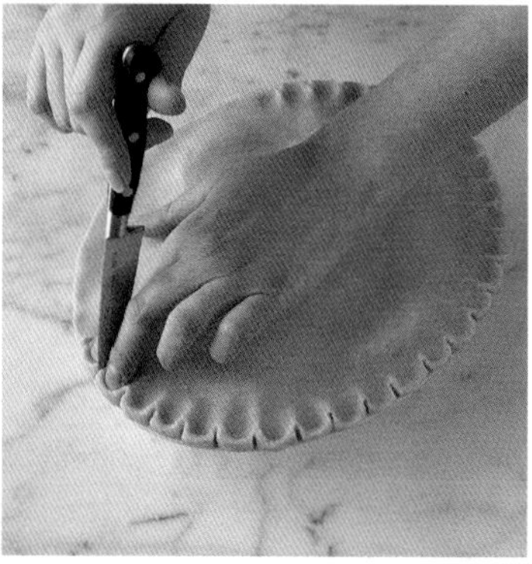

3

Covering a deep pie dish

1 Roll out the dough to an oval about 7.5 cm/3 in larger than the dish. Cut a strip the same width as the rim of the dish and long enough to cover the rim. Brush the rim with water, and lay the strip in place.

2 Dampen the dough strip with water. Roll the rest of the dough around the rolling pin, and unroll it over the dish. Press gently to seal the pastry lid to the strip of dough, and trim off the excess.

3 Make a scalloped edge as shown. Make a small hole in the centre of the lid, over the funnel. If you like, stick on shapes cut from dough trimmings, using a little egg glaze.

of dough and fold the edges over to enclose the butter. Flour the work surface, and roll out the parcel of dough into a rectangle measuring about 20 x 40 cm/8 x 12 in. Sprinkle a little flour on any places where the dough breaks or the butter seeps out. Fold the rectangle into three, like a business letter, then give it a quarter turn (45 degrees). Repeat the rolling out and folding twice more – three times altogether.

Put the folded dough back into the plastic bag and place it in the refrigerator to chill for 1 hour, then repeat the three rollings and foldings. Chill for another hour. The dough is now ready to use, or you can roll and fold it one more time if you like, to make nine times altogether.

Baking blind

To prevent the bottom of a pastry case being rather under-cooked and soggy, it is a good idea to bake the case 'blind' before you put in the filling. To do this, line the tart or flan tin with the pastry dough, prick the bottom with a fork and then cover the pastry with baking parchment, greaseproof paper or foil, bringing it up the sides of the tin. Fill the tin to the brim with dried beans (dried broad beans are excellent) or special ceramic baking beans. Bake in a preheated oven (220°C/425°F, gas mark 7) for 12–15 minutes. Remove the beans and paper or foil, and bake for a few minutes more or until the pastry has lost its translucent look. You can now add the filling.

CHOUX PASTRY

Use for éclairs, profiteroles and so forth.

70 g/2½ oz butter
¼ teaspoon salt
¼ teaspoon caster sugar
85 g/3 oz plain flour
3–4 free-range eggs

Put the butter, salt and sugar in a heavy saucepan and add 150 ml/¼ pint of water. Bring to the boil, stirring occasionally to help the butter melt. Remove the pan from the heat and allow the mixture to cool a little.

Sift the flour into the pan and beat with a wooden spoon until it is completely absorbed and the mixture is smooth. Return the saucepan to the heat and beat the mixture for a further 1–2 minutes or until it starts to pull away from the sides of the pan.

Remove the pan from the heat once again. Break in an egg and beat it into the mixture until it is fully absorbed, and then add the second and third eggs in the same way. Break the fourth egg into a cup and whisk it with a fork. Beat just enough of this whisked egg into the mixture to make a soft dough that holds its shape – 3 eggs may be enough if they were extra large ones. Use the remainder of the fourth egg, beaten with a pinch of salt, to glaze the choux pastries before baking them.

HOT-WATER CRUST PASTRY

This type of pastry is traditionally used for making such dishes as raised pies.

450 g/1 lb plain flour
a good pinch of salt
170 g/6 oz good-quality lard
150 ml/¼ pint milk

Put the flour and salt into a bowl. Bring the lard, milk and 150 ml/¼ pint of water to the boil in a saucepan. Pour into the flour, and mix the ingredients together with a wooden spoon to make a smooth dough.

When the dough is cool enough to handle, knead it lightly and evenly with your hands – don't overhandle or it will become tough. Use the dough while it is still warm.

BLACKBERRY AND APPLE PIE

SERVES 6

450 g/1 lb fresh plump blackberries
450 g/1 lb cooking apples – preferably Bramley's, peeled, cored and sliced
85 g/3 oz granulated or light soft brown sugar
3 cloves
Shortcrust Pastry made with 170 g/6 oz flour
free-range egg yolk beaten with a few drops of water for glazing (optional)

Preheat the oven to 220°C/425°F, gas mark 7.

Put a pie funnel in the middle of a 28 x 22 cm/ 11 x 8½ in pie dish. Put in the fruit in layers, sprinkling the sugar over the layers as you go. Drop in the cloves. Roll out the pastry dough and use to cover the dish. Make a small hole in the centre of the pastry lid, over the pie funnel, and decorate with the pastry trimmings, making apple and leaf shapes. Glaze with the egg yolk, brushed on with a pastry brush. Or, if you prefer, brush the pie with water and sprinkle it with a little sugar instead.

Bake the pie for 12–15 minutes, then turn the heat down to 180°C/350°F, gas mark 4. Bake for a further 30 minutes. If the top of the pie is becoming too brown, cover it loosely with foil. Serve the pie hot with plenty of cream.

ALTERNATIVE: Fill with apples alone (a mixture of Bramley's and Cox's or Golden Delicious is very good), and add some grated orange or lemon zest with the sugar. Or, use apples with fresh or dried blueberries or cranberries. Rough Puff Pastry can be substituted for the shortcrust.

STRAWBERRY TART

SERVES 4

Pâte Brisée made with 85 g/3 oz flour
2–3 tablespoons seedless raspberry jelly or sieved raspberry jam
grated zest of ½ orange
450 g/1 lb strawberries, hulled and halved

Preheat the oven to 180°C/350°F, gas mark 4.

Roll out the pastry dough and cut a 25 cm/10 in round, using a plate as a guide. Transfer the round to a buttered baking sheet. Bake for 15–20 minutes or until cooked and a nice pale biscuit colour. Allow to cool slightly.

Warm the raspberry jelly or jam in a small saucepan until melted smooth. Mix in the grated orange zest. Brush the mixture over the pastry round, leaving a 1 cm/½ in margin clear all around the edge. Arrange the strawberry halves carefully on the pastry base in concentric circles.

Eat the tart while still warm, if possible, although it is still delicious cold.

ALTERNATIVE: Use raspberries instead of the strawberries, choosing firm, perfect fruit.
Lemon tart Spread the pastry base with freshly made, warm Lemon Curd.

apple 162–3
blackberry 172
covering a deep pie dish 404
lard 110
plain flour 114
raspberry 171–2
strawberry 171
sugar 210–12
zesting citrus fruits 423

baking sheet 236
pastry making equipment 237

Lemon Curd 419
Pâte Brisée 402
Rough Puff Pastry 402
Shortcrust Pastry 402

PUMPKIN PIE

SERVE 4

Shortcrust Pastry made with 170 g/6 oz flour
700 g/1½ lb pumpkin
85 g/3 oz caster sugar
½ teaspoon ground allspice
1 teaspoon ground ginger
3 free-range eggs, beaten
generous 150 ml/¼ pint creamy milk or single cream
½ teaspoon grated nutmeg

Roll out the pastry dough and use to line a 20 cm/8 in flan tin. Bake the pastry case blind.

Peel the pumpkin, discard all seeds and fibres, and cut the flesh into cubes. Put them in a wide shallow saucepan or sauté pan with 3 tablespoons of water. Cook gently, stirring from time to time, for about 40 minutes, stirring occasionally. Quite a lot of liquid will run out of the pumpkin. When the pumpkin is soft and translucent, tip it into a wire sieve to drain.

Preheat the oven to 190°C/375°F, gas mark 5.

Purée the well-drained pumpkin in a food processor or using the fine blade of a Mouli-légumes (if using the processor, press the purée through a sieve to remove all fibres). Add the sugar, allspice, ginger, eggs and milk or cream and mix until smooth and creamy. Pour into the pastry case and sprinkle the top with nutmeg. Bake for 1 hour or until the filling is just set. Cover with greaseproof paper if the pastry becomes too brown.

PECAN PIE

SERVES 4–6

Shortcrust Pastry made with 170 g/6 oz flour
85 g/3 oz unsalted butter, softened
85 g/3 oz soft light brown sugar
1 tablespoon vanilla sugar
3 free-range eggs
4 tablespoons thin honey
170 g/6 oz shelled pecans
a pinch of salt

Preheat the oven to 220°C/425°F, gas mark 7.

Roll out the pastry dough and use to line a 20 cm/8 in tart tin. Bake the pastry case blind.

Cream the butter and the sugars together until light and fluffy. Beat in the eggs one at a time. Stir in the honey, pecans and salt. Fill the pastry case with the mixture.

Bake for about 30 minutes. To test if the pie is ready, insert the point of a knife into the middle of the filling; it should come out clean. Eat the pie warm.

ALTERNATIVE: **Walnut pie** Use shelled walnuts instead of pecans.

RHUBARB AND RAISIN PIE

Serve this excellent pie hot with fresh cream.

SERVES 6

Shortcrust Pastry made with 225 g/8 oz flour
900 g/2 lb rhubarb, cut into 2.5 cm/1 in pieces
2 teaspoons plain flour
85 g/3 oz sugar
55 g/2 oz raisins soaked in 3 tablespoons port or red wine
a little top of the milk or half cream for glazing

Preheat the oven to 220°C/425°F, gas mark 7.

Roll out half of the shortcrust pastry dough and use to line a 26 cm/10 in pie plate. Put in the rhubarb and sprinkle with the flour and most of the sugar. Spread the raisins over the top and pour on the port or red wine used for soaking them. Roll out the rest of the pastry dough and lay over the filling. Press the edges together to seal. Flute the edge, and make several cuts in the pastry lid. Brush with top of the milk or half cream and sprinkle with the remaining sugar.

Bake for 12–15 minutes, then lower the temperature to 180°C/350°F, gas mark 4. Bake for a further 20–25 minutes, covering loosely with foil if the pastry looks as if it is becoming too brown.

TRADITIONAL CUSTARD TART

This is a great favourite in the annals of British puddings.

SERVES 4

For the pastry:
115 g/4 oz plain flour
a pinch of salt
55 g/2 oz butter, diced
1 free-range egg yolk
a little beaten egg yolk for glazing

For the custard filling:
300 ml/½ pint milk
300 ml/½ pint double cream
½ vanilla pod, split lengthways
2 free-range eggs
4 free-range egg yolks
85 g/3 oz caster sugar
a pinch of salt
freshly grated nutmeg

baking blind 404
honey 210
lining a tart or flan tin 403
milk 97–8
nutmeg 198
pecan 188
pumpkin 155, 157
raisin 182
rhubarb 170, 174
spices 196–9
sugar 210–12
vanilla pod 198
vanilla sugar 198, 211
walnut 188

food processor 238
Mouli-légumes 226
pastry making equipment 237
sieves 226–7

Shortcrust Pastry 402

RHUBARB AND RAISIN PIE

baking blind 404
infuse 422
lining a tart or flan tin 403

graters 224, 226
ladle 227
pastry making equipment 237

APRICOT TART

To make the pastry put the flour and salt in a bowl and rub in the butter until the mixture resembles fine crumbs. Mix in the egg yolk and 1–2 tablespoons iced water using a fork or knife. When the mixture clumps together, gather it into a ball. Place in a plastic bag and chill for at least 1 hour before rolling out.

Preheat the oven to 180°C/350°F, gas mark 4.

Roll out the pastry dough as thinly as possible and use it to line a 20 cm/8 in flan or tart tin that is 4 cm/1½ in deep. Bake the pastry case blind for 15–20 minutes. Remove the beans and paper or foil. Lightly brush the inside of the pastry case with beaten egg yolk, which will form a seal and prevent any leaks of filling. Return to the oven to bake for a further 10 minutes or so, until it is golden and crisp and well cooked all through, particularly the base. Remove the pastry case and set aside. Lower the oven temperature to 170°C/325°F, gas mark 3.

Heat together the milk, cream and vanilla pod until bubbles appear around the edge. Stir briefly, then remove from the heat and cover the pan. Leave to infuse for 30 minutes.

Beat together the whole eggs, egg yolks and sugar. Strain in the flavoured milk. Add the salt and stir to mix everything together thoroughly. Leave to stand for 5 minutes, and then skim off any froth with kitchen paper. Carefully ladle almost all the custard mixture into the cooked pastry case. Set on the middle shelf of the oven, then add the rest of the filling (this is a good way to avoid spillage). Bake for 30 minutes; the custard filling should still be slightly wobbly. Grate plenty of nutmeg over the surface. Return the tart to the oven and finish cooking for a further 10 minutes. Serve warm.

FRENCH ALMOND TART

This shining brown puff, called a *Pithiviers*, is often seen in French pâtisseries, the top decorated with one of a thousand different geometric designs, and the almond filling varying from a smooth honey-coloured paste to a solid, granular marzipan. It makes a delicious dessert and is equally good for tea.

SERVES 6–8

115 g/4 oz unsalted butter, softened
115 g/4 oz caster sugar plus extra for sprinkling
3 free-range egg yolks
225 g/8 oz ground almonds
5 tablespoons double cream, whipped
2 teaspoons dark rum or ½ teaspoon grated lemon zest
Flaky Pastry made with 225 g/8 oz flour
free-range egg beaten with a little milk for glazing

Cream the butter and sugar together until pale and light. Add the egg yolks and beat for 2 minutes. Lightly mix in the almonds, cream and rum or lemon zest.

Preheat the oven to 200°C/400°F, gas mark 6.

Divide the pastry dough in two, one portion slightly larger than the other. Form the smaller of the two pieces into a ball, then roll it out into a round the thickness of a penny, leaving it untrimmed; the round will be about 22 cm/8½ in diameter. Transfer it to a large dampened baking tray. Spread the almond mixture evenly over the pastry round, leaving a margin of about 2.5 cm/1 in clear around the edge.

Roll out the second piece of the pastry dough into a round slightly larger and thicker than the first one. Dampen the margin of the bottom round, then lay the other round over the top and press the edges together lightly. Trim and notch the edge. Glaze the top with egg and milk and mark a pattern of lines over it with a knife. Bake for 35–40 minutes or until the pastry is puffed and golden brown. Take it out of the oven and sprinkle the top with a little extra caster sugar.

APRICOT TART

SERVES 4

450 g/1 lb apricots, fresh or canned
Flaky Pastry made with 115 g/4 oz flour
55 g/2 oz caster sugar
55 g/2 oz unsalted butter

Preheat the oven to 220°C/425°F, gas mark 7.

If using fresh apricots, cut them in half and remove the stones. If using canned apricots, drain them very thoroughly in a sieve.

Roll out the pastry dough into a rectangle about 20 x 30 cm/8 x 12 in. Trim the edges very neatly with a sharp knife – if it is not cleanly cut the pastry won't rise properly. Put the pastry rectangle on to a dampened baking sheet. Press the apricot halves, cut side up, into the pastry in rows, leaving a 1 cm/½ in margin clear round the outside edges. Sprinkle the apricots with the sugar and dot the butter all over the top.

Bake for 10 minutes, then turn down the heat to 200°C/400°F, gas mark 6. Bake for a further 20–30 minutes or until the pastry and apricots are glazed with melted butter and sugar, and starting to blacken on the very tips. Eat hot or cold.

ALTERNATIVE: **Apple tart** Arrange neat rows of thinly sliced dessert apples instead of the apricots.

PROFITEROLES

MAKES 8–10

Choux Pastry made with 85 g/3 oz flour
1 free-range egg beaten with a pinch of salt for glazing
300 ml/½ pint double cream
1 teaspoon vanilla sugar

For the icing:

115 g/4 oz good-quality dark chocolate, chopped
2 teaspoons rum
115 g/4 oz unsalted butter, softened

Preheat the oven to 180°C/350°F, gas mark 4.

Dampen two large baking sheets. Put rounded dessertspoons of the choux pastry, well spaced out, on the baking sheets. Or, better still, put the dough in a piping bag fitted with a 1 cm/½ in nozzle and pipe out rounds about 4 cm/1½ in across and 2.5 cm/1 in high. Brush the tops with the egg glaze. Lightly flatten the profiteroles with a pastry brush.

Bake for 20 minutes or until firm and golden. Transfer to a wire rack to cool. While they are still warm prick a small hole in the base of each profiterole to let the steam escape.

Whip the cream lightly with the vanilla sugar.

When the puffs are cool and crisp, open them a little and fill them with the whipped cream. Alternatively pipe in the cream through the hole in the base.

To make the icing, melt the chocolate with the rum in the top of a double boiler. Remove from the heat and add the butter, a little at a time, stirring until each addition has melted. Set the base of the saucepan in cold water and beat the icing until it is thick enough to spread. Spoon it on top of the profiteroles. Allow the icing to cool and set before serving.

ALTERNATIVES: **Croquembouche** Make smaller profiteroles and, if you like, after filling, stick them together with melted caramel into a pyramid.
Eclairs Pipe the choux pastry in fingers about 7.5 cm/3 in long. Bake, fill and ice as above.

almond 186–7
apple 162–3
apricot 170
butter 99–100
chocolate 212–12
cream 99–100
toasting and grinding nuts 423
vanilla sugar 198, 211
whipping cream 423

baking sheet 236
pastry making equipment 237
piping bag and nozzle 237

Choux Pastry 404
Flaky Pastry 402

Cakes and Biscuits

butter 99–100
candied peel 184–5
chocolate 212–13
citron 165
cornflour 116
cream of tartar 119
eggs 96–7
self-raising flour 114
sugar 210–12
vanilla sugar 198, 211
whipping cream 423
whisking egg whites 423

cake tins 236–7
electric mixers 238–9
flour sifter 237
roasting tin 236
rubber spatula 228
whisks 227

White Frosting 415

SUMMER SPONGE CAKE

This is a white, light, fluffy cake.

MAKES A 25 CM/10 IN SANDWICH CAKE

- 4 free-range eggs, separated
- ½ teaspoon cream of tartar
- 340 g/12 oz granulated sugar
- 2 teaspoons vanilla sugar
- 225 g/8 oz self-raising flour
- a pinch of salt
- icing sugar

For the filling:

- 4 heaped tablespoons home-made jam, such as damson
- 120 ml/4 fl oz double or whipping cream, whipped

Preheat the oven to 150°C/300°F, gas mark 2. Butter and flour a medium-deep 25 cm/10 in round cake tin.

Whisk the egg whites with the cream of tartar, preferably using a hand-held electric mixer, until they are stiff. In a separate bowl, beat the egg yolks with 3 tablespoons of cold water for at least 3 minutes, until the yolks start to turn pale. Gradually add the granulated and vanilla sugars and then 150 ml/¼ pint of boiling water in a thin stream, beating with the mixer.

Sift the flour with the salt. Using a rubber spatula or large metal spoon, gradually fold the flour into the egg yolk mixture. Then fold in the whisked egg whites, gently but thoroughly. Turn the mixture into the cake tin. Bake for 1½–2 hours or until a skewer inserted into the centre comes out clean. Allow to cool on a wire rack.

Cut the cake in half horizontally. Spread the jam over the cut surface of the bottom half, and the whipped cream over the cut surface of the top half. Sandwich the two halves together. Sift a little icing sugar over the top or drizzle with glacé icing.

ALTERNATIVES: Sandwich the cake with chocolate cream filling (see Devil's Food Cake) rather than jam and whipped cream, and cover with White Frosting.

RICH CHOCOLATE CAKE

This recipe for flour-less chocolate cake may well have come about when someone decided to cook chocolate mousse to see what would happen. The result is very rich and has a texture not unlike a mousse

SERVES 8–10

- 340 g/12 oz bittersweet chocolate, broken into chunks
- 170 g/6 oz unsalted butter
- 200 g/7 oz caster sugar
- 6 free-range eggs

Preheat the oven to 150°C/300°F, gas mark 2. Lightly butter and flour a shallow 23 cm/9 in round cake tin (not loose-bottomed). Line the bottom with a circle of greaseproof or non-stick silicone paper.

Melt the chocolate with the butter in a bowl set over a pan of hot but not boiling water. Beat with a whisk until completely smooth. Keep warm.

Put the sugar in a small heavy-based saucepan with 100 ml/3½ fl oz of water. Heat, stirring to dissolve the sugar, then bring to the boil and boil for 2–3 minutes. Remove from the heat.

Using an electric mixer (this is essential), beat the eggs until they are thick and fluffy. With the motor still running, pour in the hot sugar syrup in a continuous thin stream, beating until the mixture is very thick; this can take 5–10 minutes. Switch off the beaters for a moment and add the chocolate and butter mixture to the bowl. Then, very gently, at extremely low speed, turn the beaters through the two mixtures so that they become completely homogeneous. A final folding action with a rubber spatula will reach right to the bottom of the bowl to ensure that there are no streaks.

Pour the mixture into the cake tin and set in a roasting tin. Pour enough hot water into the roasting tin to come at least three-quarters of the way up the cake tin. Bake for 40–45 minutes or until firm and springy to the touch.

Remove from the oven. Leave the cake tin in the water and allow the cake to cool in the tin. Then carefully run a knife around the side of the cake, being careful not to ruck up the paper underneath it, and turn out on to a plate. Cut into wedges and serve with thick cream.

MADEIRA CAKE

This good, plain, moist-textured cake is excellent in the middle of the morning with a glass of wine or a cup of coffee or tea.

MAKES A 15 CM/6 IN CAKE

- a large piece of candied citron peel or a large slice of candied lemon or orange peel
- 115 g/4 oz unsalted butter, softened
- 140 g/5 oz caster sugar
- 140 g/5 oz self-raising flour
- 30 g/1 oz cornflour
- a pinch of salt
- 2 free-range eggs
- 2 tablespoons milk

Preheat the oven to 180°C/350°F, gas mark 4. Butter and flour a deep 15 cm/6 in round cake tin.

Soften the citron peel, if using, by soaking it in a little warm water.

Cream the butter and sugar together until pale and creamy. Sift the flour and cornflour together and add the salt. Add one egg to the creamed butter and sugar and beat. Stir in half the flour and stir, then the remaining egg and flour alternately. Finally, stir in the milk.

Turn the mixture into the prepared tin. Bake in the middle of the oven for 1¼ hours or until a skewer inserted into the centre comes out clean. After 30 minutes, decorate the top of the cake with strips of peel arranged in a star shape in the middle.

ALTERNATIVE: **Cherry cake** Add 225 g/8 oz glacé cherries, lightly tossed in flour, to the mixture before turning it into the tin. Cover the cake with White Frosting, and decorate the top with 55 g/2 oz halved glacé cherries. This is a good tea-time treat for children and is not too rich.

DEVIL'S FOOD CAKE

MAKES A 20 CM/8 IN SANDWICH CAKE

- 85 g/3 oz good-quality dark chocolate, chopped
- 310 g/11 oz soft dark brown sugar
- 1 teaspoon vanilla sugar
- 2 tablespoons dark rum
- 115 g/4 oz unsalted butter, softened

RICH CHOCOLATE CAKE

- 2 free-range eggs
- 225 g/8 oz self-raising flour
- 4 tablespoons milk

For the chocolate cream filling:

- 85 g/3 oz best-quality dark chocolate, chopped
- 30 g/1 oz unsalted butter
- 150 ml/¼ pint double cream
- 140 g/5 oz icing sugar, sifted
- a tiny pinch of salt

Put the chopped chocolate, 140 g/5 oz of the brown sugar, the vanilla sugar and the rum into a small saucepan. Add 2 tablespoons of water. Heat gently, stirring all the time, until the mixture becomes smooth. Allow to cool.

Preheat the oven to 180°C/350°F, gas mark 4. Grease three 20 cm/8 in sandwich tins.

Cream the butter with the remaining brown sugar until light and fluffy. Beat in the eggs, one at a time. Add the cold chocolate and rum mixture and beat again. Add the flour and milk and mix them in lightly with a wooden spoon. Divide the mixture among the tins.

Bake for 20–25 minutes or until a skewer inserted into the centre of a cake comes out clean. Allow to cool in the tins for 5–10 minutes before turning out on to wire racks.

butter 99–100
chocolate 212–13
cream 99–100
eggs 96–7
glacé cherry 185
sugar 210–12
vanilla sugar 198, 211

cake tins 236–7
cooling rack 231
electric mixers 238–9
flour sifter 237

White Frosting 415

almond 186–7
blanching almonds 189
butter 99–100
candied peel 184–5
coffee 214–15
eggs 96–7
glacé cherry 185
spices 196–9
sugar 210–12
sultana and currant 182–3
toasting and grinding nuts 423
walnut 188
wheat flours 114–15

cake tins 236–7
electric mixers 238–9
food processor 238
flour sifter 237
palette knife 228
whisks 227

White Frosting 415

To make the filling, melt the chocolate and butter together in a bowl set over a pan of hot water. Allow to cool. Mix in the cream, icing sugar and salt, and whisk until the filling is thick (8–10 minutes with an electric mixer, or a little longer if using a balloon whisk).

When the cakes are completely cold, sandwich them together with chocolate cream filling. If you like, cover the cake with White Frosting.

WALNUT CAKE

MAKES A 15 CM/6 IN SANDWICH CAKE

- 170 g/6 oz unsalted butter, softened
- 170 g/6 oz caster sugar
- 3 free-range eggs
- 170 g/6 oz self-raising flour
- a pinch of salt
- 85 g/3 oz shelled walnuts, coarsely chopped, plus a few walnut halves
- White Frosting

For the filling:

- 75 g/2½ oz unsalted butter, softened
- 170 g/6 oz icing sugar
- 3 tablespoons strong black coffee

Preheat the oven to 170°C/325°F, gas mark 3. Grease a deep 15 cm/6 in round cake tin.

Cream the butter with the sugar until light and fluffy. Beat in the eggs one at a time; add a tablespoon of the flour after you have beaten in the second egg to prevent the mixture from curdling. Lightly stir in the rest of the flour and the salt, using a wooden spoon or rubber spatula. Do not use an electric mixer as too much beating toughens the flour. Stir in the walnuts.

Turn the mixture into the cake tin. Bake for 1 hour or until a skewer inserted into the centre comes out clean. Leave to cool in the tin. When the cake is cold, cut it in half horizontally.

To make the filling, put all the ingredients into a bowl or food processor and beat or whizz them to a smooth cream. Use to sandwich the cake together.

Pour the warm white frosting over the cake and smooth it over the top with a palette knife. Cover the sides too, if you wish. Decorate with halved walnuts. Leave to set for several hours before serving.

DUNDEE CAKE

MAKES A 20 CM/8 IN CAKE

- 170 g/6 oz plain flour
- 1 teaspoon mixed spice
- a pinch of salt
- 170 g/6 oz unsalted butter, softened
- 170 g/6 oz soft brown sugar
- 4 free-range eggs, beaten
- 115 g/4 oz blanched almonds
- 115 g/4 oz ground almonds
- 115 g/4 oz glacé cherries
- 115 g/4 oz chopped candied peel
- 225 g/8 oz currants
- 225 g/8 oz sultanas
- 225 g/8 oz seedless raisins

Preheat the oven to 170°C/325°F, gas mark 3. Grease and line a deep 20 cm/8 in round cake tin.

Sift the flour with the mixed spice and add the salt. Cream the butter with the sugar until pale and fluffy. Add the flour and eggs alternately to the creamed mixture, beating between each addition. Cut all but about 8 of the blanched almonds into slivers. Add the slivered almonds to the mixture, together with the ground almonds, cherries and candied peel. Shake the currants, sultanas and raisins in a little extra flour to coat them lightly, and stir them in.

Turn the mixture into the cake tin, and decorate the top with a star-shape of whole blanched almonds. Bake for 2½–3 hours or until a skewer inserted into the centre comes out clean. Cover the top of the cake lightly with foil about halfway through the baking time, to prevent it from becoming too brown. Allow to cool in the tin.

TWELFTH DAY CAKE

Twelfth Day is 6 January and is, according to old custom, a day of kings, cakes and wassailing. A Twelfth Day cake was traditionally lavishly decorated with coloured confectionery designed as stars, palaces and dragons. It should have a bean and a pea inside – the person who finds the bean in their piece of cake is king for the night and the one who finds the pea is queen.

MAKES 2 CAKES, EACH 1.35–1.8 KG/3–4 LB

- 450 g/1 lb self-raising flour
- 1 teaspoon mixed spice
- 1 teaspoon ground ginger
- 1 teaspoon grated nutmeg
- 450 g/1 lb unsalted butter, softened
- 450 g/1 lb soft dark brown sugar
- 6 free-range eggs
- 225 g/8 oz candied peel, chopped
- 340 g/12 oz currants
- 340 g/12 oz sultanas
- 340 g/12 oz large seedless raisins
- 225 g/8 oz glacé cherries, halved
- 115 g/4 oz ground almonds

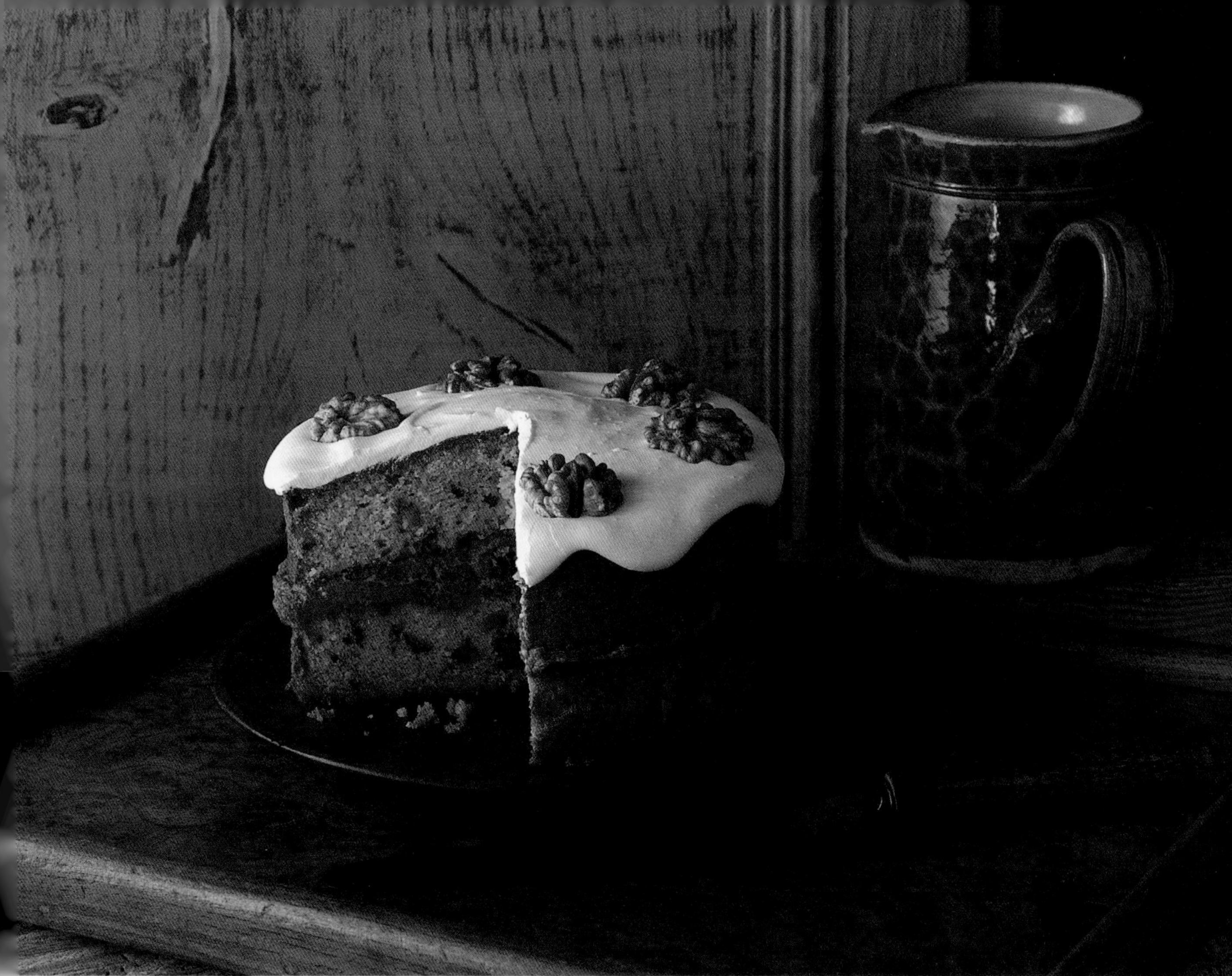

115 g/4 oz blanched almonds or pecans, cut into slivers
120 ml/4 fl oz Madeira or brandy
120 ml/4 fl oz milk

Preheat the oven to 180°C/350°F, gas mark 4. Butter two deep 20 cm/8 in round cake tins with removable bases, and line the bottom and sides. Wrap foil around the outside of the tins.

Sift the flour and spices together. Cream the butter with the sugar until pale and fluffy. Beat in the eggs, one at a time; add a tablespoon of the flour after each egg. Add the remaining flour and mix it in with a wooden spoon. Stir in the peel, fruit, almonds, Madeira or brandy and milk.

Divide the mixture between the tins. Bake for 2½–3 hours or until a skewer inserted into the centre comes out clean. Check the cakes from time to time, and turn them around if they are rising unevenly. Cover them with foil when they are starting to brown and before they start to blacken. Leave to cool in the tins.

ALTERNATIVE: **Christmas cake** Cover the cooled cake with Marzipan and Royal Icing.

WALNUT CAKE

HAZELNUT CAKES

These have a delicious rich flavour. They should be soft in the centre but with a slight crunch to them.

MAKES 12–18

3 free-range egg whites
170 g/6 oz caster sugar
170 g/6 oz ground hazelnuts

Preheat the oven to 180°C/350°F, gas mark 4. Line a baking tray or tin with foil and dust lightly with flour.

Whisk the egg whites to a stiff snow. Fold in the sugar and ground hazelnuts lightly but thoroughly. Spread the mixture 1–2 cm/½–¾ in thick on the foil-lined tray. Bake for about 20 minutes or until lightly browned and crisp on top.

Cut into squares and turn them over carefully. Return the tray to the oven and reduce the heat to 140°C/275°F, gas mark 1. Let the cakes dry out for 10–15 minutes. Cool on a wire rack.

hazelnut 188
whisking egg whites 423

cake tins 236–7
cooling rack 229
flour sifter 237

Marzipan 415
Royal Icing 415

almond 186–7
butter 99–100
cocoa powder 210, 212–13
golden syrup 210
honey 210
maple syrup 210
molasses 211
oats 116
pecan 188
spices 196–9
sugar 210–12
toasting and grinding nuts 423
walnut 188
whisking egg whites 423

cake tins 236–7
flour sifter 237
madeleine tray 237
rolling pin 237

FLAPJACKS

MAKES 16–20

- 85 g/3 oz unsalted butter
- 85 g/3 oz caster sugar
- 2 tablespoons golden syrup or maple syrup
- 140 g/5 oz rolled oats

Preheat the oven to 180°C/350°F, gas mark 4.

Combine the butter, sugar and syrup in a small saucepan and melt over a gentle heat. Stir in the oats, mixing well. Spread the mixture 5–10 mm/¼–½ in thick in a lightly buttered Swiss roll tin. Bake for 15–20 minutes or until golden. Allow to cool a little, then mark into rectangles with a knife and break into pieces. Cool completely before eating or storing.

GINGERBREAD MEN AND WOMEN

MAKES 15–20

- 55 g/2 oz unsalted butter, softened
- 115 g/4 oz caster sugar
- 4 tablespoons molasses
- 340 g/12 oz self-raising flour
- 2 teaspoons ground ginger
- ½ teaspoon ground cinnamon
- ½ teaspoon ground cloves
- a pinch of salt

For the icing:

- 2–3 tablespoons icing sugar
- a few drops of lemon juice or water

Preheat the oven to 180°C/350°F, gas mark 4.

Cream the butter and sugar until pale and fluffy. Add the molasses and 4 tablespoons of water, and blend well. Sift together the flour, spices and salt. Add to the butter and molasses mixture and blend together quickly until the mixture is like fine crumbs. Gather together and work into a dough with your hands. Add a little more water if the dough feels too dry.

Roll out the dough, half at a time, on a lightly floured surface to about 5mm/¼in thickness. Cut out gingerbread men and women shapes using a knife or a cutter. Transfer them carefully to a greased baking sheet. Bake for 8–10 minutes. Allow to cool on a rack.

Mix the icing sugar to a paste with a few drops of lemon juice or water. Use this icing to decorate the gingerbread people, using a wooden cocktail stick.

ALTERNATIVE: The gingerbread men and women can be decorated before they are baked, using currants, raisins and bits of candied peel to provide them with eyes, buttons and hair.

HONEY MADELEINES

You will need traditional madeleine trays with their shell-shaped indentations for these delicious little sponges. Serve them with Blackcurrant Jelly.

MAKES 12

- 115 g/4 oz unsalted butter
- 200 g/7 oz caster sugar
- 55 g/2 oz plain flour, sifted
- scant 55 g/2 oz ground almonds
- 3 free-range egg whites
- 1 tablespoon runny honey

Melt the butter in a saucepan and continue heating until it turns pale golden brown. Pour it into a metal bowl to cool. In another bowl, mix together the sugar, flour and ground almonds. Whisk the egg whites until light and foamy. Add the sugar and almond mixture and fold in gently but thoroughly. Lightly stir in the honey and browned butter.

Brush the indentations in the madeleine trays with melted butter, then dust with flour and tap out any excess. Spoon about 1 tablespoon of the mixture into each indentation; they should be filled to the brim. Refrigerate for 1 hour.

Preheat the oven to 190°C/375°F, gas mark 5.

Bake the madeleines for 15 minutes or until puffed up and firm to the touch. Leave them to cool in the trays for a few minutes, then lift out.

BROWNIES

MAKES 16

- 85 g/3 oz white vegetable fat or unsalted butter
- 45 g/1½ oz cocoa powder
- 225 g/8 oz caster sugar – preferably vanilla sugar
- 2 extra large free-range eggs
- 55 g/2 oz plain flour
- ½ teaspoon baking powder
- ¼ teaspoon salt
- 115 g/4 oz walnuts or pecans, chopped (optional)

Preheat the oven to 180°C/350°F, gas mark 4.

Melt the fat or butter in a saucepan. Remove from the heat and stir in the cocoa and sugar. Add the eggs one at a time, beating them in thoroughly. Sift together the flour and baking powder and add the salt. Stir into the mixture in the pan, beating gently but thoroughly. Stir in the nuts, if using.

Pour the mixture into a greased 20 cm/8 in square cake tin. Bake for 30 minutes or until a skewer inserted into the centre comes out clean. Cool in the tin. Cut into 5 cm/2 in squares when cold.

COFFEE BUTTER ICING

MAKES ENOUGH TO FILL AND COVER A LARGE CAKE
170 g/6 oz unsalted butter, softened
170 g/6 oz icing sugar, sifted
1 teaspoon very strong black coffee

Beat the butter and sugar together until smooth and light. Beat in the coffee.

ALTERNATIVES: **Orange or lemon butter icing** Use orange or lemon juice instead of coffee. A little grated zest can be added for a stronger flavour.
Chocolate butter icing Use cocoa powder, dissolved in a little water, instead of coffee.

ORANGE GLACÉ ICING

Use for sponge cakes.

MAKES ENOUGH TO COVER A 20 CM/8 IN CAKE OR THE TOP OF A 25 CM/10 IN CAKE
225 g/8 oz icing sugar
juice of ½–1 orange

Sift the icing sugar into a bowl. Add the juice of ½ orange, stirring it in well until the sugar has completely blended with the juice. If you want a thin, translucent glaze add more orange juice.

Spread the icing over the cake with a palette knife.

ALTERNATIVE: **Lemon glacé icing** Use lemon juice instead of the orange juice.

WHITE FROSTING

This is very white and light. It should be used while still warm, and will harden after 2 days.

MAKES ENOUGH TO COVER THE TOP AND SIDES OF A 20–25 CM/8–10 IN CAKE
30 g/1 oz vanilla sugar
200 g/7 oz granulated sugar
1 free-range egg white

Put the sugars into a small saucepan with 5 tablespoons of water and stir over a low heat until the sugar has dissolved completely. Bring to the boil and continue to boil until the syrup reaches a temperature of 120°C/240°F, at which point a little of the syrup will make a soft ball when dropped into a cup of cold water. Remove the pan from the heat.

Whisk the egg white in a clean bowl until it is stiff. Pour in the hot sugar syrup in a thin stream, whisking all the time. Continue to whisk until the mixture is very thick.

Pour or spread the warm frosting over the cold cake and tidy it up with a palette knife.

ALTERNATIVE: Use 225 g/8 oz granulated sugar instead of the two sugars, and add a drop or two of vanilla essence, to taste, to the egg white and sugar syrup mixture while whisking.

MARZIPAN

MAKES ENOUGH TO COVER A 1.35–1.8 KG/3–4 LB CAKE
225 g/8 oz icing sugar, sifted
225 g/8 oz caster sugar
340 g/12 oz ground almonds
2 free-range eggs
1 teaspoon rum or brandy

Mix together the sugars and almonds thoroughly in a bowl. Beat the eggs in a small bowl with the rum or brandy. Add most of the egg mixture to the dry ingredients. Work everything together thoroughly to make a paste, using a wooden spoon at first and then your hands. Add more of the egg mixture if the paste is too crumbly – it should be firm enough to handle but pliable enough to roll out.

To use for covering a cake, sift some icing sugar on to a work surface, to prevent the marzipan from sticking too much, and roll out the marzipan to 5 mm/¼ in thick.

ALTERNATIVES: For a pronounced almond flavour, add a few drops of almond essence to the mixture. Instead of rum or brandy, marzipan can be flavoured with a few drops of rosewater or orange-flower water.

ROYAL ICING

This is the icing to use for covering Christmas cake.

MAKES ENOUGH TO COVER A LARGE CAKE
2 free-range egg whites
a pinch of salt
2 teaspoons lemon juice
450 g/1 lb icing sugar, sifted

Whisk the egg whites with the salt until thick and soft. Add the lemon juice. Gradually whisk in the sugar to make a smooth, thick icing. Use the icing straight away, spreading it on to the cake with a palette knife. Leave it to dry overnight before cutting the cake.

almond 186–7
butter 99–100
coffee 214–15
lemon 167
orange 165–6
sugar 210–12
toasting and grinding nuts 423
vanilla sugar 198, 211
whisking egg whites 423
zesting citrus fruits 423

juice extractors 227, 239
palette knife 228
rolling pin 237
sugar thermometer 241
whisks 227

Preserves

MAKING JAM, MARMALADE AND JELLY

Making good preserves does not necessarily mean an afternoon's devotion to the preserving pan. Small quantities are perfectly practical and do not take long. But before you start, it is as well to be aware of a few golden rules.

Preparation Have everything ready and scrupulously clean. You can warm the sugar slightly in a low oven before adding it to the fruit; this will help it to dissolve more quickly.

Pectin This is the substance, present in certain fruits, that together and in balance with sugar and fruit-acid ensures a good set. Fruit that is slightly unripe contains more pectin than ripe fruit; and fruits that are tart even when ripe – apples, quinces, redcurrants, blackcurrants, gooseberries, Seville oranges and lemons – are particularly rich in pectin. When making preserves with fruit that is low in pectin, such as strawberries, the setting can be helped along with the addition of lemon juice or fresh redcurrant juice. For a really firm but less good result, commercial pectin made from apple pulp can be added.

Setting point Test the jam, marmalade or jelly frequently after it has boiled for about 10 minutes. To establish whether the setting point has been reached, cool a little of the hot mixture on a cold plate and then nudge it with your finger: if it wrinkles and clings to the spot, it is ready. Skim it at this point, to remove scum and froth.

The jars When setting point has been reached, remove the pan from the heat and allow the mixture to cool a little, to prevent the fruit from rising to the top, before pouring it into heated clean, dry jars. If using cellophane covers with rubber bands for jam, put a greaseproof disc on top of the hot jam to seal it off from contact with the air. To ensure a tight fit, moisten the cellophane on the outside before putting the covers on the cool jars.

Storing Store your home-made preserves in a cool, dark and dry place.

STRAWBERRY JAM

Strawberry jam never sets quite as well as other jams unless, as here, you add some form of acid- and pectin-forming fruit such as lemon.

MAKES 2.7 KG/6 LB

1.8 kg/4 lb preserving sugar
1.8 kg/4 lb firm strawberries
juice of 2 lemons

STRAWBERRY JAM

Warm the preserving sugar in a low oven. Put the strawberries and lemon juice in a preserving pan and let them soften over a very gentle heat. The juice will gradually run out of the fruit – stir from time to time to help it along.

When the strawberries are floating in their own juice, which may take 20–30 minutes, add the warmed sugar and stir until it dissolves. Bring to a rapid boil, stirring frequently, and boil until the jam reaches setting point. Take the pan off the heat. Draw the scum on the surface to the sides and skim it off carefully. Allow the jam to cool a little before ladling it into heated clean, dry jars.

GOOSEBERRY JAM

Gooseberry jam has a particularly beautiful colour.

gooseberries
preserving sugar

Top and tail the gooseberries. Put them in a preserving pan or heavy saucepan with 150 ml/¼ pint of water for every 450 g/1 lb of fruit. Bring to the boil, then reduce the heat to low and let the fruit soften for about 15 minutes.

Add 450 g/1 lb preserving sugar for each 450 g/1 lb of fruit used and stir to dissolve it. Bring back to the boil, and boil steadily and rather fast for 11–12 minutes or until the jam reaches setting point. Gooseberry jam, because it gets very thick, has a tendency to burn. To avoid this, stir it with a wooden spoon while it boils, or stand the preserving pan or saucepan on a heat-diffusing mat.

Skim quickly and carefully to remove all scum and froth, then pour the jam into heated clean, dry jars and cover immediately.

BLACKCURRANT JAM

This makes a soft and thick jam. So often blackcurrant jam is hard, or has little chewy currants that feel disagreeable between the teeth, but simmering before the bulk of the sugar goes in softens the fruit completely.

MAKES 3–3.6 KG/7–8 LB

1.8 kg/4 lb blackcurrants
1.8 kg/4 lb preserving sugar

With a fork, pull the currants from their stalks. Discard any green fruit. Put the currants in a preserving pan with 225 g/8 oz of the sugar and 600 ml/1 pint of water. Bring slowly to the boil and simmer for 10–15 minutes. Add the remaining sugar

blackcurrant 173
gooseberry 172
preserving sugar 212
strawberry 171

juice extractors 227, 239
ladle 227
preserving equipment 241

crabapple 163–4
making jam, marmalade and jelly 417
medlar 163–4
preserving sugar 212
quince 163–4
redcurrant 173
Seville orange 165

preserving equipment 241

and stir until it has dissolved before starting the simmering again. Then simmer for 15 minutes or until the jam reaches setting point. Skim well. Stir, then pour into heated clean, dry jars and cover.

SEVILLE ORANGE MARMALADE

Use unsprayed, unwaxed fruit if possible.

MAKES ABOUT 1.35 KG/3 LB

- 1.35 kg/3 lb Seville oranges
- 2 lemons
- about 2.7 kg/6 lb preserving sugar

Scrub the oranges and lemons with a vegetable brush. Peel them and cut the peel into fairly coarse strips. Chop the orange and lemon pulp, and remove the pips and any pith. Tie the pith and pips in a muslin bag – they contain the pectin that sets the marmalade, so don't leave out this step. Put the peel and flesh in a preserving pan with the bag of pips and add 3.5 litres/6 pints of water. Simmer gently until the volume has reduced by about one-third.

Squeeze the bag of pips over the pan to press out all the juice, and discard it. Measure the cooked pulp in a measuring jug and return it to the preserving pan. Add 450 g/1 lb preserving sugar to each 600 ml/1 pint pulp. Stir over a gentle heat until the sugar has dissolved. Then bring to the boil and boil until setting point is reached.

Allow the marmalade to cool a little, to prevent the peel from rising to the top of the jars. Then ladle into heated clean, dry jars. Keep a week or two, or longer, before eating.

CLEAR QUINCE JELLY

This delicate jelly is an exquisite clear red, and is delicious both on bread and with pork.

MAKES 1.35–1.8 KG/3–4 LB

- 900 g/2 lb ripe golden quinces
- about 900 g/2 lb preserving sugar

Wash the quinces and cut them up into coarse pieces. Put them into a saucepan with 1.8 litres/3 pints of water. Bring to the boil and simmer gently until the fruit is completely soft.

Pour the cooked quinces into a muslin cloth or jelly bag suspended over a bowl and strain out the juice. Don't squeeze the bag at all – just let the juice drip, so that it runs through a clear pale pink. When it has stopped dripping, discard the quince pulp. Measure the strained juice into a large saucepan or preserving pan. Add 450 g/1 lb of preserving sugar for every 600 ml/1 pint of juice. Bring to the boil slowly, stirring to dissolve the sugar completely before the liquid starts to boil, then boil rapidly until the jelly reaches setting point.

Skim any scum and froth from the surface. Pour the jelly into heated clean, dry jars and then cover.

ALTERNATIVES: **Crabapple jelly** Use crabapples instead of quinces. Eat this delightful sweet-tart jelly with cold meats and poultry.
Medlar jelly Use medlars instead of quinces. Because medlars will yield much less juice, the quantity of jelly made is about 700–900 g/1½–2 lb. Medlar jelly, which is a clear pink and has a slightly tart flavour, is delicious with game or lamb.

REDCURRANT JELLY

This method is very extravagant, but makes such superb jelly that if you have plenty of redcurrants it is well worth while. Choose some slightly unripe ones as these have more acid and help set the jelly.

- redcurrants
- sugar

Push the currants into large preserving jars and cover them tightly. Put the jars in a large saucepan of water. Bring the water to the boil and let it seethe until the currants have sunk in the jars and their juice has run out. This will take 2–3 hours.

Pour the fruit and juice into a jelly bag or fine muslin cloth suspended over a bowl. Let the juice drip through overnight.

Measure the juice and put it in a preserving pan. Add 450 g/1 lb of sugar for each 600 ml/1 pint of juice. Stir over a low heat until the sugar dissolves completely, then bring to the boil. Boil rapidly until setting point is reached. Skim off all froth and scum, and pour quickly into heated clean, dry jars. Cover when cool, and do not tip or shake the jars while the jelly is cooling.

ALTERNATIVE: If the method described above seems too wasteful, you can mash the berries to extract more of the juice before putting them into the jelly bag. However, doing this will slightly darken the colour of the finished jelly.

PEACH CONSERVE

This is a good way of using up bruised or second-grade peaches.

MAKES 1.35 KG/3 LB
- about 1.1 kg/2½ lb peaches
- juice of 1 lemon
- 450 g/1 lb preserving sugar
- 60 ml/2 fl oz brandy

Dip each peach into boiling water for half a minute, then peel off the skin with a blunt knife. Cut the peaches in half and take out the stones. Cut away any bruised flesh. Put the fruit into a large pan and add 1 tablespoon of water. Simmer very gently for 45 minutes.

Remove from the heat and measure the cooked peaches in a measuring jug; you want to have about 900 ml/1½ pints. Return the cooked peaches to the preserving pan and add the lemon juice and preserving sugar. Set the pan over a gentle heat and stir until the sugar has dissolved. Then turn up the heat and boil for 6 minutes. Remove the pan from the heat, cover it and leave in a cool place overnight.

The next morning return the pan to the heat and bring the peach pulp to the boil. Stir in the brandy. Ladle the conserve into heated clean, dry jars. Allow to cool and then cover in the usual way.

LEMON CURD

MAKES ABOUT 450 G/1 LB
- 2–3 lemons
- 115 g/4 oz unsalted butter, melted
- 225 g/8 oz caster sugar
- 2–3 free-range eggs, beaten

Pare the zest from the lemons very thinly. Squeeze the juice from the lemons and strain it. Put the lemon zest and juice in the top of a double boiler, or in a stone jar standing in a pan of hot but not boiling water. Add the butter, sugar and eggs and mix together. Cook gently, stirring from time to time, until the mixture is thick enough to coat the back of the spoon. Strain the curd and bottle it in heated clean, dry jars.

GREEN TOMATO SOUR

Despite its name, green tomato sour is in fact not at all sour but quite sweet, with an interesting mellow flavour.

MAKES 3.6 KG/8 LB
- 2.7 kg/6 lb small green tomatoes, thinly sliced
- 900 g/2 lb onions, chopped
- salt
- 3 green peppers, seeded and chopped
- 700 g/1½ lb soft light brown sugar
- 3 tablespoons mustard seed
- 1 tablespoon coriander seed
- ½ teaspoon celery seed
- 2 teaspoons turmeric
- 1.2 litres/2 pints distilled vinegar

Layer the tomatoes and onions in a large earthenware bowl, sprinkling each layer with plenty of salt. Let them stand overnight.

Drain off the liquid, and put the tomatoes and onions in a preserving pan. Add the green peppers, sugar, spices and vinegar – the vinegar should barely cover the vegetables, so add more or less as necessary. Simmer for 2 hours. Pour the mixture into the earthenware bowl and allow to stand overnight.

The next day, simmer the chutney for about half an hour or until there is just enough thickish liquid to cover the vegetables when they are packed together. Ladle the chutney into heated clean, dry jars. Keep for at least 3 weeks before opening and eating.

SWEET PEPPER CHUTNEY

This excellent chutney is a good accompaniment for all cold meats and game.

MAKES 900 G/2 LB
- 4 tablespoons olive oil
- 3 onions, coarsely chopped
- 2 red peppers
- 2 green peppers
- salt
- ½ teaspoon ground ginger
- 1 teaspoon mixed spice
- 12 allspice berries, coarsely crushed
- 1 garlic clove, chopped
- 450 g/1 lb tomatoes, skinned and chopped
- 115 g/4 oz seedless raisins
- 170 g/6 oz sugar
- 150 ml/¼ pint white wine vinegar

Heat the oil in a preserving pan and soften the onions. Meanwhile, remove the cores and seeds from the peppers and cut them into flat pieces about the size of a postage stamp. When the onions are tender, add the peppers, a little salt, the ginger, mixed spice, allspice and garlic. Cook gently for 10 minutes. Stir in the tomatoes and raisins and cook for 10 more minutes. Add the sugar and wine vinegar and stir to dissolve the sugar. Bring to a simmer and simmer for 2 hours or until the chutney is rather thick and bronze in colour.

Ladle into heated clean, dry pots and seal them. Keep in a cool, dry place for at least 2 weeks before opening and eating.

butter 99–100
eggs 96–7
lemon 167
peach 169
peeling peaches 423
raisin 182
skinning and seeding tomatoes 423
spices 196–9
sugar 210–12
sweet pepper 152
tomato 150–1
vinegars 204–5
zesting citrus fruits 423

juice extractors 227, 239
ladle 227
potato peeler 224
preserving equipment 241
sieves 226–7

Planning menus

Memorable meals come in all shapes and sizes. From a casual picnic on a perfect summer's day to a celebratory dinner party, from a quiet night in without the children to a classic Sunday lunch with all the family. Good company, a comfortable and attractive environment, a relaxed and happy atmosphere will all shape our experience of a meal, but generally the cornerstone will be the food itself.

The emphasis of this book, quite deliberately, is on the quality and availability of ingredients. If you know what to look for when you are shopping; if you select from produce in season that is at its best and full of flavour; and if you know how to identify the good from the average from the bad then you have already won half the battle. If you are like me, you will take great pleasure in going shopping and planning a meal around just what happens to be available: you might see some wonderful cod in the fishmonger, and this might inspire you to buy some ginger and spring onions so that you can cook it in a slightly different and more interesting way.

Of course, some people prefer to go shopping armed with a list of ingredients for the dishes they have decided to cook, and here the season should give you a good idea of what to expect: asparagus and lamb in spring, for example, or game and berries in autumn. But whichever method you adopt, you have to consider how the various ingredients will combine in a dish, and how the various dishes will complement each other. Garlic, for example, has a capacity to overwhelm other flavours, and, indeed, it's the garlic we taste first and foremost when it is served with snails or frog's legs or mushrooms; but when you think about it, the subtlety of the snails or frog's legs or mushrooms remains and produces something quite different in each case.

Still other foods act as a vehicle for the ingredients with which they are combined. Chicken is a fine example: depending on how it's cooked, you get amazingly diverse results – Coq au Vin is vastly different from roast chicken, and neither are remotely similar to chicken that has been used as the basis for a curry or one that has been cooked with soy sauce and sesame for a Sichuan Chicken Salad.

This confidence in handling and balancing ingredients is something that comes with experience, not just of cooking but of eating out in restaurants or at other people's houses. The true cook develops an instinct for combining ingredients in the right quantities to produce something exceptional: I don't know who it was who first thought of combining hare and chocolate – it sounds so unpromising, and yet it works wonderfully well. As culinary influences circle the world in search of new and exciting ingredients and recipes, the repertoire of combinations at our disposal becomes ever-more eclectic.

The care we apply to the combination of ingredients in a single dish applies equally to the balance of dishes that makes up a meal. Only a greedy child, I suspect, would want to follow up a rich starter with an equally rich main course, finishing the meal with a rich chocolate pudding and lashings of cream. Most of us prefer to balance flavours and courses according to the time of year and the type of occasion – even, perhaps, the day of the week.

When it comes to presentation of the food on the plate, balance is equally important. Most of us, from time to time, succumb to the temptations of 'comfort food', piling the plate with a favourite dish. Yet I sigh when confronted by the classic Sunday roast with its many elements on one messy plate. Each item on its own is often quite delicious, but they lose their individual flavours and qualities, heaped together as if in a Five Nations' scrum. Although the faddish precision of nouvelle cuisine (the opposite extreme) is now, largely, a thing of the past, we have undoubtedly taken from it some important lessons about presentation. A good-looking dish excites the eyes and gets the taste-buds going just as surely as tempting smells from the kitchen.

The recipes in this book cover food for every occasion, from converting winter broths to light summer salads, pasta dishes that can be brought to the table within minutes, to stews and roasts that repay the preparation time in their wonderful combination of textures and flavours.

Above all, food is for pleasure. In the last twenty years, we have thankfully become less concerned with pretentious social niceties: pressures of space at home and pressures on time at work mean that a dinner party is just as likely to take place around the kitchen table as it is in a separate dining-room. A sense of pleasure in the rituals of serving dinner is simply and easily suggested: home-made food, large white napkins, plain cutlery, a couple of well-shaped wine glasses each, good wine and perhaps a bunch of fresh flowers are, for me, all the accompaniments you need.

TERENCE CONRAN

SPRING

Artichokes alla romana
Grilled polenta
or
Stewed broad beans with butter and tarragon
Grilled polenta

Asparagus soufflé
Spinach and walnut salad

Grapefruit sorbet

Garlic mushroom soup with cream
Rye bread

Marinated roast quails with honey and ginger
Spiced lentils

Jamaican baked bananas
Coconut ice-cream

Spinach frittata

Stuffed baby squid
Green salad with herb vinaigrette with balsamic vinegar

Rhubarb and raisin tart
Crème chantilly

Soused herrings

Peppered steak
Chips

Fresh raspberry pavlova

Seviche

Wyvern's chicken curry with coconut
Pilau rice

Vermicelli milk pudding with cardamom and saffron

SUMMER

Chilled cucumber soup with mint

Melanzane alla parmigiana
Rocket and walnut salad

Apricot tart
Raspberry ice-cream

Red peppers with anchovies
Toasted saffron bread

Steamed cod with ginger and spring onion
Sesame spinach

Summer pudding

Sorrel soup

Roast duck
Peas with lettuce hearts

Peach Melba

Stuffed courgettes

Grilled prawns in bacon
Spiced and fried new potatoes with minted yogurt dressing

Blackcurrant jelly
Honey madeleines

Salade niçoise

Grilled mackerel with green paste
Cool and hot cucumber salad

Coffee granita

AUTUMN

Garlic mushrooms
Warm cheese bread

Grilled polenta with poached eggs, fontina and chive cream
Frisée salad (without bacon)

Blackberry and apple pie
Crème chantilly

Green bean salad with anchovy-cream dressing

Quick-fried chicken with garlic and chilli
Plainly cooked spaghetti or pappardelle

Cherry clafoutis

Sechuan chicken salad

Shrimp and fennel risotto

Fresh orange jelly

Whitebait

Simple roast grouse
Bread sauce and redcurrant jelly
Glazed turnips
Pommes rissolées

Crème brûlée
Fresh raspberries

Spinach gnocchi with butter and sage

Roast woodcock
Cumberland game sauce
Mashed swedes

Rich chocolate cake
Chocolate ice-cream

WINTER

Celery and Parmesan salad

Spinach with chick-peas

Marmalade Queen of puddings

Oysters Rockefeller

Goose with apple stuffing
Roast potatoes
Sprouts with chestnuts
Sugar-glazed carrots

Pumpkin pie
Coconut ice-cream

Ravioli con funghi porcini

Costolette milanese
Fennel au gratin

Custard pancakes
Vanilla ice-cream

Thinly-sliced Chinese belly pork salad with bok choy

Chinese egg noodles with browned garlic, chillies and parsley

Spiced pears in red wine

Hot and sour shellfish broth

Lyonnaise calf's liver with onions
Artichokes and spinach
Creamed potatoes with parsley

Apple crumble
Custard

Glossary

Measurements

In this book, both metric and Imperial measurements have been given. As the equivalents are not exact (one ounce equals 28.350 grammes, for example), follow only one set of measurements when preparing a recipe. Spoon measures are level unless otherwise specified; 1 tablespoon is equivalent to 15 ml and 1 teaspoon to 5 ml. In some instances, liquid and butter measurements have been given in non-standard terms because the amount used largely depends on the personal preference of the cook. As a guideline, however, a wineglass traditionally holds 115 ml/4 fl oz, and a knob of butter is about the size of a walnut. Unless otherwise specified, use large eggs (previously size 3) when preparing the recipes.

Cookery terms

acidulated water: water to which lemon juice or vinegar, preferably white wine vinegar, is added, and in which certain vegetables, such as celeriac, salsify and globe artichokes, are immersed to prevent discoloration.
à la meunière: refers to a mixture of browned butter, lemon juice and parsley served with food such as fish.
al dente: Italian term (literally 'to the tooth') used to describe the texture of food, mainly pasta, when it is properly cooked and just firm to the bite.
antipasto: literally meaning 'before the pasta', this is the Italian equivalent of hors d'oeuvres and may consist of slices of salami, vegetables grilled or marinated in oil, and seafood salads.
aspic: jelly used to cover or glaze cold foods. Usually the jelly has been clarified so that decorations such as herb leaves, red peppers, olives or truffles can be seen shining through. An aspic may also refer to a savoury jelly served as a salad.
au gratin: refers to dishes that are sprinkled with cheese and/or breadcrumbs, then grilled or cooked in the oven just long enough to brown the top.
bain-marie: also known as a water bath, this consists of a large pan such as a roasting tin filled with water in which baking dishes, saucepans or bowls containing food are set (ideally on a special trivet). The bain-marie may be used to keep prepared foods hot and moist, but its most useful purpose is to ensure that certain delicate foods such as custards and sauces cook at a constant low temperature without drying out, curdling or scorching. The advantage of a bain-marie over a double boiler is that the former ensures that the food remains moist while cooking and cooks evenly, due to the surrounding steam caused by evaporation.
bard: originating from the old French word *barde*, which was a horse's iron armour, this means to wrap thin sheets of fat, usually pork fat, around meat, poultry or game to prevent the flesh from drying out while roasting.
baste: to spoon cooking juices or another liquid over food while it cooks to keep it moist.
battuto: Italian term for a mixture of very finely chopped vegetables and pancetta or bacon which is cooked and then used for flavouring sauces, stews and soups.
beurre manié: flour and softened butter worked together to a paste, used to thicken soups, sauces and stews.
beurre noir: refers to a sauce for skate and other fish, made by cooking butter until nut brown (not black, despite the name) and mixing in vinegar, parsley and optional capers.
beurre noisette: butter cooked until just brown; lemon juice and seasoning may be added.
bind: to add egg, liquid or a thickening agent to a mixture to hold it together. Foods such as pâtés, rissoles and stuffings sometimes require binding.
bisque: thick creamy soup usually based on seafood – especially lobster, crayfish or shrimp – but sometimes game or poultry.
blanch: to immerse food briefly in boiling water to soften it, to keep it white, to help remove its skin (as for almonds and some fruits and vegetables), or to remove excess salt or bitterness.
braise: to cook food slowly, after it has been browned, in a minimum of liquid under a tight cover.
brine: salt-water solution used to preserve or flavour meat, fish or vegetables.
canapés: small appetizers made of bread – fresh, fried or toasted – topped with various savoury mixtures, or other small foods that can be eaten with the fingers, to be served with drinks.
charcuterie: French term that refers to the wide assortment of pork products – sausages, pâtés, hams etc – sold in specialist shops called charcuteries.
chine: to loosen the backbone (chine) from the ribs of a joint of meat to allow easier carving.
choucroute garnie: dish from Alsace of sauerkraut garnished with sausages, pig's ears or trotters, ham, pickled pork knuckles and similar meats.
chowder: thick soup that takes its name from the French word for pot or cauldron, *chaudière*.
chutney: Indian relish, cooked or uncooked, of fruits or vegetables and spices, served with curries, cold meats and other dishes.
clarify: to remove impurities from fats – particularly from butter for cooking – and from stocks and consommés.
cocotte: small ovenproof dish used for baking individual mousses, soufflés or egg dishes.
compote: fruit cooked in a sugar syrup.
confits: fruits candied in sugar, often with brandy added; or meat or poultry preserved in its own fat, such as *confit d'oie* (goose) and *confit de canard* (duck).
cream: to beat butter or butter and sugar to a light consistency.
croquette: cork- or oval-shaped mixtures of chopped meat, fish, eggs or vegetables, egg-and-breadcrumbed and then deep fried.
curd: coagulated substance that is produced in milk when it is soured.
dariole: both a small cylindrical mould and the food – usually a pudding – that is baked in it.
daube: French stew of braised meat and vegetables.
deglaze: to scrape browned solidified cooking juices off the bottom of a roasting tin, frying pan or saucepan, loosening them with the help of a liquid such as wine, brandy or stock.
dégorger: to salt vegetables such as aubergine and cucumber to draw out their bitter juices; also to soak certain foods, such as sweetbreads, in water to remove a strong flavour and blood or to improve colour.
devil: to season foods with spicy ingredients, usually mustard, cayenne and Worcestershire sauce, often in the form of a sauce.
dredge: to coat foods lightly with flour, icing sugar or another fine powder.
duxelles: finely chopped mushrooms, often mixed with chopped shallots or onions, sautéed in butter and used for stuffings and garnishes.
emulsion: mixture such as mayonnaise in which fat or oil is held in suspension.
en croûte: refers to cooking food, particularly pâté and meat, entirely encased in pastry.
en papillote: refers to cooking food, and often serving it, in paper cases (*papillote* is the French for curl-papers).
escabeche: Portuguese, Spanish and Latin American way of preparing fish, poultry and game by cooking it and then marinating it.
farce: a savoury stuffing for meat, fish or vegetables.
filo, phyllo pastry: paper-thin pastry dough sheets, very similar to strudel pastry. Filo is usually brushed with butter and then layered; sweet or savoury fillings may be layered with the pastry, or wrapped in it, before baking.
flan: open pie or tart, normally cooked in a metal flan ring. In Spain and Mexico flan is a baked caramel custard.
forcemeat: mixture of minced meat, vegetables or bread used as a stuffing.
galantine: boned and stuffed poultry, game or meat, often glazed with aspic, decorated and served cold.
glaze: to make food shiny by coating it with a sugar syrup, aspic, beaten egg, milk etc.
gluten: elastic protein found in some grains, such as hard or strong wheat, that develops with kneading and in the presence of water, and helps to trap the air bubbles produced by fermenting yeast, making a light, well-risen bread.
granita: Italian water ice with a granular texture, flavoured with fruit, coffee etc.
hang: to suspend meat or game from hooks for a period of time to make them more tender and allow their flavour to mature.
infuse: to extract flavour from food by steeping in a hot liquid – the resulting liquid is an infusion. This technique is usually applied in making tea, coffee and tisanes. Milk is infused with onion and other flavourings for béchamel sauce or with vanilla for custard.
julienne: thin matchstick strips of vegetables, ham etc, often used as a garnish.
lard: to insert strips of fat (lardons) into meat to be roasted, using a special needle, to make the meat more succulent.
lardons, lardoons: strips of fat bacon or pork fat.
liaison: thickening for a sauce or soup, which may be a starch such as flour or cornflour, or a mixture of egg yolk and cream; or an emulsion such as oil and egg yolk in mayonnaise.
macedoine: mixture, cooked or uncooked, of fruits or vegetables cut into small cubes.
macerate: to steep in liquid, often spirits or liqueurs, so that the food (usually fruit) becomes infused with the liquid's flavour.
marc: substance left after the pressing of fruits, especially applied to grapes in wine-making. Also a clear alcohol made from the pressed grapes after wine-making.
marinate: to soak raw meat, fish or vegetables in a seasoned liquid (a marinade) to make it more tender and/or flavourful.
mezzes: Middle Eastern hors d'oeuvres, often including olives, grilled cheese, small spiced

meatballs, cooked vegetables, salads and purées, and nuts such as pistachios and almonds.
mirepoix: diced vegetables, such as carrots, onions and leeks used as a basis for a braise or sauce, or, cooked in butter, as a garnish for cutlet or fish dishes.
navarin: French lamb or mutton stew made with a large proportion of turnips, carrots, onions and potatoes, and in spring with peas and young vegetables, to become *navarin printemps*.
pâté: savoury mixture of chopped meat or game, usually containing a proportion of pork and pork fat, which is baked either with or without a casing of pastry and served cold. The word is extended also to cover mixtures that are not baked, such as fish pâtés.
poach: to cook food immersed in gently simmering liquid.
purée: raw or cooked food, usually vegetables or fruit, that is mashed and then sieved, or worked in a food processor, blender or Mouli-légumes until smooth.
quenelles: lightly cooked dumplings made of finely chopped fish or meat.
quiche: a savoury custard tart, originally from Lorraine.
ragoût: French stew of meat and vegetables.
ragù: Italian term for a meat stew or sauce.
ramekin: small, round ovenproof dish for individual servings.
reduce: to concentrate or thicken a liquid by evaporation through rapid boiling.
refresh: to rinse or immerse hot food (usually green vegetables) in very cold or iced water to stop further cooking and to set the colour of the food.
render: to melt animal fat slowly to a liquid. It is then strained to eliminate any residue.
risotto: Italian savoury rice dish, usually with a creamy consistency.
rissole: small patty made of cooked meat or fish, sometimes with rice or vegetables, bound together and fried.
roux: cooked mixture of flour and fat, usually butter, used as the basis for savoury sauces.
rub in: to mix flour or other dry ingredients with fat, usually butter or lard, using the fingertips to give a crumbly rather than a smooth result. This technique is especially important in the making of pastry and scones.
sauté: to cook briskly in a small amount of fat in a shallow pan, shaking the pan to make sure that the pieces being fried are evenly browned.
scald: to heat liquid, usually milk, to just below boiling point, until bubbles form round the edge.
score: to make shallow cuts over the surface of food. Steaks may be scored before they are grilled or fried to tenderize them (by cutting through the fine connecting tissues), and some whole fish are scored before grilling so that they will cook through quickly and evenly.
seviche: a dish of raw fish marinated in lemon or lime juice, the acidity of which 'cooks' the fish.
simmer: to keep a liquid at just below boiling point so that it remains gently 'shivering'.
souse: to pickle in vinegar or brine, a method most often applied to oily fish such as herrings.
steam: to cook food in steam, usually in a perforated container set above boiling water.
stir-fry: to cook food quickly in a little oil or lard over a high heat, stirring and tossing constantly. A wok is the best pan for this as the rounded shape distributes the heat evenly and a lot of food can be fried in a very little fat.
stock: well-flavoured broth in which meat, poultry or vegetables or a combination of these have been cooked. It is used instead of water in many dishes, particularly soups and sauces, to enhance their flavour.
sweat: to soften vegetables, particularly onions, by cooking them gently so that they release their juices but do not brown.
tapas: snacks traditionally served in Spanish bars, consisting of marinated vegetables, olives, meats, slices of cold Spanish omelette and the like.
tart: open-faced pie, normally filled with fruit or other sweet fillings but also savoury custards.
terrine: both a deep, rectangular or oval mould used for cooking pâté, and the pâté itself.
timbale: both a cup-shaped earthenware or metal mould and the food cooked in such a mould, usually containing rice or pasta.
whey: watery liquid that separates out when milk or cream curdles.
zest: oily, coloured skin of citrus peel, used as a flavouring agent.

Basic cookery techniques

making beurre manié: mash together equal weights of softened butter and flour to make a paste. Add this in small pieces to a hot sauce, soup, etc at the end of cooking, whisking in enough beurre manié to thicken the liquid.
clarifying butter: melt butter over low heat, then continue to heat gently, without allowing the butter to colour, until the milk solids separate and fall to the bottom of the pan. Remove from the heat and allow to settle for 10 minutes, then strain through a sieve lined with moist paper towels. Clarified butter can be kept in the refrigerator, tightly covered, for several weeks or it can be frozen.
whipping cream: pour chilled cream into a chilled bowl. Use a whisk, a rotary whisk or electric beaters to whip the cream until it is thickened or stiff enough to pipe, according to recipe instructions. A tablespoon or two of iced water can be added to lighten the cream.
making crème fraîche: stir 5 tablespoons buttermilk into 600 ml/1 pint whipping or double cream and keep in a warm place (24–29°C/75–85°F) for about 8 hours or until thickened and slightly soured in flavour. Store in the refrigerator.
whisking egg whites: if using an electric mixer, start at low speed (or slowly with a whisk). When the egg whites are foamy, increase the speed (to high for an electric mixer) and whisk until stiff peaks will form. If adding sugar, whisk the whites until soft peaks form, then whisk in the sugar gradually and continue whisking until the mixture will hold stiff, shiny peaks.
coating with egg and crumbs: dip food to be coated into seasoned flour, turning to coat both sides, then shake off excess flour; dip next into beaten egg, moistening both sides; finally, dip into fine crumbs, coating both sides and pressing lightly so the crumbs will adhere.
dissolving gelatine: for powdered gelatine, sprinkle it over liquid as specified in the recipe and leave to soak for about 5 minutes, then heat gently, without stirring, until the gelatine has completely dissolved. For gelatine leaves, soak in cold water for a few minutes, until soft and soggy, then drain, add to a warm mixture and stir until melted.
skinning and seeding tomatoes: cut a small cross in the base of each tomato, then plunge into boiling water. Leave for about 10 seconds or until the skin begins to peel away from the cuts, then lift out the tomatoes and immerse in cold water. As soon as the tomatoes are cool enough to handle, drain them and slip off the skin. To remove the seeds, cut each tomato in half crosswise. Gently squeeze each half and shake out the seeds; remove any remaining seeds with the tip of a teaspoon or your finger.
skinning peppers: grill or roast the peppers until the skin is blistered and blackened all over (turn the peppers as necessary). Put the peppers in a plastic bag and leave to cool. Peel off the skins with the help of a small knife.
seeding chillies: cut each chilli in half lengthways, then scrape out the seeds and cut away the white ribs with a small knife. Take care not to touch your eyes or any other sensitive area when handling chillies, and be sure to wash your hands thoroughly in hot soapy water when you have finished.
crushing and chopping garlic: put a cook's knife flat on top of the garlic clove and bang the knife with the side of your fist to crush the garlic slightly. This will loosen the skin, which can then be peeled off. Crush the garlic further under the side of the knife, to flatten it completely. Then, according to the recipe instructions, chop the garlic coarsely or finely with the knife blade.
cooking pulses: most dried pulses need to be soaked for at least 8 hours or overnight before cooking (lentils and split peas are exceptions). Drain off the soaking water and replace with fresh water. If cooking red kidney beans, bring to the boil and boil for an initial 10 minutes (to destroy any harmful toxins that may be present), then drain and add fresh water. To cook all pulses, simmer in plenty of unsalted water until they are tender. The cooking time will vary according to the age and dryness of the pea or bean, but in general most need 1½–2 hours; split peas and lentils require less time.
peeling peaches: as for tomatoes
zesting citrus fruits: for large strips of zest use a vegetable peeler to shave off just the coloured part (the strips can then be cut into very thin shreds with a knife); for small, curled strips use a canelle knife; for very fine filaments use a citrus zester. Zest can also be grated off.
toasting and grinding nuts: spread the nuts on a baking sheet and toast in a preheated 180°C/350°F, gas 4 oven, or under a moderate grill, stirring occasionally, until golden brown; or toast in a dry frying pan over moderate heat, stirring frequently. Grind nuts in a nut mill, clean coffee grinder or food processor, taking care not to over-grind the nuts to an oily paste (adding a little sugar or flour will help prevent this).
making coconut milk: mix equal quantities of grated fresh or desiccated coconut and boiling water, then leave to cool; strain through muslin, squeezing to extract all the liquid. Canned coconut milk will normally separate into a thin milk with a thick layer at the top (which can be spooned off to use as coconut cream). For a thicker coconut milk, shake the can well before opening.

Index

page numbers in **bold** refer to illustrations

abalone **43**, 44
acidulated water 422
adzuki bean, dried **127**, 128
alcohol, cooking 208–9
ale, cooking 208
allspice **197**, 198
almond 186–7, **187**
  blanching 189, **189**
  almond oil **112**, 113
  French Almond Tart 408–9
amaranth 134
anchovy **15**, 16, 31
  essence 206
  paste 206, **206**
  salted **32**
andouille 74, **74**
andouillette 74, **74**
angelica **192**, 194
  crystallized 185, **185**
angler fish *see* monkfish
Angostura bitters 207
anise 196, **196**
anise chervil *see* sweet cicely
anise pepper *see* Sichuan pepper
Anjou pear **164**, 165
antipasto 422
Appenzeller **104**, 105
apple 162–3, **163**
  choosing 162
  cooking 162–3
  dried **183**, 184
  purée 162
  raw 163
  storing 162
  Apple Crumble 387
  Apple Fritters 387
  Apple Sauce 260
  Apple Tart 409
apricot **168**, 170
  dried **183**, 184
  Apricot Tart **408**, 409
arachide oil *see* groundnut oil
Arbroath smokie 30, **30**
arrowroot 118
artichoke *see* globe artichoke, Jerusalem artichoke
asafoetida **198**, 199
Asiago cheese 103
Asian pear **164**, 165
asparagus 137–8, **137**
  Asparagus Risotto 349
  Asparagus Soufflé 328–9
atherine 16
aubergine 153, **154**
  Aubergine, Pepper and Tomato Pizza with Thyme 361–2
  Aubergine Tart 327–8
  Lebanese Aubergine Salad 365–6
  Stir-Fried Aubergines with Chilli and Coriander 384
avocado 153–4, **154**
  Guacamole 365

back fat 110
bacon
  breakfast 70
  cuts 69, 70
  fat 69
  types 69–70, **70**
  Bacon Omelette 324
bagel 119, **119**
bakeware *see* ovenware
baking
  bread 356–8, **356–8**
  fish 261
  potato 147
baking powder 118–19
baking sheet 236
balm 193, 194
bamboo shoot 140
banana fig *see* banana, dried
banana 178, **179**
  dried 183, **183**
  Jamaican Baked Bananas 391–2
barbecues 240–1, **240**
  accessories **240**, 241
  types 240–1, **240**
barley 116, **117**
barracuda 17
basil 192, **192**
bass 14, **14**
  freshwater **24**, 25
  Sea Bass Pipérade 264, **265**
bath chaps 70
bay leaf **192**, 193
  see also bouquet garni
Bayonne ham 69
bean sprout **140**, 142
beans 140, **140–1**, 142
  dried 126–8, **127**
bear 81
Béarnaise Sauce 255
beater 226
Béchamel Sauce 255
bêche de mer 45
beechwheat *see* buckwheat
beef
  choosing 51
  cooking 51
  cuts 51–3, **52**, 63, **63**
  dried 71, **71**
  preparing 63, **63**
  salted 71, **71**
  Beef in Beer 284
  Blade Steak with Shallots 282
  Burgundian Beef Stew 282–3, **283**
  Golden Beef Stock 244–5
  Peppered Steak 282
  Rich Brown Beef Stock 245
  Slow-Cooked Brisket of Beef with Soy, Sake and Oysters 284–5
  Steak and Kidney Pudding 283–4
beet greens 133, **133**
beetroot 149, **150**
  Hot Red Beet Salad 379
Bel Paese cheese 107, **107**
belly, pork **59**, 60
berries 170–4, **171**, **173**
  dried **183**, 184
betel nut 187–8, **187**
Beurre Blanc 256
Beurré Bosc pear 165, **165**
Beurré Hardy pear 165
bicarbonate of soda 118–19
bierwurst sausage 76, **76**
bilberry 173
biltong 71, **71**
biscuits 414
black Barbados *see* sugar
black bean, dried 126–7, **127**
black pudding 74, **75**
black trumpet *see* horn of plenty
black-eyed bean, dried 127, **127**
blackberry **171**, 172
  Blackberry and Apple Pie 405
blackcurrant 173, **173**
  Blackcurrant Jam 417–18
  Blackcurrant Jelly **390**, 391
blade
  beef **52**, 53
  pork **59**, 60
bleak 25
blenders 238, **238**
Bleu de Corse cheese 108
Bleu des Causses cheese 109, **109**
blewit 160
bloater 29–30, **30**
blood sausage 74, **75**
blow torch 229, **231**
Blue Wensleydale cheese 109, **109**
blueberry 173, **173**
bluefish 15, **15**
blutwurst sausage 74
boar 81
board 227, **228**, 237
bockwurst sausage 73, **74**
boiling
  beef 52, 53
  meat 50
  mutton 56–7
  pork 59
  potatoes 146–7
  veal 55, 56
boiling fowl 87, **88**
boiling ham 68–9, **68**
bommaloe fish, Bombay duck 31
boning
  duck 94–5, **94–5**
  knives 222, **223**
  lamb 65–6, **65–6**
  round fish 28, **28**
bonito 16
Bonne Louise pear 165
borage **193**, 194
borlotti bean, dried 127, **127**
Borscht **248**, 249
Boston Baked Beans 354
bottle opener 229
boudin blanc *see* white pudding
bouquet garni 190, **191**
bowls 230, **231**
boysenberry **171**, 172
braising
  beef 52
  lamb 56, 57
  meat 50
  pork 59
  veal 55, 56
Bramley's Seedling apple 162, **163**
bran 114, **115**
brassica 134–137, **134–5**
bratheringe 31, **32**
bratwurst sausage 72, **72**
brazier 241
Brazil nut **187**, 188
Bread and Butter Pudding 394–5
bread machine 239
Bread Sauce 257
Breadcrumbs *see* Crumbs
breadfruit **180**, 182
bread 119–20, **119**, **120**
  baking 356–8, **356–8**
  recipes 358–64, **360**, **363**
  shaping **357–8**
breakfast bacon 70
bream 14, **14**, 25
breast
  lamb **57**, 58
  veal **54**, 56
bresaola 71, **71**
Bresse Bleu cheese 109, **109**
Brick cheese 106
Brie cheese 106, **107**
brill **11**, 12
brioche 119, **119**
  Brioche Loaf 359–61
brisket **52**, 53
brisling 30
  canned 32
broad bean **141**, 142
  dried 127, **127**
  Broad Beans and Bacon 378
  Stewed Broad Beans with Butter and Tarragon 378
broccoli **135**, 136
brooklime 134
Brownies 414
Brussels sprout **135**, 136–7
  Brussels Sprouts with Chestnuts 375
buckling 30
buckwheat 117–18, **117**
  buckwheat pasta 123, **123**
  Buckwheat Kasha 351
buffalo 81
buffalofish 25
bulb baster 229, **231**
bulgur wheat *see* burghul wheat
bullace **168**, 169
bun sheet **235**, 237
bündnerfleisch 71, **71**
burbot 25
burghul wheat 114, **115**
  Burghul Pilaf 351
burnet **193**, 194
butter 99–100, **100**
  Garlic and Herb Butter 257
  Horseradish Butter 257
  Maître d'Hôtel Butter 257
butter bean, dried 126, **127**
buttermilk 98–9, **98**, 100

cabbage 134–6, **134–5**
  Chinese **134**, 136
  choosing 134–5
  cooking 135–6
  storing 134–5
  Braised Red Cabbage 374–5
  Cabbage with Chestnut Stuffing 374
  Cumin-Spiced Cabbage 375
cabbage greens 133, **133**
cacciatore salami **77**, 78

caciocavallo cheese 105
cactus pear *see* prickly pear
Caerphilly cheese 103, **105**
caillette *see* cayette
cake tester 229, **231**
cakes 410–13, **411**, **413**
  equipment **235**, 236–7
  icing 415
Camembert cheese 106, **107**
can opener **228**, 229
candied peel 184–5, **185**
canelle knife **223**, 224
cannelloni 335
Cantal cheese 103, **104**
cantaloupe melon 176, **177**
Cape gooseberry **180**, 181
  dried 184
capercaillie 84
caper 207, **207**
capon 86, **88**
cappuccino 216
carambola *see* star fruit
caraway seed **196**, 197
cardamom **198**, 199
cardoon 140
carob 212, 213, **213**
carp 23, **24**
carragheen **45**, 46
carrot 148, **149**
  Delicate Carrot Soup 246
  Sugar-Glazed Carrots 382
cashew 186, **187**
cassava 147–8, **148**
casserole 236, **232**
cassia 197–8
catfish 23, **24**
caul fat **61**, 62
cauliflower **135**, 136
  Cauliflower au Gratin 375
  Cauliflower Soup 254
cauliflower fungi 159–60
cavalo nero 133
caviare 31–2, **32**
cayenne pepper 201, **201**
cayette 75
celeriac 148–9, **150**
celery 138, **138**
  seed **196**, 197
  Celery and Parmesan Salad 365
celtuce 129
cep 158–9, **158–9**
cervelas sausage 73
cervelat sausage 76, **76**
Chakchouka 323
channel bass *see* red drum
chanterelle **158**, 159
chaource cheese **107**, 108
chapati 120, **120**
char 22, **22**
chayote 156–7, **156**
Cheddar-type cheeses 103–4, **104–5**
cheese
  blue 108–9, **109**
  fresh 101–2, **102**
  goat's 108, **108**
  hard 102–5, **104–5**
  recipes 329–331, **331**
  semi-firm 105–6, **106**
  soft 106–8, **107**
  Cheesecake 395–6
  Cheese Omelette 324
  Cheese Tart 327–8
  Mozzarella in Carrozza 330, **331**
  Swiss Fondue 329
cheese knife 225
cheese wire 225
cherry
  choosing 169
  cooking 169
  dried **183**, 184
  glacé 185, **185**
  storing 169
  types 168–9, **168**
  Cherry Cake 410–11
  Cherry Clafoutis 388, **389**
chervil 190, **191**
  see also fines herbes
Cheshire cheese 103, **104**
Chester cheese *see* Cheshire cheese
chestnut **187**, 188
  peeling 189, **189**
chick-pea, dried 127–8, **127**
chicken 86–7, **88**
  cooking 87
  eggs 96–7, **96**
  jointing 92, **92**
  livers 90
  stuffing of 93, **93**
  trussing 91, **91**
  Chicken with Almonds and Raisins 306
  Chicken on a Bed of Garlic 306
  Chicken with Black Olives and Tomatoes 306–7
  Chicken Pie with Cream and Mushrooms 317
  Chicken Stock 244
  Cold Chicken and Ham Pie 314–15, **315**
  Coq au Vin **304**, 305
  Grilled Chicken Kebabs 307
  Old-Fashioned Chicken Broth 249
  Poulet Paysanne 307
  Quick-Fried Chicken with Garlic and Chilli 305
  Roast Chicken with Marjoram 305–6
  Roast Marinated Chicken Breasts 310, **310**
  Sichuan Chicken Salad 372, **373**
  Tarragon Chicken with Mushrooms 308
  Wyvern's Chicken Curry with Coconut 308, **309**
chickweed 134
chicory 129–30, **130**
  Chicory in Butter and Cream 372
chilli *see* chilli pepper
chilli pepper 152–3, **152**
  chilli flakes 201
  chilli powder 201, **201**
  chilli sauce 206, **206**
Chinese artichoke *see* crosne
Chinese Belly Pork Salad with Bok Choy 371–2
Chinese Egg Noodles with Browned Garlic, Chillies and Parsley 345
Chinese noodles 125
Chinese sausage 74, **74**
chinois **223**, 226
chip cutter 225
chive 190, **191**
  see also fines herbes
chocolate 212–13, **213**
  Chocolate Butter Icing 415
  Chocolate Orange Mousse 394
  Rich Chocolate Cake 410, **411**
  Rich Chocolate Mousse 394
chorizo salami 78
Choux Pastry 404–5
chow mein 125
Christmas Pudding 396
christophene *see* chayote
chrogi *see* crosne
chuck, beef **52**, 53
chump end
  lamb 57, **57**
  pork **59**, 60
  veal **54**, 55
chutney 207, **207**, 422
  recipes 419
ciabatta 120, **120**
ciccorio *see* radicchio
Cider Barbecue Sauce 257
cinnamon 197–8, **197**
citron 165
citrus fruit 165–7, **166–7**
  preparing 167, **167**
citrus zester **223**, 224
clam **37**, 38
  shucking 41, **41**
Clear Quince Jelly 418
cleaver 222, **223**
clementine 166, **166**
cloud ear 161, **161**
cloudberry 172
clove 197, **197**
coalfish *see* coley
cob nut *see* hazelnut
cockle **37**, 38
cocoa 210, 212–13, **213**
coconut **187**, 188–9, 423
  splitting 189, **189**
  Coconut Ice-Cream 399
cod 12–13, **13**
  cod family 12–14, **13**
  dried 31, **32**
  roe 30, **30**
  Fish Cakes 265
  Salt Cod with Potatoes 274
  Steamed Cod with Ginger and Spring Onion 264
coffee 214–15, **215**
  additives 216
  beans 214–15, **215**
  brewing 216
  decaffeinated 216
  grinding 215–16, **215**
  instant 216–17
  roasting 215, **215**
  Coffee Butter Icing 415
  Coffee Granita 401
  Coffee Ice-Cream 398
coffee grinder 226
  electrical **238**, 239
coffee machine, electrical **238**, 239
colander **228**, 229
Colby cheese 105, **106**
Colcannon 374
Cold Game Pie 316
coley 13, 14
collards *see* cabbage greens
collet, veal 56
colourings 206, 207
Comice pear 164, **164**
Comté cheese 104–5, **105**
conch 44
condiments 206–7, **206–7**
Conference pear 164, **164**
confit de canard 71
confit d'oie 71, **71**
Consommé 250
cooling rack 229, **231**
coppa ham **68**, 69
corer 225
coriander 191–2, **191**
  seed **198**, 199
corkscrew **228**, 229
corn 115–16, **115**
Corn Bread 362–3
corn oil 112, **112**
corn salad 129, **131**
cornflour 116
Cornish Pasties 317
Cornish Saffron Bread **360**, 361
cotechino sausage 73, **74**
courgette 156, **156**
  Courgettes au Gratin 385
  Courgettes with Dill and Sour Cream 384–5
  Stuffed Courgettes 385–6
Cox's Orange Pippin apple 162, **163**
crab 33, **33**
  picking a cooked crab 40–1, **40–1**
  Crab Cakes 275
  Crab Salad with Thai Flavours 368
  Dressed Crab 275
crabapple 163–4, **163**
  Crabapple Jelly 418
cranberry 173, **173**
  dried **183**, 184
  Fresh Cranberry Sauce 260
crawfish 34, **34**
crayfish 34–5, **35**
cream **98–9**, 99–100
cream of tartar 119
Crème Brûlée 394
Crème Caramel 392
crème double *see* crème fraîche
crème fraîche **98**, 99
Crêpes Suzette 396–7
Crespolini 341–2
cress 130–31, **131**
crispbread 120, **120**
Crispin apple 162, **163**
croissant 119, **119**
Croquembouche 409
crosne 150
Croûtons 364
Crudités with Aïoli 365
Crumbs 364
crumpet 119, **119**
crusher **223**, 226

crystallized foods
flowers 185
fruit 185, **185**
cucumber 155, **155**
Chilled Cucumber Soup with Mint 254
Cool and Hot Cucumber Salad 367
culatello ham 69
Cumberland Game Sauce 260
Cumberland sausages 72
cumin **198**, 199
curing
meat 71, **71**
poultry 71, **71**
currant 172–3, **173**, 182–3, **183**
cusk 14
Custard Pancakes 397
custard-apple **180**, 181
cuts, meat
bacon 69, 70
beef 51–3, 52, 63, **63**
lamb 56–8, **57**, 65–7, **65–7**
pork 58–60, **59**, 64, **64**
veal 54–6, **54**, 64, **64**
cutter **223**, 225
cuttlefish **43**, 44

dab **11**, 12
dace 25
daikon *see* mouli
dairy foods
butter 99–100, **100**
cheeses 101–9, **102**, **104–9**
cream 99, **99**
eggs 96–7, **96**
home-made 100
milk 97–9, **98**
damson **168**, 169
danbo cheese 105, **106**
dandelion **132**, 133
Danish Blue cheese 109, **109**
Dark Chocolate Mousse 394
date **180**, 182
dried 183–4, **183**
deep-fryer 239
defrosting
chicken 86
meat 51
turkey 87
demi-sel cheese 102
demitasse 216
desserts 387–409, **389–90**, **393**, **403–4**, **406**, **408**
Devil's Food Cake 411–12
dewberry 172
dhal, dried 128
Lentil Dhal 355
Dijon mustard 202, **202**
dill 191, **191**
seed 196, **196**
dishes **232**, 236
pastry **235**, 237
dolphin fish **18**, 19
dorado *see* dolphin fish
Dorset Blue Vinny cheese 109, **109**
Dover sole 11, **11**
dredger 237
dried foods
beans 126–8, **127**
beef 71, **71**
fruit 182–4, **183**
peas 126–8, **127**, **128**
dripping 110–11
Dublin Bay prawn *see* langoustine
duck 89–90, **89**
boning 94–5, **94–5**
cooking 90
egg **96**, 97
foie gras 90
liver 90
stuffing of 94–5, **94–5**
wild 82, **83**
Duck with Coconut Cream and Green Curry Paste 313–14
Duck with Green Olives 313
Galantine of Duck 320, **321**
Roast Duck 312–13
dulse **45**, 46
dumpling 124
recipes 344–5
Dundee Cake 412

ears 62
eaux-de-vie, cooking 208
Eclairs 409
Edam cheese 104, **105**
eel **20**
conger 20, **20**
freshwater **24**, 25
jellied 32, **32**
smoked 30–1, **30**
egg 96–7, **96**
cooking 96–7
flat omelettes 325
hard-boiled 322
omelette fillings 324
poached 322
recipes 322–9, **326**
scrambled 322
soft-boiled 322
tart fillings 327–8
Aïoli 259
Bacon and Egg Tart **326**, 327
Curried Eggs 322
Egg Mayonnaise 327
Egg Mousse 327
Eggs Benedict 323
Eggs with Spinach and Cheese 323
Herb Mayonnaise 259
Mayonnaise 259
Oeufs en Cocotte à la Crème 324
Oeufs sur le Plat 323
Omelette Arnold Bennett 325–6
Omelette Fines Herbes 324
Omelette with Artichokes and Parsley 324–5
Rolled Omelettes with Spiced Greens 325
egg pasta 121–22, **122**
eggplant *see* aubergine
Egremont Russet apple 162, **163**
Egyptian brown bean *see* ful medame
Egyptian Falafels 353–4
elderberry **173**, 174
Elderflower Sorbet 401
electrical appliances 238–9, **238**
elver 25
Emmental cheese 105, **105**
Empire apple 162, **163**
endive 129–30, **130**
enoki 161, **161**
Epoisses cheese 108
equipment 222–41
bowls 230, **231**
cake making **235**, 236–7
cleaning 225–6
cutting implements 222–6, **223**
decorating **235**, 237
electrical appliances 238–9, **238**
knives 222–24, **223**
mashers **223**, **226**, 227
measuring 230–3, **231**
mincer **223**, 226
ovenware **232**, 235–6
pans **232**, 233–5
pastry making **235**, 236, 237
sieves 223, 226
storing 225–6
escalope, veal 55, 64, **64**
escarole 129–30, **130**
espresso 216

faggot 75
farfalle **334**, 335
fats
see also oils
bacon 69
cooking 110–11, **111**
goose 89
feathered game 82–5, **83–5**
feet 62
feijoa **181**, 182
fennel 137, **137**, 191, **191**
seed 196, **196**
Fennel au Gratin 375–6
fenugreek **198**, 199
feta cheese 102, **102**
fiddlehead fern 140
fig **180**, 181
dried 183, **183**
figue de mer 44–5
filbert *see* hazelnut
filleting
flat fish 26, **26**
knives 224
round fish 27, **27**
fillet
beef 52–3, **53**, 63, **63**
pork **59**, 60
fines herbes 190
finnan haddie 29, **30**
Creamed Finnan Haddie 275
finocchio *see* fennel
fish
canned 32, **32**
choosing 10, **10**
cod family 12–14, **13**
cooking 261
dried 29, 31, **32**
flat 11–12, **11**
freezing 10
freshwater 21–25, **22**, **24**
glazing 10
great 16–17, **17**
oily 15–16, **15**
pickling 31, **32**
preparing 26–8, **26–8**
preserving 29–32, **30**, **32**
recipes 261–81
salting 29, 31–2, **32**
saltwater 11–20, **11**, **13–15**, **17–18**
sauce 206, **206**
shellfish 33–42, **33–7**, **39–42**
small fry 15–16, **15**
smoking 29, **30**
storing 10
Fish Fumet 246
New England Fish Chowder 252
fish slice *see* turner
five-spice powder 196
Flaky Pastry 402–4
flambéing 208
flank
beef **52**, 53
veal **54**, 56
Flapjacks 414
flat fish 11–12, **11**
preparing 26–8, **26**
flavouring essences 206, 207
flounder 11–12, **11**
flour
barley 116
carob 213, **213**
cornflour 116
rice 117
rye 116
thickening agent 118
type 00 114
wheat 114–15, **115**
flowers 195, **195**
crystallized 185
focaccia 120, **120**
fontainebleau cheese 102
fontina cheese 105, **105**
food mill *see* Mouli-légumes
food processor 238, **238**
foreleg, beef 53
forks 228–9
Fourme d'Ambert cheese 109, **109**
frankfurters 73, **74**
freezing
duck 90
meat 50–1
French Cheddar *see* Cantal
French Toast *see* Pain Perdu
Fresh Egg Pasta 332
freshwater fish 21–25, **22**, **24**
Frisée and Bacon Salad 366–7
Frittata 325, 326–7
frog's legs 46
fromage blanc cheese 101, **102**
fruit
berries 170–4, **171**, **173**
candied 182, 184–5, **185**
citrus 165–7, **166–7**
crystallized 185, **185**
dried 182–4, **183**
grapes 174–6, **175**

Mediterranean 177–82, **178–81**
melons 176–7, **177**
stoned 167–70, **168**
tropical 177–82, **178–81**
frying
beef 51, 52–3
fish 261
lamb 56
meat 49–50
oils 110, 111–13, **112–13**
pan **232**, 234
pork 59
potatoes 147
veal 54–5
ful medame, dried 127, **127**
fungi 158–61, **158–59**, **161**
funnel 229, **231**, 241
furred game 79–81, **80–1**

gage **168**, 169
Gala apple 162, **163**
galangal **197**, 199
game
feathered 82–5, **83–5**
furred 79–81, **80–1**
recipes 294–303, **296**, **299**, **300**, **303**
smoked 71
gammon 68
garam masala 196
garfish **18**, 19
Mediterranean Garfish 270–1
garlic **143**, 145
garlic press **223**, 227
garlic sausage 76, **77**
Gazpacho 254
gelatine 62
gendarmes salami 78
geranium leaf 195, **195**
ghee 100, **100**
gherkin 155
gigot, lamb 57
ginger **197**, 199
crystallized 185, **185**
Gingerbread Biscuits 414
glacé fruit 185, **185**
globe artichoke **137**
preparing 138–9, **139**
Artichokes alla Romana 376, **377**
Gloucester cheese 103, **104**
Gnocchi Romana 344
gnocchi **122**, 124
goatfish *see* mullet
goat's cheese 108, **108**
Goat's Cheese and Courgette Filo Tart 330
Golden Delicious apple 162, **163**
Gomost cheese 101
goose 88, **89**
cooking 89
eggs **96**, 97
fat 110–11, **111**
foie gras 90
liver 90
neck, stuffed 73–4
wild 82
Goose with Apple Stuffing 312
gooseberry **171**, 172
Gooseberry Fool 388
Gooseberry Jam 417
goosefoot 134
Gorgonzola cheese 108–9, **109**
Gouda-type cheeses 104, **105**
grains 114–18, **115–17**
recipes 350–2, **350**, **353**
Grana cheeses 103
Grana Padano cheese 103
Granny Smith apple 162, **163**
grape
choosing 175
seedless 174, **175**
serving 175–6
storing 175
grapefruit **166**, 167
Grapefruit Sorbet **400**, 401
grapeseed oil **112**, 113
grater **223**, 224, 226
Gratin of French Beans with Chives 378–9
gravlax 31, **32**
gravy strainer 229, **231**
grayling 22–23, **22**
Greek Avgolemono Soup 250–1
green bean **141**, 142
Green Bean Salad with Anchovy-Cream Dresssing 367–8
greens 132–4, **132–3**
wild 134
Grilled Polenta with Poached Eggs, Fontina and Chive Cream 352
grilling
beef 51, 52–3
fish 261
lamb 56
meat 49
pork 59
veal 54–5
grissini 120, **120**
groundnut oil 112, **113**
grouper 14–15, **14**
grouse 84–5, **84**
Simple Roast Grouse 301
Gruyère-type cheeses 104–5, **104–5**
guava 179, **179**
gudgeon 25
guinea fowl 85, **85**
Stuffed Guinea Fowl with Leek Purée 302
gull egg 97
gurnard 19, **20**
gurnet *see* gurnard

haddock 13, **13**
Arbroath smokie 30, **30**
smoked *see* finnan haddie
Fish Pie 266
haggis 74–5, **75**
hake 13, **13**
halibut **11**, 12
preparing 26, **26**
smoked 29, **30**
Baked Halibut 263–4
Halibut Salad with Capers 368–70
ham
boiling 68–9, **68**
raw **68**, 69
Ham Omelette 324
hand and spring, pork **59**, 60
hare 79–80, **80**, **81**
Hare in Sour Cream 295
haricot bean, dried 126, **127**
harusame 125
Harvey sauce 206
havarti cheese 105
hazelnut **187**, 188
skinning 189, **189**
Hazelnut Cakes 413
heads 62
hearts 62
hedgehog fungi **158**, 160
herbs, types 190–5, **191–3**, **195**
Herb Vinaigrette with Balsamic Vinegar 259
herring 15–16, **15**
Bismarck herring 31, **32**
bloater 29–30, **30**
bratheringe 31, **32**
brisling 30, 32
hareng saur 29–30
Maatje herring 31, **32**
pickled 31
rollmop 31, **32**
salted 31, **32**
sild 30, 32
soused 31, **32**
sprat 30, 32
Herrings in Oatmeal 267
Soused Herrings 267
hibachi 240, **240**
hijiki **45**, 46
hindleg, beef 53
hogget *see* lamb
hoisin sauce 206, **206**
Hollandaise Sauce 255–6
Holsteinerwurst sausage 76
hominy 115, **115**
honey 210, **210**
Honey Madeleines 414
hop shoot 140
horn of plenty **158**, 159
horse mackerel 15, **15**
horseradish **192**, 194
Horseradish Sauce 258
Hot and Sour Shellfish Broth 253–4
Hot-Water Crust Pastry 405
huckleberry 173
Hummus with Tahina 353
Hungarian brawn sausage 76, **76**

ice-cream
recipes 398–9
maker **238**, 239
scoop 229–30, **231**
icing 415
icing sugar 212, **212**
Indian date *see* tamarind
Indian fig *see* prickly pear
Indian Millet 351–2
Irish moss *see* carragheen
Israeli Falafels 353–4

jack rabbit *see* hare
jagdwurst sausage 76
jaggery 212
jam
making 417–19
recipes **416**, 417–18
storing 417
Jamaica pepper *see* allspice
jambonneau 69
jambon de Grisons 69
jamón serrano 69
Japanese artichoke *see* crosne
Japanese horseradish
paste 207
powder 207
Japanese medlar *see* loquat
Japanese noodles 125, **125**
Japanese Noodles with Char-Grilled Beef 345
Jarlsberg cheese 105, **105**
jelly
making 417
recipes 418
storing 417
jellyfish **43**, 45
jerky 71, **71**
Jerusalem artichoke 150, **150**
Jerusalem Artichokes with Cream and Parsley 382–3
jícama 150, **150**
John Dory 19, **20**
Braised John Dory with Tomatoes and Fennel 268–70
jointing, chicken 92, **92**
juice extractor **223**, 227
electrical **238**, 239
juniper berry 196–7, **196**

kabanos salami **77**, 78
kaiserfleisch **68**, 69
kale 133, **133**
kasseler **68**, 69
katenrauchwurst sausage 76
kelp **45**, 46
dashi 46
keta 32
ketchups 206, **206**
kettle 239
kid, cooking 58
kidneys 61–2, **61**
Kidneys with Mustard 293
kielbasa sausage **72**, 73
Kilkenny Brown Soda Bread 362
king 166
kipper 29, **30**
kiwi fruit **178**, 180
knackwurst sausage 73, **74**
kneading, dough 356, 357, **357**
knives 222–4, 228, **228**
care 224
materials 222
quality 222
sharpening 224
specialist **223**, 225
storing 224
types 222–4, **223**
knotroot *see* crosne
kohlrabi 149–50, **150**
kosher salt 200, **200**
kumquat 166–7, **166**

labrusca 174
lachsschinken ham 69
ladle 227, **228**

lamb
choosing 56
cooking 56–8
cuts 56–8, **57**, 65–7, **65–7**
kid 58
kidneys 61
liver 61
preparing 65–7, **65–7**
sweetbreads 61
Garlic-Braised Lamb Shanks with Yellow Peppers 290
Lamb Korma 289–90
Navarin of Lamb with Potatoes 288
Spiced Stuffed Leg of Lamb 288–9, **289**
lamb's lettuce *see* corn salad
lamprey **20**
landjäger salami 78
langoustine 35, **36**
Grilled Langoustines 276
lantern flounder *see* megrim
lard 110, **111**
lard de poitrine 70, **70**
larding needle 230
lasagne 122, **123**, 335
Lasagne al Forno 339–40
Lasagne with Mushrooms, Bacon and Artichokes 340–1, **340**
laver 45–6
Lawyer's Wig *see* shaggy ink cap
Laxton's Superb apple 162, **163**
leberkäse sausage 78, **78**
leek **143**, 145
Leek Tart 327–8
Leeks in Cream 379
Leeks with Truffles 379
leg
beef **52**, 53
lamb 57, **57**, 66–7, **66–7**
pork 59–60, **59**
veal **54**, 55
Leicester cheese 104, **104**
lemon **166**, 167
Lemon Butter Icing 415
Lemon Court-Bouillon with Parsley 245–6
Lemon Curd 419
Lemon Tart 405
lemon balm *see* balm
lemon grass 194, **195**
lemon sole **11**, 12
lentils 128, **128**
Lentil Dhal 355
Lentil Soup 248–9
Spiced Lentils 354–5
lettuce 129, **130**
Leyden cheese 104
Lido Pasta Salad 371
lima bean 142
Limburger cheese 107, **107**
lime **166**, 167
lime leaf 195, **195**
limpet 44
ling 14
liptauer cheese 101
liptol cheese *see* liptauer cheese
liqueurs, cooking 208
liquidizer 238, **238**
liquorice **198**, 199
livarot cheese 106, **107**
liver 61, **61**
Braised Liver with Bacon 292
Lyonnaise Calf's Liver with Onions 292
Sautéed Chicken Livers with Sage 292–3
liver sausage 78, **78**
lobster 33–4, **34**
preparing 39, **39**
Boiled Lobster 276
Grilled Lobster with Butter 276
lobster tools 229, **231**
loganberry **171**, 172
loin
beef 52–3, **52**
lamb 57, **57**
pork **59**, 60
veal **54**, 55
loquat **180**, 181
loukanika sausage 73, **74**
lovage **193**, 194
luganega sausage **72**, 73
lumpfish, roe 32, **32**
lychee **180**, 181
lythe *see* pollack

macadamia nut 186, **187**
macaroni 121, **122**
Macaroni Cheese with Ham 338
mace 198, **198**
McIntosh apple 162, **163**
mackerel 15, **15**
preparing 27, **27**
smoked 30, **30**
Grilled Mackerel with Green Paste 266–7
Spiced Marinated Mackerel 266
Madeira Cake 410–11
mahi mahi *see* dolphin fish
maizemeal *see* corn
makrut *see* lime leaf
Malt Loaf 362, **363**
maltagliate 335
Malted Ice-Cream 398–9
Manchego cheese 105–6, **106**
mandarin 166
mandoline **223**, 225–6
mangetout pea 141–2, **141**
mango 178, **179**
dried 184
Mango Coulis 260
mangosteen **180**, 181
manioc root *see* cassava
margarine 110, **111**
marigold 195, **195**
marinades 207, 208
marinating, fish 261
marionberry 172
marjoram 192–3, **193**
marlin 16–17
marmalade
making 417
recipes 418
storing 417
Marmalade Queen of Puddings 395
Maroilles cheese 106–7, **107**
Maroilles Cheese Tart 329–30
marrow, beef 53
marrow, vegetable 156, **156**
Marzipan 415
mascarpone cheese 102, **102**
masher **223**, 226
mashing, potatoes 147
matsutake 161, **161**
matzo cracker 120, **120**
Maytag Blue cheese 109, **109**
measuring equipment 230–3, **231**
measuring cups 231, **231**
measuring jugs 231, **231**
measuring spoons 231–3, **231**
meat
see also cuts, meat
ageing 48
beef 51–3, **52**
choosing 48–9, 51
cooking 49–50, 51
cured 71, **71**
freezing 50–1
glazes 244
lamb 56–8, **57**
offal 61–2
pork 58–60, **59**
preparing 63–7, **63–7**
recipes 282–93, **283**, **289**, **293**
storing 48–9, 51
tenderness 48
veal 54–6, **54**
meat tenderizer 226
medlar 163–4, **164**
Medlar Jelly 418
megrim 12
Melanzane alla Parmigiana 383–4
Melba Toast 364
melon 176–7, **177**
choosing 176
serving 176–7
storing 176
Melon Sorbet **400**, 401
mettwurst sausage 76, **76**
mezzaluna **223**, 224
milk
fresh 97–8
long-life 98
soured 98–9, **98**, 100
substitutes 98
millet **117**, 118
Mimolette cheese 104
mincer **223**, 226
mincing, knives **223**, 224
minneola 167
mint **193**, 194
Mint Sauce 258
mirliton *see* chayote
miso 207
mixer, electrical 238–9, **238**
mizuna 132
molasses syrup 211, **211**
monkfish 17–18, **18**
monosodium glutamate 200
Monterey Jack cheese 105, **106**
mooli *see* mouli
Moors and Christians 354, **355**
morcilla sausage 74
morel **158**, 159
Mornay Sauce 255
mortadella sausage 75–6, **76**
mostarda di Cremona *see* mostarda di frutta
mostarda di frutta 203, **203**
mostarda di Voghera 203
mouli 131, **131**
Mouli-légumes **223**, 226
mozzarella cheese 102, **102**
muffin 119, **119**
mulberry 172
mullet 18–19, **18**
preparing 26, **26**
roe 31
Grilled Grey Mullet with Fennel 270
Red Mullet en Papillote 270
mung bean, dried **127**, 128
Munster cheese 107, **107**
murcott 166
muscadine 174–5
muscat 174, **175**
mushroom 158–61, **158–9**, **161**
Chinese 161, **161**
cultivated **158–9**, 160–61
Japanese 161, **161**
ketchup 206
wild 158–60, **158–9**
Chanterelles Fried with Dill 386
Garlic Mushroom Soup with Cream 246
Garlic Mushrooms 386
Mushroom Omelette 324
Mushroom Risotto 348
Mushroom-Filled Pancakes 328
muskellunge 23
mussel **36**, 38
Moules à la Marinière 279–81
Thai Mussels **280**, 281
mustard 131, **131**, 202–3, **202–3**
American 203, **203**
English 202–3, **203**
French 202, **202**
German 203, **203**
home-made 203
preserves 203, **203**
Mustard Sauce 255–6
mustard greens 133, **134**
mustard seed oil 113
mutton
choosing 56
cooking 56–8
smoked 71
Mysost cheese 101, **102**

naan bread **119**, 120
nasturtium 195, **195**
neck
beef **52**, 53
lamb 57–8, **57**
veal **54**, 55–6
nectarine **168**, 170
needlefish *see* garfish
nettle **132**, 134

Neufchâtel cheese 102, **102**
noodles
Chinese 124–5, **125**
Japanese 125, **125**
recipes 345
Normandy Fish Stew **262**, 263
Norway Lobster *see* Dublin Bay prawn
nouilles *see* nudels
nudels 124
nutcrackers 229, **231**
nutmeg 198, **198**
nuts
preparing 189, **189**
types 186–9, **187**

oatflake 116
oats **115**, 116
ocean perch *see* redfish
octopus 43–4, **43**
offal 61–2, **61**
oil
cooking 110–13, **112–13**
flavoured 113
refined 112
unrefined 111
okra **141**, 142
olive 154–5, **154**
olive oil 112, **112**
omelettes 323–5
onion 143–4, **143–4**
French Onion Soup 249–50
Onion Sauce 255
Spanish Onion Tart 327–8
opah 16–17
orange roughy 20, **20**
orange 165–6, **166**
Orange Butter Icing 415
Orange Glacé Icing 415
Orange Granita 401
Orange Sorbet 399–401, **400**
oregano **192**, 193
Orleans Reinette apple 162, **163**
ormer *see* abalone
ortanique 166
ortolan 82–3
ostrich 90
egg 97
ovenware **232**, 235–6
materials 235
types **232**, 236
ox kidney 62
oxtail **61**, 62
oyster 36–7, **36**
sauce 206
shucking 42, **42**
Oysters Rockefeller 278–9
oyster plant *see* salsify
oyster of veal *see* shoulder of veal

paan 187–8
Packham's Triumph pear 164
Paella 346, **347**
Pain Perdu 364
palette knife 228, **228**
palm heart 140
Pan Catalan 364
Pancake 328
pancetta 69–70
pans 233–5
choosing 234
materials 233–4
preserving 241
storing 234
type **232**, 234–5
papaya 178–9, **178**
dried 184
pappardelle 335
Pappardelle with Hare Sauce 339
paprika 201, **201**
paratha 120, **120**
Parmesan cheese 103, **104**
parsley 190, **191**
see also fines herbes, bouquet garni
parsnip 148, **149**
partridge 83–4, **84**
Partridge with Celeriac 297–8
Roast Partridge with Chicken Liver Toasts 297
Passe Crassane pear 165
passion fruit **178**, 180–1
pasta 121–4, **122–3**
buckwheat 123, **123**
coloured 122–3
cooking 335
flavoured 122–3
making 332–5, **333–4**
recipes 332–45, **333–4**, **340**, **343**
sauces 124
serving 335
for soups 124
stuffed **122**, 123–4, **123**
types 121–4, **122–3**
wholewheat 123, **123**
Pasta e Fagioli 251–2
pasta machine 229, **231**
electrical 239
pastes 206, **206**
pastrami 71, **71**
pastry 402–9, **406**, **408**
equipment **235**, 236–7
making **403–4**
pastry wheel 225
pâté
recipes 314, 317–20, **318**, **321**
Pâté Brisée 402
Pâté in a Crust 319
Pâté de Campagne 318–19, **318**
paté-type sausage 78, **78**
pattypan squash 156
pawpaw *see* papaya
pea
dried 126–8, **127**, **128**
fresh 140–2, **141**
Green Pea Soup 254
Peas an Indian Way 378
Peas with Lettuce Hearts 376
Yellow Split Pea Soup 248–9
peach **168**, 169
choosing 170
cooking 170
dried **183**, 184
leaves 195
storing 170
Peach Conserve 418–19
Peach Melba 399
peanut 187, **187**
peanut oil *see* groundnut oil
Peanut Sauce 258
pear 162
choosing 165
cooking 165
dried **183**, 184
types 164–5, **164**
Spiced Pears in Red Wine 387
pecan **187**, 188
Pecan Pie 407
pecorino cheese 103, **104**
pectin 417
peeler **223**, 224
penne 121, **123**
Penne with Ham and Tomato Sauce 339
penny bun *see* cep
pepper 200–1, **201**
pepper mill **223**, 226
peppercorn *see* pepper
pepperoni **77**, 78
pepper 152–3, **152**
pimiento 152
Sweet Pepper Salad 366
perch 23, **24**
periwinkle *see* winkle
persimmon **179**, 180
pestle and mortar **223**, 226
Pesto alla Genovese 336
petit salé 70
Petit Suisse cheese 102, **102**
petit pois 141
pheasant 85, **85**
egg 97
Normandy Pheasant with Apples and Calvados 298
Pheasant with Chestnuts 298, **299**
piccalilli 203
pickerel 23
pickles 207, **207**
pickling spice 196
pie funnel 237
pies
recipes 314–17, **315**, 319, 321
sweet **404**, 405–7, **406**
pigeon 83, **84**
Braised Pigeons and Cabbage 302, **303**
Pigeon Pie 321
pike 23, **24**
Fish Mousselines 274
Quenelles 274
pike perch 23
pilchard, canned 32
pine kernal *see* pine nut
pine nut 186, **187**
pineapple 178, **179**
pinto bean, dried 127, **127**
piping bag **235**, 237
pipo crème cheese 109
Pissenlits au Lard 366–7
pistachio nut 187, **187**
pitta 119–20, **120**
pizza
base 358, **358**
recipes 361–2
plaice **11**, 12
Fried Plaice 264
Plain White Loaf 358–9
plantain 178, **180**
plockwurst sausage 76, **76**
plover egg 97
plum **168**, 169
sauce 206
poitrine fumé 70
pole flounder *see* witch
polenta 115, **115**
Grilled Polenta with Poached Eggs, Fontina and Chive Cream 352
Soft Polenta with Butter and Parmesan 352, **353**
pollack 14
pomegranate **178**, 179–80
pomelo **166**, 167
pomfret 19
pompano **18**, 19
Pont-l'Evêque cheese 106, **107**
poppadom 120, **120**
poppy seed **196**, 197
pork 58–60
choosing 58
cooking 58–60
cured 68–70, **68**, **70**
cuts 58–60, 64, **64**
escalope 64, **64**
kidneys 61
liver 61
preparing 64, **64**
salted 70
sucking-pig 60
sweetbreads 61
Boiled Bacon and Sausage with Haricot Beans and Garlic Purée 291
Fried Pork Chops 291
Gigot d'Agneau with Haricot Beans 287–8
Glazed Gammon 292, **293**
Old-Fashioned Pork Pie 315–16
Pork Fillet with Juniper 290
Rillettes of Pork 319–20
Roast Loin of Pork 290–1
Port-Salut cheese 107, **107**
Portuguese Omelette 324
pot roasting
beef 52, 53
lamb 56
meat 50
pork 59
veal 55, 56
potato 145
chips 147
choosing 146
cooking 146–7
storing 146
sweet 147
types **144**
Creamed Potatoes with Parsley 381
New Potatoes Baked with Saffron, Cream and Garlic **380**, 381
Pommes Dauphinoise 381
Pommes Rissolées 379
Roast Potatoes 379
Spiced and Fried New

Potatoes with Minted Yogurt Dressing 381–2
poularde 86
poulet 86
poultry
cured 71, **71**
giblets 90
livers 90
preparing 91–5, **91–5**
recipes **304**, 305–14, **309–10**
smoked 71, **71**
types 86–90, **88–9**
poussin 86, **88**
prawn 35–6, **35**
preparing 41, **41**
Grilled Prawns Wrapped in Bacon 276, **277**
Marinated Thai Prawns 278
Prawn and Cucumber Curry 278
Prawn and Fennel Risotto 348–9
Prawn and Fennel Soup 252–3
Prawn Omelette 324
preserves
equipment 241
making 417
recipes **416**, 417–19
storing 417
pretzel **119**, 120
prickly pear **180**, 181
Profiteroles 409
Provençal Soupe au Pistou 250, **251**
provolone cheese 105, **106**
prune **183**, 184
ptarmigan 84
pudding sausage 74–5, **75**
puddings 387–409, **403–4**, **406**, **408**
puffball, giant **159**, 160
pulses 126–8, **127**, **128**
recipes 353–5, **355**
pultost cheese 101
pumpernickel bread 119, **119**
pumpkin 155, 157, **157**
Pumpkin Pie 407
Pumpkin Soup with Basil 247–8
purslane **132**, 133–4

quail 82, **83**
egg **96**, 97
Marinated Roast Quails **300**, 301
Quails with Thyme and Orange 301–2
quatre épices 196
quetsch 169
quince 163–4, **164**
Quinces in Lemon Syrup 387
quinoa grain **117**, 118

rabbit 80–1, **80**, **81**
Braised Rabbit with Tomatoes 295
Rabbit with Prunes and Red Wine **296**, 297
radicchio 129, **130**
radish 131, **131**
Ragù alla Bolognese 336
raisin 182, **183**
rambutan 181
rapeseed oil 113, **113**
raspberry 171–2, **171**
Fresh Raspberry Pavlova 388
Pouding de Framboises 388–91
Raspberry Fool 388
Raspberry Granita 401
Ratatouille 383
ravioli **334**
Ravioli con Funghi Porcini 342, **343**
ray *see* skate
Reblochon cheese 107, **107**
red caviare *see* keta
Red Delicious apple 162, **163**
red drum 19–20, **20**
red kidney bean, dried 126, **127**
Red Peppers with Anchovies 383
red sea bass *see* red drum
red snapper **18**, 19
Red and Yellow Pepper Tart 327–8
redcurrant 173, **173**
Redcurrant Jelly 418
redfish 20
relishes 207
rhubarb 170, **173**, 174
Rhubarb and Raisin Pie **406**, 407
rib
beef **52**, 53
veal 55–6
Ribollita 252
rice 116–17, **116**
recipes 346–9, **347**
Brown Rice Pilau 346
Pilau Rice 346–8
Plain Boiled Rice 346
ricer 227
Rich Vanilla Ice-Cream 398
Rich Vegetable Stock 245
ricotta cheese 101, **102**
Rigatoni all'Amatriciana 337
Risotto alla Milanese 348
roach 25
roasting
beef 51–3
lamb 56, 57–8
meat 50
pork 59
potatoes 147
sucking-pig 60
veal 55
roasting chicken 87, **88**
Rock Cornish game hen 86, **88**
rocket **130**, 131
Rocket and Walnut Salad 367
rockfish *see* redfish
rock lobster *see* crawfish
roe
salted 31–2
smoked 30, **30**
Taramasalata 275
Rolled Omelettes with Spiced Greens 325
rolling pin **235**, 237
rollmop 31, **32**
Rome Beauty apple 162, **163**
root vegetables 145–50, **146**, **148–50**
Roquefort cheese 108, **109**
Roquefort Soufflé 329
rose hip **173**, 174
rosemary **192**, 193
rose 195, **195**
rosette salami **77**, 78
Rough Puff Pastry 402
Rouille 258–9
rowanberry 174
Royal Icing 415
rump, beef **52**, 53
rye 116
Rye Bread 359

Sabayon Sauce for Fish 256
safflower oil 113, **113**
saffron **198**, 199
Saffron Bouillabaisse with Rouille 253
sage **192**, 193–4
Sage Derby cheese 104
sago **117**, 118
sailfish 16–17, **17**
sailfluke *see* megrim
Saint Nectaire cheese **107**, 108
St Peter's fish *see* John Dory
saithe *see* coley
salad basket 229, **231**
Salade Niçoise 368, **369**
salads
potato 147
recipes 365–72, **366**, **369–70**, **373**, 379
tomato 151
vegetable 129–132, **130–1**
salami 76–8, **77**
salmon 21, **22**
canned 32
escalopes 28, **28**
gravlax 31
keta 32
preparing 28, **28**
smoked 29, **30**
Poached Whole Salmon 272
Salmon Coulibiac 271
Salmon Escalopes with Chanterelles 271
Salmon Pâté 317–18
Soy-Marinated Salmon Brochettes 273, **273**
Spicy Green Fish 272–3
salmon trout 21–2, **22**
Salsa Cruda 258
Salsa di Pomodoro 335–6
Salsa Verde 258
salsicce 73
salsicha salami **77**, 78
salsify 148, **150**
Glazed Salsify 382
salt 200, **200**
salt of hartshorn 119
salt mill **223**, 226
salted foods
beef 71, **71**
pork 70
saltpetre 200
saltwater fish 11–20, **11**, **13–15**, **17–18**
samphire 45–6, **45**
samsoe cheese 105
sand-smelt *see* atherine
sander *see* pike perch
saracen corn *see* buckwheat
sardine **15**, 16
canned 30, 32
satsuma 166, **166**
Sauce Tartare 259
sauces 206–7, **206**
pasta 124
recipes 255–60
saucisse 73
saucisson de Lyon **77**, 78
Saucisson de Toulouse **72**, 73
sausage meat 75
sausage 72–8, **72**
American 72
casings 75
cervelat 76, **76**
English 72
fresh 72–3, **72**, **74**
home-made 75
paté-type 78, **78**
preserved 73–4, **74**
pudding 74–5, **75**
salami 72, 76–8, **77**
slicing 75–6
sautéeing, potatoes 147
savory **193**, 194
sbrinz cheese 103
scad *see* horse mackerel
scales 230–1, **231**
scaling, fish 26, **26**
scallop 37–8, **37**
preparing 42, **42**
Pan-Fried Scallops with Garlic 279
Scallops with Saffron Vinaigrette, Basil and Tomato 279
scampi *see* langoustine
schabzieger cheese 103
scissors 225
Scones 364
scorzonera *see* salsify
scrag
lamb **57**, 58
veal 56
sea anemone 44
sea cucumber *see bêche de mer*
sea lamprey 20
sea robin *see* gurnard
sea slug *see bêche de mer*
sea urchin **43**, 44
Seafood Salad 370–1, **370**
seakale 139–40
seakale beet 140
seaweed 45–6, **45**
Seckel pear **164**, 165
sel gris 200, **200**
semolina 114, **115**
sesame seed **196**, 197
sesame oil 112, **113**
Seville Orange Marmalade 418
shad 23–24, **24**
shaggy ink cap **158**, 160
shallot **143**, 144–5
shark 17, **17**
shark's fin, dried 31, **32**
shears **223**, 225

shellfish 33–42, **33–7**, **39–42**
preparing 39–42, **39–42**
recipes 275–81, **277**, **280**
Sherry Trifle 392, **393**
shin
beef **52**, 53
veal 56
shoots 137–40, **137–9**
Shortcrust Pastry 402, 403, **403**
shortening 111, **111**
shoulder
beef 53
lamb **57**, 58, 65, **65**
pork **59**, 60
veal **54**, 56
shrimp 35–6, **35**
paste 206, **206**
Sichuan pepper 201, **201**
sieve **223**, 226–7
sifter **235**, 237
sild 30
canned 32
silverside **52**, 53
sirloin steak **52**, 53
Six-Vegetable Couscous 350–1, **350**
skate 18, **18**
Skate with Black Butter 268
skimmer 228
skirt **52**, 53
slicer **223**, 225
slicing sausages 75–6, **76**
sloake *see* laver
sloe **168**, 169
smelt **15**, 16
smoked foods
fish 30–1, **30**
game 71
mutton 71
poultry 71, **71**
roes 30, **30**
smoking equipment 241
snail 46
snipe 82–3
soba 125, **125**
Soft Polenta with Butter and Parmesan 352, **353**
sole 11, **11**
Fried Sole with Butter and Parsley 261
somen 125, **125**
sorbets, recipes 399–401, **400**
sorghum grain 118
sorrel **132**, 133
Spring Sorrel Soup 247
soumaintrain cheese 108
soup pasta 124
soups, recipes 246–54, **248**, **251**
soured cream 99
soy sauce 207
soya bean oil 113, **113**
soya bean, dried **127**, 128
spaghetti 121, **123**
Spaghetti alla Carbonara 337
Spaghetti alla Rustica 337
spaghetti marrow 156, **156**
spareribs, pork **59**, 60
spatchcocking, poultry 91, **91**
spatula 228, **228**
spearfish 16–17
speck 70, **70**
spelt 115
spices 196–9, **196–8**
mixtures 196
types 196–9, **196–8**
spinach 132–3, **132**
Sesame Spinach 372–3
Spinach and Bacon Salad 366–7
Spinach and Cheese Omelette 324
Spinach and Chick-Peas 373–4
Spinach Frittata 326–7
Spinach Gnocchi with Butter and Sage 344–5
Spinach and Ricotta Ravioli 342–4
Spinach Soup 247
Spinach Tart 327–8
Spinach and Walnut Salad **366**, 367
spinach beet *see* beet greens
spiny lobster *see* crawfish
spirits, cooking 209
split pea, dried 128, **128**
spoon 227, **228**
sprat **15**, 16, 30
canned 32
spring roll 124
squashes 155–7, **156–7**
Squash Fritters with Yogurt and Garlic Dressing 386
squid 43, **43**
preparing 47, **47**
Stuffed Baby Squid 281
squirrel 81
stalks 137–40, **137–9**
star anise 196, **196**
star fruit **181**, 182
steamer clam **232**, 235
steaming, fish 261
Stewed Artichokes with Spinach 376
stewing
beef 53
meat 50
veal 55
Sticky Golden Sponge Pudding 396
Stilton cheese 109, **109**
stockfish *see* cod, dried
stocks
jellied 244
recipes 244–6, 250
stone fruit 167–70, **168**
stoner 225
strawberry 171, **171**
Strawberry Fool 388
Strawberry Granita 401
Strawberry Ice-Cream 398
Strawberry Jam **416**, 417
Strawberry Tart 405
stuffing
of chicken 93, **93**
of duck 94–5, **94–5**
of turkey 87, 93, **93**
stuffing sausages 75, **76**
sturgeon 24–25, **24**
roe 31–2
smoked 30, **30**
sucking-pig 60
suet 110, **111**
sugars 210, 211–12, **212**
Sugo di Carne Toscano 336–7
sultana 182–3, **183**
sulzwurst sausage 76
Summer Minestrone 251–2
Summer Pudding 391
Summer Sponge Cake 410
sunflower oil 112–13, **113**
swede 149, **150**
Mashed Swedes 382
sweet cicely 192, **192**
see also bouquet garni
sweet cumin *see* anise
Sweet Pepper Chutney 419
sweet potato 147
Caramelized Sweet Potatoes 382
sweet woodruff **192**, 194
sweetbreads 61, **61**
sweetcorn 140, **140–1**, 142
sweeteners 210–13, **210–13**
sweetwater 174
Swiss chard **138**, 140
swordfish 16, **17**
Syllabub 394
sylte 70
syrups 210–11, **211**
Szechwan pepper *see* Sichuan pepper

Tabasco sauce 206
Tabbouleh 351
tagliarini 335
Tagliarini with Fresh Artichokes and Gremolata 338
tagliatelle 122, **122**, **334**, 335
Tagliatelle alla Panna 338
tahina 206, **206**
tails 62
Taleggio cheese 107, **107**
tamari 207
tamarillo **181**, 182
tamarind **198**, 199
tangelo **166**, 167
tangerine 166, **166**
tangor 166
tapioca **117**, 118
taro 147–8, **148**
tarragon 190–1, **191**
see also fines herbes
tarts **403**, 405–7, **408**
tayberry **171**, 172
tea
black 217–18, **217**
blended 218–19, **218**
green **217**, 218
herbal 219, **219**
oolong 218, **218**
teewurst sausage 78, **78**
telapia *see* tilapia
tench 25
tenderloin 52–3
teriyaki marinade 207
terrine 236, 314
thermometer **231**, 233, 241
thick flank, beef **52**, 53
thickening agents 118–19
Thuringer sausage 76
thyme **192**, 194
see also bouquet garni
tilapia 20, **20**
tilsit cheese 105, **106**
timer 233
tins
cakes **235**, 236–7
pastry 237
roasting **232**, 236
tisanes 219, **219**
toaster **238**, 239
Toasts 364
tocino 70
tomate de mer 44
tomatillo **151**, 152
tomato paste *see* tomato purée
tomato 150–1, **151**
choosing 151
cooking 151
ketchup 206, **206**
purée 206, **206**
salad 151
storing 151
Delicate Tomato Sauce 256
Fresh Sauce Grelette 257
Green Tomato Sour 419
Roasted Tomato Sauce 256–7
Stuffed Tomatoes 384, **385**
Tomato and Leek Soup 246–7
tommes cheese 107–8, **107**
tongue **61**, 62
top rump **52**, 53
topside **52**, 53
Torbay sole *see* witch
torsk *see* cusk
Torta Dolcelatte cheese 109, **109**
tortilla 120, **120**, 325
Traditional Custard Tart 407–8
treacle, black 211
tree tomato *see* tamarillo
Trinity Cream 394
tripe **61**, 62
trout 21–22, **22**
smoked 30, **30**
Trout Marinated in Vermouth 273–4
Trout in White Wine Jelly 273
truffle 161, **161**
trussing equipment 230
tubers 145–50, **146**, **148–50**
tuna 16, **17**
canned 32
Grilled Tuna with Anchovy 267–8
Tuna in a Packet with Red Sauce 268, **269**
turbinado sugar 211
turbot **11**, 12
Seviche 263
Turbot Poached in Cider 261–3
turkey **89**
cooking 87–8
stuffing of 87, 93, **93**
timing 311–12
trussing 93, **93**
wild 85
Roast Turkey with Two Stuffings 311–12
White Devil 312
turmeric **198**, 199

turner 228, **228**
turnip 149, **150**
Glazed Turnips 382
turntable 237
Tuscan Pasta 332
Twelfth Day Cake 412–13
type 00 flour 115

udon 125, **125**
ugli fruit **166**, 167

Vacherin cheese 106
vanilla 198, **198**
veal
choosing 54
cooking 54–5
cuts 54–6, **54**, 64, **64**
kidneys 61, **61**
liver 61, **61**
preparing 64, **64**
sweetbreads 61, **61**
Costolette Milanese 285–7
Golden Veal Stock 244–5
Osso Bucco with Lemon Gremolata **286**, 287
Rich Brown Veal Stock 245
Veal with Apples and Cream 285
Veal with Mushrooms 285
vegetable fruit 150–7, **151–2**, **154–7**
vegetable oil 113
vegetable spaghetti *see* spaghetti marrow
vegetables
greens 132–4, **132–3**
recipes 365–86, **366**, **369–70**, **373**, **377**, **380**, **385**
root 145–50, **146**, **148–50**
salad 129–32, **130–1**
shoots 137–40, **137–9**
stalks 137–40, **137–9**
tubers 145–50, **146**, **148–50**
Velouté Sauce 255
venison 79, **80**
Char-Grilled Venison 294
Roast Haunch of Venison with Pepper Sauce 294–5
Sweet-Braised Spiced Venison 294
vermicelli 121, 125, **125**
Vermicelli Milk Pudding with Cardamom and Saffron 395
Vichyssoise with Chives 254
Vinaigrette 259
vine leaf 195, **195**
vinegar
flavoured 205
types 204–5, **204–5**
violet *see figue de mer*
vollkornbrot bread 119
Vouvrillonne Sauce 255

waffle iron **238**, 239
wakame **45**, 46
walnut **187**, 188
ketchup 206
walnut oil **112**, 113
Walnut Bread 358
Walnut Cake 412, **413**
Warm Cheese Bread 363–4
wasabi *see* Japanese horseradish
watercress 130–1, **131**
Light Watercress Soup 247
watermelon 177, **177**
wax gourd 157
weakfish 19–20
weisswurst sausage 72
Wensleydale cheese 103, **105**
West Coast sole *see* megrim
wheat 114–15, **115**
wheat germ oil 113
whelk **43**, 44
whiff *see* megrim
whisk 227, **228**
White Frosting 415
white pudding 74, **75**
White Soda Bread 362
white sole *see* megrim
whitebait **15**, 16
Fried Whitebait 267
whitecurrant 173, **173**
whitefish, freshwater **24**, 25
whiting 13–14, **13**
preparing 27, **27**
whiting (American) *see* hake
Wholemeal Bread 358
wholewheat pasta 123, **123**
wildfowl 82
Williams' Bon Chrétien pear 164, **164**
wines, cooking 208–9
winkle **43**, 44
witch 12
wok **232**, 235
wonton *see* dumpling
wood grouse *see* capercaillie
woodcock 82–3, **83**
Roast Woodcock 299
Worcester Pearmain apple 162, **163**
Worcestershire sauce 206

yam bean *see* jícama
yam 147, **148**
yeast 118
dough 356, **356–7**
yogurt 99, 100
Yogurt and Garlic Dressing 259–60
Yogurt and Spring Onion Dressing 259–60
youngberry 172

Zabaglione 394
zampone sausage 73, **74**
zucchini *see* courgette
zungenwurst sausage 76, **76**

ACKNOWLEDGMENTS

The Authors would like to thank the following:
Sophie Grigson, Dee MacQuillan and Robert Neild

The Publisher would like to thank the following for their invaluable assistance in preparing this book:

Lewis Esson, for first suggesting a new edition of *The Cook Book*

Editorial
Jenny Linford, Kate Quarry, Jane Royston, Judith Sutton (American consultant), Susanna Tee, Kate Whiteman (contributing editor), Sarah Widdecombe, Simon Willis, Jeni Wright, Indexing Specialists.

Photography, Illustration and Design
Susan Campbell/King and King (meat cut artworks), Amanda Hills (ingredients buyer and stylist), Meg Jansz (recipe home economist), Dave King and Allison Tyler (USA ingredients photography), Andrew McConochie (jacket conceptualization), Róisín Neild (recipe stylist), Denys Ovenden (new fish artworks), Nato Welton (equipment stylist).

Ingredients
City Herbs, New Spitalfields Market; C. Lidgates, London W11; Jarvis & Co., Kingston; R.A. Bevan & Son, Kingston; Harrods Food Halls; Brogdale Horticultural Trust; Wild Harvest Mushrooms, London; Henry Doubleday Research Association; Harvey Nichols Food Halls; Selfridges Food Halls; Idencroft Herb Nursery, Staplehurst; Yaohan Oriental Supermarket, Colindale; G.M. & E.A. Innes, Newmachar, Aberdeen; Winterwood Soft Fruit Farm, Nr Maidstone; Remfresh, Colchester; E.W. King's, Chertsey; Garson Farm, Esher; Potato Marketing Board; Vivians, Richmond; Mrs Tee's Wild Mushrooms, Haslemere; C.R. Upton Pumpkins & Squashes, Arundel; Tawana Supermarket, London; Syon Park Garden Centre.

Equipment and Props
Braun, The Conran Shop, Le Creuset, Divertimenti, Kenwood, Krups, Petra (Beam Group Ltd), Sabatier, Salter.

Contributors to the Original Edition of the Book
Maria Kroll, Ann Sayer (contributors), Clive Corless (photography), Ingrid Jacob, Andrew Davidson, Paul Brooks (illustrators).